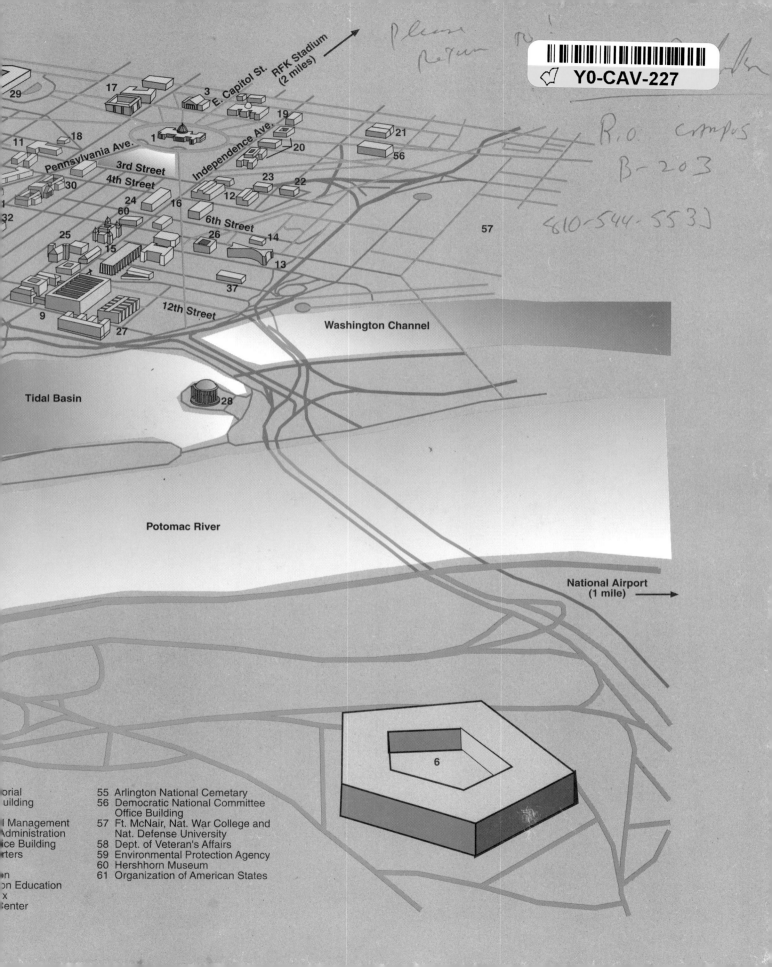

Y0-CAV-227

29

17

3   E. Capitol St.   RFK Stadium
(2 miles)

11   18

1

Pennsylvania Ave.   3rd Street
4th Street

30

32

24

60

25   16

15

9

27

12th Street

37

Independence Ave.

19

20

21

56

23   22

12

6th Street

26   14

13

57

Washington Channel

Tidal Basin   28

Potomac River

National Airport
(1 mile)

6

orial
uilding

l Management
Administration
ce Building
rters

n
on Education
x
enter

55 Arlington National Cemetary
56 Democratic National Committee
    Office Building
57 Ft. McNair, Nat. War College and
    Nat. Defense University
58 Dept. of Veteran's Affairs
59 Environmental Protection Agency
60 Hershhorn Museum
61 Organization of American States

GOVERNMENT BY THE PEOPLE

BASIC VERSION

Sixteenth Edition

James MacGregor Burns
*University of Maryland, College Park
and Williams College*

J.W. Peltason
University of California

Thomas E. Cronin
Whitman College

David B. Magleby
Brigham Young University

Prentice Hall, Englewood Cliffs, New Jersey 07632

Library of Congress Cataloging-in-Publication Data

Government by the people / James MacGregor Burns ... [et al.]. — 16th
ed., basic version.
    p.   cm.
    Includes bibliographical references and index.
    ISBN 0-13-301250-6
    1. United States—Politics and government. I. Burns, James
MacGregor.
JK274.B8525 1995
320.473—dc20

94-36426
CIP

Editorial director: Charlyce Jones Owen
Editor in chief: Nancy Roberts
Acquisitions editor: Mike Bickerstaff
Editorial/production supervision: Serena Hoffman
Copy editor: Ann Grogg
Design director: Anne Bonanno Nieglos
Interior design: Jerry Votta and Rosemarie Paccione
Illustrations: Gary Moore
Cover design: Bruce Kenselaar/Jerry Votta
Formatting supervision: Mike Bertrand
Page layout: Joh Lisa
Photo editor: Lorinda Morris-Nantz
Photo researcher: Joelle Burrows
Editorial assistant: Nicole Signoretti
Marketing manager: Kris Kleinsmith
Buyer: Bob Anderson
Cover and title page photos: Peter Gridley/FPG International

© 1995, 1993, 1990, 1989, 1987, 1985, 1984, 1981, 1978, 1975,
1972, 1969, 1966, 1963, 1960, 1957, 1954, 1952 by Prentice-Hall, Inc.
A Simon & Schuster Company
Englewood Cliffs, New Jersey 07632

All rights reserved. No part of this book may be
reproduced, in any form or by any means,
without permission in writing from the publisher.

Printed in the United States of America
10 9 8 7 6 5 4 3 2 1

ISBN 0-13-301250-6

Prentice-Hall International (UK) Limited, *London*
Prentice-Hall of Australia Pty. Limited, *Sydney*
Prentice-Hall Canada Inc., *Toronto*
Prentice-Hall Hispanoamericana, S.A., *Mexico*
Prentice-Hall of India Private Limited, *New Delhi*
Prentice-Hall of Japan, Inc., *Tokyo*
Simon & Schuster Asia Pte. Ltd., *Singapore*
Editora Prentice-Hall do Brasil, Ltda., *Rio de Janeiro*

BRIEF CONTENTS

CONTENTS

FEATURES

From Coast to Coast

A Closer Look

We the People

You Decide!

A MESSAGE FROM THE AUTHORS

With the 1992 and 1994 elections, the agenda of American politics shifted to domestic affairs, especially the economy and social policy. Across a range of issues—health care, crime control, welfare, education—Congress and the president focused on "reinventing government." The debate on the future direction of social policy and the role of government became a media event, as television, radio, and print advertisements promoted the point of view of various interest groups, who urged people to write or phone their elected officials and express their opinions. The mid-'90s also became a time of reassessment of the role of the United States in international affairs, a role that has changed with the collapse of the Soviet Union. This text is geared to analyzing these changes in terms of how the institutions and processes of American government deal with such far-reaching and contentious issues.

Even in the twentieth century, constitutional democracy has been the exception rather than the rule. In the past, most people lived under autocratic or tyrannical regimes in which a small group imposed their will on everyone else. And today, less than one-third of the nation-states around the globe exist as viable, healthy democracies. This is a testing time for new democracies as well as old ones. Contempt for government and politics is being expressed here in the United States and abroad. Yet politics and partisan competition are the lifeblood by which free people can achieve the ideals of a government by and for the people.

Constitutional democracy—the kind we have in the United States—is exceedingly hard to win, equally hard to sustain, and often hard to understand without rigorous study. The form of constitutional democracy that has emerged in the United States requires continual participation by caring, tolerant, and informed citizens. The framers of our Constitution warned that we must be vigilant in safeguarding our rights, liberties, and political institutions. But to do this, we first have to understand these institutions and the forces that have shaped the United States' political and constitutional systems.

We hope you will come away from reading this book with a richer understanding of American politics and government, and we hope that in the years to come, many of you will participate actively in making our constitutional democracy more vital and responsive to the urgent problems of the twenty-first century.

REVIEWERS

The writing of this book has profited from the informed professional, and often sharp, critical suggestions of our colleagues around the country. This and previous editions have been considerably improved as a result of reviews by the following individuals, for which we thank them all:

David Gray Adler, Idaho State University
James Anderson, Tulane University
David Barnum, De Paul University
Robert Bartlett, Purdue University
Robert C. Benedict, University of Utah
Thad Beyle, University of North Carolina
Gary Bryner, Brigham Young University
Jeanne Clarke, University of Arizona
Leif Carter, University of Georgia
Morgan Chawawa, De Kalb College
Richard Chesteen, University of Tennessee
Gary Cornia, Brigham Young University
Gary Covington, University of Iowa
Douglas Crane, De Kalb College
Richard Davis, Brigham Young University

James D. Decker, Macon College
Lois Lovelace Duke, Clemson University
Pat Dunham, Duquesne University
Robert Elias, University of San Francisco
Steven Finkel, University of Virginia
Mark Gibney, Purdue University
L. Tucker Gibson, Trinity University
Jim Graves, Kentucky State University
Paul Herrnson, University of Maryland
Marjorie Hershey, Indiana University
Michael J. Horan, University of Wyoming
Ronald J. Hrebenar, University of Utah
Diane P. Jennings, De Kalb College
J. Landrum Kelly, Georgia Southern University
Donnald F. Kettl, University of Wisconsin

Dwight Kiel, Central Florida University
Ron King, Tulane University
Michael E. Kraft, University of Wisconsin
Fred A. Kramer, University of Massachusetts
Paul Light, University of Minnesota
William Louthan, Ohio Weslyan University
Richard Matthews, Lehigh University
Robert McCalla, University of Wisconsin
Max Neiman, University of California
David Nice, Washington State University
Richard Pacelle, University of Missouri
Glen Parker, Florida State University
Kelly D. Patterson, Brigham Young University
George Pippin, Jones County College
John Portz, Northeastern University

Pamela Rodgers, University of Wisconsin
David Rosenbloom, American University
Alan Rosenthal, Rutgers University
H.E. Scruggs, Brigham Young University
Henry Shockely, Boston University

Steven Shull, University of New Orleans
Christine Marie Sierra, University of New Mexico
Robert W. Small, Massasoit Community College
Gregory W. Smith, Gettysburg College
Richard Smolka, American University

Neil Edward Snortland, University of Arkansas
Roy Thoman, West Texas A&M University
John Tierney, Boston College
Richard Valelly, Massachusetts Institute of Technology
R. Lawson Veasey, University of Arkansas

ACKNOWLEDGMENTS

We wish to acknowledge the help we have received from our colleagues, research assistants, and support staff, who have helped each of us in the preparation of this sixteenth edition. Thus we thank Patricia Pelfrey at the University of California for her superb editorial assistance and her creative and active participation in this revision. We are also indebted to Andrea Campbell for her persistence and skill in tracking down sources and for her command of the political science literature, and to Kristine Fowler and Cecile Cuttitta for their careful proofreading and for calling attention to errors large and small. At Whitman College, we thank Rob Neal and Bob Schwed for their editorial assistance, and JoAnn Collins and Donna Jones for their proofreading and technical assistance. At Brigham Young University, we give particular thanks to research assistants Nathanael Austin, Steven Davis, Marianne Holt, Quin Monson, Paul Peterson, Scott Baxter, and Liz Romney.

Our very special thanks go to our production editor, Serena Hoffman, who once again brilliantly guided us in the rewriting of this book. We also thank our Prentice Hall friends Ed Stanford, Will Ethridge, Charlyce Jones Owen, Nancy Roberts, Mike Bickerstaff, and Kris Kleinsmith. We must also thank the many other skilled professionals at Prentice Hall who assisted in the publication of this edition: Ann Grogg, for meticulous copy editing; Jerry Votta, Anne Bonanno Nieglos, and Joh Lisa for their superb design and layouts; Lorinda Morris-Nantz and Joelle Burrows for photo research; Gary Moore for our edifying new illustrations; and Nicole Signoretti, editorial assistant, for keeping track of things.

Finally, we thank the dozens of students and professors who have sent us letters with suggestions for improving *Government By The People*. We welcome your notes or calls concerning any errors or ways we can further improve the book. Please write us care of the Political Science Editor at Prentice Hall, Englewood Cliffs, New Jersey 07632, or to us directly.

James MacGregor Burns
Williams College
Williamstown, MA 01267

J.W. Peltason
University of California
300 Lakeside Drive
Oakland, CA 94612

Thomas E. Cronin
Whitman College
Walla Walla, WA 99362

David B. Magleby
Brigham Young University
Provo, UT 84602

A MESSAGE FROM THE PUBLISHER

The gratifying success *Government By The People* has enjoyed over the years results from a distinguished authorship team who always write a superb book with a distinctive combination of features. Treating each new edition as a fresh challenge—and, in many ways, a virtually new book—the authors capture American government and politics as the dynamic ventures they are.

Comprehensive and Balanced Presentation

Known for its balanced coverage of constitutional principles, political processes, and central political institutions, this latest edition offers the best of previous editions *and* exciting changes in content that include:

- A thematic examination of constitutional democracy—its ideals, its conditions, and the American struggle to realize its possibilities and potential. The American political experiment is frequently assessed in a comparative light.

- A new chapter in the *National, State, and Local Version* covers current policy priorities in health care, welfare, crime, and education. Past policy initiatives, such as the New Deal and the Great Society, as well as current debates on health and welfare reform, crime control, and education policies, are examined and compared.

- A unique chapter, "The American Political Landscape," examines social and economic diversity in American society and some of the political consequences of living in an increasingly multicultural nation. This chapter provides the framework of the social fabric of our nation, which needs to be put in context before students can fully appreciate the role that public opinion, interest group politics, and voting behavior play in America.

- In-depth analysis of the successes and failures of the Clinton presidency and the expanded role Hillary Clinton has undertaken as First Lady. Former Chapter 16, "Congress and the President," has been integrated into the discussions on Congress (Chapter 14) and the Presidency (Chapter 15).

- Full integration of the results of the 1994 elections, with analysis of party control of the House and Senate and how the 1994 elections will affect the 1996 presidential election.

- Discussion of the "new" Supreme Court, including the nominations of Justices Ginsburg and Breyer and the politics of their selection and confirmation, with

full updates and integrated analysis of recent 1994 Supreme Court cases.

- The *National, State, and Local Version* discusses the changing character of United States foreign and defense politics, including our greater involvement in the United Nations and other multinational peacekeeping organizations. Chapter 21 combines two chapters in the previous edition, reflecting the changing focus of our government in the post-cold war era and the increasing interdependence of foreign and defense policies.

- Complete incorporation of 1990 census data. Once a decade we get a thorough examination of the American polity, and these data are integrated where appropriate throughout the book.

- Innovative treatment of political ideology and culture, political participation and voting turnout, voting behavior, and campaign financing.

- Expanded coverage of state and local politics in the *National, State, and Local Version*, and a new *Texas Version*, including full updates on 1994 election results and, in the Texas version, seven chapters devoted to government and politics of the state of Texas.

- The examples in *Government By The People* are drawn from a wide range of current and historical sources. While fully reflecting recent political events, examples are also included from earlier eras to provide the important historical context within which current events can be better understood. Complete lists of suggested readings at the end of each chapter and detailed footnotes at the back of the book highlight sources of lasting and recent importance.

New Illustration Program

In addition to the features described above, this new edition of *Government By The People* includes a completely redesigned art program that is sure to increase student interest. The charts, graphs, figures, and graphics have all been reworked—many in a three-dimensional format—to enhance their content and clarity, as well as the visual appeal of the text.

Accessible and Engaging Features for the Student

Written with the student in mind by experienced scholars and teachers, *Government By The People* has always been admired for its elegant, yet engaging narrative style. To assist accessibility, key terms appear on first use in the text in bold-faced type, followed by a precise definition. These terms are also listed in the full Glossary at the end of the book.

Of particular appeal to students will be the wealth of boxed features offered in the sixteenth edition. Boxes in the margins provide amusing anecdotes and historical, biographical, and additional facts of interest about American politics that will enhance student learning. Several special features reinforce this goal as well:

You Decide! This participatory question-and-answer feature is designed to strengthen students' critical thinking skills as well as introduce interesting and challenging issues and ideas about American politics for students to ponder. A question is presented on the left page, and on the facing page a Thinking It Through discussion examines possible answers (although, as in real life, not all questions have definitive answers). This unique feature has been a long-standing favorite among the many students who have used them.

A Closer Look These journalistic-style boxes combine text, tables, photographs, and art on relevant issues of high student appeal. Like a good lecture, they provide a pause in the narrative where appropriate, to allow the pursuit of a particular topic beyond the scope of the material at hand. Some of the topics include: "Rap Lyrics and Free Speech," "Juries on Trial," "Minor Parties in American Politics," "Health Care in Advanced Industrial Democracies," "The Effect of the Deficit on Savings," "Race as an Issue in Local Elections," and "Victim's Rights."

We the People These unique boxes are designed to reflect the concerns and experiences of ethnic and minority groups in American politics. Some of the topics include: "Where We Learn the American Political Culture," "Distribution of Education in the United States," "Problems Faced by Women Bureaucrats," "Equal Justice," and "Minority Judges." The *We the People* feature, plus Chapter 8 on "The American Political Landscape" and the many instances in the text where ethnic and minority concerns, histories, and stories are told have made *Government By The People* the strongest and most complete text available that integrates *all* Americans into the story of American politics.

From Coast to Coast This new collection of four-color maps provides visual state-by-state comparisons on a broad range of topics, such as "The Uninsured," "Party Control of State Legislatures," "Fiscal Capacity to Raise Revenue Through Taxes," and "Unequal Welfare Benefits in the States." The comparisons give students the opportunity to understand how states are affected differently by many factors.

Supplements for the Instructor

Government By The People is the core of a complete learning package that includes a wide range of proven, as well as new, instructional aids. The supplements have been completely revised, not only to incorporate material new to the sixteenth edition, but also to ensure the highest quality and accuracy possible.

Instructor's Resource Manual Provides the following resources for each chapter of the text: summary, review of major concepts, lecture suggestions and topic outlines, suggestions for classroom discussions, additional resource materials, and a detailed content outline for lecture planning. New to this edition is a guide to media resources section in each chapter that identifies specific transparencies, video clips, laserdisk segments, and/or simulations available with the text that are appropriate for the content of that chapter. The Instructor's Resource Manual was prepared by Michael F. Digby and Larry Elowitz, both of Georgia College.

Electronic Instructor's Resource Manual An ASCII file version of the printed manual allows coordination of chapter resources on computer. Available for IBM PCs and Macintosh.

Strategies for Teaching American Government: A Guide for the New Instructor This unique guide offers a wealth of practical advice and information to help new instructors face the challenges of teaching courses in American Government. From setting course goals, conducting the class, constructing and evaluating tests or written assignments, to advising students, many of the issues and questions related to teaching are covered. The guide was written by Fred Whitford, Montana State University.

Test Item File The sixteenth edition test item file has been thoroughly reviewed and revised to ensure the highest level of quality and accuracy. Over 3,000 questions in multiple choice, true/false, and essay format are provided, covering factual, conceptual, and applied material from the text.

Prentice Hall Test Manager A computerized version of the test item file, this program allows full editing of questions and the addition of instructor-generated items. Other special features include random generation, scrambling question order, and test preview before printing. Available for IBM and Macintosh computers.

Telephone Test Preparation Service Prentice Hall will provide tests (with questions from our test item file) on bond paper or ditto master. We will send the exam, an alternate version if requested, and an answer key within 48 hours of a request. Complete information about this service and the toll free number are include in the printed test item file, or ask your local representative for more details.

Grade Manager The Prentice Hall gradebook/class file program allows for an unlimited number of students and classes and includes complete student information: calculating grades, displaying and printing grade-point averages as either letters or numbers, curving test grades, displaying performance graphs for each student and/or test, and printing test grades or final grades for posting. Available for IBM PCs.

American Government Transparencies, Series II and Series III These sets of 75 to 100 four-color transparency acetates reproduce illustrations, charts, and maps from the text as well as from additional sources.

Instructor's Guide to American Government Transparencies, Series II and Series III This brief guide provides descriptions, teaching suggestions, and discussion questions for each transparency. There is a separate guide for each set of transparencies.

ABC News/Prentice Hall Video Libraries Prentice Hall and ABC News bring an innovative video collection to the classroom through this series of video libraries on the newsworthy topics and pressing issues that relate to concepts covered in American Government courses. The libraries consist of feature segments from such award-winning programs as *Nightline, 20/20, World News Tonight/The American Agenda, Primetime Live,* and *This Week with David Brinkley.*

- **1992 Primaries** covers the initial campaign and primaries of the 1992 presidential election.
- **1992 Elections** covers the Democratic and Republican conventions and the November election.
- **Images in American Government** shows the conflicts of past presidential campaigns and elections plus segments on current issues.
- **Issues in American Government** provides multiple segments on issues such as health care and welfare reform, environment, crime and violence, foreign policy, the federal budget, and government waste.

Instructor's Guide to ABC News/Prentice Hall Video Libraries Provides a brief synopsis and discussion questions for each segment in the video libraries.

Prentice Hall Laserdisks The story of American Government is vividly illustrated through this exciting technology. Each laserdisk comes with a guide for using the material in the classroom.

- **1992 Primaries and Elections** includes the segments from the ABC/News video library.
- **Images in American Government** includes approximately 500 still images and segments from ABC News.
- **Issues in American Government** is a laserdisk version of the ABC News video library.

Annenberg Audiocassette Series Twelve half-hour audio programs feature distinguished guests who are actively engaged in national political life.

Supplements for the Student

Study Guide Each chapter includes outlines, study notes, a glossary, practice tests, Political Science Today study assignments, and data analysis worksheets that reinforce student learning. The guide was prepared by Dorothy Palmer of Indiana University of Pennsylvania and Larry Elowitz of Georgia College.

Study Manager A computerized study guide that generates random quizzes, provides text page references for review, and prints the corrected quiz for further study and/or submission to the instructor. All objective questions correspond to material found in the study guide. Available for IBM PCs.

Multimedia Study Guide Students can now take advantage of the exciting world of technology to study American Government with this new supplement from Prentice Hall. This unique student resource provides text, video, simulations, quizzes, timelines, and study guide tools in a CD-ROM format to engage students in the study of government and politics. Available at a reasonable price, this study resource can be used not only to reinforce comprehension of text content, but also to expand student knowledge of issues of American Government. Available for IBM PCs and Macintosh. Prepared by G. David Garson, North Carolina State University.

American Government Simulation Games, Series II Seven unique simulations engage students in various role-playing situations: Bill of Rights, House of Representatives, Presidential Budget, Secretary of State, Supreme Court, Washington Ethics, and Crime and Social Policy. Available for DOS, Windows, and Macintosh platforms and in CD-ROM format. The simulations were created by G. David Garson, North Carolina State University, and programmed by Electronic Courseware Systems, Inc., Champaign, Illinois.

A Guide to Civic Literacy This brief booklet provides suggestions for getting students involved in politics. It includes nine political activities for individuals or groups on agenda building, coalition building, registering and mobilizing voters, education, and increasing accountability. The guide was written by James Chesney and Otto Feinstein, both of Wayne State University.

The Write Stuff: Writing as a Performing and Political Art, Second Edition This brief booklet, written by Thomas E. Cronin, provides ideas and suggestions on writing style and methods in Political Science.

***Themes of the Times* Supplement** Prentice Hall and *The New York Times* expand students' knowledge beyond the classroom and into the world we live in. Users of *Government By The People* can receive a complimentary newspaper supplement containing recent articles pertinent to American Government. These articles, featuring the best in reporting and journalistic integrity associated with *The New York Times*, update the text material and contribute real-world applications to the topics covered in the course.

Prentice Hall Critical Thinking Audiocassette This 60-minute cassette teaches students how to develop their critical thinking and study skills. The first 50 minutes concentrate on critical thinking skills, specifically on how to ask the right questions. The final 10 minutes offer helpful tips on how to study, take notes, and be a more active, effective learner.

ABOUT THE AUTHORS

James MacGregor Burns is a Distinguished Scholar in Leadership, University of Maryland, College Park, and Woodrow Wilson Professor Emeritus of Government at Williams College. He has written numerous books, including *The Power to Lead* (1984), *The Vineyard of Liberty* (1982), *Leadership* (1979), *Roosevelt: The Soldier of Freedom* (1970), *The Deadlock of Democracy: Four-Party Politics in America* (1963), and *Roosevelt: The Lion and the Fox* (1956). His most recent book is *A People's Charter: The Pursuit of Rights in America* (1991), which he wrote with his son, Stewart Burns. Burns is a past president of the American Political Science Association and winner of numerous prizes, including the Pulitzer Prize in Writing.

J.W. Peltason is a leading scholar on the judicial process and public law. He is Professor of Political Science at the University of California, Irvine. As past president of the American Council on Education, Peltason has represented higher education before Congress and state legislatures. His writings include *Federal Courts in the Political Process* (1955), *Fifty-Eight Lonely Men: Southern Federal Judges and School Desegration* (1961), and *Understanding the Constitution* (1993). Among his awards are the James Madison Medal from Princeton University and the American Political Science Association's Charles E. Merriam Award.

Thomas E. Cronin is a leading student of the American presidency, leadership, and policy-making processes. He served recently as president of the Western Political Science Association. He teaches at and serves as President of Whitman College. He served as a White House Fellow and a White House aide. His writings include *The State of the Presidency* (1980), *U.S. v. Crime in the Streets* (1981), *Direct Democracy: The Politics of Initiative, Referendum, and Recall* (1989), and *Colorado Politics and Government* (1993). Cronin is a past recipient of the American Political Science Association's Charles E. Merriam Award.

David B. Magleby is nationally recognized for his expertise on direct democracy, voting behavior, and campaign finance. He is Professor of Political Science and department chair at Brigham Young University. He has taught at the University of California, Santa Cruz, and the University of Virginia. His writings include *Direct Legislation* (1984), *The Money Chase: Congressional Campaign Finance Reform* (1990), and *The Myth of the Independent Voter* (1992). He is currently president of Pi Sigma Alpha, the national political science honor society, and was commended by the Carnegie Endowment for the Advancement and Support of Education.

CONSTITUTIONAL DEMOCRACY

I t is the week before an American election, the culmination of an intense, year-long campaign. During this last week, television and the newspapers are full of political ads: "A vote for Gabrillino is a vote for the people!" one says under a picture of Frank Gabrillino, the Democratic candidate for governor. He is shown with Mrs. Gabrillino, a successful real-estate broker. There are pictures of the Gabrillinos' three children. Gabrillino's campaign themes have stressed that he is not a politician, just a man of the people. He accuses his opponent, Sarah Wong, who has been in office for two terms, of being soft on criminals and blames her for the state's economic downturn. Gabrillino insists that if Wong is reelected, the state is doomed. Wong—behind in the polls, although recently catching up—emphasizes her experience, her concern for all the people, and her willingness to defy the special interests. She is a Republican, but she plays down her party affiliation since in this state a majority of the voters have been Democrats in the past.

The two candidates have accused each other of all kinds of misdeeds. As the campaign progresses, their ads become more negative, more focused on personality than on political issues and positions. Gabrillino makes much of the fact that 20 years ago Wong indicated she had doubts about the morality and efficacy of the death penalty, even though as governor she has not commuted any death sentences and has allowed two people to be executed. Wong's supporters charge that Gabrillino is fuzzy-hearted, soft-headed, and a tool of left-wing professors. There are endorsements in the newspapers: Professors for Wong, Teachers for Gabrillino, Students for Wong, Chicanos for Gabrillino, Asians for Gabrillino. Each candidate carefully plants letters to the editor in all the newspapers. Local radio and television talk shows feature the candidates, and the candidates' organizations supply callers to attack their opponents.

Election day: Only half the eligible voters bother to vote, and exit interviews indicate that the race is too close to call. That night, projections based on 5 percent of the vote make it clear that Gabrillino will get 48 percent of the vote, Wong 46 percent, and minor parties the rest. At 11:00 P.M., Wong calls Gabrillino, congratulates him on his victory, makes a concession speech before her disappointed workers, and thanks them for their support. Gabrillino speaks to his cheering supporters at another hotel ballroom, stating that his election was a great victory for the people.

Elections are a familiar process that Americans take for granted. Many people look upon elections with disdain, saying, "It's all politics." But in fact, American elections are remarkable. They conclude with what in the course of human history is a rare event: the peaceful transfer of political power. What is unusual is what is *not* happening. Even though the day before the election Wong and her followers were insisting that if Gabrillino became governor there would be chaos and corruption, once the vote was counted there was no thought by anybody in any political party that Gabrillino should not become governor. When her term was up, Wong did not resist turning power over to the man she had called corrupt. It never crossed her mind to try to stay in office by calling on the state police to keep Gabrillino from taking power. None of Wong's supporters considered taking up arms or going underground or leaving the country. (Actually, they concentrated on how they could win the next election.) Nor did Gabrillino or his followers ever give any thought to punishing Sarah Wong and her supporters once they gained power. The Democrats wanted to throw the Republicans out of office, not in jail.

It was just a routine election—democracy at work. Most of the time in most nations, those in power got there either because they were born to the right family or because they killed or jailed their opponents. During most of human history, no one, and most especially not an opposition political party, could openly criticize their government. During most of human history, a political opponent was an enemy.

In this chapter, we begin our exploration of this unique American experiment by taking a closer look at the meaning of democracy and the historical events that created the constitutional democracy of the United States. **Constitutional democracy*** as used here refers to a government that regularly enforces recognized limits on those who govern and allows the voice of the people to be regularly heard through free and fair elections. **Constitutionalism** refers to how power is granted, dispersed, and limited.

DEFINING DEMOCRACY

The word "democracy" is nowhere to be found in the Declaration of Independence or in the U.S. Constitution, nor was it a term used by the founders of the Republic. Democracy is hard to define. It is both a very old term and a new one. It was used in a loose sense to refer to various undesirable things: "the masses," mobs, lack of standards, and a system that encourages **demagogues** (leaders who gain power by appealing to the emotions and prejudices of the rabble).

Because we are using the term *democracy* in its political sense, we will be more precise. The distinguishing feature of democracy is that government derives its authority from its citizens. In fact, the word comes from two Greek words: *demos* (the people) and *kratos* (authority or power). Thus **democracy** means government by the people, not government by one person (the monarch, the dictator, the priest) or government by the few (an oligarchy or aristocracy).

Ancient Athens and a few other Greek cities had a **direct democracy**, in which citizens came together to discuss and pass the laws and select the rulers by lot. These Greek city-states did not last, and most turned to mob rule and then resorted to dictators. When the word "democracy" came into English usage in the seventeenth century, it denoted this kind of direct democracy and was a term of derision, a negative word, usually used to refer to mob rule.

James Madison, writing in *The Federalist*, No. 10, reflected the view of many of the framers of the U.S. Constitution when he wrote "such democracies [as the Greek and Roman] . . . have ever been found incompatible with personal security, or the rights of property; and have in general been as short in their lives, as they have been violent in their deaths" (*The Federalist*, No. 10 appears in the Appendix). Democracy has taken on a positive meaning only in the last one hundred years.

These days it is no longer possible, even if desirable, to assemble the citizens of any but the smallest towns to make their laws or to select their officials directly from among the citizenry. Rather, we have invented a *system of representation*. Democracy today means **representative democracy** or, in Plato's term, a **republic** in which those who have governmental authority *get and retain* authority directly or indirectly as the result of winning free elections in which all adult citizens are allowed to participate.

The framers preferred to use the term "republic" to avoid any confusion between direct democracy, which they disliked, and representative democracy, which they liked and thought secured all the advantages of a direct democracy while curing its weaknesses. Today, and in this book, *democracy* and *republic* are often used interchangeably.

"The Athenians are here, Sire, with an offer to back us with ships, money, arms, and men—and, of course, their usual lectures about democracy."

Drawing by Ed Fisher. ©1983 The New Yorker Magazine, Inc.

*Words that appear in boldfaced type throughout the text are defined in the Glossary at the end of the book.

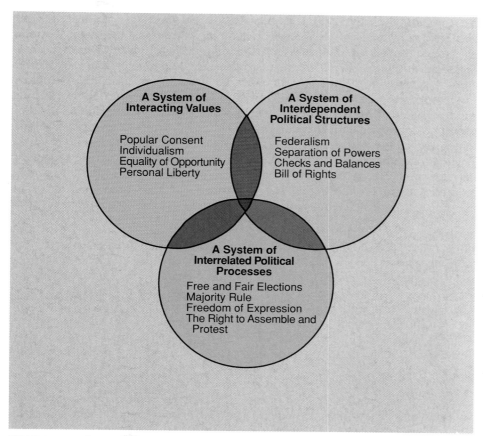

FIGURE 1-1 The Contributing Elements of Constitutional Democracy

Like most political concepts, democracy encompasses many ideas and has many meanings. Democracy is a way of life, a form of government, a way of governing, a type of nation, a state of mind, and a variety of processes. We can divide these many meanings into three broad categories: democracy as a system of interacting values, a system of interrelated political processes, and a system of interdependent political structures (see Figure 1-1).

Democracy as a System of Interacting Values

As we approach the twenty-first century, the democratic faith may be as near a universal faith as the world has. A belief in human dignity, freedom, liberty, individual rights, and other democratic values is widely shared in most corners of the world. The essence of democratic values is contained in the ideas of popular consent, respect for the individual, equality of opportunity, and personal liberty.

POPULAR CONSENT The animating principle of the American Revolution, the Declaration of Independence, and the resulting new nation was **popular consent**, the idea that a just government must derive its powers from the consent of the people it governs. A commitment to democracy thus entails a community's willingness to participate and make decisions in government. Intellectually these principles sound unobjectionable, but in practice they mean that certain individuals or groups may not get their way. A commitment to popular consent must involve a *willingness to lose* if most people vote the other way.

RESPECT FOR THE INDIVIDUAL Popular rule in a democracy flows from a belief that every individual has the potential for common sense, rationality, and a notion of fairness. Individuals, democrats insist, have important rights; collectively, those rights are the source of all legitimate governmental authority and power. These notions pervade all democratic thought. They are woven into the writings of Thomas Jefferson, especially in the Declaration of Independence: "All men . . . are endowed by their Creator with certain unalienable rights" (the Declaration of Independence appears in the Appendix). Constitutional democracies make the person—rich or poor, black or white, male or female—the *central* measure of value. The state, the union, and the corporation are measured in terms of their usefulness to individuals. Not all political systems, of course, put the individual first. Some promote **statism**, considering the state supreme. Democrats, however, believe that the state, or even the community, is *less important* than are the individuals who compose it.

EQUALITY OF OPPORTUNITY The importance of the individual is enhanced by the democratic value of *equality:* "All men are created equal and from that equal creation they derive rights inherent and unalienable, among which are the preservation of liberty and the pursuit of happiness." So reads Jefferson's first draft of the Declaration of Independence, and the words indicate the primacy of the concept. Alexis de Tocqueville, James Bryce, Harold Laski, and other international visitors who investigated American democracy have all been struck by the strength of egalitarian thought and practice in both our political and our social lives.

But what does equality mean? What kind of equality? Economic, political, legal, social, or some other kind of equality? Equality for whom? For blacks as well as whites? For women as well as men? For Native Americans, descendants of the Pilgrims, and recent immigrants? And what kind of equality? *Equality of opportunity* (almost all Americans say they want that), but also *equality of condition*? This last question is the toughest. Does equality of opportunity simply mean that everyone should have the *same place at the starting line*? Or does it mean an effort should be made to equalize most or all the factors that during the course of a person's life might determine how well he or she fares economically or socially?

President Herbert Hoover posed the issue this way: "We, through free and universal education, provide the training of the runners; we give to them an equal start; we provide in government the umpire of fairness in the race."[1] Franklin D. Roosevelt also sought to answer the question by proclaiming a "second Bill of Rights" that announced **Four Freedoms**—freedom of speech and expression, freedom of worship, freedom from want, and freedom from fear. Roosevelt's New Deal and its successor programs had tried to advance the egalitarian notions and basic security that he asserted were the rights of human beings everywhere. (We'll return to the question of equal rights in Chapter 5.)

PERSONAL LIBERTY Liberty has been the single most powerful value in American history. It was for "life, liberty, and the pursuit of happiness" that independence was declared; it was to "secure the Blessings of Liberty" that the Constitution was drawn up and adopted. Even our patriotic songs extol the "sweet land of liberty." *Liberty* or *freedom* (used interchangeably here) means that all individuals must have the opportunity to realize their own goals. The essence of liberty is *self-determination.* Liberty is not simply the absence of external restraint on a person *(freedom from)*; it is the individual's *freedom to act* positively to reach his or her goals. Moreover, both history and reason suggest that individual liberty is the key to social progress. The greater the people's freedom, the greater the chance of discovering better ways of life.

DEMOCRATIC VALUES IN CONFLICT   The basic values of democracy do not always coexist happily. Individualism may conflict with collective welfare or the public good. Freedom as *liberation* may become freedom as *alienation*. Self-determination may conflict with equal opportunity. The right of General Motors to run its automobile factories to maximize profit, as compared to the right of automobile workers in those factories to join unions or share in the running of the plants, illustrates this type of conflict in everyday life.

Liberty and equality interlock and stimulate each other at some points and oppose each other at others. Sometimes they do not relate at all. At the extreme, the pursuit of liberty might become license for unbridled selfishness or anarchy, while the pursuit of equality might mean a leveling to dull mediocrity and even the erosion of liberty. Much of our political combat revolves around how to strike a balance among democratic values—how to protect the Declaration of Independence's unalienable rights of life, liberty, and the pursuit of happiness while permitting government to "form," as the Constitution announces, "a more perfect Union, establish Justice, insure domestic Tranquility, provide for the common defence, promote the general Welfare, and secure the Blessings of Liberty to ourselves and our Posterity" (see the Preamble to the Constitution).

Over the years the American political system has clearly moved toward greater freedom and more democracy. A commitment to democracy is in many ways a twentieth-century idea. People throughout the world are more attracted to democracy today than ever before. Recent events in China, Germany, Poland, the Czech Republic, Slovakia, Russia, and South Africa are evidence that the dream of freedom and democratic government is universal.

Far more people dream about democracy than ever experience it, and many new democracies fail. To be successful, democratic government requires a political process as well as a governmental structure. In both areas, the American experiment is instructive.

Democracy as a System of Interrelated Political Processes

To become reality, democratic values must be incorporated into a *political process,* a set of arrangements for making decisions and managing the public's business. The essence of the democratic process is respect for the rules of fair play, which can be seen in the tradition of free and fair elections, majority rule, freedom of expression, and the right to assemble and protest.

FREE AND FAIR ELECTIONS   Democratic government is based on free and fair elections held at intervals frequent enough to make them relevant to policy choices. Elections are one of the most important devices for keeping officials and representatives accountable.

We previously defined *representative democracy* to mean a system of government in which those who have the authority to make decisions with the force of law acquire and retain this authority either directly or indirectly as the result of winning free elections in which the great majority of adult citizens are allowed to participate. Crucial to modern-day definitions of democracy is the idea that *opposition political parties* can exist, can run candidates in elections, and can at least have a chance to replace those who are currently holding public office. Thus political competition and choice are crucial to the existence of democracy.

While all citizens should have equal voting power, free and fair elections do not imply everyone must or will have equal political influence. Some people, because of wealth, talent, or position, have more influence than others. How much extra influence key figures should be allowed to exercise in a democracy is an ongoing question for democrats. But at the polls a president or a pick-and-shovel laborer, a newspaper publisher or a lettuce picker, casts only one vote.

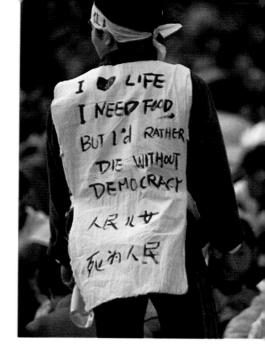

The ideal of liberty still inspires people today, as it did in the Tiananmen Square demonstrations in China that were repressed so brutally.

The Declaration of Independence committee set down on paper the ideas and goals that would later be incorporated in the Constitution. Shown here are (*left to right*) Thomas Jefferson, Roger Sherman, Benjamin Franklin, Robert Livingston, and John Adams.

MAJORITY (PLURALITY) RULE The basic rule of a democracy is that those with the most votes take charge of the government, at least until the next election, when a new majority may be voted in to take charge. In practice, *majority rule* is often *plurality rule,* in which the largest bloc takes charge, even though it may not constitute a true majority, with more than half the votes. While in charge, those elected have no right to curtail the attempts of political minorities to use all peaceful means to become a majority. So even as the winners take power, the losers can go to work to try to get it back at the next election.

The American system of constitutional democracy allows people a say in who will decide important issues. Through the system of representation, people can participate indirectly in the great debates and decisions about laws and public policies.[2]

Should the will of the majority prevail in all cases? Americans answer this question in a variety of ways. Some insist majority views should be enacted into laws and regulations. But perhaps the more widely held view is that an effective representative democracy involves far more than simply ascertaining and applying the statistical will of the people. It is a more complicated and often untidy process by which the people and their agents inform themselves, debate, compromise, and arrive at a decision, and do so only after thoughtful deliberation.

The Constitution reflects the framers' fear of tyranny by majorities, especially momentary majorities that spring from temporary passion. The framers wanted to guard society against any one part acting unjustly toward any other part. To accomplish this end, they insulated certain rights and institutions from popular choice. The effective representation of the people, the framers insisted, could not and should not be an unthinking mouthpiece for parochial interests or for each shifting breeze of opinion.

FREEDOM OF EXPRESSION Free and fair elections depend on access to information relevant to voting choices. Voters must have access to facts, competing ideas, and the views of candidates. Free and fair elections require a climate in which competing, nongovernment-owned newspapers, radio stations, and television stations can flourish. Expression by such media should be protected from government censorship.

Here again, the extent to which different ideas actually receive equal attention is determined by the nature of the media, an incumbent's special access to television and the press, and costs beyond the reach of lower-income people to make their ideas known. Still, the principle and practice of free competition of ideas during elections are essential.

THE RIGHT TO ASSEMBLE AND PROTEST Citizens must be free to organize for political purposes. Obviously, individuals can be more effective if they join with others in a party, a pressure group, a protest movement, or a demonstration. The right to oppose the government, to form opposition parties, and to have a chance of defeating incumbents is not only vital; it is a defining characteristic of a democracy.

Democracy as a System of Interdependent Political Structures

Democracy is, of course, more than values and processes. It also entails a system of political structures that safeguard these values and processes. In this country, the Constitution and Bill of Rights create an ingenious structure—one that both grants and checks government power. This constitutional structure is reinforced by a political system of parties, interest groups, media, and other institutions that mediate between the electorate and those who govern and thus help to maintain democratic stability.

This structure is remarkable for four elements: One is *federalism,* the division of powers between the national and state governments. Another is the *separation of powers* among the legislative, executive, and judicial branches. Liberty is further safeguarded by a system of *checks and balances,* which gives each branch its own powers as well as the "necessary constitutional means and personal motives to resist the encroachments of the others."[3] This combination of separation of powers and checks and balances was the supreme creation of the framers in 1787. The fourth element, the *Bill of Rights,* is also important, for it is a *written, explicit* guarantee of individual liberties and due process before the law. The chapters that follow will explain both the principles and the architectural features of democracy American-style in more detail.

MAKING DEMOCRATIC PRINCIPLES A REALITY

New democracies often fail. It is one thing to espouse democratic values, another to put them into practice. Some people, for instance, believe in democracy until they lose power in an election. Or the citizens grow weary of the political wrangling that comes with democracy and long for a strong leader who can solve problems. Such a leader, sometimes referred to as the "man on the white horse," is usually a military leader of heroic proportions. Leaders like Napoleon or Adolf Hitler promise to make the country work more smoothly, often by disbanding democratic institutions. Citizens may turn to such leaders when they face economic difficulties or are under threat from a foreign power. Sectional differences can also pull apart the fabric of democracy. Parts of a country that have a distinctive racial, religious, or ethnic composition often distrust the national majority and seek guarantees or special concessions—as French-speaking residents of Quebec have in Canada.

Vladimir Zhironovsky, an antisemitic demagogue who offers Russians simple solutions to the economic and political chaos they are facing, is true to the style of "the man on the white horse."

Because democracies face many pressures, comparatively few have lasted long. More than half the world's constitutions have been written in the past three decades. One can survey the entire continent of Asia and find no democracy that predates World War II, when a democratic constitution was imposed on Japan. In Africa, the oldest democracy is Botswana, which has had free elections and a multiparty system since 1966 (see Figure 1-2).

Conditions Conducive to Constitutional Democracy

How do we explain the relatively low number of long-lived, strong democracies? Although it is hard to specify the precise conditions that are essential for the establishment and maintenance of a democracy, here are a few things we have learned.

EDUCATIONAL CONDITIONS Clearly, the exercise of voting privileges takes some level of education on the part of the citizenry. But a word of caution: A high level of education does not "cause" or "guarantee" democratic government, as the example of Nazi Germany readily illustrates, and there are some democracies, such as India, where large numbers of people are still illiterate. Still, voting makes little sense unless a considerable number of the voters can read and write and express their interests and opinions. The poorly educated and illiterate get left out in a democracy.

ECONOMIC CONDITIONS A relatively prosperous nation, with an equitable distribution of wealth, provides the best context for democracy. Starving people, by contrast, are more interested in food than in voting. Where economic power is concentrated, political power is likely to be concentrated. Thus well-to-do nations have a greater chance of sustaining democratic governments than do those with widespread poverty. The reality is that extremes of wealth and poverty undermine the possibilities for a healthy constitutional democracy.

Some measure of private ownership of property and a relatively favorable role for the market economy are also related to the creation and maintenance of democratic institutions. Democracies can range from heavily regulated economies with public ownership of many enterprises, such as Sweden, to those in which there is little government regulation of the marketplace. But there are no examples of a democracy with a command economy and little private ownership of property, although there are many examples of nations with a market economy and no democracy. There are no truly democratic communist states, nor have there ever been any.

SOCIAL CONDITIONS Economic development generally makes democracy possible, yet political leadership and proper social conditions are necessary to make it real. In a society fragmented into warring groups that differ fiercely on fundamental issues, government by discussion and compromise is difficult. When ideologically separated groups consider the issues at stake to be vital, they may prefer to fight rather than accept the verdict of the ballot box. But in a society that consists of many overlapping associations and groupings, individuals are not as likely to identify completely with a single group and give their allegiance to it. For example, Joe Brown is a Baptist, an African American, a southerner, a Democrat, an electrician, and a member of the National Rifle Association, and he makes $50,000 a year. On some issues Joe thinks as a Baptist, on others as a southerner, and on still others as an African American. Sue Jones is a Catholic, a Republican, an auto dealer, a member of the National Organization for Women, and from a Polish background, and she makes $100,000 a year. Sometimes she acts as a Republican, sometimes as an American of Polish descent, and sometimes as a member of NOW. Jones and Brown differ on some issues yet agree on others. In general, the differences between them are not likely to be greater than their common interest in maintaining a democracy.[4]

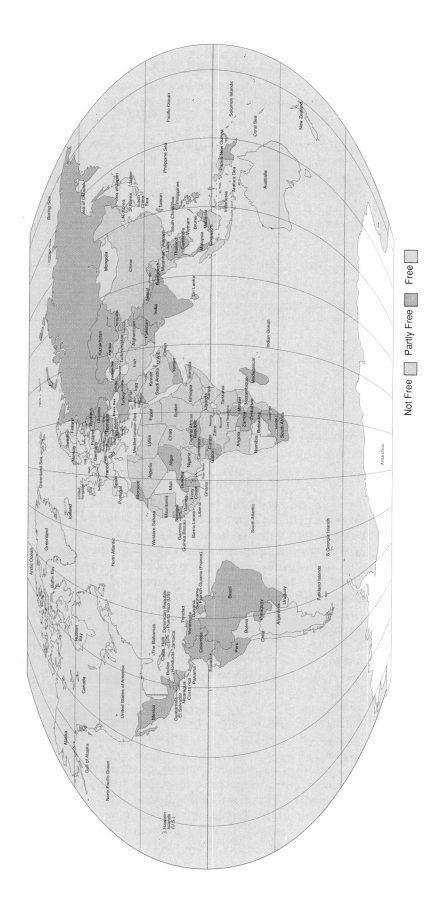

FIGURE 1-2　The Map of Freedom

Not Free ☐　Partly Free ☐　Free ☐

SOURCE: *Freedom Review*, January–February 1994, pp. 41–42. © 1994 by Freedom House.

What are the basic goals of a constitutional democracy?

Give some thought to what goals you consider most important. Then prepare a short list of the essential goals and means necessary to attain a constitutional democracy.

Democracy is also more likely to survive where other social institutions reinforce democratic habits. The family, the church, and the school are all institutions regulating important areas of life affected by and affecting government. If these institutions support and reinforce the idea of government by democratic procedures, then the habits of discussion, compromise, and respect for differences are strengthened by constant use.

IDEOLOGICAL CONDITIONS   **Ideology** refers to our basic beliefs about power and government and political practices—beliefs that arise out of the educational, economic, and social conditions we experience. Out of these educational, economic, and social conditions must also develop a general acceptance of the ideals of democracy, the willingness of a substantial portion of the people to agree to proceed democratically. This quality is sometimes called the *democratic consensus*. A well-known student of democratic ideas writes:

> Prior to politics, beneath it, enveloping it, restricting it, conditioning it, is the underlying consensus on policy that usually exists in a society among a predominant portion of the politically active members. Without such a consensus, no democratic system would long survive the endless irritations and frustrations of elections and party competition.[5]

In sum, a society that offers the best chances for democratic success is one with an educated and fairly prosperous electorate, without extreme concentrations of wealth, relatively free from intense class, ethnic, religious, or sectional antagonisms, with many private loyalties and associations, with other social institutions that buttress the principles and practices of democracy, all tending to produce a democratic consensus. Civilian control over the military is also essential. But no one of these conditions—or even all of them—guarantees democracy. There is no foolproof double-your-money-back guarantee for freedom.

The American Example

To most Americans the workings of democratic government are a dull matter. We take democracy for granted. We somehow consider it inevitable. We take pride in our ability to make it work, yet we have essentially inherited a going system. Its establishment was the work of others, eight or more generations ago. The challenge for us is not just to keep it going but to improve it. But first we must understand it, and this requires careful consideration of our democratic and constitutional roots.

The United States provides an important contrast to dictatorship, tyranny, and anarchy. It also contradicts the general tendency of democracies to fail. There were many reasons one might have expected our system to fail. The thirteen states (formerly colonies) were independent and could have gone their separate ways. Critical sectional differences based on economics and slavery were an obvious problem. Religious, ethnic, and racial diversity, which poses so many challenges to governments around the world today, existed in substantial degree in the United States during its formative years. The driving ambition of the "man on the white horse" to solve the country's problems is a constant in any society, and our country has had its share.

Given these potential problems, how has democracy survived? How did this nation establish democratic principles for its government? How did it limit the potential abuses of democracy? These questions are of importance not only to Americans but to all who value freedom and democracy everywhere. To begin to answer them, we now turn to our country's formative period of nation building.

The Pilgrims signing the Mayflower Compact aboard their ship on November 11, 1620.

OUR CONSTITUTIONAL ROOTS

The framers of the U.S. Constitution had experience to guide them. For almost two centuries, Europeans had been sailing to the New World in search of liberty—especially religious liberty—as well as land and work. While still aboard the *Mayflower*, the Pilgrims drew up a compact to protect their religious freedom and to make possible "just and equale laws." In the American colonies editors found they could speak out freely in their newspapers, dissenters could distribute leaflets, and agitators could protest in taverns or in the streets. But the picture of freedom in the colonies was a mixed one. The Puritans in Massachusetts soon established a **theocracy**, a system of government in which religious leaders claimed divine guidance. Not all religious sects were granted equal religious liberty. Dissenters were occasionally chased out of town, and some printers had their shops closed or were even physically attacked.

In short, the colonists in those early centuries were struggling with the basic questions of the balance of unity and diversity, stability and dissent, order and liberty. Puritan theocrats continued to worry "about what would maintain order in a society lacking an established church, an attachment to place, and the uncontested leadership of men of merit."[6] Nine of the thirteen colonies eventually set up a state church. Throughout the 1700s Puritans in Massachusetts barred certain men from voting on the basis of church membership. To the Anglican establishment in Virginia, campaigns for toleration were in themselves subversive. Women could not vote at all.

Still, most colonial Americans enjoyed a wide array of liberties. When John Peter Zenger, a New York newspaper printer, was jailed in 1734 by royal authority on the charge of seditious libel, Zenger's attorney appealed to a jury and won a "not guilty" verdict. The case helped establish freedom of the press. Increasingly, the question arose as to how the people could secure their liberties, rather than leave them in the hands of mobs, sheriffs, or religious establishments. The answer was to bind liberties tightly into colonial laws and constitutions. The Maryland Act for the Liberties of the People legislated that "all the inhabitants of this

Thinking it Through

Goals

Not everyone agrees with the goals we list here, and you may weigh them differently, according to your own values. How would you rank these goals? Are some more essential than others?

- Government by popular consent
- Liberty—personal, religious, economic
- Protection for property rights
- Justice—fairness and equality before the law
- Equality of economic opportunities
- Peace and stability

Means and Protections

- Constitutional democracy backed by a written constitution enumerating government powers and their limits
- Federalism
- Separation of powers
- Checks and balances
- Free and frequent elections
- Freedom of speech and press
- Competitive political parties
- Majority rule
- Government protection of minority rights, tolerance for diversity and dissent
- Right to petition government and courts for redress of grievances
- Rule of law, granting citizens due process and making government officials subject to impeachment and criminal prosecution
- Civilian control over the military

Province being Christians (slaves excepted) should have such rights, liberties, immunities, privileges, and free customs" as any natural-born subject of England. The Massachusetts Body of Liberties of 1641, which served as a model for later New York and Pennsylvania charters, guaranteed freedom of speech and petition at public meetings, right of counsel, trial by jury, "the same justice and law" for every person.[7]

The Rise of Revolutionary Fervor

As feeling against the British mounted during the 1770s and revolutionary fervor rose, Americans were determined to fight against the British for their rights and their liberties. A year after the fighting broke out in Lexington, Concord, and other areas, the Declaration of Independence proclaimed in ringing tones that all men are created equal, endowed by their Creator with certain unalienable rights; that among those are "life, liberty, and the pursuit of happiness"; that to secure those rights governments are instituted among men; and that whenever a government becomes destructive of those ends, it is the right of the people to alter or abolish it. (Read the Declaration of Independence in the Appendix.)

We all know these great ideals so well we almost take them for granted; yet the revolutionary leaders did not. They were deadly serious about these rights and willing to fight and pledge their lives, fortunes, and sacred honor for them. They determinedly set about guaranteeing liberty in the constitutions the states adopted as they broke away from the Crown. All the bills of rights in the new state constitutions guaranteed free speech, freedom of religion, and the natural rights to life, liberty, and property. All the declarations spelled out rights of persons accused of crime, such as knowing the nature of the accusation, being confronted by their accusers, and receiving a timely and public trial by jury.[8] Moreover, these guarantees were in *written* form, a sharp contrast to the unwritten British constitution.

American colonists, resentful of crushing taxes and the denial of their basic liberties by the British, flung boxes of tea into Boston harbor in what we now know as "The Boston Tea Party."

Toward Unity and Order

The quest for liberty could go only so far. As the war against the British widened, the need arose for a stronger central government that could pull together the colonies and conduct a revolutionary war. For a time the Continental Congress, which had led the way toward revolution, tried to direct hostilities against the British, but it took a man of George Washington's iron resolve to unify and direct the war effort. Sensing the need for more unity, Congress established a new national government under a written document called the **Articles of Confederation**. At first hardly worthy of the term "government," the Articles were not approved by all the state legislatures until 1781, after Washington's troops had been fighting for six years.

This new Confederation was a move toward a stronger central government, but a limited and inadequate one. Having fought a war against a strong central government in London, Americans were understandably reluctant to create another one. The Articles established more of a fragile league of friendship than a national government. From 1777 to 1788, Americans made progress under this Confederation, but with the end of the war in 1783, the sense of urgency that had produced unity began to fade. Within the states, conflict between creditors and debtors grew intense. And foreign threats by no means disappeared with the defeat of the British. Territories ruled by England and Spain surrounded the new nation, which—internally divided and lacking a strong central government—made a tempting prize.

As pressures on the Confederation mounted, many leaders became convinced it would not be enough merely to revise the Articles of Confederation. To create a union strong enough to deal with internal diversity and factionalism, as well as resist external threats, a stronger central government, with adequate powers, was needed. Yet while many Americans recognized the need to give Congress authority to regulate commerce and collect limited taxes, they were still suspicious of strong central government.

In August 1786, under the leadership of Alexander Hamilton, those who favored a truly national government took advantage of the **Annapolis Convention**, a meeting in Annapolis, Maryland on problems of trade and navigation, attended by delegates from five states, to issue a call for a convention that would have full authority to consider basic amendments to the Articles of Confederation. The delegates in Annapolis asked the legislatures of their states to appoint commissioners to meet in Philadelphia on the second Monday of May 1787, "to devise such further provisions as shall appear to them necessary to render the Constitution of the Federal Government adequate to the exigencies of the Union." The convention they called for became the **Constitutional Convention**.

For a short time all was quiet. Then, late in 1786, messengers rode into George Washington's plantation at Mount Vernon with the kind of news he and other leaders had dreaded. Farmers in western Massachusetts, crushed by debts and taxes, were rebelling against foreclosures, forcing judges out of their courtrooms, and freeing debtors from jails. Washington was appalled. Ten years before, he had been leading Americans in a patriotic war against the British, and now Americans were fighting Americans!

"What, gracious God, is man?" Washington exclaimed. Clearly, liberty—as license—had been allowed to go too far. Indeed, such disorder was a threat to liberty itself. If government could not check such disorders, Washington wrote to his friend James Madison, "what security has a man for life, liberty or property?" Without a stronger central government, "thirteen Sovereignties pulling against each other, and all tugging at the federal head will soon bring ruin on the whole."

Weaknesses of the Articles of Confederation

1. Congress could not levy taxes to support the army and navy or to carry out its other activities. It could only request funds from the states.
2. Congress could not regulate trade between the states or with other nations. States taxed each others' goods and even negotiated their own trade agreements with other nations.
3. Congress could not forbid the states from issuing their own currencies, further complicating interstate trade and travel.
4. Because there was no executive branch, Congress had to handle all administrative duties.
5. The lack of a judiciary system meant that the national government had to rely on state courts to enforce national laws and settle disputes between the states. In practice state courts could overturn national laws.

Under the leadership of Daniel Shays, a group of farmers forcibly restrained the Massachusetts courts from foreclosing their mortgages. The uprising was known as Shays's Rebellion.

Not all Americans reacted as Washington did to what became known as **Shays's Rebellion**, for its leader Daniel Shays. When Abigail Adams, the politically knowledgeable wife of John Adams, sent news of the rebellion to Thomas Jefferson, the Virginian replied, "I like a little rebellion now and then," noting also that the "tree of liberty must be refreshed from time to time" with "the natural manure" of the blood of patriots and tyrants.

Shays's Rebellion petered out after the farmers attacked an arsenal and were cut down by cannon fire. Yet this "little rebellion" sent a stab of fear into the established leadership. It also acted as a catalyst. The message now was plain: Action must be taken to strengthen the machinery of government. Spurred on by Shays's Rebellion, seven states appointed commissioners to attend a convention in Philadelphia to strengthen the Articles of Confederation. Congress, rightly suspicious, finally issued a cautiously worded call to the states to appoint delegates for the "sole and express purpose of revising the Articles of Confederation." The cautious legislators specified that no recommendation would be effective unless approved by Congress and confirmed by all the state legislatures, as provided by the Articles.

At this point in the long American search for the balance between liberty and order, between diversity and unity, the impulse was decidedly toward order and unity.

THE CONSTITUTIONAL CONVENTION, 1787

The delegates who assembled in Philadelphia that May were presented with a condition, not a theory. They had to establish a national government powerful enough to prevent the young nation from dissolving. What these men did continues to have a major impact on how we are governed. It also provides an outstanding lesson in political science for the world.

The Delegates

Seventy-four delegates were appointed by the various states, but only 55 arrived in Philadelphia. Of these, approximately 40 took a real part in the work of the convention. It was a distinguished gathering. Many of the most important men of the nation were there: successful merchants, planters, bankers, lawyers, and former and present governors and congressional representatives (39 of the delegates had served in Congress). Most had read the classics of political thought. Most had participated vigorously in the practical task of constructing local and state governments. Many had also worked hard to create and direct the national Confederation of the states.

The convention was as representative as most political gatherings at the time: the participants were all white male landowners. These well-read, well-fed, well-bred, and often well-wed delegates were mainly state or national leaders, for in the 1780s ordinary people were not likely to participate in politics. Even today farm laborers, factory workers, and truck drivers are seldom found in Congress, although a haberdasher, a self-styled peanut farmer, and a movie actor have made their way to the White House. While most of those in attendance eventually supported the Constitution in the ratification debates, only eight of the 56 signers of the Declaration of Independence were present at the Constitutional Convention.

Several of the participants at the convention stand out as the prime movers. Alexander Hamilton had been the engineer of the Annapolis Convention, and as early as 1778 he had been urging that the national government be made stronger. Hamilton had come to the United States from the West Indies and while still a college student had won national attention for his brilliant pamphlets in defense of the Revolutionary cause. During the war he served as General Washington's aide, and his experiences confirmed his distaste for a Congress so weak it could not even supply the Revolution's troops with enough food or arms.

From Virginia came two of the leading delegates: George Washington and James Madison. Although active in the movement to revise the Articles of Confederation, Washington had been reluctant to attend the convention. He accepted only when persuaded that his prestige was needed for its success. He was selected unanimously to preside over the meetings. According to the records, he spoke only twice during the deliberations, yet his influence was felt in the informal gatherings as well as during the sessions. The assumption that Washington would become the first president under the new constitution inspired confidence in it. James Madison was only 36 years old at the time of the convention, yet he was one of the most learned members present. He had helped frame Virginia's first constitution and had served both in the Virginia Assembly and in the Confederation's Congress. Madison was also a leader of those who favored the establishment of a stronger national government.

The proceedings of the convention were kept secret. To encourage everyone to speak freely, delegates were forbidden to discuss the debates with outsiders. It was feared that if a delegate publicly took a firm stand on an issue, it would be harder for him to change his mind after debate and discussion. The delegates also knew that if word of the inevitable disagreements got out, it would provide ammunition for the many enemies of the convention. There were critics of this secrecy rule, but without it, agreement might not have been possible.

Consensus

The Constitutional Convention is usually discussed in terms of its three famous compromises: the compromise between large and small states over representation in Congress, the compromise between North and South over the regulation and taxation of foreign commerce, and the compromise between North and South over the counting of slaves for taxation and representation. There were many other important compromises, however, and on many significant issues most of the delegates were in agreement.

Although a few delegates might have personally favored a limited monarchy, all supported a republican form of government. This was the only form seriously considered and the only form acceptable to the nation. Equally important, all the delegates were constitutionalists who opposed arbitrary and unrestrained government.

The common philosophy accepted by most of the delegates was that of *balanced government.* They wanted to construct a national government in which no single interest would dominate. Because most of the delegates represented citizens who were alarmed by the tendencies of desperate farmers to interfere with or abuse the property rights of others, they were primarily concerned with balancing the government in the direction of protection for property and business. Most of them respected the remark of Elbridge Gerry, delegate from Massachusetts: "The evils we experience flow from the excess of democracy. The people do not want virtue, but are dupes of pretended patriots." Likewise, there was substantial agreement with Gouverneur Morris's statement that property was the "principal object of government."

Benjamin Franklin, the 81-year-old delegate from Pennsylvania, favored extending the right to vote to all white males, but most of the delegates believed that owners of land were the best guardians of liberty. James Madison voiced the fear that those without property, if given the right to vote, would either combine to deprive property owners of their rights or would become the "tools of demagogues." The delegates agreed in principle on restricted franchise, or voting rights, but differed

The Framers: Hamilton and Madison

In the Constitution the framers offered perhaps the most brilliant example of collective intellectual genius—of combining both theory and practice—in the history of the Western world. How could a country 70 times smaller in population than it is today produce several dozen men of genius in Philadelphia, and probably another hundred or so equally talented political thinkers who did not attend? The lives of two prominent delegates, Alexander Hamilton and James Madison, help explain the origins of this collective genius.

Like most of the other framers, Hamilton and Madison were superbly educated. Both had extensive private tutoring—a one-to-one teacher-student ratio. Like scores of other thinkers of the day, both combined extensive practical experience with their schooling. Both were active in their political and religious groups; both took part in political contests and electoral struggles; both helped build political coalitions.

Both men were "moral philosophers" as well as political thinkers. They had strong views on the supreme value—liberty—as well as on current issues. Instead of simply sermonizing about liberty, they *analyzed* it; they debated what *kind* of liberty, how to *protect* it, how to *expand* it. They also thought hard about other values enshrined in the Declaration of Independence, such as the virtues and dangers of equality and what kind of "happiness" Americans should pursue.

James Madison

Alexander Hamilton

On Reading The Constitution

More than two hundred years after its ratification, our Constitution remains the operating charter of our republic. It is neither self-explanatory nor a comprehensive description of our constitutional rules. Still, it remains the starting point. Yet many Americans who swear by the Constitution have never read it seriously. Copies can be found in the back of most American government and American history textbooks.

Justice Hugo Black, who served on the Supreme Court for 34 years, kept a copy of the Constitution with him at all times. He read it often. Reading the Constitution as amended would be a good way for you to begin (and then reread again to end) your study of the government of the United States. Thus, we have included a copy of it at this point in the book. Please read it carefully.

over the kind and amount of property one must own in order to vote. Because the states were in the process of relaxing qualifications for the vote, the framers recognized they would jeopardize approval of the constitution if they made the right to vote in federal elections more restricted than the franchises within the states. As a result, each state was left to determine the qualifications for electing members of the House of Representatives, the only branch of the national government in which the electorate was given a direct voice.

Within five days of its opening, the convention—with only Connecticut dissenting—voted that "a national government ought to be established consisting of a supreme legislative, executive, and judiciary." This decision to establish a national government that rested on and exercised power over individuals profoundly altered the nature of the central government and changed it from a loose league of states to a national government.

Few dissented from proposals to give the new Congress all the powers of the old Congress plus all other powers necessary to ensure that the harmony of the United States would not be disrupted by the exercise of state legislation. The framers agreed that a strong executive, which had been lacking under the Articles, was necessary to provide energy and direction. An independent judiciary was also accepted without much debate. Other issues, however, sparked considerable conflict.

Conflict and Compromise

There were serious differences among the various groups, especially between the delegates of the large and small states. One of the most contentious issues was the distribution of the land extending to the Mississippi, land that had been secured through the Revolution. Several large states asserted claims to these western lands, but the small states generally refused to go along. The large states also favored a strong national government (which they expected they could dominate), while the delegates from the small states were anxious to avoid being dominated.

This tension surfaced in the first discussions of representation in Congress. Franklin favored a single-house national legislature, but most states had had two-chamber legislatures since colonial times, and the delegates were used to the system. **Bicameralism**—the principle of the two-house legislature—also implemented the delegates' belief in the need for balanced government. The smaller chamber would represent the aristocracy and offset the larger, more democratic House of Representatives.

THE VIRGINIA PLAN   The Virginia delegation took the initiative. It had met during the delay before the convention and, as soon as the convention was organized, presented 15 resolutions. These resolutions, the **Virginia Plan**, called for a strong central government. The legislature was to be composed of two chambers. The members of the more representative chamber were to be elected by the voters; those of the smaller and more aristocratic chamber were to be chosen by the larger chamber from nominees submitted by the state legislatures. Representation in both houses was to be on the basis of either wealth or numbers, which gave the more populous and wealthy states—Massachusetts, Pennsylvania, and Virginia—a majority in the national legislature.

The Congress thus created was to be given all the legislative power of its predecessor under the Articles of Confederation, as well as the right "to legislate in all cases in which the separate States are incompetent." Further, it was to have the authority to veto state legislation in conflict with the proposed constitution. The Virginia Plan also called for a national executive to be chosen by the legislature and a national judiciary with rather extensive jurisdiction. The national Supreme Court, along with the executive, was to have a qualified veto over acts of Congress.

THE NEW JERSEY PLAN   For the first few weeks the Virginia Plan dominated the discussion. But by June 15 additional delegates from the small states had arrived,

The Constitution of the United States of America

THE PREAMBLE

We the People of the United States, in Order to form a more perfect Union, establish Justice, insure domestic Tranquility, provide for the common defence, promote the general Welfare, and secure the Blessings of Liberty to ourselves and our Posterity, do ordain and establish this Constitution for the United States of America.

ARTICLE I—THE LEGISLATIVE ARTICLE

Legislative Power

Section 1   All legislative Powers herein granted shall be vested in a Congress of the United States, which shall consist of a Senate and House of Representatives.

House of Representatives: Composition; Qualifications; Apportionment; Impeachment Power

Section 2   The House of Representatives shall be composed of Members chosen every second Year by the People of the several States, and the Electors in each State shall have the Qualifications requisite for Electors of the most numerous Branch of the State Legislature.

No Person shall be a Representative who shall not have attained to the Age of twenty five Years, and been seven Years a Citizen of the United States, and who shall not, when elected, be an Inhabitant of that State in which he shall be chosen.

Representatives and direct Taxes[1] shall be apportioned among the several States which may be included within this Union, according to their respective Numbers, *which shall be determined by adding to the whole Number of free Persons, including those bound to Service for a Term of Years, and excluding Indians not taxed, three fifths of all other Persons.*[2] The actual Enumeration shall be made within three Years after the first Meeting of the Congress of the United States, and within every subsequent Term of ten Years, in such Manner as they shall by Law direct. The Number of Representatives shall not exceed one for every thirty Thousand, but each State shall have at least one Representative; and until each enumeration shall be made, the State of New Hampshire shall be entitled to chuse three, Massachusetts eight, Rhode-Island and Providence Plantations one, Connecticut five, New-York six, New Jersey four, Pennsylvania eight, Delaware one, Maryland six, Virginia ten, North Carolina five, South Carolina five, and Georgia three.

When vacancies happen in the Representation from any State, the Executive Authority thereof shall issue Writs of Election to fill such Vacancies.

The House of Representatives shall chuse their Speaker and other Officers; and shall have the sole Power of Impeachment.

Senate Composition: Qualifications, Impeachment Trials

Section 3   The Senate of the United States shall be composed of two Senators from each State, *chosen by the Legislature thereof,*[3] for six Years; and each Senator shall have one Vote.

Immediately after they shall be assembled in Consequence of the first Election, they shall be divided as equally as may be into three Classes. The Seats of the Senators of the first Class shall be vacated at the Expiration of the second Year, of the second Class at the Expiration of the fourth Year, and of the third Class at the Expiration of the sixth Year, so that one third may be chosen every second Year; *and if Vacancies happen by Resignation, or otherwise, during the Recess of the Legislature of any State, the Executive thereof may make temporary Appointments until the next Meeting of the Legislature, which shall then fill such Vacancies.*[4]

No person shall be a Senator who shall not have attained to the Age of thirty Years, and been nine Years a Citizen of the United States, and who shall not, when elected, be an inhabitant of that State for which he shall be chosen.

The Vice President of the United States shall be President of the Senate, but shall have no Vote, unless they be equally divided.

The Senate shall chuse their other Officers, and also a President pro tempore, in the Absence of the Vice President, or when he shall exercise the Office of President of the United States.

The Senate shall have the sole Power to try all Impeachments. When sitting for that Purpose, they shall be on Oath or Affirmation. When the President of the United States is tried, the Chief Justice shall preside: And no Person shall be convicted without the Concurrence of two thirds of the Members present.

Judgment in Cases of Impeachment shall not extend further than to removal from Office, and disqualification to hold and enjoy any Office of honor, Trust or Profit under the United States; but the Party convicted shall nevertheless be liable and

[1]Modified by the 16th Amendment
[2]"Other Persons" refers to black slaves. Replaced by Section 2, 14th Amendment

[3]Repealed by the 17th Amendment
[4]Modified by the 17th Amendment

subject to Indictment, Trial, Judgment and Punishment, according to law.

Congressional Elections: Times, Places, Manner

Section 4   The Times, Places and Manner of holding Elections for Senators and Representatives, shall be prescribed in each State by the Legislature thereof; but the Congress may at any time by Law make or alter such Regulations, except as to the Places of chusing Senators.

The Congress shall assemble at least once in every Year, *and such Meeting shall be on the first Monday in December, unless they shall by Law appoint a different Day.*[5]

Powers and Duties of the Houses

Section 5   Each House shall be the Judge of the Elections, Returns and Qualifications of its own Members, and a Majority of each shall constitute a Quorum to do Business; but a smaller Number may adjourn from day to day, and may be authorized to compel the Attendance of absent Members, in such Manner, and under the Penalties as each House may provide.

Each House may determine the Rules of its Proceedings, punish its Members for disorderly Behaviour, and, with the Concurrence of two thirds, expel a Member.

Each House shall keep a Journal of its Proceedings, and from time to time publish the same, excepting such Parts as may in their Judgment require Secrecy; and the yeas and Nays of the Members of either House on any question shall, at the Desire of one fifth of those Present, be entered on the Journal.

Neither House, during the Session of Congress, shall, without the Consent of the other, adjourn for more than three days, nor to any other place than that in which the two Houses shall be sitting.

Rights of Members

Section 6   The Senators and Representatives shall receive a Compensation for their Services, to be ascertained by Law, and paid out of the Treasury of the United States. They shall in all Cases, except Treason, Felony and Breach of the Peace, be privileged from Arrest during their Attendance at the Session of their respective Houses, and in going to and returning from the same; and for any Speech or Debate in either House, they shall not be questioned in any other Place.

No Senator or Representative, shall, during the time for which he was elected, be appointed to any civil Office under the authority of the United States, which shall have been created, or the Emoluments whereof shall have been encreased during such time; and no Person holding any Office under the United States, shall be a Member of either House during his Continuance in Office.

Legislative Powers: Bills and Resolutions

Section 7   All Bills for raising Revenue shall originate in the House of Representatives; but the Senate may propose or concur with Amendments as on other Bills.

Every Bill which shall have passed the House of Representatives and the Senate, shall, before it become a Law, be presented to the President of the United States; if he approve he shall sign it, but if not he shall return it, with his Objections to that House in which it shall have originated, who shall enter the Objections at large on their Journal, and proceed to reconsider

[5]Changed by the 20th Amendment

it. If after such Reconsideration two thirds of that House shall agree to pass the Bill, it shall be sent, together with the Objections, to the other House, by which it shall likewise be reconsidered, and if approved by two thirds of that House, it shall become a Law. But in all such Cases the Votes of both Houses shall be determined by yeas and Nays, and the Names of the Persons voting for and against the Bill shall be entered on the Journal of each House respectively. If any Bill shall not be returned by the President within ten Days (Sundays excepted) after it shall have been presented to him, the Same shall be a Law, in like Manner as if he had signed it, unless the Congress by their Adjournment prevent its Return, in which Case it shall not be a Law.

Every Order, Resolution, or Vote to which the Concurrence of the Senate and House of Representatives may be necessary (except on a question of Adjournment) shall be presented to the President of the United States; and before the Same shall take Effect, shall be approved by him, or being disapproved by him, shall be repassed by two thirds of the Senate and House of Representatives, according to the Rules and Limitations prescribed in the Case of a Bill.

Powers of Congress

Section 8   The Congress shall have Power To lay and collect Taxes, Duties, Imposts and Excises, to pay the Debts and provide for the common Defence and general Welfare of the United States; but all Duties, Imposts and Excises shall be uniform throughout the United States;

To borrow Money on the Credit of the United States;

To regulate Commerce with foreign Nations, and among the several States, and with the Indian Tribes;

To establish an uniform Rule of Naturalization, and uniform Laws on the subject of Bankruptcies throughout the United States;

To coin Money, regulate the Value thereof, and of foreign Coin, and fix the Standard of Weights and Measures;

To provide for the Punishment of counterfeiting the Securities and current Coin of the United States;

To establish Post Offices and post Roads;

To promote the Progress of Science and useful Arts, by securing for limited Times to Authors and Inventors the exclusive Right to their respective Writings and Discoveries,

To constitute Tribunals inferior to the supreme Court,

To define and punish Piracies and Felonies committed on the high Seas, and Offences against the Law of Nations;

To declare War, grant Letters of Marque and Reprisal, and make Rules concerning Captures on Land and Water;

To raise and support Armies, but no Appropriation of Money to that Use shall be for a longer Term than two Years;

To provide and maintain a Navy;

To make Rules for the Government and Regulation of the land and naval Forces;

To provide for calling for the Militia to execute the Laws of the Union, suppress Insurrections and repel Invasions;

To provide for organizing, arming, and disciplining, the Militia, and for governing such Part of them as may be employed in the Service of the United States, reserving to the States respectively, the Appointment of the Officers, and the Authority of training the Militia according to the discipline prescribed by Congress;

To exercise exclusive Legislation in all Cases whatsoever, over such District (not exceeding ten Miles square) as may, by

Cession of particular States, and the Acceptance of Congress, become the Seat of the Government of the United States, and to exercise like Authority over all Places purchased by the Consent of the Legislature of the State in which the Same shall be, for the Erection of Forts, Magazines, Arsenals, dock-Yards, and other needful Buildings;—And

To make all Laws which shall be necessary and proper for carrying into Execution the foregoing Powers, and all other Powers vested by this Constitution in the Government of the United States, or in any Department or Officer thereof.

Powers Denied to Congress

Section 9 The Migration or Importation of such Persons as any of the States now existing shall think proper to admit, shall not be prohibited by the Congress prior to the Year one thousand eight hundred and eight, but a Tax or Duty may be imposed on such Importation, not exceeding ten dollars for each Person.

The privilege of the Writ of Habeas Corpus shall not be suspended, unless when in Cases of Rebellion or Invasion the public Safety may require it.

No Bill of Attainder or ex post facto Laws shall be passed.

No Capitation, or other direct, Tax shall be laid, unless in Proportion to the Census or Enumeration herein before directed to be taken.[6]

No Tax or Duty shall be laid on Articles exported from any State.

No Preference shall be given by any Regulation of Commerce or Revenue to the Ports of one State over those of another; nor shall Vessels bound to, or from, one State, be obliged to enter, clear, or pay Duties in another.

No Money shall be drawn from the Treasury, but in Consequence of Appropriations made by Law; and a regular Statement and Account of the Receipts and Expenditures of all public Money shall be published from time to time.

No Title of Nobility shall be granted by the United States; And no Person holding any Office of Profit or Trust under them, shall, without the Consent of the Congress, accept of any present, Emolument, Office, or Title, of any kind whatever, from any King, Prince, or foreign State.

Powers Denied to the States

Section 10 No State shall enter into any Treaty, Alliance, or Confederation; grant Letters of Marque and Reprisal; coin Money; emit Bills of Credit; make any Thing but gold and silver Coin a Tender in Payment of Debts; pass any Bill of Attainder, ex post facto Law, or Law impairing the Obligation of Contracts, or grant any Title of Nobility.

No State shall, without the Consent of the Congress, lay any Imposts or Duties on Imports or Exports, except what may be absolutely necessary for executing it's inspection Laws: and the net Produce of all Duties and Imposts, laid by any State on Imports or Exports, shall be for the Use of the Treasury of the United States; and all such Laws shall be subject to the Revision and Controul of the Congress.

No State shall, without the Consent of Congress, lay any Duty of Tonnage, keep Troops, or Ships of War in time of Peace, enter into any Agreement or Compact with another State, or with a foreign Power, or engage in War, unless actually invaded, or in such imminent Danger as will not admit of Delay.

[6]Modified by the 16th Amendment

ARTICLE II—THE EXECUTIVE ARTICLE
Nature and Scope of Presidential Power

Section 1 The executive Power shall be vested in a President of the United States of America. He shall hold his Office during the Term of four Years and, together with the Vice President, chosen for the same Term, be elected as follows

Each State shall appoint, in such Manner as the Legislature thereof may direct, a Number of Electors, equal to the whole Number of Senators and Representatives to which the State may be entitled in the Congress: but no Senator or Representative, or Person holding an Office of Trust or Profit under the United States, shall be appointed an Elector.

The Electors shall meet in their respective States, and vote by Ballot for two Persons, of whom one at least shall not be an Inhabitant of the same State with themselves. And they shall make a List of all the Persons voted for, and of the Number of Votes for each; which List they shall sign and certify, and transmit sealed to the Seat of the Government of the United States, directed to the President of the Senate. The President of the Senate shall, in the Presence of the Senate and House of Representatives, open all the Certificates, and the Votes shall then be counted. The Person having the greatest Number of Votes shall be the President, if such Number be a Majority of the whole Number of Electors appointed; and if there be more than one who have such Majority and have an equal Number of Votes, then the House of Representatives shall immediately chuse by Ballot one of them for President; and if no person have a Majority, then from the five highest on the List the said House shall in like Manner chuse the President. But in chusing the President, the Votes shall be taken by States, the Representation from each State having one Vote; A quorum for this Purpose shall consist of a Member or Members from two thirds of the States, and a Majority of all the States shall be necessary to a Choice. In every Case, after the Choice of the President, the person having the greatest Number of Votes of the Electors shall be the Vice President. But if there should remain two or more who have equal Vote, the Senate shall chuse from them by Ballot the Vice President.[7]

The Congress may determine the Time of chusing the Electors, and the Day on which they shall give their Votes; which Day shall be the same throughout the United States.

No Person except a natural born Citizen, or a Citizen of the United States, at the time of the Adoption of this Constitution, shall be eligible to the Office of President; neither shall any Person be eligible to that Office who shall not have attained to the Age of thirty five Years, and been fourteen Years a Resident within the United States.

In Case of the Removal of the President from Office, or of his Death, Resignation, or Inability to discharge the Powers and Duties of the said Office, the same shall devolve on the Vice President, and the Congress may by Law provide for the Case of Removal, Death, Resignation, or Inability, both of the President and Vice President, declaring what Officer shall then act as President, and such Officer shall act accordingly, until the Disability be removed, or a President shall be elected.[8]

The President shall, at stated Times, receive for his Services, a Compensation, which shall neither be encreased nor diminished during the Period of which he shall have been elected, and he shall not receive within that Period any other Emolument from the United States, or any of them.

[7]Changed by the 12th and 20th Amendments
[8]Modified by the 25th Amendment

3

Before he enter on the Execution of his Office, he shall take the following Oath or Affirmation:—"I do solemnly swear (or affirm) that I will faithfully execute the Office of President of the United States, and will to the best of my Ability, preserve, protect and defend the Constitution of the United States."

Powers and Duties of the President

Section 2 The President shall be the Commander in Chief of the Army and Navy of the United States, and of the Militia of the several States, when called into the actual Service of the United States, he may require the Opinion, in writing, of the principal Officer in each of the executive Departments, upon any Subject relating to the Duties of their respective Offices, and he shall have the Power to grant Reprieves and Pardons for Offences against the United States, except in Cases of Impeachment.

He shall have Power, by and with the Advice and Consent of the Senate to make Treaties, provided two thirds of the Senators present concur; and he shall nominate, and by and with the Advice and Consent of the Senate, shall appoint Ambassadors, other public Ministers and Consuls, Judges of the supreme Court, and all other Officers of the United States, whose Appointments are not herein otherwise provided for, and which shall be established by Law: but the Congress may by Law vest the Appointment of such inferior Officers, as they think proper, in the President alone, in the Courts of Law, or in the Heads of Departments.

The President shall have Power to fill up all Vacancies that may happen during the Recess of the Senate, by granting Commissions which shall expire at the End of their next Session.

Section 3 He shall from time to time give to the Congress Information of the State of the Union, and recommend to their Consideration such Measures as he shall judge necessary and expedient; he may, on extraordinary Occasions, convene both Houses, or either of them, and in Case of Disagreement between them, with Respect to the Time of Adjournment, he may adjourn them to such Time as he shall think proper; he shall receive Ambassadors and other public Ministers; he shall take Care that the Laws be faithfully executed, and shall Commission all the Officers of the United States.

Section 4 The President, Vice President and all civil Officers of the United States, shall be removed from Office on Impeachment for, and Conviction of, Treason, Bribery, or other High Crimes and Misdemeanors.

ARTICLE III—THE JUDICIAL ARTICLE

Judicial Power, Courts, Judges

Section 1 The judicial Power of the United States, shall be vested in one supreme Court, and in such inferior Courts as the Congress may from time to time ordain and establish. The Judges, both of the supreme and inferior Courts, shall hold their Offices during good Behaviour, and shall, at stated Times, receive for their Services, a Compensation, which shall not be diminished during their Continuance in Office.

Jurisdiction

Section 2 The judicial Power shall extend to all Cases, in Law and Equity, arising under this Constitution, the Laws of the United States, and Treaties made, or which shall be made, under their Authority;—to all Cases affecting Ambassadors, other public Ministers and Consuls;—to all Cases of admiralty and maritime Jurisdiction;—to Controversies to which the United States shall be a Party;—to Controversies between two or more States; *between a State and Citizens of another State;*[9]—between Citizens of different States;—between Citizens of the same State claiming Lands under Grants of different States, and between a State, or the Citizens thereof, and foreign States, Citizens, or Subjects.

In all Cases affecting Ambassadors, other public Ministers and Consuls, and those in which a State shall be Party, the supreme Court shall have original Jurisdiction. In all the other Cases before mentioned, the supreme Court shall have appellate Jurisdiction, both as to Law and Fact, with such Exceptions, and under such Regulations as Congress shall make.

The Trial of all Crimes, except in Cases of Impeachment, shall be by Jury; and such Trial shall be held in the State where the said Crimes shall have been committed; but when not committed within any State, the Trial shall be at such Place or Places as the Congress may by Law have directed.

Treason

Section 3 Treason against the United States, shall consist only in levying War against them, or in adhering to their Enemies, giving them Aid and Comfort. No Person shall be convicted of Treason unless on the Testimony of two Witnesses to the same overt Act, or on Confession in open Court.

The Congress shall have Power to declare the Punishment of Treason, but no Attainder of Treason shall work Corruption of Blood, or Forfeiture except during the Life of the Person attainted.

ARTICLE IV—INTERSTATE RELATIONS

Full Faith and Credit Clause

Section 1 Full Faith and Credit shall be given in each State to the public Acts, Records, and judicial Proceedings of every other State. And the Congress may by general Laws prescribe the Manner in which such Acts, Records and Proceedings shall be proved, and the Effect thereof.

Privileges and Immunities; Interstate Extradition

Section 2 The Citizens of each State shall be entitled to all Privileges and Immunities of Citizens in the several States.

A person charged in any State with Treason, Felony or other Crime, who shall flee from Justice, and be found in another State, shall on Demand of the executive Authority of the State from which he fled, be delivered up to be removed to the State having jurisdiction of the Crime.

No person held to Service or Labour in one State, under the Laws thereof, escaping into another, shall, in Consequence of any Law or Regulation therein, be discharged from such Service or Labour, but shall be delivered up on Claim of the Party to whom such Service or Labour may be due.[10]

Admission of States

Section 3 New States may be admitted by the Congress into this Union; but no new State shall be formed or erected within the Jurisdiction of any other State; nor any State be formed by

[9] Modified by the 11th Amendment
[10] Repealed by the 13th Amendment

the Junction of two or more States, or Parts of States, without the Consent of the Legislatures of the States concerned as well as of the Congress.

The Congress shall have Power to dispose of and make all needful Rules and Regulations respecting the Territory or other Property belonging to the United States; and nothing in this Constitution shall be so construed as to Prejudice any Claims of the United States, or of any particular State.

Republican Form of Government

Section 4   The United States shall guarantee to every State in this Union a Republican Form of Government, and shall protect each of them against Invasion; and on Application of the Legislature, or of the Executive (when the Legislature cannot be convened) against domestic Violence.

ARTICLE V—THE AMENDING POWER

The Congress, whenever two thirds of both Houses shall deem it necessary, shall propose Amendments to this Constitution, or, on the Application of the Legislatures of two thirds of several States, shall call a Convention for proposing Amendments, which, in either Case, shall be valid to all Intents and Purposes, as Part of this Constitution, when ratified by the Legislatures of three fourths of the several States, or by Conventions in three fourths thereof, as the one or the other Mode of Ratification may be proposed by the Congress; Provided that no Amendment which may be made prior to the Year One thousand eight hundred and eight shall in any Manner affect the first and fourth Clauses in the Ninth Section of the first Article; and that no State, without its Consent, shall be deprived of its equal Suffrage in the Senate.

ARTICLE VI—THE SUPREMACY ACT

All Debts contracted and Engagements entered into, before the Adoption of this Constitution, shall be as valid against the United States under the Constitution, as under the Confederation.

This Constitution, and the Laws of the United States which shall be made in Pursuance thereof; and all Treaties made, or which shall be made, under the Authority of the United States, shall be the supreme Law of the Land; and the Judges in every State shall be bound thereby, any Thing in the Constitution or Laws of any State to the Contrary notwithstanding.

The Senators and Representatives before mentioned, and the Members of the several State Legislatures, and all executive and judicial Officers, both of the United States and of the several States, shall be bound by Oath or Affirmation, to support this Constitution; but no religious Test shall ever be required as a Qualification to any Office or public Trust under the United States.

ARTICLE VII—RATIFICATION

The Ratification of the Conventions of nine States, shall be sufficient for the Establishment of this Constitution between the States so ratifying the Same.

done in Convention by the Unanimous Consent of the States present the Seventeenth Day of September in the Year of our Lord one thousand seven hundred and Eighty seven and of

the Independence of the United States of America the Twelfth. *In Witness whereof We have hereunto subscribed our Names.*

THE BILL OF RIGHTS

[The first ten amendments were ratified on December 15, 1791, and form what is known as the "Bill of Rights"]

AMENDMENT 1—RELIGION, SPEECH, ASSEMBLY, AND POLITICS

Congress shall make no law respecting an establishment of religion, or prohibiting the free exercise thereof; or abridging the freedom of speech, or of the press; or the right of the people peaceably to assemble, and to petition the Government for a redress of grievances.

AMENDMENT 2—MILITIA AND THE RIGHT TO BEAR ARMS

A well regulated Militia, being necessary to the security of a free State, the right of the people to keep and bear Arms, shall not be infringed.

AMENDMENT 3—QUARTERING OF SOLDIERS

No Soldier shall, in time of peace be quartered in any house, without the consent of the Owner, nor in time of war, but in manner to be prescribed by law.

AMENDMENT 4—SEARCHES AND SEIZURES

The right of the people to be secure in their persons, houses, papers, and effects, against unreasonable searches and seizures, shall not be violated, and no Warrants shall issue, but upon probable cause, supported by Oath or affirmation, and particularly describing the place to be searched, and the persons or things to be seized.

AMENDMENT 5—GRAND JURIES, SELF-INCRIMINATION, DOUBLE JEOPARDY, DUE PROCESS, AND EMINENT DOMAIN

No person shall be held to answer for a capital, or otherwise infamous crime, unless on a presentment or indictment of a Grand jury, except in cases arising in the land or naval forces, or in the Militia, when in actual service in time of War or public danger; nor shall any person be subject for the same offence to be twice put in jeopardy of life or limb; nor shall be compelled in any criminal case to be a witness against himself, nor be deprived of life, liberty, or property, without due process of law; nor shall private property be taken for public use, without just compensation.

AMENDMENT 6—CRIMINAL COURT PROCEDURES

In all criminal prosecutions, the accused shall enjoy the right to a speedy and public trial, by an impartial jury of the State and district wherein the crime shall have been committed, which district shall have been previously ascertained by law, and to be informed of the nature and cause of the accusation; to be confronted with the witnesses against him; to have compulsory process for obtaining Witnesses in his favor, and to have the Assistance of Counsel for his defence.

AMENDMENT 7—TRIAL BY JURY IN COMMON LAW CASES

In Suits at common law, where the value in controversy shall exceed twenty dollars, the right of trial by jury shall be preserved, and no fact tried by a jury shall be otherwise re-examined in any Court of the United States, than according to the rules of the common law.

AMENDMENT 8—BAIL, CRUEL AND UNUSUAL PUNISHMENT

Excessive bail shall not be required, nor excessive fines imposed, nor cruel and unusual punishments inflicted.

AMENDMENT 9—RIGHTS RETAINED BY THE PEOPLE

The enumeration in the Constitution, of certain rights, shall not be construed to deny or disparage others retained by the people.

AMENDMENT 10—RESERVED POWERS OF THE STATES

The powers not delegated to the United States by the Constitution, nor prohibited by it to the States, are reserved to the States respectively, or to the people.

PRE-CIVIL WAR AMENDMENTS

AMENDMENT 11—SUITS AGAINST THE STATES

[Ratified February 7, 1795]

The Judicial power of the United States shall not be construed to extend to any suit in law or equity, commenced or prosecuted against one of the United States by Citizens of another State, or by Citizens or Subjects of any Foreign State.

AMENDMENT 12—ELECTION OF THE PRESIDENT

[Ratified July 27, 1804]

The Electors shall meet in their respective states, and vote by ballot for President and Vice-President, one of whom, at least, shall not be an inhabitant of the same state with themselves; they shall name in their ballots the person voted for as President, and in distinct ballots the person voted for as Vice-President, and they shall make distinct lists of all persons voted for as President, and of all persons voted for as Vice-President, and of the number of votes for each, which lists they shall sign and certify, and transmit sealed to the seat of the government of the United States, directed to the President of the Senate;—The President of the Senate shall, in presence of the Senate and House of Representatives, open all the certificates and the votes shall then be counted;—The person having the greatest number of votes for President, shall be the President, if such number be a majority of the whole number of Electors appointed; and if no person have such majority, then from the persons having the highest numbers not exceeding three on the list of those voted for as President, the House of Representatives shall choose immediately, by ballot, the President. But in choosing the President, the votes shall be taken by states, the representation from each state having one vote; a quorum for this purpose shall consist of a member or members from two-thirds of the states, and a majority of all states shall be necessary to a choice. And if the House of Representatives shall not choose a President whenever the right of choice

shall devolve upon them, *before the fourth day of March next following,* then the Vice-President shall act as President, as in the case of the death or other constitutional disability of the President.[11] The person having the greatest number of votes as Vice-President, shall be the Vice-President, if such a number be a majority of the whole numbers of Electors appointed, and if no person have a majority, then from the two highest numbers on the list, the Senate shall choose the Vice-President; a quorum for the purpose shall consist of two-thirds of the whole number of Senators, and a majority of the whole number shall be necessary to a choice. But no person constitutionally ineligible to the office of President shall be eligible to that of Vice-President of the United States.

CIVIL WAR AMENDMENTS

AMENDMENT 13—PROHIBITION OF SLAVERY

[Ratified December 6, 1865]

Section 1   Neither slavery nor involuntary servitude, except as a punishment for crime whereof the party shall have been duly convicted, shall exist within the United States, or any place subject to their jurisdiction.

Section 2   Congress shall have power to enforce this article by appropriate legislation.

AMENDMENT 14—CITIZENSHIP, DUE PROCESS, AND EQUAL PROTECTION OF THE LAWS

[Ratified July 9, 1868]

Section 1   All persons born or naturalized in the United States, and subject to the jurisdiction thereof, are citizens of the United States and of the State wherein they reside. No State shall make or enforce any law which shall abridge the privileges or immunities of citizens of the United States; nor shall any State deprive any person of life, liberty, or property, without due process of law; nor deny to any person within its jurisdiction the equal protection of the laws.

Section 2   Representatives shall be apportioned among the several States according to their respective numbers, counting the whole number of persons in each State, excluding Indians not taxed. But when the right to vote at any election for the choice of electors for President and Vice President of the United States, Representatives in Congress, the Executive and Judicial officers of a State, or the members of the Legislature thereof, is denied to any of the male inhabitants of such State, being twenty-one[12] years of age, and citizens of the United States, or in any way abridged, except for participation in rebellion, or other crime, the basis of representation therein shall be reduced in the proportion which the number of such male citizens shall bear to the whole number of male citizens twenty-one years of age in such State.

Section 3   No person shall be a Senator or Representative in Congress, or elector of President and Vice President, or hold any office, civil or military, under the United States, or under any State, who, having previously taken an oath, as a member of Congress, or as an officer of the United States, or as a member of

[11]Changed by the 20th Amendment
[12]Changed by the 26th Amendment

any State legislature, or as an executive or judicial officer of any State, to support the Constitution of the United States, shall have engaged in insurrection or rebellion against the same, or given aid or comfort to the enemies thereof. But Congress may by a vote of two-thirds of each House, remove such disability.

Section 4   The validity of the public debt of the United States, authorized by law, including debts incurred for payment of pensions and bounties for services in suppressing insurrection or rebellion, shall not be questioned. But neither the United States nor any State shall assume or pay any debt or obligation incurred in aid of insurrection or rebellion against the United States, or any claim for the loss or emancipation of any slave; but all such debts, obligations and claims shall be held illegal and void.

Section 5   The Congress shall have power to enforce, by appropriate legislation, the provisions of this article.

AMENDMENT 15—THE RIGHT TO VOTE

[Ratified February 3, 1870]

Section 1   The right of citizens of the United States to vote shall not be denied or abridged by the United States or by any State on account of race, color, or previous condition of servitude.

Section 2   The Congress shall have power to enforce this article by appropriate legislation.

AMENDMENT 16—INCOME TAXES

[Ratified February 3, 1913]

The Congress shall have power to lay and collect taxes on incomes, from whatever source derived, without apportionment among the several States, and without regard to any census or enumeration.

AMENDMENT 17—DIRECT ELECTION OF SENATORS

[Ratified April 8, 1913]

The Senate of the United States shall be composed of two Senators from each State, elected by the people thereof, for six years; and each Senator shall have one vote. The electors in each State shall have the qualifications requisite for electors of the most numerous branch of the State legislatures.

When vacancies happen in the representation of any State in the Senate, the executive authority of such State shall issue writs of election to fill such vacancies: *Provided*, That the Legislature of any State may empower the executive thereof to make temporary appointment until the people fill the vacancies by election as the legislature may direct.

This amendment shall not be so construed as to affect the election or term of any Senator chosen before it becomes valid as part of the Constitution.

AMENDMENT 18—PROHIBITION

[Ratified January 16, 1919   Repealed December 5, 1933 by Amendment 21]

Section 1   After one year from the ratification of this article the manufacture, sale, or transportation of intoxicating liquors within, the importation thereof into, or the exportation thereof from the United States and all territory subject to the jurisdiction thereof for beverage purposes is hereby prohibited.

Section 2   The Congress and the several states shall have concurrent power to enforce this article by appropriate legislation.

Section 3   This article shall be inoperative unless it shall have been ratified as an amendment to the Constitution by the legislatures of the several states, as provided in the Constitution, within seven years from the date of the submission hereof to the States by the Congress.[13]

AMENDMENT 19—FOR WOMEN'S SUFFRAGE

[Ratified August 18, 1920]

The right of the citizens of the United States to vote shall not be denied or abridged by the United States or by any State on account of sex.

Congress shall have power, by appropriate legislation, to enforce the provision of this article.

AMENDMENT 20—THE LAME DUCK AMENDMENT

[Ratified January 23, 1933]

Section 1   The terms of the President and Vice President shall end at noon on the 20th day of January, and the terms of the Senators and Representatives at noon on the 3rd day of January, of the years in which such terms would have ended if this article had not been ratified; and the terms of their successors shall then begin.

Section 2   The Congress shall assemble at least once in every year, and such meeting shall begin at noon on the 3rd day of January, unless they shall by law appoint a different day.

Section 3   If, at the time fixed for the beginning of the term of the President, the President elect shall have died, the Vice President elect shall become President. If a President shall not have been chosen before the time fixed for the beginning of his term, or if the President elect shall have failed to qualify, then the Vice President elect shall act as President until a President shall have qualified; and the Congress may by law provide for the case wherein neither a President elect nor a Vice President elect shall have qualified, declaring who shall then act as President, or the manner in which one who is to act shall be selected, and such person shall act accordingly until a President or Vice President shall have qualified.

Section 4   The Congress may by law provide for the case of the death of any of the persons from whom the House of Representatives may choose a President whenever the right of choice shall have developed upon them, and for the case of the death of any of the persons from whom the Senate may choose a Vice President whenever the right of choice shall have devolved upon them.

Section 5   Sections 1 and 2 shall take effect on the 15th day of October following the ratification of this article.

Section 6   This article shall be inoperative unless it shall have been ratified as an amendment to the Constitution by the legislatures of three-fourths of the several States within seven years from the date of its submission.

[13]Repealed by the 21st Amendment

AMENDMENT 21—REPEAL OF PROHIBITION
[Ratified December 5, 1933]

Section 1 The eighteenth article of amendment to the Constitution of the United States is hereby repealed.

Section 2 The transportation or importation into any State, Territory, or Possession of the United States for delivery or use therein of intoxicating liquors, in violation of the laws thereof, is hereby prohibited.

Section 3 This article shall be inoperative unless it shall have been ratified as an amendment to the Constitution by conventions in the several States, as provided in the Constitution, within seven years from the date of the submission hereof to the States by the Congress.

AMENDMENT 22—NUMBER OF PRESIDENTIAL TERMS
[Ratified February 27, 1951]

Section 1 No person shall be elected to the office of the President more than twice, and no person who has held the office of President, or acted as President, for more than two years of a term to which some other person was elected President shall be elected to the Office of the President more than once. But this Article shall not apply to any person holding the office of President when this article was proposed by the Congress, and shall not prevent any person who may be holding the office of President, or acting as President, during the term within which this Article becomes operative from holding the office of President or acting as President during the remainder of such term.

Section 2 This Article shall be inoperative unless it shall have been ratified as an amendment to the Constitution by the legislatures of three-fourths of the several states within seven years from the date of its submission to the States by the Congress.

AMENDMENT 23—PRESIDENTIAL ELECTORS FOR THE DISTRICT OF COLUMBIA
[Ratified March 29, 1961]

Section 1 The District constituting the seat of Government of the United States shall appoint in such manner as the Congress may direct:

A number of electors of President and Vice President equal to the whole number of Senators and Representatives in Congress to which the District would be entitled if it were a State, but in no event more than the least populous State; they shall be in addition to those appointed by the States, but they shall be considered, for the purposes of the election of President and Vice President, to be electors appointed by a State; and they shall meet in the District and perform such duties as provided by the twelfth article of amendment.

Section 2 The Congress shall have power to enforce this article by appropriate legislation.

AMENDMENT 24—THE ANTI-POLL TAX AMENDMENT
[Ratified January 23, 1964]

Section 1 The right of citizens of the United States to vote in any primary or other election for President or Vice President, for electors for President or Vice President, or for Senator or Representative in Congress, shall not be denied or abridged by the United States or any State by reason of failure to pay any poll tax or other tax.

Section 2 The Congress shall have power to enforce this article by appropriate legislation.

AMENDMENT 25—PRESIDENTIAL DISABILITY, VICE PRESIDENTIAL VACANCIES
[Ratified February 10, 1967]

Section 1 In case of the removal of the President from office or his death or resignation, the Vice President shall become President.

Section 2 Whenever there is a vacancy in the office of the Vice President, the President shall nominate a Vice President who shall take the office upon confirmation by a majority vote of both houses of Congress.

Section 3 Whenever the President transmits to the President pro tempore of the Senate and the Speaker of the House of Representatives his written declaration that he is unable to discharge the powers and duties of his office, and until he transmits to them a written declaration to the contrary, such powers and duties shall be discharged by the Vice President as Acting President.

Section 4 Whenever the Vice-President and a majority of either the principal officers of the executive departments, or of such other body as Congress may by law provide, transmit to the President pro tempore of the Senate and the Speaker of the House of Representatives their written declaration that the President is unable to discharge the powers and duties of his office, the Vice President shall immediately assume the powers and duties of the office as Acting President.

Thereafter, when the President transmits to the President pro tempore of the Senate and the Speaker of the House of Representatives his written declaration that no inability exists, he shall resume the powers and duties of his office unless the Vice President and a majority of either the principal officers of the executive departments, or of such other body as Congress may by law provide, transmit within four days to the President pro tempore of the Senate and the Speaker of the House of Representatives their written declaration that the President is unable to discharge the powers and duties of his office. Thereupon Congress shall decide the issue, assembling within 48 hours for that purpose if not in session. If the Congress, within 21 days after receipt of the latter written declaration, or, if Congress is not in session, within 21 days after Congress is required to assemble, determines by two-thirds vote of both houses that the President is unable to discharge the powers and duties of his office, the Vice President shall continue to discharge the same as Acting President; otherwise, the President shall resume the powers and duties of his office.

AMENDMENT 26—EIGHTEEN-YEAR-OLD VOTE
[Ratified July 1, 1971]

Section 1 The right of citizens of the United States, who are eighteen years of age, or older, to vote shall not be denied or abridged by the United States or by any State on account of age.

Section 2 The Congress shall have power to enforce this article by appropriate legislation.

AMENDMENT 27—CONGRESSIONAL SALARIES
[Ratified May 7, 1992]

No law, varying the compensation for the services of the Senators and Representatives, shall take effect, until an election of Representative shall be intervened.

From Coast to Coast

Land Disputes in the New Republic

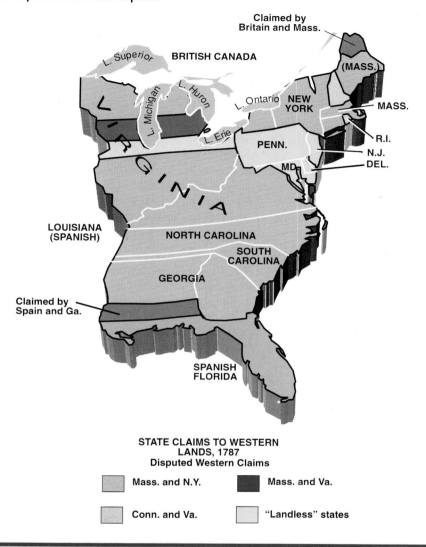

Claimed by
Britain and Mass.

BRITISH CANADA

L. Superior

L. Michigan

L. Huron

L. Ontario

L. Erie

(MASS.)

NEW
YORK

MASS.

R.I.

PENN.

N.J.

DEL.

MD.

VIRGINIA

LOUISIANA
(SPANISH)

NORTH CAROLINA

SOUTH
CAROLINA

GEORGIA

Claimed by
Spain and Ga.

SPANISH
FLORIDA

**STATE CLAIMS TO WESTERN
LANDS, 1787**
Disputed Western Claims

Mass. and N.Y.

Mass. and Va.

Conn. and Va.

"Landless" states

SOURCE: Bureau of the Census, Release CB 91-677, June 12, 1991.

and they began a counterattack. They rallied around William Paterson of New Jersey, who presented a series of resolutions known as the **New Jersey Plan**. Paterson did not question the need for a strengthened central government, yet he was concerned about how this strength might be used. The New Jersey Plan would give Congress the right to tax and regulate commerce and to coerce states, yet it would retain the single-house legislature (as under the Articles of Confederation) in which each state, regardless of size, would have the same vote. The plan contained the germ of what eventually came to be a key provision of our Constitution: the *supremacy clause.* The national Supreme Court was to hear appeals from state judges, and the supremacy clause would require all judges—state and national—to treat laws of the national government and the treaties of the United States as superior to the constitutions and laws of each of the states.

"Remember, gentlemen, we aren't here just to draft a constitution. We're here to draft the best damn constitution in the world."

Drawing by Steiner. ©1982 The New Yorker Magazine, Inc.

Paterson maneuvered to force concessions from the larger states. He favored a strong central government, but not one the big states could control. Further, he raised the issue of practical politics. To adopt the Virginia Plan—which would create a powerful national government dominated by Massachusetts, Pennsylvania, and Virginia and eliminate the states as important units of government—would all but guarantee that the states would reject the new constitution. Still, the large states resisted, and for a time the convention was deadlocked. The small states believed all states should be represented equally in Congress, at least in the upper house. The large states insisted representation in both houses be based on population or wealth and that national legislators be elected by the voters rather than by state legislatures. Finally, a Committee of Eleven was elected to devise a compromise. On July 5 it presented its proposals.

THE CONNECTICUT COMPROMISE   Because of the prominent role of the Connecticut delegation, this plan has since been known as the **Connecticut Compromise**, or as it is sometimes called, the Great Compromise. It called for one house in which each state would have an equal vote and a second house in which representation would be based on population and in which all bills for raising or appropriating money would originate. This proposal was a setback for the large states, which agreed to it only when the smaller states made it clear this was their price for union. After equality of state representation in the Senate was accepted, most objections to establishing a strong national government dissolved.

NORTH-SOUTH COMPROMISES   Other issues at the convention split the delegates North and South. Southerners were afraid a northern majority in Congress might discriminate against southern trade. They had some basis for this concern. John Jay, secretary of foreign affairs for the Confederation, had proposed a treaty with Great Britain that would have given advantages to northern merchants at the expense of southern exporters. To protect themselves, the southern delegates insisted a two-thirds majority be required in the Senate before presidents could ratify treaties.

Differences between the North and South were also evident on the issue of representation in the House of Representatives. The question was whether to count slaves for purposes of apportioning seats in the House. The South wanted to count slaves and thereby enlarge its number of representatives; the North resisted. After heated debate, the delegates agreed on the **three-fifths compromise**. Each slave would be counted as three-fifths of a free person for the purposes of apportionment in the House and of direct taxation. The explanation for "three-fifths," as opposed to some other fraction, was that it maintained a balance of power between the North and South. The issue of "balance" would recur in the early history of our nation as territorial governments were established and territories applied for statehood.

OTHER ISSUES   The delegates found other issues about which to argue. Should the national government have lower courts, or would one federal Supreme Court be enough? This issue was resolved by postponing the decision; the Constitution states that there shall be one Supreme Court and that Congress *may* establish inferior courts. How should the president be selected? For a long time the convention accepted the idea that the president should be elected by Congress. Yet the delegates feared Congress would dominate the president, or vice versa. Election by the state legislatures was rejected because these bodies were distrusted. Finally, the electoral college system was devised. This was perhaps the most novel and contrived contribution of the delegates; today it is one of the more criticized provisions in the Constitution.[9] (Consult Article II, Section 1, of the Constitution.)

After three months the delegates stopped debating. On September 17, 1787, they assembled for the impressive ceremony of signing the document they were recommending to the nation. All but three of those still present signed; others who opposed the general drift of the convention had already left. Their work well done, delegates adjourned to the nearby City Tavern to relax and celebrate.

TO ADOPT OR NOT TO ADOPT?

The delegates had gone far. They had not hesitated to disregard Congress's instruction to do no more than revise the Articles or to ignore Article XIII of the Articles of Confederation. This article declared the Union to be perpetual and prohibited any alteration of the Articles unless agreed to by Congress and *by every one of the state legislatures,* a provision that had made it impossible to amend the Articles. The convention delegates, however, boldly declared that their newly proposed Constitution should go into effect when ratified by *popularly elected conventions in nine states.* They turned to this method of ratification for practical considerations as well as for reasons of principle. Not only were the delegates aware that there was little chance of securing approval of the new Constitution in all state legislatures; many also believed the Constitution should be ratified by an authority higher than a legislature. A constitution based on popular approval would have higher legal and moral status. The Articles of Confederation had been a compact of state governments, but the Constitution was to be a "we the people." Nevertheless, even this method of ratification would not be easy. The nation was not ready to adopt the Constitution without a thorough debate.

Federalists versus Antifederalists

Supporters of the new government, by cleverly appropriating the name **Federalists**, took some of the sting out of charges they were trying to destroy the states and establish an all-powerful central government. By calling their opponents **Antifederalists**, they pointed up the negative character of the arguments of those who opposed ratification.

The split was in part geographical: seaboard and city regions tended to be Federalist strongholds; backcountry regions from Maine (a part of Massachusetts) through Georgia, inhabited by farmers and other relatively poor people, were generally Antifederalist. But as in most political contests, no single factor completely accounted for the division between Federalists and Antifederalists. Thus in Virginia the leaders of both sides came from the same general social and economic class. New York City and Philadelphia strongly supported the Constitution, yet so did predominantly rural New Jersey.

The great debate was conducted with pamphlets, papers, letters to the editor, and speeches. The issues were important, but in the main the argument was carried on in a quiet and calm manner. Out of the debate came a series of essays known as *The Federalist*, written by Alexander Hamilton, James Madison, and John Jay to persuade the voters of New York to ratify the Constitution. *The Federalist* is still, said Charles Beard, "widely regarded as the most profound single treatise on the Constitution ever written and as among the few masterly works in political science produced in all the centuries of history."[10] (Three of the most important *Federalist* essays, Nos. 10, 51, and 78, are found in the Appendix of this book; we urge you to read them.) The great debate stands even today as an outstanding example of free people using public discussion to determine the nature of their fundamental laws.

The Antifederalists' most telling criticism of the proposed Constitution was its failure to include a bill of rights.[11] The Federalists believed a bill of rights unnecessary. They contended that the proposed national government had only the specific powers delegated to it by the states and people, so there was no need to specify that Congress could not, for example, abridge freedom of the press because it had no power to regulate the press. Moreover, the Federalists argued, to guarantee *some* rights might be dangerous, because it would then be thought that rights *not* listed could be denied. The Constitution already protected some important rights—trial by jury in federal criminal cases, for example. Hamilton and others also insisted that paper guarantees were weak supports on which to depend for protection against governmental tyranny.

Creating the Republic

April 1775 American Revolution begins at Lexington and Concord

June 1775 George Washington assumes command of Continental forces

July 1776 Declaration of Independence approved

November 1777 Articles of Confederation adopted by Continental Congress

March 1781 Articles of Confederation ratified by the states

October 1781 British defeated at Yorktown

April 1784 Congress ratifies peace treaty with British

Late 1786 Shays's Rebellion in western Massachusetts

May 1787 Constitutional Convention opens in Philadelphia

September 1787 Constitution for the United States adopted by Convention

June 1788 Constitution ratified by nine states

Early 1789 First national elections

March 1789 United States Congress meets for the first time in New York

April 1789 George Washington inaugurated as first president

September 1789 John Jay becomes first chief justice of the United States

September 1789 Congress proposes Bill of Rights

December 1791 Bill of Rights (first 10 amendments) ratified as part of the U.S. Constitution

Note: It took about 15 years to win independence, form an interim government that tried to govern, fashion a "more perfect union," and actually get a national government, with functioning legislative, executive, and judicial branches.

The Antifederalists were unconvinced. If some rights were protected, what could be the objection to providing constitutional protection for others? Without a bill of rights, what was to prevent Congress from using one of its delegated powers to abridge free speech? If bills of rights were needed in state constitutions to limit state governments, why was a bill of rights not needed in the national constitution to limit the national government? This was a government farther from the people, they contended, with a greater tendency to subvert natural rights.

The Politics of Ratification

The absence of a bill of rights in the proposed constitution dominated the struggle over its adoption. "There is no Declaration of Rights" was the first sentence of an attack on the document by Virginia delegate George Mason. In taverns and church gatherings and newspaper offices up and down the eastern seaboard, people were muttering, "No bill of rights—no constitution!" This feeling was so strong that some Antifederalists, who were far more concerned with *states'* rights than *individual* rights, joined forces with bill of rights advocates in an effort to defeat the proposed Constitution.

The Federalists were first off the mark in the struggle over the Constitution that opened as soon as the delegates left Philadelphia in mid-September 1787. The Federalists' immediate tactic was to secure ratification in as many states as possible before the opposition had time to organize. The Antifederalists were handicapped. Most newspapers were owned by supporters of ratification. Moreover, Antifederalist strength was concentrated in rural areas, which were underrepresented in some state legislatures and difficult to arouse to political action. They needed time to perfect their organization and collect their strength. The Federalists, composed of a more closely knit group of leaders throughout the colonies, moved in a hurry.

In most of the small states, now satisfied by equal Senate representation, ratification was gained without difficulty. Delaware was the first state to ratify. By early 1788, Pennsylvania, New Jersey, Georgia, and Connecticut had also ratified. In the view of the grass-roots political observer Mercy Warren of Massachusetts, there seemed to be few Americans who did not "unite in the general wish for the restoration of public faith, the revival of commerce, arts, agriculture, and industry, under a lenient, peaceable and energetic government."[12]

Reports were coming in from Massachusetts, however, that opposition was broadening, especially in the hinterland of the state. The position of such key leaders as John Hancock and Samuel Adams was in doubt. The debate in the ratifying convention in Boston pitched some of the most polished Federalist leaders against an array of eloquent but plainspoken Antifederalists. The debate raged for most of January 1788 and into February. At times it looked as though the Constitution would lose, as Antifederalists raised the cry of "Why no Bill of Rights?" and other objections. But in the end the Constitution was narrowly ratified in Massachusetts, 187 to 168 (see Table 1-1).

The Federalists were elated, yet in fact both sides had won. To gain votes for the Constitution, the Federalists had had to make a deal, one of the most important compromises in U.S. history. The Federalists adopted the strategy of accepting their opponents' most convincing argument—the lack of a bill of rights—and offered to add a bill of rights to the Constitution, but only *after* the new government under the Constitution was set up. Thus the Federalists sidetracked proposals for a *second* convention, which might have turned into a "runaway" gathering. In turn, the Antifederalists, led by such notables as Samuel Adams, won a promise for bill of rights amendments—a promise later honored by Madison and his fellow Federalist leaders. John Hancock, it was said, came over to the Federalist side after hints he might be selected vice-president under the new government.

TABLE 1.1

Ratification of the U.S. Constitution

State	Date
Delaware	Dec. 7, 1787
Pennsylvania	Dec. 12, 1787
New Jersey	Dec. 19, 1787
Georgia	Jan. 2, 1788
Connecticut	Jan. 9, 1788
Massachusetts	Feb. 6, 1788
Maryland	April 28, 1788
South Carolina	May 23, 1788
New Hampshire	June 21, 1788
Virginia	June 25, 1788
New York	July 26, 1788
North Carolina	Nov. 21, 1789
Rhode Island	May 29, 1790

The struggle over the Constitution continued through the spring of 1788. By June 21, Maryland, South Carolina, and New Hampshire had ratified, putting the Constitution over the top in the number (nine) required for ratification. But two big hurdles remained: Virginia and New York. Virginia was crucial, as the most populous state, the home of Washington and other heroes, a link between North and South. The Virginia ratifying convention rivaled the Constitution Convention in the caliber of its delegates. Madison, who had only recently switched to favoring the bill of rights position after saying earlier it was unnecessary, captained the Federalist forces. The fiery Patrick Henry led the opposition. In an epic debate, Henry cried that liberty was the issue—"Liberty, the greatest of earthly possessions . . . that precious jewel!" But Madison quietly rebutted him and then played his trump card, a promise that a bill of rights embracing the freedoms of religion and speech and assembly would be added to the Constitution. At a critical moment, Washington himself tipped the balance with a letter urging ratification. News of the Virginia vote, 89 for the Constitution and 79 opposed, was rushed to New York.[13]

The great landowners along the Hudson, unlike their southern planter friends, were opposed to the Constitution. They feared federal taxation of their holdings, and they did not want to abolish the profitable tax New York had been levying on the trade and commerce of other states. When the convention assembled, the Federalists were greatly outnumbered, but they were aided by the strategy and skill of Hamilton and by word of Virginia's ratification. New York approved by a margin of three votes. Although North Carolina and Rhode Island still remained outside the Union (the former ratified in November 1789, and the latter six months later), the new nation was created. In New York, a few members of the old Congress assembled to issue the call for elections under the new Constitution. Then Congress adjourned without setting a date for reconvening.

INTO THE TWENTY-FIRST CENTURY

A constitution that is to endure must reflect both the hard experiences and high hopes of the people for whom it is written. Those who framed our Constitution did not, of course, complete the task of constitution making. That process began long before the Constitutional Convention, and it continues still. Constitutions, even written ones, are growing and evolving organisms.

In the past decade this nation celebrated the two-hundredth anniversary of the Constitution and of the Bill of Rights. Yet this period of commemoration and celebration has also been a period of questioning. Questions about constitutional democracy have no easy answers, no single logical response; these are basic questions that deal with value choices. The questions in the Closer Look box may help stimulate your thinking as you proceed to a more detailed investigation of our Republic.

You must remember, as you consider these questions, that the framers did not favor a government in which the mass of people would participate directly, or one that would always be representative of or responsive to the people at large. Rather, they sought to control both the spirit of faction and the emotional or ill-considered thrusts of majorities. Their prime concern was how to design a viable yet limited government. The framers had not seen a political party in the modern sense, and they would not have liked it if they had. They did not favor an arousing, mobilizing kind of leadership, but preferred instead a stabilizing, balancing, magisterial leadership, the kind George Washington was expected to (and generally did) supply.

Today we have high-intensity politics characterized by vigorously organized groups and political action committees, potent and volatile public opinion dominated by opinion-making leaders, political parties vying to mobilize nationwide majorities, and celebrity officials intimately covered by the national networks,

The Grand Union—1776

First Stars and Stripes—1777

The Great Seal—1782

Constitution Flag—1789

CHALLENGES FOR OUR CONSTITUTIONAL DEMOCRACY

1. *"All men are created equal":* What kinds of equality are—and should be—protected by the Constitution, and by what means?

2. *"Government by the people":* Does the evolving constitutional system, including political parties and interest groups, strengthen fair and effective representation of the people?

3. *National power:* Too much or too little? Are the limits on the federal government's powers realistic and enforceable, given the intense pressures on the government?

4. *Federalism:* Does our form of it work? Does the Constitution provide for an efficient and realistic balance between national and state power?

5. *Checks and balances:* Are there too many? Does the constitutional separation of powers between the president and Congress create an ungovernable system, notably in economic policy?

6. *Women's rights:* Are they adequately protected by the Constitution today?

7. *Safeguarding minorities:* Does the Constitution adequately protect the rights of African Americans, Native Americans, Hispanic Americans and other ethnic groups, and recent immigrants?

8. *Suspects' rights:* Can representative government protect its citizens and yet uphold the rights of the criminally accused?

9. *Individual liberties:* Are they adequately protected in the Constitution?

10. *The judicial branch:* Is it too powerful? Are the federal courts exceeding their proper powers as interpreters of the Constitution?

11. *War and peace:* Is the Constitution adequate for the nuclear age?

12. *Constitutional responsibilities:* Are Americans participating adequately in our democratic system? Do citizens in the United States take civic responsibilities too lightly? Is democracy in jeopardy?

CNN, and C-SPAN. How responsive are our governing processes to fast-moving changes in public attitudes and moods? Will our Constitution and the political system it created be able to deal with the problems of our third century?

According to an old story, Benjamin Franklin was confronted by an older woman as he left the last session of the Constitutional Convention in Philadelphia in September 1787.

"What kind of government have you given us, Dr. Franklin?" she asked. "A Republic or a Monarchy?"

"A Republic, Madam," he answered, "if you can keep it."

SUMMARY

1. *Democracy* is an often misused term, and it is used by many people to mean many different things. We use it here to refer to a system of interacting values, interrelated political processes, and interdependent political structures. The vital principle of democracy is that a *just* government must derive its powers from the consent of the people, and that this *consent* must be regularly renewed at free and fair elections.

2. Stable constitutional democracy is encouraged by various conditions, such as an educated citizenry, a healthy economy, and overlapping associations and groupings within a society in which major institutions interact to create a certain degree of consensus about the importance of democratic procedures. Civilian control over the military and a general acceptance of the ideals of democracy are also essential.

3. Democracy developed gradually. A revolution had to be fought before a system of representative democracy could be tried and tested. It took several years before a national constitution could be written, and almost another year to be ratified. It took still another two years before a Bill of

Rights could be adopted and ratified. It has taken more than two hundred years for democratic institutions to be refined and for systems of competition and choice to be hammered out. Democratic institutions in the United States are still evolving.

4. *Constitutionalism* is a general label we apply to those arrangements such as checks and balances, federalism, separation of powers, due process, and the Bill of Rights that force our leaders and representatives to listen, think, deliberate, bargain, and explain before they act and make laws. And a constitutional government enforces recognized and regularly applied limits on the powers of those who govern.

5. A *constitutional democracy* is a governing process in which the voice of the people is regularly heard through free and fair elections. It is also a government in which recognized limits are regularly applied to those who govern. Constitutional democracy remains in many ways a goal rather than an achievement, and, as we enter the twenty-first century, a number of questions remain about its vitality and its capacity to mature.

FURTHER READING

BERNARD BAILYN, ed., *The Debate on the Constitution: Federalist and Antifederalist Speeches, Articles, and Letters During the Struggle over Ratification* (2 vols. Library of America, 1993).

JAMES MACGREGOR BURNS, *The Vineyard of Liberty* (Knopf, 1982).

JAMES MACGREGOR BURNS AND STEWART BURNS, *The People's Charter* (Knopf, 1991).

THOMAS E. CRONIN, *Direct Democracy: The Politics of the Initiative, Referendum, and Recall* (Harvard University Press, 1989).

ROBERT A. DAHL, *Democracy and Its Critics* (Yale University Press, 1989).

ALEXANDER HAMILTON, JAMES MADISON AND JOHN JAY, *The Feder-*

alist Papers, ed. Clinton Rossiter (New American Library, 1961). Also in several other editions.

SAMUEL P. HUNTINGTON, *The Third Wave: Democratization in the Late Twentieth Century* (University of Oklahoma Press, 1991).

RICHARD B. MORRIS, *Witnesses at the Creation: Hamilton, Madison and Jay, and the Constitution* (Holt, Rinehart and Winston, 1985).

ALEXIS DE TOCQUEVILLE, *Democracy in America* , 2 vols., 1835 (Vintage, 1955).

GORDON S. WOOD, *The Creation of the American Republic, 1776–1787* (University of North Carolina Press, 1969).

See also the *Journal of Democracy.*

THE LIVING
CONSTITUTION

The original, unamended Constitution was a skinny document of only some 4,543 words (you can carry it around in your coat pocket), yet it packed a powerful punch. It was intended to be only a framework for governing; it was a document into which citizens could, if optimistic, read their hopes, or, if pessimistic, their fears. Most of them would be surprised to learn that more than two hundred years later we still have not written another constitution—let alone two or three!

With the adoption of the Constitution, prosperity returned. Markets for American goods were opening in Europe, and business was pulling out of its postwar slump. Such events seemed to justify Federalist claims that adoption of the Constitution would correct the nation's problems. Within a surprisingly short time the Constitution lost its partisan character; both Antifederalists and Federalists honored it. Politicians differed less and less over whether the Constitution was good; they began to argue over what it meant.

The 1791 adoption of the Bill of Rights made the Constitution more popular than ever.[1] As the Constitution won the support of Americans, it began to take on the aura of natural law, law that defines right from wrong, law that is higher than human law. "The Fathers grew ever larger in stature," wrote Max Lerner, "as they receded from view; the era in which they lived and fought became a Golden Age; in that age there had been a fresh dawn for the world, and its men were giants against the sky."[2] This early Constitution worship helped bring unity to the diverse new nation. Like the Crown in Britain, the Constitution became a symbol of national loyalty, evoking both emotional and intellectual support from all Americans, regardless of their differences. The framers' work became part of the American creed.[3] It stood for liberty, equality before the law, limited government—indeed, for just about whatever anyone wanted to read into it.

The Constitution, however, is more than a symbol. It is also a supreme and binding law that both grants and limits powers. "In framing a government which is to be administered by men over men," wrote James Madison in *The Federalist*, No. 51, "the great difficulty lies in this: you must first enable the government to control the governed; and in the next place oblige it to control itself." (Take a look at *The Federalist*, No. 51, which appears in the Appendix of this book.) The Constitution is both a *positive* instrument of government, which enables the governors to control the governed, and a *restraint* on government, which enables the ruled to check the rulers.

In what ways does the Constitution limit the power of the government? In what ways does it create governmental power? How has it managed to serve as a great symbol of national unity and at the same time a somewhat adaptable and changing instrument of government? The secret is an ingenious separation of powers and a system of checks and balances that combine to check power with power.

CHECKING POWER WITH POWER

It may seem strange to begin by stressing the ways in which the Constitution limits governmental power, but we must keep in mind the dilemma the framers faced. They wanted a *stronger and more effective* national government than they had under the Articles of Confederation. At the same time, they

"And there are three branches of government, so that each branch has the other two to blame everything on."

Dunagin's People by Ralph Dunagin. © 1978 Field Newspaper Syndicate. By permission of the News America Syndicate.

were keenly aware that the people would not accept too much central control. Efficiency and order were important concerns, but they were not as important as *liberty*. The framers wanted to ensure domestic tranquillity and prevent future rebellions, but they also wanted to forestall the emergence of a homegrown King George III. Accordingly, they allotted certain powers to the national government and reserved the rest for the states, thus establishing a system of *federalism* (whose nature and problems we take up in Chapter 3). Even this was not enough. They believed they needed additional means to limit the national government.

The most important way to make public officials observe the constitutional limits on their powers is through *regular and fair elections*; voters have the ability to throw out of office those who abuse power. Yet the framers were not willing to depend solely on such political controls, because they did not fully trust the people's judgment. "Free government is founded on jealousy, and not in confidence," said Thomas Jefferson. "In questions of power, then, let no more be heard of confidence in man, but bind him down from mischief by the chains of the Constitution."[4]

Even more important, the framers feared that a majority faction might use the new central government to deprive minorities of their rights. "A dependence on the people is, no doubt, the primary control on the government," Madison admitted in *The Federalist*, No. 51, "but experience has taught mankind the necessity of auxiliary precautions." What were these "auxiliary precautions" against popular tyranny?

Separation of Powers

The first step was the **separation of powers**, that is, the allocation of constitutional authority to each of the three branches of the national government. In *The Federalist*, No. 47, Madison wrote, "No political truth is certainly of greater intrinsic value, or is stamped with the authority of more enlightened patrons of liberty, than that . . . the accumulation of all powers, legislative, executive, and judiciary, in the same hands . . . may justly be pronounced the very definition of tyranny." (Chief among the "enlightened patrons of liberty" to whose authority Madison was appealing were John Locke and Montesquieu, whose works were subscribed to by most educated Americans.)

The intrinsic value of the principle of dispersion of power does not by itself account for its incorporation into our Constitution. Such dispersion of power had been the general practice in the colonies for more than one hundred years. Only during the Revolutionary period did some of the states and the Articles of Confederation concentrate authority in the hands of the legislature, and that unhappy experience confirmed the framers' belief in the merits of separation of powers. Many attributed the evils of state government and the lack of energy in the central government to the fact that there was no strong executive both to check legislative abuses and to give energy and direction to administration.

Still, separating power was not enough. There was always the danger—from the framers' point of view—that different officials with different powers might pool their authority and act together. Separation of powers by itself might not prevent governmental branches and officials from responding to the same pressures—from the demand of an overwhelming majority of the voters to suppress an offensive book, for example, or to impose confiscatory taxes on rich people. If separating power was not enough, what else could be done?

Checks and Balances: Ambition to Counteract Ambition

The framers' answer was a system of **checks and balances**. "The great security against a gradual concentration of the several powers in the same department," wrote Madison in *The Federalist*, No. 51, "consists in giving to those who administer each department the necessary constitutional means and personal motives to resist encroachments of the others. . . . Ambition must be made to counteract ambition."

Each branch therefore has a role in the actions of the others (see Figure 2-1). We have a "government of separated institutions sharing powers."[5] Congress enacts laws, yet the president can veto them. The Supreme Court can declare laws passed by Congress and signed by the president unconstitutional, but the president appoints the justices and all the other federal judges with the Senate's approval. The president administers the laws, but Congress provides the money. Moreover, the Senate and the House of Representatives have an absolute veto over each other in the enactment of a law, because bills must be approved by both houses.

Not only does each branch have some authority over the others, but each is *politically independent of the others*. The president is selected by electors (now popularly elected). Senators are now chosen by the voters in each state, and

FIGURE 2-1   The Separation of Powers and Checks and Balances

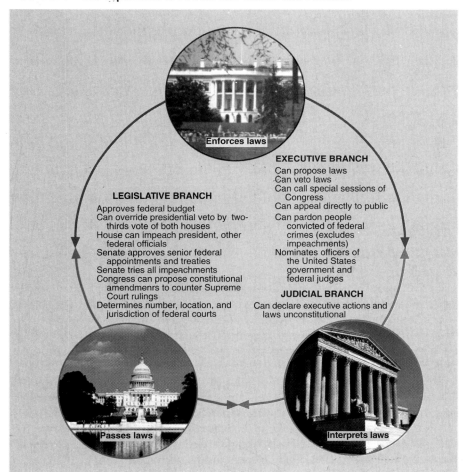

members of the House are chosen by voters in their districts. And although federal judges are appointed by the president with the consent of the Senate, once in office they hold terms virtually for life.

The framers also ensured that a majority of the voters could win control over only part of the government at one time. Although a popular majority might take control of the House of Representatives in an off-year (that is, a nonpresidential) election, the president, representing a previous popular majority, would still have two years to go. Further, senators are chosen for six years. Finally, independent national courts, which have developed their own powerful checks, were also provided. In fact, judges have become so important in our system of checks and balances that they deserve special attention.

JUDICIAL REVIEW AND THE "GUARDIANS OF THE CONSTITUTION"

Judges did not claim the power of **judicial review**—the power of a court to *refuse* to enforce a law or a government regulation that in the opinion of the judges conflicts with the Constitution—until some years after the Constitution was in operation. From the beginning, however, judges were expected to restrain legislative majorities. "The independence of judges," wrote Alexander Hamilton in *The Federalist*, No. 78 (which appears in the Appendix), "may be an essential safeguard against the effects of occasional ill humors in the society."

Judicial review is a contribution of the United States to the art of government, a contribution adapted in part in recent years in other nations such as Canada and Germany. (The Canadian constitution's "notwithstanding" provision allows either a provincial legislature or the national parliament in effect to override certain sections of the Charter of Rights for a renewable period of six years.)[6] If British or American citizens are thrown into prison without cause, they can appeal to the courts of their respective countries for protection. But no British judge may declare a law duly enacted by Parliament null and void because the judge believes it violates the British constitution; Parliament is the guardian of the British constitution. In the United States the courts, ultimately the Supreme Court, are the keepers of the constitutional conscience—not Congress and not the president. How did judges get this tremendous responsibility?

Origins of Judicial Review

The Constitution says nothing about who should have the final word in disputes that might arise over its meaning. Whether the delegates to the Constitutional Convention of 1787 intended to give the courts the power of judicial review is a question long debated. The framers clearly intended for the Supreme Court to have the power to declare *state* legislation unconstitutional, but whether they intended to give it the same power over *national* legislation is not clear. The late Edward S. Corwin, the outstanding authority on the American Constitution, concluded that unquestionably "the framers anticipated some sort of judicial review. . . . But it is equally without question that the ideas generally current in 1787 were far from presaging the present vast role of the court."[7] Why, then, did the framers not specifically provide for judicial review? Probably because they believed the power could readily be inferred from certain general provisions.

The Federalists—those who wrote the Constitution and controlled the national government until 1801—generally supported a strong role for federal courts and favored judicial review. Their opponents, the Jeffersonian Republicans (called Democrats after 1832), were less enthusiastic. In 1798 and 1799 Jefferson and Madison (who by this time had left the Federalist camp), with the Virginia and Kentucky Resolutions, came close to the position that state legislatures—and not the Supreme Court—had the ultimate power to interpret the Constitution. These resolutions seemed to question even whether the Supreme Court had the final authority to review state legislation, something about which there had been little doubt.

When the Jeffersonians defeated the Federalists in the elections of 1800, it was still undecided whether the Supreme Court would actually exercise the power of judicial review. The idea was in the air, logical reasons to support a doctrine of judicial review were at hand, and some precedents could even be cited; nevertheless judicial review was not an established power. Then in 1803 came *Marbury v Madison*, one of the most famous Supreme Court decisions of all time.[8]

Marbury versus Madison (1803)

The elections of 1800 marked the rise to power of the Jeffersonian Republicans. President John Adams and fellow Federalists did not take their defeat easily. Indeed, they were greatly alarmed at what they considered to be the "enthronement of the rabble." Yet there was nothing much they could do about it before leaving office—or was there? The Constitution gives the president, with the consent of the Senate, the power to appoint federal judges to hold office during "good Behaviour." With the judiciary in the hands of good Federalists, thought Adams and his associates, they could stave off the worst consequences of Jefferson's victory.

The lame duck Federalist Congress created dozens of new federal judicial posts. (**Lame duck** is the term applied to elected officials who have recently been defeated for office but are serving out the rest of their term before being replaced by their successors.) By March 3, 1801, Adams had appointed, and the Senate had confirmed, loyal Federalists to all these new positions. Adams signed the commissions and turned them over to John Marshall, the secretary of state in the Adams administration, to be sealed and delivered. Marshall had just received his own commission as chief justice of the United States, but he was continuing to serve as secretary of state until Adams's term as president expired. Working right up until nine o'clock on the evening of March 3, Marshall sealed, but was unable to deliver, all the commissions. The important ones were taken care of, however, and the only ones left were for the justices of the peace for the District of Columbia. The newly appointed chief justice left these commissions for his successor to deliver.

Jefferson, now inaugurated as president, was angered by this "packing" of the judiciary. When he discovered that some of the commissions were still lying on a table in the Department of State, he instructed a clerk not to deliver them. Jefferson could see no reason why the District needed so many justices of the peace, especially Federalist justices.[9]

Among the commissions not delivered was one for William Marbury. After waiting in vain, Marbury decided to seek action from the courts. Searching through the statute books, he came across Section 13 of the Judiciary Act of 1789, which authorized the Supreme Court "to issue writs of *mandamus*, in cases warranted by the principles and usages of law, to . . . persons holding office under

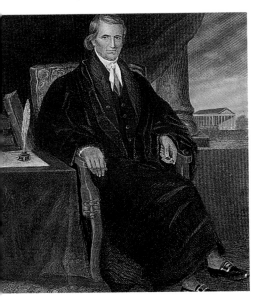

Chief Justice John Marshall (1755–1835), our most influential Supreme Court justice. Appointed in 1801, Marshall served until 1835. Earlier he had been a staunch defender of the U.S. Constitution at the Virginia ratifying convention, a member of Congress, and a secretary of state. He is one of those rare people who served in all three branches of government.

the authority of the United States." A **writ of *mandamus*** is a court order directing an official, such as the secretary of state, to perform a ministerial duty, a duty about which the official has no discretion, such as delivering a commission. So, thought Marbury, why not ask the Supreme Court to issue a writ of *mandamus* to force James Madison, the new secretary of state, to deliver the commission? Marbury and his companions went directly to the Supreme Court, and, citing Section 13, they made the request.

What could Marshall do? If the Court issued the writ, Madison and Jefferson would probably ignore it. The Court would be powerless, and its prestige, already low, might suffer a fatal blow. On the other hand, by refusing to issue the writ, the judges would appear to support the Jeffersonian Republicans' claim that the Court had no authority to interfere with the executive. Would Marshall issue the writ? Most people thought so; angry Republicans even threatened impeachment if he did so.

On February 24, 1803, the Supreme Court delivered its opinion. The first part was as expected. Marbury was entitled to his commission, said Marshall, and Madison should have delivered it to him. Moreover, a writ of *mandamus* could be issued by the proper court against even so high an officer as the secretary of state, the president of the United States' own agent.

Then came the surprise. Although Section 13 of the Judiciary Act seems to give the Supreme Court original jurisdiction in cases such as that in question, this section, said Marshall, is contrary to Article III of the Constitution, which gives the Supreme Court original jurisdiction *only* when an ambassador or other foreign minister is affected or when a state is a party. Even though this is a case of original jurisdiction, Marbury is neither a state nor a foreign minister. If we follow Section 13, wrote Marshall, we have jurisdiction; if we follow the Constitution, we have no jurisdiction.

Marshall then posed the question in a more pointed way: Should the Supreme Court enforce an unconstitutional law? Of course not, he concluded. The Constitution is the supreme and binding law, and the courts cannot enforce any action of Congress that conflicts with it.

The real question remained unanswered. Congress and the president had also read the Constitution, and according to their interpretation, which was also reasonable, Section 13 was compatible with Article III. Where did the Supreme Court get the right to say they were wrong? Why should the Supreme Court's interpretation of the Constitution be preferred to that of Congress and the president?

Paralleling Hamilton's argument in *The Federalist*, No. 78, Marshall reasoned: The Constitution is law: judges—not legislators or executives—interpret law. Therefore, judges should interpret the Constitution. "If two laws conflict with each other, the courts must decide on the operation of each," he said. Case dismissed.

Jefferson fumed. For one thing, Marshall had said that a court with the proper jurisdiction could issue a writ of *mandamus*, even against the secretary of state, one of the president's closest advisers. Yet there was little Jefferson could do about what he thought was Marshall's arrogance. There was not even a court order he could refuse to obey. In a single stroke, Marshall had lectured the Jeffersonian Republicans for failing to perform their duties, and he had gone a long way toward acquiring the power for the Supreme Court to review acts of Congress. And he had done it in a manner that made it difficult for the Republicans to challenge.

Marbury v Madison is a masterpiece of judicial strategy. Marshall went out of his way to declare Section 13 unconstitutional. He could have interpreted the section to mean that the Supreme Court could issue writs of *mandamus* in those cases in which it did have jurisdiction. He could have interpreted Article III to mean that Congress could add to, though not subtract from, the original jurisdiction the Constitution gives to the Supreme Court. He could have dismissed the case for want of jurisdiction without discussing Marbury's right to his commission. But none of these would have suited his purpose. Marshall was fearful for the Supreme Court's future; unless the Court spoke out, he reasoned, it would become subordinate to the president and Congress.

Marshall's decision, important as it was, did not by itself establish the Supreme Court's power to review and declare acts of Congress unconstitutional. Not until the *Dred Scott* case in 1857 did the Supreme Court declare another act of Congress unconstitutional,[10] and not until after the Civil War did the modern use of judicial review become established.

Marbury v Madison might have been interpreted by subsequent generations in a very limited way, so that the Supreme Court had the right to determine the scope of its *own* powers under Article III, but that Congress and the president had the authority to interpret *their* own powers under Articles I and II, respectively. One scholar insists that is what Marshall intended and that the more expansive interpretation of *Marbury v Madison* is part of a myth designed to perpetuate judicial dominance.[11] However, Marshall's decision has not been interpreted in this way. On the contrary, building on Marshall's precedent over the decades, the Court has taken the commanding position as the authoritative interpreter of the Constitution.

Perhaps if Marshall had not spoken when he did, the Court might not have been able to assume the power of judicial review. He created the precedent. This is a classic example of constitutional development through judicial interpretation. The Constitution gives no specific authorization for the Court to declare congressional enactments null and void; yet today this practice is a vital part of our constitutional system.

Several important consequences follow from the acceptance of Marshall's argument that judges are the official interpreters of the Constitution. The most important is that even a law enacted by the Congress and approved by the president may, under many circumstances, be challenged by a single person. Simply by bringing a lawsuit, those who lack the clout to get a bill through Congress or influence a federal agency may often secure a judicial hearing. And organized interest groups often find that policy goals unattainable by legislation can be achieved by litigation. Litigation thus supplements, and at times takes precedence over, legislation as a way to make public policy.[12]

CHECKS AND BALANCES: DOES IT WORK?

What if a majority of the people gain control of all branches of government and force through radical measures? If a great majority of the voters want to take a certain step, the framers knew that nothing could stop them—nothing, that is, except despotic government, and that the framers did not want. They reasoned that all they could do—and this is quite a lot—is to prevent, temporarily, full control by the popular majority.

Distrustful of both the elites and the masses, the framers deliberately built *inefficiency* into our political system. They designed the decision-making process so that the national government can act decisively only when there is a general agreement, a consensus, among most of the interest groups and after all sides have had a chance to have their say.

Two hundred years after the ratification of the Constitution, Americans continue to debate the desirability of these limits under the vastly different

In 1857 the Supreme Court denied Dred Scott his freedom by ruling that slaves were property and protected as such by the Constitution. This decision declared an act of Congress—the Missouri Compromise—to be unconstitutional. This decision was later overruled by the Fourteenth Amendment.

gridlock

Should we change our Constitution?

Of the more than 170 constitutions in the world, the Constitution of the United States is the oldest and one of the most admired. Yet the two-hundredth birthday celebrations of the writing of the Constitution (1787), its ratification (1788), and the drawing up and ratification of the Bill of Rights (1789–91) directed our attention to how we might improve it. Do you, in the spirit of the Constitution's framers, have any amendments you would like to see become part of the Constitution?

The Exercise of Checks and Balances, 1789–1994

Vetoes

The president has vetoed about 2,500 acts of Congress.

Congress has overridden presidential vetoes about 100 times.

Judicial Review

The Supreme Court has ruled close to 150 congressional acts or parts thereof unconstitutional. Its 1983 decision on legislative vetoes (*INS v Chahda*) affects another 200 provisions.

Impeachment

The House of Representatives has impeached 16 federal officials, including 13 federal judges; of these, the Senate has convicted 7.

Confirmation

The Senate has refused to confirm 9 cabinet nominations, and many other cabinet and subcabinet appointments were withdrawn because of likely Senate rejection.

---

conditions of our times. Crucial questions remain: Are these checks necessary or sufficient to prevent abuses of political power? Is the greater danger that governments will not do the right things, or that they will do the wrong things? Do these limitations work to prevent abuses, or do they result in a "deadlock of democracy," making coherent governmental action for the general welfare difficult, if not impossible?

Modifications of Checks and Balances

Even though fragmentation of political power remains, several developments have modified the way the system of checks and balances works.

1. *The rise of national political parties.* Political parties can serve as unifying factors—at times drawing together the president, senators, representatives, and sometimes even judges behind common programs. Yet the parties, in turn, can be splintered and weakened by having to work through a system of fragmented governmental power, so they never become strong or cohesive. Moreover, when one party controls the Congress and the other the White House, as has generally been the case since the end of World War II, parties may intensify checks and balances, rather than moderate them, to the point that no definitive action can be taken on some major issues.[13]

   Divided government may lead to such competition between the two branches that we find "each institution protecting and promoting itself through a broad interpretation of its constitutional and political status, even usurping the other's power when the opportunity presents itself."[14] Thus, we have had battles over presidential impoundments, budgeting deadlocks, and unseemly and angry confirmation hearings for the appointment of federal judges, especially for the justices of the Supreme Court. Divided government also makes it difficult for the voters to hold anybody or any party accountable. "Presidents blame Congress . . . while members of Congress attack the president. . . . Citizens genuinely can not tell who is to blame."[15]

   Yet when all the shouting dies down, concluded Professor David R. Mayhew after a careful review of the evidence, "control by one party has not made all that much difference." There have been just as many congressional investigations and just as much important legislation passed when one party controls Congress and another controls the presidency as when the same party controls both branches.[16]

   President Bill Clinton's election in 1992 ushered in the first era of same-party control of the White House and the Congress since the Carter administration, 1976–80. The Democratic Senate gave President Clinton's presidential appointments somewhat smoother treatment than it gave President George Bush's, but not without serious questioning of credentials. Tension between the White House and Congress over who decides when and under what conditions American military forces should be deployed may have been moderated by the same party's controlling both branches, but, if so, the moderation is slight. Contention between the president and Congress over the budget, the North American Free Trade Agreement, health care reform, gun control, and criminal violence continues to reflect the vigor of the checks and balances system and demonstrates that same-party control only tempers interbranch strife.

2. *Expansion of the electorate and changes in electoral methods.* The framers wanted the president to be chosen by wise, independent citizens free from

popular passions and hero worship. Almost from the beginning, however, presidential electors have pledged prior to elections to cast their votes for their parties' presidential candidates. Further, senators, originally elected by state legislatures, are today chosen directly by the people.

The "people" entitled to vote has expanded from white property-owning males to all citizens over 18 years of age. During the past century, American states have expanded the role of the electorate within the states by adopting **direct primaries**, in which voters select party nominees, and by permitting voters in about half the states to vote directly on laws (**initiative** and **referendum**) and even to remove elected state and local officials from office (**recall**). At the national level the electorate has been given a major voice in choosing party nominees not merely for the House and the Senate but even for president.

3. *Establishment of agencies deliberately designed to exercise legislative, executive, and judicial functions.* When the national government began seriously to regulate the economy, it issued detailed rules on such complex matters as railroad safety, bank and stock exchange practices, employment conditions, union negotiations, and oil and gasoline emissions. It has been difficult to assign regulatory responsibilities without blending the powers to make and apply rules and to decide disputes. Beginning in 1887 Congress created independent regulatory commissions such as the Interstate Commerce Commission and the Federal Communications Commission, and in this century it established independent executive agencies such as the Environmental Protection Agency.

4. *Changes in technology.* The system of checks and balances operates differently today from the way it did in 1787. Back then there were no televised congressional committee hearings, no electronic listening devices, no *Larry King Live* or radio talk shows, no *New York Times*, *Wall Street Journal*, *USA Today*, CNN, C-Span, no nightly news programs with national audiences, no presidential press conferences, and no live coverage of wars and of Americans being held hostage in foreign lands. Nuclear bombs, television, computers, cellular telephones, fax machines, public opinion polls—these and other innovations, including the "information superhighway," create conditions very different from those of two centuries ago. In some ways these new technologies have added to the powers of presidents by, among other things, permitting them to appeal directly to millions of people and giving them immediate access to public opinion. These new technologies have also added leverage to organized interests by making it easy for them to target thousands of letters and calls at Congress, to organize letters to the editor, and to stage media events. New technologies have also given greater independence and influence to nongovernmental agencies such as the press. They have made it possible for rich people like Ross Perot and religious leaders like Pat Robertson, who have access to large resources, to bypass political parties and carry their message directly to the electorate.

5. *The emergence of the United States as a world power and the existence of recurrent crises.* Today, problems anywhere in the world—China, Bosnia, the Persian Gulf, Somalia—often become crises for the United States. The need to deal with perpetual emergencies has concentrated power in the hands of the chief executive and the presidential staff. The president's role as the most significant player on the world stage and the immediate coverage of summit conferences with foreign leaders enhance his status as domestic leader. Headline-producing ceremonial, as well as substantive,

Independent Regulatory Agencies

Thinking it Through

Although most of us do not think we should change our Constitution very often, in recent years some members of Congress have suggested amendments that would:

Prevent Congress from increasing tax rates retroactively

Give Congress and the states the power to make flag desecration illegal

Require a balanced federal budget

Permit state-sponsored prayers in public schools

Provide for equal rights under the law for women

Abolish the electoral college and provide for the direct election of the president

Permit citizens to participate directly in national law making by initiative petitions, to be approved or rejected by a direct vote of the people

Provide for a single, non-renewable six-year term for the president

Give the president an item veto over appropriations (a veto over part of a bill while accepting the rest)

Impose a twelve-year limit on the terms of members of the House of Representatives and the Senate.

events give the president a visibility no congressional leader can achieve. The office of the president has sometimes served to impose some measure of national unity. Drawing on constitutional, political, and emergency powers, the president has sometimes been able to overcome restraints imposed by the Constitution on the exercise of cohesive governmental power—to the applause of some, and the alarm of others.

The British and American Systems: A Study in Contrasts

Although many Americans question the usefulness and functions of some government institutions, we tend to take the system of checks and balances for granted, considering it necessary for constitutional government. Like Madison, we view the amassing of power by any one branch of government as leading to tyranny, especially since scandals such as Watergate, in which President Richard Nixon tried to use federal agencies to suppress evidence of his administration's involvement in a break-in at Democratic party headquarters, and the Iran-Contra affair, in which the Reagan administration worked covertly to sell arms to Iran in order to get around congressional limitations on giving aid to the Nicaraguan government.

Yet it is quite possible for a government to be constitutional without these checks and balances. The British system is a good example (see Figure 2-2). Under the British system, voters elect members of Parliament from districts throughout the nation, much as we elect members of the House of Representatives. Members of the House of Commons have almost complete constitutional power. Leaders of the majority party serve as executive ministers, who collectively form the cabinet, with the prime minister as its head. The prime minister, like the other cabinet members, represents a constituency (a district) and is in effect chosen by the majority party. When the executive officers lose the support of the majority in the Commons on a major issue, they must resign or call for new elections. Formerly the House of Lords could check the Commons, but it is now almost powerless. There is no high court with the power to declare acts of Parliament unconstitutional. The prime minister cannot veto them, although he or she may ask the Crown to dissolve Parliament and call new elections for members of the House of Commons.

The British system is based on *majority* (51 percent) or *plurality rule* (largest number); that is, a plurality of the voters elects a parliamentary majority. Like us, the British elect legislators from districts, and the party with the most votes in that district wins the seat, so that even with three or more parties, a plurality of the popular vote usually results in a majority of the parliamentary seats. So long as the parliamentary majority stays together, it can enact into law the majority party's program. British parties are cohesive and disciplined; party members vote together and support their parliamentary leaders. In Britain the party that wins an election has a very good chance of seeing its *platform*, or policy goals, enacted. Our system usually depends on the agreement of many elements of society. The party that wins a presidential or congressional election or even one that controls both these branches will still have a tough time carrying out its platform promises. The British system *concentrates* control and responsibility in the legislature; ours *diffuses* control and responsibility among several organs of government.

We have a written document called the Constitution; Britain has no such single document. Yet both systems are constitutional in the sense that the rulers are subject to regular restraints. The limits our written Constitution and the conventions the unwritten British constitution impose rest on underlying values and attitudes.

FIGURE 2-2   A Comparison of the British and American Systems

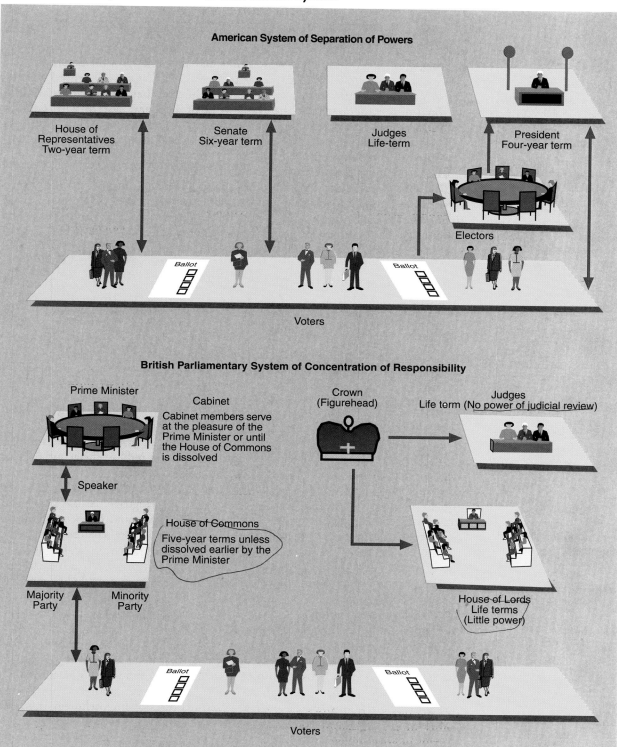

American System of Separation of Powers

House of Representatives
Two-year term

Senate
Six-year term

Judges
Life-term

President
Four-year term

Electors

Ballot

Ballot

Voters

British Parliamentary System of Concentration of Responsibility

Prime Minister

Cabinet
Cabinet members serve at the pleasure of the Prime Minister or until the House of Commons is dissolved

Crown
(Figurehead)

Judges
Life term (No power of judicial review)

Speaker

House of Commons
Five-year terms unless dissolved earlier by the Prime Minister

Majority Party

Minority Party

House of Lords
Life terms
(Little power)

Ballot

Ballot

Voters

How the Amending Power Has Been Used

To Add or Subtract National Government Power

The Eleventh took some jurisdiction away from the national courts.

The Thirteenth abolished slavery and authorized Congress to legislate against it.

The Sixteenth enabled Congress to levy an income tax.

The Eighteenth authorized Congress to prohibit the manufacture, sale, or transportation of liquor.

The Twenty-first repealed the Eighteenth and gave states the authority to regulate liquor sales.

The Twenty-seventh limited the power of Congress to set members' salaries.

To Limit State Government Power

The Thirteenth abolished slavery.

The Fourteenth granted national citizenship and prohibited states from abridging privileges of national citizenship; from denying persons life, liberty, and property without due process; and from denying persons equal protection of the laws. This amendment has come to be interpreted as imposing restraints on state powers in every area of public life.

To Expand the Electorate and Its Power

The Fifteenth extended the suffrage to all male African Americans.

The Seventeenth took the right to elect their United States senators from state legislatures and gave it to the voters in each state.

The Nineteenth extended suffrage to women.

The Twenty-third gave voters of the District of Columbia the right to vote for president and vice-president.

The Twenty-fourth prohibited any state from taxing the right to vote (the poll tax).

The Twenty-sixth extended the suffrage to otherwise qualified persons 18 years of age or older.

To Reduce the Electorate's Power

The Twenty-second took from the electorate the right to elect any person to the office of president for more than two full terms.

THE CONSTITUTION AS AN INSTRUMENT OF GOVERNMENT

As careful as the Constitution's framers were to limit the powers they gave the national government, the main reason they had assembled in Philadelphia was *to create a stronger national government*. Having learned that a weak central government, incapable of governing, is a danger to liberty, they wished to establish a national government within the framework of a federal system with enough authority to meet the needs of all times. They made general grants of power, leaving it to succeeding generations to fill in the details and organize the structure of government in accordance with experience.

Hence our formal, written Constitution is only the skeleton of our system. It is filled out by numerous rules that must be considered part of our constitutional system in its larger sense. In fact, it is primarily through changes in our informal, *unwritten* Constitution that our system is kept up to date. These changes are to be found in certain basic statutes and historical practices of Congress, presidential practices, customs and usages of the nation, and decisions of the Supreme Court.

Congressional Elaboration

Because the framers gave Congress authority over many of the structural details of the national government, it is not necessary to amend the Constitution every time a change is needed. Rather, Congress can act from year to year. Examples of congressional elaboration appear in such legislation as the Judiciary Act of 1789, which laid the foundations of our national judicial system; in the laws establishing the organization and functions of all federal executive officials subordinate to the president; and in the rules of procedure, internal organization, and practices of Congress.

IMPEACHMENT AND REMOVAL POWER   A dramatic example of congressional elaboration of our constitutional system is the use of the impeachment and removal power. An **impeachment** is a formal accusation against a public official and the first step in removal from office. Constitutional language is sparse. Take a look at your copy of the Constitution, and note that according to Article I—the Legislative Article—it is up to Congress to give meaning to that language. Article I gives the House of Representatives the sole power of impeachment, and the Senate the sole power to try all impeachments. When sitting for that purpose, senators "shall be on Oath or Affirmation." In the event the president is being tried, the chief justice of the United States presides. Article I also requires conviction on impeachment charges to have the agreement of two-thirds of the senators present. Judgments shall extend no further than removal from office and disqualification from holding any office under the United States, but a person convicted shall also be liable to indictment, trial, judgment, and punishment according to the law. In Article II—the Executive Article—the Constitution provides that the "President, Vice President and all civil Officers of the United States, shall be removed from Office on Impeachment for, and Conviction of, Treason, Bribery, or other High Crimes and Misdemeanors." This article also exempts cases of impeachment from the president's pardoning power. Article III—the Judicial Article—exempts cases of impeachment from the jury trial requirement. That is all the relevant constitutional language. We must look to history to answer most questions about the proper exercise of these powers.[17]

Fortunately, our experiences have triggered few acute constitutional disputes about the interpretation of impeachment procedures, and there is little history to go on. The House of Representatives has investigated 66 individuals for possible impeachment and has impeached 16 (one resigned after the impeachment resolutions were adopted, so the House voted on articles of impeachment for only 15);

the Senate has convicted seven (all federal judges). The recent spate of impeachment proceedings—three since 1986—caused the Senate to decide, not without controversy, that the responsibility to hear evidence can be delegated to a committee. The Supreme Court has ruled that the Senate may so delegate and, in fact, that the House and Senate possess the constitutional authority to decide what the impeachment process shall be, subject to little, if any, judicial review.[18]

Only one president—Andrew Johnson—was impeached, in 1868, but the Senate failed by one vote to muster the two-thirds necessary to support the charges. Another president—Richard Nixon—resigned on August 9, 1974, to avoid impeachment after the House Judiciary Committee recommended three articles of impeachment against him. The House did not press the matter further, but the articles of impeachment were submitted by the committee and were "accepted" by the House.

Even though congressional precedents have rejected the *broadest* view—that the Constitution authorizes removal of officers by impeachment because of *political* objections to them or because of their unpopularity (a view that might have moved us more in the direction of a parliamentary type of government)—Congress has also rejected the *narrowest* construction: that impeachable offenses are *only* those that involve violations of the criminal laws. Rather, the firmly established position is that impeachment and conviction are only justified if there have been serious violations of constitutional responsibilities and a clear dereliction of duty.[19]

Presidential Practices

Although the president's formal constitutional powers have not changed, the office is dramatically more important and more central today than it was in 1789. Vigorous presidents—George Washington, Thomas Jefferson, Andrew Jackson, Abraham Lincoln, Theodore Roosevelt, Woodrow Wilson, Franklin Roosevelt, Harry Truman, Lyndon Johnson, Bill Clinton—have boldly exercised their political and constitutional powers, especially during times of national crisis. Such presidential practices have become important precedents, building the power and influence of the office. Even John Tyler made his contribution to constitutional elaboration. Upon becoming president through vice-presidential succession, Tyler established the precedent that the vice-president becomes the president, not merely the acting president.

Presidential practices include **executive privilege** (the right of the president to withhold information), **impoundment** of funds previously appropriated by Congress, the right to send our armed forces into hostilities, and, most important, the right to propose legislation and work actively to secure its passage by Congress. President Clinton, for example, has placed health care reform on the national agenda by pushing it before the nation and Congress as a priority for legislative action.

Foreign and economic crises as well as nuclear-age realities add force to the president's role as the nation's "final arbiter." Political scientist Richard Neustadt says, "When it comes to action risking nuclear war, technology has modified the Constitution: the President, perforce, becomes the only such man in the system capable of exercising judgment under the extraordinary limits now imposed by secrecy, complexity, and time."[20] The presidency has also become the pivotal office for regulating the economy and protecting the general welfare. Plainly, the president has also become a chief legislator as well as the nation's chief executive.

Custom and Usage

Custom and usage round out our governmental system. Although not specifically mentioned in the Constitution, certain practices are now fundamental. It has been primarily the development of structures outside the formal Constitution—

How the Amending Power Has Been Used (continued)

To Make Structural Changes in Government

The Twelfth corrected deficiencies in the operation of the electoral college that were revealed by the development of a two-party national system.

The Twentieth altered the calendar for congressional sessions and shortened the time between the election of presidents and their assumption of office.

The Twenty-fifth provided procedures for filling vacancies in the vice-presidency and for determining whether presidents are unable to perform their duties.

Andrew Johnson is the only American president to be impeached, but the charges failed to receive the necessary two-thirds vote in the Senate. Impeachment charges were also brought against Richard Nixon, who resigned to avoid appearing before the House Judiciary Committee.

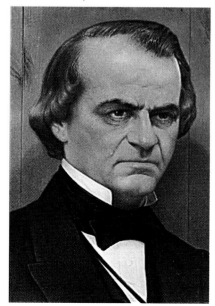

such as national political parties or the extension of the suffrage within the states—that democratized our Constitution. Through these developments, the president has become responsive to the people and has a political base different from that of Congress, so the constitutional relationship between the branches today is considerably different from that envisaged by the framers.

What is the difference between a custom and a usage? Not much. One could distinguish between them by reserving **custom** to refer to practices of non-governmental institutions such as political parties or of the electorate—not nominating or voting for persons who are not residents of the district they wish to represent—and reserving **usage** to refer to long-standing practices of Congress, the president, and the courts. The two terms are used together to refer both to customs of nongovernmental agencies and usages of governmental institutions, a usage we adopt here. Do not worry about the distinction—that is, unless your teacher does.

Judicial Interpretation

Judicial interpretation of the Constitution, especially by the Supreme Court, has played an important part in keeping the constitutional system up to date. As social and economic conditions have changed and new national demands have developed, the Supreme Court has changed its interpretation of the Constitution accordingly. In the words of Woodrow Wilson, "The Supreme Court is a constitutional convention in continuous session." Because the Constitution adapts to changing times, it does not require frequent formal amendment.

The advantages of this flexibility may be appreciated by comparing the national Constitution with the rigid and often overly specific state constitutions. Many state constitutions, more like legal codes than basic charters, are so detailed that they excessively tie the hands of the public officials. Such constitutions must be amended frequently or replaced every generation or so.

A Rigid or Flexible Constitution ?

The idea of a constantly changing system disturbs many people. How, they contend, can you have a constitutional government when the Constitution is constantly being twisted by interpretation and changed by informal methods? This view fails

Presidential nominating conventions are not mentioned in the Constitution, but they are a fundamental custom of our political system today.

AMENDING THE CONSTITUTION

The framers set up two ways to propose amendments and two ways to ratify them, and they saw to it that amendments could not be adopted by simple majorities. Each amendment must be both proposed and ratified.

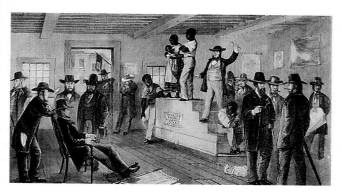

The Thirteenth, Fourteenth, and Fifteenth Amendments put an end to slave auctions like this and granted basic rights to all races.

The Nineteenth Amendment extended the right to vote to women.

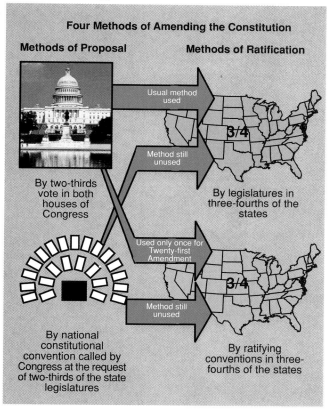

Four Methods of Amending the Constitution

Methods of Proposal — **Methods of Ratification**

Usual method used

Method still unused

By two-thirds vote in both houses of Congress

By legislatures in three-fourths of the states

3/4

Used only once for Twenty-first Amendment

Method still unused

By national constitutional convention called by Congress at the request of two-thirds of the state legislatures

By ratifying conventions in three-fourths of the states

3/4

The 27 Constitutional Amendments and Their Times for Ratification

Amendment	Time to Ratify	Ratified	Amendment	Time to Ratify	Ratified
1-10. Bill of Rights	2 years, 2½ months	1791	19. Women's suffrage	1 year, 2½ months	1920
11. Lawsuits against states	3 years, 10 months	1795	20. Terms of office	11 months	1933
12. Presidential elections	8½ months	1804	21. Repeal of prohibition	9½ months	1933
13. Abolition of slavery	10½ months	1865	22. Limit on presidential terms	3 years, 11½ months	1951
14. Civil rights laws	2 years, 11½ months	1868	23. Washington, D.C., vote	9 months	1961
15. Suffrage for all races	1 year, 1 month	1870	24. Abolition of poll taxes	1 year, 5½ months	1964
16. Income tax	3 years, 7½ months	1913	25. Presidential succession	1 year, 6½ months	1967
17. Senatorial elections	1 year, ½ month	1913	26. 18-year-old suffrage	4 months	1971
18. Prohibition	1 year, 1½ months	1919	27. Congressional salaries	202 years, 7½ months	1992

Is a constitutional convention to consider a Balanced Budget Amendment desirable?

In recent years Congress has received petitions for a convention to propose amendments to permit states to encourage prayer in public schools, to reverse Supreme Court decisions relating to abortions, to prohibit busing as a means of achieving integration in public schools, and to change the amending process to permit state legislatures to propose amendments without the intervention of Congress. Perhaps the most active campaign for a convention has been sponsored by the National Taxpayers Union on behalf of a Balanced Budget Amendment. Thirty-two state legislatures have petitioned Congress on this issue, although some petitions are of questionable validity.

Why has Congress been so reluctant to call a convention? Perhaps members recall what happened two hundred years ago when a reluctant Confederation Congress called into being a Constitutional Convention for the sole purpose of considering amendments to the Articles of Confederation, only to have that Convention ignore its instructions and create an entirely new Constitution.

to distinguish between two aspects of the Constitution. As an expression of *basic and timeless personal liberties*, the Constitution does not and should not change. For example, a government cannot destroy free speech and still remain a constitutional government. In this sense the Constitution is unchanging. But when we consider the Constitution as an *instrument of government* and a positive grant of power, we realize that if it does not grow with the nation it serves, it will soon be pushed aside. The framers could not have conceived of the problems faced by a government of a large, powerful, and wealthy nation of about 265 million people in the last decade of the twentieth century. Although the general purposes of government remain the same—to establish liberty, promote justice, ensure domestic tranquillity, and provide for the common defense—the powers of government adequate to accomplish these purposes in 1787 are simply insufficient two hundred years later.

"We the people"—the people of today and tomorrow, not just the people of 1787—ordain and establish the Constitution. "The Constitution," wrote Jefferson, "belongs to the living and not to the dead." So firmly did he believe this that he suggested there might be a new constitution for every generation. New constitutions have not been necessary, however, because in a less formal way each generation has taken part in the process of developing and changing the original Constitution. Because of its remarkable adaptability, the Constitution has survived democratic and industrial revolutions, the turmoil of civil war, the tensions of major depressions, and the dislocations of world wars.

CHANGING THE LETTER OF THE CONSTITUTION

The framers knew that future experiences would call for changes in the text of the Constitution and that some means for formal amendment was necessary. In Article V they gave responsibility for amending the Constitution to Congress and to the states; the president has no formal authority over constitutional amendments. Presidential veto power does not extend to them, although presidential political influence is often crucial in getting amendments proposed by Congress and ratified by the states. Nor may governors veto ratification of amendments.

Proposing Amendments

The first method for proposing amendments—and the only one used so far—is by a two-thirds vote of both houses of Congress. Dozens of resolutions proposing amendments are introduced in every session. Thousands have been introduced since 1789, most of them during the last two decades. Few make any headway. Throughout our history Congress has proposed only 33 amendments (21 plus the Bill of Rights, including the Twenty-seventh, which was originally part of the Bill of Rights but took more than two hundred years for ratification).

In recent years there has been a flurry of congressional consideration of constitutional amendments. None has been formally proposed by both chambers; many are currently under consideration. One being given serious consideration is the so-called Balanced Budget Amendment. It has the support of a majority in both the House and the Senate, but so far not the required two-thirds necessary for passage. In 1986 the Senate came within one vote of proposing such an amendment, and in March of 1994 a similar proposal fell four votes short of the necessary two-thirds vote in the Senate. Although it would not have made any difference, the House of Representatives also took up the amendment a few days later. It failed by twelve votes in the House to get the necessary two-thirds. The 1994 version would have required a balanced budget by 2001 and provided for both a wartime exception and an override of the requirement for a balanced budget by a three-fifths majority of both houses.

Why has proposing amendments to the Constitution become such a popular pastime? In part because interest groups unhappy with Supreme Court decisions seek to overturn them. In part because groups frustrated by their inability to get things done in Congress—balancing the budget, for example—hope to bypass the Congress. And in part because scholars or interest-group representatives (not necessarily mutually exclusive categories) seek to change the procedures and process of government to make the system more responsive.[21]

The second method for proposing amendments—by a convention called by Congress at the request of the legislatures in two-thirds of the states—has never been used. This method presents some difficult questions.[22] First, can state legislatures apply for a convention to propose specific amendments on one topic, or must they request a convention with full powers to revise the entire Constitution?[23] How long do state petitions remain alive? How should delegates be chosen? How should a convention be run?

Congress has considered bills to answer some of these questions but has not passed any, in part because most members do not wish to encourage a constitutional convention for fear that once in session it might propose amendments on any and all topics. Most proposals call for Congress to set the date and place for a convention whenever both chambers conclude that legislatures in two-thirds of the states have petitioned about a particular subject closely enough in time to one another to reflect a "contemporaneous national request" for action. Under Article V of the Constitution, Congress could call for such a convention without the concurrence of the president, who is not part of the amendatory process at all. Under most proposals, each state would have as many delegates to the convention as it has representatives and senators in Congress. Finally—a crucial point—the convention would be *limited to considering only the subject specified* in the state legislative petitions and described in the congressional call for the convention. Scholars are divided, however, on whether Congress has the authority to so limit what a constitutional convention might propose.[24]

Despite several organized efforts to force Congress to call a constitutional convention (or else to propose the amendment itself), Congress has never done so.[25] We came close to a convention in 1967, when the thirty-third state legislature—only one short of the required number—petitioned Congress to call a convention to propose an amendment to set aside a Supreme Court ruling that both chambers of a state legislature must be apportioned on the basis of population. A thirty-fourth state never petitioned for a convention, and as state legislatures completed the process of reapportionment, pressures for an amendment abated.

Ratifying Amendments

After an amendment has been proposed, it must be ratified by the states. Again, two methods are provided: approval by the legislatures in three-fourths of the states, or approval by specially called ratifying conventions in three-fourths of the states. Congress determines which method is used. All amendments except one—the Twenty-first (to repeal the Eighteenth, the Prohibition Amendment)—have been submitted to the state legislatures for ratification.

Seven state constitutions specify that their state legislatures must ratify a proposed amendment to the U.S. Constitution by majorities of three-fifths or two-thirds of each chamber. Although a state legislature may change its mind and ratify an amendment after it has voted against ratification, the weight of opinion is that once a state has ratified an amendment, it cannot "unratify" it.[26]

Submitting amendments to legislatures rather than ratifying conventions allows changes to be made in the Constitution without any direct expressions by the voters. Legislators may have been elected before the proposed amendments were submitted to the states. In any event, state legislators are chosen because of

Thinking it Through

A constitutional convention to consider the Balanced Budget Amendment is necessary and desirable because:

1. The fiscal excesses of the federal government threaten irreparable damage to the nation.

2. We must correct this situation through constitutional reform with a tax limitation or balanced budget amendment. But Congress has refused to propose a constitutional amendment to control its fiscal practices.

3. The framers provided the people with a direct method of proposing amendments to the Constitution.

4. Thirty-two states have passed resolutions calling for a constitutional convention. Completion of this process is essential to the future of our nation.

No constitutional convention should be called because:

1. The Constitution does not define or limit the scope of such a convention.

2. Our only precedent, the 1787 Constitutional Convention, broke every legal restraint the Confederation Congress had designed to limit its power.

3. Assurances that limits can now be imposed are without substance; if a convention meets, it will do whatever the majority wants it to do. A number of secondary agendas have already been suggested.

4. Assurances that the threat of a convention, when backed by 33 states, will force Congress to pass an amendment limiting its spending are historically unsound and legally suspect.

SOURCE: Lewis K. Uhler, president of the National Tax-Limitation Committee, Roseville, Cal., and Linda Rogers-Kingsbury, president of Citizens to Protect the Constitution, Washington, D.C. Quoted in *Liberty* (March/April 1991), pp. 2, 3.

The Twenty-seventh Amendment: Is Two Hundred and Three Years a Reasonable Time?

In March 1982, Gregory Watson, a student at the University of Texas writing a paper on the Equal Rights Amendment, came across an amendment proposed in 1789 as part of the Bill of Rights that would prohibit a pay raise for members of Congress until the intervention of an election for members of the House. He found that only 6 of the original 13 states had ratified it, and that during the intervening years only 3 more states had done so.

Watson decided to start a ratification movement. He got some publicity for his efforts and, with the help of Texas Republican State Representative Don Mielke, persuaded 6 more state legislatures to ratify this long-forgotten proposed amendment. (By the way, Watson only got a C on his paper, although he "is credited with influencing 26 state legislatures to ratify the congressional amendment."*)

After Congress tried unsuccessfully in 1989 to avoid public heat by delegating the decision to increase congressional salaries to an independent commission, anti-Congress sentiment began to grow, and the ratification movement began to pick up steam. On May 7, 1992, the Michigan legislature became the thirty-eighth state to ratify it, and on May 18, 1992, the United States archivist certified that the amendment was part of the Constitution and had it printed in the *Federal Register*.

The first reaction of some congressional leaders was to question this action because the Supreme Court had made it clear that amendments must be ratified within a "reasonable time." However, when members of Congress realized that the issue could be used against them in the next election, they declared the Twenty-seventh Amendment to be "valid as part of the Constitution of the United States." The vote was not even close: 99 to 0 in the Senate, 414 to 3 in the House. Only the representative from Iowa spoke against ratification. He told his colleagues, "The principle of contemporary consensus . . . is just too important to ever waive just because it appears popular at the moment."

*Ruth Ann Strickland, "The Twenty-seventh Amendment and Constitutional Change by Stealth," *P.S. Political Science and Politics* (December 1993), p. 720.

their views on schools, taxation, or other matters, or because of their personal popularity. They are almost never elected because of their stand on proposed constitutional amendments, although the candidates' position on the Equal Rights Amendment (ERA) did surface as a key issue in several state legislative elections.

Procedures can make a difference. The decision to submit the Twenty-first Amendment repealing Prohibition to ratifying conventions came about because the "wets" rightly believed that repeal had a better chance of success with conventions than with the rural-dominated state legislatures. For similar tactical reasons, southern Democrats joined with eastern Republican conservatives in an unsuccessful effort to submit the Nineteenth Amendment to give women the vote, also called the Susan B. Anthony Amendment, to ratifying conventions. Let the voters decide—the male voters, that is—they argued.[27] For the Twenty-first Amendment, Congress left it up to each state legislature to determine how the ratifying conventions would be organized and delegates elected. State delegates ran at large on tickets that pledged they would vote for or against ratification. As a result, when state conventions were called to order, they quickly ratified the decision the voters had already made. In effect, ratification had been submitted to the voters.

The Supreme Court has said that ratification must take place within a "reasonable time." It suggested that it is up to Congress to police this requirement. Congress, at the time it proclaims the amendment to be part of the Constitution, must decide whether an amendment has been ratified within a reasonable time so that it is to "sufficiently contemporaneous to reflect the will of the people."[28] However, since Congress has approved ratification of the Twenty-seventh Amendment, which had been before the nation for almost 203 years, there seems to be no limit to what it will consider to be a reasonable time for ratification to take place. It is conceivable, but not likely, the Supreme Court could some day rule that the Twenty-seventh Amendment had not been properly ratified.[29]

The question of reasonableness of time for ratification is not likely to become an issue with respect to other amendments. At the time it "certified" the ratification of the Twenty-seventh Amendment, the Senate declared the other three outstanding amendments to be "dead." For future amendments Congress will probably continue the current practice of stipulating that an amendment will not become part of the Constitution unless ratified by the necessary number of states within seven years from the date of its submission. In fact, ratification ordinarily takes place rather quickly.[30]

Ratification Politics

Before the submission of the Equal Rights Amendment (ERA) and the D.C. Amendment, the Child Labor Amendment was the only formally proposed amendment since the Civil War that failed to be ratified. Ordinarily the existence of a political coalition sufficient to get an amendment proposed by Congress reflects enough support in the nation to ensure ratification. The failure of the ERA and the D.C. amendments to be ratified makes it clear this is not always the case.

THE EQUAL RIGHTS AMENDMENT   The ERA received overwhelming support in both houses of Congress and in both national party platforms; not until 1980 did one party (the Republican) adopt a stance of neutrality. Every president from Harry Truman to Ronald Reagan, and many of their wives, endorsed the amendment. By the end of the campaign for ratification, more than 450 organizations with a total membership of more than 50 million were on record in support of the ERA.[31]

Soon after submission of the amendment in 1972, many legislatures ratified quickly—sometimes without hearings—and by overwhelming majorities. By the end of 1972, 22 states had ratified the amendment.[32] It appeared that the ERA would soon become part of the Constitution. Then the opposition organized under the articulate leadership of Phyllis Schlafly, a prominent spokesperson for conservative causes, and the ERA became controversial.

Opponents argued that "women would not only be subject to the military draft but also assigned to combat duty. Full-time housewives and mothers would be forced to join the labor force. Furthermore, women would no longer enjoy existing advantages under state domestic relations codes and under labor law."[33] The ERA also became embroiled in the controversy over abortion. Many opponents contended that its ratification would jeopardize the power of states and Congress to regulate abortion in any way and would compel public funding of abortions.[34]

After the ERA became controversial, state legislatures held lengthy hearings, and floor debates became heated. Legislators hid behind parliamentary procedures and avoided making a decision for as long as possible. Opposition to ratification arose chiefly in the same cluster of southern states that had opposed ratification of the Nineteenth Amendment.

As the opposition grew more active, proponents redoubled their efforts. The National Organization for Women (NOW) called for an economic boycott of cities in nonratifying states, and many organizations refused to hold their conventions in Chicago, Kansas City, Las Vegas, Miami, Atlanta, and New Orleans. In the autumn of 1978 it appeared that the ERA would fall three short of the necessary number of ratifying states before the expiration of the seven-year limit—March 22, 1979. After an extended debate, and after voting down provisions that would have authorized state legislatures to change their minds and rescind prior ratification, Congress, by a simple majority vote, extended the time limit until June 30, 1982. It was argued that because the time limit was in the accompanying enabling legislation, not in the body of the proposed amendment, it was subject to congressional modification by simple majority. Nonetheless, by the final deadline the amendment was still three state legislatures short. Its failure to be ratified made moot the pending court test of the extension's constitutionality.

The framers intended that amending the Constitution should be difficult. The ERA ratification battle demonstrates how well they planned.[35]

THE D.C. AMENDMENT The Constitution vests in Congress the right to exercise exclusive legislation over the seat of the government of the United States, that is, the District of Columbia. Congress has delegated considerable power of home rule to those who live in Washington, D.C., or the District, as it is usually called. People who live in Washington pay federal taxes and D.C. taxes and are subject to federal laws. Under the Twenty-third Amendment, they also have three electoral votes. Yet the District's only congressional voice is a nonvoting delegate who serves on committees, attends sessions, and may participate in all debates. In 1993 Congress allowed the District delegate to vote in committees and on the floor but stipulated that the delegate's vote could never make the decisive difference on any issue.

An amendment proposed in 1978 would have given the 600,000 people of the District of Columbia two senators and the same number of representatives (one, under current law) in the House of Representatives it would have if it were a state. It would also have given the District a vote in the ratification of constitutional amendments and three electoral votes, with the possibility of more if its population grew to warrant it. It has three already, under the Twenty-third Amendment. Finally, it would have repealed the Twenty-third Amendment. Congress—in contrast to what it did with ERA—pointedly reverted to earlier practice and placed the seven-year limit for ratification in the text of the amendment, thus precluding extending the time limit by a simple majority of both houses.

Although their initial hopes for ratification were high, advocates of the amendment knew that ratification would be difficult. Many people in many states view

We The People

EQUAL RIGHTS AMENDMENT (ERA)

Proposed March 22, 1972. Died June 30, 1982, three state legislatures shy of the thirty-eight needed for ratification.

Section 1. Equality of rights under the law shall not be denied or abridged by the United States or by any State on account of sex.

Section 2. The Congress shall have power to enforce, by appropriate legislation, the provisions of this article.

Section 3. This amendment shall take effect two years after the date of ratification.

the District as "too urban, too liberal, and too Democratic." Moreover, the coalition that pushed the D.C. Amendment through Congress failed to maintain its cohesion during the ratification struggle. Even though the D.C. Amendment passed both chambers of Congress by large margins and with impressive bipartisan support in 1978, it had been ratified by only 16 states by its deadline of August 22, 1985.

Proponents of the amendment, after giving up hope it would be ratified, turned their attention to persuading Congress to admit the District to the Union as a state—except for a small portion that would remain the "seat of the Government of the United States." Statehood for the District of Columbia would accomplish all that the D.C. Amendment could have done, and more. Moreover, it would require only a simple majority vote of both houses of Congress and the approval of the president to accomplish.

Only about 8 percent of the District's voters are registered Republicans. Statehood for the District would, in all probability, produce two Democratic senators,[36] one of whom might well be the Reverend Jesse Jackson, the so-called "unofficial senator" from the District who was elected in November 1988 to serve as an unpaid nonvoting representative of the District and to lobby in behalf of statehood.[37] The Democratic party platform of 1992 pledged support for statehood for the District, and President Clinton declared, "It is fundamentally unfair that residents of the District are denied full representation and participation in our national life."[38] With the White House in the hands of a Democrat, the chances for statehood for the District of Columbia were considerably greater than when Republicans were in charge; nonetheless the House of Representatives on November 21, 1993, voted 227 to 153 against statehood. Statehood was supported by only 151 of the 258 House Democrats. Eleanor Holmes Norton, the District's nonvoting delegate to the House, and other statehood proponents declared a victory in that they got committee hearings, a floor debate, and a vote on the bill. They consider that the "issue now has national visibility."[39]

SUMMARY

1. Our Constitution both grants and limits powers. The framers established a government to be operated by ordinary people. They did not anticipate Americans would be so virtuous and civic minded that they could be trusted to operate a government without checks and balances. The framers were suspicious of people, especially of those having political power, so they separated and distributed the powers of the newly created national government in a variety of ways.

2. The framers were also concerned that the national government be strong enough to solve national problems. They wanted it to be responsive to the wishes of the people and to carry out those wishes, that is, the matured and refined wishes of the people. Thus they gave the national government substantial grants of power. But these grants were made with such broad strokes that it has been possible for the national government and the constitutional system to remain flexible and adapt to changing conditions.

3. Although the American governmental system has its roots in British traditions, our separation of powers and

checks and balances systems differ sharply from the British system of concentrated responsibility. It is also different because our courts have the power of judicial review.

4. The system of checks and balances has been modified over time. The Constitution has been adapted to new conditions through congressional elaboration, modern presidential practices, customs and usages, and judicial interpretation.

5. Although adaptable, the Constitution itself needs to be altered from time to time, and the document provides a procedure for its own amendment. An amendment must be both proposed and ratified: proposed by either a two-thirds vote in each chamber of Congress or by a national convention called by Congress on petition of the legislatures in two-thirds of the states; ratified either by the legislatures in three-fourths of the states or by specially called ratifying conventions in three-fourths of the states. The Constitution has been formally amended 27 times. The usual method has been proposal by two-thirds vote in both houses of Congress and ratification by the legislatures in three-fourths of the states.

FURTHER READING

BRUCE A. ACKERMAN, *We the People* (Harvard University Press, Belknap Press, 1991).

WILBOURN E. BENTON, ED., *1787: Drafting the U.S. Constitution* (Texas A&M Press, 1986).

RICHARD B. BERNSTEIN, *Amending America: If We Love the Constitution So Much Why Do We Keep Trying to Change It?* (Time, 1993).

JAMES BRYCE, *The American Commonwealth*, vols. 1 and 2 (Macmillan, 1889).

JAMES MacGREGOR BURNS, *The Vineyard of Liberty* (Knopf, 1982).

RUSSELL L. CAPLAN, *Constitutional Brinkmanship: Amending the Constitution by National Convention* (Oxford University Press, 1988).

ROBERT LOWRY CLINTON, *Marbury v. Madison and Judicial Review* (University Press of Kansas, 1989).

CHARLES HARDIN, *Constitutional Reform in America: Essays on the Separation of Powers* (Iowa State University Press, 1989).

LIBRARY OF CONGRESS, CONGRESSIONAL RESEARCH SERVICE, *The Constitution of the United States of America: Analysis and Interpretation*, Senate Document 100-9 (U.S. Government Printing Office, 1991).

BARBARA B. KNIGHT, *Separation of Powers in the American Political System* (George Mason University Press, 1989).

DONALD G. MATHEWS AND JANE SHERRON DE HART, *Sex, Gender, and the Politics of ERA: North Carolina and the Nation* (Oxford University Press, 1990).

DREW R. McCOY, *The Last of the Fathers: James Madison and the Republican Legacy* (Columbia University Press, 1989).

FORREST McDONALD, *Novus Ordo Seclorum: The Intellectual Origins of the Constitution* (University Press of Kansas, 1985).

J. W. PELTASON, *Understanding the Constitution*, 13th ed. (Harcourt Brace, 1994).

BARBARA A. PERRY, *Unfounded Fears: Myths and Realities of a Constitutional Convention* (Greenwood Press, 1989).

JAMES L. SUNDQUIST, *Constitutional Reform and Effective Government* (Brookings Institution, 1986).

JOHN R. VILE, *Rewriting the United States Constitution: An Examination of Proposals from Reconstruction to the Present* (Praeger, 1991).

JOHN R. VILE, *The Constitutional Amending Process in American Political Thought* (Praeger, 1992).

AMERICAN
FEDERALISM

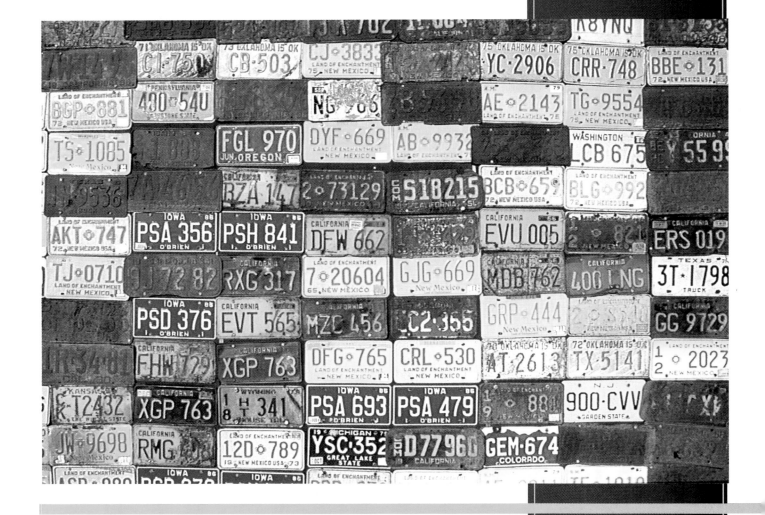

That ours is a federal system, a system in which governmental power is divided between the national government and the states, makes a lot of difference, even if we are not always aware that this is the case. Almost every aspect of our lives is affected by several layers of government. Consider your college or university. About half the students are likely to be receiving some form of national or state financial assistance to help pay their tuition and fees. The institution itself is chartered by the state. Most of the funds that pay for the teachers, staff, and buildings at public institutions come from state appropriations, state bonds, private gifts encouraged by national tax laws, or a combination of national, state, and private sources. Faculty research, especially in the sciences, is likely to be supported by some combination of national, state, and private (yet tax-deductible) dollars. The conditions under which students are admitted, how their grades are posted and reported, and how faculty and staff are appointed and evaluated are subject to national and state regulations. Experiments on animals are subject to governmental supervision, and national and state inspectors check to make sure laboratories properly dispose of used chemicals.

Federalism—the constitutional division of powers between the national government and the states—is central to the workings of American government, as it was when our Constitution was being written. Most early Americans put at the top of their worry list a fear that governments might threaten their liberties. Questions about how powers were to be divided between the new national government and their states were much on their minds.

Today Americans often take federalism for granted and do not think about it. Throughout much of the rest of the world, however, federalism issues have come to the top of the political agenda. In Canada, for example, the very nature of the federal system is at stake as the French-speaking province of Quebec demands special status and a considerable measure of autonomy.[1] The former Soviet Union, a highly centralized government that was federal only in form but not in fact, has broken apart into 15 independent nations. Russia itself is going through struggles between Moscow and the provinces. Throughout Central Europe tensions erupt into violence as nations divide and subdivide. Even in the United Kingdom there are calls for a rethinking of the relationship between Scotland and England.

At our beginnings federalism was hailed as a potent barrier against tyranny. If the newly formed national government threatened people's liberties, the states would protect them—and vice versa. Federalism issues did not end with the founding period. In 1861, men and women fought and died for Virginia or Texas or for the Union (although it would be a mistake to think of the Civil War as merely a particularly heated debate over the principles of federalism). And although not at the forefront of the politics of our time, federalism issues remain an important part of our political agenda, not merely in national elections but in Congress and before the courts of our land.[2]

Today the debates are not likely to be about the constitutional division of authority between the national government and the states. The national government's constitutional authority to deal with issues affecting the nation is clearly established, whether they concern civil rights, highway speed limits, or the sale of holiday lights. Nonetheless, we still argue about some aspects of the division of responsibilities between the national and state governments. We debate: whether Congress intended to regulate a subject completely or to leave some regulation to state discretion; whether, in the absence of congressional action, states may deal with subjects that affect commerce or people in other states; whether Congress

Interpretations of Federalism

Federalism is a powerful but elusive concept, leading both scholars and politicians to add adjectives that reflect their ideas:

Dual Federalism interprets the Constitution as giving a limited list of powers—primarily foreign policy and national defense—to the national government, leaving most power to sovereign states. Each level of government is dominant within its own sphere. The Supreme Court serves as the umpire between the national government and the states in case of a dispute over which government is in charge of a particular activity. During our first hundred years, dual federalism was the favored interpretation most of the time by the Supreme Court.

Cooperative Federalism stresses federalism as a system to deliver governmental goods and services to the people and calls for cooperation among various levels of governments in "getting the job done."

Marble Cake Federalism, coined by political scientist Morton Grodzins in 1960, conceives federalism as a marble cake in which all levels of government are involved in a variety of issues and programs, rather than a layer cake with uniform divisions between layers or levels of government.[a]

Competitive Federalism, a term created by political scientist Thomas R. Dye, brings to the fore the fact that federalism provides us with a national government, 50 states, and thousands of other units, each competing with the others in the way in which they put together packages of services and taxes and vying for the support of citizens. Applying the analogy of the marketplace, Dye emphasizes that at the state and local levels we have some choice which state and city we want "to use," just as we have choices about which automobile we wish to drive.[b]

Permissive Federalism implies that although federalism provides "a sharing of power and authority between the national and state government, the states' share rests upon the permission and permissiveness of the national government."[c]

New Federalism, favored by Presidents Richard Nixon, Ronald Reagan, and George Bush emphasized their view that we should return fiscal resources and management responsibilities to the states in the form of large block grants and revenue sharing, and that we should more rationally sort out functions between national and state governments.

[a] Morton Grodzins, "The Federal System," in *Goals for Americans: The Report of the President's Commission on National Goals* (Columbia University Press, 1960).
[b] Thomas R. Dye, *American Federalism: Competition Among Governments* (Lexington Books, 1990), pp. 13–17.
[c] Michael D. Reagan and John G. Sanzone, *The New Federalism* (Oxford University Press, 1981), p. 175.

should regulate completely the conditions of employment in the workplace or leave some room for the states to do so.

Although couched in terms of federalism, such arguments reflect differences among various interests. The national and state governments are the arenas in which, and through which, clashes take place between consumers and producers, workers and employers, airlines and railroads, pro-choice and right-to-life advocates, progrowth and antigrowth forces, and all the other contending groups that make up our political system.

In this chapter we will begin by defining federalism and discussing its advantages and disadvantages. Next we will look at the constitutional basis of our federal system. Then we will see how the Supreme Court and political developments have shaped—and continue to shape—our modern system of federalism.

DEFINING FEDERALISM

Scholars have argued and wars have been fought about what federalism really means. One scholar counted 267 definitions.[3] **Federalism**, as we define it, is a form of government in which a constitution distributes powers between a central government and subdivisional governments—usually called states or provinces or republics—giving to both the national government and the regional governments substantial responsibilities and powers, including the power to collect taxes and to pass and enforce laws regulating the conduct of individuals.

The mere existence of both national and state governments does not make a system federal. What is important is that a *constitution divides governmental powers between the national government and the constituent governments* (called *states* in the United States), giving substantial functions to each. Neither the central nor the constituent government receives its powers from the other; both derive them from a common source—a constitution. This constitutional distribution of powers cannot be changed by the ordinary processes of legislation—by, for example, an act of either a national or a state legislature. Both levels of government operate through their own agents and exercise power directly over individuals. Other countries with federal systems include Canada, Switzerland, Mexico, and Australia. "Nearly 40 percent of the people of the world now live in nations with a federal form of government. Another third live in countries that use some elements of federalism."[4]

Constitutionally, the federal system of the United States consists of only the national government and the 50 states. "Cities are not," the Supreme Court has reminded us, "sovereign entities." But in a practical sense, we are a nation of almost 87,000 governmental units—from the national government to the school board district (see Table 3-1). This does not make for a tidy, efficient, easy-to-understand system; yet, as we shall see, it does have its virtues.

Alternatives to Federalism

Among the alternatives to federalism are **unitary systems** of government in which a constitution vests all governmental power in the central government. The central government, if it so chooses, may delegate authority to constituent units, but what it delegates it may take away. Britain, France, Israel, and the Philippines have unitary governments. In the United States, state constitutions usually create this kind of relationship between the state and its local governments.

At the other extreme are **confederations** in which sovereign nations by a constitutional compact create a central government but carefully *limit* the power of the central government and do not give it the power to regulate the conduct of individuals directly. The central government makes regulations for the constituent governments, but it exists and operates only at their direction. The 13 states under the Articles of Confederation operated in this manner, as did the southern Confederacy during the Civil War (see Figure 3-1).

To complicate this matter, the framers of our Constitution used the term "federal" to describe what we would now call a *confederate* form of government. Moreover, today the term "federal" is frequently used as a synonym for national; people often refer to the government in Washington as "the federal government." But it is the states and the national government *together* that make up our federal system.

Why Federalism?

In 1787, federalism was an obvious choice. Confederation had been tried and found wanting, but a unitary system was out of the question. Most of the people were too deeply attached to their state governments to permit subordination to central rule. Federalism was, and still is, thought to be ideally suited to the needs of a heterogeneous people spread over a large continent, suspicious of concentrated power, and desiring unity but not uniformity. Federalism offered, and still offers, many advantages for such a people.[5]

FEDERALISM CHECKS THE GROWTH OF TYRANNY Although in the rest of the world federal forms have not been notably successful in preventing tyranny and many unitary governments are democratic, Americans tend to associate freedom with federalism.[6] As James Madison pointed out in *The Federalist*, No. 10: If "factious leaders . . . kindle a flame within their particular states," national leaders can check the spread of the "conflagration through the other states." Shays's Rebellion was a dramatic example. Moreover, when one political party loses control of the national government, it is still likely to hold office in a number of states. It can then regroup, develop new policies and new leaders, and continue to challenge the party in power at the national level.

Such diffusion of power creates its own problems. It makes it difficult for a national majority to carry out a program of action, and it permits those who control a state government to frustrate the consensus expressed through Congress and national agencies. To some of our Constitution's framers, these obstacles were an advantage. They were more fearful that a single-interest national majority might capture the national government and attempt to suppress the interests of others than that minority interests might frustrate the national will. Of course the size of the nation and the many interests within it are the greatest obstacles to the formation of a single-interest majority, a point often overlooked today but emphasized by Madison in *The Federalist*, No. 10. If such a majority were to occur, having to work through a federal system would act to check its power.

FEDERALISM ALLOWS UNITY WITHOUT UNIFORMITY National politicians and parties do not have to iron out every difference on every issue that divides us, whether it be abortion, divorce, gun control, gambling, capital punishment, education financing, or comparable worth. (**Comparable worth**, which mandates comparable pay for jobs requiring comparable skills, has been advanced as one way to correct pay inequities between higher-paying, male-dominated fields, such as plumbing, and lower-paying, female-dominated fields, such as teaching.) Instead, these issues are debated in state legislatures, county courthouses, and city halls. This advantage of federalism is becoming less significant as more local issues become national and as events and outcomes in one state immediately affect policy debates at the national level.

FEDERALISM ENCOURAGES EXPERIMENTATION Supreme Court Justice Louis Brandeis pointed out that state governments provide great "laboratories" for

TABLE 3-1

Number of Governments

States	50
Counties	3,043
Municipalities	19,296
Towns	16,666
School Districts	14,556
Special Districts	33,131
Total	86,742

SOURCE: U.S. Department of Commerce, Bureau of the Census, *1992 Census of Governments.*

FIGURE 3-1   A Comparison of Federalism and Confederation

Government under the Articles of Confederation: 1781-1788

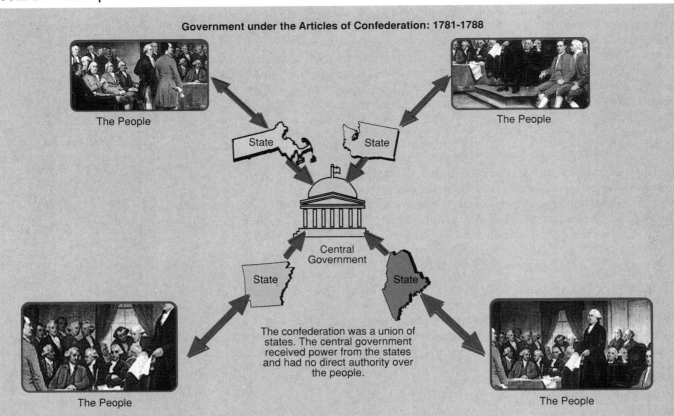

The People

State   State

Central Government

The confederation was a union of states. The central government received power from the states and had no direct authority over the people.

The People

The People

The People

Government under U.S. Constitution (Federation): 1789-

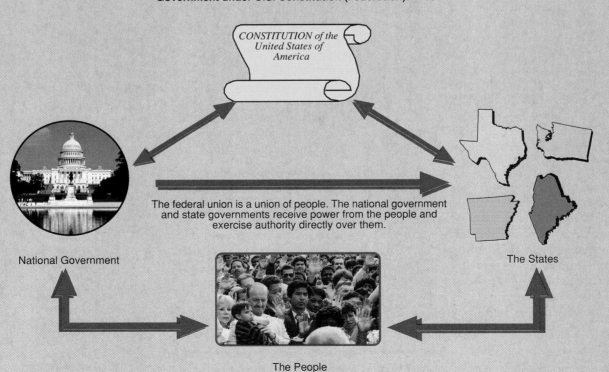

CONSTITUTION of the United States of America

The federal union is a union of people. The national government and state governments receive power from the people and exercise authority directly over them.

National Government

The States

The People

public policy experimentation, with states serving as proving grounds. If they adopt programs that fail, the negative effects are limited; if programs succeed, they can be adopted by other states and by the national government. Georgia, for example, was the first state to permit 18-year-olds to vote; New York has been vigorous in its assault on water pollution; California has pioneered air pollution control programs, especially automobile emission standards. After federal leadership on environmental matters waned in the 1970s, New Jersey initiated programs to handle toxic wastes, radon gas testing, and mandatory recycling. Many states legalized abortion under certain conditions before the Supreme Court acted. (Whether these laws and regulations are progress or regression depends, of course, on one's values, as do so many questions of politics.) "Sunset laws" (requiring periodic reauthorization for programs), equal housing, no-fault insurance, and "lemon laws" (providing consumer protection for faulty automobiles) are other examples of programs that originated in the states. Oregon and Hawaii are pioneers in creating new systems for the delivery of health care. Nevada is the only state, so far, to legalize statewide gambling, but some aspects of legalized casino gambling are now found in more than half the states. Not all innovations, even those considered successful, are widely adopted; Nebraska is the only state, for example, to use the unicameral legislature.

The states' role as laboratories of democracy has become even more important as the federal government in the 1990s faces "fiscal and political limits . . . and as the nation confronts such matters as . . . the revolution in family life, including, for example, surrogate motherhood, test-tube babies, adoption, and care of the elderly."[7]

FEDERALISM KEEPS GOVERNMENT CLOSER TO THE PEOPLE By providing numerous arenas for decision making, federalism involves many people and helps keep government closer to the people. Every day thousands of Americans are busy serving on city councils, school boards, neighborhood associations, and planning commissions. And since they are close to the issues and have firsthand knowledge of what needs to be done, they may be more responsive to the problem than the experts in Washington.

We should be cautious, however, about generalizing that state and local governments are necessarily "closer to the people" than is the national government. True, more people are involved in local and state politics than in national affairs, and in recent years confidence in the ability of state governments has gone up while respect for national agencies has diminished (see Figure 3-2). Yet national and international affairs are often more on people's minds than are state or even local politics. Fewer voters participate in state elections than in congressional and presidential elections; still, states and their local units remain an important part of the political life of those concerned with public affairs.

THE CONSTITUTIONAL STRUCTURE OF AMERICAN FEDERALISM

Dividing powers and responsibilities between the national and state governments requires thousands of court decisions, hundreds of books, and endless speeches to explain—and even then the division lacks precise definition.

Powers of the National Government

The Constitution, chiefly in the first three articles, delegates legislative, executive, and judicial powers to the national government. In addition to these **express powers**, such as the power to appropriate funds, the Constitution delegates to

Neighborhood associations such as this provide firsthand knowledge of what needs to be done on local issues.

FIGURE 3-2 The Most Popular Level of Government

SOURCE: Advisory Commission on Intergovernmental Relations, *Changing Public Attitudes on Governments and Taxes, 1991* (Government Printing Office, 1992), p. 7.

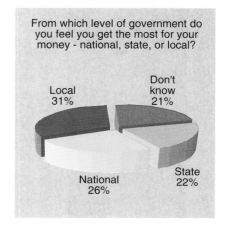

From which level of government do you feel you get the most for your money - national, state, or local?

Local 31%

Don't know 21%

National 26%

State 22%

The formal constitutional framework of our federal system may be stated relatively simply:

1. The national government has only those powers *delegated* to it by the Constitution (with the important exception of the inherent power over foreign affairs).
2. Within the scope of its operations, the national government is supreme.
3. The state governments have the powers not delegated to the central government, except those *denied* to them by the Constitution and their state constitutions.
4. Some powers are specifically denied to *both* the national and state governments; others are specifically denied *only* to the states; still others are denied *only* to the national government.

Congress **implied powers**, such as the power to create banks, which may be inferred from express powers. (We will see an example when we discuss the landmark case of *McCulloch v Maryland*.) The constitutional basis for the implied powers of Congress is the **necessary and proper clause** (Article I, Section 8, Clause 18). This clause gives Congress the right "to make all Laws which shall be necessary and proper for carrying into Execution the foregoing Powers, and all other Powers vested . . . in the Government of the United States."

In the field of foreign affairs the Constitution gives the national government **inherent powers**, so that the national government has the same authority to deal with other nations as if it were the central government in a unitary system. These inherent powers do not depend on specific constitutional grants. For example, the government of the United States may acquire territory by discovery and occupation, though no specific clause in the Constitution allows such acquisition. Even if the Constitution were silent about foreign affairs—which it is not—the national government would have the right to declare war, make treaties, and appoint and receive ambassadors.

Together, these express, implied, and inherent powers create a flexible system that has allowed the Supreme Court, Congress, the president, and the people to expand the central government's powers to meet the needs of a modern industrial nation operating in a global economy. This expansion of central government functions has rested on four constitutional pillars.

NATIONAL SUPREMACY ARTICLE   One of the most important pillars is found in Article VI of the Constitution: "This Constitution, and the Laws of the United States which shall be made in Pursuance thereof; and all Treaties made . . . under the Authority of the United States, shall be the supreme Law of the Land; and the Judges in every State shall be bound thereby; any Thing in the Constitution or Laws of any State to the Contrary notwithstanding." All officials, state as well as national, are bound by constitutional oath to support the Constitution of the United States. States may not use their reserved powers to override national policies; this restriction also applies to local units of government since they are agents of the states. National laws and regulations of federal agencies *preempt* the field, so that conflicting state and local rules and regulations are unenforceable.

THE WAR POWER   The national government is responsible for protecting the nation from external aggression and, when necessary, for waging war. In today's world military strength depends not only on troops in the field but also on the ability to mobilize the nation's industrial might and to apply scientific knowledge to the tasks of defense. The national government has the power to wage war and to do what is necessary and proper to do so successfully. Thus the national government has the power to do almost anything not in direct conflict with constitutional guarantees.

THE POWER TO REGULATE INTERSTATE AND FOREIGN COMMERCE   Congressional authority extends to all commerce that affects more than one state and to all those activities, wherever they exist or whatever their nature, whose control Congress decides is necessary and proper to regulate interstate and foreign commerce. *Commerce* includes the production, buying, selling, renting, and transporting of goods, services, and properties.[8] The **commerce clause**—Article 1, Section 8, Clause 3—packs a tremendous constitutional punch; it gives Congress the power "to regulate Commerce with foreign Nations, and among the several States, and with the Indian Tribes." In these few words the national government has been able to find constitutional justification for regulating a wide range of human activity, including agriculture, transportation, finance, product safety, labor-relations, and the workplace. Few, if any, aspects of our economy today affect commerce in only one state and are thus outside the scope of the national government's constitutional authority.

The commerce clause can also be used to sustain legislation that goes beyond commercial matters. When the Supreme Court upheld the 1964 Civil Rights Act forbidding discrimination because of race, religion, or national origin in places of public accommodation, it said: "Congress's action in removing the disruptive effect which it found racial discrimination has on interstate travel is not invalidated because Congress was also legislating against what it considers to be moral wrongs." Discrimination restricts the flow of interstate commerce; therefore, Congress could legislate against the discrimination. Moreover, the law could be applied even to local places of public accommodation because local incidents of discrimination have a substantial and harmful impact on interstate commerce. "If it is interstate commerce that feels the pinch, it does not matter how local the operation that applies the squeeze."[9]

THE POWER TO TAX AND SPEND Congress lacks constitutional authority to pass laws solely on the ground that they will promote the general welfare, but it may raise taxes and spend money for this purpose. This distinction between *legislating* and *appropriating* makes little difference most of the time. Congress, for example, lacks constitutional power to regulate education or agriculture directly, yet it does have the power to appropriate money to support education or to pay farm subsidies. By attaching conditions to its grants of money, Congress may thus regulate what it cannot directly control by law.

When Congress puts up the money, it determines how the money will be spent. By withholding or threatening to withhold funds, the national government can influence or control state operations and regulate individual conduct. For example, Congress has stipulated that federal funds should be withdrawn from any program in which any person is denied benefits because of race, color, or national origin; subsequently the categories of sex and physical handicap were added. Congress has also used its power of the purse to force states to raise the drinking age to 21 by tying such a condition to federal dollars for highways.

Congress frequently requires states to do certain things—for example, provide services to indigent mothers and take action to clean up the air and water—or else Congress will impose even more stringent federal regulations. These requirements are called **federal mandates**. Often, Congress does not supply the funds required to carry out these mandates.

These four constitutional pillars—the national supremacy clause, the war power, the power over interstate commerce, and, most especially, the power to tax and spend for the general welfare—have permitted a tremendous expansion of federal functions, so much so that the national government has in effect almost full power to enact any legislation that Congress thinks will promote the general welfare, so long as it does not conflict with those provisions of the Constitution designed to protect individual rights.

Powers of the States

The Constitution *reserves for the states* all powers not granted to the national government, subject only to the limitations of the Constitution. Powers not given *exclusively* to the national government, by provision of the Constitution or by judicial interpretation, may be concurrently exercised by the states, as long as there is no conflict with national law. Each state has **concurrent powers** with the national government, such as the power to levy taxes and regulate commerce internal to each state (see Table 3-2).

Precisely how federalism limits the states' taxing powers is not simple to explain or understand. In general, a state may levy a tax on the same item as the

An Expanding Nation

A great advantage of federalism—and part of the genius and flexibility of our constitutional system—has been the way in which we acquired territory and extended rights and guarantees by means of statehood, commonwealth, or territorial status, and thus grew from 13 to 50 states.

Louisiana Purchase	1803
Florida	1819
Texas	1845
Oregon	1846
Mexican Cession	1848
Gadsden Purchase	1853
Alaska	1867
Hawaii	1898
Philippines	1898–1946
Puerto Rico	1899
Guam	1899
American Samoa	1900
Canal Zone	1904
U.S. Virgin Islands	1917
Pacific Islands Trust Territory	1947

The power to regulate interstate commerce allowed Congress to forbid discrimination in places of public accommodation in the 1964 Civil Rights Act.

Should Puerto Rico become a state?

Should Puerto Rico, with more than 3.6 million citizens, be admitted as our fifty-first state? It would be the twenty-fifth largest state, with two senators and at least six representatives. With the House membership fixed at 435, unless Congress increased it there would have to be a reduction in the representation from six of the smaller states. Puerto Rico currently has commonwealth status. President Bill Clinton has said that he will support whatever Puerto Ricans want.

Even though Puerto Ricans are U.S. citizens, they cannot vote in presidential elections while living there; they have no senators and no voting members in our House of Representatives. Its citizens are exempt from federal income taxes, and its businesses enjoy tax breaks that have lured more than two thousand manufacturing plants there during the past 30 years. Spanish is the language used in schools and in government circles.

Do you favor or oppose statehood for Puerto Rico? What problems do you think granting Puerto Rico statehood raises?

national government, but a state cannot, by a tax, "unduly burden" commerce among the states, or interfere with a function of the national government, or complicate the operation of a national law, or abridge the terms of a treaty of the United States. Who decides whether a state tax is an "undue burden" on a national function or commerce among the states? Ultimately, the Supreme Court decides.

Federalism issues are even more complicated when states act to protect the environment and the public health and well-being. Where Congress has not pre-empted the field, states may even regulate interstate businesses, provided these regulations do not cover matters requiring uniform national treatment or unduly burden interstate commerce. Who decides what matters require uniform national treatment or what actions might place an undue burden on interstate commerce? Congress does, subject to final review by the Supreme Court. When Congress is silent or does not clearly state its intentions, courts—ultimately the Supreme Court—decide if there is a conflict with the national Constitution or if there has been federal preemption by law or regulation.

Constitutional Limits and Obligations

To make federalism work, the Constitution imposes certain restraints on both the national and the state governments. States are prohibited from:

1. Making treaties with foreign governments
2. Authorizing private persons to prey on the shipping and commerce of other nations—what the Constitution refers to as granting letters of marque and reprisal, a practice common during times of war in the eighteenth century
3. Coining money, issuing bills of credit, or making anything but gold and silver coin a tender in payment of debts

Nor may states without the consent of Congress:

1. Tax imports or exports
2. Tax foreign ships
3. Keep troops or ships in time of peace (except the state militia, now called the National Guard)

TABLE 3-2

The Federal Division of Powers

Types of Powers Delegated to the National Government	Types of Powers Reserved for the States	Some Concurrent Powers Shared by the National and State Governments
• Express powers stated in Constitution • Implied powers that may be inferred from express powers • Inherent powers that allow nation to present a united front to foreign powers	• To create a republican form of government • To charter local governments • To conduct elections • To exercise all powers not delegated to the national government or denied to the states by the Constitution	• To tax citizens and businesses • To borrow and spend money • To establish courts • To pass and enforce laws • To protect civil rights

4. Enter into compacts with other states or foreign nations that "tend to increase the political power in the States, which may encroach upon or interfere"[10] with the supremacy of the national government

5. Engage in war, unless invaded (an invasion of one state would be an invasion of the United States itself) or in such imminent danger as will not admit of delay.

The national government, in turn, is required by the Constitution to refrain from exercising its powers, especially its powers to tax and to regulate interstate commerce, in such a way as to interfere substantially with the states' abilities to perform their responsibilities. Making this generalization about how the principles of federalism limit national powers is easier than citing modern-day examples of the Supreme Court's striking down actions of the national government because they interfere with state sovereignty. Today, whatever protection states have comes from the political process—in restraints that our system provides because individuals elected from the states participate in the decisions of Congress—rather than from judicially enforced limitations.[11]

The Constitution also requires the national government to guarantee to each state a *republican form of government*. The framers used this term to distinguish a republic from a monarchy, on the one side, and from a pure, direct democracy, on the other. Congress, not the courts, enforces this guarantee and determines what is or is not a republican form of government. By permitting the congressional delegation of a state to take its seat in Congress, Congress, in effect, acknowledges that the state has the republican form of government guaranteed by the Constitution.

In addition, the national government is obliged by the Constitution to protect states against *domestic insurrection*. Congress has delegated to the president the authority to dispatch troops to put down such insurrections when so requested by the proper state authorities. If there are contesting state authorities, the president decides which are the proper ones.[12] The president does not have to wait, however, for a request from state authorities to send federal troops into a state to enforce federal laws. Today it is hard to imagine a situation of domestic insurrection against a state that would not also involve federal laws.

Horizontal Federalism: Interstate Relations

Three clauses in the Constitution, taken from the Articles of Confederation, require states to give full faith and credit to one another's public acts, records, and judicial proceedings; to extend to one another's citizens the privileges and immunities of their own citizens; and to return persons who are fleeing from justice.

FULL FAITH AND CREDIT The **full faith and credit clause** (Article IV, Section 1), one of the more technical provisions of the Constitution, requires that state courts enforce the civil judgments of the courts of other states and accept their public records and acts as valid. (It does not require states to enforce the criminal laws of other states; in most cases, for one state to enforce the criminal laws of another would raise constitutional issues.) The clause applies especially to noncriminal judicial proceedings, such as enforcement of judicial settlements and court awards.

INTERSTATE PRIVILEGES AND IMMUNITIES Under Article IV, Section 2, states must extend to citizens of other states the privileges and immunities granted to their own citizens, including the protection of the laws, the right to engage in peaceful occupations, access to the courts, and freedom from discriminatory taxes. Further, because of this clause, states may not impose unreasonable

Thinking it Through

On November 15, 1993, after a spirited debate, Puerto Ricans voted 48.4 percent in favor of continuing as a commonwealth, with 46.2 percent favoring statehood and 4.4 percent supporting independence.

What explains the outcome? Puerto Rico's economic circumstances may have been the key factor. Even though there has been great economic progress in the past generation, per capita income in Puerto Rico is only half that of our poorest state, and unemployment is almost double that in the United States. Many Puerto Ricans fear the loss of business tax breaks, and citizens would have to pay federal income taxes if Puerto Rico became a state. Some worry, too, that they would be forced to make English the language used in government and in education. Congress forced several states, including Louisiana, New Mexico, and Arizona, to require English as the official language upon admission to the Union.

The commonwealth option that won the support of the voters by a close vote called for some additional benefits, but it will be up to Congress to decide whether to grant them.

Secessionism Lives On

Secession—an effort by a local region to break away from the parent state—recurs periodically in American and world history. England fought an unsuccessful war to prevent the 13 colonies from forming an independent nation. The United States waged the Civil War to prevent secession by the southern states. The Soviet Union dissolved after failing to hold its member republics together. And Yugoslavia has been violently torn apart by ethnic hatreds.

In 1992 the citizens of southwestern Kansas called for a constitutional convention to withdraw from Kansas and form the fifty-first state. The citizens of Staten Island recently voted to secede from New York City; the New York legislature is now considering the issue. In past years, citizens of Alaska, Nantucket, Virginia, Nebraska, Colorado, and California have also made unsuccessful attempts to secede. A northern California legislator is pushing for a statewide referendum to break California into three separate states. Texas, when admitted into the Union, received congressional consent to break into five states if it ever should wish to do so.

durational residency requirements, that is, withhold rights to American citizens who have recently moved to the state and thereby have become citizens of that state. For example, a state may not set unreasonable time limits to withhold state-funded medical benefits from new citizens or to keep them from voting. How long a residency requirement may a state impose? A day seems about as long as the Court will tolerate to withhold welfare payments or medical care, 50 days or so for voting privileges, and one year for eligibility for in-state tuition for state-supported colleges and universities.

EXTRADITION   In Article IV, Section 2, the Constitution asserts that when individuals charged with crimes have fled from one state to another, the state to which they have fled is to deliver them to the proper officials upon the demand of the executive authority of the state from which they fled. This process is called **extradition**. "The obvious objective of the Extradition Clause," the courts have claimed, "is that no State should become a safe haven for the fugitives from a sister State's criminal justice system."[13] Congress has supplemented this constitutional provision by making the governor of the state to which fugitives have fled the agent responsible for returning them.

Despite the use of the word "shall" in the Constitution, an 1861 Supreme Court decision, based on an antiquated view of federalism, controlled extradition until 1987, and federal courts would not order governors to surrender (extradite) persons wanted in other states. This is no longer so, since the 1861 decision has been reversed.[14] Usually federal courts do not become involved, and extradition is a routine matter. Recently, however, disputes over the custody of children that sometimes lead to criminal charges of parental kidnapping have complicated extradition procedures.

Despite their constitutional obligation, governors of asylum states have on occasion refused to honor a request for extradition. So far in modern times no federal judge has had to try to enforce an extradition request. When the governor of Indiana refused to extradite Bobby Knight, the celebrated Indiana University basketball coach who had been convicted in absentia by a Puerto Rican court of assaulting a police officer during the Pan-American Games in Puerto Rico, the governor of Puerto Rico decided to drop the matter.

INTERSTATE COMPACTS   The Constitution also requires states to settle disputes with one another without the use of force. States may carry their legal disputes to the Supreme Court, or they may negotiate **interstate compacts**. More often interstate compacts are used to establish interstate agencies to handle interstate problems. Before most interstate compacts become effective, congressional approval is required. After a compact has been signed and approved by Congress, it becomes binding on all signatory states, and its terms are enforceable by the Supreme Court. A typical state belongs to 20 compacts dealing with such subjects as environmental protection, crime control, water rights, and higher education exchanges.[15]

THE POLITICS OF FEDERALISM

This outline of the constitutional structure of federalism is oversimplified and even misleading—especially in terms of the division of powers between the national government and the states. The formal structures of our federal system have not changed much since 1787, but the political realities, especially during the last half-century, have greatly altered how federalism works. To understand these changes, we need to look at some of the trends that continue to fuel the debate about the meaning of federalism.

The Growth of Big Government

Over the past two hundred years there has been a drift of power from other institutions—families, churches and synagogues, the marketplace—to governments, and especially to the national government. "No one planned the growth," explains the Advisory Commission on Intergovernmental Relations, "but everyone played a part in it."[16] How did this come about? For a variety of reasons. One is that many of our problems have become national in scope. Much that was local in 1789, in 1860, or in 1930 is now national—even global. State governments could supervise the relations between small merchants and their few employees, but only the national government can supervise relations between an international industry and its thousands of employees, all organized in national unions.

As industrialization proceeded, powerful interests made demands on the national government. Business groups called on the government for aid in the form of tariffs, a national banking system, and subsidies to railroads and the merchant marine. Farmers learned that the national government could give more aid than the states, and they, too, began to demand help. By the beginning of this century, urban groups in general, and organized labor in particular, pressed their claims. Big business, big agriculture, and big labor all add up to big government.

The growth of the national economy and the creation of a national transportation and communications network altered people's attitudes toward the national government. Before the Civil War, the national government was viewed as a distant, even foreign, government. Today, in part because of television, most people identify as closely with Washington as with their state capitals. We are apt to know more about our president than about our governor, more about our national senators and representatives than about our state legislators or even the local officials who run our cities and schools.

The Great Depression of the 1930s stimulated extensive national action on such issues as relief, unemployment, and agriculture surpluses. World War II brought federal regulation of wages, prices, and employment, as well as national efforts to allocate resources, train personnel, and support engineering and inventions. After the war the national government helped veterans obtain college degrees and inaugurated a vast system of support for university research. The United States became the most powerful leader of the free world, maintaining substantial military forces even in times of peace. The Great Society programs of

Qualifying for In-State Tuition

Financially independent adults who move into a state just before enrolling in a state-supported university or college may be required to prove that they have become citizens of that state and intend to remain after finishing their schooling by supplying such evidence of citizenship as tax payments, a driver's license, car registration, voter registration, and a continuous, year-round off-campus residence. Students who are financially dependent on their parents remain citizens of the state of their parents.

One of the Great Society programs that has survived and is seen as successful is Head Start. Here a Head Start teacher reads to a class.

Should the national government be made stronger or weaker?

Look closely at the operation of your state and city governments. Do the facts as you know them support the centralists' demand for increasing federal control over state and local issues? Or are the decentralists correct that government that is closer to the people is the best and should be as free of national government constraint as possible?

the 1960s poured out grants-in-aid to states and localities. City dwellers who had migrated from the rural South to northern cities began to seek federal funds for—at the very least—housing, education, and mass transportation.

Although economic and social conditions created many of the pressures for expansion of the national government, so did political claims. Members of Congress, presidents, federal judges, and federal administrators have actively promoted federal initiatives. And until the recent years of overwhelming budget deficits, Congress in particular encouraged this trend. True, when there is widespread conflict about what to do—how to reduce the federal deficit, adopt a national energy policy, reform Social Security, provide health care for the indigent—Congress waits for a national consensus. But when an organized constituency wants something and there is no counterpressure, Congress "responds often to everyone, and with great vigor."[17] Once established, federal programs generate groups with vested interests in promoting, defending, and expanding them. Associations are formed, alliances are made. "In a word, the growth of government has created a constituency of, by, and for government."[18]

As we approach the end of this century, our federal debt stands at $4.4 trillion. We have annual deficits of over $250 billion, between 4 and 5 percent of the gross domestic product. These deficits have become a major constraint on the expansion of federal programs. Annual outlays for **entitlements** increase each year. Entitlements are programs, such as Social Security and Medicare, in which Congress has promised to provide all the funds necessary to all individuals who qualify. Moreover, for most of these entitlement programs Congress has also promised to provide an annual cost-of-living adjustment, a COLA. As a consequence, there is not much room for the federal government to undertake additional programs, even with the hoped-for reduction of defense expenditures following the end of the cold war.

Despite the pressure for the national government to "do something" about urban poverty and crime in the streets, fear of an increase in federal taxes, or a reduction in other federal programs, or expansion of the national debt with its threat of future economic crisis, has served to moderate—at least for the moment—the expansion of national government spending. Even so total federal outlays for fiscal 1995 are $1,519 trillion.[19] That is big government by any measure.

The Great Debate—Centralists versus Decentralists

The growth of big government was not without constitutional controversy. During the Great Depression of the 1930s, the nation debated whether Congress had the constitutional authority to enact legislation on agriculture, labor, education, housing, and welfare. Only 30 years ago some questioned the constitutional authority of Congress to legislate against racial discrimination. The debate continues between **centralists**, those who favor national action (or as we used to call them, *nationalists*) and **decentralists**, those who favor action at the state and local levels (or by the old-fashioned name, *states' righters*). The victory for the nationalists is relatively recent and not likely to be the last word. Throughout our history and into the present, powerful groups have favored states' rights, and they still do today.

The constitutional arguments revolving around federalism grew out of specific political issues: Did the national government have the authority to outlaw slavery in the territories? Did states have the authority to operate racially segregated schools? Could Congress regulate labor relations? The debates were frequently phrased in constitutional language, with appeals to the great principles of federalism. But they were also arguments over who gets what, where, and how.

Among those favoring the decentralist or states' rights interpretation, with varying emphasis, were Thomas Jefferson, John C. Calhoun, the Supreme Court from the 1920s to 1937, and more recently, Ronald Reagan, George Bush, Chief

Justice William H. Rehnquist, and Justice Sandra Day O'Connor. Most decentralists contend the Constitution is a treaty among sovereign states that created the central government and gave it carefully limited authority. As a result, the national government is nothing more than an agent of the states, and every one of its powers should be narrowly defined. Any question about whether the states have given a particular function to the central government or have reserved it for themselves should be resolved in favor of the states.

Decentralists hold that the national government should not be permitted to exercise its delegated powers in a way that interferes with activities reserved for the states. The Tenth Amendment, they claim, makes this clear: "The powers not delegated to the United States by the Constitution, nor prohibited by it to the States, are reserved to the States respectively, or to the people." Decentralists insist state governments are closer to the people and reflect the people's wishes more accurately than does the national government. The national government, they add, is inherently heavy-handed and bureaucratic; to preserve our federal system and our liberties, central authority must be kept under control.

The centralist position has been supported by Chief Justice John Marshall, Abraham Lincoln, Theodore Roosevelt, Franklin Roosevelt, and throughout most of our history by the Supreme Court. Chief Justice Rehnquist and Justice O'Connor, two of the strongest "defenders of states' sovereignty on the U.S. Supreme Court" of the last half century, were on the verge of winning enough converts from the Reagan and Bush appointees to veer the current Court back to a more decentralist position. The election of President Bill Clinton and his selection of more liberal-oriented justices such as Ruth Bader Ginsburg and Stephen Breyer makes a return to earlier interpretations of the Constitution somewhat less likely. However, President Clinton is an avid supporter of fewer congressional controls on the states, and if Congress continues to ignore the problems of the states, there could be a political and judicial reaction.[20]

Centralists reject the whole idea of the Constitution as an interstate compact. Rather, they view the Constitution as a supreme law established by the people. The national government is an agent of the people, not of the states, because it was the people who drew up the Constitution and created the national government. The sovereign people gave the national government sufficient power to accomplish the great objectives listed in the Preamble to the Constitution. They intended that the central government's powers should be liberally defined and that the central government should be denied authority only when the Constitution clearly prohibits it from acting.

Centralists argue that the national government is a government of all the people and that each state speaks for only some of the people. Although the Tenth Amendment clearly reserves powers for the states, as Chief Justice Harlan Stone said, "The Tenth Amendment states but a truism that all is retained which has not been surrendered."[21] The amendment does not deny the national government the right to exercise to the fullest extent all the powers given to it by the Constitution. On the other hand, the supremacy of the national government, it is argued, restricts the states, because governments representing part of the people cannot be allowed to interfere with a government representing all of them.

THE ROLE OF THE FEDERAL COURTS

Congress and the results of the political process ultimately decide how power will be divided between the national and the state governments. Still, the federal courts—and especially the Supreme Court—have often been called on to umpire the ongoing debate about which level of government should do what, for whom,

Centralists' Arguments

1. State and local officials tend to be less competent than national officials.

2. State and local officials tend to be concerned only with the interests of their own areas.

3. State and local governments are unable or unwilling to raise taxes needed to carry out vital government functions.

4. State and local governments are more apt to reflect local racial and ethnic biases as well as the biases of dominant local industries.

5. State and local governments are afraid to regulate industries for fear the industries will move elsewhere.

Decentralists' Arguments

1. Increased urbanization has made states more responsive to the needs of city people.

2. In recent years state and local governments have shown greater willingness to raise taxes than the national government.

3. State and local governments have become as sensitive to the needs of the poor and minorities as is the national government.

4. State and local governments have reformed and modernized and thus become more effective governments.

and to whom. This role for the Courts was claimed in the celebrated case of *McCulloch v Maryland*.

McCulloch versus Maryland

In *McCulloch v Maryland* (1819), the Supreme Court had the first of many chances to choose between a centralist and a decentralist interpretation of our federal system.[22] Maryland had levied a tax against the Baltimore branch of the Bank of the United States, a semipublic agency established by Congress. James William McCulloch, the cashier of the bank, refused to pay on the grounds that a state could not tax an instrument of the national government. Maryland's attorneys responded that, in the first place, the national government did not have the power to incorporate a bank, but even if it did, the state had the power to tax it.

Maryland was represented before the Court by some of the country's most distinguished lawyers, including Luther Martin, a delegate to the Constitutional Convention. Martin left the convention early when it became apparent that a strong national government was in the making. Basing his argument on the states' rights view of federalism, Martin said the power to incorporate a bank is not expressly delegated to the national government. He maintained that the necessary and proper clause gives Congress only the power to choose those means and to pass those laws absolutely essential to the execution of its expressly granted powers. Because a bank is not absolutely necessary to the exercise of any of its delegated powers, Congress has no authority to establish it. As for Maryland's right to tax the bank, Martin's position was clear: The power to tax is one of the powers reserved to the states; they may use it as they see fit.

The national government was represented by equally distinguished counsel, chief among whom was Daniel Webster. Webster conceded the power to create a bank is not one of the express powers of the national government. However, the power to pass laws *necessary and proper* to carry out Congress's express powers is specifically delegated to Congress. This delegation of implied powers should be interpreted to mean Congress has authority to enact any legislation convenient and useful for carrying out its delegated national powers. Therefore, Congress may incorporate a bank as an appropriate, convenient, and useful means of exercising the granted powers of collecting taxes, borrowing money, and caring for the property of the United States.

Although the power to tax is reserved to the states, Webster argued that states cannot use their reserved powers to interfere with the operations of the national government. The Constitution leaves no room for doubt; in cases of conflict between the national and state governments, the national government is supreme.

Speaking for a unanimous Court, Chief Justice John Marshall rejected every one of Maryland's contentions. He wrote:

> We must never forget that it is a constitution we are expounding . . . a constitution intended to endure for ages to come, and consequently, to be adapted to the various crises of human affairs. . . . The government of the Union, then, . . . is, emphatically, and truly, a government of the people. In form and substance it emanates from them. Its powers are granted by them, and are to be exercised directly on them, and for their benefit. . . . It can never be to their interest and cannot be presumed to have been their intention, to clog and embarrass its execution, by withholding the most appropriate means.

Marshall summarized his views on the powers of the national government in these now-famous words: "Let the end be legitimate, let it be within the scope of the Constitution, and all means which are appropriate, which are plainly adapted to that end, which are not prohibited, but consist with the letter and spirit of the constitution, are constitutional."

Having thus established the doctrine of implied national powers, Marshall set forth the doctrine of **national supremacy**. No state, he said, can use its reserved taxing powers to tax a national instrument. "The power to tax involves the power to destroy. . . . If the right of the states to tax the means employed by the general government be conceded, the declaration that the Constitution, and the laws made in pursuance thereof, shall be the supreme law of the land, is empty and unmeaning declamation."

The long-range significance of *McCulloch v Maryland* in providing support for the developing forces of nationalism cannot be overstated. The arguments of the states' righters, if accepted, would have strapped the national government in a constitutional straitjacket and denied it powers needed to handle the problems of an expanding nation.

An Expanding Role for the Federal Courts

The authority of federal judges to review the activities of state and local governments has expanded dramatically in recent decades because of modern judicial interpretations of the Thirteenth, Fourteenth, and Fifteenth Amendments (especially the Fourteenth) and the congressional legislation enacted to implement these amendments. Today almost every action by state and local officials is subject to challenge before a federal judge as a violation of the Constitution or of federal law.

In carrying out their judgments, federal judges sometimes have, in effect, taken over the supervision of state prison systems, public hospitals, public schools, and other public facilities. The Supreme Court has gone so far as to sustain a federal judge's right to order a local school board in Missouri to ignore the state's constitutional constraints and to raise taxes and sell bonds to fund the operation of a racially integrated magnet school. In his dissent, joined by Chief Justice Rehnquist and Justices Antonin Scalia and O'Connor, Justice Anthony M. Kennedy charged that the Court majority disregarded "fundamental precepts for the democratic control of public institutions," with its "casual embrace of taxation imposed by the unelected, life-tenured federal judiciary."[23]

One of the major instruments for opening these issues for federal court review is the Supreme Court's revitalization—some would say rewriting—during recent decades of an 1871 civil rights act originally written to combat the Ku Klux Klan. This act (now called Section 1983 after its designation in Title 42 of the United States Code) permits individuals to go into federal court to sue cities and counties for damages or seek injunctions against any person acting under the color of law—that is in an official capacity—who they believe has deprived them of any right secured by the Constitution or by any one of the several thousands of federal laws.[24] Although federal judges can order states to stop acting in a manner that violates the federal Constitution or laws or treaties, the Eleventh Amendment constrains federal courts from hearing damage suits against the states, but not against local government officials.

Federal judges have also become agencies to enforce federal mandates. Any citizen can now sue a state to make it carry out these duties. For example, doctors and hospitals may sue a state to force it to provide "reasonable" reimbursement as required by federal Medicare law.[25] Parents may sue a state for allegedly failing to provide their disabled children with a "free appropriate public education" or otherwise reimburse such parents for tuition in a private school.[26]

Federal judges spend a considerable portion of their time deciding cases in which the central issue is whether some provisions of federal laws have preempted state and local action. **Preemption** occurs when a federal law or regulation takes over and precludes enforcement of a state or local law or regulation. State and local laws are preempted not only when they conflict directly with

About 15 Ku Klux Klan members, protesting the Martin Luther King holiday in January 1994 in Tallahassee, Florida, were outnumbered by over 200 counterdemonstrators. Similar Klan protests in Columbus, Ohio, Little Rock, Arkansas, and Austin, Texas, were also drowned out.

federal laws and regulations, but also if they touch a field in which the "federal interest is so dominant that the federal system will be assumed to preclude enforcement of state laws on the same subject."[27] Examples of federal preemption include the Coast Guard Authorization Act directing the secretary of transportation to develop standards for determining when people are considered intoxicated while operating a marine recreational vessel; dozens of laws regulating hazardous substances, water quality, and clean air standards; and many civil rights acts, most especially the Civil Rights Act of 1964 and the Voting Rights Act of 1965.

Over the years federal judges, under the leadership of the Supreme Court, have favored national powers (including their own). However, recently the Supreme Court has returned to the states several explosive political issues. Perhaps most notably in 1989 in *Webster v Reproductive Health Services,* and in 1992 in *Casey v Planned Parenthood,* the Court gave states considerable latitude to regulate abortion, setting off intense clashes between pro-choice and right-to-life groups in the state legislatures.[28]

Despite the Supreme Court's bias in favor of national over state authority, few would deny the Supreme Court the power to review and set aside state actions. As Justice Oliver Wendell Holmes once remarked: "I do not think the United States would come to an end if we lost our power to declare an Act of Congress void. I do think the Union would be imperiled if we could not make that declaration as to the laws of the several States."[29]

FEDERALISM AND THE USE OF FEDERAL GRANTS

Congress authorizes programs, establishes general rules for how the programs will operate, and decides whether and how much room should be left for state or local discretion. Most important, Congress appropriates the funds for these programs and, until recently, has had deeper pockets than even the richest states. One of Congress's most potent tools for influencing policy at the state and local levels has been the federal grant.

Types of Federal Grants

There are four types of federal grants: categorical-formula grants, project grants, block grants (or as the Clinton administration calls them, flexible grants), and revenue sharing.

CATEGORICAL-FORMULA GRANTS   Congress appropriates funds for specific purposes—welfare, school lunches, the building of airports and highways. The funds are allocated by formula and are subject to detailed federal conditions, often on a matching basis; that is, the government receiving the federal funds must put up some of its own dollars. There are hundreds of grant programs, but two dozen, including Medicaid and Aid to Families with Dependent Children, account for almost 85 percent of total spending for categoricals.[30]

PROJECT GRANTS   Congress appropriates a certain sum, but the dollars are allocated to state and local units and sometimes to nongovernmental agencies, based on applications from those who wish to participate. Examples are grants by the National Science Foundation to universities and research institutes to support the work of scientists or grants open to states and localities to support training and employment programs.

BLOCK GRANTS   These grants, favored by recent Republican presidents and most governors but opposed by most Democratic members of Congress and big city mayors, are broad grants to states for prescribed activities—elementary and secondary education, social services, preventive health, and health services—with only a few specific strings attached. During the first year of his presidency, Ronald Reagan was able to convince Congress to consolidate 57 categorical grant programs, constituting 10 percent of federal aid to state and local governments, into 9 block grants. But that was as far as Congress was willing to go. President Clinton has advocated following Vice-President Al Gore's National Performance Review recommendation that 55 categorical grants consisting of $12.9 billion be combined into 6 flexible block grants in such areas as water quality, training, environment, defense conversion.[31]

Big city mayors oppose proposals for block grants because such grants threaten to take both dollars and discretion from them. They also deprive members of Congress of the opportunity to announce and take credit for grants to their particular districts.[32] As a result, most proposals for block grants do not get too far.

REVENUE SHARING   This program involved federal grants to state and local governments to be used at their discretion and subject only to very general conditions. From 1972 to 1987, substantial revenue-sharing funds were given to state and local governments. When in the second Reagan administration federal budget deficits soared and "there was no revenue to share," revenue sharing was terminated—to the states in 1986 and to local governments in 1987.

The Politics of Federal Grants

Arguments about the forms of federal aid involve more than questions of efficiency. They reflect differences about what constitutes desirable public policy, where power should be located, and who will gain or lose by the various types of grants. And the debate is not just a dispute over whether state and local governments can be trusted to spend federal dollars wisely. It is also a debate about *which* state and local officials should be given control over the spending.

Specialists who work for state and local governments often have more in common with their fellow specialists working for the national government than they do with their own governors, mayors, or state legislators. These specialists

A Message from Garcia: Federalism as a Political and Not a Legal Constraint

In 1985, by a 5 to 4 vote, in *Garcia v San Antonio Metro*, the Supreme Court said in essence that the federal courts should get out of the business of protecting the states from congressional interference. Congress, not the courts, said the court majority, decides which actions of the states should be regulated by the national government. The Court, in this case, upheld the application of the federal minimum wage and hours regulations to the employees of the San Antonio transit system.[*]

The message from *Garcia* is not the final word on this matter. Congress's 1993 action, in limiting the power of states to apply their general welfare legislation to religious practices, is such an unusual interference with the power of the states as to present the justices with difficult federalism issues. Nonetheless, if federal courts do resume the task of protecting the states from congressional legislation, as even the justices most concerned about the rights of states have acknowledged, the type of activities protected by state sovereignty from the reach of the national government "may well be negligible."[†]

Can Congress be counted on, as the Court argued in *Garcia*, to protect the states from being overwhelmed by the national government? Members of Congress are no longer dependent on state political parties for funds or help at election time. Congressional voting on federalism issues shows only moderate support of federalism.[**] And although a few senators have suggested a constitutional amendment to reverse *Garcia*, the movement to do so has not generated much support.

[*]*Garcia v San Antonio Metro. Transit Authority*, 469 US 528 (1985).
[†]Justice O'Connor, dissenting in *Garcia v San Antonio Metro*.
[**]Rodney E. Hero, "The U.S. Congress and American Federalism: Are 'Subnational' Governments Protected?" *Western Political Quarterly* 42 (March 1989), p. 103. For greater skepticism, see also Martha Derthick, "Preserving Federalism: Congress, the States, and the Supreme Court," *Brookings Review* 4 (Winter/Spring 1986), pp. 32–37.

Goals of Federal Grants

Federal grants serve four purposes, of which the most important is the fourth:

1. To supply state and local governments with revenue
2. To establish minimum national standards for such things as highways and clean air
3. To equalize resources among the states by taking, through federal taxes, money from people with high incomes and spending it, through grants, in states where the poor live
4. To attack national problems yet minimize the growth of federal agencies.

(highway engineers, welfare administrators, educators) confer at meetings, read common journals, and jointly defend the independence of their programs from attempts by "politicians" (elected national or state officials) to regulate them.[33] When interest groups, congressional committee staffers, and federal bureaucrats (who in turn are connected to state and local bureaucrats) join forces, they create powerful guilds.[34] These are often referred to as **issue networks or iron triangles**, and they can be very effective in protecting programs.

Republican presidents "have consistently favored fewer strings, less federal supervision, and the delegation of spending discretion to the state and local governments."[35] Democratic presidents before Clinton have been less supportive of general grants. Congress has divided similarly, with Democrats generally voting for more detailed federal regulations and Republicans for maximum state and local discretion. As a former governor of Arkansas and a self-styled "new Democrat," and as part of his program of "Reinventing Government," President Clinton strongly advocates giving states and localities more, rather than less, discretion. When it came to specific legislation, Clinton's Republican predecessors, despite their avowed support for local discretion, honored this principle more in the breach than in true observance. Clinton's record on this matter is yet to be established.

Chief executives—governors and presidents from both major parties—generally tend to urge the consolidation of categorical-formula grants into larger blocks. Legislators who prefer to decide where the funds are to go and groups that benefit from existing programs are likely to resist such consolidations, most of the time successfully. Consider the battle over libraries. The administration "proposed the consolidation of several narrow library grants. Congress resisted, and the reason was simple and can be expressed quantitatively: 99.99 percent of the public is not interested in library grant reform. Of the .01 percent who are interested, all are librarians and oppose it."[36] Or in another example, President Clinton's proposed consolidation of 150 different education and training programs, costing $24 billion each year, is meeting resistance. "The federal bureaucracy is woven together with agency employees and congressional committees who zealously guard every corner of their turf. To please them all, training dollars must be spread thin across the federal universe diluting their effectiveness."[37]

Even when Congress provides for block grants, it tends to impose more and more rules on their use, a practice known as *recategorization*. To get around congressional unwillingness to give up control over and resist pressure from those who want to protect categorical grants, President Clinton has proposed to Congress that it delegate to the state and local governments the right to mix funds from different programs and to select one agency's set of rules in spending the money.[38] If Congress should do so, it would be in fact, and not just in language, "reinventing federalism."

The battle over the appropriate level of national government control of the funds it grants to the states tends to be cyclical. A scholar of federalism explains, "Complaints about excessive federal control tend to be followed by proposals to shift more power to state and local governments. Then, when problems arise in state and local administration—and problems inevitably arise when any organization tries to administer anything—demands for closer federal supervision and tighter federal controls follow."[39]

At the moment, the national government is having such acute budgetary problems that the pressures are toward the elimination or reduction of federal grants and the return of many functions to the states. The number of federal grants hit a low of 404 in 1984 but went back up again to 557 in 1992. The percentage of federal dollars as part of state and local spending was 26.5 percent in 1978, but by 1989 it had dropped to 17.3 percent. That percentage edged back up again to

20.5 percent in 1991, but the reason for the increase is that the national government was giving a greater percentage of federal dollars directly to individuals through programs such as Medicare.[40] Funds available for spending by state and local governments, despite an increase in the number of grant programs, continue to decline (see Figure 3-3).

REGULATORY FEDERALISM AND FEDERAL MANDATES

Fewer federal dollars has not meant fewer federal controls. On the contrary, the federal government continues to impose mandates on states and local governments, often without any offsetting federal funds. State and local officials complain that these new federal regulatory devices are far more intrusive than the old-fashioned conditions they used to complain about as part of federal grant programs.[41] As one observer concludes, "In sum, the role of Congress with respect to subnational governance has changed since 1965 from a generous supplier of funds to a preemptor imposing costs that have the potential for bankrupting many small rural local governments and fiscally strained cities by the year 2000."[42] One study by Price Waterhouse estimates that unfunded federal mandates will cost localities $90 billion over the next five years.[43] State and local officials have organized protests against unfunded federal mandates, even organizing a NUM Day—National Unfunded Mandates—on October 27, 1993. The day before, President Clinton signed an executive order prohibiting federal agencies from issuing regulations that impose unfunded mandates on states and localities.[44] Issuing this directive was one of the recommendations that emerged from Vice President Gore's National Performance Review.[45] But such an order cannot stop the flow of such mandates. The Americans with Disabilities Act, for example, calls on state and local governments to build ramps and alter curbs—renovations that will cost millions. The Environmental

FIGURE 3-3   The Curtailment of Federal Aid

SOURCE: Advisory Commission on Intergovernmental Relations, *Significant Features of Fiscal Federalism*, Vol. 2 (Government Printing Office, 1992), p. 60.

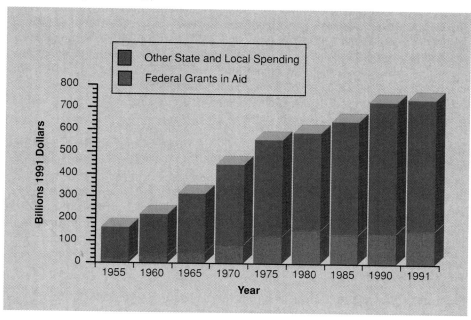

Improved cooperation between the federal government and state and local government is critical to the success of our nation in the years ahead. First of all, we must reestablish the federal-state partnership. For too long, Washington has passed on mandates and requirements to the states without supplying the resources to pay for them. As a result, state and local governments have had to substantially increase taxes to provide the required services. In a Clinton administration, we will ensure that the federal government resumes its responsibilities, instead of just passing the buck on to others.

   Second, I think we need to reassess the ways in which the federal government can help state and local governments carry out tasks that are traditionally state and local responsibilities. For instance, I believe the federal government can play a greater and more effective role in education, by passing federal standards and requiring national examinations of every American student.

SOURCE: *Civic Action* (newsletter of the National Civic League), March/April 1992.

From Coast to Coast

Fiscal Capacity to Raise Revenue Through Taxes

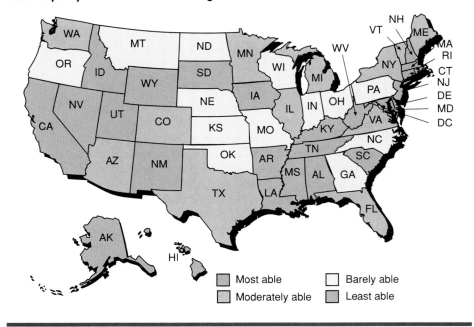

Most able
Moderately able
Barely able
Least able

SOURCE: Advisory Commission on Intergovernmental Relations, *Significant Features of Fiscal Federalism*, Vol. 2, (Government Printing Office, 1992), p. 268.

Protection Agency regulations requiring states to build automobile pollution-testing stations and take other actions to reduce pollution carry no corresponding federal dollars.[46]

New Techniques of Federal Control

DIRECT ORDERS   In a few instances, federal regulation takes the form of direct orders that must be complied with under threat of criminal or civil sanction. Examples are the Equal Opportunity Act of 1982, barring job discrimination by state and local governments because of race, color, religion, sex, and national origin, and the Marine Protection Amendments of 1977, prohibiting cities from dumping sewage into the ocean. Because such direct orders raise mild constitutional concerns and more serious political ones, Congress favors other techniques for imposing the federal will on the states.

CROSS-CUTTING REQUIREMENTS   The first and most famous of these requirements (so-called because a condition on one federal grant is extended to all activities supported by federal funds regardless of their source) is Title VI of the 1964 Civil Rights Act, which holds that no person may be discriminated against in the use of federal funds because of race, color, national origin, sex, or handicapped status. More than 60 cross-cutting requirements concern the environment, historic preservation, contract wage rates, access to governmental information, the care of experimental animals, the treatment of human subjects in research projects, and so on.

CROSS-OVER SANCTIONS   These sanctions permit the use of federal dollars in one program to influence state and local policy in another. One example is the

Emergency Highway Energy Conservation Act of 1974, which prohibits the secretary of transportation from approving federal funding for highway construction in states having a speed limit in excess of 55 miles per hour (since amended to allow the limit to be raised to 65 miles per hour in less-congested areas). Another example is a 1984 act that threatened to reduce federal highway aid by up to 15 percent for any state that failed to adopt a minimum drinking age of 21 by 1987.

TOTAL PREEMPTION   This kind of control rests not on the national government's power to spend but on its powers under the supremacy and commerce clauses to preempt conflicting state and local activities. Building on this constitutional authority, federal law in certain areas just preempts state and local governments from the field. "There are fourteen types of total preemption laws, ranging from ones removing all regulatory powers from the states to ones authorizing states to cooperate in enforcing a statute."[47]

PARTIAL PREEMPTION   In these instances federal law establishes basic policies but requires states to administer them. Some programs give states an option to participate, but if a state chooses not to do so the national government then steps in and directly runs the programs. Even worse from the state's point of view is *mandatory partial preemption*, in which the national government requires the state to act on peril of losing other funds but provides no funds to support the state action. The Clean Air Act of 1990 is an example of mandatory partial preemption; the federal government sets national air quality standards and requires states to devise plans and pay for their implementation and enforcement.[48] If a state fails to adopt air pollution plans that are deemed to be adequate, so-called hammer provisions require federal implementation plans to be imposed on the state.[49] State violations of the clean air requirements can be "punished" by a variety of sanctions, including withholding of federal funds for a variety of purposes. Medicaid is another example of the national government providing some dollars but mandating states to provide services that cost more than the federal funds cover.

These new forms of federal regulation accelerated during the 1970s and abated only slightly during the 1980s. More than half the federal statutes preempting state and local authority have been enacted in the last two decades[50] (see Figure 3-4). Despite the Reagan-Bush emphasis on retrenchment of federal regulations, their administrations sought national controls to force states to adopt drunk-driving legislation, to cut off federal funds to cities enacting rent controls, and to force on states and localities certain busing, abortion, and school prayer policies.[51] President

FIGURE 3-4   Increases in Federal Laws that Preempt State Authority

SOURCE: Based on U.S. Advisory Commission on Intergovernmental Relations 1992 estimate. Copyright © 1992 by The New York Times Company. Reprinted by permission.

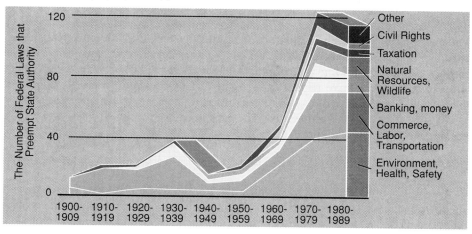

Clinton pledged to give state and local governments more discretion. "My view," he told the National Governors' Association, "is that we ought to give more elbow room to experimentation." However, unlike his immediate predecessors, who looked upon an active national government as a problem, Clinton favors a positive role for the national government.[52]

Liberals and conservatives alike tend to favor fewer federal controls over state and local officials in the abstract, yet are willing to make exceptions in policy areas when they feel strongly something must be done to correct or prevent an injustice. Because there are plenty of injustices, federal regulation of state and local governments remains a continuing feature of our political system.

POLITICS AND FEDERALISM: A LOOK TO THE FUTURE

The ongoing debate about federalism can be understood on several levels. On one level, it is an argument about which government can most effectively deal with a particular problem—the national government or the states. On another level, it is an attempt by interest groups to find the forum—Washington or their state capitals—where they have the greatest chance of a sympathetic hearing. And on yet another level, it is a debate about the best way to protect liberty and promote equality.[53]

Until the civil rights revolution of the 1960s, for example, segregationists feared that national officials—responding to different political majorities—would work for racial integration. Thus they praised local government, emphasized the dangers of overcentralization, and argued that the protection of civil rights was not a proper function of the national government. As one political scientist observes, "Federalism has a dark history to overcome. For nearly two hundred years, states' rights have been asserted to protect slavery, segregation, and discrimination."[54]

Today the politics of federalism, even with respect to civil rights, is more complicated than in the past.[55] With changing political power distributions, the national government is not necessarily more favorable to the claims of minorities than most state or city governments. With the Supreme Court's abandonment of rigorous constitutional protection for women's right to abortions and its refusal to extend marital privacy rights to gays and lesbians, some state constitutions and state courts now provide more protection for these rights than does the U.S. Constitution. State and local governments also "have become the principal agents for advancing the cause of comparable worth. This role challenges the conventional wisdom that only centrist alternatives can advance equal opportunity and civil rights for all citizens."[56]

As states more actively regulate the economy, some business interests have been arguing that conflicting state regulations are unduly burdening interstate commerce and are asking for preemptive federal regulation to save them, not only from stringent state regulations but from having to adjust to 50 different state laws.[57] "One national dumb rule is better than 50 inconsistent rules of any kind," says a lawyer who represents trade groups in the food industries and medical devices.[58]

The Reemergence of the States

When the national government slowed the rate of growth of its domestic spending, the states took over some of its responsibilities.[59] But, "instead of getting government off the backs of the American people," Reagan "presided over a huge growth of big government at the state level."[60] Not only were the programs shifted to the states, so were the costs of running them. For example, in 1970 Medicaid cost the states about 4 percent of their budgets; by 1995 it may be in excess of 20 percent.[61]

Abandoned by the national government, cities and counties have also turned again to their own state capitals. States have responded to this reduction in federal funding for urban governments with mixed results. Some states—Florida, Massachusetts, New Jersey, New York, and Oklahoma—tried with some success to replace the withdrawn federal funds for their cities and schools until they, too, fell upon hard times in the early 1990s. Other states—California, for example—made little effort to replace the federal dollars or keep up the cut programs.[62]

By the 1990s, states were staggering under these additional burdens and being forced to raise taxes, lower the level of services, or use mandates to make local governments provide additional services without state aid.[63] These fiscal realities and the economic recession of the early 1990s "have stalled the states' resurgence."[64] Their costs for education, for welfare, for prisons, for health care are now going up much faster than their revenues. The rate of growth of state governments has slowed. The rate of growth of the problems they face has not.

The Newest Federalism
Herblock, *Through the Looking Glass* (Norton & Company, 1984), p. 42. Reprinted by permission.

The Future of Federalism

In 1933, seeing state governments helpless during the Great Depression, one writer stated, "I do not predict that the states will go, but affirm that they have gone."[65] Those prophets of doom were wrong. States are stronger than ever. Most have improved their governmental structures, taken on greater roles in funding education, launched programs to help distressed cities, and—despite new constitutional limitations—expanded their tax bases. Able men and women have been attracted to many governorships. "Today, states, in formal representational, policymaking, and implementation terms at least, are more representative, more responsive, more activist, and more professional in their operations than they ever have been. They face their expanded roles better equipped to assume and fulfill them."[66]

The national government, however, is not likely to retreat to a pre-1930 posture or even a pre-1960 one. The underlying economic and social conditions that generated the demand for federal action have not substantially altered. On the contrary, in addition to such traditional issues as helping people find jobs and preventing inflation and depressions that still require national action, countless new issues have been added to the national agenda by the growth of a global economy based on high technology, service, and information. It is worth remembering that in terms of gross domestic product, many American states are larger than many nations—California, for example, has an economy larger than that of Great Britain—yet most states still lack the jurisdiction by themselves to clean up the air, modernize the air traffic control system, regulate the economy, prevent pollution of rivers, deal with drug abuse, or prevent the spread of AIDS and find its cure. And there are issues such as the lack of decent housing and access to health care for inner-city African Americans and Hispanics and the skyrocketing costs of health care for all Americans that are beyond the capacity of the states to solve alone.

Most Americans have strong attachments to our federal system—in the abstract. They remain loyal to their states and show a healthy skepticism about the national government. Yet most of the time for most of the people, the concerns are about more immediate problems—clean air, safety in the streets, relations between men and women, jobs, the cost of medical care, heating fuel for their homes, and gasoline for their cars. They are not much concerned about the nature of federal grants or arguments about the virtues of national versus state action. They are willing to use whatever governmental agencies or combinations of agencies they feel can best serve their needs and represent their interests.

American federalism has modified, and been modified by, the political and social issues facing us during the last two hundred years. It will continue to shape our society. Our federal system remains firmly rooted in our political system as well as our constitutional democracy. We are not about to abolish it or modify it drastically. But just as the federalism of today is as different from that of 1787 as a jet airplane is from a stagecoach, so federalism will continue to evolve as we move into the twenty-first century.

SUMMARY

1. Our federal constitutional system has evolved into something only slightly different in form, yet significantly different in operation, from the 1789 version.

2. It is not possible to find neat and clear and noncontroversial divisions between the functions of the national and state governments.

3. Today the national government has the constitutional authority to do whatever Congress thinks is necessary and proper, and there are few if any judicially enforced limits to restrain Congress from interfering with the actions of the states.

4. The centralization of constitutional power at the national level does not mean that federalism is dead. Political power remains dispersed, and states remain active and significant political realities.

5. Ideological bias in favor of either national or state action is likely to reflect concrete political objectives. Conservative support for states' rights and the liberal preference for national action are no longer as predictable. Shifting political issues continue to lead to shifting allegiances among the various levels of government.

6. The drift toward increasing federal action has been fueled more by underlying economic and social changes than by concerns about federalism, but we detect a vigorous trend toward the view that federalism as a political principle is worthy of being preserved.

7. The major instrument of federal intervention has been various kinds of grants-in-aid, of which the most prominent are categorical-formula grants, project grants, block grants, and revenue sharing.

8. Additional forms of federal intervention to control the activities of state and local governments have become more important in recent decades. These include direct orders, cross-cutting requirements on federal funds, crossover sanctions in the use of federal funds, total preemption, and partial preemption.

9. Beginning in the 1970s, accelerating in the 1980s, and continuing into the 1990s, there has been a substantial return of policy responsibilities to the states and a pause in the expanding role of the national government.

10. Today we no longer spend so much time debating the *law* of federalism; we have moved to the *politics* of federalism. As now interpreted, the Constitution gives us the option to decide through the political process what we want to do, who is going to pay, and how we are going to get it done.

FURTHER READING

ADVISORY COMMISSION ON INTERGOVERNMENTAL RELATIONS, *Intergovernmental Perspective* (U.S. Government Printing Office, published four times a year).

THOMAS J. ANTON, *American Federalism and Public Policy* (Temple University Press, 1989).

RAOUL BERGER, *Federalism: The Founders' Design* (University of Oklahoma Press, 1987).

SAMUEL H. BEER, *To Make a Nation: The Rediscovery of American Federalism* (Harvard University Press, Belknap Press, 1993).

CENTER FOR THE STUDY OF FEDERALISM, *Publius: The Journal of Federalism* (Temple University, published quarterly; one issue is an "Annual Review of the State of American Federalism").

TIMOTHY J. CONLAN, *New Federalism: Intergovernmental Reform from Nixon to Reagan* (Brookings Institution, 1988).

THOMAS R. DYE, *American Federalism: Competition Among Governments* (Lexington Books, 1990).

DANIEL J. ELAZAR, *Exploring Federalism* (University of Alabama Press, 1987).

MICHAEL FIX AND DAPHNE A. KENYON, *Coping with Mandates* (Urban Institute Press, 1990).

AL GORE, *From Red Tape to Results—Creating a Government That Works Better and Costs Less: Report of the National Performance Review* (U.S. Government Printing Office, 1993).

CHRISTOPHER HAMILTON AND DONALD T. WELLS, *Federalism, Power and Political Economy* (Prentice Hall, 1990).

JOHN KINCAID, ED., "American Federalism: The Third Century," *Annals of the American Academy of Political and Social Science* 509 (May 1990).

SUE O'BRIEN AND MARSHALL KAPLAN, *The Governors and the New Federalism* (Westview Press, 1991).

VINCENT OSTROM, *The Meaning of American Federalism* (ICS Press, 1991).

WILLIAM H. RIKER, *The Development of American Federalism* (Academic Publishers, 1987).

HARRY N. SCHEIBER, *Federalism and the Judicial Mind: Essays on American Constitutional Law and Politics* (Institute of Governmental Studies, University of California at Berkeley, 1992).

WILLIAM H. STEWART, *Concepts of Federalism* (Center for the Study of Federalism and University Press of America, 1984).

THOMAS R. SWARTZ AND JOHN E. PECK, *The Changing Face of Fiscal Federalism* (M. E. Sharpe, 1990).

JOSEPH F. ZIMMERMAN, *Contemporary American Federalism: The Growth of National Power* (Praeger, 1992).

JOSEPH F. ZIMMERMAN, *Federal Preemption: The Silent Revolution* (Iowa State University Press, 1991).

FIRST AMENDMENT RIGHTS

4

"Congress shall make no law," declares the First Amendment, "respecting an establishment of religion, or prohibiting the free exercise thereof; or abridging the freedom of speech, or of the press, or the right of the people peaceably to assemble, and to petition the Government for a redress of grievances." In this one sentence our Constitution lays down the fundamental principles of a free society: freedom of conscience and freedom of expression.

Although it was the framers who wrote the Constitution, in a sense it was the people who drafted our basic charter of liberties. As we have seen, the Constitution drawn up in Philadelphia included guarantees of a few basic rights, but it lacked a specific bill of rights similar to that found in most state constitutions. This omission aroused widespread suspicion among the people. In order to persuade delegates to the state ratification conventions to vote for the Constitution, the Federalists had to promise to correct this deficiency. In its first session, the new Congress proposed twelve amendments, ten of which were ratified by the end of 1791 and became part of the Constitution. These ten amendments are known as the Bill of Rights.[1] (As we saw in Chapter 2, another of those proposed amendments was ratified 202 years later and became the Twenty-seventh Amendment.)

Note that the Bill of Rights literally applies *only to the national government*. As John Marshall held in *Barron v Baltimore* (1833), the Bill of Rights limits the national, not the state governments.[2] Why not the states? The people were confident they could control their own state officials, and most of the state constitutions already had bills of rights. It was the new and distant central government they feared. As it turned out, those fears were largely misplaced. The national government—responsive to tens of millions of voters from a variety of races, creeds, religions, and economic interests—has shown less tendency to curtail civil liberties than have state and local governments. Until recently, for the most part, state judges have not used the bills of rights in their respective state constitutions to protect civil liberties.

When the Fourteenth Amendment, which *does* apply to the states, was adopted in 1868, some contended its **due process clause**—which states that no person shall be deprived of life, liberty, or property without due process of law—limits states in precisely the same way the Bill of Rights limits the national government. At least, they argued, freedom of speech should be protected by the Fourteenth Amendment. For decades the Supreme Court refused to interpret the Fourteenth Amendment in this way. Then in 1925, in *Gitlow v New York*, the Court announced: "For present purposes we may and do assume that freedom of speech and of the press—which are protected by the First Amendment from abridgment by Congress—are among the fundamental personal rights and 'liberties' protected by the due process clause of the Fourteenth Amendment from impairment by the States."[3]

THE NATIONALIZATION OF THE BILL OF RIGHTS

Gitlow v New York was a revolutionary decision. For the first time, the U.S. Constitution protected freedom of speech and of the press from abridgment by state and local governments. By the 1940s the other provisions of the First Amendment—religion, assembly, petition—had been brought within the scope of the Fourteenth Amendment. Today the First Amendment's restraints are applied to all who exercise governmental authority, at national, state, or local levels.

If the First Amendment applies to the states, why not the other parts of the Bill of Rights, most of which have to do with the rights of persons accused of crimes and with restraints on police procedures? Beginning in the 1930s, and continuing at an accelerated pace during the 1960s, the Supreme Court **selectively incorporated** provision after provision of the Bill of Rights into the due process clause.[4] Today the Fourteenth Amendment imposes on the states all the provisions of the Bill of Rights except those of the Second, Third, Seventh, and Tenth Amendments, and the grand jury requirements of the Fifth Amendment. When we talk about the Bill of Rights today, we are really talking about limits on the power of all who govern, whether they do so on behalf of the national government, the states, or local units of government.

How are we to distinguish between those provisions of the Bill of Rights that are incorporated into the Fourteenth Amendment—that is, made to limit state and local governments—from those that are not? The rights *not* incorporated are those the Supreme Court has concluded could be replaced by other procedures without necessarily resulting in a denial of justice or liberty. Whereas no nation could be considered free without freedom of speech, for example—which is why it is incorporated as part of the due process clause of the Fourteenth Amendment—justice could be done without necessarily requiring a grand jury indictment before bringing people to trial. That is why this provision in the Fifth Amendment has not been incorporated.

In addition to the rights specifically protected by the Constitution, the Supreme Court has found constitutional protection for other fundamental rights. For example, the rights of association and of privacy, as well as the right to travel, are not mentioned anywhere in the Constitution. Yet these important but unexpressed rights have nonetheless been found to share constitutional protection in common with explicit guarantees.[5]

After the Supreme Court incorporated most of the national Bill of Rights into the Fourteenth Amendment, little attention was paid by state judges—or anybody else—to the bills of rights in their respective state constitutions. "The Supreme Court took such complete control of the field that state judges could sit back in the conviction that their part was simply to await the next landmark decision."[6] Recently, however, stimulated in part by the U.S. Supreme Court's more limited interpretation of some provisions of the national Bill of Rights, there has been a renewal of interest in state constitutions as independent sources of additional protection for civil liberties and civil rights.[7]

Advocates of what has come to be called **new judicial federalism** contend that the U.S. Constitution should set minimum but not maximum standards to protect our rights. There is nothing, they argue, to keep state courts from using similar provisions of the bill of rights in their own state constitutions to provide more protection for rights than is to be found in the U.S. Constitution. Moreover, state bills of rights sometimes have language that encourages a more expansive protection of rights than does the national Bill of Rights. For example, a dozen states have an equal rights amendment in their constitutions, and eleven explicitly protect the right of privacy.[8] The Louisiana state constitution prohibits age discrimination; 35 state constitutions affirm the right of free speech; 36 state constitutions have clauses that could easily be construed as going beyond the Second Amendment in protecting the right to bear arms.[9]

Thirty-two state supreme courts have found some rights protected to a greater extent than the Supreme Court of the United States has found to be secured by the national Bill of Rights.[10] Nevertheless, state court decisions extending rights beyond the limits secured by the U.S. Constitution are exceptions and are to be found in a substantial manner in relatively few states, such as California, Alaska, Florida, and Massachusetts.[11]

If a state supreme court goes too far beyond public sentiment in its own state, its decisions run the risk of being overturned by an amendment to the state constitution.

In 1990, for example, in California and Alaska, after their respective state courts extended to criminal defendants some rights beyond those provided by the U.S. Constitution, "victims' rights" amendments were added to these state constitutions to reverse the effect of those decisions and to forbid state judges from so extending the rights of criminal defendants beyond those provided by the U.S. Constitution. And since most state judges lack lifetime tenure and are subject to electoral contests, state judges "who stray too far from most of the people of their state's understanding of their state constitutions are likely to get chucked out of office,"[12] as happened in California in 1988 with the defeat of Chief Justice Rose Bird and two other liberal justices. Thus, despite the revival of interest in state bills of rights, the U.S. Supreme Court and the national Bill of Rights remain the dominant protectors of civil liberties and civil rights.

CONGRESS SHALL MAKE NO LAW RESPECTING AN ESTABLISHMENT OF RELIGION

The first words of the First Amendment are emphatic and brief: "Congress shall make no law respecting an establishment of religion." The framers were reacting to the English system, wherein the Crown was the head not only or the government but also of the established church—the Church of England—and public officials were required to take an oath of support for the established church as a condition of holding office.

Since 1947 the Supreme Court has construed the **establishment clause** to erect a *wall of separation between church and state,* to prohibit any law or governmental action designed to confer any benefit on religion, even if all sects are treated the same.[13] As Justice Souter recently restated it for the Court, "the heart of the Establishment Clause [is] that government should not prefer one religion to another, or religion to irreligion."[14] That view is under attack by Chief Justice William Rehnquist, Justice Antonin Scalia, and Justice Clarence Thomas, who hold to a *nonpreferentialist* position.[15] They believe the Constitution simply prohibits favoritism toward a particular religion, but does not prohibit governmental encouragement of religious activities or even some support for religious organizations, so long as individuals are not *legally* coerced into participating in religious activities.

The establishment clause does not prevent governments from *accommodating* to religious needs. To what extent and under which conditions governments may accommodate to these needs is at the heart of much of the debate among the justices in interpreting the clause. For example, Justice Anthony Kennedy interprets the clause to forbid governments from imposing any pressure on persons to participate in religious activities, even if such pressure falls short of legal compulsion, such as prayer at high school graduations.[16] Justice Sandra Day O'Connor's test is one of *endorsement;* that is, she believes the clause forbids any governmental action that endorses religious activities, even if there is no coercion. Justice John Paul Stevens adheres to a strict *separationist* view. Justices Souter and Ginsburg would appear to be closer to the separationist than the accommodationist interpretation. Justice Stephen Breyer's views are yet to be revealed.

Despite criticism of the so-called *Lemon* test, first put forward in the case of *Lemon v Kurtzman,* and despite the fact that in Justice O'Connor's words, "the slide away from *Lemon's* unitary approach is well under way,"[17] the test remains as the prevailing guide in interpreting the establishment clause. Under this three-part test, (1) a law must have a secular legislative purpose; (2) its primary effect must neither advance nor inhibit religion; (3) it must avoid "excessive government entanglement with religion." The establishment clause is designed to prevent three evils: "sponsorship, financial support, and active involvement of the sovereign in religious activity."[18]

Forms of Citation

In this and the next several chapters, we discuss constitutional rules at length, and to talk about the Constitution is to talk about Supreme Court decisions. Many of these decisions are cited in the notes at the back of the book so that you can look them up if you wish. Two forms of citation are used:

1. Official Supreme Court reports are cited as: *Gitlow v New York,* 268 US 652 (1925). This means that this case can be found in the 268th volume of the *United States Supreme Court Reports* on page 652, and it was decided in 1925. These reports are published by the U.S. Government Printing Office.

2. For more recent cases, see the advance sheets of *United States Supreme Court Reports,* published by the Lawyers' Cooperative Publishing Company of Rochester, New York. An example is a case involving First Amendment issues, *Campbell v Acuff-Rose Music,* in which 2 Live Crew's commercial parody of "Pretty Woman" was upheld as "fair use" of the original Roy Orbison song. It is cited as: 127 L Ed 2d 500 (1994). This means that it can be found in volume 127 of the Lawyers' Edition, second series, starting on page 500, and it was decided in 1994.

Do nativity scenes on public property violate the establishment clause?

The Supreme Court has applied the *Lemon* test to determine the constitutionality of displays on public property of religious symbols such as nativity scenes, menorahs, and crosses. Do these displays have a secular purpose? Is their primary effect neither to advance nor inhibit religion? And do they involve excessive government entanglement with religion?

You Decide!

Because of the establishment clause, states (and, of course, other units of government such as state universities, colleges, and school districts) may not introduce any kind of devotional exercises into the public school curriculum. However, the Supreme Court has not, as it is sometimes said, prohibited prayer in public schools. It is not unconstitutional for people to pray in a school building. What is unconstitutional is *sponsorship or encouragement* of prayer by public school authorities.[19] In 1992 the Court extended the ban against school-endorsed prayer in public schools to forbid the use of a nondenominational prayer at primary and secondary school graduations. The Court concluded that such a practice coerces students into participating in religious ceremonies.[20]

Devotional reading of the Bible, recitation of the Lord's Prayer, and posting of the Ten Commandments on the walls of classrooms in public schools are also prohibited by the Constitution. Nor may a state forbid the teaching of evolution or require the simultaneous teaching of "creation science"—that is, the belief that human life did not evolve but rather was created by a single act of God.[21]

Tax exemptions for church property, along with that of other nonprofit institutions, are constitutional. State legislatures and Congress may hire chaplains to open each day's legislative session—a practice that has continued without interruption since the first session of Congress. But if done in a public school, this practice would be unconstitutional. Apparently, the difference is that legislators, as adults, are not "susceptible to religious indoctrination or peer pressure."[22] Also, as the joke goes, legislators need the prayer more.

Parochial School Aid

A troublesome area involves attempts by many states to provide financial assistance to parochial schools. The Supreme Court has tried to draw a line between permissible public aid to students, including those in sectarian schools, and impermissible public aid to religion.

At the college level the problems are relatively simple. Tax funds may be used to construct buildings and operate educational programs at church-related schools, as long as the money is not spent directly on buildings used for religious purposes or on teaching religious subjects. Even if students choose to attend religious schools and become ministers, governmental aid to these students is permissible. Such aid has a secular purpose; its effect on religion is the result of individual choice, "and it does not confer any message of state endorsement of religion."[23]

At the elementary and secondary level, however, the constitutional problems become more complicated, and "the current law on government aid to religious schools is a quagmire."[24] Here the secular and religious parts of institutions and instruction are much more closely interwoven. Students are younger and more susceptible to indoctrination, and the chances are greater that aid given to church-operated schools might seep into aid for religion.

Despite the constitutional obstacles, some states have attempted to provide tax credits or deductions for those who send their children to private, largely church-affiliated schools. Deductions or credits available only to parents of children attending nonpublic schools are unconstitutional, but allowing tax-paying parents to deduct or take a credit from their state income taxes for what they paid for tuition and other costs to send their children to school—public or private—is constitutionally permissible, even if most of the benefit goes to those who send their children to private religious schools.[25]

The Supreme Court has also approved using tax funds to provide students attending primary and secondary church-operated schools (except those that deny admission because of race or religion) with textbooks, standardized tests, lunches, transportation to and from school, diagnostic services for speech and hearing problems, and other kinds of remedial help—provided such services take place outside

Children may pray in public schools, provided the prayer is not organized, authorized, or endorsed by the school authorities.

The courts have allowed the use of public funds to provide books and remedial services to parochial schools.

of the school building and away from the "pervasively sectarian atmosphere of the church-related schools."[26]

Tax funds may not be used in religious schools to pay teachers' salaries, purchase equipment, provide counseling for students, produce teacher-prepared tests, repair facilities, or transport students on field trips. School authorities may not permit religious instructors to come into public school buildings during the school day to provide religious instruction on a voluntary basis.

However, in 1993 the Court upheld the assignment of a sign-language interpreter, paid for by public funds, to accompany a deaf child to a parochial school. The Court held that this was aid to a student, not to a religion. In the context of a state program that made such services generally available, there could be no danger that such a practice could be construed as an endorsement of religion. The minority contended that since the interpreter would be obliged to follow the deaf student throughout his day, including attendance at Mass, "the interpreter's every gesture would be infused with religious significance."[27]

Why is it constitutional for state governments to pay for books but not for maps? For bus trips but not for field trips? For standardized tests but not for tests prepared by teachers? For a sign-language interpreter, but not for teachers? Those on the "approved" side meet the three-part *Lemon* test, but those on the "forbidden" side fail one of the requirements. Thus, transportation to and from school, which is permitted, involves a routine trip that every student makes every day; it is unrelated to any aspect of the curriculum. Field trips, which cannot be paid for by tax funds, are controlled by teachers and are aids to instruction. Books and standardized tests, which can be bought by tax funds, can be easily evaluated to ensure that they are not designed to promote religion, whereas maps or teacher-prepared tests cannot be so readily checked. And in cases involving teaching by public teachers in parochial schools, the supervision to ensure avoidance of religious influences creates excessive entanglement of church and state, whereas a sign-language interpreter does no more than accurately interpret whatever material is presented to the class as a whole.

Right to Worship as One Chooses

The Constitution not only forbids the establishment of religion but also forbids Congress and the states from passing any law "prohibiting the free exercise thereof." This is the **free exercise clause**. "The Court has struggled to find a neutral course between the two religion clauses, both of which are cast in absolute terms, and either of which, if expanded to a logical extreme, would tend to clash with the other."[28] Thus a law that requires people to do something contrary to the teachings of their religion may interfere with their free exercise of religion. Yet to exempt them from the law because of their religious convictions could favor religious activities in such a way as to offend the establishment clause.

What is a church? What is a religion? The Constitution provides no definition, and the Supreme Court has been reluctant—understandably—to get into these questions. Unconventional religions are entitled to the same constitutional protection as are the more traditional ones. The free exercise clause extends to those who act on sincerely held religious beliefs, not just to those who respond to a specific command of a particular church. But, although the Court does not "underestimate the difficulty of distinguishing between religious and secular convictions and determining whether a professed belief is sincerely held,"[29] only beliefs rooted in a *religion* are protected by the free exercise clause.

The right to hold any or no religious *belief* is one of our few absolute rights. No government has authority to compel the acceptance of any creed or to censor it. A state may not compel a religious belief or deny persons any right because of their beliefs or lack of them. Requiring religious oaths as a condition of public

Thinking it Through

The answer to these questions depends on the *context*; that is, whether the particular physical setting of the display and what is included with it makes it appear that government is transmitting a religious or a secular message. If the display appears to endorse religious beliefs, it is unconstitutional; if it does not have such an effect, it is constitutional.

A display in a public space of a nativity scene was upheld because Santa's house and other symbols of the Christmas season appeared along with it. A Hanukkah menorah on the steps of the Pittsburgh City Hall was upheld because it was located next to a Christmas tree. The Court majority concluded that these displays had a secular purpose of celebrating both the religious and secular dimensions of the winter holidays and provided little or no benefit to religion in general or to the Christian or Jewish faiths in particular.

The Constitution, said the Court in the first of these decisions, "does not require complete separation of church and state; it affirmatively mandates accommodation, not merely tolerance of all religions, and forbids hostility toward any." On the other side, the Court ruled that the Constitution does *not* permit an unadorned display of the nativity scene in a courthouse, for in this context the impression conveyed was that the county government was endorsing the display's specific religious message.*

*Lynch v Donnelly, 465 US 668 (1984); County of Allegheny et al. v American Civil Liberties Union, 488 US 816 (1989).

Does federally supported sex education violate the establishment clause?

In the Adolescent Family Life Act of 1981 Congress provided for grants to charitable organizations, including religious organizations, to teach teenagers about "sexual prudence." Does such a law violate the establishment clause? Do grants of money or supplies to religious organizations under the law violate the establishment clause?

You Decide!

employment or as a prerequisite to running for public office is unconstitutional. In fact, the *only time* the Constitution mentions the word religion is to state: "No religious Test shall ever be required as a Qualification to any Office or public Trust under the United States" (Article VI).

Although carefully protected, the right to *practice* a religion has had less protection than the right to hold particular beliefs. Religious convictions do not ordinarily exempt one from obeying an otherwise valid and nondiscriminatory law or government regulation. Prior to 1990 the Supreme Court applied what is known as the *compelling interest test* and carefully scrutinized laws alleged to infringe on religious practices. The Court insisted that the government provide some compelling public purpose to justify the infringement: "Only those interests of the highest order and those not otherwise served can overbalance legitimate claims to the free exercise of religion."[30] In other words, the Constitution was thought to throw "a mantle of protection" around religious practices, and the burden was on the government to justify interfering with them.

Then, in 1990, the Rehnquist Court significantly altered the interpretation of the free exercise cause. In *Employment Division v Smith*, the Court discarded the compelling interest test, except as it applied to laws denying people unemployment compensation. Outside of this narrow field, so far as the Constitution is concerned, a government no longer has to show a compelling interest in order to apply its general laws to religious practices. As long as a law does not single out and ban religious practices because "they are engaged in for religious reasons, or only because of the religious belief they display," a general law may be applied to conduct even if it is religiously inspired. In this particular instance, Oregon was allowed to deny unemployment benefits to two Native Americans who were fired because they used peyote as part of their religious rituals.[31]

Three years later, however, the city of Hialeah, Florida, was told that it could not apply its ordinances forbidding the slaughtering of animals as part of religious rituals to the Santeria religious services since other forms of animal slaughtering are allowed, and it was clear that these ordinances had been designed *specifically* to forbid the slaughter of animals as part of religious rituals in the Santeria religion.[32] Similarly, in 1993 the Court declared unconstitutional a public school practice that made its facilities available after school hours to any organization except religious ones. The Court struck down this practice more as a content-based restriction on speech than as an interference with religious freedom, but it also held that to allow religious groups the same right to use school facilities outside of school hours as any other group did not violate the establishment clause.[33]

Even prior to *Employment Division v Smith*, when the Supreme Court was using the compelling interest test, it nonetheless upheld laws and regulations outlawing business activities on Sunday, as applied to Orthodox Jews, and forbidding military officers to wear headgear while indoors, as applied to an Orthodox Jew's wearing of a *yarmulke* (skullcap). Congress subsequently intervened to make such practices permissible. The Court has also sustained an Internal Revenue Service regulation denying tax exemption to religious schools that admit members of only one race.[34] The Forest Service was allowed to construct a road through a portion of national forest held sacred by Native Americans and used by them for religious ceremonies.[35]

On the other hand, a state may not require Jehovah's Witnesses (or anyone else, for that matter) to participate in public school flag-salute ceremonies. Although a state may compel parents to send their children to some kind of accredited school, parents have a constitutional right to send their children to a church-sponsored rather than to a public school. Similarly, a state's compulsory school laws cannot compel the Amish to send their children to school beyond the eighth grade. Through the eighth grade the interests of the state in ensuring that all children

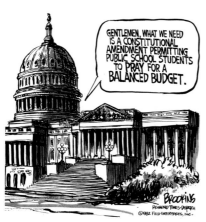

GENTLEMEN, WHAT WE NEED IS A CONSTITUTIONAL AMENDMENT PERMITTING PUBLIC SCHOOL STUDENTS TO PRAY FOR A BALANCED BUDGET.

Brookins, *Richmond Times Dispatch*. © 1982 Field Enterprises, Inc.

Compulsory education laws cannot force Amish children to attend public schools beyond eighth grade.

learn basic skills overbalance religious convictions; after the eighth grade, religious convictions are given priority.

In 1993 Congress passed and President Bill Clinton signed the Religious Freedom Restoration Act, which was explicitly designed to reverse *Employment Division v Smith* and restore the use of the compelling interest test. The Religious Freedom Restoration Act exempts people from laws and governmental actions that burden their religious freedom, even if the burden results from "a rule of general applicability," except where the government can demonstrate that the burden is "the least restrictive means of furthering a compelling interest." By the terms of this law, "A person whose religious exercise" has been violated by a law or regulation may "assert that violation as a claim or defense in a judicial proceeding and obtain appropriate relief against [the] government."[36] It is not clear precisely how in practice one asserts this right.

In signing the bill, President Clinton said that reversing a decision of the Supreme Court "is a power that is rightly hesitantly and infrequently exercised by the United States Congress. But this is an issue in which that extraordinary measure was clearly called for."[37] That Congress can confer such a defense for persons who refuse to comply with federal laws and regulations is one thing; but that it can confer such a right on persons who do not comply with their own state and local laws and regulations raises interesting questions of federalism. It is not clear by what authority Congress can so diminish the power of state governments and restrict their power to legislate. If a religion permits individuals, under some circumstances, to avoid laws applied to others, it is predictable that people will claim this status, even though they may not be acting because of religious convictions or because of the commands of a church.

FREE SPEECH AND FREE PEOPLE

Government by the people is based on every person's right to speak freely, to organize in groups, to question the decisions of the government, and to campaign openly against it. Only through free and uncensored expression of opinion can government be kept responsive to the electorate and political power be transferred peacefully. Elections, separation of powers, and constitutional guarantees are meaningless unless all persons have the right to speak frankly and to hear and judge for themselves the worth of what others have to say.

Despite the fundamental importance of free speech to a democracy, some people seem to believe speech should be free only for those who agree with them.

Thinking it Through

Not necessarily, said the Supreme Court by a 5 to 4 vote. In *Bowen v Kendrick*, 487 US 589 (1988), Chief Justice William H. Rehnquist delivered the opinion of the majority of the Court. He applied the three-pronged *Lemon* test but with a strong accommodationist twist. The act was, he held, clearly motivated by a legitimate *secular purpose*: the elimination or reduction of the problems caused by teenage sexuality and pregnancy. Its effect has not been to promote religion, to advance substantial federal funds to churches, or to create a crucial symbolic link between government and religion; and finally, there has been no *excessive governmental entanglement* with religion.

Justice Sandra Day O'Connor, in a concurring opinion, joined with the Chief Justice and Justices Antonin Scalia, Anthony M. Kennedy, and Byron R. White in upholding the law on its face, but gave her vote only on the condition that the case be returned to the trial court to be sure that the law as applied had not in fact been used to permit "public funds to promote religious doctrine."

The Best Test of Truth

Justice Oliver Wendell Holmes, Jr., dissenting in *Abrams v United States*, wrote:

Persecution for the expression of opinions seems to me perfectly logical. If you have no doubt of your premises or your power and want a certain result with all your heart, you naturally express your wishes in law and sweep away all opposition. . . . But when men have realized that time has upset many fighting faiths, they may come to believe even more than they believe the very foundations of their own conduct that the ultimate good desired is better reached by free trade in ideas—that the best test of truth is the power of the thought to get itself accepted in the competition of the market, and that truth is the only ground upon which their wishes safely can be carried out. That at any rate is the theory of our Constitution. It is an experiment, as all life is an experiment.

SOURCE: *Abrams v United States*, 250 US 616 (1919).

Americans overwhelmingly support principles of tolerance when such principles are presented in general, abstract fashion—for example, "Do you believe in freedom of speech?" They are less tolerant, however, when the speech is directed to them or is critical of their race, religion, or ethnic origin.

Free speech is not simply the personal right of individuals to have their say; it is also the right of the rest of us to hear them. John Stuart Mill, whose *Essay on Liberty* (1859) is the classic defense of free speech, put it this way:

The peculiar evil of silencing the expression of opinion, is that it is robbing the human race. . . . If the opinion is right, they are deprived of the opportunity of exchanging error for truth; if wrong, they lose what is almost as great a benefit, the clearer perception and livelier impression of truth, produced by its collision with error.[38]

And freedom of speech is, as Justice Robert H. Jackson said, "freedom to differ as to things that touch the heart of the existing order."[39]

Yet some who say they believe in free speech draw the line at ideas they consider dangerous. What is a dangerous idea? Who decides? In the realm of political ideas, who can find an objective, eternally valid standard of right? Or as Chief Justice William H. Rehnquist put it for the Supreme Court, "The First Amendment recognizes no such thing as a 'false' idea."[40] The search for truth involves the possibility—even the inevitability—of error. The search cannot go on unless it proceeds freely in the minds and speech of all. This means, in the words of Justice Oliver Wendell Holmes Jr., "not free thought for those who agree with us but freedom for the thought that we hate."[41]

Even though the First Amendment explicitly denies Congress the power to pass *any* law abridging freedom of speech, the amendment has never been interpreted in such absolute terms. Like almost all rights, freedom of speech and of the press is limited. In discussing the constitutional power of government to regulate speech, it is useful to distinguish among *belief*, *speech*, and *action*.

At one extreme is the right to believe as we wish, a right as absolute as any can be for people living in an organized society. Despite occasional deviations in practice, the traditional American view is that *thoughts* are inviolable. No government has the right to punish a person for beliefs or to interfere in any way with freedom of conscience.

At the other extreme is *action*, which is usually restrained. The Constitution protects from governmental regulation our right to *believe* we should drive an automobile 75 miles an hour, but we have no constitutional *right* to drive 75 miles an hour. As has been said, "The right to swing your arm ends where the other person's nose begins."

Speech stands somewhere between belief and action. It is not an absolute right as is belief, but neither is it as exposed to governmental restraint as is action. Some kinds of speech—obscenity, child pornography, libel, sedition, or speech that constitutes fighting words—although not "entirely invisible to the Constitution"[42] are not entitled, in most circumstances, to any constitutional protection, and in a few circumstances to only a little constitutional protection. Many problems arise in distinguishing between what does and does not fit into these categories of "unprotected speech." All other speech is entitled to full constitutional protection, but are there any limits?

Historic Constitutional Tests

It is useful to start with the three constitutional tests developed earlier in this century, for they continue to reflect basic judicial and public attitudes toward governmental regulation of speech. These are the *bad tendency doctrine*, the *clear and present danger doctrine*, and the *preferred position doctrine*.

THE BAD TENDENCY DOCTRINE According to the adherents of the **bad tendency doctrine,** legislative bodies, and not courts, have the primary responsibility to determine when speech should be outlawed. The Constitution, they argue, authorizes legislatures to forbid speech that has a tendency to lead to illegal action. Moreover, "the legislature cannot reasonably be required to measure the danger from every . . . utterance in the nice balance of a jeweler's scale. . . . It may, in the exercise of its judgment, suppress the threatened danger in its incipiency."[43]

This doctrine, which stems from the common law, has not had the support of the Supreme Court since *Gitlow v New York* in 1925. Nonetheless, many legislators, city council members, and others (including some state courts as late as 1982) appear to hold this position.[44] It also appears to be the view of many college students who want to see their institution punish student colleagues or faculty who express "hateful" or "offensive" ideas.

Suppose a city council or the trustees of a public university decide that public utterances of abusive racial remarks or insulting sexual taunts are dangerous because they could lead to violence, and these officials make such remarks illegal or grounds for discipline. Those who hold to the bad tendency test argue that, because it is not totally unreasonable that abusive racial or insulting sexual remarks could provoke violence or inflict injury on individuals, such a law or regulation would be constitutional.

THE CLEAR AND PRESENT DANGER DOCTRINE Justice Oliver Wendell Holmes, Jr., announced this celebrated doctrine in *Schenck v United States:* "The question in every case is whether the words are used in circumstances and are of such a nature as to create a clear and present danger that they will bring about substantive evils that Congress has a right to prevent."[45] Justice Louis D. Brandeis further elaborated in a later case, "No danger flowing from speech can be deemed clear and present, unless the incidence of the evil" that will result from that speech "is so imminent that it may befall before there is opportunity for full discussion."[46]

Supporters of the **clear and present danger doctrine** concede that speech is not an absolute right. Yet they believe free speech to be so fundamental to the operations of a constitutional democracy that no government should be allowed to restrict any particular speech unless it can demonstrate that there is such a close connection between the speech and an illegal action that the speech itself takes on the character of the action. To shout "Fire" *falsely* in a crowded theater is Justice Holmes's famous example. A government should not be allowed to interfere with speech unless it can prove, ultimately to a skeptical judiciary, that the particular speech in question presented an immediate danger of a major evil; for example, speech leading to a riot, destruction of property, corruption of an election, or direct interference with recruitment of soldiers.

Consider our previous example of public university hate-speech codes and city ordinances against abusive or insulting language. Advocates of the clear and present danger doctrine would argue that, even though a legislature had made it illegal to make abusive racial or insulting sexual remarks in public or the public university had made it grounds for disciplining a student, the regulation could not be applied constitutionally to any person for anything he or she said or wrote, unless the government or university presents convincing evidence that the particular remarks made by the particular individual might clearly and presently have led to a riot or to direct physical injury to specific individuals or be the direct cause of some other serious activity the government has a right to make illegal or the university to punish.

THE PREFERRED POSITION DOCTRINE Those who hold to the **preferred position doctrine,** such as the late Justice Hugo L. Black, come close to the position that

Justice Hugo Black, a former U.S. Senator from Alabama and a member of the Supreme Court from 1937 to 1971, was a noted champion of First Amendment rights.

freedom of expression—that is, the use of words and pictures—may never be curtailed. This does not mean that there is nothing left for judges to decide, for a line must still be drawn between speech and nonspeech.

The preferred position interpretation of the First Amendment gives these freedoms a preferred position in our constitutional hierarchy. Judges have a special duty to protect these freedoms and should be most skeptical about laws trespassing on them. Legislative majorities are free to experiment with and to adopt various schemes regulating our lives in general, but when they tamper with freedom of speech, they interfere with the channels of the political process. Only if the government can show that limitations on speech are absolutely necessary to avoid imminent and serious substantive evils are such limitations to be allowed.

If we apply the preferred position doctrine to our example of a law against abusive racial or insulting sexual remarks, the law itself would be declared unconstitutional. Restraints on such abusive speech are not absolutely necessary to prevent riots or other social disturbances. Whatever danger may come from such remarks does not justify restricting free comment. Moreover, supporters of the preferred position doctrine contend that the law itself, by imposing a *chilling effect* on speech and not merely its application, violates the Constitution.

Current Constitutional Tests

The three historic doctrines just discussed still provide the background for debates on freedom of speech. Today, however, the Supreme Court is more apt to use the following doctrines to measure the limits of governmental power.

PRIOR RESTRAINT Of all the forms of governmental interference with expression, judges are most suspicious of those that impose **prior restraint**—restraints prior to publication. Prior restraints include licensing requirements before a speech can be made, a motion picture shown, or a newspaper published. The Supreme Court has refused to declare all forms of prior censorship unconstitutional, but a "prior restraint on expression comes to this court with a 'heavy presumption' against its constitutionality. . . . The Government thus carries a heavy burden of showing justification for the enforcement of such a restraint."[47] Except as applied to motion pictures, most of the few examples of the Court's actual approval of prior restraints relate to military and security matters. The Court has also upheld the right of high school authorities to exercise "editorial control over the style and content of student speech" in school newspapers and other "school-sponsored expressive activities so long as their actions are reasonably related to legitimate pedagogical concerns."[48]

VAGUENESS Any law is unconstitutional if it "either forbids or requires the doing of an act in terms so vague that men of common intelligence must necessarily guess at its meaning and differ as to its application."[49] Laws touching First Amendment freedoms are required to pass even more rigid standards regarding vagueness. These laws must not allow those who administer them so much discretion that they could discriminate against those whose views they dislike. The law must also not be so vague that people are afraid to exercise protected freedoms. Such vague and overbroad laws have a *chilling effect* on freedom of speech. The Supreme Court has struck down laws that condemn "sacrilegious" movies or publications of "criminal deeds of bloodshed or lust . . . so massed as to become vehicles for inciting violent and depraved crimes."[50]

OVERBREADTH Closely related to the vagueness doctrine is the overbreadth doctrine, the requirement that a statute relating to First Amendment freedoms cannot be so broad that it sweeps within its prohibitions protected speech as well as non-protected activities—for example, a loyalty oath that endangers protected forms of association along with illegal activities. Because the very existence of overbroad statutes tends to repress protected speech, such statutes may be declared unconstitutional on their face, that is, entirely and not in some particular application of the law.

LEAST DRASTIC MEANS   Even for an important purpose, a legislature may not choose a law that impinges on First Amendment freedoms if there are other ways to handle the problem. To illustrate, a state may protect the public from unscrupulous lawyers, but it may not do so by forbidding organizations to make legal services available to their members or by forbidding attorneys from advertising their fees for simple services. The state could adopt other ways to protect the public from such lawyers that do not impinge on freedom of association or speech; for example, providing for the disbarment of lawyers who misled their clients.

CONTENT NEUTRAL   Content-neutral laws are much less likely to be struck down than those that restrict speech because of its content. As the Court wrote, "Regulations which permit the Government to discriminate on the basis of the content of the message cannot be tolerated under the First Amendment."[51] For example, a law forbidding posting of handbills on telephone poles has been sustained. Yet a law prohibiting posting of handbills advocating racism or sexism would, in all probability, be declared unconstitutional because it would relate to what is being said rather than where and how it is being said.

The lack of content neutrality was the grounds for the Court striking down a St. Paul, Minnesota, ordinance that forbade burning crosses or displaying Nazi swastikas or other "fighting words" to arouse anger, alarm, or resentment on the basis of race, color, creed, religion, or gender because St. Paul did not forbid such displays to arouse anger on the basis of other matters, for example, political affiliation, union membership, or homosexuality. Said Justice Antonin Scalia for the Court, "Aspersions upon a person's mother . . . would seemingly be usable . . . in the placards of those arguing *in favor* of racial, color, etc., tolerance and equality, but could not be used by that speaker's opponents."[52]

CENTRALITY OF POLITICAL SPEECH   "Not all speech is of equal First Amendment importance. It is speech on 'matters of public concern that is at the heart of the First Amendment's protection.'"[53] There is some contradiction between content neutrality and centrality of political speech. Legislatures and city councils are supposed to pass laws that are content neutral, but in determining whether or not those laws violate the Constitution, judges may take into account what kind of speech is involved.

COMMERCIAL SPEECH   Commercial speech is speech that "proposes a commercial transaction."[54] The mere fact that it is uttered for a profit—for example, charitable solicitations—does not make it commercial speech. Even though commercial speech is constitutionally protected, common-sense differences exist between commercial and other kinds of speech. Commercial speech is, therefore, subject to much more regulation than other speech. For example, advertising the sale of anything illegal may be forbidden, as can false and misleading commercial advertising. However, a law forbidding false and misleading political speech or political advertising is clearly unconstitutional because government does not have the right to forbid anyone from expressing ideas because they are thought to be false or misleading.

Who Decides?

Plainly, neither doctrines nor constitutional tests decide cases; judges do. Doctrines are judges' starting points; each case requires a judge to weigh a variety of factors: What was said? Where was it said? How was it said? What was the intent of the person who said it? Which government is attempting to regulate the speech—a city

Does the press have a right to withhold information?

Although most reporters have challenged the right of the government to withhold information, they claim a right to do so themselves, including the right to keep information from grand juries and legislative committees. Without this right, they say, they cannot assure their sources of confidentiality, and they will not be able to get the information they need to keep the public informed.

council speaking for a few people, or the Congress speaking for many? Few acts of Congress have ever been struck down because of conflict with the First Amendment. How is the government attempting to regulate the speech? By prior censorship? By punishment after the speech? Why is the government acting? To preserve the public peace? To prevent criticism of those in power? These and scores of other considerations are involved in the never-ending process of determining what the Constitution permits and what it forbids.

FREEDOM OF THE PRESS

Freedom of the press is the same as freedom of speech, except that the clause relating to speech protects oral communications and the phrase relating to the press embraces written ones. When we speak of "the press," most people, including most journalists, think only of the print media.[55] Yet "the liberty of the press is not confined to newspapers and periodicals. . . . The press in its historic connotation comprehends every sort of publication which affords a vehicle of information and opinion."[56]

Although we still utilize street corner meetings and public rallies to communicate ideas and influence public policies, today most of us rely on television, newspapers, radio, movies—the mass media—to tell us what is happening in the world. The press thus includes electronic media—radio, television, even electronic mail. Differing constitutional rules apply, however, to each kind of media. Print media are largely unregulated; the electronic media are subject to limited regulation.

Some newspeople contend that the press, especially the written press, should have more freedom of speech than do nonjournalists. Former Chief Justice Warren Burger acknowledged that media representatives have a valid claim to function as "surrogates for the public and thus may be provided special seating and priority of entry [at trials] so that they may report what people in attendance have seen and heard."[57] "Media defendants" have more protection against libel suits than "nonmedia defendants."[58] The Supreme Court has been careful to protect the press from some kinds of tax burdens even when there is no evidence of any evil intent on the part of the taxing authorities.[59] And news corporations are not subject to the same kinds of limitations as other corporations on how they may spend corporate dollars to influence elections.

Still, the prevailing view is: "The First Amendment does not 'belong' to any definable category of persons or entities; it belongs to all who exercise its freedoms."[60] Representatives of the press continue to argue otherwise. They also claim not merely the constitutional right to publish but also a right of access, a right to protect their sources, and a right to secure their files against search warrants.

The Student Press

The First Amendment does not provide the same protection for the student press as it does for nonschool papers. The Supreme Court, although agreeing that the First Amendment was involved, nonetheless sustained the right of a St. Louis area high school principal to impose prior censorship upon a school newspaper written and edited by a journalism class. The paper was not a public forum, open by policy or practice "for indiscriminate use by the general public" or by student organizations. Rather, it was a school-sponsored paper and part of the school's educational program, and thus could be regulated by school authorities.[61]

Does the Press Have the Right to Know?

Courts have carefully protected the press's right to publish information, no matter how the journalists got it. But reporters, editors, and others argue that this is not enough. If reporters are excluded from places where public business is being conducted or denied access to information in government files, they are not able to perform their historic function of keeping the public informed. The Supreme Court has refused to acknowledge a right to know, although it did concede there is a First Amendment right for the press, along with the public, to be present at criminal trials.[62]

Although they have no constitutional obligation to do so, many states have adopted *sunshine laws* requiring public agencies to open their meetings to the public and the press. Congress, too, requires most federal executive agencies to open hearings and meetings of advisory groups to the public. Congress, in fact, holds most of its committee meetings in public. Federal and state courtroom trials are open, but judicial conferences are not.

Congress has authorized the president to establish a classification system to keep some public documents and governmental files secret, and it is a crime for any person to divulge such classified information. So far, however, although they have been threatened, no newspapers have been prosecuted for doing so.

EXECUTIVE PRIVILEGE   Most presidents have claimed a constitutional right to withhold information not only from the press but from Congress and the courts if, in the president's judgment, its release would jeopardize national security or interfere with the confidentiality of advice. This claim is referred to as **executive privilege.** In the celebrated case of *United States v Nixon* (1974), the Supreme Court ruled that executive privilege does not shield a president from a judicial subpoena for material relevant to a criminal prosecution.[63] This historic decision, which marked the second time the Supreme Court decided a matter directly involving the president as a party to a case, rejected a claim of absolute executive privilege. The Court did, however, recognize that a president's "singularly unique role" gives the office a limited executive privilege to which judges should show the "utmost deference."

Free Press versus Fair Trials

When newspapers and television report in vivid detail the facts of a crime, interview prosecutors and police, question witnesses, and hold press conferences for defendants and their attorneys, as in the O. J. Simpson case, they may so inflame the public that finding a panel of impartial jurors and conducting a fair trial is difficult. In England, strict rules determine what the media may report, and judges do not hesitate to punish newspapers that comment on pending criminal proceedings. In the United States, in contrast, free comment is emphasized. Yet the Supreme Court has not been indifferent to protecting persons on trial from inflammatory publicity. Its remedies have been to order new trials or to instruct judges to impose sanctions on prosecutors and police, not on reporters. "Lawyers representing clients in pending cases may be regulated under a less demanding standard than that established for regulation of the press."[64] They may be disciplined for their comments prior to or during a trial even if the comments do not present a clear and present danger but merely if they are "substantially likely to have a materially prejudicial effect."

Federal rules of criminal procedure forbid radio or photographic coverage of criminal cases in federal courts, but most states now permit televising of courtroom proceedings. Such TV programs have become very popular. Defendants, however, have the right to present evidence that television interfered with their trial, prevented fair hearings, and deprived them of due process.[65]

OTHER MEDIA AND OTHER MESSAGES

When the Constitution was written, freedom of "the press" referred to leaflets, newspapers, and books. The Constitution also protects other media, such as the mails, motion pictures, billboards, radio, television, cable, telephones, fax machines,

National Public Radio commentator Nina Totenberg refused to reveal her sources for stories about sexual harrassment allegations against Justice Clarence Thomas.

Thinking it Through

The Supreme Court has declared that reporters, and presumably scholars, have no constitutional right to ignore legal requests and withhold information from judicial authorities. If any privilege is to be given to newspeople, said the Court, it should be done by act of Congress and of the states.[*] Congress has not yet responded to this suggestion, but many states have passed so-called "shield laws" that provide some protection from state court subpoenas.

Branzburg v Hayes, 408 US 665 (1972).

The 1966 Freedom of Information Act

The Freedom of Information Act (FOIA) of 1966, as amended, liberalized access to nonclassified government records. This act makes the records of federal executive agencies available subject to certain exceptions, such as private financial transactions, personnel records, criminal investigation files, interoffice memoranda, and letters used in internal decision making. If federal agencies fail to move promptly on requests for information, persons are entitled to speedy judicial hearings. The burden is on an agency to explain its refusal to supply material, and if the judge decides the government has improperly withheld information, the government has to pay the legal fees. Since the inception of FOIA, more than 250,000 people have requested information, and more than 90 percent of these requests have been granted.

Some critics are concerned that FOIA has had an adverse effect on our ability to carry out confidential investigations and that its implementation costs too much. Others are concerned that FOIA may be used by businesses to obtain competitors' secrets. But most observers, especially newspaper reporters and scholars, believe that FOIA gives real meaning to the citizen's right to know.

SOURCE: Page Putnam Miller, "Status Report on the Freedom of Information Act," *PS: Political Science and Politics* (Winter 1988), pp. 87–90.

other electronic media, as well as expressive conduct. Because each form of communication entails special problems, each needs a different degree of protection.

The Mails

More than 70 years ago, Justice Oliver Wendell Holmes, Jr., wrote in dissent: "The United States may give up the Post Office when it sees fit, but while it carries it on, the use of the mails is almost as much a part of free speech as is the right to use our tongues."[66] In 1965, the Court adopted Holmes's views by striking down the first congressional act ever held to conflict with the First Amendment. That act had directed the postmaster general to detain foreign mailings of "communist political propaganda" and to deliver these materials only upon the addressee's request.[67] The Court has also set aside federal laws authorizing postal authorities to exclude from the mails materials they consider obscene.

Although government censorship of mail is unconstitutional, household censorship is not. The Court has sustained a law giving any householder the absolute right to ask the postmaster to order mailers to delete names in the household from all mailing lists and to refrain from sending any advertisements that householders, in their sole discretion, believe to be "erotically arousing or sexually provocative."[68] It makes no constitutional difference if a householder includes a dry-goods catalog in such a category. Moreover, Congress may forbid—and has forbidden—the use of mailboxes for any materials except those sent through the United States mails.

Motion Pictures and Plays

Films may be treated differently from books or newspapers, and prior censorship of films to prevent the showing of obscenity is not necessarily unconstitutional. However, laws calling for submission of films to a government review board are constitutional only if there is a prompt judicial hearing. The burden is on the government to prove to the court that the particular film in question is in fact obscene. Prior censorship of films through review boards used to be a rather common in some places—for example, Massachusetts and Maryland and in some cities.

Live performances, such as plays and revues, are also entitled to constitutional protection.[69] Yet live theater is subject to greater regulation than either the printed page or the motion picture. The First Amendment, especially in view of the Twenty-first Amendment repealing prohibition, does not protect liquor licensees from state regulations forbidding sexually suggestive performances in places where liquor is sold.[70]

Handbills, Sound Trucks, and Billboards

Religious and political pamphlets, leaflets, and handbills have been historic weapons in the defense of liberty, and their distribution is constitutionally protected. So, too, is the use of their more contemporary counterparts—sound trucks and billboards. A state, for example, cannot restrain the distribution of leaflets merely to keep its streets clean; nor can it ban handbills that do not carry the name and address of the author. However, reasonable, content-neutral regulations specifying where publications may be sold are permissible. As for sound trucks, those that emit loud and raucous noises may be banned. Furthermore, content-neutral regulations detailing the time, place, and manner in which amplification devices may be used for musical performances such as rock concerts are also acceptable. Billboards, too, are entitled to constitutional protection, especially those used for noncommercial purposes.

Radio and Television

Television today is the most important means of distributing news as well as the primary forum for appealing for votes. Yet of all the mass media, broadcasting has received the least First Amendment protection. Congress established a system of commercial broadcasting, supplemented by the Corporation for Public Broadcasting, which provides funds for public radio and television. The entire system is regulated by the Federal Communications Commission (FCC). The FCC grants licenses for limited periods and makes regulations for their use. Broadcasters, using publicly owned airwaves, have no constitutional right to use these facilities without licenses.

The First Amendment would prevent censorship if the FCC tried to impose it. Yet the First Amendment does not prevent the FCC from imposing sanctions on stations that broadcast *filthy words,* as the FCC did in 1993 when it fined Infinity Broadcasting for allegedly indecent remarks by "shock jock" Howard Stern, even though such indecencies are not legally obscene. Nor does the First Amendment prevent the FCC from refusing to renew a license if in its opinion a broadcaster has not served the public interest.

The First Amendment did not prevent the FCC from adopting what came to be known as the **fairness doctrine,** requiring broadcasters to cover issues of public significance and to reflect differing viewpoints, as was done from 1949 to 1987. Thus, if licensees made editorial statements or endorsed candidates, they had to give persons representing a different point of view an opportunity to respond. Congress has imposed an additional **equal-time requirement,** requiring licensees to be sure that all candidates for public office had equal air time. Later Congress modified this requirement to make possible presidential debates between candidates of only the two major parties.[71]

The major argument in favor of allowing more government regulation of broadcasters than of newspaper and magazine publishers is that the public owns the limited number of airwaves, and those who have access to these airwaves have control over a limited resource. In a footnote to a 1984 decision, the Court noted, "The prevailing rationale for broadcast regulation has come under increasing criticism in recent years" because such technological changes as cable, direct-beam broadcast, and videotapes may be undermining the assumption that the scarcity of channels justifies government regulation. "We are not prepared, however," wrote Justice William J. Brennan, Jr., for the majority, "to reconsider our long-standing approach without some signal from Congress or the FCC that technological developments have advanced so far that some revision of the system of broadcast regulation may be required."[72] So far Congress has not signaled its desire for change. On the contrary, it opposed, although unsuccessfully, steps by the FCC under the Reagan and Bush administrations to move toward more deregulation of television.

Cable Television and the Right of Access

As new means of communication are invented, they raise the old issues in new forms. Cable television is a good example. In the 1984 Cable Act, Congress allowed, but did not require, free public access to channels. As a condition for getting a license, cable firms in many cities had to agree to provide access to one or more channels on a first-come, first-served basis. Such public access channels, it was argued, would be the town meetings of the next century. In 1992 Congress revised the law to authorize cable operators to ban "obscene materials, sexually explicit conduct or material soliciting or promoting unlawful conduct,"[73] but the courts have barred the FCC from enforcing this law until its constitutionality is resolved. In June 1994, in *Turner Broadcasting System, Inc., v FCC,* the Supreme Court ruled that cable television is entitled to more protection than broadcast television.

Telephones, Fax, E-Mail, and the Information Superhighway

Now that fax machines are in widespread use, states are beginning to pass "junk fax laws," making it illegal to fax unsolicited advertisements. Similar legislation is proposed to restrict autodialers, which send computer telephone messages into homes.

Buying the Airwaves

Do political parties, candidates for office, or interest groups have a right to radio or television time if they are willing to pay for it? The answer divides champions of free speech. Although a unanimous Supreme Court concluded that governments could not force newspapers to accept advertisements or print replies from persons they have criticized, judges had a much harder time finding the "right answer" to similar questions about broadcasting.

The justices concluded that Congress may impose an obligation on broadcast licensees to sell time to legally qualified candidates for Congress, and the Federal Communications Commission may supervise how they do so. Seven justices concluded that neither the First Amendment nor the Federal Communications Act gives *everybody* the right to buy air time; however, the Court could not muster a majority behind any single opinion.

Chief Justice Warren Burger noted that if broadcasters had to accept the offers of all who wished to buy air time, those with the most money could monopolize radio and television. He said that although the First Amendment gives no one a right of access to broadcasting facilities, Congress or the FCC could provide such access.

Justice William O. Douglas, long-time advocate of an expansive interpretation of the First Amendment, argued that refusal by broadcasters—with the sanction of the FCC—to accept paid political advertisements violates the First Amendment rights of those who are denied access to audiences.[*]

[*]*Red Lion Broadcasting Co. v Federal Communications Commission,* 395 US 367 (1969).

Does every group have a constitutional right to say anything it wishes on public access TV?

For example, does the Ku Klux Klan have a right to put on a program advocating racial supremacy? Does Tar-Har, "whose group prophesies a racial war in which blacks will avenge their enslavement,"* have a right to make racial threats? Does the First Amendment give any person the right to say or do on public television what they can say or do on a street corner? What if a state or a city abolishes public access channels, as Kansas City, Missouri, did in 1988 to keep the Klan off the air? What of the First Amendment rights of the cable operators? Does the Constitution protect their right not to provide access to those whose views they find objectionable? And where does the FCC fit in?

*Joseph Berger, "Forum for Bigotry and Racist Hate? Fringe Groups on Public-Access TV," The New York Times, May 23, 1993, p. A13.

You Decide!

New technologies like video games have opened up the question of whether the government can constitutionally control or censor material aimed at young children.

A dozen states and Congress have either banned or restricted the use of autodialers, and these regulations are being challenged in the courts on First Amendment grounds.[74] Although federal laws protect against eavesdropping on telephone conversations, including those conveyed by cellular phones, these laws do not as yet extend to walk-around phones that transmit messages via radio waves. Moreover, enforcing laws against electronic eavesdropping on cordless phones is difficult, if not impossible.[75]

As Congress and the states begin to deal with these problems, they and the judges who will be reviewing these actions as subsequent lawsuits are filed will have to apply traditional constitutional principles to new situations. For example, what about pornography and obscenity over telephones and E-mail? Congress, reflecting concern about "dial-a-porn," especially as directed to persons under 18, imposed a total ban on obscene and indecent interstate commercial telephone messages to any person, whatever their age. The Court found no constitutional obstacles to the law as it relates to "obscene" messages but declared unconstitutional the provision relating to "indecent" messages. Justice Byron R. White wrote for the Court:

> It may well be that there is no fail-safe method of guaranteeing that never will a minor be able to access the dial-a-porn system, . . . but from all we know . . . the FCC's technological approach to restricting dial-a-porn messages to adults who seek them would be extremely effective, and only a few of the most enterprising and disobedient young people will manage to secure access to such messages.[76]

The Court also distinguished between the limited ban on indecent messages over the airwaves that it had previously sustained[77] and the ban on such messages over telephones. Because of the unique attributes of broadcasting, its messages are readily available to children and can intrude into the privacy of the home without prior warning. Telephone messages, on the other hand, are available only to people who want to hear them. It also may be possible, as the Court suggested, to deny minors access to indecent telephone messages more readily than to indecent broadcasting, excepting, of course, "enterprising and disobedient young people."

Following the Court's decision against allowing Congress to ban indecent telephone calls, Congress passed a law narrowly tailored to protect minors from exposure to such materials. Based on that law, the FCC adopted regulations requiring telephone companies that bill customers for 900 calls to block pornographic services to all households except those that specifically request access. The Supreme Court, by refusing to review a decision of a court of appeals upholding the constitutionality of this law and implementing regulations, cleared the way for its enforcement.[78]

What of the thousands of electronic bulletin boards on which people communicate with each other by computer? May those who provide these billboard services be held responsible for obscene messages, and do they have a right to exclude from the boards hate messages or racially or sexually offensive matter? And if government agencies are involved, to what extent do the First and Fourteenth Amendments limit the ability of the agencies to control the content of the messages?[79] These are some more of the unanswered constitutional questions being presented by the information superhighway.

Picketing

Picketing of employers is a normal trade union practice, and such picketing is constitutionally protected, as is picketing and protesting for various causes. A law forbidding all picketing would be an unconstitutional invasion of speech. However, "picketing involves elements of both speech and conduct, i.e., patrolling," and "because of this intermingling of protected and unprotected elements, picketing can be subject to controls that would not be constitutionally permissible in the case of pure speech."[80]

African Americans in New York City organized picketing of a Korean-owned grocery, claiming the owner had mistreated a young black customer.

When picketing becomes coercive and interferes with the rights of customers to go into or out of a place of work, or keeps employees from going through a picket line, or interferes with people going into and out of places to which they are entitled to go, such as an abortion clinic, it may be regulated. Since First Amendment questions are involved, such regulations are subject to close judicial scrutiny. While indicating that it might not sustain a ban on all residential picketing, the Court upheld an ordinance that forbids picketing "before or about a single residence."[81] On the other hand, while upholding a congressional prohibition on "hostile congregating" within 500 feet of a foreign embassy, the Court struck down a prohibition on "hostile picketing" in front of such embassies.[82]

Expressive Conduct

People express their views by many other means than just talking or writing. They raise flags, wave banners, march in parades, wear political buttons, carry signs. These various forms of expression, this *symbolic speech* (or as it is coming to be called, *expressive conduct*) is constitutionaly protected. "We cannot accept the view," Chief Justice Earl Warren wrote, "that an apparently limitless variety of conduct can be labeled speech whenever the person engaged in the conduct intends thereby to express an idea."[83] Similarly, Chief Justice Warren Burger wrote:

> Conduct that the State police power can prohibit on a public street does not become automatically protected by the Constitution merely because the conduct is moved to . . . a "live theatre" stage, any more than a "live" performance of a man and woman locked in a sexual embrace at high noon in Times Square is protected by the Constitution merely because they simultaneously engaged in a political dialogue.[84]

Except when the government interest is directly aimed at the symbolic character of the conduct, such as laws forbidding flag burning, the burden is on those who engage in expressive conduct to show that the First Amendment applies. In reviewing laws that regulate expressive conduct, the Court uses a four-part test, first announced in *United States v O'Brien*.[85] The government may forbid or regulate expressive conduct if: (1) the regulation is within the constitutional power of the government; (2) it furthers an important government interest; (3) the governmental interest is unrelated to the suppression of expression; and (4) the incidental

Thinking it Through

The courts are beginning to supply the answers to these new constitutional questions, and they are doing so by applying traditional doctrines, moving slowly, watching actual experiences, and taking their cues from the FCC. The Supreme Court has recently held that regulations of cable television are subject to more rigorous scrutiny than are those that apply to broadcast television.[†]

As David A. Kaplan pointed out, "It is an exquisitely vexing debate over cable television and the First Amendment. Trouble is, the First Amendment seems to be on both sides."*

†*Turner Broadcasting System, Inc., v FCC,* June 27, 1994.

*David A. Kaplan, "Is the Klan Entitled to Public Access?" *The New York Times,* July 31, 1988, p. A24.

restriction on alleged First Amendment freedom is no greater than is essential to the furtherance of the interest.[86]

Applying these tests, the Supreme Court has concluded that the government cannot forbid the burning of the American flag as a form of political protest, for the interest of the government is directly aimed at the suppression of expressive conduct. Nor can a city make it a crime to burn a cross or display a Nazi swastika when such displays create anger, alarm, or resentment based on racial, ethnic, gender, or religious bias. However, the Court has strongly hinted that a carefully drawn, content-neutral ordinance might be sustained.[87]

On the other side, burning a draft card in violation of a congressional regulation is not a constitutionally protected form of expressive conduct because Congress, when it made the protection and presentation of such cards a requirement, was not trying to prohibit conduct because of its communicative attributes but was working to implement the draft laws. In the same fashion, the National Park Service was allowed to forbid persons from sleeping overnight in Lafayette Park across from the White House as a way to protest the government failure to protect the rights of the homeless.[88] And although acrobatic and ballroom dancing are not entitled to First Amendment protection, when nude dancing is performed as entertainment in order to express erotic thoughts, such dancing is "within the outer perimeters of the First Amendment." Said Chief Justice Rehnquist for the Court, "We view such dancing as only marginally so." (At least he did not say "barely so.") Nonetheless, the Court upheld the application of a state's public indecency statute to such dancing, requiring dancers to wear pasties and a G-string.[89]

NONPROTECTED SPEECH

As we have noted, some kinds of speech are not entitled to constitutional protection. This does not mean that the constitutional issues relating to these kinds of speech are simple. On the contrary, how we prove *libel*, how we define *obscenity*, and how we determine which words are *fighting words* are hotly contested issues.

Libel

At one time newspaper publishers and editors had to take considerable care about what they wrote, for fear they might be prosecuted for **libel**—written defamation—by the government or sued for money damages by individuals. Today, through a progressive raising of constitutional standards, it has become more difficult to win a libel suit against a newspaper or magazine.

In *The New York Times v Sullivan* and subsequent cases, the Supreme Court established the guidelines for libel cases. The Constitution severely limits a state's power to award damages in a libel action brought by a public official against critics of official conduct. Neither *public officials* nor *public figures* can collect damages for any comments made about them, unless they can prove with "convincing clarity" the comments were made with "actual malice."[90] *Actual malice* means not merely that the defendant had bad motives, but that the "statements were made with a reckless disregard for the truth," which in turn means that the defendant must have made the false publication with a "high degree of awareness of probable falsity."[91]

Public figures cannot collect damages even when subject to outrageous, clearly inaccurate, and false cartoons. Such was the case when *Hustler Magazine* printed a cartoon parodying the Reverend Jerry Falwell; the Court held such cartoons cannot reasonably be understood as describing actual facts or actual events.[92] Nor does the mere fact a public figure is quoted as saying something that he or she did *not* say amount to a libel. "Unless the alteration" in what the person has said "results in material change," the mere fact the words were deliberately altered does not equate with the constitutionally required knowledge of falsity.[93]

Constitutional standards for libel charges brought by *private* persons are not so rigid. State laws may permit private persons to collect damages without having to prove actual malice if they can prove the statements made about them are false and negligently published.

Obscenity

Today, fears about obscenity and pornography have replaced seventeenth-century fears about heresy and 1950s fears about communism.[94] Obscene publications are not entitled to constitutional protection, but members of the Supreme Court, like everybody else, have great difficulty in defining obscenity. Almost 100 separate opinions have been written on the matter.

In *Miller v California* (1973), the Court was finally able to assemble a majority opinion. Speaking for five members of the Court, Chief Justice Warren Burger once again tried to clarify a constitutional definition of **obscenity.** A work may be considered legally obscene provided: (1) the average person, applying contemporary standards of the particular community, would find that the work, taken as a whole, appeals to a prurient interest in sex (that is, patently offensive interests "over and beyond those that would be characterized as normal"[95]); (2) the work depicts or describes in a patently offensive way sexual conduct specifically defined by the applicable law or authoritatively construed; and (3) the work, taken as a whole, lacks serious literary, artistic, political, or scientific value.[96] Chief Justice Burger specifically rejected part of the previous test—the so-called *Memoirs v Massachusetts* (1966) formula: No work should be judged obscene unless it is "utterly without redeeming social value."[97] He argued such a test would make it impossible for a state to outlaw hard-core pornography.

Does the *Miller* decision mean that local communities can ban whatever a prosecutor could persuade a jury is obscene? Many hoped they could; many others feared they would. But how far could a jury go? Could it decide to ban "Little Red Riding Hood"? After all, who really knows what went on in that bedroom? A year after the *Miller* decision, the Supreme Court warned: "It would be a serious misreading of *Miller* to conclude that juries have unbridled discretion in determining what is patently offensive." Appellate courts, said Justice Rehnquist speaking for the Court, should review jury determinations to ensure compliance with constitutional standards. And the Supreme Court itself, after such review, ruled that the movie *Carnal Knowledge* was not obscene, contrary to the conclusion of a jury in Albany, Georgia.[98]

Obscenity, then, is not entitled to constitutional protection. But governments must proceed under laws that specifically define the kinds of sexual conduct forbidden in word or picture. Moreover, it is not a crime for booksellers to offer obscene books for sale; they must be shown to have done so *knowingly*. Otherwise, booksellers would tend to avoid placing on their shelves materials that some authorities might consider objectionable, and the public would be deprived of an opportunity to purchase anything except some person's determination of the "safe and sanitary." The mere private possession of obscene materials is not a crime either.

What about X-rated movies that fall short of the constitutional definition of obscenity? They are entitled to some constitutional protection, but less protection than political speech, and they are subject to greater government regulation. "The state may legitimately use the content of these materials as the basis for placing them in a different classification from other motion pictures."[99] Cities may also regulate, by zoning laws, where so-called adult motion picture theaters may be located.

RAP LYRICS AND FREE SPEECH

The inflammatory and degrading messages in some popular records and on music television have aroused many groups to action. Starting several years ago with Tipper Gore's campaign for ratings on sexually explicit records to keep them out of the hands of children, protests were also heard from parent groups who asked television networks to monitor the violence in programs targeted for young children. "Gangster rap," and in particular a recording by Ice T calling for attacks on the police, brought out protests from police organizations and parents throughout the country and boycotts of the recording company. Women's groups voiced resentment of the portrayal of women as willing victims of brutal sex acts and the insulting language used to describe them in music videos.

Carol Moseley Braun, newly elected Illinois senator, presided over a hearing of the Juvenile Justice Subcommittee of the Judiciary Committee on the violent and vulgar lyrics of rap music. In their defense, music stations, recording companies, and rap singers cited the guarantees of free speech and maintained that they were speaking the truth as people in the ghettos saw it.

The rap group Ice T's records encourage killing cops and abusing women.

Senator Carol Moseley Braun looks on as young rappers prepare to testify before the Senate Judiciary Committee.

Sexually explicit materials either about minors or aimed at them are *not* protected by the First Amendment. Provided they act under narrowly drawn statutes, state and local governments can, for example, ban the knowing sale of "adult" magazines to minors, even if such materials would not be considered legally obscene if sold to adults. And governments can make it a crime to depict sexual conduct by children, even if the depicted behavior would not be considered obscene if performed by adults.

Pornography

Pornography used to be merely a synonym for *obscenity*. Pressure for regulating pornography came primarily from political conservatives and religious fundamentalists concerned that it undermines moral standards. More recently, many feminists have joined them, arguing that "pornography is central in creating and maintaining sex as a basis for discrimination."[100] They contend pornography promotes sexual abuse of individual women and perpetuates social subordination of women as a class. Feminists define pornographic materials as sexually explicit pictures or words that depict women as sexual objects enjoying pain and humiliation or that present abuse of women as a sexual stimulus for men. Some have argued that the line should be drawn to permit regulation of "depictions of sexuality that involve rape and violence against women."[101]

Advocates of regulation of pornography argue that just as sexually explicit materials about minors are not entitled to First Amendment protection, so should there be no such protection for pornographic materials. They propose that civil penalties be imposed on pornographers, and that women—and others who have had pornography forced upon them—be given the right to file complaints and sue for damages. The Senate Judiciary Committee has proposed the Pornography Victim's Compensation Act allowing crime victims to sue producers, distributors, and exhibitors of a book, magazine, movie, or lyric "that the victim believes triggered the crime."[102]

Women and men have differed significantly in their attitudes about pornography (see Table 4-1). Men are less likely than women to think pornography damages adults who read it, and women are twice as likely to favor laws banning the sale of pornography, regardless of the age of the buyer, while men tend to favor restricting the sale of pornography to minors.[103]

Not all feminists favor antipornography ordinances, yet those who do have been joined by social conservatives, and thus a new era in the battle over pornography has just begun. For this new antipornography coalition to be successful, a substantial alteration in constitutional doctrine will be required.[104] The Canadian Supreme Court has redefined obscenity to include materials that degrade women, and several cities in the United States have been considering the adoption of antipornography ordinances.[105] Only Indianapolis has passed such a law, which was declared unconstitutional in a decision affirmed by the Supreme Court without opinion.[106]

Censorship of films and books may be imposed by a variety of means other than formal action. In some cities, such local groups as the Legion of Decency may pressure authorities. Feminists, by threats of boycott, have pressured some stores to stop selling magazines they believe depict women in a demeaning and pornographic manner. Local police have been known to threaten booksellers with criminal prosecution if they persist in showing films or selling books of which some local people disapprove.

Fighting Words

Governments may punish certain well-defined and narrowly limited classes of speech that "by their very utterance inflict injury or tend to incite an immediate breach of peace."[107] These so-called **fighting words** "have a direct tendency to cause acts of violence by the person to whom, individually, the remarks are addressed."[108] That the words are abusive, harsh, or insulting, or that they create anger, alarm, or resentment based on racial, ethnic, gender, or religious basis is not sufficient. Thus, a four-letter word worn on a sweatshirt was not judged to be a fighting word in the constitutional sense, at least when it is not directed to any specific person.[109]

The "fighting words" category has taken on additional significance in recent years in view of the attempts by many state universities and colleges to regulate insulting racial, ethnic, and sexual slurs. The Constitution limits how public universities and colleges may punish students for what they say, and cases challenging these so called "hate codes" are working their way through the courts. That speech may be insulting or racially offensive or sexist does not mean that it lacks constitutional protection. As the Court has said, "If there is a bedrock principle underlying

TABLE 4-1

Attitudes Toward Pornography, 1992

	Yes	No	DK/NA*
Sexual materials lead to a breakdown of morals.			
Men	56%	36%	8%
Women	65	27	8
Sexual materials lead people to commit rape.			
Men	53	37	10
Women	63	27	10

	Men	Women
There should be laws against the distribution of pornography, whatever the age.	39%	47%
There should be laws against the distribution of pornography to persons under 18.	56	49
There should be no laws forbidding the distribution of pornography.	4	3
DK/NA*	1	1

SOURCE: National Opinion Research Center, University of Chicago, *General Social Surveys, 1992.*

*DK/NA = Don't Know or No Answer.

the First Amendment, it is that the Government may not prohibit the expression of an idea simply because society finds the idea offensive or disagreeable."[110]

The Supreme Court has gone out of its way to warn governments and public universities against moving to punish fighting words by codes designed to protect people against insults solely because of their race, sex, or religion. "The First Amendment does not," wrote Justice Antonin Scalia for the Court, "permit [governments] to impose special prohibitions on those speakers who express views on disfavored subjects."[111] But in the role of landlord for residence halls, universities and colleges may have greater authority to impose reasonable time, place, and manner regulations against insulting racial, sexual, or religious slurs directed toward fellow residents.

The speech of faculty and staff at public universities and colleges is also protected by the Constitution, but a university has more leeway in regulating the speech of its employees than it has of its students. Thus, a university's constitutional discretion in controlling offensive or sexist speech by faculty and staff is greater than its discretion for students.

Private universities and colleges are not subject to these constitutional limitations on how they may regulate the speech of their students. However, state governments may protect the speech of students against undue regulation by these institutions, and colleges and universities that receive federal funds may find that their freedom to regulate the use of offensive speech by students is limited by federal laws and regulations. Federal and state laws regulating the responsibilities of employers to provide a workplace free from sexual harassment apply to universities, private and public.

RIGHT TO ASSEMBLE AND TO PETITION THE GOVERNMENT

Freedom of Assembly

In the winter of 1977, Frank Collins, "a self-avowed Nazi," threatened to lead his small band, dressed in brown shirts and carrying swastikas, in a jack-booted march through the streets of Skokie, Illinois, a Chicago suburb with a large Jewish population.[112] Skokie's citizens included survivors of Hitler's extermination camps; many of them had relatives who lost their lives in the Holocaust. Many people, including the officials of Skokie and a local judge, argued that Collins and his followers should not be allowed to march. They argued that this would be like shouting "Fire!" in a crowded theater, and that to permit such a use of the streets presented a clear and present danger of inciting people to violence. These same arguments were put forward to contend that Iranian followers of the late Ayatollah Khomeini should not be allowed to protest publicly in Washington, D.C., at a time when most Americans were angry about Khomeini's illegal and brutal treatment of innocent American hostages in Tehran. The right to assemble peaceably, they said, should not be extended to Iranian aliens who were abusing this right to provoke Americans to violence.

In both cases judicial authorities defended the rights of these unpopular minorities to demonstrate. (Collins never actually marched in Skokie, but he did march in another part of the Chicago area.[113]) But it is not always the "bad guys" whose rights have to be protected by the courts. It also took occasional judicial intervention in the 1960s to preserve for Martin Luther King, Jr., and for those who marched with him, the right to demonstrate in the streets of southern cities in behalf of civil rights for African Americans.

Such incidents present the classic free speech problem of the "heckler's veto," when the audience becomes so abusive that it is impossible for the speaker to be heard. It is almost always easier, and certainly politically more prudent, to maintain order by curbing public demonstrations of unpopular groups than by moving against those who are threatening them. On the other hand, if police did not have the right to order groups to disperse, public order would be at the mercy of those who resort to street demonstrations just to create tensions and provoke street battles.

Public Forums and Time, Place, and Manner Regulations

The Constitution protects the right to speak, but it does not give persons the right to communicate their views to everyone, every place, at any time they wish. No one has the right deliberately to incite others to violence, to block traffic, or to hold parades or make speeches in public streets or on public sidewalks whenever he or she wishes. Governments may not specify what can or cannot be said, but they can make reasonable *time, place, and manner* regulations for the holding of assemblies or protests or gatherings. The extent of government regulation varies with where the assembly takes place.

Our Constitution defends the right of Ku Klux Klan members, neo-Nazis, skinheads, and others to express unpopular opinions, but the public is free to disagree with them.

The Supreme Court has divided public property into three categories: public forums, limited public forums, and nonpublic forums. The extent to which governments may limit access depends on the kind of forums involved. *Public forums* are those public places historically associated with the free exercise of expressive activities, such as streets, sidewalks, and parks. Courts look closely at time, place, and manner regulations as they apply to these traditional public forums to ensure that they are being applied evenhandedly and that action is not taken because of what is being said rather than how and where or by whom it is being said.[114] Further, in these traditional public forums, no restrictive laws are permitted unless they are viewpoint neutral and the government in question can prove that they are necessary to serve a compelling government interest.

Other kinds of public property, such as designated rooms in a city hall or after-hour use of school buildings, may be designated as *limited public forums*, available for assembly and speech for limited purposes, a limited amount of time, and even for a limited class of speakers (such as only students, only teachers, or only employees), provided the distinctions between those allowed access and those not allowed access are viewpoint neutral.

Nonpublic forums include public facilities such as libraries, courthouses, schools, swimming pools, and government offices that are open to the public but are not public forums. As long as persons use such facilities within the normal bounds of conduct, they may not be constitutionally restrained from doing so. However, persons may be excluded from such places as a government office or a school if they engage in activities for which the facilities were not created. They have no right to interfere with programs or try to appropriate facilities—especially facilities such as a university president's office—in order to stage a political protest.

Does the right of peaceful assembly and petition include the right to violate a law nonviolently but deliberately? We have no precise answer. But in general, *civil disobedience*—even if peaceful—is not a protected right. When Dr. Martin Luther King, Jr., and his followers refused to comply with a state court's injunction forbidding them to parade in Birmingham without first securing a permit, the Supreme Court sustained their conviction, even though there was serious doubt about the constitutionality of the injunction and the ordinance on which it was based. Justice Potter Stewart, speaking for the five-member majority, said: "No man can be judge in his own case, however exalted his station, however righteous his motive, and irrespective of his race, color, politics, or religion." Persons are not "constitutionally free to ignore all the procedures of the law and carry their battles to the streets."[115] The four dissenting justices insisted that one does have a right to defy peacefully an obviously unconstitutional statute or injunction.

The First Amendment rights of right-to-life protesters to picket on the public streets in front of abortion clinics and the right of access to abortion clinics came in conflict as a result of Operation Rescue's campaign to shut down abortion clinics. Congress passed the Freedom of Access to Clinic Entrances Act of 1994. That act makes it a federal crime to use force, threats, or physical obstruction to interfere with anyone providing or receiving abortions and other reproductive health services. It imposes fines and prison terms up to 18 months for nonviolent offenses and up to 10 years for violent ones. It allows abortion clinic employees and clients or the Department of Justice to sue for damages and seek federal injunctions against violators. Although the act explicitly exempts conduct protected by the free speech and assembly clauses, such as peaceful picketing and passing out leaflets, opponents of the legislation contend that this act interferes with the anti-abortion movement's right to engage in picketing and protesting. They maintain that the act imposes punishment far more severe than state laws and city ordinances for blocking sidewalks and sit-ins.[116]

Assembly on Private Property

What of private property? The right to assemble does not include the right to trespass on private property. A state may protect property owners against those who attempt to convert property to their own uses, even if they are doing so to express ideas.

The profusion of large, privately owned shopping malls that cover many acres and are larger than some towns presents some difficult constitutional issues. The Supreme Court has set the following guidelines: Privately owned shopping malls are neither public streets nor places of public assembly; no one has a constitutional right to use such a mall to hand out political leaflets, to picket for political purposes, or otherwise to exercise First Amendment freedoms. On the other hand, states and cities may legally obligate the owners of such centers to permit their use for peaceful political purposes such as distributing handbills or getting people to sign petitions. In other words, although people have no constitutional right to engage in political action in a nonpublic shopping center, neither do the owners of such centers have a constitutional right to close them to political action in the face of reasonable state or local regulations providing for access that does not interfere with their primary commercial purposes.[117]

Freedom of Association

The right to petition the government for redress of grievances is specifically guaranteed by the Constitution. The right to organize to promote political and other causes is not expressly mentioned in the Constitution, but "it is beyond debate that freedom to engage in association for the advancement of beliefs and ideas is an inseparable aspect of the 'liberty' assured by the Due Process clause of the Fourteenth Amendment which embraces freedom of speech."[118]

The Supreme Court has written of freedom to associate in two distinct senses. In one line of decisions it has protected people's right to enter into and maintain "certain intimate human relationships" against "undue intrusion by the State. . . . In this respect, freedom of association receives protection as a fundamental element of personal liberty."[119] The other aspect relates to activities protected by the First Amendment: speech, assembly, petition, the redress of grievances, and the free exercise of religion.

Some troublesome constitutional questions arise from congressional and state regulation of the amount of money that candidates, political parties, and interest groups can raise and spend for political purposes. Is money speech? If so, then is government regulation of its use constitutionally suspect? Or is money more like action, and therefore open to governmental regulation?[120] In *Buckley v Valeo*, the Court sustained limits on the amount of money people may *contribute to candidates* and their campaign committees on the grounds that such limits only marginally restrict contributors' abilities to express political views.[121] But it struck down limits on the amounts that may be contributed to *associations* formed to support or oppose ballot measures submitted to popular vote.

Limits on what people can *spend*, in contrast to what they can contribute, have fared even less well. Governments may not set limits on the amounts that people (including candidates) can spend on political matters. Presidential candidates, such as Ross Perot in 1992, who have access to their own wealth and who choose not to take federal funds for their campaigns may not be limited in what they spend. Limits on what presidential candidates can spend apply only to expenditures by the candidate's party organizations and "coordinated groups," not to "independent groups or committees," who have a constitutional right to spend as much as they wish to further the candidate's election.[122]

SUBVERSIVE CONDUCT AND SEDITIOUS SPEECH

"If there is any fixed star in our constitutional constellation," Justice Robert Jackson said, "it is that no official, high or petty, can prescribe what shall be orthodox in politics, nationalism, religion, or other matters of opinion."[123] Any group can champion whatever position it wishes: vegetarianism, feminism, sexism, communism, fascism, black nationalism, white supremacy, Zionism, anti-Semitism, Americanism.

It is one thing to punish persons for what they *do*; it is another to punish them for what they *say*. The story of the development of constitutional democracy is in large measure the story of making this distinction clear.

The Sedition Act of 1798

The adoption of the Constitution and the Bill of Rights did not result in a quick, easy victory for those who wished to establish free speech in the United States.[124] In 1798, only seven years after the First Amendment had been ratified, Congress passed the first national law aimed against **sedition**—attempting to overthrow the government by force or to interrupt its activities by violence. Those were perilous times for the young Republic, for war with France seemed imminent. The Federalists, in control of both Congress and the presidency, persuaded themselves that national safety required some suppression of speech.

The Sedition Act marked a considerable advance over English common law in that it made truth a defense and allowed the jury, not a judge, to decide the fact of sedition as well as the fact of publication. It did, however, make it a crime to utter false, scandalous, or malicious statements intended to bring the government or any of its officers into disrepute or "to incite against them the hatred of the good people of the United States."[125]

Popular reaction to the Sedition Act helped defeat the Federalists in the elections of 1800. They had failed to grasp the democratic idea that a person may criticize the government of the day, oppose its policies, and work for its downfall, but still be loyal to the nation.

The Smith Act of 1940

The first peacetime sedition law since the Sedition Act of 1798 was the Smith Act of 1940. The Smith Act forbids persons to advocate overthrow of the government with the intent to bring it about; to distribute, with disloyal intent, matter teaching or advising the overthrow of government by violence; and to organize knowingly or to help organize any group having such purposes.

In *Dennis v United States* (1950), the Court agreed that the Smith Act could be applied to the leaders of the Communist party, who had been charged with conspiring to advocate the violent overthrow of the government.[126] Since then the Court has substantially modified its holding. Congress may not outlaw the mere advocacy of the abstract doctrine of violent overthrow: "The essential distinction is that those to whom the advocacy is addressed must be urged to do something now or in the future, rather than merely to believe in something."[127] Moreover, advocacy of the use of force may not be forbidden "except where such advocacy is directed to inciting or producing imminent lawless action and is likely to incite or produce such action."[128]

In short, seditious speech, if narrowly defined to cover only the advocacy of immediate and concrete acts of violence, is not constitutionally protected. Such narrow interpretation of the sedition laws means people are free to work for their political objectives as long as they abandon the use of force—or its specific and immediate advocacy—as a means of bringing it about.

SUMMARY

1. First Amendment freedoms—freedom of religion, freedom from the establishment of religion, freedom of speech, freedom of the press, freedom of assembly and petition, and freedom of association—are at the heart of a healthy constitutional democracy.

2. Since World War I, the Supreme Court has become the primary branch of government for giving meaning to these constitutional restraints. And since 1925 these constitutional limits have been applied not only to Congress but to all governmental agencies—national, state, and local.

3. Clashes about First Amendment freedoms are not usefully thought of as battles between the "good guys" and the "bad guys" or as dramas in which judges rush to the rescue of liberty. Rather, these are arguments over conflicting notions of what is in the public interest.

4. Over the years, the Supreme Court has taken a practical approach to First Amendment freedoms. It has refused to make them absolute rights above any kind of governmental regulation, direct or indirect, or to say that they must be preserved at whatever price. But the justices have recognized that a constitutional democracy tampers with these freedoms at great peril. They have insisted upon compelling justification before permitting these rights to be limited. How compelling the justification is, in a free society, will always remain an open question.

FURTHER READING

ELLEN ALDERMAN AND CAROLINE KENNEDY, *In Our Defense: The Bill of Rights in Action* (Morrow, 1991).

STEPHEN BATES, *Battleground* (Poseidon Press, 1993).

LEE C. BOLLINGER, *Images of a Free Press* (University of Chicago Press, 1991).

JAMES MACGREGOR BURNS AND STEWART BURNS, *A People's Charter: The Pursuit of Rights in America* (Knopf, 1991).

T. BARTON CARTER, MARC A. FRANKLIN, AND JAY B. WRIGHT, *The First Amendment and the Fourth Estate*, 5th ed. (Foundation Press, 1991).

ZECHARIAH CHAFEE, JR., *Free Speech in the United States* (Harvard University Press, 1941).

ELLIS COSE, *The Press* (William Morrow, 1989).

DONALD L. DRAKEMAN, *Church-State Constitutional Issues: Making Sense of the Establishment Clause* (Greenwood Press, 1991).

TERRY EASTLAND, ED. *Religious Liberty in the Supreme Court: The Cases That Define the Debate over Church and State* (Ethics and Policy Center, 1993).

IRA GLASSER, *Visions of Liberty: The Bill of Rights for All Americans* (Arcade, 1991).

MARK A. GRABER, *Transforming Free Speech: The Ambiguous Legacy of Civil Libertarianism* (University of California Press, 1991).

EDWARD DE GRAZIA AND ROGER K. NEWMAN, *Banned Films: Movies, Censors and the First Amendment* (R. R. Bowker, 1982).

MARJORIE HEINS, *Sex, Sin and Blasphemy : A Guide to America's Censorship Wars* (New Press, 1993).

NAT HENTOFF, *The First Freedom: The Tumultuous History of Free Speech in America*, 2d ed. (Delacorte, 1988).

EUGENE W. HICKOK, JR., ED., *The Bill of Rights: Original Meaning and Current Understanding* (University Press of Virginia, 1991).

JAMES E. LEAHY, *The First Amendment, 1791–1991: Two Hundred Years of Freedom* (McFarland & Co., 1991).

ANTHONY LEWIS, *Make No Law: The Sullivan Case and the First Amendment* (Random House, 1991).

LEONARD W. LEVY, *The Establishment Clause: Religion and the First Amendment* (Macmillan, 1986).

MARTHA M. MCCARTHY, *A Delicate Balance: Church, State, and the Schools* (Phi Delta Kappan Educational Foundation, 1983).

JOHN STUART MILL, *Essay on Liberty* (1859), in *The English Philosophers from Bacon to Mill*, ed. Arthur Burtt (Random House, 1939), pp.949–1041.

WILLIAM LEE MILLER, *The First Liberty: Religion and the American Republic* (Knopf, 1986).

MELVILLE B. NIMMER, *Nimmer on Freedom of Speech: A Treatise on the Theory of the First Amendment* (Mathew Binder, 1987).

DAVID M. O'BRIEN, *The Public's Right to Know: The Supreme Court and the First Amendment* (Praeger, 1981).

J. W. PELTASON, *Understanding the Constitution*, 13th ed. (Harcourt Brace, 1994).

LUCAS A. POWE, JR., *American Broadcasting and the First Amendment* (University of California Press, 1987).

LUCAS A. POWE, JR., *The Fourth Estate and the Constitution: Freedom of the Press in America* (University of California Press, 1991).

JONATHAN RAUCH, *Kindly Inquisitors: The New Attacks on Free Thought* (University of Chicago Press, 1993).

RODNEY A. SMOLLA, *Free Speech in an Open Society* (Knopf, 1992).

JOHN D. STEVENS, *Shaping the First Amendment: The Development of Free Expression* (Sage Publications, 1982).

GEOFFREY R. STONE, *The Bill of Rights in the Modern State*, Richard A. Epstein and Cass R. Sunstein, eds. (University of Chicago Press, 1992).

CASS R. SUNSTEIN, *Democracy and the Problems of Free Speech* (Free Press, 1993).

WILLIAM W. VAN ALSTYNE, *Interpretations of the First Amendment* (Duke University Press, 1984).

ROBERT J. WAGMAN, *The First Amendment Book* (World Almanac, 1991).

RONALD C. WHITE, JR., AND ALBRIGHT G. ZIMMERAN, EDS., *An Unsettled Arena: Religions and the Bill of Rights* (William B. Eerdmans, 1990).

JOHN F. WILSON, ED., *Church and State in America*, 2 vols. (Greenwood Press, 1987).

EQUAL RIGHTS UNDER THE LAW

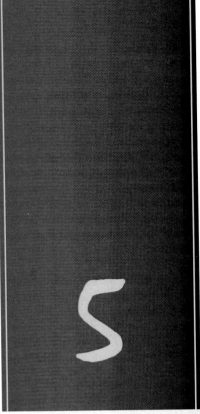

Let's consider again the ringing words of the Declaration of Independence: "We hold these truths to be self-evident, that *all* men are created equal, that they are endowed by their Creator with certain unalienable Rights, that among these are Life, Liberty, and the pursuit of Happiness." In this one sentence the Declaration affirmed the precious rights of *equality* and *liberty* and appeared to rate equality at least on a par with liberty. The Declaration does not talk about equality of white, Christian, or Anglo-Saxon men, but of *all* men. Undoubtedly, if the Declaration were to be written today, the framers would speak of "persons" rather than "men." This creed of individual dignity and equality is older than our Declaration of Independence; its roots go back into the teachings of Judaism and Christianity.

What about the Constitution? What was the framers' attitude toward liberty and equality? We know that the builders of our constitutional system cherished liberty as their highest ideal. And although you will not find any reference to the idea of *equality* (not even the word itself is in the Constitution or in the array of liberties that form the Bill of Rights), we know the framers believed that all men—at least all white men—were equally entitled to life, liberty, and the pursuit of happiness (the framers changed "pursuit of happiness" to "property" in the Bill of Rights). They felt strongly that there should be no noble or privileged class under the law. Like the Declaration, the Constitution refers to "men" or "him," not to women, and none of its lofty sentiments applied to slaves, who enjoyed neither liberty nor equality.

The framers resolved their ambiguity about what kind of equality and for whom by creating systems of government designed to protect what they called **natural rights**. Today we speak of **human rights**, but the idea is the same: All citizens are entitled to their dignity and worth. By equal rights the framers meant that every person has an equal right to protection against arbitrary treatment, an equal right to the liberties guaranteed by the Bill of Rights, and an equal right to protection by any laws passed by the new national government.

The Constitution itself provides two ways of protecting civil rights. First, it ensures that government imposes no discriminatory barriers, and, second, it grants national and state governments authority to protect civil rights against interference by private individuals. This chapter is concerned with both the protection of our rights from abuse *by* government and the protection *through* government of our rights, to be free from abuse by our fellow citizens. In this chapter we focus on the struggles of women, Native Americans, Hispanics, Asian Americans, and African Americans to secure the basic civil rights to vote, to an education, to a job, and to a place to live on equal terms with their fellow citizens.

EQUALITY AND EQUAL RIGHTS

Americans are committed to equality. "Equality," however, is an elusive term, and "few issues have sparked more controversy or held more sway over the course of history."[1] Part of the difficulty is that "equality" lacks precise meaning. The concept for which there is the greatest consensus, and that is most clearly written into the Constitution, is that everybody should have *equality of opportunity* regardless of race, ethnic origin, religion, and, in recent years, sex. Ensuring this equality of opportunity is what we mean by the struggle for civil rights.

A variation of the concept of equal opportunity is *equality of starting conditions*. There is not much equal opportunity if one person starting the race is born into a

"Treat people as equals, and the first thing you know, they believe they are."

Drawing by Mulligan. © 1982 The New Yorker Magazine, Inc.

well-to-do family, lives in a quiet suburb, is well fed, and receives a good education, while another is born into a poor, broken family, lives in an inner-city neighborhood, and attends inferior schools. Thus, it is argued, if we are to have equality of opportunity in a meaningful sense, we must compensate the disadvantaged through federal programs such as Head Start, which provides children from poor families with preschool experiences to prepare them for elementary school and to ensure that they have true equality of opportunity to learn.

Compensating people so they will have equality of conditions can be accomplished by ensuring that individuals are not placed at a disadvantage because of prejudice or poverty. But such action sometimes shades into a concept of *equality among groups*. Traditional emphasis has been upon individual achievement. When large disparities in wealth and advantage exist among groups—as between blacks and whites or between women and men—equality becomes a highly divisive political issue. The disadvantaged tend to emphasize those common traits that exclude them from the mainstream. They champion programs like affirmative action that are designed to provide special help to people based upon their group memberships. Whether such programs promote or deny equality is one of the most controversial current debates.

Finally, equality sometimes means *equality of results*. One perennial debate, especially among college students, is whether social justice and "genuine" equality can coexist in a nation in which some people have so much money and so many good things in life and others have so little. Socialists and some others say social justice and genuine equality cannot coexist with such wide disparities in income. Yet such a view has had little support in the United States. There is considerable support for guaranteeing a minimum floor—a "safety net"—below which no one should be allowed to fall, but insistence on equality of results would greatly restrict or undermine equality of opportunity. The American Dream is not that everybody should have the same amount of material goods, but that all people should be able to hope and to strive to improve their lot and, especially, to assume that the opportunities for economic advancement will be even greater for their children. Thus, whatever a person's economic status for the moment, that person should be able to think things will get better and that hard work and risk taking will be rewarded.

It is within the context of these concerns for equality that we look at the struggle for civil rights. The first phase took two hundred years. The struggle is not over yet, but we have largely achieved equality under the law. To put into perspective the court decisions, laws, and other governmental actions relating to civil rights for women and minorities, we review next the political and social contexts in which these constitutional issues are raised. Constitutional questions do not involve only court decisions, laws, and constitutional amendments; they encompass the entire social, economic, and political system. Although the struggles of all groups are interwoven, they are not identical, so we comment briefly and separately on each.

Women's Rights

The struggle for equal rights for women has long been intertwined with the battle to secure such rights for blacks. The Seneca Falls Women's Rights Convention (1848), which launched the women's movement, involved men and women who had long been active in the campaign to abolish slavery.

As the Civil War approached, women were urged to abandon their cause, at least temporarily, and devote their energies to getting rid of slavery.[2] The Civil War brought the women's movement to a halt. The Fourteenth Amendment even introduced into the Constitution a provision that overtly allowed discrimination against women; it provided that any state that kept males over 21 from voting should suffer a reduction of its representation in the House of Representatives. Women were no better served by the Fifteenth Amendment, forbidding denial of

Susan B. Anthony (*left*) and Elizabeth Cady Stanton (*right*) were the two most influential leaders of the women's suffrage movement of the nineteenth century.

the right to vote because of race. For a time the temperance movement to prohibit the sale of liquor diverted attention away from women's rights as well.

By the turn of the century, however, a vigorous campaign was underway for **women's suffrage**—the right to vote—within the states. The first victories came in western states, where Wyoming led the way. As a territory, Wyoming had given women the right to vote. It is said when members of Congress in Washington grumbled about this "petticoat provision," the Wyoming legislators replied they would stay out of the Union one hundred years rather than come in without women's suffrage. Congress gave in and admitted Wyoming to the Union, women's suffrage and all. By the end of World War I, more than half the states had granted women the right to vote in some or all elections.

To many suffragists this state-by-state approach seemed slow and uncertain. They wanted a decisive victory—a constitutional amendment that would, with one blow, force all states to allow qualified women to vote. Finally, in 1919, Congress proposed the Nineteenth Amendment. Opposition to its adoption and ratification was intertwined with opposition to the rights of blacks. Many southerners opposed the amendment. Not only would it extend the franchise to black women, but because it gave Congress enforcement power, it might also bring federal officials to investigate elections to ensure that the amendment was being obeyed, an interference that might call attention to how blacks were being kept from voting.

In 1918, Senator James Vardaman, Democrat from Mississippi, opposed the Nineteenth Amendment and called for "repeal of the Fifteenth, the modification of the Fourteenth, . . . making this a government by white men, of white men, for all men."[3] But opposition to women's suffrage was not limited to southerners. Senator William Borah, a conservative Republican from Idaho, also opposed it, again on racial grounds, saying, "There are 100,000 Japanese and Chinese women in the Pacific states, and I have no particular desire to bestow suffrage upon them."[4]

With the ratification of the Nineteenth Amendment in 1920, women won the right to vote. Still, they were denied equal pay and equal rights, and they suffered numerous legal disabilities imposed by both national and state laws. During the last several decades the ultimately unsuccessful struggle to secure the adoption of the Equal Rights Amendment occupied much of the attention of the women's movement. But there are now other goals, and the political clout of women is being mobilized increasingly behind issues that range from pay, through pensions, to peace, sexual harassment, abortion rights, and election to office.[5]

The Struggle for Racial Justice

Americans have had a painful confrontation with the problem of race before, during, and after the Civil War. As a result of the northern victory, the Thirteenth, Fourteenth, and Fifteenth Amendments became part of the Constitution. Congress also passed a series of civil rights laws to implement these constitutional provisions and established such special programs as the Freedmen's Bureau to provide educational and social services for the freed slaves.

SEGREGATION AND WHITE SUPREMACY Before Reconstruction programs had any significant effect, the southern white male political leadership was restored to power. By 1877, Reconstruction was ending, and northern political leaders abandoned blacks to their fate at the hands of their former white masters. Presidents no longer concerned themselves with the enforcement of civil rights laws, and Congress enacted no new ones. The Supreme Court either declared old laws unconstitutional or interpreted them so narrowly that they were ineffective. The Court also gave such a limited construction to the Thirteenth, Fourteenth, and Fifteenth Amendments that they failed to accomplish their intended purpose of protecting the rights of blacks.

We The People

Women's History Is Half of History

Timeline row 1 (upper labels):

Lucretia Mott, Elizabeth Cady Stanton barred from this convention

Sewing machine invented

Women's Rights Convention

Clara Barton, Mother Bickerdyke, nurses

Declaration of Sentiments, Seneca Falls

Harriet Beecher Stowe, *Uncle Tom's Cabin*

Sojourner Truth

Women's Loyal League

Ha Tu lea

1840 .... **1860**

World Antislavery Convention

Irish imigration begins

Texas admitted to the Union

Dred Scott decision

Lincoln elected

Emancipati Proclamati

Harper's Ferry

Fort Sumter

Timeline row 2:

International Council of Women

Ladies' Home Journal

Jane Addams, Hull House

Women's Trade Union League

Brandeis brief, protective legislation

General Federation of Women's Clubs

National American Women Suffrage Association

Susan B. Anthony

Florence Kelley. reformer

Charlotte Perkins Gilman, Women and Economics

Comstock laws

Nati Won Pa

1900

Samuel Gompers, American Federation of Labor

Immigration from Southern Europe

Progressive Era

Panama canal begun

Populists

Battle of Wounded Knee

Theodore Roosevelt

Wood Wils

Timeline row 3:

WACS, WAVES, WASPS. women's service corps

Dr. Spock

Title VII prohibits sex discrimination in employment

Execu Ord manda affirma actio

Rosie the Riveter

800,000 women fired by aircraft companies

Mary McCarthy, *The Group*

Betty Friedan, *The Feminine Mystique*

Suburbia

The

1940 .... **1960**

Pearl Harbor

Atomic bomb

Television

The New Frontier

Kennedy assassinated

The Great Society

Vietn

Korea

World War II ends

Eisenhower

March on Washington, Martin Luther King Jr.

Civil Rights Act

mo

Timeline row 4:

ERA deadline passed without ratification

Geraldine Ferraro, first woman nominated as vice-presidential candidate of a major political party (the Democratic party)

State of Washington adopts comparable worth for some State employees

Congress reverses impact of *Grove* decision that had limited federal civil rights laws

Sandra Day O'Connor, first woman Supreme Court justice appointed

ERA reintroduced in Congress

re

Reagan

Challenger explodes

Reagan-Gorbachev talks, INF Treaty

B

e Hymn of the
epublic,"
Ward Howe

Equal
Rights
Association

Frances Willard
Woman's Christian
Temperance Union

Clara
Barton,
Red Cross

Evaporated
milk
available

Radcliffe,
Bryn Mawr
founded

Mother Mary
Jones,
labor
organizer

Emily
Dickinson

1880

rrenders
Grant

14th Amendment
makes blacks
citizens and adds
the word "male"
to the
Constitution

15th Amendment
(provides for
black male
suffrage)

Reconstruction

Custer,
Little Big Horn

Civil service
reform

Transcontinental
railroad completed

Women's Joint
Congressional
Committee
National Council of
Defense

ists jailed
ite House
nstration

Women get
the vote

League of
Women
Voters

Alice Paul
introduces
Equal Rights
Amendment
(ERA)

Margaret Mead,
*Coming of Age in
Samoa*

The flapper

Frances Perkins,
secretary of labor

Frozen foods
introduced

Claire Booth Luce,
The Women

1920

U.S. enters
World War I

Treaty of
Versailles

19th Amendment
(Women's Suffrage)
ratified

Prohibition

Herbert
Hoover

Stock market
crash

Depression

FDR,
New Deal

Eleanor
Roosevelt

onal
zation
omen
W)

Gloria Steinem,
Ms. Magazine

National
Women's
Strike

ERA
passed by
Congress

Title IX
prohibits sex
discrimination
in education

International
Women's
Year

Supreme Court
legalizes abortion in
Roe v Wade

Women's
Educational
Equity Act
passed

Episcopalians
ordain women

National
Women's
Conference,
Houston

ERA
ratification
deadline
extended

Nancy
Kissebaum
elected to
Senate

1980

Resurrection
City

Cambodia

Moon
landing

Watergate

Carter

on

urt
Wade

Clarence Thomas
Supreme Court
confirmation hearings

Supreme Court
reaffirms core
holding of
Roe v Wade

First Lady Hillary Clinton heads Task Force
on National Health Care Reform

Ruth Bader Ginsburg appointed to
the Supreme Court

1992

1993

Middle - East Peace
talks

By 1900, white supremacy was unchallenged in the South, where most blacks lived. Blacks were kept from voting; they were forced to accept menial jobs; and they were denied educational opportunities. In 1896, in *Plessy v Ferguson*, the Supreme Court gave constitutional sanction to government-imposed racial segregation.6 Even if the Court had declared segregation unconstitutional, a decision so contrary to popular feeling and political realities would have had little impact. In 1896, blacks were lynched an average of one every four days, and few whites raised a voice in protest.

During World War I, African Americans began to migrate to northern cities to seek educational opportunities and jobs in war factories. These trends were accelerated by the New Deal and World War II, and the South, through urbanization and industrialization, became more like the rest of the nation. As migration of African Americans out of the rural South into southern and northern cities shifted the racial composition of cities, the African American vote became important in national elections. Although discrimination continued, there were more jobs and more social gains. Above all, these changes created an African American middle class opposed to segregation as a symbol of servitude and a cause of inequality. By the middle of the twentieth century, urban blacks were active and politically powerful citizens. There was a growing, persistent, and insistent demand for the abolition of color barriers.

THE NATIONAL GOVERNMENT RESPONDS   Because of the special nature of the electoral college and the dynamics of our political system, by the 1930s it became more difficult for the president—or anyone hoping to be president—to ignore the aspirations of blacks. The commitment of our presidents, and in more recent decades of our senators, to the cause of equal protection became translated into the appointment of federal judges more sympathetic to an interpretation of the Thirteenth, Fourteenth, and Fifteenth Amendments that would carry out the amendments' original purpose of securing the civil and voting rights of African Americans.

In the 1930s, African Americans began resorting to lawsuits to secure their rights and to challenge the doctrine of segregation. They emphasized litigation because they had no alternative; they lacked sufficient political power to make their demands effective before either state legislatures or Congress. After World War II, civil rights litigation began to have an impact. Under the leadership of the Supreme Court, federal judges started to use the Fourteenth Amendment to reverse earlier

During World War I, African American flyers fighting in a segregated unit established a record for bravery and effectiveness.

decisions that rendered it and federal legislation ineffective. In 1954, in *Brown v Board of Education*, the Supreme Court reversed a half-century-old precedent and declared public school segregation unconstitutional. In the years that followed, the Court outlawed all forms of government-imposed segregation and struck down most of the devices that had been used by state and local authorities to keep African Americans from voting. Presidents used their executive authority to fight segregation in the armed services and the federal bureaucracy, and they directed the Department of Justice to enforce whatever civil rights laws were available.

As the 1950s came to a close, the emerging national consensus in favor of governmental action to protect civil rights and the growing political voice of African Americans in the northern states began to have some influence on Congress. In 1957 Congress overrode a southern filibuster in the Senate and enacted the first federal civil rights laws since Reconstruction. During the 1950s the conflict was primarily an attempt by the national government to compel southern state governments to stop segregating African Americans into inferior schools, parks, libraries, houses, and jobs. Then came the momentous 1960s.

A TURNING POINT   A decade after the Supreme Court declared public school segregation unconstitutional, most black children in the South still attended segregated schools. In northern cities segregation in housing and education remained the established pattern as well. In the South most African Americans still were kept from voting, despite the fact that such action clearly violated the Constitution of the United States. Most legal barriers in the path of equal rights had fallen, yet most African Americans still could not buy houses where they wanted, secure the jobs they needed, find educational opportunities for their children, and in the South they could not eat in a restaurant or walk on the streets of so-called "white neighborhoods" without being insulted.

But times were changing. What had once been thought of as a southern problem was finally being recognized as a national challenge. By 1963 the struggles in the courtrooms were being supplemented by a massive social, economic, and political movement.

The "revolt" in 1963 was not unexpected, and its immediate background was not the struggle to desegregate the schools. In one sense it began when the first black slave was educated three hundred years earlier. Its more recent origin was in Montgomery, Alabama, on December 1, 1955, when seamstress Rosa

In 1957, federal troops had to be called in to enforce the desegregation of Central High School in Little Rock, Arkansas.

I Have A Dream . . .

Five score years ago, a great American in whose symbolic shadow we stand, signed the Emancipation Proclamation. This momentous decree came as a great beacon light of hope to millions of Negro slaves who had been seared in the flames of withering injustice. It came as a joyous daybreak to end the long night of captivity. But one hundred years later, we must face the tragic fact that the Negro is still not free. One hundred years later, the life of the Negro is still sadly crippled by the manacles of segregation and the chains of discrimination. One hundred years later, the Negro lives on a lonely island of poverty in the midst of a vast ocean of material prosperity. One hundred years later, the Negro is still languishing in the corners of American society and finds himself an exile in his own land. So we have come here today to dramatize an appalling condition. . . .

I have a dream that one day this nation will rise up and live out the true meaning of its creed: "We hold these truths to be self-evident; that all men are created equal."

I have a dream that one day on the red hills of Georgia the sons of former slaves and the sons of former slave owners will be able to sit down together at the table of brotherhood.

I have a dream that one day even the state of Mississippi, a desert state sweltering with the heat of injustice and oppression, will be transformed into an oasis of freedom and justice.

I have a dream that my four little children will one day live in a nation where they will not be judged by the color of their skin but by the content of their character.

SOURCE: Martin Luther King, Jr., address at the Lincoln Memorial, August 28, 1963.

Parks refused to give up a seat in the front of a bus and was removed from the bus. The black community of Montgomery responded by boycotting city buses. The boycott worked.[7]

Montgomery produced a charismatic national civil rights leader: the Reverend Martin Luther King, Jr. Through his Southern Christian Leadership Conference and his doctrine of nonviolent resistance, Dr. King gave a new dimension to the struggle. By the early 1960s, new organizational resources came into existence in almost every city to support and sponsor sit-ins, freedom rides, live-ins, and nonviolent demonstrations.[8] These measures were sometimes met with violence toward blacks and their civil rights allies, and at times state and local governments failed either to protect the victims or to prosecute those responsible for the violence.[9]

The forces of social discontent exploded in the summer of 1963. The explosion started with a demonstration in Birmingham, Alabama, which was countered by the use of fire hoses, police dogs, and mass arrests. It ended in a march in Washington, D.C., where at least 250,000 people heard Dr. King and other civil rights leaders speak, and countless millions listened and watched them on television. By the time the summer was over, there was hardly a city, North or South, that had not had demonstrations, protests, or sit-ins. Some also had violence.

This direct action had some effect. Civil rights ordinances were enacted in many cities, and more schools were desegregated that fall than in any year since 1956. At the national level, President John Kennedy urged Congress to enact a comprehensive civil rights bill. Late in 1963, the nation's grief over the assassination of President Kennedy, who had become identified with civil rights goals, added political fuel to the drive for federal action.[10] President Lyndon Johnson gave civil rights legislation his highest priority. On July 2, 1964, after months of debate, he signed into law the Civil Rights Act of 1964.[11]

TWO SOCIETIES? At the close of the 1960s the legal phase of the civil rights movement had come to a close, but as "things got better," discontent grew. When blacks had been completely subjugated, they had lacked resources to defend themselves. Then, as is true of almost all social revolutions, as conditions began to improve, demands became more and more insistent. Millions of impoverished African Americans demonstrated growing impatience with the discrimination that remained. This volatile situation gave way to racial violence and disorders. By 1965, the year of a brutal riot in Watts, a section of Los Angeles, racial disorders were clearly becoming part of the American scene. In 1966 and 1967 the disorders increased in scope and intensity. The Detroit riot in July 1967, the worst such disturbance up to this time in modern American history,[12] made clear the deep divisions between the races and the urgency of taking corrective action.

Native Americans

Of all the minorities in the United States, the nearly 2 million people who designated themselves as Native Americans in the 1990 census may encompass some of the greatest diversity. Almost half live on or near a reservation—a tract of land given to the tribal nations by treaty—and are enrolled as members of one of the 308 tribes within the continental United States or one of the 200 Native Alaskan communities served by the Bureau of Indian Affairs.[13] Among them, Native Americans speak 200 languages.

Native Americans speak of their tribes as "nations," yet they are not states, nor are they nations possessed of the full attributes of sovereignty. Rather, they are a separate people with power to regulate their own internal affairs, subject to congressional supervision. Congress has special responsibilities to Native Americans. States are precluded from regulating or taxing the tribes or extending the jurisdiction of their courts over the tribes unless authorized to do so by Congress.[14] Native Americans living off reservations and working in the general community pay the same taxes as everybody else.

By act of Congress, Indians are American citizens, and by acts of Congress and of the states in which they live, they have the right to vote. Off reservations they have the same rights as any other Americans. If they are enrolled members of a recognized tribe, they are entitled to certain benefits created by law and by treaty. These benefits are administered by the Bureau of Indian Affairs of the Department of the Interior. Moreover, Native Americans who belong to these federally recognized tribes have preference in employment within the bureau, a preference the Supreme Court upheld as a grant not to a "discrete racial group, but, rather, as members of quasi-sovereign tribal entities."[15]

As a result of the growing militancy of Native Americans and a greater national consciousness of the concerns of minorities, Americans are now aware that most Native Americans live in poverty. Native Americans "are in far worse health than the rest of the population, dying earlier and suffering disproportionately from alcoholism, accidents, diabetes, and pneumonia."[16] Some reservations lack adequate health care facilities, educational opportunities, decent housing, and jobs. Congress has started to compensate Native Americans for past injustices and provide more opportunities for the development of tribal economic independence. Judges are also showing a greater vigilance in the enforcement of Indian treaty rights.

Under Article I, Section 8, Congress has full power under the commerce clause to regulate Indian tribes. Although Congress abolished treaty-making with the Indians in 1871, there has been a revived interest in interpreting earlier treaties in a way to protect the independence and authority of the Indian tribes. During the period of assimilation that began in 1887 and lasted until 1934, tribal governments were weak, some reservations were dissolved, and more than 100 tribes had their relationship with the federal government severed.[17] The civil rights movement of the 1960s created a more favorable climate for the concerns of Native Americans, and their goals are to reassert treaty rights and secure greater autonomy for the tribes. Under the leadership of the Native American Rights Fund (NARF), in part a Ford Foundation-funded legal defense firm, there have been more Indian law cases brought in the last two decades than at any time in our history.[18] In 1992 Ben Nighthorse Campbell, a Democrat from Colorado, became the first Native American to be elected to Congress.

Hundreds of Sioux Indians took part in a 220-mile March of Memory to mark the 100th anniversary of the Wounded Knee massacre.

Hispanics

This East Los Angeles mural speaks for the Hispanic community: "The present is a struggle; the future is ours."

The struggle for civil rights has by no means been limited to women, African Americans, and Native Americans. Each new wave of immigrants has been considered suspect by those who arrived earlier—all the more so if its members were not white or English speaking. Formal barriers of law and informal barriers of custom have combined to deny equal rights. But as groups have established themselves—first economically, then politically—most of these barriers have been swept away, and constitutionally guaranteed rights have been asserted.

There are approximately 23 million Hispanics (or Latinos as some prefer to be called), about 9 percent of the U.S. population and an increase of 60 percent since 1980. The largest group consists of more than 14 million Mexican Americans, often called Chicanos. Most Mexican Americans live in California, Texas, Arizona, and New Mexico, but many now live in other parts of the country as well.[19]

The second largest group of Hispanics consists of the 2.7 million Puerto Ricans who reside on the mainland, primarily in the "barrios" of New York, Chicago, and other northern cities. They retain close ties with Puerto Rico and move back and forth from the island to the mainland.

The third subgroup of Hispanics consists of more than 1 million who fled from Castro's Cuba early in the 1960s and a second wave of refugees, called the Mariel refugees, who fled in the 1980s. These Cubans, who live mainly in south Florida, include a substantial number of well-educated, successful businesspeople and professionals. The fourth group includes a rapidly growing number of refugees from other nations in Central and South America who presently number about 5 million.[20]

To black power has been added "brown power"—sometimes as an ally, sometimes as a rival.[21] Yet many Hispanics lack the ties with the white power structure that provided some help for blacks before the civil rights movement—ties that, for example, helped create the historically black colleges and universities. Hispanics have also been handicapped because English, the primary language of the mainstream, is not their native tongue. Until recent decades "no provision whatsoever was made for the education of Mexican-American children" in the Southwest. "When eventually they were allowed into the schools, they were segregated from Anglo children because of their language handicap. Considered by school authorities to be children of an inferior race, they were often punished for speaking Spanish, heard their names involuntarily Anglicized, and saw their cultural background systematically ignored in textbooks."[22]

Taking their cue from African Americans, Hispanics are becoming increasingly active in politics, although they do not yet register or vote in significant numbers as compared to blacks. There are only an estimated 4 to 5 million registered Latino voters, and an immigrant Hispanic lives in the United States for 18 years, on average, before becoming a U.S. citizen, compared with the five-year average for Asian immigrants.[23]

Although Hispanics total about 9 percent of the United States population, there were only 10 Hispanic members in the 435-member U.S. House of Representatives in 1990. Hispanics used the provisions of the Voting Rights Act of 1965 to bring about the creation of more congressional districts in which Hispanics make up a majority of the voters. By the 1994 election, the total rose to 19 Hispanics in the House of Representatives.[24]

We have never had a Hispanic United States senator, and less than 1 percent of elected local officials are Hispanic. However, this situation is beginning to change. Some Hispanic members of Congress have gained seniority and occupy key roles, such as Henry B. Gonzalez (D.-Tex.), chair of the House Banking Committee. Two members of President Clinton's cabinet, Secretary of Housing and Urban Development Henry Cisneros and Secretary of Transportation Federico Peña, are Hispanic.

The number of Hispanics in local leadership positions is growing. Almost 2,000 Hispanics hold elective office in Texas.[25] Hispanic mayors preside in cities like Miami and Tampa; Florida and New Mexico recently had Hispanic governors. The Mexican-American Legal Defense and Education Fund (MALDEF), the Puerto Rican Legal Defense and Education Fund, the Southwest Voter Registration Education Project, the League of United Latin American Citizens (LULAC, an umbrella organization hoping to coordinate the Hispanic community), and the National Hispanic Leadership Agenda (NHLA) are increasingly politically active.

Asian Americans

The term "Asian" describes individuals from many different countries and many different ethnic backgrounds. Most people from Asian backgrounds do not think of themselves as "Asians" but as Americans of Chinese, Japanese, Vietnamese, Cambodian, Korean, or another specific ancestry. About 40 percent of our immigrants now are from Asia, and the 7.3 million Asians counted in the 1990 census are an increase since 1980 of almost 108 percent. They live chiefly in the West, but there has been a rapid increase in Asian Americans in New York and Texas.

Although Asian Americans are often considered a "model minority" because of their general success in education and business, the U.S. Civil Rights Commission, a federal fact-finding body of eight commissioners, half appointed by the president and half by Congress, found that "Asian-Americans do face widespread prejudice, discrimination and barriers to equal opportunity" and that racially motivated violence against them "occurs with disturbing frequency."[26]

The Chinese were the first Asians to come to the United States. Beginning in 1847, when young male peasants came here to get away from poverty and to work in mines, on railroads, and on farms, the Chinese encountered economic and cultural fears of the white majority, who did not understand them or their culture. In response, the Chinese seldom tried to assimilate but instead gravitated to "Chinatowns." Discriminatory immigration and naturalization restrictions, imposed beginning in 1882, were strengthened in the following years and were not removed until the end of World War II. Since that time, the Chinese have moved into the mainstream of American society, and they are beginning to run for and win local political offices.

The Japanese first migrated to Hawaii in the 1860s and then to California in the 1880s. Most Japanese immigrants remained in the West Coast states. By the beginning of the twentieth century, they faced overt hostility. In 1905 labor leaders organized the Japanese and Korean Exclusion League, and in 1906 the San Francisco Board of Education excluded all Chinese, Japanese, and Korean children from neighborhood schools. Some western states passed laws denying the right to own land to aliens who were ineligible to become citizens—that is, aliens of Asian ancestry. During World War II, anti-Japanese hysteria provoked the internment of West Coast Japanese, most of whom were American citizens guilty of no crimes, in prison camps, the largest of which was Manzanar, at Tule Lake, California. During this time Japanese property was often sold at confiscatory rates. Following the war, the exclusionary acts were repealed, and by congressional, presidential, and court action, laws designed to keep Japanese Americans from participating fully in American economic and political life were set aside. In 1988, President Ronald Reagan signed a law providing $20,000 restitution to each of the approximately 60,000 surviving World War II internees.

Koreans—more than 800,000 of them—are concentrated in southern California, Colorado, Honolulu, and New York City. Until recently, like other Asian Americans, they faced overt discrimination in jobs and housing. A Korean middle class has been

"Thanks for coming in. It's such a relief to be able to deny someone a loan when there's no possibility of being charged with sex, race, age, or ethnic bias."

Drawing by Ed Fisher. © 1976 The New Yorker Magazine, Inc.

growing, with many becoming teachers, doctors, and lawyers. However, many others continue to operate small family businesses such as dry cleaners, florist shops, service stations, and small grocery stores, often in inner cities.[27] As prosperous small businesspeople, they are often the target of the anger of the poor people whose neighborhoods they serve. Many Korean stores were destroyed in the 1992 Los Angeles riots.

When Filipinos first came to the United States in the early part of this century, they were considered American nationals because the United States then owned their native country. Nonetheless, they were denied their rights to full citizenship and faced discrimination and even violence, including anti-Filipino riots in the state of Washington in 1928 and later in California, where nearly one-third of the approximately 1.5 million Filipinos live.[28] Their economic status has improved, but their influence in politics remains as small as their numbers.

The newest Asian arrivals consist of more than a million Indo-Chinese refugees from Vietnam, Laos, and Cambodia, who first came to the United States in 1975 and settled in Los Angeles and California's Orange and San Diego counties. Although this group includes middle-class people who left during the fall of Saigon following the end of the Vietnam War, it also consists of large numbers of "boat people," mostly peasants in their homelands, who came to our shores without any financial resources. In a relatively short time most have established themselves economically. Although they are starting to have political influence (most apparently registered as Republicans), they remain socially and economically segregated and have not been in the United States long enough to become an effective part of the political process.

EQUAL PROTECTION OF THE LAWS: WHAT DOES IT MEAN?

The **equal protection clause** of the Fourteenth Amendment declares no state (including any subdivision thereof) shall "deny to any person within its jurisdiction the equal protection of the laws." Although there is no parallel clause limiting the national government, the Fifth Amendment's due process clause, which states that no person shall "be deprived of life, liberty, or property, without due process of law," has been interpreted to impose the same restraints on the national government. Note the restraints of equal protection apply only to the *actions of governments*, not to those of private individuals. Thus an important question is always: Is the action being challenged that of a government, that is, is it *state action*? Or is the challenged discriminatory action merely that of private persons, unsupported and detached from the actions of a government?

The equal protection clause does not prevent governments from making distinctions among people. Governments could not legislate without doing so. What the Constitution forbids is *unreasonable* classifications. In general, a classification is unreasonable when there is no relation between the classes it creates and permissible governmental goals. A law prohibiting redheads from voting, for example, would be unreasonable. On the other hand, laws denying to persons under 18 the right to vote, to marry without the permission of their parents, or to apply for a license to drive a car appear to be reasonable (at least to most persons over 18).

One of our most troublesome issues is how to distinguish between constitutional and unconstitutional classifications. The Supreme Court uses three tests for this purpose: (1) the traditional rational basis test for most laws; (2) the most stringent test of all, a strict scrutiny test for laws dealing with suspect classes and fundamental rights; (3) the heightened scrutiny test or, as it is sometimes called, middle tier or intermediate test for laws dealing with quasi-suspect classifications.

The Equal Protection Clause

THE RATIONAL BASIS TEST   The traditional test to determine whether a law complies with the equal protection requirement places the burden of proof on those attacking it. If the facts justify a classification, the law will be sustained, even if it results in some inequality. If the Supreme Court chooses to apply this *rational basis test*, the law in question will usually be upheld. For example, the Supreme Court concluded that there is a rational basis to support Minnesota's decision to ban the sale of milk in plastic nonreturnable bottles while allowing its sale in biodegradable paperboard nonreturnable cartons.[29]

SUSPECT CLASSIFICATIONS AND STRICT SCRUTINY   The most stringent test, the *strict scrutiny test*, is used when a suspect class or a fundamental right is involved. The normal presumption of constitutionality is reversed. When a law is subject to strict scrutiny, it is not sufficient that the law be a reasonable means to handle a particular problem. Rather, the courts must be persuaded that there is both a "compelling public interest" to justify such a classification and no other less restrictive way to accomplish this compelling public purpose.

A **suspect class** is a class of people subjected to deliberate unequal treatment in the past, or relegated by society to a position of such political powerlessness as to require extraordinary judicial protection.[30] Classifications based on *race* and *national origin* are suspect when they result from state and local government laws and regulations. State and local laws that treat people differently because of their race or national origin are subject to strict scrutiny. It does not make any difference if the laws are designed for so-called "benign" purposes—that is, to help persons of a particular race or national origin—rather than invidious purposes—that is, to injure or denigrate them.

State or local laws that classify people by their *religion* would also create a suspect class, although there is no specific Supreme Court decision to this effect, probably because governments seldom classify people according to religion. State or local laws that impose political limitations on *aliens* also create suspect classifications, and thus are subject to strict scrutiny.

What of *national laws* classifying people by race, national origin, or alien status? Federal laws and regulations dealing with aliens are subject, not to the strict scrutiny test, but to the slightly less stringent heightened scrutiny test.[31] Congress, unlike state and local governments, may take race, and presumably national origin, into account for benign purposes. When it does so, congressional laws are subject not to strict scrutiny but to heightened scrutiny.

QUASI-SUSPECT CLASSIFICATIONS AND HEIGHTENED SCRUTINY   The intermediate test—more difficult for a law to pass than the rational basis test and slightly less burdensome than the strict scrutiny test—is called the *heightened scrutiny test*. It applies to what the court has called "quasi-suspect" classes. A quasi-suspect class is a class to which the intermediate test applies. To sustain a law under this test, the burden is on the government to show that its classification serves "important governmental objectives" and is substantially related to these objectives.

An example of a quasi-suspect class is illegitimate children. Although some contend that laws imposing disabilities on illegitimate children should be subject to the same strict scrutiny test as state laws based on race, the Supreme Court has been unwilling to go that far. However, in view of the long history of treating illegitimate children less favorably than legitimate ones, the Court has subjected laws dealing with illegitimate children to a heightened scrutiny test.

Classifications based on gender are also subject to heightened scrutiny. Not until 1971 was any classification based on sex declared unconstitutional. Prior to that time many laws that purported to provide special protection for women—such as

---

The Equal Protection Clause: Three Tiers of Tests

1. *Rational basis:* The burden is on those attacking the law, and the courts are likely to sustain the law so long as there are some facts and plausible reasons to justify the classification.
2. *Strict scrutiny:* The government has the heavy burden of persuading a court that there is a "compelling public interest" calling for such a classification, and that there is no other, less restrictive way to accomplish this compelling public purpose.
3. *Heightened scrutiny:* The burden shifts to the government to show that the classification serves important governmental objectives and is substantially related to those objectives.

Some Governmental Actions Declared Unconstitutional by the Supreme Court Because of Sex Discrimination

- Provisions of Social Security laws providing benefits to families with unemployed fathers but not unemployed mothers
- A state law giving sons child support from their fathers until they are 21, but daughters only until they are 18
- A state law prohibiting the sale of beer to males under 21, but to females under 18
- A state law providing that husbands, but not wives, may be required to pay alimony
- A state law excluding males from enrolling in a professional nursing program designed for women, offered by a public university
- The practice of giving prosecutors the right to have people disqualified from serving on a jury solely because of their gender
  NOTE: The Constitution protects men as well as women from discrimination because of sex.

Some Governmental Actions Alleged to Be Unconstitutional Discrimination Against Persons Because of Sex but Sustained by the Supreme Court

- A state law granting a property tax exemption to widows but not to widowers
- A naval regulation giving female officers 13 years to be promoted or discharged but giving male officers only 9 years
- A provision giving larger Social Security retirement benefits to women than to men
- A federal law requiring registration for a possible draft for males but not for females

a Michigan law forbidding any woman other than the wife or daughter of a tavern owner to serve as barmaid—were upheld. As Justice William J. Brennan, Jr., wrote for the Court in 1973: "There can be no doubt that our nation has had a long and unfortunate history of sex discrimination. Traditionally such discrimination was rationalized by an attitude of 'romantic paternalism' which in practical effect put women, not on a pedestal, but in a cage."[32]

Today the Court's view is that gender classifications, although not as suspect as those based on race, are subject to the *heightened scrutiny test*; that is, to sustain a classification based on gender, the burden is on the government to show that it serves "important governmental objectives" and is substantially related to these objectives. Treating women differently from men (or vice versa) is forbidden when supported by no more substantial justification than "archaic and overbroad generalizations," "old notions," and "the role-typing society has long imposed upon women."[33] If the government's objective is "to protect members of one sex because they are presumed to suffer from an inherent handicap or to be innately inferior," that objective itself is illegitimate.[34]

The Supreme Court has struck down most, but not all, laws brought before it that were alleged to discriminate against women. Those the Court has refused to strike down include the males-only draft and veterans' preference in civil service jobs.[35]

POVERTY AND AGE The Supreme Court is being urged to designate additional categories of people as suspect or quasi-suspect classes in order to provide greater judicial protection for them. It is argued that just as racial minorities and women are entitled to special constitutional protection, so should be the poor and the elderly. The Supreme Court, however, "has never held that financial need alone identifies a suspect class for purposes of equal protection analysis."[36] Thus, a state may rely on property taxes for funds for schools, even if this means that schools in "rich" districts spend more per pupil than those in "poor" districts.

Age is neither a suspect nor a quasi-suspect class. Our laws and practices commonly make distinctions based on age: to obtain a driver's license, to marry without parental consent, to attend schools, to buy alcohol, and so on. Many governmental institutions have age-specific programs: for senior citizens, for adult students, for midcareer persons. Although the Supreme Court has refused to make age a suspect classification requiring extra judicial protection, Congress, responding to "gray power," is treating age more and more as a protected category. Congress has made it illegal for most employers to discriminate in their employment practices on the basis of old age. And except for a few exempt occupations, Congress prohibits employers from imposing mandatory age retirement requirements. About one-fourth of the court actions filed by the Equal Employment Opportunity Commission relate to claims of age discrimination.[37]

FUNDAMENTAL RIGHTS AND STRICT SCRUTINY The Court also strictly scrutinizes laws impinging on **fundamental rights**. What makes a right fundamental in the constitutional sense? It is not the importance or the significance of the right that makes it fundamental, but whether it is *explicitly or implicitly guaranteed by the Constitution*.[38] Under this test, the rights to travel and to vote have been held to be fundamental, as well as such First Amendment rights as the right to associate for the advancement of political beliefs. The rights to an education, to housing, or to welfare benefits have not been held to be fundamental. Important as these rights may be, they are not guaranteed by the Constitution, meaning that there are no constitutional provisions specifically protecting these rights from governmental regulation.

Proving Discrimination

Does the fact that a law or a regulation has a differential effect—what has come to be known as *disparate impact*—on persons of different race or sex by itself establish that it is unconstitutional? In one of its most important decisions, *Washington v Davis*

(1976), the Supreme Court said no. "The invidious quality of a law claimed to be racially discriminatory must ultimately be traced to a racially discriminatory purpose."[39] "An unwavering line of cases" from the Supreme Court "hold that a violation of the Equal Protection Clause requires state action motivated by discriminatory intent; the disproportionate effects of state action are not sufficient to establish such a violation."[40] Or, as the Court said in another case: "The Fourteenth Amendment guarantees equal laws, not equal results."[41]

What do these rulings on disparate impact mean in practical terms? They mean, for example, that city ordinances that permit only single-family residences and thus make low-cost housing projects impossible are not unconstitutional—even if their effect is to keep minorities from moving into the city—unless it can be shown that they were adopted *with the intent to discriminate against minorities.* The rulings also mean that a preference for veterans in public employment does not violate the equal protection clause, even though its effect is to keep many women from getting jobs; the distinction between veterans and nonveterans was not adopted deliberately to create a sex barrier.

Still, the disparate impact that a law or governmental practice has is not irrelevant in determining its constitutionality. In a community with a large number of African Americans or Hispanics, it would be constitutionally suspicious if only a few of them were called for jury duty. Under such circumstances, the burden of proof shifts to the state or city to demonstrate that it has not engaged in unconstitutional discriminatory conduct.

What is constitutional can nonetheless be made *illegal.* Things that are unconstitutional are always illegal, but what is illegal may not be unconstitutional. One of the most hotly contested issues of recent years has been how to interpret the various civil rights acts, especially Title VII of the Civil Rights Act of 1964, which forbids discrimination in employment on the basis of race, sex, religion, and national origin.

Congress has also intervened to make illegal some voting practices that are not necessarily unconstitutional. The Voting Rights Act of 1965 tests the legality of state voting laws and practices by their *effects* rather than by the purposes of those who passed them.

THE LIFE AND DEATH OF JIM CROW EDUCATION

Until the Supreme Court struck down such laws in the 1950s, southern states made it illegal for whites and blacks to ride in the same train cars, attend the same theaters, go to the same schools, be born in the same hospitals, or be buried in the same cemeteries. **Jim Crow laws**, as they came to be called, blanketed southern life.[42] Southern states and some places in the North enforced segregation in transportation, places of public accommodation, educational facilities, swimming pools, and parks. How could these laws stand in the face of the equal protection clause? This was the question raised in *Plessy v Ferguson.*

Segregation, Discrimination, and *Plessy v Ferguson*

In 1896 in *Plessy v Ferguson*, the Supreme Court endorsed the view that racial segregation did not constitute discrimination if "equal" accommodations were provided for the members of both races.[43] Equal accommodations were required only for public facilities such as schools and colleges and for a limited category of public utilities such as trains and buses. Although the *Plessy* decision required equality as the price for compulsory segregation, the "equal" part of the formula was meaningless. States segregated blacks into unequal facilities, and blacks lacked the political power to protest.

The passage of time did not lessen the inequalities. Beginning in the late 1930s, blacks started to file lawsuits challenging the doctrine. They cited facts to show that in practice, separate but equal always resulted in discrimination against blacks. At first the Supreme Court was not willing to upset the separate but equal doctrine, but started to undermine it.

The End of Separate but Equal: *Brown v Board of Education*

In the spring of 1954, in *Brown v Board of Education*, the Supreme Court finally reversed its 1896 holding as it applied to public schools. It ruled that "separate but equal" is a contradiction in terms. *Segregation is itself discrimination.*[44] A year later the Court ordered school boards to proceed with "all deliberate speed to desegregate public schools at the earliest practical date."[45] In the years following the *Brown* decision, federal judges struck down a whole battery of schemes designed to evade the Court's ruling. Beginning in 1963, the Supreme Court gradually reversed its decision that granted school districts time to prepare for desegregation. In 1969 the Court completed that reversal, stating: "Continued operation of racially segregated schools under the standard of 'all deliberate speed' is no longer constitutionally permissible. School districts must immediately terminate dual school systems based on race and operate only unitary school systems."[46]

In the 1960s Congress and the president joined even more directly in the battle against school segregation. Title VI of the Civil Rights Act of 1964 stipulates that federal dollars under any grant program or project must be withdrawn from an entire school or institution of higher education that discriminates "on the ground of race, color, or national origin" in "any program or activity receiving Federal financial assistance." Congress in 1972 added sex discrimination to this list; other acts have added the handicapped, the aged, Vietnam veterans, and disabled veterans. Title VI also imposes a responsibility on schools to take affirmative action to ensure that persons in the protected categories are not denied access to any federally supported program or activity.

Busing

Thurgood Marshall (*center*), George E.C. Hayes (*left*), and James Nabrit, Jr., (*right*) argued and won *Brown v Board of Education of Topeka* before the Supreme Court in 1954.

The Supreme Court endorsed busing schoolchildren out of their neighborhoods to achieve racial balance in schools as one of the tools a federal judge might use to bring about school integration, but only to remedy the consequences of officially sanctioned segregation, that is, **de jure segregation**, or segregation required or sanctioned by law. It has refused to permit busing to overcome the effects of **de facto segregation**, segregation that arises from social customs or personal choice or as the result of residential segregation.[47] In other words, if judges find that authorities had operated segregated schools in the past or had caused segregation by systematic and purposeful actions, judges could order a school district to bus pupils.[48] But judges may not, said the Supreme Court in a case involving the Detroit metropolitan area, order busing between suburbs and cities or any other interdistrict lines to overcome racial imbalances in schools where such segregation was not caused by official actions.[49]

The result has been paradoxical. Southern cities that previously operated legally segregated school systems now have more integrated schools than do large northern cities (see Table 5-1). In large metropolitan areas in the North and South, many school districts in central cities are predominantly black and/or Hispanic, partly as the result of "white flight" to the suburbs and private schools to escape court-ordered busing, but in more recent years due to higher birth rates and immigration. Without interdistrict busing it is difficult to integrate schools by judicial decree. In fact, since the Supreme Court's decision in the Detroit case, there has been little progress in school desegregation.[50] By the 1991-92 school year, "after decades of progress, schools in the South had rising concentrations of black students and those in the West had rising concentrations of Hispanic students"; furthermore, two out of every three African American public school students attend schools where the enrollment is more than 50 percent black or Latino.[51]

The Supreme Court has told federal district judges to stop enforcing desegregation decrees, even in districts that once had de jure segregation, if current school segregation is based on residential segregation that "flows from private decision making and economic factors too attenuated to be considered a consequence of the former school segregation."[52] African American leaders, while still supporting desegregation efforts, are giving more attention to improving the quality of inner-city schools than to desegregating them. As Dr. Beverly P. Cole, director of education and housing for the NAACP, has said, "At the present time, we are more concerned with the quality of education and this has to take precedence over whether schools are integrated."[53]

BARRIERS TO VOTING

States determine voting qualifications, but they do so subject to a variety of constitutional restraints. Article I, Section 4, gives Congress the power to supersede state regulations as to the "Times, Places and Manner" of elections for representatives, senators, and presidential electors. Congress has used this authority to set age qualifications and residency requirements to vote in national elections, to establish a uniform day for all states to hold elections for members of Congress and presidential electors, and to give American citizens who reside outside the United States the right to vote for members of Congress and presidential electors in the states in which they previously lived.

The major limitations on the states' power to set voting qualifications, however, are contained in the Fourteenth and Fifteenth Amendments (forbidding unreasonable qualifications and those based on race), the Nineteenth Amendment (forbidding qualifications based on sex), and the Twenty-sixth Amendment (forbidding states to deny citizens 18 years of age or older the right to vote on account of age). These amendments also empower Congress to enact the laws necessary to enforce their provisions.

Getting Around the Fourteenth and Fifteenth Amendments

Despite fierce opposition to the Nineteenth Amendment, no organized resistance to its implementation surfaced after its ratification gave women the right to vote. This was not so following ratification of the Fourteenth and Fifteenth Amendments. Black men were allowed to participate in the political life of southern states only when and because the federal government insisted upon it. As soon as federal troops were withdrawn from the South in 1877, southern Democrats regained control of state governments and set out to keep blacks from voting. They used social pressure and violence. Organized secret societies like the Ku Klux Klan engaged in such terrorist activities as midnight shootings, burnings, whippings, and lynchings to keep blacks from voting.

These measures worked. But toward the end of the nineteenth century, and for the first time since the Civil War, parts of the South had two strong political parties: the Democrats and the Populists. White supremacists were fearful the parties might compete for the black vote, and blacks might come to hold the balance of power. White supremacists also feared that continued use of excessive force and fraud to disenfranchise blacks might cause the president and Congress to intervene.

Southern leaders reasoned that if they could pass laws depriving blacks of the vote on grounds other than race, blacks would find it difficult to challenge such

TABLE 5-1

Segregation Moves North and West

States with the largest percentage of Hispanic and black students attending schools that have 90 to 100 percent minority populations.

Blacks	
1. Illinois	59.3%
2. Michigan	58.5
3. New York	57.5
4. New Jersey	54.6
5. Pennsylvania	45.7
6. Tennessee	37.3
7. Alabama	36.8
8. Maryland	36.7
9. Mississippi	36.6
10. Connecticut	36.2

Hispanics	
1. New York	58.1
2. New Jersey	44.4
3. Texas	41.7
4. California	35.4
5. Illinois	33.7
6. Connecticut	33.7
7. Florida	28.0
8. Pennsylvania	27.4
9. Indiana	19.6
10. New Mexico	18.3
11. Arizona	16.2

SOURCE: Gary Orfield, "The Growth of Segregation in American Schools: Changing Patterns of Segregation and Poverty Since 1968," a report to the National School Boards Association, reported in *The New York Times*, December 14, 1993, p. A1.

Should Congress forbid
employment tests that have a
disparate impact on ethnic
minorities and women?

What if an employer requires a test that
may be related to job performance, but
nonetheless screens out more members
of one race or sex than another? Does
this disparate impact of the test, say, on
women or African Americans, show
indirect discrimination, and does it
prove illegal discrimination?

laws in the courts. Some whites protested that such laws could be used against whites as well as blacks. But keeping poor whites from voting did not disturb the conservative leaders of the Democratic party, for they were often just as anxious to undermine white support for the Populist party as they were to disenfranchise blacks. "The disenfranchisement movement of the 1890s gave the Southern states the most impressive system of obstacles between the voter and the ballot box known to the democratic world."[54]

In the 1940s the Supreme Court began to strike down one after another of the devices used to keep blacks from voting. In 1944 (*Smith v Allwright*) the Court declared the **white primary** unconstitutional.[55] In 1960 it held that **racial gerrymandering**—the drawing of election districts so as to ensure that blacks are a minority in all districts—is contrary to the Fifteenth Amendment.[56] In 1964 the Twenty-fourth Amendment eliminated the **poll tax**—payment required as a condition for voting—in elections for members of Congress and presidential electors, and in 1966 the Court held that the Fourteenth Amendment forbade the poll tax as a condition in any election.[57]

Those wishing to deny African Americans the right to vote were forced to rely on registration requirements. On the surface these requirements appeared to be perfectly proper; it was the way they were administered that kept blacks from the polls. They were often applied by white election officers while white police stood guard, with white judges hearing appeals from decisions of registration officials. These officials often seized on the smallest error in an application blank as an excuse to disqualify a voter. In one parish in Louisiana, after four white voters filed affidavits in which they challenged the legality of the registration of black voters on the grounds that these voters had made an "error in spilling" (*sic*) in their applications, registration officials struck 1,300 out of approximately 1,500 black voters from the polls.[58]

In many southern areas, **literacy tests** were used to discriminate against blacks. Some states, either as an additional requirement or as a substitute, required applicants to demonstrate to the satisfaction of election officials that they understood the national and state constitutions and, furthermore, that they were persons of good character. Although poor whites often avoided registration out of fear of embarrassment from failing a literacy test, the tests were more often used to discriminate against blacks.[59] Whites were often asked simple questions; blacks were asked questions that would baffle a Supreme Court justice. "In the 1960s southern registrars were observed testing black applicants on such matters as the number of bubbles in a soap bar, the news contained in a copy of the *Peking Daily*, the meaning of obscure passages in state constitutions, and the definition of terms such as *habeas corpus*."[60] In Louisiana, 49,603 illiterate white voters were able to persuade election officials they could understand the Constitution, but only two illiterate black voters were able to do so.

The Voting Rights Act of 1965

For two decades after World War II, under the leadership of the Supreme Court, federal judges carefully scrutinized voting laws and procedures in cases brought before them. Yet this approach did not open the voting booth to African Americans, especially those living in rural areas of the Deep South. Finally Congress began to act. The Civil Rights Act of 1964 set aside, for elections for members of Congress and the president, literacy tests for persons who had completed the equivalent of the sixth grade and prohibited denial of the right to vote because of minor errors on application forms.

The Civil Rights Act of 1964 had hardly been enacted when events in Selma, Alabama, dramatized the inadequacy of depending on the courts to prevent racial barriers in polling places. A voter-registration drive in that city, led by

Martin Luther King, Jr., produced arrests, marches on the state capital, and the murder of two civil rights workers. But still there was no dent in the color bar at the polls.

Responding to events in Selma, President Lyndon Johnson made a dramatic address to Congress and the nation calling for federal action to ensure that no person would be deprived of the right to vote in any election for any office because of color or race. Congress responded with the Voting Rights Act of 1965.[61]

The Voting Rights Act goes beyond merely protecting the right to vote, especially as amended in 1982 to protect minorities against the dilution of their voting power.[62] What precisely constitutes "dilution" and how it is to be measured are the subject of much litigation. The Supreme Court has broadly construed Section 5, requiring Department of Justice preclearance of changes in voting qualifications or practices in states and districts covered by the law. Examples include changes in the location of polling places; changes in candidacy requirements and qualifications, such as changes in filing deadlines; changes in the composition of the electorate, such as changes from ward to at-large elections or changes in boundary lines of voting districts; and changes that affect the creation or abolition of an elective office. The Court refused, however, to extend the act to cover changes in the distribution of power among officials after two Alabama counties altered the power of county commissioners in such a way as to reduce the authority of recently elected black commissioners.[63]

The Voting Rights Act, combined with the redistricting required as a consequence of the 1990 census, substantially increased the number of election districts represented by African Americans and Hispanics. The Department of Justice, working with organizations representing these groups, has rejected most redistricting plans that fail to draw as many districts as possible in which minorities constitute a majority. The federal courts are also moving along these same lines. Most of these districts tend to be Democratic. Concentrating black and Hispanic voters in districts to ensure that they are in a majority will result in leaving other districts heavily white and Republican. The consequence will be more minority districts and more safely Republican districts.[64]

States may take race into account in the drawing of electoral districts; in fact, in order to comply with the Voting Rights Act they have to do so. However, they may not make race the *sole* reason for drawing district lines. A state violates the Constitution if it draws district lines, even if its purpose is to comply with the Voting Rights Act, that result in districts of such bizarre shape that it is clear they were drawn for the purpose of separating voters by race, disregarding traditional districting principles such as compactness, contiguity, and respect for political subdivisions. When North Carolina, in response to urgings of the attorney general of the United States, drew a district 160 miles long and in some places only an interstate highway in width, the Court held that white voters had grounds to raise the issue of an unconstitutional use of race and sent the case back to the district judge for his consideration of their claims. States comply with the Voting Rights Act if they provide for districts roughly proportional to the minority voters' respective shares in the voting-age population.[65]

Results of the New Laws

Millions of African Americans now participate in our political life. More than 8,000 blacks hold national, state, or local office. More than 300 are mayors, including in such key cities as Atlanta, Birmingham, Denver, Baltimore, Oakland, Detroit, and Washington, D.C. There are blacks in all southern legislatures, and there are more blacks in the U.S. House of Representatives than at any time since Reconstruction. There is an African American United States Senator, and Virginia recently had an African American governor.

In 1971, in *Griggs v Duke Power* concerning the requirement of a high school diploma for becoming a janitor, the Supreme Court held that showing the disparate impact of an employment practice was sufficient to shift the burden of proof to the employer to show that this practice or test was job related.[*] Eighteen years later, in *Wards Cove v Antonio*, the Supreme Court more or less gutted the *Griggs* test. The Court placed the burden on those charging discrimination to show that a challenged practice—say, a test—had a significantly disparate impact and was not connected with a business goal. Then, in the Civil Rights Act of 1991, Congress stepped in to provide that once those charging discrimination show that a test or a physical requirement for a job results in reducing the number of women, or minorities, or handicapped, or persons of a particular religion eligible for that job, then the employer must "demonstrate that the challenged practice is job related for the position in question and consistent with business necessity."

SOURCE: This discussion is based on a summary of the Civil Rights Act of 1991 prepared by David S. Tatel of Hogan & Hartson, December 18, 1991.

Griggs v Duke Power, 401 US 424 (1971).

FULFILLING THE PROMISE OF THE VOTING RIGHTS ACT

The Voting Rights Act—enacted almost a century after the Fifteenth Amendment was ratified—finally made it possible for blacks to register and vote in every district in the United States. The act has been extended and strengthened three times, most recently in 1982. Since its passage, African Americans have the right to vote, and they are doing so. Federal observers have been sent to more than 60 counties—some as late as 1983—to ensure that blacks were not being intimidated, although it has been unnecessary to appoint federal examiners in most areas because the mere threat to send them has been enough.*

*Richard L. Engstrom, "Racial Vote Dilution: The Concept and the Court," in *The Voting Rights Act: Consequences and Implications*, ed. Lorn S. Foster (Praeger, 1985), p. 13. See also Mack H. Jones, "The Voting Rights Act as an Intervention Strategy for Social Change: Symbolism or Substance?" in Foster, pp. 63–84, for the view that the Justice Department failed to enforce these provisions with appropriate vigor.

Major Provisions of the Voting Rights Act of 1965 as Amended in 1974 and 1982 and Interpreted by the Supreme Court

Black Elected Officials in 1993

Federal	42
State	533
County	913
Municipal	3,903
Judicial and Law Enforcement	922
Education	1,689
Total	8,002

SOURCE: *Black Elected Officials: A National Roster, 1993* (Washington, D.C.: Center for Political and Economic Studies Press, 1994), p. xxii.

Section 2

Forbids *any* government to use any procedures related to voting, regardless of intent, that result in the denial of vote to any person because of race or color or the *dilution* of the voting power of members of a protected class.

Sections 3, 6, and 7

In the areas covered by the law, those that have had a long history of discrimination against blacks, mostly but not exclusively in the South, federal courts and the United States attorney general may appoint federal examiners to register voters and to ensure that all persons' votes are counted.

Section 4

Abolishes English literacy requirements for any person who has gone beyond the sixth grade. In addition, in areas where more than 5 percent of the citizens are members of a single language minority, ballots and other written materials relating to the vote are to be printed in that language.

Section 5

Requires governmental units covered by the law, mostly southern states that prior to 1965 had a long history of discriminating against blacks, to submit for preclearance all proposed changes in their voting laws or practices to the United States attorney general or to the United States Court of Appeals for the District of Columbia. (Note that approval of the local federal district judge will not do. Congress did not want to entrust this responsibility to anyone who might be subject to local political pressures—even a federal judge.) These changes are not to be approved until reviewed to assure that the change has neither the *purpose* nor the *effect* of denying the vote to any person because of race or color or of *diluting* the voting power of any person because of race or color. The Department of Justice has up to 120 days to preclear any change in election procedure; it reviews an average of 17,000 electoral changes each year.* Sixteen states had to preclear part of and nine states had to secure approval for their entire redistricting plans following the 1990 census changes.

Section 10

Abolishes the poll tax as a precondition of voting in any governmental election.

Clark v Roemer, 114 L Ed 2d 691 (1991).

Has all this made any difference? "A significant disillusionment with the franchise is said to be evident among many blacks today."[66] For example, Katherine Tate concludes, "At most, the new black political representation has benefited middle-class blacks, providing new economic opportunities through government employment and minority contracting in city governments."[67] The precise influence of black voting is a subject of much study, but the results are not clear

A federal registrar helps African Americans register to vote, as required by the 1965 Voting Rights Act.

Wellington Webb (*left*) being congratulated when he became the first African American in the history of Denver, Colorado, to be elected mayor.

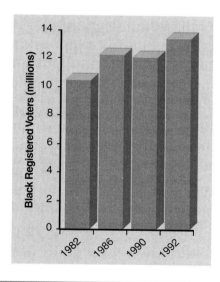

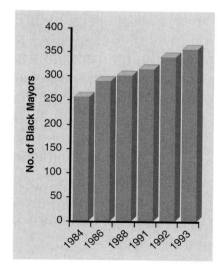

and the patterns are changing.[68] Most scholars are coming to the conclusion that "if blacks (and Hispanics) organize, compete in the electoral arena, and elect one or more of their number to city council, they can lay claim to a larger slice of the public pie."[69] In effect, minorities can convert their voting potential into public policy if they mobilize their members. Yet despite the fact that many of our largest cities have black mayors, black police chiefs, and black superintendents of schools, they have been unable to bring about major improvements in the social, economic, and educational conditions for large numbers of inner-city blacks, in large part because cities lack resources and powers to deal with the root causes.

The consequences of greater participation by blacks in the political process need to be measured by other means in addition to the number of black officeholders.[70] When the influence of black voters is distributed over a larger number of districts, black voters may provide the margin of victory to a white candidate, even if they are unable to elect a black officeholder. As long as candidates of any race believe they have a chance of getting enough black votes to win, they will probably find it politically profitable to be concerned about the interests of black constituents.[71] In fact, there is evidence that representatives in some districts with a majority of whites are as "strongly supportive of black interests as are representatives of majority black districts."[72] Since the passage of the Voting Rights Act of 1965, governors and senators, especially in areas with large numbers of black voters, have become much more sympathetic to the concerns of black voters. The views of black constituents have become a fact of political life and have to be taken into account by policy makers, including presidents who appoint and senators who confirm federal judges.

The significance of this political fact was demonstrated by the Senate's rejection in 1987 of Robert Bork's nomination to the Supreme Court. Judge Bork was a member of the Court of Appeals for the District of Columbia and a respected constitutional authority. But his constitutional views aroused the opposition of many, including the leaders of civil rights and women's groups. Among those voting against his confirmation were many "senators from southern states, where once, not too long ago, blacks could not register to vote. [They] voted against Bork . . . to protect the seats an enfranchised black electorate helped them to win."[73]

BARRIERS TO PUBLIC ACCOMMODATIONS, JOBS, AND HOMES

As we have noted, the Fifth and Fourteenth Amendments apply only to *governmental action*, not to private discriminatory conduct. Moreover, our Constitution creates "a zone of privacy which precludes government from interfering with private clubs or groups. The associational rights which our system honors permit all-white, all-black, all-brown, and all-yellow clubs to be established. They also permit all-Catholic, all-Jewish, or all-agnostic clubs. . . . Government may not tell a man or a woman who his or her associates must be. The individual may be as selective as he desires."[74]

Families, churches, or private groups organized for political, religious, cultural, social, or expressive purposes are constitutionally different from large associations organized along other lines, such as the United States Jaycees (the Junior Chamber of Commerce) or a large law partnership. The Supreme Court, for example, has upheld the application of state and local human relations and public accommodations laws forbidding sex or racial discrimination to organizations such as the Jaycees, the Rotary Club, and large (in this case more than 400 members) private eating clubs. Such associations and clubs are not small intimate groups. Nor were they able to demonstrate that allowing women or minorities to become members would change the content or impact of their purposes.[75]

This segregated drinking fountain was typical of the widespread discrimination that faced African Americans in this country as recently as the 1960s.

Until recent decades the fact that the Fourteenth Amendment is inapplicable to private conduct hindered Congress's ability to regulate against non-state-sanctioned discriminatory conduct. In 1883 the Supreme Court declared unconstitutional an act of Congress that made it a federal offense for any operator of a public conveyance, hotel, or theater to deny accommodations to any person because of race or color on the grounds that the Fourteenth Amendment does not give Congress authority to legislate against discrimination by private individuals.[76]

Since the 1960s, however, the constitutional authority of Congress to legislate against discrimination by private individuals is no longer an issue. The Court has so broadly construed the commerce clause, which gives Congress the power to regulate interstate and foreign commerce, that it alone justifies almost any action that Congress might want to take against discriminatory conduct by individuals.

The Court has also reinterpreted the Thirteenth Amendment, at least as far as racial discrimination is concerned, to sustain congressional legislation against discrimination. In addition to the Thirteenth and the Fourteenth Amendments, Congress may use, and has used, the power to tax and spend to prevent not only racial discrimination but also discrimination based on ethnic origin, sex, disability, and age. It may also use the power to regulate interstate commerce, as it did in the most important and sweeping Civil Rights Act—that of 1964.

The Civil Rights Act of 1964

With this law, for the first time since Reconstruction, Congress authorized the massive use of federal authority to combat privately imposed racial discrimination.

TITLE II: PLACES OF PUBLIC ACCOMMODATION   Title II makes it a federal offense to discriminate against any customer or patron in a place of public accommodation because of race, color, religion, or national origin. It applies to any inn, hotel, motel, or lodging establishment (except establishments with fewer than five rooms and occupied by the proprietor—in other words, small boardinghouses); to any restaurant or gasoline station that serves interstate travelers or serves food or products, of which a substantial portion have moved in interstate commerce; and to any movie house, theater, concert hall, sports arena, or other place of entertainment that customarily presents films, performances, athletic teams, or other sources of entertainment that are moved in interstate commerce.

Title II has been vigorously enforced, and African Americans organized programs to test it. The Department of Justice filed more than 400 lawsuits. Within a few months after its adoption, the Supreme Court, in *Heart of Atlanta Motel v United States*, unanimously sustained its constitutionality.[77] As a result, public establishments, including those in the South, have opened their doors to all customers.

TITLE VII: EMPLOYMENT   The Constitution and numerous congressional laws forbid *governments* to deny persons employment because of race, color, religion, or sex. By Title VII of the Civil Rights Act, Congress has made it illegal for any employer or trade union in any industry affecting interstate commerce and employing 15 or more people (and, since 1972, any state or local agency such as a school or university) to discriminate in employment practices against any person because of race, color, national origin, religion, or sex.[78] Title VII forbids discrimination with respect to compensation, terms, conditions, or privileges of employment. The intent is to "strike at the entire spectrum of disparate treatment,"

Major Civil Rights Laws

CIVIL RIGHTS ACT, 1957: The first civil rights law since Reconstruction, PL 85-315 makes it a federal crime to prevent persons from voting in federal elections and authorizes the attorney general to bring suit when a person was deprived of his or her voting rights.

CIVIL RIGHTS ACT, 1964: The most sweeping antibias law, PL 88-352 bars discrimination in employment on the basis of race, color, religion, sex, or national origin and in public accommodations and federally funded programs on the basis of race, color, religion, or national origin. It also created the Equal Employment Opportunity Commission.

VOTING RIGHTS ACT, 1965: PL 89-110 authorizes the appointment of federal examiners to register voters in areas found to have been discriminating and strengthens penalties for those who interfered with others' right to vote.

AGE DISCRIMINATION IN EMPLOYMENT ACT, 1967: PL 90-202 prohibits job discrimination against workers or job applicants ages 40 through 65. It was amended in 1975 (PL 94-135) to bar age bias in federally assisted programs and in 1986 (PL 99-592) to prohibit mandatory retirement in most jobs.

FAIR HOUSING ACT, 1968: PL 90-284 prohibits discrimination on the basis of race, color, religion, or national origin in the sale or rental of most housing. It also includes provisions to protect civil rights workers from injury or intimidation and provides for federal penalties for those convicted of rioting or encouraging others to do so.

TITLE IX. EDUCATION AMENDMENT OF 1972: PL 92-318 provides that "No person . . . shall, on the basis of sex, be excluded from participation in, be denied the benefits of, or be subjected to discrimination under any education program or activity receiving Federal financial assistance."

REHABILITATION ACT, 1973: Primarily a reauthorization of programs to rehabilitate the handicapped, PL 93-112 carries two little-noted provisions whose importance became clear only after the fact. Section 503 requires that recipients of federal grants greater than $2,500 institute affirmative action programs to hire and promote "qualified handicapped individuals," while Section 504 states, "No otherwise qualified handicapped individual . . . shall, solely by reason of his handicap, be excluded from the participation in, be denied the benefits of, or be subjected to discrimination under any program or activity receiving federal financial assistance."

CIVIL RIGHTS RESTORATION ACT OF 1988: Overriding President Ronald Reagan's veto, Congress in PL 100-259 overturned a 1984 Supreme Court ruling that anti-sex discrimination provisions of the 1972 Education Act

which includes requiring people to work in a discriminatorily hostile or abusive environment.[79] Employers have an obligation to create workplaces which avoid such abusive environments. Other legislation makes it illegal to engage in discriminatory activities that affect those with physical handicaps, veterans, or persons over 40.

There are a few exceptions. Religious institutions such as parochial schools may use religious standards. Age, sex, or handicap may be considered where occupational qualifications are absolutely necessary to the normal operation of a particular business or enterprise.

In 1991, Congress amended Title VII to set aside several Supreme Court decisions and to make it easier to challenge employment practices—tests, qualifications, conditions—that, whatever the intent, have a disparate adverse impact on women and minorities.

Title VII was passed to protect minorities and women; nonetheless, employers who discriminate against white males also violate its provisions. Moreover, when Congress adopted Title VII, it stated that the act should not be used to require any employer to grant preferential treatment to any individual or to any group on account of racial or sexual imbalance that might exist in the employer's work force. Title VII, however, does not preclude employers, public or private, from adopting race-sensitive affirmative action programs designed to overcome past discrimination against minorities and women.

Title VII has several special features. Not only do aggrieved persons have a right of private action to sue for damages for themselves, but they can do so for other persons similarly situated in a *class action*. In addition, Congress created the Equal Employment Opportunity Commission (EEOC) to enforce its provisions. The commission, which consists of five members appointed by the president with the consent of the Senate, works together with state authorities to try to bring about compliance with the act and may seek judicial enforcement of complaints against private employers. The attorney general prosecutes Title VII violations by public agencies. The vigor with which the EEOC and the attorney general have acted has varied over the years, depending on the commitment of the president in office.[80]

Title VII is supplemented, indeed in some instances even supplanted, by a 1965 presidential executive order requiring all contractors of the federal government, including universities, to adopt and implement affirmative action programs to correct for "underutilization" of women and minorities. Such programs may not establish racial or ethnic quotas for minorities or women, but they do call on contractors to establish timetables and goals; to follow open recruitment procedures; to keep records of applicants by race, sex, and national origin; and to explain why their labor force does not reflect the same proportion of persons in the covered categories that exist within the appropriate labor market pools. Failure of contractors to file and implement an approved affirmative action plan may lead to loss of federal contracts or grants.

Housing: The Civil Rights Acts of 1966, 1968, and 1988

Housing is the last frontier of the civil rights crusade, the area in which progress is slowest and genuine change most remote. "Blacks at every economic level are significantly segregated from whites of similar economic status."[81] "Housing segregation is serious because it is at the root of many other forms of segregation and inequality."[82] "Segregated housing contributes mightily to a vicious circle that also includes educational and employment discrimination. . . . Because of poor schools for many minorities, they cannot find well-paying jobs. Without such jobs they often cannot afford to live in nicer neighborhoods with decent housing. And because of their location in less desirable communities, good educational systems are less likely to be available."[83]

In 1948, in *Shelley v Kraemer*, the Supreme Court held that judges could no longer enforce racially **restrictive covenants** (a provision in a deed to real property restricting its sale).[84] In 1968 Congress passed the Fair Housing Act. This act, amended in 1988, is now known as the Fair Housing Amendments Act. It covers all housing offered for rent or sale except that owned by private individuals who own no more than three houses, who sell or rent these houses without the services of an agent, and who do not indicate any preference or discrimination in their advertising; dwellings that have no more than four separate living units, in which the owner maintains a residence (so-called "Mrs. Murphy boardinghouses"); and religious organizations and private clubs housing their own members on a noncommercial basis. For all other housing, the act forbids owners to refuse to sell or rent to any person because of race, color, religion, national origin, sex (since 1974), and handicap or because a person has children (since 1988). Housing for older persons is exempted from this family provision. No discriminatory advertising is permitted.

The weakest link in the 1968 act turned out to be the sections dealing with enforcement. Prior to the 1988 amendments, primary responsibility fell upon those injured by discriminatory housing practices. Now the Department of Housing and Urban Development (HUD) is obliged to investigate and process complaints. The Department of Justice must provide an attorney for complainants who are unable to afford one. Even more important, complainants may now bring their allegations of discrimination before administrative law judges within HUD.

The Department of Justice has filed hundreds of cases, especially those involving large apartment complexes. The courts have built up such "a formidable body of precedent that almost anyone who can prove discrimination, and has the determination and money to do so, can get the house he wants and even substantial damage awards."[85] And the addition, in 1988, of administrative enforcement procedures gives this federal law considerably stronger teeth. "Nevertheless, the present system is fundamentally flawed because it continues to rely on victims detecting discrimination against them and then filing suit."[86]

Most African Americans and Hispanics continue to be discriminated against when they attempt to rent apartments or to buy houses. Realtors continue to steer blacks and Hispanics toward neighborhoods that are not predominantly white, to require larger rental deposits for minorities than for whites, and even to refuse outright to sell or rent to minorities.[87] Less than 1 percent of these discriminatory actions are complained about because they are often so subtle that victims are not even aware that they are being discriminated against. "While blacks and other minorities have made strides in voting rights, education and jobs, the homes they return to each night are in communities still largely defined by race."[88]

AFFIRMATIVE ACTION: IS IT CONSTITUTIONAL?

Prior to 1954, when white majorities were using state power to segregate blacks and discriminate against them, civil rights advocates cited with approval the words of Justice John Marshall Harlan, dissenting in *Plessy v Ferguson*: "Our Constitution is color-blind and neither knows nor tolerates class among citizens."[89] It was not until

Major Civil Rights Laws (continued)

Amendments applied only to the specific program or activity receiving federal aid and not to the entire institution. In reversing *Grove City College v Bell*, Congress also specified that antibias provisions of three other laws applied to entire institutions if any segment received federal funding. The three were the 1964 Civil Rights Act, Section 504 of the 1973 Rehabilitation Act, and the 1975 Age Discrimination Act.

FAIR HOUSING ACT AMENDMENTS, 1988: PL 100-430 gives the Department of Housing and Urban Development greater authority to enforce the 1968 law and prohibits housing bias against the handicapped and families with children.

AMERICANS WITH DISABILITIES ACT, 1991: PL 102-119 prohibits discrimination based on disability in employment, places of public accommodations, and public services and requires that facilities be designed to make them accessible and usable by those with disabilities and to the extent feasible be redesigned to do so.

THE CIVIL RIGHTS ACT OF 1991: PL 102-166 counters the effects of nine Supreme Court decisions. It places a greater burden on employers to justify practices that negatively affect women and minorities by requiring employers to justify such practices as being job related for the position in question, being a business necessity, or showing that there are no alternative practices which would have a less negative impact on the protected group. It authorizes limited compensatory damages for intentional discrimination and punitive damages if the defendant acted with malice or reckless indifference to the rights of the individual based on sex, religion, or disability. (Unlimited damages are allowed for racial or ethnic bias under a Reconstruction civil rights law.) It amends the 1866 civil rights law, now 42 USC 1981, to prohibit not merely racial discrimination in initial hiring but other forms of race bias in the workplace, for example, in promotions. It prohibits "race norming" of tests used for employment or promotion—that is, setting different cutoff scores on the bases of race or ethnic origin. The act also establishes a commission, appointed by the president and Congress, to examine the "glass ceiling" that seems to keep women from becoming executives and to make recommendations on how to increase promotion of women and minorities to management positions.

SOURCE: Adapted from *Social Policy*, May 13, 1989, p. 1122.

PL means Public Law, and the number following is the number of the Congress; thus PL 85-315 means it was enacted by the 85th Congress.

Alan Bakke, who won a historic affirmative action suit, is surrounded by reporters as he leaves class after his first day at the University of California medical school.

1954 that Justice Harlan's views triumphed. In *Brown v Board of Education* the Court called racial classifications "odious to our system" and made race a suspect class. In the years immediately following, the Court also established that although the Fourteenth Amendment was adopted to protect blacks, its provisions extend to other minorities, to women, and to white males. The Court emphasized that the rights protected belong to each and every individual, not to the group to which he or she may belong.

By the 1960s there was a new set of constitutional and national policy debates. Many people began to assert that government neutrality was not enough. If governments and universities and employers merely stop discriminating against blacks, Hispanics, and women, yet change nothing else, those previously discriminated against are still kept from equal participation in American life. They have been so handicapped by past discrimination that in the competition for openings in medical schools or for skilled jobs or for their share of government grants and contracts, they suffer disabilities not shared by white males.

By the 1960s governments started to respond to these arguments. Presidents issued executive orders, Congress adopted programs, state legislatures created requirements, cities adopted ordinances, and university trustees issued policies. Although the details vary (and the details are constitutionally significant), these programs call on governments, governmental contractors, and in some instances private employers to take **affirmative action** to redress imbalances in work forces and governmental contracts in order to reflect more accurately the racial, sexual, and ethnic diversity of employment pools and to give opportunities to minority and women contractors. These race-, ethnic-, and sex-conscious remedies to overcome the consequences of past discrimination against blacks, Hispanics, Native Americans, and women may be known as *affirmative action* programs by those who support them, but they are regarded as *reverse discrimination* by those who oppose them.

What of the constitutionality of affirmative action programs resting on race and sex classifications, motivated by a desire to help persons handicapped by individual and institutional racism and sexism? The questions have been raised most directly with respect to affirmative action programs for African Americans.

The first major statement of the Court came in a celebrated case relating to university admissions. Allan Bakke, a white male and a top student at Minnesota and Stanford universities, as well as a Vietnam War veteran, applied both in 1973 and 1974 to the medical school of the University of California at Davis. In each of those years the school admitted 100 new students, 84 in a general admissions program and 16 in a special admissions program created for African Americans, Chicanos, Asian Americans, and Native Americans—groups who had been underrepresented until the special admissions program was established. Bakke's application was rejected each year, but students with lower grade-point averages, test scores, and interview ratings were admitted under the special admissions program. After his second rejection, Bakke brought a suit in federal court claiming he had been excluded because of his race, contrary to requirements of the Constitution and Title VI of the Civil Rights Act of 1964.

In *University of California Regents v Bakke* (1978), the Supreme Court ruled the Davis plan was unconstitutional.[90] But in an opinion by Justice Lewis Powell, which no other member of the Court completely shared, the Court also declared that affirmative action programs are not necessarily unconstitutional. In order to achieve a diversified student body, a state university may properly take race and ethnic background into account as one of several factors in choosing students. However, the university's goal may not be to redress past misconduct by the society or to ensure that more minority members become doctors. The problem with the California plan was it created a category of admissions from which whites were excluded solely because of their race.

Following *Bakke*, the Court dealt with a variety of affirmative action programs, sustaining most, but not all of them. Yet as Justice Byron White said, "Agreement upon a means for applying the Equal Protection Clause to an affirmative-action program has eluded this Court every time the issue has come before us."[91] In *Richmond v Croson* in 1989, a Court majority, over the bitter dissents of Justices Thurgood Marshall, William J. Brennan, Jr., and Harry Blackmun, struck down a plan of the city of Richmond requiring nonminority city contractors to subcontract at least 30 percent of the dollar amount of their contracts to one or more minority business enterprises. Said Justice Sandra Day O'Connor for the Court, in language that seemed to call into question the validity of most state and local government affirmative action plans, "Race-sensitive remedial measures are to be justified only after a strong basis in evidence has established that remedial action is necessary to overcome the consequences of past discriminatory action." Justice Thurgood Marshall in dissent contended that there is "a profound difference separating governmental actions that themselves are racist, and governmental actions seeking to remedy the effects of prior racism." The proper test, he wrote, for race-conscious classifications designed to further remedial goals is merely that they have to be justified as serving important governmental objectives and must be substantially related to the achievement of those objectives. The majority, he said, "sounds a full-scale retreat from the effort to deliver on the century-old promise of equality and scuttled the efforts of a city to surmount its discriminatory past."[92]

Although *Richmond v Croson* was interpreted to signal a hardened attitude by the Court toward affirmative action, on the last day of the 1989-90 term, to the surprise of most, Justice William J. Brennan, Jr., speaking for four other justices, in *Metro Broadcasting v Federal Communications Commission*, rejected the strict scrutiny test in favor of the less rigid middle-tier, heightened scrutiny test for governmental laws and regulations creating race classifications *so far as the national government is concerned*. Further, the national government is not, said the Court, limited to using race-sensitive measures to overcome past discrimination but may use them for other legitimate governmental objectives. The Court upheld the right of the Federal Communications Commission, in response to congressional mandates, under certain conditions to limit the transfer of certain existing radio and television broadcast stations *only* to minority-controlled firms. Justice Brennan's language sustaining this action was sweeping: "Benign race-conscious measures mandated by Congress—even if those measures are not remedial in the sense of being designed to compensate victims of past governmental or societal discrimination—are constitutionally permissible to the extent that they serve important governmental objectives within the power of Congress and are substantially related to achievement of those objectives." We find, he wrote, "that a congressionally mandated benign race-conscious program that is substantially related to the achievement of an important governmental interest is consistent with equal protection principles so long as it does not impose *undue* burdens on nonminorities." Justice O'Connor, the author of the *Croson* opinion, wrote in dissent, "'Benign' racial classification is a contradiction in terms. Governmental distinctions among citizens based on race or ethnicity, even in the rare circumstances permitted by our cases, exact costs and carry with them substantial dangers. To the person denied an opportunity or right based on race, the classification is hardly benign. The right to equal protection of the laws is a personal right."[93]

Outside of the employment and contract context the Court has reaffirmed, again with respect to states, its hostility toward the use of race even for remedial purposes and in a case relating to the drawing of electoral district lines where the injury to non-protected groups is much less a concern, the Court, again by a 5 to 4 vote, this time with Justice O'Connor speaking for the Court, emphasized that any use of race for whatever purposes is subject to strict scrutiny.[94]

These decisions are not the last judicial word. They do not relate directly to private employers or to programs based on sex. There are more decisions to come as the Court—and the nation—engage in the never-ending business of clarifying constitutional guidelines.

Where does all this leave us, at least for the moment, with respect to the constitutionality of governmental affirmative action programs?

1. All racial classifications in *state and local laws*, including those justified for benign or remedial purposes, are suspect and are subject to the strict scrutiny test to ensure that they are neither motivated by illegitimate notions of racial inferiority or simple racial politics.

2. Congress has much greater discretion than do states or local governments in fashioning race-sensitive remedial measures because it is empowered by Section 5 of the Fourteenth Amendment to do what is necessary and proper to enforce equal protection guarantees.

3. At the state and local levels, "When a legislative body chooses to employ a suspect classification, it cannot rest upon a generalized assertion as to the classification's relevance to its goals."[95] Race-sensitive remedial measures are to be justified only after a strong basis in evidence has established that remedial action is necessary to overcome the consequences of past discriminatory action.

4. A race-sensitive state and local remedy must be narrowly tailored to remedy the specific prior discrimination.

5. When a state and local government can identify in fact racial discrimination within its jurisdiction it may adopt "in the extreme case, some form of narrowly tailored racial preference . . . necessary to break down patterns of deliberate exclusion."[96]

6. The Supreme Court in a 5 to 4 opinion in which three of the five justices are no longer on the Court, held that Congress could adopt benign race-sensitive laws in order to promote governmental purposes.

EQUAL RIGHTS TODAY

After the Detroit and other racial disturbances of 1967, President Lyndon Johnson appointed a special Advisory Commission on Civil Disorders to investigate the origins of the riots and to recommend measures to prevent or contain such disasters in the future. When the commission (called the Kerner Commission after its chair, then-Governor Otto Kerner of Illinois) issued its report, it said in stark, clear language: "What white Americans have never fully understood—but what the Negro can never forget—is that white society is deeply implicated in the ghetto. *White institutions created it, white institutions maintain it, and white society condones it.*" The basic conclusion of the commission was that "our nation is moving toward two societies, one black, one white—separate and unequal" and that "only a commitment to national action on an unprecedented scale" could change this trend.[97]

The commission made sweeping recommendations on jobs, education, housing, and the welfare system. But other events diverted attention from these recommendations, at least temporarily: the Vietnam War, the partial calming of racial tensions, the election of Ronald Reagan and George Bush (especially the former), who were skeptical of governmental actions designed to enforce civil rights; and a growing skepticism about the effectiveness of governmental action.[98] As one commentator summarized the central themes of the administrations of Reagan and Bush: (1) change is very complex; (2) there are often negative and unanticipated consequences of well-intended reforms; (3) things will get better if the government stops trying to intervene; (4) inequality arises not from prejudice but from cultural deficiencies that are made worse by governmental paternalism.[99] The Clinton administration is much more sympathetic toward the use of governmental power to deal with issues of inequality, but because of budgetary constraints, it has been unable or unwilling to promote any major initiatives directly aimed at the problems of our inner cities.

Today legal barriers have been lowered, if not removed, by civil rights legislation, executive orders, and judicial decisions. African Americans and other minorities can vote, get a meal where they want, and stay at hotels. Hundreds of thousands have entered the middle class. Although some people still find ways to circumvent or obstruct the force of civil rights laws, especially those that apply to housing, by and large the government's action in the 1960s opened the legal system and provided blacks with equal rights under the law. Important as these victories are, "They were victories largely for the middle class—those who could travel, entertain in restaurants and stay in hotels. Those victories did not change life conditions for the mass of blacks who are still poor."[100]

More than a generation after the Kerner Commission issued its report, life for inner-city blacks is worse. As middle-class blacks have moved out of the inner city, the remaining *underclass*, as they are coming to be called, has become even more isolated from the rest of the nation.[101] Children are growing up on streets where drug abuse and crime are everyday events. These Americans live in "separate and deteriorating societies, with separate economies, diverging family structures and basic institutions, and even growing linguistic separation within the core ghettos. The scale of their isolation by race, class, and economic situation is much greater than it was in the 1960s, impoverishment, joblessness, educational inequality, and housing insufficiency even more severe."[102]

In November 1991, the entire world watched four white Los Angeles police officers beat Rodney King, an African American, on television, while taking him into custody as other members of the Los Angeles Police Department stood by and made no attempt to interfere. In April 1992 an all-white jury, after a long trial, failed to convict those officers for what appeared to almost all who saw the videotape as excessive use of force and police brutality. The three days of rioting in Los Angeles and other cities that followed the announcement of these acquittals resulted in over 50 deaths and millions of dollars lost from looting and destruction. This outburst brought home the fact that the problems highlighted by the Kerner Commission three decades ago are still with us, and the sense of hopelessness and anger felt by many inner-city African Americans and Hispanics is as great today as ever.

Despite the lack of improvement in social conditions, the push for integration has lessened. "In fact, power on both sides of the color line is based to some extent on acceptance of segregation. On the black side of the color line, it is advantageous to keep blacks within black electoral areas and keep black-controlled resources within black institutions: integrationist policies are often viewed as posing larger threats than they actually do. On the white side of the line . . . some residents in outlying suburbs see critical advantages in their almost all-white and all middle-class status."[103]

Some contend attention should be paid to the plight of the underclass, and that instead of focusing on issues of race, what is needed is a policy of increasing jobs.[104] Others say there has to be a reviving of the civil rights crusade, a restoration of vigorous civil rights enforcement, a metropolitan approach, job training, and above all, an attack on residential segregation.[105] In the 1990s the issue of race is still one of our dominant domestic issues. "The issue, more specifically, is the yet unsettled matter of the role of the black man in a white society."[106] Race appears to be "transforming the American political landscape,"[107] especially yet not exclusively in the nation's largest cities.

SUMMARY

1. Americans are committed to *equality*, an elusive term, with most support for *equality of opportunity*, some for *equality of starting conditions*, and some for *equality of results*.

2. The crusade for women's rights was born partly out of the struggle to abolish slavery. Similarly, the modern women's movement learned and gained power from the civil rights movements of the 1950s and early 1960s. The fate of these two social movements has long been intertwined. Recently, concern for equal rights under the law has been expanded to include the rights of Native Americans, Hispanics, and Asians.

3. Progress in securing civil rights for blacks was a long time in coming. After the Civil War the national government briefly tried to secure some measure of protection for the freed slaves and to enforce the Thirteenth, Fourteenth, and Fifteenth Amendments and the civil rights laws passed to implement them. But when federal troops withdrew from the South in 1877, the national government withdrew from the field and blacks were left to their own resources. The rights granted by the Constitution became meaningless. Not until 1954, in *Brown v Board of Education*, did the Supreme Court reverse an 1896 decision upholding racial segregation and announce that enforced racial segregation in public education was unconstitutional. Eventually Congress and the president threw their weight behind a major effort to prevent racial segregation and discrimination against blacks.

4. The Supreme Court uses a three-tiered approach to evaluate the constitutionality of laws challenged as violating the equal protection clause. Laws touching economic concerns are sustained if they are rationally related to the accomplishment of a legitimate government goal. Laws that classify people because of sex or illegitimacy are subject by the courts to the constitutional test known as *heightened scrutiny* and are sustained only if they serve important governmental objectives and are substantially related to achieving those objectives. The most stringent constitutional test, or *strict scrutiny*, is used to review laws that touch fundamental rights or classify people because of race or ethnic origin. Such laws will be sustained only if the government can show a *compelling public interest*.

5. After a long, struggle women achieved the right to vote with the adoption of the Nineteenth Amendment in 1920. With the rebirth of the women's movement in the 1960s, federal courts began for the first time to interpret constitutional provisions to protect women against sex discrimination.

6. Most recently older Americans have joined with women, African Americans, Hispanics, Native Americans, and Asian Americans to secure legislative protection for their special concerns.

7. The desirability and constitutionality of affirmative action programs that provide special benefits to those who have been subjected to past discrimination divide the nation and the Supreme Court. Remedial programs, especially those designed by Congress, closely tailored to overcome specific instances of disadvantage due to past discrimination, are likely to pass the Supreme Court's suspicion of race, national origin, and sex classifications. However, such state and local governmental programs are subject to the more exacting strict scrutiny test, and fewer of them are likely to survive.

FURTHER READING

JANET K. BOLES, ED., "American Feminism: New Issues for a Mature Movement," *Annals of the American Academy of Political and Social Science* (May 1991).

TAYLOR BRANCH, *Parting the Waters: America in the King Years, 1954–1963* (Simon & Schuster, 1988).

STEPHEN L. CARTER, *Reflections of an Affirmative Action Baby* (Basic Books, 1991).

CHANDLER DAVIDSON AND BERNARD GROFMAN, EDS., *Quiet Revolution in the South* (Princeton University Press, 1994).

LAURA L. CRITES AND WINIFRED L. HEPPERLE, *Women, the Courts, and Equality* (Sage Publications, 1987).

JANET DEWART, ED., *The State of Black America* (National Urban League, published annually).

GERTRUDE EZORSKY, *Racism and Justice: The Case for Affirmative Action* (Cornell University Press, 1991).

RONALD J. FISCUS, *The Constitutional Logic of Affirmative Action* (Duke University Press, 1992).

ANDREW HACKER, *Two Nations: Black and White, Separate, Hostile, Unequal* (Charles Scribner's Sons, 1992).

FRED R. HARRIS AND ROGER W. WILKINS, *Quiet Riots: Race and Poverty in the United States—The Kerner Report Twenty Years Later* (Pantheon Books, 1988).

RICHARD KLUGER, *Simple Justice* (Knopf, 1976).

OREN LYONS ET AL., *Exiled in the Land of the Free: Democracy, Indian Nations, and the U.S. Constitution* (Clear Light Publishers, 1992).

SUSAN GLUCK MEZEY, *In Pursuit of Equality: Women, Public Policy, and the Federal Courts* (St. Martin's Press, 1992).

GARY ORFIELD AND CAROLE ASHKINAZE, *The Closing Door: Conservative Policy and Black Opportunity* (University of Chicago Press, 1991).

J W. PELTASON, *Fifty-eight Lonely Men: Southern Federal Judges and School Desegregation* (University of Illinois Press, 1971).

PETER SKERRY, *Mexican Americans: The Ambivalent Minority* (Free Press, 1993).

SHELBY STEELE, *The Content of Our Character: A New Vision of Race in America* (St. Martin's Press, 1990).

MAURILIO E. VIGIL, *Hispanics in American Politics: The Search for Political Power* (University Press of America, 1987).

RIGHTS TO LIFE, LIBERTY, AND PROPERTY

Throughout the world men and women are rebelling against the police state under which they live, against governments in which police are unrestrained in how they go about finding, capturing, and punishing so-called "enemies of the people." When we in the United States get impatient about the time-consuming steps that must be followed before our criminals are taken off the streets, or about the endless rounds of appeals and reviews available to those charged with crimes, we need to remember how lucky we are to live in a society that values **due process**—established rules and regulations that restrain those who exercise governmental power.

Public officials in the United States do have great power. Under certain conditions they can seize our property, throw us into jail, and—in extreme circumstances—even take our lives. It is necessary to give power to those who govern. It is also dangerous. It is so dangerous that to keep officials from becoming tyrants, we are unwilling to depend on the ballot box alone. We know political controls mean little when an elected majority uses its power to deprive unpopular minorities of their rights. Because public power can be dangerous, we parcel it out in small chunks and surround it with restraints. No single official can decide to take our lives, liberty, or property. Moreover, officials must act according to the rules. If they act outside the scope of their authority or contrary to the law, they have no claim to our obedience. These are the precious rights of all who live under the American flag—rich or poor, young or old, black or white, man or woman, alien or citizen. In this chapter, we will take a closer look at the safeguards that protect the rights to life, liberty, and property.

CITIZENSHIP RIGHTS

Every nation has rules that determine nationality and define who is a member of, owes allegiance to, and is a subject of the nation-state. But in a democracy, citizenship is more than nationality, more than being merely a subject.[1] Citizenship is an office, and, like other offices, it carries with it certain powers and responsibilities. How citizenship is acquired and retained should therefore be a matter of considerable importance to everyone.

How Citizenship Is Acquired and Lost

This basic right of citizenship was not given constitutional protection until 1868, when the Fourteenth Amendment was adopted. The Fourteenth Amendment states: "All persons born or naturalized in the United States, and subject to the jurisdiction thereof, are citizens of the United States and of the State wherein they reside." This means that all persons born in the United States, except children born to foreign ambassadors and ministers, are citizens of this country regardless of the citizenship of their parents. (Congress has defined the United States for this purpose to include Puerto Rico, Guam, the Northern Marianas, and the Virgin Islands.) Although the Fourteenth Amendment does not make Native Americans citizens of the United States and of the states in which they live, Congress has done so.

The Fourteenth Amendment confers citizenship according to the principle of *jus soli*—by place of birth. In addition, Congress has granted, under certain conditions, citizenship at birth according to the principle of *jus sanguinis*—by blood. A child born to an American citizen living abroad is an American citizen if the

American parent has lived in the United States for ten years, including two after age 14.

NATURALIZATION Citizenship may also be acquired by either collective or individual **naturalization**, a legal action conferring citizenship upon an alien. The granting of citizenship to the people of the Northern Marianas in 1977 by an act of Congress is an example of collective naturalization. Individual naturalization requirements are determined by Congress. Today, with minor exceptions, nonenemy aliens over age 18 who have been lawfully admitted for permanent residence and who have resided in the United States for at least five years and in the state in which they are residing for at least six months are eligible for naturalization, which is finally conferred by a court. Any state or federal court of record in the United States or the Immigration and Naturalization Service (INS) can grant citizenship. The INS makes the necessary investigations. Any person denied citizenship after a hearing before an immigration officer may seek a *de novo* (completely new) hearing before a federal district judge.

Citizenship is granted if the judge or hearing officer is satisfied that the applicant has met all the requirements, renounces allegiance to his or her former country, swears to support and defend the Constitution and laws of the United States against all enemies, and promises to bear arms on behalf of the United States when required to do so by law. Those whose religious beliefs prevent them from bearing arms are allowed to take an oath swearing that, if called to duty, they will serve in the armed forces as noncombatants or will perform work of national importance under civilian direction. The court or INS then grants a certificate of naturalization.

Naturalized citizenship may be revoked by court order if the government can prove citizenship was secured by deception. In addition, citizenship, however acquired, may be renounced voluntarily. But citizenship cannot be taken from people because of what they have done—for committing certain crimes, for example, voting in foreign elections, or serving in foreign armies. Some actions, however, such as taking out citizenship in another country or swearing allegiance to another nation, may be taken into account as "highly persuasive evidence of a purpose to abandon citizenship." Even so, the government must prove that the citizen "not only voluntarily committed the expatriating act prescribed in the statute, but also intended to relinquish his citizenship."[2]

DUAL CITIZENSHIP Because each nation has complete authority to decide for itself the question of nationality, it is possible for a person to be considered a citizen by two or more nations. Dual citizenship is not unusual, especially for persons from nations that do not recognize the right of the individual to choose his or her own nationality, called the **right of expatriation**. (One of the issues of the War of 1812 was that England did not recognize sailors born in England as having abandoned their English citizenship on becoming naturalized American citizens.) Children born abroad to American citizens may also be citizens of the nation in which they were born. Children born in the United States of parents from a foreign nation may also be citizens of their parents' country. Dual citizenship carries negative as well as positive consequences; a person with dual citizenship may, for example, be subject to national service obligations and taxes in both countries.

Rights of American Citizens

An American citizen becomes a citizen of one of our states merely by residing in that state. "Residence," as used in the Fourteenth Amendment, means the place one calls home. The legal status of residence should not be confused with the fact of physical presence. A person may be living in Washington, D.C. but be a citizen of California—that is, consider California home and vote in that state. Residence is primarily a question of *intent*.

THE RIGHT OF CITIZENSHIP

Although natural-born Americans tend to take citizenship for granted, most naturalized citizens cherish it, for it represents hard work and a sincere commitment on their part. Would natural-born Americans appreciate citizenship more if they had to meet the same standards as foreign-born applicants?

Naturalization Requirements

An applicant for naturalization must:

1. Be over age 18.
2. Be lawfully admitted to the United States for permanent residence, and have resided in the United States for at least five years and in the state in which they are residing for at least six months.
3. File a petition of naturalization with a clerk of a court of record (federal or state) verified by two witnesses.
4. Be able to read, write, and speak English.
5. Possess a good moral character.
6. Understand and demonstrate an attachment to the history, principles, and form of government of the United States.
7. Demonstrate that he or she is well disposed toward the good order and happiness of the country.
8. Demonstrate that he or she does not now believe in, nor within the last ten years has ever believed in, advocated, or belonged to an organization that supports opposition to organized government, overthrow of government by violence, or the doctrines of world communism or any other form of totalitarianism.

Albert Einstein (1879–1955), his daughter *(right)*, and his secretary *(left)*, take the oath of American citizenship. A brilliant physicist known for formulating the theory of relativity, Einstein was born in Germany. Because he was Jewish, the Nazi government confiscated his property and revoked his citizenship in 1934, at which time he immigrated to the United States.

THE RIGHT TO TRAVEL ABROAD   Although the right of interstate travel is virtually unqualified, the right to international travel can be regulated within the bounds of due process. Under current law it is unlawful for citizens to leave or enter the United States without a valid passport (except as otherwise provided by the president, as has been done for travel to Mexico, Canada, and parts of the Caribbean). The president, acting through the secretary of state, may refuse to grant or may revoke a passport if the government concludes that a holder's activities in foreign countries are causing or are likely to cause serious damage to our national security or foreign policy.

THE RIGHT TO LIVE IN THE UNITED STATES   This right, which is not subject to any congressional limitation, is perhaps the most precious aspect of American citizenship. Aliens have no such right. They may be stopped on the high seas or at the borders and turned away if they fail to meet the terms and conditions stipulated by the Congress for admission into the United States. Today millions of people around the world are begging to come and live in the United States, but only American citizens have a constitutionally *guaranteed* right to do so.

Rights of Aliens

President Franklin Roosevelt, reminding us of our heritage as a haven for people fleeing religious and political persecution, opened his address to a convention of the Daughters of the American Revolution with the salutation, "Fellow immigrants and revolutionaries." Some Americans, however, are concerned that admitting so many people from abroad will dilute American traditions. Throughout our history debates have flared among those wishing to open our borders and those wishing to close them.

Congress has wide discretion in setting the numbers, terms, and conditions under which aliens can come and stay in the United States. By 1882 it began to restrict the entry of persons alleged to be "undesirable," such as prostitutes and revolutionaries. During World War I, Congress, for the first time, set limits on the number of aliens who could be admitted each year. The Immigration Act of 1924 created a system that discriminated against immigrants from southern Europe and southeastern Asia on the basis of national origin.

The United States has always drawn immigrants seeking opportunity and freedom. Here men, women, and children crowd the deck of the S.S. *Patria* as it approaches New York in December 1906.

In 1965, after years of debate, a new immigration law was adopted. It remains the basic legislation, although it has often been amended and was thoroughly revised in 1990. It is again under congressional review, and new basic legislation is likely in the near future.

The law sets an annual ceiling of 700,000 for nonamnesty, nonrefugee aliens allowed to come here as *permanent residents* until fiscal 1996, when the total is to be reduced to 675,000. Preference is given to immediate relatives of United States citizens and of permanent residents. There is an annual limit on immigrants from any single country of no more than 70 percent for family connection visas and employment-based immigrants (see Figure 6–1).

Prior to the 1990 amendment, quotas were filled almost exclusively on the basis of family reunification. To rectify this situation, the 1990 act created a "diversity" category to provide visas for immigrants from 34 countries, chiefly but not exclusively European, whether or not they already have relatives living in the United States. About 70 percent of all the permanently admitted aliens in the U.S., however, still come under a family reunification preference.

The law makes provision for granting 140,000 visas a year to people who have special job skills or who are needed to fill jobs for which U.S. workers are not available. The law also provides for special treatment for Hong Kong nationals, especially executives

FIGURE 6-1   Coming to America

SOURCE: Steven Kearsley, *San Francisco Chronicle*, June 21, 1993, p. A7.

Family-based immigrants — **445,000**
Spouses, children and siblings of U.S. citizens

Employment-based immigrants — **119,000**
Foreign workers, their spouses and children

Humanitarian — **227,000**
Political refugees who claim political asylum

Other categories — **76,000**
Amerasian children of U.S. servicemen, residents of Ireland and other nations whose quotas previously were reduced, employees of U.S. businesses operating in Hong Kong and displaced Tibetans.

Amnesty legalizations — **163,000**
Undocumented immigrants who took advantage of the 1986 amnesty program.

Illegal immigrants — **200,000**
The Census Bureau estimates that the U.S. population rises about 200,000 a year because of illegal immigrants.

We The People

Foreign-Born Population of the United States

- Never have so many immigrants lived in this country, although the foreign-born proportion of the population was larger earlier in this century, when the U.S. population was smaller.
- The place of birth of most immigrants has shifted from Europe to Asia and Latin America.
- 19.7 million, or just under 8 percent of the U.S. population, are foreign-born.
- Nearly 32 million persons speak a language other than English at home, and more than 40 percent of them say they do not speak English very well.
- The number of immigrants from Mexico and from Asia has more than doubled in the last decade.
- Projected population percentages for Los Angeles County for the year 2000 are 40 percent Hispanic, 34 percent white, 16 percent Asian, and 10 percent black.
- The Los Angeles Unified School District (the second largest in the nation) serves more than 625,000 students speaking 80 different languages, more than 83,000 of them foreign-born.

SOURCES: U.S. Department of Commerce, Bureau of the Census, and Barbara Vobejda, "A Nation in Transition: Census Reveals Striking Stratification of U.S. Society," *The Washington Post*, May 29, 1992, pp. A1, A18–A19.

and managers from U.S. companies in Hong Kong, who are facing the 1997 transfer of Hong Kong from the United Kingdom to China. Another provision allows for the admission of some well-to-do persons—"millionaire immigrants"—who are willing and able to invest a substantial sum in the United States to create or support a business that will provide jobs for Americans. There have been few takers for admission under this provision.

In addition to regularly admitted permanent resident aliens, more than 100,000 *political refugees* are admitted each year. Political refugees are defined by law as persons who have well-founded fears of persecution in their own countries based on their race, religion, nationality, social class, or political opinion. Although the number of political refugees allowed is 50,000 annually, after consultations with Congress the president may set, and has been setting, a higher number.

The attorney general, acting through the U.S. Immigration and Naturalization Service, may also grant *asylum* to persons already in the United States, at ports of entry, or in countries other than their own, if the attorney general agrees with the applicants that they, like political refugees, have well-founded fears of persecution in the country to which they would otherwise be returned, based on their race, religion, nationality, membership in a particular social group, or political opinion. It is not enough, however, that applicants face the same conditions, no matter how terrible, that all other citizens of their country face, or that they wish to escape from bad economic or political conditions. They must show *individual* danger of persecution. Where political conditions are extremely fluid, the Department of Justice can grant an individual "temporary protected status" while it tries to determine the peril the applicant actually faces at home.

The Immigration and Naturalization Service may turn back at the border persons seeking asylum when it considers their requests insubstantial, or it may even hold them in detention camps.[3] Further, the president may order the Coast Guard—as both George Bush and Bill Clinton did with respect to Haitian refugees—to stop persons on the high seas before they enter the territorial waters of the United States and return them to the country from which they have fled without determining whether they qualify as refugees.[4] Aliens do not have a constitutional right to enter the United States. Nonetheless, many people are willing to risk great danger to get here and detention once they arrive, just for the chance of being granted asylum.

Once in the United States, aliens are "subject to the full range of obligations, including the payment of taxes, imposed by the states' civil and criminal laws."[5] Aliens are counted in the census for the purpose of apportioning seats in the United States House of Representatives among the states. Aliens enjoy considerable constitutional protection while in the United States—no matter how they get here. Most provisions of the Constitution speak of the rights of persons, not just of citizens. States, for example, have no greater authority to interfere with an alien's freedom of religion than with a citizen's. State and local regulations directed at aliens must ensure that they receive the equal protection of the laws to which they are constitutionally entitled.

Undocumented Aliens: The Immigration Reform and Control Act of 1986

How should we deal with the millions of aliens, mostly from Mexico and other nations in Central and South America, who have illegally crossed our borders, not because they fear political persecution but because they see greater economic opportunity in the United States?[6] It is not a question of constitutional power, for "over no conceivable subject is the legislative power of Congress more complete than it is over the admission of aliens."[7] Rather, the problems are political and practical. The Immigration and Naturalization Service does not have the money or staff to patrol the thousands of miles of our southern and northern borders. Moreover, it is very difficult to track down undocumented aliens inside the United States, round them up, and expel them in a fashion consistent with practices and policies of a free society.

Once here, undocumented aliens do not find it hard to become invisible, especially in our larger cities, or to find jobs. Some employers prefer to hire them because they work for less money than those who are here lawfully, and they are also unprotected. Justice John Paul Stevens quoted one of the sponsors of the Immigration Reform and Control Act of 1986 as describing the vulnerability of this "subculture of human beings who are afraid to go the cops, afraid to go to a hospital, afraid to go to their employer who says, 'One peep out of you, buster, and you are down the road.'"[8]

Congress has been faced with conflicting pressures: from Hispanic groups concerned that making it illegal to hire undocumented workers will make employers hesitate to hire any Hispanics; from employers who do not want to keep costly records and have to investigate the legal status of everybody they hire; from employers of farm workers who want to be sure that they will have enough farm laborers to pick seasonal crops; from American workers who do not want undocumented workers being used to keep wages low; from city and local governmental officials who have to find the funds to provide social services for undocumented aliens. To deal with these conflicting pressures, in 1986 Congress enacted the Immigration Reform and Control Act, often known as Simpson-Mazzoli.

Today immigration policy is once again before the nation. In California, Florida, Texas, New York, and Illinois, where most of the undocumented aliens live, governors and legislators are calling on the national government to shoulder a greater share of the costs of social services for these aliens. Pressures are building to exclude undocumented aliens from admission to universities and colleges, from welfare programs, and from health care. But others insist that the contributions of undocumented aliens, as well as humanitarian considerations, oblige us to provide health care, welfare, and other social services. In 1982 the Supreme Court declared that states cannot constitutionally exclude children of undocumented aliens from the public schools or charge their parents a tuition fee.[9] Since it did so by a 5 to 4 vote, the issue is likely to be revisited.

We tend to consider U.S. immigration policy a purely internal matter, yet it clearly affects our relations with other nations, most especially with Mexico, as the lengthy negotiations over the North American Free Trade Agreement (NAFTA) demonstrated. Whereas officials of the United States view immigration policy as a matter of sovereignty, "Mexicans see it as a bilateral process that requires a bilateral policy."[10]

PROPERTY RIGHTS

Constitutional Protection of Property

Property does not have rights. People do. **Property rights** are the rights of an individual to own, use, rent, invest in, buy, and sell property. Historically, the close connection between liberty and ownership of property, between property and power, has been emphasized in American political thinking and American political institutions.

A major purpose of the framers of the Constitution was to establish a government strong enough to protect people's rights to use and enjoy their own property. At the same time, the framers wanted to limit government so it could not endanger that right. As a result, the framers included in the Constitution a variety of clauses regarding property.

When the Chinese ship *Golden Venture* ran aground off Rockaway Beach, New York, its cargo of 350 illegal aliens swam ashore or died in the attempt. Their urge to come to the United States was so strong that they had agreed to work under slave labor conditions to pay back the smugglers who brought them here.

The Simpson-Mazzoli Act

- Undocumented aliens who had lived continuously in the United States since January 1, 1982, were permitted to apply for amnesty for a limited time.
- Employers who knowingly hire illegal aliens may be fined from $250 to $5,000 per alien, and repeat offenders may be given a prison term of up to six months.
- Employers are subject to penalty if they discriminate against legal residents because they are foreign born.
- A certain number of aliens are allowed to come into the United States to serve as temporary farm workers.

Of the estimated 2 to 3 million aliens eligible for amnesty under the act, about 1.8 million applied for it by the May 4, 1987, deadline. Others did not apply because of costs, inability to document their status, or fear that they might expose family members to deportation. Although passage of the act was followed by a brief decrease in the number of undocumented aliens coming across our borders, it has not accomplished its objective of stemming the flow. Large numbers of undocumented aliens continue to live and work here, and the number continues to increase.

SOURCES: Dianna Solis, "Illegal Immigration by Mexicans, Despite Reform Laws, Nears '86 Record Level," *The Wall Street Journal,* June 3, 1991, p. A6; Ashley Dunn, "Phony Papers Destroy Immigration Control," *Los Angeles Times,* December 27, 1991, p. A3.

THE LEGAL TENDER AND CONTRACT CLAUSES Of special concern to the framers were the efforts of some state legislatures to protect debtors at the expense of their creditors by a variety of means, including issuing paper currency and setting aside private contracts. To prevent these practices, the Constitution forbids states from making anything except gold or silver *legal tender* for the payment of debts and from passing any "Law impairing the Obligation of Contracts."

The *contract clause*, Article I, Section 10, was designed to prevent states from extending the period during which debtors could meet their payments or otherwise get out of contractual obligations. The framers had in mind an ordinary contract between private persons. However, beginning with Chief Justice John Marshall, the Supreme Court expanded the coverage of the clause to prevent states from altering privileges previously conferred on corporations. In effect, the contract clause was used to protect property and to maintain the status quo at the expense of the power of the states to guard the public welfare. In the 1880s, however, the Court gradually began to restrict the coverage of the contract clause and to subject contracts to what in constitutional law is known as **police powers**—the power to protect the public health, safety, welfare, and morals. By 1934 the Supreme Court actually held that even contracts between individuals—the very ones the contract clause was intended to protect—could be modified by state law in order to avert social and economic catastrophe.[11] Although the contract clause is still invoked occasionally to challenge a state regulation of property, it is no longer a significant limitation on governmental power.

The Power of Eminent Domain:
What Happens When the Government Takes Our Property?

Both the national and state governments have the power of **eminent domain**—the power to take private property for public use—but the owner must be fairly compensated. This limitation, contained in the Fifth Amendment, was the first provision of the Bill of Rights to be *incorporated* within the Fourteenth Amendment—to be enforced as a limitation on state governments as well as on the national government. (For a discussion of incorporation, see Chapter 5.)[12]

What constitutes a "taking" for purposes of eminent domain?[13] The clause does not require compensation merely because governmental action may result in property loss. For example, if a zoning regulation restricts an area to single-family residential use and thus lowers the value of a particular property, no compensation is due. Ordinarily, but not always, the taking must be *direct*, and a person must lose title and control over the property. Sometimes, especially in recent years, the courts have found that a governmental regulation has gone "too far" and must be deemed a "taking" for which the government must pay compensation to its owners, even when title is left in the hands of the owners.[14] These are called **regulatory takings.** Thus, if a government creates landing and takeoff paths for airplanes over property adjacent to an airport, making the land no longer suitable for its prior use (say, raising chickens), compensation is warranted.

Nor is "just compensation" always easy to define. In case of a dispute, the final resolution is made by the courts. By and large, "the owner is entitled to receive what a willing buyer would pay in cash to a willing seller at the time of the taking."[15] An owner is not entitled to compensation for the personal value of an old, broken-down house that is loved dearly. It will still bring compensation only for an old, broken-down house.

The *taking clause* has received renewed judicial attention in the last several years as many state and local units strive to protect the environment and quality of life by regulating the terms and conditions under which land may be developed. In the late 1980s the Supreme Court began using the taking clause to review these governmental regulations. For example, the Supreme Court held that if a government has prevented a property owner from developing property by regulations that turned out to be unconstitutional, the owner is entitled to just compensation for the temporary taking, even if the government finally withdraws the regulation.[16] The Court also ruled that a government has engaged in a taking if it imposes an unrelated condition before issuing a building permit—requiring, for example, that the owner of a beach-front home allow the public to walk across the property to the beach as a condition for receiving a permit to enlarge the house.[17]

Due Process : New and Old

Perhaps the most difficult parts of the Constitution to understand are the clauses in the Fifth and Fourteenth Amendments that forbid national and state governments *to deny any person life, liberty, or property without due process of law.* These **due process clauses** have resulted in hundreds of Supreme Court decisions. Even so, it is impossible to explain due process precisely. In fact, the Supreme Court has refused to give *due process* a precise definition and has emphasized that "due process, unlike some legal rules, is not a technical conception with a fixed content unrelated to time, place and circumstances."[18]

PROCEDURAL DUE PROCESS   There are two kinds of due process: procedural and substantive. **Procedural due process** generally refers to the methods by which a law is enforced. But a law itself, as enacted, may violate the procedural due process requirement if it is too vague or if it creates an improper presumption of guilt. A *vague statute* fails to provide adequate warning and does not contain sufficient guidelines for law enforcement officials, juries, and courts.

A statute that creates an improper presumption of guilt denies due process by shifting the burden of proof from the government to the accused person. Laws presuming, for example, that all marijuana or cocaine in a person's possession must have been obtained illegally have been declared unconstitutional. But the Court did uphold a presumption with respect to heroin. As virtually all heroine is illegally imported, it is therefore not unreasonable to presume that a person who possesses heroin obtained it illegally.[19]

Traditionally, however, procedural due process refers not to the law itself but to the way in which a law is *applied*. To paraphrase Daniel Webster's famous definition, it requires a procedure that *hears* before it condemns, proceeds upon inquiry,

The Pitfalls of Law Making

When faced with vexing social problems, we often mutter, "There ought to be a law." But devising clear laws and procedures in accordance with the Constitution and its guarantees of due process is easier said than done, as these examples show.

Some Statutes Declared Void for Vagueness

- A statute making it a crime to treat "contemptuously" the American flag.
- A vagrancy ordinance classifying vagrants as "rogues and vagabonds," "dissolute persons who go about begging," "common night walkers," and so on.
- An ordinance requiring persons who loiter or wander the streets to provide "credible and reliable" identification and to account for their presence when required by a police officer.

A Statute Not Considered Vague

- An ordinance requiring a license for businesses selling any items "designed or marketed for use with illegal cannabis or drugs"—what are commonly known as "headshops."

Some Laws Declared to Deny Substantive Due Process

- A school board regulation requiring teachers to cease teaching past the fourth month of pregnancy and barring them from returning to the classroom until three months after the birth of a child.
- A state law permitting confinement of nondangerous mentally ill persons against their wishes.

The Coast Guard confiscates cocaine off the coast of South Florida. The ship that smuggled the drug was also confiscated, and the money derived from its sale was applied toward drug prevention programs.

Is a college education a constitutional right?

Scott E. Ewing was dismissed by the University of Michigan from a six-year combined undergraduate and medical educational program after failing an examination required to qualify for the final two years. His request to retake the examination was denied. He brought an action in a federal district court, alleging that, because every other medical student who had failed the examination had routinely been given at least a second chance to take the test, he had a property interest in his continued enrollment in the program. He contended his dismissal was arbitrary and capricious and was thus in violation of his substantive due process rights guaranteed by the Fourteenth Amendment. The university said he had been dismissed for proper academic reasons, that no one has a constitutional right to a second examination, and that what it had done was perfectly reasonable.

Did Ewing have a due process property interest to continued enrollment free from arbitrary state action?

Did the state of Michigan violate Ewing's substantive property right in this instance?

You Decide!

"What's so great about due process? Due process got me ten years."
Drawing by Handelsman. © 1972 The New Yorker Magazine, Inc.

and renders judgment only after a trial or some kind of hearing. Originally, procedural due process was limited to criminal prosecutions, but it now applies to most kinds of governmental proceedings. It is required, for instance, in juvenile hearings, disbarment proceedings, proceedings to determine eligibility for welfare payments, revocation of drivers' licenses, and disciplinary proceedings in state universities and public schools.

Procedural due process has taken on new importance with the expanded interpretation of the words "liberty" and "property." The liberty that is protected is more than freedom from being thrown into jail, and the property that is secured goes beyond the mere ownership of real estate, things, or money. Rather, liberty includes "the right of the individual to contract, to engage in any of the common occupations of life, to acquire useful knowledge, to marry, to establish a home and bring up children, to worship God according to the dictates of his own conscience, and generally to enjoy those common law privileges long recognized as essential to the orderly pursuit of happiness by free men."[20] The property protected by due process includes a variety of rights that may be conferred by state law, such as certain kinds of licenses, protection from being fired from some jobs except for just cause (for example, incompetence) and according to certain procedures, protection from deprivation of certain pension rights, and so on.

This expansion of the meanings of liberty and property has blurred the distinctions between liberty rights and property rights. Moreover, it has lessened the difference between a *right* and a *privilege*. Today public welfare, housing, education, employment, professional licenses, and so on, are increasingly becoming matters of entitlement, that is, a legal right. Their denial thus may raise some due process questions.

Nevertheless, "the range of interests protected by procedural due process is not infinite." Not every "grievous loss visited upon a person by the State is sufficient to invoke the procedural protections of the due process clause."[21] Whether or not an interest is protected by due process depends on the nature of the interest, not its importance to the individual. Faculty members in public institutions, for instance, are not entitled to procedural due process before being denied tenure because they have no constitutional right to teaching jobs. However, if public employees, including teachers, are given tenure rights by *law or institutional policies*, they are entitled to due process before they may be deprived of property rights or jobs.[22] Since the due process clause applies only to the action of governments, faculty members at private institutions are not entitled to due process, but they, along with other employees, public and private, are protected by provisions of federal and state civil rights laws.

"Once it is determined that due process applies, the question remains what process is due." What is *due* varies with the kind of interest involved, the reliability of the procedures used, and the governmental purposes to be served.[23] In a federal courtroom, due process requires the careful observance of the provision of the Bill of Rights as outlined in Amendments Four through Eight. In a state courtroom, due process requires the careful observance of all provisions of the Bill of Rights except indictment by grand jury and jury trials in civil cases. The question of what is *due* in other kinds of proceedings is what must be done to ensure *fundamental fairness*. It is hard to generalize because many kinds of proceedings are involved, but at a minimum the person involved must have adequate notice and an opportunity to be heard.

SUBSTANTIVE DUE PROCESS   Procedural due process places limits on *how* governmental power may be exercised; **substantive due process** places limits on *what* a government may do. Procedural due process pertains to the *procedures* of the law, substantive due process to the *content* of the law. Procedural due process mainly limits the executive and judicial branches; substantive due process mainly limits the legislative branch. Substantive due process means that an "unreasonable" law, even if properly passed and properly applied, is unconstitutional. It means that there are certain things governments *should not be allowed to do*, no matter how they do it.

Before 1937, substantive due process was used primarily to protect *liberty of contract*—that is, business liberty, or the right of employers to make contracts with employees freely, without government interference. Indeed, the adoption of the doctrine of substantive due process and the simultaneous expansion of the meaning of liberty and property made the Supreme Court, for a time, the final judge of our economic and industrial life. During this period the Supreme Court was dominated by conservative jurists who considered almost all social welfare legislation unreasonable. They used the due process clause to strike down laws setting maximum hours of labor, establishing minimum wages, regulating prices, and forbidding employers to fire workers for union membership.

The trouble with the substantive interpretation of due process is that what a person, including a judge, thinks is a "reasonable" law depends on economic, social, and political views rather than on legal doctrine. In democracies, elected officials are supposed to accommodate opposing notions of reasonableness and to decide what regulations of liberty and property are needed. When the Supreme Court substitutes its own ideas of reasonableness for those of the legislature, it acts like a superlegislature.

In response to this criticism, the Supreme Court since 1937 has largely refused to apply the doctrine of substantive due process in reviewing laws regulating the economy. The court is now of the view that deciding what constitutes reasonable regulations of business and commercial life is a legislative, not a judicial, responsibility. As long as the justices find a conceivable connection between a law regulating business and the promotion of the public welfare, the Supreme Court will not interfere.

Substantive due process, resting on the notion that laws must be reasonable, has deep roots in concepts of natural law and a long history in the American constitutional tradition. For most Americans most of the time, it is not enough merely to say that a law reflects the wishes of the popular or legislative majority. We also want our laws to be just, and we continue to rely heavily on judges to decide what is just. In Chapter 16 we look again at the tensions between democratic procedures and judicial uses of substantive due process to review the constitutionality of the acts of elected officials.

PRIVACY RIGHTS

The most important extension of substantive due process in recent decades has been its expansion to protect the right of privacy, especially marital privacy. Although there is no mention of the right of privacy in the Constitution, the Supreme Court has put together some elements from the First, Fourth, Fifth, Ninth, and Fourteenth Amendments to recognize that personal privacy is one of the rights protected by the Constitution.

There are three aspects of this right: (1) the right to be free from governmental surveillance and intrusion, especially in marital matters; (2) the right not to have private affairs made public by the government; and (3) the right to be free in thought and belief from governmental compulsion.[24]

Congress showed concern about the first kind of privacy in the Family Educational Rights Act of 1974 and the Privacy Act of 1974. These laws limit record-keeping and record-disclosing activities of schools and universities that receive federal funds; place restraints on files kept by federal agencies; and, under certain conditions, give individuals access to government files in order to correct

Computers and Privacy Rights

- Do the First and Fourth Amendments protect persons from having seized computers "searched"?
- Are electronic data bases of personal information subject to Fourth Amendment protection from governmental search and seizure?
- Does the public have the right of access to computerized governmental files?
- Does the government have the right to censor pornographic electronic transmissions?
- Does the government have the right to prosecute computer hackers?

Thinking it Through

Eight members of the U.S. Supreme Court said that even if it is assumed that Ewing had such a right, the responsibility for determining academic matters belongs to the faculty, and judges should interfere only if there is "a substantial departure from accepted academic norms as to demonstrate that the faculty did not exercise professional judgment and acted clearly in an arbitrary and capricious manner."

Justice Lewis F. Powell, Jr., concurred, but would not even concede that Ewing might, for purposes of the decision, have a substantive due process property right not to be dismissed by a state university in an arbitrary manner. You might want to read this short opinion. You can find it in many libraries. Give this citation to the librarian: *Regents of the University of Michigan v Ewing*, 474 US 214 (1985).

Drug Testing

In recent years Fourth Amendment questions have been raised about the constitutionality of testing blood and urine for drugs. Although agreeing that such tests intrude upon expectations of privacy and are searches within the meaning of the Fourth Amendment, the Supreme Court held that the federal regulations requiring such tests for railroad workers involved in accidents do not violate the Fourth Amendment, even as used without any warrant requirement. Justice Thurgood Marshall, bitterly dissenting, wrote, "The majority's acceptance of a dragnet blood and urine testing ensures that the first, and worst, casualty of the war on drugs will be the precious liberties of our citizens."*

*Skinner v Railway Labor Executives, 489 US 602 (1989).

One controversial aspect of constitutional protection of privacy relates to government control of abortions.

information about themselves. But privacy, although highly valued in the abstract, has often run afoul of other rights, such as freedom of the press. When in conflict with these other rights, it has not fared well before either Congress or the courts.

Abortion Rights

The most controversial aspect of constitutional protection for privacy relates to the extent of state power to regulate abortions. In *Roe v Wade*, decided in 1973, the Supreme Court ruled: (1) during the first trimester of a woman's pregnancy, it is an unreasonable and therefore unconstitutional interference with her liberty and privacy rights for a state to set any limits on her choice to have an abortion or on her doctor's medical judgments about how to carry it out; (2) during the second trimester, the state's interest in protecting the health of women becomes compelling, and a state may make a reasonable regulation about how, where, and when abortions may be performed; and (3) during the third trimester, when the life of the fetus outside the womb becomes viable, the state's interest in protecting the unborn child is so important that the state can proscribe abortions altogether, except when necessary to preserve the life or health of the mother.[25]

After two decades of heated public debate and attempts by both Presidents Ronald Reagan and George Bush to select Supreme Court justices who could be expected to vote to reverse *Roe v Wade,* on the final day of the 1991–92 court term the decision was reaffirmed. A bitterly divided Rehnquist Court, by a five-person majority (O'Connor, Kennedy, Souter, Blackmun, and Stevens) upheld the view that the due process clauses of the Constitution protect a woman's liberty to chose an abortion prior to viability. The Court, however, held that the right to have an abortion prior to viability is subject to state regulation that does not "unduly burden" it. In other words, states may make *reasonable* regulations on how a woman exercises her right to an abortion so long as "the State does not prohibit any woman from making the ultimate decision to terminate her pregnancy before viability."[26]

Applying the undue burden test, the Court held, for instance, that states can prohibit the use of state funds and facilities for performing abortions, that a state may make a minor's right to an abortion conditional on her first notifying at least one parent or a judge, that a state may condition an abortion on a 24-hour waiting period during which a doctor must inform the woman about alternatives in a

state-prescribed talk. On the other hand, a state may not condition a woman's right to an abortion on her first notifying her husband.[27]

Sexual Orientation Rights

Although there is debate as to how much constitutional protection is provided for marital privacy, the Supreme Court has refused to extend any such protection to relations between homosexuals. By a 5 to 4 vote, the Court refused to declare unconstitutional a Georgia law that criminalized consensual sodomy as practiced by homosexuals. That homosexual conduct occurs in the privacy of the home, said the majority, does not affect the result. Justice Harry A. Blackmun, in dissent, wrote that the "Constitution embodies a promise that a certain private sphere of individual liberty will be kept largely beyond the reach of government," that the Court has long recognized that certain "decisions are properly for the individual to make," and that there are certain places, such as the home, where the government should intrude only in extreme circumstances.[28]

Because of the strong emotions on both sides of this issue, the right of privacy as an element of substantive due process is one of the developing edges of constitutional law, one about which people both on and off the court have strong feelings. How the Supreme Court handles privacy issues has become front page news.

RIGHTS OF PERSONS ACCUSED OF CRIMES

Freedom from Unreasonable Searches and Seizures

According to the Fourth Amendment "The right of the people to be secure in their persons, houses, papers, and effects, against unreasonable searches and seizures, shall not be violated, and no Warrants shall issue, but upon probable cause, supported by Oath or affirmation, and particularly describing the place to be searched, and the persons or things to be seized." Despite what we sometimes see in television police dramas and read in the press, law enforcement officers have no general right to break down doors and invade homes. They are not supposed to search people except under certain conditions, and they have no right to arrest them except under certain circumstances.[29]

Seizures, or what we now call police detentions and arrests, are in fact given less protection than searches of our property. Police may arrest people without warrants in public places, provided there is *probable cause*—a fair probability that the persons in question have committed or are about to commit crimes. No later than two days after making an arrest, the police must take the arrested person to a magistrate so that the latter—not just the police—can decide whether probable cause existed to justify the warrantless arrest.[30] Probable cause, however, does not, except in extreme emergencies, justify a warrantless arrest of people in their own homes.

Not every time the police stop a person to ask questions or even to seek that person's consent to a search is there a seizure or detention requiring probable cause or a warrant. If all that happens is that the police ask questions or even seek consent to search that individual's person or possessions in a noncoercive atmosphere, there is no detention. "So long as a reasonable person would feel free 'to disregard the police and go about his business,' the encounter is consensual and no reasonable suspicion is required. The encounter will not trigger Fourth Amendment scrutiny unless it loses its consensual nature." But if the person refuses to answer questions or consent to a search, and the police, by either physical force or a show of authority, restrain the movement of the person, even though there is no arrest, the Fourth Amendment comes into play.[31] For example, if police approach people in airports and request identification, this act by itself does not constitute a detention. The

Deadly Force

Under the common law, police officers apprehending a fleeing, suspected felon can use weapons that might result in such a felon's serious injury, even death. But the Fourth Amendment places substantial limits on the use of what is called "deadly force." It is unconstitutional to shoot at an apparently unarmed, fleeing, suspected felon unless the officer has probable cause to believe that the suspect poses a significant threat of death or serious injury to the officer or others. Also, when feasible, the officer must first warn the suspect: "Halt or I'll shoot."

Police often have reason to stop cars and check their passengers and contents. If the police use physical force to detain a person, then the Fourth Amendment may come into play, but here the young driver cooperates with the trooper who stopped him.

same is true if police ask bus passengers for consent to search their luggage for drugs. But if the police do more, especially after consent is refused, then their actions create an "in-custody detention" that requires them to have some objective justification for the search beyond mere suspicion.

The Constitution does not forbid searches, only "unreasonable" ones. "It is a cardinal principle that searches conducted outside the judicial process, without prior approval by a judge or a magistrate, are per se unreasonable under the Fourth Amendment—subject only to a few specially established and well-delineated exceptions."[32] In fact, however, the number of exceptions keeps growing, and they are not well delineated. And there are various administrative searches by nonpolice government agents, such as teachers and health officials, not designed to uncover crimes. Rules governing the conduct of such administrative searches are more lenient than are those for searches by police investigating crimes.

Where the Fourth Amendment applies, the exceptions to the general rule against warrantless searches and seizures of what is found by police and customs officials are as follows:

1. *The Automobile Exception:* The exception is justified in part because of the mobility of automobiles and in part because persons are not entitled to the same expectations of privacy in their automobiles as in their homes or other places. If officers have probable cause to believe that an automobile is being used to commit a crime, even a traffic offense, or that it contains persons who have committed crimes, or that it contains evidence of crimes or contraband, they may stop the automobile, detain the persons found therein, and search them and any containers or packages found inside the car.[33]

2. *The Terry Exception:* First discussed in *Terry v Ohio*, these brief investigatory stops and searches were originally justified only when officers had reason to believe they were dealing with armed and dangerous persons, but they have subsequently been expanded to cover stops when the police have reason to believe that a person has committed or is about to commit a criminal offense. The intrusion permitted under a *Terry* search is limited to a quick pat-down to check for weapons that might be used to assault the arresting officer, to check for contraband, to determine identity, or to maintain briefly the status quo while obtaining more information.[34] If an officer stops and frisks a suspect to look for weapons and finds criminal evidence that might justify an arrest, then the officer can make a full search.[35] To illustrate: An officer, acting on an informer's tip, approached a man sitting in a car. The officer ordered the suspect to get out of the car, but the suspect merely rolled down the window. The officer saw a bulge on the suspect's waistband. He reached over into the car and removed a gun from the suspect's waistband. The officer arrested the suspect, although the mere possession of a weapon is not a crime, made a search, and found heroin.[36]

3. *Searches Subsequent to Valid Arrest:* When making a lawful arrest, either with an arrest warrant or because of probable cause, police may make a warrantless search of persons involved, the areas under their immediate control, and all the possessions they take with them to the place of detention. And police may make a protective sweep of the immediate area to be sure it does not harbor other dangerous persons.[37]

4. *Searches for Evidence:* When there is probable cause to make an arrest, even if one is not made, limited searches are permitted if necessary to preserve easily-disposed-of evidence, such as scrapings under fingernails.[38]

5. *Inventory Searches:* Searches that are part of the routine procedures of an arrest are permissible, provided there are established rules for inventory searches so

that such a search does not become "a ruse for a general rummaging in order to discover incriminating evidence."[39]

6. *Consent:* Searches based on voluntary consent are allowed, even if the persons who give the consent are not told they have a right to refuse to grant permission.[40]

7. *Border Searches:* Searches of persons and the goods they bring with them are permissible at border crossings.[41] The border search exception also permits officials to open mail entering the country if they have "reasonable cause" to suspect it contains merchandise imported contrary to the law.[42] (The border search exception does not extend to searches by Puerto Rican authorities of persons coming from the continental United States; such persons are not making an international crossing.)[43]

8. *Plain-View Exception:* The plain-view exception permits officers to seize evidence without a warrant if: (1) they are lawfully in a position from which the evidence can be viewed; (2) it is immediately apparent to them that the items they observe are evidence of a crime or are contraband; and (3) they have probable cause—a reasonable suspicion will not do—that the evidence uncovered is contraband or evidence of a crime.[44]

9. *Exigent Circumstances:* Searches are permissible under "exigent circumstances," that is, when officers do not have time to secure a warrant before evidence is destroyed, or a criminal escapes capture, or when there is need "to protect or preserve life or avoid serious injury." An example of exigent circumstances is that fire fighters and police may enter a burning building without a warrant and may remain there for a reasonable time to investigate the cause of the blaze after the fire has been extinguished. However, after the fire has been put out, the emergency is not to be used as an excuse to make an exhaustive, warrantless search for evidence not in plain sight.[45] Films, books and other materials that might be protected by the First Amendment may be seized under the exigent-circumstances exception only if there are multiple copies of the seized materials, most of which are left undisturbed.

"The court finds itself on the horns of a dilemma. On the one hand, wiretap evidence is inadmissible, and on the other hand, I'm dying to hear it."
Drawing by Handelsman. © 1972 The New Yorker Magazine, Inc.

Outside these exceptions, a police search without consent is constitutionally unreasonable unless it has been authorized by a valid **search warrant,** issued by a magistrate after the police indicate under oath that they have *probable cause* to justify its issuance. Magistrates must perform this function in a neutral and detached manner and not serve merely as rubber stamps for the police.

The Constitution not only ordinarily requires a search warrant, but it also requires a specific one because *general search warrants*—warrants that authorize police to search a particular place or person without limitation—are unconstitutional. When a magistrate issues a warrant, the warrant must describe: (1) what places are to be searched, and (2) what things are to be seized. And a warrant is needed to search a person in any place he or she has an "expectation of privacy that society is prepared to recognize as reasonable," for example, in a hotel room, in a rented home, in a friend's apartment.[46] In short, the Fourth Amendment protects people, not places, from unreasonable governmental intrusions.

Wire Tapping and Electronic Surveillance

Scientific inventions have confronted judges with new problems in applying the Fourth Amendment. Obviously, the writers of the Fourth Amendment intended such physical objects as books, papers, letters, and other kinds of documents to be protected from seizure by the government except in cases in which magistrates had issued search warrants. But what of overhearing phone conversations by tapping

Does the Fourth Amendment protect against judicially ordered surgery?

At 1:00 A.M. on July 18, 1982, Ralph E. Watkinson was closing his shop for the night, when someone pointing a gun came toward him. Watkinson drew his own gun and fired, the fire was returned, and Watkinson was hit in the leg. He watched his assailant flee, apparently wounded on the left side. Later that night Rudolph Lee, Jr., suffering from a gunshot wound to his left chest, was identified by Watkinson as the man who shot him. Lee was charged with the crime. Shortly thereafter the Commonwealth of Virginia moved in a state court for an order directing Lee to undergo surgery to remove (in effect, search for) an object thought to be a bullet lodged under his left collarbone.

Does such a search violate the Fourth Amendment?

phone wires, or using electronic devices to eavesdrop, or using secret video cameras to make videotapes? In *Olmstead v United States* (1928) a bare majority of the Supreme Court held there was no unconstitutional search unless seizure of physical objects or actual physical entry into a premise was involved. Justices Oliver Wendell Holmes and Louis D. Brandeis, in dissent, argued that the Constitution should keep up with the times; the "dirty business" of wiretapping produced the same evil invasion of privacy the framers had in mind when they wrote the Fourth Amendment.[47]

Forty years later, in *Katz v United States* (1967), the Supreme Court adopted the Holmes-Brandeis position:

> The Fourth Amendment protects people—and not simply "areas"—against unreasonable searches and seizures. Wherever a man may be [subsequently modified and limited to those places where a person has a legitimate expectation of privacy that society is prepared to recognize as reasonable],[48] he is entitled to know that he will remain free from unreasonable searches and seizures.[49]

The Exclusionary Rule

Combining the Fourth Amendment prohibition against unreasonable searches with the Fifth Amendment injunction that persons shall not be compelled to be witnesses against themselves, the Supreme Court ruled, in *Mapp v Ohio* (1961), that evidence obtained unconstitutionally cannot be used in a criminal trial as part of the government's main case against persons from whom it was seized.[50] This is what is called the **exclusionary rule**. It was adopted in large part to prevent police misconduct. Because police are seldom prosecuted for making illegal searches and often can't afford to pay civil damages, the justices believed the exclusionary rule was the best—and maybe the only—sanction.

Critics of the exclusionary rule, including Chief Justice William H. Rehnquist, question why criminals should go free just because of police misconduct or ineptness. So far the Supreme Court has refused to abandon the rule. It has started making some exceptions to it, however, such as in cases in which police have relied in good faith on a search warrant that subsequently turned out to be improperly granted.[51]

The exclusionary rule covers only trials of those from whom the evidence was unconstitutionally seized, as one citizen, Jack Payner, found out. Internal Revenue Service agents, aided by a private investigator and operating in the best tradition of television police dramas, broke into Payner's banker's hotel room after a female undercover agent had lured the banker out to dinner. The agents "borrowed" the banker's briefcase, photographed documents, put the original documents back, and returned the briefcase. This "caper" was clearly a deliberate intrusion into the banker's privacy and a violation of his Fourth Amendment rights. Nonetheless, the evidence was allowed to be used to convict Payner, one of the banker's customers, of income tax evasion. Payner could expect neither privacy in his banker's briefcase nor any ownership of the documents taken from it.[52]

The Right to Remain Silent

During the seventeenth century, certain special courts in England forced confessions of heresy and sedition from religious dissenters. The British privilege against self-incrimination developed in response to these practices. Because they were familiar with this history, the framers of our Bill of Rights included in the Fifth Amendment the provision that persons shall not be compelled to testify against themselves in criminal prosecutions. This protection against self-incrimination is designed to strengthen a fundamental principle of Anglo-American justice: No person has an obligation to prove innocence. Rather, the burden is on the government to prove guilt.

The privilege against self-incrimination applies literally only in criminal prosecutions, but it has always been interpreted to protect any person subject to questioning by any agency of government, such as a congressional committee. It is not enough, however, to contend that answers might be embarrassing or might lead to loss of a job or even to civil suits; persons must have a reasonable fear that the answers might support a criminal prosecution or "furnish a link in the chain of evidence needed to prosecute" a crime.[53]

Sometimes authorities would rather have information from witnesses than prosecute them. Congress has established procedures so that prosecutors and congressional committees may secure a *grant of immunity* for such a witness. After immunity has been granted, a witness no longer has a constitutional right to refuse to testify. A person granted this immunity can still be prosecuted for crimes subject to such investigations, but the government cannot use the information directly derived from the compelled testimony in any subsequent prosecution. This grant of immunity can be a formidable bar to successful prosecution, as was indicated by the government's inability to prosecute successfully Oliver North and others involved in the Iran-Contra affair.

The Miranda Warning

Police questioning of suspects is a key procedure in solving crimes. It can, however, be easily abused. Police officers sometimes forget or ignore the constitutional rights of suspects, especially those who are frightened and ignorant. Unauthorized detention and lengthy interrogation to wring confessions from suspects, common practice in police states, until recently were not unknown in the United States.

What good is the presumption of innocence if, long before the accused are brought before the court, they are detained and forced to prove their innocence to the police? Judges have done much to stamp out such police brutality. The Supreme Court has ruled that admission into evidence of a coerced confession violates the self-incrimination clause, deprives a person of the assistance of counsel guaranteed by the Sixth and Fourteenth Amendments, deprives a person of due process, and undermines the entire proceeding.[54]

Federal and state laws require police officers to take those whom they have arrested before magistrates right away so that the magistrates may inform them of their constitutional rights and allow them to get in touch with friends and seek legal advice. Despite these requirements, police were often tempted to quiz suspects first, trying to get them to confess before a magistrate informed them of their constitutional right to remain silent.

To put an end to such practices, the Supreme Court, in *Miranda v Arizona* (1966), announced that no conviction—federal or state—could stand if evidence introduced at the trial had been obtained by the police during "custodial interrogation," unless suspects have been: (1) notified that they are free to remain silent; (2) warned that what they say may be used against them in court; (3) told that they have a right to have attorneys present during questioning; (4) informed that if they cannot afford to hire their own lawyers, attorneys will be provided for them; and (5) permitted to terminate any stage of the police interrogation. If suspects answer questions in the absence of an attorney, the burden is on the prosecution to demonstrate that suspects knowingly and intelligently gave up their rights to remain silent and to have their own lawyers present. Failure to comply with these requirements leads to reversal of a conviction, even if other evidence is sufficient to establish guilt.[55]

Critics of the *Miranda* decision believe the Court has unnecessarily and severely limited the ability of the police to bring criminals to justice. The importance of pretrial interrogations is underscored by the fact that roughly 90 percent of all criminal convictions result from guilty pleas and never reach a full trial. Nevertheless, despite sustained attack, the Supreme Court has refused to reverse *Miranda*, although it has modified its original ruling to some extent. In order to deter *perjury* (lying under oath), evidence obtained contrary to the *Miranda* guidelines can be used to attack the credibility of defendants who offer contradictory testimony at their trials.

Thinking it Through

The Supreme Court previously sustained the right of a state, under proper circumstances and for proper reasons, to compel persons to submit to blood tests. In the Watkinson case, there was no question about lack of proper judicial and legal procedures: The state had more than a warrant for this "search"; it had a valid order of a state judge. Nonetheless, a unanimous Court found this to be an unreasonable search. The state failed, the Court concluded, to demonstrate such a compelling need for the bullet to justify so substantial an intrusion upon the suspect's privacy and security interests.*

In this rare example, a search was declared unconstitutional not because of improper procedures but because it intruded, under the circumstances, beyond the realm of the government's proper concerns.

What does such a case tell you about the guidelines for interpreting the Constitution? Did the Court follow the literal words of the Constitution, the intentions of the framers, or were the justices applying their interpretations of the current sense of justice? Which intentions of which framers? (Remember the framers did not intend the Fourth Amendment to apply to the states at all.) How is the Court to know which interpretation of the current sense of justice to follow?

*Winston v Lee, 470 US 753 (1985).

The Minibill of Rights: Rights in the Original Constitution

1. Writ of *habeas corpus*
2. No bills of attainder
3. No *ex post facto* laws
4. No titles of nobility
5. Trial by jury in national courts
6. Protection for citizens as they move from one state to another, including the right to travel
7. Protects against use of crime of treason to restrict other activities and limits punishment for treason
8. Guarantee that each state has a republican form of government
9. No religious test oaths as a condition for holding a federal office.

Even though most of the framers did not think a Bill of Rights was necessary, they considered certain rights important enough to be included in the original Constitution. These include the right of a writ of *habeas corpus* and protection against *ex post facto* laws and bills of attainder.

The Writ of *Habeas Corpus*

Foremost among constitutional rights is the guarantee that the **writ of *habeas corpus*** will be available unless suspended in time of rebellion or invasion. Literally meaning, "produce the body," this writ is a court order directing any official having a person in custody to produce the prisoner in court and to explain to the judge why the prisoner is being held. Permission to suspend the writ is found in the article setting forth the powers of Congress so, presumably, only Congress has the right to suspend it.

As originally used, the writ was merely a court inquiry to determine whether a person was being held in custody as the result of an act of a court with proper jurisdiction. But over the years it has developed into a remedy "available to effect discharge from any confinement contrary to the Constitution or fundamental law."[56] Persons being held apply, usually through an attorney, for release and state why they believe they are being held unlawfully. The judge then orders the jailer to show cause why the writ should not be issued. If a judge finds a petitioner is being detained unlawfully, the judge may order the prisoner's immediate release. Although state judges lack jurisdiction to issue writs of *habeas corpus* to find out why national authorities are holding persons, federal district judges may do so to find out if state and local officials are holding people "in violation of the Constitution or laws or treaties of the United States."[57]

In recent years a controversy has erupted between those who believe federal judges should be given wide discretion to issue writs of *habeas corpus* in order to protect constitutional rights and those who believe the writ has been abused by state prisoners to touch off an endless and unessential round of reviews, which sometimes lead to convictions being set aside by a federal judge *after* the matter has been carefully reviewed by at least two state courts. As evidence, critics point to the many prisoners on death row who have successfully used *habeas corpus* to raise objection after objection, delaying the execution of their sentence for years.

Partly because of this criticism, partly from concern for maintaining the principles of federalism, and partly in response to a growing overload on the federal courts, the Supreme Court, under the leadership of Chief Justice Rehnquist, has severely restricted the use of *habeas corpus* by federal judges. For example, if a state court has already provided an opportunity for persons to present the argument that the evidence used against them was unconstitutionally obtained in violation of the Fourth Amendment, a federal district judge may no longer review that question again.[58] The Supreme Court has also instructed federal judges not to entertain a second *habeas corpus* petition from a state court that would raise again an issue that could have been presented in a first petition unless the petitioner can demonstrate *cause and prejudice*; that is, the burden is on petitioners to show that there was a valid reason why they had not raised their complaints at the time of their first petition, and that they have actually been prejudiced by the failure of the courts to consider their arguments about why they have been denied due process.[59]

Ex Post Facto Laws and Bills of Attainder

The Constitution forbids both the national and the state governments from passing *ex post facto* laws and enacting bills of attainder (Article I, Sections 9 and 10).

An ***ex post facto* law** is a retroactive criminal law that works to the disadvantage of an individual. Examples would include a law making a particular act a crime that was

The "Miranda" warning is read to suspects by a police officer before questioning them to inform them of their rights, such as the right to remain silent and the right to have an attorney present.

not a crime when committed, increasing punishment for a crime after the crime was committed, or lessening proof necessary to convict for a crime after it was committed. The prohibition does not prevent the passage of retroactive penal laws that work to the benefit of an accused—a law decreasing punishment, for example. Nor does the prohibition prevent passage of retroactive civil laws. Income tax rates as applied to income already earned, for example, may be increased, as was done in 1993.

A **bill of attainder** is a legislative act inflicting punishment, including deprivation of property, without judicial trial on named individuals or members of a specified group. For example, Congress enacted a bill of attainder in conflict with this prohibition when it named three federal employees in an appropriations bill and declared they should receive no compensation from the federal treasury, other than for military or jury services, unless reappointed to office by the president with the consent of the Senate.

THE SHORT AND NOT TOO HAPPY LIFE OF JOHN CROOK

Evidence in the popular press affirms that many people consider the rights of persons accused of crime to be less important than other civil liberties. But, as Justice Felix Frankfurter observed, "The history of liberty has largely been the history of observance of procedural safeguards." Further, these safeguards have frequently "been forged in controversies involving not very nice people."[60]

The rights of persons accused of crime by the national government can be found in the Constitution and in the Fourth, Fifth, Sixth, and Eighth Amendments. To gain some idea of how these constitutional safeguards are applied, let us follow the fortunes and misfortunes of a fictitious character, John Crook, as he is prosecuted for a federal crime.

John Crook sent circulars through the mail selling shares in a nonexistent gold mine—an action contrary to dozens of federal laws. When postal offices uncovered these activities, they went to the district court and secured from a United States magistrate a warrant to arrest Crook and another warrant to search his home for copies of the circulars. They found Crook at home and read the *Miranda* warning to him, emphasizing especially his *right to remain silent* and *to have the assistance of counsel.* They showed him the warrant, arrested him for using the mails to defraud, and found and seized some of the circulars mentioned in the search warrant.

The Preliminary Hearing and Right to Counsel

Crook was promptly brought before a federal district judge, who again emphasized that Crook had a constitutional right to assistance of counsel. Judges have a positive obligation to ensure that all persons subject to any kind of custodial interrogation are represented by lawyers.[61] Unless the record clearly shows that the accused were fully aware of what they were doing and gave up the right to counsel, or intelligently exercised the right to represent themselves, the absence of counsel will render criminal proceedings unconstitutional. The right extends to all hearings for all offenses for which an accused could be deprived of liberty, whether or not a jury trial is required. Trials in which fines are the only penalty are exempt from the assistance-of-counsel requirement. This assistance is required at every stage of a criminal proceeding after the initiation of formal charges—preliminary hearings, bail hearings, trial, sentence, and first appeal. When Crook told the judge he could could not afford to hire his own counsel, the judge appointed an attorney paid for by the federal government to represent him.

At this point Crook had not been convicted of anything. In fact, he had not even been formally charged with any crime, and he was entitled to be free without

1. Makes it a crime for any unauthorized person to tap telephone wires or to use or sell, in interstate commerce, electronic bugging devices.

2. Empowers the United States attorney general to secure a warrant from a federal judge authorizing federal agents to engage in bugging in order to track down persons suspected of certain federal crimes.

3. Permits wiretaps without prior court approval for 48 hours in emergency situations involving certain crimes, such as child pornography, illegal currency transactions, offenses against crime witnesses, or immediate danger of death or serious injury.

4. Authorizes the principal prosecuting attorney of any state or political subdivision to apply to a state judge for a warrant approving wiretapping or other oral intercepts for felonies. (Most state and local jurisdictions allow such intercepts.)

5. Permits judges to issue warrants only if they decide probable cause exists that a crime is being, has been, or is about to be committed, and that information relating to that crime may be obtained only by wiretapping.

What is a bill of attainder?

As a condition of receiving federally funded student financial aid, men must attest that they have complied with the registration requirements of the Selective Service Act. Is this a bill of attainder?

You Decide!

having to pay *excessive bail*. (Note the Eighth Amendment does not require that bail be set, but forbids imposition of *excessive* bail.) Suspects are entitled to a hearing within five days, and judges or magistrates must explain in writing why they believe there is clear and convincing evidence that pretrial release might endanger the safety of other persons and the community.[62] The judge set Crook's bail at $5,000, and Crook was held over until the convening of the next federal grand jury. After hiring a professional bondsman, who posted the bail and collected a 10 percent fee, Crook was free as long as he remained within the judicial district.

The Indictment

Except for members of the armed forces, the national government cannot require anyone to stand trial for a serious crime except *on grand jury indictment*. Grand jurors are concerned not with a person's guilt or innocence but merely with *whether there is enough evidence to warrant a trial*. The **grand jury** has wide-ranging investigatory powers and "is to inquire into all information that might bear on its investigations until it is satisfied that it has identified an offense or satisfied itself that none has occurred."[63] The strict rules that govern jury proceedings do not apply. The grand jury may admit hearsay evidence, and the exclusionary rule to enforce the Fourth Amendment does not apply. If a majority of the grand jurors agree that a trial is justified, they return what is known as a *true bill,* or *indictment*.

When the next grand jury was convened, the United States district attorney brought evidence before the 23 jurors to indicate that Crook had committed a federal crime. In Crook's case the grand jury was in agreement with the United States district attorney and returned a true bill against Crook.

After a copy of the indictment was served on Crook, he was again ordered to appear before a federal district judge. The Constitution guarantees the accused *the right to be informed of the nature and cause of the accusation* so that he or she can prepare a defense. Consequently, the federal prosecutor took care that the indictment clearly stated the nature of the offense, and she saw to it that copies were properly served on Crook and his lawyer.

Actually, prior to his hearing, Crook's attorney discussed with the United States attorney's office the possibility of Crook's pleading guilty to the lesser offense of false representation in return for which he would not have to stand trial for the more serious charge of using the mails to defraud. Prosecutors, faced with more cases than they can handle, like this kind of **plea bargaining.** Likewise, defendants are often willing to "cop a plea" to a lesser offense to avoid the risk of more serious punishment.

When defendants plead guilty, they are usually forever prevented from raising objections to their convictions. That is why, before accepting guilty pleas, judges question defendants to be sure that their attorneys have explained the alternatives and that they know what they are doing. It never came to this in Crook's case, however. After discussing the matter with his attorney, Crook elected to stand trial on the charge and entered a plea of not guilty.

The Trial

After indictment, Crook's bail was raised to $20,000. Now the federal government was obligated to give him a *speedy and public trial*. Do not, however, take the word "speedy" too literally. Crook had to be given time to prepare his defense. Defendants, in fact, often ask for delays, because delay often works to their advantage. If, in contrast, the government denies the accused a speedy trial in a constitutional sense, the remedy is drastic. Not only is the conviction reversed, but the case must be dismissed outright.

Crook's lawyer pointed out that under the Sixth Amendment, Crook had a right to trial before an *impartial jury* selected from the state and district in which the alleged crime was committed because he was being tried for a serious crime, that is,

"I'm not crazy about the way the judge said he would try to scrounge up a jury of my peers."
Dave Carpenter, *The Wall Street Journal,* June 1, 1994.

one punishable by more than six months in prison or a $500 fine.[64] Although federal law requires juries of 12, the Constitution requires only that juries consist of at least six persons. Conviction in federal courts must be by unanimous vote. (The Constitution permits state courts to render guilty verdicts by nonunanimous juries, provided such juries consist of six or more persons.) An impartial jury, and one that meets the requirements of due process and equal protection, consists of persons who represent a fair cross-section of the community. Although defendants are not entitled to juries on which there are necessarily members of their own race, sex, religion, or national origin, they are entitled to be tried by juries from which jurors have not been excluded because of these categories. Such discriminatory action also violates the civil rights secured by the equal protection clause of those denied the opportunity to serve on juries. Government prosecutors cannot strike persons from juries because of race or gender, and neither can defense attorneys use what are called *peremptory challenges* to keep people off juries because of race, ethnic origin, or sex.[65]

Crook told his lawyer he had dinner with George Witness on the night on which he was charged with sending the damaging circulars. The attorney took advantage of Crook's constitutional *right to obtain witnesses in his favor* and had the judge subpoena Witness to appear at the trial and testify. Although Witness could have refused to testify on the grounds that his testimony would tend *to incriminate* him, he agreed to appear. Crook himself, however, chose to use his constitutional right *not to be a witness against himself* and refused to take the stand. He knew that if he did so, the prosecution would have a right to cross-examination, and he was fearful of what might be uncovered. To protect Crook's right against *self-incrimination,* the judge conducting the trial was required to caution the jury against drawing any conclusions from Crook's decision not to testify. All prosecution witnesses appeared in court and were available for defense cross-examination; the Constitution also insists that accused persons have the *right to be confronted with the witnesses* against them.

The Sentencing

At the conclusion of the trial, the jury brought in a verdict of guilty. The judge then raised Crook's bail to $50,000 and announced that she would hand down a sentence on the following Monday. The Eighth Amendment forbids the levying *of excessive fines* and the *inflicting of cruel and unusual punishments.*

The ban against cruel and unusual punishments limits government in three ways:

1. It limits the kinds and methods of punishment that may be imposed, prohibiting, for example, torture, intentional denial of medical care, inhumane conditions, unnecessary or wanton inflicting of pain, and deliberate indifference to medical and other needs of prisoners.[66]

2. It prohibits punishments grossly disproportionate to the severity of the crime. However, outside the context of capital punishment—where the Court has limited the death penalty to crimes in which a life has been taken—the Court has been "reluctant to review legislatively mandated terms of imprisonment,"[67] and "successful challenges to the proportionality of particular sentences will be exceedingly rare."[68]

3. It limits the power of the government to decide what can be made a criminal offense. For example, the mere act of being a chronic alcoholic may not be made a crime because alcoholism is an illness. However, being drunk in public may be a criminal offense.

What of *capital punishment?* After much soul searching, and many cases, the Supreme Court has ruled that the death penalty is not necessarily cruel and unusual punishment when imposed for conviction of the crime of murder. The death

Thinking it Through

A federal district judge thought so, but the Supreme Court did not. Chief Justice Warren Burger, speaking for the Court, pointed out that any student who wished to apply for aid could become eligible for it at any time by registration. In addition to not singling out an identifiable group, as is characteristic of a bill of attainder, the registration requirement, said the Court, did not impose punishment because the sanction was a mere denial of a noncontractual government benefit.*

*Selective Service System et al. v. Minnesota Public Interest Research Group, 468 U.S. 841 (1984).

penalty may, however, be imposed only on those convicted of crimes that have resulted in a victim's death.

Back to Crook. His case did not involve a capital offense. The judge, following the guidelines set down by the United States Sentencing Commission, gave Crook the maximum punishment of a $25,000 fine and three years in the penitentiary. Such a sentence could not be considered cruel and unusual. Crook could have appealed both his sentence and his conviction to the court of appeals, but he chose not to do so.

John Crook and the State Government

While still in the federal penitentiary, Crook was taken by federal authorities before the state courts to answer charges that when he solicited shares in his nonexistent gold mine, he had also violated several state laws. Through his state-appointed attorney, Crook protested he had already been tried by the federal government for using the mails to defraud. He pointed to the Fifth Amendment provision that no person shall be "subject for the same offense to be twice put in jeopardy of life or limb."[69] The judge answered: "The Supreme Court has said that **double jeopardy** prevents two criminal trials by the *same* government for the same criminal offense." Double jeopardy does not prevent punishment by the national and the state governments for the same offense or for successive prosecutions for the same crime by two states.

What constitutional rights can Crook claim in the state courts? First, every state constitution contains a bill of rights listing practically the same guarantees found in the national Bill of Rights. Until recently, most state judges were less inclined than federal judges to interpret the constitutional guarantees of their own state constitutions liberally in favor of those accused of crime. Although, as we noted in Chapter 4, some state judges now are being more liberal in using the bills of rights in their own state constitutions to protect the rights of persons accused of crimes, most cases still turn on the application of the provisions of the Bill of Rights of the U.S. Constitution.

To what extent does the U.S. Constitution protect courtroom procedures from state actions? As noted, the Bill of Rights does not directly apply to the states, but the Fourteenth Amendment does. As the result of a series of Supreme Court decisions interpreting the Fourteenth Amendment, it now imposes on the states all the provisions of the Bill of Rights except those of the Second, Third, Seventh, and the Tenth Amendments, and the grand jury requirements of the Fifth Amendment. No specific Supreme Court decision applies the excessive bail and fine limitation to the

Three Strikes And You're Out

Although the crime rate is actually going down, public concern about crime is going up. At both the national and state level, presidents, governors and legislators are vying with one another to show their toughness about crime. Laws have been proposed to require judges to impose lifetime sentences upon persons convicted of three felonies. In some states, the felonies have to be for violent crimes; in others any three felonies will do.

Scholars are skeptical that "Three Strikes and You're Out " laws will reduce the crime rate; it will certainly require great expenditures of public funds to construct more jails and take care of aging felons.

Under the Sixth Amendment, a person has a right to trial before an impartial jury. An impartial jury consists of people who represent a fair cross-section of the community and from which jurors have not been excluded because of race, sex, religion, or national origin.

states. However, almost by definition, if a bail or fine is excessive, its imposition is likely to be considered a denial of due process.

The Supreme Court will probably not incorporate additional provisions of the Bill of Rights into the Fourteenth Amendment; most lawyers, political scientists, and other observers believe states should be allowed to continue to conduct civil trials before judges without juries and to indict persons for serious crimes by means other than grand juries. Many states provide for some civil trials without juries. A number no longer require grand juries for any crimes; even more require them only for felonies; and less than a dozen require them for all except minor offenses. Other provisions in the Second, Third, and Tenth Amendments not incorporated are really not applicable to the states.

HOW JUST IS OUR SYSTEM OF JUSTICE?

What are the major criticisms of the American system of justice? How have they been answered?

Too Many Loopholes   Some observers argue that by overprotecting the innocent and placing too much of a burden on the government not to make any mistakes, we delay justice, encourage disrespect for the law, and allow guilty persons to go unpunished. Justice should be swift and certain without being arbitrary. But under our procedures criminals may go unpunished because: (1) the police decide not to arrest them; (2) the judge decides not to hold them for a trial; (3) the prosecutor decides not to prosecute them; (4) the grand jury decides not to indict them; (5) the jury decides not to convict them; (6) the judge decides not to sentence them; (7) an appeals court decides to reverse the conviction; (8) a judge decides to release them on a *habeas corpus* writ; or (9) if retried and convicted, the executive decides to pardon, reprieve, or parole them. As a result, the public never knows whom to hold responsible when laws are not enforced. The police can blame the prosecutor, the prosecutor can blame the police, and they can all blame the juries and judges.

Others take a different view and point out that there is more to justice than simply securing convictions. All the steps in the administration of criminal laws have been developed over centuries of trial and error, and each step has been constructed to protect against particular abuses. History warns against entrusting the instruments of criminal law enforcement to a single officer. For this reason, responsibility is vested in many officials.

Too Unreliable   Critics who say that our system of justice is unreliable often point to trial by jury as the chief source of trouble. Trial by jury, they argue, leads to a theatrical combat between lawyers who base their appeals on the prejudices and sentiments of the jurors. "Mr. Prejudice and Miss Sympathy are the names of witnesses whose testimony is never recorded, but must nevertheless be reckoned with in trials by jury." [70] No other country relies as heavily on trial by jury as does the United States. Jury trials are also time consuming and costly.

Defenders of the jury system reply that trial by jury provides a check by non-professionals on the actions of judges and prosecutors. Moreover, there is no evidence that juries are unreliable. On the contrary, decisions of juries do not systematically differ from those of judges.[71] Moreover, the jury system helps to educate citizens and enables them to participate in the application of their own laws.

The grand jury system has also come under attack. In theory, the grand jury has two functions: (1) to protect the innocent from having to stand trial by requiring prosecutors to demonstrate behind closed doors that they have enough evidence to justify trial; and (2) to provide an independent agency, not controlled by those in

The Nationalization of the Bill of Rights

1890   No taking of property without just compensation (*Chicago, Milwaukee and St. Paul Ry v Minnesota*, 134 US 418, 1890)

1925   Freedom of speech (*Gitlow v New York*)

1931   Freedom of press (*Near v Minnesota*)

1932   Fair trial (*Powell v Alabama*)

1934   Free exercise of religion (*Hamilton v Regents of California*, confirmed in 1940 by *Cantwell v Connecticut*)

1937   Freedom of assembly (*De Jonge v Oregon*)

1942   Right to counsel in capital cases (*Betts v Brady*)

1947   Separation of church and state; establishment of religion (*Everson v Board of Education*)

1948   Right to a public trial (*In re Oliver*)

1949   Right against unreasonable searches and seizure (*Wolf v Colorado*)

1958   Freedom of association (*NAACP v Alabama*)

1961   Exclusionary rule (*Mapp v Ohio*)

1962   Right against cruel and unusual punishments (*Robinson v California*)

1963   Right to counsel in felony cases (*Gideon v Wainwright*)

1964   Right against self-incrimination (*Mallory v Hogan*)

1965   Right to confront witnesses (*Pointer v Texas*)

1965   Right of privacy (*Griswold v Connecticut*)

1966   Right to an impartial jury (*Parker v Gladden*)

1967   Right to a speedy trial (*Klopfer v North Carolina*)

1967   Right to compulsory process for obtaining witnesses (*Washington v Texas*)

1968   Right to a jury trial for all serious crimes (*Duncan v Louisiana*)

1969   Right against double jeopardy (*Benton v Maryland*)

1972   Right to counsel for all crimes involving a jail term (*Argersinger v Hamlin*)

JURIES ON TRIAL

Criticism of the role of juries has increased in recent years as the general public learned the intimate details of some notorious trials because of around-the-clock television coverage and front-page newspaper attention. Resentment and bewilderment followed when juries failed to convict persons for what appeared to the general public as obvious crimes. Examples include the 1992 acquittal of Los Angeles police officers whose extended beating of Rodney King had been videotaped and then witnessed by the entire nation (two officers were subsequently convicted of federal crimes); the 1993 trial of Damian Williams, whose brutal beating of truck driver Reginald Denny in the Los Angeles riots following the acquittal verdict in the King case was also captured on video, but who also received a relatively light sentence; the 1993–94 trial of the Menendez brothers, who confessed to the killing of both their parents but whose long trials resulted in hung juries that could not agree as to the precise nature of their crime; and the 1994 trial of Lorena Bobbitt for mutilating her husband, which resulted in her acquittal for reasons of temporary insanity as a result of her husband's brutality.

 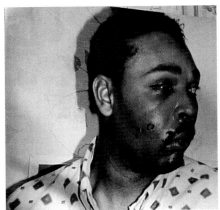

power, to investigate wrongdoing. Critics charge, however, that the grand jury has become a tool of the prosecutor. Said Justice William O. Douglas, "It is, indeed, common knowledge that the grand jury, having been conceived as a bulwark between the citizen and the Government, is now a tool of the Executive." [72]

During the 1960s critics on the left of the political spectrum charged that grand juries had become instruments to intimidate radicals, blacks, and antiwar militants. However, by the 1970s grand juries were being used to investigate the executive branch. In the Watergate investigation of the Nixon administration, it was through the use of the grand jury that the special prosecutor was able to present to the courts his contention that the president had no constitutional right to withhold information about wrongdoing. In recent years, there are calls to reform the federal grand jury system and remove some of the limitations on the right of federal jurors to make public comments, so that such juries might more effectively investigate allegations of wrongdoing by federal officials and look into social problems. As one advocate of such a reform has written, "Federal grand juries with broad investigatory powers would give citizens a new tool and a new platform. The public would be far more likely to listen to what the grand jurors said than to what the experts said." [73]

Too Discriminatory During the last several decades, the Supreme Court has worked particularly hard to enforce the ideal of equal justice under the law. Persons accused of crime who cannot afford attorneys must be furnished them at government expense. If transcripts are required for appeals, such transcripts must be made available to those who cannot afford to purchase them. If appeals are permitted, the government must provide attorneys for at least one appeal of the decision of the trial court. Poor people cannot be imprisoned because of inability to pay a fine. Nor, once sentenced, can poor persons be kept in jail beyond the term of the sentence because they cannot afford to pay a fine. Even for civil proceedings—divorce proceedings, for example—fees cannot be imposed that deny poor persons their fundamental rights, such as the right to obtain a divorce. A state has no obligation, however, to waive fees for those seeking to be declared bankrupt. The Court apparently believes that people have a constitutional right to be absolved of the ties that bind but not of their debts.

Despite all these protections, it remains true that racial and ethnic discrimination in the criminal justice system, especially outside the courtroom, persists. How much it persists is hard to measure. The editors of the *Harvard Law Review* believe it is significant. "Racism still pervades the United States criminal justice system," they charge, including police conduct, prosecutorial actions, among jurors, and in the sentencing process. [74] The editors blame the persistence of racism in the criminal justice system in part on the Supreme Court's requirement that, except in cases involving juror selection, litigants cannot legally prove racism through general evidence about racism in the system. They must show through direct evidence relating to their particular cases the discriminatory intent of the decision maker and the adverse consequence flowing from this intent to their case. [75]

One expert close to the subject comes to a different conclusion. He reports:

about 80 percent of the black overrepresentation in prison can be explained by differential involvement in crime and about 20 percent by subsequent racially discriminatory processes....[76] "That is not at all to say that racial discrimination within the criminal justice system is unimportant; it certainly is important. What is suggested is only that it is relatively less important than other discriminatory pressures"[77] in society in general outside of the criminal justice system.

One of the more acute problems of our society is the tension between the police and the African American and Hispanic communities congregated in the ghettos and barrios of our large cities. Such tensions were evident in the Rodney King beating and the 1992 Los Angeles riots. Many members of minorities do not believe they have

One way to improve relations between police and minority communities reformers say, is to recruit more African Americans, Hispanics, and women.

equal protection under the law. "Whether the stated belief is well founded or not is at least partly beside the point. The existence of the belief is damaging enough."[78] Blacks consider the police to be enforcers of white law. Studies proving prejudice on the part of some white police officers and examples of rough, if not brutal, police treatment of blacks are ample evidence to support this viewpoint. The general pattern, however, is that minorities are being shot by the police at rates approximately proportional to rates of minorities in street crime, but "there is a slight added increment and all you can conclude is the data support what common observation and folk tales make very clear—there is an element of racial prejudice in police shooting at minorities."[79]

In recent decades action has been taken to recruit more African Americans, Hispanics, and women as police officers, including appointment to command posts. Community relations programs have been established. Considerable progress has been made, and relations between police and minority communities in some cities appear to be improving.

THE SUPREME COURT AND CIVIL LIBERTIES

Clearly, judges—especially those on the Supreme Court—play a major role in enforcing constitutional guarantees. This combination of judicial enforcement and written guarantees of enumerated liberties is one of the basic features of the American system of government. As Justice Robert H. Jackson wrote:

> The very purpose of a Bill of Rights was to withdraw certain subjects from the vicissitudes of political controversy, to place them beyond the reach of majorities and officials and to establish them as legal principles to be applied by the courts. One's right to life, liberty, and property, to free speech, a free press, freedom of worship and assembly, and other fundamental rights may not be submitted to vote: they depend on the outcome of no elections.[80]

This emphasis on constitutional limitations and judicial enforcement is an example of the "auxiliary precautions" James Madison believed were necessary to prevent arbitrary governmental action. In other free nations citizens rely more on elections and political checks to protect their rights; in the United States we appeal to judges when we fear our freedoms are in danger.

Such reliance on judicial protection of our civil liberties focuses attention on the Supreme Court. Yet only a small number of controversies are actually carried to the Supreme Court, and a Supreme Court decision is not the end of the policy-making process. Lower-court judges as well as police, superintendents of schools, local prosecutors, school boards, state legislatures, and thousands of others give reality to the Court's doctrines.

The Supreme Court can do little unless its decisions over time reflect a national consensus. Judges by themselves cannot guarantee anything; neither can the First Amendment. As Justice Jackson once asked:

> Must we first maintain a system of free political government to assure a free judiciary to guarantee free government?…It is my belief that the attitude of a society and of its organized political forces, rather than its legal machinery, is the controlling force in the character of free institutions.…Any court which undertakes by its legal processes to enforce civil liberties needs the support of an enlightened and vigorous public opinion.[81]

Thus, the Bill of Rights—and the other procedural and substantive liberties of our Constitution—cannot rest on a foundation merely of tradition. The preservation of these rights depends on wide, continuing, and knowledgeable public support. Inevitably that public support will be tested—sometimes sorely tested—in the years to come.

SUMMARY

1. One of the basic distinctions between a free society and a police state is that in a free society there are effective restraints on the way public officials, especially law enforcement officials, perform their duties. In the United States these constitutional restraints are judicially enforceable.

2. The Constitution protects the acquisition and retention of citizenship. It protects the basic liberties of citizens as well as aliens.

3. The Constitution protects our property from arbitrary governmental interference, although debates about which interferences are reasonable and which are arbitrary are not easily settled.

4. The Constitution imposes limits not only on the procedures government must follow but also on the ends it may pursue. Some actions are out of bounds no matter what procedures are followed. Legislatures have the primary role in determining what is reasonable and what is unreasonable. However, the Supreme Court continues to exercise its own independent and final review of legislative determinations of reasonableness, especially on matters affecting civil liberties and civil rights.

5. The framers knew from their own experiences that in their zeal to maintain power and to enforce the laws, public officials are often tempted to infringe on the rights of those accused of crimes. To prevent such abuse, the Constitution imposes detailed procedures federal officials must follow in making searches and arrests and in bringing people to trial.

6. The Supreme Court interprets the Constitution, especially the Fourteenth Amendment, to impose on state and local governments almost the same restraints in the administration of justice as it imposes on the national government.

7. The Supreme Court continues to play a prominent role in developing public policy to protect the rights of the accused, to ensure that the innocent are not punished, and to guarantee that the public is protected against those who break the laws. The Court's decisions influence what the public believes and how police officers and others involved in the administration of justice behave. But the Court alone cannot—and should not—guarantee fairness in the administration of justice.

FURTHER READING

JAMES V. CALVI AND SUSAN COLEMAN, *American Laws and Legal Systems* (Prentice Hall, 1989).

GEORGE F. COLE, *The American System of Criminal Justice,* 5th ed. (Brooks/Cole, 1989).

GEORGE F. COLE, *Criminal Justice: Law and Politics,* 6th ed. (Wadsworth, 1993).

ROGER H. DAVIDSON AND WALTER J. OLESZEK, *Governing: Readings and Cases in American Politics,* 2d ed. (Congressional Quarterly Press, 1992).

RICHARD EPSTEIN, *Bargaining with the State* (Princeton University Press, 1993).

GEORGE T. FELKENES, *Constitutional Law for Criminal Justice,* 2d ed. (Prentice Hall, 1988).

MACKLIN FLEMING, *The Price of Perfect Justice* (Basic Books, 1974).

LOUIS FISHER, *American Constitutional Law* (McGraw-Hill, 1990).

NATHAN GLAZER, ed., *Clamor at the Gates: The New American Immigration* (ICS Press, 1985).

JOHN GUINTHER, *The Jury in America* (Facts-on-File Publications, 1988).

MARY M. KRITZ, ed., *U.S. Immigration and Refugee Policy* (Heath, 1982).

WAYNE R. LaFAVE, *Search and Seizure: A Treatise on the Fourth Amendment,* 2d ed. (West Publishers, 1987).

LEONARD W. LEVY, KENNETH L. KARST, AND DENNIS J. MAHONE, *Criminal Justice and the Supreme Court* (Macmillan, 1990).

ROBERT E. LITAN, ed., *Verdict: Assessing the Civil Jury System* (Brookings, 1993).

STUART NAGEL, ERIKA FAIRCHILD, AND ANTHONY CHAMPAGNE, *The Political Science of Criminal Justice* (Thomas, 1983).

J. W. PELTASON, *Corwin and Peltason's Understanding the Constitution,* 13th ed. (Harcourt Brace 1994).

GERALD D. ROBIN, *Introduction to the Criminal Justice System,* 4th ed. (Harper and Row, 1990).

JUDITH N. SHKLAR, *American Citizenship: The Quest for Inclusion* (Harvard University Press, 1991).

MARTHA S. SIEGEL, *The Insiders' Guide, 1991–1992* (Sheridan Chandler, 1991).

SPECIAL COMMISSION ON CRIMINAL JUSTICE IN A FREE SOCIETY, *Criminal Justice in Crisis* (American Bar Association, 1988).

ROBERT W. TUCKER, CHARLES B. KEELEY, AND LINDA W. RIGLEY, eds., *Immigration and U.S. Foreign Policy* (Westview Press, 1990).

NORMAN L. ZUCKER AND NAOMI FLINK ZUCKER, *The Guarded Gate: The Reality of American Refugee Policy* (Harcourt Brace Jovanovich, 1987).

POLITICAL CULTURE AND IDEOLOGY

7

The Jones family lives in a middle-class neighborhood not far from State College. To supplement their income, they decide to remodel their basement and rent it out to college students. The Joneses advertise their apartment in the local newspaper and on campus. Many inquire about the apartment, and the Joneses decide to rent to two undergraduates, Frank and Sam. Much to their surprise, Mr. and Mrs. Jones learn about a month later that Frank and Sam are gay.

The sexual preference of their renters is a concern because Mr. and Mrs. Jones view homosexuality as a sin, and they do not want practicing homosexuals living in their home in close proximity to their three children. They decide to ask the students to find another apartment. They assume it is their right to choose their tenants.

Frank and Sam react angrily to the request that they find another place to live simply because of their sexual orientation. They contact a gay and lesbian support group at State College and hire an attorney. Their rights to equal treatment are protected, they assume, because the city has recently passed an ordinance protecting gays and lesbians from discrimination. However, their attorney informs them that the Jones are permitted under the law to evict people simply because of their sexual preferences. Homosexual rights ordinances, where they exist, apply to apartment buildings but not to apartments in homes. Frank and Sam decide to find another apartment rather than pursue their case.

The issues raised by this hypothetical story go much further than the status of current housing law. This case is an example of the long-standing tension between individual liberty and equal opportunity. Mr. and Mrs. Jones say that their individual liberty permits them to decide whether or not to rent to homosexuals. Frank and Sam feel that they should be entitled to the same treatment as heterosexuals, and that the Joneses should not be allowed to discriminate against them because of their sexual preference.

As this example illustrates, our values and ideals are often in conflict. We want people to have as much liberty as possible, and we want people to to be treated equally. Frank and Sam's desire not to be discriminated against as well as their desire for personal liberty conflicts with the personal liberty of the Joneses not to have to rent to people whose conduct and behavior they disapprove of. How Americans resolve such conflicts tells us a lot about our political culture. How we propose to reconcile such conflicts and similar issues depends on our **ideology**—our ideas and beliefs about the proper role of government and political power. In this chapter, we will look at the political culture that unites us as well as the ideologies that sometimes divide us.

THE AMERICAN POLITICAL CULTURE

Political scientists use the term **political culture** to refer to a set of widely shared beliefs, values, and norms concerning the relationship of citizens to government and to one another. The American political culture is the sum of our most cherished shared values. American democratic values include liberty, equality, individualism, democracy, justice, the rule of law, and economic freedom. There is, however, no definitive listing of American political values, and, as we noted in Chapter 1, these widely shared democratic values overlap and sometimes conflict.

Values We Share

Most Americans are patriotic and share a sense of civic responsibility: 88 percent say they are "very patriotic," 94 percent feel it is their "duty to always vote," and nearly three in four Americans think voting gives them some say in how the government runs things.

Some Americans distrust government: 58 percent think "government regulation of business usually does more harm than good," and two out of three think that "when something is run by the government, it is usually inefficient and wasteful." Americans are more distrustful of the federal government than of local government: 77 percent think "the federal government should run only those things that cannot be run at the local level."

Most Americans believe in providing equal opportunity: 94 percent believe "our society should do what is necessary to make sure that everyone has an equal opportunity to succeed."

Most Americans believe government should help those in need: 62 percent believe "it is the responsibility of government to take care of people who can't take care of themselves," and 73 percent think "the government should guarantee every citizen enough to eat and a place to sleep."

A large number of Americans are religious: 88 percent believe in the existence of God, and 80 percent see prayer as an important part of their daily life.

Most Americans say they see family and marriage as important: 81 percent say they have "old-fashioned values about family and marriage," and nearly three out of four think "too many children are being raised in daycare centers these days."

Most Americans distrust large corporations: 72 percent of Americans think "too much power is concentrated in the hands of a few big companies," and 63 percent think "business corporations make too much in profit."

Americans are generally optimistic: 59 percent think that the United States "can always find a way to solve our problems and get what we want."

SOURCE: Times Mirror Center for the People and the Press, *The People, the Press, and Politics, 1990: A Times Mirror Political Typology* (October 11, 1990), (December 4, 1991), pp. 21–29, pp.66–73, and *The Vocal Minority in American Politics* (July 16, 1993), pp. 103–8.

Shared Values

The values and beliefs described here as part of the American political culture are grounded in a philosophical tradition called **classical liberalism.** This tradition influenced the founders of our Republic and continues to be important to democratic movements around the world today. Classical liberalism, which is not the same as modern-day liberalism, stresses the importance of the individual and of freedom, equality, private property, limited government, and popular consent. All these elements, you will remember, are part of what we have described as the political culture of the United States.

Before the American and French Revolutions, these were radically new and different ideas. Europe had been dominated by aristocracies, had experienced centuries of political and social inequality, and had been ruled by governments that were unconstrained and often arbitrary in the exercise of power. Liberal political philosophers rebelled against these traditions and instead postulated the principles of classical liberalism. They claimed individuals have certain **natural rights,** and that the state (or government), as a primary threat to these rights, must be limited and controlled. At the same time, the economic system was changing from mercantilism to capitalism. People began to think they could improve their lot in life. The principles of a free market system were accepted and adopted, and these ideas clearly influenced the thinking of the founders of our nation.

The American Revolution, based on values like individual liberty and popular consent, has often served as a focal point of the American political culture. The Fourth of July celebrations held in every corner of the country salute freedom and liberty. The Constitution, like the Revolution, also defines our nation and its values.

LIBERTY Americans have always been united by a commitment to liberty or freedom. No value in the American political culture is more revered. "We have always been a nation obsessed with liberty. Liberty over authority, freedom over responsibility, rights over duties—these are our historic preferences," wrote the late Clinton Rossiter, a noted political scientist. "Not the good man, but the free man has been the measure of all things in this 'sweet land of liberty'; not national glory but individual liberty has been the object of political authority and the test of its worth."[1]

EQUALITY Jefferson's famous words in the Declaration of Independence express the primacy of our views of equality: "We hold these truths to be selfevident, that all men are created equal, that they are endowed by their Creator with certain unalienable rights, that among these are life, liberty, and the pursuit of happiness." We have always believed in social equality. In contrast to the Europeans, our nation shunned aristocracy. For example, we explicitly banned titles of nobility in our Constitution. Instead of having sharp distinctions between an upper and a lower class, our nation is characterized by its large middle class.

Equality also refers to *political equality*, the idea that every individual has a right to equal protection under the law and equal voting power. While political equality is a goal, it has not always been a reality. African Americans, Native Americans, and women have been denied political equality in the past.

Equality encompasses the idea of equal opportunity, especially with regard to improving economic status. Americans believe that social background, should not limit our opportunity to achieve to the best of our ability, nor should race, gender, or religion. The nation's commitment to public education—programs like Head Start for underprivileged preschool children, state support for public colleges and universities, and federal financial aid for higher education—reflects our belief in equality. Other government programs motivated by this same desire include Medicaid and the Federal National Mortgage Association (Fannie Mae).

INDIVIDUALISM   The United States is characterized by a persistent commitment to the individual. Under our system of government, individuals have both rights and responsibilities. The individual's importance and dignity are enhanced by our views of political equality.

Concern for preserving individual freedom of choice and what limits, if any, to place on individual choice often generate intense political conflict. The debate over legalized abortion is often framed in terms of individual choice versus limits on that choice prescribed by law. While we Americans agree with the idea of individual rights and freedom, we also understand that such rights often come into conflict with other rights or with the government's need to maintain order.

As Americans, we have faith in the common sense of the ordinary person. The tradition of Abraham Lincoln and Harry Truman, that anyone can become president, has been a bold one. We prefer action to reflection; we are generally antitheoretical, anti-expert, and indeed anti-intellectual. The emphasis on practicality and "common sense" has become part of our image. Poets like Walt Whitman, Stephen Vincent Benét, and Carl Sandburg, and storytellers like Mark Twain, Will Rogers, Eudora Welty, and Garrison Keillor have helped shape this idea into tradition. This reverence for the common man and woman helps to explain our ambivalence toward power, politics, and government authority. In the United States, government is often viewed as a necessary evil.

DEMOCRACY, GOVERNMENT, AND THE CONSTITUTION   The American political culture includes attitudes and beliefs about principles of government, procedures, documents, and institutions. A *democratic consensus*—a fairly widespread agreement on fundamental principles of governance and the values that undergird them—is

Government efforts to enforce the laws and maintain order must be done within certain clearly specified limits. After a 51-day standoff between federal law enforcement agents and members of The Branch Davidian religious cult in Waco, Texas, FBI agents attacked the stronghold, which quickly became engulfed in flames. Seventy-five persons, including at least 25 children, died from the fire or from gunshot wounds inflicted by fellow cult members. Attorney General Janet Reno accepted responsibility for the actions of federal law enforcement officers. Later the head of the Department of Alcohol, Tobacco and Firearms was dismissed, and the top five advisers were suspended.

essential to the maintenance of democracy and the other values we discuss here. We Americans have deeply rooted ideas about who has power to do what, how people acquire power, and how they are removed from power. These are fundamental "rules of the game" in which widespread consensus is important.

We believe in *majority rule,* yet we also believe that people in the minority should be free to try to win majority support for their opinions. We also strongly favor a two-party system and regular elections. Our institutions are based on the principle of representation and the consent of the governed. We believe in *popular sovereignty*—that the ultimate power resides in the people themselves. Government, from our perspective, should exist to serve the people rather than the other way around. The means by which the government learns the will of the people is through elections, perhaps the most important expression of popular consent. One of the most important jobs of government is to maintain order, something many of us take for granted.

Many of the limits on government are specified in the Constitution and the Bill of Rights. The Constitution is worshiped as a national symbol, and Americans view being "unconstitutional" as exceedingly close to being "un-American." Yet we often differ over what certain constitutional provisions require or over the precise meaning of the framers' original intentions.

We Americans honor many of these rights more in the abstract than in particular situations (see Table 7-1). Fifty percent of us, for instance, think that books with dangerous ideas should be banned from public school libraries. Intolerance of dissenting or offensive views is amply demonstrated in many public opinion polls and is observed clearly on college and university campuses as well. Still, Americans can ordinarily be characterized as affirming support for democratic and constitutional values.

JUSTICE AND THE RULE OF LAW   Inscribed over the entrance to the U.S. Supreme Court are the words "Equal Justice under Law." The rule of law means that government is based on a body of law applied equally and by just procedures, as opposed to rule by an elite in which the whims of those in power decide policy or resolve disputes. Chief Justice John Marshall succinctly summarized this principle: "The government of the United States has been emphatically termed a government of laws, not of men."[2] We Americans believe strongly in the principle of fairness: all individuals are entitled to the same legal rights and protections.

TABLE 7-1

It Depends on What You Mean by Rights and Freedoms

	Agree	Disagree	Don't Know
The government ought to be able to censor news stories that it feels threaten national security. (1990)	62%	34%	4%
Books that contain dangerous ideas should (1990) be banned from public school libraries. (1993)	50 52	45 44	5 4
The police should be allowed to search the houses of known drug dealers without a court order. (1990)	57	41	2
School boards ought to have the right to (1990) fire teachers who are known homosexuals. (1993)	49 34	45 60	6 6

SOURCE: Times Mirror Center for the People and the Press, *The People, The Press, and Politics, 1990: A Times Mirror Political Typology,* October 11, 1990, pp. 126–27, and *The Vocal Minority in American Politics,* July 16, 1993, p. 108.

TABLE 7-2

Public Optimism in Switzerland and the United States

Survey respondents were asked to rate whether they were looking forward to the year 2000 very optimistically, rather optimistically, rather pessimistically, or very pessimistically in terms of their personal future, the future of their country and that of the world.

| | Percent Very or Rather Optimistic | |
	Switzerland	United States
Personal future	89%	82%
Future of the country	62	71
Future of the world	47	66

SOURCE: Survey Research Consultants International, Inc., *Index to International Public Opinion, 1990–1991*, p. 611.

NATIONALISM, OPTIMISM, AND IDEALISM   Americans are also highly nationalistic. We are proud of our past and tend to deemphasize, or even forget, our nation's intolerance, diplomatic and military setbacks, the shame of slavery, and the denial of suffrage to women for more than a century. We are optimistic—about people, but not about government. We are also optimistic about opportunity, choice, options, individualism, and most of all, about freedom to improve ourselves and to achieve success with as little interference as possible from others or the government.

We know our system is not perfect. We often grumble that our elected officials have lost touch with the common people. We are disgusted by too many scandals, and impatient with the slowness of the system to solve problems like health care and crime. Yet we have an abiding faith in government by the people and in our ability to solve problems. As Table 7-2 indicates, Swiss and U.S. citizens are similarly optimistic about their personal futures, but the greater optimism among Americans is based in their views of their country's future as well as the future of the world.

There remains a remarkable belief that our nation is better, stronger, and more virtuous than other nations. Doubtless this sense of mission is a source of discipline, a builder of morale, and a fortifier of nationalism. But an excessive or wrongheaded sense of mission can also cause problems. Like every country, the United States has interests and motives that are selfish as well as generous, squalid as well as idealistic. We, too, are part of human history. Still, our idealism persists, and our efforts in support of human needs and rights throughout the world are evidence of this idealism.

Political and Economic Change

Our political values are clearly affected by historical developments and by economic and technological growth. The Declaration of Independence and our Constitution identify such important political values as individual liberty, property rights, and limited government.[3] In the early years we also emphasized separation of powers, checks and balances, states' rights, and of course the Bill of Rights. It took an additional generation or two before we also began to take seriously the ideal of democratic governance, the expansion of suffrage, and competitive nominations and elections. Notions of political equality and effective participation emerged during the presidency of Andrew Jackson and matured in the course of the nineteenth century. By the century's end, populists and suffragists turned ideals into action and formed large-scale movements to achieve more democratic forms of participation and more responsive forms of governance.

THE INDUSTRIAL TRANSFORMATION   By the late nineteenth century, the agrarian society the framers knew was largely replaced by industrial capitalism and the growth of large corporations. With these changes, American ideology was irreversibly transformed. We committed ourselves to encourage economic growth by fostering privately owned corporations. The changed economic order had profound consequences for our political values—for how we viewed the role of government and how we related to one another. No one captures the implications of this shift better than political scientist Robert A. Dahl:

> One of the consequences of the new order has been a high degree of inequality in the distribution of wealth and income—a far greater inequality than had ever been thought likely or desirable under an agrarian order by Democratic Republicans like Jefferson and Madison, or had ever been thought consistent with democratic or republican government in the historic writings on the subject from Aristotle to Locke, Montesquieu, and Rousseau. Previous theorists and advocates had, like many of the framers of our own Constitution, insisted that a republic could exist only if the citizen body continued neither rich nor poor. Citizens, it was argued, must enjoy a rough equality of conditions.[4]

Thus, although constitutionalism and the democratic ideal embodied American political values in this nation's first century and remained undiminished into the next century, a commitment to capitalism and free enterprise became an additional widely shared political value.

With the rise and success of the American industrial economy came the accumulation of great wealth in the hands of a few—the robber barons or tycoons. Many had taken great risks and earned their fortunes through inventions and efficient production practices. As disparities of income grew, so did disparities in political resources. Economic resources can be converted into political resources, and

> economic advantages increase one's chances of getting an education, gaining higher status, and having more time available for politics. . . . Economic advantages also help in providing psychological resources such as confidence and optimism, which strengthens both the incentives to participate in politics and the willingness to acquire political skills.[5]

The rise of the large corporation and concentrated individual wealth in the United States created divisions and fostered resentment. The growth of monopolies prompted passage of antitrust legislation and unsafe work conditions led to regulation of the workplace. More important, at the turn of the century, muckraking journalists charged that the robber barons behind the huge corporations were using their power to exploit workers and limit competition. Only the national government, it seemed, had the power to ensure fair treatment in the marketplace. This sentiment not only gave rise to the nation's first antitrust legislation but also sowed the idea that government could—and should—as the Constitution asserts, "promote the general welfare" by doing more to regulate the workings of business.

THE GREAT DEPRESSION AND NEW DEAL   Then came the Great Depression and the near-collapse of the capitalistic system. Unrestrained capitalism and the unregulated market were faulted by many as a cause of the Depression. In any event, when it came, it brought the nation to the brink of disaster. There was no unemployment compensation, no guarantee on bank savings, no federal regulation of the securities exchanges, no Social Security. Americans turned to government to improve the lot of the millions of jobless and homeless citizens. With Franklin D. Roosevelt's New Deal, the idea gained widespread acceptance that government should use its powers and resources assertively to ensure some measure of equal opportunity and social justice.

The use of child labor in factories was one aspect of the inequality between rich and poor in the industrial era.

Today free enterprise is no longer unbridled; instead government regulations, antitrust laws, job safety regulations, environmental standards, and minimum wage rates all balance the freedom of enterprise against the rights of individuals. That most of us support a semiregulated or mixed free enterprise system is one of our nation's greatest sources of stability (see Table 7-3).

In a sense the *rights revolution* of the 1780s and 1790s has never ended. The protection of property rights from an overly powerful government was followed by the quest for political rights, voting rights, black emancipation, and economic rights. Today we witness fights for gender rights, children's rights, gay rights, animal rights, the rights of trees and endangered species, and victim's rights, to name a few.

President Franklin Roosevelt's State of the Union Address in 1944 articulated an expanded "Second Bill of Rights" for all citizens. Roosevelt declared that this nation must make a firm commitment to "economic security and independence." Included in his Second Bill of Rights were:

- The right to a useful and remunerative job in the industries, shops, farms, or mines of the nation
- The right to earn enough to provide adequate food and clothing and recreation
- The right of every farmer to raise and sell his products at a return which will give him and his family a decent living
- The right of every business man, large and small, to trade in an atmosphere of freedom from unfair competition and domination by monopolies at home or abroad
- The right of every family to a decent home
- The right to adequate medical care and the opportunity to achieve and enjoy good health
- The right to adequate protection from the economic fears of old age, sickness, accident, and unemployment
- The right to a good education.[6]

Roosevelt's proclamation and later efforts by Kennedy and Johnson in the 1960s to pass landmark civil and voting rights legislation and launch a War on Poverty have defined the ideological political fights of the last half of the twentieth century. Modern-day liberalism and conservatism turn, in large measure, on how much one

TABLE 7-3

Attitudes on Business and Welfare, 1993

	Agree	Disagree	Don't Know
There is too much power concentrated in the hands of a few big companies.	72%	25%	3%
Business corporations make too much profit.	63	32	5
The government should help more needy people, even if it means going deeper in debt.	43	52	5
We have gone too far in pushing equal rights in this country.	43	54	3
It is the responsibility of the government to take care of people who can't take care of themselves.	62	35	3

SOURCE: Times Mirror Center for the People and the Press, *The Vocal Minority in American Politics*, July 16, 1993, pp. 103–4.

We The People

Where We Learn the American Political Culture

The Family

One of the important sources of political culture in the United States and other nations as well is the family. Children are taught from an early age what it means to be an American. They are curious about why people vote, what the president does, and whether Grandpa fought in World War II. The questions may vary somewhat from family to family, but the themes of authority, freedom, equality, liberty, and partisanship are common.* Families are the most important reference groups, and compared to families in other cultures, American families are much more egalitarian.

The Schools

Public schools are another source of the American political culture. Children and teachers often begin the school day by saluting the flag, reciting the Pledge of Allegiance, or singing the National Anthem. Teaching American political and economic values is part of the curriculum. Not only are values taught in U.S. history class, but they are put into practice in school elections and newspapers and in encouraging students to participate in small-scale economic ventures.

Colleges and universities also play a role in fostering the American political culture. Students who attend college are often more confident than other persons in dealing with bureaucracy and politics generally, more likely to participate in politics and vote, and more knowledgeable about government. Many states, including large ones like California and Texas, require college students to take courses in American government or state government, in part to instill a sense of civic duty while imparting knowledge about state and national governments.

During the Depression of the 1930s, widespread poverty prompted President Roosevelt's "Second Bill of Rights," which included the right to a decent home. In the 1990s, however, many are still homeless.

believes in Roosevelt's Second Bill of Rights: how much government assistance one thinks is owed to minorities, women, or others who have suffered discrimination or have been left behind by the industrial or technological revolutions of the twentieth century. Passage of Johnson's Great Society programs of the 1960s gave renewed emphasis to this expanded view of rights. President Bill Clinton's efforts to provide health care to all Americans can be seen as an application of this approach to expanded rights. In calling for health care reform, Clinton referred to Roosevelt's Second Bill of Rights, asserting that "health care is a basic right all should have."[7]

The American Dream

Many of our political values come together in the **American Dream**, a complex set of ideas about the economy and its relation to individuals. Whether we realize it or not, this American Dream speaks to our most deeply held hopes and goals. The essence of the American Dream can be found in our endorsement of **capitalism**, an economic system characterized by private property, competitive markets, economic incentives, and limited government involvement in the production and pricing of goods and services.

The concept of private property enjoys extraordinary popularity in our political culture. In many European democracies, the state owns and operates transportation systems, the media, and other businesses that are privately owned and operated in the United States. Whether it be a farm, a humble bungalow, a highrise condominium, a factory, or a shopping mall, Americans cherish the dream of acquiring property. Moreover, most of us believe that those who own property have the right to decide how it is to be used.

The right to private property is just one of the economic incentives that cement our support for capitalism and fuel the American Dream. We believe that this is the land of opportunity for the enterprising. Here the competitive, practical go-getter can make a fortune or build a dream home. People who have more ability or work extremely hard, we hold, should get ahead, should earn more, and should enjoy economic rewards. We also believe that those who earn a lot of money should be able to pass most of what they have earned along to their children and relatives. Even the poorest Americans oppose high inheritance taxes or limits on how much someone can earn. In fact, the widespread support of the American Dream is clearly more important than the number of people who actually achieve it.

We Americans believe our mixed free enterprise system gives almost everyone a fair chance, that this system is necessary for free government to survive, and that our freedom depends on it. We reject communism and even modified forms of socialism and take pride in the reality that not only has communism not worked around the world, but that most formerly communist nations are shifting toward free enterprise systems in the 1990s.

In the United States, both individuals and corporations have acquired great wealth and, at the same time exercised great political clout. Their power has, in turn, bred a certain amount of resentment. An increasing number of us believe the political system too often favors the rich over the poor. It is widely believed that when it comes to taxes, corporations and wealthy people do not pay their fair share. President Clinton used this argument in selling his 1993 tax package which included higher taxes on the rich.

This conflict in values between a *competitive economy*, in which individuals should be free to reap large rewards for their initiative and hard work, and a *democratic society*, in which everyone should be able to earn a decent living, carries over into our politics. How the public resolves this tension can change over time. For instance, social programs that sought to extend equality of opportunity enjoyed broad support in the 1960s. During the 1980s they were attacked and partially dismantled as Ronald Reagan sought to implement a more conservative, procapitalist policy.

As important as the American Dream is to our national consciousness, we must admit to certain realities. Many millions in this country are still denied equality of opportunity because of race, ethnic background, or gender. An underclass persists in the form of impoverished families, ill-nourished and ill-educated children, and people living in the streets.[8] Many cities are actually two cities, in which some live in luxury while others live in squalor. The gap between rich and poor has grown in recent years. The gap between rich farms and marginal farms has deepened. And a sharp difference between white and black income persists tenaciously. Far more than we want to admit, people's chances for success still depend on the neighborhood they grow up in or the college they attend.

IDEOLOGY AND PUBLIC POLICY

Ideology refers to the structure of a person's ideas or beliefs about political values and the role of government. It includes the views people develop as they mature about how government should work and how it actually works. Ideology links our basic values to the day-to-day operations or policies of government.

Two major, yet rather broad, schools of political thinking dominate American politics today: *liberalism* and *conservatism*. Two lesser, but more defined, schools of thought, *socialism* and *libertarianism*, also help define the spectrum of ideology in the United States. We turn now to a more detailed description of these approaches.

Liberalism

In the seventeenth and eighteenth centuries, classical liberals fought to minimize the role of government. They stressed individual rights and perceived of governments as the primary threat to these rights and liberties. Thus they favored a limit-

Religious and Civic Organizations

Many other factors are also important to the formation and maintenance of the American political culture. Religious freedom and diversity have played a part. American churches and temples have long fostered "a common set of moral understandings about good and bad, right and wrong, in the realm of individual and social action."[†] Freedom, including freedom of religion, individualism, pluralism, and civic duty, have all been fostered by churches. As churches do not all take the same positions on political issues, their impact is sometimes mitigated, but they have been important to such major social and political movements as abolition of slavery, expansion of civil rights, and opposition to war. Other organizations like the Boy Scouts, 4-H, League of Women Voters, Rotary Club, and Chamber of Commerce encourage citizen participation and pride in community and nation.

The Mass Media

In modern times the mass media have taken over some functions previously performed by the family. By the time they are adults, children will probably have spent more time watching television than in conversation with their parents. They may have had more political instruction from MTV than from their parents or their schools.

Political Activities

Finally, Americans educate each other about political values in the workplace, at the PTA meeting, or in more expressly political activities.

* Fred I. Greenstein, *Children and Politics* (Yale University Press, 1965), p. 44.
† Robert N. Bellah, *The Broken Covenant: American Civil Religion in Time of Trial* (Seabury Press, 1975), p. ix. See also Charles W. Dunn, ed., *Religion in American Politics* (CQ Press, 1989) and Kenneth D. Wald, *Religion and Politics in the United States* (CQ Press, 1992).

"He's trustworthy, loyal, obedient, cheerful, and all that, but he leans to the left."

Drawing by Dedini. © 1988 The New Yorker Magazine, Inc.

ed government and sought ample guarantees of protection from governmental harassment. Over time the emphasis on individualism has remained constant, but the perception of the need for government has changed. Nowadays, liberals view government as protecting individuals from being abused by a variety of governmental and nongovernmental forces such as market vagaries, business decisions, and discriminatory practices.

In its modern American usage, **liberalism** refers to a belief in the positive uses of government to bring about justice and equality of opportunity. Modern-day liberals wish to preserve the rights of the individual and the right to own private property, yet they are also willing to have the government intervene in the economy to remedy the defects of capitalism and a market economy. Contemporary American liberalism has its roots in Franklin Roosevelt's New Deal programs, designed to aid the poor and to protect people against unemployment and bank failures. Today, liberals also seek protection against inadequate or deficient medical assistance and inadequate or deficient housing and education. They generally believe in affirmative action programs, regulations that protect workers' health and safety, tax rates that rise with income, and the right of unions to organize as well as to strike.

On a more philosophical level, liberals generally believe in the possibility of progress. They believe things can be made to work, that the future will be better, that obstacles can be overcome. This positive set of beliefs may explain some of their willingness to believe in the potential benefits of governmental action, a willingness to alter or even negate the old Jeffersonian notion that "government governs best when it governs least." Liberals contend that the character of modern technology and the side effects of industrialization cry out for at least limited governmental programs to offset the loss of liberties suffered by the less well-to-do and the weak. Liberals frequently stress the need for a compassionate and affirmative government.

Both liberals and conservatives are active in projects like Habitat for Humanity, which uses volunteers in the construction of decent homes for lower income families. Here Yale University students and the family that will live in the house join in finishing the job.

Liberals contend that conservatives will usually rule in their own interest and are motivated by the maxim, "Let the government take care of the rich, and the rich in turn will take care of the poor." Liberals, on the other hand, prefer that government take care of the weak, for the strong can nearly always take care of themselves. "We have rejected the discredited theory that the fortunes of the nation should be in the hands of a privileged few," said President Harry Truman. "Instead, we believe that our economic system should rest on a democratic foundation and that wealth should be created for the benefit of all. . . . Every segment of our population and every individual has a right to expect from his government a fair deal."[9]

In the liberal view, all people are equal. Equality of opportunity is essential, and, toward that end, discriminatory practices must be eliminated. Some liberals favor the reduction of great inequalities of wealth that make equality of opportunity impossible. Most favor a certain minimum level of income. Rather than placing a cap on wealth, they want a floor placed beneath the poor. In short, liberals have sought "to lessen the harsh impact of oligarchical rule in economic life, to introduce a measure of democracy within or democratic controls over the industrial-technological process, to assure freedom from arbitrary command within the economic no less than within the political sphere."[10] They ask: How can citizens be equal and free if they are dependent on and necessarily servile to the powers that be?

TYPES OF LIBERALS   Liberals, it should be emphasized, come in many varieties. Some stress civil rights or women's rights or high-quality public education. Others urge government to adopt a more progressive tax system and do more to help the homeless, the handicapped, and society's "have-nots." Still others decry militarism and crusade for treaties and alliances that might bring about a world without terrorism and war. And yet other liberals are preoccupied with environmental or consumer issues. Some liberals embrace all these issues, placing them on an equal plane.

In a sense, liberals who emphasize economic issues may be called *New Deal liberals*; others are *social liberals* or *peace liberals*. If this is not confusing enough, there are those who call themselves **neoliberals.** Neoliberals believe in liberty, justice, and a fair chance for everyone, and they argue that the truly down-and-out must have government assistance. Yet they do not automatically favor unions and big government, nor do they automatically criticize big business or the military. Neoliberals are best characterized as liberals who have lost faith in many welfare programs and are skeptical about the efficiency and responsiveness of large, Washington-based bureaucracies. They are better at diagnosing some of the deficiencies of old liberalism than they are at pointing out what should be done. A sample of neoliberal thinking regularly appears in *The Washington Monthly*.[11]

CRITICISMS OF LIBERALISM   Not everyone, by a long shot, is convinced that liberals in whatever form have the answers for the problems of the 1990s. Critics of liberalism, old and new, say they place too much reliance on governmental solutions, higher taxes, and bureaucrats. Opponents of liberalism say that somewhere along the line liberals forgot that government, to serve our best interests, has to be limited. Power tends to corrupt, they add, and too much reliance or dependence on government can corrupt the spirit, can undermine self-reliance, and can make us forget about those cherished personal freedoms and property rights our Republic was founded to secure and protect. When we get too much government, it tends to start dictating to us, and then our rights and liberties are at risk. Further, too many governmental controls or regulations and too much taxation undermine the self-help ethic that has "made America great." In short, critics of liberalism contend that the welfare and regulatory state pushed by liberals will ultimately destroy individual initiative, the entrepreneurial spirit, and the very engine of economic growth that might lead to true equality of economic opportunities.

Some liberals admit that Ronald Reagan and George Bush redefined the issues in the 1980s and 1990s in such a way that liberalism sounded unnecessary and dated, if not wholly harmful. Wrapping themselves in the symbols of nationalism and patriotism, conservatives took a strong stand in favor of business, the death penalty, and prayer in schools—issues popular with most voters. Liberals, on the other hand, wrapped themselves in the symbols of compassion, fairness, equality, and social justice, also popular issues, but perhaps more relevant in races for Congress than for the White House.

The 1992 election contest between Bill Clinton and George Bush centered on the economy. Hanging in Clinton's campaign headquarters was a poster that read, "It's the economy, stupid!" reminding the Clinton campaign that it would be stupid to let the campaign stray from that issue. George Bush, on the other hand, wanted to stress his experience in defense and foreign policy, his success in the war against Iraq, and his more conservative position on issues like abortion and school prayer. In the end, the economic concerns were too great for Bush to counter, and Clinton won the election.

Kevin Phillips believes that economic divisions will be the major theme of politics in the 1990s:

> One could reasonably assume that the 1990s would be a time in which to correct the excesses of the 1980s, for the dangers posed by excessive individualism, greed and insufficient concern for America as a community went beyond the issue of fairness and, by threatening the ability of the United States to maintain its economic position in the world, created an unusual meeting ground for national self-interest and reform.[12]

But Michael Barone, a well-regarded political observer, disputes the view that economics is the most important dimension of American politics. Rather, he says, cultural divisions matter most: "Civil rights, the Vietnam War, drugs, abortion, policy toward the Soviets and the Third World tended to divide Americans more often on cultural than on economic lines."[13]

Is it possible to reconcile these two positions? Politics in the United States has several focal points. As those change, so do the electoral fortunes of liberals and conservatives. Still, elections often turn on how the economy is doing, with voters blaming the party of the president if it is doing poorly or responding positively if it is doing well. This tendency is true both in presidential elections and mid-term elections.

Liberals were defeated in presidential elections in 1972, 1984, and 1988, yet they won in many state and congressional elections. On a long list of issues—the environment, Social Security, women's rights, unemployment assistance, military spending, arms control, and new programs for the homeless—liberal positions helped elect state and local politicians. Perhaps even more important, the winning candidates often were incumbents running with the advantages of incumbency, and they had maintained close relations with their constituents. Still, a number of allegedly liberal positions are out of favor. National surveys indicate what Americans want from government is lower taxes, less government regulation, less reliance on bureaucracies, a strong defense, stronger anticrime measures, less permissiveness, and a return to prayer in the schools. These are conservative positions.

As the agenda of American politics changes, so does the popularity of liberal or conservative positions. With the collapse of communism many Americans are now less concerned about defense spending and more inclined to focus on solving problems at home. Yet the fiscal constraints imposed by the tax cuts of 1981 and the crushing budget deficit changed the debate about government solutions because few are willing to raise taxes to fund new programs or new ideas. Moreover as the North American Free Trade Agreement (NAFTA) demonstrates, we live in a global economy, and our jobs and economic progress are linked to our neighbors and other countries around the world. The net effect of these changes is our national government, while focusing on domestic issues like health care, crime, and welfare, does so in a context much more aware of the constaints of the budget deficit and the unpopularity of tax increases.

Conservatism

American **conservatism** has its roots in the political thinking of John Adams, Alexander Hamilton, and many of their contemporaries. They believed in limited government and encouraged individual excellence and personal achievement. Private property rights and belief in free enterprise are cardinal attributes of contemporary conservatism. In contrast to liberals, conservatives want to keep government small, except in the area of national defense. However, because conservatives take a more pessimistic view of human nature than liberals do, they maintain that most people need strong leadership institutions, firm laws, and strict moral codes to keep their appetites under control. Government, they think, needs to ensure order. Conservatives are also inclined to believe that those who fail in life are in some way the architects of their own misfortune and thus must bear the main responsibility for solving their own problems. Conservatives have a preference for the status quo and desire change only in moderation. A sample of conservative thinking can be found in *The National Review,* a weekly magazine.

Most conservatives opposed the New Deal programs of the 1930s and the War on Poverty in the 1960s, and they have seldom favored aggressive civil rights and affirmative action programs. Human needs, they say, can and should be taken care of by families and charities. Equal treatment can be achieved by encouraging citizens to be more tolerant. Conservatives place substantial faith in the private sector, and they consider social justice to be essentially an economic question. They dislike the tendency to turn to government, especially the national government, for solutions to societal problems. Government social activism, they say, has been highly inflationary and counterproductive. Conservatives also prize stability—stability of the dollar, stability in international affairs, and stability in political and economic affairs. They prefer private giving and individual voluntary efforts targeted at social and economic problems rather than government programs.

TRADITIONAL CONSERVATIVES Traditional conservatives recognize that government must exist, yet insist it should be limited in what it does, and that within its proper sphere of action, it should be strong and resolute. "The purpose of government is to maintain the framework of order within which other private institutions can operate effectively."[14] The traditional conservative applauds the heartfelt compassion implicit in Franklin Roosevelt's Second Bill of Rights but believes that to turn to the federal government to solve those problems is to guarantee a too powerful, intrusive, and expensive government.

Liberals favor national action and a stronger central government. Conservatives, however, contend that centralization means higher taxes, that the freedom of the majority would greatly diminish, and that the initiative and risk-taking entrepreneurial impulses of inventors, capital investors, and ingenious business leaders would be irreversibly discouraged.[15]

Former U.S. Senator Barry Goldwater, the Republican candidate for president in 1964 and an outspoken conservative, condemned "government welfarism" as one of the greatest evils of the twentieth century:

Let welfare be a private concern. Let it be promoted by individuals and families, by churches, private hospitals, religious service organizations, community charities and other institutions that have been established for this purpose. If the objection is raised that private institutions lack sufficient funds, let us remember that every penny the

Rush Limbaugh: A New Voice for Conservatism

Sixteen million Americans provide an audience for political commentator, talk show host, and former disc jockey Rush Limbaugh. His syndicated radio program earns him an estimated $5 million per year, and his total estimated income from his books, speeches, and broadcasting activities is about $20 million. Known for his outspoken attacks on Bill and Hillary Clinton, feminist groups, and other liberal groups, he has also become a best-selling author of books *The Way Things Ought to Be,* and *See, I Told You So.*

Some of Limbaugh's more memorable quotes include:

Limbaugh on the women's movement:
    "I love the women's movement, especially when I'm walking behind it."
Limbaugh on the Clinton administration:
    "America's latest hostage situation."
Limbaugh on himself:
    "I'm the most dangerous man in America."

Limbaugh is so controversial that Time/CNN commissioned a poll of public opinion on the conservative commentator. Here are the words respondents used to describe him:

Intelligent	71%
Obnoxious	66
Tells it like it is	65
Offensive	59
Demeaning to women	47
Demeaning to blacks and minorities	34
Irresponsible	33

Conservative groups openly seek his endorsement and support. The National Rifle Association (NRA), for instance, hosted a banquet at which Limbaugh spoke. Seats were $125 each. The NRA sold 5,000 tickets, and another 5,000 watched the speech on a televised hook-up.

SOURCES: Kurt Andersen, "Big Mouths," *Time,* November 1, 1993, pp. 60–66; Eric Morganthaler, "A Common Touch: Dittoheads All Over Making Rush Limbaugh Superstar of the Right," *The Wall Street Journal,* June 28, 1993, p. A-1; *Time/CNN Poll,* October 26, 1993.

Barry Goldwater, Republican candidate for president in 1964, was seen by many voters as too conservative. On the other hand, George McGovern, Democratic candidate for president in 1972, was seen by many voters as too liberal.

federal government does not appropriate for welfare is potentially available for private use—and without the overhead charge for processing the money through the federal bureaucracy.[16]

In addition to fighting the welfare state, traditional conservatives, in the name of freedom, have been emphatically pro-business. Thus, they oppose higher taxes and resist all but the most necessary antitrust, trade, and environmental regulations on corporations. The functions of government should be, say conservatives, to encourage family values, protect us against foreign enemies and criminals, preserve law and order, enforce private contracts, foster competitive markets, and encourage free and fair trade.

Traditional conservatives have customarily favored dispersing power broadly throughout the political and social systems, precisely to avoid concentration of power at the national level. They favor having the market, rather than the government, distribute goods. Traditional conservatives subordinate economic and social equality to liberty and freedom. To allow the worst-off to take advantage of the best-off is to hurt both groups in the end.

THE NEW RIGHT   Another brand of conservatism—sometimes called the New Right, ultraconservatism, or even the Radical Right—emerged in the past generation. The New Right shares the love of freedom shown by the traditional conservatives and, during the 1980s, backed an aggressive effort to combat international communism, especially in Central America. It has also developed an activist public policy agenda that it would like implemented by conservatives in Congress and in the White House. The New Right favors the return of organized prayer in the public schools and renewal of covert operations by the Central Intelligence Agency. It wants strict limits on abortion; it opposes policies like job quotas, busing, and any tolerance of pornography. In short, a defining characteristic of the New Right is a strong desire to impose various social controls.

One driving force in the New Right is the Religious Right. Leaders of this group include Pat Robertson, a candidate for the presidency in 1988, and Jerry Falwell, who founded and promoted the Moral Majority in the 1980s. Much of the Religious Right's agenda overlaps that of the New Right—a concern with moral issues like abortion, homosexuality, and prayer in public schools and public meetings. Adherents of the Religious Right have been especially active at the state and local levels, in political parties and initiative campaigns and on school boards. The 1992 initiative in Colorado to overturn ordinances protecting gays and lesbians from discrimination was placed on the ballot largely through their efforts.[17] The Colorado law was later declared unconstitutional by the state supreme court.

Senator Jesse Helms (R.-N.C.) is one of the most influential leaders of the New Right. Helms built an impressive coalition in the South and elsewhere by uniting various groups: fundamentalist Christians worried about "secular humanism" and in favor of official school prayer; conservative Catholics opposed to abortion; white parents opposed to drugs, pornography, and forced busing; small business owners resentful of government intrusion; and manufacturers in favor of less governmental regulation and more defense spending. Patrick Buchanan tried to rally the New Right in his 1992 presidential campaign, but rarely got above 30 percent of the Republican primary vote, and those votes appeared to be based more on opposition to George Bush than on ideology.[18] The New Right remains an important but not dominant part of conservatism in the United States.

Some conservatives question the moralistic tone of the New Right. For example, Barry Goldwater worries that too much prominence and influence have been granted to the New Right, especially the Moral Majority and those he calls the "checkbook clergy." Our Constitution, Goldwater says, seeks to allow freedom for everyone, not merely those professing certain moral or religious views of ultimate right. Goldwater points to the bloody divisions in Northern Ireland, the holy wars in Lebanon, and the pernicious religious righteousness in Iran as examples of the politicalization of churches. "The Moral Majority has no more right to dictate its moral and political beliefs to the country than does any other group, political or religious," says Goldwater. "The same is true of pro-choice, abortion, or other groups. They are free to persuade us because this land is blessed with liberty, but not to assign religious or political absolutes—complete right or wrong."[19] Goldwater fears that the great danger of the New Right is that instead of broadening its base, it will tear his beloved Republican party apart. He also, one gathers, opposes moral absolutes—the kind the Moral Majority thrives on.

NEOCONSERVATIVES   The past generation has also witnessed the emergence of people who call themselves **neoconservatives.** Many are former Democrats who admired FDR and Harry Truman but left the Democratic party over Vietnam, busing, and the decisions of the liberal (overly liberal in their view) Earl Warren Supreme Court. They want to continue programs that work and are truly necessary, but reject the rest. An example of a successful program they would be inclined to keep is Head Start, the federally funded program for disadvantaged preschool children. Neoconservatives believe that too many government programs will lead to a paternalistic state. Though willing to interfere with the market for overriding social purposes, neoconservatives prefer finding market solutions to social problems. An example of neoconservative writing can be found in *Commentary*, a monthly magazine.

Neoconservatives favor larger military expenditures than do liberals. They remain skeptical of the intentions of some of the republics of the Commonwealth of Independent States as well as other nations. Conservatives also favor sufficient military spending to permit the United States to play a role in mediating conflicts around the world, especially in settings where U. S. interests are involved. But conservatives are not always united in their support for the use of military force, as indicated by the opposition of some conservatives to the use of American troops in Somalia, Bosnia, and Haiti in the 1990s. They also favor the death penalty and are more worried about crime than about the homeless. They say the courts have gone too far in protecting the rights of the criminal and are too little concerned about the rights of the victims of crime.

Neoconservatives are credited with various original writings on social policy, supply-side economics, education, and the role of "national interest" in foreign affairs. *Supply-side economics* (which during the 1980s was often called "Reaganomics") is the belief that lower taxes will encourage economic growth, new jobs, and ultimately new tax revenues. The United States, in the neoconservative view, should use its power to shape events; it cannot retreat into isolationism. Thus neoconservatives heartily approved Reagan's invasion of Grenada, his bombing of Libya, and U.S. assertiveness in Central America.[20] More recently they strongly supported the use of military force in Panama and Kuwait.

CRITICISMS OF CONSERVATISM   Not everyone agreed with Ronald Reagan's statement that "government is the problem."[21] Indeed, critics of conservatism before and during the Reagan-Bush era saw hostility to government as counterproductive and inconsistent. Conservatives, they argued, have a selective opposition to government. They want more government when it serves their needs—by regulating pornography and abortion, for example—but are opposed to it when it serves somebody else's. Critics point out that government spending, especially for defense, grew during the 1980s when the conservatives were in control. Conservatives are often criticized for insensitivity to the social needs of the homeless and mentally ill.

**Differences In Political Ideology:
Conservative, Moderate, Liberal**

| | Self-Classification | | |
	Conservative	Moderate	Liberal
Sex			
Male	36%	44%	20%
Female	25	55	20
Race			
Black	14	63	23
White	32	47	20
American			
Indian	40	44	16
Asian	44	44	12
Hispanic	22	64	14
Age			
18–24	21	55	23
25–34	29	48	24
35–44	33	40	27
45–54	37	44	19
55–64	29	58	13
65+	28	60	12
Education			
Less than high			
school	19	70	12
High school			
graduate	26	59	15
Some college	32	45	23
Bachelor's			
degree	46	25	30
Advanced			
degree	36	23	40
Religion			
Protestant	33	50	17
Catholic	30	51	19
Jewish	16	32	52
Party Identification			
Republican	55	39	6
Independent	20	54	26
Democrat	17	52	31

SOURCE: 1992 American National Election Studies, Center for Political Studies, University of Michigan.

Note: We have combined with the moderates persons who do not know their ideology or had not thought much about it. For the party identification, we have combined Independent leaners with their respective parties. Rows may not add up to 100% due to rounding.

Conservatives place great faith in our market economy—critics would say too much faith. This posture often puts them at odds with labor unions and consumer activists and in close alliance with business people, particularly large corporations. Hostility to regulation and a belief in competition are some of the reasons conservatives pushed deregulation in the 1980s. These changes did not always have the intended positive effects, as the collapse of many savings and loans revealed.[22] During the same decade, according to some critics, the Reagan administration's decision not to pursue antitrust actions encouraged a flurry of mergers and acquisitions that diverted our economy from more productive economic activity.[23] Conservatives counter that relying on "market solutions" and encouraging the free market are still the best course of action in most policy areas.[24]

Consistent with the conservative hostility to government was the policy of the Reagan years of lowering taxes. In his 1981 address to the nation on the state of the economy, Reagan likened government to children who spend more than their parents can afford. He mentioned that such extravagance could be cured by "simply reducing their allowance."[25] Implied was the idea that government spending could be controlled by reducing the amount government was allowed to spend. Many conservatives embraced the idea that if we lower taxes on the rich, their economic activity will "trickle down" to the poor. This view was criticized by many Democrats in the 1992 election campaign, who pointed out that the growth in income and wealth in the 1980s was largely concentrated among the well-to-do.[26]

Conservatives are also criticized for their failure to acknowledge and endorse policies that deal with racism and sexism in the United States. Their opposition to the civil rights laws in the 1960s and their opposition to affirmative action in the 1990s are examples of this perspective. Not only have conservatives opposed new laws in these areas, they have hampered the activity of the executive branch when in power, and have sought to limit the activity of the courts in these matters as well.

Socialism and Libertarianism

Our review of American political ideology would not be complete without a brief comment on socialism and libertarianism.

SOCIALISM **Socialism** is an economic and governmental system based on public ownership of the means of production and exchange. Karl Marx once described socialism as a transitional stage of society between capitalism and communism. In a capitalist system, the means of production and most of the property are privately owned, whereas in a communist or socialist system, property is "owned" by the state in common for all the people. In the ultimate socialist country, justice is achieved by having participants determine their own needs and take what is appropriate from the common product of society. Marx's dictum was, "From each according to his ability, to each according to his needs."[27]

In one of the most dramatic transformations in recent times, Russia, its sister republics, and its former European satellites abandoned their version of socialism—communism—and are now attempting to establish free markets. These countries had previously rejected capitalism, preferring state ownership and centralized government planning of the economy. But by the 1990s the disparities in economic well-being between capitalist and communist nations produced a tide of political and economic reform that left communism intact in only a few countries, such as Cuba.

American socialists—of whom there are very few outspoken or prominent examples—favor a greatly expanded role for the government. They would nationalize certain industries, institute a public jobs program so that all who want work would be put to work, and place a much steeper tax burden on the wealthy. In short, American socialists favor policies to help the underdog by means of income redistribution programs. They also favor stepped-up efforts toward greater equality in property rights. American socialists would drastically cut defense spending as well.[28] Most of the democracies of Western Europe are far more influenced by socialist ideas than we are in the United States, but they remain, like the United States, largely market economies.

Representative Bernard Sanders of Vermont is the only socialist in the U.S. Congress. He has run as an Independent.

LIBERTARIANISM   **Libertarianism** is an ideology that cherishes individual liberty and insists on a sharply limited government. It carries some overtones of anarchism, of the classical English liberalism of the past, and of a 1930s-style conservatism. The Libertarian party has gained a modest following among people who believe that both liberals and conservatives lack consistency in their attitude toward the power of the national government. Libertarians preach opposition to government and just about all its programs. They favor massive cuts in government spending, an end to the Federal Bureau of Investigation and the Central Intelligence Agency and most regulatory commissions, and a minimal defense establishment (one that would defend the United States only if directly attacked). They oppose *all* government regulation, including, for example mandatory seat-belt and helmet laws. A poster at one of their recent national conventions read, "U.S. out of Latin America; U.S. out of North America!" Libertarians favor eliminating not only welfare programs but also programs that subsidize business, farmers, and the rich. They opposed government-backed guaranteed loans for Chrysler and other businesses and would turn the functions of the Postal Service over to private companies. Unlike most conservatives, libertarians would repeal laws that regulate personal morality, including abortion, pornography, prostitution, and recreational drugs.

A Libertarian party candidate for president has been on the ballot in all 50 states in recent presidential elections, although never obtaining more than 1 percent of the vote. The Libertarian candidate for president in 1992, André Marrou, ran on a platform that emphasized elimination of corporate subsidies, social welfare, and foreign military welfare; decriminalization of drugs; abolition of the Federal Reserve Board and return of the gold standard; withdrawal of the overseas military from Japan, Korea, the Philippines, Germany, and elsewhere; and abolition of the Internal Revenue Service and the income tax. Libertarian positions are rarely timid; at the very least, they prompt intriguing political debates.

A Word of Caution

Political labels have different meanings across national boundaries as well as over time. To be a liberal in certain European nations is to be on the right; to be liberal in the 1990s in the United States is to be on the left. In recent elections, "liberal," which back in FDR's day had been popular, became "the L-word," a label most politicians sought to avoid. George Bush found it helpful in his 1988 campaign to charge Michael Dukakis and congressional Democrats with being "liberal," which he equated with supporting high taxes, being "soft on crime," and advocating too much government interference in the economy.

During the 1992 election, Bill Clinton attempted to distance himself from the liberal positions of previous Democratic presidential candidates by asserting that he was a "different kind of Democrat." His emphasis on investment, personal responsibility, new jobs and economic growth, and an end to permanent welfare system, were offered as evidence. While his concern for health care reform and his prochoice stance on abortion were in tune with the liberal wing of his party, Clinton avoided the label of "liberal Democrat." The future reputation of liberals will be defined in part by Clinton's successes or failures. Conservatives will continue to

André Marrou was the Libertarian candidate for president in 1992.

attempt to label his programs and proposals "liberal," and Clinton will continue to attempt to avoid the label because he wants to build as broad a coalition as possible.

It is also important to appreciate that ideology both causes events and is affected by them. Just as the Great Depression resulted in almost a tidal wave of ideological change, so did our involvement in World War II, Korea, and Vietnam, each in its own way. World War II, with its positive example of how government can work to defend freedom, strengthened positive views about the role of the national government. The Vietnam War probably had the opposite effect—disillusionment with government. The antigovernment sentiment in recent presidential elections is undoubtedly related to Vietnam, the Watergate scandal, and the Iran-Contra affair.

Debates about communist expansionism are increasingly dated and irrelevant in American politics. In the 1990s there is little fear that the United States will become communist, and the communist threat around the world is greatly diminished. But people of varying ideologies do indeed worry about whether the United States is becoming too soft and losing ground in the global economy. Today we are more likely to debate what will make us beat, or at least compete with, "those capitalists from Japan" and other Pacific Rim nations. Ideological controversy centers on how we can improve our schools, encourage a stronger work ethic, and stop the flow of drugs into the country; whether to permit openly gay people into the military or sanction gay marriages; and the best ways to instill religious values, build character, and encourage cohesive and lasting families.

Do social programs and job-training programs make things better or worse? Is reliance on the marketplace or on government planners a better way to make long-term policy decisions for the nation? What is the best way to balance the budget and curb inflation? Are foreign investors and international conglomerates shaping our lives as well as our economic policy decisions? Ideological debate and differences are always with us, but the nature of the issues changes. There are likely to be even more changes as we approach the end of the century.

IDEOLOGY AND THE AMERICAN PEOPLE

Despite the twists and turns of American politics, the distribution of ideology in our nation has been remarkably consistent in the past 20 years (see box). There are more conservatives than liberals, but the proportion of conservatives did not increase substantially with the decisive Republican presidential victories of the 1980s. Survey questions used to ascertain ideology permit respondents not only to answer "moderate" but also to indicate that they "don't know" their ideology or "have not thought much about it." The combined "moderate" and "don't know" categories are consistently much larger than either the conservative or liberal group and constitute a cluster more interested in pragmatism than ideology. These people vote for liberals in some races and conservatives in others because they simply prefer one candidate over another. Indeed there are more who indicate no ideology than indicate liberal and conservative combined. In sum, most Americans are unconstrained by a consistent ideology.[29]

One other important fact about ideology in the United States is that very few people see themselves as extreme conservatives or extreme liberals. In 1992, only 3 percent of the population saw themselves as extreme conservatives, and an even smaller percentage, 2 percent, saw themselves as extreme liberals. These percentages also have changed very little over time. When given the option to describe themselves as "conservative" or "slightly conservative," 15 percent say "slightly conservative" and only 13 percent say "conservative."[30] The same tendency is true of liberals. (We analyze party identification in Chapter 10, but it is important to note here that there are liberal and conservative wings in both parties.)

HOW AMERICANS DEFINE THEIR IDEOLOGY

Most Americans are not deeply "ideological." They lack an internally consistent and coherent set of beliefs about politics and public issues. The average citizen does not spend a lot of time thinking about government and public policies. Still, many Americans have ideological moorings, and some hold them fiercely. Politically, Americans are often said to be moderate and pragmatic rather than ideological. The most common measure of ideology is simply to ask people where they would place themselves on a liberal/conservative scale.

What the Public Thinks It Means to Be a Liberal or a Conservative

Q: What sort of things do you have in mind when you say someone's political views are Liberal? (top five responses)

Accept change	38%
Favor social programs	20
Favor government spending/spend freely	17
Favor abortion	14
Favor freedom to do as one chooses/ not interested in setting moral standards	11

Q: What sort of things do you have in mind when you say someone's political views are Conservative? (top five responses)

Resist change or new ideas	44%
Spend less freely/tight economic policy	18
Are slow or cautious in response to problems/do nothing	14
Support free enterprise/capitalism	13
Oppose abortion.	11

SOURCE: 1992 National Election Study, Center for Political Studies, University of Michigan.

Ideology Curve

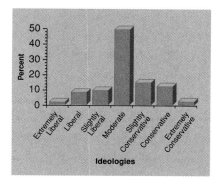

SOURCE: 1992 National Election Study, Center for Political Studies, University of Michigan.

Ideology over Time

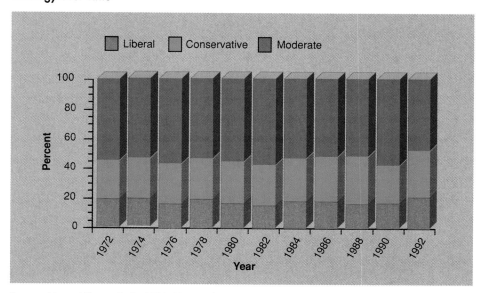

SOURCES: National Election Study, 1952–88, Cumulative Data File; 1990 National Election Study and 1992 National Election Study, Center for Political Studies, University of Michigan.

"There's no justice in the world, Kirby, but I'm not convinced that this is an entirely bad thing."

Drawing by Handelsman. © 1986 The New Yorker Magazine, Inc.

For those who have a liberal or conservative preference, ideology provides a lens through which to view politics. It helps simplify the complexities of politics, policies, personalities, and programs. An ideology may be an accurate or an inaccurate description of reality, yet it is still the way a person thinks about people, power, and society. For these reasons, it is important to understand how people view candidates, issues, and public policy. Among legislators, lobbyists, and party activists, ideology is even more important. Their ideologies shape our social and political institutions and help determine public policies and constitutional change.

An alternative to the liberal/conservative self-identification measure of ideology is to ask people about their attitudes toward politicians and public policies. Most Americans do not organize their attitudes systematically. A voter may want increased spending for defense but vote for the party that is for reducing defense spending because he or she has always voted for that party or prefers its stand on the environment. Or a person may favor adoption of the North American Free Trade Agreement and government-financed health care for all and still support Ross Perot.

Consistency among various attitudes and opinions is often relatively low. Much of the time people view political issues as isolated matters and do not apply a general standard of performance in evaluating parties or candidates. Indeed, many citizens find it difficult to relate what happens in one policy situation to what happens in another. This problem becomes worse as government gets into more and more policy areas. Hence, most people, not surprisingly, have difficulty finding candidates who reflect their ideological preferences across a range of issues.

The absence of widespread and solidified liberal and conservative positions in the United States makes for politics and policy-making processes that are markedly different from those in many European and other nations. Our policy making is characterized more by coalitions of the moment than by fixed alignments that pit one set of ideologies against another. And our politics is marked more by moderation, pragmatism, and accommodation than a prolonged and strained battle between two, three, or more competing philosophies of government. Elsewhere, especially in countries where a strong Socialist or Christian Democratic party exists, things are different.

By no means, however, does this mean that policies or ideas are not elements in our politics. Such issues as affirmative action, NAFTA, the Supreme Court's abortion rulings, and options for health care reform, gun control, and environmental protection have aroused people who previously were passive about politics and political ideas.

IDEOLOGY AND TOLERANCE

Is there a connection between support for civil liberties and tolerance for racial minorities and the ideologies of liberalism and conservatism? Some political scientists assert that conservatives are generally less tolerant than liberals. This view is stoutly contested by conservatives, who have charged liberals with trying to impose a "politically correct" position on universities and the media. "Conservatives," observe Herbert McClosky and Alida Brill, "have repeatedly shown their fear of political and social instability. With rare exceptions, the conservatives have been the party of tradition, stability, duty, respect for authority, and the primacy of 'law and order' over all competing values."[31]

Liberals share many of these views but place a different emphasis on the interpretation. They have more faith in government and readily turn to government to help achieve greater equality of opportunity. Liberals are usually more tolerant of dissent and the expression of unorthodox opinions. However, liberals, too, can be intolerant—of antiabortion forces, for example, or the National Rifle Association, or the views of Rush Limbaugh.

Tolerance for the homosexual lifestyle is often a litmus test of liberal or conservative ideology. This Lesbian and Gay March on Washington in October 1993 brought some 200,000 people out in support of removal of discriminatory laws against gays.

Most liberals are strongly opposed to crime and lawbreaking, yet they are as concerned about the roots or causes of crime as they are about the punishment of criminals. Perhaps for this reason, liberals exhibit somewhat greater concern than conservatives for the rights of the accused and are more willing to expand the rights of due process. Conservatives usually take a harder line and, in recent years, have won widespread popular support for their greater concern for the victims of crime than for the rights of the accused.

Such differences are most evident in the responses of liberals and conservatives to questions of civil rights and civil liberties. Research in the early 1980s found that, despite our common political culture and despite our widespread allegiance to constitutionalism and the Bill of Rights, many Americans sharply disagree on some basic political matters. Liberals are ordinarily more willing than conservatives to defend the rights of those who are in the minority, who may be wrong, or who take unorthodox or unpleasing stands.

In the area of free speech, conservatives were once seen as less willing to permit speech that was out of the political or cultural mainstream. Perhaps conservatives were less tolerant because those who claimed to be exercising the right of free speech often attacked established values. Now the argument that liberalism is correlated with tolerance is more complicated and the evidence less persuasive.

Conservatives believe that the United States has become too permissive. Many conservatives, especially in the New or Religious Right, are highly critical of homosexuals, drug users, prostitutes, unwed mothers, and pornography. They worry about what they claim has been a decline in moral standards and, interestingly, call on government to help reverse these trends. Liberals, on the other hand, generally accept nonconformity in conduct and opinion as an inescapable by-product of freedom:

> Like John Stuart Mill, contemporary liberals tend to perceive the free exchange of divergent views and attempts at social experimentation as potential harbingers of social improvement and progress. They regard the dangers to society from unorthodox beliefs and behavior as minimal compared with their potential benefits—a small price to be paid for social advancement."[32]

In this regard, liberals are like libertarians.

It is these sharp cleavages in political thinking that stir opposing interest groups into formation and action. Groups such as the Moral Majority, the American Civil Liberties Union, Amnesty International, Mothers Against Drunk Driving, Queer Nation, and countless others promote their views of what is politically desirable. It is also these differences in ideological perspectives that reinforce party loyalties and that divide us at election time. Policy fights in Congress, between Congress and the White House, and during judicial confirmation hearings also have their roots in our uneasily coexisting ideological values.

Ideologies have consequences. Although Americans share many ideas in common, we as a people also hold many contradictory ideas. Our hard-earned rights and liberties are never entirely safeguarded; they are fragile and are shaped by the political, economic, and social climate of the day. In the next chapters we examine the interest groups and political parties that are ever-present to advance their values and compete in the always-evolving American political culture. Before turning to those topics, we will examine the social and economic diversity of the American political landscape in Chapter 8 and see why agreement on shared democratic values is all the more remarkable.

SUMMARY

1. The United States, like every other nation or society, has a distinctive political culture. It consists of a widely held set of fundamental political values and accepted processes and institutions that permit us to manage conflict and resolve problems. In the United States, there is, at least in the abstract, a widespread reverence for the Constitution, the Bill of Rights, a two-party system, and the right to elect officials on the basis of majority rule. Our belief in social equality has fostered acceptance of the notion that government should guarantee equality of opportunity through programs like education and job training.

2. Americans share a widespread commitment to classical liberalism, which embraces the importance of the individual and of freedom, equality, private property, limited government, and popular consent.

3. Perhaps the most notable tension in the American political culture is that we simultaneously believe in free market economics and a democratic society based on political equality. We want our economy to be relatively free from government controls and want major economic decisions to be shaped by the marketplace; yet we also want every American to enjoy the possibility of an equal voice in

shaping our laws and policies, an ideal that may require government intervention.

4. American political values have been affected by the industrial transformation, the development of large corporations and other large institutions, the Great Depression, the rights revolution, and a global economy.

5. The sources of the American political culture include the family, the schools, religious and civic organizations, the mass media, and political activities.

6. Although many Americans are nonideological and are guided primarily by moderate pragmatism, a significant segment of Americans are conservatives or liberals.

7. There are at least four dimensions that shape a person's conservative or liberal views: the economy, civil rights and civil liberties, foreign and defense policy, and lifestyle.

8. Our ideological orientation has a bearing on how tolerant we are of the views and conduct of others. Liberals tend to be more permissive, whereas conservatives generally favor tradition, stability, and greater levels of "law and order." These differences have consequences for electoral contests, judicial interpretation, and policy development in our political system.

FURTHER READING

Leon P. Baradat, *Political Ideologies: Their Origins and Impact,* 4th ed. (Prentice Hall, 1991).

William F. Buckley and Charles R. Kesler, *Keeping the Tablets: Modern American Conservative Thought* (Harper & Row, 1988).

James MacGregor Burns, *Uncommon Sense* (Harper & Row, 1972).

Louis Hartz, *The Liberal Tradition in America* (Harcourt, Brace, 1955).

Samuel Huntington, *American Politics: The Promise of Disharmony* (Harvard University Press, Belknap Press, 1981).

Irving Kristol, *Reflections of a Neo-Conservative: Looking Back, Looking Ahead* (Basic Books, 1983).

Robert Kuttner, *The End of Laissez-Faire: National Purpose and the Global Economy after the Cold War* (Knopf, 1991).

Herbert McClosky and John Zaller, *The American Ethos: Public Attitudes Toward Capitalism and Democracy* (Harvard University Press, 1984).

Kevin Phillips, *Boiling Point: Democrats, Republicans, and the Decline of Middle-Class Prosperity* (Random House, 1993).

Laurence Shames, *The Hunger for More: Searching for Values in an Age of Greed* (Times Books, 1989).

THE AMERICAN POLITICAL LANDSCAPE

The Constitution of the state of Arizona requires all government officials and employees to use English when performing government business. This provision is more specific and restrictive than the laws in some other states that require English to be the official language. In 1990, the Arizona "English only" provision was challenged by Maria-Kelley Yniguez, a state insurance claims administrator who found it necessary to use Spanish with clients. Yniguez felt caught between her commitment as a public employee to uphold the state constitution and her desire to help people who speak only Spanish. The U.S. District Court for Arizona ruled the provision unconstitutional because it violated the free speech protection of the First Amendment of the U.S. Constitution.[1]

The Arizona case raises important issues involving language, culture, and politics. During the 1980s, voters in Arizona, Colorado, California, and Florida enacted initiatives to make English the official language. Nearly three out of four Californians voted for this measure. In Florida the result was even more decisive—84 percent approved. All but three states have considered similar measures.

The controversy over language reflects our long history as a nation of immigrants. From the Germans in the 1700s and 1800s to the Hispanic and Asian newcomers of the 1980s and 1990s, the nation has had to accommodate many cultures and languages, and the controversy persists today over whether to encourage bilingual education in American schools. Bilingual education raises many of the same issues as the effort to designate English as the official language.

It is difficult for political scientists—and for college students and everyone else—to overcome the tendency to generalize from their own experience. Most of us do not stop to consider how people from other backgrounds might see things differently. This **ethnocentrism**—selective perception based on individual background, attitudes, and biases—is not uncommon among college students, who often assume that others share their economic opportunities, social attitudes, sense of civic responsibility, and self-confidence.

Albert Einstein once said few people are capable of expressing opinions that differ much from the prejudices of their social upbringing.[2] In this chapter we examine Einstein's view that the social environment explains or at least shapes our opinions and prejudices. It would be a mistake to contend that a person's social environment and background define his or her political behavior in totality. People change, learn, and grow. Yet, as we will see, the impact of social and economic factors is powerful.

Politics and government involve more than laws and legal institutions; they involve *people,* and while people in this nation have many things in common, they can also be very different. This chapter describes American diversity and the implications of geographic, social, and economic divisions for politics and government. Specifically, it explores the effects of regional or state identity on political perspectives; the implications of differences in race, ethnicity, gender, sexual orientation, religion, wealth and income, occupation, and social class for opinions on issues and voting choices; and the relationship between age and education and political participation.

WHERE ARE WE FROM?

You may have often been asked, "Where are you from?" In certain settings you answer the United States; in others, you may say Illinois, California, or Idaho; and in still others, Dallas, Brooklyn, or North Las Vegas. Where you are from can be important to your personal political identity, attached at the levels of town, city, state, and nation. Where you are from is also important to politics, because the history, economy, and social makeup of cities, states, and regions differ.

Geography and National Identity

The United States is a geographically large and historically isolated country. As Alexis de Tocqueville observed in 1830, the country has no major political or economic powers on its borders "and consequently [has] no great wars, financial crises, invasions, or conquests to fear."[3] Geographic isolation from the major powers of the world during our government's formative period helps explain American politics. The Atlantic Ocean served as a barrier to foreign meddling, giving us time to establish our political tradition and develop our economy.

In our entire history we have fought only one foreign enemy on our own soil— England in the War of 1812. (The war with Mexico of 1846–48 was fought on Mexican land, some of which became American land as a result of the war. The only other war fought on our soil was, of course, the Civil War.) In contrast, during the same period, Poland was invaded and eventually partitioned by Austria, Prussia, and Russia. The difference is largely explained by location: Poland was surrounded by Europe's great powers. Had the United States been closer to Europe, it may have been overrun like Poland, and our Constitution and institutions repeatedly changed to suit the invaders. Having powerful and aggressive neighbors makes it difficult for relatively weak nations to nurture democracy.

Scholars who study new democracies have found it generally takes more than two generations for democratic norms and values to become deeply rooted enough to withstand strong antidemocratic pressures, like military coups or economic depressions. The United States is fortunate that its geographic position gave it time to develop democratic norms and values.

The United States is a large country. Its land mass exceeds that of all but three nations in the world. In contrast, India has a population more than three times larger than the United States on a land mass one-third the size. Geographic space gave the expanding population of the United States room to spread out. This meant that some of the political conflicts arising from religion, social class, and national origins were diffused because groups could isolate themselves from one another. (See James Madison, *The Federalist*, No. 10, in the Appendix, for a development of the large republic idea.) Moreover, the large and accessible land mass helped foster the perspective that the United States had a **manifest destiny** to be a continental nation with coasts on both the Atlantic and Pacific oceans. This notion that the United States was "destined" to expand all the way to the Pacific was used to justify taking land once occupied by Native Americans and to justify our entry into the Mexican American War.

The United States is a land of abundant natural resources. We have rich farmland, which not only feeds our population but makes us one of the three major exporters of food in the world. We are rich in such natural resources as coal, iron, uranium, and many precious metals. All these resources enhance economic growth, provide jobs, and stabilize government. "The physical causes, unconnected with laws, which can lead to prosperity are more numerous in America than in any other country at any other time in history," observed Alexis de Tocqueville. "In the United States not legislation alone is democratic, for Nature herself seems to work for the people."[4]

Geography also helps explain our diversity. Parts of the United States are wonderfully suited to agriculture, others to mining or ranching, and still others to shipping. These differences produce different regional economic concerns, which in turn influence politics. For instance, a person from the agricultural heartland may

Part of our national identity is bound up with the physical isolation many families endured as pioneers. This family was seeking a new home in Custer county, Nebraska, in 1886.

have a different perception of foreign trade than an automobile worker in Detroit. In addition, that automobile worker may be African American, a fact that may be more important than what he does or where she lives. To understand American politics, we must recognize these differences.

In the United States—unlike Canada, Eastern Europe, and India—geography does not define an ethnic division. All the Serbs do not live in one place, all French-speaking Catholics in another, and all German immigrants in another. Sectional differences in the United States are primarily geographic, not ethnic or religious.

Sectional Differences

The most distinct section of the United States remains the South, although differences from other regions are diminishing. From the beginning of the Republic, the agricultural South differed from the industrial North, but the most important difference between the regions was the southern institution of slavery. Northern opposition to slavery, which grew increasingly intense in the middle of the nineteenth century, reinforced the sectional economic interests that divided the nation. The eleven Confederate states, by virtue of their decision to secede from the Union, reinforced a common political identity that persists more than a century after the Civil War.

Sectional differences were strengthened by the policy of Reconstruction, the region's common economic interests, and especially the problems of race relations. The Civil War was fought over the issue of state self-determination in such matters as slavery. When the North won the war, African Americans were emancipated, but they were not politically, socially, or economically integrated. They did not, for example, have equal voting rights; as recently as 1960, only 5 percent of African Americans in Mississippi were registered to vote.[5]

Things have changed in the last 35 years, and as a result the South is becoming less distinct today. The large migration of persons from outside the region who have moved to the sun belt has diminished somewhat the sense of regional identity. But the South has also undergone tremendous change. The civil rights revolu-

TABLE 8-1

Voting Patterns in the Eleven
Former Confederate States

Average Republican Vote for President	
1980	50%
1984	62
1988	59
1992	43

Average Republican Vote for State Legislature	
1980	17%
1984	21
1988	26
1992	30

SOURCE: U.S. Bureau of the Census, *Statistical Abstract of the United States, 1991* (Government Printing Office, 1991), pp. 252, 265; U.S. Bureau of the Census, *Statistical Abstract of the United States, 1989* (Government Printing Office, 1989), p. 254.

FIGURE 8-1
Population Gains by Region, 1970–1990.

SOURCE: U.S. Bureau of the Census, *Statistical Abstract of the United States, 1992* (Government Printing Office, 1993), p. 48.

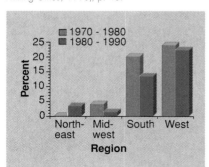

tion gave African Americans the right to vote, opened up new educational opportunities, and helped to integrate the South into the national economy. African Americans still lag behind whites in voter registration, but the gap is now no wider in the South than elsewhere and is explained more by differences in education than by race. In economic terms, the South still falls below the rest of the country in per capita income and education, but much less so than 50 years ago. The religious and moral conservatism of the South remain notable.

Until recently, political observers spoke of the "solid South," a region that voted for Democrats at all levels. The reason for the connection between the South and Democrats is simple: "The Civil War made the Democratic party the party of the South, and the Republican party, the party of the North."[6] While the South remains solidly Democratic in local, state, and most congressional elections, it is not as uniformly Democratic as it once was and is now competitive in presidential elections. Recently, except for 1992, when two southerners were on the Democratic ticket, Republicans won rather solidly in presidential races.[7] Republicans have also made inroads in some statewide and congressional elections. Still, Democrats command a large majority in state legislatures in the eleven former Confederate states (see Table 8-1). What explains this continued Democratic dominance? The answer is apparently that the disaffection of whites with the Democratic party is concentrated at the presidential level, and the addition of African American Democratic voters has only reinforced party strength at the state and local levels.

Other sectional differences have political importance. Alexis de Tocqueville saw the New England Puritan spirit as significant.[8] More recently, the West has developed an identity of individualism, hostility to government intervention, and belief in self-sufficiency. It was especially fertile ground for Ronald Reagan, who seemed to personify western values.

Another common sectional division is the sun belt/frost belt (see map).Sun belt states have been growing in population much more rapidly than the rest of the country, in part because they are attractive places for retirees. As a result of population shifts revealed by the 1990 census, the sun belt states gained 17 seats in the U.S. Congress, while frost belt states lost 15 seats. However, population growth in the South and West is occurring in different age groups. In the South population growth is largest among those over 65, while in the West it is younger persons who provide the growth. Sun belt states have also experienced greater economic growth as industries headed south and southwest, where land is cheaper and more abundant, and where labor is cheaper as well (see Figure 8-1).

State and Local Identity

Americans move often, and they quickly become identified with the politics of the state in which they now live. Mention Wyoming, Mississippi, Oregon, New York, or Kansas, and it brings to mind a certain type of politics. The same is true for many other states. Like most stereotypes, these images are often misleading, but they reflect the fact that there is a sense of identity to states as political units. These state identities are reinforced by our electoral rules and other laws.

In American politics today, one state—California—stands out. One out of ten Americans is a Californian. In terms of economic and political importance, California is in a league by itself; its 52 members of the House of Representatives exceed the total number of representatives in the smallest 21 states. No presidential candidate can afford to lose California's 54 electoral votes.[9] Californians like Richard Nixon and Ronald Reagan have helped deliver these electoral votes to the Republicans in several elections since 1952. Hard hit by the recession, California went

From Coast to Coast

Sun Belt/Frost Belt States

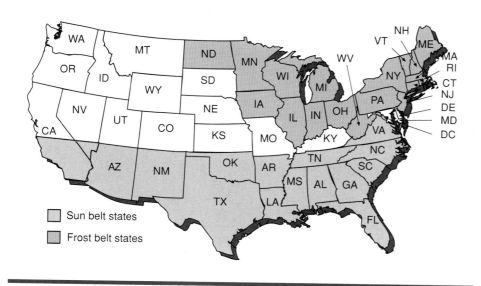

Sun belt states

Frost belt states

---

solidly for Clinton in 1992, helping to push him to victory. Clinton's political future is very much related to whether California recovers from its recession before the 1996 election.

Americans live in four types of places—central cities, suburbs, smaller communities, and rural areas. Most Americans, 75 percent of them, now live in central cities and their suburbs—what the Census Bureau calls *metropolitan areas.* During the early twentieth century, the movement of population was from rural areas to central cities, but the movement since the 1950s has been to the suburbs. During the 1970s and 1980s Americans kept moving farther and farther out from the central cities to new suburbs. Today the most urban state is California (92.6 percent); Vermont is the least urban, with only 32.2 percent living in cities or suburbs. Regionally, the West and Northeast are the most urban, the South and Midwest the most rural. The 75 percent of the population that now lives in cities and suburbs occupies only 2.5 percent of the nation's land (see Figure 8-2). Nine of the largest 25 cities lost population over the previous decade,[10] a continuation of trend since World War II.

There are many reasons people left the cities to move to the suburbs—better housing, new transportation systems that make it easier to get to work, the desire for cleaner air and safer streets, and "white flight," the movement of whites away from the central cities so that their children could attend predominantly white schools and avoid being bused for racial integration. The white, middle-class migration to the suburbs has meant that American cities have become increasingly poor, increasingly African American, and increasingly Democratic (see Table 8-2). Half of all African Americans now live in central cities, as opposed to only about one-quarter of whites. The proportions are very nearly reversed for suburbs, where more than half of all white Americans reside. Almost one-third of American suburbanites are now African Americans, up from one in five in 1980. [11]

FIGURE 8-2
A Changing Landscape as America Becomes Urban

SOURCE: U.S. Bureau of the Census, U.S. Population Reports P 23. no.185, *Population Profile of the United States, 1993* (Government Printing Office, 1993), p. 8.

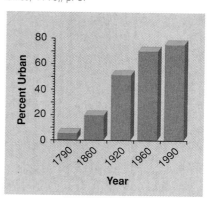

TABLE 8-2

Cities with Populations 100,000 or More that Are at Least 50 Percent African American, 1990

City	Total Population	African American
Atlanta, Georgia	394,017	67%
Baltimore, Maryland	736,014	59
Birmingham, Alabama	265,986	63
Detroit, Michigan	1,027,974	76
Gary, Indiana	116,646	81
Inglewood, California	109,602	52
Jackson, Mississippi	196,637	56
Macon, Georgia	106,612	52
Memphis, Tennessee	610,337	55
Newark, New Jersey	275,221	58
New Orleans, Louisiana	496,938	62
Richmond, Virginia	203,056	55
Savannah, Georgia	137,560	51
Washington, D.C.	606,900	66

SOURCE: U.S. Bureau of the Census, *1990 Census of Population and Housing, Summary Population and Housing Characteristics* (Government Printing Office, 1991).

In such large cities as Washington, D.C., Detroit, Baltimore, Atlanta, and New Orleans, the city population is now more than 50 percent African American. Hispanics comprise more than half of the population of Miami and San Antonio. As population shifts occur, the tax base of cities declines because the richer people have gone to the suburbs, where they now pay local sales and property taxes. At the same time, service needs in the cities have grown as the remaining less affluent population must pay for education, police protection, and health care.

Metropolitan areas are much larger than central cities. More than four times as many people live in metropolitan Los Angeles than actually live in the city.[12] Half the nation's population live in the 39 largest metropolitan areas of more than 1 million in population.[13] While people from the Chicago metropolitan area have some things in common—like an affinity for the Chicago Bulls basketball team—the characteristics of metropolitan areas as a whole can be quite different from the characteristics of the city.

Suburbs vary in relative affluence. Many older ones now face the same problems as the inner cities, but their populations typically have higher per capita income, have fewer minorities, and are typically more Republican. Companies employing professionals or engaging in high-tech or service activities frequently relocate in the suburbs to avoid city congestion and to be closer to the bedroom communities of their workers. Political boundaries, which define local governments and delineate responsibility for services, create understandable tensions among cities, suburbs, and rural areas. Tax revenues, legislative representation, zoning laws, and governmental priorities are hotly contested issues on the local level.

A LAND OF DIVERSITY

Most nations consist of groups of people who have lived together for hundreds of years and who speak the same language, share the same concept of deity, and share a common history. Japan, for example, has some people from other nations, but most of its citizens are Japanese in the fullest sense of the word, and it is the same in Germany, Sweden, Saudi Arabia, China, and France. The United States is different. We are largely a land of immigrants. We attract the poor and oppressed from all over the world, and we have been more open to accepting these people than have other nations.

One reason so many people want to come to the United States is because it is a land that holds a promise of religious, political, and economic freedom. It is also a place of opportunity for the enterprising. Our economic system has provided widespread (but not universal) opportunity for individuals to improve their economic standing. The American Dream—that everyone can "make it big"— is widely shared.

Some elements of our diversity become traditions that have political significance. Sectional differences persist between the South and the rest of the country, in part because of tradition. Third- or fourth-generation Americans may retain an identity with the native land of their ancestors, even though their spouses and neighbors do not share that identity. Holding onto our differences is often the result of socialization in our families, churches, and other closely knit groups. **Political socialization** is the process by which parents and others teach children about the values, beliefs, and attitudes of a political culture. This teaching occurs during interaction in the family, on the playground, in the neighborhood.

Because where we live and what we are in terms of our religion and occupation affect how we vote, many who study voting and make predictions about it do so in terms of these factors—what are called **demographics.** A political predisposition is a characteristic of individuals that is predictive of political behavior. While demographics can be important, as this chapter and those that follow will demonstrate, there are large individual differences within socioeconomic and demographic categories.

When social and economic differences coincide, they reinforce each other and make the differences more important. Social scientists call these differences **reinforcing cleavages**, and experience predicts that when these happen, political conflict becomes more intense and there is greater polarization in society. Nations can also have **cross-cutting cleavages**, instances when differences do not reinforce each other. To illustrate, let's look at religion and income. If in a society all the better-off individuals were of one religion and the poor another, we would have reinforcing cleavages and political conflict would be intensified. But if there were rich and poor in all religions, and if people sometimes voted on the basis of their religion and sometimes on the basis of their wealth, then we would say the divisions are cross-cutting. American diversity has generally been more of the cross-cutting type than the cleavage type, lessening political conflict because individuals have multiple allegiances.

In some societies, politics centers largely around passions over economic and religious differences. In Northern Ireland, for instance, the religious differences between Catholics and Protestants are a violent division. Although socioeconomic differences are important to understanding American government and politics, they are not as central to the form and structure of politics as religion is in Bosnia or race is in South Africa. Understanding this distinction is also important.

Americans, in the past as well as today, are not always tolerant of those from a different religion, class, or race. We often associate only with people "like us" and are suspicious of people "like them." From hostility towards German-speaking immigrants in the early colonies to the anti-immigration movements of the late 1800s and early 1900s, Americans have sometimes exhibited ethnocentrism. For much of our history, minorities have been excluded from full participation in American political and economic life. Recently, Americans have begun to take greater pride in their racial, ethnic, and religious traditions and cultures. As discussed at the beginning of this chapter, language is increasingly seen as part of a group's identity, an identity that minorities want to protect legally. Conflict over the extent to which a group seeks assimilation or maintenance of a strong group identity continues to mark American politics.

These five aliens were the first in New England to become eligible for legal permanent residence under the 1986 Immigration Reform and Control Act.

Race and Ethnicity

Among the most important distinctions in American politics are race and ethnicity. Our history as a nation of immigrants and our struggle with race relations have reinforced the importance of these differences, and they have become part of our political debate. **Race** can be defined as a grouping of human beings with common characteristics presumed to be transmitted genetically. **Ethnicity** is a social division based on national origin, religion, and language, often within the same race, and includes a sense of attachment to that group. In the United States, race issues focus on African Americans, Asians, and Hispanics, although Hispanics can be of any race. What are the racial divisions?

About three out of four Americans are white, according to 1992 census population estimates. The largest nonwhite racial group is African Americans. There are more than 31 million African Americans in the United States, roughly 12 percent of the population. Asian Americans constitute just under 3 percent of the population, and Native Americans just under 1 percent. Most American Hispanics are classified as white by the Census Bureau. The Census Bureau estimates that there are 22.1 million American Hispanics, constituting over 9 percent of the population.[14]

The racial and ethnic diversity of the American polity will only increase over time, due to different birth rates across different groups as well as different immigration rates. Between 1981 and 1991 the white population experienced a natural increase (births minus deaths) of just under 5 percent, while American Indians, Asians and Pacific Islanders, and Hispanics all had natural increase rates of around 20 percent. African Americans were in between, at 14 percent.[15] The Census Bureau has projected that by the year 2050, whites will decline from over 75 percent of the total population today to just over half. The political system will have to accommodate this transformation.

AFRICAN AMERICANS   Folklore tells us that people came to this country because it was a land of freedom and opportunity. For many it was, but for most African Americans it was the opposite. They came as slaves. African Americans were freed as a result of the Civil War, but race relations and racial divisions have been enduring issues of American politics.[16] (Many of the important civil rights cases and controversies are described in Chapter 5.)

Until 1900, more than 90 percent of all African Americans lived in the South;[17] in 1992 the figure was 54 percent.[18] Put another way, about 20 percent of the people in the South are African American. South Carolina, Georgia, Alabama, Mississippi, and Louisiana are more than 25 percent African American. Two-thirds of the citizens of the District of Columbia are African American.

Many African Americans left the South after the turn of the century, hoping to improve their lives by settling in the large cities of the Northeast, Midwest, and West. The migration from the South was substantial: 4.5 million more left the South than migrated to it between the mid-1940s and late 1960s.[19] By the 1960s, many African Americans were living in poverty in large cities, without the economic and social resources to take advantage of recently won legal opportunities. More recently, African Americans have been returning to the South, especially to its urban areas.

In economic terms, African Americans are much worse off than whites in the United States. African American median family income in 1991 was $21,550, compared to $37,780 for whites. Nearly one-third of African Americans are below the poverty level, compared to 9 percent of whites and 14.2 percent of all others.[20] Another way to measure economic well being is in terms of assets or wealth. African American's net wealth is only one-tenth that of whites, and Hispanics have only slightly more wealth than African Americans (see Figure 8-3). As a result, African

We The People

Percent of the Population by Race and Hispanic Origin

	1990	2000	2025	2050
White	75.7%	71.6%	62.1%	52.7%
African American	12.3	12.9	14.5	16.2
Amer. Indian, Eskimo, Aleut	0.8	0.9	1.0	1.2
Asian and Pacific Islander	3.0	4.5	7.8	10.7
Hispanic	9.0	11.1	16.2	21.1

SOURCE: U.S. Bureau of the Census, U.S. Population Reports, P 23 no.185, *Population Profile of the United States, 1993* (Government Printing Office, 1993), p. 5.

Americans and Hispanics have fewer resources to fall back on in hard times, and they are less likely to have the savings to help a child pay for college.[21] Some African Americans have become relatively prosperous: 13.0 percent of African American households had earnings in 1992 of over $50,000, a proportion still less than half of that for whites of non-Hispanic origin.[22] Some African Americans have risen to the top in earnings in their fields of endeavor. Athletes like Larry Johnson and Barry Bonds and entertainers like Bill Cosby, Arsenio Hall, and Oprah Winfrey are examples. Oprah Winfrey, who earned $98 million during 1991–92, was the highest paid entertainer in the world during this time, more than doubling the income of her closest competitor.

Middle-class African Americans provide role models and leadership to the civil rights movement, yet their comparatively small number in the past serves as a reminder that most African Americans remain behind whites in an economy that relies more and more on education and job skills. About 22 percent of whites graduate from college, whereas only about 12 percent of African Americans do.[23] For 18 to 24-year-old high school graduates, 39 percent of whites went on to college, 31 percent of Hispanics, and only 28 percent of African Americans.[24] Finally, the African American population is much younger than the white population; the 1992 median age for whites was 34.3, compared to 28.2 for African Americans.[25] The combination of the younger African American population, the lower level of education among African Americans, and the concentration of African Americans in economically hard-pressed urban areas has resulted in a much higher unemployment rate for young African Americans; unemployment, in turn, leads to social problems like crime and drug abuse.

African Americans have had limited rights and little political power for most of the period since emancipation. Owing their freedom to the "party of Lincoln," most African Americans initially identified with the Republicans.[26] This loyalty started to change with Franklin Roosevelt, who insisted on equal treatment for African Americans in his New Deal programs.[27] In the period after World War II, African Americans came to see the Democrats as the party of civil rights. This perception was reinforced by the 1964 presidential campaign, in which the Democratic nominee, Lyndon Johnson, took credit for the Civil Rights Act of 1964, which his Republican opponent, Barry Goldwater, had voted against. The 1964 Republican platform position on civil rights espoused states' rights—then the creed of southern segregationists—in what appeared to be an effort to win the support of Southern white voters.[28] Virtually all African Americans voted for Johnson in 1964; and in presidential elections since 1964, their Democratic vote has averaged over 91 percent.

Recently, African Americans have become much more important politically because of their increased level of voter participation and their concentrated population. African Americans constitute 0.3 percent of the population in Montana, Vermont, and Idaho, but 36 percent in Mississippi. African Americans make up 5 percent of the West, but 20 percent of the South.[29] Southern senators and representatives, for instance, can no longer afford to ignore the African American vote.[30] Evidence of growing African American political power is the dramatic growth in the number of African American state legislators, a number that rose from 168 in 1970 to 460 in 1992.[31]

In the 1993 gubernatorial election in New Jersey, African American turnout became an issue when Ed Rollins, campaign manager of the successful gubernatorial candidate Christine Todd Whitman, boasted he had distributed $500,000 to African American community leaders and Democratic activists to get them to dampen turnout. Rollins later modified his statement, but the controversy only highlighted the role African Americans can play in competitive elections in states outside the South.

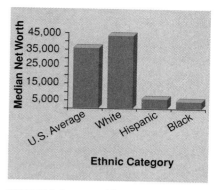

FIGURE 8-3 Wealth Distribution in the United States by Race

SOURCE: U.S. Department of the Census, Current Population Report P 70, no.34, *Household Wealth and Asset Ownership* (Government Printing Office, 1991), Table H.

TABLE 8-3

The Ethnic Asian Population in the United States

	1980	1990
	(thousands)	
Japanese	715	848
Chinese	810	1,645
Indian	385	815
Korean	355	799
Filipino	780	1,406
Vietnamese	245	615

SOURCE: U.S. Bureau of the Census, *Statistical Abstract of the United States, 1993* (Government Printing Office), p.18.

If You Eat the Tamale, Remove the Corn Husk!

During the 1976 presidential election, President Gerald Ford made a campaign appearance at the Alamo in San Antonio, Texas. During the rally he was served a tamale. Ford apparently had not eaten a tamale before, or at least not one wrapped in a corn husk. With television cameras and still photographers recording the scene, Ford bit into the tamale, corn husk and all. *The New York Times* placed the story on the front page. Ethnic food, distinctive clothing and hats, and an effort to speak the native language remain a part of presidential campaigns in the United States.

SOURCE: "Campaigning in Texas," *The New York Times,* April 10, 1976, p. 1. Copyright © 1976 by The New York Times Company. Reprinted by permission.

ASIAN AMERICANS   Asian Americans are a heterogeneous group of persons classified together by the census for statistical purposes but with significant differences in culture, language, and political experience in the United States. The group includes persons of Chinese, Japanese, Korean, Vietnamese, and Filipino origin, as well as persons from the Pacific Islands (see Table 8-3). In 1992, the United States was home to approximately 7.2 million Asian Americans, residing primarily in the western states, especially Hawaii, California, and Washington. Asian Americans are the most successful racial group economically and educationally. Nearly two out of every five Asian Americans have graduated from college, compared to just over one of every five white Americans.[32]

The numbers of Asian Americans grew during the 1970s and 1980s, largely as a result of Southeast Asian immigration. In the 1990 census, persons from Asia had climbed to one of four of all foreign-born persons living in the United States, and the Philippines was surpassed only by Mexico as the country of birth for foreign-born persons living in this country. Immigrants from the Pacific Islands more than doubled during the 1980s, and most persons in this group reside in three states—California, New York, and Hawaii. Pacific Islanders are also a diverse group in terms of language and culture. In states with heavy concentrations of Asian immigrants, these groups are now becoming more politically important and visible in politics. For instance, an Asian American, Michael Woo, ran for mayor of Los Angeles in 1993. Robert Matsui (D.-Calif.) was a leader of the coalition supporting the North American Trade Agreement (NAFTA) in the House and is seen as a likely future leader in that chamber.

NATIVE AMERICANS   Centuries ago, explorers sailed west looking for another passage to India. Colonists followed, often holding grants of land from their own government—grants they believed gave them a right to land in the New World. However, by virtue of prior usage the land belonged to "Indians," the tribal peoples who had long inhabited the land. As settlers moved west, colonial leaders dealt with Indian representatives to obtain land for colonists and to reserve certain lands for these Native Americans.

The Native American population today is nearly 2 million. Native Americans have incomes well below those of other Americans, and Native American families are generally twice as likely to be below the poverty level as African Americans or whites.[33] Native Americans are below the rest of the nation in the proportion of persons completing high school; and the proportion completing college is roughly half that of the rest of the population.[34]

HISPANICS/LATINOS   Hispanics (persons of Spanish-speaking descent) are defined by the U.S. Census Bureau as an ethnic group, and they can be of any race. For example, the president of Peru, Alberto Fujimori, is Hispanic of Japanese ancestry. Even if the Spanish-speaking descent is one or more generations removed (grandparents or great grandparents), that person is still considered Hispanic.

The terms "Latino" and "Chicano" are preferred by some persons of Spanish-speaking descent, in part because they lack association with Spain, a colonial power against which many in Latin America fought wars of independence. "The term 'Hispanic' emphasizes the white European culture of Spain because it refers to lovers of Spanish culture."[35] "Hispanic" is a term most widely used by government agencies and the media, while "Latino" appears more popular to leaders of the group. "Chicano" is often associated with the politically active Mexican-American movement of the 1960s and 1970s. Most Mexican Americans, Puerto Rican Americans, and Cuban Americans prefer to be called American rather than Latino or Hispanic.[36] The derogatory references to Mexicans by Ross Perot in his campaign against NAFTA in 1993 reinforced anger among Hispanics about how persons from Latin America are perceived and may also strengthen anti-American feelings in those countries.

TABLE 8-4

Persons of Hispanic Origin in the United States, 1992

	Number (in millions)	Percent
Mexican	14.1	63.6%
Puerto Rican	2.4	10.6
Cuban	1.0	4.7
Central and South American	3.1	14.0
Other	1.6	7.1
Total	22.1	100.0

SOURCE: U.S. Bureau of the Census, U.S. Population Reports P 23, No.185, *Population Profile of the United States, 1993* (Government Printing Office, 1993), p. 36.

Latinos are not a monolithic group, and while they share a common linguistic heritage, they often differ from one another, depending on which country they immigrated from (see Table 8-4). Cuban Americans, for instance, tend to be Republicans, while Mexican Americans and Puerto Ricans are disproportionately Democrats.[37] Socioeconomically, Cuban Americans approximate the white population, while Puerto Rican Americans and Mexican Americans are generally at the lower end of the scale.[38] Socially, Latinos divide up along these lines as well, and there can be intense rivalry among Hispanic groups. Politically, Latinos can differ on their levels of support, depending on whether the candidate is from Puerto Rico, Cuba, or Mexico. A recent study of Latinos found differences between Latinos of Mexican, Puerto Rican, and Cuban descent in partisanship, ideology, and rates of participation but widespread support for a liberal domestic agenda, including increased spending on health care, crime and drug control, education, the environment, child services, and bilingual education.[39]Given the overall growth of the Latino population, it is not surprising that both major parties have aggressively sought to cultivate Hispanic candidates.

The divisions within Latinos became more important because of the tendency of the groups to settle in different areas. Nearly two-thirds of Cuban immigrants live in Florida, especially greater Miami. Puerto Rican immigrants are concentrated in or around New York City, and Mexican American immigrants in the Southwest and California. The Census Bureau estimated in the 1990 census that more than 7.7 million Hispanics live in California alone.[40]

The Ties of Ethnicity

Except for Native Americans, all Americans are immigrants or are descended from immigrants. The largest number of immigrants came between 1900 and 1924, when 17.3 million people relocated to the United States—by far the largest immigration to one country in any quarter-century in human history. From 1981 to 1990, there were more than 7.3 million immigrants.[41] This new wave of immigrants came primarily from Latin America, especially the Caribbean and Mexico, and Asian countries such as the Philippines, Vietnam, and China. The foreign born proportion of the U.S. population increased during the 1980s, rising from 14 million in 1980 to 20 million in 1990, the largest number of foreign-born in U.S. history. Table 8-5 shows the origin of foreign-born population in 1980 and 1990. Note that among U.S. foreign born, the proportion of Asian and Mexican immigrants has pulled even with or surpassed the number of Europeans.

Anger Against Immigrants Overflows

In his greasy auto mechanic's clothing and beat-up Datsun pickup truck, Eddie Cortez hardly looks like the mayor of a large American city.

So when Immigration and Naturalization Service agents pulled him over, little did they suspect that the brown-skinned man they were threatening to deport was not only a citizen but the first Latino mayor of Pomona, California.

"I actually got pulled over and harassed, rousted, questioned, and threatened," said Cortez, a Mexican American and a conservative Republican, "If I hadn't identified myself, I was going to get thrown in the van with—as they put it—'the rest of them.'"

Cortez's story is echoing through immigrant and civil rights organizations in California and sounding a chord with many citizens and immigrants, legal and illegal. Up and down the coast, people are talking about the insults and indignities they are suffering as the anti-immigration movement explodes. . . .

• On May 20, Heriberio Camargo, a 16-year-old San Diego resident, was stopped by border officials as he was walking out of a corner store. When he failed to show them his birth certificate, they handcuffed him and placed him in a van. Neighbors alerted his mother, who came running down the street with his birth certificate. He was then released. A complaint is pending with the U.S. Justice Department.

• Also in May, Ralph Lepe, a twenty-year-old from Santa Barbara, was questioned as he worked on his parents' roof. "I told them I was an American citizen but they didn't believe me," he said. While his sister frantically searched the house for his birth certificate, Lepe answered questions about where he was born and what high school he attended. Although he had suitable answers, Border Patrol agents would not wait for his sister to produce the birth certificate. Later, at the Border Patrol detention center, Lepe signed a paper without reading it closely and was soon deported to Mexico. Lepe says that the officers told him he should carry his birth certificate with him at all times.

• On April 21, Irma Munoz, a 20-year-old engineering student at the University of California at Davis, was reportedly attacked by two white males. "They insulted me. They beat me, and they wrote things on my arms and leg (that) they said I should always remember, (such as) 'Go home illegal wetback,'" Munoz said. An investigation by university police is pending.

SOURCE: Suzanne Espinosa, Benjamin Pimentel, Susan Yoachim, and Nanette Asimov, *San Francisco Chronicle*, August 27, 1993, pp. 1,6; also *San Francisco Chronicle*, October 22, 1993, pp. 1, 4.

TABLE 8-5

Origin of Foreign-Born Population: 1980 and 1990

	1980	1990
European	36.6%	22.0%
Asian	18.0	25.2
Mexican	15.6	21.7
Caribbean	8.9	9.8
Central American	2.5	5.7
South American	4.0	5.2
African	1.4	1.8
Other	13.0	8.6

SOURCE: U.S. Bureau of the Census, U.S. Population Reports, P 23, no.185, *Population Profile of the United States, 1993* (Government Printing Office, 1993), p. 40.

Having large numbers of immigrants can pose challenges to any political and social system. They are often the source of social conflict as they compete with more established groups for jobs, rights, political power, and influence.

Among the most prominent ethnic groups in the United States are Irish Americans, Italian Americans, German Americans, Polish Americans, Hispanics, and Greek Americans. The country's early settlers were generally English-speaking Protestants; in fact, people of English, Scottish, and Welsh background make up the largest ethnic group in the United States. Irish immigrants, largely Catholics, started coming before the potato famine in the 1840s and came in even larger numbers after it. They experienced economic exploitation and religious bigotry. The Irish American response was often to retreat among themselves, forming a strong ethnic group consciousness. Other ethnic groups that followed—Italians, Greeks, Chinese—each experienced a similar cycle: flight from their homeland and happy arrival here, discrimination, exploitation, residential clustering, and the formation of a strong group identity.

Ethnic group identity is often persistent. In certain ethnic sections of large cities, people still converse in their native languages. Ethnic groups gain in political importance as they become more affluent; eventually they support candidates "of their own kind," ultimately electing mayors, governors, or even presidents. Irish Americans understandably were proud of the election to president of John F. Kennedy; and most Greek Americans identified with Michael Dukakis, the Democratic presidential nominee in 1988.

Gender

For most of U.S. history, politics and government were men's business. As discussed in Chapter 5, women gained the right to vote primarily in the western territories, beginning with Wyoming in 1869 and Utah in 1870, and then in Colorado and Idaho before the turn of the century.[42] The right was extended nationally with passage of the Nineteenth Amendment in 1920. The fears of some opponents of woman suffrage—that women would form their own party and vote largely for women or otherwise tilt politics in a different direction—have not been realized. During Susan B. Anthony's suffrage campaign, Jonas H. Upton, editor of the *Democratic Salem Monitor* in Salem, Oregon, contended that women, if given the right to vote, would combine to vote for war because they were exempt from the draft.[43] Others said women would unite to vote for prohibition.[44]

Instead of voting as a bloc, women have typically divided their vote between the two major political parties. However, in 1992, women were more likely than men to vote for Clinton and less likely to vote for Perot (see Figure 8-4). For most of the period since gaining the right to vote, they have voted at a lower rate than women in other Western democracies, but this trend appears to be changing.[45] Since 1976, women have voted at nearly the same rate as men, meaning that in recent elections, because females in the population outnumber males, the female vote has outnumbered the male vote.[46] Women have chosen to work within the existing political parties and do not overwhelmingly support female candidates, especially if they must cross parties to do so. The numbers of women elected to public office have been low; since 1917, less than 6 percent of representatives in the House have been women. The high point so far came after the 1992 election, when the number of women elected to the House of Representatives reached 47, and the number of women in the U.S. Senate rose to six. The success of so many women in the 1992 elections led some to label the election the "Year of the Woman."[47]

One of the groups that has most aggressively promoted women as candidates is EMILY's List, a group that funds pro-choice, Democratic candidates. EMILY is an acronym for *Early Money Is Like Yeast*, meaning that campaign contributions

Charges of sexual harassment by women employees of Senator Bob Packwood led to an investigation by the Senate Ethics Committee.

given to candidates early in their campaigns can help raise more money, just as yeast helps dough to rise. Republicans have duplicated EMILY's List with their own political action committee, Wish List, which gives to female candidates who are pro-choice on abortion.

The women's movement in American politics encompasses a comprehensive agenda, including voting and political rights but also extending to other basic liberties of the Bill of Rights and Fourteenth Amendment. In addition to rights and liberties, women seek equal opportunity, education, jobs, skills, respect, and self-esteem in what has been a male-dominated system.[48] There are serious inequalities between men and women in areas such as income. Nearly twice as many women as men earn only the minimum wage, and 40 percent of working women earned less than $10,000 in 1990.[49] While women earn on average only about 70 cents for every dollar earned by men, this figure has improved from the 60 cents for every dollar in 1980.[50] Because an increasing number of women today are the sole breadwinners for their families, the implications of this low income level are even more significant. The problem of lower pay for women is not restricted to working mothers. Among college graduates ages 18 to 24, women earn an average of 92 cents for every dollar earned by men of the same age and education.[51] As age increases, the earnings gap widens, so that 55 to 64-year-old college-educated women earn only 54 cents for every dollar earned by men of the same age and education.[52] Increasing women's income is an important issue to the women's movement.

There is a **gender gap**—significant differences between men and women—in public opinion and voting. Women are more likely to oppose violence in any form—death penalty, new weapons systems, or the possession of handguns. Evidence suggests that women as a group are more compassionate than men, and so are more likely to favor government that provides health insurance and family services. Women are more concerned about women's rights, enforcement of child support, sexual abuse and rape, unequal treatment of women in the legal system, the environment, peace, and pornography than men. These so-called gender issues are becoming increasingly important. American women identify such work and family issues as day care, prenatal and postnatal leave policy, and equality of treatment on the job as important.[53] Other gender issues, some of them focal points in recent U.S. Senate elections, include reproductive rights and sexual harassment.[54]

Providing a workplace in which people are not subject to sexual harassment came to the top of the political agenda after being raised during the confirmation of Supreme Court Justice Clarence Thomas (see Chapter 16) and again because of charges raised against U.S. Senator Bob Packwood. Former staff workers had accused Packwood of sexual harrassment after his reelection in 1992. More than two years later, the Senate Ethics Committee still had not held hearings or issued a report.

The Supreme Court and Congress, as we noted in Chapter 5, have provided legal protections against such harassment, and the number of lawsuits filed is on the increase (see Table 8-6).

Sexual Orientation

The 1990s have seen a growing visibility and increased awareness of diversity in sexual orientation. Gays and lesbians have more aggressively pursued their political agenda of antidiscrimination laws, access to legally sanctioned homosexual marriages, rights to custody of children and the ability to adopt children, and access to employee benefits for homosexual partners. Groups like Queer Nation, Act Up, and the National Gay and Lesbian Task Force have organized marches and otherwise sought to heighten gay awareness.

During the 1992 election, the question of gays in the military became an issue. Candidate Bill Clinton promised to drop the ban on homosexuals, and early in his

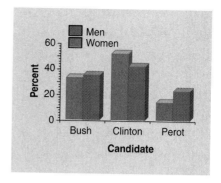

FIGURE 8-4
Gender and the Vote for President, 1992

SOURCE: 1992 National Election Study.

TABLE 8-6

Harassment in the Workplace

	1991	1993
Cases Filed	6,892	12,537
Cases Resolved	6,706	9,965
Compensation	$7.1 Million	$25.7 Million

SOURCE: "Harassment Cases: Keeping Score," *U.S. News & World Report,* November, 22, 1993, p.11.

administration he set out to fulfill this campaign promise. However, military leaders, including the Joint Chiefs of Staff, opposed the idea, as did key members of the congressional committees dealing with the armed forces. A slight majority of the public did not approve of "Bill Clinton's decision to ease the ban on homosexuals in the armed forces."[55] In the face of the intense and well-organized opposition and a possible defeat in Congress, the Clinton administration abandoned its original proposal and settled for a compromise policy of "don't ask, and don't tell"—meaning that the military will no longer ask recruits if they are homosexual, and military personnel are under no obligation to divulge their sexual orientation. Some remnants of the old policy remain, however, including an understanding that practicing homosexuals will be discharged from the military if their homosexuality is discovered.

One focal point of the politics of sexual orientation has been AIDS. Acquired Immune Deficiency Syndrome, or AIDS, has disproportionately affected the homosexual community and motivated gays and lesbians to become more politically active, visible, and well organized. Public fear of AIDS was behind a 1986 California ballot initiative to quarantine all persons with the disease, a measure that was defeated.

As the homosexual rights movement has grown in visibility and power, an opposition movement has also become part of American politics. During the 1970s, voters in some cities and states voted on measures targeted either to protect or limit homosexual rights. One unsuccessful measure in California, for instance, would have removed suspected homosexuals from the public school classroom until a hearing could be held. In 1992 and 1993, voters in Colorado, Oregon, and scattered cities, including Cincinnati, Ohio, voted on ballot measures to remove special protections previously granted to homosexuals. Similar measures were on the ballot in several states in 1994. These plebiscites reflect a backlash against what their sponsors see as laws legitimizing homosexuality. Not surprisingly, the campaigns and debates over these votes become heated. The consequence of these votes has been to put gays and lesbians on the defensive, fighting to hold onto the advances they had made in the 1980s.

Religion

In some parts of the world, religious differences can be a source of violent conflict. In Northern Ireland, Protestants and Catholics have been at war for more than four hundred years. The war in Bosnia-Herzegovina is a religious and ethnic battle among Muslims, Serbs, and Catholics. Countries like Lebanon, India, and Sri Lanka have also experienced intense religious conflict. The United States has not been immune, despite its principle of religious freedom. In 1838, Governor Lilburn W. Boggs of Missouri issued an extermination order against the Mormons.[56]

Although the intensity of religious conflict varies, it can become especially strong if there is one predominant or official faith. This is one reason why the framers did not sanction a national church in the United States. In fact, James Madison wrote in *The Federalist*, No. 51, "In a free government the security for civil rights must be the same as that for religious rights. It consists in the one case in the multiplicity of interests, and in the other in the multiplicity of sects."

The absence of an official American church does not mean that religion is unimportant in American politics. Indeed there were established state churches until the 1830s. Politicians frequently refer to God in their speeches or demonstrate their piety in other ways. And many share John Conway's view that "at the root of American political and social values . . . is the distinctive Puritanism of the early New England settlers."[57] Many Americans take their religious beliefs seriously, more so than peoples of other industrial democracies.[58] Two-thirds of Americans attend

RELIGION AND POLITICS

At one time we thought a Catholic could not be elected president. With the election of 1960 that issue was resolved. John F. Kennedy directly confronted the question of whether a Catholic would put aside religious teachings if they conflicted with constitutional obligations. He said, "I am not the Catholic candidate for President. I am the Democratic Party's candidate for President who happens also to be Catholic. I do not speak for my church on public matters, and the church does not speak for me." A candidate's religion may still become an issue if religious convictions on sensitive issues such as abortion threaten to conflict with public obligations.

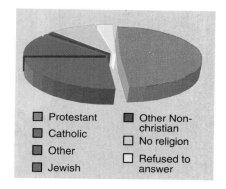

- Protestant
- Catholic
- Other
- Jewish
- Other Non-christian
- No religion
- Refused to answer

Religious Denominations of Americans, 1990

SOURCE: From a telephone survey of 113,000 households in the 48 contiguous states, conducted from April 1989 to April 1990 by the Graduate School of the City University of New York.

houses of worship at least occasionally, and 46 percent attend nearly every week or more often.[59] Religion, like ethnicity, is a shared identity—people identify themselves as Baptist, Catholic, or Buddhist. Sometimes church attendance or nonattendance is more important than differences between religions in explaining attitudes. "Among both Catholics and Protestants, frequent church-goers are less likely to support abortion than those who rarely or never attend."[60]

Religion can be an important catalyst for social change, as it was in the overthrow of communism in Central Europe[61] and in the leadership of the black church in the American civil rights movement. As writer Taylor Branch explains, the black

A LAND OF RELIGIOUS DIVERSITY

Religious observance in this country is as diverse as the population. African Americans celebrate Kwanza in December as a reminder of their African heritage and traditions. Jewish Americans celebrate Hanukkah as a testament to religious freedom that was fought for by the Maccabees. Muslim Americans obey the call to prayer daily in mosques throughout this nation.

church "served not only as a place of worship but also as a bulletin board to a people who owned no organs of communication, a credit union to those without banks, and even a kind of people's court."[62] African American ministers, like the Reverend Martin Luther King, Jr., became leaders of the civil rights movement; others, like the Reverend Jesse Jackson, have since run for office. Hence religion can be important not only as a source of personal values and attitudes but as a means of political activity and organization.

In recent years there has been an increase in political activity among fundamentalist Christians. Led by ministers like Jerry Falwell and Pat Robertson, they have supported political organizations like the Moral Majority and Christian Crusade. During the 1980s they sought to influence the national agenda, and Robertson ran for president in the Republican party in 1988. More recently, they have focused attention at the local level—school boards, city councils, mayorships, and local GOP leadership.[63] Their agenda includes the return of school prayer, the outlawing of abortion, restrictions on homosexuals, and opposition to gun control. They achieved some successes in the elections of 1993 and 1994 and are seen as an important political force in some parts of the country.

One defining characteristic of religion in the United States is the tremendous variety of denominations. About half the people in the United States describe themselves as Protestant. The largest Protestant denomination is Baptist, followed by Methodists, Lutherans, Presbyterians, and Episcopalians. Because there are so many different Protestant churches, Catholics have the largest single membership in the United States, constituting more than one-quarter of the population. Jews constitute less than 2 percent of the population. Protestants came to the United States first; most Catholics and Jews immigrated after the 1840s. It was not until 1960, however, that Americans elected a Catholic president.

In recent presidential elections, most Protestants voted Republican, while most Catholics and Jews voted Democratic.[64] The perception among many Catholics and Jews that the Democratic party is more open to them partly explains the strength of their Democratic identification. The Democrats won the loyalty of many Catholics by their willingness to nominate Al Smith for the presidency in 1928 and John Kennedy in 1960. Southern Protestants are Democrats for different reasons, largely having to do with the sectional issues discussed earlier. Religious groups vary in their rates of participation. Jews have the highest rate of reported voter turnout, 79 percent in 1992, while those who claim no religious affiliation have the lowest, 62 percent. Catholics voted at a slightly higher rate than Protestants.[65]

Religion is especially important in American politics because of the clustering of populations. Hence Catholics make up only 26 percent of the U.S. population, yet they are more than 50 percent of the population of Rhode Island, Massachusetts, and Connecticut. Baptists represent 19 percent of the U.S. population, yet they are more than 50 percent of the population of Mississippi, Alabama, and Georgia. Mormons are only 2 percent of the U.S. population, yet they are more than 70 percent of the population of Utah. The South is the most Protestant—61 percent. The state of New York has the highest percentage of Jews, 7 percent; New York City is 14 percent Jewish.

Religious differences can be related to other politically important characteristics. For instance, Jews are the most prosperous and best educated of any ethnic or religious group. More than 46 percent graduated from college, compared to 22 percent of Protestants and 20 percent of Catholics. In this example, as in others, religion is a cross-cutting cleavage in American politics; the differences do not reinforce one another. On the basis of income and education, Jews predictably would be Republicans, but 43 percent of American Jews are Democrats, while only 22 percent are Republicans.[66] Similarly, southern Protestants would predictably be heavily Republican, but many of them are Democrats.

Wealth and Income

The United States is a wealthy nation in a world of scarcity and intense economic conflict over the distribution of wealth. Indeed, to some knowledgeable observers, "the most striking thing about the United States has been its phenomenal

INCOME DISTRIBUTION IN THE UNITED STATES

The bar chart on the left demonstrates that most of the population is what we might call middle class, with 65 percent of American families having incomes ranging from $15,000 to $75,000, with the median income $30,786. Political scientists term such a distribution "normal" because it bows out in the middle. In some societies, notably developing countries, most people are either in the high or low income ranges, giving two "peaks" to the distribution. Though the bar chart shows a large middle class, the pie chart on the right indicates that the richest 20 percent earn twelve times more than the poorest 20 percent, or nearly half of all income.

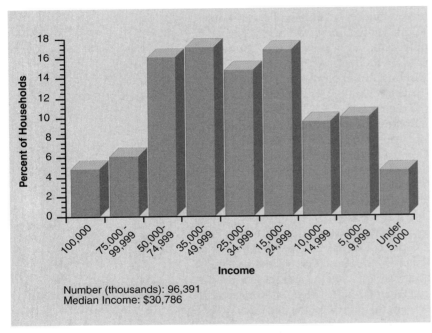

Number (thousands): 96,391
Median Income: $30,786

Total Money Income of Households, 1992

Source: U.S. Bureau of the Census, Current Population Reports P-60, no. 184, *Money Income of Households, Families, and Persons in the United States, 1992* (Government Printing Office, 1993), p. B-3.

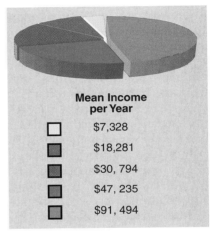

Mean Income per Year

☐	$7,328
▨	$18,281
▨	$30, 794
▨	$47, 235
▨	$91, 494

Share of Aggregate Income Received by Fifths of Households, 1992

SOURCE: U.S. Bureau of the Census, Current Population Reports P-60, no. 184, *Money Income of Households, Families, and Persons in the United States, 1992* (Government Printing Office, 1993), p. B-6.

"To the rich, the very rich, and the super rich! Have I left anybody out?"

Drawing by Mirachi. © 1988 The New Yorker Magazine, Inc.

wealth."[67] A large proportion of the people in the United States lead comfortable lives in terms of housing, nutrition, and medical care and enjoy a standard of living beyond the reach of many who live in other countries. But even in affluent societies, the distribution of wealth and income can result in important political divisions and conflicts. *Wealth* encompasses the things of economic value (savings, stocks, property) you possess; *income* is how much money you make from your job or investments. "The most common and durable source of factions has been the various and unequal distribution of property," wrote James Madison, in *The Federalist*, No. 10. He continued, "Those who hold, and those who are without property, have ever formed distinct interests in society" (see Appendix). Madison was right: economic differences often lead to conflict, and Americans remain divided politically along economic lines. Aside from race, income may be the single most important factor in explaining views on issues, partisanship, and ideology. Most rich people are Republicans, and most poor people are Democrats, and this has been true since at least the Great Depression of the 1930s.

The distribution of income within a society can have important consequences for democratic stability. If there is a perception that only the few at the top of the economic ladder can hope to earn enough for an adequate standard of living, then domestic unrest and revolution may follow. Income is related to participation in politics. Poor people who need the most help from government are the least likely to participate. They are also the most likely to favor social welfare programs.

Income has been rising in the United States. Even after adjusting for inflation, income doubled in the period between 1952 and 1991,[68] but the tendency for income to rise has slowed down. Economists debate the causes for this change; some cite higher energy costs, low levels of personal savings, and the worldwide slowdown in productivity growth.[69] In terms of income, the Northeast is the most prosperous region and the South the least prosperous. Compared to other nations, our purchasing power is higher than that of any other advanced democracy, including Japan.[70]

Most college students come from the top quarter of American families in income—those earning $50,000 a year or more. In fact, students from these families graduate from college at nearly twice the rate as those from the bottom 75 percent of the socioeconomic ladder.[71]

At the other end of the economic continuum are the poor. For twenty-five years, roughly one in every ten Americans comes from a family whose income is below the poverty line. In 1993 the official poverty level for a family of four was income below $14,335.[72] Most persons classified as below the poverty line are in families in which adults of working age either do not have jobs or work in jobs with low pay. Families headed by a female have three times the chance of falling below the poverty line.[73] African Americans are three times as likely to be poor than whites, and Hispanics are two and a half times as likely to be poor than whites. Thirty-eight percent of the poor are children, and many appear trapped in a cycle of poverty.[74]

The definition of poverty is itself political. The poverty-level figure of $14,335 identifies persons who cannot meet a minimum standard in such basics as housing, food, and medical care. Regardless of how one defines poverty, however, the poor are a minority who lack political power. During the Reagan years of the 1980s there was increasing inequality between rich and poor, a trend quite different from the 1960s, when the gap between rich and poor narrowed.[75] While there are even fewer persons over the age of 65 than there are poor people, older Americans are a much more potent force in American politics.[76] The poor vote less and are less confident and organized in dealing with politics and government.

Wealth is more concentrated than income. The wealthiest families hold most of the property and other forms of wealth like stocks and savings. Traditionally, one of the problems with concentrated wealth has been that it fosters an aristocracy. Jeffer-

Missing Persons

The 1990 census was surrounded by charges of a severe undercount. President George Bush's secretary of commerce admitted that real population in 1990 was about 259 million, instead of the 254 million reported by the Census Bureau. Still, he resisted calls to revise the count to reflect more accurately the distribution of the population among states, cities, and neighborhoods, saying that such adjustments were "unreliable."

Why is undercounting so controversial? Federal funding to cities and states totaling $59 billion is often allocated on the census population counts. The undercounting appears to have been most pronounced among minority populations and in central cities. New York's former mayor, David N. Dinkins, called the undercounting nothing less than "statistical grand larceny," because it resulted in a substantial loss in federal funds to the city.

Undercounting also has important political consequences. If the estimates had been adjusted upward, Arizona and California would have each gained another congressional seat, while Pennsylvania and Wisconsin would have each lost one.

SOURCE: Felicity Barringer, "U.S. Won't Revise 1990 Census, Says Chief of Commerce," *New York Times*, July 16, 1991, pp. A1. Copyright ©1991 by The New York Times Company. Reprinted by permission.

"It's like this. If the rich have money, they invest. If the poor have money, they eat."

Drawing by Dana Fradon. ©1992 The New Yorker Magazine.

FIGURE 8-5
Occupational Distribution in the United States, 1900-1990

SOURCE: Data for 1900–70: U.S. Bureau of the Census, *Bicentennial Statistics, Pocket Data Book, USA* (Government Printing Office, 1976), pp. 386–87; data for 1910: U.S. Bureau of the Census, *Histotical Statistics of the United States: Colonial Times to 1970,* (Government Printing Office, 1976), p. 139; data for 1980: U.S. Department of Labor, *Employment and Earnings,* vol. 28, no.1 (Government Printing Office,January 1981), p. 42; data for 1990; U.S. Department of Labor, *Employment and Earnings,* vol. 38, no.1 (Government Printing Office,January 1991), p. 36.

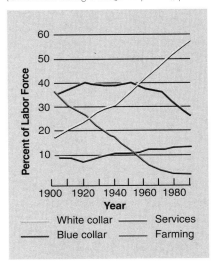

son sought to break up the "aristocracy of wealth" by changing from laws based on *primogeniture* (the eldest son's exclusive right to inherit his father's estate) to laws that encouraged people to divide their estates equally among all their children, the result being smaller landholding. He sought to foster an "aristocracy of virtue and talent" through a public school system open to all for primary grades and for the best students through the university level.[77] Education has been one of the most important means for Americans to achieve economic and social mobility. Those with an education are wealthier, and those with wealth are more inclined to get an education.

Occupation

Americans at the time of Thomas Jefferson and for several generations after worked primarily in agriculture. In 1800, 83 percent of the entire U.S. labor force was engaged in farming.[78] The agrarian period was characterized by a large number of independent, landowning farmers with little formal schooling.

By 1920, the United States had become the world's leading industrial nation. This dramatic transformation also resulted in the expansion of American cities as large numbers of workers moved there to find jobs. Labor conditions, including child labor practices, became important political issues. The invention and application of technology, such as Henry Ford's assembly line, when combined with abundant natural and human resources, meant that the U.S. gross domestic product (GDP) rose by more than 700 percent in real terms over the 55-year period from 1935 to 1990.[79]

The United States has now entered what Daniel Bell, a noted sociologist, has labeled the "post-industrial phase of our development." "A post-industrial society, being primarily a technical society, awards less on the basis of inheritance or property . . . than on education and skill."[80] Knowledge is the organizing device of the post-industrial era. Post-industrial societies have greater affluence and a class structure less defined along traditional labor versus management lines.

The changing dynamics of the American labor force can be seen in Figure 8-5, which shows the percent of the U.S. labor force in various occupations since 1900. As it demonstrates, there has been tremendous growth in the white-collar sector of our economy, rising from under 20 percent of the work force at the turn of the century to more than half by 1980. The white-collar sector includes managers, accountants, and lawyers as well as professionals and technicians in such rapid growth areas as communications, finance, insurance, and research. This shift has been accompanied by a dramatic decline in the number of people engaged in agriculture and a more modest decline in the number of people who produce goods (the manufacturing sector). Today less than one in three working Americans produces goods, and only 3 percent work on farms.

Governments are among the biggest employers. About one-fifth of our GDP is produced by federal, state, and local governments. Indeed, education is one of our largest industries; there are 3.5 million teachers.[81] The Department of Defense employs nearly 3 million civilian and military personnel.[82]

Women and racial minorities have distinct occupational patterns (see Figure 8-6). Women are much less likely than men to work in blue-collar jobs and more likely to work as professionals and technicians in white-collar jobs. More than one in four working women are employed as clerical workers, and another 18 percent are in service occupations. As noted earlier, women generally earn less than men of the same age and education. Occupations in which women predominate, like teaching and clerical work, are generally lower paying than industrial or management jobs.

Like women, African Americans and Hispanics tend to have occupations different from those of white males. African Americans are more likely than whites or Hispanics to be engaged in clerical work or service sector jobs. Large numbers of Latinos work as operators and laborers, in service jobs, and on farms. Even in

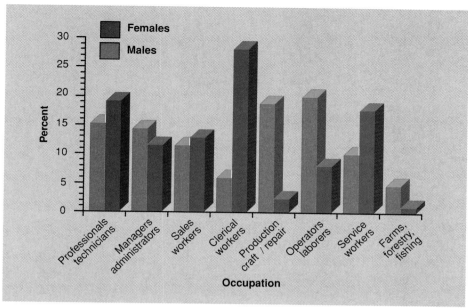

FIGURE 8-6
Occupational Distribution by Gender, 1991

Source: U.S. Department of Labor, *Employment and Earnings*, vol. 38, no.1 (Government Printing Office, January 1991), p. 29.

occupations in which African Americans or Hispanics have done better at finding jobs, they run into barriers. The courts and Congress have confronted some of these barriers.[83] The 1991 Civil Rights Act gives workers more protection against discrimination and greater monetary damages and the reimbursement of legal costs for those who can convince courts of employment bias.[84]

Social Class

Many commentators have questioned why Americans are not divided into social classes in the European sense. American workers have not formed their own political parties, nor does class help to explain much about our political life. Marxist categories of *proletariat* (those who sell their labor) and *bourgeoisie* (those who own or control the means of production) are not as important here as they are in Europe. But we do have social classes and what social scientists call **socio-economic status (SES)**—a division of the population based on occupation, income, and education. Such measures help explain some citizen behavior in American politics, but these categories have some obvious inconsistencies. For instance, some individuals perform working-class tasks (such as plumbing), but their income is middle class or even upper middle class. A schoolteacher's income is below that of many working-class jobs, but in terms of status, the job ranks at least with middle-class fields.

Most Americans, when asked what class they belong to, say "middle class." The second most frequently mentioned category is "working class." Very few Americans see themselves as lower class or upper class. But what constitutes "middle class" is highly subjective. As vice-president, George Bush once defined "middle class" as persons making over $50,000.[85] Actually, only 5.7 percent of Americans had that much income.[86] In many other industrial democracies, large proportions of the population think of themselves as working class instead of middle class.[87] In England, nearly three out of five persons see themselves as working class.[88] But to many Americans there is something undesirable about the label "working class."

One explanation for Americans' responses may be the elements of the American Dream that involve upward mobility. Or this may reflect the hostility many feel toward organized labor, which solidifies workers. European labor unions are stronger than American labor unions. In any case, compared to many countries, class divisions in the United States are less defined and less important to politics. As political scientist Seymour Martin Lipset has written, "The American social structure and values foster an emphasis on competitive individualism, an orientation that is not congruent with class consciousness, support for socialist or social democratic parties, or a strong union movement."[89]

Age

Americans are living longer, a phenomenon that has been called the "graying of America." Not only are we living longer, but fewer babies are being born proportionate to the population. This demographic change will eventually have important consequences; it will increase the demand for medical care, retirement benefits, and a host of other age-related services. The growing population of older persons was most pronounced in the West during the 1980s, but Florida remains the state with the largest proportion of persons over age 65. Persons over the age of 65 constitute 11 percent of the population but use 32 percent of all medical services.[90]

Older Americans as a group have a political agenda, and they vote. Figure 8-7, which plots voter turnout rate by age, shows a clear relationship: as age increases, so does the propensity to vote. In recent presidential elections, less than half of all 18- and 19-year-olds voted. In contrast, four out of every five 68 and 69 year olds turned out to vote.[91] As a group, they fight to ensure that Social Security is protected; they value Medicare and favor catastrophic health insurance. Despite their desire for services that benefit themselves, they also are the group most in favor of tax cuts. Past legislative victories have changed the lives of older citizens. For instance, the poverty rate among this age group dropped from 35 percent in 1959 to 12 percent in 1991, a change partly due to improved medical benefits passed during the 1960s. [92]

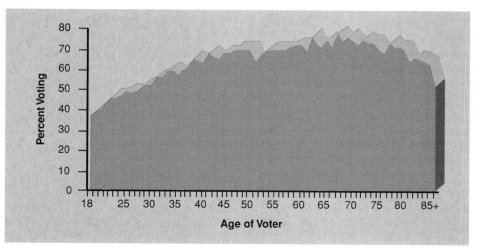

FIGURE 8-7
Percent Voting in the 1992 Presidential Election by Age

Source: U.S. Bureau of the Census, Current Population Reports P 20, no. 446, *Voting and Registration in the Election of November 1992* (Government Printing Office, 1993).

The "gray lobby" not only votes in large numbers but also has four other political assets that make it politically powerful—disposable income, discretionary time, a clear focus on issues, and effective organization—factors not found in any other age group. When older Americans compete for their share of the budget pie, the young, minorities, and the poor often lose out to the "gray lobby."

President Clinton sought the support of older Americans for his health care reform package by promising no reduction in benefits for older Americans and reduced overall costs.[93] The American Association of Retired Persons (AARP), the largest and most powerful arm of the "gray lobby," disappointed President Clinton by refusing to endorse his health care reform bill. Instead, they, like other interested groups, sought to make their own case before the Congress.

Age is important to politics in two additional ways: life cycle and generation. Examples of life-cycle effects are that as people become middle-aged they become more politically conservative, less mobile, and more likely to participate in politics. As they age further and become senior citizens who rely more on the government for services, they tend to grow more liberal.[94]

There are also *generational effects* in politics that arise when a particular generation has had experiences that make it politically distinct. An example is the experience of the Great Depression, which, for those who lived through it, shaped lifelong views of parties, issues, and political leaders. Some of this generation saw Franklin Roosevelt as the person who saved the country by pulling it out of the Depression, while others felt he sold the country down the river by launching too many government programs. A more recent generation that shared a common and distinctive political experience is the Vietnam generation. Americans who came of age politically during the Vietnam War experienced not only an unpopular war but also the civil rights movement. As with the Great Depression, not everybody saw the Vietnam War and related issues in the same way. Such differences do not diminish the importance of the issue in shaping a generation's perspective on politics and government.

Education

Education has long been linked to citizenship and civic virtue. Thomas Jefferson wrote of education, "Enlighten the people generally, and tyranny and oppressions of body and mind will vanish like evil spirits at the dawn of day."[95] The vast majority of people in the United States are educated in public schools. Nine out of every ten students in kindergarten through high school attend public schools, and four out of five students in college are in public institutions.[96]

The U.S. population has a wide range of number of years of school completed. There are, for instance, more Americans with less than a high school education than there are college graduates. High school dropout rates have declined in the last decade, yet African Americans, Hispanics, and individuals from low income families still have higher than average dropout rates. Roughly two-thirds of Americans have not gone to college, though many college students assume that the college experience is widely shared.

Still, Americans are becoming more educated. In a 50-year period, the number of Americans 25 years and older with four or more years of college has gone from only 5 percent in 1940 to more than 21 percent in the early 1990s.[97] Impressive gains have been made by all groups in the proportion graduating from high school, yet racial and ethnic minorities still lag behind whites in completing four or more years of college. African Americans have increased their rate of completion of four or more years of college tenfold since 1940, and Hispanics have almost doubled their college attendance since 1974, when data were first collected. To compete for jobs in a post-industrial society, more education, especially technical education, is necessary.

We The People

Distribution of Education in the United States (in percent)

	4 Years of High School	1–3 Years of College	4+ Years of College	Total
Total	38.6%	18.4%	21.4%	78.4%
Male	36.0	18.2	24.3	78.5
Female	41.0	18.6	18.8	78.3
White	39.1	18.6	22.2	79.9
African American	37.7	17.5	11.5	66.7
Hispanic	29.3	12.3	9.7	51.3
Other	29.7	15.5	33.5	78.7
Age				
25–34	40.8	21.6	23.7	86.1
35–44	37.6	22.6	27.5	87.7
45–54	40.1	17.9	23.2	81.2
55–64	40.5	14.5	16.9	71.9
65–74	38.2	12.1	13.2	63.5
75+	28.2	10.4	10.5	49.0

SOURCE: U.S. Bureau of the Census, Current Population Reports, P 23, no.185, *Population Profile of the United States, 1993* (Government Printing Office, 1993), p. 15.

Compared to persons in other industrial democracies, Americans and Canadians are more likely to go to college.[98] But the experience of higher education has not been uniformly shared. The proportion of whites who are college graduates is nearly double that for African Americans or Hispanics; roughly 35 percent of African Americans and nearly half of all Hispanics stopped their schooling before completing high school. Part of the difference among whites, African Americans, and Hispanics in years of school completed is a function of age. Older African Americans and Hispanics are much less likely to have completed high school. One in five African Americans and 27 percent of Hispanics over the age of 65 stopped school before the fifth grade. In contrast, younger African Americans (those under the age of 29) are more likely than whites to have stayed in school through the eighth grade, but they then have a higher dropout rate than whites in high school. Hispanics, on the other hand, have high rates of dropout, even in the lower grades. Twelve percent did not go beyond the fourth grade, and one in three did not go to high school.[99] These differences in education affect not only economic well-being but political participation and involvement.

Education is one of the most important variables in predicting political participation, confidence in dealing with government, and awareness of issues. Education is also related to the acquisition of democratic values. Those who have failed to learn the "prevailing norms" of American society are far more likely to express opposition to democratic and capitalist ideals than those who are well educated and politically knowledgeable.[100] Education is, in short, a factor we will return to again and again in subsequent chapters as we study government and politics by the people.

UNITY IN A LAND OF DIVERSITY

As remarkable as American diversity is, the existence of a strong and widely shared sense of national unity and identity may be even more remarkable. Writing about the United States some years ago, a famous reporter, John Gunther, summarized his extensive travels across the United States by saying:

Whoever invented the motto E Pluribus Unum [one out of many] has given the best three-word description of the United States ever written. The triumph of America is the triumph of a coalescing federal system. Complex as the nation is almost to the point of insufferability, it interlocks. Homogeneity and diversity—these are the stupendous rival magnets. . . . Think of the United States as an immense blanket or patchwork quilt solid with different designs and highlights. But, no matter what colors burn and flash in what corners, the warp and woof, the basic texture and fabric is the same from corner to corner, from end to end.[101]

Americans have always been united by their commitment to liberty. Equally important has been the belief that government should exist to serve the people, rather than the reverse. What shapes our political culture is the persistent commitment to the individual. One author recently concluded that "equality, individualism and openness are the crucial values of American politics in the 1990s."[102]

Part of the explanation for our unity is the unifying effect of the American Dream—the belief that this is the land of opportunity for enterprising individuals. Unity in the midst of diversity has also been enhanced by a sense of a common fate, often highlighted by a crisis. Social and economic differences become less important, for example, when we fight wars. World War II drew many Americans to experience life in different parts of the country and confirmed the patriotism of diverse groups. One question for the late 1990s will be: Can we maintain the same degree of unity in a world with fewer foreign enemies and only one military superpower? Finally, the United States has achieved a measure of unity through residential mobility, intermarriage, the mass media, and a common culture.

Social scientists sometimes speak of the *melting pot*, meaning that as minorities, especially ethnic groups, associate with other groups, they are assimilated into the rest of American society and come to share democratic values like majority rule, individualism, and the notion that America is the land of opportunity. Recently the melting pot idea has been criticized as assuming that differences between groups are to be discouraged. In its place, critics propose the notion of the *salad bowl*, in which "though the salad is an entity, the lettuce can still be distinguished from the chicory, the tomatoes from the cabbage."[103] As we have seen, important differences persist among groups, and in that sense the salad bowl analogy is accurate. But in another way, our society has achieved a unity of commitment to democratic values and processes—a political culture—that is at least in part a consequence of such elements of the melting pot theory as public schools, a common language, and hope for a better life for one's children. While ethnic divisions in the United States have posed

It is not unusual to see signs that say "Will work for food." But this sign reminds us that with the difficult economic changes of the 1990s even college graduates may be in trouble.

This piece of "neon art," entitled *Nation of Nations,* includes many of the cultures that make up the ethnic complexity of the United States.

challenges to the institutions and processes of government, the public has generally accepted diversity in political appointments, government jobs and contracts, and other aspects of policy. This is a sharp contrast to the problems of ethnicity in Canada, India, and the former Yugoslavia and Soviet Union. But what is the appropriate balance among recognition, preservation, and representation of ethnic groups and the needs for assimilation, common commitments, and a shared identity?

The United States is part of a global political landscape in which many of the same variables are important—race, religion, wealth, and the distribution of income. The changing world landscape has served, and will serve, to remind us of the challenges that diversity poses to governments. Racial, religious, and ethnic strife and historical divisions in many of the new democracies of Central Europe and the Commonwealth of Independent States have fostered insecurity within and between many nations. Other countries that are not yet democratic, like most in the Middle East, face similar challenges. While our effort to meld a single nation out of many diverse groups has not been without its failures, achieving some measure of unity is one of our governmental system's most important accomplishments.

SUMMARY

1. The character of a political society, its social and economic divisions, its traditions, and its sectional and local identifications are important to understanding public opinion, participation, voting, interest groups, political parties, and the communications process. It is often a mistake to generalize solely from one's own experience, background, beliefs, and values.

2. Geography, room to grow, abundant natural resources, our wealth, and our relative isolation from "foreign entanglements" help to explain American politics and traditions, including the notions of manifest destiny, ethnocentrism, and isolationism.

3. The South has been the most distinct region in the United States, in large part because of the issue of slavery and race relations. Other important sections include the frost belt/sun belt division.

4. Americans moved from farms to cities and more recently from cities to suburbs. Population movements were largely responses to economic opportunities, including the large migration of African Americans from the South. Today, large cities are increasingly poor, African American, and Democratic, surrounded by suburbs that are primarily middle class, white, and Republican.

5. The United States is a land of tremendous diversity in race, ethinicity, religion, wealth and income, occupation, social class, age, and education. Divisions by gender and sexual orientation have recently become more important. This diversity is often important to our politics.

6. Race has been among the most important of the differences in our landscape. We fought a civil war on the issue of freedom for African Americans, and the issue of racial equality was largely postponed until the latter half of this century. Race remains an important issue in our politics

and government. Ethnicity, including the rising numbers of Hispanics, continues to be a factor in politics, as demonstrated by the controversy over English as the official language. Religion is a difference that helps explain political behavior both in terms of persons from different religions behaving differently, but also differences between those who are religious and those who are not.

7. Gender is important in American politics. Women have gradually acquired political rights, they now play important roles in our government, and they differ from men in their attitudes on some issues. Sexual orientation is also a distinction increasingly important to politics and policy.

8. While the United States is a land of wealth and is known for its large middle class, not everyone has an adequate share in the American economic success. Poverty has grown over the past decade, and it is most concentrated among African Americans, Native Americans, Hispanics, and single-parent households. Women as a group continue to earn less than men, even in the same occupations. Differences in income and wealth remain important.

9. Age and education are important to understanding American politics. Our aging population poses important challenges to public policy. Because they participate so much more than young voters, older Americans are a potent political force. Education not only opens up economic opportunities in America but also explains many important aspects of political participation.

10. Despite our diversity, Americans share an important unity. We are united by our shared commitment to democratic values, economic opportunity, the work ethic, and the American Dream. Our national experiences like wars, olympic teams, and global economic competition have also unified us.

FURTHER READING

DANIEL BELL, *The Coming of Post-Industrial Society: A Venture in Social Forecasting* (Basic Books, 1973).

DAVID H. BENNETT, *The Party of Fear* (University of North Carolina Press, 1990).

SARAH H. EVANS, *Born for Liberty: A History of Women in America* (Free Press, 1989).

RODOLFO O. DE LA GARZA ET AL., *Latino Voices: Mexican, Puerto Rican, and Cuban Perspectives on American Politics* (Westview Press, 1992).

DENNIS GILBERT AND JOSEPH A. KAHL, *The American Class Structure: A New Synthesis*, 3d ed. (Dorsey Press, 1987).

ANDREW HACKER, *Two Nations: Black and White, Separate, Hostile, Unequal* (Charles Scribners, Sons, 1992).

SEYMOUR MARTIN LIPSET, *Continental Divide: The Values and Institutions of the United States and Canada* (Routledge, 1990).

———, *Political Man* (Doubleday, 1963).

PETER NABOKOV, ED., *Native American Testimony: A Chronicle of Indian-White Relations from Prophesy to the Present, 1492–1992* (Viking, 1991).

KEVIN PHILLIPS, *The Politics of Rich and Poor: Wealth and the American Electorate in the Reagan Aftermath* (Random House, 1990).

PAULA RIES AND ANNE J. STONE, *The American Woman, 1992–93: A Status Report* (W.W. Norton, 1992).

STEVEN J. ROSE, *Social Stratification in the United States: The American Profile Poster Revised and Expanded* (New Press, 1992).

ARTHUR M. SCHLESINGER, JR., *The Disuniting of America* (W.W. Norton, 1992).

STUDS TERKEL, *Race: How Blacks & Whites Think and Feel About the American Obsession* (W. W. Norton, 1992).

ALEXIS DE TOCQUEVILLE, *Democracy in America*, ed. J. P. Mayer, trans. George Lawrence (Doubleday and Company, 1969).

INTEREST GROUPS: THE POLITICS OF INFLUENCE

9

The vote in the House of Representatives on the North American Free Trade Agreement (NAFTA) came on November 17, 1993, after weeks of intense lobbying by labor unions, business groups, environmental interests, and the president. The agreement lowers all tariffs between the United States, Mexico, and Canada—some immediately and some over a ten-year period. The urgency of debate was amplified by a deadline; it had to be ratified during 1993 or negotiations would have to start over. While the issue had been raised during the 1992 presidential election and had long been part of the U.S. foreign policy agenda, NAFTA did not become a "hot" political issue until a few weeks before the congressional vote. The issue grew in visibility and importance with an unprecedented televised debate between Vice-President Al Gore, who vigorously supported NAFTA, and Ross Perot, former presidential contender who was one of the outspoken opponents of the agreement.

The NAFTA fight illustrates the central role interest groups play in American politics. Although some members of Congress have strong personal beliefs on trade issues, many of the votes on NAFTA could be traced back to the members' ties with various interest groups, both for and against NAFTA. Opponents included labor unions, some environmental organizations, human rights groups, Ross Perot, Pat Buchanan, and most of the Democrats in the House of Representatives, including Majority Leader Richard Gephardt (D.-Mo.) and Majority Whip David Bonior (D.-Mich.). Supporting NAFTA was an association of business groups united under the name USA*NAFTA, the U.S. Chamber of Commerce, most economists (including 12 Nobel Prize winners), many state governors, House Speaker Thomas Foley (D.-Wash.), and most House Republicans. One visible and active supporter of NAFTA was Lee Iacocca, who had just retired as the chief executive officer of Chrysler. The agreement was also supported by all living former presidents, as well as by President Clinton.

Opponents of NAFTA, led by the labor unions, launched an all-out effort to defeat the agreement. Long a major financial supporter of many House Democrats, unions told these members, "If you vote to ship jobs of our members out of this country, we're not going to support you anymore."[1] President Clinton called some of the union tactics "roughshod and musclebound." To build popular support for their position, opponents of NAFTA ran television and radio advertisements suggesting it would cost American jobs.

Interest groups that supported NAFTA sponsored their own commercials, countering the claims of treaty opponents and contending that NAFTA would create jobs. Much of the lobbying activity for the agreement was organized out of the "war room," offices in a building near the White House where staff and interns worked to mobilize popular and congressional support. As the vote neared, Clinton himself became actively involved in lobbying, holding face-to-face meetings with dozens of undecided lawmakers and spending hours on the telephone. Failure to approve NAFTA, Clinton argued, would damage his ability to win further trade concessions with other countries and weaken his presidency. He also made some key concessions to win votes. Both sides organized letter writing and telephoning campaigns to attempt to influence the decision. On the day of the vote in the House of Representatives, lobbyists for each side converged on House office buildings and set up command posts, where they directed the fight until the end.

The final vote count in the House was 234 for NAFTA and 200 against it. Those who supported it believed that economic growth comes with free trade and that Mexico and Canada would also experience economic growth as a consequence

Some Facts about Interest Groups

In the United States there are:

- 68 million families
- 90 religions with at least 50,000 adherents
- 250,000 religious congregations
- 2,000 trade associations
- 3,000 organizations with offices in Washington, D.C., one-quarter of them founded since 1970
- more than 4,000 political action committees (PACs)

In Washington, D.C., there are:

- 29 percent of all national nonprofit associations
- representatives of more than 4,000 individual corporations
- more than 37,000 lawyers

of the agreement opposed. Those who opposed it feared that the United States would lose jobs to Mexico, that the environment would suffer because of Mexico's more lax environmental laws, and that Mexico's lower paid workers would drive down wages for U.S. workers.

The battle over NAFTA was especially interesting because of the unexpected coalitions it generated. Many well-known political personalities who are normally opposed to each other temporarily put their differences aside to work together. Conservative Pat Buchanan and billionaire Ross Perot joined with the AFL-CIO and Greenpeace to oppose NAFTA. Similarly, President Clinton and House Speaker Foley worked closely with House Republican leaders and the U.S. Chamber of Commerce to ensure that NAFTA would pass.

If the coalitions in the fight over NAFTA were unusual, the clash of interest groups was not. It occurs often in American politics at all levels. In this chapter we examine the tremendous variety of such interest groups. We begin by discussing their roles and types, then turn to one of their most important activities—lobbying government. Finally, we examine the problems interest groups pose and ways to regulate them.

INTEREST GROUPS PAST AND PRESENT

One of the enduring features of democracy is the interplay of interests. Freedom and democracy seem to go hand in hand, with individuals acting politically on their perceived interests. Concern about what to do to limit the tendency of self-interested persons to seek more political power is also enduring. From the founding of our Republic to the present time, students of government have debated how to limit zealous political interests without damaging essential freedom.

The Mischiefs of Faction

What we call *interest groups* today, James Madison called **factions**. Madison also thought of political parties as factions. For Madison and the other framers of the U.S. Constitution, the daunting problem was how to establish a stable and orderly constitutional system that at the same time would respect the liberty of free citizens. Madison warned of the tendency of popular government toward the "vice" of faction, toward "instability, injustice, and confusion." Still, he would not sacrifice the liberty that led to the formation of factions. How could this dilemma be resolved?

Madison, a good practical politician and a brilliant theorist, offered both a diagnosis and a solution. The solution had already taken concrete form in the new Constitution that Madison firmly believed would control the effects of factionalism; Madison summarized this solution in *The Federalist,* No. 10 (reprinted in the Appendix).

Part of the genius of *The Federalist,* No. 10, lies in the manner in which Madison describes the factions of the day. He begins with a fundamental proposition: "The latent causes of faction are thus sown in the nature of man." He does not take a simplistic approach to faction. Factions are not merely religious, economic, or political but a combination of these, and factions can be divided into subfactions. Thus, property owners may be divided into landed, manufacturing, mercantile, and moneyed subfactions. Madison demonstrated that Americans lived in a maze of group interests, or factions. Yet he went on to argue that the "most common and durable source of factions has been the various and unequal distribution of property."

A Nation of Interests

The United States has been described as a nation of joiners. Europeans sometimes make fun of us for setting up all sorts of organizations, and we ourselves are often amused by the behavior of our groups—the noisy conventions of veterans' associations, the solemn rites of great fraternal organizations, and the oratory of patriotic societies. Yet most of these groups have serious goals and play an important role in politics.

How many groups are there in the United States? There is no way to give an accurate count. The family is the most basic and important group, and there are more than 68 million families in the United States. There are also one-quarter million religious congregations, diverse farm groups and labor unions, and more than two thousand trade associations. As we noted in Chapter 8, Americans naturally form groups according to their race, gender, ethnic background, age, occupation, and so forth. All these are groups in the broadest sense of the term; that is, their members share some common outlook or attitude, and they interact with one another in some way.

Interest groups are groups of people who share a common concern. Interest groups usually work within the framework of government and employ tactics such as lobbying to achieve their goals. They are increasing in number. Sometimes referred to as "special interests," they are viewed by many as selfish, concerned only with promoting their own well-being. Indeed, for many, the discussion of interest groups conjures up images of powerful or moneyed interests pressuring legislators to retain tax loopholes, or groups such as the National Rifle Association lobbying against gun control. Yet even such special interests would claim that their actions promote common national interests. Frequently the power of these special interests angers Americans. In the 1930s and 1940s, labor unions were often seen as greedy and power hungry. Today the image of labor unions may be even worse, and corporate conglomerates more often come under attack. Occasionally—perhaps when a powerful corporation squares off against a strong union, as in the transportation field—the public may utter a "curse on both your houses."

The definition of "special interest" can be highly subjective: "The specialness of an interest lies in the eye of the beholder."[2] Part of the politics of interest groups is to persuade the public that your group's interest is better, broader, more beneficial, more general, and at the same time to label groups that oppose yours as "special interests." For this reason we choose to use the neutral term "interest groups" in the textbook discussion.

Social Movements

Interest groups seek to work inside the existing political channels. They try to influence elections and then to influence public officials. This is the ordinary and continuing way we do business in the United States.

Different from interest groups—but often shading into them—are movements. A **movement** is a large body of people who are interested in a common issue, idea, or concern of continuing significance and who are willing to take action on that issue. Examples of movements include civil rights, environmental, antitax, and women's rights. Each of these movements represented or represents groups who felt "left out" of government. They often arise at the grass-roots level and evolve into national groups. Movements tend to see their causes as morally right and the positions of the opposition as morally wrong.

THE WOMEN'S MOVEMENT   American women in the 1770s, like their sisters in Western Europe, were dependents of their fathers and husbands. Women could not make legal arrangements or contracts, earn wages separate from those of their husbands, or vote. By marrying, they forfeited to their husbands legal custody of themselves as well as custody of all property and children.[3] Lacking the right to vote, women could not turn to electoral politics to overcome discrimination.

Groups: Straightening Out the Terms

Categories: People with certain characteristics in common: country music lovers, 16-year-olds, women, blacks, the elderly.

Groups: People who share common goals and who interact with one another: union leaders, your family, the senior class of your college.

Interest groups: People who share common goals, interact with one another, and are organized to press claims on government: veterans, soybean growers, bankers. Interest groups tend to operate within the framework of government and the existing two-party system, to use the political tactics of lobbying, to build policy coalitions within the legislative and executive branches, to strive for consensus outside of government, and to advance their goals as beneficial to all groups—not just their own.

Associations: Formal organizations created by interest groups: the National Association for the Advancement of Colored People (NAACP), National Organization for Women (NOW), AFL-CIO, National Rifle Association (NRA).

Movements: People united but loosely organized around a central idea whose goal is to change attitudes or institutions, not just policy: the civil rights movement, women's movement, antiabortion movement. People in movements tend to feel "left out" of government, to conduct political action at the grass-roots level, to put pressure on government from the outside, to build coalitions among mobilized publics, to see their causes as morally right and the opposition as wrong—even evil—and to thrive on social and political conflict.

Political action committees (PACs): The political arms of interest groups, which are legally entitled to raise and spend campaign contributions. PACs include those representing professional associations like the American Medical Association (AMPAC), labor unions, ideological groups, and corporations like Ford Motor Corporation.

Women in the United States have been involved in a long struggle for their rights, from the suffragettes who campaigned for the right to vote, to rallies and marches in recent years for the Equal Rights Amendment.

Rather, they "determined to ferment a rebellion," in Abigail Adams's words, for "we would not hold ourselves bound by any laws in which we have no voice or representation."[4]

The women's movement grew in response to this sense of powerlessness as well as to social problems that concerned women, such as illiteracy, slavery, and liquor. An 1848 convention in Seneca Falls, New York, called for equal rights in marriage, property, contracts, trades, professions, and universities; the convention also called for female suffrage. The right to vote was gradually extended to women and was finally included in the Constitution with the passage of the Nineteenth Amendment in 1920.

Having achieved one of its most important goals, the women's movement shifted its attention to other issues, like child welfare, voter education, prison reform, antilynching measures, and peace. One issue of continuing importance has been women's rights. But the women's movement, like all movements, has competing concerns and interests. Should it focus on women's rights only, or on the needs of other disadvantaged groups like African Americans, children, and low-paid workers? Which right should be most aggressively pursued: the right to an education, to legal protection, to equal pay, to a decent job? The answer is that the women's movement is not just one movement but several movements that share some, but not all, concerns. Those who see themselves as part of the movement sometimes disagree on tactics even though they may agree on goals.

One of the most important women's issues in the 1970s and 1980s was the Equal Rights Amendment. As discussed in Chapter 2, the proposed amendment sought to guarantee "equality of rights under the law" regardless of gender. While most women's groups, most women, and the Democratic party remain committed to the ERA, the amendment has not been the driving concern it once was. In its place have come issues like abortion, affirmative action for women, and the changing of particular laws that discriminate against women. Abortion has been seen as a women's issue because it is women whose bodies and lives are affected. As Justice

SOME MOVEMENTS IN THE UNITED STATES

Abolitionist	Gay rights
Suffragist	Moral Majority
Temperance	Nuclear freeze
Peace	Animal rights
Single tax	Earth First
Populist	Antitax
Civil rights	Term limits
Anti-Vietnam war	

Individuals who share a common identity or concern form movements to advance their rights or issues. The agenda and success of these movements vary widely. Some accomplish their goals and go away, others evolve into concern for other issues, and some become established interest groups that persist over time. Movements polarize opinion, but they also persuade some people to change their attitudes, and they raise public consciousness about social issues that government might otherwise ignore.

In many countries movements are viewed as a threat to government, and indeed they may be, as the governments of South Africa, China, Czechoslovakia, Russia, and others have learned. To a marked degree, our Constitution continues to protect the liberties and independence of movements. The Bill of Rights guarantees movements, whether popular or unpopular, free assembly, free speech, and due process. Hence militants do not have to engage in terrorism or other extreme activities in the United States, as they do in some countries, and they need not fear persecution for demonstrating. In a democratic system that restricts the power of those in authority, movements have considerable room to operate *within* the constitutional system.

Harry A. Blackmun said in *Roe v Wade*, "Freedom of personal choice in matters of marriage and family life is one of the liberties protected by the due process clause of the Fourteenth Amendment. . . . That right necessarily includes the right of a woman to decide whether or not to terminate her pregnancy."[5] But both women and men are divided on the issue of abortion, and there are women's groups on both sides of the issue.

The story of women's movements in the United States is one of a group whose members originally lacked political power, developed a sense of group consciousness, entered politics despite countless frustrations and setbacks, and, after long struggles, achieved some of their major political goals. Unresolved issues that concern and affect women continue to make the women's movement important to American politics.

TYPES OF INTEREST GROUPS

Interest groups vary widely from business organizations to public interest groups. Some are formal associations or organizations; others have no formal organization. Some are organized primarily to lobby; some have other goals, such as securing wage increases, conducting research, or broadly influencing public opinion by publishing reports and mass mailings.

Interest groups can be categorized into several broad types: economic, including both business and labor; ideological; public interest; foreign policy; and even government. Obviously these categories are not mutually exclusive; some business groups are also ideological and economic. The variety and overlapping nature of interest groups in the United States have been described as *interest group pluralism,* and the competition among open, responsive, and diverse groups has been credited with preserving democratic values and limiting the concentration of power in any single group.

Large groups are often made up of alliances of several small groups. As Alexis de Tocqueville observed long ago, Americans form associations for every conceivable purpose and function. And as government has become more central to Americans' lives, these groups have turned their attention to government. In Washington today, interest groups rival the federal bureaucracy in number, size, and complexity.

Economic Interest Groups

Madison pointed out that some of the most common and durable factions derive from property interests, or how we make our living and manage what we own. There are thousands, even tens of thousands, of economic interests—agriculture, skilled laborers, students, plumbers, northern businesses, southern businesses, labor unions, the airplane industry, landlords, developers, bondholders, savings and loan investors, and so on.

BUSINESS　　The most familiar business institution is probably the large corporation. Corporations range from small, one-person enterprises to large multinational entities. Large corporations—General Motors, AT&T, and Fortune 500 companies—exercise considerable political influence, as do hundreds of smaller corporations.

In the last century, both the national and state governments began to regulate business practices. Antitrust legislation was adopted to limit monopolies; labor laws were enacted to protect workers. The 1980s brought the need to regulate business and financial institutions back to the forefront as a result of leveraged buy-outs and savings and loans scandals. In the mid-1990s, corporate power and the implications of a changing domestic and global economy make corporations and their practices important political issues.

Businesses with similar interests in these regulations and other issues join together as **trade associations**. They are as diverse as the products and services they provide. Take a look in your *World Almanac;* you will find a national association for almost everything from life insurance to tire manufacturers to restaurants to real estate dealers and moviemakers. In addition, businesses of all types are organized into large, nationwide business associations such as the Conference Board, the Business Roundtable, the Business Higher-Education Forum, and the Chamber of Commerce.

The broadest business trade association is the Chamber of Commerce of the United States. Organized in 1912, the chamber is a federation of several thousand local chambers of commerce representing tens of thousands of business firms. Loosely allied with the chamber on most issues is the National Association of Manufacturers, which, since its founding in the wake of the depression of 1893, has tended to speak for the more conservative elements of American business. Large nationwide business associations often take up issues that involve many industries. One such group is the 120,000 Independent Insurance Agents of America, which launched an intensive lobbying campaign to combat banking reform that would permit banks to sell insurance across state lines.[6] In the endless battle of factions, however, even the influence of well-funded and politically focused interests is limited when strong competing interests exist.

LABOR The American work force is the least unionized of any industrial democracy, but many employees belong to some kind of association or another. These workers' associations have a range of interests, from professional standards to wages and working conditions. Labor unions are one of the most important groups representing workers.

Probably the oldest "unions" in the United States were farm organizations. The largest farm group now is the American Farm Bureau Federation, which is especially strong in the corn belt. Originally organized around government agents who helped farmers in rural counties, the federation today is almost a semigovernmental agency, but it retains full freedom to fight for such goals as price supports and expanded credit. A number of other farm organizations are based on the interests of producers of specific commodities, such as the American Soybean Association.

Other workers, too, have long been organized. Throughout the nineteenth century, workers organized political parties and local unions. Their most ambitious effort at national organization, the Knights of Labor, claimed 700,000 members. By the beginning of this century, the American Federation of Labor (AFL), a confederation of strong and independent-minded national unions mainly representing craftworkers, was the dominant organization. During the ferment of the 1930s, unions organized by industries broke away from the AFL, which was seen as more responsive to workers organized by trade, and formed a rival national organization for workers organized by industry, the Congress of Industrial Organizations (CIO). Later the AFL and CIO reunited in the organization that exists today, but some industrial union leaders contend that the AFL-CIO has become too conservative.

For some years the Committee on Political Education (COPE) of the AFL-CIO was one of the most respected—and most feared—political organizations in the country. In the Kennedy-Johnson years it won a reputation for political effectiveness. It encouraged and supervised grass-roots political activity, and at the national level it prepared and adopted a platform, 50 to 60 pages long, which spelled out labor's position on the issues. Labor contributed money to candidates, ran registration and get-out-the-vote campaigns, and otherwise supported its favorites. More recently organized labor has sputtered and faltered. Because the AFL-CIO is a federation of powerful and independent national unions, state and local groups or federations of unions have sometimes been politically divided. Leadership of the AFL-

A bitter ten-month strike by employees of the *New York Daily News* in 1990 ended with the loss of many jobs and the capitulation to most of the owner's demands.

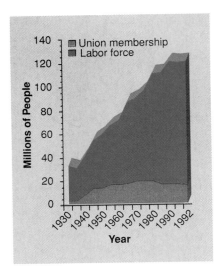

FIGURE 9-1
Labor Force and Union Membership,
1930–1992

SOURCE: Data from *World Almanac and Book of Facts, 1994* (Funk & Wagnalls, 1993), p. 141.

TABLE 9-1

PACs That Gave the Most to Federal Candidates in 1992

	(millions)
Realtors Political Action Committee	$2.9
American Medical Association Political Action Committee	2.9
Democratic Republican Independent Voter Education Committee	2.4
Association of Trial Lawyers of America Political Action Committee	2.3
National Education Association Political Action Committee	2.3
United Auto Workers Voluntary Community Action Program (UAW-V-CAP)	2.2
American Federation of State, County, and Municipal Employees (AFSCME)	1.9

SOURCE: Federal Election Commission, press release, April 29, 1993.

CIO had been in the hands of only a few men who, once elected, held office for a long time.

In 1984 the AFL-CIO took the unusual step of endorsing Democratic presidential candidate Walter F. Mondale, before the presidential primaries had begun. Mondale's campaign repeatedly had to respond to the charge that he was the candidate of special interest. In recent elections COPE has had a fair but not spectacular record of wins for its endorsed House and Senate candidates.[7] Labor unions invested heavily in the 1992 fight against NAFTA and lost, a loss that further reduced their political influence with Congress.

Organized labor's political and lobbying muscle is obviously limited, and the prospects for increasing influence in the future are dim. One reason for labor's declining influence is that unionized membership is dwindling relative to the increase in the national work force (see Figure 9-1). The AFL-CIO by no means speaks for all workers; union labor represents only about 16 percent of the nation's work force, and AFL-CIO membership amounts to about 80 percent of the total number of those organized.[8] Union membership is optional in states whose laws permit the **open shop**, where union membership cannot be required as a condition of employment. (In states that permit the **closed shop**, all workers can be required to join the union.) In an open-shop setting the union represents only those workers who choose to affiliate when it negotiates for its members, but any concessions it gains from management are shared by all employees—union and nonunion. Many workers choose not to affiliate with the union when they can secure the same pay without incurring the costs associated with union membership. The decline in the proportion of union membership is also explained in part by the shift from an industrial to a service economy.

PROFESSIONAL ASSOCIATIONS   Professional people have organized some of the strongest "unions" in the nation. Some are well known, such as the American Medical Association and the American Bar Association. Others are divided into many subgroups. Teachers, for example, are organized into large groups such as the National Education Association, the American Federation of Teachers, and the American Association of University Professors, but they are also organized into subgroups based on specialties, such as the Modern Language Association and the American Political Science Association. Many professions are dependent on and regulated by government, especially on the state level. Lawyers, for example, are licensed by states, which have set up, often as a result of pressure from lawyers themselves, certain standards of admission to the state bar. Associations also use the courts to pursue their agenda. In the area of medical malpractice, for example, medical doctors lobby hard for limited liability laws, while the trial lawyers association resists such efforts. Teachers, hair stylists, or marriage therapists work for legislation or regulations of concern to them. It is not surprising, then, that among the largest donors to political campaigns through political action committees are those representing professional associations such as the American Medical Association and the American Realtors Association (see Table 9-1).

Ideological Interest Groups

Virtually all interest groups convince themselves that they are devoted to the public welfare and not merely to their own self-interests. The Council for a Livable World, for example, campaigns for liberal candidates and issues, while the Conservative Victory Action Committee works for conservative ones. Countless groups have organized around specific issues, such as civil liberties, birth control, abortion, environmental protection, nuclear energy, and nuclear arms.[9] One of the best-known ideological groups is the American Civil Liberties Union (ACLU), with roughly one-quarter million members committed to the protection of civil liberties.[10] Some highly ideological groups are thriving in the otherwise pragmatic, pluralistic politics of the 1990s.[11]

Public Interest Groups

Public interest groups arose out of the political ferment of the 1960s. Common Cause, founded in 1970 by independent Republican John W. Gardner and later led by noted Watergate prosecutor Archibald Cox, campaigns for electoral reform and for making the political process more open. Its Washington staff raises money through direct mail campaigns, oversees state chapters, issues a flood of research reports and press releases on current issues, and lobbies on Capitol Hill and in major government departments. Ralph Nader started a conglomerate of consumer organizations that investigates and reports on governmental and corporate action—or inaction—relating to consumer interests. Public Interest Research Groups (PIRGs), founded by Ralph Nader, today number among the largest interest groups in the country, with a national membership of more than 400,000, and they have become major players on Capitol Hill. Chapters of these groups exist on many college campuses and are active in promoting environmental issues, safe energy, consumer protection, and good government.

"There's getting to be a lot of dangerous talk about the public interest."
The Herblock Gallery (Simon & Schuster, 1968).

Ideological and public interest groups behave very much like economic interest groups. They may not be motivated by a desire to make money but a desire to ban guns, save guns, or save the environment. Some of these groups are *single-issue* groups, often highly motivated on their issue and seeing politics primarily as a means to pursue their issue. Such groups are often adamant about their position and unwilling to negotiate compromises.

A specific type of public interest group is the *tax exempt public charity,* also called a 501(c)(3) organization because it is organized under section 501(c)(3) of the Internal Revenue Code. Examples include the American Heart Association, the Girl Scouts, and the American Cancer Society. Organizations must meet certain conditions to qualify for this preferred status, such as educational or philanthropic objectives. Not only are public charities tax exempt, but donations to these organizations are tax deductible and the organizations are not required to disclose information about their donors publicly. These organizations cannot participate in elections or support candidates, nor can they exist for the benefit of an individual or small group. Despite these limitations, 501(c)(3) organizations have been very active in voter registration efforts and advertising campaigns designed to influence public opinion. According to an analysis of 1988 financial disclosure forms for federal legislators, 51 Senators and 146 members of Congress were founders, officers, or directors of tax exempt organizations.[12] Former Senator Alan Cranston helped organize a voter registration foundation, and Senator Robert Dole actively supports the Dole Foundation, an organization that promotes the employment of the disabled.[13]

Foreign Policy Interest Groups

Issues of domestic policy are not the only matters of concern to interest groups. More and more, groups are organizing to promote or oppose certain foreign policies. Among the most prestigious (although not uncontroversial) foreign affairs group is the Council on Foreign Relations in New York. The council publishes a highly regarded journal, *Foreign Affairs.* Other groups, devoted to narrower areas of American foreign policy, exert pressure on legislators to enact specific policies. Among these are formal lobbies for both Israel and the Arab nations—the American Israel Public Affairs Committee and the National Association of Arab-Americans, respectively—that compete to influence policy makers in Washington. Both organizations make their cases on the basis of U.S. national interests. These lobbies have been particularly articulate in debates over proposed arms sales to Israel and the Arab nations, and the complexities of Middle East peace arrangements. Interest group pressure has also influenced U.S. policy toward South Africa and played a role in South Africa's decision to abandon apartheid. Groups ranging from student organizations to national lobbies like the American Committee on Africa have urged divestment, sanctions, or other policy measures in seeking to promote change in South Africa from the outside.

Government Interest Groups

Government itself is the source of important interest groups. Some may think that odd, but as the size of government has grown and the scope of its activity has expanded, so has governmental lobbying. Many cities and most states retain Washington lobbyists; cities hire lobbyists to represent them at the state legislature. Governors are organized through the National Governors' Association, cities through the National League of Cities, and counties through the National Association of Counties.

Government is an important source of interest groups in other ways as well. Public employees form a large and well-organized group. The National Education Association (NEA), for example, claims more than 2.75 million members. Public employers are also important to organized labor. The fastest growing unions in the AFL-CIO are public employee unions.[14]

Other Interest Groups

Americans are often emotionally and financially involved in a variety of groups: veterans groups such as American Legion or Veterans of Foreign Wars; nationality groups such as the multitude of German, Irish, Hispanic, and Korean organizations; or religious organizations such as the Knights of Columbus or B'nai B'rith. More than 150 nationwide organizations are based on national origin alone.

TABLE 9-2

Some Environmental Groups and How They Do Business

Group	Membership	Issues	Style
Greenpeace USA	2.3 million (worldwide)	Whales, oceans, toxics	Media events; mass mailings; door-to-door canvassing; does not lobby government
Natural Resources Defense Council	168,000	Energy, air and water pollution, nuclear waste	Lobbies; litigates; employs lawyers and scientists to compete with experts from agencies and industry
Sierra Club	650,000 (one-third in California)	Wildlands, pollution, endangered species	Grass-roots action; liberal, Democratic politics; hierarchy of 382 local groups making up 55 U.S. and 2 Canadian chapters; fierce internal debates
Wilderness Society	370,000	Strictly public lands	No local chapters; once a backpacker advocacy group, now has a more general, Washington-insider focus

SOURCE: *Governing*, April 1992, p. 35.

In recent years there has been a virtual explosion in the number and variety of interests and associations.[15] This is especially true for single-interest groups. Such associations are not new; the Anti-Saloon League of the 1890s was single-mindedly devoted to barring the sale and manufacture of alcoholic beverages. The League did not care whether legislators were drunk or sober as long as they voted dry. Today, single-issue groups crusade tirelessly for or against politically "hot" issues, such as the sale of firearms or abortion. Numerous environmental-protection groups press for legislation at all levels of government. Table 9-2 offers a sample of these groups.

CHARACTERISTICS AND POWER OF INTEREST GROUPS

The United States has long been known for the number and diversity of its interest groups. Most Americans belong to a number of interest groups, some of which they are aware of and others of which they may not be. For instance, older citizens may not be aware that their interests are represented by the American Association of Retired Persons (AARP). Others may not know that when they join the American Automobile Association (AAA), they not only purchase travel assistance and automobile towing when needed, but they also join a group that lobbies Congress and the Federal Highway Administration on behalf of motorists.

Groups vary in their goals, methods, and power. Among the most important group characteristics are size, resources, cohesiveness, leadership, the political and social system in which they operate, and methods being used to activate members. Interest groups also differ in the ways they attempt to influence government.

Size and Resources

Obviously size is important to political power; an organization representing 5 million voters has more influence than one speaking for 50,000. Perhaps even more important than size is the extent to which members are actively involved and focus on the attainment of policy objectives. Many people join an organization for reasons that have little to do with its political objectives. They may want to obtain group insurance, take advantage of travel benefits, participate in professional meetings, or get a job. If organizational leaders can depend on the political backing of their followers, the organization is able to put its full strength into pursuing its aims and will have an enormous advantage in the political arena. If the leaders cannot motivate the members, the organization will not be nearly as effective.

While the size of an interest group is often important, so, too, is its *spread*—the extent to which membership is concentrated or dispersed. Automobile manufacturing is concentrated in Michigan and a few other states, and as a result its influence does not have the same spread as that of the American Medical Association, which has an active chapter in virtually every congressional district. An association consisting of 3 million supporters concentrated in a few states will usually have less influence than another group consisting of 3 million supporters spread out in a large number of states. A group whose goals are contrary to widely accepted values will have a more difficult time than a group that can present its demands as in the public interest. Most interest groups cultivate specific and recognizable identities.[16]

Interest groups also differ in the extent to which they preempt a policy area or share it with other groups. Doctors and the AMA have effectively preempted the health care policy area because they play such an important role in the delivery of health care, while in the transportation policy area, railroads must compete with interstate trucking and even air-freight companies.

One of the most powerful interest groups in the country is the American Association of Retired Persons (AARP). They and the Grey Panthers exerted their influence on legislation on Social Security, Medicare, and health care reform.

Groups also differ in their *resources,* which include money, volunteers, expertise, and reputation. Some groups have the ability to influence many centers of power—both houses of Congress, the White House, federal agencies, the courts, and state and local governments—while others cannot.

Although members of a group all have a common interest in obtaining the collective benefit of group action, they do not all share a common interest in paying the cost of securing that benefit, whether it be a sacrifice of time or a membership fee to finance the group's activities. People will not usually participate unless the benefits of joining outweigh the costs. This observation helps explain the relative success of small groups compared to large groups. Members of large groups might rationally choose not to contribute to an organization that represents them because their individual contribution is so small and would probably "not make a difference anyway." However, in a small group, in which each member gets a substantial proportion of the total gain, a common interest must be achieved through the voluntary, self-interested action of the group's members.[17] An individual who does not join an interest group representing his or her interests, yet naturally receives the benefit of the influence the group achieves, is known as a **free rider**.

How do associations motivate potential members to join them? The answer becomes clear when we contrast the success of some large organizations, such as unions or the American Association of Retired Persons, with the weakness of consumer groups. Individuals will not always join an organization for the benefits of collective action. Organizations must provide selective incentives, material or otherwise, that are compelling enough to attract the potential free rider.[18] Unions are organized not just for lobbying but also to perform other important services for their members. They derive much of their strength from their negotiating position with corporations, which they use to obtain wage increases or improved safety standards. Similarly, the AARP, in addition to lobbying against social security cuts and speaking out on other issues of concern to older citizens, offers incentives such as a free subscription to its magazine, *Modern Maturity,* and member discounts at certain hotels. This combination of size and strength sets these groups apart from other large organizations in their effectiveness, as members derive numerous benefits from joining.

Large groups often become organized only when an important issue excites the public or when effective leadership can guide the organization. The mobilization of business interests has been successful in recent years in large part because of the interest of the nation's corporations and trade associations in the outcome of the legislative and elective process.[19]

Cohesiveness

Because Americans are frequently members of many associations, their loyalties are divided. This *overlapping membership* has an effect on the *cohesiveness* of an association and can create problems for organizational leaders. For example, suppose a union official asks a dozen members to come to a meeting. Several may say they will come. But two belong to a club that bowls that night, two others may have to stay home with their families, and another may have to attend a church supper. Even those who attend the meeting may not be 100 percent supporters. Perhaps they are asked to vote for a particular candidate in a coming election. Some will. But one may decide to vote for the other candidate because she is a neighbor, and another will vote for her because they are both Italian Americans. Political party loyalties or American Legion membership may also interfere with a union request. Or perhaps one member will be unsure about what to do and will not vote at all. Obviously, the unity of the membership is a key element, as is the ability to act quickly and decisively. Unity, however, is easier to achieve in a small group that focuses on a relatively specific and concrete concern that does not noticeably affect others—such as a tariff on steel pins.

Usually a mass-membership organization is made up of three types of members.[20] The first type comprises a relatively small number of formal leaders who may hold full-time, paid positions or at least devote much of their extra time, effort, and money to the group's activities. The second includes persons intensely involved in the group, organizationally and psychologically. They identify with the group's aims, attend meetings, faithfully pay dues, and do a lot of the legwork. The third type comprises people who are members in name only. They do not participate actively, they do not look on themselves as Teamsters or Rotarians or Legionnaires, and they cannot be depended on to vote in elections or otherwise act as the leadership wants. In a typical large organization, for every top leader there might be a few hundred hard-core activists and ten thousand essentially inactive members.

Another factor in group cohesiveness is organizational structure and ability to commit numbers to action. Some associations have no formal organization. Others consist of local organizations that have joined together in some sort of loose state or national federation. The local organizations retain a measure of separate power and independence, just as the states did when they entered the Union. A sort of separation of powers may be found as well. The national assembly of an organization establishes, or at least ratifies, policy. An executive committee meets more frequently. A president or director is elected to head and speak for the group, and permanent, paid officials form the organization's bureaucracy. Power may be further divided between the organization's main headquarters and its Washington office. An organization of this sort tends to be far less cohesive than a centralized, disciplined group such as the army or some trade unions.

Leadership

Closely related to cohesion is the nature of the leadership. In a group that embraces many attitudes and interests, leaders may either weld the various elements together or sharpen their disunity. The leader of a national business association, for example, must tread cautiously between big business and small business, between exporters and importers, between chain stores and corner grocery stores, and between the producers and the sellers of competing products. Yet leaders must not be at the mercy of different interests, for above all they must lead. They must show how to achieve organizational goals. The group leader is in the same position as a president or a member of Congress; he or she must know when to lead followers and when to follow them.

Techniques

Interest groups seeking to wield influence choose from a variety of political weapons and targets. As a result, they carefully monitor federal agencies and departments, both houses of Congress, the White House staff, and state and local governments. They also become involved in litigation. Other techniques include persuasion, litigation, rule making, election activities, and lobbying.

PUBLICITY AND MASS MEDIA APPEALS Interest groups exploit the communications media—television, radio, newspapers, leaflets, signs, direct mail, and word of mouth—to influence voters during elections and to motivate constituents to contact their representatives between elections. Business enjoys a special advantage in this arena, and businesspeople have the money to communicate. As large-scale advertisers, they know how to deliver their message effectively or to find an advertising agency to do it for them. Most important, they generally have easy access to the means of disseminating their message, such as the press. Interest groups for and

We The People

Some Associations with an Ethnic, Religious, Racial, or Gender Interest

- American-Arab Relations Committee
- American Gay/Lesbian Atheists
- American Jewish Congress
- Anti-Defamation League of B'nai B'rith
- Black Women Organized for Educational Development
- Buddhist Peace Fellowship
- Catholic War Veterans of the U.S.A.
- Chinese Alliance for Democracy
- Committee on South Asian Women
- Confederation of Independent Aryan Organizations
- Cowboys for Christ
- Dutch Family Heritage Society
- Episcopal Peace Fellowship
- Gray Panthers
- Greek Orthodox Young Adult League
- Men's Rights Association
- National Conference of Christians and Jews
- National Council of Churches
- National Organization for Women
- Pacific Islands Association

The National Rifle Association has a large mailing list. Here is a recent solicitation for new members.

against NAFTA and health care reform launched major media campaigns on these issues to mobilize public opinion to their point of view.

MASS MAILING   New technologies have increased the reach and effectiveness of interest groups. One of these new technologies is computerized and targeted *mass mailing*.[21] For many decades, interest groups have been sending out huge mailings to people whose names are on lists culled from telephone directories and other sources. Some of these mailings are sent out indiscriminately. Mass mailing is used by all kinds of interest groups, but it has been especially refined by so-called public interest groups, which are sometimes accused of being a small headquarters with a good mailing list. Today's technology can produce personalized letters targeted to specific groups. Speaking of the National Rifle Association, the late Congressman William J. Hughes (D.-N.J.) said, "It's a lobby that can put 15,000 letters in your district overnight and have people in your town hall meeting interrupting you."[22] Such targeted letters can also appeal to people who share a common concern, such as environmental groups.

LITIGATION   When groups find the usual political channels closed to them, they may turn to the courts.[23] The National Association for the Advancement of Colored People (NAACP), through its Legal Aid and Defense Fund, has initiated and won numerous court cases in its efforts to improve legal protection for blacks. In recent decades, urban interests and environmental groups, feeling underrepresented in state and national legislatures, have also turned to the courts to influence the political agenda.[24]

Women's groups—such as the National Organization for Women and the American Civil Liberties Union's Women's Rights Project—are examples of groups that have used the courts to pursue their objectives.[25] Despite the general impression that association litigants achieve great success in the courts, groups are no more likely than individuals to win their cases at the district court level.[26] In addition to initiating lawsuits, associations can gain a forum for their views in the courts by filing **amicus curiae briefs** (literally "friend of the court") in cases in which they are not direct parties.

INFLUENCE ON RULE MAKING   Groups have ready access to the rule-making process through which executive and regulatory agencies write the rules that implement laws. Agencies publish proposed regulations in the *Federal Register* and invite responses and reactions from all interested persons before the rules are finalized. (The *Federal Register* is published every weekday. You can find it in your school or public library.) Well-staffed associations and corporations peruse the *Register*, ever alert for proposed agency actions that will affect their interests. Lobbyists, who are often lawyers, prepare written responses to the proposed rules, draft alternative rules, and appear at the hearing to make their case. These lobbyists seek to be on good terms with the staff of the agencies so that they can learn what rules are being considered long before they are released publicly and thus have input in the early stages. Administrative rules are defined over time through legal cases and agency modifications, so even if an interest group fails to get what it wants, it can fight the rules in court or press for a reinterpretation when the agency leadership changes hands.

Finally, an interest group can seek to modify rules it does not like by going back to Congress to change the legal mandate for the agency or have the agency's budget reduced, making enforcement of existing rules difficult. In short, interest groups and lobbyists never really quit fighting for their point of view.

An example of lobbyists trying to use U.S. senators to alter administrative regulations is the case of Charles Keating and the failed Lincoln Savings and Loan. Five U.S. senators were accused of taking campaign money from Keating, then owner of the Lincoln Savings and Loan, including nearly $1 million given to California Senator Alan Cranston for his nonprofit voter registration efforts. These senators in turn lobbied savings and loan regulators.[27] After extensive research and televised hearings, the Senate did not seriously punish any of the five senators, but the negative publicity may have been a factor in three of the five deciding not to seek reelection.

ELECTION ACTIVITIES   Although nearly all large organizations say they are nonpolitical, almost all are politically involved in some way. What group leaders usually mean when they say they are nonpolitical is that they are *nonpartisan*. A distinguishing feature of organized interest groups is that they often try to work through both parties, usually for individual candidates.

Labor usually but not always favors Democrats. In the presidential elections, the AFL-CIO has supported Democrats Hubert Humphrey, Jimmy Carter, Walter Mondale, Michael Dukakis, and Bill Clinton. The Teamsters Union during this period endorsed Richard Nixon, Gerald Ford, Ronald Reagan, and George Bush. But in 1992 the Teamsters reversed this pattern and endorsed Democrat Bill Clinton. Clinton also benefited from the endorsement and support of the National Education Association, a group with more than 2.75 million members, most of them teachers.

Business groups generally endorse the incumbent but favor Republicans when no incumbent is running. Some organizations are prevented from taking a firm position by the diversity of their members. A local retailers' group, for example, might be composed equally of Republicans and Democrats, and many of its members might refuse to take an open position on a candidate for fear of losing business. In such cases more subtle means may be equally effective. Word may be passed around at meetings that candidate *X* is sound from the organization's point of view; perhaps that candidate also receives a campaign contribution from the organization's political action committee.

Ideological groups, on the other hand, may "target" certain candidates, seeking to change the candidates' positions, or failing that, to influence voters to vote against that candidate. Americans for Democratic Action and the American Conservation Union publish ratings of incumbents on a number of liberal and conservative issues, as do the U.S. Chamber of Commerce and the AFL-CIO.

How effective is electioneering by interest groups? Everything depends on the factors we have been discussing: group size, cohesiveness, objectives, political resources, leadership, and the political context. In general, though, the mass-membership organizations' power to mobilize their full strength in elections has been exaggerated in the press. Too many cross-pressures are operating in the pluralistic politics of the United States for any one group to assume a commanding role. Some groups reach their maximum influence only by allying closely with one of the two major parties. They have placed their members on local, state, and national party committees and have helped send them to party conventions as delegates. But such an alliance means losing some independence and singleness of purpose.

FORMING A POLITICAL PARTY   Another interest group strategy is to form a new political party. These parties are organized less with the intent to win *elections* than to publicize a *cause*. The Free Soil party was formed in 1848 to propagandize against the spread of slavery, and the Prohibition party was organized 20 years later to ban the sale of liquor. Farmers have formed a variety of such parties. In 1991 the National Organization for Women (NOW) announced it was forming a political party to call attention to issues of concern to its membership, but the party never became very active and no longer exists. More often, however, interest groups prefer to work through existing parties.

COOPERATIVE LOBBYING   Interest groups often form alliances. An example is the Food Group, a 30-year-old informal conference group in Washington that has represented more than 60 business and trade associations. In addition, it spawned an Information Committee on Federal Food Regulations to fight "truth-in-packaging" legislation. Although the Food Group has been fairly effective, it does run into the predictable problem of differences among members over goals and priorities and has found it difficult to put strong and unified pressure on Congress and government agencies.

Other like-minded groups have also joined together as cooperative groups. The Leadership Conference on Civil Rights brought together many black and other group interests and was a leader in the battle to defeat the nomination of Robert Bork to the U.S. Supreme Court.[28] Different types of environmentalists work together, as do consumer and ideological groups on the right and on the left. Women continue to be represented by a large variety of groups that reflect diverse interests; many of these banded together to support passage of the ERA. But the larger the coalition, the greater the chance that women, like other groups, may divide over such issues as abortion.

THE INFLUENCE OF LOBBYISTS

Despite their negative public image, lobbyists perform useful functions for government. They provide information for the decision makers of all three branches of government, they help educate and mobilize public opinion, they help prepare legislation and testify before legislative hearings, and they contribute a large share of the costs of campaigns. Yet many people are concerned that lobbyists have too much influence on government and add to the gridlock problems by being able to stop action on pressing problems.

Who Are the Lobbyists?

The typical image of interest groups in action is that of powerful, hard-nosed lobbyists who skillfully employ a combination of knowledge, persuasiveness, personal influence, charm, and money to influence legislators and bureaucrats. A few years ago two *Wall Street Journal* reporters described the corridor outside the House Ways and Means Committee office as "Gucci Gulch."[29] It was there, said the authors, that the 1986 tax act took shape—in a "shoot out" between lobbyists sporting expensive designer shoes and briefcases. Who are these well-dressed people, and what do they do?

Lobbyists are the employees of associations who try to influence policy decisions and positions in the executive and especially in the legislative branches of our government. They are experienced in the ways of government, often having been public servants before going to work for an organized interest group or association or corporation. They might start as staff in Congress, perhaps on a congressional committee. Later, when their party wins the White House, they gain an administration post, often in the same policy area as their congressional committee work. After a few years in the administration, they are ready to make the move to lobbying, either by going to work for one of the interests they dealt with while in the government or by obtaining a position with a lobbying firm. The salary for a lobbyist who has extensive contacts in Congress and the administration can be two to three times what a member of Congress earns.

This employment cycle from government to interest group is known as the **revolving door**. Contacts gained during government service are crucial to effective lobbying, and many former members of Congress make good use of their

Lobbyists in Washington await the results of a vote in Congress.

congressional experience as full-time lobbyists. Immediately upon leaving the White House staff, Michael Deaver, one of Ronald Reagan's principal advisers, became a lobbyist representing corporations like CBS and TWA as well as the governments of South Korea, Singapore, and Canada. The Republic of South Korea paid him $1.2 million over three years to protect its interests.[30]

The revolving door between government and interest groups contributes to the formation of issue networks among people who care about an issue such as energy policy or child welfare. These networks among interest groups, congressional committees and subcommittees, and the government agencies that share a common policy concern have been described as **iron triangles**. (Iron triangles or issue networks are explained in more detail in Chapter 17.) These relationships are powerful and mutually beneficial. Retired military officers can go to work for defense contractors after leaving the military but are banned for life from selling Department of Defense contracts. This does not preclude such persons from providing advice to corporations on how best to compete for defense projects.

What Do Lobbyists Do?

Lobbying, one of the best-known weapons of group influence, is probably also the oldest; it is certainly one of the most criticized. Generations of Americans have been angered by exposés of an "invisible government," accusations that unelected interest groups are the ones really making the decisions. From the time of the Yazoo land frauds two hundred years ago, when a whole state legislature was bribed and the postmaster general was put on a private payroll as a lobbyist, to the latest interest-peddling scandals in Congress, Americans have denounced lobbyists.

Today lobbying is far more extensive and sophisticated, though not necessarily more effective. Thousands of lobbyists are active in Washington, but few of them are as glamorous or as unscrupulous as the media suggest, nor are they necessarily influential. One limit on their power is the competition among interest groups. Rarely does any one group have a policy area all to itself. For example, transportation policy involves airplanes, trucks, cars, railroads, consumers, suppliers, state and local governments—the list goes on and on.

To members of Congress, the single most important thing lobbyists provide is *funding* for their next reelection campaign. "Reelection underlies everything else," writes political scientist David Mayhew.[31] Money from interest groups has become instrumental in this driving need of incumbents. Interest groups also provide volunteers for campaign activity. Their lack of support for the opposition can enhance the incumbent's chances of being reelected. Less frequently, interest groups mount their own independent campaigns for or against a candidate. But when they do, it is often in much larger chunks and is more likely to be remembered by the incumbent.

Beyond their central role in campaigns and elections, interest groups provide another essential commodity to legislators: information of two important types, political and substantive. The political information provided by lobbyists includes such matters as who supports or opposes legislation and how strongly they feel.[32] The legislator gains important substantive information on the impact of proposed laws that might not be available from any other source. Lobbyists often provide technical assistance on the drafting of bills and amendments, identify persons to testify at legislative hearings, and formulate questions to ask of administration officials at oversight hearings.

Legal and political skills, along with specialized knowledge, have become so crucial in executive and legislative policy making as to become a form of power in themselves. Elected representatives increasingly depend on their staffs for guidance,

Why Are They Called Lobbyists?

Lobbyists, as noted, are individuals, groups, and organizations that seek to influence legislative and administrative actions. Ever since governments existed, individuals and groups have petitioned their rulers. And this is an especially cherished right in constitutional democracies such as the United States.

The terms "lobbying" and "lobbyists" were not generally used until around the middle of the nineteenth century in the United States. The root in these words refers to the "lobby" or "anteroom" outside chambers in the U.S. Capitol. It was also used to refer to hotel lobbies in Washington, where the petitioners and agents of influence congregated. Thus a senator coming out of the Senate chamber might be accosted politely by several lobbyists seeking to influence his vote on some measure. Or a president might be dining at the Old Willard Hotel, a few blocks from the White House, and make reference to the number of "lobbyists" hanging around in the hotel lobby.

More recently, the noun "lobby" has been turned into a verb in this political context. Thus "to lobby" is to seek to influence legislators and government officials, and we call this "lobbying" even if there is no lobby in sight. It has become a generic term even though it originally took its meaning from the location of the activity in question.

"Please understand. I don't sell access to the government. I merely sell access to the guys who *do* sell access to the government."

Drawing by Ed Lieber. © 1986 The New Yorker Magazine, Inc.

On Being a Lobbyist

"My mother has never introduced me to her friends as "my son, the lobbyist." My son the Washington representative, maybe. Or the legislative consultant. Or the government-relations counsel. But never as the lobbyist. I can't say I blame her. Being a lobbyist has long been synonymous in the minds of many Americans with being a glorified pimp."

SOURCE: Jeffrey H. Birnbaum, *The Lobbyists: How Influence Peddlers Get Their Way in Washington* (Times Books, 1992), p. 7.

FIGURE 9-2
PAC Contributions to Congressional Candidates, 1978–1992

SOURCE: Federal Election Commission Press Releases from 1979 to 1993.

The FEC has two other categories of PACs: cooperatives and corporations without stock. In 1992 they constituted 4 and 3.4 percent of all PACs.

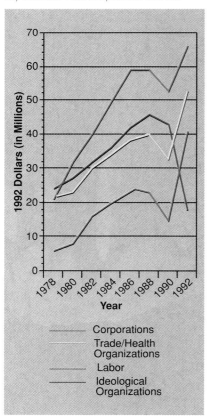

and these staffs in turn are linked with the staffs of executive departments and of lobbyists. Issue specialists know more about Section 504 or Title IX or the amendment of 1972—and who wrote that amendment and why—than most political and administrative leaders, who are usually generalists. It is in this gray area of policy making that many interest groups and lobbyists play a vital role, as people move freely from congressional or agency staff to association staff and perhaps back again.

MONEY AND POLITICS

Technically, a **political action committee (PAC)** is simply the political arm of a business, labor, trade association, or other interest group that is legally entitled to raise funds on a voluntary basis from members, stockholders, or employees in order to contribute funds to favored candidates or political parties.[33] Because PACs link two vital techniques of influence—giving money and other political aid to politicians, and persuading officeholders to act or vote "the right way" on issues—we now look at PACs more broadly as the means by which interest groups seek to influence who will be elected and what they will do once they take office.[34]

PACs can be categorized according to the type of interest they represent: corporations, trade and health organizations, labor, and ideological organizations. Figure 9-2 represents campaign contributions to congressional candidates for various types of PACs since 1978.

In 1978 there was little difference in the level of campaign activity of PACs representing corporations, labor unions, or trade associations.[35] By 1990 that had changed, with corporate PACs spending more than the others and ideological PACs at roughly half the level of spending of trade and labor PACs.

Let's look at some specific cases. In the 1992 election cycle, Congressman John Murtha of Pennsylvania raised a war chest of $935,000, with $540,000 of it coming from PACs; Congressman Jack Fields of Texas raised just over $750,000, with $453,000 coming from PACs; and Congressman Thomas Bliley of Virginia raised $721,000, with more than 60 percent of his funds coming from PACs. Congressman Murtha was unopposed and Congressmen Fields and Bliley did not face significant opposition in 1992. In the Senate, Democratic Whip Wendell Ford (D.-Ky.) raised $1.3 million from PACs out of a total campaign of $2.3 million, and Republican leader Bob Dole raised $1.2 million from PACs out of the $2.4 million he raised.[36] Neither Ford nor Dole faced significant opposition in their campaigns. PACs in 1992 made a total donation of $179 million to House and Senate candidates, up 19 percent from 1990.

The Growth of Pacs

Ironically, considering that the explosion of PACs has occurred mainly in the business world, it was organized labor that invented this device. In the 1930s, John L. Lewis, president of the United Mine Workers, set up the Nonpartisan Political League as the political arm of the newly formed Congress of Industrial Organizations. When the CIO merged with the American Federation of Labor, the new labor group established the Committee on Political Education (COPE). This unit came to be the model for most political action committees: "From the outset, national, state, and local units of COPE have not only raised and distributed funds, but have also served as the mechanism for organized and widespread union activity in the electoral process, for example, in voter registration, political education, and get-out-the-vote drives."[37] Some years later, manufacturers formed the Business-Industry Political Action Committee, but this committee, and the few other PACs in the 1960s, played a limited role.

The 1970s brought a near revolution in the role and influence of PACs, ironically as the result of post-Watergate reforms. The number of PACs increased dramatically, from about 150 to more than 4,000 today. Corporations and trade associations contributed most to this growth; today their PACs constitute the majority of all PACs. Labor PACs, on the other hand, increased only slightly in number, representing less than 10 percent of all PACs. But the increase in the number of PACs is less important than the intensity of recent PAC participation in elections and in lobbying.

How PACs Invest Their Money

In response to reporters' questions concerning the influence of money in politics, Charles Keating once stated, "One question, among the many raised in recent weeks, [has] to do with whether my financial support in any way influenced several political figures to take up my cause. I want to say in the most forceful way I can: I certainly hope so."[38] PACs take part in the entire election process, but their main influence lies in their capacity to contribute money to candidates. Candidates today need big money to wage election or reelection campaigns. It is no longer uncommon for House candidates to spend more than a million dollars, and many senators or would-be senators to spend ten times that amount.[39]

As corporate and industrial PACs increase rapidly in number, their influence grows accordingly. What counts is not so much the amounts they give but to whom they give: the more influential incumbents. In recent elections, top PAC recipients have included former Energy and Commerce Committee chair John D. Dingell (D.-Mich.) as well as House Democratic leaders Richard Gephardt (former majority leader) and Dan Rostenkowski (former chair of the Ways and Means Committee). All ten of the top PAC recipients in 1990 were Democrats, and only five of the top 50 were Republicans. Newt Gingrich, formerly Republican party whip and now Speaker of the House, made it to the top five House PAC recipients. When Republicans won control of the House in 1994, they won all chairmanships and the opportunity to cash in with PACs.

Despite reports of freewheeling spending by big corporations, most business PACs proceed cautiously.[40] In deciding which candidates to help and with how much, PACs first consider the candidate's record and the likelihood of his or her voting as the PAC wishes. But other factors are also important: the likelihood that the candidate will win; the difference money will make in the campaign; whether the candidate is an incumbent (and hence would reasonably have more chance of winning); and the PAC's access to the candidate if he or she is elected. Party is not a major criterion for corporate-related PACs, although they do contribute slightly more to Republican candidates than to Democratic ones. Labor PACs, on the other hand, give overwhelmingly to Democrats.

PACs, like individuals, are limited by law in the amount of money they can contribute to any single candidate in an election cycle. The Federal Election Campaign Act of 1971 limits PACs to $5,000 per election or $10,000 per election cycle (primary and general elections). Individuals have a $2,000 per candidate per election cycle limit. PACs have found some creative ways around this limit. They can host fund-raisers attended by other PACs to boost their reputation with the candidate, or they can "bundle" contributions. In 1986, ALIGNPAC, the political action committee of independent insurance agents, "collected contributions of more than $250,000 from individual insurance agents and presented them in a bundle to Senator Robert Packwood, who was chairman of the Senate Finance Committee."[41] Through bundling, PACs and interested individuals can increase their clout with elected officials.

The role of foreign lobbyists and PACs for companies owned by foreigners have received recent attention as the result of attempts by various foreign countries to influence American policy. Under current law, foreign-owned corporations can engage in election activities as long as the individuals making the allocation decisions are U.S. citizens, and the foreign corporations or foreign citizens do not provide funds for the PAC.[42]

The Effectiveness of PACs

How much does PAC money, especially corporate PAC money, influence election outcomes, legislation, and representation? One critic has written, "When politicians start to see a dollar sign behind every vote, every phone call, every solicitation, those other factors sometimes weighed during governance like the public good and equal access to government, become less and less important."[43] An organization called Citizens Against PACs publishes attacks on members of Congress who, in their opinion, accept too many out-of-state PAC contributions. In this area, as in others, money obviously talks. But it is easy to exaggerate that influence. While a candidate may receive a great amount of PAC money, only a fraction of that total comes from any single interest. In addition, it is debatable how much campaign contributions affect election outcomes and uncertain that winning candidates will be willing and able to "remember" their financial angels or that the money in the end produces a real payoff in legislation. So even big corporate PACs have learned to be patient. Bernadette A. Budde, political education director of the Business-Industry PAC, declared, "You know you're not going to make 10 yards on the first down, so you try to make 2 or 3 or 4 yards at a time."[44]

Much depends, however, on the context in which money is given and received. Many campaigns—especially congressional and state and local campaigns—are small-scale undertakings in which a sizable amount of money seems to make a difference. Amid all the murk of campaigning, a candidate may feel grateful for so tangible and convertible a contribution as money. Recent studies demonstrate a significant relationship between PACs giving money and receiving favorable treatment in congressional committee.[45]

PACs are pragmatic. They give largely to incumbents, and in so doing win friends. Politicians, from local officials to the president of the United States, want to be reelected. But Congress has come to embody the "career politician" perhaps more than any other institution. Incumbents need money to ensure their reelection, and PACs, sensing this opportunity, have been happy to assist.[46] By giving four out of five dollars to incumbents in recent elections, and 10 percent or less to challengers, PACs have not only helped incumbents but severely damaged the chances of challengers.[47]

PACs, like individuals, influence the outcome of elections through **independent expenditures**—money spent for or against a candidate that is not connected to the campaign of the candidate or his or her opponent. Independent expenditures can be made by individuals or PACs and can be spent in any way the spender wishes—TV spots, billboards, newspaper advertisements. In 1992, more than $10 million was spent as independent expenditures in federal elections.[48] The largest such individual expenditure so far was over $1 million in a successful effort to defeat Illinois Senator Charles Percy in 1984.[49] This was unusual, however, since independent expenditures are most often used to help someone win an election rather than targeting an opponent. This kind of spending does not preclude the group also giving the maximum permitted contribution to the candidate they wish to help. Independent expenditures are different from **soft money**, which is money given to a state or local party and often not disclosed because of lax disclosure laws at that level. But soft money and independent expenditures are alike in the sense that they are unlimited by federal law.

The expansion of PAC activity, including independent expenditures, means that interest groups can organize a "triple-threat" offensive: skillful mobilization of public opinion through large, well-financed public relations campaigns; direct assistance to friendly candidates (usually incumbents) in the form of campaign contributions as well as "education" of the voters by independent expenditures on mailings, advertisements, and the like; and direct influence on officeholders through lobbying.

CURING THE MISCHIEFS OF FACTION— TWO HUNDRED YEARS LATER

If James Madison were to return today, more than two hundred years after writing *The Federalist*, No. 10, he would not be surprised by the existence of interest groups. Nor would he be surprised by the variety of interest groups. He *might* be surprised, however, by the intense expression of factionalism—the varied weapons of group influence, the deep involvement of interest groups in the electoral process, and the vast number of lobbyists in Washington and the state capitals. And doubtless Madison, were he alive today, would be concerned about the power of faction, especially its tendency toward instability and injustice.

Concern about the evils of interest groups has been a recurrent theme throughout U.S. history. President Ronald Reagan in his farewell address warned of the power of "special interests."[50] Reagan, however, defined his iron triangle differently to include the news media rather than executive agencies. This is an unusual change because, as Reagan himself pointed out, "special interests" prefer their "cozy relationship" to be kept as far from the public eye—the news media—as possible.[51] President Reagan was not alone in warning about the problems of cozy relationships between special interests and policy makers. President Dwight Eisenhower used his farewell address to warn against the *military-industrial complex.*

Single-interest groups, which are intensively organized for or against particular policies—abortion, handgun control, tobacco subsidies, animal rights—have aroused much concern in recent years. "It is said that citizen groups organizing in ever greater numbers to push single issues ruin the careers of otherwise fine politicians who disagree with them on one emotional issue, paralyze the traditional process of governmental compromise, and ignore the common good in their selfish insistence on getting their own way."[52] But which single issues reflect narrow, selfish interests? Women's rights—even a specific issue such as the Equal Rights Amendment—are hardly "selfish," women's rights leaders contend, because they would help over half the population. Peace groups, too, claim that they represent the whole population, as do those who support prayer in schools. These issues may seem quite different from those related to subsidies to dairy farmers, for example. But some doubt the feasibility of distinguishing between narrower and broader issues or between "special" and "general" interests.

Some Americans tend to overreact to organized groups, especially to ones they oppose. They view such groups as vast, well organized, well financed, and all but irresistible in political action. They should remember, however, that large and relatively well-organized groups have weaknesses as well as strengths. The larger the group, the greater the likelihood of crisscrossing interests that drain it of unity, energy, money, and singleness of purpose.

What should be done, if anything? For decades Americans have tried to find ways to keep interest groups in check. They have agreed with James Madison that the "remedy" of suppressing factions would be worse than the disease; it would be absurd to abolish liberty simply because it nourished faction. And the existence and activity of interest groups and lobbies are solidly protected by the Constitution. But by safeguarding the value of *liberty,* have Americans allowed interest groups to threaten *equality,* the second great value in our national heritage? The question remains: How can interest groups be regulated in a way that does not threaten their constitutional liberties?

The Trouble with Special Interests

Americans generally are worried about the power of factions or special interests. Their concerns can be summarized as follows:

1. The struggle among factions is not a fair fight; narrower, more highly organized, and better-financed single-issue groups hold a decided advantage over more general groups.
2. The interest-group battle leads to great inequities, because lower-income people are grossly underrepresented among interest groups as compared to richer, more highly organized people, many of whom are represented by a multitude of organizations and lobbyists.
3. Even though the organization of hundreds of single-issue groups has reinforced the diffusion of power and fragmentation in government that the Constitution's framers so desired, it has led to incoherent policies, waste and inefficiency, endless delays, and the inability to plan ahead and anticipate crises.
4. The role of interest groups in elections has made incumbents more secure (diminished electoral competition) and enhanced the power of these groups in relation to Congress and state and local government.

Federal and State Regulation

Americans have generally responded to this question by seeking to regulate lobbying in general and political money in particular. Lobbying is dealt with by registration and disclosure. Concern over the use of money—especially corporate funds—to influence politicians goes back well over a century, to the Credit Mobilier scandals during the administration of Ulysses S. Grant. In 1877, Georgia simply wrote into its constitution the provision that lobbying is a crime, but that provision was removed as violating the U.S. Constitution. By the turn of the century the liberal press was charging that corporations were pouring millions into the presidential campaigns of candidates like Benjamin Harrison and William McKinley. During the "progressive" first two decades of this century, Congress legislated against corporate contributions in federal elections and required disclosure as to the use of money.

In 1925, responding to the Teapot Dome scandal during Warren G. Harding's administration, Congress passed the Federal Corrupt Practices Act. It required disclosure reports, both before and after elections, of receipts and expenditures by Senate and House candidates and by political committees that sought to influence federal elections in more than one state. Note that these were *federal* laws applying to *federal* elections; regulation of state lobbying and elections was left to the states.

Federal legislation, including the 1946 Federal Regulation of Lobbying Act, has not been very effective. It was, in fact, largely unenforced. Many candidates filed incomplete reports or none at all. The reform mood of the 1960s brought basic changes, "nurtured by the ever-increasing costs of campaigning, the incidence of millionaire candidates, the large disparities in campaign spending between various candidates and political parties, some clear cases of unique influence on the decision-making process by large contributors and special interests, and the apparent disadvantages of incumbency in an age of mass communications with a constant focus on the lives and activities of office-holders."[53] The upshot was the Federal Election Campaign Act (FECA) of 1971, which supplanted the earlier legislation.

FECA, which has been amended three times, establishes reporting or disclosure requirements for all candidates for the U.S. House of Representatives, the Senate, and the presidency and their political parties and campaign committees. It also requires disclosure of the amounts spent to influence federal elections by others, including individuals and political action committees. The act established partial public financing for presidential candidates, financed by a voluntary checkoff on federal income tax forms. *Spending by candidates* for Congress is not limited, but *contributions to these candidates* and to presidential candidates is limited.

There have been notable problems with the act, including the soft money loophole discussed earlier in this chapter and a weak and ineffective Federal Election Commission. The act has had its critics, and Congress has frequently debated reforming campaign financing. We discuss these reform proposals in greater detail in Chapter 12.

There has also been significant state involvement in regulating interest-group activity in elections at the state level. Some states, like Wisconsin, Minnesota, and Hawaii, provide for public financing of state offices and state legislative races; others, like Michigan, New Jersey, and Massachusetts, provide partial public financing of gubernatorial elections; a dozen more help underwrite parties with public funds.[54]

The Effects of Regulation

What have been the effects of recent campaign-finance reforms on interest groups? Ironically, that impact was not to decrease or restrict such groups but to enlarge their number and importance. The strategy of the 1971 law was to authorize direct and open participation by both labor and corporate organizations in elections and lobbying in the hopes that a visible or proper role for interest-group activity, backed by effective enforcement, would be constitutional under the First Amendment and effective in the world of practical politics. The 1971 act allowed unions and corporations to communicate on political matters to members or stockholders, to conduct registration and get-out-the-vote drives, and to spend union and company funds to set up "separated segregated funds" (PACs) to use for political purposes.

At last corporations could be sure that their open and regulated political activities were wholly legal, and they made the most of it. But what changed the rules of the game even more for corporate interests was passage in 1974 of limits on individual contributions, something not part of the 1971 act. An explosion of corporate PACs followed this 1974 amendment.[55] But as organized labor, which had previously enjoyed the right to set up its PACs, had less need of the act (except to legitimize what it was already doing), there has been little increase in the number of labor PACs. The result, labor leaders contend, is a greater imbalance than ever between the political action and organization of a relatively small number of corporation executives and stockholders, and the large membership, and potential membership, of labor unions.

One of the most important results of the recent efforts at regulation of interest-group activity is greater disclosure of how politicians fund their campaigns. With the important exception of soft money, we have a much better idea now of how much money candidates raise and how they spend it. Without disclosure, much of what we have written here about PACs, for instance, would not be public knowledge. Disclosure permits the press and the public to assess the implications of how candidates finance their campaigns.

Candidates and some appointed officials must also provide statements about their personal finances, which permits voters and the press to see what investments and resources candidates have that may affect their ability to be impartial. Such public disclosure of personal worth, the value of property owned, and outstanding debts no doubt discourages some persons from entering public life, but it also makes officeholders accountable for certain obligations and actions once they take office.

To Reform Further?

Will Congress reform the PACs and campaign finance in general? Not only is reform itself complex and difficult, but it is doubtful that Congress really *wants* reform. Many members of Congress thrive on the present arrangements, and the leaders and members of both parties actually compete for PAC dollars. When the National Association of Home Builders, a richly funded lobby, began to give more and more money to Republican candidates, Democratic leaders of the House warned that the lobby had better help Democrats, too, or its "good relationship" with the Democrats might be "damaged." One reason members of Congress become entrenched in their seats is that they become increasingly funded by PACs. Some of them are reluctant to give up such a cozy relationship. Thus the real question may not be whether Congress can reform the interest-group lobbies, but whether Congress can reform itself.[56]

In recent Congresses, campaign finance reform legislation has been passed by one and sometimes both houses, but because both houses have not agreed to the same bill, no changes have been enacted. During the 1980s and early 1990s, Presidents Reagan and Bush pledged to veto campaign finance reform bills passed by a Democratic Congress. Bill Clinton promised during his campaign to push for campaign finance and lobbying reform, and Ross Perot was an even more outspoken proponent of change. But Clinton chose to defer to congressional leaders from his party and did not press hard on the issue. The legislation, like lobbying reform generally, died in a Republican filibuster in the Senate in 1994.

U.S. Senate elections in some sparsely populated states like North and South Dakota are examples of the role of interested money from out of state. In total spending nearly $25 was spent per voter in South Dakota in 1986, a figure well in excess of the national average of $2.81. PACs provided much of this money, but large individual contributions are also important. In his successful 1988 reelection campaign, North Dakota Senator Quentin Burdick raised 99 percent of his large individual contributions from persons outside his state.[57] This level of campaign underwriting from individuals and groups outside a state raises important issues of representation.

Some people defend lobbyists as a kind of "third house" of Congress. Whereas the Senate and House are set up on a geographical basis, lobbyists represent people on the basis of main interests: jobs or other economic interests, issue positions, and ideological leanings. Small but important groups can sometimes get representation in the "third house" when they cannot get it in the other two. In a nation of vast and important interests, this kind of functional representation, if it is not abused, is a most useful supplement to geographical representation. Should the former kind of representation supplant the latter? Most analysts say no, because legislative institutions are needed to represent people in the totality of their lives and needs.

There are other arguments for "hands off" the lobbyists. PACs support both Democratic and Republican candidates and hence do not favor just one party. Another argument is that the increase in PAC corporate spending is not as great as it appears. In fact, much of the PAC money may be "old wine in new bottles"—that is, money given publicly that used to be given in the form of legal or illegal personal campaign contributions by business chiefs.[58] One argument against reform is that it is impossible in a free society to restrict the flow of money. Laws can be passed to limit or regulate the flow of money in politics, but money will find an alternative way to accomplish its purpose of influencing elections. In the spirit of the Bill of Rights, whatever the evils, no action should be taken that may remotely threaten the liberties and autonomy of corporations or interest groups in general.

Some believe that the main problem lies not in interest groups but in the way public opinion is formed, managed, and manipulated—above all, by the barons of the electronic media in a new age of communications politics. These observers urge Congress to limit what commercial television stations can charge for political advertising, to discourage so-called "negative targeting" of candidates in political advertising, and to sponsor candidate debates.

Strengthening political parties would be one way to reduce the power of special interests. If campaign contributions were directed more to parties than to candidates, then candidates would be more accountable to the parties and less tied to any particular interest. Parties are also more likely to invest in challengers than PACs are. Finally, because parties must seek to broaden their appeal, they cannot risk becoming captive of a particular narrow interest.

With Republicans winning a majority in both houses of Congress in 1994, campaign finance reform is not likely to be a priority issue. Republicans can now reap the same benefits Democrats enjoyed from PACs interested in enhancing their legislative contacts with committee chairs and the majority party leadership. Speaker Newt Gingrich has been a successful PAC fundraiser and has not supported campaign finance reform, and such reforms were not part of the Republicans' "Contract with America." Democrats missed their opportunity to reform campaign finance when they controlled both houses of Congress and the White House, and they now face a Republican party that has always been better at raising money.

SUMMARY

1. Interest groups exist to make demands on government. The dominant interest groups are economic or occupational, but a variety of other groups—religious, racial, ideological, gender, ethnic—have memberships that cut across the big economic groupings, thus their influence is both reduced and stabilized.

2. Movements of large numbers of people who are frustrated with government policies have always been with us in the United States. Blacks, women, Native Americans, and the economic underdogs have at various times organized themselves into movements.

3. The key components of movements are negative perceptions of the political system; group consciousness of mistreatment; organization and leadership; and direct actions involving large numbers of group members and supporters. Movements are protected by the Constitution, which permits them to work within our system of government.

4. The long-standing women's movement has been important in the expansion of suffrage and the framing of social issues, and it continues to press for equal rights.

5. Elements in interest-group power include size, resources, unity, singleness of purpose, organization, leadership, and the ability to contribute to candidates and political parties as well as the ability to fund lobbyists. Interest groups vary in the extent to which they have these characteristics and in their ability to apply these resources in particular institutional or political settings.

6. For many decades, interest groups have engaged in lobbying, but these efforts have become far more pervasive and significant as groups become more deeply involved in the electoral process, especially through the expanded use of political action committees (PACs). Interest groups also take their messages directly to the public through mass mailings, advertising campaigns, and cooperative lobbying.

7. Concern for PACs centers on their ability to raise money and spend it on elections in behalf of endorsed candidates, typically incumbents. This concern has led to proposals to ban PACs or more strictly limit their authority. Yet their existence and rights are protected, many believe, by our First Amendment.

8. The key issue today in "controlling factions" is whether to allow groups to proliferate and so balance each other, to try to regulate groups, or to seek reforms outside the groups by fostering balanced power in political parties or elsewhere.

FURTHER READING

JEFFREY BERRY, *The Interest Group Society,* 2d ed. (Little, Brown and Company, 1989).

JEFFERY H. BIRNBAUM, *The Lobbyists: How Influence Peddlers Get Their Way in Washington* (Times Books, 1992).

TAYLOR BRANCH, *Parting the Waters: America in the King Years, 1954–63* (Simon & Schuster, 1988).

ALLAN J. CIGLER AND BURDETT A. LOOMIS, eds., *Interest Group Politics,* 3d ed. (Congressional Quarterly Press, 1991).

AMITAI ETZIONI, *Capital Corruption: The New Attack on American Democracy* (TransAction, 1988).

ALLEN D. HERTZKE, *Representing God in Washington: The Role of Religious Lobbies in the American Polity* (University of Tennessee Press, 1988).

RONALD J. HREBENAR AND RUTH K. SCOTT, *Interest Group Politics in America,* 2d ed. (Prentice Hall, 1990).

DAVID B. MAGLEBY AND CANDICE J. NELSON, *The Money Chase: Congressional Campaign Finance Reform* (Brookings, 1990).

ANDREW S. McFARLAND, *Common Cause: Lobbying in the Public Interest* (Chatham House, 1984).

MANCUR OLSON, *The Logic of Collective Action* (Harvard University Press, 1965).

MARK P. PETRACCA, ed., *The Politics of Interests: Interest Groups Transformed* (Westview Press, 1992).

KAY L. SCHLOZMAN AND JOHN T. TIERNEY, *Organized Interests and American Democracy* (Harper and Row, 1985).

JACK L. WALKER, JR., *Mobilizing Interest Groups in America: Patrons, Professions, and Social Movements* (University of Michigan Press, 1991).

POLITICAL PARTIES: ESSENTIAL TO DEMOCRACY

10

I magine you are voting in an election for the junior college board of trustees for your area. The board has seven members, all to be selected in the election. The election is nonpartisan, and each voter has seven votes. Any registered voter can run if he or she pays the $50 filing fee and gathers 500 valid signatures on a petition supporting the candidacy; 133 candidates have qualified for the ballot. How would you decide how to cast your votes in such a wide field?

This election actually happened in Los Angeles in April 1969, and offers a useful case study of what politics would be like without political parties, which generally narrow the field of candidates and thereby simplify the voting choice. In this election a second voting cue was absent: incumbency. Because the junior college board of trustees was newly created, none of the candidates were incumbents.

What explained how people voted in this unusual context? Primarily, ballot order. Candidates were listed alphabetically, and those whose names began with the letters A to F did better than those who come later in the alphabet. Being well known helped. One of the candidates, E. G. ("Jerry") Brown, Jr., was the son of a former governor and benefited from his father's popularity. Endorsements by *The Los Angeles Times* influenced the outcome, as did the activity of a conservative campaign group and a Mexican-American surname.[1]

Rarely are American voters asked to choose from among 133 candidates. That is because political parties facilitate voting by organizing elections and simplifying choices. E. E. Schattschneider, a noted political scientist, once said, "The political parties created democracy, and modern democracy is unthinkable save in terms of the parties."[2] This provocative statement is true. The view that parties are essential to democracy runs counter to a long-standing and deep-seated American fear and distrust of parties. Yet few of us would prefer a democracy in which we were asked to choose from among a large number of candidates for each office on the ballot. To most Americans, then, parties are a "necessary evil."

This chapter begins by examining the purposes parties serve that make them so vital to the functioning of democracy. We then examine the evolution of American political parties in our democratic experience. Although American political parties have changed over time, they remain important in three quite different settings: as institutions, in government, and in the electorate. It is important to understand how parties facilitate democracy in all three settings. Finally, we will turn to a discussion of the strength of parties today and the prospects for party reform and renewal.

WHAT PARTIES DO FOR DEMOCRACY

Political parties are essential to make democracy work, as the new democracies springing up around the world are quickly learning. Parties need not be strong and cohesive like those in Western Europe and Britain, or weak like those in the United States, but without some kind of party system, even one that is embryonic and lacking in structure, these democracies are not likely to survive.

Party Functions

American political parties serve a wide variety of political and social functions, some obvious and some not so obvious. They perform some of them well, and others not so well, and how they perform them differs from place to place and time to time.

Party Functions

- Organize the competition within elections by registering and activating voters and by providing resources to candidates
- Simplify the choices facing the electorate
- Determine who shall hold office and exercise legitimate power
- Unify the electorate and moderate conflicts
- Translate public preferences into policy
- Help organize government
- Bridge the separation of powers, and foster coordination and cooperation in our system of checks and balances
- Provide a loyal opposition to elected officials at the national, state, and local levels

ORGANIZE THE COMPETITION   One of the most important functions of parties is to organize the competition, an important task we often take for granted. To organize the competition, parties do many things: they recruit and nominate candidates for office; they register and activate voters; and in some places they help candidates by training them, raising money for them, providing them with research and voter lists, and enlisting volunteers to work for them. Parties have been replaced in some of these functions by campaign consultants and professionals.

A party's ability to organize the competition is influenced by how states organize their ballots. In many states, candidates are listed in party columns, called the **party column ballot**, or Indiana ballot, which makes it somewhat easier for voters to vote a **straight ticket**—for all party candidates. Some states permit voters to do the same thing by flipping one switch in the voting machine. Other states organize the ballot by office—the so-called **office block ballot** or Massachusetts ballot—which makes it somewhat harder to cast a vote for all the candidates of a single party.

Getting the party's name on the ballot reduces but does not eliminate the need for parties to help candidates during an election. In some states for some elections, there are no party labels. Many elections for judges use a nonpartisan ballot, as do many local government elections.

DETERMINE WHO HOLDS OFFICE   Elections have important consequences. They determine who shall hold office and have political power. Parties are an integral part of making elections run, and elections serve the vital task of deciding who can legitimately exercise political power. We take for granted the peaceful transfer of power from one elected official to another, from one party to another, yet in new democracies the transfer of power following an election is often problematic. Bill Clinton is powerful and important because he won the election, and George Bush and Ross Perot have much less influence because they lost the election.

UNIFY THE ELECTORATE   Parties help unify the electorate and bring together voters from different ethnic backgrounds, parts of the country, and political ideologies. Thus they also help moderate conflicts within the body politic. When the Democratic party fell apart over the issue of slavery in 1860, and could no longer hold together its northern and southern wings, the very fabric of this nation was torn apart. For more than a century since the Civil War, however, Republicans and Democrats have held domestic conflict within acceptable bounds. Party leaders and candidates for public office appeal to diverse groups and sections, if only because these groups represent a large number of votes. Groups such as women, gays, blacks, and Jews have seen parties as allies in their fights for social justice and equality.

Even when the differences between the parties are intense over controversial social issues—such as civil rights, abortion, and the Equal Rights Amendment—there have nonetheless been sufficient differences *within* each of the two parties so that the conflict *between* the two parties has stayed within the limits of tolerance. For example, the Democratic party platform in recent years has endorsed the right of women to choose to have an abortion, whereas the Republican party platform has opposed abortion. But within each party, there are those who differ on this issue, and party candidates often do their best to conceal rather than intensify the differences.

TRANSLATE PREFERENCE INTO POLICY   In this country, parties that win power in an election are supposed to run the government and translate the policy preferences of the voters into public policy. We do not have the cohesive parties of Great Britain, for example, in which after the election the party that wins takes over the entire government, and all party members are expected to support the party and enact its promises into law. Although American parties are important in translating voter preference into public policy, the consequences of winning an election are not so dramatic. Because party views are moderate, elections do not call for 180-degree policy shifts, but the outcome of elections does change policy and policy focus, as the election of Bill Clinton in 1992 demonstrated.

Among the most important ways in which parties help translate voter preference into policy is that the winning party gets the patronage. Presidents, governors, mayors, and legislators all make party a primary consideration in the appointment of staff and key decision makers. They are limited only by civil service regulations that restrict patronage typically to the top posts, but these posts number in the thousands in the federal government, including most people who work for Congress, and they are numerous at the state and local levels. Party considerations are also important in the appointment of judges at all levels.

Political parties work to register voters before the election, and then to get them out to the polls on election day. In some states with liberal absentee voting laws, they may also encourage voters friendly to the party to obtain absentee ballots.

HELP ORGANIZE GOVERNMENT   Parties help organize the machinery of government and influence the men and women they have helped put into office. The president serves as party leader; Congress is organized on party lines; even bureaucrats are supposed to respond to new party leadership. Governors and legislative majorities serve in the same way in the states. Thus parties may help to bridge the separation of powers and foster coordination and cooperation in our system of constitutional checks and balances.

American parties have had only limited success in setting the course of national policy, however, especially when compared with traditionally strong European parties.[3] The European model of party government, what has been called a *responsible party system*, assumes that parties discipline their members through their control over nominations and campaigns. Politicians in party-centered systems like these are expected to act according to party wishes or they will not be allowed to run again under the party label. Moreover, candidates run on fairly specific party platforms and are expected to implement those policies if they win control in the election.

Because American parties do not tightly control nominations, they are unable to discipline persons with views contrary to those of the party. The American system is *candidate centered*; politicians are nominated largely on the basis of their qualifications and personal appeal, not party loyalty. In fact, it is more correct to say that we have candidate or officeholder politics rather than party politics. As a consequence, party leaders cannot guarantee passage of their program, even if they are in the majority.

PROVIDE A LOYAL OPPOSITION   Parties provide a loyal opposition. This role was first played by the Jeffersonians during the Washington administration. After a polite interval following an election—the **honeymoon**, the first months during which the administration is inaugurated and its policies are proposed—the opposition party begins to criticize the party that controls the White House, especially when the opposition party controls one or both houses of the Congress.[4]

Every now and then, for example early in President Clinton's administration, when his budget and economic stimulus recommendations did not receive a single Republican vote, the two parties in Congress divide cleanly along party lines. A few Democrats voted against Clinton's proposals, and it took Vice-President Al Gore to break the tie on the budget in the Senate. On important issues most, but not all, Democrats vote together, as do most, but not all, Republicans. And then there are times, rather unusual but not unprecedented, when a president of one party receives more votes from the opposing party than from his own, as President Clinton did on the 1992 North American Free Trade Agreement (NAFTA) vote in the House.

Nominating Candidates

From the very beginning, parties have been the mechanism by which candidates for public office are chosen. The earliest method, the **caucus**—a closed meeting of local leaders—was used in Massachusetts only a few years after the *Mayflower* landed, and it played an important part in pre-Revolutionary politics. For several decades after the United States was established, party groups in the national and state legislatures served as the caucus. The legislators in each party simply met separately to nominate candidates. Our first presidential candidates were chosen by senators and representatives who met as party delegates.

As early as the 1820s, the legislative caucus brought charges of "secret deals" and "smoke-filled rooms." Moreover, it could not be representative of the people from an area where a party was in a minority or nonexistent, as only officeholders were members. Efforts were made to make the caucus more representative. The *mixed caucus* brought in delegates from districts in which the party had no elected legislators.

Then, during the 1830s and 1840s, a system of **party conventions** was instituted. Delegates, usually chosen directly by party members in towns and cities, selected the party standard-bearers, debated and adopted a platform, and built party spirit, perhaps by celebrating a bit. But the convention method soon came under criticism. The charge was that the convention was subject to control by the party bosses and their machines. Delegates were freely bought and sold, instructions from rank-and-file party members were ignored, and meetings got completely out of control.

In response to this criticism of the convention and to encourage more participation by ordinary citizens, Wisconsin introduced the direct primary statewide in 1903. A **direct primary** election is one in which people vote directly for the party's nominees for office. Primaries spread rapidly after their introduction in Wisconsin—in the North as a Progressive Era reform and in the South as a way to bring democracy to a region that had seen no meaningful general elections, due to one-party rule by the Democrats since the end of Reconstruction. By the end of Woodrow Wilson's second administration in 1920, direct primaries were used for at least some offices in almost all states.

Today the direct primary is the typical method of picking party candidates. However, primaries vary significantly from state to state. They differ in terms of: (1) who may run in a primary and how one qualifies for the ballot; (2) whether the party organization can or does endorse candidates before the primary; (3) who may vote in a party's primary—that is, whether a voter must register with a party in order to vote; and (4) how many votes are needed for nomination—a plurality, a majority, or some other number determined by party rule or state law. The differences among primaries are not trivial; they have an important impact on the role played by party organization and on the strategy used by competing candidates.[5]

In **open primaries**, any voter, regardless of party, can participate in whichever primary he or she may choose. This kind of primary permits **crossover voting**—Republicans and Independents helping to determine who the Democratic nominee will be, and vice versa, for example. Some states use **closed primaries**, in which only persons already registered in a party may participate.

Direct primaries were introduced in large part to reduce the influence of party leaders, which they have done, but many believe that this change has had more undesirable than desirable consequences. Leaders have less influence over who gets to be the party's candidate, and candidates are less accountable to the party for what they do, both during the election and after it. Along with modern communications and fund-raising techniques, direct primaries have really cut out most of the influence of leaders of political parties.

The rise of direct primaries has not meant the death of caucuses or conventions. In fact, caucuses have reappeared in a number of states as a step in nominating presidential and other candidates. But they have returned in a much more participatory form, open to *all* party members. Party caucuses choose delegates to higher party gatherings, which in turn select delegates to state and national conventions to nominate the party candidate for offices. The Iowa caucuses, in which hundreds of thousands of Iowans participate, have often been the first important test of potential presidential nominees.[6]

In a few states, conventions still play a role in the nominating process. In Connecticut, for example, convention choices become the party nominees unless they are challenged. Candidates who attain at least 20 percent of the vote in the convention have an automatic right to challenge, but they do not always exercise this right.[7] In other states, convention nominees are designated as such on the primary ballot; they may or may not receive help from the party organization. In still other states, conventions are used to invigorate the party faithful by enabling those who work for the party nominees to hear from their leaders.

The major party nominees for president and vice-president of the country are formally chosen at **national party conventions**. Although they once played decisive roles in determining the nominees, presidential conventions today almost always ratify the results of earlier primaries and caucuses. National conventions are still important as gatherings of the party, as occasions for uniting divided factions, as forums for emerging party leaders to be tested before a national audience, and as a place at which future courses are charted.[8]

A central feature of the American party system today is that party leaders no longer control party nominations. They may participate and influence others, but they do not dominate the nominating process. The invention and spread of the direct primary took this most important function out of the hands of the party organization and put it in the hands of the voters. Candidates are also more independent of the parties because they largely fund their own campaigns, use their own communications staff to communicate with voters, and hire their own pollsters, consultants, and managers.

Nomination by petition without party designation is available in all but a few states, but it is seldom used. The campaign of Ross Perot in 1992 demonstrated, however, that candidates with sufficient volunteers or resources can get on the ballot without a party. Perot used his own millions to build an organization of volunteers who got his name on the ballot as a candidate, not of any political party but of his own organization—United We Stand, America. Ted Turner, owner of CNN and other television stations, also considered this approach to a presidential candidacy in 1992. Should Perot's methods be imitated, the trend could produce a longer ballot and a crowded general election field, with the major party candidates competing against unaffiliated candidates who get on the ballot by petition.

Party Systems

We have a **two-party system,** an electoral system in which two parties dominate. Most democracies have a **multiparty system.** These systems usually arise in countries with strong parliamentary systems, where the legislature is the most important branch of government and the head of government (often called the prime minister or premier) is the leader of one of the major parties in the legislature. This head of government often assembles a coalition of parties with sufficient votes in the legislature to give the coalition a majority in the legislature. Such coalition governments are common in countries like Israel and Italy. Minor parties can gain concessions—positions in a cabinet or particular policies that they want implemented—in return for their participation in a coalition. But major parties need the minor parties in order to form governing coalitions and are therefore willing to bargain. Thus the system favors the existence of minor parties by giving them incentives to persevere. England, however, has a strong two-party system even though it is a parliamentary system. Most democracies with strong legislatures also have somebody who serves as president or chief of state, often only in ceremonial functions.

In multiparty parliamentary systems, legislators are frequently elected by **proportional representation** in which parties receive a proportion of the legislators

- Nominate the national ticket
- Attempt to unify the party's diverse factions
- Adopt the party platform
- Showcase past and future party leaders
- Elect officers
- Attack the opposition party
- Use the free television time to appeal for mass support
- Inspire party activists to organize and get out the vote
- Raise money for state and national candidates
- Decide upon party rules

Political parties have always been the subject of humor, from Will Rogers's line that he was a member of no organized political party, being a Democrat, to this student's endorsement of the two-party system—one on Friday and one on Saturday.

Straightening Out the Terms

Major parties: Democrats and Republicans, the two parties that win almost all American elections at the national, state, and local levels.

Minor parties: parties that are often based on a single idea or principle. Many have been around for decades but only win occasionally at the state or local levels. Examples include the Libertarian party, which was on the ballot in all 50 states and the District of Columbia in 1992, the Socialist party, and the Conservative party of New York.

Minor parties often solicit a protest vote against one or both of the major parties. They occur most often at the presidential level but also arise occasionally in gubernatorial elections. Examples include Roosevelt's Bull Moose party in 1912 and George Wallace's American Independent party in 1968.

Independent candidates: it is possible to become a candidate by petition without a political party. It happens occasionally at the state and local level and in 1992 it happened at the national level, when Ross Perot made much of the fact that his United We Stand, America, was not to be considered a party. John Anderson's National Unity party in 1980 is another example of a party organized to promote a candidate.

corresponding to the proportion of the vote cast for their party in an election. In our **winner-take-all** system, the candidate with the most votes in a district or state takes office. Because a party does not gain anything by finishing second, minor parties can rarely overcome the assumption that a vote for them is a wasted vote.[9] Even if a third-party candidate can keep either major party candidate from receiving more than 50 percent (a *majority*) of the vote, the candidate with the most votes wins (a *plurality*). The winner-take-all system of dividing electoral votes pertains in all states except Maine, which uses a district system.

In multiparty systems, parties at the extremes are apt to have more influence than in our two-party system, and their legislatures more accurately reflect the full range of the views of the electorate. Their political parties can be more doctrinaire than ours because they do not have to appeal to masses of people. Parties that do not become part of the governing coalition of parties have little to say in setting government policy. In contrast, our two-party system tends to create centrist parties that appeal to moderate elements and suppress the views of extremists in the electorate. Moreover, once elected, our parties do not form as cohesive a voting block as do the ideological parties.

Another consequence of multiparty parliamentary systems is that they make governments unstable, as coalitions form and collapse. In addition, the swings in policy when party control changes can be quite dramatic. Two-party systems lead to majority governments that tend to be stable and centrist. As a result, policy shifts occur more incrementally.

Minor Parties: Persistence and Frustration

Two-party politics is the American norm, but **minor parties**—sometimes called **third parties**—have also played a role. Minor parties are of two basic types—those that arise around a candidate and usually disappear when the charismatic personality does, and those that are organized around a goal or ideology that persists over time. Communist, Prohibition, or Libertarian parties are of this second type. Minor parties of both types come and go, but there are usually several minor parties running in any given presidential election, and some are involved in state and local elections as well. Minor parties have occasionally been important: the Abolitionists, the Populists, and the Prohibitionists, Theodore Roosevelt's Bull Moose party, George Wallace's American Independent party, and John Anderson's National Unity party, to name a few.[10] In 1992 Ross Perot received 19 percent of the vote—the most for any nonmajor candidate since Theodore Roosevelt in 1912.

In 1980, John Anderson split from the Republican party, favoring many of its economic stands but taking liberal positions on social issues; he garnered 6.6 percent of the national vote but no electoral votes.

A minor party currently somewhat active on the national scene is the Libertarian party. Founded in 1972, this party wants to turn all, or almost all, government services over to the private sphere. It would end the welfare state, reduce the military to a bare minimum, terminate foreign commitments (including membership in the United Nations), and abolish laws legislating morality, such as laws dealing with prostitution, drugs, gambling, abortion, and gay rights. In 1980 the party polled more than 1 million votes, but its strength slipped later in the 1980s, leading some to think that Ronald Reagan had partially stolen some of its support and agenda.

Ross Perot and the 1992 Presidential Election

Before the primary elections had run their course in 1992, Ross Perot, a wealthy Texas businessman, made known his interest in running for president. Perot was initially "interested" but "not committed" to running and indicated that if citizens were successful in getting his name on the ballots of all 50 states, then he would run.

MINOR PARTIES IN AMERICAN POLITICS

Minor parties have succeeded in calling attention to controversial issues by organizing groups such as the antislavery and anti–civil rights movements. They boast, sometimes correctly, that they are champions not of lost causes but of causes yet to be won. But they have never won the presidency or more than a handful of congressional seats. They have never shaped national policy from *inside* the government. And their influence on national policy in general and on the platforms of the two major parties has been limited.

Theodore Roosevelt.

Eugene Debs.

George Wallace.

Year	Party	Candidate	Percent of Vote	Electoral Votes
1832	Anti-Masonic	William Wirt	8	7
1856	American (Know-Nothing)	Millard Fillmore	22	8
1860	Democratic (Secessionist)	J.C. Breckinridge	18	72
1860	Constitutional Union	John Bell	13	39
1892	People's (Populist)	James B. Weaver	9	22
1912	Bull Moose	Theodore Roosevelt	27	88
1912	Socialist	Eugene V. Debs	6	0
1924	Progressive	Robert M. La Follette	17	13
1948	States' Rights	Strom Thurmond	2	39
1948	Progressive	Henry A. Wallace	2	0
1968	American Independent	George C. Wallace	14	46
1980	National Unity	John Anderson	7	0
1992	United We Stand, America	Ross Perot	19	0

Who was Perot? He had founded and managed a successful computer firm (Electronic Data Systems) that ultimately made him very rich. Estimates of his net worth were between $2.5 and $3.5 billion. During the primaries, Perot created a high profile for himself on national television interviews. He recruited campaign professionals from both parties and built a nationwide network of paid and volunteer workers. As the bitter Republican and Democratic presidential primaries were nearing an end in early summer, Perot achieved front-runner status in a number of national polls. As it appeared certain that a tight three-way race was about to develop, the news media and the political parties began to question some of Perot's past business and personal dealings. Perot abruptly quit the race, a decision announced on the day before Bill Clinton's acceptance speech at the Democratic National Convention.

In October, Perot reentered the race and was successful in securing a place for himself and his running mate, Admiral James Stockdale, in the televised presidential and vice-presidential debates. Both Republican and Democratic parties were not certain how to campaign against Perot; they were anxious to avoid offending his supporters and yet fearful that he might further erode their standing in the polls. In an unusual twist at the end of the campaign, Perot claimed his earlier withdrawal from the race had been to avoid a "dirty trick" planned by the Bush campaign to disrupt his daughter's wedding. The charges and countercharges raised new questions about Perot.

Perot's defeat in the election did not remove him from the stage of national politics. In 1993 he lobbied hard against NAFTA and even debated Vice-President Al Gore on CNN's *Larry King Live*. Perot continued to call for campaign finance and lobbying reform, putting pressure on Clinton and Congress to take action on this issue before the 1994 elections. After losing on NAFTA, Perot again made himself part of the national political process with his strong opposition to the Clinton health care reform proposal.

A BRIEF HISTORY OF AMERICAN POLITICAL PARTIES

American political parties have evolved and changed over time, but some underlying characteristics have been constant. We have historically had a two-party system with minor parties. Our parties are moderate and accommodative—meaning that they are open to people with diverse outlooks. Political scientist V. O. Key and others argue that our party system has been shaped in large part by *realigning elections*, critical elections or turning points that define the agenda of politics and the alignment of voters within parties.[11] These periods were responses to historic changes in the economy and society. Realigning elections are characterized by intense electoral involvement by the voters, disruptions of traditional voting patterns, changes in the relations of power within the community, and the formation of new and durable electoral groupings. They have occurred cyclically, not randomly.[12] These elections tend to coincide with expansions of the suffrage or changes in the rate of voting.[13] We focus here on four realigning elections: 1824, 1860, 1896, and 1932.

Our First Parties

To the leaders of the young Republic, parties usually meant bigger, better organized, and more fierce factions, and they did not want that. Benjamin Franklin worried about the "infinite mutual abuse of parties, tearing to pieces the best of characters." In his farewell address, George Washington warned against the "baneful effects of the Spirit of Party." And Thomas Jefferson said, "If I could not go to heaven but with a party, I would not go there at all."[14]

How, then, did parties get started? Largely out of practical necessity. The same early leaders who so frequently stated their opposition to political parties also recognized the need to organize officeholders who shared their views so that government could act. To get its measures passed through Congress, the Washington administration had to fashion a coalition among factions. This job fell to Treasury Secretary Alexander Hamilton, who built an informal Federalist party, while Washington stayed "above politics." Secretary of State Jefferson and other officials, many of whom despised Hamilton and his aristocratic ways as much as they opposed the policies he favored, were uncertain about how to deal with these political differences. The overriding concern for most was the success of the new government; personal loyalty to Washington was a close second. Thus Jefferson stayed in the cabinet, despite his opposition to administration policies, during most of Washington's first term. When he left the cabinet at the end of 1793, many who joined him in opposition to the administration's economic policies remained in Congress, forming a group of legislators opposed to Federalist fiscal policies and eventually to Federalist foreign policy, which appeared "soft on Britain." This party was later known as Republicans, then as Democratic-Republicans, then as Democrats.

Andrew Jackson, organizer of a people's coalition of voters, celebrated his arrival at the White House with an inaugural party open to all that nearly tore the place down.

1824 : Andrew Jackson and the Democrats

Party politics was invigorated following the election of 1824, in which the leader in the popular vote—the hero of the battle of New Orleans, Democrat Andrew Jackson—failed to achieve the necessary majority of the electoral college and was defeated by John Quincy Adams in the runoff election in the House of Representatives. Jackson, brilliantly aided by Martin Van Buren, a veteran party builder in New York State, later knit together a winning combination of regions, interest groups, and political doctrines to win the presidency in 1828. The Whigs succeeded the Federalists as the opposition party. By the time Van Buren followed Jackson in the White House in 1837, the Democrats had become a large, nationwide movement with national and state leadership, a clear party doctrine, and grass-roots organization. The Whigs were almost as strong; in 1840 they put their own man, General William Henry Harrison ("Old Tippecanoe") into the White House. A two-party system had been born. We have had that two-party system ever since—one of few such systems worldwide.

1860 : The Civil War and the Rise of the Republicans

Out of the crisis over slavery evolved a new party: the second Republican party—ultimately the "Grand Old Party" (GOP).[15] Abraham Lincoln was elected in 1860 with the support not only of financiers, industrialists, and merchants, but also of large numbers of workers and farmers. For 50 years after 1860, the Republican coalition won every presidential race, except for Grover Cleveland's victories in 1884 and 1892. The Democratic party survived with its durable white male base in the South.

1896 : A Party in Transition

The Republican party's response to industrialization and hard times for farmers transformed it in the late 1800s. A combination of western and southern farmers and western mining interests sought an alliance with workers in the East and Midwest to "recapture America from the foreign moneyed interests responsible for industrialization. The crisis of industrialization squarely placed an agrarian-fundamentalist view of life against an industrial-progress view."[16] This realignment of 1896 differs from the others, however, in that party power did not change hands. In that sense it was a converting realignment because it reinforced the Republican majority status that had been in place since 1860.[17]

The **Progressive Era**, the first two decades of this century, was a period of political reform led by the Progressive wing of the Republican party. Much of the agenda of the Progressives focused on the corrupt political parties. Civil service reforms shifted some of the patronage out of the hands of party officials. The direct primary election took control of nominations from party leaders and gave it to the rank-and-file. And in a number of cities, nonpartisan governments were instituted, totally eliminating the role of a party. With the ratification of the Seventeenth Amendment to the Constitution in 1913, United States senators came to be popularly elected. Women obtained the right to vote when the Nineteenth Amendment was ratified in 1920. Thus within a short time, the electorate changed, the rules changed, and even the stakes of the game changed. Democrats were unable to build a durable winning coalition during this time. In fact, they remained the minority party until the early 1930s, when the Hoover administration was overwhelmed by the Great Depression.

1932 : Franklin Roosevelt and the New Deal Alignment

The 1932 election, like critical elections before it, was a turning point in American politics. In the 1930s the United States faced a devastating economic collapse. After a century of sporadic government action, the New Dealers stepped in and fundamentally altered the relationship between government and society. Between 1929 and 1932, the gross national product fell over 10 percent per year and unemployment rose from 1.5 million to more than 15 million, with millions more working only part time. Herbert Hoover and the Republican majority in Congress had responded to the Depression by arguing that the problems with the economy were largely self-correcting and that their long-standing policy of *laissez-faire*, a hands-off approach to the economy, was appropriate. Voters wanted more. Franklin D. Roosevelt and the Democrats were swept into office in 1932 by a tide of anti-Hoover and anti-Republican sentiment. Roosevelt rode this wave and labeled his response to the Depression as the New Deal; he rejected *laissez-faire* economics and instead relied on Keynesian economics, which asserted that government could influence the direction of the economy through its fiscal as well as monetary policy.

The central issue on which the Republicans and Democrats disagreed in this New Deal period was the role of government regarding the economy. Roosevelt Democrats argued that the government had to do something to pull the country out of the Depression. Republicans disagreed with the scope of government activity and of its intrusion into the economy. This central division about whether the national government should play an active role in regulating and promoting our economy remains one of the most important divisions between the Democratic and Republican parties today, although, with time, the country and both parties accepted many of the New Deal programs. For the two decades following the 1932 election, the Republican party was relegated to watching the majority Democrats—a new coalition of union households, immigrant workers, and those most hurt by the Great Depression—implement their domestic policies. During the Second World War, both parties cooperated in embracing a bipartisan foreign policy.

Republican Presidents/Democratic Congresses

During the period since 1952, Republicans became something of a "presidential" party, often winning presidential elections with landslide margins. Part of the explanation is their ability to attract popular candidates like Dwight Eisenhower and Ronald Reagan. Republicans also reaped the rewards of Democratic party divisiveness and generally weaker Democratic presidential candidates. Republicans benefited from the breakup of the once solidly Democratic South in presidential voting when the Democratic party decided in the 1950s and 1960s to take a strong stand on civil rights that offended many white southern Democrats. Yet many of these "presidential Republicans" did not give up their Democratic allegiance when voting for candidates for the Senate, the House, or for governor or other state and local officials.

Republican victories in presidential elections between 1952 and 1992 have been achieved only with the support of elements of Roosevelt's New Deal coalition. New Deal programs that benefited these very groups and expanded the middle class made possible the conservative "hold onto what we've got" thinking of voters in the 1980s and 1990s. The deviation from this pattern occurred in the 1980 election, when Ronald Reagan's coattails helped secure victories in enough U.S. Senate elections to create a Republican majority in the U.S. Senate for the first time since 1954. But in 1986 the Democrats regained their majority in the U.S. Senate and have held it since then.

Bill Clinton won back many so-called Reagan Democrats as he assembled his winning coalition in 1992. Democrats also held on to majorities in both houses, giving the Democrats control over both the legislative and executive branches for the first time since Jimmy Carter's presidency. Many of the new members elected to Congress in 1992, like Clinton, had run on the theme of change, especially with regard to the economy, health care, and the deficit. However, many of those new members were defeated in 1994—again on the theme of change—but this time with the Republicans exploiting popular discontent with Clinton and Congress.

The Republican's victory in 1994 was far reaching, securing a majority for their party in both houses of Congress, winning control of seven of the eight largest states, and making substantial inroads in state governorships and legislatures as well. More than most elections, 1994 was an election with a partisan agenda. During the campaign, at the instigation of Newt Gingrich and other House Republican leaders, the Republicans had issued a Contract with America (see accompanying box) that described a legislative agenda the Republicans would carry out if they took control of Congress. Republicans also benefited from a well-funded and talented group of candidates who put the Democrats on the defensive.

In the months before the 1994 election, Republicans chose to use the filibuster in the Senate to block passage of the Clinton legislative agenda. Their astounding success in 1994 left Clinton and the Democratic minority in Congress with a dilemma. Should they compromise and help enact some of the Republican legislative agenda? Or should they adopt the same strategy the Republicans used in 1993 and 1994 of trying to block or veto the actions of the majority party? In either event, American politics entered a period of intensified partisan behavior in Congress.

AMERICAN PARTIES TODAY

As we have noted, political parties are less and less important in selecting candidates and running elections. American political scientists have been worrying about weak and undisciplined parties for decades. Since the founding of the Republic, parties have operated within our constitutional system of separation of powers and checks and balances, which limits parties' ability to dominate our government.[18]

Most Americans have a strong antiparty bias. Parties are, in a word, distrusted. Some see parties as corrupt institutions, interested in the spoils of politics. Critics also charge that the parties evade the issues; that they fail to deliver on their promises; that they have no new ideas; that they follow public opinion rather than lead it; or that they are just one more special interest.

At the same time, Americans see the parties as *necessary*. Most Americans want party labels kept on the ballot, think of themselves as Democrats or Republicans, and typically vote for candidates from their party. They contribute millions of dollars to the two major parties. More individual contributions go to the Republicans than to

---

Major Elements of the Contract with America

- Enact a Balanced Budget Amendment.
- Enact the line-item veto.
- Reduce Congressional staff by one third.
- Stop welfare payments after two years.
- Pass a $500 per child tax credit.
- Pass a capital gains tax cut.
- Limit death penalty appeals.
- Prohibit U.S. troops being placed under United Nations command.
- Pass term limits for members of Congress.

Some Realities about American Parties

- Parties began as soon as people started taking sides in the debate over ratifying the U.S. Constitution, although it took a few years for them to organize into formal bodies.
- Political parties, and especially our two-party system, have persisted over the course of our history.
- Ours has almost always been a two-party system, differentiating us from most nations, which have a one-party or multi-party system.
- Since 1830 we have witnessed reasonably effective competition in our national party system.
- Our parties have historically been decentralized and fragmented. Parties are organized around units of competition (states, congressional districts, countries, cities), which in our governmental structure make state parties the most important units. State parties can be quite different from one another.
- Winning office and power have been more important to party leaders than specific issues or platforms; political parties in the United States are primarily organized to win or obtain political power.
- Our parties can be characterized as moderate, centrist, and pragmatic, with only modest ideological cohesion and voting discipline, especially when compared to European political parties.

Republican national chairman Haley Barbour.

the Democrats.[19] Americans believe, at least vaguely, that you cannot run a big democracy without parties.

Both parties are *moderate* in their policies and leadership.[20] Each party usually takes its extremist supporters more or less for granted and seeks out the voters in the middle. Successful party leaders must be diplomats; to win presidential elections and congressional majorities, they must find a middle ground among more or less hostile groups so that they can reach agreement on general principles.

The major parties are *decentralized*, organized around the units of competition—elections in states, cities, or congressional districts. Like the government itself, they have national, state, and local organizations.

Parties as Institutions

Edmund Burke, the frequently cited English political philosopher, writing more than two centuries ago, defined a political party as "a body of men united, for promulgating by their joint endeavors the national interest, upon some particular principle in which they are all agreed."[21] A modern theorist has expressed a much less idealistic view of parties as "a group whose members propose to act in concert in the competitive struggle for political power."[22] In the United States, parties have demonstrated both tendencies—the pursuit of principle and power. **Political parties**, then, are organizations that seek political power by electing people to office so that their positions and philosophy become public policy. Like other institutions of American government—Congress, the presidency, the courts—parties have rules, procedures, and organizational structure, and they make policy. What are the institutional characteristics of political parties?

NATIONAL PARTY LEADERSHIP   The supreme authority in both major parties is the national party convention, which meets every four years to nominate candidates for president and vice-president, to ratify the party platform, and to adopt rules. The delegates have only four days in which to accomplish their business, although many key decisions have been made ahead of time. For example, conventions now ratify the presidential aspirant already chosen in the presidential primaries and caucuses.

More directly in charge of the national party is the *national committee*. In recent years both parties have strengthened the role of the national committee and enhanced the influence of individual committee members. The committees are now more representative of the party rank-and-file. But in neither party is the national committee the center of party leadership.

The *national party chair* is the top official of each of the two major parties. The chair is formally elected by the national committee but in reality is the choice of the presidential nominee. Although they are the heads of their national party apparatus, they remain largely unknown to the voters. The chair may play a major role in running the national campaign. After the election, the power of the national chair of the victorious party tends to dwindle. Even though he or she serves as a liaison between the party and the White House, the chair actually serves at the pleasure of the president and does the president's bidding with the national party. The chair of the party without an incumbent president has considerable independence and yet works closely with the party's congressional leadership. The national committee usually elects a new head after electoral defeats.

Winning the White House is the major focus of the national party committees, while winning congressional elections is the concern of the *congressional and senatorial campaign committees*. Republican and Democratic senatorial campaign committees are composed of senators chosen for two-year terms by their fellow party members in the Senate; congressional campaign committees are chosen in the same manner by the House. The chairs of these committees, appointed by their party leadership, have much more to say about which candidates get campaign funds.

These committees once offered only token contributions to selected candidates, but today they play an important role in recruiting candidates, training them, and assisting with campaign finance. Republicans saw the potential for these committees earlier than did Democrats. In the late 1970s, in coordination with the Republican National Committee, they developed extensive fund-raising lists and raised enough money to help fund most Republican candidates for the House or the Senate.[23] Democrats in the House and Senate copied the tactic and have closed fund-raising gaps and made their campaign committees more effective.

National party organizations only rarely try to influence party nominations. Politicians invest in personal organizations and expect the party to remain neutral during the primary campaign. Although heated primary contests often preclude having a united party in the general election, national parties are helpless to prevent them.[24]

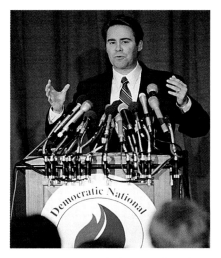

Democratic national chairman David Wilhelm.

PARTIES AT THE GRASS ROOTS   Party organization at the state and local levels is structured much like the national level. Each state has a *state committee*, headed by a *state chair*. State law determines the composition of the state committees and sets rules regulating them. Members of the state committees are usually elected from local areas, but party auxiliaries such as the Young Democrats or the Federation of Republican Women are sometimes represented as well. In many states these committees are dominated by governors, senators, or coalitions of local elected business and ethnic leaders. State chairs are normally elected by the state committees, although approximately one-quarter are chosen at state conventions. When the party controls the governorship, chairs are often agents of the governor, but some can be quite independent.[25]

Some powerful state parties have developed in recent years. Despite much state-to-state variation, the trend is toward stronger state organizations, with Republicans typically much better funded.[26] Third, and in some states fourth, parties play a role in local elections. New York, for instance, has both a Liberal and a Conservative party in addition to Democratic and Republican parties. The role these parties play in statewide elections can be important, even though they rarely win office themselves.

Below state committees are *county committees*, which vary widely in function and power. The key role of these committees is recruiting candidates for such offices as county commissioner, sheriff, and treasurer; but the recruiting job often involves finding a candidate for the office, not deciding among competing contenders. For the party that almost never wins an election, the county committee struggles to find someone willing to run. When the job is valued by those seeking it, however, primaries, not the party leaders, usually decide the winner.[27]

Many county organizations maintain a significant level of activity, placing campaign literature, organizing telephone campaigns, distributing posters and lawn signs, and canvassing door-to-door. In many areas county committees do not function at all, and many party leaders are just figureheads.

In recent years the efforts of state and county organizations have been aided by financial assistance from the party's national committee, which has distributed millions of dollars in so-called **soft money**—money that does not have to be reported under the Federal Election Campaign Act. This money must be spent for the *benefit of the party*, rather than for a particular congressional, senatorial, or presidential candidate.

At the base of the party pyramid—at the city, town, ward, and precinct level—we find the grass roots of the party, if we are to find any party activity at all (see Figure 10-1). In a few places, local ward and precinct leaders still do favors for constituents, from fixing parking tickets, to organizing clambakes, to obtaining horse-racing passes in a state like Arkansas. But strong local party organization is

FIGURE 10-1   The Party Pyramid

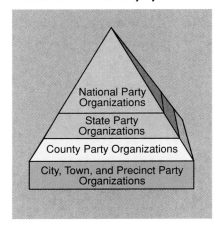

Would government work better without parties?

American government may be intensely partisan—some think much too partisan. In Congress or state legislatures the two parties often battle over legislation, investigations, and rewarding loyal districts. When legislatures become intensely partisan, they may be more concerned with advancing their own party's fortunes in the next election than with finding an acceptable compromise on legislation that would serve the public. And when a governor or president is from a party different from the legislative majority, that difference sometimes leads to partisan deadlock. Finally, partisanship in judicial or executive branch appointments means that qualified people may be excluded from consideration on the basis of party affiliation.

You decide! Would we be better off as a political system if we did not have political parties?

rare. Most local committees are poorly financed and inactive except during the few weeks before election day.[28]

What does all this party organization amount to? Not much. Party organizations and leaders play some role in winning elections, but the fact is their role is becoming less significant, most especially at the state and local levels, where candidate's organizations are superseding party organizations. Candidates for office—to become the mayor of a large city, a governor, or a member of the House or Senate—rely less and less on the party structure and more and more on the personal organizations that they themselves put together.

PARTY DIFFERENCES   If you read the **party platforms**, or official statements, you will note policy differences, but platforms are not a good place to find out about these differences. Because platforms help parties win elections, party leaders use them to try to *conceal* differences in order to appeal to as many voters as possible. Party platforms are dull and ponderous documents that few people ever see or take seriously, despite the fact that party members often fight bitterly to get their particular "plank" into the platform.

Many politicians contend platforms rarely help elect anybody, but platform positions can hurt a presidential candidate. Because the platform-writing process is not always controlled by the nominee, it is possible for presidential candidates to disagree with their own party platform. Jimmy Carter ended up with a platform in 1980 that was more liberal than his administration had been.[29]

Once elected, politicians are rarely reminded of what their platform position was on a given issue. One major exception to this was President Bush's promise not to raise taxes if elected in 1988 with his memorable "Read my lips—no new taxes." Clinton and Perot repeatedly raised this broken promise in the 1992 campaign. Clinton had to backpeddle on his 1992 promise that if elected he would lower taxes on the middle class; his budget and tax recommendations raised taxes on wealthy Americans but did not lower taxes on the middle class.

Differences at the national level between the two major parties were most sharp just before the Civil War. Again during the New Deal, the differences between Democrats and Republicans were clear to everyone. Voters were loyal to their political party because of how they felt about Franklin Roosevelt's response to the Depression. Those who approved of his programs or were helped by them favored the Democrats and thought Roosevelt a hero; those who did not like Roosevelt and saw his program as "social engineering" favored Republicans. Later, as much of the New Deal philosophy came to be accepted by both parties, the lines between the parties blurred in the eyes of many. Typically, both parties have been moderate, expressing support for a strong defense, a stable Social Security system, and economic growth.

Yet voters generally see their own party as well as the opposing party as standing for something. Thus most business and professional people sense that the Republican party best serves their interests, while workers tend to view Democrats as more helpful. The proportion of voters discerning important differences increased sharply during the Reagan years, when parties seemed to become more polarized.[30] Reagan's program emphasized lower taxes, lower spending on social programs, and increased spending for defense. In winning the presidency in 1980, Reagan drew millions of religious fundamentalists and social conservatives—pro-life, pro-prayer, and pro-defense activists—into the GOP, as well as opponents of integration, busing, racial quotas, and gay rights. Although Reagan failed to convert many of his conservative ideas into law, he did move his party toward conservatism.

In 1992, the Democratic party platform attempted a moderate tone, stating, "We believe in an activist government, but it must work in a different, more responsive way." Democrats attempted to steer a course between what they called the "*laissez-faire* capitalism of the Republicans" and the image Republicans had used to characterize them as "supporters of a welfare state." Republicans, sensitive to the role social issues had played in the Reagan and Bush coalitions, said in their platform, "We believe in traditional family values and in the Judeo-Christian heritage."[31] Differences between 1992 Democratic and Republican platforms are highlighted in Table 10-1.

Our two major parties accommodate all kinds of people and all kinds of views: there are conservative Democrats and liberal Republicans; there are rich Democrats and poor Republicans; there are African Americans, Jews, and Catholics who are Democrats, and there are African Americans, Jews, and Catholics who are Republicans. That is why the Democratic and Republican parties survive as major parties. Nevertheless, as we learned in Chapter 8, there is a group dynamic to partisan choice, and party labels do have content. Democratic leaders are more liberal than Republicans. Democrats are more likely to be progovernment in the sense that they believe government can and should have a role in civil rights, social programs, and economic fairness. But a serious question arises over how liberal the Democrats of the future will be. Look at the U.S. Senate, where the Democratic party is home to liberals like Ted Kennedy, moderates like Bill Bradley and Bob Kerrey, strong defense advocates like Sam Nunn, and southern conservatives like Howell Hefflin and John Breaux. Increasingly, southern conservatives are finding their home in the Republican party; two Republican senators—Phil Gramm of Texas and Richard Shelby of Alabama—switched parties from Democrat to Republican. Shelby switched within days after the 1994 election as Republicans took control of the U.S. Senate.

As a rule, Democrats are ideologically more diverse than Republicans. The Democratic umbrella encompasses the conservative Coalition for a Democratic Majority, the moderate Democratic Leadership Council (dominated by an array of southern governors and senators), and the liberal Americans for Democratic Action. The Democratic coalition embraces activists in the civil rights and other liberal-left movements.

Parties in Government

Despite the organizational weakness of political parties, they remain central to the operation of government in the United States. Parties, again as organizations, play a more important role after the election in the operation of government than they play in the elections themselves.

IN CONGRESS Members of Congress take their partisanship seriously, at least while they are in Washington, D.C. Their power and influence are determined in part by whether their party is in control of the House or Senate. They also have a stake in which party controls the White House. The chairs of all standing committees come from the majority party. The presiding officials of both chambers come from the majority party, except when the vice-president is in attendance at the Senate. Members of both houses sit with fellow partisans on the floor and in committee, leading to the expression often heard in floor debate, "the other side of the aisle."

Members of the congressional staff are also partisan. From the volunteer intern to the senior staffer, members of Congress expect their staff to be loyal first to them and then to their party. Should you decide to go to work for a representative or senator, you would be expected to identify yourself with that person's party and would have some difficulty working for persons from the other party later. Employees of the House and Senate—from elevator operators to the Capitol Hill police and even including the chaplain—hold patronage jobs. With few exceptions, such jobs go to persons from the party that has a majority in the House or the Senate.

Thinking it Through

It is naive to believe that the removal of parties will negate conflict, self-interest, or ambition. A political system without parties would be a society without the means to deal with disagreements over policies, economics, or social values. Americans expect legislatures to be partisan, to be contentious, and to make the most of partisan opportunities. Divided government may be less efficient, but it clearly has not bothered voters, who routinely have elected legislators from one party and governors or presidents from another. Finally, people with judicial or administrative ambitions understand the role that parties play in appointments, giving them an incentive to get involved in a party. This is not all bad because, as we have seen, it is possible for idealistic individuals to redefine and reshape a party.

TABLE 10-1

Key Party Differences: Excerpts from Republican and Democratic Party Platforms, 1992

Democratic	Republican
Deficit and Taxes: Addressing the deficit requires fair and shared sacrifice of all Americans for the common good. In 12 Republican years a national debt that took 200 years to accumulate has been quadrupled. In place of the Republican supply-side disaster, the Democratic investment, economic conversion and growth strategy will generate more revenues from a growing economy.	**Deficit and Taxes**: As the deficit comes under control, we aspire to further tax rate cuts. We will cut the capital gains tax rate to 15 percent...and index it so government cannot profit from inflation by taxing phantom capital gains, literally stealing from savings and pensions. We reject the notion advanced by the Democrats that this enhances the wealthy. To the contrary, it would...contribute to economic expansion. [Bill Clinton] has proposed the largest tax increase in American history.
Economy: The American people are hurting. The American dream of expanding opportunity has faded. Middle class families are working hard, playing by the rules, but still falling behind. An expanding, entrepreneurial economy of high-skill, high-wage jobs is the most important family policy, urban policy, labor policy, minority policy and foreign policy America can have.	**Economy**: We launched an era of growth and prosperity such as the world had never seen: 20 million new jobs in the longest peacetime economic expansion in the history of the Republic. Inflation has fallen to its lowest level in 30 years. Interest rates dropped 15 percentage points. Productivity has sharply risen. Exports are booming. Despite a global downturn in late 1990, real economic growth resumed last year. Unlike the Democrats, we believe the private sector, not the federal government, should set prevailing wage rates.
Education: We oppose the Bush Administrations' efforts to bankrupt the public school system—the bedrock of democracy—through private school vouchers. We support education reforms such as site-based decision-making and public school choice, with strong protections against discrimination. Governments must end the inequalities that create educational ghettos among school districts...and ensure that teachers' pay measures up to their decisive role in children's lives.	**Education**: Parents have the right to choose the best school for their children. [President Bush] has shown unprecedented leadership for the most important education goal of all: helping middle and low income families enjoy the same choice of schools—public, private, or religious—that families with more resources already have.
Environment: We will protect our old growth forests, preserve critical habitats, provide a genuine "no net loss" policy on wetlands,...conserve the critical resources of soil, water and air, oppose new offshore oil drilling and mineral exploration and production in our nation's many environmentally critical areas.	**Environment**: Environmental progress must continue in tandem with economic growth. Clearly we have led the world in investment in environmental protection. Environmental progress is integrally related to economic development.
Foreign Affairs: The United States must be prepared to use military force decisively when necessary to defend our vital interests...and should encourage multilateral peacekeeping through the United Nations and other international efforts. The United States cannot be strong abroad if it is weak at home. Restoring America's global economic leadership must become a central element of our national security policies.	**Foreign Affairs**: Never in this century has the United States enjoyed such security from foreign enemies. With President Bush leading the free world, the Soviet empire has collapsed...into the dustbin of history. Eastern Europe is liberated. Germany is peacefully united. The former Soviet armies are returning home. Nuclear arsenals are being cut to fractions of their former size.
Gun Control: It is time to shut down the weapons bazaars. We support a reasonable waiting period to permit background checks for purchase of handguns, [and a ban on] the possession, sale, importation and manufacture of the most deadly assault weapons. We do not support efforts to restrict weapons used for legitimate hunting and sporting purposes.	**Gun Control**: Republicans defend the constitutional right to keep and bear arms. We call for stiff mandatory sentences for those who use firearms in a crime. We note that those who seek to disarm citizens in their homes are the same liberals who tried to disarm our Nation during the Cold War and are today seeking to cut our national defense below safe levels.
Homosexuality: [We will] provide civil rights protection for gay men and lesbians and an end to Defense Department discrimination.	**Homosexuality**: We support the continued exclusion of homosexuals from the military as a matter of good order and discipline.
Health Care: All Americans should have universal access to quality, affordable health care—not as a privilege, but as a right. We will enact a uniquely American reform of the health care system to control costs and make health care affordable.	**Health Care**: Americans receive the finest medical care in the world. Republicans believe government control of health is irresponsible and ineffective. We believe health care choices should remain in the hands of the people, not government bureaucrats.
Abortion: Democrats stand behind the right of every woman to choose, consistent with *Roe v Wade*, regardless of ability to pay, and support a national law to protect that right. It is a fundamental constitutional liberty that individual Americans...can best take responsibility for making...decisions regarding reproduction.	**Abortion**: We believe the unborn child has a fundamental individual right to life which cannot be infringed. We therefore reaffirm our support for a human life amendment to the Constitution... [and] we oppose using public revenues for abortion.

IN THE EXECUTIVE BRANCH   The presidency is no less partisan. Rarely will a senior White House official be selected from the opposing party. However, part way through President Clinton's first year in office, he named a prominent Republican, David Gergen, to a White House position to handle his chaotic and ineffective press relations. Gergen was later moved to the State Department as an adviser on public relations. Presidents typically surround themselves with advisers who have campaigned with them and proven their loyalty. President Clinton's advisers and cabinet officers who fit this description include George Stephanopoulos (managed media relations in the campaign and went on to be a senior White House adviser), Ron Brown (national chair of the Democratic party who became secretary of commerce), and Mickey Kantor (worked on the campaign and was then appointed Clinton's trade negotiator).

Partisanship is also important in presidential appointments to the highest levels of the federal bureaucracy. Following the 1992 presidential election, the victorious party had more than 4,000 noncareer positions to fill.[32] Included in these positions were cabinet-level appointments and ambassadorships around the world. Party commitment, including making campaign contributions, is expected of persons who seek these positions.

Sometimes it is not enough to have been a good partisan; you must also be acceptable to a particular wing of the party. Conservative Republicans in the Reagan and Bush administrations attempted to influence political and judicial appointments in an ideological as well as partisan direction.

IN THE JUDICIAL BRANCH   The judicial branch of the national government, with its lifetime tenure and political independence, is designed to operate in an expressly nonpartisan manner. Judges, unlike Congress, do not sit together by political party. But the appointment process for judges has been partisan from the very beginning. The landmark case establishing the principle of judicial review, *Marbury v Madison* (1803), concerned the efforts of one party to stack the judiciary with fellow partisans before leaving office. Today party remains an important consideration in the naming of federal judges. While the party of the nominee is not called for on any form, those responsible for the screening and evaluating of candidates certainly take party and ideology into account.

STATE AND LOCAL LEVELS   The importance of party in the operation of local government varies somewhat among states and localities. In some states, such as New York and Illinois, local parties play an even stronger role than at the national level. In others, such as Nebraska, parties play almost no role at all. In Nebraska, the state legislature is expressly nonpartisan, though factions perform like parties and still play a role. Parties are likewise unimportant in the government of Minneapolis. But in most states and many cities, parties are important to the operation of the legislature, governor, or mayor. Judicial selection in most states is a partisan matter.

In short, political parties are important to the operation of American government. They play an important role in filling senior executive branch and judicial positions. They are the organizing device in legislatures. And for the party of the president or governor, they provide a bridge that spans the separation of powers between the executive branch and legislative branches.

Parties among the Voters

Political parties would be of little significance if they did not have meaning to the voters. Parties remain important to voters for all of the reasons described earlier in this chapter: they organize the competition, simplify the voting choices, and provide a link between the people and their government. Among voters we find all sorts of involvement with political parties, ranging from little or none to intense. But what does it mean when your answer to the question, "What is your party?" is Republican, Democratic, or Independent? We call this *party identification,* and it is very important to your political attitudes and behavior. There is also the question of *party registration*—which party you are enrolled in by law and thus entitled to participate in its primaries.

PARTY REGISTRATION   For citizens in many states, "party" has a particular legal meaning—**party registration**. At the time voters register to vote in these states, they are asked to state their party preference; they then become *registered* Democrats, Republicans, Libertarians, or whatever. Voters can subsequently change their party registration. Why do some states have party registration? One reason is to limit the participants in primary elections to persons from that party; such elections are called *closed primaries*. Hence in states like California, only registered Democrats can vote in the Democratic primary. States that have *open primaries* generally do not have party registration and permit voters to choose which party primary they wish to vote in on election day.

PARTY ACTIVISTS   This group tends to fall into three broad categories: party regulars, candidate activists, and issue activists. *Party regulars* value the party first. They value winning elections and understand that compromise and moderation are often important to that objective. They also realize that in our system it is important to keep the party together as much as possible, because a fractured party only helps the opposition.

Candidate activists are followers of a particular candidate who see the party as the means to place their candidate in power. Politicians who generate followings often see the political party as the means to achieve their electoral objectives. Candidate activists are often not concerned with the other operations of the party—with nominees for other offices, for example, or with raising money for the party.

People who supported David Duke in his Louisiana contest for governor and his unsuccessful run for the presidency in 1992 would be classified as candidate activists. Duke, a former Ku Klux Klan leader with an antiblack and antisemitic record, disavowed his past and tried to win support as a Republican from enough voters to become governor of Louisiana. He generated national attention and, while ultimately losing the gubernatorial election, made himself visible and well known. Candidate activists, like those who supported Duke, fade in interest and involvement when their candidate loses and leaves the political scene.

Issue activists wish to push the parties in a particular direction on a single issue or narrow range of issues like abortion, taxes, school prayer, the environment, or civil rights. To issue activists, the party platform is an important battleground because they seek the party endorsement for their position. Issue activists are also often candidate activists if they can find a candidate willing to embrace their position.

Both issue activists and candidate activists have been called purists because they see politics and the party as a battle over their issue, and they insist on making their "statement" on that issue or for their candidate, regardless of the electoral consequences. Such purists do not want to compromise. They prefer to lose the election rather than accept less than what they want accomplished.

Party activists thus include a diverse group of people who come to the political party with different objectives. It is not surprising, then, that some of the most interesting politics you will observe are over candidate selection and issue positions *within the political parties!* These fights over strategy and party position are conducted in open meetings and under democratic procedures. Political parties foster democracy not only by competition between the parties but through competition within the parties as well.

PARTY IDENTIFICATION Unfortunately, the vast majority of Americans are mere spectators to this kind of party activity. They lack the partisan commitment and interest needed for this level of involvement. This is not to say that parties are irrelevant or unimportant to them. For them, partisanship is what political scientists call **party identification**—an informal and subjective affiliation with a political party that most people acquire in childhood.[33] In many ways it is a standing preference for one party over another. Plainly, in particular contests for president, governor, or some other office, a voter sometimes will vote for a candidate from the other party. Yet in the absence of a compelling reason to do otherwise, most Americans vote their party identification.

Party identification is the single best predictor of how people will vote. Unlike candidates and issues, which come and go, party identification is a long-term element in voting choice. The strength of party identification is also important in predicting participation and political interest. Strong Republicans and Strong Democrats participate more actively in politics than any other groups and are generally more knowledgeable and informed. Pure Independents, on the other hand, are just the opposite; they vote at the lowest rates and have the lowest levels of interest and awareness of any of the categories of party identification. This evidence runs counter to the notion that persons who are strong partisans are unthinking party adherents.[34] Party identification is something generally acquired in childhood from parents and often reinforced by peers and early political experiences. It is part of the political socialization process described in Chapter 7.

To say that most persons have the same partisanship as their parents is not to say that some people do not identify with the other party. There are lots of Democratic children of Republican parents and vice versa, but that is not typical. People do not change parties as often as they change their attitudes on issues or enthusiasm for candidates or politicians. To define party identification as a stable, long-term force in voting does not preclude change in the underlying support for the parties or a major realignment.

PARTISAN CHANGE, REFORM, AND RENEWAL

Partisan Realignment and Dealignment

The New Deal and the critical election of 1932—events more than 60 years ago—still provide the basic structure of our party alignments. When will there be another **realignment**—an election that dramatically changes the voters' partisan identification? Whether a realignment has occurred is frequently debated in the literature of political science, but most political science researchers believe we have not experienced any major realignment since 1932.[35] Partisan identification for the past four decades has been stable, and while new voters have been added to the electorate—blacks and 18-to-21-year-olds—the basic character of the party system has not changed dramatically.

In presidential voting, Republicans have done well, winning five of the last seven presidential elections. The victory of Bill Clinton in 1992 demonstrated, however, that Democrats still have the ability to assemble a winning coalition. Many so-called Reagan Democrats returned to the Democratic party to vote for Bill Clinton, especially in heavily populated states. Yet strong support for Ross Perot could be seen as an indication of weakening party ties, or at least displeasure with the parties' standard-bearers. Perot

We The People
Portrait of the Electorate

Sex	Repub.	Dem.	Ind.
Male	42%	45%	13%
Female	34	54	11
Race			
White	42%	46%	12%
Black	8	79	13
Hispanic	27	61	11
Age			
18–24	36%	46%	17%
25–34	40	46	14
35–44	38	51	11
45–54	40	50	11
55–64	36	54	10
65+	39	53	8
Income			
Less than $10,000	28%	56%	16%
$10,000–$19,999	30	59	11
$20,000–$29,999	30	56	14
$30,000–$39,999	42	48	10
$40,000–$59,999	45	47	8
$60,000+	54	37	10
Religion			
Jewish	9%	86%	5%
Catholic	33	55	11
Protestant	44	45	11
Ideology			
Liberal	14%	77%	9%
Moderate/Don't Know	31	53	16
Conservative	65	28	7
Region			
Northeast	32%	55%	13%
Midwest	43	45	12
South	34	53	13
West	44	49	8
Total	38	50	12

SOURCE: 1992 American National Election Study, Center for Political Studies, University of Michigan.

We have classified Independents who lean toward a party with that party.

PARTY IDENTIFICATION

Party identification is measured by the answers to the following question:

Generally speaking, in politics do you usually think of yourself as a Republican, a Democrat, an Independent, or what?

Persons who answer Republican or Democrat to this question are then asked:

Would you call yourself a strong or a not very strong Republican/Democrat?

Persons who answered Independent to the first question are asked this follow-up question:

Do you think of yourself as closer to the Republican or the Democratic party?

Persons who did not indicate Democrat, Republican, or Independent to the first question rarely exceed 2 percent of the electorate and include persons who are apolitical or who identify with one of the minor political parties. Because of their consistently small numbers, they are typically not very important to election outcomes.

The party identification question thus produces seven categories of persons: Strong Democrats, Weak Democrats, Independent-leaning Democrats, Pure Independents, Independent-leaning Republicans, Weak Republicans, and Strong Republicans. Over the 40-year period during which political scientists have been asking these questions, the partisan preferences of the American public have been remarkably stable. The following table presents the party identification breakdown for the period from 1952 to 1992.

Party Identification, 1952–1992

	Strong Democrat	Weak Democrat	Independent-leaning Democrat	Pure Independent	Independent-leaning Republican	Weak Republican	Strong Republican	Apolitical
1952	22%	25%	10%	6%	7%	14%	14%	3%
1956	21	23	6	9	8	14	15	4
1958	27	22	7	7	5	17	11	4
1960	20	25	6	10	7	14	16	3
1962	23	23	7	8	6	16	12	4
1964	27	25	9	8	6	14	11	1
1966	18	28	9	12	7	15	10	1
1968	20	25	10	11	9	15	10	1
1970	20	24	10	13	8	15	9	1
1972	15	26	11	13	11	13	10	1
1974	18	21	13	15	9	14	8	3
1976	15	25	12	15	10	14	9	1
1978	15	24	14	14	10	14	8	2
1980	18	23	11	13	10	14	9	3
1982	20	24	11	11	8	14	10	2
1984	17	20	11	11	12	15	12	2
1986	18	22	10	12	11	15	11	2
1988	18	18	12	11	13	14	14	2
1990	17	19	12	11	13	17	11	2
1992	18	18	14	11	12	14	11	1

SOURCE: American National Election Studies.

Public Confidence in the Parties

Which political party, Republican or Democratic, do you think would do a better job with each of the following?

	Republican	Democratic
Unemployment	20%	65%
Environmental issues	24	59
Health care policy	20	62
Foreign affairs	64	25
Tax policy	30	49
National defense	57	28
Economic conditions	24	58
Race relations	22	58
Abortion	26	56
Education	25	60

What political party do you think would more likely keep the United States out of World War III?

33%	45%

What political party will do a better job of keeping the country prosperous?

42%	38%

Which party is best able to deal with the most important problems facing this country today?

34%	40%

SOURCE: *The Gallup Poll Monthly*, April 1992, July 1992.

How to Tell 'em Apart

- Republicans usually wear hats. Democrats usually don't.
- Democrats buy banned books. Republicans form censorship committees and read them.
- Democrats eat the fish they catch. Republicans hang them on the wall.
- Republicans study the financial pages of the newspaper. Democrats put them on the bottom of the bird cage.
- On Saturday, Republicans head for the golf course, the yacht club, or the hunting lodge. Democrats get a haircut, wash the car, or go bowling.
- Republicans have guest rooms. Democrats have spare rooms filled with old baby furniture.
- Republicans hire exterminators. Democrats step on the bugs.
- Republicans sleep in twin beds—some even in separate rooms. That is why there are more Democrats.

SOURCE: Adapted from the National Republican Congressional Committee newsletter.

"*Very* Republican. I love it."
Drawing by Tobey. © 1986
The New Yorker Magazine, Inc.

received 36 percent of his vote from Democrats, 44 percent from Republicans, and 17 percent from Independents.[36] That so much of his support came from both parties will prolong the realignment debate.

Further evidence of a voting realignment came in the early 1980s, when Republicans won several close Senate elections and gained a majority in that body. Democrats, however, won back the Senate in 1986, and until 1994 they seemed to have a permanent majority in the House. All of that seemed to change with the 1994 election as Republicans were swept into office with a tidal wave of victories. Including Senator Shelby's post-election change of party, Republicans had a net gain of nine seats. In the House the change was even more dramatic, given the fact that the Democrats had held a majority for 40 years. Republicans made major inroads in the South and strengthened their share of the vote among white males. Political scientists will be debating for years whether 1994 was indeed a realignment or only a transitory rejection of Bill Clinton and an unfocussed campaign by the Democrats.

What, then, should we make of recent voting behavior and a possible realignment? One argument, often espoused by Democrats, is that Republican success in presidential elections is the result of their stronger candidates and better campaigns. Republican presidential candidates have generally been seen in more positive terms than Democratic candidates. Voters have liked them more. Republican presidential campaigns have also done a better job of focusing the campaign on issues and themes that benefit their candidates and hurt Democrats. An exception to this was Clinton's keeping the focus of the 1992 election on the economy (It's the economy, stupid!), which helped him and hurt Bush. Clinton may not have been able to sustain this focus had it not been for Perot's stressing the deficit and economic issues.

Many who vote Democratic at the state and local levels and for Congress vote Republican for president. During the 1980s, these were called the Reagan Democrats. But large numbers of Democrats voting for the Republican presidential candidate while remaining loyal to other Democrats is not a realignment; rather, it suggests that if Democrats run stronger candidates and better campaigns, they should be able to win presidential elections as well.

Some think that, instead of a realignment, we are experiencing the rejection of partisanship in favor of becoming Independents. There has indeed been an increase in the number of persons who characterize themselves as Independents. Hedrick Smith, formerly of *The New York Times*, expresses a widespread view: "The most important phenomenon of American politics in the past quarter century has been the rise of independent voters who have at times outnumbered Republicans."[37] The implications of this contention have been speculated about by many political scientists.[38]

The **dealignment** argument—that people have abandoned both parties to become Independents—would be more persuasive were it not that two-thirds of all Independents are really partisans in their voting behavior and attitudes. One-third of the people who claim to be Independents lean toward the Democratic party and vote Democratic election after election. Another one-third of Independents lean Republican and just as predictably vote Republican. The remaining one-third, who appear to be genuine Independents and who do not vote predictably for one party, turn out to be people with little interest in politics. Despite the reported growth in Independents, there were proportionately about the same number of Pure Independents in 1992 as there were in 1956.[39] Table 10-2 summarizes voting behavior in contests for president in 1988 and 1992 and for U.S. House of Representatives in 1990.

Strong partisans are loyal to their party. Since 1952, Strong Republicans have voted Republican on average over 95 percent of the time, and Strong Democrats have voted Democratic more than 85 percent of the time. Weak and Independent-leaning Democrats have voted Democratic roughly two-thirds of the time over the past 40 years. Weak and Independent-leaning Republicans are even more predictably partisan, with more than 85 percent voting Republican on average since 1952. Weak and

Independent-leaning Republicans defect from their party more when voting for the U.S. House; about 1 in 3 votes Democratic. The elections summarized in Table 10-2 and the data going back to 1952 both clearly show that Independent-leaning Democrats vote as Democrats and Independent-leaning Republicans as Republicans. Pure Independents are volatile, voting heavily Republican for president in 1988 yet giving a plurality of their vote to Clinton (41 percent) in 1992.

Because most Independents are really closet partisans in their voting behavior and have been so for a long time, much of the case for the dealignment theory fails. Something about the parties inhibits most Independents from labeling themselves as partisans. However, it is a mistake to assume that all Independents see the political world in similar terms and constitute a monolithic force. There are instead at least three groups, and most of them are predictably partisan.

Why has realignment moved so slowly? Why aren't all conservatives now happily ensconced in the Republican party and all liberals gladly lodged in the Democratic party? Americans do not casually cross party lines. If you grew up in a conservative New Hampshire family whose forebearers voted Republican for a century, you are pretty much conditioned to stay with the GOP. Even if that party took a direction you disliked, you might continue to register as a Republican but quietly vote Democratic to avoid friction in the family. Or if you come from a "yellow dog" Democratic family in Texas (meaning your family would vote for a "yellow dog" before it would vote for a Republican), you might continue to vote for Democrats locally even though you disliked various Democratic candidates for president or U.S. senator. Evidence indicates that this pattern is common throughout the South.

The other reason for slow realignment is the local nature of the party. For decades, conservative Democrats in the South have been voting for Republican candidates for president—not only Bush and Reagan but for Nixon and even Eisenhower—without changing their identification from the Democratic party to

TABLE 10-2

Voting Behavior of Partisans and Independents, 1988-1992

| | Percent of Democratic Vote | | |
	President (1988)	U.S. House (1990)	President (1992)
Strong Democrats	93%	90%	93%
Weak Democrats	67	79	68
Independent-leaning Democrats	88	79	70
Pure Independents	32	61	41
Independent-leaning Republicans	14	32	11
Weak Republicans	16	39	14
Strong Republicans	2	17	3

SOURCE: American National Election Studies, Center for Political Studies, University of Michigan.

the Republican. Why? Partly because they still see themselves as Democrats, but partly because the Democratic party remains much stronger at the state and local level in the South. So if candidates and voters want to have an impact on local politics, in which the only meaningful elections may be in the Democratic primaries, they retain their Democratic affiliation. In 1992 Bill Clinton and Al Gore, both southerners, won their own states of Arkansas and Tennessee, as well as Georgia and Louisiana, and mounted a competitive campaign elsewhere in the South.

Are Political Parties Dying ?

The American party system faces three main charges: (1) parties do not take meaningful and contrasting positions on issues, especially the issues of the 1990s; (2) party membership is essentially meaningless, so that parties neither define issues critically nor are able to prosper organizationally; and (3) parties are so concerned with accommodating those on the middle of the ideological spectrum that they are incapable of serving as an avenue for social progress. How valid are these charges today?

Some experts fear parties are so weak they may be mortally ill, or at least in a long decline. They point first to the long-run impact of the Progressive reforms early in this century, reforms that robbed party organizations of their control of the nomination process by allowing masses of independent and "uninformed" voters to enter the primaries and vote for candidates who might not be acceptable to party leaders. They also point to nonpartisan elections in cities and towns and the staggering of national, state, and local elections that made it harder for parties to influence the election process. Legislation limiting the viability and functions of parties was bad enough, say the party pessimists, but parties suffer from further ills today.

The rise of television and videocassette campaigns and the parallel rise in campaign, media, and direct-mail consultants may have made parties irrelevant in educating, mobilizing, and organizing the electorate. (See Chapter 13 for more on the media in this role.) In addition, partly as a result of media influence, the most powerful electoral forces today are candidate organizations, not party organizations. Office seekers, supported by money and media, organize their personal following to win nominations (while the party leaders are supposed to stand by neutrally). If they win office, they are far more responsive to their personal following than to the party leadership, which means that the party lacks clout over politicians and policy.[40]

Advocates of strong parties concede parts of this diagnosis are correct: the demise of political machines at the local level, the decline in strong partisan affiliations, the weakness of grass-roots party membership. Yet they see signs of party revival they think the pessimists ignore. The national party organizations—the national committees and the congressional and senatorial campaign committees—are significantly better funded than they were in earlier days; they even own permanent, modern headquarters in Washington, D.C. Moreover, the parties are more capable of providing assistance to candidates and to state and local party organizations because of their strong financial base and because they have defined their role as providing expertise to those who need it but cannot otherwise obtain it. Optimists hope these advances will give the national parties some leverage over the positions that office seekers and officeholders take on party issues.[41]

How can the "party doctors" differ so widely in diagnosing the condition of the "patients"? Party pessimists have concentrated mostly on the Democratic party, which has been much weaker nationally than the Republican party, and on presidential elections, where the Democrats are weakest, rather than on congressional or gubernatorial results. With Clinton in the White House, Democrats show signs of rebirth as a viable national organization. Optimists, seeing what Republicans have been able to do for some years, have predicted correctly that Democrats would follow suit.

During the first year of the Reagan administration, the Republican party in Congress demonstrated a remarkable ability to vote together on issues of importance to the president's program. This trend can be measured by the *party unity score*, defined as the percentage of members of a party who vote together on roll call votes in Congress on which a majority of the members of one party vote against a majority of the members of the other party. Clinton had the highest party unity scores from his party in 1993 than any party in the past 40 years—88 percent of the Democrats voted together, while 87 percent of the Republicans voted together.[42] Clinton needed the strong support from his party in key votes on the budget and tax proposals but benefited also from strong Republican support on the NAFTA vote.

One other measure of party unity is a president's ability not to have to use the veto power, something Clinton was able to avoid in his first year in office—only the second time a president has done so in more than 60 years. Thus, while rank-and-file voters do not seem to be returning to strong partisan ties, party organizations and the party in government do show distinct and significant signs of strength.

Party Reform and Renewal

By the 1870s, William Marcy ("Boss") Tweed of the New York City party machine had been dethroned and jailed, but his image lived on—the image of a crooked power wielder at the center of a vast web of influence, buying votes from legislators and city councilors, handing out spoils to party henchmen, bribing officials when he could not control them outright, making corrupt deals with business interests, living off kickbacks from contractors, and commanding a following of "toughs" and strong-arm men. The essence of the boss's power lay in his control of nominations, which he accomplished by packing conventions with his own people.

REFORMS OF THE PROGRESSIVE MOVEMENT   As we have seen, by the dawn of the twentieth century, middle-class reformers, part of the Progressive movement, took the nominating process "back to the people" by means of the party primary, the direct election of U.S. senators, nonpartisan local elections, and civil service reforms. But many party experts hold the primary responsible for the downfall not only of the party bosses but also of parties themselves as responsible and efficient organizations. The conventions were not just a way to pick candidates; they also organized the grass-roots leadership of the party. In most cities and some states, the convention—and with it much of the leadership—simply disappeared.

REFORM AMONG THE DEMOCRATS   A second wave of party reform occurred after the 1968 election, when the Democrats, responding to the disarray during their Chicago convention and disputes about the fairness of delegate selection procedures, agreed to a process that led to greater use of direct primaries and greater representation of younger voters, women, and minorities among elected delegates. Another reform was the abolition of the rule that a winner of a state's convention or primaries got all the states' delegates. This rule was replaced by a system of proportionality in which candidates received delegates in rough proportion to the votes they received in the primary election.

Chicago's mayor Richard Daley, father of the current mayor of Chicago, and many other party stalwarts argued that these reforms would make the party reflective of the views of college professors and intellectuals, and not working-class people, unionists, elderly, and others. Some of those others included elected officials who either chose not to participate in the new processes or in some cases were not elected. Responding to this criticism, the party created "superdelegate" positions for such elected officials and party leaders.

REFORM AMONG THE REPUBLICANS   Republicans were not immune to criticism that their party conventions and party procedures were keeping out the rank-and-file. During this period they did not make changes as drastic as the Democrats, but they did give the national committee more control over presidential campaigns in an effort to avoid Watergate-type excesses, and state parties were urged to encourage broader participation by all groups, including women, minorities, youth, and the poor. While making these concessions to reformers within their own party, Republicans put more of their emphasis on improving the party structure to win elections. The Republican party entered the 1980s with a party organization far superior to that of the Democrats. The GOP emphasized grass-roots organization and membership recruitment. Seminars were held to teach Republican candidates how to make speeches and hold press conferences, and weekend conferences were organized for training young professionals. Both parties now conduct training sessions with candidates on campaign planning, advertising, fund raising, using phone banks, recruiting volunteers, and campaign scheduling.[43]

PARTY RENEWAL   Some politicians and scholars, both Republican and Democrat, are more interested in party *renewal* than party reform. In their view, the party system must be strengthened more than reformed. Those pushing for party renewal focus on the need to turn the party into a better structured, more active, more effective, and more policy-oriented organization.

The leadership of both parties may be strengthened by complex campaign laws and finance legislation, as well as sophisticated and expensive election technology, which led candidates at all levels to turn increasingly to the national party for technical advice and financial assistance. Although the national GOP remains a federation of state parties in theory, in practice national headquarters continues to gain more visibility and influence from its expanded services. The victory of Bill Clinton in 1992 and his campaign's ability to raise money may result in a strengthened Democratic party organization. One analyst observed that the parties have developed a division of labor between the national and state parties as well as between the national party and the congressional campaign committees that "requires a significant degree of coordination."[44]

SUMMARY

1. Political parties are essential to providing the choices, organizing the resources, and facilitating the representation needed in a modern constitutional democracy.

2. Political parties serve a wide variety of political and social functions. The most important of these are organizing the competition, simplifying choices, determining who shall hold office and exercise legitimate power, unifying the electorate, translating public preferences into policy, helping to organize government bridging the separation of powers by fostering coordination and cooperation among branches of government, and providing loyal opposition.

3. American parties are decentralized and organized around the unit of competition (states, congressional districts, countries, cities), which is usually at the state and local levels. Parties have declined both in organizational strength and in the esteem they hold among many Americans since the days in which they were described as strong political forces. Parties throughout our history have been seen as corrupting and are often feared. Yet both parties, at the national level and within state and local governments, have shown renewed signs of vitality.

4. American political parties are moderate. Our two major parties maintained their ascendancy in the past by bringing factions and interests together in coalitions broad enough to win the presidency and congressional elections.

5. Third parties have not been notably successful.

6. Parties are vital in the operation of government. Congress is organized around parties, and judicial and many executive branch appointments are based in large part on partisanship.

7. The two major parties have been criticized as being too much alike; yet this criticism is overstated if one looks at the policies they favor, their leadership, and their performance when in power. The parties are also said to be poorly organized and financed, a criticism that was more valid a decade ago than it is today.

8. American parties have experienced critical elections and realignments. Most political scientists agree the last realignment occurred in 1932. There has been in the period since the 1970s a growth in the number of persons who call themselves Independents—what is sometimes called dealignment. But most Independents are closet partisans who vote for the party toward which they lean.

FURTHER READING

MICHAEL BARONE, *Our Country: The Shaping of America from Roosevelt to Reagan* (Free Press, 1990).

JOHN F. BIBBY, *Politics, Parties and Elections in America* (Nelson-Hall, 1992).

THOMAS BYRNE EDSALL AND MARY D. EDSALL, *Chain Reaction: The Impact of Race, Rights, and Taxes on American Politics* (Norton, 1991).

LEON EPSTEIN, *Political Parties in the American Mold* (University of Wisconsin Press, 1986).

PAUL S. HERRNSON, *Party Campaigning in the 1980s: Have the National Parties Made a Comeback as Key Players in Congressional Elections?* (Harvard University Press, 1988).

WILLIAM J. KEEFE, *Parties, Politics, and Public Policy in America*, 6th ed. (Congressional Quarterly Press, 1991).

BRUCE E. KEITH, DAVID B. MAGLEBY, CANDICE J. NELSON, ELIZABETH ORR, MARK WESTLYE, AND RAYMOUND E. WOLFINGER, *The Myth of the Independent Voter* (University of California Press, 1992).

SIDNEY M. MILKIS, *The President and the Parties: The Transformation of the American Party System Since the New Deal* (Oxford University Press, 1993).

KEVIN PHILLIPS, *The Politics of Rich and Poor: Wealth and the American Electorate in the Reagan Aftermath* (Random House, 1990).

STEVEN J. ROSENSTONE, ROY L. BEHR, AND EDWARD H. LAZARUS, *Third Parties in America: Citizen Response to Major Party Failure* (Princeton University Press, 1984).

JAMES SUNDQUIST, *Dynamics of the Party System: Alignment and Realignment of Political Parties in the United States*, rev. ed. (Brookings Institution, 1983).

MARTIN P. WATTENBERG, *The Decline of American Political Parties, 1952–1988* (Harvard University Press, 1990).

PUBLIC OPINION, PARTICIPATION, AND VOTING

At the end of a nationally televised presidential debate in 1980, ABC News conducted a "call-in-your-vote" poll to determine the winner of the debate. Ted Koppel introduced the poll at 11:30 p.m. (Eastern Time) by saying:

> Good evening. The great presidential debate of 1980 is now history. For the past half-hour, and continuing throughout this broadcast,…ABC News is conducting a massive computerized telephone poll, nationwide. There will be no scientifically selected sample; only the votes of those who call in will be counted….The telephone company is charging 50 cents a call which will be added to your bill….A few of you are calling in and complaining that although you are calling for one candidate, you are receiving a recorded message confirming your vote for another candidate. We have checked that out with the telephone company; they assure us that the system is in fact working. It's the telephone company's system; we have to take their word for it.
>
> If you haven't called yet and would like to, here's how you can register your opinion as to who gained the most from tonight's debate: If you think President Carter gained the most, simply dial 1-900-590-1800. If you believe Governor Reagan gained more, dial 1-900-590-7400.[1]

Koppel stated that multiple calls from one telephone would not be recorded. At the end of the program Ronald Reagan had won. He had received 67 percent of the vote, compared to Jimmy Carter's 33 percent. The ABC-News Poll was cited by newspapers the next day as the first poll that declared Reagan the winner.[2]

Was this a valid poll? Did it correctly measure public opinion on the presidential debate? The answer is clearly no. The poll was flawed in a number of ways. First, the sample was self-selecting and not likely to be representative of the public or even of people who watched the debate on television. Despite ABC's claim, multiple voting may well have taken place. The timing of the poll also may have skewed the results. Many of Carter's supporters in his home region would have gone to bed before the poll began at 11:30 p.m., while in Reagan's home base of California it was only 8:30 p.m. Given the costs involved, poor people and those with less interest would have been discouraged from calling. It is also difficult to know whether the reports of switched recordings indicate that votes were miscounted. Finally, Koppel changed the wording of the question during the program from "Who won tonight's debate?" to "Who gained the most in tonight's debate?" This slight change could have brought different responses from some viewers.

This ABC call-in-your-vote poll is not the only example of how *not* to measure public opinion. Many local television news programs interview people on the street to assess local public opinion. Some major daily newspapers conduct weekly call-in polls that ask intentionally provocative questions. Even a straw poll of a meeting of Iowa hog farmers can generate national news.

In this chapter we will look at the nature of public opinion and how to measure it, how we formulate our political beliefs, the factors that affect the formation of our opinions, the nature and level of political participation in the United States, and why people vote as they do.

PUBLIC OPINION

Governments of all types must be concerned with public opinion, for unrest and protest can topple them. But in a constitutional democracy like ours, public opinion plays an even larger role. As we discussed in Chapters 1 and 7, our widely shared values include a belief in popular sovereignty, political equality, and majority rule.

Demonstrations and protest marches are an intense form of participation and can activate spectators whose attitudes have not yet been formed.

Individuals have opinions and express those opinions in a variety of ways, including protest demonstrations, letters to newspaper editors, and voting in free and regularly scheduled elections. Elected officials refer often to public opinion as a basis for their actions. In short, democracy and public opinion go hand in hand.

What Is Public Opinion?

We define **public opinion** as the distribution of individual preferences or evaluations of a given issue, candidate, or institution within a population. *Distribution* means the proportion of the population that holds one opinion or viewpoint as compared to those with opposing opinions or those with no opinion at all. For instance, had ABC pollsters conducted a scientific poll in 1980, they might have found 47 percent who felt Ronald Reagan had won the debate, 37 percent who felt Jimmy Carter had won, and 16 percent who did not know who won. This would be the distribution. The distribution in the last pre-election poll done by Gallup in 1992 was Clinton 44 percent, Bush 37 percent, Perot 14 percent, and undecided 5 percent. *Individual preferences* means that when we measure public opinion, we are asking individuals—not groups, elected officials, or journalists—about their opinions. The *universe* or *population* is the relevant group of people for the question. Public opinion can be classified not only according to distribution but according to the intensity with which individuals hold opinions, whether individuals hold opinions that they are not fully cognizant of (latent opinions), and the salience of the issue on which we are measuring opinion. We will explore each of these characteristics.

DISTRIBUTION Considering the electorate as a whole, we may find some issues on which most people agree or most people disagree. When a substantial percentage of a sample agree on an issue—for example, that schools should be racially integrated—there is a *consensus*. But on most issues, opinions are divided in various proportions. When a large portion of each side feels intensely about an issue, voters are said to be *polarized*. Vietnam in the 1960s and abortion in the 1990s are polarizing issues (see Table 11-1).

INTENSITY This factor produces the brightest and deepest hues in the fabric of public opinion. The fervor of people's beliefs varies greatly. For example, some individuals mildly favor gun-control legislation, while others mildly oppose it; still others are emphatically for or against it. Some people may have no interest in the matter at all; still others may not even have heard of it. Intensity is typically measured by asking people to indicate how strongly they feel on an issue or about a politician. Such a question is often called a *scale*.

LATENCY Latency refers to political opinions that exist merely as a potential; they may not have crystallized yet. But they are still important, for they can be evoked by leaders and converted into action. Latent opinions set rough boundaries for leaders who know that if they take certain actions they will trigger either opposition or support from millions of people. If leaders have some understanding of latent opinions, or people's real wants, needs, and hopes, they will know how to mobilize them and draw them to the polls on election day. Many who lived in communist Poland, East Germany, or Czechoslovakia must have had latent opinions favorable to democracy—opinions supporting majority rule, freedom, meaningful elections. The speed with which the public embraced democratic reforms was possible because leaders found widespread support for these ideas.

SALIENCE What causes opinions to be stable or fluid, intense or latent? A major factor is salience. By **salience** we mean the extent to which people feel that issues are relevant to them. Your next-door neighbor may feel intensely about abortion or gun control or Bill Clinton, whereas you may get excited about health care or

TABLE 11-1

How Opinions Differ on Abortion

| | Percent Saying Abortion Should Be | | | |
	Legal Under Any Circumstances	Legal Under Certain Circumstances	Illegal in All Circumstances	Don't Know
Total Adults	31%	53%	14%	3%
Age				
18–29 years	34	48	15	2
30–49 years	33	55	12	1
50–65 years	26	53	15	5
65 and over	22	53	18	7
Sex				
Men	28	55	13	4
Women	32	51	15	2
Education				
Less than high school	12	56	26	7
High school graduate	29	57	11	3
Some college	39	45	14	2
College graduate	42	47	10	1
Race				
White	31	53	13	3
Nonwhite	27	50	22	2
Black	21	52	26	1
Religion				
Protestant	29	54	15	3
Catholic	28	59	13	2
Political Philosophy				
Liberal	47	40	13	—
Moderate	29	57	11	4
Conservative	27	55	17	2
Party Identification				
Republican	27	56	13	5
Independent Republican	34	48	18	—
Independent	35	51	13	2
Independent Democrat	40	48	11	1
Democrat	31	52	16	1
Income				
Less than $20,000	26	54	17	4
$20,000–$29,000	26	61	10	4
$30,000–$49,999	33	51	15	—
More than $50,000	43	45	12	—

SOURCE: National survey by the Gallup Organization, January 1992. Figures may not add up to 100 percent due to rounding.

unemployment. Most people are more concerned about personal issues like paying the bills and keeping their jobs than about national issues. But if their personal concerns are connected with national issues, salience rises sharply.

Salience may change over time. During the Great Depression of the 1930s, Americans were mainly concerned about jobs, wages, and economic security. By the 1940s, foreign issues came to the fore. In the 1960s, problems of race and

"It should be a 'yes' or 'no' or 'undecided'—we don't accept a 'don't give a damn answer!'"

The Wall Street Journal, December 12, 1990.

poverty aroused intense feeling. Vietnam and then Watergate riveted the people's attention. By the 1990s, concern about jobs, drugs, street crime, welfare, health care, and the state of the environment had become salient issues.

How Do We Get Our Political Opinions and Values?

No one is *born* with political views. We learn them from many teachers. The process by which we develop our political attitudes, values, and beliefs is called **political socialization**. As we discussed earlier, this process starts in childhood, and the family and the schools are probably the two most important political teachers. A noted child psychologist concluded that children learn the content of our culture in childhood and adolescence but reshape it as they live their lives.[3] Socialization also lays the foundation for political beliefs, values, ideology, and partisanship.

One common element of political socialization in all cultures is **nationalism**, a consciousness of the nation-state and of belonging to that entity. Robert Coles describes nationalism:

> As soon as we are born, in most places on this earth, we acquire a nationality, a membership in a community. . . . A royal doll, a flag to wave in a parade, coins with their engraved messages—these are sources of instruction and connect a young person to a country. The attachment can be strong, indeed even among children yet to attend school, wherever the flag is saluted, the national anthem sung. The attachment is as parental as the words imply—homeland, motherland, fatherland. . . . Nationalism works its way into just about every corner of the mind's life.[4]

Political attitudes often stem from religious, racial, gender, ethnic, and economic beliefs and values. The sources of our views are immensely varied in the pluralistic political culture of the United States. But we can make at least one generalization safely: *We form our attitudes in groups,* not only in groups such as schools and social organizations but especially in close-knit groups like the family. When we identify closely with the attitudes and interests of a particular group, we tend to see politics through the "eyes" of that group.[5]

Group affiliation does not necessarily mean that individual members of the group do not think for themselves. Each member brings his or her own emotions, feelings, memories, and resistances to groups. The extent to which people are captive to groups is indeed a running argument among scholars from different disciplines. Sociologists tend to emphasize the pervasive influence of groups over their members. Certain schools of psychology focus more on the developmental stages within individuals that alternately prompt them to be joiners or loners. Political scientists have traditionally tended to agree more with the sociological approach.[6] Political psychologists seek to combine both approaches.

The considerable variation in the factors that influence our political beliefs produces a wide array of attitudes in society. However, children in the United States at an early age adopt common values that provide continuity with the past and legitimize the American political system. Young children know what country they live in, and their loyalty to the nation develops early. Although the details of our political system may still elude them, most young Americans acquire a respect for the Constitution and for the concept of participatory democracy as well as an initially positive view of the most visible figure in our democracy, the president.

FAMILY American children typically show political interest by the age of ten or even earlier, and by the early teens their interest may be fairly high. Learning experiences gradually shape the values and beliefs people acquire in childhood. Consider your own political learning process. You probably formed your picture of the world by listening to a parent at dinner or by absorbing the tales your older brothers and sisters brought home from school. Perhaps you heard about politics from grandparents, aunts, and uncles. You, in turn, influenced your family, if only by bringing some of your own hopes and problems home from school. What we first learn in the family is not so much specific political opinions as basic attitudes that shape our opinions—attitudes toward our neighbors, political parties, other classes or types of people, particular leaders (especially presidents), and society in general.

Studies of high school students indicate a high correlation between the political party of the parents and the partisan choice of the child. And this relatively high degree of correspondence continues throughout life. Such a finding raises some interesting questions: Does the *direct* influence of parents create the correspondence? Or are parents and children equally influenced by living in the same *social environment*—neighborhood, church, socioeconomic groups? The answer is both, and one influence often strengthens the other. A daughter of Democratic parents growing up in a small southern town with strong Democratic leanings will be affected by friends, by other adults, and perhaps by youngsters in a church group, all of whom may reinforce the attitudes of her parents.[7]

SCHOOLS Schools also mold young citizens' values and attitudes. American schools see part of their purpose as preparing students to be citizens and active participants in governing their communities and nation. At an early age, schoolchildren begin to pick up specific political values and acquire basic attitudes toward our system of government. Education, like the family, prepares Americans to live in society. It is a massive enterprise.

From kindergarten through college, children generally develop political values that will enhance their citizenship and legitimize the American political system. In their study of American history, schoolchildren are introduced to our nation's heroes and heroines, the important events in our history, and the ideals of our society. Other aspects of the student's experience, such as the daily Pledge of Allegiance, usually reinforce respect of country. In school, children also often gain practical experience in the workings of democracy through elections for class or school officers and student government. In some colleges, state legislatures or college trustees have made a course or courses in U.S. history or American government a graduation requirement.

Do school influences give young people greater faith in political institutions? Yes and no. A classic study examined relationships among community leaders'

Nationalism is reinforced by patriotic activities such as the Pledge of Allegiance in school.

Taking the Pulse of the People

Public opinion polls of varying types have long been part of American politics, but the advent of computers and modern social science techniques enormously expanded the use of survey research. The hallmarks of scientific polls are proper sampling, unambiguous and fair questions, professional interviewing, and thorough analysis and reporting of the results.

Proper sampling is based on random choices of the appropriate set of people. *Random choice* means that every individual has an equal chance of being selected. For instance, a survey of 18-to-24 year olds should not be done solely among college students, since roughly three-quarters of this age group are not college students. The accuracy of poll results depends largely on securing an appropriate sample representative of the universe of people.

The art of asking questions is also important to scientific polling. The wording of questions can influence the answers given. Good questions are fair, have been pretested, and are delivered by trained and professional interviewers who read the questions exactly as written and without any intonation in their voices. Questions are worded in different ways to measure factual knowledge, opinion on issues or controversies, intensity of opinion, or views on hypothetical situations. The order of questions can also alter the responses, making it important to know all the questions asked in a poll before evaluating the responses to any given question. Questions that permit the respondents to answer in their own words are called *open-ended* questions.

Thorough analysis and reporting of the results are expected of scientific polls. When polls are conducted in person or on the telephone, the results can be immediately analyzed and released. Scientific polls must indicate the sample size, the margin of expected statistical error for a standard question, and when the poll was conducted.

attitudes, civics texts, and students' attitudes in three Boston communities—one upper-middle class, one lower-middle class, and one working class. The school texts in all three communities stressed the right of citizens to try to influence government, but only the texts used in the upper-middle-class community stressed politics as conflict and as a process for adjusting differing group demands. And only the upper-middle-class community had leaders who underscored politics as a *conflict* process, thus reinforcing the lessons in the texts. Edgar Litt, a political scientist, concluded that the lower-middle-class students were learning that government was a process carried out by institutions in their behalf, while the upper-middle-class students were learning that the political process was something they could influence.[8]

How does *college* influence political opinions? One study suggests that students planning to attend college are more likely to be knowledgeable about politics, more in favor of free speech, and more likely to talk and read about politics.[9] Reflecting national trends, campus conservatism and Republicanism increased in the 1980s; but there are indications from the same study that college students in the 1990s were again more liberal.[10] Is this the influence of the professors, the curriculum, or the students? It is difficult to generalize. Parents sometimes fear professors have too much influence on their college-age children; however, most professors doubt they have significant influence over students. The debate about whether there is peer pressure on college campuses to conform to certain acceptable ideas—so-called *political correctness* (PC)—reinforces the point that college is a time when attitudes and values are confronted and defined.

MASS MEDIA   Family and school are not the only influences on children and adolescents. The mass media also serve as agents of socialization by providing a link between individuals and the values and behavior of others. For example, the mass media present information about our society, and when we watch, listen, and read, we discover which values and role models are considered important. Events that get intensive media coverage often focus our attention on certain issues, as, for example, the televised Senate hearings of the Clarence Thomas confirmation for the Supreme Court. Those hearings directed widespread attention to the issue of sexual harassment in the workplace. The role of the mass media as a socializing force is discussed in greater detail in Chapter 13.

OTHER INFLUENCES   Religious and ethnic attitudes also serve to shape opinions, both within and outside the family. Historically, Protestant families tend to be more conservative than Catholics on economic and welfare issues, whereas Jewish families tend to be more liberal on both economic and noneconomic issues than either Catholics or Protestants. Protestants vary widely on certain social issues. Evangelicals–whose numbers include a small percentage of Catholics but are mainly made up of Protestants from the more fundamentalist sects—are generally much more socially conservative than nonevangelicals.[11]

Generalizations about how people vote are useful, but we have to be careful about stereotyping people. True, Jewish families tend to be more liberal on both economic and noneconomic issues than either Catholics or Protestants, but there are lots of conservative Jewish families and liberal Catholic and Protestant ones. It is dangerous to assume that because we know a person's religious preferences or ethnic background we can know his or her political opinions. Moreover, all persons are subject to **cross-pressures**—racial, religious, ethnic, or other group pressures that pull an individual in different directions.

What happens when a young person's parents and friends disagree? One study revealed that when high school students were cross-pressured in this way, they tended to go along with parents rather than friends on party affiliation; with friends rather than parents on issues like the death penalty or gun control; and somewhere in between on their actual votes in presidential elections.[12]

Stability and Change in Public Opinion

Most of us do not change our opinions very often. Even if the world changes rapidly around us, we are slow to change our minds about things that matter to us or to shift our loyalties. In general, people who remain in the same place, in the same occupation, and in the same income group throughout their lives tend to have more stable opinions. But people can carry their attitudes with them. Families who move from cities to suburbs often retain their big-city attitudes long after they have moved.

Adults are not simply the sum of all their early experiences, however. Political analysts are becoming more interested in the ways in which adults modify their views *after* completing school or college. A major factor may be a harsh experience, such as a war, economic depression, or loss of a job, that shocks people out of their existing attitudes. A clear example of how public opinion change can lead to policy change is the issue of troop withdrawal from Vietnam. "Public opinion had a substantial impact on the rate of troop withdrawals."[13]

In the recent Persian Gulf War, opposition to the use of U.S. forces was greatly reduced after a few days of success in the air and ground war. When American forces were dispatched to Somalia in Operation Restore Hope in January 1993, 79 percent approved of the use of troops to ensure the delivery of humanitarian aid, food, and medical provisions. But when U.S. soldiers were killed and dragged through the streets of Mogidishu, support fell to only 17 percent in October of the same year.[14]

Sometimes even the strongest and most stable opinions are subject to change. One of the "sacred cows" of American politics in the 1950s and 1960s was non-recognition of the People's Republic of China. A powerful lobby, composed of leaders of both major parties, carried on a militant campaign against admitting mainland China to the United Nations. Then President Richard Nixon, who had earlier opposed the recognition of the People's Republic, made a dramatic trip to China and promoted a policy of conciliation toward Beijing. Many Americans, responding to Nixon's leadership, shifted their own position toward friendlier relations with China. But, with the massacre of students in Tiananmen Square in 1989, American attitudes toward the *government* of China hardened again.

Public Opinion and Public Policy

An important issue regarding polling is the question of leadership. Walter Lippmann's classic book *Public Opinion* raises the concern that political leaders could defer too much to public opinion rather than informing and leading it.[15] Edmund Burke, a political philosopher and member of Parliament writing in the 1770s, distinguished between officials who saw their job as *following* public opinion (a group he called *delegates)* and officials who believed they had been elected to *lead* (a group Burke called *trustees*).

For much of human history it has been difficult to measure public opinion. "What I want," Abraham Lincoln once said, "is to get done what the people desire to be done, and the question for me is how to find that out exactly." Another president, Woodrow Wilson, once complained to the newspapers that they had no business saying what people thought: "You do not know, and the worst of it, since the responsibility is mine, I do not know, what they are thinking about. I have the most imperfect means of finding out, and yet I have got to act as if I knew."

Politicians in our day do not face the uncertainty about public opinion faced by Lincoln and Wilson. They can and do know what public opinion is on all major policy issues. But public opinion is not always stable and consistent. On many issues, public opinion can change once the public learns more about the issue or perceives

How You Ask It Shapes How You Answer It

How you ask a polling question makes a lot of difference in the responses people give, as demonstrated by the way three different polls asked about special interests and campaign finance. The first question was written by Ross Perot's own organization, and not an individual survey researcher. It was included in a mail survey prior to the 1992 presidential campaigns and was published in *TV Guide* and asked individuals to send in their answers. Perot's survey was criticized widely by survey organizations for its skewed sample and biased questions. The second and third questions were part of national surveys conducted by professional polling firms using random samples.

1. Should laws be passed to eliminate all possibilities of special interests giving huge sums of money to candidates?
Yes   99%

2. Should laws be passed to prohibit interest groups from contributing to campaigns, or do groups have a right to contribute to the candidate they support?
Prohibit contribution   40%
Groups have right   55%

3. Please tell me whether you favor or oppose the proposal: The passage of new laws that would eliminate all possibility of special interests giving large sums of money to candidates.
Favor   70%
Oppose   28%

SOURCE: Daniel Goleman, "Pollsters Enlist Psychologists in Quest for Unbiased Results," *The New York Times*, September 7, 1993, pp. C1, C11.

"Young man, I am no random sample."
© Punch/Rothco.

Despite pollsters' predictions that his opponent, Thomas E. Dewey, would be elected president, and despite the Chicago Tribune headline to that effect, Harry Truman won the 1948 election.

there is another side to the question. It is on these issues that politicians can help shape attitudes. Consider the issue of racial segregation in housing. Had legislators and judges in many states only followed public opinion, open housing laws would not have been passed by legislatures or affirmed by the courts. But current public opinion on this question is very different from what it was 25 years ago, in part because some politicians at that time were willing to risk their political careers by attempting to change public opinion.

More typically, elected officials seek to follow public opinion. Gaining reelection has been found to be a driving motive for most members of Congress.[16] There is evidence that "legislators show greater attention to public opinion as election day looms," and the closeness of fit between constituent opinion and roll-call voting reflects that connection.[17] Candidates use polls to determine where to campaign, how to campaign, and even whether to campaign. In the years and months preceding a national convention, politicians watch the polls to determine who among the hopefuls has political appeal. Have polls become more important than voters in influencing who can mount a viable campaign?

The accuracy of some political polls is suspect. More than 80 percent of newspapers and half of television stations conduct or commission their own polls.[18] These media polls are often not conducted as carefully as the academic polls conducted at major universities, but they play a major role in shaping public opinion.[19]

One such type of poll is *election forecasting*—the use of polls to predict in advance how an election will turn out. During the campaign pollsters submit regular "returns" on the standings of the candidates. On the whole, the record of the leading forecasters in "day-before" polling has been good, as Table 11-2 shows.

The most sensational slip in election forecasts came in 1948, during the presidential battle between President Harry Truman and New York Governor Thomas E. Dewey. Most polls indicated Truman was running far behind, and most pollsters stood pat on their predictions Governor Dewey would win. Early in September one of them actually announced the race was over. Gallup gave the president only 45 percent of the popular vote in his final forecast, and Roper predicted 37 percent.

Preelection polls charted an up-and-down course for Republican George Pataki's campaign to replace New York's three-term incumbent governor, Democrat Mario Cuomo. At the start of the campaign, Pataki trailed by a large margin, then caught up and passed Cuomo. In the final days, polls showed Cuomo winning, but on election night, Pataki was victorious.

TABLE 11-2

Presidential Winners Forecast by the Pollsters (by percentage)

Year	Actual Vote	Roper Poll	Gallup Poll	Harris Poll
1944	54%	54%	53%	—
1948	49	37	45	—
1952	45*	43	46	—
1956	42	40	40	—
1960	49	47	49	—
1964	61	—	61	—
1968	43	—	40	43
1972	38	—	35	35
1976	51	51	46*	46*
1980	41	—	44	41
1984	41	45	41	48
1988	46	—	45	48
1992**	43	—	44	44

*In 1976 both Gallup and Harris said it was a "toss-up" and refused to make a prediction. They also reported that more people than usual had not made up their minds.

**In 1992, CBS/New York Times, The Washington Post, USA Today/CNN, and Wall Street Journal/NBC all predicted Bill Clinton would win with 44 percent of the vote; ABC predicted his vote as 43 percent

On election day, Truman won 49 percent of the popular vote, and the pollsters were subjected to general ridicule. Their mistake lay in not selecting a representative sample of the universe; instead, they relied on a nonrandom sample to make their predictions. Since then pollsters have been more careful in their methods and more cautious in making predictions.[20]

Surely polls are no substitute for elections. Faced with a ballot, voters must translate opinions into concrete decisions between personalities and parties. They must decide what is important and what is not. Democracy is more than the expression of views, more than a simple mirror of opinion. It also involves choosing among leaders, taking sides on certain issues, and selecting the governmental actions that may follow. Democracy is the thoughtful participation of people in the political process; it means using heads as well as counting them. Elections, with all their failings, at least establish the link between the many voices of "We the People" and the decisions of their leaders. In Chapter 12 we will examine the biggest, fairest, and most decisive "public opinion poll" of all—elections. Before examining who votes and why they vote as they do, we need to understand more about citizen awareness and interest.

AWARENESS AND INTEREST

For most people, politics is of secondary importance to earning a living, raising a family, and having a good time, and some Americans are more concerned about which team wins the Superbowl than they are about who wins the school board elections, who gets to be mayor, even who gets to be president of the United States. Most people find politics complicated and difficult to understand. And they should, for democracy *is* complicated and difficult to understand. But it helps to understand the mechanics and structures of our government: how the government operates, how the electoral college works, how many chambers there are in Congress, the length of terms for the president and for members of the Senate and House of Representatives, for example. These aspects of government are typically best known by younger persons, who remember learning them in school.

The general adult public, however, fares poorly when quizzed about elected officials (see Table 11-3). Less than half of Americans are able to recall the name of their member of Congress, and only 60 percent can name even one of their U.S. senators.[21] With so many voters not knowing who represents them in Congress, it is not surprising that "on even hotly debated congressional issues, few people know where their Congress member stands."[22]

Although the public's knowledge of institutional and candidate issues is poor, its knowledge of important public policy issues is worse. In the 1948 presidential election, candidates Dewey and Truman debated the Taft-Hartley Act throughout the entire campaign, and the two parties took opposite positions. Yet at the time of the election, 30 percent of the voters had never heard of the act and had no opinion on it. Thirty years later, in the midst of an energy crisis, 40 percent of adult Americans did not know that the United States imported oil. In 1982, after years of debate over ratification of the Equal Rights Amendment, nearly one-third of the adults in the United States indicated they had never heard of it. In late August 1993, several weeks before the vote in Congress on the North American Free Trade Agreement (NAFTA), 6 out of 10 Americans reported they were not following the NAFTA story at all.[23]

Fortunately, not all Americans are uninformed or uninterested. Since 1960, about 25 percent of the public have been interested in politics most of the time. They are the *attentive public*, people who know and understand how the government works, vote in most elections, read a daily newspaper, and "talk politics" with their families and friends. They tend to be better educated and more committed to democratic values than are other Americans.

TABLE 11-3

Political Participation and Awareness in the United States

Vote in presidential elections	50%
Vote in congressional elections	35–40
Know name of congressional representative	36
Know names of both U.S. senators	29
Occasionally contact local officials	28
Vote in local elections	10–30
Occasionally attend public meetings	19
Occasionally contact federal or state officials	16
Know name of state senator	13
Give money to candidate or party	13
Know name of state representative	12

SOURCES: Selected polls, including Gallup, Denver Post, National Election Studies at the University of Michigan, and *The New York Times*.

At the opposite end of the spectrum are *nonvoters*–people who are rarely interested in politics or public affairs and rarely vote. Since 1960, about 35 percent of Americans have indicated that they have little interest in politics or are only occasionally interested.[24] A subset of this group might be called *chronic political know-nothings*. These individuals not only avoid political activity but have little interest in government and limited knowledge about it.

Between the attentive public and the nonvoters are the *part-time citizens*, roughly 40 percent of the American public. These individuals participate selectively in elections, voting in presidential elections but usually not in others. Politics and government do not greatly interest them; they pay only minimal attention to the news, and they rarely discuss candidates or elections with others. Figure 11-1 shows the varying participation in politics.

Our democracy can probably survive with a large number of citizens being passive about politics and little interested in it. In fact, a good case can be made that democracies are more stable when interest in politics does not become too intense. Yet there is evidence that we do need a substantial number of people to be concerned about policy issues and involved in politics.

PARTICIPATION: TRANSLATING OPINIONS INTO ACTION

Americans can influence their government's actions in several different ways, many of which are protected by the Constitution. Destruction of property and physical violence fall into a category of unlawful participation, but our political system is remarkably tolerant of protest that is not destructive or violent. Boycotts, picketing, sit-ins, and marches are all legally protected. Rosa Parks and Martin Luther King, Jr., used the peaceful breaking of the law to protest what they saw to be problems with that law. The number of Americans who participate in such protests is small, but the impact of their actions in shaping public opinion can be substantial.

A distinguishing characteristic of a democracy is that citizens can influence government decisions by participating in politics. In totalitarian societies, participation is very limited, forcing people who want to influence government to violence or revolution. When the Soviet Union refused to use its forces to put down candlelight protests by East Germans in Leipzig and other cities in 1989, 20 years of communist rule collapsed. But protests and responses are not always peaceful or successful. The protest of Chinese students in Tiananmen Square failed to stop the onslaught of tanks and the repression that followed. Americans sometimes forget that our democracy was born of this kind of revolution, and that the creation of a constitutional democracy is much more difficult and demanding of public participation than is maintaining one. The people of Haiti, Russia, and the former Yugoslavia are experiencing these difficulties firsthand during the 1990s.

Even in an established democracy, people may feel so strongly about an issue that they would rather fight than accept the verdict of an election. Our most classic example is the Civil War. Following the election of 1860 the South took up arms, sensing a popular tide against slavery. War marked the breakdown of democracy. Examples in our own time include antiabortion groups that use violence to press their political agenda.

In the 1960s a larger number, but still a distinct minority of Americans, actively sought to influence government policy in Vietnam by writing letters to public officials and editors of their local newspapers, circulating petitions to present to the president and Congress, joining or contributing to interest groups, and attending political meetings, and marches. Participation in these ways takes time and a sense of confidence about influencing government. Most Americans choose not to get

FIGURE 11-1 Level of Interest in Politics, 1992

SOURCE: 1992 American National Election Study, Center for Political Studies, University of Michigan Ann Arbor.

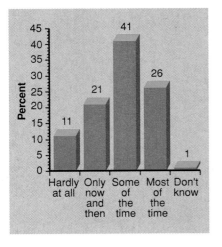

involved in these ways, sometimes because they lack confidence that their effort will make a difference or because they lack the time or means to invest in this type of participation.

Large numbers of Americans routinely participate in such rituals of democracy as singing the National Anthem or reciting the Pledge of Allegiance. They communicate about government and politics to their children and grandchildren. They serve as jurors in courtrooms and enlist in the military. They express concern about the involvement of American military forces in foreign hostilities. They complain about taxes and government regulations. And each year millions of Americans visit Washington, D.C., and other historic sights.

VOTING

Voting is the type of political activity most often engaged in by Americans. The United States is a constitutional democracy with many decades of free and open elections and a tradition of the peaceful transfer of power between competing groups and parties.

Originally the Constitution left the individual states free to determine the crucial question of who could vote, and the qualifications for voting differed considerably from state to state. All states barred women from voting, many did not permit blacks to vote, and property ownership was sometimes a requirement. By the time of the Civil War, the franchise had been extended to all white male citizens in every state. Since that time, the ability of states to set eligibility standards for voting has been restricted by four constitutional amendments (see box on Expanding the Franchise).[25]

The civil rights movement in the 1960s, which made voting rights a central issue, secured adoption of the Twenty-fourth Amendment and passage of the 1965 Voting Rights Act. The Voting Rights Act banned literacy tests, eased registration requirements, and provided for the replacement of local election officials with federal registrars in areas where the denial of the right to vote had been most blatant. Its passage resulted in a dramatic expansion of black registration and voting. Once blacks were permitted to register to vote "the focus of voting discrimination shifted . . . to preventing them from winning elections."[26] In southern legislative districts where blacks are in the majority, however, there has been a "dramatic increase in the proportion of black legislators elected."[27]

Turnout

Americans hold more elections for more offices than do citizens of any other democracy. In most states citizens can vote in a general election, one or more primary elections, and special elections on local matters. For example, in a two-year period, voters in Pasadena, California, had the option of voting in as many as five elections (see Table 11-4).

In part because there are so many elections, American voters tend to pick and choose which elections to vote in. Americans elect officeholders in general elections, determine party nominees in primary elections, and conduct special elections to replace senators who have died or left office. Elections held in years when the president is on the ballot are called *presidential election years*. If the election is held midway between presidential elections, it is called a *midterm election*. Elections held in odd calendar years are often called *off-year elections*. Midterm elections like the one in 1994 elect about one-third of the U.S. Senate, all members of the House of Representatives, most governors and other statewide officeholders, as well as large numbers of state legislators. Many local elections are held in the spring of odd-numbered years in which voters elect city councils and mayors.

We The People

Expanding the Franchise

1870 Fifteenth Amendment forbade states from denying the right to vote because of "race, color, or previous condition of servitude."

1920 Nineteenth Amendment gave women the right to vote.

1924 Congress passed law granting Native Americans citizenship and voting rights.

1964 Twenty-fourth Amendment prohibited the use of poll taxes.

1965 Voting Rights Act removed restrictions that kept blacks from voting.

1971 Twenty-sixth Amendment extended the vote to citizens age 18 and older.

Americans vote frequently and for a wide variety of public offices, as these voters in Centerville, Massachusetts, are doing.

TABLE 11-4

Voter Participation in Pasadena, California, 1990–1992

	Number	Percent
1990 voting age population	102,608	
Average voter registration	63,324*	62%
Turnout		
1990 statewide primary election****	24,692	24
1990 statewide general election****	34,909**	34
1991, March, school board primary election	16,169***	16
1991, April, school board general election	6,397***	6
1992 statewide primary election****	23,193	23
1992 statewide general election*****	47,346	46
1993, March, school board primary election	40,134	38
1993, April, school board general election	10,626	10
1993 statewide special election	18,303	17
1994 statewide primary election****	17,236	16
1994 statewide general election****	31,225	30

SOURCES: Beatrice Valdez, assistant registrar, Los Angeles County; Marrell Herren, Pasadena City Clerk; census data from Department of Finance, California State Data Center

*Average of voter registration for 1990–91.

**Absentee ballots not counted at city level; county-wide average of 14 percent added for estimate of in-person and absentee voting.

***Pasadena vote calculated on the basis of 62 percent of registered voters in school district residing in Pasadena.

****Includes candidates for state and federal offices.

FIGURE 11-2 Voter Turnout in Presidential and Midterm Elections, 1990–1994

SOURCE: U.S. Bureau of the Census, *Statistical Abstract of the United States*, 1993 (Government Printing Office, 1993) p. 284. For 1994, Committee for the Study of the American Electorate.

Turnout—the proportion of the voting-age public that votes—is highest in presidential general elections (see Figure 11-2). It is higher in general elections than in primary elections and higher in primary elections than in special elections. Turnout is higher in presidential general elections than in midterm general elections and higher in presidential primary elections than in midterm primary elections.[28] Turnout is higher in elections in which candidates for federal office are on the ballot (U.S. senator, member of the House of Representatives, president) than in state elections in years when there are no federal contests. Some states elect their governor and other state officials in odd-numbered years to separate state from national politics. The result is generally lower turnout. Finally, local or municipal elections have lower turnout than state elections, and municipal primaries have even lower rates of participation.

Voting laws also affect rates of voting. One peculiarly American legal requirement—voter registration—discourages voting. Most other democracies have automatic voter registration. As Table 11-5 indicates, turnout in American elections is lower than in most other democracies. This was not always the case. In fact, in the 1800s, turnout in the United States was much like that of Europe today. Turnout began to drop significantly around the turn of the century, in part as a result of election reform (see Figure 11-3).

In the 1800s ballots were prepared by the parties, often using different colors of paper that allowed them to monitor how people had voted. In some areas charges of multiple voting generated a reform movement that substituted the **Australian ballot**, a secret ballot printed by the state, for the party ballots and initiated **voter registration** to reduce multiple voting and limit voting to those who had previously established their eligibility.

Voter Registration

Registration laws vary by state, but in every state except North Dakota registration is required in order to vote. Three states permit election-day voter registration. The most important provision regarding voter registration may be the closing date. A few years ago it was not uncommon for closing days to be six months before the election; now, by federal law, no state can stop registration more than 30 days before an election.[29] Voter registration places a responsibility on voters to take an extra step—usually filling out a form at the county courthouse or with a roving registrar—some days or weeks before the election. Other important

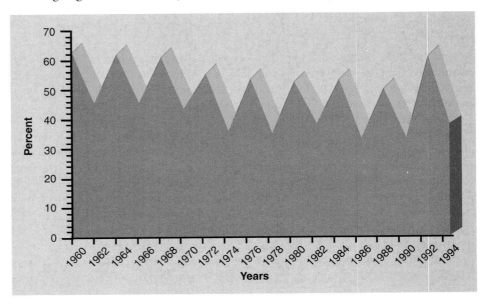

TABLE 11-5

Registration and Voting in the World's Democracies

	Average Turnout as Percent of Eligible Vote	Compulsion Penalties*	Automatic Registration**
Australia	88%	Yes	No
Austria	88	No	Yes
Belgium	88	Yes	Yes
Canada	68	No	Yes
Denmark	85	No	Yes
Finland	82	No	Yes
France	78	No	No
Ireland	77	No	Yes
Israel	80	No	Yes
Italy	94	Yes	Yes
Japan	72	No	Yes
Netherlands	82	No	Yes
New Zealand	83	No	No
Norway	82	No	Yes
Spain	78	No	Yes
Sweden	88	No	Yes
Switzerland	44	No	Yes
United Kingdom	75	No	Yes
United States	54	No	Yes
West Germany	85	No	Yes

SOURCE: G. Bingham Powell Jr., "American Voter Turnout in Comparative Perspective," *American Political Science Review* 80 (March 1986), p. 38.

*Compulsion penalties are fines or other possible state actions against nonvoters.

**Automatic registration utilizes other forms of citizen identification like a driver's license.

FIGURE 11-3   Voter Turnout in Presidential Elections, 1800–1992

SOURCES: For 1800 to 1992, Walter Dean Burnham, "The Turnout Problem," in *Elections American Style*, ed. A. James Reichley (Brookings, 1987), pp. 113–114; for 1960 to 1992, U.S. Bureau of the Census, *Statistical Abstract of the United States, 1993* (Government Printing Office, 1993), p. 284.

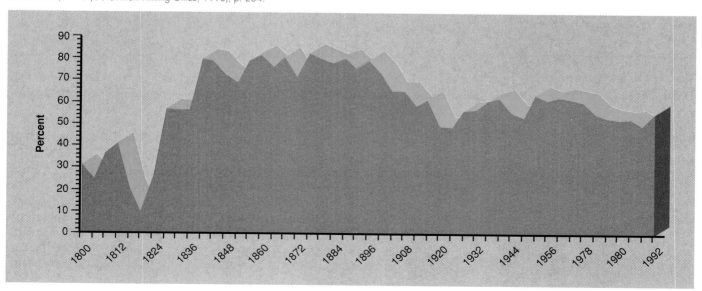

President Bill Clinton and House Speaker Tom Foley admire a T-shirt presented to them after the signing of the Motor Voter bill on May 20, 1993. The bill allows people to register to vote at any motor vehicle office in the country.

provisions include places of registration, and hours of registration. Each provision limits turnout. If registration were simply extended until the day of the election, turnout would probably increase by 6 percent,[30] and if this extension were combined with other reforms, it is estimated the rate of voting could be increased by more than 9 percent.[31]

Turnout over Time

In 1960, turnout peaked at almost 63 percent, but it has since declined.[32] Turnout should have gone up since 1960 because the Voting Rights Act of 1965 added large numbers of African Americans to the pool of registered voters. Women, another historically underrepresented group, have also increased their voting levels to the point where turnout among women since 1988 actually exceeds that of men.[33] Finally, our electorate has grown richer and more educated since the 1960s, and since wealth and education are related to voting, we should have seen an increase instead of a decrease in voting. However, 85 million Americans have failed to vote in recent presidential elections; the nonvoting figures are even higher for congressional, state, county, and local elections.[34] Voting did increase in 1992, rising by 5 percent over 1988—a result of the high level of interest in that particular election.

The Motor-Voter Bill

After many years of debates, voter registration procedures were eased a bit when, on May 20, 1993, President Bill Clinton signed the National Voter Registration Act, the "motor-voter" bill, so called because it allows people to register to vote while applying for or renewing a driver's license. It also requires states to designate offices that provide welfare and disabled assistance to facilitate voter registration. States have the option to include public schools, libraries, and city and county clerks' offices as registration sites. The law also requires states to allow registration by mail using a standardized form. It does not allow removal of names from voting rolls for nonvoting, but only for a change in residence or death.

Proponents of the law say it will reach the 49 million Americans of voting age with driver's licenses or identification cards but who have not registered to vote. Opponents claim the new law is another federal mandate that does not appropriate money to pay for the costs involved. They also assert it will increase election fraud because of the difficulty in removing names from voting rolls.

Why Is Turnout So Low?

If almost half of all eligible voters are not participating in elections, they too are expressing an opinion. Who fails to vote? Why? Is low voter turnout a serious problem in a democracy? If so, what can be done about it?

The simplest explanation for low turnout is that people are lazy. The problem is not that simple. Of course, some people are apathetic, but the vast majority of Americans are not. Paradoxically, we compare favorably with other nations in political interest and awareness,[35] but for a variety of institutional and political reasons, we fail to convert these qualities into votes (see Table 11-6).

The cost of voting is higher in the United States than in other industrial democracies, while the perceived benefits are lower.[36] By "cost" we mean the expenditure of time and effort required to vote. In our system, individuals face tough institutional obstacles to voting, and they must make sense of a range of political alternatives that do not necessarily meet their interests. Voter registration, already examined, appears to be the major block to voting.[37]

TABLE 11-6

Why People Don't Vote

Did not register	42%
Do not like the candidates	17
Are not interested in politics	5
Are sick or disabled	8
Are not U.S. citizens	5
Are new residents in area	4
Are away from home	3
Cannot leave job	3
Have no way to get to polls	1
Other reasons	2
No particular reason	10

SOURCE: Gallup poll, 1980.

Another factor in the decline of voter turnout since the 1960s is the Twenty-sixth Amendment, which lowered the voting age to 18. It increased the number of eligible voters, but among the group that is least likely to vote. With ratification of the amendment in 1971, turnout fell from 61 percent in 1968 to 55 percent in 1972.[38] The effect of adding this low turnout group to the electorate has been to lower the overall turnout rate.

In other large industrialized democracies, the political parties shoulder much of the burden of persuading people to vote. American parties are too weak to take on this task; in particular, the Democratic party, which has an enormous stake in a heavy voter turnout from lower-income Americans, seldom achieves the voting participation it wants.

Another factor in low turnout is the absence of real competition in many election contests. Many cities and regions have a "one-and-a-half party" system—as in Chicago, Boston, Washington, Rhode Island, Utah, Hawaii, and Kansas. In such cities or states one party dominates while the other party only competes occasionally.

Some Americans believe it makes no difference who wins. They claim that there is no real choice between candidates or parties, that winning candidates and parties fail to carry out their promises, and that the same people run the government no matter who wins.

Other critics say the reason people do not vote is that our political leaders do not appeal to the voters. Candidates, it is argued, do not offer "real" choices; they are not exciting or avoid taking positions on important issues. Yet in several recent elections there have been important differences between the candidates that included different stands on such salient issues as abortion, welfare, and jobs. During the 1992 election campaign there was much discussion of voter anger and frustration with government. Widespread concern with the economy, interest generated by Ross Perot's candidacy, and the perception that there was a need for change in the government motivated a record number of Americans to vote in the 1992 elections. More than 10 percent of the people who voted in 1992 were voting for the first time, and these new voters generally supported Bill Clinton. Turnout rose by 5 percentage points over the 1988 election, and in some states, the increase was as much as 10 percent. Was this increase a response to the unusual nature of the 1992 election or an indication of a trend of greater voter interest and participation that will continue when we do not have a tightly contested three-way presidential race?

College students have comparatively low rates of voting, which may be because they are involved in matters other than politics. Older citizens are more likely to vote and participate in the political process.

What If They Held an Election and No One Voted?

Such an election actually happened in Centreville, Mississippi, in 1993. Candidate Danny Jones appeared to be a sure winner for a seat on the board of aldermen (city council), in part because he was the only candidate. But no one actually voted, including Jones, who had to work late on election day. State law requires winners to get at least one vote, so a special election had to be held, at which Jones received 45 votes.

SOURCE: *Parade Magazine*, January 2, 1994, p. 4.

Who Voted in 1994?

Race

White	79%
Black	13
Hispanic	5

Sex

Men	49%
Women	51

Education

Not High School graduate	5%
High School Graduate	22
Some college	32
College graduate	22
Postgraduate	19

VOTED IN 1992 FOR:

Clinton	45%
Bush	37
Perot	12

THIS COUNTRY IS:

Going in the right direction	37%
Off on the wrong track	59

SOURCE: Mitofsty International, *New York Times*, November 10, p. B4.

Turnout in 1994 was higher than in the preceding midterm elections of 1986 and 1990. According to exit polls, voters in 1994 were about twice as likely to be conservative as liberal. There were more Democrats than Republicans among voters in 1994, and a plurality said they had voted for Clinton in 1992. Turnout may have been a partial explanation for the defeat suffered by Democrats in 1994, but it is only a partial explanation.

Who Votes?

The extent of voting varies widely among different groups. The *level of education* especially helps predict whether people will vote. Those who finish elementary school are more likely to vote than those who do not; those who graduate from high school tend to turn out more than those who finish elementary school; and those who graduate from college turn out more than those who graduate from high school.[39] "Education increases one's capacity for understanding complex and intangible subjects such as politics," according to one study, "as well as encouraging the ethic of civil responsibility. Moreover, schools provide experience dealing with a variety of bureaucratic problems, such as coping with requirements, filling out forms, and meeting deadlines."[40] Race and ethnic background are linked with different levels of voting in large part because they have less education. Blacks in general turn out at lower rates than whites. The poor and less educated are more likely not to show up at the polls on election day.

Income and *age* are also important factors. Those with higher family incomes are more likely to vote than those with lower incomes. Income, of course, corresponds to occupation, and those with higher-status careers are more likely to vote than those with lower-status jobs. Older people, unless they are very old and perhaps infirm, are more likely to vote than younger people. Persons 18 to 24 years of age have a poor voting record; so do persons over 70. Women's increasing turnout generally is attributed to higher levels of education.[41]

How Serious Is Nonvoting?

Some political scientists argue that nonvoting is not a critical problem. "Nonvoting is not a social disease," contends Austin Ranney, a noted student of politics. He points out that legal and extralegal denial of the vote to African Americans, women, Hispanics, persons over 18, and other groups has now been outlawed, so nonvoting is *voluntary*. He quotes the late Senator Sam Ervin: "I don't believe in making it easy for apathetic, lazy people to vote."[42] Apathy and low levels of voting can also be seen as some indication of acceptance of things as they are, and therefore why spend the time and effort involved in voting?

Those who say that nonvoting is a critical problem cite the "class bias" of those who do vote. The social makeup and attitudes of nonvoters are significantly different from those of voters and hence greatly distort the representative system. Nonvoters tend to be the low-income, younger, blue-collar, less educated, "less white" Americans, as noted earlier. The "very poor, those with incomes below $5,000 a year, have about two-thirds the representation among voters than their numbers would suggest." Thus the people who need the most help from the government lack their fair share of electoral power to obtain it. And, it is argued, this situation is growing worse.[43]

Others reject this class-bias argument. They admit nonvoters are demographically different, yet they cite polls showing that nonvoters' attitudes are not much different from voters' attitudes. One study, comparing the party identification of voters with that of all Americans, found the proportion of Democrats was nearly identical (51.4 percent of all citizens and 51.3 percent of voters), while Republicans as voters were slightly overrepresented (36 percent of citizens and 39.7 percent of voters). All other political differences are considered to be much smaller than

From Coast to Coast

Average Turnout Percentage in General Elections by State, 1980–92

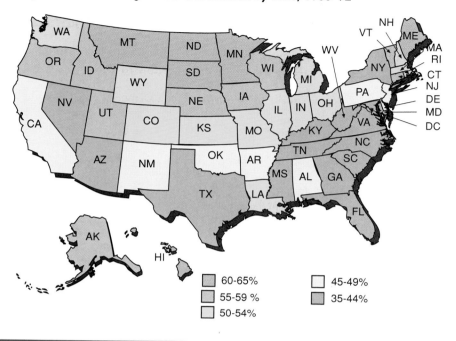

60-65%
55-59 %
50-54%
45-49%
35-44%

SOURCE: Royce Crocker, "Voter Registration and Turnout: 1948–1990," *Congressional Research Service*, August 11, 1992, pp. 20–31; and Royce Crocker, "Voter Turnout in the Presidential Election of 1992: The States," *Congressional Research Service*, January 26, 1993.

this 3.7 percent gap. Further, voters are not "disproportionately hostile" to social welfare policies.[44]

Another study asserts that the typical nonvoter is no longer just poor or a high school dropout but is dispersed among socioeconomic and other categories. In 1960, 72 percent of nonvoters had less than a high school education, and 60 percent were poor. In 1992, half of those who did not vote had not attended school beyond the eighth grade, and of those with incomes in the bottom third, 55 percent did not vote.[45]

Those who see a class bias defend their observations. Low voting, they say, reflects "the underdevelopment of political attitudes resulting from the historic exclusion of low-income groups from active electoral participation." In short, part of the problem of low-income, less-educated people is their failure to be conscious of their real interests. Dynamic leadership or strong party organization, or both, would not only attract the poor to the polls but make clear their "class grievances and aspirations."[46]

What effect might increased voter turnout have in national elections? It might make a difference, since there are partisan differences between different demographic groups, and candidates would have to adjust to the demands of the expanded electorate. A noted political scientist, while acknowledging that no political system could achieve 100 percent participation, pointed out that the entire balance of power in the political system could be overturned if the large nonvoter population decided to vote.[47] However, others argue that the difference may not be as pronounced. Nonvoters are not more in favor of government ownership or control of

A Closer Look

MEASURING PARTISAN IDENTIFICATION

Partisan identification is a long-term attachment or identification with a political party. Individuals are asked the following question to determine their party identification:

> Generally speaking, do you usually think of yourself as a Democrat, a Republican, an Independent, or what?

If the respondent answers "Democrat" or "Republican," the interviewer follows up with:

> Would you call yourself a strong Democrat [Republican] or a not very strong Democrat [Republican]?

If the respondent answers "Independent," the interviewer probes:

> Do you think of yourself as closer to the Republican party or to the Democratic party?

These questions permit researchers to classify the public into eight categories:

Strong Democrat
Weak Democrat (persons who said they were not very strong Democrats)
Independent Democrat (Independents who said they were closer to the Democratic party)
Independent
Independent Republican (Independents who said they were closer to the Republican party)
Weak Republican (persons who said they were not very strong Republicans)
Strong Republican
Other (persons who said they belonged to no party, were apolitical, or identify with a different party)

SOURCE: 1990 American National Election Study, Center for Political Studies, University of Michigan, Ann Arbor; Bruce E. Keith, David B. Magleby, Candice J. Nelson, Elizabeth Orr, Mark C. Westlye, and Raymond E. Wolfinger, *The Myth of the Independent Voter* (University of California Press, 1992), pp. 14, 68, 72.

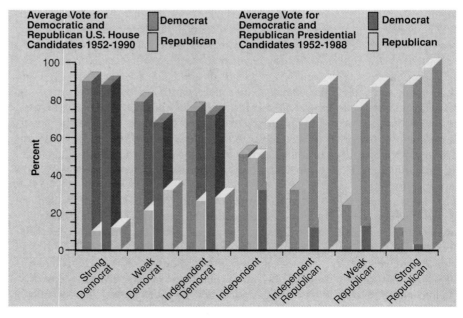

industry, and they are not more egalitarian. Nonvoters are, however, more inclined to favor additional spending on welfare programs.[48]

Another way to think of low voter turnout is to see it as a sign of approval with things as they are, whereas high voter turnout would signify disapproval and widespread desire for change. Even on the subject of how to interpret low turnout there is disagreement.

VOTING CHOICES

Why do people vote as they do? Political scientists have identified three main elements of the voting choice: *partisan identification, candidate appeal,* and *issues.* These elements overlap. Partisan identification has a lot to do with one's evaluation of the candidates and often predicts a person's stand on issues. It is part of our national mythology that Americans vote for the person and not the party, but, as we will see, the person we vote for is most often from our party.

Partisan Identification

Partisan identification is the subjective sense of identification or affiliation that a person has with a political party, a long-standing preference for one party over the other. Partisanship is typically acquired in childhood or adolescence as a result of the socialization process in the family, then reinforced by peer groups in adolescence. In the absence of reasons to vote otherwise, people depend on this preference or identification to simplify their voting choices. Partisan identification is *not* party registration; it is not party membership in the sense of being a dues-paying, card-carrying member, as in some European parties. Rather, it is a psychological sense of attachment to one party or another.

Political scientists measure party identification by asking if one considers himself or herself a Republican, a Democrat, an Independent, or what? All but a few answer Republican, Democrat, or Independent; less than 3 percent on average have indicated any other preference (see A Closer Look box). Those who indicate a partisan preference are asked a follow-up question that measures the strength of their identification. Independents are asked if they are closer to one or the other of the political parties.[49] The point to reinforce here is the continuing importance of partisanship as the best single predictor of the vote. In situations of less electoral significance or when voters have little information, the importance of party is amplified.

There has been a dramatic increase in the number of Independents beginning in the mid-1970s. Nominally there are more Independents in the electorate today than Republicans. But two-thirds of all Independents are, in fact, partisans in their voting behavior. Independent Democrats are predictably Democratic in their voting behavior, and Independent Republicans vote heavily Republican. Independent-leaners are thus very different from each other and from the Pure Independents. Pure Independents have the lowest rate of turnout but generally do side with the eventual winner in presidential elections. These data on Independents only reinforce the importance of partisanship as an explanation of voting choice, because when we consider Independent Democrats and Independent Republicans as Democrats and Republicans respectively, there were only 13 percent Pure Independents or others without a party in 1992, and the average for the period 1952–92 was only 13 percent.[50]

Although partisan identification has fluctuated somewhat in the past 40 years, it remains more stable than attitudes about issues or political ideology. Fluctuations in partisan identification appear to come in response to economic conditions and political performance, especially of the president.[51] It remains a long-term

How important are issues when voting for president?

With the media and public demanding more straightforward stands on specific problems, what part do issues play in an election? What were the most important issues in 1992? How about 1994 and 1996?

attachment for most people, especially when Independent-leaners are included among the partisans.

While long-term partisan identification is important, it clearly is not the only factor in voting choices; otherwise the Democrats would have won every presidential election since the last realignment in 1932. In fact, Republicans have been more successful in winning the White House during this period than Democrats. The answer to this puzzle is largely found in a second major explanation of voting choice—candidate appeal.

Candidate Appeal

Republican nominees for president have typically been the more popular candidates, with the exception of 1992, when Democrat Bill Clinton was seen in more positive light than George Bush. "Rather than signaling the birth of a new Republican era, however, the elections of the 1980s mark a critical threshold in the emergence of the candidate-centered era in American electoral politics. The change in focus from parties to candidates is an important historical trend, which has been gradually taking place over the last several decades."[52] Clinton's election reinforces the importance of candidates. He was especially popular among younger voters, women, and African Americans, but he also persuaded many "Reagan Democrats"—those who had defected to the Republicans in the 1980s—to return to their party.

Positive aspects of candidate appeal include experience, leadership, good judgment, competence, strength, and energy. Negative candidate appeal includes the opposite of these attributes, plus aspects like extremism, dishonesty, and lack of knowledge. An example of a candidate with positive appeal is Dwight Eisenhower, who was well known from his leadership of the Allied effort in World War II. Not all generals are successful in politics. It was Ike's unmilitary manner, his moderation, his personal charm, and his lack of a strong party position that made him appealing across the ideological spectrum.

Ronald Reagan generated positive candidate appeal by asserting values the public found lacking in Jimmy Carter—leadership and strength. But Reagan also openly sought to relate to Democrats in his acceptance speech at the Republican National Convention by describing himself as a "card-carrying union member." Reagan's union, the Screen Actors Guild, is hardly blue-collar, but he made the point that he understood and could represent unionized labor, typically a Democratic stronghold. Reagan also attempted to broaden his appeal in his acceptance speech in 1980 by conspicuously quoting Franklin D. Roosevelt, role model of the modern Democratic party.

Reagan's effort to generate positive candidate appeal was successful. Carter had hoped that Reagan would behave more like Barry Goldwater, who in his acceptance speech in 1964 had said, "Extremism in the defense of liberty is no vice....Moderation in the pursuit of justice is no virtue."[53] Lyndon Johnson, Goldwater's opponent, benefited from public perception that Goldwater and those who nominated him were out of the mainstream of American politics. This perception was confirmed when Goldwater's supporters at the convention refused for several minutes to let Governor Nelson Rockefeller speak.[54]

George McGovern, like Goldwater, was a candidate with negative appeal. Many of his supporters, by their "hippie" dress and manner, appeared out of the mainstream of American politics, but most damaging to McGovern was the way he handled Missouri Senator Tom Eagleton, whom he had chosen for his running mate, only to discover 12 days later that Eagleton had been hospitalized three times between 1960 and 1966 for treatment of emotional exhaustion and depression. McGovern initially responded that he stood behind Eagleton "1,000 percent." As press coverage and criticism of McGovern's lack of investigation into Eagleton's past grew, McGovern dropped Eagleton from the ticket and named a new running mate, Sargent Shriver. To the public, the episode reflected poorly on McGovern's judgment and his ability to stand by his word in the face of opposition. In the end, "only about one-third of the public thought he could be trusted as president."[55]

Candidate appeal can have positive or negative components; it can include something as simple as being well known. Generating name identification or recognition is a centerpiece of most campaigns. Increasingly, our politics focuses on the negative elements of candidates, and opponents or third parties are quick to point out the limitations or problems of any given candidate. Many saw the 1988 election as a very negative presidential campaign, in which the Bush-Quayle ticket called attention to the alleged errors of Governor Michael Dukakis—furloughing criminals like Willie Horton and not stopping pollution in Boston harbor. The Dukakis campaign did not reciprocate, thereby permitting Bush both to define Dukakis in negative terms and to define himself positively.

Candidate appeal often involves an assessment of a candidate's character. Is the candidate honest? Is the candidate a patriot? Is the candidate dedicated to "family values"? Does the candidate have religious or spiritual commitments? The American press in recent elections has sometimes played the role of "character cop," often asking, as candidates Gary Hart and Bill Clinton learned, questions about private lives and lifestyles. The press asks these questions because voters are interested in a presidential candidate's background—perhaps even more interested in a candidate's character than in his position on hard-to-understand health care or regulatory policy issues.

The 1992 election was somewhat more positive than those that preceded it. Bush did his best to attack Clinton's unwillingness to serve in the Vietnam War, and Perot and Clinton attacked Bush's economic record. Both Bush and Clinton, however, were gentle toward Perot, as they both hoped to get his endorsement or his supporters' votes.

Issues

Analysts of voting behavior heatedly debate the role of issues in voters' choices. Most scholars agree that issues, while important, are not as central to the decision process as partisanship and candidate appeal.[56] Part of the reason is that candidates often intentionally obscure their positions on issues, an understandable strategy.[57] Richard Nixon asserted that he had a plan to end the Vietnam War in 1968, clearly the most important issue in that year, but would not reveal the specifics of that plan. By not detailing his plan, he stood to gain votes from those who wanted a more aggressive war effort as well as those who wanted a cease-fire.

Voting on the basis on issues presumes a level of interest in issues that only a few voters have. For issue voting to occur, the issue must be important to voters, opposing candidates must take opposing stands on the issues, and voters must know these positions and vote accordingly. Rarely do candidates focus on only one issue. Voters often will agree with one candidate on one issue and with the opposing candidate on another. In such an instance, issues will likely not be the determining factor. But lack of interest by voters in issues does not mean candidates can take any issue position they wish.[58]

Voting a certain way because of candidate positions on specific policy questions, such as how to lower health care costs or whether to lower the capital gains tax, is an unrealistic expectation. More likely than *prospective issue voting* (voting based on

Thinking it Through

During the 1980s, Republicans were able to capitalize on issues such as foreign policy, taxes, and fear of the Soviet Union. In Bill Clinton's campaign in 1992, the Democrats framed new issues to their advantage. They addressed the economy, the deficit, and health care—the three most important issues in 1992. Clinton's campaign headquarters hung a sign saying, "It's the economy, stupid!" to remind the staff of the most important issue in the election.

This table shows which issues mattered most to voters in the 1992 presidential election.

Economy/jobs	43%
Deficit	21
Health care	19
Family values	15
Taxes	14
Education	13
Abortion	12
Foreign Policy	8
Environment	6

SOURCE: Voter Research and Surveys, Exit Poll of Voters, November 3, 1992.

what a candidate pledges to do about an issue if elected) is *retrospective issue voting* (holding incumbents, usually the president's party, responsible for performance on issues such as the economy or foreign policy).[59] In times of peace and prosperity, voters will reward the incumbent; if the nation falls short on either, voters will elect the opposition.

Scholars have also found that voter approval or disapproval of the performance of an outgoing president like Ronald Reagan in 1988 can have an impact on the vote for a presidentially endorsed successor. For example, 92 percent of those who strongly approved of Reagan's handling of the economy voted for George Bush in 1988.[60] But by 1992, Bush's handling of the economy came to be the most important issue in his defeat to Bill Clinton. More than two-thirds of Americans responding to exit polls described the economy in negative terms.

The 1992 Bush campaign attempted to divert attention away from the economy to issues of character, experience, and trust. But voters were more concerned about change than about these generalized qualities. Nearly half of Americans thought Clinton was lying about his draft record, but they did not consequently vote for Bush. In fact more than half of all veterans voted for Clinton. Dan Quayle sought to make "family values" an issue, but only one in six voters thought the issue important in deciding their vote. In fact, Republican attacks on nontraditional families may have alienated more voters than they attracted. Abortion, another issue many thought would be important to the election outcome, was cited by only 12 percent of voters as important in their voting decisions.[61]

Federal annual deficits and the national debt were the central issues Ross Perot raised. Change was the underlying theme—change from the Bush administration and change from politics as usual. Although Perot criticized Clinton about his record as governor of Arkansas and for his lack of business experience, most of his criticism centered on George Bush. In the end, Perot kept the focus of the campaign on the economy, an issue that clearly helped Clinton win the election.

The state of the economy is often the central issue in midterm elections as well. Several studies have found a positive relationship between the state of the economy and "out" party gains (and "in" party losses) in congressional seats.[62] Political scientists have also been able to locate the sources of this effect in individual voter's decision making. Voters tend to vote against candidates of the "in" party, including incumbents, if the voters perceive a decline or standstill in their personal financial situations.[63] Voters see responsibility for the economy resting more with the president and Congress than with governors or local officials.[64] Socioeconomic status is also important. Less-educated and low-income voters tend to judge a candidate on the basis of their personal financial condition. Upper-status voters, who personally tend to suffer less when economic conditions decline, are more likely to watch the overall performance of the economy and to judge candidates on that basis.[65]

Despite generally good economic news and success in lowering the federal budget deficit, Democrats suffered a substantial defeat in 1994. Why? Part of the explanation lies in Bill Clinton's low approval ratings. Despite his efforts to improve his popularity by trips to the Middle East shortly before the election, the public continued to have doubts about his leadership. Clinton, who had won election two years earlier on the theme of change, found that he and Democrats in Congress were targets of the same voter frustrations they had directed at George Bush. Republicans in Congress had used the filibuster and other tactics to defeat much of the Clinton and Democratic legislative agenda and then succeeded in arguing that Congress was in need of wholesale change. Republicans captured the "change" theme by presenting their "Contract With America," which included a commitment to provide a Balanced Budget Amendment, term limits for members of Congress, and other reforms. This strategy kept Democrats off balance and enabled Republicans to take advantage of voter anger in 1994.

SUMMARY

1. Public opinion is not a solid unit but a loose and complex combination of views and attitudes individuals acquire through various influences from childhood on. Public opinion takes on qualities of stability, fluidity, intensity, latency, consensus, or polarization—each of which is affected by people's feelings about the salience of issues.

2. Not all public opinion polls are accurate or scientific. Question wording and order, sampling problems, misinterpretation, and the timing of the survey can all make polls inaccurate.

3. The American public has a generally low level of interest in politics, and most people do not follow politics and government closely. One subset of the public—the attentive public—has high levels of political interest and awareness.

4. The vast majority of Americans do not engage in such forms of political participation as working in campaigns, writing letters to newspaper editors or elected officials, or even attempting to influence how another person will vote.

5. Better-educated, older, and party- and group-involved people tend to vote more; the poor tend to vote the least.

6. Voter turnout tends to be higher in national than in state and local elections, and higher in presidential than in midterm elections.

7. Party identification remains an important element in the voting choice of most Americans. It represents a long-term attachment and is a "lens" through which voters view candidates and issues as they make their voting choices. Voters decide their vote less frequently on the basis of issues.

FURTHER READING

HERBERT ASHER, *Polling and the Public*, 2d ed. (Congressional Quarterly Press, 1992).

M. MARGARET CONWAY, *Political Participation in the United States*, 2d ed. (Congressional Quarterly Press, 1991).

PAT DUNHAM, *Electoral Behavior in the United States* (Prentice Hall, 1991).

ROBERT S. ERIKSON, NORMAN R. LUTTBEG, AND KENT L. TEDIN, *American Public Opinion*, 4th ed. (Macmillan, 1991).

WILLIAM H. FLANIGAN AND NANCY H. ZINGALE, *Political Behavior of the American Electorate*, 8th ed. (Congressional Quarterly Press, 1994).

BRUCE E. KEITH, DAVID B. MAGLEBY, CANDICE J. NELSON, ELIZABETH ORR, MARK C. WESTLYE, AND RAYMOND E. WOLFINGER, *The Myth of the Independent Voter* (University of California Press, 1992).

V. O. KEY, JR., *Public Opinion and American Democracy* (Alfred A. Knopf, 1961).

W. RUSSELL NEUMAN, *The Paradox of Mass Politics* (Harvard University Press, 1986).

BENJAMIN I. PAGE AND ROBERT Y. SHAPIRO, *The Rational Public: Fifty Years of Trends in Americans' Policy Preferences* (University of Chicago Press, 1992).

FRANK R. PARKER, *Black Votes Count: Political Empowerment in Mississippi after 1965* (University of North Carolina Press, 1990).

SAMUEL L. POPKIN, *The Reasoning Voter: Communication and Persuasion in Presidential Campaigns* (University of Chicago Press, 1991).

JOHN ZALLER, *The Origins and Nature of Mass Opinion* (Cambridge University Press, 1992).

See also *Public Opinion Quarterly; The American Journal of Political Science;* and *The American Political Science Review.*

CAMPAIGNS AND ELECTIONS: DEMOCRACY IN ACTION

I n her first year in Congress, Representative Marjorie Margolies-Mezvinsky (D.-Pa.) cast the deciding vote on President Bill Clinton's deficit reduction package. During her campaign in 1992 she had promised to vote against higher taxes, a pledge she had renewed as recently as the day before. But House Democratic leaders thought they had a commitment from Ms. Margolies-Mezvinsky to support the president if hers would be the deciding vote. When she entered the House chambers, the president's bill was two votes short of passage, with three votes remaining to be cast. Before she could vote, Representative Ray Thornton (D.-Ark.) voted no, leaving Representative Margolies-Mezvinsky and Representative Pat Williams (D.-Mont.) as the deciding votes. Williams voted yes and Margolies-Mezvinsky followed, giving the president a one-vote victory margin. Democrats cheered, while Republicans reportedly chanted, "Goodbye, Marjorie," waving at her as if she had just fouled out of a basketball game. Her reversal in favor of the president's budget package, which contained higher taxes, was a decision to support her party and the administration over her previous commitments to her constituents.

Margolies-Mezvinsky had won election in 1992 by just 1,373 votes in an affluent suburban Philadelphia district that had not elected a Democrat in 76 years. Before seeking office she had been a television journalist and author of a best-selling book on dating. She is known to many of her constituents as "3M," because they become tongue-tied over her name.

Originally, Margolies-Mezvinsky had planned to vote against Clinton's plan. She had even prepared a statement for a news conference to explain to her constituents why she voted no. However, before she entered the floor of Congress, President Clinton personally asked Representative Margolies-Mezvinsky to change her vote. She writes:

> I knew at the time that changing my vote at the eleventh hour may have been tantamount to political suicide. So the vote resolved itself into one simple equation and ultimately, one simple question: Was my political future more important than the agenda that the President had laid out…? It hit me that if I turned him down, if I let him down, I would personally be cutting a President off at the knees in his first seven months in office.[1]

Following her critical vote, Margolies-Mezvinsky returned to her district and attended a town meeting of constituents. She told them, "I do not regret my vote nor do I apologize. I do regret that this vote may mean I will be a one-term member of Congress." Half the room is reported to have cheered and the other half to have shouted, "No way!"[2]

Representative Margolies-Mezvinsky became better known as a result of her vote. When Pope John Paul II visited Denver about a week later, Pat Schroeder (D.-Colo.) was asked what she planned to tell the pontiff. Her reply, "We're going to tell him to pray for Marjorie Margolies-Mezvinsky."[3] President Clinton fulfilled his pledge to support Representative Margolies-Mezvinsky by visiting her district and holding hearings on how to lower entitlement spending.[4]

Republicans in Pennsylvania and Washington, D.C. targeted Margolies-Mezvinsky for defeat in 1994. Even without her decisive vote on the budget, her original margin of victory would have made her vulnerable in a midterm election. Like many other Democrats who supported Clinton, she was defeated in the Republican tide that swept the country in 1994. Of the twenty-four women first elected to Congress in 1992, including Margolies-Mezvinsky, six were defeated in 1994.

The amount of attention focused on this one race is a bit unusual, but voting and elections in the United States are a centerpiece of our politics. Americans vote more often and for more offices than do the citizens of any other democracy. In 1994 we elected 33 U.S. senators, 35 state governors, and all 435 members of the U.S. House of Representatives. In 1996 we shall elect not only a president and vice-president but governors in 12 states, 35 U.S. senators, and all 435 members of the U.S. House of Representatives. At the state level we elect people to serve as insurance commissioners, secretaries of state, and, in most states, judges. We hold thousands of elections for everything from community college directors to county sheriffs. About half a million persons hold elected state and local offices.[5] In addition to voting for people, in 27 states citizens can place laws or constitutional amendments on the ballot by petition. In all states except Delaware, voters must approve all changes in the state constitution. Issues decided directly by voters include limiting automobile insurance rates, lowering taxes, and setting term limits for elected officials.

In this chapter we begin by explaining the implications of different election rules. We note four important problems that deserve attention: the lack of competition for some offices, problems associated with nominating presidential candidates, the complexities and distorting consequences of the electoral college, and the influence of money in our elections. We will also discuss proposed reforms in each of these problem areas.

THE RULES OF THE GAME

The rules of the game—the electoral game—make a difference. Although the Constitution sets certain conditions and requirements, and Congress has been exercising this power with greater frequency, most electoral rules remain matters of state law.

Regularly Scheduled Elections

In our system, elections are held at fixed intervals that cannot be changed by the party in power. It does not make any difference if the nation is at war or in the midst of a crisis; when the calendar calls for an election, the election is held. In many parliamentary democracies, such as Great Britain and Canada, the date of the election is open, so long as the election is held within five years of the previous election. In our system, the timing of elections is set in advance and at fixed intervals. Elections for members of Congress occur the first Tuesday after the first Monday in November of even-numbered years. Although there are some exceptions (special elections or peculiar state provisions), participants know in advance just when the next election will be.

Fixed Terms

Since our system holds elections at fixed intervals, elected officials have *fixed terms* of office, meaning that the length of a term in office is set, not indefinite. The Constitution has set the term of office for the U.S. House of Representatives at two years, the Senate at six years, and the presidency at four years. Fixed terms of office mean that politicians can anticipate the next election for a given office and plan for it.

Our system also has *staggered terms* for some offices; not all offices are up for election at any one time. All House members are up for election every two years, but only one-third of the senators are up for election at the same time. Because House members are perpetually campaigning, many have expressed support for lengthening their terms to four years. Also, House members must now give up their seats to run for the Senate; with a four-year term, they could run for the Senate at the middle of their term and, if they lost, still retain their House seat.

Most senators oppose giving their colleagues in the House a four-year term, even though senators can run for president without having to give up their seats if the presidential election occurs two or four years into their six-year term. When the senatorial term expires, senators are not allowed to campaign for both offices, except in Texas. Lyndon Johnson had state law changed in 1960 to permit him to run for both vice-president and the Senate. Lloyd Bentsen benefited from this rule when he ran for both offices in 1988.

Term limitation is another electoral rule with important consequences. The Twenty-second Amendment to the Constitution, adopted in 1951, limits persons elected president to two terms. Knowing that a president cannot run again changes the way the Congress, the opposing party, and the press regard the president. A politician who cannot, or has announced he or she will not, run again is called a **lame duck**. Efforts to limit the terms of other politicians have become a major issue in several American states. The most frequent targets have been state legislators.

Winner-Takes-All

One of the most important features of our electoral system is the **winner-takes-all** rule.[6] In most American electoral settings, the candidate with the most votes wins. The winner does not necessarily need to have a *majority* (more than half the votes cast); in a multicandidate race the winner may have only a *plurality*—the largest number of votes. Most American election districts are also **single-member districts**, meaning that in any district for any given election— senator, governor, U.S. House, state legislative seat—the election determines one representative or official.[7]

An important consequence of the winner-takes-all and the single-member district rules is that they tend to create a two-party system in which the differences between the two parties are not very great. The best way to win an election is to assemble a large *coalition* that leads to a majority or at least a plurality.

The winner-takes-all system is very different from **proportional representation** systems, in which political parties secure legislative seats and power in proportion to the number of votes they receive in the election. Let's assume a hypothetical state has three representatives up for election. In each of the three contests, the Republican defeats the Democrat, but in one district by only a very narrow margin. If you add up the statewide vote, the Republicans get 67 percent and the Democrats 33 percent. Under our winner-takes-all with its single-member district system, the Republicans get all three seats. But under a system of proportional representation, the Democrats would receive one seat because they got roughly one-third of the vote. Proportional representation thus rewards minor parties and permits them to go their separate ways. Countries that practice some form of proportional representation include Germany, Israel, and Japan.

Other examples of election practices that are significant are nominating party candidates by direct primaries rather than by party elites, electing U.S. senators by a vote of the people rather than by the state legislature (prohibited by the Seventeenth Amendment), and the form of the ballot adopted by the state.

The Electoral College

When it comes to electing our president and vice-president, we do so by a rather unusual, and some would say clumsy, device known as the **electoral college**, a system the framers devised to remove the choice from a direct vote by the people.

The electoral vote for the president in the election of 1876 was disputed in three southern states. Here the commission created to determine how to count those electoral votes makes its report. The winner was Rutherford B. Hayes.

Under this system each state has as many electors as it has representatives and senators. Thus California, for instance, has 54 electoral votes, and Vermont has 3. Electors are often longtime party workers who are appointed by the parties and are pledged to cast their electoral votes for their party's candidates for president and vice-president.

The Twelfth Amendment requires electors to vote separately for president and vice-president. To demonstrate how this works, if you voted for Bill Clinton for president in 1992, you were actually voting for electors pledged to vote for Clinton for president and Albert Gore for vice-president; if you voted for Bush and Quayle, you were in fact voting for electors pledged to them. Hence, who the electors are does not make a difference in the outcome, and few people pay any attention to who the electors are.

Candidates who win a plurality of the popular vote in a state secure *all* that state's electoral vote. The winning electors go to their state capital on the first Monday after the second Wednesday in December to cast their ballots. These ballots are then sent to Congress, and, early in January, Congress formally counts the ballots and declares to the world what everybody already knows—who won the election for president and vice-president.

It takes a majority of the electoral votes to win. If no candidate gets a majority of the electoral votes for president, the House chooses among the top three candidates, with each state delegation having one vote. If no candidate gets a majority of the electoral votes for vice-president, the Senate chooses among the top two candidates, with each senator casting one vote.

The emergence of Ross Perot as a possible third-party candidate brought considerable attention to the electoral college in 1992. People began to ask questions like: Which Congress casts the vote, the one now serving or the new one just elected? The answer is the new one, the one elected in November and taking office the first week in January. But what happens if a state's delegation cannot agree on a candidate? Then its vote does not count. Would it be possible to have a president of one party and a vice-president of another? Yes, if the election were thrown into the House and Senate.

The operation of the electoral college, with its statewide winner-takes-all rule—a candidate wins either *all* of a state's electoral votes or *none*—sharply influences the presidency and presidential politics. To win a presidential election, a candidate must appeal

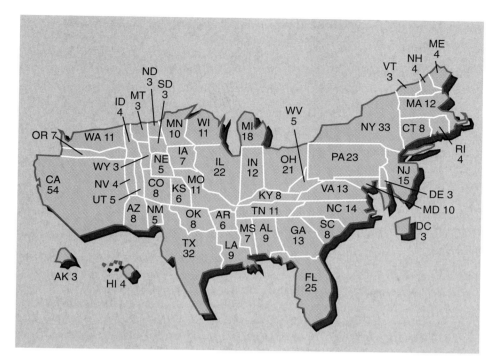

FIGURE 12-1 State Size Based on the Number of Electoral Votes

SOURCE: Holly Idelson, "Count Adds Seats in Eight States," *Congressional Quarterly Weekly Report* 48 (December 29, 1990), p. 4220.

successfully to urban and suburban groups in such big states as California, Texas, Ohio, and Illinois.[8] In 1992, California's total electoral vote of 54 exceeded the combined electoral votes of the 14 least populated states plus the District of Columbia. Figure 12-1 provides a visual comparison of state size according to electoral votes.

Presidential candidates do not ordinarily waste time campaigning in a state unless they have at least a fighting chance of carrying that state; nor do they waste time in a state in which their party is a sure winner. Richard Nixon in 1960 was the last candidate to promise to campaign in all 50 states. He did so, but lost valuable time traveling to and from Alaska, while John Kennedy focused on the more populous states. The contest usually narrows down to the medium-sized and big states, where the balance between the parties tends to be fairly even.

The fact that less populous states enjoy extra strength in the electoral college makes it possible for a person to receive a majority of the national popular vote but not a majority of the electoral vote. This happened in 1824, when Andrew Jackson won 12 percent more of the vote than John Quincy Adams; in 1876, when Samuel Tilden received more popular votes than Rutherford B. Hayes; and again in 1888, when Grover Cleveland received fewer electoral votes than Benjamin Harrison. It almost happened in the close elections of 1960 and 1976; the shift of a few votes in a few key states would have resulted in the election of a president without a popular majority, and in a year with a serious minor party candidate could result in the election of a president without a plurality of the vote.

RUNNING FOR CONGRESS

How candidates run for Congress depends largely on the nature of their district, who the candidate is, and the candidate's ability to raise money. A first-term representative is likely to run a race for reelection that differs from that of a veteran of Congress or a novice who has never run for office before. Despite these differences, we can make five generalizations about most House and Senate elections.

First, most congressional elections are not close. In districts where most people belong to one party or where incumbents are popular and enjoy fund-raising and

The House Decides

When there are only two major candidates for the presidency, the chances of an election being "thrown into the House" are remote. But twice in our history the House has had to act: in 1800, before the Twelfth Amendment was written, the House had to choose in a tie vote between Thomas Jefferson and Aaron Burr; in 1824 the House picked John Quincy Adams over Andrew Jackson and William Crawford. Henry Clay, who was forced out of the race when he came in third, threw his support behind Adams. When Adams was elected, he made Clay his secretary of state.

The 1824 vote in the House was especially contentious. Jackson, winner of the popular vote, was passed over when the vote went to the House. This infuriated the supporters of Jackson, who won the electoral college vote by a wide margin four years later.

other campaign advantages, there is often little competition.[9] Defenders of constitutional democracy are concerned by the fact that so many officeholders have safe seats. When officeholders do not have to fight to retain their seat, elections are not performing their proper role.[10]

Congressional elections tend to be more competitive than state legislative elections. Mayoral elections are often hotly contested because politicians view the prize as more valuable. Competition is also more likely when funding is adequate for both candidates. Elections for governor and for the U.S. Senate are more seriously contested and adequately financed than those for the U.S. House of Representatives.

Second, the extent of presidential popularity affects both House and Senate elections during presidential election years as well as midterm elections. The impact of presidential popularity in a presidential election is the **coattail effect**, the boost candidates from the president's party get from a popular presidential candidate running in the same election. Winning presidential candidates do not always provide such a boost. The Republicans suffered a net loss of six seats when George Bush won the presidency in 1988, and the Democrats suffered a net loss of ten seats when Bill Clinton won the 1992 presidential election.[11]

Figure 12-2 presents the number of seats in the House of Representatives gained or lost by the party controlling the White House in mid-term elections since 1938. In each of these elections, the party controlling the White House *lost* seats in the House. The range of losses, however, is quite wide, from a low of 4 seats for the Democrats in 1962 to a high of 71 seats (again for the Democrats) in 1938.

Republicans did better in 1994 than in any midterm election since 1946, picking up 53 seats. The Republican sweep included the defeat of House Speaker Tom Foley, the first sitting Speaker to be defeated since 1860, and other senior Democrats such as Dan Rostenkowski and Jack Brooks. The Republican tide was not isolated to the House, but included a net gain of nine seats in the Senate, counting the post-election switch of Alabama Senator Shelby to the Republican party. Republicans also won major victories in governors' races.

The number of seats lost is partly a function of how well the president's party did in the preceding presidential election. Lyndon Johnson's landslide victory in 1964 may have helped produce a net gain of 47 Democratic seats that year, the exact number of seats that the Democrats lost back to Republicans two years later. Other presidential elections do not result in large gains for the president's party.

Third, technology is increasingly influential in all campaigns. Congressional candidates need campaign managers, opinion pollsters, direct-mail fund-raisers, computer

FIGURE 12-2 Seats Lost by the President's Party in Midterm Elections for the House of Representatives, 1938–1994

SOURCE: Based on Norman J. Ornstein, Thomas E. Mann, and Michael J. Malbin, *Vital Statistics on Congress, 1993–1994* (Congressional Quarterly, 1994), p. 53.

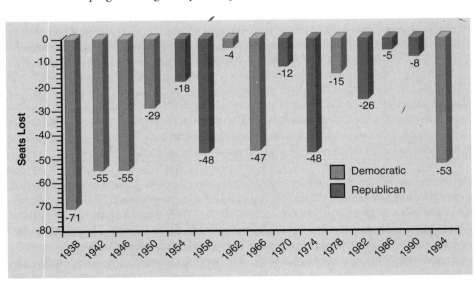

experts, media specialists, and many other consultants. Much effort is centered on television, especially television advertising. Because television time is so expensive, the cost of campaigns has soared and the importance of money has increased. Television advertising is less efficient for House candidates whose districts are in large cities where their ads reach more people outside their district than in it. In these districts House candidates use direct mail or other forms of advertising instead of television.

A fourth characteristic is the use of negative campaigning—focusing on an opponent's alleged failings. Negative campaigning has been with us since the beginning, but in recent years it has become more the norm than the exception, not only in congressional campaigns but in campaigns for president and governor. In 1994, the U.S. Senate contest in Virginia saw Oliver North (R) emphasize Chuck Robb's (D) marital indiscretions, and Robb reminded Virginians of North's perjury before Congress. Republican candidates George Bush in Texas, Jeb Bush in Florida, and Pete Wilson in California tried to depict their Democratic opponents as soft on crime through emotional ads.

And finally, politics in the 1990s is more candidate-centered, as opposed to issue- or party-oriented, and increasingly dependent on the mass media. Politicians essentially nominate themselves for office by winning votes in the primary election. To do this, candidates must rely on name identification and campaign funds spent on advertising.[12] Once elected, politicians are driven by the desire for reelection.[13] Their responsibilities in governing often seem less important than winning reelection or positioning themselves to run for a higher office. In 1994, Democrats sought to downplay their partisanship and distance themselves from Clinton, while Republicans sought to link the Democrats with Bill and Hillary Clinton. One commercial even had the face of a Democratic candidate transformed into the face of Bill Clinton to reinforce this connection.

"My former opponent is supporting me in the general election. Please disregard all the things I said about him in the primary."

Dunagin's People by Ralph Dunagin. Reprinted with special permission of NAS, Inc.

The House of Representatives

Every two years, as many as 1,000 candidates—including approximately 400 incumbents—campaign for Congress. After deciding to take the plunge, candidates must first plan a primary race unless they face no opponents for the party's nomination. Incumbents are rarely challenged for renomination from within their own party, and when they are, the challenges are seldom serious. In 1988 and 1990, for example, only one House incumbent was defeated in a primary election. Challengers running against entrenched incumbents rarely encounter opposition in their own party.[14]

In 1992 more candidates were defeated in primaries or decided not to seek reelection than had been the case for many years. Part of the explanation is that the 1990 redistricting placed some incumbents in the same congressional district as other incumbents. In addition, the negative publicity surrounding bounced checks from the House Bank inflamed an anti-incumbent mood in 1992 and convinced many incumbents not to run the risk of being defeated in the primaries.

The 1994 elections resulted in substantial turnover, with a net gain of more than fifty seats for the Republicans in the House and nine seats in the Senate. House Republicans, led by Newt Gingrich, had chosen to make Bill Clinton the focus of their campaign and had promised such changes as term limitations, a Balanced Budget Amendment, and a substantial reduction in congressional staff.

MOUNTING A PRIMARY CAMPAIGN The first step for challengers in contested primaries or for those seeking open seats is to build a *personal* organization. The *party* organization usually stays neutral until the nomination is decided. A candidate can build an organization while holding another office, such as a seat in the state legislature, or by deliberately getting to know people, serving in civic causes, helping other candidates, and being conspicuous without being controversial.

The next steps are to raise funds, hire campaign managers, place television ads, and conduct polls. All these things depend on raising funds, which few can-

Important Factors in Winning an Election

Uncontrollable Factors

- Incumbent running
- Strength of party organization
- National tides or landslide possibility
- Socioeconomic makeup of district

Organizational Factors

- Registration drives
- Fund-raising machinery
- Campaign organization
- Volunteers
- Media campaign
- Direct-mail campaign efforts
- Get-out-the-vote efforts

Candidate's Personal Leadership Factors

- Personal appeal
- Knowledge of issues
- Speaking and debating ability
- Commitment and determination
- Ability to earn free, positive media coverage

didates are able to do before the primaries. Most primary campaigns are run on low budgets.

Now the major hurdle is to become visible. Candidates scheme to get their names in the newspapers or mentioned on television. As the old cliché goes, "It doesn't matter what they say about you as long as they spell your name right." In large cities with many campaigns, congressional candidates are frequently lost in media "noise," and in rural areas the press often plays down political news. Candidates rely on personal contacts, on hand shaking and door-to-door campaigning, and on identifying likely supporters and courting their favor—the same techniques used in campaigns for lesser offices. The turnout in primaries tends to be low, except in campaigns in which large sums of money are expended on advertising.

CAMPAIGNING FOR THE GENERAL ELECTION   General election campaigns can usefully be divided into four types: incumbent campaigns, serious challenger campaigns, weak challenger campaigns, and open seat campaigns.

Most incumbent members of Congress win reelection.[15] Since 1970, over 90 percent of incumbent House members seeking reelection have won. Incumbents tend to win because they are popular, and those who run against them run weak, underfunded campaigns.[16] Knowing the advantage of incumbency, potential challengers, often choose not to run, thereby helping the incumbent further.[17] In recent House elections incumbent's outspent their challengers roughly 3 to 1; in the Senate the difference was closer to 2 to 1.[18] Most challengers spend little money, run campaigns that are not significantly more visible than primary campaigns, contact few voters, and lose badly.

A few challengers in each election mount serious challenges because of the incumbent's perceived vulnerability, the challenger's own wealth, party, or political action committee efforts, or a combination of factors. Often their campaign expenditures rival the incumbents, yet most of them lose. In 1988, only 6 challengers defeated incumbents; only 40 others polled more than 40 percent of the votes in the November election. The number of challengers defeating incumbents rose to 15 in 1990; just under 4 percent of incumbents seeking reelection were defeated. In 1992, however, many incumbents chose to retire or run for other offices, and others were denied reelection.

The Republican sweep of 1994 removed as many as thirty House and two Senate Democratic incumbents from office, and other incumbents won by very close margins. Republican incumbents fared much better, as no Republican House or Senate incumbents were defeated in 1994. When Democratic defeats were added to the seats Democrats lost due to retirements, control of both chambers went to the Republicans.

Why is keeping a House seat so much easier than gaining it? Incumbents have a host of advantages that help them gain reelection. These "perks" include free mailings to constituents (the *franking privilege*), free use of broadcast studios to record radio and television tapes to be sent to local media outlets, and, perhaps most important of all, a large staff to perform countless favors and send a stream of press reports and mail, in the member's name, back to the district. All help a House member build not only name recognition but also a positive image.[19] Representatives also try to win committee posts, even on minor committees, that relate to the needs of their districts and build connections with constituents.[20] Congressional careers are built on a variety of personal contacts: shaking hands, canvassing homes, emphasizing local problems, remembering people's names, doing favors.[21] If an incumbent is successful at building "constituent trust," he or she will win reelection again and again.[22]

If incumbents win so often, how do we get any significant turnover in the House of Representatives at all? The turnover comes when incumbents die, decide to retire, or seek some other office. Redistricting, which happens once each decade, can lead to high turnover, as it did in 1992 when incumbents were forced to run against each other in new districts. Incumbents may decide that the new district is less friendly to them and run for another office or retire. Potential candidates for the House as well as political action committees and political party committees all watch open seat races closely. Hence open seat races tend to be more competitive.

One solution to the problem of the "permanent Congress" is to limit the number of terms a person can serve (see Figure 12-3). To apply term limits to the U.S. Congress will probably require an amendment to the Constitution. A Washington state initiative that limited congressional terms was declared unconstitutional by the district court and will be appealed to the U.S. Supreme Court.[23] Typically, the proposed limit is 12 years: 6 two-year House terms, 2 six-year U.S. Senate terms, and 3 four-year state Senate terms.

Voters in eight states and the District of Columbia voted on term limits in 1994, and only in Utah were they defeated. Voters in Washington voted on term limits twice, enacting them the second time they were on the ballot.

The Senate

Running for the Senate is big-time politics. The six-year term and the national exposure make a Senate seat a glittering prize, so competition is usually intense. Senate campaigns generally feature state-of-the-art campaign technology; a race normally costs millions of dollars.[24] Still, Senate races tend to be much like those for the House. The essential tactics include focusing on a simple campaign theme, getting others involved, making as many personal contacts as possible (especially in states with small populations), and avoiding giving the opposition positive publicity.

Incumbency is also an advantage for senators, although not as much as for representatives. Incumbent senators are more widely known through the media. Because senators and Senate candidates are far more visible than House candidates, they cannot easily duck tough issues. Much of what citizens hear about House members, in contrast, is generated from the members' own offices. Further, senators normally face tougher competition—challengers who frequently are already well known or who raise and spend significant amounts of money.[25]

When there is a chance to alter party control of the Senate, as was the case twice in the 1980s and again in 1994, more good candidates run and the number of competitive elections increases. But the cost of Senate campaigns can vary greatly. California has 69 times the number of potential voters as Wyoming, and the political culture and nature of their media markets differ dramatically. When party control of the U.S. Senate is up for grabs, a seat from Wyoming is much cheaper than a seat from California. Still, disproportionately large amounts of money may be spent in small states, as the stakes of controlling the Senate are high. It is not surprising that Senate elections in less-populated states have become battlegrounds.[26]

RUNNING FOR PRESIDENT

There are actually two campaigns for the presidency. One is the *mass media election*, which we will examine in Chapter 13.[27] The other is the *formal election*, which involves seeking the nomination of a major party and then amassing enough votes on the first Tuesday after the first Monday in November to win a majority in the electoral college. The formal campaign has three stages: winning delegates, capturing the convention, and campaigning in the fall.

Stage 1: Winning Delegates

Presidential hopefuls must make a series of critical tactical decisions. The first is when to start campaigning. Some candidates begin almost as soon as the last presidential election is over. Campaigning begins well before any actual declaration of candidacy, as candidates try to line up supporters to win caucuses or primaries in

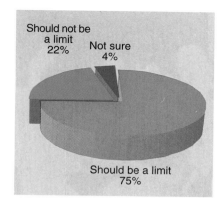

FIGURE 12-3   Support for Term Limits

SOURCE: NBC/Wall Street Journal Poll. Averages for polls between January 1990 and 1992.

Who Has Enacted Term Limits?

Alaska	1994
Arizona	1992
Arkansas	1992
California	1992
Colorado	1990*
Florida	1992
Idaho	1994
Maine	1994
Massachusetts	1994
Michigan	1992
Missouri	1992
Montana	1992
Nebraska	1994
Nevada	1994
North Dakota	1992
Ohio	1992
Oklahoma	1994
Oregon	1992
South Dakota	1992
Utah	1994**
Washington	1992
Wyoming	1992

Voters rejected term limits in:

Washington	1991
Utah	1994

*Colorado voters modified their 1990 term limits initiative in 1994 to shorten the possible terms for U.S. House of Representatives from six terms (12 years) to three terms (6 years).

**The Utah State Legislature approved term limits contingent upon 25 other states also enacting them. A 1994 ballot initiative to have term limits take effect immediately failed.

Bill Clinton outlasted all of his opponents in the 1992 primaries to secure the nomination before the last primary in California.

key states and to raise money for their nomination effort. The 1992 campaign developed much later than usual, in part because the popularity of George Bush in 1991 deterred potential rivals.

Candidates must calculate how to deal with the crazy array of presidential primaries and caucuses that constitute our delegate selection system. Although the process is limited somewhat by federal regulation of campaign financing and national party rules, states can set up, within broad limits, the systems they prefer. The result is a complex maze that critics call flawed.[28]

PRESIDENTIAL PRIMARIES   State **presidential primaries**, unknown before this century, have become the main method of choosing delegates. Today more than two-thirds of the states, including most of the larger states and hence the vast majority of voters, use presidential primaries. In 1992 primaries selected 80 percent of the Democratic delegates and 83 percent of the Republican delegates. The rest of the states use caucuses or conventions.

Presidential primaries have two main features: a "beauty contest," in which voters indicate which candidate for president running in the primary they prefer, and the selection of delegates who will actually attend the convention and vote for the nominee. Different combinations of these two features have produced the following systems:

1. *Proportional representation*: Delegates to the national convention are allocated on the basis of the votes candidates win in the "beauty contest." This system has been used in most of the states, including several of the largest ones. The Democrats now mandate a proportional representation rule for all their primaries.[29]

2. *Winner-takes-all*: In the Republican party, in some states there is a winner-takes-all rule that whoever gets the most votes wins all that state's delegates, as George Bush did in the California Republican primary in 1992.

3. *Delegate selection*: In several states, large and small, voters choose delegates who may or may not have pledged how they will vote in the national party convention. The names of the presidential hopefuls do not appear separately on the ballot and there is no presidential preference. Under this arrangement, delegates are more likely to feel free to exercise their independent judgment at the convention. This system is used only by the Republicans.

4. *Delegate selection and separate presidential poll*: In several states, including New Hampshire (where for many years the first presidential primary has been held), voters decide twice: once to state their choice for president, and once to choose delegates pledged, or at least favorable, to a presidential candidate. This is one of the oldest kinds of presidential primary.[30]

CAUCUSES AND CONVENTIONS   About a dozen states use a caucus and/or convention system for choosing delegates.[31] This is the oldest method of choosing delegates and is fundamentally different from the primary system because it centers on the *party organization*. In principle, the caucus and convention system is far simpler than the primary method. Delegates to the national party conventions are chosen by delegates to state or district conventions, who themselves are chosen earlier in county, precinct, or town caucuses. A **caucus** is a meeting of party members and supporters of various candidates. The process starts at local meetings open to all party members, who discuss and take positions on candidates and issues and elect delegates to represent their views at the next level. This process repeats until national nominating convention delegates are chosen by conventions of delegates throughout a district or state.

There are many variations of the caucus and convention system, because they are regulated by each state's parties and legislature. Iowa holds its caucuses in

March before any primary or other caucus. As a result it gets much national attention, and in most presidential elections candidates give great importance to doing well there. In 1992 Iowa was less important because Iowa's Senator Tom Harkin was running for president and was almost certain to win his home state. The same may be true in 1996 for Republicans if Senator Bob Dole from neighboring Kansas runs in Iowa.

Whoever runs in 1996, on a Monday evening in early February of that year, Iowans will hold hundreds of Democratic and Republican precinct meetings. Large numbers of voters will attend these small town meetings. Although an even larger number of Iowans would doubtless vote in a primary if one were held, the thousands attending these caucuses will have a chance to meet and exchange views on issues and candidates, rather than merely pulling a lever in a voting booth or placing an *X* on a ballot. A special feature of the Iowa meetings is that college students can attend local caucuses in their college or hometowns, as they prefer, with a minimum degree of hassle.

STRATEGIC CONSIDERATIONS Strategies for gaining delegates to the national convention have changed over the years. Some candidates think it wise to skip some of the earlier contests and enter first in states where their strength lies. This strategy was challenged by the "go everywhere" plan Jimmy Carter pursued in winning the 1976 Democratic nomination. Most candidates choose to run hard in Iowa and New Hampshire, hoping that early showings in these states, which receive a great deal of media attention, will move them into the spotlight for later efforts. The victory of Paul Tsongas in New Hampshire in 1992 and Republican candidate Patrick Buchanan's better-than-expected showing gave both candidates substantial media attention.

Sometimes strategies are determined by events beyond the candidates' control. Straw polls, conducted well in advance of the opening caucuses and primaries, may be interpreted by the press in ways that give some relatively unknown candidates advantages. Thus, since journalists deem it so, participation in many such events becomes important. Similarly, debates—often televised—have become an important feature of the nominating process.

During this phase, candidates win or lose by their ability to adapt their own strengths to changing circumstances: the number of candidates running, the ideological splits among the candidates, the calendar of events, the amount of money available for the campaign, the ways in which the media cover a particular state, and events that disrupt planning. Especially important is the ability of candidates to manage the media's expectation of their performance. Lyndon Johnson actually won the New Hampshire primary in 1968, but because Eugene McCarthy did better than the press had expected, McCarthy was interpreted as the "winner." Winning in the primaries thus becomes a game of expectations, and candidates may intentionally downplay their expectations so that "doing better than expected" might generate momentum for their campaign.

Stage 2: Capturing the Convention

National party conventions bring together all delegates elected in primaries, caucuses, or state conventions to nominate the party's presidential and vice-presidential candidates. The first convention was held in 1808, when a few Federalist leaders met secretly in New York to nominate candidates for president and vice-president. In the early 1830s, under the leadership of Democrats Andrew Jackson and Martin Van Buren, the first "open" convention was held by a major party. Historically, delegates arrived at national nominating conventions with differing degrees of commitment to presidential candidates. Some delegates were pledged to no candidate at all, others to a specific candidate for one or two ballots, and others firmly to one candidate only.

The 1992 national nominating conventions were filled with typical campaign hoopla. Democrats Al Gore and Bill Clinton (*left*) struck a homey, emotional tone in their acceptance speeches, but George Bush (*right*) took a more defiant approach and called again for tax cuts.

Recent conventions have merely ratified decisions already made in the primaries and caucuses, in part because delegates were required to pledge themselves to a specific presidential hopeful (in the Democratic party) or because one candidate has been able to amass the necessary number of delegates in advance. And because of "reforms" encouraging delegates to stick with the person to whom they are pledged, there has been less room to maneuver at conventions. National party conventions used to be events of high excitement because they determined who would be the party nominees, but in every election since the Republican convention of 1948 and the Democratic convention of 1952, the nominee has been chosen on the *first* ballot.

Still, conventions get national attention. There is a slim possibility that the first ballot may not be decisive, and there is excitement generated by the presidential nominee's selection of a vice-presidential running mate. National party conventions also provide the public with an opportunity to watch the major parties define their platforms.

A convention can launch the general election campaign in either a positive or negative way. How delegates behave and what the party decides are covered by batteries of cameras and battalions of newspersons. Selected incidents at the convention are carried to millions in this country and around the world. The convention is very much a party affair, even though nominating or confirming the nomination of a president is the main event.

Conventions have their own rules, routines, and rituals. Usually the first day is devoted to a keynote address and other speeches touting the party and denouncing the opposition; the second day to committee reports, including party and convention rules and the party platform; the third day to presidential balloting; and the fourth to choosing a vice-presidential nominee and winding up with the presidential candidate's acceptance speech.[32] Balloting for president used to be the highlight of the proceedings, but dramatic struggles can occur over the adoption of the rules and the platform. Not long ago sharp encounters occurred over credentials—that is, over which delegates should be seated. The matter was most often in dispute when southern states sent all-white delegations to the Democratic convention. Credential fights have decreased since standard procedures for choosing delegates have been enforced and African Americans have secured the right to vote.

THE PARTY PLATFORM   Delegates to national nominating conventions sometimes spend hours debating their platforms. Why? Critics have long pointed out that the party platform is binding on no one and is more likely to hurt than help a candidate. But presidential candidates take the platform seriously because it gives an indication of the general direction a party wants to take. Most presidents make an effort to implement their party's platform.[33] In recent years the parties have been successful in working out their platform before the convention so that delegates seldom debate and vote on more than a couple of controversial issues.

THE VICE-PRESIDENTIAL NOMINEE   The choice of the vice-presidential nominee has become increasingly important. The just-elected presidential nominee dictates the choice of a running mate; this practice is now taken for granted. Rarely does a person actually "run" for the vice-presidential nomination because only one vote counts, but there is a good deal of maneuvering to capture that one vote. Sometimes the choice of a running mate is made by the presidential nominee at the convention—not a time conducive to careful and deliberate thought. More often the choice is made before the convention, but the announcement is delayed until the convention as speculation about the choice often adds drama. However, presidential contender Ronald Reagan announced his choice in 1976 before the convention, as did Bill Clinton in 1992.

Traditionally the presidential nominee chooses a running mate who will "balance the ticket." Walter Mondale raised this tradition to a dramatic new height in 1984 by selecting a woman, Representative Geraldine A. Ferraro, to run with him. Mondale's bold decision was an effort to strengthen his appeal to women voters. Presidential candidates sometimes ignore the idea of a balanced ticket, as Bill Clinton did in 1992 when he chose another southern white male, Al Gore, to be his running mate.

THE VALUE OF CONVENTIONS   Why do the parties continue to have conventions if the nominee is known in advance and the vice-presidential nominee is the choice of one person? What role do conventions play in our system? For the parties, they are a time of "coming together" to endorse a party program and to build unity and enthusiasm for the fall campaign. For future candidates, they are a chance to capture the national spotlight and further their political ambitions. Speeches in recent conventions by Mario Cuomo, Pat Buchanan, and Jack Kemp generated interest in them as future presidential candidates. When Governor Bill Clinton spoke to the 1988 Democratic convention, he spoke for over 35 minutes and nominated Michael Dukakis. His nominating speech was so long that he got more than the normal media attention, some of it critical. For nominees, they are an opportunity to define themselves in positive ways. The potential is there to heal wounds festering from the primary campaign and move into the general election united. Of course, the potential is not always achieved. Many campaign managers in recent elections have seen conventions as potentially dangerous to their candidate and coalition. As a result, they work at damage control as well as celebration.

NOMINATION BY PETITION   There is a way to run for president of the United States that avoids the grueling process of primary elections and conventions—if your are rich enough or well known enough. H. Ross Perot took this route in 1992. Independent candidates Perot in 1992 and John Anderson in 1980 met the

To Thy Candidate Be True?

How tightly should convention delegates be bound to the presidential candidates to whom they were pledged in the primaries? This question dominated the first day of proceedings at the 1980 Democratic convention. Delegates supporting President Jimmy Carter, who had won most of the primaries, argued that if delegates could violate their "pledges," primaries would be a farce and conventions undemocratic and unrepresentative. Delegates backing Senator Edward Kennedy contended that such a rule would make delegates into "pawns" and conventions into "rubber stamps." Why have a convention at all, they asked, if delegates could not act in a deliberative—rather than merely a representative—capacity, especially because months had gone by since many delegates had been selected and conditions had changed? A majority of the convention supported Carter's position, and party rules appeared to require that "delegates elected to the national convention pledged to a presidential candidate shall in all good conscience reflect the sentiments of those who elected them."*

Delegate Selection Rules for the 1984 Democratic National Convention (Democratic National Committee, 1982), p. 13.

Without a political party to nominate him for president, Ross Perot gathered enough signatures on petitions throughout the country to make him a viable candidate.

The Hard Life of a Campaigner

No one has captured the spirit of presidential campaigning better than Adlai E. Stevenson, the unsuccessful Democratic candidate in 1952 and 1956:

You must emerge, bright and bubbling with wisdom and well-being, every morning at 8 o'clock, just in time for a charming and profound breakfast talk, shake hands with hundreds, often literally thousands, of people, make several inspiring, "newsworthy" speeches during the day, confer with political leaders along the way and with your staff all the time, write at every chance, think if possible, read mail and newspapers, talk on the telephone, talk to everybody, dictate, receive delegations, eat, with decorum—and discretion!—and ride through city after city on the back of an open car, smiling until your mouth is dehydrated by the wind, waving until the blood runs out of your arm, and then bounce gaily, confidently, masterfully into great howling halls, shaved and all made up for television with the right color shirt and tie—I always forgot—and a manuscript so defaced with chicken tracks and last-minute jottings that you couldn't follow it, even if the spotlights weren't blinding and even if the still photographers didn't shoot you in the eye every time you looked at them. (I've often wondered what happened to all those pictures!) Then all you have to do is make a great, imperishable speech, get out through the pressing crowds with a few score autographs, your clothes intact, your hands bruised, and back to the hotel—in time to see a few important people.

But the real work has just commenced—two or three, sometimes four hours of frenzied writing and editing of the next day's immortal mouthings so you can get something to the stenographers, so they can get something to the mimeograph machines, so they can get something to the reporters, so they can get something to their papers by deadline time. (And I quickly concluded that all deadlines were yesterday!) Finally sleep, sweet sleep, steals you away, unless you worry—which I do.

Today photocopy machines have replaced stenographers, and speech writers draft the "immortal mouthings" for many candidates. The assassination of President John Kennedy in 1963 ended motorcades on the backs of open cars, but campaigning is still an exhausting effort. All those who listened to the hoarse voice of Bill Clinton or saw George Bush's fatigue in the 1992 campaign will recognize how demanding running in a presidential campaign still is.

SOURCE: Adlai E. Stevenson, *Major Campaign Speeches, 1952* (Random House, 1953), pp. XI–XII. Copyright © 1953 by Random House, Inc.

various state petition requirements or paid the $500 filing fee in Louisiana and made it onto the ballot in all fifty states. The petition process can be as simple as submitting the signatures of 200 registered voters in Washington state, or as difficult as getting the signatures of 3 percent of registered voters (63,000 signatures) in Maryland. Perot and Anderson have demonstrated that you do not need a political party to run for president.

They also demonstrated that you do not need a political party to run a visible campaign that is taken seriously by your opponents and the American people. In 1992, Perot and his running mate, James Stockdale, got nearly one-fifth of the popular vote. Perot was not nominated by any political party, did not run in any primaries, and had not sought any office before. How did he do it?

He did it by spending about $65 million of his own money to promote himself as a candidate. His candidacy was unusual because it generated so much media attention; he skillfully used free media, like the television program *Larry King Live* on which he opened his campaign and appeared many times during its course. Perot's anti-politician, anti-Washington, and anti-deficit message struck a responsive chord in the American public. His folksy and often humorous manner of communicating reinforced his appeal.

Despite some early mistakes and difficulties with his staff, Perot ran a respectable campaign and played an important role in defining the issues. In fact, during part of the campaign, there was the possibility that he might come in second in the race or win enough electoral votes to throw the election into the House of Representatives. Perot did come in second in two states—Utah and Maine—and he garnered almost 20 million votes. However, he won no electoral votes.

Following the election Perot continued to be courted by both Republicans and Democrats, who hoped to win back his supporters for the 1994 and 1996 elections. His influence fell after the televised debate over the North American Free Trade Agreement (NAFTA) with Vice-President Al Gore, in which Perot was widely seen as testy, whiney, and a "bossy, old billionaire bully."[34]

Stage 3: Campaigning in the Fall

The national nominating convention adjourns immediately after the presidential and vice-presidential candidates deliver their acceptance speeches to the delegates and the national television audience. The time between the conventions and Labor Day is traditionally a time for resting, binding up convention wounds, gearing the party for action, and planning campaign strategy. In recent elections, however, the campaigns have hardly paused after the convention.[35]

Strategy differs from one election to another, but politicians, pollsters, and political scientists have collected enough information to agree broadly that a number of basic factors affect election outcomes. Whether the nation is prosperous or not probably has the most to do with who wins a presidential election, but, as we have noted, most voters vote on the basis of party and candidate appeal.[36] Much depends on voter turnout as well. The Democrats' advantage in number of people who identify themselves as Democrats is mitigated by the higher voter turnout among Republicans. Republicans also usually have better access to money.

THE MEDIA AND THE IMAGE   The question of candidate definition is central. Candidates ask: How can I keep the focus of the campaign on themes and issues favorable to me? Should the opposition be attacked or ignored when it attacks me and my record? What image do I wish to project? There was a major, and evidently highly effective, effort by the Richard Nixon's campaigners in 1968 to help the candidate shed his old image of divisiveness and failure.[37] In 1992, Clinton's campaign team, led by political strategist James Carville, succeeded in keeping the focus of the campaign on the economy rather than on foreign policy or elements of

Clinton's background like his Vietnam era draft status or his involvement with a failed real estate development in Arkansas.

PRESIDENTIAL DEBATES Televised presidential debates are now a major feature of presidential elections. The 1960 debate between John Kennedy and Richard Nixon boosted Kennedy's campaign and elevated the role of television in our politics.[38] In 1964 and 1972, incumbents Lyndon Johnson and Nixon refused to debate their challengers. In 1976, President Gerald Ford debated Jimmy Carter and mistakenly said, while defending his record of negotiating with the Soviet Union, that each country in Eastern Europe "is independent, autonomous, it has its own territorial integrity, and none was under Soviet domination." That mistake damaged his credibility.

Adlai Stevenson.

In 1980 the question arose whether to include third-party candidate John Anderson in the televised debates, as it did again in 1992 with Ross Perot. Perot and his running mate, James Stockdale, were included in all presidential and vice-presidential debates. The 1992 debates generated large viewing audiences, averaging over 80 million for each debate (around 110 million people watched the 1994 football Superbowl). Each debate used a different format, one of which had undecided voters asking the presidential candidates questions. The debates did not result in large numbers of voters changing their minds about the candidates; rather, they reinforced voters' prior choices and brought additional attention to Ross Perot.

Although some journalists are quick to express their dissatisfaction with presidential candidates for being so concerned with makeup and rehearsed answers, and although the debates have not always had telling effects on the election outcomes, they have provided important opportunities for candidates to distinguish themselves and for the public to weigh their qualifications. Candidates who do well in these debates are at a great advantage. They have to be quick on their feet, well rehearsed, and have a personality that comes across positively on television. But doing well in the debates does not guarantee a successful presidency. Even a Washington or a Lincoln might not have campaigned effectively on television.

IMPROVING ELECTIONS

Concern over how we choose presidents now centers on two issues: (1) the rise in the number, timing, and representativeness of presidential primaries, and (2) the role of the electoral college, including the possibility that a presidential election might be thrown into the House of Representatives, with possibly controversial results.[39] Electoral reform focuses on encouraging greater turnout and changing the way we finance elections, which is the subject of the final section in this chapter.

The Pros and Cons of Presidential Primaries

The main argument in favor of presidential primaries is that they open the nominating process to more voters than do caucus or convention methods. Today the media play up the primary in every important state, and voters follow the races in other states as well as their own. In so doing, they can judge the candidates' political qualities: their abilities to organize campaigns, communicate through the media, stand up under pressure, avoid making mistakes (or recover if they do make them), adjust their appeals to shifting events and to different regions of the country, control their staffs as well as utilize them, and be decisive, articulate, resilient, informed, and ultimately successful in winning votes. In short, supporters claim, primaries test candidates on the very qualities they must exhibit in the presidency.[40]

British Elections: A Contrast

British general elections offer an interesting contrast to elections in the United States:

1. The election campaign lasts only three weeks.

2. Candidates for the House of Commons, the most critical election in Britain, are allowed to raise and spend only $15,000. If they spend more they are disqualified.

3. Each candidate gets the same amount of free air time, and each candidate is allowed one free election leaflet mailed to each voter in the constituency.

4. About 75 percent of voters turn out, and about 95 percent of eligible voters are registered to vote.

5. At the voting booth, the voter is handed a slip of paper with the names of three or four candidates for the House of Commons. No other offices or ballot questions are presented at the same time.

SOURCE: Adapted from Dudley Fishburn (a candidate for Parliament in 1992), "British Campaigning—How Civilized!" *The New York Times,* April 14, 1992, p. 25.

Primaries are not only the most participatory but also the most *representative* way to choose our presidents. With millions of voters participating in more than 30 state primaries,[41] more people take part than was the case before the use of primaries expanded in the 1970s. As primaries take place, some aspirants drop out. With the number of entrants thus narrowed, the public focuses its attention on the remaining candidates. Thus in 1992 the number of candidates for the Democratic nomination got smaller and smaller until toward the end it was narrowed to ex-governor Jerry Brown of California and Bill Clinton.

Critics of primaries grant that more voters take part in primaries than in the caucus and convention methods of choosing delegates, but they question the quality of the participation. For one thing, supporters of the different candidates have no opportunity to deliberate together in public. Voters in primaries must depend largely on the news media and advertising for their information and basis for judgment. Voters in presidential primaries tend to be more interested in, and influenced by, candidates' personalities and media skills than their positions on vital issues.[42] Participation has been low in recent years. In 1992 primaries turnout was generally under 30 percent of the voting age population, and it declined as the primary season progressed and the field of candidates narrowed.[43]

Low levels of turnout in primaries open the possibility that extreme groups will have a disproportionate say; the "selectorate" replaces the electorate. In addition, candidates are forced to appeal to highly motivated voters, usually from the conservative wing of the Republican party and the liberal wing of the Democratic party. As a result, candidates often take ideologically extreme positions during the primaries.

The primary voting mechanism—each citizen casting one vote for one candidate, often in a multicandidate field—does not allow voters to express relative preferences. In 1976, for instance, a number of liberal Democratic candidates ran in the New Hampshire primary. Jimmy Carter was the only one seen as moderate or conservative. Liberal candidates split the liberal vote; Carter received the moderate and conservative vote. Liberal voters had no opportunity to say they preferred any of the liberal candidates over Carter. Such an electoral system does not allow for rank ordering that may be necessary to reflect what the electorate actually wants.[44]

Another criticism is that the primaries are badly scheduled and the primary season lasts too long.[45] As we have noted, the media give a lot of attention to the first primary.[46] Twenty states, including most southern states, hold their primaries on the same day—Super Tuesday—in March. The intention of this schedule is to enhance the position of the South in the nominating process, helping moderate candidates or candidates from the region. Super Tuesday gave Bill Clinton's campaign a boost in 1992. Primaries in some of the larger states, such as Pennsylvania, Illinois, New York, and California, are traditionally held later in the spring. In many recent election years, contests in both parties had been virtually decided before the primaries in these populous states took place. As a result, some voters claim they have no "say" in determining the presidential candidates, and California has considered moving its presidential primary from June to March.

Moreover, the length of the nominating campaign exhausts the candidates and tries the patience of the voters. The "primary season" lasts more than three months, and during that period, primaries are held at least twice a month, and at times weekly. Candidates often campaign for months and sometimes years in advance of the Iowa caucus and New Hampshire primary, and victory might go to the candidates with the greater stamina.[47]

Finally, some critics directly contradict those who say that primaries test the qualities needed to be president. Instead, candidates have only to win "the media game" in which they must be witty, resourceful, attractive, and articulate. These may not be the most important qualities to be a good president. Thomas Jefferson,

From Coast to Coast

Voter Turnout in the 1992 Primaries

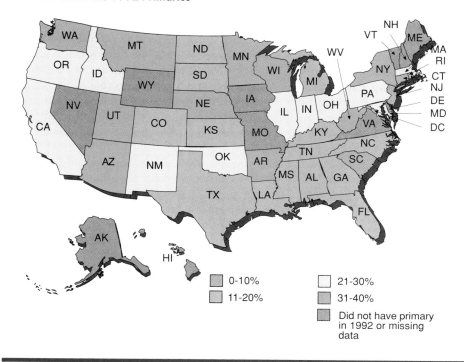

Legend:
- 0-10%
- 11-20%
- 21-30%
- 31-40%
- Did not have primary in 1992 or missing data

Abraham Lincoln, and Harry Truman were able presidents, but they did not have great "media appeal." Critics are disturbed by the gap between the qualities required to carry primary contests and the qualities needed to organize an administration, get support on issues, and deal with congressional leaders, governors, and mayors. Yet no system guarantees that the candidate who would make the best president will win.

Reforming the Nominating Process

What could be substituted for state presidential primaries? Some argue in favor of a *national presidential primary.* This would take the form of a single nationwide election, probably held in May or September, or of separate state primaries held in all the states on the same day. Supporters contend that a one-shot national presidential primary (though a runoff might be necessary) would be simple, direct, and representative. It would cut down the wear-and-tear on candidates, and it would attract a large turnout because of intensive media coverage. Opponents argue that this "reform" would make the present system even worse. It would enhance the role of showmanship and gamesmanship; and, being enormously expensive, it would hurt the chances of candidates who lack strong financial backing.[48] More generally, voting mechanisms that promote candidates with certain minimum levels of support and eliminate those with less support more accurately reflect voter preferences than mechanisms that give all candidates, no matter how poor their showing, a proportionate share of the delegates.

A more modest proposal is to hold *regional primaries,* possibly at two-or three-week intervals across the country—in other words, expand on the Super Tuesday idea. Regional primaries might bring more coherence to the process, encourage more emphasis on issues of regional concern, and cut down on wear-and-tear. But such primaries would retain most of the disadvantages of the present system—especially the emphasis on money and media. Clearly, they would give an advantage to candidates from whatever region held the first primary, and this advantage would encourage regional candidates and might increase polarization among sections of the country.

A quite different proposal is to cut down drastically on the number of presidential primaries and make more use of the *caucus* system. The huge turnout of voters in the Iowa caucuses in recent elections shows that participation can be high; the time participants spent discussing candidates and issues shows that such participation can be thoughtful and informed. In caucus states, candidates are less dependent on the media and more dependent on their abilities to reach political activists. By centering delegate selection in party meetings, the caucus system would also, some say, enhance the role of the party.[49]

Still another idea—used by Colorado for nominations to state officers and by Utah for nominations to federal and state office—would turn the process around. Beginning in May, local caucuses and then state conventions would be held in every state. They would then send delegates—a certain percentage of whom would be unpledged to any presidential candidate—to the national party conventions, which would be held in the summer. The national conventions would select two or three candidates to compete in a national primary to be held in September. In this Colorado plan, or *national preprimary caucus and convention* plan, voters registered by party would be allowed to vote for their party nominee in the September primaries.[50]

How we choose nominees for president is determined by a combination of party rules and state laws. Reformers agree that the current process is flawed but disagree over which aspects of it require change. Democrats have been most unhappy with the current system because, until 1992, it had produced nominees who did not fare well in the general election. Some blamed the rules for these defeats, but others, like Ronald Brown, Democratic National Committee chair from 1989 to 1992, expressed doubt that a change of rules would result in more successful Democratic candidates. The election of Bill Clinton in 1992 put the debate to rest because the Democratic party would focus on reelecting Clinton in 1996. The debate now will probably shift to the Republican party, where the race for the 1996 election may include a fight over nominating rules and procedures.

Reforming the Electoral College

Americans have long been critical of the nature and workings of the electoral college.

1. Critics contend that small states and large "swing" states are overrepresented.
2. The winner-takes-all aspect distorts equal representation of all voters, so that a candidate who receives fewer popular votes than an opponent can still be elected.
3. Electors can (and do) vote for a person other than the candidate for whom they were pledged to vote.
4. If no candidate wins a majority of the electoral vote (as Ross Perot's independent candidacy might have produced in 1992), the issue is thrown into the House of Representatives, where each state delegation, no matter how large or small, has one vote, thus distorting the representative process even more.

The possibility of three viable presidential candidates in 1992 once again put reform of the electoral college on the national agenda. Defenders say that opponents exaggerate the possible dangers; the system has not broken down so far, and it probably never will. This is the "if it ain't broke, don't fix it" school of thought. If the electoral college is anti-popular or anti-majoritarian, so what? "The electoral college avoids uncertainty when the popular vote is extremely close (as in 1960, 1968, and 1976) and prevents candidates with narrow appeal from making it to the White House."[51]

The most frequently proposed reform of the electoral college system is *direct popular election* of the president. Presidents would be elected directly by the voters just as are governors; the electoral college and individual electors would be abolished. Such proposals usually provide that, if no candidate receives at least 40 percent of the total popular vote, a **runoff election** will be held between the two contenders with the most votes. Supporters argue that direct election would give every voter the same weight in the presidential balloting. Winners would take on more credibility or "legitimacy" because their victories would reflect the will of the voters. The dangers and complications of the present electoral system would be replaced by a simple, visible, and decisive method. Opponents contend that the plan would require a national election system and thus would further undermine federalism; that it would encourage unrestrained majority rule and hence political extremism; and that it would hurt the smaller states, which would lose some of their present influence. Some also fear that the plan would make presidential campaigns more remote from the voters; candidates might stress television and give up their present forays into shopping centers and city malls.[52]

An ingenious proposal for a *national bonus plan* has been worked out by a group of scholars and politicians. Under this plan the electoral college would be retained, but it would be heavily weighted toward the winner of the popular vote. A pool of 102 electoral votes (two for each state and the District of Columbia) would automatically be granted to the candidate who gained the most popular votes. These bonus votes would be added to that candidate's electoral college vote. If these votes totaled a majority in the electoral college, the candidate would be elected. If not, a runoff would be held between the two candidates who won the most popular votes. The largely ceremonial position of elector would be formally eliminated. Proponents contend the plan would ensure that the popular vote winner would also be the electoral vote winner. They also claim the plan would encourage increased voter turnout and two-party competition in one-party states and do away with the elector who votes against the decision in his or her state.[53] Opponents say minor parties and independent candidates would be discouraged by such a system.

From time to time, Congress considers proposals for a constitutional amendment to elect presidents directly. Such proposals, however, seldom get far because of the strong opposition of various interests that believe they may be disadvantaged by such a change. Groups such as African Americans and farmers, for example, fear they might lose their *swing vote* power—their ability to make a difference in key states that may tip the electoral college balance.

The failure of the effort to change the system of elections—like the failure of the attempt to change the nominating process—points to an important conclusion about procedural reform: Americans normally do not focus on procedures. Only after a major electoral college crisis is any significant change likely. Then citizens will focus on problems of the electoral system, not on hypothetical problems discussed by political scientists and democratic theorists, but on the real problems facing them.

Some reformers have suggested the elimination of electoral college meetings such as this one on December 19, 1988, by the Republican electors of the state of Virginia to cast their votes for George Bush and Dan Quayle, who had won the popular vote in November.

MONEY IN AMERICAN ELECTIONS

Campaigns cost money. Campaign money can come from a variety of sources: a candidate's own wealth, political parties, interested individuals, or interest groups. Money is contributed to candidates for a variety of reasons, ranging from altruism

The costs of congressional elections have risen dramatically over the past fifteen years, while the rates of reelection have risen. Part of the explanation for the success incumbents have enjoyed is their "special" relationship with Political Action Committees (PACs).

1. The Permanent Congress

Between 1980 and 1990, about 90 percent of House incumbents seeking reelection have been returned to office, leading critics to charge that what we have in Washington is the "permanent Congress."

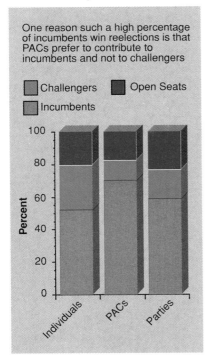

2. Rising Campaign Costs

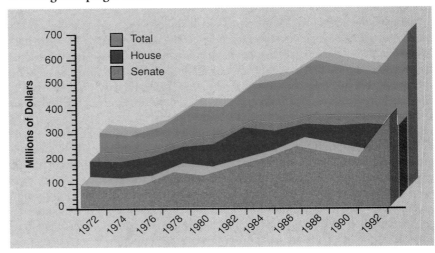

3. Incumbents' Dependence on PAC Money

One reason such a high percentage of incumbents win reelections is that PACs prefer to contribute to incumbents and not to challengers

Presidential candidate Jerry Brown refused to accept PAC money in his 1992 campaign and frequently mentioned the toll-free number people could call to make contributions.

Money figured largely in the bitter 1994 campaign in Virginia between Oliver North and Chuck Robb for the U.S. Senate. Both spent large sums on a barrage of negative ads, with much of North's money coming from out-of-state conservative and religious groups.

to self-interest. Concern about campaign finance stems from the possibility that candidates, in their pursuit of campaign funds, will decide it is more important to represent their contributors rather than their conscience or the views of the voters. The potential corruption that results from politicians' dependence on **interested money**—money given by persons or groups in the hope of influencing the outcome of an election and subsequently influencing policy—concerns many observers of American politics.

Concern about money influencing policy is not new. In 1925, responding to the Teapot Dome scandal in which a cabinet member was convicted of accepting bribes, Congress passed the Corrupt Practices Act, which required disclosure of campaign funds but was "written in such a way as to exempt virtually all of them [members of Congress] from its provisions."[54] Concerns about money buying influence are still with us. The 1972 Watergate scandal, in its most limited sense, was the illegal break-in of Democratic party headquarters by persons associated with the Nixon campaign to steal campaign documents and plant listening devices. But, as news reporters and congressional investigators discovered, large amounts of money from corporations and individuals were "laundered" in secret bank accounts outside the country for political and campaign purposes. Nixon's 1972 campaign spent more than $60 million, more than twice what it had expended in 1968. Investigators discovered that wealthy individuals made large contributions to influence the outcome of the election or secure ambassadorships and administrative appointments.

In the early 1990s Charles Keating and his failed Lincoln Savings and Loan spotlighted the possibility that undue influence comes with large contributions. Keating asked five U.S. senators, all of whom had received substantial campaign contributions or other "perks" from him, to intervene on his behalf with federal bank regulators looking into his savings and loan business. These senators came to be called the Keating Five. The reelection campaign of California Senator Alan Cranston, in particular, had clearly benefited from the more than $1 million Keating had contributed to a voter registration and get-out-the-vote effort run by the senator's son. Watergate and the Keating Five illustrate the problems that arise because politicians need money to run campaigns, and corporations and individuals are all too happy to provide it.

The high costs of campaigns diminish the ability of challengers to mount visible campaigns. Declining competition in our democracy is in part explained by the difficulty challengers have in raising money. Incumbents have a substantial advantage in raising interested money from wealthy individuals and **political action committees (PACs)**, the political arms of interest groups that are allowed to make political contributions. Hence it is not only the source of campaign money that is a problem but the pattern of unequal distribution as well.

Approaches to Reform

Big, long campaigns—especially presidential campaigns—have required big money for some time. Neil O. Staebler, who observed politics for more than half a century as a state committee member, a state chair, a national committee member, a member of Congress, and eventually a member of the Federal Election Commission, commented, "Money corruption has been present in politics for 170 or 180 years. We've been actively working at it since Teddy Roosevelt started back in 1907. But for sixty years practically nothing useful was done....Politics was very much the art of figuring out what you could get away with."[55]

In the past, reformers have tried three basic strategies to prevent abuse in political contributions: (1) imposing limitations on the giving, receiving, and spending of political money; (2) requiring public disclosure of the sources and uses of political money; and (3) giving governmental subsidies to presidential candidates,

Some Provisions of the Federal Election Campaign Act, 1974

- Establishes a Federal Election Commission appointed by the president with the advice and consent of the Senate to regulate the campaign financing of candidates for president, senator, and representative.

- Requires all candidates to designate one principal campaign committee to report all contributions and expenditures.

- Provides for public financing of presidential general election campaigns (with funds from the tax checkoff) and for partial public financing (on a matching basis) of presidential nominating campaigns.

- Provides for subsidies to the two national parties for their convention expenses and to any minor party that polled 5 percent of the total vote in the previous presidential election.

- Limits spending by candidates for presidential nominations (on a state-by-state basis and in total) and in the presidential general elections for those candidates who accept public funding.

- Limits the amounts that national parties may spend on presidential campaigns and on individual congressional and senatorial campaigns.

- Sets a limit of $1,000 on the amount that any individual can give to a candidate for the U.S. Senate or for the U.S. House of Representatives in the primary election, a limit of $1,000 per candidate in the general election, and a limit of $5,000 per candidate per election ($5,000 in primary and $5,000 in general election) for multicandidate organizations (political action committees).

- Sets an overall limitation of $25,000 on the amount that any individual can donate to all candidates for federal office in an election cycle (no similar limitation applicable to political action committees).

- Sets no limit on the amount a candidate can spend on his or her campaign.

- Sets no limit on the amount that individuals or groups can spend independently (that is, on activities not coordinated with a candidate's campaign).

campaigns, and parties, including incentive arrangements. Recent campaign finance laws have tended to use all three strategies for dealing with a problem that sometimes seems insolvable.

THE FEDERAL ELECTION CAMPAIGN ACT   In 1971 Congress passed two significant laws dealing with campaign funding. The Federal Election Campaign Act (FECA) limits amounts that candidates for federal office can spend on media advertising, requires the disclosure of the sources of campaign funds as well as how they were spent, and requires political action committees active in federal campaigns to register with the government and report all major contributions and expenditures. This 1971 law also provided a tax checkoff that allowed taxpayers, by checking a box on their income tax form, to direct $1 of general revenue to a fund to subsidize presidential campaigns.

POST-WATERGATE REFORMS   Further campaign funding reform was prompted by Watergate and widespread public concern about money in elections. In 1974 Congress passed and President Gerald Ford signed the most sweeping campaign reform measure in U.S. history. This legislation established more realistic limits on contributions and spending, tightened disclosure, and provided for public financing of presidential campaigns. The amount of the public subsidy rises with inflation.

The law had to be extensively amended after the 1976 *Buckley v Valeo* decision, which overturned several of its provisions on grounds that they violated the First Amendment.[56] However, the basic outline of the act, emphasizing limitations on contributions and full and open disclosure of all activities by candidates for the House of Representatives and the Senate and public financing of presidential campaigns, remains unchanged. Similarly, later amendments adjusted reporting requirements and encouraged volunteer activities, but they have not altered the philosophy behind the regulation of campaign money.[57]

The campaign finance reform system has worked rather well. All presidential candidates except millionaire John Connally, who sought the Republican nomination in 1980, and billionaire independent H. Ross Perot in 1992, have accepted the voluntary limitations on spending that come with partial public financing of presidential campaigns. Even Ronald Reagan, who opposed public financing, accepted public subsidies in all three of his major presidential campaigns. But the system is not without problems. The number of taxpayers checking off on their income tax forms that they want $1 of their taxes to be directed to the presidential campaign fund has been declining, although enough did so to cover all the costs of the 1992 elections. The Federal Election Commission, designed to oversee the process, is prone to unending partisan deadlock, and in recent years the commission has not been given sufficient funds to maintain its full disclosure activity.

THE UNSOLVED PROBLEM OF SOFT MONEY   The most serious problem with the presidential campaign finance system is the use of **soft money**—funds given to state and local parties by political parties, individuals, or PACs for voter registration drives and party mailings. No limits are set on the amount of such contributions. The money is called "soft" because federal law does not require disclosure of its source or use. Although such money is supposed to benefit *only state and local parties*, it influences federal elections. Presidential candidates in both parties have made raising soft money a high priority. In 1988 at least 375 people contributed $100,000 in soft money to the Democratic and Republican parties.[58] Soft money has risen in presidential campaigns from roughly $19 million in 1980 and 1984, to $45 million in 1988, to a record high $66 million in 1992.[59] If the soft money loophole is not closed, it is likely to undermine most other FECA provisions, including disclosure requirements, spending limitations, and contribution limitations.

Consequences of Current Campaign Financing Practices

Complicated as it is to regulate how presidential campaigns are financed, it is more difficult to get consensus about what, if anything, should be done about congressional campaigns. The problem is easy to identify. Dramatically escalating costs, a growing dependence on PAC money, decreasing visibility and competitiveness of challengers (especially in the House), the ability of wealthy individuals to fund their campaigns, and the danger of large contributions altering election outcomes are all related to current campaign financing practices.

RISING COSTS OF CAMPAIGNS   Since the FECA became law in 1972, total expenditures by candidates for the House have more than doubled after controlling for inflation, and they have risen even more in Senate elections.[60] Television advertising is expensive, limiting the field of challengers to those who have sufficient time or desire to spend more than a year raising money. The American ideal that anyone—a person from humble beginnings or of modest wealth—can seek and hold high public office is no longer true. And rising costs mean incumbents need to spend more time fund raising and therefore less time legislating and representing their districts.

Candidates for federal office and related party activity spent an estimated $1.9 billion in 1992, of which $678 million was spent on congressional campaigns.[61] These are big sums, but they must be put into perspective. The $1.9 billion spent on national elections is but a fraction of a percent of the total cost of government. One Trident submarine, for example, costs hundreds of millions of dollars. In the 1988 presidential campaign, the candidates collectively spent around $500 million. In 1992, slightly more money was spent by presidential candidates. Spending was down in the nomination phase of the 1992 election, but during the general election phase, it increased largely due to the lavish media campaign waged by Ross Perot, who spent roughly $65 million from his own vast fortune.[62]

DECLINING COMPETITION   Unless something is done to help finance challengers, incumbents are likely to continue to have the advantage in seeking reelection.[63] Challengers in both parties are typically underfunded, often largely "invisible."[64] House Republican challengers averaged $92,000 in spending in 1992. In today's world of expensive campaigns, candidates are indeed invisible if they can only spend $100,000. Democratic challengers fared even worse (see Table 12-1). Incumbents in both parties can and do spend much more, and if they feel seriously challenged they can raise even more money.

The high cost of campaigns also dampens competition by discouraging individuals from running for office. Potential challengers look at the fund-raising advantages enjoyed by incumbents, at incumbents' campaign bank accounts (which sometimes have $1 million before the campaign even starts), and at the time it will take for them to raise enough money just to launch a minimal campaign, and then decide to direct their energies elsewhere. Moreover, unlike incumbents, who are being paid while campaigning and fund raising, most challengers have to support themselves and their families for the period of the campaign, which for the House and Senate now is roughly two years.

The high rates of incumbent reelection, especially to the U.S. House of Representatives, have led some to decry the "permanent Congress." While some reformers point to automatic term limits as a way to foster turnover in the House at 12-year intervals, providing challengers sufficient funds to be visible and competitive might have the same effect.

INCREASING DEPENDENCE ON PACs AND WEALTHY DONORS   Where does the money come from to finance these expensive election campaigns? For most House incumbents the answer is political action committees. In 1988, for instance, 255 of the 408 incumbents seeking reelection raised more money from PACs than from individuals. In 1992, that number grew to 197 of 371.[65] Senators are somewhat less

Hard and Soft Money, 1980–1992

A 1979 law allows political parties to raise and spend money for general political activities outside the limits on federal contributions for generic party advertisements, billboards, and bumper stickers as well as for the development of volunteer lists and to pay for office space. This is called "soft money."

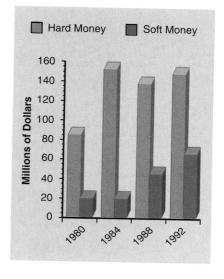

SOURCE: Beth Donovan, "Parties Turned Soft Money Law into Hard and Fast Spending," *Congressional Quarterly Weekly Report* 51 (May 15, 1993), pp. 1196–97.

THE VOTE THAT REALLY COUNTS

By permission of Bill Mauldin and Wil-Jo Associates.

Should PACs be abolished?

As a member of Congress who almost lost out to a heavily PAC-financed candidate in the last election, you are urged by constituents to take a bold and simple step: vote to abolish all PACs. A bill is introduced that would simply abolish all such committees on the grounds that through financial contributions to candidates they are gaining excessive influence over politics and policy. How do you vote?

dependent on PACs in the percentage of their total fund raising, but because they spend so much more, they raise even more money from PACs than House incumbents. Challengers for seats in either chamber receive little from PACs because PACs do not want to offend politicians in power, and politicians in power want to stay in office. This marriage of interests has meant that congressional incumbents court PAC contributions, and PACs are happy to oblige.

Politicians also turn to individual donors who can contribute $500 or $1,000 to their campaigns. Persons who make such contributions are giving interested money; they hold the expectation that legislators they have helped win will respond to their concerns. Given congressional incumbents' preoccupation with reelection, contributions from PACs or large individual contributions are likely to be remembered.

To be sure, PACs and individuals give political money for many reasons. But the American Medical Association's PAC, the realtors' PAC, the foreign auto dealers' PAC, the public employees' PAC, and those individuals who write checks totaling $25,000 per year share something in common: They want certain laws to be passed or repealed, certain funds appropriated, or certain administrative decisions rendered. At a minimum they want access to officeholders, a chance to talk with members before key votes.

Defenders of PACs often point out that there is no demonstrable relationship between contributions and roll call votes. But influence in the legislative process

---

TABLE 12-1

Average Campaign Expenditures of Candidates for the House of Representatives, by Party and Candidate Status, 1974–1992

Party and Year	Amount Spent (rounded and in thousands)		
	Incumbent	Challenger	Open Seat
Republican			
1974	$213.3	$ 54.8	$214.4
1976	210.3	122.6	234.1
1978	252.4	154.3	379.1
1980	281.4	220.7	355.6
1982	389.9	220.1	426.5
1984	350.9	240.3	468.9
1986	436.6	131.2	581.8
1988	451.6	109.8	553.1
1990	397.6	109.8	443.4
1992	543.0	92.0	163.3
Democrat			
1974	102.9	157.3	264.8
1976	168.5	106.5	334.5
1978	207.4	142.1	424.5
1980	250.8	148.0	286.1
1982	335.7	191.7	347.1
1984	351.4	156.7	441.4
1986	372.1	170.3	499.2
1988	395.8	158.6	510.1
1990	400.4	108.7	520.3
1992	611.2	66.3	175.1

SOURCE: David B. Magleby and Candice J. Nelson, *The Money Chase: Congressional Campaign Finance Reform* (Brookings Institution, 1990) p. 38; Norman J. Ornstein, Thomas E. Mann, and Michael J. Malbin, *Vital Statistics on Congress, 1991–1992* (Congressional Quarterly Press, 1992), pp. 74–75. Federal Election Commission, 1992.

depends on access to staff and members of Congress. Access is obviously not possible for everyone, and such access is a large advantage. Most agree that campaign contributions give the donors unusual access. PACs influence the legislative process in other ways as well. Their access helps them structure the legislative agenda with friendly legislators and influence the drafting of legislation or amendments to existing bills. These are all advantages that, reformers claim, others do not have.

CANDIDATES' PERSONAL WEALTH AND THE PROBLEM OF INDEPENDENT EXPENDITURE

The FECA has been roundly criticized for what it fails to do. Campaign finance legislation cannot constitutionally restrict rich candidates—the Rockefellers, the Kennedys, the Perots—from giving heavily to their own campaigns. Big money makes a big difference, and wealthy candidates can afford to spend that kind of money. In presidential politics this advantage can be most meaningful in the period before the primaries begin. There may be no constitutional way to limit how much money people can spend on their own campaigns.

Similarly, the FECA does not constrain **independent expenditures** by groups or individuals who are separate from political candidates. This loophole has been permitted by the Supreme Court on free speech grounds. Groups sympathetic to, but independent of, candidates are allowed to raise and spend funds to help elect them or to defeat their opponents. For example, in 1984 Michael Goland, a Californian, spent $1,100,740 as an independent expenditure to defeat Illinois Senator Charles Percy.[66] As long as there is no collusion between the independent spender and the candidate, an individual or PAC can spend an unlimited amount of money for or against a candidate. Independent expenditures are not soft money; they are fully disclosed. Soft money is given to state parties for "party building." It is not limited and, if state law does not require disclosure, not disclosed.

Some also contend that the law fails in that it provides vast sums for presidential campaigns and relatively little—mainly for convention costs—to the national parties. Helping candidates at the expense of parties, it is said, intensifies the growing trend toward more personalized, fragmented, and individualized politics. Some favor greater subsidies to parties until they can be self-supporting. It was in response to the needs of parties that the soft money exemption was created.

Prospects for Reform

For the 12 years Ronald Reagan and George Bush controlled the White House, campaign finance reform always faced a likely veto from the president. Neither president was supportive of a comprehensive change that Congress was considering or that was advocated by Common Cause. Opposition to such reforms as limiting PACs, providing public funding, and restricting soft money was also evident in Congress. Democratic incumbents who benefit the most from PACs had reservations about removing their financial support base, Republicans were philosophically opposed to public financing of congressional elections, and both parties had benefited from soft money in one way or another. The House and Senate had different perspectives on reforming campaign finance. One group for whom reform is critically important—challengers— had no vote because the changes would be enacted entirely by incumbents. This situation created the danger that any change would be "an incumbent protection bill."

In his first few months in office, President Clinton proposed comprehensive campaign finance reform—including partial public financing of congressional elections, limitations on the amount of money congressional candidates could accept from PACs, and virtual elimination of soft money in presidential elections. Not surprisingly, Democrats and Republicans in Congress objected and quickly embarked on their own campaign finance reform agendas. House Democrats were less eager for change than Clinton was, and the president was forced to downplay his campaign promise for change.

Michael Huffington spent over $25 million of his own money in an unsuccessful race for the U.S. Senate from California in 1994. Diane Feinstein also spent heavily and defeated him by a slim margin in the most expensive Senate campaign in U.S. history.

Thinking it Through

Because you "know your Constitution," you probably vote against the bill on the grounds it would threaten the right to form an association for political purposes—a right protected under the Bill of Rights. Instead, you might bring in a substitute bill—perhaps setting a limit of, say, $2,500 on the amount a PAC could contribute to any one candidate or party. Such a limit would work to curb the influence of PACs without impairing the right of citizens to set up the PAC. But you would introduce your substitute bill knowing that it might someday be declared unconstitutional by the Supreme Court.

Clinton also had to worry about Ross Perot's frequent charge that "running up and down the halls of Congress all day, everyday, are the organized special interests who have the money that makes it possible to buy the television time to campaign to get reelected next year."[67] Clinton thus found himself in a cross fire with his own proreform campaign promises and Perot's rhetoric coming at him from one side and his own party leaders in Congress opposed to many reforms on the other.

INTERPRETING THE 1992 AND 1994 ELECTIONS

Even though he won election by a margin of only 5 percent of the total popular vote, Bill Clinton swept to a landslide victory in the electoral college. Clinton ran as a "different kind of Democrat" in 1992, arguing that he was different from Walter Mondale and Michael Dukakis. Part of his strategy was to avoid the "liberal Democrat" label that Bush and Reagan had attached to Democratic nominees. Exit polls demonstrated that Clinton succeeded in recapturing more than half of the Democrats who voted for George Bush in 1988.[68]

Bill Clinton's ability to attract Democratic voters and most Independents helps explain his strong showing in the industrial Northeast and Midwest, as well as in the Pacific Coast states. Clinton did especially well among African Americans, receiving three-quarters of the vote, and among Catholics and women, getting roughly half of the vote—a marked improvement over Democratic candidates in 1980, 1984, and 1988. Evidence that Clinton was able to avoid the "liberal" label was found in his strong showing among moderates; he picked up more than half of these voters.

The glue that held this Clinton coalition together was agreement on the need for change and a stronger economy. Try as George Bush did to shift attention from this topic, he was unable to do so. Attacks on Clinton's lack of experience in foreign policy, his explanation of his draft record, or the Republican party's commitment to "family values" did not overcome the bad news about the economy. Ross Perot's insistence that the candidates talk about the federal deficit, the national debt, and the stagnant economy only made it more difficult to change the focus of the campaign.

The 1992 elections were labeled by the media as the "year of the woman" because of the large number of female candidates for congress. Those elected in 1992 included a record number of women and minorities, including the first African-American woman senator, Carol Mosely-Braun (D.-IL), and the first Native American senator in 60 years, Ben Nighthorse Campbell (D.-CO). There were more than the average number of retirements in 1992, and redistricting meant that there were more than the average number of districts without incumbents in the House. Among the incumbents who sought reelection, the success rate was again very high—over 90 percent of House incumbents reelected.

In 1994 Republicans won stunning victories in contests for Congress, governor, and state legislatures across most of the country. Democrats lost control of both houses of Congress for the first time since 1954; Tom Foley was the first sitting Speaker to be defeated since 1860; and prominent Democrats like Dan Rostenkowski, Jack Brooks, and Jim Sasser were defeated. The Republicans won control of governorships that had been Democratic in New York, Texas, Pennsylvania, Tennessee, Alabama, and Idaho. Republicans gained an additional 450 seats in state legislatures and achieved control of 15 state legislative chambers.

The shift to Republicans was especially pronounced in the South, which had tended to vote Republican for president in recent elections but remained Democratic in Congress. Republicans changed that in 1994, picking up a net gain of two Republican senators and 16 House members in the eleven confederate states. Republicans also enjoyed a net gain of three governors in this once solidly Democratic region.

Part of the explanation for the Republican success is a very good set of candidates, often well financed. Two sons of former President George Bush ran for governor in 1994; George W. Bush was elected in Texas and Jeb Bush lost narrowly in Florida. Other examples of strong Republican candidates included Mitt Romney, who gave Ted Kennedy a race in Massachusetts, and Olympia Snowe, who won a Senate seat in Maine.

Republicans also capitalized on the strong antigovernment sentiment in the country. Much of this anger was directed at the Congress, because of the check-cashing scandal, corruption in the House Post Office, and a sense that the institution was not working. Republicans were successful in arguing that change was needed because of the 40-year period of Democratic dominance in Congress.

SUMMARY

1. Our electoral system is based on winner-takes-all rules, with typically single-member district or single-officeholder arrangements. These rules foster a moderate two-party system. That we have fixed and staggered terms of office adds predictability to our electoral system.

2. The electoral college is the means by which presidents are actually elected. To win a state's electoral votes, a candidate must have a plurality of votes in that state. The winner takes all. Thus candidates cannot afford to lose the popular vote in the most populous states. The electoral college also gives disproportionate power to the smallest states and holds within it the potential for defeat of the popular vote winner. Reform efforts have been unsuccessful because the system has worked in the past.

3. Many House, state, and local races are not seriously contested. The extent to which a campaign is likely to be hotly contested varies with the importance of the office and the chance a challenger has of winning. Senate races are more likely to be contested, though most incumbents win.

4. The race for the presidency actually takes place in three stages: winning delegate support in presidential primaries and caucuses, gaining the formal party nomination at the presidential convention (usually predetermined by the first stage), and winning a majority of the electoral college.

5. The present presidential selection system is under criticism because of its length and expense and because it seems to test candidates for media skills less needed in the White House than the ability to govern, including the capacity to form coalitions and make hard decisions.

6. Even though presidential nominations today are usually decided weeks or months before the national party conventions, these conventions still have an important role in setting the parties' direction, unifying their ranks, and firing up enthusiasm. They also influence nominations in future years.

7. Because large campaign contributors are suspected of improperly influencing public officials, Congress has long sought to regulate political contributions. The main approaches of reform have been: (1) imposing limitations on giving, receiving, and spending money; (2) requiring public disclosure of the sources and uses of political money; and (3) giving governmental subsidies to presidential candidates, campaigns, and parties, including incentive arrangements. Present regulation includes all three approaches.

FURTHER READING

LARRY M. BARTELS, *Presidential Primaries and the Dynamics of Public Choice* (Princeton University Press, 1988).

EARL BLACK AND MERLE BLACK, *The Vital South: How Presidents Are Elected* (Harvard University Press, 1992).

ALAN EHRENHALT, *The United States of Ambition: Politicians, Power, and the Pursuit of Office* (Times Books, 1991).

LINDA FOWLER AND ROBERT MCCLURE, *Political Ambition: Who Decides To Run for Congress* (Yale University Press, 1989).

GARY C. JACOBSON, *The Politics of Congressional Elections*, 3d ed. (HarperCollins, 1992).

JOHN KESSEL, *Presidential Campaign Politics*, 4th ed. (Brooks Cole, 1992)

ROBERT D. LOEVY, *The Flawed Path to the Presidency, 1992: Unfairness and Inequality in the Presidential Selection Process* (State University of New York Press, 1994)

DAVID B. MAGLEBY AND CANDICE J. NELSON, *The Money Chase: Congressional Campaign Finance Reform* (Brookings Institution, 1990).

NELSON W. POLSBY AND AARON WILDAVSKY, *Presidential Elections: Contemporary Strategies of American Politics*, 8th ed. (Free Press, 1991).

SAMUEL L. POPKIN, *The Reasoning Voter: Communication and Persuasion in Presidential Campaigns* (University of Chicago Press, 1991).

FRANK J. SORAUF, *Inside Campaign Finance: Myths and Realities* (Yale University Press, 1992).

STEPHEN J. WAYNE, *The Road to the White House, 1992: The Politics of Presidential Elections*, 4th ed. (St. Martin's Press, 1992).

THE MEDIA AND AMERICAN POLITICS

W̲hen George Bush first learned of the success of American bombing of Baghdad in January 1991, it was likely from watching the Cable News Network (CNN). The dramatic broadcast by two American journalists from a Baghdad hotel room announced to the world that the coalition offensive against Iraq had begun. As the war progressed, people everywhere watched live television reports of Scud missile attacks by Iraq on Saudi Arabia, the use of American Patriot missiles as a counter-Scud weapon, and daily press briefings from both sides of the Kuwait-Saudi Arabian border. Not only did George Bush turn to CNN on the first night of the bombing and thereafter for information on what was happening in Iraq, but it is believed that Saddam Hussein also watched CNN to learn of developments in his own country.

The news media are just as important in domestic politics. When Bill Clinton sought support for his budget and health care program, he spoke to the nation on television, showed up on talk shows, and used the radio. These appearances were an effort to mobilize public opinion to pressure Congress to respond.

Americans have more ways to find out what is going on in the world than do citizens of any other democracy. We have widespread access to television. We get constant around-the-clock news. Our magazines reflect all kinds of different opinions and perspectives and promote every conceivable cause. We have some of the world's greatest newspapers. Although during wartime we have had some censorship of the news, with very few exceptions people are free to say or write whatever they wish.

This is not to say that press coverage of politics and government in the United States is without problems. Our Constitution guarantees a free press, not a responsible one. People often blame the media for many of our ills—for increasing tension between the races, for biased attacks upon public officials, for sleaze and sensationalism, and for being more interested in making money than in conveying information. Media bashing has become something of a national pastime, and there is considerable merit to all these charges. But "the media" at times is simply an abstraction for those who prefer criticizing the messenger to avoid dealing with the message. Comments like, "It is the media's fault that we have lost our social values," or "The media's preoccupation with negative traits of candidates turns Americans off to politics" are overly broad assertions. The media do have certain tendencies that affect American politics and public policy, but, as we shall see, far more problems are blamed on the media than they deserve.

No discussion of American politics today is complete without assessing the role of the media. The media provide the major source of information, even for the most important policy makers. A free press is also essential for the maintenance of democracy. This chapter examines the media's role in American politics, beginning with the factors promoting the rise of the media as an independent force, continuing with a discussion of the media's influence on each of us as citizens and on our election campaigns, and culminating in an appraisal of the media's influence on the governance of our nation.

THE INFLUENCE OF THE MEDIA

Is the influence of the media in politics real or a myth? The media, in particular the print media, have been called "the other government," "the fourth estate," and "the fourth branch of government."[1] Evidence that the mass media influence our culture and politics is plentiful. Before we can examine that influence, however, we must

Some Key Terms

When we refer to "the media," what do we mean? Years ago the only means of communication to large numbers of people was through the press. With the advent of radio and television, we adopted the term the "mass media," a general term that refers to television, newspapers, and magazines.

- *Media*—a general term that refers to all forms of communication. The term "the media" is an abstraction that often lacks precision.
- *Mass media*—communication by the media on a large scale.
- *Media event*—activity undertaken to generate news coverage and publicity that would not be done if news reporters or cameras were not present.
- *The press*—the news media, in popular language often limited to print media.
- *News media*—print and broadcast coverage of the news.
- *Journalist*—a news reporter who writes news for the press or broadcasts news via electronic media.
- *Fourth estate*—the press and news media in general. In medieval Europe the three estates were nobility, clergy, and commons; the news reporters have been called the fourth estate.
- *Fourth branch of government*—the news media are sometimes referred to as supplementing the three traditional branches of government—executive, judicial, and legislative.

Television brought the Persian Gulf War into the homes of millions of Americans. Here the Cable News Network (CNN) shows an Iraqi bomb shelter that allegedly had been destroyed by allied missiles.

define some terms. The **mass media** are means of communication that reach the mass public; they include newspapers and magazines, radio, television (broadcast, cable, and satellite) and films, recordings, and books.[2] The news media emphasize news, but the distinctions are not clear-cut. Some media critics contend there is now a combination of the two—a medium called "infotainment" that uses entertainment techniques to present the news. As evidence, they point to evening news programs featuring "happy talk" between news anchors and to prime-time programs such as *60 Minutes, Primetime, 20/20*, and talk shows with hosts like Rush Limbaugh, Larry King, Phil Donahue, and Oprah Winfrey.

By definition, the mass media disseminate their message to a large and often heterogeneous audience at the same moment. Because they must have broad appeal, their messages often are simplified, stereotyped, and formulaic. Certainly the mass media are big business. They live off high audience ratings and substantial advertising revenues, which are essential to their "bottom line" of big profits. But does profit spell political clout? Two factors are important here: the media's pervasiveness and their role as a linking mechanism.

The Pervasiveness of Television and Radio

Almost all Americans see television every day, and most homes have at least two sets, each turned on for an average of seven hours per day. While television is primarily an entertainment medium, most Americans use it for news as well. Three out of four Americans watch television news regularly.[3]

For several decades the three network evening news programs captured more than 90 percent of the audience for television news, and national news was available only at set times in the morning and early evening hours. Today, many options exist for broadcast news information, and Americans rely more and more on these alternative sources. One-quarter of Americans say they are regular viewers of CNN, while two out of five say they regularly watch network prime-time newsmagazine shows like *60 Minutes*.[4]

Television has not displaced radio. On the contrary, radio continues to reach more American households than does television. Only one household in a hundred does not have a radio. Nine out of ten Americans listen to the radio every day.[5] Cars and radios seem to go together.

Americans get more than "the facts" from radio and TV. They also get analysis of the news. Following major speeches or news events, on talk shows and on magazine programs like *60 Minutes*, media personalities provide interpretations and assessments of the news. Many people will not decide "what to think" before they have heard from their favorite commentators. In the 1992 presidential elections Bill Clinton and George Bush saw their messages being immediately analyzed and dissected by news commentators. Some commentators themselves become important political figures, as Patrick J. Buchanan did in 1992; his regular participation on CNN's *Crossfire* increased his public visibility before he ran for the presidency.

The Continuing Importance of Newspapers

Recent technological advances have created intense competition for advertising revenues and have contributed to sweeping changes in the manner in which news is transmitted and received. Satellites, cable television, computers, and videocassette recorders (VCRs) make vast amounts of political information available 24 hours a day; satellites eliminate the obstacles of time and distance; computers increase the volume of information that can be stored and retrieved; and cable channels and VCRs increase viewing options.

Despite vigorous competition from the broadcast media, many Americans still read newspapers. Newspaper circulation has held steady at about 63 million nationwide—or about one copy for every four people—for the past 20 years. Another indication of the media's pervasiveness is the rise of national newspapers. *The Wall Street Journal*, with a circulation of nearly 2 million, has long acted as a national newspaper with a specialization in business and finance. Other newspapers with more general interests have emerged. *USA Today*, created in 1982 by the Gannett Corporation, now has a circulation of nearly 1.5 million. In addition, *The New York Times* has a national edition and is read by more than 1 million people (see Table 13–1).

A Linking Mechanism

The pervasiveness of the media alone does not prove their political influence. But it does place the media in a position to be influential because they can reach so much of the American public so quickly. With a large population scattered

TABLE 13-1

Top Newspapers in Circulation, 1993*

1. Wall Street Journal	1,818,652
2. USA Today	1,494,929
3. New York Times	1,141,366
4. Los Angeles Times	1,089,690
5. Washington Post	813,908
6. New York Daily News	764,070
7. Newsday	747,890
8. Chicago Tribune	690,842
9. Detroit Free Press	566,116
10. San Francisco Chronicle	544,253

SOURCE: USA Today Research, December 6, 1993.

*Total Monday-through-Saturday circulation for six-month period ending September 30, 1993.

Before the advent of television and radio, people relied primarily on newspapers for information. Here a group of newsboys in 1909 prepare to deliver their papers.

over a continent, both the reach and speed of the modern media elevate their importance.

The media have become the primary linking mechanism in American politics—a way of connecting policy makers, candidates, and the public in a national, largely electronic, communication network. Candidates talk to voters. Voters respond to candidates. Policy makers and constituents interact. And policy makers and other elite groups—such as interest groups and policy experts—communicate with each other through the media. The media do more than pass along information. The information transmitted can change voters' perceptions of social reality, and it affects their responses to those perceptions. Candidates also may tap voter sentiment from media polls. Policy makers assess policy effectiveness in part through media coverage. And the people rely on the media to evaluate governmental performance and policy.

The Rise of an Autonomous Press

Back in the eighteenth century, not only was there no television or radio, there were only a few newspapers, and those that did exist were run by political parties. Their purpose was not to distribute the news but to defend their own party and attack the other party. The framers relied heavily upon pamphlets and essays to get their messages to the public.

POLITICAL MOUTHPIECE   At the time of the ratification of the Constitution, newspapers consisted of a single sheet, often printed irregularly by store owners to hawk their services or goods. Newspapers rarely lasted more than a year, due to delinquent subscribers and high costs.[6] But the framers understood the important role the press should play as a watchdog of politicians and government.

The new nation's political leaders, such as Alexander Hamilton and Thomas Jefferson, recognized the need to reach the people. Political party organizations as we know them did not exist, but the active role of the press in supporting the Revolution had fostered a growing awareness of the political potential of newspapers. Hamilton recruited staunch Boston Federalist John Fenno to edit and publish a newspaper in the new national capital of Philadelphia. Jefferson responded by attracting Philip Freneau, a talented writer and editor and a loyal Republican, to do the same for the Republicans. (Jefferson's Republicans later became the Democratic party.)

Although the two newspapers competed in Philadelphia for several years, their lasting significance was as a model for future partisan newspapers. They became the nucleus of competing partisan newspaper networks throughout the nation. Federalist and Republican newspapers in the various states relied on the national newspapers for national government news and editorials. The free mailing of newspapers among editors allowed by the U.S. Post Office encouraged this usage.

The linkage between newspaper editors and politicians was maintained through several methods. Politicians loaned or gave money to partisan editors to set up newspapers. Hamilton and other prominent Federalists gave $1,000 each for the start-up of the *New York Evening Post*[7] and helped solicit subscriptions from among party supporters. Government patronage appointments were extended to favorite editors. John C. Calhoun, for example, while serving as secretary of war, hired his favorite editor as federal superintendent of Indian trade. One means of financial support was designation as a government newspaper duly authorized to print the text of laws, reports, speeches, and treaties.[8]

The early American press served as a political mouthpiece for political leaders. Its close connection with politicians and political parties offered the opportunity for financial stability, but at the cost of journalistic independence.

FINANCIAL INDEPENDENCE   The Jacksonian era of the 1820s and 1830s was characterized by increased mass participation in American politics through rallies, bonfires, and local political clubs. As the vehicle for communication with the public, the press began to shift its appeal away from elite readers and toward large masses of less educated and less politically interested readers. This movement was reinforced by rising literacy rates that supported greater circulation for newspapers. These two forces—increased political participation by the common people and the rise of literacy among Americans—began to alter the relationship between politicians and the press.

Some newspaper publishers began to experiment with a new financing structure. They charged a penny a paper, paid on delivery, instead of the traditional annual subscription fee of eight to ten dollars, which was beyond the ability of most readers to pay. Through expanded circulation and more emphasis on advertising, newspapers could become financially independent. The plan for a new "penny press" not only worked, it became a common model for the press thereafter.

The effect of this new independence on the political role of the press was not immediate; in keeping with the strong partisanship of the nineteenth century, many publishers continued to promote partisan causes and candidates anyway. However, some began to criticize their own party. Republican Horace Greeley, editor of the *New York Tribune*, felt at liberty to criticize Abraham Lincoln during the Civil War. Several Republican newspapers abandoned their party's candidate for president in 1884.[9]

The changing finances of newspapers also affected the definition of what constituted news. Before the "penny press," news was political—speeches, documents, editorials—directed at a politically interested readership. The "penny press" reshaped the definition of news as it sought to appeal to the less politically aware with human interest stories, sports, crime and public trials, and social activities.

As news about politics began to constitute a smaller proportion of the newspaper, politicians searched for alternative ways to communicate with the public. In the 1850s, members of Congress used their mail privileges—the franking privilege—to distribute copies of their speeches. During the first half of 1858, for example, members of Congress mailed 800,000 copies of their speeches without charge.[10]

"OBJECTIVE JOURNALISM"   The death knell of the partisan press sounded with the rise of "objective journalism." Many journalists began to argue that the press should be independent of the political parties. *New York Tribune* editor Whitelaw Reid eloquently expressed this sentiment:

> Independent journalism! That is the watchword of the future in the profession. An end of concealments because it would hurt the party; an end of one-sided expositions...; an end of assaults that are not believed fully just but must be made because the exigency of party warfare demands them...that is the end which to every perplexed, conscientious journalist a new and beneficent Declaration of Independence affords.[11]

Journalists also began to view their work as a profession and established professional associations with codes of ethics and publication of journals. This professionalization of journalism reinforced the notion that journalists should be independent of partisan politics—a notion that still pertains today. The rise of the wire services as the primary source for national news (they were politically neutral in order to attract more customers) further strengthened the trend toward objectivity.

THE IMPACT OF BROADCASTING   Radio and television changed the media's role in politics by nationalizing and personalizing the news. Radio did it first, beginning with the creation of networks in the 1920s. Radio dominated national politics until the rise of television after World War II.

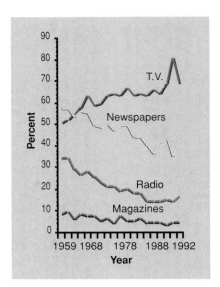

FIGURE 13-1 Where Americans Get Most of Their News

SOURCE: Surveys by the Roper Organization for the Television Information Office, 1959–1992. Numbers do not equal 100 percent due to multiple responses.

President Franklin Roosevelt showed how to use radio effectively. Before 1933 most radio addresses were treated like commencement speeches and major orations, but Roosevelt spoke to his audience on a personal level and showed that radio could be used as a one-to-one conversation. Roosevelt's "fireside chats" established a standard for presidential use of the broadcast media still followed today. Frances Perkins, secretary of labor, recalled that when Roosevelt began speaking over the microphone, he would visualize the average citizen in front of him. "His face would smile and light up as though he were actually sitting on the front porch or in the parlor with them."[12]

Radio was also used for political speeches, campaign advertising, and coverage of political events, such as national nominating conventions. Members of Congress used radio extensively. During the 1930s, more than one thousand speeches were made by members of Congress on one network alone.[13]

Radio provided a means to bypass the editorial screening of the press, since politicians could speak directly to listeners without editing. It also contributed to increased interest in national and international news, since activities outside a listener's local area could be heard as if one were actually there.

Television added a visual dimension, which greatly contributed to rising audience interest in national events. Audience interest grew to the point that by 1963, two major networks doubled the length of their evening news broadcast from 15 to 30 minutes. With the advent of cable television, the coverage of news expanded as well as the range of possible programs. Viewers now can watch news programs 24 hours a day. Specialized cable stations give substantial coverage to Congress and the courts, and some local cable stations provide live coverage of city councils and other public meetings. As we learned during the Persian Gulf War, American cable news coverage is watched around the world for instantaneous coverage of news stories. Coverage of news-related issues in the prime evening hours is provided in programs like *60 Minutes*, *20/20*, and *Crossfire*.

MOST IMPORTANT NEWS SOURCE What is the most important source of news for most Americans? In 1959, when this question was first asked, the proportion who answered newspapers was 6 percent higher than television; the remaining group said they used both television and newspapers (see Figure 13–1). Today, television is the most important source of news by a margin of 3 to 2. Television is now the most trusted source of the news. Generally about two-thirds of Americans indicate that television is one of their most important news sources. This number climbed to over 80 percent in early 1991, when television coverage of the Persian Gulf War kept the nation glued to their TV sets night after night. Newspapers have dropped and are most trusted by about 1 in 4 Americans. Newspapers are the preferred news sources for local candidates.

MEDIA CONGLOMERATES Television can be profitable. One reason is that governmental limitations on competition permit monopoly ownership of broadcast licenses. Radio networks and newspapers were the first to purchase the new medium and establish cross-ownership patterns that persist today. For example, in 1992 the Gannett Corporation owned 81 daily newspapers, 10 television stations, and 15 radio stations. Media conglomerates with large financial resources now dominate the media business and have contributed to the centralization of news. The Federal Communications Commission in 1992 relaxed ownership rules permitting one owner to control up to 30 AM and 30 FM radio stations.

Are a few media conglomerates likely to provide sufficient competition of ideas to support a democratic system?[14] And without them, can local populations scattered around the country, depending only on local media, find out what is happening in the nation's capital? Why not have government-owned media carry out educational and information functions as well as entertainment functions, as they do in Great Britain and France?[15] The answer is that Americans put great stock in an independent press and news media; Americans find centralized government-owned media unacceptable.

Another concern has been the gobbling up of American communication assets by foreign interests. Local newspapers, radio, and television stations used to be owned primarily by local firms; today this is not the case. Large firms, many of them foreign, have acquired ownership of many newspaper and broadcasting stations. A national press—*USA Today*, *The Wall Street Journal*, and *The New York Times*—has also developed. The remaining local outlets depend heavily on news that is gathered, edited, and distributed by national organizations like United Press International and Associated Press. As a result, some people contend that information these days is more diluted, homogenized, and moderated than it would be if the newspapers and broadcast stations were locally owned and the news was gathered and edited locally.[16]

THE NEW JOURNALISM A new sense of professionalism among news reporters has given the press greater autonomy. By the 1960s, schools of journalism were attracting students who wanted to contribute to social change.[17] Press autonomy was enhanced by a press corps self-confident enough to feel equal to politicians. A consequence of objective journalism was the creation of a press that acted as a "common carrier" of information between government and the public. Some journalists, however, challenged this role by arguing they should be more than mere conduits of official information; they should provide their own analysis and interpretation of events to balance the government's position. Others went so far as to advocate that journalists should side with those who are less powerful in society and unable to speak for themselves—a practice termed *advocacy journalism*.[18] A related trend was toward *adversarial journalism*—the practice of challenging government and serving as the opposition to public officials, particularly the president.[19] Notable examples include the reporting of Seymour Hersh of *The New York Times*, who exposed secret documents which came to be known as the *Pentagon Papers* on how the United States became involved in the Vietnam War; Robert Woodward and Carl Bernstein of *The Washington Post*, who played an important role in uncovering the Watergate conspiracy; and Nina Totenberg of National Public Radio, whose reporting on sexual harassment charges helped force the Senate Judiciary Committee to extend the hearings on the confirmation of Clarence Thomas to the U.S. Supreme Court. The growth in this type of journalism was in part a consequence of the types of people choosing journalism as a profession.

A New Mediator in American Politics

Political parties and interest groups have long been seen as political mediators between private individuals and the government—mediators who help to organize the world of politics for the average citizen. This is less so today because the media now serve that function, and political parties have lost their exclusive control over the nominating process. Moreover, there is much greater attention given today to judging candidates not so much in terms of party affiliations and platforms, but in terms of character and competence. The press, not the parties, is performing this evaluative function.

News media have taken over the role of "speaking for the people." Journalists tell politicians what "the people" want and think, and then they tell the people what politicians and policy makers are doing. Politicians understand this, and they know how dependent they are on the media in getting their message out to voters. They know a hostile press can hurt them. Clearly, today's politicians have to spend much of their time cultivating the press. President Clinton, after a rocky start with

We The People

Who Follows the News?

	Serious Users*	Moderate Users and Nonusers
Sex		
Male	58%	42%
Female	45	55
Race		
White	51	49
Nonwhite	52	48
Age		
Under 30	45	55
30–49	51	49
50+	56	44
Education		
College graduate	72	28
Some college	55	45
High school graduate	46	54
Less than high school graduate	38	62
Total	51	49

SOURCE: Times Mirror Center for the People and the Press, *The American Media: Who Reads, Who Listens, Who Watches, Who Cares*, July 15, 1990.

* This category combines "News Sophisticates" and "Other Serious News Consumers."

"We find the defendant guilty as charged by the media."

Drawing by Chon Day. © 1978 The New Yorker Magazine, Inc.

the White House press corps, hired David Gergen to help him improve his press relations and coverage. Gergen had previously worked for Republican presidents, most notably Ronald Reagan, and is credited with improving Clinton's performance in this area. At Gergen's suggestion, the president hosted a media picnic in the White House Rose Garden, invited radio talk show hosts to broadcast from the White House during the budget and economic stimulus package votes in Congress, and provided "photo opportunities" with reporters at receptions. Gergen also allowed reporters more immediate access to himself and others in the press office. These moves are credited with an improved relationship between the press and president.

Journalists now contend they have a proper function of screening candidates and looking into their characters—a function that once belonged to party leaders. Thus in recent presidential elections, candidates have been subjected to investigative reporters looking into their sex and drug practices as well as going through their records all the way back to college to see if there is anything that might be considered "improper." During the 1992 campaign as well as after his election, the media reported charges of President Clinton's alleged extramarital affairs and his business dealings with a failed savings and loan involving the Whitewater Development Corporation.

THE MEDIA AND PUBLIC OPINION

Scholars, journalists, politicians, and political pundits have long debated the power of the media over public opinion. Do the media shape opinions? Do they alter people's behavior? Can they even affect our core values? For a long time, analysts tended to play down the influence of the news media in American politics as compared with the influence of use of the media by political leaders. The impact of Franklin D. Roosevelt's "fireside chats" symbolized the power of the politician against that of the news editor. Roosevelt spoke directly to his listeners over the radio in a way and at a time of his own choosing, and no network official was able to block or influence that direct connection. President John Kennedy's use of the television press conference represented a similar direct contact with the public. President Ronald Reagan was nicknamed the "Great Communicator" because of his ability to take an issue directly to the people through television. Ross Perot emerged on the national scene because of skill in using television talk shows.

The news media are now so important that elected officials and politicians spend considerable time trying to learn how to use them. Presidential events and "photo opportunities" are planned with the evening news and its format in mind.[20] Members of Congress use Capitol Hill recording studios to tape messages for local television and radio stations. And the media often respond positively to these activities by politicians. White House press briefings are frequently included in the evening news, and Congress has excellent access to local media. How government officials use the press, how the press uses government officials, and to what extent the press and television can and should be regulated are critical questions for study.

In recent years many entertainment shows have broken the stereotypes about women and minorities and shown them as major figures in their own persona. In the past such shows tended to show African Americans, Hispanics, and gays and lesbians in stereotypical gender and race roles that subtly reinforced cultural values of sexual and racial inequality. Subtle political messages are found in all types of programming; for example, every sports event begins with the National Anthem, which encourages people to be proud of their country. Many entertainers feature

"VALUES" AND THE MEDIA

For decades conservatives have claimed that the mass media in this country are too liberal—advancing a liberal agenda and attacking traditional values. This issue surfaced again in 1992 when former Vice-President Dan Quayle attacked the "cultural elite" of the nation as mocking families, religion, and patriotism. Quayle went on to say, "Talk about right and wrong, and they'll mock us in newsrooms, sitcom studios, and faculty lounges across America." Quayle charged the television series *Murphy Brown* with "mocking the importance of fathers by bearing a child and calling it 'just another lifestyle choice.'"

Studies show that moviemakers and journalists are more liberal than the general public. A 1992 survey of 104 top television writers and executives found that many of their attitudes toward moral and religious questions are not shared by their audience.

Believe adultery is wrong	
Hollywood	49%
Everyone else	85
Have no religious affiliation	
Hollywood	45%
Everyone else	4
Believe homosexual acts are wrong	
Hollywood	20%
Everyone else	76
Believe in a woman's right to an abortion	
Hollywood	97%
Everyone else	59

SOURCE: The Center for Media and Public Affairs, as reported in *Newsweek*, July 20, 1992.

jokes about political figures and institutions like the Congress. Clearly the media play an important role in reinforcing norms and attitudes.

Audience

People are not just empty vessels into which politicians pour information and ideas. How we interpret political messages depends on a variety of factors: political socialization, selectivity, needs, and the individual's ability to recall and comprehend the message.

POLITICAL SOCIALIZATION   Although we would like to believe we consume the news with an open mind, the reality is that we employ a set of filters or screens to help us interpret and integrate the information. When we watch television or read newspapers, magazines, and books, we bring with us values and attitudes that have been shaped by family, peers, school, and the groups to which we belong.[21] We develop our political attitudes, values, and behavior through an education process that social scientists call **political socialization**. (See Chapter 11 for more detail on this process.) The media, particularly television, may influence our values and attitudes, but they are not as important in the formation of our political attitudes as is our family.[22] Face–to–face contacts often have far more impact on us than the more impersonal television or newspaper. Strong identification with a party also acts as a powerful filter.[23] A conservative Republican from Arizona might watch the "liberal Eastern networks" night after night and year after year and complain about the biased news coverage while sticking to his or her own opinions.

SELECTIVITY   People practice **selective exposure**—screening out those messages that do not conform to their own biases. They subscribe to newspapers or magazines that already support their views. People also practice **selective perception**—perceiving what they want to in media messages and disregarding the rest.[24] One dramatic example is viewers' varying responses to Professor Anita Hill and Judge Clarence Thomas in the 1991 Senate hearings on Thomas's nomination to the Supreme Court. Those who believed Anita Hill's testimony on sexual harassment perceived Thomas as untruthful, while those who believed Thomas's denials discounted Hill's testimony. A similar example of selective perception was the supportive way conservatives generally responded to Paula Jones's charge that Bill Clinton had made sexual advances, as compared to the defensive reactions of Clinton's liberal supporters.

NEEDS   Another mitigating factor in how the media influence opinions is the use to which people put media messages. People read newspapers, listen to the radio, or watch television for very different reasons—sometimes because they are bored, tired, or have nothing better to do, sometimes to get information.[25] People who want to gain information and cultivate an interest in politics are affected differently from those who use media primarily for entertainment.[26] For those who are most interested in entertainment, gossip about President Clinton's alleged affairs, Senator Bob Packwood's diary entries, or George Bush's dislike of broccoli is more important than Clinton's, Packwood's, or Bush's political opinions or deeds. Thus, events like rape trials of prominent individuals are likely to draw more attention than foreign policy speeches by presidential candidates. Members of the broader audience will also more likely follow news that directly affects their lives, such as interest rate changes.[27]

RECALL AND COMPREHENSION   Still another limitation on media influence on public opinion is the extent to which the audience can recall the stories or comprehend their importance. Candidates and officials send out tons of information designed to influence what people think and do, especially how they vote. But people forget or fail to comprehend much of it.[28] The fragmentary and rapid mode of presentation of television news contributes to the problem.

Do the media behave responsibly in reporting riots?

Millions of Americans were shocked by the brutal beating of Rodney King in 1991 by Los Angeles police. The incident, captured on tape by an amateur videocamera operator, was played again and again on the television news during the days immediately following the incident. Then, in a surprising verdict, a jury acquitted the police officers of brutality and other charges, and the nation watched in horror as riots broke out in Los Angeles. Here as well, the media repeatedly showed clips of random acts of violence, beatings, and burnings.

Did the media behave responsibly in their coverage of the Rodney King case and the Los Angeles riots? Did media coverage exacerbate racial tensions and encourage people to riot, both in Los Angeles and in other cities? How should the media behave in such explosive situations?

You Decide!

Given all the information available to people about politics and government, it is not surprising most pick and choose which media source—television, radio, newspapers—to pay attention to and which news stories are important. One scholar who studied the process of selecting which news to pay attention to and remember found that comprehension varied widely, "depending on the nature of stories, the use of visuals, and the concerns and lifestyles of the audience."[29] The best predictor of retention of news stories was political interest. People tend to fit today's news stories into more general assumptions or beliefs about government, politicians, or the media itself.

Bias

There is continuous debate over whether newspapers, radio commentators, television reporters, magazine writers, and especially the mass media are biased. Americans believe they are.[30] Conservatives complain the media are too liberal; liberals claim the media represent the interests of the establishment; and politicians complain they cannot get their messages across. People in general blame many things either on the politicians or on the media.

How can we assess the political bias of the news media? Some contend that television networks are large corporations whose first and foremost concern is profit.[31] For many critics of the media, this observation defines the peculiar nature of the press. It is dedicated, on the one hand, to the impartial reporting of "fact" and, on the other, to boosting ratings and pleasing circulation managers, advertisers, sponsors, and stockholders. Somewhere along the line, the search for truth may get lost, although news organizations pride themselves on their objectivity.[32]

It is becoming more and more difficult to distinguish news from entertainment. Political jokes abound on late-night comedy shows, and we get pungent political messages from the cartoon pages, prime-time network shows, and Hollywood. Actors have become politicians, and politicians have become

Reporter Sam Donaldson is also a commentator on ABC's news magazine show, in which he expresses his personal opinions of events. Do Donaldson's views bias his reporting of the news? Does the public see him as objective?

TABLE 13-2

Samples of the Revolving Door between Journalism and Government Service

	Press Job	Government Job
Ken Bode	TV news reporter ←	Press secretary
Patrick Buchanan	TV commentator ←	Speechwriter and presidential candidate
Hodding Carter	TV commentator ↔	Assistant secretary of state
John Chancellor	TV news anchor ↔	Director, U.S. Information Agency
Leslie Gelb	Newspaper columnist ←	Assistant secretary of state
David Gergen	Newsmagazine editor → and TV commentator	Presidential communications counselor
Chris Matthews	Newspaper columnist ←	Press secretary
Bill Moyers	Newspaper editor ← and TV commentator	Press secretary
William Safire	Newspaper columnist ←	Speechwriter
Pierre Salinger	TV news reporter ←	Press secretary
Diane Sawyer	TV news anchor ←	White House aide
Carl Stern	TV reporter ←	Director of Public Affairs, Justice Department
John Sununu	TV commentator ←	White House chief of staff
Strobe Talbott	Newsmagazine editor and reporter ←	Deputy secretary of state

Thinking it Through

In a free society, the media are the judge of what is newsworthy. The videotape of the Rodney King beating clearly constituted news. The fact that it reinforced perceptions in the African American community of unfair treatment by police could not be avoided. It may be possible that some people engaged in looting and violence in other cities as a result of what they saw on television, but the media were only reporting important events. People's responses to such events are much more likely to be driven by previous beliefs, attitudes, and values than by media coverage. Months later in a second trial the media also reported convictions under federal civil rights statutes against the police officers involved in the beatings.

The Infomercial

In the final days of the 1992 presidential campaign, Ross Perot turned to a form of advertising used infrequently in previous presidential elections. He purchased television time in 30-minute segments and used it to talk about the deficit, the national debt, and governmental reform—especially term limits and the elimination of political action committees. Perot also used this "infomercial" format to introduce himself to the American public. One infomercial was essentially a video biography of Perot, replete with testimonials from Perot family, friends, and employees.

The infomercials were successful. One infomercial had almost 20 million viewers and captured an audience share greater than one of the two competing networks. The novelty of these advertisements attracted viewers, which in turn generated media attention and elevated Perot to a serious contender in the presidential election.

actors. Political analysis creeps onto the front pages of most papers, and many fear that the politics of the editorial page influences coverage of the news.

David Broder of *The Washington Post* voices similar concerns about the confusion of roles by journalists who have served in government (see Table 13–2). According to Broder, a line must divide objective journalism from partisan politics, but many in the print and television media have crossed this line. Broder opposes the idea of journalists becoming government officials and vice versa.[33] Others argue that, because of their government service, journalists with close working relationships with politicians can give us a valuable perspective on government without losing their professional neutrality.

Equally disturbing to some observers is the media's alleged political bias, whether liberal or conservative. But to whom are these critics referring? To reporters, writers, editors, producers, or owners of TV and newspapers? Do they assume a journalist's personal politics will be translated into biased reporting? And does the public think so?

Conservatives say the press is too liberal. They criticize the press for advocating liberal social causes and ignoring the conservative viewpoint.[34] Journalists usually are more liberal than the population as a whole, while editors tend to be a bit more conservative than their reporters, and media owners are more conservative still. Twenty-three percent of the public describe themselves as liberal, compared to 38 percent of college-educated professionals, from whose ranks most journalists are drawn. But even among the professionals, journalists' liberalism stands out. Fifty-five percent describe themselves as liberals.[35]

The far left also accuses the media of bias. Leftist critics contend the mainstream press is purely a propaganda device of the ruling class, creating the boundaries of acceptable thinking and thereby shutting out left–wing viewpoints. Leftist critics see the mass media as capitalist enterprises that dislike airing anticapitalist sentiments. As well as being a tool of the business class, according to these critics, the media are also a tool of government propaganda that seeks to distort the facts. Others see this "conspiracy theory" as merely a rationalization by leftists who are disgruntled over the failure of their views to take hold with the American people.[36]

Another theory of bias has to do with the possible cultural bias of journalists. Elite journalists—those who work for national news media organizations—tend to share a similar culture—cosmopolitan, urban, upper class. Their approach to the events and issues they cover is governed by their common world view. Part of this bias may be derived from their professional training.[37] The result is an almost unconscious perspective that produces bias because elite journalists give greater weight to the side of issues that corresponds to their own version of reality.[38] Newspapers and television news often set a tone of dissatisfaction with the performance of the national government and a cynicism about politics and politicians. A critical tone may be an inevitable element in the mind set of the press.

But to whose benefit does that critical tone work? Conservatives and the far left are not the only ones who perceive bias. Liberals point to newspaper endorsements of Republican presidential candidates to support their claim that newspapers are biased toward conservative policies and candidates. Daily newspapers tend to endorse Republicans over Democrats for president by a ratio greater than 2 to 1.

The critical question is not how the press is biased but whether the press bias, whatever the direction, seeps into the content of the news. The answer to that question is still not settled. Some empirical studies of news content have failed to find the expected bias.[39]

TALK SHOWS: THE NEWEST FORUM

Every day, around the clock, in homes all over the United States, talk shows provide a kind of 1990s American town meeting. With an audience of millions, hosts, hostesses, and their guests analyze the day's news events and vent their feelings from all political perspectives. Radio and television are today's major political arenas.

All three presidential candidates appeared frequently on television and radio talk shows during the 1992 campaign. Ross Perot became identified with the *Larry King Live* show, and Bill Clinton played his saxophone on Arsenio Hall's show and appeared on MTV. George Bush preferred early morning talk shows such as NBC's *Today* and ABC's *Good Morning, America*. All three candidates were seen frequently on public television and C–SPAN.

Televised talk shows continued to be major media events after the election. Vice-President Al Gore and Ross Perot debated the merits of the North American Free Trade Agreement (NAFTA) on a special 90-minute edition of *Larry King Live*. The debate was watched by 11.2 million people (a CNN audience second only to that of the Persian Gulf War) and played a role in the subsequent vote on NAFTA.[*] As in other televised call-in shows, the callers and their questions were almost forgotten in the vivid clash of personalities in the debate.

[*]"The King of Cable," *Entertainment Weekly*, December 10, 1993, p. 65.

Should the government censor
movie and TV violence?

Complaints about excessive and graph-
ic violence portrayed on TV have been
voiced by a broad spectrum of people
in this country. In particular, people
have been concerned about the effect
of such viewing on young children, who
might model their attitudes and behavior
on what they see. Would you favor having government censor violence on television programs? Should such restrictions pertain to all programming, or only
to shows targeted to young viewers?

Public Opinion

The media can make a big difference in what Americans believe. Television, because of its visual dimension, is especially important in shaping opinion, and television news exposure cuts across age groups, educational levels, social classes, and races. Television, with all its concreteness and drama, has an emotional impact that print cannot hope to match.[40] As a result, the media are a potent influence in agenda setting and issue framing.

AGENDA SETTING   The power to set the public agenda is significant, and by calling public attention to certain issues, the media help to determine what topics will become the subject of public debate.[41] However, the agenda-setting function of the media is not uniformly pervasive. It is limited by the audience and the nature of the issue.[42]

One politician who effectively used the media for agenda setting was Ronald Reagan. More than any other president before him, Reagan and his advisers carefully crafted the images and scenes of his presidency to fit the role of television. Thus television became an "electronic throne." According to former Vice-President Walter Mondale, "If I had to give up…the opportunity to get on the evening news or the veto power,…I'd throw the veto power away. [Television news] is the President's most indispensable power."[43]

Agenda setting has significant political consequences. It focuses public attention on certain aspects of American politics and ignores others.[44] In assessing governmental or candidate performance, the media can affect the ultimate choice of policy or candidate.[45] One example of agenda setting during the 1992 presidential primaries was press attention to Bill Clinton's rumored extramarital affairs and draft record instead of his stands on policy questions.

ISSUE FRAMING   The context given an issue or event in a news story can affect public perceptions.[46] For example, when United States involvement in Bosnia was framed in news stories as a repetition of Vietnam, Clinton administration officials were understandably anxious about vanishing public support for U.S. involvement. When George Bush sought support for the Persian Gulf War, he compared Suddam Hussein to Adolf Hitler so as to frame the conflict differently. The same kind of framing has been part of the abortion debate, with those favoring abortion defining their position in terms of freedom of choice as a positive way to frame the issue. Similarly, when voters decide ballot questions, the side that most effectively defines the issue generally wins.[47]

Regulation

The charges of media bias and the importance of agenda setting and issue definition are only some of the reasons why some urge government to regulate the media. Traditionally, newspapers have not been regulated because of our First Amendment guarantee of freedom of the press and because competition among newspapers has been seen as a way to limit bias. Critics of the growth of media conglomerates propose that newspaper chains be broken up through antimonopoly legislation.

Regulation of the broadcast media has existed in some form since its inception. Because of the limited number of television and radio frequencies, government has overseen matters like licensing, financing, and even content. One such regulation required "fairness" in news programming.[48] As written into law and interpreted by the Federal Communications Commission, the **fairness doctrine** imposed on radio and television license holders an obligation to ensure that differing viewpoints were presented about controversial issues or persons. With the advent of cable television and the Reagan administration's antiregulatory perspective, extension of the doctrine was repealed in 1987.

The media are criticized for sensationalism, overemphasis on "theater" and spectacles, obsession with violence, lack of self-criticism, lack of objectivity, and superficial reporting. They have been urged to provide more explanation, interpretation, and analysis; to look at how they report on activities of the government; to depend less on "packaged" news handed out by government bureaucracies; to be more aggressive in covering the White House; and to become better educated themselves about what really goes on in the Congress.[49]

Critics hesitate to propose harsh or sweeping remedies for the failures of press, television, and radio—lest controls threaten First Amendment liberties. But critics are also uncertain about how serious the problem really is and how improvement can best be accomplished.[50] Moreover, the seriousness of the problem varies widely with the situation. For example, in closely balanced election races, in which media influence or bias might be strong enough to tilt the outcome one way or the other, the opinions put forth by major press and networks may be crucial. But others argue that in our pluralistic nation, which comprises an enormous variety of groups and movements, Americans have so many "filters" through which to observe events that it is extremely difficult to influence public opinion.

THE MEDIA AND ELECTIONS

Do news stories determine who wins or loses elections, who gets nominated for office, or which referenda get passed? News stories probably have more influence today because of the shift to greater direct democracy in our political system by which primaries nominate candidates, with little role left for parties. In addition, voters decide many important issues directly through initiatives and referendums.

While the influence of the media may be greater due to these changes, there is little evidence such influence controls elections. Generally, the more visible the campaign, the less likely voters are to be swayed by any one source. Hence, news coverage is more likely to be important in a city referendum than in an election for president or the Senate.

Diversification of the news media also lessens the ability of any one medium to dominate politics. Newspaper publishers who were once seen as very important in state and local politics now know that politicians and their media advisers can communicate their message through television, radio, direct mail, videocassettes, and cable television. Hence, while the news media remain an important means of communication, there is now more competition among the various media, and politicians and candidates can get their message out regardless of what the editor of the state's largest newspaper may think.

The Electoral Campaign

Campaigns are run differently today than they were a generation ago. During the 1960 election, John Kennedy's effort to attract media attention by winning early primaries was considered novel; today it is standard operating procedure.

CHOICE OF CANDIDATES   The role of the media begins with the decision of who will run. Television greatly affects the list of preferred traits for presidential candidates. A hundred years ago, successful candidates needed a strong pair of lungs. Today it is a "telegenic" appearance, a pleasing voice, and no obvious physical

Thinking it Through

In the spring of 1994 a congressional hearing solicited testimony from parent groups, psychologists, and law enforcement representatives on the effects of viewing murders, rapes, beatings, and torture on the minds of both children and adults. Experts showed a correlation between aggressive behavior and the depiction of violent acts in movies and TV. "Copycat" killings were also attributed to seeing such crimes portrayed. TV violence, it was agreed, fosters attitudes of indifference to violence and social acceptance of violent behavior.

In response, representatives of the movie, TV, and cable industries maintained that they could police themselves and establish standards to moderate the amount of violence in their programs. They proposed a grading system for TV shows that would indicate to parents what ages the shows were suitable for. Attorney General Janet Reno warned the industry that if they did not clean up their act, the government would step in to set limits on what could be shown.

Some object to the idea of censorship because it is contrary to the ideals of a democratic society and places too much power in the hands of the government. Should the cruelty of the wicked stepmother in Hansel and Gretel be considered objectionable? Whose standards should be applied? If some movies are too vicious for children to see, should adults also be denied the right to see them? The situation is complex and does not lend itself to simple solutions.

impairments. Back in the 1930s, the press chose not to show Franklin Roosevelt in his wheelchair or using braces, whereas today the country knows every intimate detail of the president's health.

The importance of the public's perception of these traits is evident in the ridicule directed at candidates who lack them. In 1988, Michael Dukakis was derided for his boring speaking style and Richard Gephardt for his blond eyebrows that vanished on television screens. Paul Tsongas, in 1992, was criticized for his dull speaking. The emergence of candidates like Tsongas, who lack the preferred traits, suggests that not having them has not deterred "unmedia" types from running. But the absence of these characteristics has become a formidable obstacle for a candidate.

If the news media pay no attention to a candidate, he or she is not likely to win any elections. Although the media insist that they pay attention to all who have a chance to win, they also influence who has such a chance. Some candidates have come up with creative ways to generate media attention. Lawton Chiles, running for the U.S. Senate from Florida, captured media attention by walking across the state. The novelty of the idea meant that reporters gave Chiles lots of free media coverage. Sometimes candidates can make their advertisements generate news coverage. Paul Wellstone used creative advertisements in his Minnesota Senate campaign in which he said that he did not have much money to pay for ads, so he would have to talk fast to cram what he had to say into fewer commercials. The witty way he did this became a news event itself—and got Wellstone additional coverage.

CAMPAIGN EVENTS   Because of the importance of media attention for communicating with voters, candidates schedule media events—talk shows, press conferences, interviews, and "photo opportunities" with various groups and in visual settings that reinforce the verbal message. Even the national party conventions have become less focused on the responsibility of actually choosing the nominee than on serving as the first media event of the general election campaign.[51] In the wake of declining

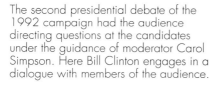

The second presidential debate of the 1992 campaign had the audience directing questions at the candidates under the guidance of moderator Carol Simpson. Here Bill Clinton engages in a dialogue with members of the audience.

viewership of the conventions, the political parties have sought to regain audience interest by reliance on "movie stars, entertainment routines, and professionally produced documentaries in their convention proceedings."[52] Coverage of the 1992 national political conventions was scaled back to key personalities a few hours each night on the major networks, and only C-SPAN broadcast the entire proceedings of both conventions.

MEDIA TECHNOLOGY   Thanks to new media technology, candidates finally can be in more than one place at a time. Satellites allow candidates to conduct local television interviews without actually traveling to the area or to communicate with party workers across the country. Specific voter groups can be targeted through cable television systems or low-power television stations that reach homogeneous neighborhoods or small towns. Videocassette tapes with short messages from the candidates further extend the campaign's reach.[53] Bill Clinton used this tool effectively during the early 1992 presidential primaries.

The expense associated with media technology has contributed to the skyrocketing costs of campaigning (discussed in Chapter 12). Candidates wonder if they are really getting "the bang for their buck." Political scientist Michael J. Robinson concludes that paid advertising has little effect on voters in primary contests. It is most useful as a means to respond to other candidates' advertisements and as a measure of candidate viability to the press.[54]

Technology permits campaign staffers to cover their own candidate, following the candidate around with cassette recorders and minicams and taping anything he or she does that resembles news. These tapes are then delivered to radio and television stations and cable systems. Speed and low cost permit campaign staffs to make these electronic actualities, or *soundbites*, available to the media, and these reports are often broadcast intact and, in many instances, without much editorial comment.[55]

"Hey, do you want to be on the news tonight or not? This is a sound bite, not the Gettysburg Address. Just say what you have to say, Senator, and get the hell off."

Drawing by Zeller. © 1989 The New Yorker Magazine, Inc.

Image Making

Do the media tend to prefer image over issues? Actually, image has always been an important part of presidential campaigns.[56] Themes such as "Tippecanoe and Tyler Too" and "Abe the Rail Splitter" were not issue oriented. The new kinds of media have expanded this "defining" role, which in turn has affected candidates' vote-getting strategies and the ability to communicate messages. Television is especially important here because of the power of the visual image. Edmund Muskie crying while defending his wife's reputation in 1972, Ronald Reagan taking charge of a debate against George Bush in 1980, and Ross Perot speaking in down-home language in 1992 are all examples.

Candidates recognize that their messages about policy are often ignored or given little attention. The press tends to emphasize goofs and gossip, or tensions within the campaign or among party leaders. For example, the press focused on the momentary tension in 1992 between Bill Clinton and Jesse Jackson stemming from Clinton's appearing before an African American audience to criticize a rap singer for her alleged racist comments.

Media Consultants

Attention to image making has been a contributing factor in the rise of a new player in campaign politics—the consultants, media campaign professionals who provide candidates with advice and services such as media relations, advertising strategy, and opinion polling.[57] In the 1992 election, for instance, consultants attempted

TABLE 13-3

Themes of Election News Coverage

Horse race: winning and losing, strategy and tactics, fund raising	32%
Campaign issues: facts and rumors of scandals, allegations of dirty or low-level campaigning	13
Campaign images: candidates' style of campaigning, posturing, likability	15
Governing images: leadership ability, trustworthiness	7
Policy issues: foreign policy and domestic economy	17
Candidates' orientation: personal and political background, ideology, group support	16
Total	100%

SOURCE: Thomas E. Patterson, "The Press and Its Missed Assignment," in *The Elections of 1988*, ed. Michael Nelson (Congressional Quarterly Press, 1989), p. 98.

to counter the impression that Hillary Clinton was too assertive by having her discuss her cookie-making skills, drop her maiden name in campaign references, and play the role of the supportive spouse.[58]

Some media consultants have been credited with propelling candidates to success. Republican consultants like Roger Ailes and Stuart Spencer, and Democratic consultants like Patrick Caddell and Robert Squier, have acquired powerful reputations among political activists. But media consultants also have been blamed for the negative themes of recent presidential campaigns. The classic example is a 1988 ad linking Michael Dukakis to Willie Horton, a convicted murderer who murdered again while on a prison furlough program.

Media consultants have taken over the role formerly played by party politicians. Before World War II, candidates for office at all levels from president to dog catcher were advised by party professionals. Such leaders made their judgments about possible candidates on the basis of long observation of the candidates' performances under fire, decisiveness, conviction, political skill, and other "presidential" qualities (in addition to their chances of victory). Party professionals told candidates which party and interest-group leaders to placate, which issues to stress, and which topics to avoid. Today, candidates are more interested in the advice of a media consultant. Consultants think more in terms of the candidates' images, television techniques, flexibility, "salability," and the like. Consultants report the results of *focus groups* (small sample groups of people who are asked questions about candidates and issues in a discussion setting) and public opinion polls, which in turn determine what the candidate says and does. Some critics allege that political consultants have become a new "political elite" who can virtually choose candidates by determining in advance which men and women have the right images, or at least images that can be restyled for the widest popularity.[59]

Political consultants who specialize in media advertising and image making realize their own limitations in packaging candidates. As one media consultant put it, "It is a very hard job to turn a turkey into a movie star; you try instead to make people like the turkey."[60] Media consultants have even attempted to create antipackaging images for their candidates. Michael Dukakis and Paul Simon in 1988 and Ross Perot in 1992 ran campaigns based on the image that they were not creatures of their media consultants.

Voter Choice

The media play an especially important role during political campaigns because they are depended on as the most important means of communication by candidates to get their message across, and by voters to find out what are the issues, learn about the candidates, and for advice on how to vote.

INFORMATION ABOUT CANDIDATES What voters know about candidates is largely based on media coverage. If the media have not covered a candidate, the voters generally do not know him or her. The images voters acquire from the media tend to be more stylistic than issue oriented. Journalists are more likely to comment on a candidate's personal background, style of campaigning, or standing in the polls compared to other candidates—in what is sometimes called the "horse race"[61] (see Table 13–3). "Many stories focus on who is ahead, who is behind, who is going to win, and who is going to lose, rather than examining how and why the race is as it is."[62] Reporters focus on the tactics and strategy of campaigns because they perceive that the public is interested and influenced by such coverage.[63] The media also seem to alternate between a kind of "gee whiz" attitude toward their current hero and a tendency to pounce on a candidate's ill-chosen remarks.

INFORMATION ABOUT ISSUES The media's propensity to focus on the "game" of campaigns displaces coverage of issues. When there is a scarcity of issue information on television news, voters tend to learn more about issue positions from televised political advertisements or newspapers.[64] Such advertising is becoming increasingly negative in tone. A rule of thumb in the "old politics" was to ignore the charges of the opposition, thus according one's rival no importance or standing. That practice seems to be changing, however, as candidates trade charges and countercharges increasing in viciousness and character assassination.

Political advertising may be even more important to campaign workers, contributors, and the reporters and analysts who cover the election.[65] Recent evidence suggests that expensive media campaigns fostering negative impressions of the candidates contribute to lower turnout.[66] In referendum elections, advertising is the most important source of information in voter decision making.[67]

THE DECISION Newspapers and television seem to have more influence in determining the outcome of primaries than of general elections.[68] This is probably because voters are less likely to know about the candidates and have fewer clues about how they stand in a primary. By the time of the November general election, however, party affiliation, incumbency, and other factors moderate the impact of media messages. The mass media are more likely to influence undecided voters, voters who in a close election can determine who wins and who loses.

ELECTION NIGHT REPORTING Does election night reporting affect the outcome of elections? Election returns from the East come in three hours before the polls close on the West Coast. As major networks often project the presidential winner well ahead of poll closings in western states, some western voters have been discouraged from voting. As a result, voter turnout in congressional and local elections has been affected. In a close presidential election, however, such early reporting may well stimulate turnout because voters will know their vote could determine the outcome. In short, it is only in elections in which one candidate appears to be winning by a large margin that television reporting makes voters feel their vote is meaningless.[69]

THE MEDIA AND GOVERNANCE

Walter Lippmann termed the media's influence on public affairs the "beam of a searchlight that moves restlessly about, bringing one episode and then another out of darkness into vision."[70] The searchlight lands on a policy issue because of a combination of factors, including "the efforts of political actors who seek to illuminate the process for their own purposes, as well as the particular news values of the media."[71]

The press serves as both observer and participant.[72] As observer, the press records and transmits information to and from actors in policy making. But as participant, the press acts as watchdog or critic and serves as the "eyes and ears" of the general public. It helps set the agenda of policy issues and serves as a check on the abuse of power.

But the press's role as participant is limited by its own news values. The policy stage at which the press is most powerful is that of agenda setting. The press brings problems to the fore and challenges policy makers to address them but rarely follows the policy process to its conclusion. Rather, it leaves the issue at the doorstep of

TABLE 13-4

Presidential News Conferences with White House Correspondents

President	Average per Month	Total Number
Herbert Hoover (1929–33)	5.6	268
Franklin D. Roosevelt (1933–45)	6.9	998
Harry Truman (1945–53)	3.4	334
Dwight Eisenhower (1953–61)	2.0	193
John Kennedy (1961–63)	1.9	64
Lyndon Johnson (1963–69)	2.2	135
Richard Nixon (1969–74)	0.5	37
Gerald Ford (1974–77)	1.3	39
Jimmy Carter (1977–81)	0.8	59
Ronald Reagan (1981–89)	0.5	44
George Bush (1989–93)	3	142
Bill Clinton (1993–94)	3.8	84

SOURCE: Samuel Kernell, *Going Public* (Congressional Quarterly Press, 1986), p. 69; *Public Papers of the Presidents, Ronald Reagan*, Book II, 1988–89 (Government Printing Office, 1991), p. C-8; *Public Papers of the Presidents, George Bush*, Book II, 1992–93 (Government Printing Office, 1993), p. C-7; *Weekly Compilation of Presidential Documents*, Vol. 29 Annual Index, p. C-17.

public officials. By the time the issue reaches the stages of policy formulation and implementation, the press has moved on to another issue. While policies are being formulated and implemented, decision makers are at their most impressionable;[73] yet the press has little impact at this stage.

Lack of media interest in policy implementation explains the lack of coverage of the bureaucracy. Bureaucratic activities rarely constitute news. Only in the case of a scandal, such as the savings and loan debacle in the early 1990s or the Housing and Urban Development disclosures of abuse in 1989, does the press take notice. Some agencies, however, prefer bureaucratic anonymity. After his study of government press offices, Stephen Hess wrote, "Most executives would be satisfied with a press strategy of no surprises. All their press officers need do to be doing their job is provide a rudimentary early warning system [for crises] and issue routine announcements."[74] But the assumption of most policy makers, even those handling classified national security information, is that their actions will leak out sooner or later.

Some media critics contend a negative consequence of the media's searchlight approach to policy coverage is the media's pressure on policy makers to resolve a problem once the searchlight is focused on it. Foreign policy may be in particular danger from such quick responses due to media attention. Presidential adviser Lloyd Cutler asserts the press's pressure on a president can be difficult to resist:

> If an ominous foreign event is featured on TV news, the president and his advisers feel bound to make a response in time for the next evening news broadcast....If he does not have a response ready by the late afternoon deadline, the evening news may report that the president's advisers are divided, that the president cannot make up his mind, or that while the president hesitates, his political opponents know exactly what to do.[75]

Political Institutions and the Press

The president has become a star of media coverage, particularly television, and has made the media his forum for setting the public agenda and achieving his legislative aims. Presidential news conferences command attention (see Table 13–4). Every public activity, both professional and personal, is potentially newsworthy. A presidential cold or sickness can become front page news.

A president attempts to manipulate news coverage to his benefit. Speeches are used to set the national agenda or spur congressional action. Travel to foreign countries usually boosts popular support at home, thanks to the largely favorable news coverage. Better yet for the president, most coverage of the president—either while at home or abroad—is favorable or at worst neutral.[76]

Congress, on the other hand, has suffered at the hands of the media. News coverage of Congress is typically negative and portrays a badly fragmented body unable to act quickly on much of anything.[77] Congress's problem is that it does not meet news imperatives. Unlike the presidency, it lacks an ultimate spokesperson—a single individual who can speak for the whole institution.[78] Congress does not organize its work for the press. While the White House engages in the "care and feeding" of the press corps, Congress does not arrange its schedule to suit the media; floor debates, for example, might compete with both committee hearings and press conferences.[79] By its nature, Congress does not act quickly. Singularly dramatic actions are nearly impossible for the Congress, but such actions constitute news for the press. The press, therefore, turns to the president to describe federal government activity on a day-to-day basis and treats the Congress largely as a foil to the president. Most coverage of the Congress is of its reaction to the initiatives of the president.[80]

Presidents use the news conference to get certain information out to the public, but run the risk of having to respond to criticism and challenges by reporters.

The federal institution least dependent on the press is the Supreme Court, which relies little on public communication for political support. Rather, it relies indirectly on public opinion for continued deference and compliance with its decisions.[81] The Court has strong incentives to avoid the perception of direct manipulation of the press, so it retains an image of aloofness from politics and public opinion. Thus, manipulation of press coverage of the Court is far more subtle and complex than for the other two institutions.[82]

The news media's greatest role as a participant in the governing process may be at the local level. Most of us have multiple sources for finding out what is happening in Washington that act as a check on the biases and limitations of reporters who cover national government and policy. But when it comes to finding out about the city council, the school board, or the local water district, most of us are dependent on the work of a single reporter. Consequently the media's influence is much greater when there are fewer news sources.

THE MEDIA AND CONSTITUTIONAL DEMOCRACY

Indisputably, the media have acquired a role as a major, highly autonomous force in American politics. They mold political attitudes and behavior, organize debate, affect electoral outcomes, help shape policy, and influence the behavior of institutions. The question for our constitutional democracy is: Are the news media doing a good job of bringing information to the citizens and providing a forum in which to debate complex issues?

Scholars, politicians, media critics, and even some journalists have chided the press for failure to fulfill adequately certain roles in a democratic society. There is no shortage of critics with suggestions as to how newspeople might do better, such as greater specialization by journalists by policy area and more stringent separation between the entertainment and news functions of a network, newspaper, or magazine. Others, chiefly political scientists, have suggested that journalists should show less interest in the "game" aspect of campaigns. However, Thomas Patterson, a political scientist, does not think these reforms will work or make any significant difference. The problem, according to Patterson, is that the news business cannot, no matter how hard it tries, perform the functions once carried out by our political parties. It is not that the journalists are not doing their job, but that political parties no longer function as the chief connection between candidates and voters.[83] Newspeople now play that role and have made parties less necessary.

Other critics believe that the influence of the press has been vastly overstated. They claim parties, interest groups, and the personalities of politicians are more important influences. City, state, and federal governments, they assert, have far more impact on a person's politics than does television or the press. Religion, friends, family, teachers, wars, depressions, and assassinations are all more important than the media, which can only reflect the nation's wants, cater to its needs, and sometimes illuminate its troubles or successes.

Not all those who think the media are powerful agree that their power is harmful. After all, they argue, the media perform a vital educative function. Further, they continue, almost 70 percent of the public think the press is a watchdog that keeps government leaders from doing bad things[84] (see Table 13–5). At the very least, the media have the power to mold the agenda of the day; and at most, in the words of the late Theodore White, they have the power to "determine what people will talk and think about—an authority that in other nations is reserved for tyrants, priests, parties, and mandarins."[85]

TABLE 13-5

Confidence in Institutions

Question: As far as people running these institutions are concerned, would you say you have a great deal of confidence, only some confidence, or hardly any confidence in them at all?

	Great deal	Quite a lot	Some	Very little	No opinion
The military	32%	35%	23%	8%	1%*
Church or organized religion	29	24	29	14	3
Police	22	30	35	11	-
Television news	19	27	36	16	2
The presidency	19	24	32	20	3
The U.S. Supreme Court	18	25	37	15	2
Public schools	14	25	37	21	2
Banks	14	24	42	19	1
The medical system	14	20	34	28	3
Newspapers	12	19	42	22	3
Television	11	10	43	31	3
Organized labor	9	17	41	26	3
Congress	8	11	40	35	4
Big business	7	16	44	28	3
The criminal justice system	6	11	38	39	4

Source: *The Gallup Poll Monthly*, April 1993.

*Figures might not add up to 100% due to rounding.

SUMMARY

1. The news media include newspapers, television, radio, magazines, and books in all of their forms. These means of communication have been called "the fourth branch of government."

2. The news media are a pervasive feature of American politics, and the popular media more generally help to define our culture. Moreover, the rise of new communications technologies has made the media more influential throughout American society. The news media provide a "linking" function between politicians and government officials and the public, and vice versa.

3. The influence of the mass media over public opinion is significant yet not overwhelming. People may not pay much attention to the media or believe all they read or see or hear. They may be critical or suspicious of the media and hence resistant to it. People tend to "filter" the news in part through their political socialization, their selectivity, their interest and attention, and their ability to recall or comprehend the content of the news.

4. Presidential campaigns are dominated by media coverage during both the pre– and postconvention stages. One effect of media influence is that most people seem more interested in the contest as a "game" or "horse race" than as an occasion for serious discussion of issues and candidates.

5. A major effect of mass media news is agenda setting, that is, determining what problems will become salient issues for people to form opinions about and to discuss. The media are also influential in defining issues.

6. The media are criticized as biased both by conservatives (who charge that reporters are too liberal) and by liberals (who claim that the media are captive of corporate interests). The mass media are big business, but their product is information, which is protected under the First Amendment. Little evidence exists of actual, deliberate bias in news reporting.

7. The media are under attack for sensationalism, superficial reporting, biased coverage, and overemphasis on the "theatrical." Any efforts at comprehensive reform will be frustrated, however, by at least two factors: reformers do not agree on what course to follow; and they, and virtually all other Americans, fear taking any action that might threaten the freedom of the press.

NOAM CHOMSKY AND EDWARD S. HERMAN, *Manufacturing Consent: The Political Economy of the Mass Media* (Pantheon Books, 1988).

TIMOTHY COOK, *Making Laws and Making News: Press Strategies in the U.S. House of Representatives* (Brookings Institution, 1990).

RICHARD DAVIS, *The Press and American Politics: The New Mediator* (Longman, 1992).

————, ED., *Politics and the Media* (Prentice Hall, 1994).

CAROL FELSENTHAL, *Power, Privilege and "The Post": The Catherine Graham Story* (Putnam, 1993).

SUZANNE GARMENT, *Scandal: The Culture of Mistrust in American Politics* (Time Books, 1991).

STEPHEN HESS, *The Government/Press Connection* (Brookings Institution, 1984).

————, *Live from Capitol Hill! Studies of Congress and the Media* (Brookings Institution, 1991).

SHANTO IYENGAR AND DONALD R. KINDER, *News That Matters* (University of Chicago Press, 1987).

KATHLEEN HALL JAMIESON, *Dirty Politics: Deception, Distraction, and Democracy* (Oxford University Press, 1992).

S. ROBERT LICHTER, STANLEY ROTHMAN, AND LINDA S. LICHTER, *The Media Elite* (Adler and Adler, 1986).

MARTIN LINSKY, *Impact: How the Press Affects Federal Policymaking: Six Case Studies* (Norton, 1986).

JOHN ANTHONY MALTESE, *Spin Control: The White House Office of Communications and the Management of Presidential News* (University of North Carolina Press, 1992).

DOROTHY D. NESBIT, *Videostyle in Senate Campaigns* (University of Tennessee Press, 1988).

THOMAS E. PATTERSON, *Out of Order* (Knopf, 1993).

TOM ROSENSTEIL, *Strange Bedfellows: How Television and the Presidential Candidates Changed American Politics, 1992* (Hyperion, 1993).

WILLIAM RUSHER, *The Coming Battle for the Media* (William Morrow, 1988).

SIMON SEFATY, *The Media and Foreign Policy* (St. Martin's Press, 1990).

DARRELL M. WEST, *Air Wars: Television Advertising in Election Campaigns, 1952-1992* (Congressional Quarterly, 1993).

CONGRESS: THE PEOPLE'S BRANCH

14

The 104th Congress (1995–1997) witnessed a Republican takeover in both chambers of Congress. Republicans claimed they would work constructively with President Clinton, yet the "Contract with America" that most House Republicans pledged to uphold guaranteed at least as much conflict as cooperation between the branches.

Democrats had had their chance in the 103rd Congress, and they had passed family leave and voter registration legislation, a major crime control bill, the North American Free Trade Agreement, and considered more than 6,700 bills and resolutions. Experts called it one of the most productive legislative sessions in recent years, but most Americans either disliked what Congress had been doing or felt it would have no positive effect on the nation.[1]

Congress is one of the most democratic and representative institutions in our system of constitutional democracy, yet it fails to win the enduring respect of most Americans. Less than 20 percent of Americans in one recent poll told pollsters they had "a lot" or "a great deal" of confidence in Congress, and more than one-third said they had "very little" confidence in Congress. The military, organized religion, and even the Supreme Court and the presidency fared significantly better in the views of most Americans.[2] Perhaps we hold unrealistic expectations for the Congress. Perhaps because it does its work in the full view of media and public scrutiny, Congress cannot look dignified. That a score or more of its members have had serious ethical or legal troubles in recent years raises further public doubts.

Now, more than two hundred years after the First Congress met in New York, the men and women we elect to Congress are striving to make this "people's branch" work. In many ways, this challenging task seems guaranteed to draw criticism, but it needs to be understood. We begin this chapter by looking at the way senators and representatives are elected. We then examine the job of law making and the most frequently heard criticisms of Congress.

CONGRESSIONAL ELECTIONS

Members of Congress get their job by winning an election, the outcome of which depends on many factors. By far the most important is the nature of the state or district in which the candidate runs. Is it a **safe seat**—one that is predictably won by one party or the other—or is it a highly competitive one? Other factors affecting winning elections are personal appeal of the candidate, whether the opponent is an incumbent or a newcomer, local issues, campaign strategies, the fundraising abilities of the candidate, and occasionally, national tides, such as the 1964, 1974, and 1980 elections.

Incumbents have traditionally enjoyed a great advantage over challengers. In recent years, however, incumbency has become less of an advantage, if not a downright handicap. Critics like Ross Perot, Ralph Nader, and Rush Limbaugh have targeted the "Washington insiders" and created a climate of antagonism toward Congress as an institution.

Districting and Apportionment

Congress has given state legislatures control over the drawing of congressional districts. Senators, of course, represent entire states, but House seats are distributed among the states according to population; each state receives at least one seat. State legislatures, subject to a gubernatorial veto, draw the district lines for the House of Representatives. The party in control of the state legislature traditionally draws the

The word *gerrymandering* comes from the name of a governor of Massachusetts, Elbridge Gerry, and the salamander-shaped district that was created to favor his party.

lines to enhance their political fortunes. This is known as **gerrymandering**, after Governor Elbridge Gerry of Massachusetts, who, in 1811, reluctantly signed a redistricting bill that created a distinctly partisan district shaped like a salamander.

State legislatures are free to draw congressional districts pretty much as they wish, subject to some constitutional limitations. First, each district must be equal in population, or as equal as possible.[3] To accommodate population shifts, **redistricting** occurs once a decade, after each national census. Because population shifts also occur between states, it is necessary once a decade to reapportion seats for the U.S. House of Representatives. Thus, in 1990, 13 states lost representatives and 8 gained new seats in the House.

A state legislature must not be overzealous in favoring one party at the expense of another. The Supreme Court has held that grossly partisan gerrymandering is, under certain circumstances, unconstitutional.[4]

Finally, although a state legislature may design congressional districts to virtually guarantee the election of a member of a particular minority, it must be careful not to do so in a fashion that focuses only on racial considerations and ignores such matters as county lines and city boundaries.[5]

A Profile of Members of Congress

The entire membership of the House of Representatives (435) is elected to two-year terms in even-numbered years. Elections for the six-year Senate terms are staggered, so that one-third of the Senate's 100 members are chosen every two years. Members of the House of Representatives must be 25 years old and have been citizens for seven years. Senators must be at least 30 and have been citizens for nine years.

Nearly 90 percent of our national legislators are male. Most are well-educated, middle-aged, and come from upper-middle or upper income backgrounds. Until recently, they were also mainly white Anglo-Saxon Protestants (WASPs). Larger numbers of Roman Catholics and many Jews now bring Congress's religious makeup closer in line with the general population.[6] But there are still far fewer African Americans and women in Congress than in the general public, and only a handful of Asian Americans and Hispanics, as well as one Native American. Nearly 40 percent of our national legislators are lawyers. There are also some farmers,

The new members of Congress reflect greater diversity in the large number of women, African Americans, Hispanics, and other ethnic groups who came to Washington in 1992.

teachers, clergy, business people, a veterinarian, and even a few former college professors. Few members come from blue-collar occupations. That most members are the products of middle- and upper-class families does not necessarily mean they are interested only in improving the position of that portion of the population. Senators like Edward Kennedy (D.-Mass.) and Jay Rockefeller (D.-W.Va.) for instance, are affluent white males but strong advocates of legislation to protect women, minorities, and poor people.

Issues of special interest to women have received increased attention in Congress lately, no doubt due in part to the doubling of the number of women in Congress in the 1990s. Thus, Congress has enacted laws to combat violence against women and to improve medical research on diseases that affect women. Congress has also made it a crime to block access to abortion clinics by force.

THE STRUCTURE AND POWERS OF CONGRESS

The most important fact about Congress is it is **bicameral**, that is, made up of two houses. Few national legislatures are genuinely bicameral. Many have two houses, but one is usually largely ceremonial. In the United States, the Senate and the House each have an absolute veto over the other's law making. Each chamber runs its own affairs, sets its own rules, and conducts its own investigations. The law-making role, however, is shared. Each must be seen as a separate institution, even though both houses reflect similar political forces and share common organizational patterns.

As James Madison explained in *The Federalist*, No. 51, the protection against giving too much power to the legislature "is to divide the legislature into different branches; and to render them, by different modes of election and different principles of action, as little connected with each other as the nature of their common functions, and their common dependence on the society will admit." (*The Federalist*, No. 51, is reprinted in the Appendix.) The House of Representatives was expected to reflect the popular will of the average citizen, whereas the Senate was to provide for stability, continuity, and in-depth deliberation. Many of the framers hoped the Senate would stem any rash populist impulses of the other chamber.

In Article I, the Constitution outlined the structure, powers, and responsibilities of Congress, giving it "All legislative Powers herein granted": the power to spend and tax in order to "provide for the common Defence and general Welfare of the United States"; the power to borrow money; the power to regulate commerce with foreign nations and among the states; the power to declare war, raise and support armies, and provide and maintain a navy; the power to establish post offices; and the power to set up the federal courts under the Supreme Court. As a final catchall, the Constitution gives Congress the right "to make all Laws which shall be necessary and proper for carrying into Execution" the powers set out. Several nonlegislative functions were also granted, such as participating in the process of constitutional amendment and impeachment (given to the House) and trying an impeached federal officer (given to the Senate).

The Constitution confers additional responsibilities on the Senate. The Senate has the power to confirm many presidential nominations—sometimes as many as 500 key executive and judicial nominees a year. In a two-year Congress there may be more than 5,000 civilian nominations and 90,000 military nominations needing senatorial approval. The Senate must also give its consent, by a two-thirds vote of the senators present, before a president may ratify a treaty.

Although the Seventeenth Amendment to the Constitution (1913), which provides for direct election of U.S. senators, altered the character of the Senate's

Why Do Incumbent Members of Congress Usually Win?

- *They enjoy better name recognition*, and to be known at all is generally to be known favorably. Challengers are almost always less well known.
- *They enjoy free mailings* (called the franking privilege) to every household in the state or district. These mailings—which often resemble campaign brochures—portray members as hard-working and influential.
- *They have greater access to the media.*
- *They raise campaign money more easily than challengers*, because lobbyists and political action committees (PACs) seek their ears and their favors. Also, many campaign contributors know that incumbents are more likely than challengers to get reelected, so they give to those they know will win. Indeed $8 out of every $10 of PAC money is now given to incumbents.
- *They usually have had more campaign experience*, and they can claim to have had more experience in Congress and in Washington.
- *They have large staffs* to help with case-work and constituency services for the folks back home.
- *They take credit for federal monies* that get allocated to their regions.
- They are in a better position than challengers to *take advantage of government research staffs*, new government studies, and even classified information.

No one of these factors can guarantee a member's reelection, but skillful use of them makes it difficult to unseat a healthy incumbent.

"Please, Senator Fairchild, you have to leave. You lost."

Drawing by Sauers. © 1983 The New Yorker Magazine, Inc.

We The People

A Profile of the 104th Congress
(1995–1997)

SENATE: 53 Republicans
47 Democrats
Sex: 8 women
92 men
Race: 1 African American
2 Asian-Pacific
1 Native American
Average Age: 58
Religion: 20 Catholic
14 Episcopalian
11 Methodist
10 Baptist
9 Jewish
8 Presbyterian
4 Lutheran
3 Mormon

HOUSE: 231 Republicans
203 Democrats
1 Independent
Sex: 48 women
387 men
Race: 38 African American
18 Hispanic
4 Asian-Pacific
Average Age: 51
Religion: 125 Catholic
57 Baptist
50 Methodist
47 Presbyterian
34 Episcopalian
24 Jewish
15 Lutheran
10 Mormon

TABLE 14-1

Differences between the House of Representatives and the Senate

House of Representatives	Senate
Two-year term	Six-year term
435 members	100 members
Smaller constituencies	Larger constituencies
Fewer personal staff	More personal staff
Equal populations represented	States represented
Less flexible rules	More flexible rules
Limited debate	Unlimited debate
More policy specialists	Policy generalists
Less media coverage	More media coverage
Less prestige	More prestige
Less reliance on staff	More reliance on staff
More powerful committee leaders	More equal distribution of power
Very important committees	Less important committees
22 standing committees	16 standing committees
Nongermane amendments (riders) not allowed	Nongermane amendments (riders) allowed
Important Rules Committee	Special treaty ratification power
Some bills permit no floor amendments (closed rule)	Special confirmation power

membership, the two chambers still have many differences (see Table 14-1). However, the two houses are more similar today in their membership and operations than they were two hundred or even one hundred years ago.

The House has some distinctive responsibilities, yet these have not proved to be as important as those given to the Senate. For example, although all revenue bills must originate in the House, this practice does not give the House much advantage, as the Senate has freely amended these bills, sometimes changing everything except the title.

The framers did not intend Congress to be all-powerful. They reserved certain authority for the states and for the people and gave other powers to the executive and judicial branches of the national government. As time passed, Congress gained power in some respects and lost it in others. The power of Congress also changes with the times and the president. As the role and authority of the national government have expanded, so, too, have the policy-making and oversight responsibilities of Congress. Still, Congress has not kept pace with its great rival, the presidency, which in many respects today holds the place in our national government that many of the framers desired for Congress. The president's national security responsibilities, preparation of the budget, media visibility, and agenda-setting influence have all enhanced the position of the presidency. The growth of executive authority may be part of a worldwide trend. Legislative bodies almost everywhere have become subordinate to the executive at all levels of government.

Despite its sometimes secondary role in recent decades, Congress still performs these seven important functions:

1. *Representation* involves expressing the diversity and conflicting views of the regional, economic, social, racial, religious, and other interests in the United States.

2. *Law making* is enacting measures to help solve substantive problems.

3. *Consensus building* is the bargaining process by which these interests are reconciled.

4. *Overseeing the bureaucracy* means ensuring that laws and policies approved by Congress are faithfully carried out by the executive branch and that they accomplish what was intended.

5. *Policy clarification* (or policy incubation, as it is sometimes called) is the identification and publicizing of issues.

6. For the Senate, *confirming* presidential appointees and ratifying treaties.

7. *Investigating* the operation of government agencies or other problems.

The House of Representatives

The organization and procedures in the House are different from those in the Senate, if only because the House is more than four times as large as the Senate. *How* things are done affects *what* is done. The House assigns different types of bills to different calendars. For instance, finance measures—tax or appropriations bills—are put on a special calendar for quicker action. The House has other ways to speed up law making, including electronic voting. Ordinary rules may be suspended by a two-thirds vote, or immediate action may be taken by unanimous consent of the members on the floor. By sitting as the *committee of the whole*, the House is able to operate more informally and more quickly than under its regular rules. A quorum in the committee of the whole is composed of only 100 members, rather than a majority of the whole chamber, and voting is quicker and simpler. Members are limited in how long they can speak, and debate may be cut off simply by majority vote.

Senator Ben Nighthorse Campbell (D.-Colo) and Senator Carol Moseley Braun (D.-Ill), elected in 1992, were, respectively, the first Native American and the first African American woman to win seats in the U.S. Senate.

THE SPEAKER AND OTHER LEADERS The **Speaker** is the presiding officer in the House of Representatives.[7] The Constitution mandates that the House of Representatives shall choose its Speaker, yet it does not say anything about duties or powers of the office. This officer is formally elected by the House but is actually selected by the majority party; it is usually someone with broad appeal in the party. Revolts in 1910 by the rank-and-file Progressives stripped Speakers of much of their power, including control over who served on which congressional committees. As the highest-ranking officer in Congress, the Speaker represents it on ceremonial occasions. Third in line of succession to the presidency (in case of death, resignation, or impeachment), the Speaker must keep the White House informed about his whereabouts at all times.

The routine powers of the Speaker include recognizing members who wish to speak, ruling on questions of parliamentary procedure, and appointing members to select and conference committees—that is, temporary committees, not standing committees. In general, the Speaker directs business on the floor of the House. More significant, of course, is a Speaker's political and behind-the-scenes influence. (When Democrats are in the majority, the Speaker chairs the influential Democratic Steering and Policy Committee, which consists of about 24 members: the Speaker's lieutenants, four others appointed by the Speaker, and 12 elected by regional caucuses within the House Democratic party. The Steering and Policy Committee devises and directs party strategy.) The Speaker has the authority to refer legislation to the relevant committee and to select most members and the chair of the House Rules Committee.

The late Representative Thomas P. ("Tip") O'Neill (D.-Mass.), who served as Speaker from 1977 until 1987, held that he not only had to represent the major party in Congress and continue to represent his own constituents (from the Cambridge, Massachusetts, area) but also had to be, in his words, the "guiding force behind both the development of legislation and the process of winning enough votes to get it passed." Further, O'Neill added, the "most important power is to set the agenda." If the Speaker genuinely does not want a bill to come up for a floor vote, it generally does not.[8]

The late Thomas (Tip) O'Neill, long-time Speaker of the House of Representatives. Although he could wheel and deal when necessary, he generally kept the best interests of his constituents uppermost in his mind.

The Speaker is assisted by a **majority leader,** who helps plan party strategy, confers with other party leaders, and tries to keep members of the party in line. The minority party elects a **minority leader,** who usually steps into the speakership when his or her party gains a majority in the House. These positions are also sometimes called *majority and minority floor leader.* Assisting each floor leader are the party **whips.** (The term comes from the "whipper-in," who in fox hunts keeps the hounds bunched in a pack.) The whips serve as liaison between the House leadership of each party and the rank-and-file. They inform members when important bills will come up for a vote, prepare summaries of the bills, do nose counts for the leadership, exert mild pressure on members to support the leadership, and try to ensure maximum attendance on the floor for critical votes.

At the beginning of the session and occasionally afterward, each party holds a **caucus** of all its members (called a **conference** by Republicans) to elect party officers, approve committee assignments, elect committee leaders, discuss important legislation, and perhaps try to agree on party policy.

THE HOUSE RULES COMMITTEE   The House, unlike the Senate, has a Rules Committee that helps regulate the time of floor debate for each bill as well as limitations on floor amendments. In the normal course of events, a bill does not come up for action on the floor without a *rule* from the Rules Committee; the rule sets the length of debate and specifies whether the bill can or cannot be amended. By failing to act or refusing to grant a rule, the committee can delay consideration of a bill. A **closed rule** prohibits amendments altogether or provides that only members of the committee reporting the bill may offer amendments; closed rules are usually reserved for tax and spending bills. An **open rule** permits debate within the overall time allocated to the bill.

Until the mid-1960s, the Rules Committee was dominated by a coalition of Republicans and conservative Democrats. Liberals denounced it as unrepresentative, unfair, and dictatorial. More recently, the Rules Committee membership has come to reflect the views of the total membership of the majority party. The Rules Committee today is usually an arm of the leadership, and rather than block legislation, it offers a "dress rehearsal" opportunity to those trying to press for new measures.

The Senate

The Senate has the same basic committee structure, elected party leadership, and decentralized power as the House, but because the Senate is a smaller body, its procedures are more informal, and it permits more time for debate. Television has made the Senate an even more visible and key political forum. It has become more open and outward looking, and its members today share influence more equitably than in the past. The Senate now addresses a wider range of issues than ever before.[9]

The president of the Senate (the vice-president of the United States) has little influence over Senate proceedings. A vice-president can vote only in case of a tie and is seldom consulted when important decisions are made. The Senate also elects from among the majority party a **president pro tempore**, usually the most senior member, who is official chair in the absence of the vice-president. Presiding over the Senate on most occasions is a thankless chore, so the president pro tempore regularly delegates this responsibility to junior members of the chamber.

Party machinery in the Senate is somewhat similar to that of the House. There are party caucuses (conferences), majority and minority floor leaders, and party whips. Each party has a *policy committee*, composed of the leaders of the party, which is theoretically responsible for the party's overall legislative program. In the Senate the party steering committees handle only committee assignments. Unlike the House party steering committees, the Senate's party policy committees are formally

Senate Majority Leader Robert Dole (*left*) and Speaker of the House Newt Gingrich (*right*) were elected to the top leadership posts in Congress following the Rupublican takeover in the November 1994 election.

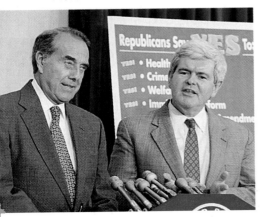

provided for by law, and each has a regular staff and a budget. Although the Senate party policy committees have some influence on legislation, they have not asserted strong legislative leadership or managed to coordinate policy.

The Senate *majority leader*—the elected leader of the majority party in the Senate—is an influential person within the Senate and sometimes nationally. As the Senate's major power broker, the majority leader has the right to be the first senator heard on the floor. In consultation with the *minority leader*, the majority leader determines the Senate's agenda and has much to say about committee assignments for members of the majority party. The position confers somewhat less authority than the speakership in the House, and its influence depends on the person's political and parliamentary skills and on the national political situation.[10] Republican Senator Robert Dole of Kansas was elected Senate Majority Leader in early 1995, a position he had held for a while in the mid 1980s when the Republicans controlled the U.S. Senate.

"Listen pal, I didn't spend seven million bucks to get here so I could yield the floor to you."

Drawing by Dana Fradon. © 1987 The New Yorker Magazine, Inc.

POLITICAL ENVIRONMENT Senators have more diverse policy interests than do members of the House, serve on more committees, and are more likely to wield power in their state parties. For these reasons, the Senate has a character different from that of the House. Even first-term senators can become visible and politically significant. This possibility for prominence is due to the smaller size of the Senate, its greater access to the media, and the larger staffs that senators enjoy.[11]

The contemporary Senate is individualistic. With the expanding role of subcommittee chairs and enlarged staff, the influence of committee chairs has declined, and key decisions are often made on the Senate floor. The Senate is a more open, fluid, and decentralized body now than it was a generation or two ago. Indeed, it is often said that the Senate has one hundred separate power centers and is so splintered that the party leaders have difficulty arranging the day-to-day schedule. "It's pretty hard to set the agenda over here," said Senator Robert Dole, Republican leader. "The leadership is powerless unless the senators are willing to give them authority."[12]

THE FILIBUSTER A major difference between the Senate and the House is that debate is much less limited in the Senate. A senator who gains the floor may go on talking until he or she relinquishes the right to talk voluntarily or through exhaustion. This right to unlimited debate may be used by a small group of senators to **filibuster**—delay Senate proceedings in order to delay or prevent a vote. At one time the filibuster was a favorite weapon of southern senators intent on blocking civil rights legislation. More recently the filibuster has been used for a wider range of issues. The Senate in 1987 had, for instance, a week-long filibuster opposing a congressional campaign finance reform bill. And in 1993, Republicans used a filibuster to kill President Clinton's economic stimulus package. A filibuster, or the threat of a filibuster, is typically most potent at the end of a congressional session, when there is a fixed date for adjournment, because it could mean that many bills that have made it to the end of the legislation process will die for lack of a floor vote. The knowledge that a bill might be subject to a filibuster is often just enough to force a compromise satisfactory to its opponents. Sometimes the leaders, knowing that a filibuster will tie up the Senate and keep it from enacting other needed legislation, do not bring a bill to the floor.

A filibuster can be defeated. Until 1917 the Senate could terminate a filibuster only if every member agreed. That same year, however, the Senate adopted its first debate-ending, or **cloture**, rule. Now, as long as the senators who are doing the talking stay on their feet, debate can be stopped only by a cloture vote. The rule of cloture specifies that two days after 16 members sign a petition, the question of curtailing debate must be put to a vote. If three-fifths of the total number

Party Shift, 1995

With the Republican landslide in the November 1994 election, committee chairs in the Senate switched to the new majority party:

• Appropriations	Mark Hatfield
• Armed services	Strom Thurmond
• Banking	Alfonse D'Amato
• Budget	Pete Domenici
• Finance	Bob Packwood
• Foreign relations	Jesse Helms
• Judiciary	Orrin Hatch
• Labor	Nancy Landon

After Bill Clinton named Lani Guiniere for the job of Assistant Attorney General for Civil Rights, he was worried that criticism in Congress of her position on affirmative action would prevent her being confirmed, so he withdrew the nomination.

of senators (60 of the 100 members) vote for cloture, no senator may speak for more than one hour. A final vote must be taken after no more than 30 hours of debate, including all delaying tactics, such as quorum calls and roll call votes on procedure. After the 30 hours of debate, the motion before the Senate must be brought to a vote.

The tactic or the threat of a filibuster is available to Senate minorities to force the majority to compromise and modify its position, and Republicans have learned to use it well in recent years. Cloture votes are also relatively rare, yet they are more common today than in earlier years, in part because the Senate reduced the number of votes needed from 67 to 60. Sponsors sometimes invoke a cloture vote, hoping to expedite floor business before debate even begins seriously.

THE POWER TO CONFIRM The Senate has the constitutional power to confirm presidential appointments to such positions as the cabinet, the U.S. Supreme Court and other federal courts, all ambassadorial positions, and many executive branch positions. As with other legislative business, the confirmation process starts in committees, with the relevant standing committee having jurisdiction. The Judiciary Committee considers judges and Supreme Court nominees; the Foreign Relations Committee considers all ambassadorial appointments. Nominees now routinely appear before the committee to answer questions, and they typically have met individually with key senators well before the hearing.

The framers of the Constitution regarded the confirmation process and its advice and consent by the Senate as an important check on executive power. Alexander Hamilton viewed it as a way for Congress to prevent the appointment of "unfit characters." Today the U.S. Senate and the president often struggle over control of top personnel in the executive and judicial branches.

The Constitution leaves the question somewhat ambiguous: "The President . . . shall nominate, and by and with the Advice and Consent of the Senate, shall appoint Ambassadors, other public Ministers and Consuls, Judges of the Supreme Court, all other officers of the United States." Presidents, however, have never enjoyed exclusive control over hiring and firing in the executive branch. The Senate jealously guards its right to confirm or reject major appointments; during the period of strong Congresses after the Civil War, presidents had to struggle to keep their power to appoint and dismiss. But for most of the twentieth century, presidents have gained a reasonable amount of control over top appointments, in part, because a growing number of people in and out of Congress believe that chief executives without compatible cabinet-level appointees of their choice cannot be held accountable.

In recent years the Senate has taken a somewhat tougher stand on presidential appointments. This was especially true when Democrats controlled the Senate and Republicans controlled the White House. Time spent evaluating and screening presidential nominations has increased. The Senate rejected several nominees of presidents George Bush and Ronald Reagan, including turning down Bush's choice for secretary of defense, John Tower. President Bill Clinton has had to withdraw nominees for attorney general and several lesser posts because of Senate opposition.

The Senate's role in the confirmation process was never intended to eliminate politics but rather to use politics as a safeguard. Some conservatives in recent years object that the Senate has occasionally rejected nominees because of their political beliefs and thus interfered with the executive power of presidents. In such instances, so this complaint goes, the Senate's decision is not a reflection of the fitness of a nominee but rather of the political strength of the president.

By the tradition called **senatorial courtesy**, a president confers with the senator or senators from the state where an appointee is to work. A nomination is less likely to secure Senate approval against the objection of these senators, especially if these senators are members of the president's party, even if his party does not control the Senate. Thus, for nearly all district court judgeships and a variety of other positions, senators can exercise what is, in fact, a veto that can be overridden only with difficulty. Further, it is usually exercised in secret and subject to little accountability. But this form of patronage is sufficiently important to senators that senatorial courtesy is likely to continue.

It is useful to note a distinction between *judicial appointments*, especially those to the Supreme Court, and *administration appointments*. The Senate plays a greater role in judicial appointments because judges serve for life and constitute an independent and, as we discuss in Chapter 16, vital branch of the government. There is an argument that when it comes to cabinet-level positions in the executive branch, a president ought to be able to choose those who will carry out the general views of the White House. In contrast, a president is not expected to enjoy partisan loyalty from those nominated to the bench.

The confirmation provisions in the Constitution have fulfilled most of the intentions of the framers. The Senate has been able to use its power to reject unqualified nominees. It has sometimes also been able to prevent those with serious conflicts of interest from taking office. In addition, senators have been able to use the confirmation process to make their views known to prospective executive officials. Indeed, the very existence of the confirmation process generally deters presidents from appointing weak, questionable, or "unfit characters."

THE JOB OF THE LEGISLATOR

Congress as a Place to Work

The elegant U.S. Capitol building is the working center of our nation's legislative process. It is flanked by a half a dozen House and Senate office buildings, the sprawling Library of Congress, and a number of other annex office buildings that help Congress do its work. Members of Congress employ about 20,000 staff aides who work directly with them in Washington, D.C., or in their districts. Nearly another 18,000 work for the General Accounting Office, the Government Printing Office, the Library of Congress, the Architect of the Capitol, and smaller agencies that work under the control of Congress.

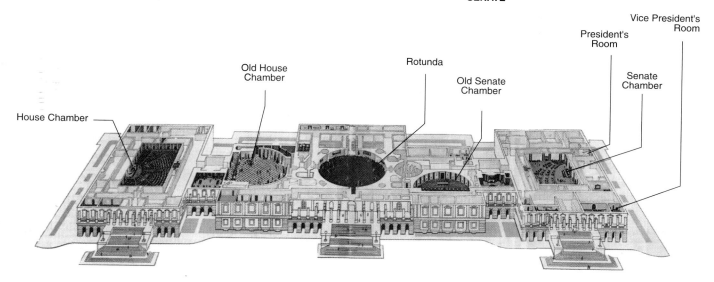

HOUSE OF REPRESENTATIVES   **SENATE**

Vice President's Room

President's Room

Old House Chamber   Rotunda   Old Senate Chamber   Senate Chamber

House Chamber

Most political scientists regard a large, competent staff on Capitol Hill as a reasonably positive development. But Ross Perot, Bill Clinton, and consumer advocate Ralph Nader have criticized "empire-building" in Congress over the past 30 years. Senator David Boren (D.-Okla.) headed up a 1993 effort to streamline and restructure the Congress, and he favored a one-third reduction in staffing on Capitol Hill. "You reach a point of diminishing returns," said Boren.[13] Saying he had grown frustrated by a Senate that had become a fragmented set of individual empires and political fiefdoms and overly partisan, Boren retired in 1995.[14]

Legislators as Representatives

Congress has a split personality. One Congress is a *law-making institution* that writes laws and makes policy for the entire nation. In this capacity, all the members are expected to set aside their personal ambitions and perhaps even the concerns of their own constituencies. But Congress is also a *representative assembly*, made up of 535 elected officials who serve as links between their constituents and the national government. The dual roles of *making laws* and *responding to constituents' demands* have forced members to balance national concerns against the specific interests of their states or districts.

For whom does a representative speak? The geographical district and its immediate interests? The party? The nation? Some special interest? His or her conscience? Congress was intended to serve as a forum for registering the interests and values of the nation. It was never intended that the legislative branch represent views identical to those of the executive. But to whom does the individual representative listen?

Members of Congress perceive their roles differently. Some believe they should serve as **delegates** from their districts. These legislators believe it is their duty to find out what "the folks back home" want and act accordingly. This orientation is often assumed by Republicans, nonleaders, nonsoutherners, or members with low seniority.

Other members see their role as that of **trustee**. Their constituents, they contend, did not send them to Congress to serve as mere robots or "errand-runners." They act and vote according to their own view of what is best for their district or state as well as the nation. As one member explained, "I have a responsibility not only to follow [my constituents], but to inform them and lead them. I'm not going

Senators and representatives like to claim credit for bringing money from the federal government to their states or districts. New York Senator Alfonse D'Amato is pictured here delivering a check for over $200 million to the Metropolitan Transit Authority of New York City.

to betray my responsibility to my constituents. I owe them not only my industry but my judgment. That's why they sent me here."[15] In this view a legislature is a place for deliberation and learning, not a mere gathering of ambassadors from localities. The trustee focus is more common among Democrats, House leaders, southerners, and high-seniority members.

Although the question of *delegate* versus *trustee* is an old one, it poses a false dichotomy. Representatives cannot follow detailed instructions from their constituents, because such instructions seldom exist. On many important policy questions, members hear nothing from their constituents. They hear most often only from those who agree with them. Still, a legislator should be able to define, or help define, the national interest, and this means trying to understand the needs and aspirations of millions of people. Most legislators shift back and forth in their role, depending on their perception of the public interest, their standing in the last and next elections, and the pressures of the moment. Overall, however, most members of Congress view themselves more as free agents than as delegates for their districts.

Legislators as Lawmakers

House members cast roughly 500 recorded votes a year, and senators about 350.[16] When voting, members of Congress are influenced by their perceptions of the problem addressed by the legislation, their perceptions of their constituents' interests, and the views of their trusted colleagues, staff, party leaders, lobbyists, and the president.[17]

POLICY AND PHILOSOPHICAL CONVICTIONS Most of the time, members vote their own ideological beliefs, knowing that constituents tend to grant them considerable leeway.[18] A liberal on social issues is also likely to be a liberal on tax and national security issues. Thus, on controversial issues such as national health insurance, taxes, or defense spending, knowing the general philosophical leanings of individual members provides a helpful guide both to how they make up their minds and how they will vote.

One voting pattern, described as the **conservative coalition**, cuts across party lines. It consists of southern Democrats and Republicans who vote together against other Democrats. In the 1950s and 1960s, the coalition formed on about one-quarter of the important roll call votes. Since the mid-1980s, the coalition has come together on roughly a dozen votes a year, and when it does, it wins more than 80 percent of the time in the House and does even better in the Senate.[19] The conservative coalition is most likely to form around domestic issues, especially social welfare legislation. But its strength in Congress cannot be measured by voting decisions alone, because some committee chairs who are members of this informal group may be able to prevent legislation they oppose from ever being voted on.

VOTERS Legislators pay attention to the views of their constituents on issues as well as their "potential views" as issues become more important.[20] Party and executive branch pressures also play a role, but when all is said and done, the members' political futures depend on how most voters in their districts feel about their performance. Rarely does a legislator consistently and deliberately vote against the wishes of the people back home. Legislators might pay more attention to voter attitudes on controversial or heavily publicized matters than on less-known issues.

A paradox is evident here. Members of Congress sometimes think that their individual law-making actions have considerable impact on constituents. Yet constituents' general ignorance of how their representatives vote implies the impact can be small. Members may think their constituents like (or dislike) what they are doing, when actually the voters have little idea of what is going on in Congress. This misperception is explained in part by the tendency of legislators to overestimate

The Many Meanings of Representation

Representation is one of the most challenging concepts in political science, yet one of the most important. These definitions may be helpful.

- *Formal representation* is the authority to act in another's behalf, gained through an institutional process or arrangement, such as free and open elections. The formal arrangement of selection, not the behavior of the representative, defines representation in this usage.

- *Descriptive or demographic representation* is the extent to which a representative mirrors the characteristics of the people he or she formally represents. According to this usage of the term, a representative legislature should be an exact portrait, in miniature, of the people.

- *Symbolic representation* is the extent to which a legislator is accepted as believable and as "one of their own" by the folks back home. This usage has a lot to do with a legislator's style and nonverbal signals.

- *Substantive representation* is a legislator's responsiveness to constituents. Do the policy and voting views of a legislator match those of constituents, or does the legislator rely primarily on his or her own judgment? This approach is that of a guardian or trustee, as opposed to a direct delegate of the citizens.

Voters brought a great deal of pressure to bear on their members of Congress both for and against passage of the North American Free Trade Agreement (NAFTA), which passed by a very close count.

their visibility; most citizens do not even know the names of their senators and representatives. Aside from periodic polls, members hear most often from the **attentive public**—those who follow public affairs carefully—rather than the general public. Still, members of Congress must constantly be concerned about how they will explain their votes, especially around election day. Even if only a few voters are aware of their stand on a given issue, this group might make the difference between victory and defeat.

COLLEAGUES Voting decisions are also affected by the advice members obtain from other representatives. Severe time limitations and the frequency with which members must make decisions force them to depend on the advice of like-minded colleagues. In particular, they look to respected members of the committee who worked on a bill, especially the committee chair or ranking member of the minority party.

Unlike voters back home, other members usually have detailed knowledge about issues before Congress. Their views are often public; they may have voted on the matter in previous sessions or in committee, and their public statements may have been placed in the *Congressional Record*. Members are sometimes influenced to vote one way merely because they know a colleague is on the *other* side of the issue. On occasion, in recent years, members say they have been impressed by watching a member's speech on C-SPAN while working in their office. More often, legislators find out how their friends stand on an issue, listen to the party leadership's advice, and take into account the various committee reports. If they are still in doubt, they consult other friends and staff. The members most often consulted are those who represent similar districts or the same region or state, like-minded members of the same party or faction, and those on the committee from which the legislation has come.

For some legislators, the **state delegation**—senators and representatives from the same state—reinforces a common identity. Texas Democrats have long been a strong and cohesive delegation. Other states, like California, have less cohesive state delegations.

A member may also vote with a colleague in the expectation that the colleague will later vote for a measure about which the member is concerned (*log rolling*). Some vote trading takes place to build coalitions so that members can "bring home the bacon" to their constituents. Other vote trading reflects *reciprocity* in congressional relations or deference to colleagues' superior information or expertise.

Many forces—regional, local, ties of friendship—can override party influence. Members are sometimes influenced by informal groups (ideological groups, ethnic caucuses, regional groupings, and even the class of colleagues with whom they were elected—for example, "the class of 1994"). Social groups in Congress ranging from the Congressional Black Caucus to the prayer group also can provide voting cues.

CONGRESSIONAL STAFF   Congress is the only legislature in the world with a huge staff, and its staff is one of its chief sources of power. For years, political scientists urged Congress to strengthen its staff. Without additional help, they said, representatives and senators were at a disadvantage in dealing with the executive branch and were overly dependent on information supplied by the White House or lobbyists. Complexity of issues and increasingly demanding schedules, too, created pressures for additional staff. Congress responded, some would say, with a vengeance. About 27,000 staff members, researchers, budget analysts, and others now work for Congress.[21] This number had increased at least threefold in the 1960s and 1970s but leveled off in the 1980s as Congress was pressured to lower government spending.

Every congressional committee, however, and every subcommittee is now at least minimally staffed. In addition, all members of Congress have increased the number of personal staff members working for them both in their Washington and home district offices. About one-third of the House of Representatives staff and one-fourth of the Senate staff are home based. These staff members help members of Congress communicate with the voters back home and provide constituency services and casework. Much of the work done in district offices is akin to a continuous campaign effort: generating favorable publicity, arranging for local appearances and newspaper interviews, scheduling, and contacting important civic and business leaders in the region. In the 1970s, Congress also added a Congressional Budget Office and an Office of Technology Assessment to its already existing Library of Congress, Congressional Research Service, and General Accounting Office staffs.

Because of the complexity of their responsibilities, members of Congress must delegate all kinds of tasks to their staffs. As a result, some members now wonder whether they or their staffs are in charge. This is especially true of senators, who tend to have a wider range of subject matter specialties than do representatives. At congressional hearings, it is often a staff member who tells the legislator what to ask. Congressional staffers become knowledgeable about special policy areas and deal on a day-to-day basis with their counterparts in the executive departments and interest groups. Indeed, some observers say that some of the most powerful people in Washington are congressional staffers. Staffers draft bills, conduct research, and often do much of the parliamentary negotiating and coalition building. Professional staffers often have the opportunity to influence legislative decisions. And certainly there is some truth to the notion that the more staffers there are, the more they look for things to do, such as preparing more legislation, suggesting more investigations, and in general making more work for themselves.

We should not exaggerate the independent power base of staffers, who can be summarily fired at the whim of those they serve. Staffers lack civil service protection. Although they cannot be dismissed because of their race, sex, or national origin, they know that if they wander too far from the views of the one person who can fire them, they will quickly be called back into line. Research suggests that when congressional aides promote a particular policy goal, they usually, if not always, do so at the request of the chair of the committee they work for or the member they serve.[22]

On the Party Connection

Party cohesion and control in the House of Representatives falls short of what is to be found in parliamentary systems or even in many state legislatures. . . . But the parties retain a central role in both the present functioning of the Congress and in periodic efforts to improve its performance.

The party structure is the most important mechanism we have to contain those excesses and impose a measure of collective responsibility on ourselves. The precise rewards and costs of party loyalty will differ for members who are differently situated, but for all, I believe, there ought to be a presumption that enables a House of disparate parts to function.

SOURCE: David E. Price, *The Congressional Experience: A View from the Hill* (Westview Press, 1992), pp. 73 and 90. Congressman Price (D.-NC) is a former professor of political science at Yale and Duke universities.

PARTY Another source of influence on legislative behavior is the political party. Naturally, there is a fair amount of agreement among party colleagues, and friendships tend to develop within the party. On some issues the pressure to conform to a party position is immediate and direct, even when a member does not believe in the party position. Members most often vote with their party; whether as a result of party pressure or natural affinity, on major bills there is a tendency for *most* Democrats to be arrayed against *most* Republicans.

Partisan voting has been increasing in the House since the early 1970s. Roughly three-fourths of all senators and House members cast *party votes* (votes on which majorities of both parties take opposite positions). House Democrats outside the South vote together nearly 90 percent of the time.[23] Party differences have been stronger over domestic, regulatory, and welfare measures than over foreign policy and civil liberty issues.

In recent years, party leaders in both chambers and parties have tried to encourage more cohesive and loyal party voting. Proponents of increased *party cohesion* (in which partisans stick together and vote with greater unity) say this is the only way to achieve collective responsibility in Congress. Senate minority leader Robert Dole has often been successful in getting Senate Republicans to stick together to oppose Bill Clinton's economic and tax measures.

INTEREST GROUPS Lobbyists represent interest groups in the legislative process. Interest groups, acting through their political action committees (PACs), make substantial contributions to congressional elections, giving largely to incumbents. In addition to their role as financiers of elections, interest groups (through their lobbyists) are important participants in the legislative process because they provide information.

THE PRESIDENT Presidents and executive branch officials also influence how legislators vote, particularly on foreign policy or national security issues.[24] President Bush benefited from a bipartisan coalition that passed the resolution authorizing the use of military force in the Persian Gulf. President Clinton benefited from strong Republican support in Congress to help win approval for the North American Free Trade Agreement, even when large numbers in his own party opposed this measure. Congress is sometimes overwhelmed by the greater public relations and persuasive abilities of a president.

Through effective use of their constitutional and political powers, presidents have become full-time partners in the legislative process. Still, members of Congress are reluctant to admit that they are influenced by pressures from the White House. On key domestic issues, legislators are more likely to be influenced by their constituents and by their own policy convictions than by what the White House wants.

THE LEGISLATIVE OBSTACLE COURSE

Congress operates under a system of multiple vetoes. The framers dispersed powers so they could not be accumulated by any would-be tyrant. In addition to the checks of bicameralism, Congress has also developed an elaborate set of customs to accompany these constitutional features that serve to distribute power. Follow a bill through the legislative process, and you clearly see this *dispersion of power* (see Figure 14-1). Procedures and rules of the Senate differ somewhat from those of the House, but in each chamber power is fragmented and influence is decentralized.

Every bill, including those drawn up in the executive branch, must be *introduced* in the House and the Senate by a member of that body. Bills are then *referred*

FIGURE 14-1   How a Bill Becomes a Law

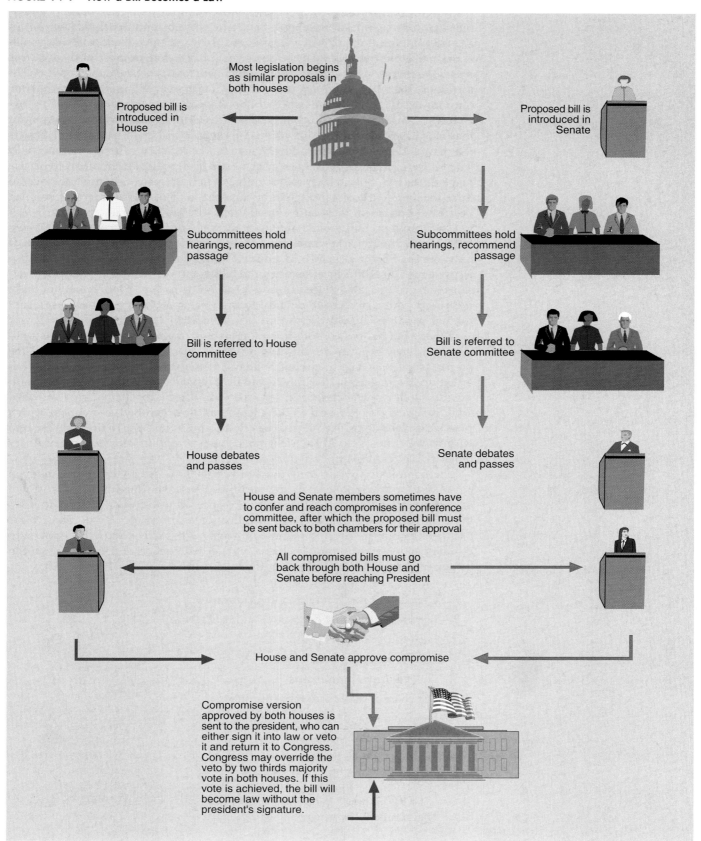

by the leadership to the appropriate standing committee. Roughly 90 percent of the bills introduced every two years die in a subcommittee for lack of support. For bills that have significant backing, a committee or subcommittee holds *hearings* to receive opinions. It then meets to *mark up* (discuss and amend) and vote on the bill. If the subcommittee and then the parent committee vote in favor of the bill, it is *reported*—that is, sent—to the full chamber, where it is debated and voted on. In the House the bill must go first to the Rules Committee for a *rule* that sets the time limit for debate and indicates whether floor amendments are allowed.

In the Senate, it is not uncommon for legislators to attach **riders**—provisions that may have little relationship to the bill they are riding on. For example, riders that have little to do with spending money can be attached to appropriations bills. The House of Representatives has stricter rules that require amendments to be germane to the bill, but no such rule is enforced in the Senate. Senators use riders to force the president to accept legislation attached to a bill that is otherwise popular, because the president must either accept the entire bill or veto it.

On most important topics (aside from taxes), both chambers consider their own bills, often at roughly the same time. There is no requirement that one act first. If only one chamber passes the bill, it dies. If both houses pass bills on the same subject but there are differences between the bills—and there often are—the two versions must go to a conference committee for reconciliation. If a bill does not make it through both chambers in identical form in the same Congress (two-year term), it must begin the entire process in the next Congress.

When a bill has passed both houses in identical form, it then goes to the president, who may sign the bill into law or veto it. If Congress is in session and the president waits ten days (excluding Sundays), then the bill becomes law without his signature. If Congress has adjourned and the president waits ten days without signing the bill, it is then defeated by a **pocket veto**. Except for the pocket veto, when a bill is vetoed it is returned to the chamber of its origin by the president with a message explaining the reasons for the veto. Congress can vote to **override** the veto with a two-thirds vote in each chamber, but assembling such an extraordinary majority is often difficult.

The complexity of the congressional system provides a tremendous built-in advantage for the opponents of any measure. Those who sponsor a bill must win at every step; opponents need to win only once. Multiple opportunities to kill a bill exist because of the dispersion of influence, and because at a dozen or more points in committee or in the House or Senate, a bill may be stopped or allowed to die (inaction is the same as killing a bill). Whether good or bad, a proposal can be delayed or rejected by any one of the following:

1. The chair of the House standing committee
2. The House standing committee and its leaders
3. The House standing committee
4. The House Rules Committee
5. The majority of the House
6. The chair of the Senate subcommittee
7. The Senate standing committee
8. The majority of the Senate
9. The floor leaders in both chambers
10. A few senators, in the case of a filibuster
11. The House-Senate conference committee, if the chambers disagree
12. The president (by veto)

Authorization and Appropriation

Congress acts by a two-step process; it *authorizes* and it *appropriates*. After Congress and the president authorize a program, Congress, with the president's concurrence, has to appropriate the funds to implement it. Appropriations are processed by a separate committee and its subcommittees. For example, the 1992 Education Act and its several titles reauthorize a variety of programs for a five-year period, including those for federal loans and grants for college students. The authorization act sets the limits on the amount that students may borrow and the conditions under which they must pay back the loan. But the authorization is useless until Congress appropriates funds and the president signs the appropriations bill into law each year. Congress is often likely to appropriate less money for student loans and grants than it has authorized.

The Importance of Compromise

Clearly, a bill does not become law unless its sponsors are willing to compromise to get the votes necessary for its passage. One tactical decision at the start is whether to push for action in the Senate first, in the House first, or in both. For example, if a bill is expected to be opposed in the Senate, its sponsors may seek passage in the House and hope that a sizable victory there will spur the Senate into action. Another decision concerns the committee to which the bill is assigned. Normally, referral to a committee is automatic. Sometimes, however, a bill involves more than one jurisdiction and can be written in such a way that it may go to a committee that will look more kindly on it.

Getting a bill through Congress requires more than a majority at any one time or place. Majorities must be mobilized over and over again—in subcommittee, in committee, in chamber, and possibly again in chamber to override a presidential veto. These majorities shift and change, and they involve different legislators in different situations at different points in time. New coalitions must be built again and again.

Effective legislators are good at building coalitions, overcoming the objections of legislators who are undecided or only slightly opposed to the bill, and reciprocating when colleagues' bills are put forward. The job of a legislator, in sum, requires the ability to compromise and to work well with others.

COMMITTEES: THE LITTLE LEGISLATURES

It is sometimes said that Congress is a collection of committees that come together in a chamber every once in a while to approve one another's actions. There is much truth in this. Congress has long relied on committees to get much of its work done. Woodrow Wilson, a teacher of political science before he became president, expressed a similar thought: "Congress in session is Congress on display. Congress in committee is Congress at work."[25] Today we would say that Congress in subcommittee is Congress at work. The main struggle over legislation takes place in subcommittees.[26] Congress also utilizes **joint committees** whose members are selected from both houses to oversee such institutions as the Library of Congress or to investigate issues like the Iran-Contra affair in the Reagan administration. Some committees organized to conduct investigations are also called **select or special committees**.

The House Democratic caucus divides standing committees into three categories. The first category is *exclusive committees* and includes Appropriations, Ways and Means, and Rules. Members who serve on one of these committees may not serve on any other standing committee. The second category is *major committees*, which include committees like Armed Services; members can serve on only one of

COMMITTEES: CONGRESS AT WORK

The 22 standing committees of the House of Representatives each have an average membership of about 35 representatives. These committees have a total of about 135 subcommittees. The committees are "the eye, the ear, the hand, and very often the brain of the House."

What Committees Do

- Study legislative proposals
- Consider communications from the executive branch
- Confirm or reject federal appointees
- Conduct hearings and investigations
- Review ongoing executive operations
- Prepare reports and surveys
- Make recommendations about corrective legislation
- Review reports, documents, and research related to committee policy
- Meet informally with public- and private-sector leaders about their committee domain
- Conduct on-site visits and inspections

Standing Committees of the House of Representatives

- Agriculture
- Appropriations
- Armed Services
- Banking, Finance, and Urban Affairs
- Budget
- District of Columbia
- Education and Labor
- Energy and Commerce
- Foreign Affairs
- Government Operations
- House Administration
- Interior and Insular Affairs
- Judiciary
- Merchant Marine and Fisheries
- Post Office and Civil Service
- Public Works and Transportation
- Rules
- Science and Technology
- Small Business
- Standards of Official Conduct
- Veterans' Affairs
- Ways and Means

Standing Committees of the Senate

- Agriculture, Nutrition, and Forestry
- Appropriations
- Armed Services
- Banking, Housing, and Urban Affairs
- Budget
- Commerce, Science, and Transportation
- Energy and Natural Resources
- Environment and Public Works
- Finance
- Foreign Relations
- Governmental Affairs
- Judiciary
- Labor and Human Resources
- Rules and Administration
- Small Business
- Veterans' Affairs

these but can add assignments to two *nonmajor committees,* such as Post Office and Civil Service or Merchant Marine and Fisheries. House members rarely serve on more than three standing committees.

Standing committees and their subcommittees are where most of the legislative work is done. Bills can be pigeonholed for weeks, amended beyond recognition, or kept in committee forever. Or a bill can go through the committee in a hurry. A committee reports out favorably only a small fraction of all the bills that come to it. Although a bill can be forced to the floor of the House through a **discharge petition** signed by a majority of the membership, legislators are reluctant to bypass committees. They regard committee members as experts in their fields. Sometimes, too, they are reluctant to risk the anger of committee leaders. And there is a strong sense of *reciprocity:* "You respect my committee's jurisdiction, and I will respect yours." Not surprisingly, few discharge petitions gain the necessary number of signatures.

The Senate has 16 standing committees, each composed of 12 to 29 members, and more than 85 subcommittees. While members of the House hold relatively few committee assignments, each senator normally serves on three standing committees and at least of seven subcommittees. Senators are more likely to serve on choice committees (committees that have clout) in part because of the *Johnson rule* (named after then-Senate Majority Leader Lyndon Johnson), which requires that no Democratic senator can have a second major committee assignment before all Democratic senators have one. Senate Republicans have implemented a similar power-sharing rule.

Among the important Senate committees are Foreign Relations, Budget, Finance, and Appropriations. Senate committees have the same powers over the framing of legislation as do those of the House, but they have somewhat less power to keep bills from reaching the floor.

Choosing Committee Members

Control and staffing of standing committees are partisan matters. The chair and a majority of each standing committee come from the majority party. The minority party is represented on each committee roughly in proportion to its membership in the entire chamber, except on some powerful committees on which the majority may want to enhance its position. Getting on a politically advantageous committee is important to members of Congress. A representative from Kansas, for example, would much rather serve on the Agriculture Committee than on the Merchant Marine and Fisheries Committee. Members usually stay on the same committees from one Congress to the next, although less senior members who have had less desirable assignments often seek better committees when places become available.

How are committee members chosen? In the House of Representatives, a Committee on Committees of the Republican membership allots places to Republican members. This committee is composed of one member from each state having Republican representation in the House; the member is almost always the senior member of the state's delegation. Because each member has as many votes in the committee as there are Republicans in the delegation, the group is dominated by senior members from the large state delegations. On the Democratic side, assignment to committees is handled by the Steering and Policy Committee of the Democratic caucus in negotiation with senior Democrats from the state delegations. In the Senate, veterans also dominate the assignment process; each party has a small Steering Committee that makes committee assignments. In making assignments, leaders are guided by various considerations: how talented and cooperative a member is, whether his or her region is already well represented on a committee, and whether the assignment will aid in reelecting the member.

One reason Congress can cope with its huge workload is that its committees and subcommittees are organized around subject matter specialties. This specialization allows members to develop technical expertise in specific areas and to recruit skilled staffs. Thus Congress is often able to challenge experts from the bureaucracy. Interest groups and lobbyists realize the great power a specific committee has in certain areas and focus their attention on its members. Similarly, members of executive departments are careful to cultivate the committee and subcommittee chairs and members of "their" committees. One powerful Senate committee chair reminded his constituents of the amount of federal tax money being spent in their state: "This does not happen by accident," the senator's campaign pamphlet said. "It takes power and influence in Congress."

Committees are not all alike. Some are powerful, others are much less important. Because of the Senate's special role in foreign policy, for example, the Senate Foreign Relations Committee is usually more influential than the House Committee on Foreign Affairs. For the two Appropriations Committees, however, the reverse is true; the House Appropriations Committee plays a more significant role than the Senate committee, although these differences are less than they used to be. We should also note that committees differ not only for institutional reasons but also according to the goals and abilities of their members.[27]

How Congress uses committees is critical in its role as a partner in policy making. In recent years progress has been made in opening hearings to the public and improving the quality of committee staffs, but it is difficult to restructure committee jurisdictions so that they do not overlap. Thus, a dozen different committees deal with energy, education, and the war on drugs. Efforts to make the committee system more efficient are often considered threats to the delicate balance of power within the chamber.

Seniority Rule

Thirty years ago committee chairs determined the total workload of committees, hired and fired staff, and formed subcommittees and assigned them jurisdictions, members, and aides. Chairs also managed the most important bills assigned to their committees. Since the mid-1970s, however, less senior members have insisted they be given more authority. Subcommittee chairs have also become more independent. It is not uncommon these days for a member of Congress of only one or two terms to be the chair of an important subcommittee, and indeed such placement is the tradition in the Senate. In recent years there have also been moves to strengthen the powers of the party leaders and caucuses at the expense of the committee chairs.

Chairs are still usually awarded on the basis of the **seniority rule.** The member of the majority party who has had the longest continuous service on the committee ordinarily becomes its chair. On some occasions, this rule has been rejected and another senior member from the majority party on that committee has been chosen. In 1975 rank-and-file House Democrats, their ranks swollen and resolve stiffened by 75 mostly liberal newcomers, removed three elderly committee chairs from their positions. In 1994 House Democrats passed over the most senior member and picked Representative David Obey (D.-Wis.) to serve as the next chair of the influential House Appropriations Committee. The seniority rule remains the "normal" way chairs are chosen, but as Speaker Thomas S. Foley noted, "The seniority system has always had great respect here, but it's never been ironclad."[28]

The seniority rule of automatic (or almost automatic) selection elevates the most experienced committee members and encourages members to stay on committees. Seniority encourages specialization and expertise. It also reduces the interpersonal politics that would arise if committee chairs were elected. Its effect is to give the most influence in Congress to states and districts that are solidly Democratic constituencies, as the Democrats have been in the majority of both houses for most of the time since the Great Depression. Until the 1970s, the seniority rule gave disproportionate power to southern Democrats; more recently, urban Democrats from safe seats control more chairs. The seniority rule lessens the influence of states or districts where the two parties are more evenly matched and where there is more turnover in who represents the state or district.

Congressional leaders support the seniority rule. Many legislators conclude: "The longer I'm here, the better I like the system." Further, those who are most anxious to change the system have the least power to produce such changes. In the past, the seniority system favored southern and rural interests and worked against organized labor, civil rights, and other urban-based interests. But today it is the liberal urban-based groups who benefit from seniority. As more women and minorities become senators and members of Congress, they, too, will likely attain chairs under the seniority custom that might be denied to them under more freewheeling selection rules.

Investigations and Oversight

The power to investigate is one of Congress's most important functions; some think it even more important than its power to legislate. Congress conducts investigations to determine if legislation is needed, to gather facts relevant to legislation, to assess the efficiency of executive agencies, to build public support, to expose corruption, and to enhance the image or reputation of its members.[29] Hearings by standing committees, their subcommittees, or special select committees are an important source of information and opinion. They provide an arena in which experts can submit their views, and statements and statistics can be entered in the record.[30] Congress's investigations are controversial, especially such well-publicized open hearings as those of the Senate Foreign Relations Committee during the Vietnam War and more recently the "Whitewater" hearings examining the Clinton family investments.

There are various kinds of investigations or hearings: routine ones conducted in the ordinary work of committees and subcommittees, and special ones conducted by special or select committees. These latter tend to be the most publicized, such as the 1987 Joint Senate-House Committee on the Iran-Contra affair. The Senate Watergate Committee's televised investigation into election practices and campaign-finance abuses in 1973 was intended less to obtain new information than to arouse citizens and promote support for electoral reforms.

Among the more important functions of congressional hearings is the oversight function—the responsibility to question executive branch officials to see whether their agencies are complying with the wishes of the Congress and conducting their programs efficiently. Authorization committees regularly hold oversight hearings, and appropriations committees, exercising "the congressional power of the purse," often use appropriations hearings to communicate committee members' views about how agency officials should carry out their business. Cabinet members have been known to dread the loaded questions of hostile members of Congress and to hate having to watch themselves on the evening news trying to explain why their agencies made some mistakes.

Conference Committees

When the framers created a two-house national legislature, they anticipated the two chambers would represent sharply different interests. The Senate was to be a small chamber of persons elected indirectly by the people to hold long, overlapping terms. It was to be a chamber of scrutiny, a gathering of wise leaders who would counsel and sanction a president—whether that president liked it or not. The House of Representatives, elected anew every two years, was to be a more direct instrument of the people.

The Senate did serve as a conservative check on the House, especially in the late nineteenth and early twentieth centuries, when it was extremely conservative and something of a rich man's club. But some factors—chiefly political—have altered the character of both the House and the Senate. Sometimes now the House is more conservative than the Senate. Executive departments and agencies, for instance, occasionally consider the Senate to be a court of appeals for appropriations that have been shot down by the House.

Given the differences between the House and the Senate, it is not surprising that the version of a bill passed by one chamber may differ substantially from the version passed by the other. Only if both houses pass an absolutely identical measure can it become law. Most of the time one house accepts the language of the other, but at least 15 percent of all bills passed (usually major ones) must be referred to a **conference committee**—a special committee of members from each chamber—that settles the differences between versions. Both parties are represented, but the majority party has more members.

The proceedings of a conference committee are usually an elaborate bargaining process. When the proposed bill is brought back to the two chambers, the conference report can be accepted or rejected (often with further negotiations ordered), but it cannot be amended. Each set of conference members must convince its colleagues that any concessions made to the other chamber were on unimportant points and that nothing basic to the original version of the bill was surrendered.

How much leeway does a conference committee have? Ordinarily members are expected to stay somewhere between the different versions. On matters for which there is no clear middle ground, members are sometimes accused of exceeding their instructions and producing a new bill. The conference committee has even been called a "third house" of Congress, one that arbitrarily revises policy. Conference committees are also criticized on the ground that they are not representative, even of the committees approving the bill, and that they disproportionately represent senior committee leaders. Critics also complain little can be done about the subtle new features that might be slipped into a bill by a conference committee. Despite such criticism, some kind of conference committee is needed for a two-house legislature to work. Conference committees integrate a bill as it comes from the two chambers.

Which chamber, House or Senate, wins more often in conference committees? On the surface it appears that the Senate's version wins more often, but this is partly because the Senate more often than not acts on its legislation after the House. Political scientist David J. Vogler concludes:

> Such an outcome does not mean that the Senate has a greater impact on the final legislative product than does the House. On the contrary, by creating the original bill and setting the agenda for debate on the issue, the House is judged to have the more real impact on the final shape of legislation as it passes through conference than does the Senate.[31]

In effect the House plays a dominant law-making role, while the Senate plays a key representational role through amendments.

CONGRESS: AN ASSESSMENT AND A VIEW ON REFORM

More than two hundred years after its creation, Congress is a much larger and very different kind of institution. Yet most of its major functions remain the same, and their responsible exercise is crucial to the health of our constitutional democracy.

We still look to Congress in the 1990s to make laws, raise revenues, represent citizens, investigate abuses of power, and oversee the executive branch, and the Senate still confirms top administrative and judicial appointees. Congress is still a bicameral organization, and its chambers still check one another as together they check and balance the executive and judicial branches of government. The interests of states and regions are still represented, debated, and brokered.

Today most members engage in continual electioneering to stay in office. So many members appear driven by their desire to win reelection that much of what takes place in Congress seems mainly designed to promote reelection. These efforts usually pay off. At the same time, this concern with reelection is generally healthy because it fosters accountability; the desire to please the voters is the link that keeps the system democratic. Congress is also characterized by internal fragmentation and diffusion of power. More and more of the work these days is done in committees or subcommittees. Multiple, successive decision points make it much easier to prevent than to pass legislation.

How does such a Congress make any progress? In an institution where most members act as individual entrepreneurs and consider themselves leaders, the task of providing institutional leadership is increasingly difficult. This is particularly true in the Senate, which prides itself on extended debate and deliberation. With limited resources, and only sometimes aided by the president, congressional leaders are asked to bring together a diverse, fragmented, and independent institution. The congressional system requires majority action and acts only when majorities can be achieved. That the framers accomplished their original objective—creating a Congress that would not move with undue haste—has been generally well realized.

Americans often characterize Congress as a bickering, timid, ignorant, selfish, or narrow-minded body. Yet we also admire the stamina and civic responsibility of members of Congress we know. Individual members of Congress are more popular than the institution. Perhaps this is because we expect Congress to solve most of our national ills, yet we judge individual members primarily on how well they serve the interests of their states and districts and on their personal appeal (see Figure 14-2).

Some of the criticism of Congress is justified. Yet critics usually forget that our national legislature is particularly exposed, and some of our expectations of it are unrealistic. First, Congress does nearly all its work directly in the public

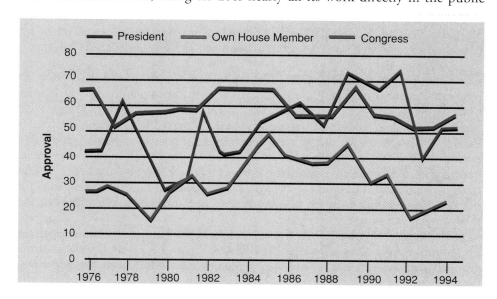

FIGURE 14-2   Presidential, Congressional, and Own House Member Approval Ratings, 1975–1994

Sources: The Gallup Poll, CBS News/New York Times Poll, ABC/Washington Post Poll, NBC News/Wall Street Journal Poll.

How would you "reform" Congress?

Which of these proposed reforms do you think should be adopted to improve Congress?

Move to a European-style parliamentary system

Extend House terms to four years

Limit House and Senate tenure to 12 years

Provide for public financing of campaigns and ban campaign contributions

Permit only people who live in a district or state to contribute to candidates for Congress

Radically reduce the number of committees and subcommittees

Strengthen the power and resources of the party leaders

Reduce the size of congressional staffs

Set and abide by an agenda agreed to at the beginning of each session

Have shorter sessions for Congress, so members can spend more time in their districts

Elect a senior senator rather than the vice-president to preside permanently over the Senate

eye. Unfortunate incidents—quarrels, name calling, evasive actions, inaccurate statements, and ethical lapses—that might be hushed up in the executive or judicial branches are almost always observed and duly reported by the news media. Second, Congress by its nature is controversial and argumentative. Its 535 members are found on both sides, sometimes on half a dozen sides, of every important question. The average citizen who holds one opinion is likely to be intolerant of other views and of the legislators holding them. There is also a considerable difference between holding an opinion and writing legislation. Moreover, during the 1990s Congress has both raised taxes and cut services—not a recipe for popularity!

Criticisms of Congress

CONGRESS IS INEFFICIENT   House and Senate procedures are, some charge, simply not suited to the needs of a modern industrial nation. Too much time is required to get bills through the complicated legislative process, and bills are often buried or defeated by procedural devices. Members are not as well informed as they should be. The dispersion of power guarantees slowness.

Some of this criticism is exaggerated. Evaluating procedure and structure is difficult to separate from evaluating policy, about which everyone has an individual preference. From the White House's vantage point, for example, Congress is inefficient when it does not process the president's bills quickly.

Congress deals with an enormous number of complex measures. Many procedures in both houses expedite handling of bills, and the committee and subcommittee system is a reasonable device for hearing arguments and compiling information. Still, the question of efficiency remains. Many members feel defeated by the system. Study groups inside and outside Congress have urged the chambers to reduce the number of committee assignments, establish better information systems, centralize more power in their leadership positions, and strengthen majority rule. Congress has done many of these things, yet the pace of legislation is not much improved.

Some of the paralysis in Congress is caused by the proliferation of subcommittees, the overlapping jurisdictions of these committees, and a congressional staff seeking to advance the agenda of individual members or subcommittees. A complicated budget process also adds to the paralysis. Better-educated and more independent-minded people are being elected to Congress, often with loose or weak ties to political parties.[32] These younger and more independent members make it difficult for party leaders to build coalitions and to maintain an efficient agenda for Congress.

CONGRESS IS UNREPRESENTATIVE   The complaint is often made that Congress represents regional or constituents' interests over the national interest. Defenders of Congress respond that representing their districts is precisely what Congress was designed to do. Legislators are described as being obsessed with staying in office—indeed, as concentrating solely on winning reelection—often at the expense of critical national issues such as the deficit, drug abuse, foreign policy, and trade. Former House Republican leader John Rhodes was perhaps too harsh when he said that "the majority of congressional actions are not aimed at producing results for the American people as much as perpetuating the longevity and comfort of the men who run Congress."[33]

Can the members of Congress, who are so much the products of upper- or upper-middle-class backgrounds, really speak for the needs of low-income groups? Can a Congress that has only 9 percent women and 5 percent black membership truly represent our female and minority populations? Moreover, the seniority system, even with its modifications, biases both houses toward conservatism. Defenders of Congress respond that there should be a strong institution to guarantee minority rights and to act as a check on mindless majority rule. Critics answer by arguing that minorities should have a right to publicize and delay what the majority proposes to do but not to defeat it.

In fact, we have a system of dual representation in which both Congress and the president can and do claim to speak for the people. But because "the people" seldom, if ever, speak with a single voice, the structure and character of the two systems tend to give us a Congress that speaks for one majority and a president who often speaks for another. Between the two, sometimes we get a balance—and sometimes deadlock.

Vocal critics of congressional fiscal irresponsibility are former presidential candidate Paul Tsongas (*left*) and former Senator Warren Rudman (*right*), who joined together to form the Concord Coalition to work for reform of Congress.

CONGRESS IS UNETHICAL   Some critics claim we have "the best Congress money can buy."[34] Many people allege that special interests and single-issue groups are stronger than ever and that they are able to fragment and often delay or block proceedings in Congress. The current system of financing congressional elections has been called a scandal. It forces members of Congress to beg for money from wealthy individuals and political action committees representing interest groups whose primary purpose is to seek support for pet legislation. Until recently, members of both houses could collect speaking fees, called honoraria, from the interest groups associated with their legislation.

Critics complain that some members of Congress are tied to the economic interests they are asked to regulate and are beholden to the political action committees that increasingly fund their campaigns. Others charge that members of Congress get too many personal privileges and that there have been too many abuses of these so-called fringe benefits. One such benefit—the House Bank's no penalty for bounced checks—became a major issue in 1992. The forced departures of Speaker Jim Wright and House Majority Whip Tony Coelho in 1989 because of ethical conflicts of interest and the indictment and conviction of a handful of other national legislators in recent years have reinforced this image. The highly public ethical or legal charges brought against Senator Bob Packwood and Representative Dan Rostenkowski in 1994 amplified this view.

In response to occasional scandals, both houses have passed ethics codes and have created ethics subcommittees. These codes require public disclosure of income and property holdings by legislators, key aides, and spouses. They also ban gifts of over $100 to a legislator, a staff member, or a legislator's family from a registered lobbyist, an organization with a political action committee, a foreign government, or a business with an interest in legislation before Congress. But these actions have not much improved the image of Congress.

CONGRESS LACKS COLLECTIVE RESPONSIBILITY   Others wonder if the problems of Congress arise because each branch can blame the other for inaction or mistakes in policy. Some suggest, for example, that we might be better served by having four-year terms for members of the House and permitting members of Congress to serve simultaneously in the president's cabinet, on the model of the British parliamentary system. A few scholars even propose that we elect presidents and members of Congress on a team ticket, that is, send a partisan team to Washington and prevent split-ticket voting. These reformers also seek means to strengthen partisan ties and efforts to link Congress and the president.[35]

Some critics see the main problem in Congress as the dispersion of power among committee and subcommittee leaders, elected party officials, factional leaders, informal caucus leaders, and other legislators. It is a "nobody's-in-charge" system.

Thinking it Through

No "reform" is neutral in terms of effects. Some groups will benefit more than others from the passage of a reform proposal. Most reforms also have unanticipated consequences that may create more problems. Still, the search goes on for practical ways to improve Congress's ability to do the people's work. Congress spent a lot of time in 1993 and 1994 trying to come up with procedure and fundraising reforms—but despite great public pressure to reform, Congress did little to alter its old ways.

Free Checking

One of the "perks" of serving in the House of Representatives until recently was access to "free checking." But here the term took on new meaning; it meant that the House Bank would lend you the money if you did not have sufficient funds, and it would cover overdrawn checks without any service charge or interest. The House Bank was unlike other banks in other ways as well; it did not pay interest on accounts, issue credit cards, or lend money. But unlimited check protection is highly unusual and was a well-kept secret until 1992, when a routine audit found that many members had written "bad" checks.

The Democratic leadership initially tried to downplay the problem, saying it was an internal matter and that only the names of the worst offenders would be released. Under substantial public pressure and with many Republicans delighting in the embarrassment Democrats faced because of their "secrecy" position, the House voted to list *all* offenders.

All told, 303 current or former members of Congress had written bad checks. Some had never done so, but others had written many; Representative Ronald V. Dellums (D.-Calif.), for example, had written 851 checks with insufficient funds. Republican House leader Newt Gingrich (R.-Ga.), wrote a bad check to pay for his 1990 federal income taxes.

The impact of the House Bank scandal had electoral consequences in 1992, as some prominent bad check writers chose not to seek reelection, several lost their renomination or reelection bids, and others lost their bids for U.S. Senate seats.

This dispersion of power means that to get things done, congressional leaders must bargain and negotiate. The result of this "brokerage" system is that laws may be watered down, defeated, delayed, or written in vague language. According to some critics, too much leeway is given to unknown bureaucrats to develop the regulations that will enforce the legislation. Accountability is confused, responsibility is eroded, and well-organized special interests that know how to work the system have an unfair advantage.

Critics worry that if Congress responds to so many single interests, it cannot speak for the great majority or for the nation as a whole. It cannot anticipate problems, plan ahead, and put together political coalitions to deal with critical problems. Some of those concerned about congressional irresponsibility do not blame the special interests alone. They argue that brokerage is mainly the result of a constitutional system that divides authority, checks power with power, and disperses political leadership. Yet other factors making it difficult for Congress to act as a unified branch arise from the fact that each chamber may be controlled by a different political party.

CONGRESS DELEGATES TOO MUCH TO THE EXECUTIVE BRANCH   Because of the complexity of modern problems and the inability to work out coalitions and compromises, there is a tendency for Congress to say to the executive branch: "Do something" about drugs; or "Do something" about AIDS and acid rain. If Congress turns a matter over to an administrative agency, the result may be that the rules and regulations issued by the administrators effectively become the law.

CONGRESS IS TOO RESPONSIVE TO ORGANIZED INTERESTS   It is also charged that the committee system is *too* responsive to organized special interests. Both houses, critics hold, overrepresent well-organized economic power structures at the expense of the average citizen. This final charge suggests that even though members of Congress are rarely bought by campaign contributions, the way Congress conducts its business—and who gets heard at its hearings and in its corridors—is influenced to too great an extent by those who can raise and disburse large sums of money as campaign contributions through political action committees. Former Senator S. I. Hayakawa (R.-Calif.) put it this way: "I'm not saying my colleagues are corrupted by the system. But it isn't hard for the recipient of a generous contribution from, let us say, the dairy industry to convince himself that what is in the interest of the dairy industry is indeed in the public interest."[36] The dependency on **interested money** is driven in part by the high cost of campaigns. Former representative, senator, and Reagan cabinet member Richard S. Schweiker said, "We've reached the point where a member has to be either a millionaire or a continual fundraiser, and that's a tragic commentary on where we are going."[37]

Defenders of Congress insist these charges are overstated. They say money would hardly influence the three dozen or more millionaires who are members of the Senate and the one hundred or so members of the House who are well-off financially. Defenders of Congress also point out that some members of Congress regularly turn down certain types of campaign contributions. Because of various campaign reform laws, candidates for Congress must now report all major campaign contributions to the Federal Election Commission. Thus, who gives what to whom is at least part of the public record. Still, the criticism is valid, and a large number of Americans are perplexed or disturbed about the degree of influence seemingly associated with campaign contributions from political action committees and wealthy individuals.

A Defense of Congress

Some criticize Congress for being both imperial and lazy—criticisms that contradict one another yet are nonetheless widespread. For example, the Bush and Reagan administrations often said Congress interfered with the president's conduct of foreign policy, was tied to parochial interests, and was too slow, too unwieldy, and too captured by sectional and special interests. Unlike the presidency, they added, Congress was more like a lawyer representing special clients than like a judge weighing the larger picture and the longer-term interests of the entire nation.

Supporters of Congress say that the president and Congress are given co-equal responsibility for shaping *both* foreign and domestic policy. The challenge that confronted the framers—how to reconcile the need for executive energy with republican liberty—is still with us. The history of constitutional democracy has always been the search for limitations on absolute power and for techniques of sharing power. Our American style of constitutionalism and separation of powers, especially in the absence of a major crisis, often means a slow-moving and sometimes inefficient decision-making system. It means a system that often hinders rather than facilitates leadership. It is a system that invites contention, division, debate, delay, and political conflict. Critics often call this *gridlock* or *deadlock* or even *paralysis*. Defenders of the Congress prefer to call it *deliberation*.

Plainly, however, members of Congress are rarely lazy. For instance, a typical day for a senator might begin with an early morning breakfast with constituents or a visiting group of businesspeople, students, or foreign dignitaries. This meeting is followed by subcommittee and committee meetings, a working lunch, several trips to the Senate floor to vote, and interviews with journalists, professors, and prospective staff in the afternoon. Then there is a dinner with other committee members to work out the details of a bill, interrupted by votes on the Senate floor. Often a senator will finish the day around 10 P.M. or later.

Some members are criticized for taking so-called "junkets," that is, trips abroad in connection with the work of their committee assignments. But most of the travel of members of Congress is hard work. They have to travel back home, generally once a month, where they speak from morning to night and meet with students, public officials, and often irate constituents. Then they get back on the plane and head for Washington, D.C. It is a demanding schedule.

Although several scandals in the early- and mid-1990s brought attacks on Congress to the forefront of American politics, attacking Congress has been a national pastime for generations. Will Rogers told some of his best jokes at the expense of Congress, as Jay Leno and David Letterman do today. Cartoonists love Congress for its unfailing ability to put its worst foot forward. Even members of Congress often "run" against Congress when they are at home in their districts.

Criticism of Congress—its alleged incompetence, its overresponsiveness, its inefficiencies—are not issues that can be dealt with outside the context of policy preferences and democratic procedures. Sometimes criticism tells us more about the critic than it does about the effectiveness of Congress. Constitutional democracy is plainly not the most efficient form of government. Congress was never intended to act swiftly; it was not created to be a rubber stamp or even a cooperative partner for presidents. Its greatest strengths—its diversity and deliberative character—also weaken its position in dealing with the more centralized executive branch. Its members will rarely be fast on their 1,070 feet. The 535 members, divided into two houses, two parties, dozens of committees, and hundreds of subcommittees, will always have a difficult time arriving at a common strategy to combat a president determined to use executive powers to the fullest.

Why One Senator Left

There was no one moment when I decided to leave the Senate. As I worked through my decision, I remembered 14-hour days: running from one room to another and one office building to another because four of my committees were meeting at the same time; lunching just off the Senate floor while waiting for my amendment to come up; dashing to the Capitol steps for photos with three groups from home and back to my offices for five appointments on pending legislation or projects—all followed by three or four hours of returning new phone calls, answering dozens of new letters, and reading a pile of urgent action memos from staff members asking directions on issues or constituent problems. Those days usually ended at 10 P.M. with dinner at my desk.

There was no time for reflection, no time to exchange ideas with fellow senators. . . . My family life and personal friendships paid a stiff price. There were only three weekends last year when I was not airborne. . . . One month it took 27 days before my wife and I could have dinner together and an unscheduled evening at home. At the end of certain days, I sometimes asked myself what I had really done to help solve the major problems facing our country. My honest answer was: not much.

SOURCE: Adapted from David L. Boren, "Why I Am Leaving the Senate," *The New York Times,* May 13, 1994, p. A15.

Congress is supposed to reflect geographical and narrow interests, to register the diversity of the United States. In *The Federalist*, No. 57, James Madison wrote: "Who are to be the electors of the Federal Representatives? Not the rich more than the poor; not the learned more than the ignorant; not the haughty heirs of distinguished names, more than the humble sons of obscure and unpropitious fortune."[38] Yet as the costs of campaigning increase, and as the body of elected officials continues to come from essentially upper or upper-middle class, we must question whether ours is the open, representative, responsive, and responsible legislative system we can point to with pride as a model for those in other parts of the world who yearn for constitutional democracy.

As Congress prepares for the twenty-first century, the following questions have to be raised: Can Congress overcome partisan bickering and agree on action? Can it have a long-range view, staying power, the span of attention, and the ability to make sensible laws for the whole nation? The real question is whether Congress is operating effectively enough most of the time to deal with crime, welfare, health, and other issues the general public feels require national action. Although our answers would differ, all of us would agree that a vital, responsive, and effective Congress is essential if we would make our constitutional democracy live up to its ideals.

SUMMARY

1. Members of Congress are largely driven by the desire to seek election and win reelection. Once elected, they are successful at staying in office. Much of what Congress does is in response to this motive. Members work hard to get favors for their districts, to serve the needs of constituents, and to maintain a high visibility in their districts or states. Incumbents have advantages that help explain their success at reelection: they have greater name recognition; they have large staffs; they are better able to raise campaign money; and they have greater access to the media. Partisanship, candidate appeal, and important issues contribute to the voters' choice for Congress.

2. Senators and representatives come primarily from upper- and middle-class backgrounds. They are better educated than Americans as a whole. The typical member of Congress is a middle-aged, white, male lawyer.

3. Congress performs these functions: representation, law making, consensus building, overseeing, investigating, policy clarification, and legitimizing. Congress as a collective body must attempt to perform these tasks even as most of its members serve as ombudsmen for their constituents and work for their own reelections.

4. Most of the work in Congress is done in committees and subcommittees. Congress has attempted in recent years to streamline its committee system and modify its methods of selecting committee chairs. Seniority practices are still generally followed, yet the threat of removal forces committee chairs to consult with younger members of the majority party. Subcommittees are now more important in an increasingly decentralized Congress.

5. The workload for Congress is considerable. Much could be done to make our national legislature perform its functions more effectively. Some improvements have been made in recent years: redistricting and reapportionment have shaped a Congress that somewhat more accurately reflects the population. The filibuster in the Senate and the Rules Committee in the House are less obstructive than they once were. The role of the Speaker and of party steering committees has been enhanced, and Congress is better staffed.

FURTHER READING

JOEL D. ABERBACH, *Keeping a Watchful Eye: The Politics of Congressional Oversight* (Brookings Institution, 1990).

BARBARA BOXER, *Strangers in the Senate* (National Press, 1993).

STEPHEN L. CARTER, *The Confirmation Mess: Cleaning Up the Federal Appointment Process* (Basic Books, 1994).

GARY COX AND MATTHEW MCCUBBINS, *Legislative Leviathan: Party Government in the House* (University of California Press, 1993).

ROGER H. DAVIDSON, ED., *The Postreform Congress* (St. Martin's Press, 1992).

ROGER H. DAVIDSON AND WALTER J. OLESZEK, *Congress and Its Members*, 4th ed. (Congressional Quarterly Press, 1994).

LAWRENCE C. DODD AND BRUCE J. OPPENHEIMER, EDS., *Congress Reconsidered*, 4th ed. (Congressional Quarterly Press, 1989).

RICHARD F. FENNO, JR., *Home Style: House Members in Their Districts* (Little, Brown, 1978).

MORRIS FIORINA, *Congress: Keystone of the Washington Establishment*, 2d ed. (Yale University Press, 1989).

FRED HARRIS, *Deadlock or Decision: The U.S. Senate and the Rise of National Politics* (Oxford University Press, 1992).

GARY C. JACOBSON, *The Electoral Origins of Divided Government: Competition in U.S. House Elections, 1946–1988* (Westview Press, 1990).

GARY C. JACOBSON, *The Politics of Congressional Elections,* 3d ed. (HarperCollins, 1992).

JOHN W. KINGDON, *Congressional Voting Decisions,* 3d ed. (University of Michigan Press, 1989).

THOMAS MANN AND NORMAN ORNSTEIN, EDS., *Renewing Congress: A Second Report* (American Enterprise Institute and Brookings Institution, 1993).

DAVID R. MAYHEW, *Congress: The Electoral Connection* (Yale University Press, 1974).

WALTER J. OLESZEK, *Congressional Procedures and the Policy Process,* 3d ed. (Congressional Quarterly Press, 1989).

DAVID E. PRICE, *The Congressional Experience* (Westview Press, 1993).

JONATHAN RAUCH, *Demosclerosis: The Silent Killer Of American Government* (Times Books, 1994).

ANDRÉE REEVES, *Congressional Committee Chairmen: Those Who Made an Evolution* (University Press of Kentucky, 1994).

DAVID SCHOENBROD, *Power Without Responsibility: How Congress Abuses the People Through Delegation* (Yale University Press, 1994).

PAUL SIMON, *Advice and Consent: Clarence Thomas, Robert Bork and the Intriguing History of the Supreme Court's Nominating Battles* (National Press Books, 1992).

BARBARA SINCLAIR, *The Transformation of the U.S. Senate* (Johns Hopkins University Press, 1989).

STEVEN S. SMITH, *Call To Order: Floor Politics in the House and Senate* (Brookings Institution, 1989).

JAMES L. SUNDQUIST, ED., *Beyond Gridlock? Prospects for Governance in the Clinton Years—and After* (Brookings Institution, 1993).

CAROL M. SWAIN, *Black Faces, Black Interests: The Representation of African-Americans in Congress* (Harvard University Press, 1993)

The Presidency: The Leadership Branch

A s he traveled slowly up the east coast from Mount Vernon to New York (the temporary seat of government) in 1789, newly elected President George Washington was showered with parades and fireworks. His whole trip was one long ovation, a celebration of the people's yearning for a strong individual who could provide continuity and leadership for the nation.

Yet Washington and his compatriots were of two minds about the power of the presidency. The framers both admired and feared leadership. They realized the country needed a more effective, centralized government, yet they were suspicious of the potential abuses of power, especially the power vested in a single individual. Given what they had lived through in the preceding decades, they had every right to these fears. Moreover, they hardly wanted to jeopardize the rights and liberties they had fought so hard to win in the recent revolution.

Americans still have not resolved their ambivalence toward the presidency. Should a president be "above politics" and merely wait for a consensus to emerge from the people and Congress? Or should the institution be clearly political, *leading* the people and *leading* Congress? Should its powers be narrowly defined, or should it be granted broad authority to respond to national and international emergencies? Is an office created over two hundred years ago in an agrarian society adequate for the post-cold war era in which the United States is challenged to play a leading role in global trade, diplomacy, peacekeeping, and environmental conservation? Can any person meet such high expectations of the presidency? And does the greatly enlarged role of the presidency under today's circumstances alter and perhaps undermine some of the fundamental checks and balances in our constitutional democracy? We'll try to answer these questions as we take a closer look at the central role of the American presidency.

WHAT WE LOOK FOR IN PRESIDENTS

The framers perceived their president in the image of George Washington, the man they expected would first occupy the office. Like Washington, the American executive was to be a wise, moderate, dignified, nonpartisan leader of all the people. Washington had served his country in a variety of ways, most notably as commander in chief of the Continental Army for eight years and as an instigator of, and later presiding officer at, the Constitutional Convention of 1787. No one commanded the trust and respect that Washington did, and he was unanimously elected as the first president of the new republic in 1789. George Washington knew the people needed to have confidence in their fledgling government, a sense of continuity with the past, a time of calmness and stability, free of emergencies and crises. He knew, too, that the new nation faced many foreign dangers.

Article II of the Constitution outlines the nature and scope of presidential power. It responded to Washington's calls for vigorous executive leadership. Washington's misgivings about his qualifications and about the scope of presidential power faded as he set precedents and fulfilled the hopes of the people.[1] He was sensitive to the fine line between providing stronger leadership and infringing on the individual rights and liberties of the people. He knew then, as every president after him has either known or learned, that Americans have a strong streak of anti-government and even anti-authority sentiment. We want strong presidential leadership when the times demand it or when it serves our favorite causes, yet we insist that no elected official or governmental agency dare infringe on our rights.

George Washington was unanimously elected as the first president and was inaugurated in New York City on April 30, 1789.

TABLE 15-1

The One Quality Voters Said They Wanted Most in a President

Honesty/integrity	43%
Leadership/ability to make decisions	11
Sense of responsibility to people	6
Believes United States rates first	5
Understanding of the poor	4
Sound economic program	4
Intelligence	2
Good judgment	2
Self-confidence	2
Experience	2
High moral standards	2
Accessibility	1
Other	3
No answer/don't know	12

SOURCE: CBS News–New York Times Poll, April 1992.

We are not at all clear about how much power we want to vest in the president. When presidents take charge and try to run the country, they are often criticized for trying to impose their will on the nation. More likely, however, they are going to be criticized because they do nothing and, even more likely, to be blamed for whatever happens to the country—for our not having a proper health policy, for a recession, for inflation, for the homeless, or for ethnic warfare in remote nations. People who like what the president is doing are champions of presidential leadership, but people who disapprove of what a president is doing point to the dangers of dictatorship.

What kind of person does it take to perform this delicate balancing act? Our Constitution establishes only three qualifications for the office: a president must be at least 35 years of age, have lived in the United States for 14 years, and be a natural-born citizen. Our "unwritten presidential job description"—the one we carry around in our heads—says a president has to be many things to many people. Every four years Americans search the national landscape for a potential heroic leader who is blessed with the judgment of a Washington, the mind of a Jefferson, the steadfastness of a Lincoln, the calm of an Eisenhower, and the grace of a John F. Kennedy.

Americans want leadership, but what kind of leadership? We want someone who can provide a sense of purpose, someone who can remind us of our shared aspirations as a constitutional democracy and a pragmatic, hardworking, generous nation. Yet we also want someone who can pay close attention to our immediate needs—jobs, peace, prosperity.

Voters sometimes place more emphasis on a presidential candidate's character and integrity than they do on a candidate's stands on social and economic issues (see Table 15-1). This emphasis is not misguided. Presidents have enormous power, especially in times of crisis. They also select the people who run the executive departments and serve on our courts, and thus they have much to do with the standards of governmental performance and ethics. Hence it is important to weigh their character and their allegiance to democratic values and to the spirit of the Constitution.

We also pick our candidates in terms of their personalities. Can they get along with members of Congress, the press, fellow party leaders, and leaders of other nations? We also ask whether the would-be president displays vision, judgment, a grasp of history, a sense of proportion, and a sense of humor. To be sure, people prefer candidates whose views on issues accord with their own; if they like a person's personality, they trust that individual's policy ideas to be acceptable. A candidate's character and policy preferences sometimes get blurred—if not reversed—in the voter's mind

In addition, the public wants a president to be tough, decisive, and competent. Voters recognize the need for strong leadership, even in a democracy. They yearn for a leader with foresight and personal strength. Moreover, people want someone who will simplify politics, symbolize the protective role of the state, and yet be concerned with them. We want *effectiveness* but also *fairness*. Do we ask too much? The novelist John Steinbeck thought so: "We give the President more work than a man can do, more responsibility than a man should take, more pressure than a man can bear. We abuse him often and rarely praise him. We wear him out, use him up, eat him up. . . . He is ours and we exercise the right to destroy him."[2]

Americans applaud presidents when things go well and blame them when things go wrong. Disasters as well as triumphs are credited to presidents—Wilson's League of Nations, Hoover's Depression, Roosevelt's New Deal, Johnson's Vietnam War, Nixon's Watergate, Bush's Persian Gulf War. An exaggerated sense of presidential wisdom and power sometimes causes us to forget there are limits to what presidents can accomplish. Although the tragedies of American involvement in Vietnam and of presidential involvement in the Watergate scandal deglamorized the presidency, the vitality of our constitutional democracy still depends in large measure on creative presidential leadership.

The Original Intent

The framers of the Constitution created a presidency of limited powers. They wanted a presidential office that would stay clear of parties and factions, enforce the laws passed by Congress, deal with foreign governments, and help states put down disorders. They wanted a presidency strong enough to match Congress but not so strong that it would overpower Congress. They seemed to have in mind that the president should be an elected king with substantial personal authority, who serves the common good and minimizes the negative influence of the worst factions. They combined the ceremonial head of government with the actual head of government. The term of office would be four years, and presidents would be indefinitely eligible to succeed themselves (the two-term limit would be added to the Constitution much later, in 1951).

Although independent from the legislature, presidents would still *share* considerable power with Congress. The essence of the arrangement would be in intermingling powers with Congress. To enact government business, the separate branches would have to cooperate and consult with one another. A president's major appointments would have to be approved by the Senate; Congress could override the chief executive's veto by a two-thirds vote of each chamber; and the president could make treaties only with the advice and consent of two-thirds of the senators. All appropriations (the power of the purse) would be legislated by Congress, not the president. But even a presidency with such limited powers, hemmed in by the system of checks and balances, worried some Americans in 1787. The framers deliberately outlined the powers of the president broadly. The president, they thought, should have discretionary power to act when other governmental branches failed to meet their responsibilities or to respond to the urgencies of the day.

The Politics of Shared Power

Our constitutional democracy was designed to be one of both shared powers and division. The framers wanted disagreement as well as cooperation because they assumed that the checks and balances within the government would prevent the president and Congress from "ganging up" against the people's liberties. The framers actually made disagreements inevitable by providing that the president, Senate, and House of Representatives would be elected by different constituencies and for different lengths of service.

The United States is unique among major world powers because it is neither a parliamentary democracy nor a wholly executive-dominated government. Our Constitution plainly invites both Congress and the president to set policy and govern the nation. Leadership and policy change are encouraged only when two, and sometimes all three, branches of government concur on the desirability of new directions. Sometimes Congress has been the dominant partner, but more recently our presidents seem to hold the upper hand, despite constitutionally specified restraints.

The politics of shared power has often been stormy, as the Persian Gulf War, Iran-Contra affair, and the Whitewater investigations illustrate. The politics of shared powers is characterized by changing patterns of cooperation and conflict depending on the partisan and ideological makeup of Congress, the popularity and skills of the president, and various events that shape the politics of the times.

The Roots of Divided Government

We can point to numerous roots of divided government in the United States, but these factors are most clearly at work: constitutional ambiguities, different constituencies, varying terms of office, divided party control of the branches (much of the time in recent years), weak political parties, and fluctuating power.

Who Were the Best Presidents?

Past surveys of *historians* have consistently obtained these results:

1. Abraham Lincoln
2. George Washington
3. Franklin D. Roosevelt
4. Andrew Jackson
5. Thomas Jefferson
6. Theodore Roosevelt
7. Woodrow Wilson

But surveys of the *public* turn out differently. A Gallup Poll asked the American people: "What three presidents do you regard as the greatest?"

1. John F. Kennedy 52%
2. Abraham Lincoln 49%
3. Franklin D. Roosevelt 45%
4. Harry Truman 37%
5. George Washington 25%
6. Dwight Eisenhower 24%

Should we have a six-year
nonrenewable term for presidents?

Several presidents (Lyndon Johnson,
Richard Nixon, Jimmy Carter) have
favored amending the Constitution to
provide for a single, nonrenewable six-
year term for president. Most experts on
the presidency oppose this proposal.
What are the merits and disadvantages
of this proposed amendment?

You Decide!

CONSTITUTIONAL AMBIGUITIES   Article I of the Constitution grants to Congress "all legislative Powers" but limits them to those "herein granted." It then sets forth in some detail the powers vested in Congress. In contrast, Article II vests in the president "the executive Power" without limiting it to such powers as are "herein granted" and then proceeds to describe these powers in very general terms. Is this difference in language between Articles I and II significant? Some scholars and most presidents have argued that a president is granted by Article II a general and undefined power to act to promote the well-being of the United States, subject only to precise constitutional limits. Therefore, they contend, a president is not limited to the powers spelled out in the Constitution, as is Congress, but has all the executive powers of the United States. Other scholars and most members of Congress say the president either has no such inherent power or has it only in extraordinary circumstances.

Whatever the language of the Constitution, the president has often exercised powers not expressly defined in it. These powers have been given a variety of names: *implied, inherent, or emergency powers.* For example, George Bush sent troops into Panama to help overthrow its government and capture General Manuel Noriega, and he did so without asking for a declaration of war and largely without consulting Congress. Bush was criticized by Congress for acting without congressional approval. Yet even the most faithful defenders of congressional prerogatives recognize that in extraordinary emergencies a president "may have to act promptly without clear constitutional or statutory support."[3] This difference between Capitol Hill and the White House over a president's general executive powers is merely one of several ambiguities in our constitutional arrangements.

DIFFERENT CONSTITUENCIES   Another root of divided government comes from the different constituencies Congress and the president represent. Members of Congress represent state and local districts, and hence reflect specific geographic, ethnic, and economic interests. James Madison and other framers of the Constitution anticipated legislators would often be pressured by local and state interests.

Presidents and their aides often think members of Congress are captives of sectional interests and local pressures. Members of Congress, of course, see sensitivity to state and local concerns as essential to their job as representatives. As a result, members of Congress—even those from a president's own party and own region—may look at problems and solutions somewhat differently from the way a president does, as a president represents a national perspective.

There is an old saying in Washington, D.C., that "where you stand depends on where you sit." President Lyndon Johnson, for example, viewed the importance of civil rights legislation differently when he was in the White House from the way he viewed it when he represented Texas in the U.S. House and Senate. And President Gerald Ford quipped, "When I was in the House for 25 years, I almost always looked down Pennsylvania Avenue at the White House, regardless of whether Democrats or Republicans were there, and wondered why they were so arrogant. Then, when I was in the White House myself, I looked up at the Congress and wondered how there could be 535 irresponsible members of Congress."[4]

VARYING TERMS OF OFFICE   Presidents serve for four years with a chance of reelection to a second term; senators have the luxury of six-year terms; members of the House of Representatives are elected for two-year terms. Different constituencies and lengths of service make these national offices responsive to different moods and points of view. Different electoral forces may have been at work in the election that elected them. A majority of the voters can win control over only part of the national government at a time—and this arrangement, too, was by design.

Presidents often act quickly to shape national priorities in their first year following the flush of their electoral victories. They act to win support for their agendas before the almost inevitable decline in public approval. Congress, on the other hand, moves more slowly; as President Bush once joked, "The way to slow down old age is to move it through Congress." Congress is inefficient in part "because it represents a vast array of local interests. Congress passes new laws slowly and reviews old ones carefully." The decision-making pace of Congress and of the president is not the same because of their different terms of office. The result is often conflict and deadlock.[5]

Moreover, members of Congress may have been in office for 10 or 20 years and perhaps look forward to serving several more terms. Some members of Congress are, in effect, career politicians and stay in office a long time. Hence they assume they will outlast the president, who has a limited term of service and is a **lame duck** in the second term. Presidents, however, think mainly about today and tomorrow.

DIVIDED PARTY CONTROL OF THE BRANCHES   Since 1952 there has been a split in partisan control of the presidency and Congress for about two-thirds of the time. Republican Presidents George Bush, Gerald Ford, and Richard Nixon had to deal with a Congress that was entirely under the control of Democrats. And Republican Presidents Ronald Reagan and Dwight Eisenhower had to deal with Congresses that most of the time were under the control of Democrats. Only Presidents John Kennedy, Lyndon Johnson, Jimmy Carter, and Bill Clinton enjoyed majority control by their own party in Congress, and even they had considerable trouble getting support for their legislative programs.

In the days, weeks, and sometimes months following the inauguration, presidents usually enjoy what has been called the **honeymoon**, a period of generally positive relations with the press and Congress, which is often thought to last about six months. Franklin Roosevelt, Lyndon Johnson, Ronald Reagan, and Bill Clinton all enjoyed legislative success in their first years in office.

The opposition party in Congress regularly mounts its own programs. It will, when possible, defeat a president's policy initiatives and substitute its own. This effort becomes all the more troublesome for a president when Congress is controlled by the opposition party.

WEAK POLITICAL PARTIES   Political parties in the United States are organizationally weak and highly decentralized. Changes in the way parties finance, organize, and televise nominations and elections have had the effect of weakening the ability of national party leaders, such as the president, to discipline party members. Most members of Congress run and finance their elections with only minimal assistance or even ties to their national party. They customarily respond to local conditions and run their campaigns independently of their party's presidential candidate or national platform. Thus they feel few obligations to go along with the president of their own party, unless whatever measure is at stake is in the interest of their home district or state.

FLUCTUATING POWER   The American public's waxing and waning support for Congress complicates the problems of divided government. We often like our own members of Congress while being highly critical of the Congress as a whole. We keep reelecting the same representatives, yet in recent years Americans have generally held presidents in higher esteem than Congress as an institution, and this fluctuating prestige has consequences. Greater prestige for the presidency often gives the incumbent in the White House an edge in battles with Congress.

Congress is viewed by most people as inefficient, in part because it has to represent local interests and respond (some think too much) to narrow pressures or parochial constituencies. Yet when presidents decline in popularity, such as after the Watergate scandal, Americans turn to Congress to hold the president and the presidency

Thinking it Through

Pro

- It might help take politics out of the presidency and thereby lessen the likelihood of scandals like Watergate.
- Four years is too short a time to get the job done.
- Presidents could concentrate on the job rather than on reelection.
- During wartime a president would not waste time campaigning.
- Budgets are already cast for about two years ahead when a president gets into office.
- Six years is enough even for the healthiest of presidents.

Con

- A six-year term would give us two more years of the "clunkers" and two fewer years of the great ones.
- Four years is long enough to tell whether a president is doing the job.
- The best way to be reelected is to do the job well, maintain majority support, and be an effective leader.
- The four-year term forces presidents to be accountable for their promises and platforms.
- Many of our great presidents served ably for more than six years: Washington, Jefferson, Wilson, FDR, and Eisenhower.
- A healthy, democratic country needs a politician in the White House, one who can bargain, persuade, build crucial political coalitions, and get diverse political factions to work together.
- We should not surrender a hard-won democratic right: to kick a leader *out* of office.

Factors that Influence a President's Success in Congress

- Same party in control of Congress
- Similar ideological interests in control of Congress
- National emergencies
- The "honeymoon" effect experienced during the first year in office
- High public approval ratings for the president
- Effective presidential lobbying of the Congress
- Threat of presidential veto
- Presidential bargaining with use of patronage powers
- Clear presidential priorities that win consensus in the nation
- President's "bully pulpit" publicity efforts, including addresses and news conferences

"Bully Pulpit"

This term was used and made popular by President Theodore Roosevelt (TR), who believed the office of president provided an enormous opportunity to inspire and even preach to a national constituency as if it were a national congregation. "Bully" is a term of approval and affirmation. TR used it as in "Bully for you," meaning terrific, great, or well done! Presidents like Woodrow Wilson, Franklin Roosevelt, John Kennedy, and Ronald Reagan have been noted for their use of the presidential "bully pulpit."

accountable. At such times the public insists Congress be strengthened and asks it to play a more equal role in governing the nation. Americans often remind themselves that they do not want presidents unilaterally dictating policies and laws. They want a Congress that does more than just rubber-stamp presidential decisions.

Although separation of powers and divided government are obstacles, they are not insurmountable barriers to good public policy making. Presidents and Congress can legislate when the leaders of both institutions bargain and compromise in ways that overcome the roots of division discussed here. In fact, while the Constitution disperses power and invites a continual struggle between these two branches, it also requires the two branches to integrate the fragmented parts of the system into a workable government. And usually these two branches of government do work together. Even when the relationship is regarded as hostile, "bills get passed and signed into law. Presidential appointments are approved by the Senate. Budgets are enacted and the government is kept afloat. This necessary cooperation goes on even when control of the White House and the Capitol is divided between the two major parties."[6]

The presidential record of dealing with Congress in recent decades is mixed. Presidents enjoy considerable success in getting most of their nominations confirmed by the Senate. Relatively few presidential vetoes are overturned by Congress. Also, most presidential budget requests eventually win approval, although Congress jealously guards its right to modify them, especially in areas such as defense and education. On the other hand, Congress approves only about 50 percent of the president's major policy recommendations. And Congress is, in fact, the source of a fair percentage of the laws identified as part of the president's program.

A relatively unified Congress could make life pretty miserable for a president. It could, for example, refuse to confirm a president's vital nominations, reduce funds for key programs, and reject treaties. It could also override the chief executive's vetoes. Yet the historical record suggests most presidents have enjoyed far greater cooperation from Congress than those possibilities might imply, and modern-day presidents are more powerful than those of the last century, even though their constitutional powers have not changed.

The Extension of Executive Power

After two centuries, our presidential track record is good. Perhaps in no other nation have leaders with so much power at their command so carefully followed the restraints imposed on them by a written Constitution. The exact dimensions of executive power at any given moment are partly the consequence of the incumbent's character and energy, combined with the needs of the time, the values of the citizenry, and the challenges to our nation's survival.[7] By and large, the history of presidential power is one of steady, if uneven, growth. Of the 36 individuals who have filled the office, about one-third have enlarged its powers. Andrew Jackson, Abraham Lincoln, and both Roosevelts, for example, strengthened both the institution and its powers by the way they responded to crises and set priorities.

In this extension of the executive power, Congress and the courts have often been willing partners. In emergencies Congress often delegates discretion to the executive branch; and the legislature sometimes seems incapable of dealing with matters that are highly technical or that require immediate response and constant management. Some people think what Congress lacks most is the will to use powers it already has. But this explanation is hardly satisfactory as the weakness of Congress is not unique among legislative bodies. During the last two centuries in all democracies, and at all levels, power has drifted from legislators to executives. The English prime minister, the French president, governors of our states, and mayors of our cities all play more dominant roles than they did, generally speaking, one hundred years ago.

Several factors have strengthened the presidency. The danger of war plainly increases a president's influence on the nation's affairs. The cold war—with its enormous standing army, nuclear weapons, and widespread intelligence and alliance operations—invited presidential dominance in national security matters. Television also contributes to the growth of presidential influence. With access to prime time, presidents take their cases directly to the people. This invitation to bypass and sometimes to ignore Congress, the Washington press, and even party leaders weakens the checks once imposed on the presidency.

Growth of the federal role in domestic and economic matters has also increased presidential responsibility and contributed to an enlarged presidential establishment. Problems not easily delegated to any one department often get pulled into the White House. When new programs concern several federal agencies, someone near the president is often asked to set a consistent policy and reconcile conflicts. White House aides, with some justification, claim the presidency is the only place in government where it is possible to establish and coordinate national priorities. And presidents constantly set up central review and coordination units that help formulate new policies, settle jurisdictional disputes among departments, and provide access for the well-organized interest groups who want their views to be given weight in decision making.

The growth of the presidency is also encouraged by public expectations. Although we may dislike or condemn individual presidents, popular attitudes toward the institution of the presidency remain positive. We want very much to believe in our presidents, perhaps because we have no royal family, no established religion, and no common ceremonial leadership. Sometimes, in an effort to live up to exaggerated expectations, presidents overextend themselves. Wanting to maintain popularity encourages them to make frequent appeals to the general public. These television appeals become bargaining chips that may help presidents temporarily improve their public images and even win occasional fights in Congress, as President Johnson did during the Vietnam War. If used too often, though, these appeals can undermine a president's relations with Congress and render the parties less important in supplying policy ideas and in keeping presidents and other elected officials accountable.[8]

Today a president is asked to play several roles that are not carefully spelled out in the Constitution. We want the chief executive to be an international peacemaker as well as a national morale builder, a politician in chief as well as a commander in chief, and a unifying representative of all the people. We want the president to be the architect of "a new world order" and to negotiate favorable trade pacts with major trading partners. We want every new president to be virtually everything all our great presidents have been, and then some.

THE JOB OF PRESIDENT

In addition to the obvious leadership responsibilities a president has in foreign policy, economics, and domestic policy, six broad functional kinds of leadership are expected of a president. These policy areas and functions permit us to develop a job profile of an American president (see Table 15-2).

Presidents as Crisis Managers

"The President shall be Commander in Chief of the Army and Navy of the United States," reads Section 2 of Article II of the Constitution. Even though this is the first of the president's powers listed in the Constitution, the framers intended the military role to be a limited one—far less than a king's. Congress would declare war and call up the army and navy. And Congress would control the power of the purse

TABLE 15-2

A Presidential Job Description

Functional Leadership	Foreign Policy	Examples of Policy Responsibilities Economics	Domestic Policy
Crisis management	Liberating Kuwait (Persian Gulf War)	FDR's handling of the Depression, 1930s	Response to urban riots
Symbolic and morale-building leadership	Clinton's trip to Europe on 50th anniversary of D-day	Being bullish on American productivity	Visiting flood and disaster victims; helping Alaska clean up oil spill
Recruitment of top officials	Selecting Joint Chiefs of Staff chair	Hiring wise economic advisers	Nominating a chief justice
Priority setting and problem clarification	Working with United Nations on peacekeeping priorities	Outlining tax-cut or revenue-producing programs	Setting priorities in environmental protection and health care
Legislative and political coalition building	Negotiating with Congress on aid to Eastern European nations	Vetoing tax legislation	Fighting for domestic spending programs
Program implementation, administration, and oversight	Making Middle East peace accords work	Monitoring Internal Revenue Service performance	Appraising the impact of federal social programs

and hence the funding of wars. Yet it was important, the framers insisted, that the people's elected representative—the president—be in charge of the military. This principle of *civilian* control over the military is an absolutely central element in our constitutional democracy.

This principle has meant that in the United States today we do not worry, as do people in many nations around the world, whether the military establishment will accept the outcome of elections. General Douglas MacArthur tested this principle of American constitutionalism late in the Korean War when he challenged President Harry Truman. Truman, an unpopular president at the time, had to tell the popular general to leave his command—and the general went. Many people consider this civilian supremacy over the military one of our most significant contributions to the survival of constitutional democracy. We put the president, a civilian, on top.

When crises and national emergencies occur, Americans instinctively turn to the chief executive, who is expected to provide not only executive and political leadership but also the appearance of a confident, "take-charge" executive who has a steady hand at the helm. Public necessity forces presidents to do what Lincoln and Franklin Roosevelt did during the national emergencies of their day: provide the stability and continuity needed to protect the union and safeguard vital American interests.

Two centuries of national expansion and recurrent crises have increased the powers of the president beyond those specified by the Constitution. The complexity of Congress's decision-making procedures, its unwieldy numbers, and its constitutional tasks make it a more public, deliberative, and divided organization than the presidency. When major crises occur, Congress traditionally holds debates and, almost as predictably, delegates authority to a president, charging that official to take whatever actions are necessary. This is essentially what Congress did when Bush asked for its support to force Saddam Hussein out of Kuwait.

The primary factor underlying this transformation in the president's function as commander in chief has been the changed role of the United States in the world, especially since World War II. In the postwar years every president from

President Clinton met with world leaders at the 1994 NATO meeting to work out plans for dealing with the crisis in Bosnia.

Truman to the present argued for and won widespread support for the position that military strength, especially military superiority over the now-defunct Soviet Union, was the primary route to national security. Nations willingly grew dependent on our assistance, which rapidly became translated into a multitude of treaties, pacts, and diplomatic agreements. From then on, nearly every threat to the political stability of our far-flung network of allies became a test of whether we would honor our commitments in good faith. These commitments, plus the fear of nuclear war and the importance of deterrence, prompted Congress to give presidents great flexibility in this area. This doesn't mean Congress will always agree with a president. Bill Clinton's wavering policies in Somalia, Bosnia, Haiti, and North Korea won him more criticism than support from Congress and the public in his first years in office.

Presidents are expected to be crisis managers in the domestic sphere as well. Whenever things go wrong, we demand presidential-level planning and problem solving. When terrorists attack U.S. citizens, people assume their president will retaliate. When a disastrous oil spill occurs, as it did off the Alaskan coast a few years ago, people expect the head of state to step in and assist. When riots occur in our cities, we ask what the president is going to do about it. In many crises, however, presidents are little more than victims of fast-breaking events and forces outside of their control. They are sometimes surprised, overtaken by developments, and placed on the defensive.

Presidents as Morale Builders

Presidents are the nation's number-one celebrities; almost anything they do is news. Merely by going to church or taking a jog, presidents command attention. By their actions they can arouse a sense of hope or despair, honor or dishonor.

The framers of the Constitution did not fully anticipate the symbolic and morale-building functions a president must perform. Certain magisterial functions, such as receiving ambassadors and granting pardons, were conferred. But over time the presidency has acquired enormous *symbolic* significance. People turn to national leaders just as tribespeople turn to shamans—for meaning, healing, empowerment, assurance, and a sense of purpose. Many people find comfort in an oversimplified image of the president as a warrior-captain at the helm of the great ship of state—liberator, prophet, defender of liberty and democracy, and spokesperson for the American Dream.

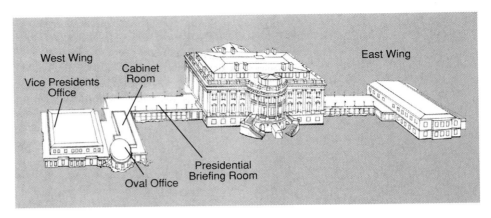

The White House is an executive office, a ceremonial mansion, and a home. Some presidents have viewed it almost as a jail, preferring to spend as much time as possible at other retreats outside Washington, but most Americans view the rather elegant White House as the center of political and social activity in the nation's capital. It is also something of a national shrine and draws millions of people from the United States and around the world to visit it each year.

Presidential head-of-state duties often seem trivial and unimportant. For example, throwing out the ceremonial first baseball of the season, promoting Easter seals, pressing buttons that start big power projects, and consoling the survivors of American victims of terrorist attacks do not require executive talents. Yet our president is continuously asked to champion our common heritage, to help unify the nation, and also to create an improved climate within which the diverse interests of the nation can work together.

In 1994, as one example, President Clinton held a historic and highly symbolic meeting with representatives of hundreds of leaders from Native American tribes to underscore their importance as well as their new stature in dealing with the federal government.

A PRESIDENTIAL DILEMMA   Some expectations for presidents are inconsistent with one another. On the one hand, the president is a party leader, spokesperson, and representative of a segment of the population loosely identified with a particular party. As such, the president not only directs the national party organization, but as chief legislator, also takes specific positions on issues for or against some groups. On the other hand, as ceremonial leader and chief of state, the president attempts to act for *all* the people. A chief executive must faithfully administer the laws, whether passed by Democratic or Republican majorities in Congress. Yet in making appointments and in applying the law, presidents often understandably think first of the interests of those who elected them.

The morale-building job of the president involves much more than just ceremonial, cheerleading, or quasi-chaplain duties. Presidential leadership, at its finest, radiates confidence and empowers people to give their best, to unleash the vast energies for good that exist in the nation. Our best leaders have been able to provide this special and often intangible element.

Presidents as Recruiters

Often a single appointment may achieve more than scores of presidential policy initiatives. President Eisenhower's nomination of Earl Warren to be chief justice of the United States may have been the single most significant decision of his administration in the area of domestic policy. Warren served for more than 15 years and presided over vast changes in civil rights and civil liberties. President Clinton's nominees Ruth Bader Ginsburg and Stephen Breyer are also likely to have long-term effects. In a similar way, selection of a secretary of state, top economic advisers, a secretary of the interior, or top White House aides can have an enormous impact on long-term national policy.

President Clinton has won both praise and criticism for his performance as a recruiter. He won praise for appointing cabinet members like Henry Cisneros and

Bruce Babbitt and White House aides like Bob Rubin and David Gergen. Yet he was faulted for his initial appointments at the defense, state, and commerce departments, and he was also criticized for his slowness in filling a large number of assistant secretary and judicial positions. Although his management style has been criticized, he has succeeded in making the cabinet and his administration "more like America"—more women, more minorities than have served under previous presidents. He is trying to carry out his campaign promises, but he is simultaneously faulted for going too fast and too slow, for trying to do too much and too little.

Presidents control more than 4,000 appointments, including hundreds of federal judgeships and top positions in the military and diplomatic service. (Note, however, that many appointments must be made with the approval of the Senate.) Effective presidents shrewdly use their appointment powers not only to reward campaign supporters and enhance ties to Congress but also to communicate priorities and policy directions. Because the top appointees are also a major link between the White House and the millions of people who serve in the federal and military career services, the chief executive needs the best possible managers and motivators in these crucial positions.

Besides identifying and recruiting them, the president must also try to keep the most talented of these officials in government as long as possible.[9] The turnover problem is acute. Many able people come to top positions—say in the cabinet or subcabinet—and stay for just two years or so. Less than one-third stay for more than three years. These top federal posts do not pay as much as similar positions in the private sector, and living in Washington is expensive.

Various financial disclosure and conflict-of-interest requirements, imposed on presidential appointees as a result of the Ethics in Government Act of 1978, discourage some potential appointees from accepting government jobs. They must fill out many forms, and they must testify at sometimes complicated, time-consuming, confusing, and embarrassing congressional hearings. Media scrutiny of citizen-leaders called to government service has also become more intensive. Recruiters for recent presidents report they often go to their second or third choice before they find someone willing to accept an appointment. "No other nation relies so heavily on noncareer personnel for the management of its government. . . . If talented Americans decline the opportunity for public service, if they endure it only for brief periods, or if they are ill-prepared for the challenges they will face in the public sector, the system will not deliver on its promise."[10]

A president must strengthen the hand of the ablest people working in the bureaucracy and promote them to higher positions at the senior reaches of the executive branch. In short, the personnel responsibilities of a president are great and require much time.

Presidents as Priority Setters

Presidents, by custom, have become responsible for proposing initiatives in the areas of foreign policy, economic growth and stability, and the quality of life in the United States. This was not always the case. But beginning with Woodrow Wilson, and especially since the New Deal, a president is expected to promote peace, prevent depressions, and propose reforms to ensure domestic progress. The long-term trend in national policy making is toward greater centralization.

New ideas to improve national policies are seized upon by a president searching for campaign issues or legislative program material, and they are refined by the executive office staff, by special presidential task forces, and by Congress.

NATIONAL SECURITY POLICY   The framers foresaw a special need for speed and unity in our dealings with other nations. As a result, presidents generally have more leeway in foreign policy and military affairs than they have in domestic matters.

The Job of President

Constitutional Responsibilities

   Act as commander in chief
   Negotiate treaties
   Receive foreign ambassadors
   Nominate top federal officials, including federal judges
   Veto bills
   Faithfully administer federal laws
   Pardon persons convicted of federal offenses
   Address Congress and the nation

Informal Roles

   Crisis manager
   World leader
   Legislative leader
   Party leader
   Morale builder
   Personnel recruiter
   Priority setter
   Budget setter
   Conflict resolver
   Coalition builder
   Bargainer and persuader

THE PRESIDENTIAL WAR POWER

The Constitution delegates to Congress the authority to declare the legal state of war (with the consent of the president), but in practice the commander in chief often starts the fighting or initiates actions that lead to war. This power has often been used by the president. From George Washington's time until Clinton's, the president, by ordering troops into battle, has often decided when Americans will fight and when they will not. When the cause has had political support, the president's use of this authority has been approved. In 1846, James K. Polk ordered American forces to advance into disputed territory; when Mexico resisted, Polk informed Congress that war existed by act of Mexico, and a formal declaration of war was soon forthcoming. Abraham Lincoln called up troops, spent money, set up a blockade, and fought the first few months of the Civil War without even calling Congress into session. William McKinley's dispatch of a battleship to Havana harbor, where it blew up, helped precipitate war with Spain in 1898. The United States was not formally at war with Germany until late 1941, but prior to the Japanese attack

Abraham Lincoln used his authority as president to call up troops during the first few months of the Civil War without even calling Congress into session.

The Constitution vests in a president command of the two major instruments of foreign policy—the diplomatic corps and the armed services. It also gives the chief executive responsibility for negotiating treaties and commitments with other nations, although Congress usually gets to vote on these matters.

Congress has also granted presidents discretion in initiating foreign policies, for diplomacy frequently requires quick action. A president can act swiftly; Congress usually cannot. The Supreme Court has upheld strong presidential authority in this area. In *United States v Curtiss Wright* in 1936, the Court referred to the "exclusive

President Franklin D. Roosevelt signed the declaration of war against Japan on December 8, 1941 as leaders of Congress looked on. It was the last time a president of the United States signed a formal declaration of war.

on Pearl Harbor, Franklin Roosevelt ordered the navy to guard convoys to Great Britain and to open fire on submarines threatening the convoys. Since World War II, presidents have sent forces without specific congressional authorization to Korea, Berlin, Vietnam, Lebanon, Grenada, Cuba, Libya, Panama, Kuwait, Somalia, and Rwanda—in short, around the world.

In 1973, Congress overrode Richard Nixon's presidential veto and enacted the War Powers Resolution, which declared that henceforth the president can commit the armed forces of the United States only: (1) after a declaration of war by Congress; (2) by specific statutory authorization; or (3) in a national emergency created by an attack on the United States or its armed forces. After committing the armed forces under the third circumstance, the president is required to report to Congress within 48 hours. Unless Congress has declared war, the troop commitment must be ended within 60 days. The president is allowed another 30 days if the chief executive claims the safety of the United States forces requires their continued use. A president is also obligated by this resolution to consult Congress "in every possible instance" before committing troops to battle. Moreover, at any time, by concurrent resolution *not subject to presidential veto*, Congress may direct the president to disengage such troops. A *concurrent resolution* is passed when both chambers of Congress wish to express the "sense" of their body on some question. Both houses must pass it in the same form. These resolutions are not sent to the president and do not have the force of law. Because of a 1983 court ruling, the question of whether Congress can remove the troops by concurrent resolution or legislative veto is now in doubt.

Not everyone was pleased by the passage of the War Powers Resolution of 1973. Nixon vetoed it because he said it encroached on presidential powers. Others said it gave away a constitutional power plainly belonging to Congress—namely, the war-making or war-declaring power—for up to 90 days. Still other observers, however much they may have thought this resolution was defective, believed nonetheless that war powers legislation was of symbolic and institutional significance because it reflected a new determination in Congress at the time. Presidents from Nixon to Clinton have not changed their behavior much, yet they have been put on notice that the commitment of American troops is subject to congressional approval. According to the resolution, presidents have to persuade Congress and the nation that their actions are justified by the gravest of national emergencies. Presidents in the future will, at least occasionally, hold back from conflict until they get what, in effect, might be a congressional declaration of war.

power of the president as the sole organ of the federal government in the field of international relations—a power which does not require as a basis for its exercise an act of Congress, but which, of course, like every other governmental power, must be exercised in subordination to the applicable provisions of the Constitution."[11] These are sweeping words.[12] Yet a determined Congress that knows what it wants to do and can agree on action does not lack power in foreign relations. It must authorize and appropriate the funds that back up our policies abroad. It is a forum for debate and criticism.

ECONOMIC POLICY   Ever since the New Deal, presidents have been expected to keep unemployment low, fight inflation, keep taxes down, and promote economic growth and prosperity. The Constitution did not place these duties on the executive, but presidents know that when the nation is not prosperous and jobs are scarce, they may suffer the fate of Herbert Hoover, who was denounced for his alleged inaction during the Great Depression. The growth and complexity of economic problems since the Depression of the 1930s have placed even more initiatives in the president's hands. The delicate balancing required to keep a modern economy operating means that presidents must regularly make key fiscal and budgetary policy decisions. Recent elections have turned largely on economics, or as Bill Clinton's staff aides put it, "It's the economy, stupid!"[13]

Although presidents sometimes get their economic advice elsewhere, their chief advisers on economic policy are the secretary of the treasury, the three members of the Council of Economic Advisers, and the director of the Office of Management and Budget. The chair of the Federal Reserve Board of Governors is often also a key White House adviser on the economy.

DOMESTIC POLICY   A leader is one who knows where the followers are. Lincoln did not invent the antislavery movement. Kennedy and Johnson did not begin the civil rights movement. Clinton was hardly the first leader to notice the unfairness of health policies. But they all, in their respective times, became embroiled in these controversies, for a president cannot long ignore what divides or inspires a nation.

The essence of the modern presidency lies in its potential to resolve societal conflicts. To be sure, much of the time a president will try to avoid conflict, seeking instead to defer, delegate, or otherwise delay controversial decisions. An effective president, however, will clarify the major issues of the day, define what is possible, and organize the governmental structure so that important goals can be realized. Clearly, a president has the ability to focus the legislative agenda on administration priorities, whatever their origins.

A president—with the cooperation of Congress—can set national goals and propose legislation. Close inspection indicates, however, that in most instances "new initiatives" in domestic policy are measures that have been under consideration in previous sessions of Congress. Just as the celebrated New Deal legislation had a fairly well-defined history extending back several years before its embrace by Franklin Roosevelt, many of Clinton's initiatives—health care and "the end of welfare as we know it"—are the fruits of long campaigns by congressional activists and interest groups.

Presidents as Legislative and Political Coalition Builders

The Constitution provides that the president "shall from time to time give to the Congress information on the State of the Union, and recommend to their Consideration such Measures as he shall judge necessary and expedient." From the start, strong presidents have exploited this power. George Washington and John Adams went in person to Congress to deliver information and recommendations. Thomas Jefferson and many presidents after him sent written messages, but Woodrow Wilson restored the practice of delivering a personal, and often dramatic, message. Franklin Roosevelt used radio talks and personal appearances to draw the attention of the whole nation to his program, as have most subsequent presidents. Bill Clinton visited Congress soon after he was elected and went back on several occasions to mingle with members of Congress or to give major reports to the nation. Clinton has also held numerous television forums to win public support for his legislative programs.

Less public, yet equally important, are the frequent written policy messages dispatched from the White House to the members of Congress on a range of public problems. These messages are important in defining the administration's position

and in giving assistance to friendly legislators. Moreover, these messages are often accompanied by detailed drafts of legislation that members of Congress may sponsor with little or no change. These White House proposals, the products of bill-drafting experts on the president's staff or in the executive departments and agencies, may be strengthened or diluted by Congress, but many of the original provisions survive.

An effective president is an effective politician—the most visible and potentially the strongest mobilizer of influence in the American system of power. "Politician" is a nasty word to many Americans; it often connotes a scheming, evasive, self-interested person. Little wonder many politicians claim they are "above politics." There is, however, a more constructive definition of "politician": one who helps manage conflict; one who knows how to negotiate, bargain, and help reconcile different views in order to make the difficult and desirable become reality. Presidents cannot escape political coalition-building tasks.[14] As candidates, they have made promises to the people. To get things done and to be reelected, they must work with many people and countless interest groups who have differing loyalties and responsibilities. Inevitably, presidents become embroiled in legislative politics, bureaucratic politics, and lobbying politics, and their approval ratings suffer as a consequence (see Figure 15-1).

An effective president is an effective politician. Here President Lyndon Johnson celebrates with Martin Luther King, Jr., the passage of civil rights legislation.

Presidents make good on more of their promises than the general public appreciates. Most presidents enjoy at least partial success on most of the initiatives they favored during their campaigns or soon after they came to the White House. Although they control most of what they decide to recommend to Congress, other institutions, especially Congress, control what presidents can achieve. Presidents may control what they initiate, at least within reason, but other political leaders often determine the fate, shape, and funding of these presidential initiatives.

Despite their formal powers, presidents can rarely command; they spend most of their time *persuading* people. Potentially, presidents have enormous persuasive

FIGURE 15-1 Presidential Approval Ratings

SOURCE: The Gallup Poll, 1994.

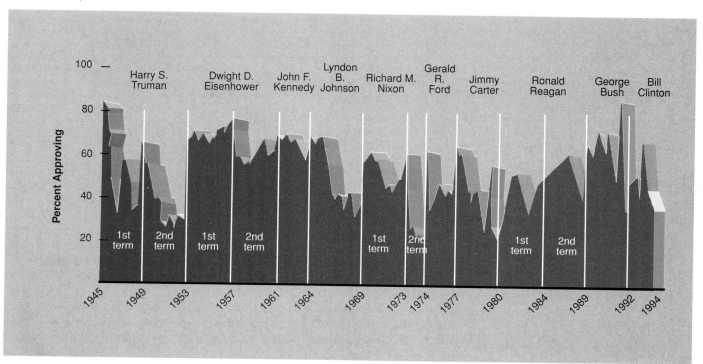

We The People

How Representative Are Our Presidents?

Sex: All male
Race: All white
Ethnic background:
All but five were of Anglo ancestry, which includes English, Irish, Scots, Welsh. Presidents whose ancestors were not from the British Isles were: Martin Van Buren (Dutch), Theodore Roosevelt (Dutch, Scots-Irish, and French Huguenot), Franklin D. Roosevelt (Dutch, French-Dutch), Herbert Hoover (Swiss-German), and Dwight D. Eisenhower (Swiss-German).

Age:
Oldest when elected: Ronald Reagan, 69 (first term), 73 (second term)
Youngest when elected: John F. Kennedy, 43
Average age at inauguration: 55

Religion:
Baptist: Warren G. Harding, Harry Truman, Jimmy Carter, Bill Clinton
Congregationalist: Calvin Coolidge
Disciples of Christ: James A. Garfield, Lyndon B. Johnson, Ronald Reagan
Dutch Reformed: Martin Van Buren, Theodore Roosevelt
Episcopalian: George Washington, James Madison, James Monroe, William Henry Harrison, John Tyler, Zachary Taylor, Franklin Pierce, Chester A. Arthur, Franklin D. Roosevelt, Gerald R. Ford, George Bush
Methodist: James K. Polk, Ulysses S. Grant, Rutherford B. Hayes, William McKinley
Presbyterian: Andrew Jackson, James Buchanan, Grover Cleveland, Benjamin Harrison, Woodrow Wilson, Dwight D. Eisenhower
Roman Catholic: John F. Kennedy
Society of Friends: Herbert Hoover, Richard M. Nixon
Unitarian: John Adams, John Quincy Adams, Millard Fillmore, William Howard Taft
No specific denomination: Thomas Jefferson, Abraham Lincoln, Andrew Johnson

SOURCE: Tim Taylor, *The Book of Presidents* (Arno Press, 1992), pp. 663, 667.

powers, but in a government of separated institutions that share powers, some congressional, bureaucratic, and military leaders are beyond the president's political reach. They have their own constituencies—a House committee, for example, or a powerful interest group. Presidents cannot simply give orders like a first sergeant.

From a president's vantage point, it is seldom helpful or wise to punish legislators from one's own party who, for whatever reason, decide not to support part of the president's legislative program. With power dispersed and decentralized in Congress, it is just too risky for a president to single out a few party "disloyalists" for retribution. White House congressional relations aides abide by the motto of "No permanent allies, no permanent enemies." Someone whose vote is lost today may cast the crucial vote on some other measure next week.

This is also true of a president's dealings with interest groups. Thus Clinton and the leaders of organized labor were on opposite sides of the North American Free Trade Agreement (NAFTA) vote in 1993, yet they were able to patch things up and work together on health reform a year later.

Presidents are sometimes in a better position to bargain and trade for votes with members of Congress than are the members themselves. In addition to receiving presidential help in their reelection campaigns, members of Congress also want federal projects for their districts, patronage for their supporters, help with their own pet legislative measures, and defense contracts and benefits for major industries in their districts or states. Thus, "among the currencies in the president's trading system are negative sanctions—threats to withhold favors from members who fail to go along."[15]

The White House has a number of resources with which to influence most members of Congress. Presidents can make stirring appeals for party unity—if their parties enjoy majorities in Congress. They can also try to educate and rally the public around their programs. Much of the time, however, a president must deal with a Congress that moves according to its own pace and that responds to a variety of constituent and organized interests above and beyond the requests and appeals coming from the White House.

Many students of the presidency think the power to persuade is the president's chief resource and that such power comes through bargaining. Bargaining, in turn, comes primarily through getting others to believe it is in their self-interest to cooperate. Hence the skill of a president in communicating and winning others over is the necessary energizing factor in moving the institutions of the national government to action. This school of thought also holds that a president cannot be above the battle or above politics. Rather, a president must enjoy the give and take of congressional-presidential relations as well as between the parties and between the White House and the press. Classic examples of effective presidential coalition building are Franklin Roosevelt's winning public support for his New Deal programs, Lyndon Johnson's getting his Great Society legislation passed, and Clinton's mobilizing public and congressional support to raise taxes, at least on the wealthy, and win approval for the North American Free Trade Agreement. President Clinton's success in getting his crime and health reform plans through Congress depended to a large degree on the coalitions he was able to forge.

The Presidential Veto

A president can veto a bill by returning it, together with specific objections, to the house in which it originated. Congress, by a two-thirds vote in each chamber, may **override** the president's veto. Another variation of the veto is known as the **pocket veto**. In the ordinary course of events, if the president does not sign or veto a bill within ten weekdays after receiving it, it becomes law without the chief executive's signature. But if Congress adjourns within the ten days, the president—by taking no action—can kill the bill.

The veto's strength lies in the difficulty Congress has in getting a two-thirds majority of both houses. From 1789 through 1994, presidents have exercised their regular veto power 1,436 times; only 103 of these vetoes have been overridden by Congress. However, when scholars separate out the vetoes of private bills (bills dealing with individual claims against the government, or land titles, or matters such as immigration and naturalization) from public bills, they find that about 19 percent of the public bill vetoes have been overridden by Congress. Still, writes Robert Spitzer, "a presidential success rate of more than 80 percent for important legislation poses a daunting challenge to anyone seeking to overturn a veto."[16]

In short, there is little Congress can do when confronted with a veto. It must either get enough votes to override the veto or modify the legislation and try again (see Table 15-3). Presidents are able to make the vast majority of their regular vetoes stick. Although Congress overrode 23 percent of Reagan's vetoes, it was only able to override one of George Bush's 46 vetoes.

Congress often manipulates legislation to reduce the chance of a presidential veto. It attaches irrelevant but controversial provisions, called **riders**, to legislation the president considers vital. Presidents must either accept or reject the whole bill, for they do not have the power to delete individual items, a power known as the **item veto**. In one appropriations bill, for example, lawmakers may combine badly needed funds for the armed forces with costly **pork-barrel** items. "Pork-barrel" refers to government benefits or programs that help the economy of a member's district—as in "bringing home the bacon."

Presidents can also use the veto power in a positive way. They can announce that bills under consideration by Congress will be turned back unless certain changes are made. They can use the threat of a veto against a bill Congress wants badly in exchange for other bills that they want. A presidential veto can also protect a national minority from hasty, unfair legislation passed in the heat of the moment. But the veto is essentially a negative weapon of limited use to a president like Clinton, who is pressing for action.

The presidential veto power has stirred little controversy. Carter vetoed only 31 bills, Nixon vetoed 43, Ford 66, Reagan 78, and Bush 46. Clinton did not veto any measures in his first two years. Still, the occasional use of the pocket veto has stirred some criticism. Some members of Congress said the framers envisioned a more limited use of the veto.

The Item Veto Debate

Several recent presidents have called for a constitutional amendment permitting presidents to have item veto power—the right to veto particular subsections or items within major appropriations bills passed by Congress. Presidents can, of course, veto an entire bill.

The item veto would work like this: Following a review of a major appropriations bill sent from Congress for presidential signature, the president might approve perhaps 94 percent of the spending but object to the remaining 6 percent as wasteful or undesirable. Or the president might just disagree with this type of spending. In any event, the White House would veto only those objectionable items. Congress would have the right, according to most of the proposed item veto amendments, to override the president's veto of these items by the same two-thirds vote required to override a general presidential veto.

One of the major reasons advanced in support of the item veto is that presidents, although responsible for the budget and accountable for budget deficits, do not have adequate authority to fight deficit spending. If they had the item veto, supporters say, they could delete waste and pork-barrel spending primarily intended to help members of Congress win reelection. Pork-barrel items are often added to necessary appropriations bills at the last minute. Items vetoed by presidents

TABLE 15-3

Presidential Vetoes, 1933–1994

President	Vetoes
Franklin D. Roosevelt	635
Harry S. Truman	250
Dwight D. Eisenhower	181
John F. Kennedy	21
Lyndon B. Johnson	30
Richard M. Nixon	43
Gerald R. Ford	66
Jimmy Carter	31
Ronald Reagan	78
George Bush	46
Bill Clinton	0

SOURCE: *Congressional Quarterly* and Office of Executive Clerk, The White House.

**Why Presidential Approval
(in Polls) Usually Declines
the Longer Presidents
Are in Office**

- Expectations that are raised in campaigns are dashed as time forecloses resources and options.

- Things that go wrong get blamed, rightly or wrongly, on presidents, whether or not presidents have the power to deal with these matters.

- Rising disapproval of incumbent presidents is often influenced by inflation and unemployment.

- Major negative events, such as the Vietnam War, Watergate scandal, Iranian hostage crisis, or Los Angeles riots, influence how people evaluate presidents.

- Press and media criticism accumulates over time and sharpens the public's dissatisfaction with a president. Perhaps, too, time in office simply wears out our welcome for a president.

Political scientists are not exactly sure of the precise relationships among these factors; different studies produce different findings. These factors are, however, plainly some of the more important ones, and some of them are doubtless interrelated.

would not likely win two-thirds support in both chambers of Congress. Hence, waste would be reduced.

Presidents also say they need the item veto because Congress often passes crucial appropriations measures near the end of congressional sessions. To veto an entire bill then might force the government to shut down. Clever legislators often add their own pet measures to legislation the White House has struggled to win, thus making it unlikely that a president would dare veto the entire package.

Proponents note that 43 state governors have the item veto power, which has worked reasonably well in most states. They also point out that the American people in nearly every survey favor giving this additional authority to presidents.

But perhaps the most compelling reason to support the item veto is the growing concern about the soaring federal debt and annual deficits. Congress has not been able to curb enough spending, raise enough revenues, or bring about the proper balance to put our economic house in order. If Congress has acted irresponsibly, why not give the president this additional clout?

Congress, not surprisingly, remains unconvinced. Most members of Congress see the item veto as an attempt by presidents to diminish the powers of Congress and add further powers to the presidency. Many opponents of the item veto say it would end even the pretense of Congress acting as an equal branch of government. In effect, they say, giving this power to the White House would allow presidents and their budget aides to "edit" the whole budget and rewrite appropriations legislation on a line-by-line basis.

Giving presidents the item veto could lead to undesirable pressure tactics and political retribution. Imagine a president who needs just a few more votes for a top-priority trade or crime bill, and just a few holdouts remain. The White House could then examine pending projects in the holdout legislators' districts and "suggest" that these members vote for the president's proposal. It does not take much imagination, legislators say, to see how much more persuasive a president would be if such calls were buttressed with a veto over individual projects and activities within their home states and districts.

Further, critics of the item veto say a president already has a number of powers to help balance the budget and fight deficits. Since it is the president who prepares the budget, a president who really wants a balanced budget should present one in the first place. Presidents also have the right, and ought to exercise it more regularly, to veto certain appropriations bills entirely. They also have the various options of sending measures back to Congress for delay, or with suggestions for specific cuts based on the grounds of efficiency. Finally, they have the splendid power of the "bully pulpit," and this, too, can be used to keep Congress honest when it comes to wasteful spending.

Opponents also object to the item veto because they view it as a convenient escape from the difficult political choices elected officials must make. The problems the item veto supposedly addresses are more political and substantive than they are structural or constitutional. Congress and presidents should have the will to curb unneeded spending and to raise taxes and balance the budget. And they should be held accountable when they fail in these responsibilities. The item veto might make Congress even less responsible by encouraging it to pass the buck to the White House more often. At the same time, many people believe the item veto would provide more power than an effective president needs—and more power than an "imperial" or a misguided president should have.

Presidents and Public Opinion

The press conference is an example of how the president can employ the machinery of communication in a systematic manner. Years ago press conferences were rather casual affairs. Franklin Roosevelt ran his get-togethers informally and was a master at withholding information as well as giving it. Under Truman the conference became an institutionalized part of the presidential communications apparatus. Kennedy authorized regular live telecasts of press conferences and used them frequently for direct communication with the people. Reagan effectively used five-minute Saturday afternoon radio chats to communicate his views, ask for support, and win Sunday morning media coverage. Clinton occasionally uses the press conference, which has aided him in his efforts to deal with Congress and the media, and he too speaks directly to the public on his Saturday morning radio broadcasts.

Presidents commission private polls to gauge public opinion; they want to be able to distinguish the public's whims, estimate the strength and direction of its thinking, and respond to its impatience. Presidents must know not only *what* to do but *when* to do it. Public opinion can be unstable and unpredictable. Lyndon Johnson recognized that his wide popular support of the mid-1960s had melted away by 1968, when he decided not to run again. Nixon's dramatic drop of nearly 45 percentage points in public opinion polls, a result of the Watergate scandal, helped force his resignation. Bush won unusual public approval during and after the successful military efforts in the Persian Gulf in early 1991, but his popular approval sharply diminished during the economic downturn that followed. Most presidents lose support the longer they are in office. Dissatisfaction sets in; interest groups grow impatient; unkept promises must be accounted for; and the president gets blamed for many of the things that go wrong.[17]

Clinton has had especially testy relations with the press. Things became so bad in his first year that he brought in Republican David Gergen to serve as his senior adviser for policy and media matters. Gergen had worked previously for Nixon, Ford, and Reagan. Clinton's relationship with the media improved for a while, but later his problems with the Whitewater affair and the Paula Jones story complicated his dealings with the press. Media references to ongoing feuds in the White House also hurt Clinton's credibility.[18]

Clinton used every available means to get his message out to the American public. He was the first president to appear on MTV, and he turned up on town meetings and talk shows with great regularity. Both he and Hillary Clinton have had to deal with the press in an era of "in your face journalism," where many of the old rules and courtesies about the separation of public and private life have disappeared, especially those having to do with marital and extramarital relations. We have to remember, however, that Jefferson, Lincoln, and Franklin Roosevelt were all vilified by the press and rarely shown much reverence in their lifetimes. Presidents are always fair game for media critics.

PARTY LEADERSHIP Another potential source of influence for the president is the political party. Most presidents since Jefferson have been party leaders, and generally the more effective the presidents, the more use they have made of party support. Wilson, the two Roosevelts, and Reagan fortified their executive and legislative influence by mobilizing support within their party. Yet presidents are led by their party as much as they lead it; no president has ever wholly dominated his party.[19]

Presidents as Administrators

The Constitution charges the president to "take Care that the Laws be faithfully executed." Because their other responsibilities demand most of their attention, however, presidents must delegate much of their administrative authority. They are, then, dependent on their subordinates. Theoretically, at least, orders flow *down* an administrative *line*: from president, to cabinet members, to bureau chiefs, to smaller offices. Like all top executives, a president is assisted by a *staff*, who advise the chief executive. This line and staff organization is typical of every large administrative entity, whether it be the army, General Motors, or the United Nations.

Presidents have come to rely heavily on their personal staffs. Nowhere else—not in Congress, not in the cabinet, not in the party—can presidents find the loyalty and single-mindedness that often develop among their closest White House aides. They come to view many cabinet heads as merely staunch advocates of their departments and the constituencies they serve. Presidents assume that their aides will provide them with neutral and objective advice, but there are substantial costs

President Clinton counted on the communication skill of his election campaign director, George Stephanopoulus, to deal with the Washington press corps, but Stephanopoulus did not establish good rapport with the savvy reporters, and Clinton called on Washington insider David Gergen. Gergen, a Republican, helped out for a year or so, yet Clinton continued to have a rough time with the press.

"Well, if you were Gergen, what would *you* tell McLarty to tell Clinton to tell Christopher to do?."

Drawing by Handes) man. © 1993 The New Yorker Magazine, Inc.

to listening only to one's closest aides. The White House can usually be thought of as a palace court in which strong presidents create an environment that weeds out any assistant who persists in presenting irritating or opposing views.

The number of employees in the presidential entourage has grown steadily since the early 1900s, when only a few dozen people served a president at a cost of less than a few hundred thousand dollars annually. Today a White House staff of about 450 operates at the cost of several million dollars a year. This staff makes up just one part of the Executive Office of the President.

THE INSTITUTIONALIZED EXECUTIVE OFFICE   Approved by Congress in 1939, the Executive Office of the President was the recommendation of Franklin Roosevelt's Committee on Administrative Management. Its intention was to provide presidents the help they obviously needed to carry out the growing responsibilities imposed by the Great Depression and by the enlarged role of government. The Executive Office of the President consists of the Office of Management and Budget, the Council of Economic Advisers, and several other staff units (see Figure 15-2).

The staff of the White House office can be categorized by functions: (1) domestic policy; (2) economic policy; (3) national security or foreign policy; (4) administration and personnel matters (as well as personal paperwork and scheduling for the president); (5) congressional relations; and (6) public relations.

Presidential aides sometimes insist they are simply the eyes and ears of the president, that they make few important decisions, and that they never insert themselves between the chief executive and the heads of departments. But the burgeoning White House staff and the inevitable emergence of a few strong White House advisers have made this traditional picture nearly obsolete. Some White House aides, impatient with bureaucratic and congressional bottlenecks or even political sabotage, come to view the presidency as if it alone were the whole government. Oliver North surely felt that way under President Reagan. Separation of powers means little to them, and they lose sight of their place within the larger constitutional system.

The **Office of Management and Budget (OMB)** continues to be the central presidential staff agency. Its director advises the president in detail about the hundreds of government agencies—how much money they should be allotted in the budget and what kind of job they are doing. OMB seeks to improve the planning, management, and statistical work of the agencies. It makes a special effort to see that each agency conforms to presidential policies in its dealings with Congress; each agency has to clear its policy recommendations to Congress through OMB first.

FIGURE 15-2   Executive Office of the President

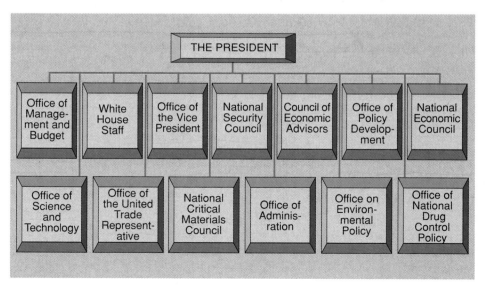

A budget is more than just a financial plan, because it reflects power struggles and indicates national priorities (and wishful thinking).[20] To the president, the budget is a means of control over administrators who may be trying to join ranks with politicians or interest groups to thwart presidential priorities. Through the long budget preparation process, presidents use OMB as a way of conserving and centralizing their own influence.

THE CABINET   It is hard to find a more unusual institution than the president's cabinet. The cabinet is not specifically mentioned by name in the Constitution (but see the Twenty-fifth Amendment). Yet since George Washington's administration, every president has had one. Washington's consisted of his secretaries of state, treasury, and war, plus his attorney general.

Today the selection of cabinet members is the first major job for the president-elect. The cabinet consists of the president, the vice-president, the officers who head the 14 executive departments, and a few others a president considers cabinet-level officials. The cabinet has always been a loosely designated body, and it is not always clear who belongs in it. In recent years, certain executive branch administrators and White House counselors have been accorded cabinet rank.

Presidents need strong and creative aides to sift through the competing advice that comes to the White House, and a staff to help them monitor the implementation of policies in the sprawling federal executive departments. But presidents also need a strong cabinet and counselors in Congress and elsewhere to provide alternative views to help ensure that they do not become isolated by an overly protective entourage.

Cabinet government as practiced in parliamentary systems—where the voice and the vote of the cabinet members count for a lot—simply does not exist in the United States. In fact, an American president is not required by the Constitution to form a cabinet or to hold regular meetings. Kennedy, Johnson, and Nixon all preferred small conferences with individuals specifically involved in a problem. Kennedy saw no reason to discuss defense department matters with his secretaries of agriculture and labor, and he thought cabinet meetings wasted valuable time for too many already busy people. Both Carter and Reagan tried to revive the cabinet, and both met often with their cabinets during their first two years. But the longer they remained in office, the less frequently they met with their cabinets as a whole. Some of Clinton's cabinet complain of too little contact with the president and of too many calls from young White House aides. This is an old problem.

The Cabinet

Vice-President

Secretary of State

Secretary of Treasury

Secretary of Defense

Attorney General

Secretary of Interior

Secretary of Agriculture

Secretary of Commerce

Secretary of Labor

Secretary of Health and Human Services

Secretary of Housing and Urban Development

Secretary of Transportation

Secretary of Energy

Secretary of Education

Secretary of Veterans Affairs

Chief of Staff at the White House

Director of the Office of Management and Budget

Counselor to the President

U.S. Trade Representative

President Clinton and his cabinet.

Line of Succession
to the Presidency

The Constitution leaves succession after the vice-president up to Congress. Thus this is the line of succession according to law passed by Congress. However, the constitutional qualifications still apply. For example, if the secretary of state was born in a foreign country of parents who were not U.S. citizens, he or she would be bypassed in this line.

1. Vice-President
2. Speaker of the House of Representatives
3. Senate President Pro Tempore
4. Secretary of State
5. Secretary of the Treasury
6. Secretary of Defense
7. Attorney General
8. Secretary of the Interior
9. Secretary of Agriculture
10. Secretary of Commerce
11. Secretary of Labor
12. Secretary of Health and Human Services
13. Secretary of Housing and Urban Development
14. Secretary of Transportation
15. Secretary of Energy
16. Secretary of Education
17. Secretary of Veterans Affairs

Presidential advisers and the heads of various White House-based cabinet-level councils or review units, such as the National Security Council and the Office of Management and Budget, have gained equal or even superior status to many of the department and cabinet secretaries. This shift has occurred in part because these people are physically located in or next door to the White House. Further, presidents believe some department heads often adopt narrow "advocate" views: the agriculture cabinet officer as a strident advocate for the farmers; the Housing and Urban Development cabinet officer as an ambassador for the housing industry and, to some extent, also for big city mayors; and so on through much of the cabinet, especially those preoccupied with domestic policy matters. As good relations between presidents and cabinet members weaken, presidents, in frustration, turn more often to trusted senior White House staff aides to settle conflicts and coordinate policy. Tension almost always builds between senior White House aides and their counterparts in the cabinet. Personal staff members remain close to the president's ear and are more influential as a result.

Recent presidents have formed various committees of certain cabinet or subcabinet members, such as Clinton's National Economic Council, in an attempt to integrate key departmental and White House advisers around major policy matters. Such committees or councils are patterned after the **National Security Council**, established in 1947 to confer with the president on matters relating to national security. These initiatives are aimed at decentralizing policy discussions while giving cabinet members a genuine feeling that they are being consulted and involved in important policy developments.

THE VICE-PRESIDENT

Although the vice-presidency is now a part of the presidential establishment, it has not been so for long. Most vice-presidents served mainly as president of the Senate. Up to the 1950s, the vice-president was at best a "fifth wheel" and at worst a political rival who sometimes connived against the president. The office was often dismissed as a joke. One reason for the vice-president's posture as an outsider was that presidential nominees prior to Clinton usually chose running mates who were geographically, ideologically, demographically, and in other ways likely to "balance the ticket." Clinton ignored the desire to balance the ticket and picked another white, male, progressive southerner.

As the Clinton-Gore example suggests, recent presidential candidates have selected more like-minded persons as their running mates and have also made more use of them. Today the vice-presidency brings both advantages and liabilities to a person who aspires to the presidency. The job surely provides exposure to the issues and challenges of the office, but it is hard to appear "presidential" while at the same time avoiding the appearance of being disloyal to or upstaging the president.[21]

Ideally, a vice-president serves several roles in addition to the ceremonial function of acting as president of the Senate. A vice-president gets to cast the tie-breaking vote if the Senate has a tie vote, but this situation usually occurs less than once a year. The vice-president is also a member of the National Security Council. Vice-president Al Gore headed a national review of the federal bureaucracy for Clinton, a temporary yet highly visible presidential assignment. In addition, Gore effectively debated Ross Perot in a widely viewed TV debate on the North American Free Trade Agreement. Gore also spearheaded various "information superhighway" initiatives for Clinton.

The real test of the role of vice-president is whether he or she is fully integrated into the decision-making process in the White House. All vice-presidents are "back-up equipment" in case something happens to the president. They can head up any number of councils, visit any number of countries, and still not be much involved in the day-to-day operations of the presidency. President Carter included Walter Mondale in the daily processes of decision making in the White House; President Reagan sometimes included George Bush in a similar way; President Clinton has clearly used Al Gore as an important adviser and confidant on domestic as well as foreign policy matters.[22]

The 1992 vice-presidential debate on network television turned into a slugfest between Republican Dan Quayle and Democrat Al Gore, with Independent Ross Perot's running mate, Admiral James Stockdale, asking, "Why am I here?"

Tensions sometimes develop between presidential aides and vice-presidents and their staffs. Part of the problem arises because most presidents seldom wish to give up any ceremonial duties for which they themselves can win credit. Neither do cabinet members like to share their responsibilities with vice-presidents, making it hard for vice-presidents to gain administrative experience. Presidents often delegate unpleasant political chores to their vice-presidents. However, the importance of the vice-presidency is underscored by the fact that nine presidents have not been able to finish their terms. Four presidents have been assassinated, four have died naturally, and one has resigned. One-third of our presidents were once vice-presidents, including Truman, Lyndon Johnson, Nixon, Ford, and Bush.

The vice-presidency has been significantly affected by two post-World War II constitutional amendments. The Twenty-second Amendment, ratified in 1951, imposes a two-term limit on presidents; consequently vice-presidents have a better chance of moving up to the Oval Office. The Twenty-fifth Amendment, ratified in 1967, confirms the prior practice of making the vice-president not an acting president, but president, in the event of the death of a president. Also of significance, this amendment provides a procedure to determine whether an incumbent president is unable to discharge the powers and duties of the office and establishes procedures to fill a vacancy in the vice-presidency. For a few hours in 1985, George Bush became the first "acting president" when the first of these provisions was invoked while President Reagan underwent a minor cancer operation. The amendment also provides that in the event of a vacancy in the office of vice-president, the president nominates a vice-president, who takes office upon confirmation by a majority vote of both houses of Congress. This procedure generally ensures the appointment of a vice-president in whom the president has confidence. Thus vice-presidents who have to take over the presidency can be expected to reflect most of their predecessor's policies.

The tension between a president and a vice-president is natural. After all, except for the vice-president, everybody who works closely with a president can be fired. It is almost certain that vice-presidents will continue to have an undefined ad hoc set of assignments, subject more to the good will and mood of the president than to any fixed description.[23]

THE FIRST LADY

A president cannot by law appoint a spouse to a federal job. But Bill Clinton enlarged the role of his wife, making her post at least as important as most cabinet positions. Hillary Rodham Clinton, a talented and successful attorney, became the most influential first lady in American history. She headed up the Clinton administration's planning

Should presidents be limited to two terms in office?

Before he left office, former President Ronald Reagan called for the repeal of the Twenty-second Amendment to the Constitution, the one that limits a president to two terms. Why do you think he opposed the amendment? What additional reasons could be put forth to persuade people to repeal this relatively new (1951) provision in the Constitution? What are the best reasons for retaining the Twenty-second?

You Decide!

Factors that Constrain Presidents

The Constitution
Federalism
Separation of powers
Congress
Federal courts
Investigative media
Public opinion
Opposing party
Opposing factions in president's party
Interest groups
Editorial opinion (and cartoonists)
Bureaucratic resistance
Opposing world powers and the international economy
World public opinion and U.N. policies
World leaders
Presidential advisers
Regularly scheduled elections
Unrealistic expectations
Party platforms
Independent counsels
The shape of the economy and the imperatives of economic development
Fear of losing next election for self or party

efforts for national health care reform. She also took an active role in the nomination of federal judges and key administrative posts. Many people, men and women, praised Hillary Clinton's assignments as well as her brilliance and political savvy. She was hailed as a first lady for our time and as a bold and appropriate symbol for our age.[24]

But a few critics said the idea of a "first ladyship" was an affront to American democracy. Critics contend that her influence over major decisions came without election or official appointment. Her ambiguous role evades antinepotism laws and avoids the responsibility that should go with authority. "It makes no difference if the spouse is knowledgeable and uses power skillfully, as Mrs. Clinton usually does," wrote A. M. Rosenthal of *The New York Times*. "However used, in a democracy, political power must not be bestowed with marriage vows."[25]

Political spouses invariably influence their husbands or wives; Mrs. Clinton's influence appeared to be larger and more regular. Earlier presidential spouses, including Dolley Madison, Edith Wilson, and Eleanor Roosevelt, counseled and lobbied their presidential husbands, yet Hillary Clinton set new precedents and has also paid the price of such pioneering.

By 1994, both because of her influence and because of her role in the Whitewater land investment, bumper stickers appeared in some parts of the country that read in large letters: "IMPEACH CLINTON" and added in small print, "and her husband too."

CONSTRAINTS ON THE PRESIDENT

Presidential power may be greater today than ever before. It is misleading, however, to infer from a president's capacity to begin a nuclear war that the chief executive has similar power to bring about solutions in policy-making areas. Seldom are presidents free agents in bringing about basic social change. As priority setter, politician, and executive, a president shares power with members of Congress, bureaucrats, and interest-group elites. The ability to set priorities is not the same as the ability to enforce laws and administer them properly. Presidents who want to be effective in implementing policy changes must know they face a number of constraints. Besides the formal system of checks and balances, effective presidents must learn to deal with media criticism, cultural challenges, and a growing number of international pressures. Presidents are also enormously shaped by their times, by the ideological leanings of the people, and by the successes and failures of their immediate predecessors.[26]

Media Criticism

Ronald Reagan once walked away from one of his news conferences and, turning to an aide, blasted the reporters, not realizing a microphone was picking up his every word. John F. Kennedy once canceled more than 50 White House subscriptions to the *New York Herald Tribune* because he was furious about the way the paper treated his decisions. Lyndon Johnson regularly planted "softball questions" (questions he could easily answer) among friendly reporters at presidential press conferences. Bill Clinton complains about "gotcha journalism," and has been especially upset at the media's rough treatment of his wife. All recent presidents have complained that the modern media misrepresent them and disproportionately report bad news.

Enjoying enormous First Amendment rights in this country, reporters usually go about their business of analyzing and criticizing presidents with gusto. Scores of media representatives are regularly stationed at the White House, and they travel everywhere the president goes, reporting on every move. Reporters from all the major networks and newspapers are assigned to be with the president 24 hours a day; they call this "the death watch." Presidential statements—even on trivial matters—are sent back to the newsrooms and immediately printed or aired. Major statements and policy initiatives are reported and subjected to analysis. The media, at the White House and elsewhere, also force issues to the forefront of national attention that might never have been discussed publicly in earlier times and that seldom are discussed in other countries. Presidents, of course, want all their initiatives printed and praised as much as possible.

But media people believe they should provide a context in which presidential statements can be understood; hence, they not only tell people what a president said but often try to explain what the statement means. This interpretation is offered primarily by columnists, editorial writers, and commentators, who are expected to agree with or to criticize a president and to explain their reasons for doing so. Further, those who manage newspapers and radio and television stations in the country want to balance their stories about what presidents say—especially in presidential speeches—with an equal amount of time for the spokespersons of the opposition party or persons who hold different points of view.

In recent years this kind of *adversarial* media coverage has often left the impression that a president's influence is more divisive than unifying. Except when a president attends a baseball game or welcomes some noted sports or arts hero to the White House, media coverage involves interpretation. No reporter has ever won a Pulitzer or any other media prize for writing a story favorable to the administration. The journalism profession invariably honors those who uncover wrongdoing.

What have presidents done about this? Typically they have been patient and respected the critical dialogue so essential in a democracy. However, presidents and their aides have also engaged in extensive public relations efforts aimed at winning admiration and support for the president and White House policies.[27] Out-of-town editors are invited in for special briefings, and extra effort is made to get the president out of Washington for meetings with local and regional media representatives, who are generally viewed as less critical than Washington-based media. White House media experts devise ways to get the president's point of view out to the public, to get the president on prime-time television, or to arrange for flattering action photos.

The modern media are indeed a formidable adversary of the modern presidency. But the presidency is not being brutally wounded, and its capacity for leadership is not being sapped because of aggressive coverage by the media. Defenders of the press like to quote Thomas Jefferson, who, although angered by the press when he was president, said: "Were it left to me to decide whether we should have a government without newspapers or newspapers without a government, I should not hesitate to prefer the latter."

Defenders of the media say presidents have too often lied or manipulated the public's understanding of the issues. The media, they contend, are obligated to cover opposition views, especially when they think a president is wrong. Even though journalists may have political sympathies, they prize their independence and seldom play the role of cheerleader. "Their fault may be the opposite: seeing politicians and their handlers up close, they have no faith in any of them and are carriers, as well as recorders, of the prevailing disenchantment."[28]

No matter who is in the White House, presidents and the media will often be in conflict. This ongoing struggle is inherent in a constitutional democracy. The Watergate scandal fortified the media through its important role in bringing the scandal to public attention. Further, because the media—especially television—are viewed as more trustworthy and believable than most other national institutions, most Americans, most of the time, believe what they hear and see on television. But the resources of the White House and the amount of free media coverage given presidents—especially communicators like Franklin Roosevelt, John Kennedy, and Ronald Reagan—provide an effective counterpoint to the media.

Cultural Challenges

Because all presidents face cultural dilemmas (for example, attitudes and values toward gay rights or abortion), they need to understand the cultural contexts and cultural values of those they would lead. Political scientists Richard Ellis and Aaron

Thinking it Through

Reagan said the people should be able to reelect a president as many times as they want, just as they now reelect House and Senate members. He also hinted that the Twenty-second Amendment might weaken a president late in his second term by making him a lame duck, less powerful because everyone knows he will not be around in a year or so. Advocates of repeal also say we may sometimes need to keep a veteran president in office during a crisis period, much as we retained Franklin Roosevelt in 1940. Others say eight years may not be enough time to resolve certain major problems.

The Twenty-second Amendment is not only a limit on the incumbent but also on the electorate, the first since the ratification of the Constitution to restrict the power of the electorate rather than expand it. It is based, advocates of repeal suggest, on the assumption that the voters cannot be trusted.

Those who favor keeping the Twenty-second Amendment cite these reasons: First, the presidency is so powerful today that we need the Twenty-second Amendment as an additional check and balance against abuse of this power. Second, the amendment encourages both parties to seek out quality candidates to succeed to office and discourages dependence on a single ruler. Third, few leaders are likely to have the health, the intellectual energy, and the new ideas needed to perform the demanding responsibilities of the presidency beyond eight years in office. Finally, Americans have always believed in citizen-leaders rather than career politicians, and this amendment encourages this ideal.

Can a president be sued?

In May of 1994, Paula Jones brought sexual harassment charges against President Bill Clinton and a former Arkansas state trooper for a 1991 incident she alleges occured in an Arkansas hotel room when Clinton was governor of Arkansas and she was a state employee.

Clinton denied the charges and hired a lawyer, who asked a federal judge in Arkansas to postpone the suit until the end of Clinton's presidency. He also asked the court to rule on whether presidents are immune from having to answer civil suits during their tenure.

Do you think presidents should be held accountable for acts that occurred prior to their term in office while they are serving the nation? Does their high office make them different from any other citizens?

You Decide!

Wildavsky contend presidents can be evaluated in terms of dilemmas confronted, evaded, created, or overcome. The "great" presidents, like Washington, Jefferson, Jackson, and Lincoln, they argue, are those who provided solutions to the cultural and societal dilemmas of their day. Borrowing from anthropologists, they suggest three competing political cultures: *hierarchical, individualist,* and *egalitarian.* "The type of leadership preferred and feared, and the kinds of support given to and demands made upon leaders, we hypothesize, vary by political culture."[29]

In a hierarchical culture, characterized by respect for authority and acceptance of formal hierarchical relations (for example, the marines or a college basketball team), leadership is relatively easy to exercise. On the other hand, those who try to provide leadership in a society that yearns for equality are invariably frustrated, for egalitarians (lovers of equality) are dedicated to diminishing differences among people. "Would-be egalitarian leaders are thus in trouble before they start," for authority and leadership inherently create inequalities.[30]

In the individualist culture, Ellis and Wildavsky see governance organized to maximize individual freedom and thus minimize the need for governmental authority. Citizens in such a culture perform a delicate balancing act between permitting leaders to arise when they are needed and getting rid of them whenever possible.

These authors note that the United States is a nation rightly characterized by its strong individualism, weak hierarchies, and only occasional bursts of egalitarianism. Thus, "with egalitarians rejecting authority, individualists desiring to escape it, and hierarchical forces too weak to impose it, presidents seeking to rely on formal authority alone are in a precarious position."[31]

One of the contributions of George Washington's leadership was his strong commitment to central government but wise appreciation for the limits of authority in the United States. Abraham Lincoln is credited with skillfully exercising executive leadership in a notably antileadership system, but doing so in a way that showed a government could provide emergency leadership in times of total war without allowing this power to lead inexorably to permanent dictatorship in peacetime.[32] Lincoln delicately balanced the need for leadership with the need for assurances that the circumstances were extraordinary.

At their best, presidential leaders are individuals who perceive what is needed and understand how to mobilize people and resources to accomplish mutual goals. Effective presidents build on strengths—their own as well as those of their followers and colleagues—and on the opportunities afforded by their culture and situation.

International Pressures

Many writers call attention to the growing number of international pressures facing any president. Historian Paul Kennedy bluntly observed that the task facing American leaders over the next few decades must be to recognize that broad trends are under way on a global scale and that "there is a need to 'manage' affairs so that *relative* erosion of the United States' position takes place slowly and smoothly."[33] Our presidents and leaders, he and others are saying, have to learn to cooperate with and persuade allies, and they must have the ability to win the support of leaders elsewhere as well.

Presidents today are forced to deal with a much stronger European Community and with the increasingly powerful economic force of Japan and other Pacific Rim nations. Multilateral action usually makes far more sense than unilateral action. Presidents have to secure not only the support of Congress and the American people; they must also win the cooperation of foreign nations. It is increasingly clear, as Bill Clinton has surely learned, that the international system, especially the international economy, is stronger than any president or prime minister.[34]

Most other nations long ago learned that to succeed in an international system requires understanding other nations as well as one's own. Current and future presidents will have to be even better prepared than in the past to take global needs, aspirations, and politics into account.

PRESIDENTIAL-CONGRESSIONAL RELATIONS

However much the public may want Congress to be a partner with the president and a major check on presidential power, public support for Congress is uneven and usually a good bit lower than it is for the president. Power is dispersed in Congress. Its deliberations and quarrels are public. The public often views Congress as "the bickering branch," especially if a persuasive activist is in the White House.

The American people believe, however, that their own members of Congress pay more attention to their views than does the president. Congress, as a forum, does represent and register the diversity of the United States. That very virtue, however, makes it difficult for Congress to provide leadership and to challenge and bargain effectively with presidents. Not surprisingly, a wary public, dissatisfied with programs that do not work and policies that do not measure up to the urgencies of the moment, will look elsewhere, often to the president or to an aspiring presidential candidate.

It is no coincidence that one's views about congressional versus presidential powers are related to which party controls these respective branches. From 1981 to 1993, when Republicans controlled the White House, Republicans, not surprisingly, liked the idea of a strong presidency and often criticized Congress for interfering in matters that should be left to the discretion of the White House. Conversely, Democrats found a strong Congress more to their liking when Richard Nixon, Gerald Ford, Ronald Reagan, or George Bush was president than when their party was in office at 1600 Pennsylvania Avenue.

Many people worry about "imperial presidents" and about the possible alienation of the people from their leaders, especially as complex issues continue to centralize responsibilities in the hands of the national government and the executive. Those who are concerned about these matters will not content themselves—nor should they—with the existing safeguards against misuse of presidential powers. It is not easy, however, to contrive devices that will check a president who would misuse powers without hamstringing a president who would use those same powers for appropriate purposes and democratically acceptable ends.

James Madison warned that our country could never trust "parchment barriers" to halt the encroaching abuse of power. In the end, constitutions live only if they embody the spirit, values, and deeply held civic beliefs of the people. As the poet Walt Whitman reminded us, tyranny is always a possibility—if the people lose their supreme confidence in themselves and their spirit of defiance. Tyranny may always enter; there is no bar or charm against it. The only bar against it is a large, resolute breed of citizens.

Too much has been made by too many presidents and too many scholars of the view that only the president is the representative of all the people. Members of Congress do not represent the people exactly as a president does, but the two houses collectively represent the people in ways a president cannot and does not.

In the end, the issue is not so much whether the presidency should be stronger than Congress or vice versa. The real issue is that Congress and the presidency must *both* be strengthened to do the pressing work required for the well-being of the American people.

LEADERSHIP IN A CONSTITUTIONAL DEMOCRACY

The most compelling restraint on presidential powers is the opinion of the American people. Citizens have more power than they realize. Presidents listen when citizens are "sending a message." Citizens can also "vote" between elections in innumerable ways—by changing parties, by organizing protests, by voting for the opposition party in off-year elections, by voting for or against issues in state referenda.

Roots Of Presidential-Congressional Conflict

- Varying terms of office
- Diverse geographical constituencies
- Conflicting responsibilities and constitutional ambiguities
- Different partisan ties
- Constitutional provisions requiring extensive sharing of power
- Congress seen as disorganized and inefficient by the president and by the public
- The White House viewed as arbitrary and insensitive by Congress
- Each wants the credit for successes, and each seeks to blame the other when things go wrong

Thinking it Through

People who believe a president should be immune from civil suits contend that a president's responsibilities are unique, and therefore a president should be protected from distractions such as civil lawsuits until he or she leaves the White House. If a president was subject to such suits, Clinton's lawyer held, this could lead to a flood of frivolous lawsuits that would distract the president from effectively conducting the nation's business. In effect, he maintained, a president should be treated as special, at least while in office, because otherwise his ability to serve the public could be seriously compromised.

The Supreme Court ruled in 1982 that presidents are immune from lawsuits for official acts, yet the court has never granted immunity to a public official for unofficial acts. Lawyers for Paula Jones argue that a president shouldn't be treated differently from any other citizen.

How would you settle the matter? Are the responsibilities of a president different from those of other elected or appointed officials? This complicated and politically explosive case will eventually be settled in the federal courts.

Unrealistic Expectations?

The presidency will surely remain one of our nation's best sources for creative policy change. Americans will continue to expect presidents to do more, not less. The presidency will almost certainly continue to be a hard-pressed office, laden with the cumulative weight of contradictory expectations. Thus, we want our presidents to be:

- Gentle and kind, but also forceful, cunning, and decisive
- A common person who can give an uncommon performance
- Above politics, yet a skilled political coalition builder
- An inspirational leader who never promises more than he or she can deliver
- A programmatic but also pragmatic and flexible leader
- Innovative and inventive, ahead of the times, yet always responsive to popular majorities
- A moral leader, yet not too preachy or moralizing
- A bipartisan leader of all the people but also a leader of one political party
- A "take charge" leader yet someone who listens a lot

We need a healthy skepticism toward presidential decisions. A lesson learned from the Watergate period is not that the powers of the presidency should be lessened, but that other institutions—parties, Congress, the courts—need constantly to be revitalized. Unless we can find ways to renew and reinvigorate our political parties, to achieve some measure of responsiveness to the electorate and party control over public policy, we may well be destined to continue the march toward an American version of how General Charles de Gaulle governed in France—a highly personalized and centralized system overly dependent on a charismatic individual.

One of the persisting paradoxes of the American presidency is that, on the one hand, the institution is always too powerful, and on the other, it is always too weak. It is too strong because in many ways it is contrary to our ideals of government by the people and decentralization of power. It is too weak because presidents seldom are able to keep the promises they make. Of course, the presidency is always too strong when we dislike the incumbent. And the presidency is always too constrained when we believe a president is striving to serve the public interest—as we define it!

Americans' mixed views of the job often put our presidents in a "no-win" situation. History suggests there is no foolproof way to guarantee our presidents will possess the appropriate administrative skills as well as the moral character the job requires. On balance, voters have chosen well. Still, James Madison's advice remains useful: "A dependence on the people is, no doubt, the primary control of the government; but experience has taught mankind the necessity of auxiliary precautions" (see *The Federalist*, No. 51 in the Appendix). We must maintain the effectiveness of these "auxiliary precautions"—Congress, parties, the courts, the press, the Bill of Rights, and concerned citizens' groups—if we are to ensure a properly balanced and constitutional presidency.

SUMMARY

1. Presidents must act as crisis-managing, morale-building, personnel-recruiting, priority-setting, coalition-building, and managerial leaders. No president can divide the job into tidy compartments. Ultimately, these responsibilities overlap.

2. The office of the president combines a huge presidential establishment, a president's personality, the cultural dilemmas of the day, high popular expectations, and the heavy demands on the chief executive. It is still being

reshaped as new presidents with ideas and styles of their own move into the White House.

3. The expansion of presidential powers has been a continual development during the past several decades. Crises, both foreign and economic, have enlarged these powers. When there is a need for decisive action, presidents are asked to supply it. Congress, of course, is traditionally expected to share in the formulation of national policy. Yet Congress is often so fragmented that it has been a willing partner in the growth of the presidency. At the same time, Congress is constantly setting boundaries on how far presidents can extend their influence. Every president must learn anew the need to work closely with the members of Congress.

4. The separation of powers and necessity of sharing decision making, especially in foreign affairs, produce a creative tension between the White House and Congress. Both presidents and Congress have occasionally overstepped their roles in recent years; the process is never neat and tidy; complete accord is only sometimes achieved. Yet the two branches do cooperate, and somehow the business of government does get done.

5. Several factors can cause conflict in our system of divided government. Among these are constitutional ambiguities, different constituencies, varying terms of office, divided party control of the different branches, weak party discipline, and fluctuating support for Congress or the president.

6. Presidents generally exercise more leadership in foreign and national security policy than does Congress, and generally, though not always, Congress is more supportive of presidential requests in these areas. These tendencies have led to the notion that there are "two presidencies"—a stronger, more successful one in foreign affairs and a weaker, less successful one in domestic policy.

7. The overriding task of American citizens is to bind presidents to the majority's will without shackling them. To expect too much of our presidents may be to weaken them in the leadership tasks we need them to perform. To require immediate accountability might paralyze the presidency. Presidential leadership, properly defined, must be more than the power to persuade and less than the power to coerce. It must be the power to achieve by democratic and constitutional means results acceptable to the people.

FURTHER READING

James David Barber, *The Presidential Character*, 4th ed. (Prentice Hall, 1992).

Jon R. Bond and Richard Fleisher, *The Presidents in the Legislative Arena* (University of Chicago Press, 1990).

Paul Brace and Barbara Hinckley, *Follow the Leader* (Basic Books, 1992).

Thomas E. Cronin, *The State of the Presidency*, 2d ed. (Little, Brown, 1980).

Thomas E. Cronin, ed., *Inventing the American Presidency* (University Press of Kansas, 1989).

Terry Eastland, *Energy in the Executive* (Free Press, 1992).

Louis Fisher, *Constitutional Conflicts Between Congress and the President*, 3d ed. (University Press of Kansas, 1991).

Louis Fisher, *The Politics of Shared Power: Congress and the Executive* (Congressional Quarterly Press, 1986).

Michael Genovese, *The Dilemmas of Presidential Leadership* (HarperCollins, 1995).

Samuel Kernell, *Going Public: New Strategies of Presidential Leadership* (Congressional Quarterly Press, 1986).

Leonard W. Levy and Louis Fisher, eds., *Encyclopedia of the American Presidency* (Simon & Schuster, 1994).

John A. Maltese, *Spin Control: The White House Office of Communications and the Management of the Presidential News* (University of North Carolina Press, 1992).

Sidney M. Milkis, *The President and the Parties: The Transformation of the American Party System Since the New Deal* (Oxford University Press, 1993).

Michael Nelson, ed., *Guide to the American Presidency* (Congressional Quarterly Press, 1989).

Richard E. Neustadt, *Presidential Power and the Modern Presidents* (Free Press, 1991).

Mark A. Peterson, *Legislating Together: The White House and Capitol Hill from Eisenhower to Reagan* (Harvard University Press, 1990).

Glenn A. Phelps, *George Washington and American Constitutionalism* (University Press of Kansas, 1993).

John Podhoretz, *Hell of a Ride: Backstage at the White House Follies, 1989–1993* (Simon & Schuster, 1993).

Richard Rose, *The Postmodern President: George Bush Meets the World*, 2d ed. (Chatham House, 1991).

Arthur M. Schlesinger, Jr., *The Imperial Presidency* (Houghton Mifflin, 1973).

Stephen Skowronek, *The Politics Presidents Make: Leadership from John Adams to George Bush* (Harvard University Press, 1993).

Robert Spitzer, *The President and Congress: Executive Hegemony at the Crossroads of American Government* (McGraw-Hill, 1993).

Bob Woodward, *The Agenda: Inside the Clinton White House* (Simon & Schuster, 1994).

THE JUDICIARY: THE BALANCING BRANCH

16

I t was not an inspiring occasion. The few people present could hardly know they were witnessing the first meeting of what was to become the most important court in the world, the Supreme Court of the United States. It began on February 2, 1790. Chief Justice John Jay from New York, Justice James Wilson from Pennsylvania, and Justice William Cushing from Massachusetts were the only three of the original six appointees who made it through the snowy roads to New York City. They met in the Royal Exchange Building, an open-air market for butchers, which was the seat of the new federal government. The term lasted ten days, there were no cases to hear, and there was no quorum. The time was devoted to the admission of lawyers to practice before the Court.[1]

Four years later, Chief Justice John Jay resigned, in part because the federal court system lacked "energy, weight, and dignity," and in part to become governor of New York. But by the end of Chief Justice John Marshall's service (1801–1835), the Supreme Court had taken its place as a coequal third branch of the federal government. In fact, foreigners are often amazed at the power Americans give their judges, especially their federal judges. In 1834, after his visit to the United States, French aristocrat Alexis de Tocqueville wrote: "If I were asked where I place the American aristocracy, I should reply without hesitation . . . that it occupies the judicial bench and bar.... Scarcely any political question arises in the United States that is not resolved, sooner or later, into a judicial question."[2] A century later the English writer Harold Laski observed, "The respect in which federal courts and, above all, the Supreme Court are held is hardly surpassed by the influence they exert on the life of the United States."[3]

Why do judges play such a central role in our political life? One reason, as we saw in Chapter 2, is that in *Marbury v Madison* (1803), Chief Justice John Marshall successfully claimed for judges the power of **judicial review,** that is, the power to interpret the Constitution authoritatively. Only a constitutional amendment or a later Supreme Court can modify the Court's doctrine. Justice Felix Frankfurter once put it tersely: "The Supreme Court is the Constitution."

Besides exercising the power of judicial review, judges—and not just those on the Supreme Court—resolve disputes involving millions of dollars, decide conflicts among interests, supervise the criminal justice system, and make rules that affect the lives of millions of people. They are not only resolvers of legal conflicts; through their equity powers they have, in effect, become managers of schools, prisons, mental hospitals, and complex businesses.[4] Sometimes, in fact, they decide the details of how these institutions should be run. Still, the role of our judges is limited by the scope and nature of judicial power.

THE SCOPE OF JUDICIAL POWER

The American judicial process rests on an *adversary system*. A court of law is a neutral arena in which two parties argue their differences and present their points of view before an impartial arbiter. The adversary system, or *fight theory*, may or may not be adequate to arrive at the truth, but it is the basis of our judicial system. The logic of the adversary system imposes formal restraints on the scope of judicial power, and its rhetoric leads us to conceive the role of the judge in a special way.

Judicial power is essentially *passive*. Judges cannot reach out and instigate a case. Furthermore, not all disputes are within the scope of judicial power. Judges decide only **justiciable disputes**—those that grow out of actual cases and are

Types of Law

Statutory Law
Law that comes from authoritative and specific law-making sources, primarily legislatures but also including treaties and executive orders.

Common Law
Judge-made law that originated in England in the twelfth century, when royal judges traveled around the country settling disputes in each locality according to prevailing custom. The common law continues to develop according to the rule of *stare decisis*, which means "Let the decision stand." This is the rule of precedent, which implies that a rule established by a court is to be followed in all similar cases.

Equity Law
Law used whenever common law remedies are inadequate. For example, if an injury done to property may do irreparable harm for which money damages cannot provide compensation, under equity a person may ask the judge to issue an injunction ordering the offending person not to take the threatened action. If the wrongdoer persists, he or she may be punished for contempt of court.

Constitutional Law
Statements interpreting the United States Constitution that have been given Supreme Court approval.

Admiralty and Maritime Law
Law applicable to cases concerning shipping and waterway commerce on the high seas and on the navigable waters of the United States.

Administrative Law
Law relating to the authority and procedures of administrative agencies as well as to the rules and regulations issued by those agencies.

Criminal Law
Law that defines crimes against the public order and provides for punishment. Government is responsible for enforcing criminal law, the great body of which is enacted by states and enforced by state officials in state courts. However, the criminal caseload of federal judges is growing.

Civil Law
Law that governs the relations between individuals and defines their legal rights. However, the government can also be a party to a civil action. Under the Sherman Antitrust Act, for example, the federal government may initiate civil as well as criminal action to prevent violations of the law.

---

capable of settlement by legal methods. Not all constitutional disputes are justiciable. Some raise **political questions,** which require knowledge of a nonlegal character, or the use of techniques not suitable for a court, or are explicitly assigned by the Constitution to Congress or the president. Which of two competing state governments is the proper one? What does the Constitution mean when it provides that the national government should guarantee to each state a republican form of state government? Which group of officials of a foreign nation should be recognized by the United States as the government of that nation?[5] These are all *political questions.*

Judges are not supposed to use their power unless there is a real *case or controversy.* "It was never thought that, by means of a friendly suit, a party beaten in the legislature could transfer to the courts an inquiry as to the constitutionality of a legislative act."[6] (This, of course, is exactly what is done in nonfriendly suits. In such cases, however, the two parties have an interest in getting the full facts before the court.) In addition, litigants must have *standing to sue;* that is, they must have sustained or be in immediate danger of sustaining a direct and substantial injury. It is not enough merely to have a general interest in a subject or to believe that a law is unconstitutional.[7]

Of increasing importance in recent years are **class action suits** in which a small number of persons are allowed to represent all other persons similarly situated—a suit on behalf of all students in a university, for example, or all patients in a hospital, or all persons who bought a particular model of an automobile. "Would-be class action litigants must show that they are proper representatives for the class of persons they seek to champion, that the types of issues they wish to raise are common to the class, and they must be able to demonstrate how a remedy can be formed that will meet the needs of the class."[8]

Do Judges Make Law?

"Do judges make law? Course they do. Made some myself," remarked Jeremiah Smith, judge of the New Hampshire Supreme Court.[9] Most judges, even today, are less candid. Judges obviously make law, but to admit it is somehow disturbing. Such statements do not conform to our notions of what a judge should do.

Why do we think judges should not make law? Many people equate a judge's role with that of a referee in a prizefight. We expect referees to be impartial and disinterested, to treat both parties as equals. We expect them to apply rules, not make them.

Laws are not made, however, in the same way as the rules of a sport, and herein lies the answer to our question. Not only *do* judges make law, but they *must.* Legislatures make law by enacting statutes, but judges apply statutes to concrete situations. In some cases, applicability is clear: "If anything is a vehicle, a motorcar is one."[10] But does the word "vehicle" in a statute include bicycles, airplanes, and roller skates? A judge is constantly faced with situations that possess some features of similar cases but lack others. Statutes are drawn in broad terms: drivers shall act with "reasonable care"; no one may make "excessive noise" in the vicinity of a hospital; employers must maintain "safe working conditions." Such broad terms must be used because legislators cannot know exactly what will happen in the future.

These problems are intensified when judges are asked—as American judges are—to apply the Constitution, which was written more than two hundred years ago. The Constitution is full of generalizations: "due process of law," "equal protection of the laws," "unreasonable searches and seizures," "Commerce … among the several States." Recourse to the intent of the framers or just to the words of the Constitution is not likely to help judges faced with cases involving electronic wiretaps, multinational corporations, or birth control pills.

Adherence to Precedent

Just because judges make policy, however, does not mean they are free to make it as they wish. They are subject to a variety of limits on what they decide—some imposed by the political system of which they are a part, some by their own professional obligations as lawyers. Among these constraints is the rule of **stare decisis,** the rule of precedent.

Stare decisis pervades our judicial system. Judges are expected to abide by all previous decisions of their own courts and all rulings of superior courts. Although adherence to precedent is normal, the doctrine of *stare decisis* is not nearly as restrictive as some people think.[11] Consider, for example, the father who, removing his hat as he enters a church, says to his son: "This is the way to behave on such occasions. Do as I do."[12] Like the judge trying to follow a precedent, the son has a wide range of possibilities open to him. How much of his father's behavior must be imitated? Does it matter if the hat is removed slowly or quickly? If the hat is put under the seat? If it is not replaced on the head inside the church? The judge can distinguish precedents by stating that a previous case does not control the immediate one because of differences in context. In addition, many areas of law have conflicting precedents, one of which can be chosen to support a decision for either party.

The doctrine of *stare decisis* is even less controlling in the field of constitutional law. Because the Constitution itself, rather than any one interpretation of it, is binding, the Court can reverse a previous decision it no longer wishes to follow, as it has done dozens of times. Supreme Court justices are, therefore, not seriously restricted by *stare decisis*. As Justice John Marshall Harlan told a group of law students, "I want to say to you young gentlemen that if we don't like an act of Congress, we don't have too much trouble to find grounds for declaring it unconstitutional."[13]

FEDERAL JUSTICE

"The judicial Power of the United States," says Article III of the Constitution, "shall be vested in one supreme Court, and in such inferior Courts as the Congress may from time to time ordain and establish." Courts created to carry out this judicial power are called *Article III* or *constitutional courts*. Congress may also establish *Article I* or *legislative courts* to carry out the legislative powers the Constitution has granted to it. The main difference between a legislative and a constitutional court is that the judges of the former need not be appointed to "hold their Offices during good Behavior" and may be assigned other than purely judicial duties.

The Constitution requires a Supreme Court. It is a necessity if the national government is to have the power to frame and enforce laws superior to those of the states. The lack of such an agency to maintain national supremacy, to ensure uniform interpretation of national legislation, and to resolve conflicts among the states was one of the glaring deficiencies of the central government under the Articles of Confederation.

Congress decides whether there will be national courts in addition to the one Supreme Court ordained by the Constitution. The Constitution also allows Congress to determine the size of the Supreme Court. The First Congress divided the nation into districts and created lower national courts for each district. That decision, though often supplemented, has never been seriously questioned.

Federal Courts of General Jurisdiction

Today the hierarchy of national courts of general jurisdiction consists of district courts, courts of appeals, and one Supreme Court (see Figure 16–1). Although the Supreme Court and its justices receive most of the attention, the workhorses of the

Types of Courts

Examples of Special Article III or Constitutional Courts

In addition to Article III courts of general jurisdiction, Congress has created constitutional courts with special jurisdiction:

UNITED STATES COURT OF INTERNATIONAL TRADE (FORMERLY U.S. CUSTOMS COURT). Consists of 9 judges who review rulings of customs collectors and conflicts arising under various tariff and trade laws.

UNITED STATES COURT OF APPEALS FOR THE FEDERAL CIRCUIT. Consists of 12 judges who sit in panels of three to hear appeals of cases from all federal courts relating to patents as well as to review decisions of the Patent Office and of the Court of International Trade.

Examples of Article I or Legislative Courts

UNITED STATES COURT OF CLAIMS. Consists of 16 judges appointed for 15-year terms who have jurisdiction over all property and contract damage suits against the United States.

UNITED STATES COURT OF MILITARY APPEALS. Consists of 5 civilian judges appointed for 15 years each by the president with the consent of the Senate. This court, created by Congress under its grant of authority to make the rules and regulations for "land and naval forces," applies military law, which is separate from the body of law that governs the rest of the federal court system.

BANKRUPTCY JUDGES. Almost 300 judges appointed by the courts of appeals to serve as adjuncts to the federal district courts for terms of 14 years each. These judges handle bankruptcy matters subject to review by federal district judges.

UNITED STATES COURT OF VETERAN APPEALS. Consists of 2 to 6 judges who hear appeals from certain administrative decisions of the Veterans Administration.

SOURCE: Lawrence Baum, "Specializing the Federal Courts: Neutral Reforms or Efforts to Shape Judicial Policy?" *Judicature* 74 (December 1990/January 1991), pp. 217-224.

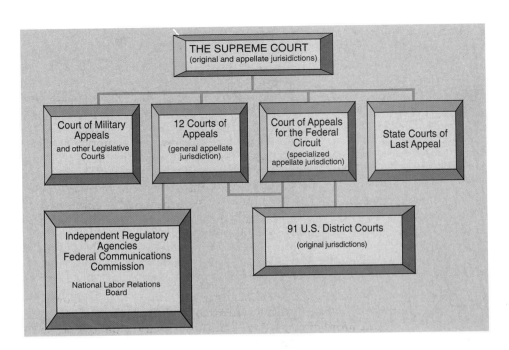

THE SUPREME COURT
(original and appellate jurisidictions)

Court of Military Appeals
and other Legislative Courts

12 Courts of Appeals
(general appellate jurisdiction)

Court of Appeals for the Federal Circuit
(specialized appellate jurisdiction)

State Courts of Last Appeal

Independent Regulatory Agencies
Federal Communications Commission
National Labor Relations Board

91 U.S. District Courts
(original jurisdictions)

FIGURE 16-1   **The Structure of the Federal Courts**

federal judiciary are the district courts within the states, in the District of Columbia, and in the territories. Each state has at least one district court. Larger states have as many as the demands of judicial business and the pressure of politics require, although no state has more than four.

There are 89 district courts in the 50 states, plus one in the District of Columbia and one in the Commonwealth of Puerto Rico. Each has at least 2 judges, but may have as many as 28. District judges normally sit separately and hold court by themselves. There are 610 permanent district judges in the 50 states, plus 15 in the District of Columbia and 7 in the Commonwealth of Puerto Rico. All district judges are nominated by the president and confirmed by the Senate. District judges, like all Article III federal judges, hold office for life.

District courts are trial courts of **original jurisdiction.** They are the only federal courts that regularly employ **grand juries** (indicting) and **petit juries** (trial). Many cases tried before district judges involve citizens of different states, and the judges apply the appropriate state laws. Otherwise, district judges are concerned with federal laws. For example, they hear and decide cases involving crimes against the United States—suits under the national revenue, postal, patent, copyright, trademark, bankruptcy, and civil rights laws.[14]

District judges are assisted by clerks, bailiffs, stenographers, law clerks, court reporters, probation officers, and United States magistrate judges. All these officials are appointed by the judges. The 374 full-time and 105 part-time *federal magistrate judges* are becoming increasingly important.[15] After being screened by panels composed of residents of the judicial districts, full-time magistrates are appointed for eight-year renewable terms, part-time magistrates for four-year renewable terms.

Magistrates "look like a judge, act like a judge, and speak like a judge."[16] Magistrates, most of whom wear robes and since 1990 are called "Judge," issue warrants for arrest, hold hearings to determine whether arrested persons should be held for action by the grand jury, and, if so, set bail. They hear motions subject to varying kinds of review by their district judges. They preside over civil trials—jury and non-jury—with the consent of both parties, and over non-jury trials for petty offenses with the consent of the defendants.[17] Under the supervision of the district judge, and with the consent of the accused, they may preside over the selection of a jury for a felony trial.[18]

"It's nothing personal, Prescott. It's just that a higher court gets a kick out of overturning a lower court."

Saturday Review, June 24, 1967.

Except for the few cases that may be taken directly to the Supreme Court, a final decision of a district court is reviewable by a *court of appeals*. The United States is divided into 12 *judicial circuits*, one of which is the District of Columbia (see map). Each has a court of appeals consisting of 6 to 28 permanent judgeships (179 in all). The Court of Appeals for the Federal Circuit has national jurisdiction. Each court of appeals normally hears cases in panels of three, but for especially important and controversial cases all judges may be present, that is, they may sit *en banc*.

Courts of appeals have only **appellate jurisdiction**, the authority to review decisions of the district courts within their circuits and also some of the actions of the independent regulatory agencies, such as the Federal Trade Commission. These courts are powerful policy makers.[19] Less than 1 percent of the cases from these courts are looked at carefully by the Supreme Court. As the policy role of federal courts has become a prominent political issue, more attention is being focused on these courts and the judges who serve on them.[20]

State and Federal Courts

In addition to federal courts, each state maintains a judicial system of its own, and many large municipalities have judicial systems as complex as those of the states. State courts have sole jurisdiction to try all cases not within the judicial power the Constitution grants to the United States.

The federal and state court systems are related, but they do not exist in a superior-inferior relationship. Except for the limited **habeas corpus** jurisdiction of the district courts (the power to release persons from custody if the judge is not satisfied that the person is being constitutionally detained), the Supreme Court is the only federal court that may review state court decisions. And it may do so only under special conditions.

Factors Constraining Federal Judges

- The Constitution
- Precedent (*stare decisis*)
- Statutory law
- Legal thought as found in books and law reviews
- Opinions of other courts
- Interest groups
- Public opinion
- Media opinion
- Views of colleagues
- Views of law clerks
- Contemporary events and general social environment
- Traditions of the law
- Actions of the legislature, past and future
- Actions of executives, past and future
- Limitations of time and staffing

These factors are not listed in any particular order. Some weigh more heavily at one time than at another, and on some judges more than on others.

From Coast to Coast

The Thirteen Federal Judicial Courts

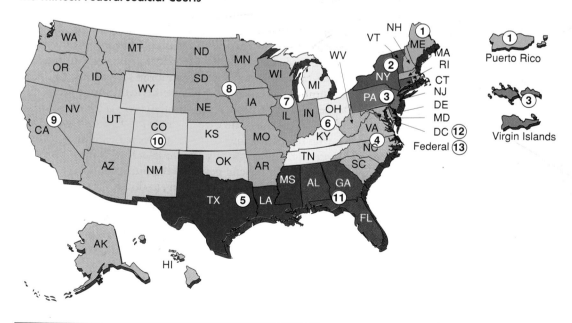

SOURCE: *The Federal Register.*

Go To the Source

The Public Affairs Video Archives at Purdue University can supply videotapes and videoguides for the Senate Judiciary Committee hearings on recent Supreme Court nominations. For information, see your local librarian or write to Public Affairs Video Archives, Stewart Center, Purdue University, West Lafayette, Ind. 47907.

Other than the original jurisdiction the Constitution vests directly in the Supreme Court, no federal court has any jurisdiction except that granted to it by act of Congress. Congress also determines whether this judicial power of the United States will be exercised exclusively by federal courts or concurrently by both federal and state courts.

PROSECUTION AND DEFENSE

Federal Lawyers

Judges decide cases; they do not prosecute persons. That job, on the federal level, falls to the Department of Justice: the attorney general, the solicitor general, the 94 United States attorneys, and some 1,200 assistant attorneys. The president, with the consent of the Senate, appoints a United States attorney for each district court. United States attorneys serve a four-year term but may be dismissed by the president at any time. These appointments are of great interest to senators, who exercise significant influence over the selection process through **senatorial courtesy**—the presidential custom of submitting the names of prospective appointees for approval to senators from the states in which the appointees reside. Because U.S. attorneys are almost always members of the president's political party, it is customary for them to resign if the opposition party wins the White House.

The attorney general, in consultation with the U.S. attorney in each district, appoints assistant attorneys. Some districts have only one; the largest, the Southern District of New York, has more than 65. These attorneys, working with the U.S. attorney and assisted by the Federal Bureau of Investigation and other federal law-enforcement agencies, begin proceedings against those alleged to have broken federal laws. They also represent the United States in civil suits.

Prosecutors and the Solicitor General

Prosecutors decide whether to charge an offense and which offense to charge. They have largely unreviewable discretion. "So long as the prosecutor has probable cause to believe that the accused committed an offense defined by statute, the decision whether or not to prosecute, and what charge to file or bring before a grand jury, generally rests entirely in his [or her] discretion."[21]

Prosecutors negotiate with the lawyers for **defendants** (those accused of an offense) and often work out a **plea bargain** whereby defendants agree to plead guilty to one offense to avoid having to stand trial for a more serious offense. Prosecutors make recommendations to judges about what sentences to impose.

Attorneys from the Department of Justice and from other federal agencies participate in well over half the cases on the Supreme Court's docket. Of special importance is the *solicitor general* (SG), who represents the government before the Supreme Court. (When the SG appears before the Supreme Court, he wears a formal dark vest, tails, and striped pants.) When the solicitor general petitions the Supreme Court and asks it to review an opinion of a lower court, the Court is likely to do so. "Overall, the government is involved in about two-thirds of all cases heard during a term, and the solicitor general's record of wins has been fairly consistent in the past decade. About 75 percent of all rulings goes his way."[22] Moreover, no appeal may be taken by the United States to any appellate court without the approval of the solicitor general.[23]

Although the solicitor general reports to the attorney general, the SG (sometimes called the "Tenth Justice") has traditionally been given some measure of independence from the White House but has always been responsive to the views of the president. The Reagan administration used the SG to carry its social policy agenda to the Supreme Court—to try to persuade the justices, for example, to limit affirmative action and to restrict the right of women to have abortions.[24] The Clinton administration's solicitor general, Drew S. Days, heads a staff of 23 lawyers and continues in the activist manner of his immediate predecessors, although on the opposite side on many issues from the Reagan and Bush administrations.[25]

A Department of Justice office that is becoming increasingly important is the *assistant attorney general*, who heads up the Office of Legal Counsel. The OLC is "the principal legal guardian in the executive branch of the constitutional prerogatives and powers of the presidency"[26] and works closely with the Office of the Counsel to the President located in the White House.

Federal Defense Lawyers

The federal government also provides lawyers for poor defendants in criminal trials. Each district court has some discretion as to how to provide this assistance. Most districts use the traditional system of assigning a private attorney. About half of the 91 judicial districts, however, have opted to use the **public defender** system. These salaried public defenders operate under the general supervision of the Administrative Office of the United States Courts. Congress is now reviewing the effectiveness of these procedures; in its March 1993 report to Congress, the Judicial Conference of the United States said the most important problem confronting the federal defender program is lack of money.[27]

Congress has also created a private nonprofit organization—the Legal Services Corporation—to provide financial assistance to organizations that furnish legal help to the poor in noncriminal legal matters. "It currently funds 4,500 lawyers in 323 programs nationwide."[28] The corporation is the center of controversy between those who would restrict its help to suing landlords, employers, husbands, or wives in traditional legal battles and those who would allow it to use class action suits to challenge the status quo. It is governed by an 11-member board of directors appointed by the president with the advice and consent of the Senate. Hillary Rodham Clinton was chair of LSC when her husband was governor of Arkansas. President Clinton has increased the budget and supported a broad mandate for the Legal Services Corporation, which, in contrast, was kept under tight controls by the Bush and Reagan administrations.

THE POLITICS OF JUDICIAL SELECTION

The selection of federal judges has always been part of the political process. It makes a difference who serves on the federal courts—a difference in how the Constitution is interpreted and how goods and services and values are distributed. It has always been so, but as the courts have come to play an even more important role in the political process, and as more and more interests—African Americans and women, for example—have become empowered to participate in that process, judicial selection politics have come front and center on the political stage.

The president selects federal judges with the advice and consent of the Senate. Political reality imposes constraints on the president's discretion, and the selection of a federal judge is actually a complex bargaining process. The principal figures involved are the candidates, the president, and the "subpresidency for judicial selection"[29] consisting of key members of the Department of Justice, United States senators, the Standing Committee on the Federal Judiciary of the American Bar Association, party leaders, and, increasingly, interest groups.

Recent presidents have inserted the White House much more directly into the process than did their predecessors. Department of Justice officials and key White House staff meet often to review proposed names. President Clinton, a former professor of constitutional law and a state attorney general, takes a special interest in judicial appointments. He takes an active role in finding and suggesting nominees to the Supreme Court and the courts of appeals, as does the First Lady Hillary Rodham Clinton, also a lawyer.[30]

Jurisdiction of the Supreme Court

Original
In all cases affecting ambassadors, other public ministers, and consuls.
In cases in which a state is a party.

Appellate
In all other cases arising under the judicial power of the United States. The Supreme Court has appellate jurisdiction—power to review decisions of other courts—except when Congress determines otherwise.

Jurisdiction of the Federal Courts

Federal Courts can hear and decide cases or controversies in law and equity if:

1. They arise under the Constitution, a federal law, or a treaty.
2. They arise under admiralty and maritime laws.
3. They arise because of a dispute involving land claimed under titles granted by two or more states.
4. The United States is a party to the case.
5. A state is a party to the case (but not if a suit was begun or prosecuted against a state by an individual or a foreign nation).
6. They are between citizens of different states.*
7. They affect the accredited representatives of a foreign nation.

*Congress has chosen to limit this *diversity jurisdiction* of federal courts, as it is called, to cases in which the amount in controversy exceeds $50,000.

The Liability Revolution: The Tort Law Explosion

In recent decades, there has been a huge increase in *tort law*, that part of civil law covering the liability of those whose conduct injures others and the compensation they must pay.

"Throughout most of American history, liability law has been an obscure legal byway . . . with little discernible effect on the wider society or economy."* Today liability has dramatically expanded, and the targets are mainly manufacturers, physicians, hospitals, towns, and counties, and their insurance carriers.

Judges have played a leading role in this liability revolution, to the praise of some who believe judges have provided protection for the weak against the powerful, to the criticism of others who believe judges have usurped legislative responsibilities and impaired the effectiveness of our economy.

This is yet another example of the important role judges play. They not only resolve disputes between individuals, but in so doing they are central policy makers.

*Walter Olson, "The Liability Revolution: New Directions in Liability Law," *Proceedings of the Academy of Political Science* 37, no. 1 (1988), p. 1.

Before the White House submits names of nominees for the federal district courts to the Senate, the president observes the practice of *senatorial courtesy* by consulting with appropriate senators. Even a senator from the opposition party is usually consulted. If negotiations are deadlocked between the senators or between the senators and the Department of Justice, a seat may stay vacant for years.[31]

President Clinton has given Democratic senators "clear guidelines about the kind of judges he wants."[32] These senators, however, take the initiative and send names to the Department of Justice, rather than wait for names to be cleared with them, and most senators consult with the screening panels.

The custom of senatorial courtesy no longer applies to Supreme Court appointments and is not often applied to the selection of judges for the courts of appeals because these judges do not serve in any one senator's domain. This difference in selection politics means that district court judges often reflect values different from those of persons appointed to the courts of appeal or the Supreme Court.[33]

The American Bar Association's Standing Committee on the Federal Judiciary plays a special role in the appointment process. Although its ratings of judicial nominees do not bind a president or the Senate, presidents are hesitant to submit for Senate confirmation a candidate rated "not qualified" by the ABA. During an earlier period, the American Bar Association was thought to introduce a bias favoring the conservative "corporation lawyer" into the selection process. In recent years, however, conservative groups have mounted an attack on the ABA's role, contending it reflects a liberal bias and gives low ratings to "sandbag conservative nominees."[34]

Liberal interest groups, such as People for the American Way and Alliance for Justice, as well as conservative groups, such as the Heritage Foundation and the Free Congress Foundation's Judicial Monitoring Project, have become active in the preliminaries, making known their views about nominees even before the names are released to the public or sent to the Senate Judiciary Committee for confirmation.[35]

The Senate: Advice and Consent

The normal presumption is that the president should be allowed considerable discretion in the selection of federal judges. Despite this presumption, the Senate takes seriously its responsibility to confirm presidential nominations, especially when the party controlling the Senate is different from that of the president, as was the case in recent years until the Clinton administration.

Most nominations, especially those for the lower federal courts, are processed without much controversy, especially when a president whose party controls the Senate nominates a highly qualified candidate. This action usually results "in a lopsided, consensual vote." When the president nominates a less well-qualified candidate, especially when the president and a majority of the Senate are from different political parties, "then a conflictual vote is likely."[36]

The major battle over judicial confirmations, if there is one, ordinarily takes place before the Senate Judiciary Committee. The Senate usually goes along with the recommendations of its Judiciary Committee without much debate. Yet floor debates are not all that rare. Overall, the Senate has refused to confirm 29 of the 138 presidential nominations for Supreme Court justices, including 7 in this century.[37]

Prior to 1955, only two nominees for the Supreme Court made personal appearances before the Senate Judiciary Committee: Harlan Fiske Stone in 1925 and Felix Frankfurter in 1939. The common practice was for the Senate to look into candidates' qualifications and background yet not examine them in person. More recently, the committee has felt free to ask judicial candidates a full range of questions, since it is now crystal clear that a candidate's political orientation is the major factor in determining how he or she will vote on the cases that come before the Court. Except for Robert Bork, nominated by President Ronald Reagan in 1987, judicial nominees have steadfastly refused to answer questions when the answer might reveal how they would decide a case likely to come up to the Supreme Court. Judge Bork had written so many articles, made so many speeches, and decided so many cases that he thought he had to clarify his constitutional views. His candor may well have contributed to the Senate's rejection of him and is likely to scare off future nominees from responding to similar questions.

The Role of Party, Race, and Sex

Presidents so seldom nominate judges from the opposing party (around 90 percent of judicial appointments since the time of Franklin Roosevelt have gone to persons from the president's party) that partisan considerations are taken for granted and partisan affiliation is rarely mentioned (see Table 16-1). Today journalists pay more attention to other characteristics, such as race and sex.

President Jimmy Carter, who had no opportunity to appoint anyone to the Supreme Court, selected more African Americans, Hispanics, and women for the lower federal courts than all other presidents combined—40 women, 38 African Americans, and 16 Hispanics. President Ronald Reagan, although the first to appoint a woman to the Supreme Court, appointed fewer minority members or women than did Carter, perhaps in part because fewer minorities and women could pass the Reagan administration's ideological screening. Twenty percent of George Bush's appointees were women, 7 percent African Americans, and 4 percent Hispanics.[38]

Bill Clinton pledged to appoint federal judges who would be more "representative" of the ethnic makeup of the United States. When he began his term, there were 115 vacancies, and Congress was under pressure to create additional judgeships. By the end of his term in 1997, he could very well fill at least half of the federal judiciary. And as Senator Joseph Biden, Jr., chair of the Senate Judiciary Committee, has said, "There will not be an ideological blood test, like there was during the Reagan and Bush years, to see if the candidate is a moderate or liberal, but there will be an insistence upon diversity."[39] President Clinton was slow in making his initial

TABLE 16-1

Party Affiliation of District and Appeals Judges Appointed by Presidents from Franklin Roosevelt to Bill Clinton

President	Party	Appointees from Same Party
Roosevelt	Democrat	97%
Truman	Democrat	92
Eisenhower	Republican	95
Kennedy	Democrat	92
Johnson	Democrat	96
Nixon	Republican	93
Ford	Republican	81
Carter	Democrat	90
Reagan	Republican	94
Bush	Republican	89
Clinton	Democrat	88

SOURCE: Sheldon Goldman, "The Bush Imprint on the Judiciary: Carrying on a Tradition," *Judicature* 74 (April/May 1991), pp. 298–99; also Sheldon Goldman and Matthew D. Saronson, "Clinton's Nontraditional Judges: The Triumph of Affirmative Action," *Judicature* 78 (September/October 1994).

NOTE: Figures for President Clinton are for nominations through June 1, 1994. Figures for other presidents are for confirmed appointments.

During televised confirmation hearings on Clarence Thomas's nomination to the Supreme Court, Anita Hill was interrogated by an all white, all male Senate Judiciary Committee about her charge of sexual harrassment by Thomas.

The Role of a Federal Judge

What is it like to be a judge? Most of the time it is very satisfying. One enjoys the prestige. Courtrooms contain every symbol of authority that a set designer could imagine. Everyone stands up when you come in. You wear a costume identifying you as, if not quite divine, someone special. Attendants twitter all around. Most striking, at every sitting, at least two highly trained lawyers, whose job it is to talk, who love to talk, allow you to interrupt them whenever you want.

There are negatives, of course. We have been known to get frivolous cases, or splendidly prepared ones that are nevertheless boring almost beyond belief. Also, the system is designed to maximize the judge's anxiety—that he has just made a mistake, or is about to. It is not just that (as the egg sorter complained about his job) it is "decisions, decisions, decisions all day long"; it is that the system is designed to ensure that the questions presented to us are the hardest to resolve. Seeking a judicial solution to a problem is usually an act of last resort.

The judicial system is the most expensive machine ever invented for finding out what happened and what to do about it. When we judges get a question, it is almost always (a) very important, and (b) a tough case that is close enough to drive one mad. Hence the craft is hard. Much tension accompanies the job of deciding the questions that all the rest of the social matrix has found too hard to answer. But the effort is worth it. For the job of adjudication is to decide those questions according to particular rules and free of the influences that often affect decisions made outside the courtroom. We represent a third value that is not, and is trusted not to be, the prisoner of either wealth or popular prejudice.

Thus all the pleasing mummery in the courtroom, all our political insulation, indeed all our power, is designed to support a message: "Whichever side you're on, we are not on your side or your opponent's side; you must persuade us not that you've got money or that you've got votes, but that your cause is lawful and just." That is a role worth fulfilling.

SOURCE: From an address by Irving R. Kaufman, chief judge of the Manhattan-based U.S. Court of Appeals for the Second Circuit, reprinted in *Time*, May 5, 1980, p. 70.

appointments, but by the end of his first year he had nominated 48 federal judges, more than half of whom were women or minorities: 23 percent African Americans, 35 percent women, and 6 percent Hispanics.[40]

The Role of Ideology

Finding a party member is not enough; presidents want to pick the "right" kind of Republican or "our" kind of Democrat to serve as judge. By and large they have been able to achieve this goal. Republican judges picked by Republican presidents tend to be judicial conservatives (with the notable exception of President Dwight Eisenhower's nomination of Chief Justice Earl Warren), and most Democratic judges picked by Democratic presidents are more likely to be liberals. Both of these orientations were tempered by the fact that judges had to go through a senatorial confirmation screen that during the administrations of Reagan and Bush was of the opposite persuasion from that of the White House.[41]

When the appointment is to the Supreme Court, the policy orientation of the nominee is likely to be foremost among presidential concerns. As President Abraham Lincoln told Congressman George S. Boutewell when he appointed Salmon P. Chase to the Supreme Court: "We wish for a Chief Justice who will sustain what has been done in regard to emancipation and legal tender."[42] Theodore Roosevelt voiced the same concern about appointing the "correct" person in a letter to Senator Henry Cabot Lodge about Judge Oliver Wendell Holmes, Jr., of the Massachusetts Supreme Judicial Court, whom he was considering for the Supreme Court: "Now I should like to know that Judge Holmes was in entire sympathy with our views, that is with your views and mine. I should hold myself guilty of an irreparable wrong to the nation if I should appoint any man who was not absolutely sane and sound on the great national policies for which we stand in public life."[43]

President Ronald Reagan's two terms made it possible for him to join Presidents Franklin D. Roosevelt and Dwight D. Eisenhower as the only presidents in modern times to appoint a majority of the federal bench. All told, Reagan appointed 346 lifetime judges. Like his predecessors, he was concerned about the ideologies of those he nominated, and his administration acted carefully to nominate only those whose views about the role of the courts and constitutional issues were consistent with Reagan's own.[44] Not only were a large number of judicial conservatives appointed, but many of them—because they were comparatively young—will continue to have an effect on judicial policy making well into the next century. (Despite the care given in their selection, there is some evidence that the Reagan judges may not be that much more conservative than judges appointed by other presidents.[45])

As President Bush's commitment to conservatism was somewhat less well established than Reagan's, conservatives and their organizations, such as the Heritage Foundation, the Pacific Legal Foundation, and the Federalist Society, focused their attention on Bush's judicial appointments, "turning on the heat . . . so that the Bush administration doesn't squander any opportunity to tip the U.S. Supreme Court further to the right or turn its back on President Reagan's legacy of appointing conservatives to the federal bench."[46] Bush, looking to lower federal and state courts for candidates, appointed 148 district judges, 37 appellate judges, and two Supreme Court justices— David Souter and Clarence Thomas. His appointees were among the most conservative in recent history.[47] Their conservative constitutional views helped consolidate the Court's "turn to the right," a turn President Bill Clinton is trying to reverse.[48]

The Role of Judicial Philosophy

What about a candidate's judicial philosophy? Does a candidate believe that judges should try to interpret the Constitution to reflect what the framers intended and what its words literally say; that is, does the candidate believe in **judicial restraint**?

Or does the candidate believe the Constitution cannot and should not be interpreted literally, but rather be adapted to reflect current conditions and philosophies; that is, does the candidate believe in **judicial activism**?

Judicial philosophy is closely related to political ideology. Throughout most of our history, federal courts have been more conservative than Congress, the White House, or state legislatures. Prior to 1937, judicial self-restraint was the battle cry of liberals who objected to judges interpreting the due process clauses of the Fifth and Fourteenth Amendments to strike down many laws passed to protect labor and women and to keep the national and state governments from regulating the economy. These judges broadly construed the words of the Constitution to prevent what they thought to be unreasonable regulations of property.

By the time of Richard Nixon, Ronald Reagan, and George Bush, however, the judicial shoe was on the other foot, and it was conservatives who were advocates of judicial self-restraint. What is wanted, they argued, are judges who will let Congress, the president, and the state legislatures do what they want, unless it clearly contravenes the precise words of the Constitution: regulate or forbid abortions, for example, adopt prayers for public schools, impose capital punishment, or authorize police to engage in wiretapping.

It would be wrong to assume that judicial philosophy is nothing more than another way to argue about political ideology. Some conservatives, for example, favor judicial activism because they want current judges to reverse the last half century of precedents and actively seek to protect property rights from government regulation. Some liberals favor judicial restraint because they believe democracy will flourish when judges stay out of policy debates. Nonetheless, most of the country understands enough about the policy-making role of judges to recognize that the debates about the proper role of the courts and about how to interpret the Constitution are reflections of differing convictions about what policy outcomes are in the public interest. The debate over the Supreme Court's role today is less about activism and restraint than it is about competing conceptions of the proper balance between government authority and individual rights.

Judicial Longevity and Presidential Tenure

Ideology and judicial philosophy affect not only presidents' nominations for the federal courts but also *when* sitting judges choose to retire. Because federal judges serve for life, they may be able to schedule their retirement to allow a president whose views they approve to nominate their successors. Chief Justice Roger B. Taney stayed on the bench long after his health began to fail to prevent President Abraham Lincoln from nominating a Republican. In 1929 Chief Justice William Howard Taft wrote: "I am older and slower and less acute and more confused. However, as long as things continue as they are, and I am able to answer in my place, I must stay on the court in order to prevent the Bolsheviki [Herbert Hoover, a conservative Republican, was in the White House] from getting control."[49]

Although former Chief Justice Warren Burger denied that he retired in 1986 in order to permit President Ronald Reagan to replace him with a constitutional conservative, his retirement did give Reagan an opportunity to rejuvenate the conservative wing of the Court by promoting the 61-year-old William H. Rehnquist, an articulate constitutional conservative, to replace the 78-year-old Burger. Reagan then picked another constitutional conservative, the 50-year-old Antonin Scalia, from the Court of Appeals for the District of Columbia, to take the seat vacated by Rehnquist.[50] Liberal Supreme Court justices William J. Brennan, Jr., and Thurgood Marshall held onto their seats well into their 80s, and many assumed that they were doing so in the hope that they might be able to stay on the Court until the time that a president more congenial to their views might be in the White House. They did not make it.

We The People

Minority Judges

Federal judges in general and the Supreme Court in particular have been a more diverse body of people than those who have lived in the White House. Catholics, Jews, African Americans, and women have served on the Supreme Court and other federal courts long before they could be elected to the White House.

	Reagan	Bush	Clinton
Women	7.6%	19.5%	35%
White	93.5	89.2	72.3
Black	1.9	6.5	23
Hispanic	4.1	4.3	6
Asian	.05	0	0

SOURCE: White House Counsel Office, published in Paul M. Barrett, "More Minorities, Women Named to U.S. Courts," *The Wall Street Journal*, December 23, 1993, p. B1. See also David G. Savage and Ronald J. Ostrow, "Women, Minorities, Outpace White Men for Jobs on Bench," *Los Angeles Times*, January 11, 1994, p. A11.

A Closer Look

Examination of recent nomination battles highlights the interplay of party, race, sex, ideology, and judicial philosophy in the process of selecting and confirming a Supreme Court justice.

The Bork Battle

When Justice Lewis F. Powell, Jr., who had had the swing vote on such critical issues as affirmative action and abortion, announced his retirement as he neared 80 years of age at the end of the term in July 1987, he made it possible for Ronald Reagan to select a justice who could have a decisive vote on many issues. President Reagan quickly nominated Judge Robert Bork, a member of the Court of Appeals for the District of Columbia and a noted jurist and legal scholar. Despite Bork's controversial writings on many current constitutional issues, his scholarly and legal qualifications made it appear initially that he would be confirmed. However, his nomination so offended women's and black organizations that they organized a campaign to block the Bork nomination. After almost four months of national debate, 12 days of acrimonious questioning by the members of the Senate Judiciary Committee, and 23 hours of debate on the Senate floor, the Senate voted 58 to 42 against Bork's confirmation.

Robert Bork.

The Souter Solution

The political bruises resulting from the Bork confirmation proceedings were traumatic. Political pundits speculated that in the future, presidents would seek noncontroversial candidates for the Supreme Court. This prediction came true in 1990 with George Bush's nominee to replace William J. Brennan, Jr., leader of the liberal bloc on the Supreme Court, who had been able to blunt the conservative impact of Rehnquist, Scalia, and Kennedy. President Bush chose David Souter, who had been on the Court of Appeals for three months and had been a member of the New Hampshire Supreme Court. Educated at Harvard and Oxford, he had written no law articles, made practically no speeches, and lived the secluded life of a sitting judge. When he appeared before the Judiciary Committee, Souter steadfastly refused to answer any questions that might reveal his orientation on abortion and privacy issues, to the frustration of the Senate Democrats. He was confirmed by an overwhelming vote.

David Souter.

The Thomas Tangle

When Justice Thurgood Marshall retired in 1991, President Bush sent to the Senate the name of a controversial jurist, Judge Clarence Thomas, then sitting on the Court of Appeals for the District of Columbia. Thomas is a conservative African American. Prior to his brief service on the Court of Appeals, he

Clarence Thomas.

Ruth Bader Ginsburg.

had served as chair of the Equal Employment Opportunity Commission (EEOC) and in the Office of Civil Rights. During five days of grueling questions about his constitutional views, Judge Thomas, as had his predecessor, refused to respond. The Senate Judiciary Committee narrowly recommended his confirmation.

Two days before the Senate was due to vote on his confirmation, documents leaked to the press revealed that a former associate of Judge Thomas, Anita Hill, had accused him of sexually harassing her when she worked for him in the Department of Education and the EEOC. Women's and liberal groups exploded in outrage. There followed three days of dramatic and emotion-charged hearings telecast to the nation in which Judge Thomas categorically denied the charges presented persuasively by his accuser. Panels of witnesses pro and con came forward to testify. Judge Thomas was confirmed by the Senate 52 to 48, the closest Supreme Court confirmation vote in modern times.

Clinton Appoints Two

Almost as soon as President Clinton took office, Justice Byron White announced he would leave the Court at the end of its 1992–1993 term. It was clear that with this appointment, Clinton could arrest the Court's conservative drift and fulfill his campaign pledge to appoint justices committed to protect the rights of privacy—that is, to preserve a woman's freedom to choose an abortion.

After several months of deliberation, including the rather public consideration of other candidates, President Clinton nominated Ruth Bader Ginsburg. Judge Ginsburg was a 13-year veteran of the Court of Appeals for the District of Columbia, to which she had been appointed by President Carter. On the Court of Appeals she had earned a reputation for fairness and moderation. She was readily confirmed by the Senate and took her seat for the opening of the 1993-1994 term.

Clinton had a second opportunity when Harry A. Blackmun, at age 85, announced his intention to leave the Court during the spring of 1994. Blackmun, best known for writing the opinion in *Roe v Wade*, was thought at first to be a judicial conservative, but by the time of his retirement, he had become the most liberal member of the Court.

The leading candidates were all sitting judges except for Interior Secretary Bruce Babbitt and Senate Majority Leader George Mitchell. After Mitchell withdrew from consideration and Senate opposition developed against Babbitt, President Clinton nominated Stephen G. Breyer, Chief Judge of the First Circuit, a noncontroversial judicial moderate who was readily confirmed by the Senate.

Should justices' political views influence their decisions?

Do you think that the political views of the Supreme Court justices, that is, whether they are liberal or conservative, ought to influence their decisions in the cases that come before them?

Reforming the Selection Process

The televised Bork and Thomas confirmation hearings aroused considerable criticism from both liberals and conservatives and created widespread complaints that "something is wrong with the process." Everybody appeared to be dissatisfied with it. Democratic senators were frustrated by their inability to get nominees to explain their judicial philosophies or to reveal their constitutional values. They argued that unless candidates respond about their constitutional philosophy, the Senate should refuse to confirm. Republican senators and the Bush White House accused Senate Democrats of improperly trying to force candidates to commit how they would decide cases and thus jeopardize the independence of the courts and compromise their ability to be impartial judges. Senators, they argued, should content themselves with checking into candidates' integrity and legal background and not ask about political and constitutional orientation or badger candidates to reveal how they might vote on cases that will come before them for decision.[51]

A group of experts agreed that judicial appointments could not and should not be free of political considerations but recommended that an attempt be made to constrain the partisan politics surrounding the confirmation process for Supreme Court justices. They recommended, among other things, that "Supreme Court nominees should no longer be expected to appear as witnesses during the Senate Judiciary Committee's hearings on their confirmation" and that the Senate return to the practice of judging nominees on their written record and on the testimony of legal experts.[52] It is unlikely, however, that there will be any fundamental alteration in the selection process. Now that Democrats control both the White House and the Senate, conservatives will closely question Clinton's nominees about their constitutional views, while Democrats will stress the virtues of judicial independence. Presidents of all persuasions are not likely to want to limit their discretion in selecting judges. As one scholar pointed out:

> The cries to depoliticize the process are not only naive, but perhaps too hastily considered. The apparent decorum of the past was achieved at the expense of participation and accountability. Few who viewed the agony and personal tragedies of the Clarence Thomas proceedings can avoid the almost instinctive desire to return to less visible and contentious proceedings, but the stakes are too high and involve the vital interests of too many forces to seek refuge in the ways of the past.[53]

The politics of judicial selection may shock those who like to think judges are picked strictly in terms of legal merit and without regard for party, race, sex, or ideology. But as a former Justice Department official has said, "When courts cease being an instrument for political change, then maybe the judges will stop being politically selected."[54]

CHANGING THE NUMBERS Partisan politics also affects decisions about the number of federal judges. One of the first actions of a political party after gaining control of the White House and Congress is to increase the number of federal judgeships. With divided government, however, when one party controls Congress and the other holds the White House, a stalemate is likely to occur and relatively few new judicial positions will be created. During Andrew Johnson's administration, Congress went so far as to reduce the size of the Supreme Court to prevent the president from filling two vacancies. After Johnson left the White House, Congress returned the Court to its former size to permit Ulysses S. Grant to fill the vacancies. In 1937, President Franklin Roosevelt proposed an increase in the size of the Supreme Court by one additional justice for every member of the Court over the age of 70, up to a total of 15 members. Ostensibly, the proposal was aimed at making the Court more

THE SUPREME COURT

1. Courtyards
2. Solicitor General's Office
3. Lawyers' Lounge
4. Marshall's Office
5. Main Hall
6. Court Room
7. Conference and Reception Rooms

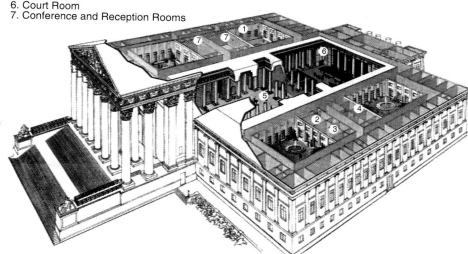

efficient. In fact, Roosevelt and his advisers were frustrated because the Court had declared much New Deal legislation unconstitutional. Despite Roosevelt's popularity, this "court-packing scheme" aroused intense opposition. Roosevelt's proposals to change the Court's size failed. He lost the battle, but he won the war, as the Court began to sustain some important New Deal legislation.

CHANGING THE JURISDICTION   Congressional control over the structure and jurisdiction of federal courts has been used to influence the course of judicial policy making. Although unable to get rid of Federalist judges by impeachment, the Jeffersonians abolished the circuit courts created by the Federalist Congress just prior to their losing control. In 1869 radical Republicans in Congress altered the Supreme Court's appellate jurisdiction in order to snatch from the Court a case it was about to review involving the constitutionality of some Reconstruction legislation.[55]

During the Reagan administration, a number of bills were introduced in Congress either to eliminate the jurisdiction of all federal courts over cases relating to abortion, school prayer, and school busing, or to eliminate the appellate jurisdiction of the Supreme Court over such matters. These bills sparked debate about whether the Constitution gives Congress authority to take such actions. Congress has not yet decided to make what could amount to a fundamental shift in the nature of the relationship between Congress and the Supreme Court.

HOW THE SUPREME COURT OPERATES

Supreme Court justices are in session from the first Monday in October through the end of June. They listen to oral arguments for two weeks and then adjourn for two weeks to consider the cases and write their opinions. By agreement, six justices must participate in each decision. Cases are decided by a majority. In the event of a tie vote, the decision of the lower court is sustained, although, on rare occasions, the case may be reargued.

Thinking it Through

A national telephone survey of 603 adults found that 23 percent of all respondents said that justices' political views *should* influence their decisions, while 69 percent disagreed. When asked how much they think justices' political views influence their decisions, 44 percent responded "a lot," 44 percent answered "somewhat," and 8 percent said "not much."

How do you think responses to these questions vary among respondents with different political views of their own? Twenty-nine percent of liberals, 19 percent of moderates, and 24 percent of conservatives think justices should bring their political views to bear on their decisions. Conservatives are most likely (52 percent) to say justices' political views influence their decisions a lot, followed by moderates at 43 percent and liberals at 39 percent; 35 percent of conservatives, 47 percent of moderates and 50 percent of liberals say justices' decisions are influenced somewhat by their political views.

SOURCE: John M. Scheb, II, and William Lyons, "Public Holds U.S. Supreme Court in High Regard," *Judicature* 77 (March-April 1994), pp. 273–274.

Don't Call Me Judge

A member of the United States Supreme Court is called "Justice," not "Judge," and the chief justice is the "Chief Justice of the United States," not the "Chief Justice of the Supreme Court." Members of the Court call him "The Chief," but nobody else should. In the years before Justice Sandra Day O'Connor was appointed to the Court, justices were often called "Mr. Justice" and were collectively known as "The Brethren." Nowadays "Justice" will do, and so will "Your Honor."

A member of the lower federal court is "Judge," not "Justice." The practice among the states varies, but members of state supreme courts are coming to be called "Justices."

SOURCE: David Margolick, "Here Comes the Chief Justice (Please Don't Call Him Judge)," *The New York Times*, April 26, 1991, p. B1.

The Rise of the Law Clerks

Beginning in the 1930s, federal judges began the practice of hiring the best recent graduates of law schools to serve as clerks for a year or two. As the judicial work load increased, more law clerks have been appointed. Today each Supreme Court justice is entitled to four clerks (circuit judges have three, and each court of appeals has "staff attorneys"). Clerks draft opinions and screen writs of *certiorari*, which determine the cases the Court will review. Justices often talk through their cases with their law clerks.

Law clerks are young and energetic, and they know how to use computers to do research and prepare drafts of opinions. As the number of law clerks and computers has increased, so has the number of concurring and dissenting opinions. Further, today's opinions are longer and have more substantive footnotes and elaborate citations of cases and law review articles. As Justice Harry A. Blackmun said about his colleague, Justice John Paul Stevens, "He uses hundreds of footnotes. Sometimes I think what he does is to outline his opinion, give it to his clerks and say, 'You put the footnotes in,' and of course there's an ego trip for the clerks and they have all kinds of footnotes."*

*Harry A. Blackmun, quoted in Stuart Taylor, Jr., "When High Court's Away, Clerks' Work Begins," *The New York Times*, September 23, 1988, p. 22.

At 10:00 A.M. on the days when the Supreme Court sits, the eight associate justices and the chief justice, dressed in their robes, file into the Court. As they take their seats—arranged according to seniority, with the chief justice in the center—the clerk of the Court introduces them as the "Honorable Chief Justice and Associate Justices of the Supreme Court of the United States." Those present in the courtroom, asked to stand when the justices enter, are seated, and counsel take their places along tables in front of the bench. The attorneys for the Department of Justice, dressed in formal morning clothes, are at the right. The other attorneys are dressed conservatively; sport coats are not considered proper. Dress and ceremony are all part of the high ritual of the Court:

> The majesty of its courtroom; the black robes of the justices; the ritual of its proceedings at oral argument and on decision day; the secrecy and isolation of its decision-making conferences; the formal opinions invoking the symbols of Constitution, precedent, and framers' intent; and all the other elements of setting and conduct distinguish the Supreme Court, a body of constitutional guardians, from all other government officials.[56]

Which Cases Reach the Supreme Court?

When citizens vow they will take their cases to the highest court of the land even if it costs their last penny, they underestimate the difficulty of securing Supreme Court review, overestimate the cost (although it costs plenty), and reveal a basic misunderstanding of the Court's role. The rules for appealing a case to the Supreme Court are established by act of Congress. Today all appellate cases come before the Court by means of a discretionary **writ of *certiorari***, a formal writ used to bring a case up to the Court. (Until 1988 there were a few types of cases the Supreme Court was obliged by law to review.) In addition, the Constitution stipulates the Supreme Court has original jurisdiction in a few specified situations. But the fact is the Supreme Court has control of its agenda and decides which cases it wants to consider. The justices closely review around 85 to 125 of the thousands of cases presented to them annually.

It is not enough, for example, that Jones thinks he should have won his case against Smith. There probably has already been at least one appellate review of the trial, either in a federal court of appeals or in a state supreme court. The Supreme Court will review Jones's case only if his claim has broad public significance. For instance, the rulings among the courts of appeals may conflict; by deciding the Jones case, the Supreme Court can establish which rule is to be followed throughout the judicial system. Or Jones's case may raise a constitutional issue on which a state supreme court has presented an interpretation with which the Court disagrees. The crucial factor in determining whether the Supreme Court will hear a case is its importance not to Jones but to the operation of the governmental system as a whole.

The Court accepts cases under the *rule of four*. If four justices are sufficiently interested in a petition for a writ of *certiorari*, the petition will be granted and the case brought forward for review. Nowadays the law clerks (called the "cert pool") read the petitions and write a memorandum on each for circulation to all the justices in the pool. Only Justice John Paul Stevens stays out of the pool, and even he, it is rumored, divides up the cert petitions among his own clerks and reads only a few of them himself.[57]

Denial of a writ of *certiorari* does not mean that the justices agree with the decision of the lower court, nor does it establish precedents. Refusal to grant such a writ may indicate all kinds of possibilities: the justices may not wish to become involved in a political "hot potato," or the Court may be so divided on an issue that it is not yet prepared to take a stand.[58]

Briefs and Oral Arguments

Before a case is heard in open court, the justices receive printed briefs, perhaps hundreds of pages long, in which each side presents legal arguments, historical materials, and relevant precedents. In addition, the Supreme Court may receive briefs from *amici curiae* (literally, "friends of the court"), who may be individuals, organizations, or government agencies that have an interest in the case and claim they have information of value to the Court. This procedure guarantees that the Department of Justice is represented if a suit between two private parties calls the constitutionality of an act of Congress into question. The *amicus curiae* brief is also used by presidents, through the Department of Justice, to see that the views of the current administration are brought to the Court's attention.[59]

Drawing by Richter. © 1983 The New Yorker Magazine, Inc.

Often organizations file *amicus curiae* briefs before the Supreme Court grants a writ of *certiorari* in order to lobby the Supreme Court to review the case. Their doing so enhances the probability that the court will take the case for review,[60] but has almost no influence on how the case is decided.[61] A brief brought by a private party or interest group may help the justices by presenting an argument or point of law that the parties to the case have not raised. Often the briefs are filed as a means of pressuring the Court to reach a particular decision. In the *Bakke* case, in which the Supreme Court dealt substantively with affirmative action issues, 37 *amicus* briefs were filed for the University of California, 16 for Allan Bakke, and 5 that did not take sides. In *Webster v Reproductive Health Services,* argued in the spring of 1989 and dealing with a Missouri law regulating abortions and a request from both Missouri and the solicitor general for the Court to reverse *Roe v Wade,* 78 *amicus* briefs were filed.[62]

Formal oratory before the Supreme Court, perhaps lasting for several days, is a thing of the past. As a rule, counsel for each side is limited to 30 minutes. Lawyers use a lectern to which two lights are attached. A white light flashes five minutes before time is up; when the red light goes on, the lawyer must stop, even in the middle of an "if."

The entire procedure is formally informal. Sometimes, to the annoyance of attorneys, justices talk among themselves or consult briefs or legal volumes during the oral presentation. Sometimes, if justices find a presentation particularly bad, they ostentatiously consult their watches. Justices freely interrupt the lawyers to ask questions and to request additional information. In recent years, especially with the addition of Justices Scalia and Ginsburg, "The justices seem barely able to contain themselves, often interrupting the answer to one question with another query."[63] The 30-minute limit is becoming a problem, especially when the solicitor general participates, since his ten minutes comes out of the time of the two parties before the Court.[64]

If a lawyer seems to be having a difficult time, justices may try to help him or her present a better case. Occasionally, justices bounce arguments off a hapless attorney and at one another. Justice Antonin Scalia is a harsh questioner. "When Scalia prepares to ask a question, he doesn't just adjust himself in his chair to get closer to the microphone like the others; he looks like a vulture, zooming in for the kill. He strains way forward, pinches his eyebrows, and poses the question, like '… do you want us to believe….'"[65] Justice Sandra Day O'Connor commented about him, "Some of our members are former law professors and haven't lost their technique of asking questions."[66] Justice Thurgood Marshall did "a terrible job of keeping his mouth away from the mike" when whispering.[67] Justice Ruth Bader Ginsburg, in her early days on the Court, was a particularly persistent questioner, frequently rivaling Justice Scalia in asking the most questions.

Behind the Curtains: The Conference

Wednesday afternoons and all day Friday the justices meet in conference. They have heard the oral arguments, read and studied the briefs, and examined the petitions. Before every conference, each justice receives a list of the cases to be discussed. Each

Justice Stephen G. Breyer

Justice Breyer is a graduate of Stanford University, Oxford, and Harvard Law School. He served as Supreme Court law clerk for Justice Arthur Goldburg and worked for two additional years in the Antitrust Division of the U.S. Justice Department. He was a member of the faculty at Harvard Law School before being appointed by President Carter as a Federal Appeals Court judge. A noted author and commentator on the law and regulatory policy, Breyer also served earlier as counsel for the U.S. Senate Judiciary Committee.

President Clinton nominated Breyer for the Supreme Court in 1994, and after a cordial hearing before the Senate Judiciary Committee on July 12 to 14, he was easily confirmed by the Senate.

Speaking before the Judiciary Committee on the law's purpose, Breyer stated:

I believe the law must work for people. The vast array of Constitution, statutes, rules, regulations, practices, procedures—that huge, vast web—has a single basic purpose. That purpose is to help the many different individuals who make up America from so many different backgrounds and circumstances, with so many different needs and hopes. Its purpose is to help them live together productively, harmoniously, and in freedom. Keeping that ultimate purpose in mind helps guide a judge through the labyrinth of rules and regulations that the law too often becomes, to reach what is there at bottom—the very human goals that underlie the Constitution and the statutes that Congress writes.

Source: *Congressional Quarterly*, July 16, 1994, pp. 1958–1959.

brings to the meeting a red leather book in which the cases and the votes of the justices are recorded. These conferences are secret affairs, although in recent years the secrecy has been penetrated. They are marked by informality and by vigorous give and take; they are both "collegial and substantive."[68] The chief justice presides, usually opening the discussion by stating the facts, summarizing the questions of law, and making suggestions for disposing of the case. Each member of the Court is then asked, in order of seniority, to give his or her views and conclusions. Recently the justices have not bothered with formal votes because they express their views when they discuss the case.[69]

The dynamics of the conference are illustrated by the maneuvering in the case of *National League of Cities v Usery,* taken up by the Court at its session on Friday, March 5, 1976.[70] (This case was reversed nine years later in *Garcia v San Antonio Metro.*)[71] The question was whether the federal minimum wage law should be applied to municipal police and fire fighters and other workers. In 1968, in *Maryland v Wirtz,* the Court had upheld the application of this same law to state hospital workers and school employees.[72] This would appear to be a binding precedent.

Chief Justice Warren Burger opened the discussion by saying that for the time being he would pass, although his "brethren," as the justices used to call each other until a year before the appointment of Justice Sandra Day O'Connor, knew he really would like to see *Wirtz* overruled. Justice William J. Brennan, Jr., next in seniority, argued that the Court was bound by the *Wirtz* precedent. Justice Potter Stewart told his colleagues that although he had dissented in *Wirtz,* he would not vote to overrule it unless five other justices wanted to do so. In other words, he did not want to be the one to cause a reversal. Justices Byron R. White and Thurgood Marshall agreed that the *Wirtz* precedent controlled. As the discussion went around the table, the vote was three for applying the federal law to city workers; Justice Stewart was prepared to go along, and the chief justice was on the fence.

Justice Harry A. Blackmun "wondered if there was some way to distinguish the case from *Wirtz* so that they could avoid the precedent." There was a way to make a distinction between the two types of employees, agreed Justices Powell and Rehnquist. They were quite ready to overrule *Wirtz* and hold the federal law should not be applied to either state hospital workers or to city police and fire fighters, if the rest of the justices would go along. Justice Stevens, the junior justice, said he thought *Wirtz* should prevail. Thus there were five votes to uphold the law as applied to the additional state and municipal employees and to reinforce the *Wirtz* decision.

The discussion was not over. Justice White chided Justice Stewart for refusing to become the fifth vote to overturn a prior decision they both thought was wrong. Justice Stewart responded: "I think you are right, I'll vote the other way." But he said he was not going to vote for some underhanded formula; he wanted a clear ruling that *Wirtz* was being overruled. The chief justice now declared he would vote to overrule, so the vote became 5 to 4 to do so. He assigned Justice Rehnquist the responsibility for drafting an opinion for the Court.

Opinions

As a general rule, Supreme Court opinions state the facts, present the issues, announce the decision, and, most important, explain the reasoning of the Court. These opinions are the Court's principal method of expressing its views to the world. Perhaps the most important function of opinions is to instruct the judges of all other state and federal courts in the United States on how to decide similar cases in the future.

Judicial opinions may be directed at Congress or at the president. If the Court regrets that "in the absence of action by Congress, we have no choice but to . . ." or insists that "relief of the sort that petitioner demands can only come from the political branches of government," it is clearly asking Congress to act.[73] The justices also use opinions to communicate with the public. A well-handled opinion may increase support among specialized groups—especially lawyers and judges—and among the general population for a policy the Court is stressing. For this reason, the Court delayed declaring school segregation unconstitutional until unanimity could be secured. The justices understood that any sign of dissension on the bench on this major social issue would be an invitation to evade the Court's ruling.

ASSIGNING OPINIONS   The justice to whom an opinion is assigned knows that he or she must influence the outcome, for no vote in conference is final. Justices are free to change their minds if persuaded by the draft opinion. When voting with the majority, the chief justice decides who drafts the opinion. When the chief justice is in the minority, the senior justice among the majority makes the assignment, often to himself or herself. Justices are free to write a **dissenting opinion** if they wish. Dissenting opinions are, in Chief Justice Charles Evans Hughes's words, "an appeal to the brooding spirit of the law, to the intelligence of a later day."[74] Dissenting opinions are quite common, as justices hope that someday these dissenting opinions will command a majority of the court. If a justice agrees with the majority on how the case should be decided but differs on the reasoning, that justice may write a **concurring opinion**.

CIRCULATING DRAFTS   Writing an opinion for the Court is an exacting task. The document must win the support of at least four—even more, if possible—intelligent, strong-willed persons, all of whom may have voted the same way but for different reasons. Assisted by the law clerks, the assigned justice writes a draft and sends it to colleagues for comments. If the justice is lucky, the majority will accept the draft, perhaps with only minor changes. If the draft is not satisfactory to the other justices, it must be redrafted and recirculated until a majority can reach agreement.

If the initial version is not acceptable to a majority, an elaborate bargaining process occurs. The opinion ultimately published is not necessarily the opinion the author would have liked to write. Like a committee report, it represents the common denominator. Justice Oliver Wendell Holmes, Jr., bitterly complained to British political scientist Harold J. Laski that he had written an opinion in terms to suit the majority of the brethren, although it did not suit him.

> Years ago I did the same thing in the interest of getting a job done. I let the brethren put in a reason that I thought bad and cut out all that I thought good and I have squirmed ever since, and swore that never again—but again I yield and now comes a petition for rehearing pointing out all the horrors that will ensue from just what I didn't want to say.[75]

The two major weapons justices can use against their colleagues are their votes and their willingness to write separate opinions attacking a doctrine the majority wishes to see adopted. Especially if the Court is closely divided, one justice may be in a position to demand that a given argument be included in, or removed from, the opinion as the price of his or her vote. Sometimes this bargaining occurs even though the Court is not closely divided. An opinion writer who anticipates that a decision will bring critical public reaction may wish to have it presented as the view of a unanimous Court and may be prepared to compromise to achieve unanimity. See Table 16-2 for a comparison of dissent rates in various Courts.

The internal battling over the opinion in *National League of Cities v Usery* is typical of what happens in many cases.[76] After the first round of voting, it appeared that Justice Brennan would assign the opinion, because he was the senior justice in what appeared to be the majority. But when Justice Stewart switched his vote, the

TABLE 16-2

Comparison of Dissent Rates

"The Great Dissenters"	Number of Dissenting Opinions
William Johnson, 1804–1834	30
John Catron, 1837–1865	26
Nathan Clifford, 1858–1881	60
John Marshall Harlan, 1877–1911	119
Oliver Wendell Holmes, Jr., 1902–1932	72
Louis D. Brandeis, 1916–1939	65
Harlan F. Stone, 1925–1946	93
Hugo Black, 1937–1971	310
Felix Frankfurter, 1939–1962	251
John Marshall Harlan, 1955–1971	242

The Burger and Rehnquist Courts	
William O. Douglas, 1969–1974	231
John Paul Stevens, 1975–1994	406
William Brennan, Jr., 1969–1990	402
Thurgood Marshall, 1969–1991	315
William H. Rehnquist, 1972–1994	272
Potter Stewart, 1969–1981	130
Byron R. White, 1969–1993	236
Harry A. Blackmun, 1970–1994	257
Antonin Scalia, 1986–1994	63
Lewis F. Powell, Jr., 1971–1987	159
Sandra Day O'Connor, 1981–1994	91
Warren Burger, 1969–1986	111
Anthony M. Kennedy, 1987–1994	39
David Souter, 1990–1994	21
Clarence Thomas, 1991–1994	19
Ruth Bader Ginsburg, 1993–1994	7

SOURCE: David M. O'Brien, *Storm Center: The Supreme Court in American Politics,* 3d ed. (W. W. Norton, 1993), with updates by authors.

Who Were the Great Justices?

Although this question is asked often, the answers are necessarily subjective and tell you as much about the values of the evaluators as they do about the merits of the justices. Nonetheless, two law professors surveyed about 65 law school deans and professors of law and political science. Respondents were asked to evaluate the performance of 96 justices who had served from 1789 to 1970. The 12 rated "best" or "great" were:

John Marshall*
Joseph Story
Roger B. Taney*
John Marshall Harlan
Oliver W. Holmes, Jr.
Charles Evans Hughes*
Louis B. Brandeis
Harlan F. Stone*
Benjamin Cardozo
Hugo Black
Felix Frankfurter
Earl Warren*

*Chief justices

SOURCE: Henry J. Abraham, *Justices and Presidents: A Political History of Appointments to the Supreme Court*, 3d ed. (Oxford University Press, 1992), p. 412. Copyright © 1992 by Henry J. Abraham. Reprinted by permission of Oxford University Press.

Chief Justice William Hubbs Rehnquist was formerly an assistant attorney general and was an associate justice of the Supreme Court from 1971 to 1986.

chief justice was with the majority, so it now fell to him to assign the opinion, which he did—to Justice Rehnquist. As Justice Rehnquist circulated his draft, Justices Stevens and Brennan each sent around strong dissents. Justice Stewart's clerks hoped that they might be able to persuade him to change his mind, so they presented him with their own critical analysis of the Rehnquist draft. Despite the pressures, Justice Stewart stood fast with Rehnquist. Justice Blackmun was wavering, and how he would go would determine the outcome. Justice Rehnquist modified his draft to take Blackmun's views into account, to be sure that he kept Blackmun's vote. Justice Brennan was also working on Blackmun. In his dissent he had written: "I cannot recall another instance in the Court's history when the reasoning of so many decisions covering so long a span of time has been discarded in such a roughshod manner." On the draft he sent to Justice Blackmun he wrote a personal note, "asking if there was anything that he could do to get his vote."

Although Justice Blackmun was disturbed by the sarcastic tone of Brennan's opinion, he still had not made up his mind to stay with Rehnquist. He "toyed with concurring in the result only," which would have meant that Rehnquist would have been denied the fifth vote for his opinion, which was necessary to make it a controlling precedent. Finally, he decided merely to write a single-paragraph concurring opinion explaining that in different situations where the federal government has a greater interest than it did in this particular case, federal intervention into the affairs of state and local governments might be justified. But because his concurrence endorsed the Rehnquist opinion, that opinion became the opinion of the Court and thus a controlling precedent. It was Justice Blackmun who, nine years later, wrote the opinion for the Court in *Garcia v San Antonio Metro*, which overturned *National League of Cities v Usery.*

The Powers of the Chief Justice

The ability of the chief justice to influence the Court has varied considerably.[77] Chief Justice Charles Evans Hughes ran the conferences like a stern schoolmaster, keeping the justices talking to the point, moving the discussion along, and doing his best to work out compromises. He tried to achieve unanimous votes in order to give decisions greater weight. Chief Justice Harlan F. Stone, on the other hand, encouraged justices to state their own points of view and let the discussions wander. Chief Justice Warren Burger devoted much of his time to judicial reform, speaking to bar and lay groups and trying to build political support for modernizing the judicial process.

Chief Justice William H. Rehnquist had 15 years of Court experience prior to his elevation to the post of Chief Justice. He had demonstrated his personal warmth and charm. He "has not utilized his position as Chief Justice to shape the decisions of the Court,"[78] but as the Reagan-Bush justices are now a majority, his constitutional views, formerly expressed only in his dissenting opinions, are now the opinions of the Court.[79] "The Chief Justiceship does not guarantee leadership. It only offers its incumbent an opportunity to lead. Optimum leadership inheres in the combination of the office and an able, persuasive, personable judge."[80]

After the Lawsuit Is Over

Victory in the Supreme Court does not necessarily mean that winning parties get what they want. As a rule, the Court does not implement its own decision but "remands," that is, sends back, the case to the lower court with instructions to act in accordance with the Supreme Court's opinion. The lower court often has considerable leeway in interpreting the Court's mandate as it disposes of the case.

Although Congress or a president has occasionally "ignored" or "construed" a Supreme Court ruling to avoid its impact, decisions whose enforcement requires only the action of a central governmental agency usually become effective immediately. Thus, when the Supreme Court held that President Harry Truman lacked constitutional authority to seize steel companies temporarily to avoid a shutdown during the Korean War, the president promptly complied. Of course, subsequent presidents have great discretion in determining how that particular precedent should be applied to them.

The impact of a particular ruling announced by the Supreme Court on the behavior of those who are not immediate parties to a lawsuit is even more uncertain. Many of the more important decisions require further action by administrative and elected officials before they become the effective law of the land. Sometimes Supreme Court decisions are simply ignored. Despite the Supreme Court's holding that it is unconstitutional for school boards to require prayers within schools, for example, some school boards continue their previous practices.[81] And for years after the Supreme Court held public school segregation unconstitutional, many school districts remained segregated.[82]

The most difficult Supreme Court decisions to implement are those that require the cooperation of large numbers of officials. For example, a Supreme Court decision announcing a new standard for warrantless searches is not likely to have an impact on the way police make arrests for some time, since not many police officers subscribe to the *United States Supreme Court Reports.* The process is more complex. Local prosecutors, state attorneys general, chiefs of police, and state and federal trial court judges must all participate to give "meaning" to Supreme Court decisions.

The Constitution may be what the Supreme Court says it is, but a Supreme Court opinion, for the moment at least, is what a trial judge or police officer or a prosecutor or a school board or a city council says it is.

JUDICIAL POWER
IN A CONSTITUTIONAL DEMOCRACY

An independent judiciary is one of the hallmarks of a free society. As impartial dispensers of equal justice under the law, judges should not be dependent on the executive, the legislature, the parties to the case, the electorate, or a mob outside the courtroom. But this very independence, essential to protect judges in their roles as legal umpires, raises basic problems when a democratic society decides—as ours has—also to make these same judges policy makers. Perhaps in no other society do the people resort to litigation as a means of making public policy as much as they do in the United States.

The involvement of our courts in politics exposes the judiciary to political criticism. Throughout our history the Supreme Court has been attacked for engaging in "judicial legislation." This is nothing new. Yet the more active role of the federal courts since 1937 on behalf of liberal causes and the Reagan and Bush administrations' frontal attack on that role have returned these issues to the forefront of public debate.

Since the end of World War II, federal courts under the Supreme Court's leadership have removed most of the constitutional restraints on government regulation of business. At the same time, they have imposed many more restraints to protect civil liberties and civil rights, especially for the poor and minorities. Since 1943 the Supreme Court has declared unconstitutional more than 50 acts of Congress as well as more than 400 acts of state legislatures and city councils. Overall, the Supreme Court has struck down over 140 acts of Congress (see Table 16-3) and almost 1,100 pieces of state legislation and state constitutional provisions. In one 1983 decision, *INS v Chadha,* it called into question 200 provisions of various federal laws.[83]

TABLE 16-3

U.S. Supreme Court Declarations of Unconstitutionality of Federal Statutes (in Whole or in Part)

Time Span	Chief Justice	Number of Declarations of Unconstitutionality
1798–1801	John Jay	0
	John Rutledge	0
	Oliver Ellsworth	0
1801–1835	John Marshall	1
1836–1864	Roger B. Taney	1
1864–1873	Salmon P. Chase	10
1874–1888	Morrison R. Waite	9
1888–1910	Melville W. Fuller	14
1910–1921	Edward D. White	12
1921–1930	William Howard Taft	12
1930–1936	Charles Evans Hughes	14
1936–1941	Charles Evans Hughes	0
1941–1946	Harlan F. Stone	2
1946–1953	Fred M. Vinson	1
1953–1969	Earl Warren	25
1969–1986	Warren Burger	34
1986–1993	William H. Rehnquist	7
Total		143

SOURCE: Adapted from Henry J. Abraham, *The Judicial Process,* 6th ed. (Oxford University Press, 1993), p. 273; also David M. O'Brien, "The Rehnquist Court and Federal Preemption," *Publius* 23 (1993), pp. 15–31.

Note: Table is arranged chronologically in accordance with tenure of chief justices as of July 1986.

Can states refuse to provide free education for undocumented aliens?

A few years ago the Texas state legislature decided Texas taxpayers should no longer provide a free public education for the children of undocumented aliens.

Then, in 1994, Californians adopted Proposition 187, which forbids schools and colleges to admit undocumented aliens and public hospitals to provide any treatment other than emergency care to them.

Setting aside for a moment whether you think such a policy is desirable, in your judgment, is there anything in the United States Constitution, especially in the *equal protection clause*, that should prevent the Texas legislature or the California electorate from making such a choice? What dilemmas of democracy does this case illustrate?

Whereas in earlier times judges occasionally told public officials what they could not do, today they often tell them what they *must* do. For example, federal judges, responding to class action complaints, have told Congress, state legislatures, and local officials that they must provide attorneys for the poor, ensure adequate care for mental patients, modernize prisons, and even break up the telephone system (in this last case the Department of Justice initiated the action). Often judges retain jurisdiction for years as they preside over the implementation of the decrees they have issued.[84] Judges have always been policy makers; that role is not a matter of choice but flows from the roles they play in deciding cases. But today they also govern.[85]

The Great Debate over the Proper Role of the Courts

Some people contend that the courts have a duty to protect the long-range interests of the public as defined in the Constitution, even against the short-range wishes of the voters (but then what is and is not defined by the Constitution is the issue). Defenders of this activist judicial role argue that if Congress, the White House, and the state legislatures are unable to resolve pressing problems when people are being denied justice and their constitutional rights, then the courts should resolve those problems. The Supreme Court, they say, should be "a leader in a vital national seminar that leads to the formulation of values for the American people."[86]

Critics of judicial activism, on the other side, contend that for the last half a century the federal courts, in their zeal to protect the people, became unhinged from their political moorings in the political and constitutional system. These critics argue that even if courts make the "right" decisions, it is not right for courts to take over the legislative responsibilities of the people's elected representatives.

Others claim the debate between those who favor judicial restraint and those who favor judicial activism oversimplifies the choices. Judges, they argue, should take a leadership role in some areas but a restrained role in others. They stand with Justice Harlan F. Stone, who argued that courts have a special duty to intervene: (1) whenever legislation restricts the political process by which decisions are made, or (2) whenever legislation restricts the rights of "discrete and insular minorities." In all other areas, the political process should be allowed to work, and judges should not set aside legislation or interfere with administrative agencies merely because judges would prefer some other policy or even some other interpretation of the Constitution.[87]

For a brief time when the Reagan and Bush jurists dominated both the Supreme Court and lower federal courts, many conservatives supported an active judicial role, and some liberals were skeptical about conservative judges using judicial power.[88] With President Clinton in a position to reverse the conservative makeup of the federal judiciary, liberals may become less skeptical about an active judiciary, and conservatives are likely to prefer more restrained judges.

The People and the Court

Whether judges are liberal or conservative, defer to legislatures or not, try to apply the Constitution as they think the framers intended, or interpret it to conform to current values, there are linkages between what the judges do and what the people want done. The linkages are not direct, and the people never speak with one mind, but these linkages are the heart of the matter.[89] In the first place, the president and the Senate are likely to appoint justices whose decisions reflect contemporary values. When the people elected George Bush, they got judges who reflected his perspectives. When they elected Bill Clinton, they got judges who reflect his values and preferences.

Bush was able to pick two Supreme Court justices—David Souter and Clarence Thomas—who, as expected, joined the Reagan appointees to complete the Court's "turn to the right." Yet at the end of the 1991–1992 term, that Court, by a 5 to 4 vote in *Planned Parenthood v Casey*, nonetheless refused to overturn *Roe v Wade* and upheld its core holding that the Constitution protects the right of a woman to an abortion, although subjecting that right to state regulations that do not unduly burden it.[90] This close vote on abortion made it clear that the 1992 election would determine whether that right would continue to be protected by the Constitution. At stake was whether it would be George Bush or Bill Clinton who would nominate new members of the Supreme Court. Clinton pledged to nominate only persons committed to the view that the Constitution protects a woman's right to choose. Bush continued to disavow that he had any "litmus test" for his nominees and insisted that it would be improper to inquire how they would vote on specific issues, but he made it clear that he would continue to appoint conservative jurists who could be expected to vote to reverse *Roe v Wade*.

Voters in 1992 had a more clear-cut choice on a specific constitutional issue than perhaps in any other presidential election. They also had an opportunity to influence the direction of constitutional interpretation by their votes for U.S. senators—the men and women who advise and consent on presidential judicial nominations. They gave control of the Senate to Democrats.

Public opinion influences what judges decide. Judicial opinions that reflect what the people want have the greatest survival value.[91] When a new political coalition takes over the White House or Congress, the old regime stays on in the federal courts, or, as one unknown wit put it: "The good presidents do dies with them, the bad lives on after them on the Supreme Court." New electoral coalitions eventually take over the federal courts, and before long, new interpretations of the Constitution reflect the dominant political ideology.

Judges have neither armies nor police to execute their rulings. Although Congress cannot reverse Supreme Court decisions that relate to constitutional interpretations, and only three Supreme Court decisions have been reversed by formal constitutional amendment, the political system alters judicial policy in more subtle ways. Decisions are binding on the parties to a particular case, but the policies involved in judicial decisions are effective and durable only if they are supported by a considerable portion of the electorate. To win a favorable Supreme Court decision is to win something of considerable political value, but the policies reflected by that decision may or may not alter the way people behave. "American courts are not all-powerful institutions."[92] If the Court's policies are too far out of step with the values of the country, the Court is likely to be "reversed." As Chief Justice William H. Rehnquist has written, "No judge worthy of his salt would ever cast his vote in a particular case simply because he thought the majority of the public wanted him to vote that way, but that is quite a different thing from saying that no judge is ever influenced by the great tides of public opinion that run a country such as ours."[93]

The American policy-making process is complex. What Congress and the White House and the state legislatures and police officers do has an effect on what the Supreme Court does, and what the Supreme Court does has an effect on what Congress and the White House and the state legislatures and the police do. Most important, what all these agencies do is related to what the various segments of "the people" want done. Consider, for example, the chain of developments that made the Constitution more reflective of the values of equal rights under the law. Changing economic and social conditions led to the growth of a black leadership, which in turn generated political power for blacks, which led presidents to care about what blacks wanted, which resulted in their appointing judges who reflected the values of civil rights advocates. And this action led to action and reaction in city councils, school boards, and state legislatures. The judges certainly played a leadership role in the development of a national civil rights consensus, and where they led the people followed. Today we are in the midst of a continuing debate about what the Constitution "means" about affirmative action. The answer is being decided only in part by what the judges say it means.

Supreme Court Decisions Reversed by Constitutional Amendment

Chisholm v Georgia, 2 Dallas 419 (1793), allowed states to be sued in federal courts; reversed by the Eleventh Amendment, ratified 1795.

Dred Scott Case, 19 Howard 393 (1857), held that African Americans were ineligible for American citizenship; reversed by the Fourteenth Amendment, ratified 1868.

Pollock v Farmer's Land & Trust Co., 157 US 429 (1895), denied Congress authority to levy an income tax; reversed by the Sixteenth Amendment, ratified 1913.

Thinking it Through

Proposition 187 is currently being challenged in the courts, but in *Plyler v Doe* (1982), five members of the United States Supreme Court ruled that the Texas law violated the equal protection clause because Texas had failed to show its action would, as alleged, protect the state from an influx of illegal immigrants, improve the overall quality of education, or save substantial sums of money. "If the state," wrote Justice William J. Brennan, Jr., "is to deny a discrete group of innocent children the free public education it offers to other children residing within its borders, that denial must be justified by a showing that it furthers some substantial state interests. No such showing was made here."

Chief Justice Warren Burger, dissenting along with Justices Byron R. White, William H. Rehnquist, and Sandra Day O'Connor, wrote: "I agree without hesitation that it is senseless for an enlightened society to deprive any children—including illegal aliens—of an elementary education. However, the Constitution does not vest in this Court the authority to strike down laws because they do not meet our standards of desirable social policy, 'wisdom,' or 'common sense.'. . . Today's cases, I regret to say, present yet another example of unwarranted judicial action which in the long run tends to contribute to the weakening of our political process."

"The people" speak in many ways and with many voices. The Supreme Court—and the other courts—represent and reflect the values of some of these people. Although the Court is not the defenseless institution portrayed by some commentators, and its decisions are as much shapers of public opinion as reflections of it, ultimately the power of the Court in our constitutional democracy rests on retaining the support of most of the people most of the time. No better standard for determining the legitimacy of a governmental institution has been discovered.

SUMMARY

1. Judges in the United States play a more active role in the political process than they do in other democracies. Federal courts receive their jurisdiction directly from Congress, which must decide the constitutional division of responsibilities among federal and state courts.

2. Federal judges apply statutory law, common law, equity, admiralty, and maritime law, and administrative law. They apply federal, criminal, and civil law. Although bound by procedural requirements, including *stare decisis,* they have to exercise discretion.

3. Partisanship and ideology are important factors in the selection of federal judges, and these factors ensure a linkage between the courts and the rest of the political system so that the views of the people are reflected, even if indirectly, in the work of the courts.

4. The Supreme Court, which has almost complete control over the cases it reviews as they come up from the state courts, the courts of appeals, and district courts, is a revered but somewhat mysterious branch of our govern-

ment. Annually its nine justices dispose of thousands of cases, but most of their time is concentrated on the 85 to 125 cases per year that establish guidelines for lower courts and the country.

5. A continuing concern of major importance is the reconciliation of the role of judges—especially those on the Supreme Court—as independent and fair dispensers of justice for the parties before them with their vital role as interpreters of the Constitution. This is an especially complex problem in our democracy because of the power of judicial review and the significant role courts play making public policy.

6. The debate about how judges should interpret the Constitution is almost as old as the Republic. More than two hundred years after the Constitution was adopted, the argument between those who contend judges should interpret the document literally and those who believe they cannot, and should not, has returned to the headlines.

FURTHER READING

HENRY J. ABRAHAM, *The Judiciary: The Supreme Court in the Governmental Process,* 7th ed. (Allyn and Bacon, 1987).

————, *Justices and Presidents: A Political History of Appointments to the Supreme Court,* 3d ed. (Oxford University Press, 1992).

ROBERT BORK, *The Tempting of America: The Political Seduction of the Law* (Macmillan, 1990).

ETHAN BRONNER, *Battle for Justice: How the Bork Nomination Shook America* (W. W. Norton, 1989).

BENJAMIN R. CARDOZO, *The Nature of the Judicial Process* (Yale University Press, 1921).

STEPHEN L. CARTER, *The Confirmation Mess: Cleaning Up the Federal Appointments Process* (Basic Books, 1994).

RICHARD DAVIS, *Decision and Images: The Supreme Court and the Press (*Prentice Hall, 1994).

JOHN HART ELY, *Democracy and Distrust: A Theory of Judicial Review* (Harvard University Press, 1980).

LEE EPSTEIN AND JOESPH F. KOBYLKA, *The Supreme Court and Legal Change: Abortion and the Death Penalty* (University of North Carolina Press, 1993).

LOUIS FISHER, *Constitutional Dialogues: Interpretation as Political Process* (Princeton University Press, 1988).

KERMIT L. HALL, ED., *The Oxford Companion to the Supreme Court of the United States* (Oxford University Press, 1992).

EUGENE W. HICKOK JR., ED., *The Bill of Rights: Original Meanings and Current Understanding* (University Press of Virginia, 1991).

PETER IRVING AND STEPHANIE GUITTON, EDS., *May It Please the Court: Transcripts of 23 Recordings of Landmark Cases as Argued Before the Supreme Court* (The New Press, 1993).

WILLIAM LASSER, *The Limits of Judicial Power: The Supreme Court in American Politics* (University of North Carolina Press, 1989).

LEONARD W. LEVY, *Original Intent and the Framers' Constitution* (Macmillian, 1988).

THOMAS R. MARSHALL, *Public Opinion and the Supreme Court* (Unwin Hyman, 1989).

JOHN MASSARO, *Supremely Political: The Role of Ideology and Presidential Management in Unsuccessful Supreme Court Nominations* (State University of New York Press, 1990).

WALTER F. MURPHY AND C. HERMAN PRITCHETT, *Courts, Judges and Politics: An Introduction to the Judicial Process,* 4th ed. (Random House, 1986).

DAVID M. O'BRIEN, *Storm Center: The Supreme Court in American Politics,* 3d ed. (W. W. Norton, 1993).

J. W. PELTASON, *Federal Courts in the Political Process* (Doubleday, 1955).

BARBARA A. PERRY, *A "Representative" Supreme Court? The Impact of Race, Religion, and Gender on Appointments* (Greenwood Press, 1991).

H. W. PERRY, JR., *Deciding To Decide* (Harvard University Press, 1991).

TIMOTHY H. PHELPS AND HELEN WINTERNITZ, *Capitol Games: Clarence Thomas, Anita Hill, and the Story of a Supreme Court Nomination* (Hyperion, 1992).

RICHARD A POSNER, *The Federal Courts* (Harvard University Press, 1985).

GERALD N. ROSENBERG, *The Hollow Hope: Can Courts Bring About Social Change?* (University of Chicago Press, 1991).

DAVID G. SAVAGE, *Turning Right: The Making of the Rehnquist Supreme Court* (John Wiley & Sons, 1992).

BERNARD SCHWARTZ, *A History of the Supreme Court* (Oxford University Press, 1993).

PAUL SIMON, *Advice and Consent: Clarence Thomas, Robert Bork, and the Intriguing History of the Supreme Court Battles* (National Press Books, 1992).

ELLIOT E. SLOTNICK, *Judicial Politics: Readings from "Judicature"* (Nelson-Hall, 1992).

LAURENCE H. TRIBE, *God Save This Honorable Court: How the Choice of Supreme Court Justices Shapes Our History* (Random House, 1985).

STEPHEN L. WASBY, *The Supreme Court in the Federal Judicial System,* 4th ed. (Nelson-Hall, 1993).

THE BUREAUCRACY: THE REAL POWER?

17

Attacking the bureaucracy is as traditional in American politics as kissing babies and marching in Fourth of July parades. Candidates for public office frequently take aim at the government bureaucracy and speak about it as an alien force whose policies appear devised by interest groups with little regard for the welfare of the average citizen. Thus one recent candidate running for the U.S. Senate boasted that if elected he would fight "the arrogant and wasteful federal bureaucracy." And some members of Congress like to joke that there is a parlor game played in the nation's capital. "It's called 'Bureaucracy,'" they say. "And there is only one rule. The first one to move loses."

Bill Clinton and his running mate, Al Gore, like virtually all candidates for the White House, attacked the federal bureaucracy and promised to make it more responsive and efficient. They also pledged to cut its size. Once elected, Clinton appointed Gore to head a team to "reinvent government." Not surprisingly, Gore found plenty of examples of bureaucracies so big and wasteful they no longer served the American public. He also found that many federal agencies are monopolies with few incentives to innovate or improve. Gore and colleagues made 800 recommendations for overhauling and streamlining the federal government, some of which we discuss later in this chapter.[1]

Ironically, at the same time, the Clinton administration was campaigning for a national health plan that would call into being a huge centralized health bureaucracy to oversee health providers and a complex health delivery system. One critic noted that it looked as though the authors of the Clinton-Gore health plan had not read the Clinton-Gore bureaucracy reform report.[2]

In this chapter we explain who bureaucrats are, examine the functions and realities of our national public bureaucracy, and explore how elected officials are trying to make our bureaucracy leaner, more responsive, and more accountable to the American people.

THE FEDERAL BUREAUCRACY

Bureaucrats, or career government employees, work in the executive branch, in the 14 cabinet-level departments, and in the more than 50 independent agencies embracing about 2,000 bureaus, divisions, branches, offices, services, and other subunits of government. Five big agencies—the Departments of Army, Navy, and Air Force, the Department of Veterans Affairs, and the U.S. Postal Service—tower over the others in size. Most agencies are directly responsible to the president, yet some, like the Postal Service, are partly independent. Agencies exist by act of Congress; legislators can abolish them either by passing a new law or by withholding funds.[3]

The terms "bureaucrat" and "bureaucracy" are of recent origin. Initially referring to a cloth covering the desks or flat writing tables of French government officials in the eighteenth century, the term "bureau" came to be linked with the suffix "ocracy" signifying rule of government (as in "democracy" or "aristocracy"). "Bureaucracy," as it came to be used 100 years ago, referred to a rational, efficient method of organization. "Bureaucracy" today can refer to a professional corps of officials organized in a pyramidal hierarchy and functioning under impersonal, uniform rules and procedures. The term "bureaucracy" typically refers to the whole body of nonelected and nonpresidentially appointed government officials in the executive branch who work for presidents and their political appointees.

Bureaucracies tend to create a lot of paperwork. Employees of a private company pose with the amount of paper they were required to file with the government in one year.

In this chapter we use the terms "bureaucracy" and "bureaucrat" in their neutral sense. Yet popular usage of these terms is typically negative: thus the wiseacre remark, "My friend doesn't work, he has a government job," or accusations that government workers are lazy, officious, buck-passing, and imperial.

Bureaucracies are public or private organizations that: "(1) are large (generally more than 100 employees); (2) are hierarchical in structure, with each employee accountable to the top executive through a chain of command; (3) provide each employee with a clearly defined role and area of responsibility; (4) base their actions and decisions on impersonal rules; and (5) hire and promote employees based on skills and training related to their specific jobs."[4] Bureaucracies in the modern sense came into being in governments to provide predictability and efficiency and to minimize the arbitrary practices that so often characterized rule under dictatorial monarchs.

Critics believe the federal bureaucracy is an overzealous guardian of the status quo and is too lazy or unimaginative to innovate or experiment. Others fear that a powerful national bureaucracy is too liberal and encourages a wasteful welfare state. Many people also think the federal bureaucracy is too large, too powerful, too unaccountable. And nearly everyone is suspicious that there is waste and "fat" in government, especially those who have heard about Defense Department procurement cost overruns, welfare fraud, and general inefficiencies. Such stereotypes are widespread, for bureaucracies have never been popular, but the skepticism and hostility toward public bureaucracies seem greater today than before.

Career public servants have no press secretaries to tell their side of the story. As with much of the oversimplified campaign talk in American politics, the "bureaucrats-are-bums" speeches are often misleading. Of course, we have a lot of red tape and overlap in our public administration process—too much. And it is proper to ask whether bureaucracy and its methods have stifled innovation and productivity. The real question, however, is less the existence of bureaucracy than whether the bureaucracy is responsive to the electorate's definition of the nation's needs and interests.

Bureaucracy is a fact of modern life. Most of us will work in some public or private bureaucracy for part, if not most, of our careers. Public bureaucracies pose special challenges because they report to competing political institutions and must function within our constitutional democracy of shared powers and multiple checks and balances.

How Did the Bureaucracy Evolve?

From 1789 until about 1829, the federal service was drawn from an upper-class, white male elite. In 1829, President Andrew Jackson called for greater participation by the middle and lower classes. He employed a **spoils system** that was followed by his successors until well into the 1890s. This system, epitomized by the phrase "to the victor belong the spoils," operated on the theory that party loyalists should be rewarded and that government would be effective and responsive only if followers of the president held most key federal posts. Besides, it was thought that government should not be complicated; almost anybody should be able to do the job. With each new president came a full turnover in the federal service.

Later in the nineteenth century, however, a sharp reaction set in against this system. In response to the various abuses of the system and most immediately to the assassination of President James Garfield in 1881 by a disappointed office seeker, Congress passed the Pendleton Act. It set up a limited **merit system** based on a testing program to evaluate candidates. Federal employees were to be selected and retained according to their "merit," not their party loyalty. Federal service was placed under the control of a three-person bipartisan board called the Civil Service Commission, which functioned from 1883 to 1978.[5]

From Coast to Coast

Federal Employment Is Widely Dispersed

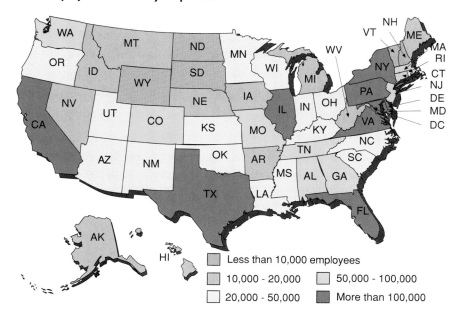

Less than 10,000 employees
10,000 - 20,000
20,000 - 50,000
50,000 - 100,000
More than 100,000

SOURCE: U.S. Census Bureau, Office of Personnel Management.

By the 1950s, coverage under the merit system had grown from 10 percent of all federal employees when it was first established to about 90 percent. In 1978 the Civil Service Reform Act abolished the Civil Service Commission and split its functions between two new agencies. This split was necessary to avoid a conflict of interest inherent in the agency that recruits, hires, and promotes employees also being the same agency that passes judgment on employee grievances about fairness and discrimination.

Today the Office of Personnel Management (OPM) administers civil service laws, rules, and regulations. An independent Merit Systems Protection Board is charged with protecting the integrity of the federal merit system and the rights of federal employees. The board conducts studies of the merit system, hears and decides charges of wrongdoing, considers employee appeals against adverse agency actions, and orders corrective and disciplinary actions against an agency executive or employee when appropriate. A special counsel, originally attached to the Merit Systems Protection Board but now independent, investigates wrongful personnel practices and prosecutes officials who violate civil service rules and regulations.

Who Are the Bureaucrats?

In this chapter we are mainly interested in the 4.6 million people (2.8 million civilians and nearly 1.8 million in the military services) who make up the executive branch of the federal government. Certain facts about these people need to be emphasized:

1. Fewer than 350,000 (or about 12 percent) of the career civilian employees work in the Washington area. The vast majority are scattered throughout the country and around the world. California alone has more federal employees than does the District of Columbia (see map).

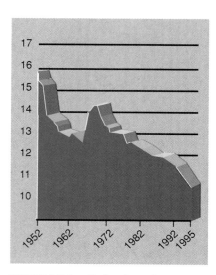

FIGURE 17-1 Federal Employment per 1,000 Americans

SOURCE: U.S. Census Bureau, Office of Personnel Management.

2. Nearly one-third of the civilian employees work for the army, the navy, the air force, or some other defense agency.

3. The welfare state may consume a sizable portion of our budget, but the size of the federal bureaucracy that administers it is relatively small. Less than 15 percent of the bureaucrats work for welfare agencies such as the Social Security Administration or the Rural Electrification Administration. Almost half of those who do work for the Department of Veterans Affairs.

4. Federal employees are not all of one type. Indeed, in terms of social origin, education, religion, and other background factors, bureaucrats are more broadly representative of the nation than are legislators or politically appointed executives.[6]

5. Federal employment per 1,000 people in the U.S. population has decreased steadily over the past generation (see Figure 17-1).

6. Bureaucrats work at an endless variety of jobs. More than 15,000 different personnel skills are represented in the federal government. Unlike Americans as a whole, however, most federal employees are white-collar workers: secretaries, clerks, lawyers, inspectors, engineers.

7. Nearly 20,000 federal civilian employees work in territories belonging to the United States, and another 100,000 in foreign nations.

The vast number of senior bureaucrats are honest professionals and experts at their business. Presidents, Congress, and other elected officials ignore the bureaucracy's advice at their peril. A compelling example is provided by the Central Intelligence Agency's (CIA) perceptive memoranda (many of them later published in the celebrated *Pentagon Papers*) arguing that the Vietnam War as President Lyndon Johnson wanted to conduct it would be a failure. This was good advice from an expert bureaucracy, but Johnson disregarded it. The Clinton White House similarly chose to ignore top State, Defense, and CIA officials who warned about the difficulty of planned U.S. initiatives in Somalia, Bosnia, and Haiti in 1993 and 1994.

What Do Bureaucrats Do?

After the president has signed a bill into law or a regulatory agency has made its rules, they must be implemented. Legislation or administrative decisions are not self-implementing. Implementation of policy is the function of the executive branch, its bureaucracy, and in some instances, state, county, and local governments as well.

More is involved in policy implementation than the literal translation of goals into practice. Indeed, it is during this stage that many key decisions are made. The coalition that pushes a bill through Congress often does not stay together after the bill has been enacted. Congress often passes ambiguous legislation that conceals serious policy differences. Because of policy differences among the supporters of a bill, Congress sets general goals and passes the responsibility for interpretation on to the bureaucrats. Legislators are frequently more concerned with the symbolic potency of legislation than with its substantive content. As a result, the bureaucracy is given considerable latitude to translate general guidelines into specific directives. Bureaucrats are sometimes blamed for confusion, yet they are merely trying to carry out deliberately unclear policies in a political atmosphere characterized by conflict and competition.

Consider civil rights legislation. Often differences among women's groups, African American groups, Latino groups, employer groups, and trade unions are momentarily resolved and a bill becomes law. But after the bill has been enacted, the coalition that supported the bill falls apart, and the resulting conflicting pressures are felt by the agencies trying to implement the policies. Employers claim that the agencies' regulations are unrealistic and interfere with their rights; women's groups contend agencies are failing to enforce the law vigorously enough; black groups claim agencies favor the women's groups but ignore African Americans. The more controversial the issue, the greater the chance of delay, as powerful interest groups clash over a program and force bureaucrats to move cautiously.

The implementation process involves a long chain of decision points. At each decision point a public official or community leader often can advance or delay the program. The more decision points a program needs to clear, the greater the chance of failure or delay. Special problems result if the successful implementation of a national program depends on the cooperation of state and local officials. One state or community may be eager to help; another may be opposed to a program and try to stop it.

A number of federal programs have failed to accomplish their desired goals because of problems that occurred in administration. Sometimes these difficulties lead to the outright failure of a program, but more often they mean excessive delay, watered-down goals, or cost overruns. John Kennedy's economic reform programs in Latin America, Lyndon Johnson's Model Cities program, Richard Nixon's and Gerald Ford's crime control programs, Jimmy Carter's human rights initiatives in foreign policy, and George Bush's antidrug crusade all faced problems of implementation. When such failures occur, it is easier to blame the original legislation rather than what happened after the bill became law. Of course, poorly written legislation and badly conceived policy yield poor results, but even the best legislation can fail because of problems encountered during implementation.

Like so much of politics, successful policy implementation cannot be guaranteed. It depends on the creation of stable routines for implementation, the ability to adjust to changing circumstances, the quality of the working relationship between implementers at various levels, the degree of conflict invoked by the policy, and the general level of public support for the program.

How Is the Bureaucracy Organized ?

FORMAL ORGANIZATION   The executive branch departments are headed by cabinet members called *secretaries* (except Justice, which is headed by the attorney general). The secretaries are directly responsible to the president. Although departments vary greatly in size, they have certain features in common. A deputy or an undersecretary takes part of the administrative load off the secretary's shoulders, and several assistant secretaries direct major programs. The secretaries have assistants who help them in planning, budget, personnel, legal services, public relations, and other staff functions.

Departments are subdivided into bureaus and smaller units, and the basis for their division may differ. The most common basis is *function*. For example, the Commerce Department is divided into the Bureau of the Census, the Patent and Trademark Office, and so on. The basis may also be *clientele* (for example, the Bureau of Indian Affairs of the Interior Department), or *work processes* (for example, the Economic Research Service of the Agriculture Department), or *geography* (for example, the Alaskan Air Command of the Department of the Air Force).

Government corporations, such as the Corporation for Public Broadcasting and the Federal Deposit Insurance Corporation, are a cross between business corporations and regular government agencies. Government corporations were designed to make possible a freedom of action and flexibility not always found in the regular agencies. These corporations have been freed from certain regulations of the Office of Management and Budget and the comptroller general. They also

Executive Branch Departments

- Department of State (1789)
- Department of the Treasury (1789)
- Department of Defense (1947, originally War, 1789)
- Department of Justice (1789)
- Department of the Interior (1849)
- Department of Agriculture (1862)
- Department of Commerce (1913, originally Commerce and Labor, 1903)
- Department of Labor (1913, originally Commerce and Labor, 1903)
- Department of Health and Human Services (1979, originally Health, Education and Welfare, 1953)
- Department of Housing and Urban Development (1965)
- Department of Transportation (1966)
- Department of Energy (1977)
- Department of Education (1979)
- Department of Veterans Affairs (1989)

Dates indicate when the department was established.

The Federal Deposit Insurance Corporation, a government corporation, was set up to protect depositors' accounts in banks and savings and loans companies. Here an FDIC poster on a bank door announces the closing of the bank and informs depositors where and how to seek restitution of their money.

have more leeway in using their own earnings. Still, because these corporations are a part of the government, the government retains control over their activities.

Government entities that are not corporations and do not fall within cabinet departments are called **independent agencies**. They consist of many types of organizations with differing degrees of independence. Many, however, are no more independent of the president and Congress than the departments. The huge General Services Administration (GSA), for example, the function of which is to operate and maintain federal properties, is not represented in the cabinet, but its director is responsible to the White House and its actions are closely watched by Congress.[7]

Another type of agency is the **independent regulatory board or commission**. Examples are the Securities and Exchange Commission, the National Labor Relations Board, and the Federal Reserve Board. Congress deliberately set up these boards to keep them somewhat free from White House influence; the president nominates them and Congress confirms them, but the president can fire them. They exercise **quasi-legislative and quasi-judicial** functions. Congress has protected their independence in several ways: the boards are headed by three or more commissioners with overlapping terms; they often have to be bipartisan in membership (that is, they must have some Democrats as well as some Republicans); and members are appointed for fixed terms in office, some for only 3 years but others for up to 14 years.

Within each of the departments, corporations, and independent agencies are many subordinate units. The standard name for the largest subunit is the **bureau**, although it is sometimes called an office, administration, or service. Bureaus are the working units of the federal government. In contrast to the big departments, which often consist of a variety of agencies, bureaus usually have fairly definite and clear-cut duties, as their names show: the Bureau of the Census in the Commerce Department, the Forest Service in the Agriculture Department, the Social Security Administration in the Department of Health and Human Services, the Bureau of the Mint in the Treasury Department, the Bureau of Indian Affairs and the Park Service in the Interior Department, and the Bureau of Prisons, Federal Bureau of Investigation (FBI), and Drug Enforcement Administration in the Justice Department.

By assigning certain functions to each unit, placing an official at the head, and holding that official responsible for performance, formal bureaucracy allows for both specialization and coordination, permits ready communication, and in general makes a large and complex organization more manageable.

INFORMAL ORGANIZATION   To look at a formal organization chart is only to *begin* to understand how an agency works, for we also need to understand the informal organization (see Figure 17-2). Bureaucrats differ in attitudes, motives, abilities, experiences, and political clout, and these differences matter. Leadership in an organization is exercised in a variety of places; some officials may have considerably more influence than others with the same formal status. Further, loyalties of officials cut across the formal aims of the agency.

Informal organization can have a significant effect on administration. A subordinate official in an agency might be especially close to the chief because they went to the same college, or they play racquetball together, or because the subordinate knows how to ingratiate himself with the chief. A staff official may have tremendous influence not because of formal authority but because of experience, fairness, common sense, and personality. In an agency headed by a chief who is weak or unimaginative, a vacuum may develop that encourages others to take over. Such informal organization and communication, cutting across regular channels, are inevitable in any organization—public or private, civilian or military.

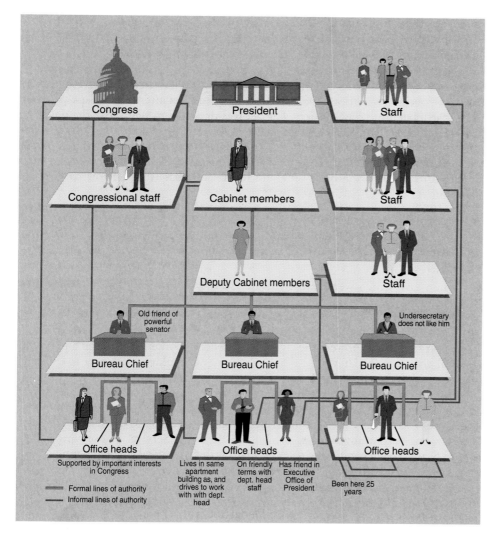

Congress

President

Staff

Congressional staff

Cabinet members

Staff

Deputy Cabinet members

Staff

Old friend of powerful senator

Undersecretary does not like him

Bureau Chief

Bureau Chief

Bureau Chief

Office heads

Office heads

Office heads

Supported by important interests in Congress

Lives in same apartment building as, and drives to work with with dept. head

On friendly terms with dept. head staff

Has friend in Executive Office of President

Been here 25 years

——— Formal lines of authority
———— Informal lines of authority

FIGURE 17-2   Hypothetical Relationships within the Executive Branch

THE BUREAUCRACY IN ACTION

Hiring Practices in the Bureaucracy

Senior government administrators work with the Office of Personnel Management in staffing their agencies. OPM acts as a policy maker for recruiting, examining, and appointing government workers. It advertises for new employees, prepares and administers oral and written examinations throughout the country, and compiles a register of names of those who pass the tests. OPM delegates to individual agencies the responsibility for hiring new personnel, subject to its standards. Individual agencies may promote people from within or transfer a civil servant already in the government. If, however, they wish to consider an "outsider," they request OPM to certify possible candidates from its roster of applicants. OPM typically certifies the top three applicants who have applied for the departmental or agency opening, and the agency normally selects one of these. However, the agency can decide to make no appointment or to request other applicants if it thinks none of the three is qualified.

These procedures are intended to protect the merit principle and to meet agencies' needs for qualified personnel. In practice, the two objectives are not the same. Trade-offs have to be made, particularly between central control by OPM

Hatch Act Rules: What Federal Civilian Employees May and May Not Do

May register and vote as they choose

May assist in voter registration

May express opinions about candidates and issues

May participate in campaigns in their off-duty activities

May contribute money to political organizations or attend political fund-raising functions

May wear or display political badges, buttons, or stickers

May attend political rallies and meetings

May join political clubs or parties

May seek and hold positions in political parties

May campaign for or against referendum questions, constitutional amendments, municipal ordinances

May not be candidates for public office in partisan elections

May not use official authority to interfere with or affect the results of an election

May not collect contributions or sell tickets to political fund-raising functions from subordinate employees

May not solicit funds or discourage the political activity of any person who has business before the employee's office

May not solicit funds or discourage political activity by any person who is the subject of an ongoing audit, investigation, or enforcement action

These rules apply to nearly all federal civil servants. Rules are stricter for military personnel and certain agencies like the FBI, CIA, and Secret Service.

SOURCE: Adapted from the U.S. Merit Systems Protection Board publications and from *Congressional Quarterly*, November 13, 1993, p. 3146.

and delegation of discretionary authority to the agencies. Further, the pursuit of both objectives is enfeebled by the introduction of additional and often incompatible objectives—the veteran preference system, for example.

THE HATCH ACT, OLD AND NEW   In 1939 Congress passed an Act to Prevent Pernicious Political Activities, usually called the **Hatch Act** after its chief sponsor, Senator Carl Hatch of New Mexico. The act was designed to neutralize the danger of a federal civil service being able to shape, if not dictate, the election of presidents and members of Congress. In essence, the Hatch Act permitted federal employees to vote, but not to take an active part in partisan politics. The Hatch Act also made it illegal to dismiss non-policy-making federal officials (those below cabinet and subcabinet rank) for partisan reasons.[8]

In 1993, Congress, with the encouragement of the Clinton administration, overhauled the old Hatch Act and made many forms of participation in partisan politics permissible. The revised Hatch Act still bars federal officials from running as candidates in partisan elections, but it does permit most federal civil servants to hold party positions and involve themselves in party fund raising and campaigning. This new law, which went into effect in 1994, was especially welcomed by those who believed the old Hatch Act discouraged political participation by over two million individuals who might otherwise be vigorous political activists.[9]

Supporters of the old Hatch Act still warn that the best way to achieve an impartial government and protect the rights of all federal workers is through a politically neutral civil service. They hold that a government employee's attempt to influence the votes of others is inconsistent with the spirit of the Constitution.

The new Hatch Act spells out many restrictions on federal bureaucrats to raise campaign funds in their agencies, and it specifically bars nearly all partisan activity for those who work in such highly sensitive federal agencies as the CIA, FBI, Secret Service, and certain divisions of the Internal Revenue Service. Those who work in the U.S. military have stricter rules regulating their political involvement.

EMPLOYEE UNIONS   Since 1962, federal civilian employees have had the right to form unions or associations that represent them in seeking to improve government personnel policies, and about one-third of them have joined such unions. Some of the more important unions representing federal employees today are the American Federation of Government Employees, the National Treasury Employees Union, the National Association of Government Employees, and the National Federation of Federal Employees. Unlike unions in the private sector, these groups lack the right to strike and are not able to bargain over pay and benefits. What can they do? They attempt to negotiate better personnel policies and practices for federal workers, and they represent federal bureaucrats at grievance and disciplinary proceedings. They also lobby Congress on measures affecting personnel changes.

Principles of Bureaucratic Management

Early in this century, several scholars developed a formal model of administration from which they derived certain principles:

1. *Unity of command.* Every officer should have a superior to whom to report and from whom to take orders.

2. *Chain of command.* There should be a firm line of authority running from the top down and responsibility running from the bottom up.

3. *Line and staff.* The staff advises the executive but gives no commands, whereas the line has operating duties.

4. *Span of control.* A hierarchical structure should be established so that no individuals supervise more agencies directly than they can effectively handle.

5. *Decentralization.* When possible, administrators should delegate decisions and responsibilities to lower levels.

Woodrow Wilson, while still a Princeton University professor, adopted many of these views in his writings. Politics and public administration, he said, should be carefully separated. Leave politics to Congress and management to administrators who adhere to the laws passed by Congress. Followers of the noted German sociologist Max Weber contended that a properly run bureaucracy could be a model of efficiency based on rational and impartial management.[10]

The Classical or Textbook Model

According to the textbook model, bureaucrats should be closely controlled by established rules and regulations. Although this is not always true in practice, it is generally the case. Administrators are not free to make any rules they wish or to decide disputes any way they please. Several kinds of limitations exist:

1. The basic legislative power of Congress compels agencies to identify the will of Congress and to interpret and apply laws as Congress would wish. Congress can amend a law to make its intent clearer, conduct oversight hearings and investigations, or restrict appropriations.

2. Congress has closely regulated the procedures to be followed by regulatory agencies. Under the Administrative Procedures Act of 1946, agencies must publicize their procedures and organization, give advance information of proposed rules to interested persons, allow such persons to present written information and arguments, and allow parties appearing before the agency to be accompanied by counsel and to cross-examine witnesses.

3. Under certain conditions, final actions of agencies may be appealed to the courts.

4. Some federal agencies are created for the specific purpose of overseeing and limiting their fellow agencies. Examples are the Office of Management and Budget (OMB) and the General Accounting Office (GAO). In addition to reviewing an agency's budget requests annually in the name of the president, OMB reviews management, organization, and administrative practices on a more or less continuous basis. GAO conducts audits of agency spending and investigates the effectiveness of alternative programs designed for similar ends.

5. Administrators are constrained by informal political checks. They must keep in mind the demands of professional ethics, the advice and criticism of experts, and the attitudes of Congress, the president, interest groups, political parties, private persons, and so on. In the long run, these informal safeguards may be the most important of all.

This classical or textbook model remains influential because it reflects reality. Laws of Congress, although not the whole story, are an important part of the story. Federal agencies and career servants are creatures of the enabling laws under which they work.

Bureaucratic Realities

Suppose Congress passes a law setting federal standards for automobile safety and designates the Department of Transportation to carry out a law that all automobiles must have air bags by 1997. Conflicts over this requirement do not stop with the adoption of the law. Or suppose a president announces that we are about to wage

We The People

Problems Faced by Women Bureaucrats

Although women constitute about 50 percent of the federal career work force, they are severely underrepresented in top positions. And they often complain that male supervisors tend to give preference to other males in hiring and promotions. Some women bureaucrats suggest that men progress more rapidly because they have more opportunities to "network" than women do.

The journal *Government Executive* surveyed 156 of the women serving in the elite Senior Executive Service and found:

- 65 percent said they have the impression that their views were not respected as much as if they were male.
- 63 percent said they have been mistaken for a secretary at a business meeting.
- 54 percent said they have felt that a male subordinate resisted taking direction from them because they were female.
- 30 percent said they felt that their personal lives were scrutinized more closely than those of their male colleagues.
- 21 percent said they have felt sexually harassed.

SOURCE: Bobbi Nodel, "Women in Government," *Government Executive,* August 1988, p. 13.

Should civil servants be given unannounced drug tests?

Some 50 million Americans have tried marijuana, and 20 million are reputed to use it regularly. About 6 million use cocaine, and about 500,000 are heroin addicts. The rise of "crack" is rapidly destroying lives and neighborhoods. Drug use and abuse cost the economy tens of billions in health and criminal justice expenses and lost productivity. The trade puts everyone at risk, not just those who use drugs. Drug use by federal employees can be particularly hazardous, especially by air traffic controllers and top governmental policy makers.

Do the consequences of drug use justify across-the-board, random, unannounced drug and urinalysis tests for policy makers, senior civil servants, and other civil servants as a condition of employment?

war on drug abuse, and Congress appropriates funds and designates the agencies to carry out programs. Politics—conflicts over who is to get what and who is to do what—continue to be important as the policy is applied to changing conditions.

Career administrators are in a good position to know when a program is not operating properly and what action is needed. But one of the major complaints about bureaucrats is that they do not go out of their way to make things better. The problem is that many bureaucrats often learn by hard experience that they are more likely to get into trouble by attempting to improve or change programs than they are if they just do nothing. Hardening of administrative arteries is more likely, some critics say, than administrative aggressiveness.

Often the fiercest battles in Washington are not over principles or programs but over jurisdictional boundaries, personnel cuts, and fringe benefits. Career employees come to believe the expansion of their organization is vital to the public interest. They sometimes become more skillful at building political alliances to protect their own organization than at building alliances to ensure the effectiveness of the programs their organization administers.

Organizations, both public and private, also tend to resist change and to resent "outside" direction, whether by a president or by other external supervisors or boards. A department head in the government, a large corporation, or a university is often likely to consider the president of the organization to be an outsider whose judgment in matters affecting his or her bureau is always suspect.

Career administrators often become involved in politics. Some of them have more bargaining and alliance-building skills than the elected and appointed officials to whom they report. In one sense, agency leaders are at the center of action in Washington. Over time, administrative agencies may come to resemble entrenched pressure groups in that they operate to advance *their own interests*. The FBI is a good example; it is always seeking more funds, new projects, and as much independence as possible from the Justice Department in which it is located.

Career bureaucrats develop a keen sensitivity to the political environment and get caught up in a network of issue experts and politicians who specialize in certain policy areas. With the growth of federal programs has come an explosion in the number of policy aides on Capitol Hill, of Washington law firms that specialize in assisting clients who are interested in policy developments, and of lobbyists (some say at least 40,000) who work with Congress and the federal bureaucracy to advance various economic and professional interests.[11] Groups that perceive real or potential harm to their interests cultivate the bureau chiefs and agency staffs of concern to their programs. They also work closely with the committees or subcommittees of Congress that authorize, appropriate, and oversee programs run by these key bureaucracies. One former cabinet member, testifying before a congressional committee, described the process this way:

> It is a fact, unknown to the general public, that some elements in Congress and some special interest lobbies have never really wanted the departmental Secretaries (cabinet members) to be strong. As everyone in this room knows but few people outside of Washington understand, questions of public policy nominally lodged with the Secretary are often decided far beyond the Secretary's reach by a trinity—not exactly a holy trinity—consisting of (1) representatives of an outside lobby, (2) middle-level bureaucrats, and (3) selected Members of Congress, particularly concerned with appropriations.
>
> In a given field these people may have collaborated for years. They may have formed deep personal and family friendships. They have traded innumerable favors. They have seen Secretaries come and go.... They have a durable alliance that cranks out legislation and appropriations in behalf of their special interest.[12]

Members of Congress cultivate bureau officials, just as special interests nurture close ties with both Congress and bureau heads. Congress controls agency budgets and has the power to approve or deny requests for relevant legislation. Bureau officials are especially careful to develop good relations with members of the congressional committees and subcommittees that handle their legislation and appropriations.

Some bureaucrats become more entangled than others with these external coalitions. Bureau chiefs are logical targets for the efforts of concerned interest groups. On the other hand, recognizing the power of interest groups, bureau chiefs frequently recruit them as allies in pursuing common goals. What these bureau officials have in common with interest groups and their allies in Congress is a shared view that more money should be spent on federal programs run by the bureau in question. These alliances—among bureaucrats, interest groups, and subcommittee members and their staffs on Capitol Hill—are sometimes described as **iron triangles**.

The executive branch is not the smooth operating hierarchy it is made to appear on an organization chart. The president, cabinet members, and their politically appointed undersecretaries and assistant secretaries have their work cut out for them as they try to impose their will on the permanent civil service. Bureaucrats, with their strong allies in Congress and the interest groups, often resist change and direction from their appointed or elected political "superiors." Some view these external relations as "administrative guerrilla warfare" and a serious roadblock to holding elected leaders accountable. Others anticipate a clash over values as inevitable in a system that provides ample opportunities for such clashes. After all, the bureaus themselves are merely one more forum for registering the many demands that make up the people's will.

The Case of Bureau Chief George Brown

The following case is fictional, yet based on actual experiences of a typical bureaucrat. (Note that not only is our main character, George Brown, fictitious, but so are the Bureau of Erosion and the Department of Conservation. Other agencies mentioned do exist.) This case illustrates some of the painful choices bureaucrats have to make.

George Brown is chief of the Bureau of Erosion in the Department of Conservation. A graduate of North Dakota State University, Brown is a career official in the federal service and a member of the Senior Executive Service. He is 47; his appointment to the post was a result of both ability and luck. When his old bureau chief retired, the president wanted to bring in an erosion expert from Illinois, but influential members of Congress pressed for the selection of a recently "retired" (actually he was defeated in the last election!) member of the House of Representatives from a farm state. After deadlock and delay, Brown, then a division head in the Bureau of Erosion, was promoted to bureau chief as a compromise.

Early in March of Brown's second year in his new post, his boss, the secretary of conservation, summoned him and the other bureau heads to an important conference and informed them that he had just attended a cabinet meeting in which the president had called on each department to make at least a 10 percent cut in spending in the coming fiscal year. The president, the secretary reported, was responding to popular demands for federal fiscal restraint.

Brown quickly calculated what this cutback would mean for his agency. For several years the Bureau of Erosion had been spending about $800 million a year to help farmers protect their farmland. Could it get along on about $700 million, and where could savings be made? Returning to his office, Brown called a meeting of his personnel, budget, and management officials. After hours of discussion, it was agreed that savings could be effected only by decreasing the scope of the program, a step that would involve terminating about 1,500 of the bureau's employees. Brown asked his subordinates to prepare a list of employees who were the least useful to the bureau. He would decide which to drop after checking with the affected members of Congress.

Unannounced drug testing raises serious Fourth Amendment questions. The idea that a group of people should be subjected to random searches without reasonable individual cause has been resisted since the outset of our life as a nation. When Congress, or the president, or the head of a federal agency requires testing as a condition of employment, even if evidence of drug use would not be used to dismiss employees, skeptical judges must be persuaded that the testing is not an "unreasonable" search and seizure.

The Supreme Court ruled in two 1989 decisions involving railway workers and U.S. Customs Service employees that mandatory blood and urine tests may be required for certain workers without a showing of "individualized suspicion." Writing for the Court in the railway workers' case, Justice Anthony Kennedy said the government's interest in testing even without a showing of individual suspicion is compelling. Employees subject to the tests discharge duties fraught with such risks of injury to others that even a momentary lapse of attention can have disastrous results.

The two cases dealt with post-accident testing of railway personnel on duty at the time of a major accident and with customs officials who carry firearms, handle classified information, or intercept drugs.

Drug testing of all federal employees, or even only those in policy-making positions, presents difficult constitutional issues. Supporters of privacy rights and civil liberties are uncomfortable with carrying this policy too far. Drug testing, some concede, may be necessary for certain individuals where public safety is genuinely involved, but it is not needed and would be an unconstitutional deprivation of privacy rights under the Fourth Amendment as a general policy.

Admiral Hyman G. Rickover, Bureaucratic Rebel

The career of the late Admiral Hyman G. Rickover points up the limits on the authority of presidents and cabinet members over some bureaucrats. Rickover served as an officer for 63 years, longer than any other naval officer in American history. Hailed for supervising the production of the nuclear-powered submarine, he often bullied subordinates, intimidated superiors, and in general attacked the naval bureaucracy. For more than 30 years Admiral Rickover worked with powerful members of Congress to build a nuclear-powered navy, often in complete and open defiance of the chief of naval operations, the secretary of defense, and the president. He outlasted 14 secretaries of defense, 14 secretaries of the navy, and at least 10 chiefs of naval operations. Time and again Congress chose to listen to Rickover rather than to his superiors, even when they had vigorous backing from various presidents. Yet Rickover was an admiral in the U.S. Navy and as such was presumably subject to the authority of many of those whom he defied.

One reason for Rickover's success was that his ships worked better than promised. Another reason was that he had unwavering support from the members of the Armed Services Committees of both the House and the Senate and from members of the Joint Committee on Atomic Energy. "Rickover's skill at cultivating Congress—he works the hallways of congressional office buildings as assiduously as any lobbyist for a cause—has given his supporters on the Hill a sense that they also played a key role in creating the nuclear fleet."*

*Juan Cameron, "Admiral Rickover's Final Battle," *Fortune*, November 1976, p. 200.

A few weeks later Brown presented a $710 million budget to Secretary Jones, who approved it and passed it along to the White House. The president then went over the figures in a conference with the director of the Office of Management and Budget, and a few weeks later the White House submitted the budget for the whole executive department, incorporating the Erosion Bureau's $710 million, to Congress.

Meanwhile Brown was running into trouble. News of the proposed budget cut had leaked immediately to the bureau's personnel in the field. Nobody knew who would be dropped if the cut went through, and some officials were already looking around for other positions. Morale fell. Hearing of the cut, farmers' representatives in Washington notified local farm organizations throughout the country. Soon Brown began to receive letters demanding certain services be maintained. Members of the farm bloc in Congress were also becoming restless.

Shortly after the president's budget went to Congress, Representative Jim Smith of Kansas asked Brown to meet with him. Smith was chair of the Subcommittee on Agriculture of the influential House Appropriations Committee and thus a powerful factor in congressional treatment of the budget. Smith said he had consulted his fellow subcommittee members, both Democratic and Republican, and they all agreed the Erosion Bureau's cut must not go through. The farmers needed even more than the usual $800 million because of severe flood conditions in some sections of the country. He warned they would rise up in arms if the program were reduced. Members of Congress from agricultural areas, Smith went on, were under tremendous pressure. Leaders of farm groups in Washington were mobilizing farmers everywhere. Besides, Smith said, the president was unfair in cutting down on the farm program; he did not understand agricultural problems, and he failed to recognize that programs designed to increase agricultural output were the best way to reduce the trade imbalance. Let the cuts in federal programs be made elsewhere.

Smith then came to the point. Brown, he said, must vigorously oppose the budget cut. Hearings on appropriations would begin in a few days, and Brown as bureau chief would, of course, testify. At that time he must insist that the cuts would hurt the bureau and undermine its whole program. Brown would not have to volunteer this statement, Smith said. He could just respond to leading questions put by committee members. Brown's testimony, Smith thought, would help clinch the argument against the cut because the committee would respect the judgment of the administrator closest to the problem. Other bureaucrats were fighting to save their appropriations. Obviously, said Smith, they are counting on public reaction to get them exemptions from the 10 percent cutback, and Brown would be foolish not to do the same.

Brown was in an embarrassing position. He had submitted his estimates to the secretary of conservation and to the president, and it was his duty to back them up. The rules of the game demanded, moreover, that agency heads defend budget estimates submitted to Congress, whatever their personal feelings might be. The president had appointed Brown to his position and had a right to expect loyalty. On the other hand, Brown was on the spot with his own agency. The employees all expected their chief to look out for them. Brown had developed cordial relations with his staff, and he squirmed at the thought of having to let more than a thousand employees go. What would they think when they heard him defend the cut? More important, he wanted to maintain friendly relations with the farmers, the farm organizations, and the farm bloc in Congress. Finally, Brown was committed to his program. He grasped its true importance, whereas the president's budget advisers did not. And he knew that his pet project—aid to poverty-stricken areas in Appalachia—would probably be sacrificed because it was not supported by a powerful constituency.

Brown turned for advice to an old friend in the Office of Management and Budget. This friend urged him to defend the president's budget. He appealed to Brown's professional pride as an administrator and career public servant. He reminded him that the chief executive must have control of the budget and that agency heads must subordinate their interests to the executive program. He said the only way to balance the budget would be for all agencies to make program cuts. As for the employees to be dropped—well, that was part of the game. Some of them might be able to get jobs in other government agencies; civil service would protect their status. Anyway, they would understand Brown's position. In a parting shot he that mentioned the president had Brown in mind for bigger things.

The next day Brown had lunch with a North Dakota senator, wise and experienced in Washington ways, who had helped him get his start in government. The senator was sympathetic. But there was no doubt about what Brown should do, the senator said. He should follow Representative Smith's plan, of course, being as diplomatic as possible about it. That way he would protect his position with those who would be most important in the long run.

"After all," the senator said, "presidents come and go, parties rise and fall, but Smith and the other members of Congress will be here a long time, and so will the farm organizations. They can do a lot for you in future years. And remember one other thing," the senator concluded. "These people are the elected representatives of the people. Constitutionally, Congress has the power to spend money as it sees fit. Why should you object if they want to spend an extra 70 or 80 million?"

Leaving the Dirksen Senate Office Building, Brown realized his dilemma was worse than ever. The arguments on both sides were persuasive. He felt hopelessly divided in his loyalties and responsibilities. The president expected one thing of him; Congress expected another. As a professional administrator, he felt obliged to side with the president. As head of a bureau, however, he wanted to protect his team and his programs. His future? Whatever decision he made, he was bound to antagonize important people and interests.

After much soul searching, Brown decided the issue involved more than loyalties, ambitions, and programs. Ultimately it boiled down to two questions: First, to whom was he, Brown, legally and administratively responsible? Formally, of course, he was responsible to the chief executive who appointed him, who was accountable to the people. Brown knew, too, that he was accountable to Congress, which after all has the power over all fiscal matters. Second, which course of action did he think was better for the welfare of all the people? Looking at the question this way, he believed the president was right in asking for fiscal restraint. As a taxpayer and consumer himself, Brown recognized the need to reduce the federal budget deficit. To be sure, Congress must make the final decision. Yet to make the decision, Congress had to act on the advice of the administration, and the administration should speak with one voice for the majority of the people, or it should not be speaking out at all.

With mixed feelings Brown decided to support the president. Being a seasoned alliance builder, however, he hedged his bets. He came out strongly for the president's budget, yet at the same time he sent friendly members of Congress some questions to be asked of him in future hearings so he could explain the impact of the cutbacks. He also circulated to some of these same members of Congress an analysis of the impact of personnel and funding cuts in their states and districts.

J. Edgar Hoover, Consummate Bureaucrat

J. Edgar Hoover (1895–1972), chief of the Federal Bureau of Investigation for almost half a century, was in theory subject to direction from the attorney general and the president of the United States. In fact, he was so popular with Congress and the public that he was practically immune to control. Part of this "popularity," we now know, came from his investigatory power, which was feared as well as abused. That immunity served the country poorly at times, such as when Hoover was able to wiretap Dr. Martin Luther King, Jr., or others he disliked, but it served the country well when Hoover was able to thwart President Richard Nixon and his aides in certain of their illegal efforts to undermine political opponents.* But how safe is a democracy when the administrative head of a major agency can defy even the elected president?

*See Anthony Summers, *Official and Confidential: The Secret Life of J. Edgar Hoover* (Putnam, 1993).

Red Tape

The term "red tape" comes from the ribbon English civil servants once used to tie up and bind legal documents. Today, along with taxes and death, we think of red tape as an inevitable aspect of bureaucratic inefficiency. We are annoyed when we have to wait in lines while officials check files or consult with their supervisors. We are furious when officials lose important documents. Red tape often takes the form of an official's punctilious adherence to rigid procedures. We may view it as a hopeless tangle of rules and regulations that keep public servants from doing anything but stamping and shuffling papers.

But these same rules and regulations help ensure that public servants act impartially. In other words, red tape stems from our desire not to give public servants too much discretion and to hold them accountable. After all, they are spending our money. Remember, too, that one person's red tape is another person's prudent system or proper cautiousness.

Our fictional account of George Brown and similar case studies leads to three important generalizations about bureaucrats:

1. **Bureaucrats are people, not robots, and are subject to many influences—the president, OMB, the cabinet, the House, the Senate, the courts, competing interest groups, public opinion, as well as their own sense of what is right.**

2. **Bureaucrats do not respond merely to orders from the top but to a variety of motives stemming from their own personalities, political attitudes, educational and professional backgrounds, formal and informal organization and communication, and the political context in which they operate.**

3. **Bureaucrats are important in government. Some of them have considerable discretion and make decisions of great significance. The cumulative effect of all their policies and actions on our daily lives is enormous.**

WHAT THE PUBLIC THINKS OF BUREAUCRATS AND THE BUREAUCRACY

Big bureaucracy in the abstract is unpopular, especially when it is out of sight and what it does is little understood. It engages in so many activities that most people find something it does offensive (like taxing them, inspecting them, or regulating them). Big bureaucracy is sometimes defined as that part of the government people dislike.

Civil servants, as individuals, are appreciated, but as a class they are not. Citizens who have dealings with federal employees on a face-to-face basis say they are pleased by employees' performance. In contrast to scorn for bureaucrats and bureaucracy in the abstract, Americans seem to approve the conduct of individual federal employees—Postal Service delivery persons, forest rangers, Veterans Affairs Department officials, or the county field agents who help with the local 4-H programs. They also admire astronauts, marines, FBI agents, and Coast Guard officers, all of whom are also federal employees.

Still, bureaucrats as a group are a favorite punching bag—a convenient scapegoat—for reporters and politicians who want to place the blame on someone for things that go wrong in government. An irreverent journal in the nation's capital, *The Washington Monthly*, rails against clumsy bureaucracy in every issue. Most newspapers and magazines feature stories and cartoons critical of the federal bureaucracy.

Red Tape and Waste

We Americans are generally skeptical of, if not cynical about, big government. We equate bigness with remoteness, incompetence, and unresponsiveness. We also assume that the bigger government gets, the less efficient it is, and the more it wastes. Perhaps the most criticized aspect of the federal bureaucracy is that career public employees seem to enjoy the closest thing to job security; they are almost as secure in their jobs as if they were confirmed for life on the Supreme Court. For all practical purposes, federal workers can neither be fairly punished nor justly rewarded. Hence most of them, critics say, perform the bare minimum.

When Thomas Jefferson was president, the federal government employed 2,120 persons: Indian commissioners, postmasters, collectors of customs, tax

THE BUREAUCRATS: PAPER SHUFFLERS OR EMPIRE BUILDERS?

One of the paradoxes of public attitudes toward bureaucrats is that some of the time we criticize federal employees for working too little, for being lazy, or for lacking initiative—for failing to abide by the so-called work ethic. Yet at the same time we view federal workers as too powerful and we accuse them of intervening in or regulating our lives far too much. Can bureaucrats in reality be both timid *and* empire builders? In fact, there are enough bureaucrats to fulfill all kinds of contrasting stereotypes, so despite the seeming contradiction, perhaps both views are valid.

Even federal employees gripe about the system. Although top federal employees say they like the challenge of their work, the opportunity to participate in forming and managing important policies, and the quality of people with whom they work, most workers dislike the rigidity, the red tape, and the frustrations of dealing with interest groups and politicians.

"Think of it. Presidents come and go, but WE go on forever!"

Berry's World. Reproduced by permission of NEA, Inc.

CRITICISMS OF FEDERAL WORKERS

BUREAUCRATS AS PAPER-SHUFFLING CLERKS ARE:

Timid and indecisive
Flabby, overpaid, and lazy
Ruled by inertia
Unimaginative
Devoted to rigid procedures
Slow to accept new ideas
Slow to abandon unsuccessful policies
Impersonal and lacking individuality
Red tape artists
On "one long coffee break"

BUREAUCRATS AS THE REAL POWER IN WASHINGTON ARE:

A self-anointed elite in our nation's capital
An oppressive foreign power
The fourth branch of government
Intolerably meddlesome
A demanding giant
The permanent government
Superbureaucrats who wield vast power
Influential enough to do great injury
Intrusive, arrogant empire builders

WHAT TOP FEDERAL CAREER EMPLOYEES LIKE LEAST AND MOST ABOUT THEIR WORK

LIKE LEAST:

Inability to take personnel actions that should be a manager's prerogative (e.g., hiring and discipline)
Inadequate resources (e.g., personnel, budget)
Personal financial sacrifice
Red tape
Frustrations in dealing with interest groups and Congress

LIKE MOST:

Challenging assignments
Opportunity to have an impact on policy programs
Opportunity for public service
Opportunity to use and expand one's knowledge and skills
Caliber of colleagues

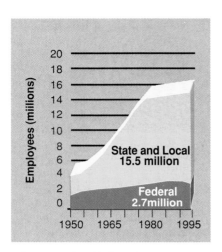

FIGURE 17-3   **Civilian Government Employees**

SOURCE: Bureau of Labor Statistics, U.S. Department of Labor.

Henry Cisneros, former mayor of San Antonio, Texas, is the secretary of Housing and Urban Development. He has worked to streamline the implementation of housing policy and ensure the integrity of HUD's contract procedures.

collectors, marshals, lighthouse keepers, and clerks. Today the president heads an executive branch of, as noted earlier, nearly 2.8 million civilians and slightly under 1.8 million military employees, who work in at least 2,000 units of federal administration (see Figure 17-3). Critics today say the federal bureaucracy is too large. One thing is certain—government bureaucracy is a major part of our society.

1. In the last 20 years, more than 250 new federal agencies or bureaus have been created; fewer than two dozen have been disbanded. One new one is the recently created office to promote national service volunteering. One disbanded one was the Office of Economic Opportunity, which had been responsible for the War on Poverty during the 1960s.

2. The national government owns one-third of the nation's land and nearly 50 percent of the land west of Denver, Colorado. The Department of Defense alone owns land equivalent to the size of the state of Virginia. The government in recent years has held title to 400,000 buildings and rented 50,000 buildings.

3. For every worker on the federal civilian payroll, three or four workers earn their living indirectly from the federal government as consultants and contractors. In other words, there may be about 8 to 10 million "invisible federal employees" as the government contracts out more of its work.

No wonder people often conclude that government is trying to do too much, in too great detail, on too many subjects, for too many separate purposes. Some people suggest that before Congress can enact a new law, it should be required to repeal two existing ones. The central problem with the bureaucracy, critics add, is not that it exists, but that we have failed to subject it to the control and discipline alleged to operate in the private sector.

A corporation president who served as secretary of the treasury said one of the lessons he learned about working in government was "that the tests of efficiency and cost-effectiveness which are the basic standards of business, are in government not the only—and frequently not even the major—criteria."[13] President Gerald Ford put it this way: "One of the enduring truths of the nation's capital is that bureaucrats *survive*. Agencies don't fold their tents and quietly fade away after their work is done. They find Something New to Do. Invariably, that Something New involves more people with more power and more paperwork—all involving more expenditures."[14]

Critics say, too, that the incentive system in the national bureaucracy seems to promote growth and inefficiency. Growth in a bureau improves employee chances for promotion and higher salaries, so a significant portion of time is devoted to its expansion. In short, one of the most common complaints is that our national civil servants seldom have any incentive to save taxpayers money. Systems that might encourage efficiency appear to be lacking; on the contrary, everything seems to tempt them in the opposite direction.

Another charge leveled against bureaucrats is that once a program is established, the people assigned to it become committed to the "cause." In the Office of Civil Rights in the Department of Education, for example, appointments generally go to those concerned about protecting the rights of women and minorities. The protection of rights is their assigned task, and in their zeal they strengthen their authority. Those assigned to the Drug Enforcement Administration are likely to be convinced that enforcement of the federal laws against narcotics is of supreme importance; in carrying out their duties, they sometimes go beyond their vested authority. Groups outside the government who want their programs carried forward pressure the agencies; women's groups and minority advocacy groups carefully watch the Office of Civil Rights, for instance.

A Positive Perspective

Bureaucracy is a function not only of governments but also of corporations, universities, and private associations. It is a reality of modern existence. The challenge in the 1990s is not to wish away or complain about big bureaucracies, but to learn how to improve their performance and make them more efficient and accountable. Recent efforts at some state and local government levels have made their bureaucracies more entrepreneurial. The cities of St. Paul, Minnesota, and Indianapolis, Indiana, and the states of Florida under Governor Lawton Chiles and Massachusetts under Governor William Weld have introduced various market incentives, rewards, and public/private partnerships that encourage efficiency and responsiveness. The strategies used in these places and elsewhere are detailed in David Osborne and Ted Gaebler's *Reinventing Government: How the Entrepreneurial Spirit Is Transforming the Public Sector.*[15] Competition and incentives can prudently be built into various government monopolies so that bureaucracies become more responsive to their customers.

A comparison of the performance of our bureaucracy with most bureaucracies in the world suggests we should be grateful for the service we get from our public employees. The U.S. Postal Service provides a good example. Although it is criticized as being the last dinosaur, it is faster, more efficient, and less costly than comparable services around the world. Another example is the United States tax system; it is the most effective such system in the world.

It may come as a surprise to those who criticize big bureaucracy and waste that the size of the federal bureaucracy has remained fairly stable for the past generation, despite population growth and the expansion of many federal programs. Some bureaucracies actually shrank. For example, both the postal and the military services have experienced major cutbacks in personnel in recent years. The growth that does occur is often due to population or workload expansion rather than Parkinson's Law of bureaucratic "empire building." Little evidence is available to support contentions that bigness necessarily creates inefficiency and rigidity. Some studies even come to the opposite conclusion. Surely the success of General Electric and Motorola in the private sector and the Universities of California and Michigan in the public sector suggest some virtues of complex bureaucracies.

Compared to most other nations, U.S. government employment has not grown. Government employment grew by more than 20 percent in Sweden in the past generation and by over 11 percent in Italy and Germany during the same period. There has been a decline in U.S. government employment during the last ten years, especially since the end of the cold war. Moreover, government employment as a percentage of total employment in the United States is 30 to 50 percent lower than in these Western European democracies.

"Reinventing Government" in the 1990s

The Clinton administration has continued the downsizing of the Defense Department, including both military and civilian employees, begun during the Bush presidency. Clinton hopes to cut the size of the federal civilian work force by over 250,000 before 1998 and cut the White House staff by 25 percent. As noted at the beginning of this chapter, Clinton assigned Vice-President Al Gore

Do Government Agencies Ever Fade Away?

Herbert Kaufman, a student of bureaucracies, set out a few years ago to study whether government agencies ever die. He began by looking at 175 agencies in selected areas of the national government that existed in 1923 and then traced them for the next 50 years. All but 27 were alive and well in 1973. In the meantime scores of new agencies had been created to work in these same areas. Death of a bureaucracy is the exception rather than the rule. The birth of new units continues, regardless of whether a Democrat or a Republican occupies the White House. Additional bureaucracies seem to be encouraged by sudden shifts in economic conditions or international tensions or by a "built-in thrust that...assists the even finer division of labor in organizations." Excessive workloads in existing agencies, pressure by groups who believe a new agency will be more sympathetic to their point of view, and a variety of societal change factors all work to create more units of government.

SOURCE: Herbert Kaufman, *Are Government Organizations Immortal?* (Brookings Institution, 1976), p. 67.

One of Bill Clinton's campaign promises was that his administration would "reinvent government" to get rid of bureaucratic waste and inefficiency. His vice-president, Al Gore, was assigned the task of working out a plan, which Clinton is shown here releasing to the public.

Can private and public organizations learn management techniques from one another?

Can management and leadership strategies used by General Electric, Apple Computers, or Prentice Hall be used as easily in the public bureaucracies of government? What do you think?

the responsibility to create a federal government that works better and costs less. Gore and his associates were guided by four principles for federal agencies: measure results; put the customer (the U.S. citizen) in the driver's seat; introduce competition and a market orientation wherever possible; and decentralize whenever possible.[16]

Gore's report on the bureaucracy's performance made 800 recommendations for encouraging efficiency, productivity, and responsiveness in government operations. Some recommendations from the 1993 Gore report were:

- Close or consolidate 1,200 field offices of the Department of Agriculture.
- Allow the sale of the Alaska Power Administration.
- Reduce the number of Department of Education programs from 230 to 189.
- Eliminate federal support payments (subsidies) for mohair, wool, and honey.
- Remove people who are no longer disabled from disability insurance rolls.
- Allow all federal agencies funds for creative innovation.
- Encourage market-based approaches to reduce pollution.
- Eliminate the Government Printing Office's monopoly on publishing government documents and reports.
- Reduce the time required to fire incompetent federal employees by half.
- Insist that all agencies survey customers, measure customer satisfaction, and establish service standards equal to the best in business.

BUREAUCRATIC RESPONSIVENESS

One of the most complex questions concerning public bureaucracies is whether they are responsive enough to the citizens and the elected officials who represent them. Being *responsive* means being quick to react and treating those who need assistance sympathetically. Determining how responsive an agency is depends on the perceptions of the person involved. A person who has had to stand for hours in a long line, whether at the post office or at a welfare agency, will complain about unresponsive bureaucrats. Someone who has a problem that a federal bureaucrat treats "by the book" rather than by common sense also develops a critical view.

Standard Operating Procedures

Bureaucracies develop routines and standard operating procedures to ensure efficiency and productivity. Unfortunately, reliance on routine reduces flexibility. Just about everyone has at one time or another been turned away from the local post office because a package to be mailed was too large, or too small, or in the wrong kind of container. It is hard on such occasions to hold back our anger: Why can't they be flexible? Why can't they be reasonable? Why can't they deal with me in a personal way?

Procedures that allow the post office, the army, or the Internal Revenue Service to perform efficiently sometimes also diminish their ability to respond to the personalized needs of individuals. Routines help to prevent chaos and allow government behavior to be consistent, uniform, and impartial. The inevitable and necessary result of big bureaucracy is often a trade-off; quick, personalized, and sympathetic service is sacrificed for order.

Privatization

Can certain problems be better handled by agencies other than government bureaucracies? For example, should the government run railways, prisons, and a public television channel, or should we encourage the private sector and free market mechanisms to handle these responsibilities?

Privatization is the process of contracting public services to private organizations. Examples of privatization include the contracting out by San Francisco of its budget analysis to a private firm, contracting out by Massachusetts of much of its tax collecting, and contracting out by the city of Chelsea, Massachusetts, of the operation of its schools to Boston University. The National Aeronautics and Space Administration contracts out most of the manufacturing of its space vehicles.

Private or nonprofit firms handle a vast array of services, from repairing ships to delivering "meals-on-wheels" to the home-bound elderly. Some people suggest that our state and federal prisons might be more effectively operated by private firms. Advocates of privatization claim it would reduce costs and provide better service than reliance on the federal bureaucracy.[17]

Critics of privatization point to the cost overruns and waste in the procurement of weapons systems as failures of privatization. Those who advocate privatization on the ideological grounds that business is always superior to government are, according to David Osborne and Ted Gaebler, "selling the American people snake oil." Privatization is one answer, they say, but not *the* answer:

> Services can be contracted out or turned over to the private sector. But *governance* cannot. We can privatize discrete [governmental programs], but not the overall process of governance. If we did, we would have no mechanism by which to make collective decisions, no way to set the rules of the marketplace, no means to enforce rules of behavior. We would lose all sense of equity and altruism: services that could not generate a profit, whether housing for the homeless or health care for the poor, would barely exist....
>
> Business does some things better than government, but government does some things better than business. The public sector tends to be better, for instance, at policy management, regulation, ensuring equity, preventing discrimination or exploitation, ensuring continuity and stability of services, and ensuring social cohesion....Business tends to do better at performing economic tasks, innovating, replicating successful experiments, adapting to rapid change, abandoning unsuccessful or obsolete activities, and performing complex or technical tasks.[18]

Would we be better off if the U.S. Postal Service were turned over to private firms? A business executive who recently served as postmaster general, Anthony Frank, says no. He praises the Postal Service for its high on-time delivery and points out that all Americans, no matter where they live, get essentially the same service at the same price. "If you privatize it," Frank pointed out in 1992, "the cost would go up for a lot of Americans. Twenty-nine cents compared to anywhere else in the world is an incredible bargain," says Frank. "It's 67 cents in Germany, 47 cents in Japan, and 42 cents in Canada. And they don't have any overnight service."[19]

BUREAUCRATIC ACCOUNTABILITY

The question of *bureaucratic responsiveness* is extremely difficult to disentangle from the question of *bureaucratic accountability*. In determining the responsiveness of the U.S. Navy or the FBI or the Department of Transportation, we must also ask who should oversee and control them.

Thinking it Through

Many similarities exist between private and public organizations. Middle-level managers in a bank and in the Internal Revenue Service, for example, have similar managerial tasks and similar organizational goals. Personnel in welfare organizations can learn from the Red Cross or a well-run private hospital how to deliver their services. The Postal Service has obviously picked up some strategies from United Parcel Service (UPS) and Federal Express. Morale building and organizational restructuring are needed in public as well as private enterprises.

Yet differences exist, too. Demands for accountability and equity are greater in the public sector than in the private corporation. Efficiency is only one of the goals of a government agency, not its primary goal. Unable to be single-minded in pursuing efficiency, a public-sector organization will seldom be as efficient as a private-sector business. "Those who focus on the similarities of public and private sectors tend to have an image of a civil service that is hierarchically subordinate to, and solely responsive to, the president and his priorities. That image is unrealistic given the structure and design of this country's government."

SOURCE: Edie N. Goldenberg, "The Grace Commission and Civil Service Reform," in *The Unfinished Agenda for Civil Service Reform*, ed. Charles H. Levine (Brookings Institution, 1985), p. 90.

To whom should bureaucrats be accountable?

One of the important challenges in American government is how to keep nonelected government workers (bureaucrats) accountable to the taxpayers. After all, whose bureaucracy is this, anyway? Part of the challenge is figuring out how accountability can be guaranteed. How should the day-to-day operations and behavior of the typical U.S. public bureaucrat be controlled? From this list of possibilities, select one or more as your preferences.

> The Constitution
> Laws and statutes
> Congress
> The president
> Their administrative superiors, including bureau chiefs and cabinet officers
> Their own view of "the public interest"
> Court rulings
> Public opinion
> Interest groups
> The media
> Their profession
> Public-employee unions
> Political parties and their platforms
> Intellectual opinion
> Their co-workers and colleagues
> Taxpayers

You Decide!

Should bureaucrats be accountable to the president's cabinet, the majority who elected the president, or the majority in Congress? Plainly, most Americans would like the bureaucracy to be responsive to the public interest. But defining the public interest is the crucial problem. The president and the House and the Senate and the committees of Congress all claim to speak on behalf of the public interest. Moreover, to whom bureaucrats should be accountable is an inherently *political* question. Certain forms of accountability favor some groups and interests over others. Accountability to the White House, for example, depends in large measure on the supporters' partisanship toward the president. Republicans, not surprisingly, favor strong presidential control over the bureaucracy when Republicans occupy the White House, as do Democrats when their party wins the White House.

To the President

Modern presidents invariably contend the president should be in charge, for the chief executive is responsive to the broadest constituency. A president, it is argued, must see that popular needs and expectations are converted into administrative action. When the nation elects a conservative president who favors cutbacks in federal programs and less governmental intervention in the economy, his policies must be carried out by the bureaucracy. The voters' wishes can be translated into action only if the bureaucrats support presidential policies.

Yet, as we have seen, under the American system of checks and balances the party winning a presidential election does not acquire control of the national government or even of the executive branch itself. Under our Constitution, the president is not even the undisputed master of the executive structure. Congress sets up the agencies, broadly determines their organization, provides money, and establishes the ground rules under which they operate. Congress constantly reviews the activities of the bureaucrats in appropriation hearings, special investigations, or informal inquiries. And, as we have also seen, the Senate confirms important cabinet-level leaders.

Presidents come into an ongoing system over which they have little control and within which they have little leeway to make the bureaucracy responsive. Still, some presidential control over the bureaucracy may be exercised through the powers of *appointment, reorganization,* and *budgeting.* More specifically, a president can attempt to control the bureaucracy by appointing or promoting sympathetic personnel, mobilizing public opinion and congressional pressure, changing the administrative apparatus, influencing budget decisions, using extensive personal persuasion, and if all else fails, shifting a bureaucracy's assignment to another department or agency (although this requires tacit if not explicit congressional approval).

Presidents appoint about 4,000 people to top positions within the executive branch; however, many of these are confidential assistants or special aides to cabinet officers. Moreover, many require Senate confirmation and are not exclusively a president's choice. Some suggest that a president's hand could be strengthened if the chief executive were able to make two or three times as many political appointments.

ASSISTANT SECRETARIES: A WEAK LINK   Although presidents can usually recruit to their cabinets people of prominence and influence, they find it much harder to hire outstanding people at the assistant secretary level. Assistant secretaries infuse the views and values of the White House into the federal bureaucracy. These citizen-leaders serve as links between the people who elect the presidents and the civil servants. Many people, however, are not willing to interrupt their professional or business careers to become assistant secretaries.

Over the last several years the position has become one of relatively low pay, little prestige in Washington, short tenure (people stay, on average, barely two years in these posts), and high cost to one's family. As a result, presidents often fill these slots with relatively young people who, from the day they arrive in Washington, are looking for their next job. These assistant secretaries, or people in comparable appointed posts, are forced to wear "kid gloves" with those they are supposed to regulate because it is from them that their next job is often likely to come. Others have strong ideological convictions but little experience in administration and congressional politics. Still others use the position as a transition to retirement.

These presidential appointees have to deal with civil servants who know their "bosses" will not be there long. Most civil servants have virtually secure jobs, and sometimes all they have to do to ignore presidentially selected assistant secretaries is to wait them out for a year or two. Moreover, in and around Washington, government workers constitute a powerful political group. Assistant secretaries who try to significantly alter the policy directions of those who are supposedly under their supervision may do so at considerable political and legal peril.

THE SENIOR EXECUTIVE SERVICE The Civil Service Reform Act of 1978 created a Senior Executive Service. This pool of more than 8,000 career officials (which can include up to 10 percent political appointees by an administration) can be filled without senatorial confirmation, and its individual members are subject to transfer from one program to another within a department according to an administration's wishes. The service was created to make senior career bureaucrats—especially those enmeshed in issue networks—more responsive to the goals and policy preferences of the White House. This new service gave presidents greater flexibility in selecting, promoting, and rewarding with financial bonuses those in the top career service who are productive and responsive.

The Civil Service Reform Act of 1978 was viewed with skepticism. Some feared an executive service would be put to political use. Others worried that without strong White House support, the noble intentions of the act would not be achieved. The Senior Executive Service has not lived up to many of its creators' expectations. It has had little impact on the federal workers it was supposed to help. Because of federal budgetary problems, the bonuses and related incentives have been less than was expected. Morale in the senior ranks of the federal bureaucracy is pretty much the same as it was before the service was created. The White House, however, has enjoyed an increase in the flexibility of assignments, and recent presidents have shrewdly used this flexibility to their advantage to influence and discipline the upper reaches of the executive branch.

THE OFFICE OF MANAGEMENT AND BUDGET Ever since Franklin Roosevelt strengthened the presidential staffs, the budget bureau (currently called the Office of Management and Budget) has been a key resource. OMB's primary task is to prepare the president's annual budget. The budget is a major vehicle for shaping a president's policy priorities. It is the place and the process that determine which programs will get more funds, which will be cut, and which will remain the same. Departments and agencies fight to win larger chunks of the president's budget projections. OMB supervises the preparation of the budget

As attorney general, Janet Reno supervises the FBI, the federal marshals, U.S. attorneys, and the team of lawyers who represent the government in federal court. She accepted responsibility for the actions of federal law enforcement agents in the fire and deaths that followed the standoff at the Branch Davidian compound in 1993.

Thinking it Through

Most bureaucrats, most of the time, follow guidelines provided either in the law or by their administrative superiors, but at times many factors come into play as bureaucrats have to exercise judgment and discretion. Many of the considerations listed in the You Decide box on the facing page shape bureaucratic behavior implicitly rather than explicitly. Much of this chapter has analyzed the question of bureaucratic accountability. Perhaps it will revise your thinking.

Why Presidents Occasionally Reorganize the Bureaucracy

- *Shake up* an organization to increase managerial control
- *Simplify or streamline* the bureaucracy or a specific agency
- *Reduce costs* by lessening overlap, duplication, inefficiencies
- *Symbolize priorities* by signaling new responsibilities in new agencies
- *Improve program effectiveness* by bringing separate but logically related programs to the same agency
- *Improve policy integration* by placing competitive or conflicting interests within a single organization
- *Downgrade* the importance of a program to weaken it
- *Increase power* over an unresponsive agency by installing their own people.

and hence assists very directly in the formulation of policy. It weighs and evaluates the merits of the countless proposals and pleas that constantly pour in upon the White House.

Ninety-six percent of OMB's staff are career officials trained to evaluate ongoing projects and new spending requests. OMB's top officials are presidential appointees, and they are often among a president's most important advisers. They help a president make critical decisions not only about the budget but also about management practices, collaborative efforts among government agencies, and legislative planning. OMB makes sure that both the departments and Congress are informed of the president's legislative preferences and plays an important role in expanding the policy and administrative options open to a president.[20]

To Congress

Congress has a number of ways to exercise control over the bureaucracy: by establishing agencies, formulating budgets, appropriating funds, confirming personnel, authorizing new programs or new shifts in direction, conducting investigations and hearings, reorganizing authority, and rebuking officials.

The foundation of this bureaucratic power is legal authority. A bureaucrat's information and expertise augment this legal authority. Ordinarily, bureaucrats know more than anyone else about their programs and the consequences of what they are doing. Recognizing this, Congress may request agency heads to make initial proposals and provide cost and price estimates. To reduce bureaucratic deception, Congress has imposed stiff penalties for providing misleading information.

Still, Congress is under fire, at least in some quarters, for encouraging the growth of federal spending and for deliberately allowing the bureaucracy to remain too independent. Members of Congress, so this reasoning goes, profit from the growth and complexity of the federal government. Most constituents, especially businesspeople, turn to their members of Congress for help as they battle federal red tape. Hence, as the federal bureaucracy and its funds grow, so does the influence of members of Congress. Members of Congress regularly earn political credit by interceding in federal agencies on behalf of their constituents.

> The brutal fact is that only a small minority of our 535 members of Congress would trade the present bureaucratic structure for one which was an efficient, effective agent of the general interest—the political payoffs of the latter are lower than those of the former. Congressional talk of inefficient, irresponsible, out-of-control bureaucracy is typically just that—talk—and when it is not, it usually refers to agencies under the jurisdiction of other legislators' committees. Why do reformers continually ignore the fact that Congress has all the power necessary to enforce the "people's will" on the bureaucracy? Congress can abolish or reorganize an agency. Congress can limit or expand an agency's jurisdiction, or allow its authority to lapse entirely. Congress can slash an agency's appropriations. Congress can investigate. Congress can do all these things, but individual congressmen generally find reasons not to do so.[21]

Congress, it is charged, anxious whenever possible to avoid conflict, adopts such sweeping legislation and delegates so much authority to the bureaucracy that bureaucrats, in effect, have become the nation's lawmakers. Congress could pass laws with precise wording, but it would get too bogged down in details to complete its work. Congress does not generally specify details. Instead, Congress declares its policy in general terms and empowers appropriate agencies to make appropriate decisions to meet varying circumstances throughout the nation.

It is not Congress as a whole that shares the direction over the bureaucracy with the president. More accurately, individual members and committees specialize in the appropriations and oversight processes. They oversee policies of a particular cluster of agencies—often the agencies serving constituents in their own districts. Some legislators stake out a claim over more general policies. Members of Congress, who see presidents come and go, come to think they know more about particular agencies than the president does (and sometimes they do). Some congressional leaders prefer to seal off "their" agencies from presidential direction to maintain influence over public policy. Sometimes their power is institutionalized; the army chief of engineers, for example, is given authority by law to plan public works and report to Congress without going through the president.

Another factor works in favor of congressional control. Every day thousands of bureaucrats are involved in making millions of decisions. A president has limited time, limited resources, and limited political influence over many of these agencies. Presidents and their staffs can become involved only in matters of significant political interest. Members of Congress, with an institutional staff of more than 40,000, however, can operate in areas far from the presidential spotlight.

So, whose bureaucracy is this anyway? Presidents and members of Congress both strive to exercise control over the bureaucracy, each in their own way. Interest groups and court rulings also influence the way the bureaucracy operates. For their part, career bureaucrats say they are responsive to the laws and statutes they work under and to their own standards of professionalism and responsibility. No one answer exists to the question of who or what controls the bureaucracy. And because of this, there is a never-ending search for improved means of ensuring bureaucratic accountability. This search and the experiments with countless instruments—reorganizations, civil service reforms, sunset practices, selective privatization, budgetary planning, and oversight hearings—continue.

It is increasingly clear, moreover, that virtually all national bureaucracies are more responsive nowadays than once was the case. Even organizations such as the FBI or the Corps of Engineers are now reasonably accountable to Congress and the White House, and ultimately to the American people. "Thanks to Freedom of Information statutes and other 'sunshine' legislation, [the bureaucracy] has become less selective, and the weakening of iron triangles has made it much more responsive to broad constituencies and much less the creature of its own clients."[22] Also, new restrictions the Clinton administration is enforcing prohibit those who leave government from working for the agency they recently left on any contractual basis.

REFORM AND REORGANIZATION

Some writers call for a radical overhaul of the civil service system. One observer, for example, calls for appointments for only 6 to 12 years—term limits for civil servants. Job security creates deadwood, he argues, so periodic reexamination of employee qualifications would greatly increase employee productivity and responsiveness. Another suggestion is to rotate professionals from outside the government or from other agencies to loosen up stiffened joints, bring new blood, and encourage breadth. Such rotation might also break up the iron triangles—

alliances that get fixed among senior civil servants, members of Congress, and outside client interest groups.

A related proposal goes to the heart of the democratic process. To ensure that bureaucrats are more responsive to the electorate, a major increase in the number of patronage positions has been proposed. But even if this is a desirable proposal, it is not likely to be adopted because of the strong support in the nation for the merit system and the conviction that political patronage is bad.

From 1949 to 1983, Congress delegated considerable discretion to presidents in reorganizing the executive departments. Each president made major reorganizing proposals, most of which Congress approved. Today presidents' proposals for reorganization must be approved by a joint resolution of the two chambers, making reorganization more difficult. President Clinton has made modernizing of the executive departments a priority, but to make any substantial changes he needs congressional approval.

Congress is always sensitive to the implications of any reorganization that may affect their committee structure. Congressional committee leaders are aware that if they restructure the executive branch, they may have to reorganize their own committee systems, and this might upset the balance of power in Congress. "A willingness to surrender turf is as rare among members of Congress as it is among cabinet secretaries."[23]

Presidents, however, still have reasonably broad powers to reorganize the bureaucracy within the various cabinet departments. Yet even here, congressional committees take an active interest in how and why these changes are implemented. Interest groups also watch proposed changes and try to calculate how they will affect pet programs. In short, changing the shape of an administration is more than a matter of efficiency and economy. It is also a matter of *policy outcomes:* who gets what, how, and why.

President Bill Clinton and Vice-President Al Gore are finding out what most of their predecessors learned: although everybody favors efficient government and restructuring bureaucracy, difficulties arise when you get specific because the specifics often upset the already established distribution of power in the Washington power system. Still, thanks to the end of the cold war and also to our continuing budget deficits, the federal bureaucracy is indeed shrinking and in many ways is also more efficient than in the past.

SUMMARY

1. We often condemn bureaucracy and bureaucrats, yet we continue to turn to them to solve our toughest problems and to render more and better services. A survey of our bureaucratic agencies, then, is also a survey of how our political system has tried to identify our most important national goals and how policies are implemented.

2. The American bureaucracy does not adhere to the textbook model of management organization, as it is not fully subordinate to any branch of government. It has at least two immediate bosses: Congress and the president. It must pay considerable attention as well to the courts and their rulings and, of course, to well-organized interest groups and public opinion. In many ways the bureaucracy is a semi-independent force—a fourth branch of government—in American politics.

3. Debates and controversy over big government and big bureaucracy, and over how to reorganize and eliminate waste in them, continue. Compared with many other nations and their centralized bureaucracies, the hand of bureaucracy rests more gently and less oppressively on Americans than on other peoples.

4. Whom and how the government hires and what discretion or powers it grants its employees are controversial topics. To work in the career public service is to have the opportunity to serve people, solve problems, and try to bring about a better society. Efforts to make the bureaucracy more responsive are enduring struggles in a constitutional democracy, and they are issues raised rightly in every presidential election.

FURTHER READING

JOEL D. ABERBACH, *Keeping a Watchful Eye: The Politics of Congressional Oversight* (Brookings Institution, 1990).

JOHN J. DILULIO JR., GERALD GARAVEY, AND DONALD F. KETTLE, *Improving Government Performances: An Owner's Manual* (Brookings Institution, 1993).

LAWRENCE DODD AND RICHARD SCHOTT, *Congress and the Administrative State* (Wiley, 1979).

ANTHONY DOWNS, *Inside Bureaucracy* (Little, Brown, 1967).

JAMES W. FESLER AND DONALD F. KETTL, *The Politics of the Administrative Process* (Chatham House, 1991).

CHARLES T. GOODSELL, *The Case for Bureaucracy,* 3d ed. (Chatham House, 1994).

AL GORE, *Creating a Government That Works Better and Costs Less: The Report of the National Performance Review* (Plume-Penguin, 1993).

LARRY HILL, ED., *The State of Public Bureaucracy* (M. E. Sharpe, 1992).

PATRICIA INGRAHAM AND DAVID ROSENBLOOM, EDS., *The Promise and Paradox of Civil Service Reform* (University of Pittsburgh Press, 1992).

HERBERT KAUFMAN, *The Administrative Behavior of Federal Bureau Chiefs* (Brookings Institution, 1981).

JACK H. KNOTT AND GARY J. MILLER, *Reforming Bureaucracy: The Politics of Institutional Choice* (Prentice Hall, 1987).

CHARLES H. LEVINE, ED., *The Unfinished Agenda for Civil Service Reform* (Brookings Institution, 1985).

DAVID OSBORNE AND TED GAEBLER, *Reinventing Government: How the Entrepreneurial Spirit Is Transforming the Public Sector* (Addison-Wesley, 1992).

B. GUY PETERS, *The Politics of Bureaucracy,* 3d ed. (Longman, 1989).

DENNIS D. RILEY, *Controlling the Federal Bureaucracy* (Temple University Press, 1987).

FRANCIS E. ROURKE, *Bureaucracy, Politics and Public Policy* (Little, Brown, 1983).

ANTHONY SUMMERS, *Official and Confidential: The Secret Life of J. Edgar Hoover* (Putnam, 1993).

JOHN T. TIERNEY, *The U.S. Postal Service* (Auburn House, 1988).

JAMES Q. WILSON, *Bureaucracy: What Government Agencies Do and Why They Do It* (Basic Books, 1989).

Four useful journals are *Journal of Policy Analysis and Management, National Journal, Public Administration Review,* and *Government Executive.*

THE
DEMOCRATIC
FAITH

The founding generation fought an eight-year revolution to secure their rights and liberty. Then they faced the challenge of creating a government, first at the Constitutional Convention and later in the first Congress, to write a Constitution and draft a Bill of Rights that would protect the rights to life, liberty, and self-government for themselves and for those who would come later. But they knew, as we also know, that passive allegiance to ideas and rights is never enough. Every generation must see itself as having a duty to nurture these ideals by actively renewing the community and nation of which it is a part.

The framers knew well the story of Athens. They were familiar with Pericles and his famed funeral oration in which he said that the person who takes no part in public affairs is a useless person, a good-for-nothing. The city's business, as Pericles and many Athenians saw it, was *everyone's* business. Athens had flourished as a shining beacon of what a civilized city might be, but it foundered when greed, self-centeredness, and smugness set in. As time went on, the Athenians wanted security more than they wanted liberty, they wanted comfort more than they wanted freedom. In the end they lost it all—security, comfort, and freedom. When they asked not what they could do for Athens but rather what Athens could do for them, then Athens ceased to be free. "Responsibility was the price every man must pay for freedom. It was to be had on no other terms."[1]

If we are to be citizens of the United States in the truest meaning of the term, our dreams must go beyond personal ambition and the accumulation of material goods. Our country needs citizens who understand that our well-being is tied to the well-being of our neighbors, community, and country.

As democracy movements around the world are gaining strength and formerly totalitarian governments are toppling, Americans are reminded of our democratic roots. Over the past few years, Chinese students, Polish Solidarity members, East German protesters, a Czech playwright, Thai citizens, and Haitian democrats have been willing to fight and even die for the democratic values Thomas Jefferson outlined in the Declaration of Independence. We have been stunned by the success these movements have seen in a short period of time, but we have also been saddened by the setbacks many of them have encountered. Translating democratic values into a working democratic government is difficult, as Boris Yeltsin has discovered. We in the United States have gained renewed appreciation for our system of constitutional democracy as we have watched these new republics struggle with social and economic divisions, federalism, the lack of an effective party system, and a poorly developed free press.

Our theme in this last chapter is simple: *Leadership and constitutional structures and protections are important, but an active, committed citizenry that can assume leadership itself is even more important.* Freedom and obligation go together. Liberty and duty go together. The answer to a nation's problems lies not in producing a perfect constitution or a few larger-than-life leaders. The answer lies in educating a *nation of citizen-leaders* who, regardless of their professional and private ambitions, will, at the very least, make the concerns of the Republic their avocation.

We are not complete persons, as the Athenians would remind us, unless we are reacting to and expressing ourselves through politics. We should participate in public affairs not out of social or civic duty or the prospect of a particular reward. It is for the completion of self, for our growth and self-definition in relation to others, and as an expression of our concern for those others, that we must act politically.[2]

More than any other form of government, the kind of democracy that has emerged under our Constitution requires a certain kind of faith—and a certain kind of skepticism. It requires faith concerning our common human enterprise, a

Thomas Jefferson, main author of the Declaration of Independence, first secretary of state, and third president of the United States.

Czech and Chinese Voices on Democratic Faith

I dream of a republic that is independent, free, and democratic; a republic with economic prosperity yet social justice; a humane republic that serves the individual and therefore hopes that the individual will serve it in turn; a republic of well-rounded people, because without such people, it is impossible to solve any of our problems...

Czech President Vaclav Havel
New Year's Day Speech,
January 1, 1990

We have awakened the people
We have seeded democracy
We will win
Our next generation will continue.
It doesn't matter
If we don't succeed.

Poem written by an anonymous
democracy demonstrator in China's
Tiananmen Square, spring 1989

This participant at a national convention is acting on the philosophy expressed by his T-shirt.

belief that if the people are informed and caring, they can be trusted with their own self-government, and an optimism that when things begin to go wrong, the people can be relied upon to set them right. But a healthy skepticism is needed as well. Democracy requires us to question our leaders and never trust any group with too much power. Although we prize majority rule, we must always be skeptical enough to ask whether or not a majority is right.

Constitutional democracy requires us to be constantly concerned about whether we really tolerate and protect the rights and opinions of others and whether democratic processes are in fact serving the principles of liberty, equality, and justice. In short, the democratic faith rests upon a peculiar blend of faith in the people and skepticism of them.

Thomas Jefferson, our best-known champion of the democratic faith, believed in the common sense of the people and in the flowering of the human spirit. Jefferson believed deeply that every government degenerates when it is trusted to its rulers alone. The people themselves, he wrote, are the only safe repositories of government. His was a robust commitment to popular control, to representative processes, and to accountable leadership. But he was no believer in the simple participatory democracy of ancient Greece or revolutionary France. The people, too, must have their power checked and balanced.

Government by the people does not require that everyone be involved in politics and decision-making. We are well aware that many citizens are apathetic toward politics and government. Yet government by the people does require a segment of the public that is attentive, interested, involved, and willing, at least on occasion, to criticize those in the government.

Our founders set up a government by *consent of the governed*, and our Bill of Rights specifically denies government authorities any legal opportunity to coerce that consent. Indeed, as Justice Robert H. Jackson wrote in a 1943 Supreme Court decision, *West Virginia Board of Education v Barnette*, "Authority here is to be controlled by public opinion, not public opinion by authority." Jackson added, "If there is any fixed star in our constitutional constellation, it is that no official, high or petty, can prescribe what shall be orthodox in politics, nationalism, religion, or other matters of opinion or force citizens to confess by word or act their faith therein."

With the breakup of the Soviet Union, the liberation of most Eastern European nations, and the strengthening of democracies in parts of Asia and Latin America in the early 1990s, there may be more people living today under conditions of political freedom than under totalitarian or authoritarian governments. Still, only about 40 percent of the people in the world live in nations considered wholly free. Throughout history, including the present, most governments have been authoritarian or tyrannical. Most people have lived in societies in which a small group at the top have imposed their will on the others. Authoritarian governments justify their actions by saying people are too weak to govern themselves; they need to be ruled. But neither in Castro's Cuba nor in the military regime of North Korea, neither in the People's Republic of China nor in Saudi Arabia, do ordinary people have a voice in the type of decisions we Americans routinely make: Who should go to college, or work in the fields, or serve in the army? How much money should be spent for schools, economic development initiatives, or environmental protection?

THE CASE FOR GOVERNMENT BY THE PEOPLE

The essence of our Constitution is that it both grants power to and withholds power from the national government. Fearing national weakness and popular disorder, the framers wanted to grant the government only enough power to do its basic jobs, such as maintaining national defense and providing financial stability. Valuing above all the principle of individual liberty, the framers wanted to protect the people from too much government. They wanted a limited government—but one that would work. The solution was to make government responsive to the people, but at the same time insulate the government from momentary and passionate majorities.

The first step was to distribute power among the three branches of government: legislative, executive, and judicial (*separation of powers*). The second was to share power among the branches, to enable them to limit or restrain each other (*checks and balances*). The third was to leave extensive authority with state and local governments (*federalism*). Public officials were also provided with different and competing constituencies. The framers assumed the constituents themselves would be divided (*pluralism*): northerners versus southerners, rich versus poor, city people versus country people. Finally, in 1791, as the ultimate protection of the people's liberties, the framers in Congress and in the state legislatures added the Bill of Rights.

This was not, of course, a very efficient system. But efficiency was not the main goal; the framers wanted a *safe* government. They wanted a government that allowed for plenty of deliberation and for consensus building—but that also avoided hasty decision making. It may have been somewhat more efficient than the system under the Articles of Confederation, but the constitutional system was not primarily designed to promote efficiency, and it will rarely measure up well against that standard.

As the decades passed, the national government came under greater pressure to perform effectively. The twentieth century brought involvement in vast global wars, depressions, and huge migrations of Europeans, Hispanics, and Asians. There were also migrations of African Americans and other rural people into cities in the North, Midwest, and West, as well as industrialization and technological changes in transportation, communications, medicine, and education. Governments with separation of powers and numerous checks and balances such as ours always have trouble pulling themselves together, but the American experiment had even more trouble. It was too easy for leaders to "pass the buck."

Certain realities also increased the power of political minorities—the influence that comes from campaign contributions to elected officials at every level of government, for example. The power of organized minorities to obstruct action sharpened the whole question of a representative republic. If leaders acting for a majority of people could not act—could not pass health care reform or control the senseless killings in our streets and schools—was this really government by the people?

Most Americans want a government that is efficient and effective and caring. We want to maintain our commitment to liberty and freedom. We want a government that acts for the majority but also protects minorities. We want to safeguard our nation and our streets in a world full of change and violence. We want to protect the rights of the poor, the elderly, and the minorities. Do we expect too much from government? Of course we do!

Constitutional democracy is a system of checks and balances. It balances values and competing dreams. We must balance all individual liberties against the collective security and needs of society; we must also balance certain individual liberties against other individual liberties. The question is always which rights of which people are to be protected by what means and at what price?

PARTICIPATION AND REPRESENTATION

In essence, the challenge to the future of democracy is whether we can make our representative process work better. No political problem is more complicated than this. For one thing, exact representation is impossible in the literal sense. Every man and woman has a host of conflicting desires, fears, hopes, and expectations, and no government can represent them all. Moreover, even if millions of voters could be

To Protect the Dissenter

When one element in a pluralistic system becomes very powerful in relation to the others, the pluralism of the system itself is in danger. Even with the best of intentions, the dominant element is likely to squeeze out the other elements or render them impotent....

So we have devised a variety of ways to protect the dissenter. Our civil liberties are a part of that system, and so are Robert's Rules of Order, and grievance procedures, and the commonly held view that we should hear both sides of an argument. In short, we have a tradition, a set of attitudes and specific social arrangements designed to ensure that points of view at odds with prevailing doctrine will not be rejected out of hand.

But why be so considerate of dissent and criticism? To answer this question is to state one of the strongest tenets of our political philosophy. We do not expect organizations or societies to be above criticism, nor do we trust the men who run them to be adequately self-critical. We believe that even those aspects of society that are healthy today may deteriorate tomorrow. We believe that power wielded justly today may be wielded corruptly tomorrow. We know that from the ranks of the critics come cranks and troublemakers, but from the same ranks come the saviors and innovators. And since the spirit that welcomes nonconformity is a fragile thing, we have not depended on that spirit alone. We have devised explicit legal and constitutional arrangements to protect the dissenter.

SOURCE: John W. Gardner, *Self-Renewal*, rev. ed. (Norton, 1981), pp. 71–72.

Why People Run for Office

- To solve problems and promote the American Dream—enhancing liberty and justice
- To advance fresh ideas and approaches
- To "throw some rascal out" whose views they dislike
- To gain a voice in policy making
- To serve as a party spokesperson
- To acquire political influence and a platform from which to influence public opinion
- To gain prominence and power
- To satisfy ego needs
- To gain opportunities to learn, grow, travel, and meet all kinds of people
- To be where the "action is"—involved in the thick of government and political life—campaigning, debating, drafting laws, reconciling diverse views, and making the system responsive

Why People Shy Away from Running for Office

- Loss of privacy
- Less time to spend with families or favorite pastimes
- Less income than in many business or professional occupations
- Exposure to partisan and media criticism
- Involvement in many things most people would rather not do—like marching in countless parades, attending county fairs, and going to endless political dinners, banquets, and service club meetings
- Meager rewards
- Fear that one may have to compromise principles because of the complexity of our adversarial system
- Expense of campaigning
- Aversion to conflict, divisiveness, and ambition
- Concern that the constitutional structure and party system make it nearly impossible to exercise meaningful leadership

represented in their billions of interests, the question of how they would be represented would remain. Through direct representation, such as a New England town meeting? Through economic or professional associations, such as labor unions or political action committees? Through a coalition of minority groups? Through a direct popular majority? Through state and national or even electronic referenda? All these, and other alternatives, can be defended as proper forms of representation in a constitutional democracy.

Some propose to bypass this thorny problem of representation by vastly increasing the role of *direct popular participation* in decision making. What many people regard as the most perfect form of democracy exists when every person within a given group has a full and equal opportunity to participate in all decisions and in all processes of influence, persuasion, and discussion that bear on that decision. Direct participation in decision making, its advocates contend, will serve two major purposes. It will enhance the dignity, self-respect, and understanding of individuals by giving them responsibility for the decisions that shape their lives. And it will act as a safeguard against undemocratic and antidemocratic forms of government and prevent the replacement of democracy by dictatorship or tyranny. This idea rests on a theory of self-protection that says interests can be represented, furthered, and defended best by those whom they concern directly.

Experience with many forms of participatory democracy, however, suggests that it has limitations as a form of decision making. In an age of rapidly growing population, increasingly complex economic and social systems, and enormously wide-ranging decision-making units of government, direct participation can work only in smaller communities or at the neighborhood level. As a practical matter, people simply cannot put in endless hours taking part in every decision that affects their lives.

Participatory democracy still has an important role in smaller units—in neighborhood associations, local party committees, and the like. And perhaps the idea of participation should be greatly extended, for example, to greater control by workers over the running of factories. But we must distinguish between democracy as participation and a greater role for participation in a democracy. One course of action is to enlarge the role of participation in representation; that is, to broaden the power of all people to take part in local decision making and in choosing their representatives in larger units of government. And this brings us back to the hard questions of indirect representation.

If we must have representatives, who shall represent whom? Although this question can be answered in countless ways, in practice there are two basic ways to organize representation. By electing representatives in a multitude of local districts, it is possible to build into representative institutions—the U.S. Congress, for example—most minority interests and attitudes found throughout the nation. The other way is through an election system that emphasizes majority representation. This system can be achieved by creating a nationwide electorate that elects one representative (the American president, for example) or by developing a strong two-party system that knits all the local constituencies into coalitions that can elect and sustain national majorities. A nation does not have to choose between these alternatives. It can have both, as does the United States.

Which is better: a government that represents coalitions of minorities or a government that represents a relatively clear-cut majority and has little or no obligation to the minority? The answer depends on what you expect from government. A system that represents coalitions of minorities usually reflects the trading, competition, and compromising that must take place in order to reach agreement among the various groups. Such a government has been called *broker rule;* the government acts essentially as a go-between, as a mediator among organized groups that have definite policy goals. Under broker rule, leaders cannot get too far ahead of the groups; they must tack back and forth, shifting in response to changing group pressures. Instead of acting for a united popular majority with a fairly definite program, either liberal or conservative, the government tries to satisfy all major interests by giving them a voice in decisions and sometimes a veto over actions. In the pushing and hauling of political groups, the government is continually involved in delicate balancing acts.

Some critics believe in full representation of minority groups—broker rule—but point out that fair representation has not been achieved in the American system. They point to the extent of nonvoting and other forms of nonparticipation in politics; the fact that low-income persons are less well organized in groups than upper-income persons; the bias of the stronger organized groups toward the status quo; the lack of competition among much of the news and opinion media, combined with the domination of television and the press by a few corporations; and the virtual monopoly of party politics by the two major parties, which do not always offer the voters meaningful alternatives. In the governmental system itself, critics note the devices in Congress that block majority will and overrepresent certain minorities; the distortion of representation embodied in the electoral college; and the power of the Supreme Court to invalidate laws demanded by popular majorities acting through the legislative and executive branches.

Such charges may be exaggerated, but they cannot be denied. Those who believe in fairer representation, however, can point to steady improvement in recent years. There have been changes in election laws to simplify voter registration and extend voting, to enforce one-person, one-vote standards, and to regulate campaign finance. And some progress has been made in Congress to strengthen majority rule.

By this point, you undoubtedly appreciate that democracy has to mean much more than popular government and unchecked majority rule. A democracy needs competing politicians with competing views about the public interest. A vital democracy, living and growing, places its faith in the voters, faith that they will elect not just people who will mirror their views but leaders who will exercise their best judgment—"faith that the people will not condemn those whose devotion to principle leads them to unpopular courses, but will reward courage, respect honor, and ultimately recognize right."[3]

The Role of the Politician

Americans in the mid-1990s have decidedly mixed views about elected officials. They realize that at their best politicians are skillful at compromising, mediating, negotiating, brokering—and that governing often requires these qualities. But can there be too much of a good thing? Americans also suspect politicians of being ambitious, conniving, unprincipled, opportunistic, and corrupt—"into politics just for what they can get out of it for themselves." Compared to people in other professions, Americans hold politicians in low esteem.

Yet we often find individual officeholders are responsive, bright, hardworking and friendly (even though we may suspect they are simply trying to get our vote). And our liking often turns into reverence after these same politicians depart or die. Surely George Washington, Abraham Lincoln, Dwight D. Eisenhower, and John F. Kennedy are acclaimed today. Harry Truman liked to say that a statesman is merely a politician who has been dead for about ten years.

Of course, we must put the problem in perspective. In all democracies the public may expect too much from politicians. Further, people naturally dislike those who wield power. Public officeholders, after all, tax us, regulate us, and conscript us. We dislike political compromisers and ambitious opportunists—even though we may need such people to get things done.

When U.S. citizens were asked what they think of the typical American politician, 80 percent of the responses were negative. Many see politicians as authoritarian, power hungry, on an ego trip, slick, two-faced, glib, talkative, superficial, evasive, self-serving, opportunistic, manipulative, preoccupied with getting elected,

Poking Fun at Politicians

"Don't vote, it only encourages them!"

"Thank God only one of them can win!"

"Old politicians never die, they just evade away."

"A politician is a person who approaches every question with an open mouth."

"Politicians are there when they need you."

"Politicians divide their time between running for office and running for cover."

"Political promises go in one year and out the other."

"In one country it is said that people can rise to public office only when they shoot a rhinoceros. In this country, people can only win public office if they shoot the bull."

"Let's run through this once more—and, remember, you choke up at Paragraph Three and brush away the tear at Paragraph Five."

Drawing by D. Reilly; © 1988 The New Yorker Magazine, Inc.

TABLE 18-1

Public Perception of Various Professions' Honesty and Ethical Standards

	Percent Answering High or Very High 1981	1993
Druggists and pharmacists	59%	65%
Clergy	63	53
College teachers	45	52
Medical doctors	50	51
Policemen	44	50
Dentists	52	50
Engineers	48	49
Funeral directors	30	34
TV reporters and commentators	36	28
Bankers	39	28
Journalists	32	26
Newspaper reporters	30	22
Business executives	19	20
Building contractors	19	20
Local officeholders	14	19
U.S. senators	20	18
Lawyers	25	16
TV talk show hosts	NA	16
Real estate agents	14	15
Labor union leaders	14	14
Members of Congress	15	14
State officeholders	12	14
Stockbrokers	21	13
Insurance salesmen	11	10
Advertising practitioners	9	8
Car salesmen	6	6

SOURCE: *The Gallup Poll Monthly*, July 1993, p. 39.
Note that members of Congress and state and local officeholders fare poorly.

responsive to voters only when they think voters might be angry enough to vote them out of office, and prone to promising what they do not intend to deliver.

When asked to describe their ideal American politician, these same people respond very differently. Their ideal politician is honest, humble, patriotic, compassionate, sensitive to the needs of others, well-informed, competent, fair-minded, outgoing, objective, intellectually honest, a good listener, candid, a good mediator, self-confident, inspiring, "a candidate of the people, not of the money," courageous enough to stand up to special interests, someone "who does not want power but leads because he or she is called upon to exercise talents for the public good," and to "do the job and get out when finished."

Why the gap between expectations about the typical and the ideal politician? The gap exists in part because we have high expectations. We want politicians to be like us, yet better than us. We want politicians to be perfect, to have all the answers, and to have all the right (in our minds) views. It is hard for anyone to live up to these ideals. Politicians, like all individuals, live in a real world in which perfection may be a goal, but compromises, ambition, fund raising, and self-promotion are necessary. Our "ideal leaders" are usually dead. The passage of time helps us put the accomplishments of our leaders in perspective. We want politicians to solve our problems, yet we also want them to serve as scapegoats for the things we dislike about government: taxes, regulations, and limits on our freedom.

Politician bashing has long been a tradition in the United States. Our greatest presidents by common consent were Washington, Lincoln, and Franklin Roosevelt, and each of them was roasted regularly by the press and opposition leaders. Today there is also relentless and often intense criticism aimed at those in Congress and in the White House. Radio and television talk show personalities and popular entertainment programs, ranging from Jay Leno, David Letterman, *Larry King Live*, *Nightline*, Rush Limbaugh, Pat Robertson, and Ross Perot to *60 Minutes* and *20/20,* routinely expose the vulnerabilities of our leaders.

To those in government it must seem that the world is full of critics. While critics are essential for a free government, without politicians and public-spirited leaders it would be wholly impossible to solve any of our problems. As potential citizen-leaders, you also have responsibilities to the political process. We trust that those of you who have worked your way through this book have a richer appreciation of the need for support and involvement in, as well as dissent and criticism of, our political system.

Politicians are absolutely necessary to run a democracy—certainly the American republic, whose fragmented powers require politicians to mediate among factions, build coalitions, and compromise among and within branches of government to produce policy. But are such politicians adequate? Don't we also need leaders who can rise above everyday "wheeling and dealing" and lead the nation through great crises—or, better yet, plan ahead to avert such crises?

Leadership for a Constitutional Democracy

An adequate democratic theory recognizes that constitutional democracy is not self-executing. A democracy needs leaders who have a sense of the past and are willing to share their varying conceptions of the public interest.

Even though one of the most universal cravings of our time is a hunger for creative and compelling leadership, defining creative leadership is a challenge in itself. Leadership can be understood only in the context of both leaders and followers—a leader without followers is a contradiction in terms. Leadership is also situational and contextual. A person is often effective in only one kind of situation. Leadership is not necessarily transferable. James Madison, for example, was a brilliant political and constitutional theorist. He was also a superb politician. Still, he was not a particularly able president. The leadership required to lead a marine platoon up a hill in battle is different from the leadership needed to change racist or sexist attitudes in city governments. The leadership required of a campaign manager differs from that required of a candidate. Leaders of thought are not always effective as leaders of action.

Although leaders are often skilled managers, they need more than just managerial skills. Managers do things the right way, whereas leaders are more concerned, or perhaps more preoccupied, with doing the right thing; that is, they are more concerned with the longer range, with the purposes and ends of a society or an organization. Put another way, managers are concerned with efficiency and process, especially routines and standard operating procedures. Leaders, on the other hand, must be concerned with effectiveness and purpose. They must be inventors, risk takers, and entrepreneurs. Further, they must be morale builders who can infuse values into the mission of their community or nation. Indeed, leaders are always defining, defending, and promoting values.

Some leaders have indispensable qualities of contagious self-confidence, unwarranted optimism, and dogged idealism that attract and mobilize others to undertake tasks they never dreamed they could accomplish. In short, they *empower others* and enable many of their followers to become leaders in their own right. Most of the significant breakthroughs in our nation (as well as in our communities) have been made or shaped by people who, while seeing all the complexities and obstacles ahead of them, believed in themselves and in their purposes so much that they refused to be overwhelmed and paralyzed by self-doubts. They were willing to gamble, to take risks, to look at things in a fresh way, and often to invent new rules.[4]

On Leadership

Mary Parker Follett back in 1923 wrote a book that summed it up well: "He is a leader who gives form to the inchoate energy in every man. The person who influences me most is not he who does great deeds but he who makes me feel I can do great deeds." That is, the leader guides the group and is at the same time guided by the group. No one can truly lead except from within. Leaders interpret our experience to us. Leaders give form to things vague, things latent, to mere tendencies and aspirations. They integrate, create communities of trust and empower the best in us not by dominating us but by expressing us and our collective energies and ideals and our yearning for liberty, freedom and social justice.

SOURCE: Mary Parker Follett, *The New State* (Longman's, 1923), pp. 229–30.

What Are the Most Important Qualities of a Leader?

No one knows—so much depends on the context, the challenge, and the need. The following qualities or skills are often cited as critically important; none guarantees leadership effectiveness.

- Self-knowledge
- Self-confidence
- Optimism/hope
- Self-discipline
- Sensitivity/empathy
- Stamina/energy
- Tenacity/persistence
- Integrity
- Vision
- Imagination
- Judgment
- Risk taking
- Morale building
- Coalition building
- Negotiating/mediating
- Communicating
- Breadth/creativity
- Concern for results
- Sense of humor
- Enjoyment of people

The Leadership of Kennedy and King

The relationship between John F. Kennedy, a coalition-building officeholder, and Martin Luther King, Jr., movement leader, exemplifies the diversity of leadership. Even though Kennedy raised civil rights issues during his campaign for the presidency in 1960, he never accorded them top priority in his program. Rather, he held off making major civil rights proposals until he could get his economic program through Congress. In the meantime King and other black leaders were protesting, demonstrating, encountering violence, appealing to northern and southern public opinion, and putting intense pressure on Kennedy and other federal officials to protect their civil rights and especially to put through legislation that would protect their right to vote.

As a result of this kind of movement pressure, by 1963 Kennedy was appealing to Congress for civil rights legislation. He worked closely with King and other civil rights leaders through his brother Robert, the attorney general, and at the same time tried to maintain old-time Democratic party coalitions of northerners and white southerners. Movement leaders like King put pressure on the government from the outside—while also working with Robert Kennedy and others from the inside.

After Kennedy's assassination, President Lyndon B. Johnson, together with congressional leaders, built a broad coalition of blacks, liberals, and moderate whites that helped to put the Civil Rights Act of 1964 and the Voting Rights Act of 1965 into law.

Leaders must recognize the fundamental—unexpressed as well as felt—wants and needs of potential followers. By bringing followers to a fuller consciousness of their needs, they help convert the resulting hopes and aspirations into practical demands on other leaders, especially leaders in government. Leaders must also sense when people are ready for action. A leader in a democracy consults and listens while educating followers and attempting to renew the goals of an organization. Leaders must also be sensitive to the distinctions between power and authority. *Power* is the strength or raw force to exercise control or coerce someone to do something. *Authority* is power that is accepted as legitimate by subordinates or constituents.

The whole issue of leadership raises countless questions about participation in and acceptance of power in superior/subordinate, or leader/led, relationships. How best can leaders earn and sustain moral and social acceptance for their authority? Americans generally prize participation in all kinds of organizations, especially in civic and political life. Yet a part of us yearns for charismatic leaders—decisive, attractive leaders who will simplify problems and relieve us of the burdens of leadership. Ironically, however, savior figures and charismatic leaders often—indeed almost always—create distance, not participation.

There is another type of political leader, one who takes the short rather than the long view, and engages in a short-term bargain: "I'll vote for your bill if you'll vote for mine," or "You raise money for my campaign and I'll help get your daughter a state job after I'm elected." Most political officeholders practice this trend of leadership as a practical necessity. It is the common means of doing business.

Leaders in politics can also be defined as agitators or coalition builders. *Agitators*, or movement leaders, arouse people's consciousness of their needs and problems, raise their hopes and expectations, organize or take leadership of political and social movements, and mobilize grass-roots pressure on government from the outside. Movement leaders are often considered crusaders or even prophets, whether they be abolitionists, women's suffrage leaders, antislavery leaders, populist proponents of tax and term limits, or environmental crusaders.

Coalition builders are usually intent on winning elections, whereas agitators are more concerned with mobilizing groups of people who may or may not take part in elections. Coalition builders—for example, effective campaign managers—must knit together a variety of groups in order to build a majority that can win elections. Hence, such leaders tend to be power brokers, widening their political appeals as broadly as possible, accommodating single-interest or single-cause groups or movements with intense concerns, and building compromise party platforms that appeal to large numbers of people.

Officeholders respond to pressure from movement leaders. Here President John Kennedy meets with organizers of the 1963 March on Washington (*left to right*): Whitney Young, National Urban League; Dr. Martin Luther King, Jr., Southern Leadership Conference; Rabbi Joachim Prinz, American Jewish Congress; Phillip Randolph, March on Washington director; President Kennedy; Walter Reuther, American Federation of Labor; and Roy Wilkins, National Association for the Advancement of Colored People.

RECONCILING DEMOCRACY AND LEADERSHIP

The American people will never be completely satisfied with their politicians, nor should they be. The "ideal politician" is truly a fictional character, for the ideal politician would be able to please everyone and to make conflicts disappear. Such a person could exist only in an extremely small community in which all the people shared the same ideas, ideals, and interests. But American liberties invite diversity and, therefore, conflict. Politicians, as well as the people they represent, have different ideas about what is best for the nation. After all, who is really to say what is good for anyone else—let alone for everyone else? That's why we have politicians and politics. To understand this is to better appreciate the delicate and crucial responsibilities entrusted to our elected politicians.

Americans are fond of saying, "It is all politics, you know." The insight is offered as profound. More important, it is offered as a negative, as if things would be improved if we did *not* have politics and politicians.

But politics is the lifeblood of democracy, and without politics there is no freedom. To conclude that politicians are interested in winning elections is about as profound as to conclude that businesspeople are interested in profits. Of course they are! We do not expect our economy to operate because the shoe store owner is motivated only by a desire to see that people have warm feet. Rather we harness the shoe store owner's desire to make money as a way to see to it that the largest number of people get the shoes they want at the lowest possible price. So also we harness the elected officials' desire for reelection as the way to ensure that elected officials do what most of the voters want them to do. It is the politician's desire to please the voters that is the indispensable link in making democracy work.

Our challenge is to reconcile democracy and leadership. Too often in the past we have held a view of leaders as hierarchical, male, and all-powerful. That conception is antithetical to our democratic aspirations. A nation of subservient followers can never be a democratic one. A democratic nation requires educated, skeptical, caring, engaged, and conscientious citizen-leaders.

Such a democratic citizen-leader appreciates that power wielded justly today may be wielded corruptly tomorrow. Democratic citizen-leaders are moved to protest when they know a policy is wrong or when other citizens find their rights diminished. Such leaders appreciate that criticism of official error is not criticism of our country. Citizen-leaders recognize as well that democracy rests solidly upon a mixed view of human nature. Our capacity for justice, as Reinhold Niebuhr observed, makes democracy possible. But our inclination to injustice makes democracy necessary.

Proud to Be a Politician

Must a politician gain public office by denouncing the profession? From the tone of many recent congressional races, it would appear that this is a growing trend. Journalist Charles McDowell of the Richmond Times-Dispatch noted this trend on the PBS series "The Lawmakers" and suggested that such a tactic "demeans an honorable and essential profession—that of the politician."

McDowell proposed that every member of Congress be required to take the following oath:

> I affirm that I am a politician. That I am willing to associate with other known politicians. That I have no moral reservations about committing acts of politics. Under the Constitution, I insist that politicians have as much right to indulge in politics as preachers, single-issue zealots, generals, bird-watchers, labor leaders, big business lobbyists, and all other truth-givers.
>
> I confess that, as a politician, I participate in negotiation, compromise, and tradeoffs in order to achieve something that seems reasonable to a majority. And, although I try to be guided by principle, I confess that I often find people of principle on the other side, too.
>
> So help me God.

Four presidents who exhibited very different leadership styles: John F. Kennedy, Lyndon B. Johnson, Dwight D. Eisenhower, and Harry S. Truman. They gathered at the funeral service for Sam Rayburn, former Speaker of the U.S. House of Representatives.

If elected politicians often seem bewildered in dealing with controversial issues in these confusing times, so are the rest of us. If elected officials sometimes make mistakes, so do the rest of us. If they sometimes postpone things rather than directly confront them, so do we all. The late Senator Everett Dirksen of Illinois offered a helpful perspective on politicians:

Politics is not something you can afford to leave to "other people." Since politics is the art of ordering the affairs of people through government, it should be the vocation of the very best in this Republic and the avocation of all.

There have been many who seem to equate politics with that which is bad, that which is corrupt, that which is venal, and that which is corrosive of our moral fiber. I find that throughout history most such disparaging remarks are made by those who never dared seek elective office.

To scorn all politicians and to decry their actions is to scorn those who elect them and support them—namely the citizen-elector.

SOURCE: Everett Dirksen, quoted in Conrad Joyner, *The American Politician* (University of Arizona Press, 1971), pp. 216–217.

Democratic politics is the forum or arena for excellence and responsibility, where—by acting together—citizens become free. In this sense, politics is not a necessary evil, it is a realistic good. It is the preoccupation of free people, and its existence is a test of freedom.[5]

Thus democratic leadership can be enabling and facilitating. Leadership, thought of as an engagement among equals, a collegial collaboration, can empower and liberate people and enlarge their opinions, choices, and freedoms. The answer for our Republic lies not in producing a handful of great, charismatic, Mount Rushmore leaders, but in educating a citizenry who can boast that we are no longer in need of great leaders because we have become a nation of citizens who believe that each of us can make a difference, and that all of us should regularly try.

Leadership is important. However, our system of government is, in many ways, designed to *prevent* strong and decisive action, lest too much political power be placed in the hands of one or a few people. Thus, while we have emphasized the role of leadership in constitutional democracies in these last few pages, the potential for abuse is checked not only by an involved citizenry but also by the very structure of our constitutional system. Thus the need for those healthy constraints—separation of powers, checks and balances, federalism, bicameral legislatures, and the rule of law so constantly emphasized throughout this book. Equally important, too, are the rights to organize opposition parties and factions and the right to dissent.

THE DEMOCRATIC FAITH

The ultimate test of a democratic system is the legal existence of an officially recognized opposition. A cardinal characteristic of a constitutional democracy is that it not only recognizes the need for the free organization of opposing views but positively encourages this organization. Freedom for political expression and dissent is basic—even freedom for nonsense to be spoken so that good sense not yet recognized gets a chance to be heard.

Crucial to the democratic faith is the belief that a constitutional democracy cherishes the free play of ideas. Only where the safety valve of public discussion is available and where almost any policy is subject to perpetual questioning and challenge can there be the assurance that both minority and majority rights will be served. To be afraid of public debate is to be afraid of self-government. "Rulers always have and always will find it dangerous to their security to permit people to think, believe, talk, write, assemble, and particularly to criticize the government as they please," said former Supreme Court Justice William J. Brennan, "but the language of the First Amendment indicates the framers weighed the risk involved in such freedoms and deliberately chose to stake this government's security and life upon preserving liberty to discuss public affairs intact and untouched by government."[6]

Your authors hold with Thomas Jefferson that there is nothing in the country so radically wrong that it cannot be cured by good newspapers and sound schoolmasters. Inform and educate the citizenry, and a major hurdle is overcome. Jefferson had boundless faith in education. He believed that people are rationally endowed by nature with an innate sense of justice; the average person has only to be informed to act wisely. In the long run, said Jefferson, only an educated and enlightened democracy can hope to endure.

Education is one of the best predictors of voting, participation in politics, and knowledge of public affairs. The public may not be equally involved or equally willing to invest in democracy. But the attentive public—frequently those like yourself who have gone to college—has the willingness and self-confidence to see government and politics as necessary and important. An educated public has an understanding of how government works, how individuals can influence decision makers, and how to elect like-minded people. Tolerance for different opinions must be a central part of a civic education.

Recent years have witnessed an increase in racial and ethnic tensions in the United States. These tensions sometimes encourage separation and antagonism toward the larger and more dominant Anglo culture. When carried to the extreme, these tensions promote various ethnicity cults that exaggerate differences, intensify resentments, and drive deep wedges between nationalities and races. "The genius of America" writes historian Arthur M. Schlesinger, Jr., "lies in its capacity to forge a single nation from peoples of remarkably diverse racial, religious, and ethnic origins." Schlesinger acknowledges that our government and society have been more open to some than to others, "but it is more open to all today than it was yesterday and it is likely to be even more open tomorrow than today." [7]

We are a restless, dissatisfied, and searching people. We are our own toughest critics. Our political system is far from perfect, but it still is an open system. People *can* fight city hall. People who disagree with policies in the nation can band together and be heard. We know only too well that the American Dream is never fully attained, and it is certainly not inherited. It is always to be achieved. Ultimately, "what joins the Americans one to another is not a common nationality, language, race, or ancestry...but rather their complicity in a shared work of the imagination." [8]

Our future will be shaped by those who care about extending and preserving our political rights and freedoms. Our individual liberties will never be assured unless there are people willing to take responsibility for the progress of the whole community, people willing to exercise their determination and democratic faith. Carved in granite on one of the long corridors in a building on the Harvard University campus are these words of American poet Archibald MacLeish: "How shall freedom be defended? By arms when it is attacked by arms; by truth when it is attacked by lies, by democratic faith when it is attacked by authoritarian dogma. Always, in the final act, by determination and faith."

Millions of Americans visit the great monuments in our nation's capital each year. They admire the beauty and are always impressed by the memorials to Washington, Jefferson, Lincoln, and the Vietnam veterans and by the Capitol, the Supreme Court, and the White House. The strength of the nation, however, resides not in these official buildings but in the hearts, minds, and behavior of citizens. If we lose faith, stop caring, stop participating, and stop believing in the possibilities of self-government, the monuments "will be meaningless piles of stone, and the venture that began with the Declaration of Independence, the venture familiarly known as America will be as lifeless as the stone." [9]

One thing is certain amid all the debates over what constitutional democracy, the Constitution, and the Bill of Rights mean, or should mean. The celebrations and the traumas, the advances and failures, the processes and institutions of "a government by the people"—as contrasted with something called "the state" in other lands—are inseparable from the daily lives and hopes and needs of the more than 260 million Americans. No one has expressed this argument more eloquently than Walt Whitman:

O I see flashing that this America is only you and me,
Its power, weapons, testimony, are you and me.
Its crimes, lies, thefts, defections, are you and me,
Its Congress is you and me, the officers, capitols, armies, ships, are you and me.
Its endless gestation of new States are you and me,
The war (that war so bloody and grim, the war I will henceforth forget),
    was you and me...
Freedom, language, poems, employments, are you and me,
Past, present, future, are you and me,
I dare not shirk any part of myself,
Nor any part of America good or bad. [10]

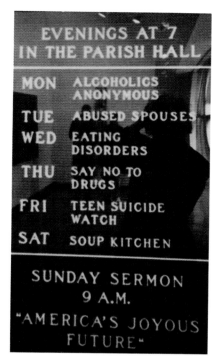

Despite the many serious problems facing our country, a spirit of optimism is still evident in our hopes for the future, as this church bulletin testifies.

Walt Whitman, legendary American poet and celebrator of the American experience.

APPENDIX

THE DECLARATION OF INDEPENDENCE

Drafted mainly by Thomas Jefferson, this document adopted by the Second Continental Congress, and signed by John Hancock and fifty-five others, outlined the rights of man and the rights to rebellion and self-government. It declared the independence of the colonies from Great Britain, justified rebellion, and listed the grievances against George the III and his government. What is memorable about this famous document is not only that it declared the birth of a new nation, but that it set forth, with eloquence, our basic philosophy of liberty and representative democracy.

IN CONGRESS, JULY 4, 1776
(The unanimous Declaration of the Thirteen United States of America)

Preamble

When, in the course of human events, it becomes necessary for one people to dissolve the political bands which have connected them with another, and to assume, among the powers of the earth, the separate and equal station to which the laws of nature and of nature's God entitle them, a decent respect to the opinions of mankind requires that they should declare the causes which impel them to the separation.

New Principles of Government

We hold these truths to be self-evident; that all men are created equal, that they are endowed by their Creator with certain unalienable rights, that among these are life, liberty, and the pursuit of happiness.

That, to secure these rights, governments are instituted among men, deriving their just powers from the consent of the governed.

That whenever any form of government becomes destructive of these ends, it is the right of the people to alter or to abolish it, and to institute new government, laying its foundation on such principles, and organizing its powers in such form, as to them shall seem most likely to effect their safety and happiness. Prudence, indeed will dictate that governments long established should not be changed for light and transient causes; and accordingly all experience hath shown that mankind are more disposed to suffer while evils are sufferable, than to right themselves by abolishing the forms to which they are accustomed. But when a long train of abuses and usurpations, pursuing invariably the same object, evinces a design to reduce them under absolute despotism, it is their right, it is their duty, to throw off such government, and to provide new guards for their future security.

Reasons for Separation

Such has been the patient sufferance of these colonies; and such is now the necessity which constrains them to alter their former systems of government. The history of the present king of Great Britain is a history of repeated injuries and usurpations, all having in direct object the establishment of an absolute tyranny over these states. To prove this, let facts be submitted to a candid world.

He has refused his assent to laws, the most wholesome and necessary for the public good.

He has forbidden his governors to pass laws of immediate and pressing importance unless suspended in their operation till his assent should be obtained; and when so suspended, he has utterly neglected to attend to them.

He has refused to pass other laws for the accommodation of large districts of people, unless those people would relinquish the right of representation in the legislature, a right inestimable to them, and formidable to tyrants only.

He has called together legislative bodies at places unusual, uncomfortable, and distant for the depository of their public records, for the sole purpose of fatiguing them into compliance with his measures.

He has dissolved representative houses repeatedly, for opposing, with manly firmness, his invasions on the rights of people.

He has refused, for a long time after such dissolutions, to cause others to be elected; whereby the legislative powers incapable of annihilation, have returned to the people at large for their exercise; the state remaining, in the meantime, exposed to all the dangers of invasion from without and convulsions within.

He has endeavored to prevent the population of these states; for that purpose obstructing the laws of naturalization of foreigners, refusing to pass others to encourage their migration hither, and raising the conditions of new appropriations of lands.

He has obstructed the administration of justice, by refusing his assent to laws for establishing judiciary powers.

He has made judges dependent on his will alone for the tenure of their offices, and the amount and payment of their salaries.

He has erected a multitude of new offices, and sent hither swarms of officers to harass our people and eat out their substance.

He has kept among us, in times of peace, standing armies, without the consent of our legislature.

He has affected to render the military independent of, and superior to, the civil power.

He has combined with others to subject us to jurisdiction foreign to our constitution and unacknowledged by our laws, giving his assent to their acts of pretended legislation:

For quartering large bodies of armed troops among us;

For protecting them, by a mock trial, from punishment for any murders which they should commit on the inhabitants of these states;

For cutting off our trade with all parts of the world;

For imposing taxes on us without our consent;

For depriving us, in many cases, of the benefits of trial by jury;

For transporting us beyond seas, to be tried for pretended offenses;

For abolishing the free system of English laws in a neighboring province, establishing therein an arbitrary government, and enlarging its boundaries, so as to render it at once an example and fit instrument for introducing the same absolute rule into these colonies;

For taking away our charters, abolishing our most valuable laws, and altering, fundamentally, the forms of our governments;

For suspending our own legislatures, and declaring themselves invented with power to legislate for us in all cases whatsoever.

He has abdicated government here, by declaring us out of his protection and waging war against us.

He has plundered our seas, ravaged our coasts, burned our towns, and destroyed the lives of our people.

He is at this time transporting large armies of foreign mercenaries to complete the works of death, desolation, and tyranny already begun with circumstances of cruelty and perfidy scarcely paralleled in the most barbarous ages and totally unworthy of the head of a civilized nation.

He has constrained our fellow-citizens, taken captive on the high seas, to bear arms against their country, to become the executioners of their friends and brethren, or to fall themselves by their hands.

He has excited domestic insurrections among us, and has endeavored to bring on the inhabitants of our frontiers the merciless Indian savages, whose known rule of warfare is an undistinguished destruction of all ages, sexes, and conditions.

In every stage of these oppressions we have petitioned for redress in the most humble terms; our repeated petitions have been answered only by repeated injury. A prince whose character is thus marked by every act which may define a tyrant is unfit to be the ruler of a free people.

Nor have we been wanting in attention to our British brethren. We have warned them, from time to time, of attempts by their legislature to extend an unwarrantable jurisdiction over us. We have reminded them of the circumstances of our emigration and settlement here. We have appealed to their native justice and magnanimity; and we have conjured them, by the ties of our common kindred, to disavow these usurpations, which would inevitably interrupt our connections and correspondence. They, too, have been deaf to the voice of justice and of consanguinity. We must, therefore, acquiesce in the necessity which denounces our separation, and hold them, as we hold the rest of mankind, enemies in war, in peace, friends.

We, therefore, the representatives of the United States of America, in General Congress assembled, appealing to the Supreme Judge of the world for the rectitude of our intentions, do, in the name and by authority of the good people of these colonies, solemnly publish and declare, that these united colonies are, and of right ought to be, free and independent states; that they are absolved from all allegiance to the British crown, and that all political connection between them and the state of Great Britain is, and ought to be, totally dissolved; and that, as free and independent states, they have full power to levy war, conclude peace, contract alliances, establish commerce, and do all other acts and things which independent states may of a right do. And, for the support of this declaration, with a firm reliance on the protection of Divine Providence, we mutually pledge to each other our lives, our fortunes, and our sacred honor.

THE FEDERALIST, NO. 10, JAMES MADISON

The Federalist, No. 10, written by James Madison soon after the Constitutional Convention, was prepared as one of several dozen newspaper essays aimed at persuading New Yorkers to ratify the proposed constitution. One of the most important basic documents in American political history, it outlines the need for and the general principles of a democratic republic. It also provides a political and economic analysis of the realities of interest group or faction politics.

To the People of the State of New York: Among the numerous advantages promised by a well-constructed union, none deserves to be more accurately developed than its tendency to break and control the violence of faction. The friend of popular governments, never finds himself so much alarmed for their character and fate, as when he contemplates their propensity of this dangerous vice. He will not fail, therefore, to set a due value on any plan which, without violating the principles to which he is attached, provides a proper cure for it. The instability, injustice, and confusion introduced into the public councils, have, in truth, been the mortal diseases under which popular governments have everywhere perished; as they continue to be the favorite and fruitful topics from which the adversaries to liberty derive their most specious declamations. The valuable improvements made by the American constitutions on the popular models, both ancient and modern, cannot certainly be too much admired; but it would be an unwarrantable partiality, to contend that they have as effectually obviated the danger on this side, as was wished and expected. Complaints are everywhere heard from our most considerate and virtuous citizens, equally the friends of public and private faith, and of public and personal liberty, that our governments are too unstable; that the public good is disregarded in the conflicts of rival parties; and that measures are too often decided, not according to the rules of justice, and the rights of the minor party, but by the superior force of an interested and overbearing majority. However anxiously we may wish that these complaints had no foundation, the evidence of known facts will not permit us to deny that they are in some degree true. It will be found, indeed, on a candid review of our situation, that some of the distresses under which we labor have been erroneously charged on the operations of our governments; but it will be found, at the same time, that other causes will not alone account for many of our heaviest misfortunes; and, particularly, for that prevailing and increasing distrust of public engagements, and alarm for private rights, which are echoed from one end of the continent to the other. These must be chiefly, if not wholly, effects of the unsteadiness and injustice, with which a factious spirit has tainted our public administrations.

By a faction, I understand a number of citizens, whether amounting to a majority of the whole, who are united and actuated by some common impulse of passion, or of interest, adverse to the rights of other citizens, or to the permanent and aggregate interests of the community.

There are two methods of curing the mischiefs of faction: the one, by removing its causes; the other, by controlling its effects.

There are again two methods of removing the causes of faction: the one, by destroying the liberty which is essential to its existence; the other, by giving to every citizen the same opinions, the same passions, and the same interests.

It could never be more truly said, than of the first remedy, that it was worse than the disease. Liberty is to faction what air is to fire, an aliment without which it instantly expires. But it could not be a less folly to abolish liberty, which is essential to political life, because it nourishes faction, than it would be to wish the annihilation of air, which is essential to animal life, because it imparts to fire its destructive agency.

The second expedient is as impracticable, as the first would be unwise. As long as the reason of man continues fallible, and he is at liberty to exercise it, different opinions will be formed. As long as the connection subsists between his reason and his self-love, his opinions and his passions will have a reciprocal influence on each other; and the former will be objects to which the latter will attach themselves. The diversity in the faculties of men, from which the rights of property originate, is not less an insuperable obstacle to an uniformity of interests. The protection of these faculties is the first object of government. From the protection of different and unequal faculties of acquiring property, the possession of different degrees and kinds of property immediately results; and from the influence of these

on the sentiments and views of the respective proprietors, ensues a division of the society into different interests and parties.

The latent causes of faction are thus sown in the nature of man; and we see them everywhere brought into different degrees of activity, according to the different circumstances of civil society. A zeal for different opinions concerning religion, concerning government, and many other points, as well of speculation as of practice; an attachment to different leaders ambitiously contending for preeminence and power; or to persons of other descriptions whose fortunes have been interesting to the human passions, have, in turn, divided mankind into parties, inflamed them with mutual animosity, and rendered them much more disposed to vex and oppress each other, than to cooperate for their common good. So strong is this propensity of mankind, to fall into mutual animosities, that where no substantial occasion presents itself, the most frivolous and fanciful distinctions have been sufficient to kindle their unfriendly passions and excite their most violent conflicts. But the most common and durable source of factions, has been the various and unequal distribution of property. Those who hold, and those who are without property, have ever formed distinct interests in society. Those who are creditors, and those who are debtors, fall under a like discrimination. A landed interest, a manufacturing interest, a mercantile interest, a moneyed interest, with many lesser interests, grow up of necessity in civilized nations, and divide them into different classes, actuated by different sentiments and views. The regulation of these various and interfering interests forms the principal task of modern legislation, and involves the spirit of the party and faction in the necessary and ordinary operations of the government.

No man is allowed to be a judge in his own cause; because his interest will certainly bias his judgment, and, not improbably, corrupt his integrity. With equal, nay, with greater reason, a body of men are unfit to be both judges and parties at the same time; yet what are many of the most important acts of legislation, but so many judicial determinations, not indeed concerning the right of single persons, but concerning the rights of large bodies of citizens? And what are the different classes of legislators, but advocates and parties to the causes which they determine? Is a law proposed concerning private debts? It is a questions to which the creditors are parties on one side, and the debtors on the other. Justice ought to hold the balance between them. Yet the parties are, and must be, themselves the judges; and the most numerous party, or, in other words, the most powerful faction, must be expected

to prevail. Shall domestic manufacturers be encouraged, and in what degree, by restrictions on foreign manufacturers? Are questions which would be differently decided by the landed and the manufacturing classes; and probably by neither with a sole regard to justice and the public good. The apportionment of taxes, on the various descriptions of property, is an act which seems to require the most exact impartiality; yet there is, perhaps, no legislative act, in which greater opportunity and temptation are given to a predominant party to trample on the rules of justice. Every shilling, with which they overburden the inferior number, is a shilling saved to their own pockets.

It is in vain to say, that enlightened statesmen will be able to adjust these clashing interests, and render them all subservient to the public good. Enlightened statesmen will not always be at the helm, nor, in many cases, can such an adjustment be made at all, without taking into view indirect and remote considerations, which will rarely prevail over the immediate interest which one party may find in disregarding the rights of another, or the good of the whole.

The inference to which we are brought is, that the causes of faction cannot be removed; and that relief is only to be sought in the means of controlling its *effects*.

If a faction consists of less than a majority, relief is supplied by the republican principle, which enables the majority to defeat its sinister views, by regular vote. It may clog the administration, it may convulse the society; but it will be unable to execute and mask its violence under the forms of the Constitution. When a majority is included in a faction, the form of popular government, on the other hand, enables it to sacrifice to its ruling passion or interest, both the public good and the rights of other citizens. To secure the public good, and private rights, against the danger of such a faction, and at the same time to preserve the spirit and the form of popular government, is then the great object to which our inquiries are directed. Let me add, that it is the great desideratum, by which alone this form of government can be rescued from the opprobrium under which it has so long laboured, and be recommended to the esteem and adoption of mankind.

By what means is this object attainable? Evidently by one of two only. Either the existence of the same passion or interest in a majority, at the same time, must be prevented; or the majority, having such coexistent passion or interest, must be rendered, by their number and local situation, unable to concert and carry into effect schemes of oppression. If the impulse and the opportunity be suffered to coincide, we well know that neither moral nor religious motives can be relied on as an adequate control. They are not found to be such on the injustice and violence of individuals, and lose their efficacy in proportion to the number combined together; that is, in proportion as their efficacy becomes needful.

From this view of the subject, it may be concluded, that a pure democracy, by which I mean a society consisting of a small number of citizens, who assemble and administer the government in person, can admit of no cure for the mischiefs of faction. A common passion or interest will, in almost every case, be felt by a majority of the whole; a communication and concert, results from the form of government itself; and there is nothing to check the inducements to sacrifice the weaker party, or an obnoxious individual. Hence, it is, that such democracies have ever been spectacles of turbulence and contention; have ever been found incompatible with personal security, or the rights of property; and have in general been as short in their lives, as they have been violent in their deaths. Theoretic politicians, who have patronized this species of government, have erroneously supposed, that by reducing mankind to a perfect equality in their political rights, they would, at the same time be perfectly equalized and assimilated in their possessions, their opinions, and their passions.

A republic, by which I mean a government in which the scheme of representation takes place, opens a different prospect, and promises the cure for which we are seeking. Let us examine the points in which it varies from pure democracy, and we shall comprehend both the nature of the cure and the efficacy which it must derive from the union.

The two great points of difference, between a democracy and a republic, are, first, the delegation of the government, in the latter, to a small number of citizens, elected by the rest; secondly, the greater number of citizens, and greater sphere of country, over which the latter may be extended.

The effect of the first difference is, on the one hand, to refine and enlarge the public views, by passing them through the medium of a chosen body of citizens, whose wisdom may best discern the true interest of their country, and whose patriotism and love of justice, will be least likely to sacrifice it to temporary or partial considerations. Under such a regulation, it may well happen, that the public voice, pronounced by the representatives of the people, will be more consonant to the public good, than if pronounced by the people themselves, convened for the purpose. On the other hand the effect may be inverted. Men of factious tempers, of local prejudices, or of sin-

ister designs, may by intrigue, by corruption, or by other means, first obtain the suffrages, and then betray the interest of the people. The question resulting is, whether small or extensive republics are most favourable to the election of proper guardians of the public weal; and it is clearly decided in favour of the latter by two obvious considerations.

In the first place, it is to be remarked that, however small the republic may be, the representatives must be raised to a certain number, in order to guard against the cabals of a few; and that however large it may be, they must be limited to a certain number, in order to guard against the confusion of a multitude. Hence, the number of representatives in the two cases not being in proportion to that of the constituents, and being proportionally greatest in the small republic, it follows, that if the proportion of fit characters be not less in the large than in the small republic, the former will present a greater option, and consequently a greater probability of a fit choice.

In the next place, as each representative will be chosen by a greater number of citizens in the large than in the small republic, it will be more difficult for unworthy candidates to practice with success the vicious arts, by which elections are too often carried; and the suffrages of the people being more free, will be more likely to centre in men who possess the most attractive merit, and the most diffusive and established characters.

It must be confessed, that in this, as in most other cases, there is a mean, on both sides of which inconveniences will be found to lie. By enlarging too much the number of electors, you render the representatives too little acquainted with all their local circumstances and lesser interests; as by reducing it too much, you render him unduly attached to these, and too little fit to comprehend and pursue great and national objects. The federal constitution forms a happy combination in this respect; the great and aggregate interests being referred to the national, the local and particular to the state legislatures.

The other point of difference is, the greater number of citizens, and extent of territory, which may be brought within the compass of republican, than of democratic government; and it is this circumstance principally which renders factious combinations less to be dreaded in the former, than in the latter. The smaller the society, the fewer probably will be the distinct parties and interests composing it; the fewer the distinct parties and interests, the more frequently will a majority be found of the same party; and the smaller the number of individuals composing a majority, and the smaller the compass within which they are placed, the more easily will

they concert and execute their plans of oppression. Extend the sphere, and you take in a greater variety of parties and interests; you make it less probable that a majority of the whole will have a common motive to invade the rights of other citizens; or if such a common motive exists, it will be more difficult for all who feel it to discover their own strength, and to act in unison with each other. Besides other impediments, it may be remarked, that where there is a consciousness of unjust or dishonourable purposes, communication is always checked by distrust, in proportion to the number whose concurrence is necessary.

Hence, it clearly appears, that the same advantage, which a republic has over a democracy, in controlling the effects of faction, is enjoyed by a large over a small republic—is enjoyed by the union over the states composing it. Does this advantage consist in the substitution of representatives, whose enlightened views and virtuous sentiments render them superior to local prejudices, and to schemes of injustice? It will not be denied that the representation of the union will be most likely to possess these requisite endowments. Does it consist in the greater security afforded by a greater variety of parties, against the event of any one party being able to outnumber and oppress the rest? In an equal degree does the increased variety of parties, comprised within the union, increase the security? Does it, in fine, consist in the greater obstacles opposed to the concert and accomplishment of the secret wishes of an unjust and interested majority? Here, again, the extent of the union gives it the most palpable advantage.

The influence of factious leaders may kindle a flame within their particular states, but will be unable to spread a general conflagration through the other states; a religious sect may degenerate into a political faction in a part of the confederacy; but the variety of sects dispersed over the entire face of it, must secure the national councils against any danger from that source: a rage for paper money, for an abolition of debts, for an equal division of property, or for any other improper or wicked project, will be less apt to pervade the whole body of the union than a particular member of it; in the same proportion as such a malady is more likely to taint a particular county or district, than an entire state.

In the extent and proper structure of the union, therefore, we behold a republican remedy for the diseases most incident to republican government. And according to the degree of pleasure and pride we feel in being republicans, ought to be our zeal in cherishing the spirit, and supporting the character of federalists.

THE FEDERALIST, NO. 51, JAMES MADISON

The Federalist, No. 51, also written by Madison, is a classic statement in defense of separation of powers and republican processes. Its fourth paragraph is especially famous and is frequently quoted by students of government.

To what expedient, then, shall we finally resort, for maintaining in practice the necessary partition of power among the several departments as laid down in the Constitution? The only answer that can be given is that as all these exterior provisions are found to be inadequate the defect must be supplied, by so contriving the interior structure of the government as that its several constituent parts may, by their mutual relations, be the means of keeping each other in their proper places. Without presuming to undertake a full development of this important idea I will hazard a few general observations which may perhaps place it in a clearer light, and enable us to form a more correct judgment of the principles and structure of the government planned by the convention.

In order to lay a due foundation for that separate and distinct exercise of the different powers of government, which to a certain extent is admitted on all hands to be essential to the preservation of liberty, it is evident that each department should have a will of its own; and consequently should be so constituted that the members of each should have as little agency as possible in the appointment of the members of the others. Were this principle rigorously adhered to, it would require that all the appointments for the supreme executive, legislative, and judiciary magistracies should be drawn from the same fountain of authority, the people, through channels having no communication whatever with one another. Perhaps such a plan of constructing the several departments would be less difficult in practice than it may in contemplation appear. Some difficulties, however, and some additional expense would attend the execution of it. Some deviations, therefore, from the principle must be admitted. In the constitution of the judiciary department in particular, it might be inexpedient to insist rigorously on the principle: first, because peculiar qualifications being essential in the members, the primary consideration ought to be to select that mode of choice which best secures these qualifications; second, because the permanent tenure by which the appointments are held in that department must soon destroy all sense of dependence on the authority conferring them.

It is equally evident that the members of each department should be as little dependent as possible on those of the others for the emoluments annexed to their offices. Were the executive magistrate, or the judges, not independent of the legislature in this particular, their independence in every other would be merely nominal.

But the great security against a gradual concentration of the several powers in the same department consists in giving to those who administer each department the necessary constitutional means and personal motives to resist encroachments of the others. The provision for defense must in this, as in all other cases, be made commensurate to the danger of attack. Ambition must be made to counteract ambition. The interest of the man must be connected with the constitutional rights of the place. It may be a reflection on human nature that such devices should be necessary to control the abuses of government. But what is government itself but the greatest of all reflections on human nature? If men were angels, no government would be necessary. If angels were to govern men, neither external nor internal controls on government would be necessary. In framing a government which is to be administered by men over men, the great difficulty lies in this: you must first enable the government to control the governed; and in the next place oblige it to control itself. A dependence on the people is, no doubt, the primary control on the government; but experience has taught mankind the necessity of auxiliary precautions.

This policy of supplying, by opposite and rival interests, the defect of better motives, might be traced through the whole system of human affairs, private as well as public. We see it particularly displayed in all the subordinate distributions of power, where the constant aim is to divide and arrange the several offices in such a manner as that each may be a check on the other—that the private interest of every individual may be a sentinel over the public rights. These inventions of prudence cannot be less requisite in the distribution of the supreme powers of the State.

But it is not possible to give to each department an equal power of self-defense. In republican government, the legislative authority necessarily predominates. The remedy for this inconveniency is to divide the legislature into different branches; and to render them, by modes of election and different principles of action, as little connected with each other as the nature of their common functions and their common dependence on the society will admit. It may even be necessary to guard against dangerous encroachments by still further precautions. As the weight of the legislative authority requires that it should be thus divided, the weakness of the executive may require, on the other hand, that it should be fortified. An absolute negative on the legislature appears, at first view, to be the natural defense with which the executive magistrate should be armed. But perhaps it would be neither altogether safe nor alone sufficient. On ordinary occasions it might not be exerted with the requisite firmness, and on extraordinary occasions it might be perfidiously abused. May not this defect of an absolute negative be supplied by some qualified connection between this weaker department and the weaker branch of the stronger department, by which the latter may be led to support the constitutional rights of the former, without being too much detached from the rights of its own department?

If the principles on which these observations are founded be just, as I persuade myself they are, and they be applied as a criterion to the several State constitutions, and to the federal Constitution, it will be found that if the latter does not perfectly correspond with them, the former are infinitely less able to bear such a test.

There are, moreover, two considerations particularly applicable to the federal system of America, which place that system in a very interesting point of view.

First. In a single republic, all the power surrendered by the people is submitted to the administration of a single government; and the usurpations are guarded against by a division of the government into distinct and separate departments. In the compound republic of America, the power surrendered by the people is first divided between two distinct governments, and then the portion allotted to each subdivided among distinct and separate departments. Hence a double security arises to the rights of the people. The different governments will control each other, at the same time that each will be controlled by itself.

Second. It is of great importance in a republic not only to guard the society against the oppression of its rulers, but to guard one part of the society against the injustice of the other part. Different interests necessarily exist in different classes of citizens. If a majority be united by a common interest, the rights of the minority will be insecure. There are but two methods of providing against this evil: the one by creating a will in the community independent of the majority—that is, of the society itself; the other, by comprehending in the society so many separate descriptions of citizens as will render an unjust combination of a majority of the whole very improbable, if not impracticable. The first method prevails in all governments possessing an hereditary or self-appointed authority. This, at best, is but a precarious security; because a power independent of the society may as well espouse the unjust views of the major as the rightful interests of the minor party, and may possibly be turned against both parties. The second method will be exemplified in the federal republic of the United States. Whilst all authority in it will be derived from and dependent on the society, the society itself will be broken into so many parts, interests and classes of citizens, that the rights of individuals, or of the minority, will be in little danger from interested combinations of the majority. In a free government the security for civil rights must be the same as that for religious rights. It consists in the one case in the multiplicity of interests, and in the other in the multiplicity of sects. The degree of security in both cases

will depend on the number of interests and sects; and this may be presumed to depend on the extent of country and number of people comprehended under the same government. This view of the subject must particularly recommend a proper federal system to all the sincere and considerate friends of republican government, since it shows that in exact proportion as the territory of the Union may be formed into more circumscribed Confederacies, or States, oppressive combinations of a majority will be facilitated; the best security, under the republican forms, for the rights of every class of citizen, will be diminished; and consequently the stability and independence of some member of the government, the only other security, must be proportionally increased. Justice is the end of government. It is the end of civil society. It ever has been and ever will be pursued until it be obtained, or until liberty be lost in the pursuit. In a society under the forms of which the stronger faction can readily unite and oppress the weaker, anarchy may as truly be said to reign as in a state of nature, where the weaker individual is not secured against the violence of the stronger; and as, in the latter state, even the stronger individuals are prompted, by the uncertainty of their condition, to submit to a government which may protect the weak as well as themselves; so, in the former state, will the more powerful factions or parties be gradually induced, by a

like motive, to wish for a government which will protect all parties, the weaker as well as the more powerful. It can be little doubted that if the State of Rhode Island was separated from the Confederacy and left to itself, the insecurity of rights under the popular form of government within such narrow limits would be displayed by such reiterated oppressions of factious majorities that some power altogether independent of the people would soon be called for by the voice of the very factions whose misrule had proved the necessity to it. In the extended republic of the United States, and among the great variety of interests, parties, and sects which it embraces, a coalition of a majority of the whole society could seldom take place on any other principles than those of justice and the general good; whilst there being thus less danger to a minor from the will of a major party, there must be less pretext, also, to provide for the security of the former, by introducing into the government a will not dependent on the latter, or, in other words, a will independent of the society itself. It is no less certain that it is important, notwithstanding the contrary opinions which have been entertained that the larger the society, provided it lie within a practicable sphere, the more duly capable it will be of self-government. And happily for the *republican cause,* the practicable sphere may be carried to a very great extent by a judicious modification and mixture of the *federal principle.*

THE FEDERALIST, NO. 78, ALEXANDER HAMILTON

The Federalist, No. 78, written by Alexander Hamilton, explains and praises the provisions for the judiciary in the newly drafted Constitution. Notice especially how Hamilton asserts that the courts have a key responsibility in determining the meaning of the Constitution as fundamental law. Hamilton is outlining here the doctrine of *judicial review* as we now know it.

We proceed now to an examination of the judiciary department of the proposed government.

In unfolding the defects of the existing Confederation, the utility and necessity of a federal judicature have been clearly pointed out. It is the less necessary to recapitulate the considerations there urged as the propriety of the institution in the abstract is not disputed; the only questions which have been raised being relative to the manner of constituting it, and to its extent. To these points, therefore, our observations shall be confined.

The manner of constituting it seems to embrace these several objects: 1st. The mode of appointing the judges. 2nd. The tenure by

which they are to hold their places. 3rd. The partition of the judiciary authority between different courts and their relations to each other.

First. As to the mode of appointing the judges: this is the same with that of appointing the officers of the Union in general and has been so fully discussed in the two last numbers that nothing can be said here which would not be useless repetition.

Second. As to the tenure by which the judges are to hold their places: this chiefly concerns their duration in office, the provisions for their support, the precautions for their responsibility.

According to the plan of the convention, all judges who may be appointed by the Unit-

ed States are to hold their offices *during good behavior;* which is conformable to the most approved of the State constitutions, and among the rest, to that of this State. Its propriety having been drawn into question by the adversaries of that plan is no light symptom of the rage for objection which disorders their imaginations and judgments. The standard of good behavior for the continuance in office of the judicial magistracy is certainly one of the most valuable of the modern improvements in the practice of government. In a monarchy it is an excellent barrier to the despotism of the prince; in a republic it is a no less excellent barrier to the encroachments and oppressions of the representative body. And it is the best expedient which can be devised in any government to secure a steady, upright, and impartial administration of the laws.

Whoever attentively considers the different departments of power must perceive that, in a government in which they are separated from each other, the judiciary, from the nature of its functions, will always be the least dangerous to the political rights of the Constitution; because it will be least in a capacity to annoy or injure them. The executive not only dispenses the honors but holds the sword of the community. The legislature not only commands the purse but prescribes the rules by which the duties and rights of every citizen are to be regulated. The judiciary, on the contrary, has no influence over either the sword or the purse; no direction either of the strength or of the wealth of the society, and can take no active resolution whatever. It may truly be said to have neither FORCE NOR WILL but merely judgment; and must ultimately depend upon the aid of the executive arm even for the efficacy of its judgments.

This simple view of the matter suggests several important consequences. It proves incontestably that the judiciary is beyond comparison the weakest of the three departments of power; that it can never attack with success either of the other two; and that all possible care is requisite to enable it to defend itself against their attacks. It equally proves that though individual oppression may now and then proceed from the courts of justice, the general liberty of the people can never be endangered from that quarter; I mean so long as the judiciary remains truly distinct from both the legislature and the executive. For I agree that "there is no liberty if the power of judging be not separated from the legislative and executive powers." And it proves, in the last place, that as liberty can have nothing to fear from the judiciary alone, but would have everything to fear from its union with either of the other departments, that as all the effects of such a union must ensue from a dependence of the former on the latter, notwithstanding a nominal and apparent separation; that as, from the natural feebleness of the judiciary, it is in continual jeopardy of being overpowered, awed, or influenced by its co-ordinate branches; and that as nothing can contribute so much to its firmness and independence as permanency in office, this quality may therefore be justly regarded as an indispensable ingredient in its constitution, and, in a great measure, as the citadel for the public justice and the public security.

The complete independence of the courts of justice is peculiarly essential in a limited Constitution. By a limited Constitution, I understand one which contains certain specified exceptions to the legislative authority; such, for instance, as that it shall pass no bills of attainder, no *ex post facto* laws, and the like. Limitations of this kind can be preserved in practice no other way than through the medium of courts of justice, whose duty it must be to declare all acts contrary to the manifest tenor of the Constitution void. Without this, all the reservations of particular rights or privileges would amount to nothing.

Some perplexity respecting the rights of the courts to pronounce legislative acts void, because contrary to the Constitution, has arisen from an imagination that the doctrine would imply a superiority to the judiciary to the legislative power. It is urged that the authority which can declare the acts of another void must necessarily be superior to the one whose acts may be declared void. As this doctrine is of great importance in all the American constitutions, a brief discussion of the grounds on which it rests cannot be unacceptable.

There is no position which depends on clearer principles than that every act of a delegated authority, contrary to the tenor of the commission under which it is exercised, is void. No legislative act, therefore, contrary to the Constitution, can be valid. To deny this would be to affirm that the deputy is greater than his principal; that the servant is above his master; that the representatives of the people are superior to the people themselves; that men acting by virtue of powers do not authorize, but what they forbid.

If it be said that the legislative body are themselves the constitutional judges of their own powers and that the construction they put upon them is conclusive upon the other departments it may be answered that this cannot be the natural presumption where it is not to be collected from any particular provisions in the Constitution. It is not otherwise to be supposed that the Constitution could intend to enable the representatives of the people to substitute their *will* to that of their constituents. It is far more rational to suppose that the courts were designed to be an intermediate body between the people and the legislature in order, among other things, to keep the latter within the limits assigned to their authority. The interpretation of the laws is the proper and peculiar province of the courts. A constitution is, in fact, and must be regarded by the judges as, a fundamental law. It therefore belongs to them to ascertain its meaning as well as the meaning of any particular act proceeding from the legislative body. If there should happen to be an irreconcilable variance between the two, that which has the superior obligation and validity ought, of course, to be preferred; or, in other words, the Constitution ought to be preferred to the statute, the intention of the people to the intention of their agents.

Nor does this conclusion by any means suppose a superiority of the judicial to the legislative power. It only supposes that the power of the people is superior to both, and that where the will of the legislature, declared in its statutes, stands in opposition to that of the people, declared in the Constitution, the judges ought to be governed by the latter rather than the former. They ought to regulate their decisions by the fundamental laws rather than by those which are not fundamental.

This exercise of judicial discretion in determining between two contradictory laws is exemplified in a familiar instance. It not uncommonly happens that there are two statutes existing at one time, clashing in whole or in part with each other and neither of them containing any repealing clause or expression. In such a case, it is the province of the courts to liquidate and fix their meaning and operation. So far as they can, by any fair construction, be reconciled to each other, reason and law conspire to dictate that this should be done; where this is impracticable, it becomes a matter of necessity to give effect to one in exclusion of the other. The rule which has obtained in the courts for determining their relative validity is that the last in order of time shall be preferred to the first. But this is a mere rule of construction, not derived from any positive law but from the nature and reason of the thing. It is a rule not enjoined upon the courts by legislative provision but adopted by themselves, as consonant to truth and propriety, for the direction of their conduct as interpreters of the law. They thought it reasonable that between the interfering acts of an *equal* authority that which was the last indication of its will should have the preference.

But in regard to the interfering acts of a superior and subordinate authority of an original and derivative power, the nature and reason of the thing indicates the converse of that rule as proper to be followed. They teach us that the prior act of a superior ought to be preferred to the subsequent act of an inferior and subordinate authority; and that accordingly, whenever a particular statute contravenes the Constitution, it will be the duty of the judicial tribunals to adhere to the latter and disregard the former.

It can be of no weight to say that the courts, on the pretense of a repugnancy, may substitute their own pleasure to the constitutional intentions of the legislature. This might as well happen in the case of two contradictory statutes; or it might as well happen in every adjudication upon any single statute. The courts must declare the sense of the law; and if they should be disposed to exercise WILL instead of JUDGMENT, the consequence would equally be the substitution of their pleasure to that of the legislative body. The observation, if it prove anything, would prove that there ought to be no judges distinct from that body.

If, then, the courts of justice are to be considered as the bulwarks of a limited Constitution against legislative encroachments, this consideration will afford a strong argument for the permanent tenure of judicial offices, since nothing will contribute so much as this to that independent spirit in the judges which must be essential to the faithful performance of so arduous a duty.

This independence of the judges is equally requisite to guard the Constitution and the rights of individuals from the effects of those ill humors which the arts of designing men, or the influence of particular conjunctures, sometimes disseminate among the people themselves, and which, though they speedily give place to better information, and more deliberate reflection, have a tendency, in the meantime, to occasion dangerous innovations in the government, and serious oppressions of the minor party in the community. Though I trust the friends of the proposed Constitution will never concur with its enemies in questioning that fundamental principal of Republican government which admits the right of the people to alter or abolish the established Constitution whenever they find it inconsistent with their happiness; yet it is not to be inferred from this principle that the representatives of the people, whenever a momentary inclination happens to lay hold of a majority of their constituents incompatible with the provisions in the existing Constitution would, on that account, be justifiable in a violation of those provisions; or that the courts would be under a greater obligation to connive at infractions in this shape than when they had proceeded wholly from the cabals of the representative body. Until the people have, by some solemn and authoritative act, annulled or changed the established form, it is binding upon themselves collectively, as well as individually; and no presumption, or even knowledge of their sentiments, can warrant their representatives in a departure from it prior to such an act. But it is easy to see that it would require an uncommon portion of fortitude in the judges to do their duty as faithful guardians of the Constitution, where legislative invasions of it had been instigated by the major voice of the community.

But it is not with a view to infractions of the Constitution only that the independence of the judges may be an essential safeguard against the effects of occasional ill humors in the society. These sometimes extend no farther than to the injury of the private rights of particular classes of citizens, by unjust and partial laws. Here also the firmness of the judicial magistracy is of vast importance in mitigating the severity and confining the operation of such laws. It not only serves to moderate the immediate mischiefs of those which may have been passed but it operates as a check upon the legislative body in passing them; who, perceiving that obstacles to the success of iniquitous intention are to be expected from the scruples of the courts, are in a manner compelled, by the very motives of the injustice they mediate, to qualify their attempts. This is a circumstance calculated to have more influence upon the character of our governments than but a few may be aware of. The benefits of the integrity and moderation of the judiciary have already been felt in more States than one; and though they may have displeased those whose sinister expectations they may have disappointed, they must have commanded the esteem and applause of all the virtuous and disinterested. Considerate men of every description ought to prize whatever will tend to beget or fortify that temper in the courts; as no man can be sure that he may not be tomorrow the victim of a spirit of injustice, by which he may be a gainer today. And every man must now feel that the inevitable tendency of such a spirit is to sap the foundations of public and private confidence and to introduce in its stead universal distrust and distress.

That inflexible and uniform adherence to the rights of the Constitution, and of individuals, which we perceive to be indispensable in the courts of justice, can certainly not be expected from judges who hold their offices by a temporary commission. Periodical appointments, however regulated, or by whomsoever made, would, in some way or other, be fatal to their necessary independence. If the power of making them was committed either to the executive or legislature there would be danger of an improper complaisance to the branch which possessed it; if to both, there would be an unwillingness to hazard the displeasure of either; if to the people, or to persons chosen by them for the special purpose, there would be too great a disposition to consult popularity to justify a reliance that nothing would be consulted by the Constitution and the laws.

There is yet a further and a weighty reason for the permanency of the judicial offices which is deducible from the nature of the qualifications they require. It has been frequently remarked with great propriety that a voluminous code of laws is one of the inconveniences necessarily connected with the advantages of a free government. To avoid an arbitrary discretion in the courts, it is indispensable that they should be bound down by strict rules and precedents which serve to define and point out their duty in every particular case that comes before them; and it will readily be conceived from the variety of controversies which grow out of the folly and wickedness of mankind that the records of those precedents must unavoidably swell to a very considerable bulk and must demand long and laborious study to acquire a competent knowledge of them. Hence it is that there can be but few men in the society who will have sufficient skill in the laws to qualify them for the stations of judges. And making the proper deductions for the ordinary depravity of human nature, the number must be still smaller of those who unite the requisite integrity with the requisite knowledge. These considerations apprise us that the government can have no great option between fit characters; and that a temporary duration in office which would naturally discourage such characters from quitting a lucrative line of practice to accept a seat on the bench would have a tendency to throw the administration of justice into hands less able and less well qualified to conduct it with utility and dignity. In the present circumstances of this country and in those in which it is likely to be for a long time to come, the disadvantages on this score would be greater than they may at first sight appear; but it must be confessed that they are far inferior to those which present themselves under the other aspects of the subject.

Upon the whole, there can be no room to doubt that the convention acted wisely in copying from the models of those constitutions which have established *good behavior* as the tenure of their judicial offices in point of duration, and that so far from being blamable on this account, their plan would have been inexcusably defective if it had wanted this important feature of good government. The experience of Great Britain affords an illustrious comment on the excellence of the institution.

Presidential Election Results 1789–1992

Year	Candidates	Party	Popular Vote	Electoral Vote
1789	George Washington			69
	John Adams			34
	Others			35
1793	George Washington			132
	John Adams			77
	George Clinton			50
	Others			5
1796	John Adams	Federalist		71
	Thomas Jefferson	Democratic-Republican		68
	Thomas Pinckney	Federalist		59
	Aaron Burr	Democratic-Republican		30
	Others			48
1800	Thomas Jefferson	Democratic-Republican		73
	Aaron Burr	Democratic-Republican		73
	John Adams	Federalist		65
	Charles C. Pinckney	Federalist		64
1804	Thomas Jefferson	Democratic-Republican		162
	Charles C. Pinckney	Federalist		14
1808	James Madison	Democratic-Republican		122
	Charles C. Pinckney	Federalist		47
	George Clinton	Independent-Republican		6
1812	James Madison	Democratic-Republican		128
	DeWitt Clinton	Federalist		89
1816	James Monroe	Democratic-Republican		183
	Rufus King	Federalist		34
1820	James Monroe	Democratic-Republican		231
	John Quincy Adams	Independent-Republican		1
1824	John Quincy Adams	Democratic-Republican	108,740(30.5%)	84
	Andrew Jackson	Democratic-Republican	153,544(43.1%)	99
	Henry Clay	Democratic-Republican	47,136(13.2%)	37
	William H. Crawford	Democratic-Republican	46,618(13.1%)	41
1828	Andrew Jackson	Democratic	647,231(56.0%)	178
	John Quincy Adams	National Republican	509,097(44.0%)	83
1832	Andrew Jackson	Democratic	687,502(55.0%)	219
	Henry Clay	National Republican	530,189(42.4%)	49
	William Wirt	Anti-Masonic		7
	John Floyd	National Republican	33,108(2.6%)	11
1836	Martin Van Buren	Democratic	761,549(50.9%)	170
	William H. Harrison	Whig	549,567(36.7%)	73
	Hugh L. White	Whig	145,396(9.7%)	26
	Daniel Webster	Whig	41,287(2.7%)	14
1840	William H. Harrison	Whig	1,275,017(53.1%)	234
	Martin Van Buren	Democratic	1,128,702(46.9%)	60
1844	James K. Polk	Democratic	1,337,243(49.6%)	170
	Henry Clay	Whig	1,299,068(48.1%)	105
	James G. Birney	Liberty	63,300(2.3%)	
1848	Zachary Taylor	Whig	1,360,101(47.4%)	163
	Lewis Cass	Democratic	1,220,544(42.5%)	127
	Martin Van Buren	Free Soil	291,163(10.1%)	
1852	Franklin Pierce	Democratic	1,601,474(50.9%)	254
	Winfield Scott	Whig	1,386,578(44.1%)	42
1856	James Buchanan	Democratic	1,838,169(45.4%)	174
	John C. Fremont	Republican	1,335,264(33.0%)	114
	Millard Fillmore	American	874,534(21.6%)	8
1860	Abraham Lincoln	Republican	1,865,593(39.8%)	180
	Stephen A. Douglas	Democratic	1,381,713(29.5%)	12
	John C. Breckinridge	Democratic	848,356(18.1%)	72
	John Bell	Constitutional Union	592,906(12.6%)	79
1864	Abraham Lincoln	Republican	2,206,938(55.0%)	212
	George B. McClellan	Democratic	1,803,787(45.0%)	21
1868	Ulysses S. Grant	Republican	3,013,421(52.7%)	214
	Horatio Seymour	Democratic	2,706,829(47.3%)	80
1872	Ulysses S. Grant	Republican	3,596,745(55.6%)	286
	Horace Greeley	Democratic	2,843,446(43.9%)	66
1876	Rutherford B. Hayes	Republican	4,036,571(48.0%)	185
	Samuel J. Tilden	Democratic	4,284,020(51.0%)	184
1880	James A. Garfield	Republican	4,449,053(48.3%)	214
	Winfield S. Hancock	Democratic	4,442,035(48.2%)	155
	James B. Weaver	Greenback-Labor	308,578(3.4%)	

Presidential Election Results 1789–1992

Year	Candidates	Party	Popular Vote	Electoral Vote
1884	Grover Cleveland	Democratic	4,874,986(48.5%)	219
	James G. Blaine	Republican	4,851,931(48.2%)	182
	Benjamin F. Butler	Greenback-Labor	175,370(1.8%)	
1888	Benjamin Harrison	Republican	5,444,337(47.8%)	233
	Grover Cleveland	Democratic	5,540,050(48.6%)	168
1892	Grover Cleveland	Democratic	5,554,414(46.0%)	277
	Benjamin Harrison	Republican	5,190,802(43.0%)	145
	James B. Weaver	Peoples	1,027,329(8.5%)	22
1896	William McKinley	Republican	7,035,638(50.8%)	271
	William J. Bryan	Democratic; Populist	6,467,946(46.7%)	176
1900	William McKinley	Republican	7,219,530(51.7%)	292
	William J. Bryan	Democratic; Populist	6,356,734(45.5%)	155
1904	Theodore Roosevelt	Republican	7,628,834(56.4%)	336
	Alton B. Parker	Democrat	5,084,401(37.6%)	140
	Eugene V. Debs	Socialist	402,460(3.0%)	
1908	William H. Taft	Republican	7,679,006(51.6%)	321
	William J. Bryan	Democratic	6,409,106(43.1%)	162
	Eugene V. Debs	Socialist	420,820(2.8%)	
1912	Woodrow Wilson	Democratic	6,286,820(41.8%)	435
	Theodore Roosevelt	Progressive	4,126,020(27.4%)	88
	William H. Taft	Republican	3,483,922(23.2%)	8
	Eugene V. Debs	Socialist	897,011(6.0%)	
1916	Woodrow Wilson	Democratic	9,129,606(49.3%)	277
	Charles E. Hughes	Republican	8,538,211(46.1%)	254
1920	Warren G. Harding	Republican	16,152,200(61.0%)	404
	James M. Cox	Democratic	9,147,353(34.6%)	127
	Eugene V. Debs	Socialist	919,799(3.5%)	
1924	Calvin Coolidge	Republican	15,725,016(54.1%)	382
	John W. Davis	Democratic	8,385,586(28.8%)	136
	Robert M. La Follette	Progressive	4,822,856(16.6%)	13
1928	Herbert C. Hoover	Republican	21,392,190(58.2%)	444
	Alfred E. Smith	Democratic	15,016,443(40.8%)	87
1932	Franklin D. Roosevelt	Democratic	22,809,638(57.3%)	472
	Herbert C. Hoover	Republican	15,758,901(39.6%)	59
	Norman Thomas	Socialist	881,951(2.2%)	
1936	Franklin D. Roosevelt	Democratic	27,751,612(60.7%)	523
	Alfred M. Landon	Republican	16,681,913(36.4%)	8
	William Lemke	Union	891,858(1.9%)	
1940	Franklin D. Roosevelt	Democratic	27,243,466(54.7%)	449
	Wendell L. Wilkie	Republican	22,304,755(44.8%)	82
1944	Franklin D. Roosevelt	Democratic	25,602,505(52.8%)	432
	Thomas E. Dewey	Republican	22,006,278(44.5%)	99
1948	Harry S. Truman	Democratic	24,105,812(49.5%)	303
	Thomas E. Dewey	Republican	21,970,065(45.1%)	189
	J. Strom Thurmond	States' Rights	1,169,063(2.4%)	39
	Henry A. Wallace	Progressive	1,157,172(2.4%)	
1952	Dwight D. Eisenhower	Republican	33,936,234(55.2%)	442
	Adlai E. Stevenson	Democratic	27,314,992(44.5%)	89
1956	Dwight D. Eisenhower	Republican	35,590,472(57.4%)	457
	Adlai E. Stevenson	Democratic	26,022,752(42.0%)	73
1960	John F. Kennedy	Democratic	34,227,096(49.9%)	303
	Richard M. Nixon	Republican	34,108,546(49.6%)	219
1964	Lyndon B Johnson	Democratic	43,126,233(61.1%)	486
	Barry Goldwater	Republican	27,174,989(38.5%)	52
1968	Richard M. Nixon	Republican	31,783,783(43.4%)	301
	Hubert H. Humphrey	Democratic	31,271,839(42.7%)	191
	George C. Wallace	American Independent	9,899,557(13.5%)	46
1972	Richard M. Nixon	Republican	46,632,189(61.3%)	520
	George McGovern	Democratic	28,422,015(37.3%)	17
1976	Jimmy Carter	Democratic	40,828,587(50.1%)	297
	Gerald R. Ford	Republican	39,147,613(48.0%)	240
1980	Ronald Reagan	Republican	42,941,145(51.0%)	489
	Jimmy Carter	Democratic	34,663,037(41.0%)	49
	John B. Anderson	Independent	5,551,551(6.6%)	
1984	Ronald Reagan	Republican	53,428,357(59%)	525
	Walter F. Mondale	Democratic	36,930,923(41%)	13
1988	George Bush	Republican	48,881,011(53%)	426
	Michael Dukakis	Democratic	41,828,350(46%)	111
1992	Bill Clinton	Democratic	38,394,210(43%)	370
	George Bush	Republican	33,974,386(38%)	168
	H. Ross Perot	Independent	16,573,465(19%)	

GLOSSARY

We have tried to write a readable book about American politics and government. We realize, however, that certain legal terms and political science phrases may not be familiar to some readers. To make such words or phrases (which appear in the text in boldface type) more understandable, we have compiled this glossary.

Administrative law Law relating to the authority and procedures of administrative agencies, as well as to the rules and regulations issued by those agencies.

Admiralty and maritime law Law derived from the general maritime law of nations, modified by Congress, applicable not only on the high seas but also on all navigable waterways in the United States. This body of law is applicable to cases concerning shipping and waterway commerce.

Advisory opinion An opinion unrelated to a particular case that gives a court's view about a constitutional or legal issue.

Affirmative action Remedial actions—originally relating to employment but now also covering college and university admissions, contracting, and other areas—designed to overcome effects of past societal and individual discrimination against minorities and women.

Amendatory veto State veto power that allows governors to return a bill to the legislature with suggested changes or amendments. The legislators must decide whether to accept the governor's recommendations or attempt to pass the bill in its original form over the veto. Also called **conditional veto.**

American Dream The widespread belief that individual initiative and hard work can result in economic success, that the next generation can have a better standard of living than the former, and that the United States is a land of opportunity.

Amicus curia ("friend of the court") brief A brief filed by an individual or organization with the permission of the court. It provides arguments in addition to those presented by the immediate parties to the case.

Annapolis Convention A convention held in August 1786 that issued the call to Congress and the states for what became the Constitutional Convention. Attended by delegates from five states, it was called to consider problems of trade and navigation.

Antifederalists Persons opposed to more nationally centralized government in general, and to the ratification of the 1787 Philadelphia Constitution in particular.

Antitrust policy Federal laws (of which the Sherman Act of 1890 is most prominent), supplemented by state laws, that try to prevent one or a few business firms from dominating a particular market through monopoly or restraint of trade.

Appellate jurisdiction Authority to review decisions of lower courts, administrative tribunals, and some independent regulatory agencies.

Articles of Confederation The first constitution of the newly independent American states. It was drafted in 1777, ratified in 1781, and replaced by the present Constitution in 1789.

Assessment The value a government places on property for purposes of taxation. The assessed value may or may not reflect the real market value.

Assigned counsel system Arrangement whereby attorneys are provided for persons accused of crime who are unable to hire their own lawyers. The judge assigns a member of the bar to provide counsel to a particular defendant.

Attentive public Those who follow public affairs fairly carefully, reading newspapers and magazines and watching television news broadcasts to keep informed about politics and world affairs.

Australian ballot A ballot printed by the state, which the voter marks and then places in a ballot box. Also called a **secret ballot.**

Bad tendency doctrine Interpretation of the First Amendment that would permit legislatures to make illegal speech that can reasonably be said to have a tendency to cause people to engage in illegal action.

Bicameral legislature Two-house legislature; form for 49 of the states as well as for the U.S. Congress.

Bill of attainder Legislative act that inflicts punishment, including deprivation of property without judicial trial, on named individuals or members of a specified group.

Bipartisanship A policy that emphasizes cooperation and a united front between the major political parties, especially on sensitive foreign policy issues.

Block grant Broad grant of funds made by one level of government to another for prescribed activities—for example, health programs or crime prevention—with few strings attached.

Broker rule Government acting essentially as a go-between or mediator among organized groups that have definite policy goals.

Bureau Generally, the largest subunit of a government department or agency.

Bureaucracy   Large private or public organizations that are hierarchical in structure, provide each employee with clearly defined responsibility, base actions and decisions on impersonal rules, and hire and promote employees based on skills and training.

Bureaucrat   Career government employee, normally one who gains office by appointment rather than election.

Capitalism   An economic system characterized by private property, competitive markets, economic incentives, and limited government involvement.

Caucus (legislative) or conference   Meeting of the members of a party in a chamber of legislature to select the party leadership in that chamber and to take party positions on pending legislative issues.

Caucus (local party)   Meeting of party members in a ward or town to choose party officials and/or candidates for public office and to decide platforms.

Centralists   Those who favor national rather than state or local action.

Charter   A city "constitution" that outlines the structure of city government, defines the authority of various officials, and provides for their selection.

Checks and balances   Constitutional grant of powers that enables each of the three branches of government—legislative, executive, and judicial—to stop some of the acts of the other branches. Ensures each branch a sufficient role in the actions of the others so that no one branch may dominate. The branches must work together if governmental business is to be performed.

City-manager plan   See Council-manager plan.

Civil law   The legal code regulating conduct between individuals and defining their legal rights. Under civil law, governments provide the forum for the settlement of disputes between private parties in such matters as contracts and business relations. The government can also be a party to a civil action.

Class action suit   Lawsuit brought by a person or group of persons on behalf of all persons similarly situated. The class may consist of a few persons or of thousands of persons. An example of a class action would be a suit by one person against an airline, alleging overcharges on behalf of that person and all others charged the same price for the same kind of flight.

Classical liberalism   A political philosophy that stresses the importance of the individual and of freedom, equality, private property, limited government, and popular consent.

Clayton Act   Act passed by Congress in 1914 that expanded governmental antitrust policy by outlawing specific abuses, such as charging different prices to different buyers in order to destroy a weaker competitor, granting rebates, making false statements about competitors and their products, buying up supplies to stifle competition, and bribing competitors' employees.

Clear and present danger doctrine   Interpretation of the First Amendment first announced by Justice Oliver Wendell Holmes. This doctrine would not let laws that directly or indirectly restrict freedom of speech be applied unless the particular speech, article, or book in question presents a clear and present danger that it will lead to acts that the government may make illegal.

Closed primary   A primary in which only persons registered in the party holding the primary may vote.

Closed rule   A procedural rule in the House of Representatives that prohibits any amendments to bills or provides that only members of the committee reporting the bill may offer amendments.

Closed shop   A company in which new employees and retained employees must be union members in good standing.

Cloture   Procedure for terminating debate (especially filibusters) in the U.S. Senate.

Coattail effect   Influence of a popular or unpopular candidate, especially a presidential candidate, on the electoral success or failure of other candidates on the same party ticket.

Collective bargaining   Method whereby representatives of the union and the employer determine wages, hours, and other conditions of employment through direct negotiation.

Commerce clause   The clause of the Constitution giving Congress the power to regulate all business activities that cross state lines or affect more than one state, and also prohibiting states from unduly burdening or discriminating against the business activities of other nations or states.

Commission charter   Form of city government in which a group of commissioners (usually five) serves as the city council, each commissioner heading a department in the municipal administration.

Common law   Body of judge-made law developed as judges decided cases; part of the English and American systems of justice.

Comparable worth   The idea that jobs should be paid at the same rate if they require comparable skills and contributions. Advocated by those who believe jobs traditionally dominated by women—nurses, secretaries, and elementary school teachers, for example—are held down in wage rates compared to equivalent type jobs traditionally dominated by men—plumbers and janitors, for example—because of discrimination and role stereotyping.

Concurrent powers   Powers the Constitution gives to both the national and state governments, such as the power to levy taxes.

Concurrent resolution   A resolution passed in the same form by both houses of Congress that expresses the "sense" of Congress on some question. Such a resolution is not sent to the president and does not have the force of law.

Concurring opinion   An opinion in which a judge explains why he or she agrees with the majority opinion but differs on the reasoning.

Conditional veto   See Amendatory veto.

Confederation   Government created when nation-states, by compact, create a new central government and limit its powers, especially the power to regulate the conduct of individuals directly.

Conference committee   Committee appointed by the presiding officers of each house of the legislature to adjust differences on a particular bill. The report of the conference committee back to each chamber cannot be amended but must be accepted or rejected as it stands.

Conglomerate Firm that owns businesses in many unrelated industries.

Connecticut Compromise Agreement by delegates to the Constitutional Convention to give each state two senators, regardless of population. This would offset the decision to allocate representatives in the House of Representatives according to population.

Consent decree Order issued by either a regulatory commission or a court in which a party, though not conceding guilt, agrees to modify future behavior. It is often used by the Federal Trade Commission to require business firms to cease anticompetitive conduct.

Conservatism Philosophical approach to the role of government that generally favors local or state governmental action over federal governmental action. Both Barry Goldwater in 1964 and Ronald Reagan in the 1980s were major proponents of this approach.

Conservative coalition A coalition in Congress of Republicans and southern Democrats who often vote together, at least in recent years, especially on social policy and welfare legislation.

Constitutional Convention The convention in Philadelphia in 1787 (May 25–September 17) that framed the Constitution of the United States. It invented the presidency, electoral college, federalism, and separation of powers—features that are still the central elements of American government. This draft had to be approved by nine states before it was ratified in 1788.

Constitutional democracy A government that enforces recognized limits on those who govern and allows the voice of the people to be heard through free and fair elections.

Constitutional home rule State constitutional authorization for local governmental units to conduct their own affairs.

Constitutional law In an American context, the authoritative interpretations of the meaning of the Constitution of the United States. Such interpretations are chiefly found in the opinions of the U.S. Supreme Court.

Constitutionalism The set of arrangements and processes—checks and balances, federalism, separation of powers, rule of law, due process, and a bill of rights—that disperses and limits the power of government officials. Constitutionalism provides for the granting as well as restraining of powers and seeks to ensure that a government's leaders and representatives are accountable to the citizens.

Convention See Party convention.

Council-manager plan Form of city government in which the city council hires a professional administrator to manage city affairs. Also known as the **city-manager plan.**

Criminal law Law that defines crimes against the public order and provides for punishment. Government is responsible for enforcing criminal law, the great body of which is enacted by states and enforced by state officials in state courts.

Cross-cutting cleavages Divisions within society that make groups more heterogeneous or different.

Crossover voting A member of one party voting for a candidate of another party. Open primaries encourage crossover voting and may

result in a situation in which nonparty members determine the party's nominee for a particular office.

Cross-pressure A pressure that pulls an individual in different directions, often related to conflicting racial, religious, ethnic, union, or other group values.

Custom Practices of nongovernmental institutions, such as political parties or the electorate, not specified in the Constitution.

De facto segregation Racial segregation that results not from governmental practices or pressures but from social customs or personal choice, including residential housing patterns.

De jure segregation Racial segregation that results from governmental actions. See also **Jim Crow laws**.

Dealignment Dramatic change in the composition of the electorate or its partisan preferences that points to a rejection of both major parties and a move to Independent status.

Decentralists Those who favor state or local action rather than national action.

Defendant In a civil action, the party defending himself or herself against charges brought by the plaintiff; in a criminal action, the person charged with the offense.

Deficit The difference between the revenues raised from sources of income other than borrowing and the expenditure of government, including paying the interest on past borrowing.

Deficit spending Spending by increasing the debt.

Delegate A view of the role of a member of a legislature which holds that, as delegates, legislators should represent the views of constituents even when personally holding different views.

Demagogue Leader who gains power by means of impassioned appeals to the prejudices and emotions of the masses.

Democracy Government by the people, either directly or indirectly, with free and frequent elections.

Demographics The study of the characteristics of populations.

Deregulation Efforts to reduce or eliminate governmental controls, rules, or regulation of economic activity.

Direct democracy A government in which citizens come together to discuss and pass laws and select rulers. May also refer to the initiative, referendum, and recall.

Direct primary Election open to all members of the party in which voters choose the persons who will be the party's nominees in the general election.

Discharge petition Petition that, if signed by a majority of the members of the House of Representatives, will pry a bill from committee and bring it to the floor for consideration.

Dissenting opinion An opinion in which a judge explains why he or she disagrees with the decision of the majority.

Divided government Governance divided between the parties, as when one controls the White House and the other Congress.

Double jeopardy Trial or punishment for the *same* crime by the *same* government. Such a practice is forbidden by the Constitution.

Due process Established rules and regulations that restrain those who exercise governmental power.

Due process clauses Clauses in the Fifth and Fourteenth Amendments that state that the national (Fifth) and the state (Fourteenth) governments shall not deprive any person of life, liberty, or property without due process of law.

Electoral college The gathering in each state of electors from that state who formally cast their ballots for their parties' candidates for president and vice-president. The electoral college is largely a formality.

Eminent domain Power of governments to take private property for public use. The Constitution requires governments to provide just compensation for property so taken.

Entitlements or Entitlement programs Programs such as Social Security, Aid to Families with Dependent Children, Medicare, and unemployment insurance to which qualified citizens are "entitled" by definitions in national legislation.

Environmental impact statement A statement required by federal law from all agencies for any project using federal funds that assesses the potential effect of the proposed project on the environment. Many states also require these statements.

Equal protection clause Clause in the Fourteenth Amendment that forbids any state to deny to any person within its jurisdiction the equal protection of the laws. By interpretation, the Fifth Amendment imposes the same limitation on the national government. This is the major constitutional restraint on the power of governments to discriminate against persons because of race, national origin, or sex.

Equal-time requirement Requirement of Congress and Federal Communications Commission that radio and television licensees must give opposing candidates for public office equal air time.

Equity Judicial remedy used whenever actions at law for money damages do not provide adequate justice.

Establishment clause Clause in the First Amendment that states that Congress shall make no law respecting an establishment of religion. By interpretation, the Fourteenth Amendment imposes the same limitation on state legislatures. It has been interpreted by the Supreme Court to forbid governmental support to any or all religions.

Ethnicity Identification with a group based upon national origin, religion, language, and often race.

Ethnocentrism A selective perception based on individual background, attitudes, and biases that leads one to believe in the superiority of one's nation or ethnic group.

Excise tax Consumer tax on a specific kind of merchandise, such as tobacco.

Exclusionary rule Rule that evidence unconstitutionally obtained cannot be used in a criminal trial as part of the government's main case against persons from whom it was seized.

Executive agreement International agreement made by a president that has the force of a treaty. It does not need the approval of the Senate.

Executive Office of the President Cluster of staff agencies created by the Reorganization Act of 1939 to help the president. Currently the Executive Office includes an Office of Management and Budget, the Council of Economic Advisers, the National Security Council, and a number of specialized offices.

Executive privilege The claim by presidents that they have the discretion to decide that the national interest will be better served if certain information is withheld from the public, including the courts and Congress. In *United States v Nixon* the Supreme Court ruled that even though presidents are entitled to the privilege, the privilege is not unlimited, and its extent is subject to judicial determination.

Ex post facto law Retroactive criminal law that works to the disadvantage of an individual.

Express powers Powers specifically granted to one of the branches of the national government by the Constitution.

Extradition Legal process whereby an alleged criminal offender is surrendered by the officials of one state to officials of the state in which the crime is alleged to have been committed.

Faction What we call "interest groups" today, James Madison called factions. He also thought of political parties as factions.

Fairness doctrine Doctrine interpreted by the Federal Communications Commission that imposed on radio and television licensees an obligation to ensure that differing viewpoints were presented about controversial issues or persons. Repealed by the FCC in 1987.

Federal mandate A requirement imposed by the federal government as a condition of receipt of federal funds.

Federal Reserve System The private-public banking regulatory system created by Congress in 1913 to establish banking practices and regulate currency in circulation and the amount of credit available. It is comprised of 12 regional banks, and its major responsibilities are supervised by a seven-member presidentially appointed Federal Reserve Board of Governors in Washington, D.C.

Federalism Constitutional arrangement whereby power is divided by a constitution between a national government and constituent governments, called states in the United States. The national and the constituent governments both exercise direct authority over individuals.

The Federalist Series of essays favoring the new Constitution, written by Alexander Hamilton, John Jay, and James Madison in 1787 and 1788, during the debate over ratification.

Federalists Persons who supported the Constitution before its ratification in 1787 to 1788. After ratification, a Federalist party developed under the leadership of Alexander Hamilton, George Washington's first secretary of the treasury. Federalists like John Adams and John Marshall generally favored a strong central government and a fiscal policy of assuming state debts and establishing a national bank.

Fee for service System of health care payment in the United States whereby patients choose their own physicians, whose bills are then covered by insurance companies.

Fighting words Words that by their very nature inflict injury upon those to whom they are addressed or cause acts of violence by them.

Filibuster Holding the floor of the U.S. Senate to delay proceedings and thereby prevent a vote on a controversial issue.

Fiscal policy Government policy that attempts to manage the economy by controlling taxing and spending.

Floating debt Short-term borrowing, often by states, to ensure that operating expenses can be met; often consists of bank loans, tax-anticipation warrants, and other notes, all of which are paid for out of current revenues.

Four Freedoms American goals proclaimed by Franklin D. Roosevelt in his message to Congress, January 6, 1941: freedom of speech, freedom of religion, freedom from want, and freedom from fear.

Franchise The right to vote.

Free exercise clause Clause in the First Amendment that states that Congress shall make no law prohibiting the free exercise of religion; extended by the Fourteenth Amendment as a limit on the states.

Free rider An individual who does not join an interest group representing his or her interests, yet receives the benefit of the influence the group achieves.

Full faith and credit clause Clause in the Constitution requiring each state to recognize the civil judgments rendered by the courts of the other states and to accept their public records and acts as valid documents.

Fundamental right Right explicitly or implicitly guaranteed by the U. S. Constitution.

Gender gap The difference between the political opinions or political behavior of men and women.

General property tax Tax levied by local (and some state) governments on real or personal, tangible property, the major portion of which is on the estimated value of one's home and land.

Gerrymandering Drawing an election district in such a way that one party or group has a distinct advantage. The strategy is to provide a close but safe margin in numerous districts while concentrating (and hence wasting) the opposition's vote in a few districts.

Government corporation Cross between a business corporation and a government agency, created to secure greater freedom of action and flexibility for a particular program.

Grand jury A jury comprising 12 to 23 persons who, in private, hear evidence presented by the government to determine whether persons shall be required to stand trial. If the jury believes there is sufficient evidence that a crime was committed, it issues an indictment.

Gross domestic product (GDP) An estimate of the total output of all economic activity in the nation, including goods and services.

Gross national product (GNP) The monetary values of all goods and services in the nation in a given year.

Habeas corpus See Writ of habeas corpus.

Hatch Act Federal statute barring federal employees from active participation in certain kinds of politics and protecting them from being fired on partisan grounds.

Honeymoon A period at the beginning of a new president's term in which the president enjoys generally positive relations with the press and Congress, usually lasting about six months.

Ideology One's basic beliefs about power, political values, and the role of government—beliefs that arise out of educational, economic, and social conditions and experiences.

Impeachment Formal accusation against a public official and the first step in removal from office.

Implied powers Powers given to Congress by the Constitution that allow Congress to do whatever is necessary and proper in order to carry out one of the express powers or any combination of them.

Impoundment Presidential refusal to allow an agency to spend funds authorized and appropriated by Congress.

Independent agency A government agency that is not part of the legislative, executive, or judicial branch, such as the Interstate Commerce Commission. The term also describes a nonregulatory agency that is not part of a cabinet department, such as the National Aeronautics and Space Administration. Members of regulatory agencies are appointed by the president, confirmed by the Senate, and removable only for some specific "cause." Also called an **independent regulatory agency.**

Independent expenditures Money spent for or against a candidate, usually by an interest group, that is not connected to the campaign of the candidate or his or her opponent.

Industrial policy Government policy that targets specific industries that might be competitive with foreign firms and helps them with tax breaks and financial incentives.

Information affidavit Certification by a public prosecutor that there is evidence to justify bringing named individuals to trial.

Inherent powers Those powers of the national government in the field of foreign affairs that the Supreme Court has declared do not depend upon constitutional grants but rather grow out of the very existence of the national government.

Initiative Procedure whereby a certain number of voters may, by petition, propose a law or constitutional amendment and get it submitted to the people for a vote. Initiatives may be direct (if the proposed law is voted on directly by the people) or indirect (if the proposal is submitted first to the legislature and then to the people, if the legislature rejects it).

Interest group A collection of people who share some common interest or attitude and seek to influence government for specific ends. Interest groups usually work within the framework of government and employ tactics such as lobbying to achieve their goals.

Interested money Financial contributions made by persons or groups in the hopes of influencing the outcome of an election and subsequently influencing policy.

Interlocking directorates Corporations in which an officer or director sits on the board of a competitor

Interstate compacts Agreements among the states. The Constitution requires that most such agreements be approved by Congress.

Iron triangle   A mutually supporting relationship among interest groups, congressional committees or subcommittees, and government agencies that share a common policy concern. Also called **Issue network**.

Item veto   Authority of the executive (usually the governor of a state) to veto parts of a legislative bill without having to veto the entire bill. Presidents do not have the power of the item veto.

Jim Crow laws   Laws that required public facilities and places of public accommodation, including those privately owned and operated, to be segregated by race.

Joint committee   Committee composed of members of both houses of a legislature. Such committees are intended to speed up legislative action. Some oversee institutions such as the Library of Congress or conduct congressional investigations.

Judicial activism   Philosophy proposing that judges cannot decide cases strictly by applying the literal words of the Constitution or by discerning the intention of the framers, but that they could and should openly recognize that judicial decision making is choosing among conflicting values. Judges should so interpret the Constitution as to keep it reflecting the current values of the American people.

Judicial interpretation   A method whereby judges can modify a constitutional provision's restrictive force by a narrow interpretation of its meaning.

Judicial restraint   Philosophy proposing that, in deciding cases, judges should declare unconstitutional only those legislative acions and executive actions that clearly violate the words of the Constitution or the intent of the framers and that constitutional changes should be left to the formal amendatory process.

Judicial review   The power of a court to refuse to enforce a law or government regulation that in the opinion of the judges conflicts with the Constitution. This authority was spelled out by Chief Justice John Marshall in *Marbury v Madison* (1803).

Jurisdictional strike   Strike arising from disputes between unions over whose members should perform a particular task.

Justiciable dispute   A dispute that grows out of an actual case and is capable of settlement by legal methods. Those constitutional disputes that are political are not justiciable.

Keynesian economics   Economic theories based on the principles advocated by John Maynard Keynes: increasing government spending during business slumps and curbing spending during booms.

Labor injunction   Court order forbidding specific individuals or groups from performing certain acts, such as striking, that the court considers harmful to the rights and property of an employer or community.

Laissez faire   Doctrine opposing governmental interference in economic affairs beyond what is necessary to protect life and property.

Lame duck   A politician in office who cannot, or has announced that he or she will not, run again.

Legislative caucus   See Caucus (legislative).

Libel   Written defamation of another person. Especially in the case of public officials and public figures, the constitutional tests designed to restrict libel actions are very rigid.

Liberalism   Philosophical approach to the role of government that generally favors the positive uses of government to bring about justice and equality of opportunity.

Libertarianism   Philosophical approach to the role of government that cherishes individual liberty and favors as limited a government as possible. Libertarians believe in free-market economics and a noninterventionist foreign policy.

Literacy test   Requirement imposed by some states that prospective voters must prove they understand national and state laws. Now illegal, such tests were used too disqualify blacks from voting in the South.

Lobby/lobbying   Activities aimed at influencing public officials, especially legislators, and the policies they enact. This is, of course, part of the citizen's right to petition the government.

Lobbyist   Person who is employed by and acts for an organized interest group or corporation to try to influence policy decisions and positions in the executive and legislative branches.

Log rolling   Mutual aid and vote trading among legislators.

Lotteries   State-sponsored and state-administered gambling used to raise money for public purposes.

Majority leader   Legislative position held by an important party member selected by the majority party in caucus or conference. The majority leader helps frame party strategy and tries to keep the membership in line. In the U.S. Senate the majority leader (in consultation with the minority leader) determines the agenda and has strong influence in committee selection.

Manifest destiny   A notion held by many nineteenth-century Americans that the United States was destined to rule the continent, from the Atlantic to the Pacific oceans.

Mass media   Means of communication that reach the mass public. The mass media include newspapers and magazines, radio and television (cable and satellite), and films, recordings, and books.

Mayor-council charter   The oldest and most common form of city government, consisting of either a weak mayor and city council or a strong mayor and council.

Medicaid   Federal program that provides medical benefits for low-income persons.

Medicare   National health insurance program for the elderly and disabled.

Melting pot   A term used to describe how persons of different nationalities or races are blended or assimilated into American society.

Merit system   A system of public employment in which selection and promotion depend on demonstrated performance rather than on political patronage.

Military-industrial complex   Alleged alliance between top military and industrial leaders who have a common interest in arms production.

Minor party   Small political party, more persistent than a third party, and generally composed of ideologues on the right or left.

Minority leader   Party leader in each house of a legislature, elected by the minority party as spokesperson for the opposition.

Missouri Plan System for selecting judges that combines features of the appointive and elective methods. The governor makes an initial appointment from a list of persons—usually three—presented by a panel of lawyers and laypersons (the panel is usually appointed by the chief judge of the state court of last resort). After the judge has served for a year, the electorate is asked at the next general election whether or not the judge should be retained in office. If a majority vote yes, the judge serves the rest of the term. At the end of the term, if a judge wishes to serve again, his or her name is once again presented to the electorate.

Monetary policy Government policy that attempts to manage the economy by controlling the money supply.

Monopoly Domination of an industry by one company.

Most-favored nation Trade policy whereby countries give each other the same favorable treatment given to other trade partners.

Movement A large body of people united around a central idea whose goal is to change attitudes or institutions, not only policies. Movements tend to feel "left out" of government and may sometimes resort to extreme measures to advance their cause.

National Labor Relations Act (1935) Guarantees workers the right to organize and bargain collectively with management. Also known as the **Wagner Act**.

National party convention The national meeting of delegates elected in primaries, caucuses, or state conventions who assemble once every four years for the purpose of nominating candidates for president and vice-president, ratifying the party platform, electing officers, and adopting rules.

National Security Council Planning and advisory board that confers with the president on matters relating to national security. Permanent members include the president, vice-president, secretary of state, secretary of defense, and the chair of the joint chiefs of staff.

National supremacy Constitutional doctrine that whenever conflict occurs between the constitutionally authorized actions of the national government and those of a state or local government, the actions of the national government take priority.

Nationalism A consciousness of the nation-state and of belonging to that entity.

Natural law God or nature's law that defines right from wrong and is higher than human law.

Natural monopoly A monopoly that is permitted because it would be inefficient to have competition in a particular industry, as in the case of a power company.

Natural rights Rights of all citizens to dignity and worth; also called **human rights**.

Naturalization Process by which persons acquire citizenship in a country other than the nation of their birth.

Necessary and proper clause Clause of the Constitution setting forth the implied powers of Congress. It states that Congress, in addition to its express powers, has the power to make all laws necessary and proper for carrying out all powers vested by the Constitution in the national government.

Neoconservativism A pragmatic form of traditional liberalism that accepts some of the welfare state but believes affirmative action has gone too far. Neoconservatives also support military spending to ensure that the United States can defend its global interests.

Neoliberal A political ideology that is left-of-center yet distrustful or skeptical of large bureaucracies and traditional welfare strategies. Neoliberals believe in relying on the marketplace and favor middle-of-the-road tax and defense policies.

New Jersey Plan Plan presented by William Paterson of New Jersey at the Constitutional Convention as a counterproposal to the Virginia Plan. The New Jersey Plan proposed only modifications in the Articles of Confederation and provided for a confederation built around powerful state governments.

New judicial federalism The practice of some state courts of using the bill of rights in their state constitutions to provide more protection for some rights than is provided by Supreme Court interpretation of the Bill of Rights in the Constitution.

North American Free Trade Agreement (NAFTA) Agreement signed by the United States, Canada, and Mexico in 1992 to form the largest free-trade zone in the world.

Obscenity Quality or state of a work that taken as a whole appeals to a prurient interest in sex by depicting sexual conduct as specifically defined by legislation or judicial interpretation in a patently offensive way and that lacks serious literary, artistic, political, or scientific value.

Office block ballot Method of voting in which all candidates are listed under the office for which they are running. Sometimes called the **Massachusetts ballot**.

Office of Management and Budget (OMB) Presidential staff agency that serves as a clearinghouse for budgetary requests and management improvements. It advises the president in detail about hundreds of government agencies—how much money they should be allotted in the budget and what kind of job they are doing—and it seeks to improve the planning, management, and statistical work of the agencies.

Oligopoly Situation in which a few firms dominate an industry.

Open primary A primary in which any voter, regardless of party, can vote.

Open rule A procedural rule in the House of Representatives that permits floor amendments within the overall time allocated to the bill.

Open shop Labor arrangement in which union membership cannot be required as a condition of employment.

Original jurisdiction The authority of a trial court to hear a case "in the first instance."

Override An action by Congress to try to reverse a presidential veto of legislation by a two-thirds vote in both chambers.

Party column ballot Method of voting in which all candidates are listed under their party designations, making it easy for the voters to cast votes for all the candidates of one party. Sometimes called the **Indiana ballot**.

Party convention A meeting of party delegates to pass on matters of policy and in some cases to select party candidates for public office. Conventions are held on county, state, and national levels.

Party identification   Subjective affiliation with a political party, usually acquired in childhood.

Party platform   The official statement of party policy.

Party registration   The act of declaring party affiliation, in some states required when one registers to vote.

Patronage   Dispensing government jobs to persons who belong to the winning political party. Also called **spoils system.**

Petit jury   The jury for the trial of a civil or criminal action.

Plea bargaining   Negotiations between prosecutor and defendant aimed at getting the defendant to plead guilty in return for the prosecutor's agreeing to reduce the seriousness of the crime for which the defendant will be convicted.

Pocket veto   Special veto power exercised by a chief executive after a legislative body has adjourned. Bills that a chief executive does not sign within ten days of adjournment do not become law and are not returned to the chamber of origin for a possible override. In effect, by such an action, a governor or president "puts the bill in his or her pocket," and the bill thus dies.

Police powers   Powers of a government to regulate persons and property in order to promote the public health, welfare, safety, and morals. In the United States, the states, but not the national government, have such general police power.

Political action committee (PAC)   The political arm of a business, labor, trade association, or other interest group that is legally entitled to raise money on a voluntary basis from members, stockholders, or employees in order to contribute to favored candidates or political parties.

Political culture   The widely shared political beliefs, values, and norms most citizens share concerning the relationship of citizens to government and to one another.

Political question   A dispute that requires knowledge of a nonlegal character or the use of techniques not suitable for a court or that are explicitly addressed by the Constitution to Congress or the president. Judges refuse to answer constitutional questions that they declare are political.

Political party   An organization that seeks political power by electing people to office so that its positions and philosophy become public policy.

Political socialization   The process by which we develop our political attitudes, values, and beliefs.

Poll tax   Payment by a person, formerly required in some states, as a condition for voting.

Popular consent   The idea that a just government must derive its powers from the consent of the people.

Populists   Adherents of a movement and political party of the 1880s and 1890s. Their geographical base was rural—in the Midwest, South, and Southwest especially. Waging "reformist" efforts against the banks, railroads, and other establishments, populists raised issues that influenced the Progressive movement and the Democratic party after 1892.

Pork-barrel   Government benefits or programs that help the economy of a member's district—as in "bringing home the bacon."

Preemption   The right of a federal law or regulation to preclude enforcement of a state or local law or regulation.

Preferred position doctrine   Interpretation of the First Amendment that holds that no law restricting expression is constitutional unless the government can demonstrate convincingly to a court that the law is absolutely necessary to prevent serious injury to the public well-being.

President pro tempore   Officer of the U.S. Senate chosen from the ranks—often a junior member of the majority party—who serves as president of the Senate in the absence of the vice-president.

Prior restraint   Restraint imposed prior to a speech's being made, a newspaper's being published, or a motion picture's being shown. The restraint may be of various kinds—for example, a requirement that a license be granted or that the approval of a censorship board be given.

Privatization   The contracting out to the "for profit" private sector of services that are typically provided by public organizations. Trash collection, ambulance, and fire protection services have been the most common privatizations of public services. The objectives are to obtain the public services at lower costs, and sometimes to shrink the public bureaucracy to encourage additional efficiencies.

Pro bono   Term used to refer to the work lawyers (or other professionals) do to serve the public good and for which they either receive no fees or decline fees.

Procedural due process   Constitutional requirement that governments proceed by proper methods.

Progressive income tax   A tax whereby upper-income citizens pay a larger fraction of their income in taxes than do lower-income citizens.

Progressives   Adherents of a "good government" movement in the first two decades of this century, who advocated measures that would open up the system and weaken party bosses. They favored nonpartisan elections, participatory primaries, and direct elections of senators.

Project grant   Federal funds given for specified purposes and based on applications.

Property rights   The rights of an individual to own, use, rent, invest in, buy, and sell property.

Property tax rate   Usually a tax per $1,000 of assessed valuation or some other such measure of the value of property.

Proportional representation   An election system in which each party running receives the proportion of legislative seats corresponding to its proportion of the vote.

Protectionism   The erecting of tariff barriers to protect domestic industry.

Public defender   Public official whose job is to provide legal assistance to those persons accused of crimes who are unable to hire their own attorneys.

Public goods   Services or commodities that individuals benefit from but that cannot be separately sold or given to individuals. Examples are clean air, national defense, and public safety.

Public opinion Cluster of views and attitudes held by people on a significant issue.

Public policy The substance of what government does. More generally, public policy reflects the intentions of a government and the subsequent actions to implement laws and other decisions of governmental bodies.

Quasi-legislative and quasi-judicial Phrase coined by the Supreme Court to permit noncourt and nonlegislative bodies to decide disputes and make rules. Decisions must, however, be subject to court review, and rules must be within the general guidelines established by the legislature.

Race A grouping of human beings with common characteristics presumed to be transmitted genetically. In the United States, race issues focus on African Americans, Asian Americans, and sometimes Hispanics, although, technically, Hispanics can be of any race.

Racial gerrymandering The drawing of election districts so as to ensure that members of a certain race are a minority in all districts.

Random sampling In public opinion polls creating a representative sample through random selection—for example, by shuffling housing tracts and interviewing individuals in every fifth, tenth, or fifteenth house.

Reaganomics Ronald Reagan's version of supply-side economics, which held that by cutting taxes and government spending in nondefense areas the economy would be stimulated enough to fund Reagan's other priority, national defense.

Realignment A dramatic change in the composition of the electorate or its partisan preferences, or both.

Recall Election in certain states or communities to determine whether an official should be removed from office before the end of his or her term. A certain number of voters, typically 25 percent of those who voted in the last election, must petition to hold a recall election.

Recidivist One who habitually relapses into crime.

Reciprocity A congressional folkway involving favors and courtesies requested and received, always with the understanding that they will be returned. Also called **log rolling**.

Redistributive policy Governmental policy that seeks to use tax revenues in such a way as to help those who have less. In effect, tax monies from the upper and middle classes are channeled into programs that assist lower income or truly needy people by redistributing some of society's wealth.

Redistricting The redrawing of congressional and other legislative district lines following the census. Also called **reapportionment**.

Reduction veto The power of a governor in a few states to reduce a particular money measure approved by the state legislature.

Referendum Practice of submitting to popular vote measures passed by the legislature or proposed by initiative. Use of the referendum may be required or optional.

Regressive tax A tax whereby lower-income citizens pay a higher fraction of their income in taxes than do higher-income citizens. In other words, a regressive tax is one that weighs most heavily on those least able to pay.

Regulation Governmental order having the force of law and designed to control or govern the behavior of a business, union, or similar organizations and individuals. Governmental regulation seeks to alter the natural workings of the open market to achieve some desired goal.

Regulatory agency, board, or commission Government agency responsible for enforcing particular statutes. Generally such an agency has quasi-legislative and quasi-judicial functions as well as executive powers.

Regulatory taking Government regulation of property so extensive that government is deemed to have taken the property and thus exercised the power of eminent domain, for which it must compensate the property owners.

Reinforcing cleavages Divisions within society that reinforce one another, making groups more homogeneous or similar.

Republic Form of government that derives its powers directly or indirectly from the people. Those chosen to govern are accountable, directly or indirectly, to those whom they govern. In contrast to a direct democracy, in which the people make rules directly, in a republic the people select representatives who make the rules. Also called **representative democracy**.

Restrictive covenant A restriction in a deed limiting to whom property may be sold and how it may be used.

Revenue sharing Program whereby federal funds are provided to state and local governments to be spent largely at the discretion of the receiving governments, subject to few and very general conditions.

Revision commission State commission that recommends changes in the state constitution. The recommendations have no force until acted upon by the state legislature and approved by the voters.

Revolving door The employment cycle in which individuals work, in turn, for governmental agencies regulating interests and then for businesses representing those interests.

Rider A provision that might not have much chance to pass on its own merits but is attached to another bill, often unrelated, to secure its legislative passage. Often bills that have little to do with spending money are attached as riders to appropriations bills, because appropriations bills are rarely defeated or vetoed.

Right of expatriation Right of an individual to choose his or her own nationality.

Right-to-work law Provision in state laws that prohibits arrangements between a union and an employer requiring membership in a union as a condition for getting or keeping a job.

Safe seat Electoral office, usually in legislature, for which the party or the incumbent is so strong that reelection is almost taken for granted.

Sales tax General tax on sales transactions, sometimes exempting food and drugs.

Search warrant A warrant that authorizes the police to search a particular place or person. A search warrant must specify the place to be searched and the objects to be seized in order to protect people from unreasonable government intrusion.

Secondary boycott Efforts by a union involved in a dispute with an employer to place pressure on a third party, who—in response to such pressure—might put pressure on the original offending employer. Such boycotts are forbidden by the 1947 Taft-Hartley Act.

Secret ballot   See Australian ballot.

Sedition   Attempting to overthrow the government by force or to interrupt its activities by violence.

Select or special committee   A congressional committee created for a specific purpose, sometimes to conduct an investigation.

Selective incorporation   The doctrine that some, but not all, provisions of the Bill of Rights should be included within the Fourteenth Amendment as a limitation on state and local governments.

Selective perception   Individuals perceiving what they want to in media messages and disregarding the rest.

Senatorial courtesy   Presidential custom of submitting the names of prospective appointees for approval to senators from the states in which the appointees reside.

Seniority rule   A practice in legislatures that assigns the chair of a committee or subcommittee to the member of the majority party who has had the longest continuous service on the committee.

Separation of powers   Constitutional division of power among legislative, executive, and judicial branches. The legislative branch is assigned the power to make laws; the executive is charged with the power to apply the laws; and the judiciary receives the power to interpret laws.

Severance tax   Tax on the privilege of "severing" natural resources such as coal, oil, and timber, charged to the companies doing the extracting or severing.

Shays's Rebellion   Rural rebellion in 1786–87 protesting mortgage foreclosures in western Massachusetts. Led by Daniel Shays, it promoted conservative support for a stronger national government.

Sherman Antitrust Act   Act passed by Congress in 1890 that attempted to foster competition and stop the growth of private monopolies by making it unlawful to form a combination that acted to restrain trade.

Shield law   Law establishing a legal right for reporters and other representatives of the media to refuse, under certain circumstances, to respond to orders of legislative committees or court subpoenas to reveal sources of information.

Single-member district   An electoral rule in which an election determines one representative or official in an electoral district.

Socialism   Philosophical approach to the role of government that favors national planning and public ownership of the means of production and exchange.

Social Security   A combination of entitlement programs paid for by employer and employee taxes. Includes retirement benefits, health insurance, and support for disabled workers and children of deceased or disabled workers.

Social stratification   The division of a community among socioeconomic groups.

Socioeconomic status (SES)   A measure of one's standing that combines in one index such factors as education, income, and occupation.

Soft money   Money contributed to a state or local political party for nonfederal uses, such as voter registration drives and party mailings, that does not have to be reported under the Federal Election Campaign Act and is often not reported because of tax disclosure laws at that level.

Speaker   The presiding officer in the House of Representatives, formally elected by the House but actually selected by the majority party. The Speaker's powers include referring legislation to committees, making appointments to the House Rules Committee, recognizing members who wish to speak, ruling on questions of parliamentary procedure, and appointing special conference committees. There is a similar office in state legislatures.

Split ticket   Voting for some of one party's candidates and some candidates from other political parties.

Spoils system   Rewarding those who support victorious candidates with profitable contracts or jobs in government; in the nineteenth century often an important incentive for political participation.

Stare decisis   The rule of precedent, whereby a rule or law contained in a judicial decision is commonly viewed as binding on judges whenever the same question is presented.

State delegation   The senators and representatives from the same state, who often help each other secure choice committee assignments, work to promote each other in leadership positions, and watch out for state interests.

Statism   Belief in the rights of the state over those of the individual—the opposite of the American tradition that the individual is exalted above the state.

Statutory law   Statutes enacted by a legislature; treaties and executive orders are also considered as statutory law.

Straight ticket   Voting for all of one party's candidates.

Strong mayor-council   Form of local government in which the public directly elects the mayor as well as the city council. However, the mayor appoints the department heads with the approval of the council, and in effect serves as the chief executive officer for the city and its administration.

Substantive due process   Constitutional requirement that governments act reasonably and that the substance of the laws themselves be fair and reasonable.

Sunset process   Process that calls for the termination of a program after a certain number of years, often six or seven, unless it is certified to be doing what it was intended to do. The word comes from the expression that "the sun should set" on programs that have outlived their usefulness.

Supply-side economics   Economic strategy of stimulating investment in businesses through tax cuts and reduced governmental regulation that would result in increased employment and eventually increased income tax revenue.

Suspect class   Racial or national origin classifications created by law and subject to careful judicial scrutiny. Suspect classifications are likely to be declared unconstitutional unless they can be justified by overwhelmingly desirable state purposes that can be achieved in no other way.

Taft-Hartley Act   Act passed by Congress in 1947 that elaborates the terms of labor-management bargaining, the conditions under which strikes can occur, and related aspects of union organization. It worked to restrict some union activities.

Tariff   Tax levied on imports to help protect a nation's industries, labor, or farmers from foreign competition. It can also be used merely to raise additional revenue.

Tax expenditure   Loss of tax revenue due to provisions of the federal tax laws that allow special exclusions, exemptions, or deductions, or that provide special credit, preferential rates of tax, or deferrals of tax liability.

Theocracy   A government by a god, or by officials claiming divine inspiration and guidance.

Third party   Temporary political parties that often arise during presidential elections.

Third-party payer   System of health care payment in the United States whereby medical bills are paid by an insurance company, or "third party."

Three-fifths compromise   North-South agreement at the Constitutional Convention of 1787 to count only three-fifths of the slave population in determining direct taxation and apportionment in the House of Representatives.

Tort law   Law, primarily judge made, dealing with damages to compensate people through a civil trial, for legal wrongs done to them, including injuries to person, reputation, or property.

Trade deficit   International trading in which the value of imports exceeds the value of exports.

Treason   Carefully defined by the Constitution to consist only of levying war against the United States, adhering to its enemies, or giving the latter aid and comfort. No person can be convicted of treason unless the accused confesses in open court or unless two witnesses testify in court that they saw the acts of treason being committed.

Trustee   A view of the function of a member of a legislature which holds that legislators may believe that they were sent to Washington or the state capitals to think and vote independently for the general welfare, and not as their constituents determine.

Trusts   Monopolies that control goods and services, often in combinations that reduce competition.

Turnout   The proportion of the voting-age public that votes.

Two-party system   Electoral system in which two major political parties dominate.

Unicameralism, unicameral legislature   One-house legislature. Nebraska and almost all cities use this form.

Union shop   A company in which new employees must join the union within a stated period of time.

Unit rule   Requirement that the whole delegation to a party convention cast its vote as the majority decides.

Unitary system or unitary government   Government with power concentrated by the constitution in a central government; also an election system in which voters elect legislators who, in turn, elect the prime minister or head of state.

Unitary tax   A state tax on the proportion of a corporation's domestic receipts earned in that state. It is a controversial tax, viewed by some as a legitimate means of securing added state revenue and by others as discouraging companies from locating in the state.

Usage   Long-standing practices of Congress, the president, and the courts not specified in the Constitution.

User charges   Fees charged directly to individuals who use certain public services on the basis of service consumed. Sometimes called a **user fee** or **user tax**.

Value-added tax (VAT)   A tax on the increased value of a product at each stage of production and distribution rather than just at the point of sale, as with a sales tax.

Veto   Rejection of proposed legislation by a president or governor.

Virginia Plan   Proposal made at the Constitutional Convention by the Virginia delegation that provided for a strong legislature with representation in each house determined by wealth or population. It thus favored the large states.

Voter registration   A system designed to reduce voter fraud such as multiple voting and to limit voting to those who have established eligibility by submitting the appropriate form.

Weak mayor–council   Form of local government in which the mayor must share most of the executive powers of a city with other elected or appointed boards and commissions. The mayor in weak-mayor cities is often mainly a ceremonial leader.

Whip   Party leader who is the liaison between the leadership and the rank-and-file in the legislature.

White primary   Under the pretense that it was not governmental action, officials of the Democratic party in the South used to admit only white persons to its primaries. Candidates of the Democratic party were the only ones with any chance of winning in the following general election; blacks were thus excluded from the only election that counted. The white primary in all its various forms was declared unconstitutional by the Supreme Court in *Smith v Allwright* (1944).

Winner-take-all   An electoral system in which the candidate with the most votes wins. In American presidential elections, the winner of the popular vote in a state receives all the electoral votes of that state.

Women's suffrage   The right of women to vote; denied in federal elections in the United States before passage of the Nineteenth Amendment in 1920.

Writ of certiorari   Writ used by the Supreme Court to review decisions of lower courts, federal and state, that are within the discretionary appellate jurisdiction of the Supreme Court. It is a formal device regularly used to bring a case up to the Court.

Writ of habeas corpus   Court order requiring explanation to a judge why a prisoner is held in custody.

Writ of mandamus   Court order directing an official to perform a nondiscretionary act as required by law.

Yellow-dog contract   Contract by an anti-union employer that forces prospective workers to promise they will not join a union after employment.

NOTES

CHAPTER 1

1. Herbert Hoover, *American Individualism* (Doubleday, 1922), p. 9. This ancient debate continues; see Robert Nozick, *Anarchy, State and Utopia* (Basic Books, 1974) and Michael Walzer, *Spheres of Justice* (Basic Books, 1983).

2. For a major theoretical work on the principle of majority rule, see Robert A. Dahl, *Democracy and Its Critics* (Yale University Press, 1989).

3. James Madison, *The Federalist*, No. 51.

4. For a discussion of the importance for democracy of such overlapping group memberships, see David Truman's seminal work, *The Governmental Process*, 2d ed. (Knopf, 1971).

5. Robert A. Dahl, *A Preface to Democratic Theory* (University of Chicago Press, 1956), p. 132.

6. Joyce Appleby, "The American Heritage: The Heirs and the Disinherited," *Journal of American History* (December 1987), p. 808.

7. Maryland and Massachusetts documents quoted in Bernard Schwartz, *Roots of the Bill of Rights* (Chelsea House, 1980), 1:68–73.

8. Richard L. Hillard, "Liberalism, Civic Humanism and the American Revolutionary Bills of Rights, 1775-1790," paper presented at the annual meeting of the Organization of American Historians, Reno, Nevada, 1988.

9. See the essays in Thomas E. Cronin, ed., *Inventing the American Presidency* (University Press of Kansas, 1989).

10. Charles A. Beard and Mary R. Beard, *A Basic History of the United States* (New Home Library, 1944), p. 136.

11. See Herbert J. Storing, ed., abridgment by Murray Dry, *The Anti-Federalist: Writings by the Opponents of the Constitution* (University of Chicago Press, 1985).

12. Mercy Warren, quoted in Pauline Maier, *The Old Revolutionaries* (Knopf, 1980), p. 284.

13. On the role of the promised bill of rights amendments in the ratifications of the Constitution, see Leonard W. Levy, *Constitutional Opinions* (Oxford University Press, 1986), chap. 6.

CHAPTER 2

1. Herbert Storing, "The Constitution and the Bill of Rights," in *Essays on the Constitution of the United States*, ed. M. Judd Harmon (Kennikat Press, 1978), pp. 36–37, points out that many Antifederalists remained unsatisfied with the Bill of Rights.

2. Max Lerner, *Ideas for the Ice Age* (Viking, 1991), pp. 241–42. See also "The American Public's Knowledge of the U.S. Constitution" (Hearst Corporation, 1987).

3. Sanford Levinson, *Constitutional Faith* (Princeton University Press, 1988), pp. 9–52.

4. Thomas Jefferson, quoted in Alpheus T. Mason, *The Supreme Court: Palladium of Freedom* (University of Michigan Press, 1962), p. 10.

5. Richard E. Neustadt, *Presidential Power* (Free Press, 1990), p. 29.

6. Robert C. Vipond, *Liberty and Community: Canadian Federalism and the Failure of the Constitution* (State University of New York Press, 1991), p. 192.

7. Edward S. Corwin, "The Constitution as Instrument and as Symbol," *American Political Science Review* (December 1936), p. 1078. J. M. Sosin argues that these earlier precedents do not support the view that judicial review was "in the air," in *The Aristocracy of the Long Robe: The Origins of Judicial Review in America* (Greenwood Press, 1989).

8. 1 Cranch 137 (1803).

9. Dumas Malone, *Jefferson the President: First Term, 1801–1805* (Little Brown and Company, 1970), p. 145.

10. *Dred Scott v Sandford*, 19 Howard 393 (1857).

11. Robert Lowry Clinton, *Marbury v. Madison and Judicial Review* (University Press of Kansas, 1989), pp. 4–42.

12. J. W. Peltason, *Federal Courts in the Political Process* (Random House, 1955).

13. James L. Sundquist, "Needed: A Political Theory for the New Era of Coalition Government in the United States," *Political Science Quarterly* (Winter 1988–89), pp. 613–35; Robert A. Godwin and Art Kaufman, eds., *Separation of Powers: Does It Still Work?* (AEI Press, 1986).

14. Charles O. Jones, "The Separate Presidency," in *The New American Political System*, ed. Anthony King, 2d ed. (AEI Press, 1990), p. 3.

15. Morris P. Fiorina, "An Era of Divided Government," *Political Science Quarterly* 107 no. 3 (1992), p. 407.

16. David R. Mayhew, *Divided We Govern: Party Control, Lawmaking, and Investigations, 1946–1990* (Yale University Press, 1991), p. 4. See also James A. Thurber, ed., *Divided Democracy: Presidents and Congress in Cooperation and Conflict* (Congressional Quarterly, 1991).

17. See Eleanore Bushnell, *Crimes, Follies, and Misfortunes: The Federal Impeachment Trials* (University of Illinois Press, 1992).

18. *Nixon v United States*, 122 L Ed 2d 1 (1993).

19. John R. Labovitz, *Presidential Impeachment* (Yale University Press, 1978).

20. Neustadt, *Presidential Power*, pp. 180–81.

21. See Committee on the Constitutional System, *A Bicentennial Analysis of the American Political Structure: Report and Recommendations of the Committee on the Constitutional System* (1987) for recommendations of a committee co-chaired by Senator Nancy L. Kassebaum, C. Douglas Dillon, and Lloyd Cutler. For critical comments, see Mark P. Petracca, "To Right What the Constitution Has Wrought or To Wrong What Is Right," presented at annual meeting of the American Political Science Association, Washington, D.C., 1988.

22. Ann Stuart Diamond, "A Convention for Proposing Amendments: The Constitution's Other Method," *Publius* (Summer 1981), pp. 113–46; Wilbur Edel, "Amending the Constitution by Convention: Myths and Realities," *State Government* 55 (1982), pp. 51–56.

23. Russell L. Caplan, *Constitutional Brinksmanship: Amending the Constitution by National Convention* (Oxford University Press, 1988) p. x.

24. Ibid.

25. For analysis of more than 40 proposals for structural change, see John R. Vile, *Rewriting the United States Constitution: An Examination of Proposals from Reconstruction to the Present* (Praeger, 1991), chap. 8.

26. Samuel S. Freedman and Pamela J. Naughton, *ERA: May a State Change Its Vote?* (Wayne State University Press, 1979).

27. Alan P. Grimes, *Democracy and Amendments to the Constitution* (Lexington Books, 1978), p. 95. See also Clement E. Vose, *Constitutional Change* (Lexington Books, 1972), pp. 342–44, which focuses on amendment politics in the case of women's suffrage, child labor, and prohibition.

28. *Dillon v Gloss*, 256 US 368 (1921).

29. William Van Alstyne, "What Do You Think About the Twenty-seventh Amendment," *Constitutional Commentary* 10, no. 1 (University of Minnesota Law School, 1993), p. 15.

30. Gregory A. Caldeira, "Constitutional Change in America: Dynamics of Ratification under Article V," *Publius* (Fall 1985), p. 29.

31. Janet K. Boles, "Building Support for the ERA: A Case of Too Much, Too Late," *PS: Political Science and Politics* (1982), p. 572.

32. Mark R. Daniels, Robert Darcy, and Joseph W. Westphal, "The ERA Won—At Least in the Opinion Polls," *PS: Political Science and Politics* (Fall 1982), p. 583.

33. Janet K. Boles, *The Politics of the Equal Rights Amendment: Conflict and Decision-Making Powers* (Longman, 1979), p. 4.

34. Gilbert Y. Steiner, *Constitutional Inequality: The Political Fortunes of the Equal Rights Amendment* (Brookings Institution, 1985), p. 64. See also Mary Frances Berry, *Why the ERA Failed: Politics, Women's Rights, and the Amending Process of the Constitution* (Indiana University Press, 1986).

35. Margery L. Elfin, "Learning from Failures Present and Past," and Marian L. Palley, "Beyond the Deadline," *PS: Political Science and Politics* (Fall 1982), pp. 582–92. See also Mark R. Daniels and Robert E. Darcy, "As Time Goes By: Arrested Diffusion of the ERA," *Publius* (Fall 1985), p. 51; Joan Hoff-Wilson, ed., *Rights of Passage: The Past and Future of the ERA* (Indiana University Press, 1986).

36. Clifford D. May, "Rumblings Rise Anew on Status of Capital," *The New York Times*, January 11, 1989, p. B6.

37. Richard L. Berke, "Behind-the-Scenes Role For a 'Shadow' Senator," *The New York Times*, March 27, 1991, p. A8.

38. Bill Clinton, quoted in B. Drummond Ayres, Jr., "District of Columbia Is Denied Statehood," *The New York Times*, November 22, 1993, p. A8.

39. Mark Plokin, commentator on District Affairs for WAMU, Washington, D.C., quoted in ibid.

CHAPTER 3

1. Ronald L. Watts, "Canadian Federalism in the 1990's: Once More in Question," *Publius* 21 (Summer 1991), pp. 169–90; Robert C. Vipond, "The Canadian Constitutional Crisis: Who's Right on Rights?" *Intergovernmental Perspective* (Fall 1991), pp. 49–52; Robert C. Vipond, *Liberty and Community: Canadian Federalism and the Failure of the Constitution* (State University of New York Press, 1991).

2. For background and theory, see Samuel H. Beer, *To Make a Nation: The Rediscovery of American Federalism* (Harvard University Press, Belknap Press, 1993).

3. William H. Stewart, *Concepts of Federalism* (Center for the Study of Federalism and University Press of America, 1984). See also Edward L. Rubin and Malcolm Feeley, "Federalism: Some Notes on a National Neurosis," *UCLA Law Review* 41 (April 1994), pp. 903–952.

4. Daniel J. Elazar, *Exploring Federalism* (University of Alabama Press, 1987), p. 6.

5. See also Beer, *To Make a Nation.*

6. William H. Riker, *The Development of American Federalism* (Academic Publishers, 1987), pp. 14–15. Riker contends that not only does federalism not guarantee freedom but that the framers of our federal system, as well as those of other nations, were not animated by considerations of safeguarding freedom but by practical considerations of preserving unity.

7. John Kincaid, "State Constitutions in the Federal System," *Annals of the American Academy of Political and Social Sciences* 496 (March 1988), p. 17. See also David Osborne, *Laboratories of Democracy* (Harvard Business School Press, 1990), p. 1.

8. *Gibbons v Ogden*, 9 Wheaton 1 (1824).

9. *Heart of Atlanta Motel v United States*, 379 US 241 (1964).

10. *US Steel Corporation v Multistate Tax Commission*, 434 US 452 (1978).

11. *Garcia v San Antonio Metro*, 469 US 528 (1985); James R. Alexander, "State Sovereignty in the Federal System," *Publius* 16 (Spring 1986), pp. 1–15.

12. *Luther v Borden*, 7 How. 1 (1849).

13. *California v Superior Court of California*, 482 US 400 (1987).

14. *Puerto Rico v Brandstadt*, 483 US 219 (1987); Kenyon Bunch and Richard J. Hardy, "Continuity or Change in Interstate Extradition? Assessing *Puerto Rico v Brandstadt,*" *Publius* (Winter 1991), pp. 51–67.

15. David C. Nice, "State Participation in Interstate Compacts," *Publius* 17 (Spring 1987), p. 70.

16. Advisory Commission on Intergovernmental Relations, *Restoring Confidence and Competence* (ACIR, 1981), p. 30.

17. Cynthia Cates Colella, "The Creation, Care and Feeding of the Leviathan: Who and What Makes Government Grow," *Intergovernmental Perspective* (Fall 1979), p. 9.

18. Aaron Wildavsky, "Bare Bones: Putting Flesh on the Skeleton of American Federalism," in Advisory Commission on Intergovernmental Relations, *The Future of Federalism in the 1980s* (ACIR, 1981), p. 79.

19. David Wessel, "Federal Deficit Shrank in Fiscal 1993 to Below Predictions of Two Agencies," *The Wall Street Journal,* October 29, 1993, p. A2.

20. David O'Brien, "Federalism as a Metaphor in the Constitutional Politics of Public Administration," *Public Administration Review* 49 (September/October 1989), p. 411.

21. *United States v Darby,* 312 US 100 (1941).

22. 4 Wheaton 316 (1819).

23. *Missouri v Jenkins,* 495 US 33 (1990).

24. *Oklahoma City v Tuttle,* 471 US 808 (1985); *Mainer v Thiboutot,* 488 US (1980); *Monell v New York City Dept. of Social Welfare,* 436 US 658 (1978).

25. David Rapp, "The FEDS: Washington and the States: The Politics of Distrust," *Governing,* September 1, 1992, p. 67.

26. *Florce County School District Four v Carter,* 93 C.D.O.S. 8329 (November 9, 1993); *School Comm. of Burlington v Department of Ed. of Mass.,* 471 US 359 (1985).

27. Joseph F. Zimmerman, "Federal Preemption under Reagan's New Federalism," *Publius* 21 (Winter 1991), pp. 7–28:

28. *Webster v Reproductive Health Services,* 492 US 490 (1989); *Casey v Planned Parenthood,* 120 L Ed 2d 674 (1992). See also Ann O'M. Bowman and Michael A. Pagano, "The State of American Federalism, 1989–1990," *Publius* 20 (Fall 1990), pp. 12–13.

29. Oliver Wendell Holmes, Jr., *Collected Legal Papers* (Harcourt, 1920), pp. 295–96.

30. George J. Gordon, *Public Administration in America,* 4th ed. (St. Martin's Press, 1992), p. 91.

31. Al Gore, *From Red Tape to Results—Creating a Government That Works Better and Costs Less: Report of the National Performance Review* (U.S. Government Printing Office, 1993), p. 38.

32. Kitty Dumas, "Governors, State Legislators Offer Block Grants," *Congressional Quarterly* 49 (April 13, 1991), p. 923.

33. Deil S. Wright, *Understanding Intergovernmental Relations,* 3d ed. (Brooks-Cole, 1982).

34. Harold Seidman and Robert Gilmour, *Politics, Position and Power,* rev. ed. (Oxford University Press, 1985).

35. John E. Chubb, "The Political Economy of Federalism," *American Political Science Review* 79 (December 1985), p. 1005.

36. Richard P. Nathan, "Special Revenue Sharing: Simple, Neat, and Correct," unpublished paper.

37. Kevin G. Salwen and Paulette Thomas, "Job Programs Flunk at Training but Keep Washington at Work," *The Wall Street Journal,* December 16, 1993, p. A1.

38. Neil R. Peirce, "Reinventing Federalism," *The Baltimore Sun,* September 27, 1993.

39. Donald F. Kettl, *The Regulation of American Federalism* (Johns Hopkins University Press, 1987), pp. 154–55.

40. Brenda Avoletta and Philip M. Dearborn, "Federal Grants-in-Aid Soar in the 1990s: But Not for Local or General Government Purposes," *Intergovernmental Perspective* (Summer 1993), p. 32; U.S. Bureau of the Census, *Statistical Abstract of the United States: 1993* (Washington, D.C., 1993), p. 295.

41. Norman Beckman, "Developments in Federal-State Relations," *The Book of the States: 1990–91* (Council of State Governments, 1990), p. 528.

42. Joseph F. Zimmerman, "Congressional Regulation of Subnational Governments," *PS: Political Science and Politics* 26 (June 1993), p. 180.

43. Ron Suskind, "Health-Care Reform May Seem Like a Bitter Pill to Localities Sick of Unfunded Federal Mandates," *The Wall Street Journal,* December 21, 1993.

44. Bill Clinton, "Enhancing the Intergovernmental Partnership," Executive Order 12875, October 26, 1993.

45. Gore, *From Red Tape to Results,* p. 37.

46. Suskind, "Health-Care Reform."

47. Zimmerman, "Congressional Regulation of Subnational Governments," p. 179.

48. Mel Dubnick and Alan Gitelson, "Nationalizing State Policies," in *The Nationalization of State Government,* ed. Jerome J. Hanus (D.C. Heath, 1981), pp. 56–57.

49. Timothy J. Conlan, "And the Beat Goes On: Intergovernmental Mandates and Preemption in an Era of Deregulation," *Publius* 21 (Summer 1991), p. 46.

50. John Kincaid, "American Federalism: The Third Century," *Annals of the American Academy of Political and Social Sciences* 509 (May 1990), p. 9. See

also Zimmerman, "Federal Preemption under Reagan's New Federalism," pp. 7–28.

51. Michael A. Pagano, Ann O'M. Bowman, and John Kincaid, "The State of American Federalism, 1990–1991," *Publius* 21 (Summer 1991), p. 4.

52. Bill Clinton, quoted by Kenneth H. Bacon, "Washington's Relations with Local Governments Improve as Clinton Puts Emphasis on Flexibility," *The Wall Street Journal,* May 4, 1993, p. A20. See also Jonathan Walters, "Reinventing the Federal System," *Governing,* January 1994, pp. 49–53.

53. Thomas R. Dye, *American Federalism: Competition Among Governments* (Lexington Books, 1990), p. 199.

54. Ibid., p. 26.

55. Daniel J. Elazar, *American Federalism: A View from the States,* 3d ed. (Harper and Row, 1984), p. 241.

56. Debra A. Stewart, "State Initiatives in the Federal System: The Politics and Policy of Comparable Worth in 1984," *Publius* (Summer 1985), p. 83.'

57. Martha M. Hamilton, "If You Want Something Done Right, Do It Yourself," *Washington Post National Weekly Edition,* September 5–11, 1988, p. 31.

58. Edward Felsenthal, "Firms Ask Congress to Pass Uniform Rules," *The Wall Street Journal,* May 10, 1993, p. B4.

59. John Herbers, "The New Federalism: Unplanned, Innovative, and Here to Stay," *Governing* 1 (October 1987), pp. 28–34.

60. Virginia I. Pastrel, "States' Rights, or Dereliction of Duty?" *Washington Post National Weekly Edition,* July 22–28, 1991, p. 23.

61. Beverly A. Cigler, "Challenges Facing Fiscal Federalism in the 1990s, *PS: Political Science and Politics* 26 (June 1993), p. 183; Bowman and Pagano, "State of American Federalism, 1989–1990," p. 7; U.S. General Accounting Office, *Federal-State-Local Relations: Trends of the Past Decade and Emerging Issues* (GAO, March 1990).

62. Richard P. Nathan, "Federalism: The Great Composition," in *The New American Political System,* ed. Anthony King, 2d ed. (AEI Press, 1990), pp. 234–35.

63. Brad C. Johnson, "Washington Should Look at the Damage It's Doing," *Washington Post National Weekly Edition,* July 22–28, 1991, p. 24; Susan A. MacManus, "Mad about Mandates: The Issue of Who Should Pay for What Resurfaces in the 1990s," *Publius* 21 (Summer 1991), pp. 59–75.

64. Cigler, "Challenges Facing Fiscal Federalism," p. 183.

65. Luther Gulick, "Reorganization of the States," *Civil Engineering* (August 1933), pp. 420–21.

66. Osborne, *Laboratories of Democracy,* p. 363.

CHAPTER 4

1. Craig Smith, *To Form a More Perfect Union: The Ratification of the Constitution and the Bill of Rights, 1787–1791* (University Press of America, 1993).

2. *Barron v Baltimore,* 7 Peters 243 (1833).

3. *Gitlow v New York,* 268 US 652 (1925).

4. Ibid.

5. *Richmond Newspapers Inc. v Virginia,* 448 US 555 (1980).

6. "Project Report: Toward an Activist Role for State Bills of Rights," *Harvard Civil Rights–Civil Liberties Law Review,* vol. 8 (March 1973), p. 274.

7. Stanley H. Friedelbaum, ed., *Human Rights in the States: New Directions in Constitutional Policy Making* (Greenwood Press, 1988); Shirley S. Abrahamson and Diane S. Gutmann, "The New Federalism: State Constitutions and State Courts," *Judicature* (August/September 1987), pp. 88–99; Stanley H. Friedelbaum, "Independent State Grounds: Contemporary Invitations to Judicial Activism," in *State Supreme Courts: Policy Makers in the Federal System,* eds. Mary Cornelia Porter and G. Alan Tarr (Greenwood Press, 1982), p. 46.

8. Peter J. Galie, "State Supreme Courts, Judicial Federalism and the Other Constitutions," *Judicature* (August/September 1987), pp. 100–110. See

also Jeff Rosen, "Altered States: Liberals and Forgotten Constitutions," *The New Republic,* July 1, 1991, p. 19; Steven Pressman, "Protecting Rights in State Courts," *Editorial Research Reports, Congressional Quarterly,* 1, no. 20 (1988), p. 277; Dorothy Beasley, "State Bills of Rights: Dead or Alive?" *Intergovernmental Perspective* (June 1989), pp. 13–17.

9. Rosen, "Altered States," p. 20.

10. Miranda S. Spivack, "How States' Rights Can Rectify the Wrongs of the Supreme Court," *Los Angeles Times,* June 16, 1991, p. M2.

11. Barry Latzer, "The Hidden Conservatism of the State Court 'Revolution,'" *Judicature* (December 1990/January 1991), p. 193.

12. Ibid.

13. *Everson v Board of Education,* 333 US 203 (1947); Leonard W. Levy, *The Establishment Clause: Religion and the First Amendment* (Macmillan, 1986).

14. *Board of Education of Kiryas Joel Village School District v Grumet,* 129 L Ed 2d 546 (1994).

15. *Bowen v Kendrick,* 487 US 589 (1988); *Texas Monthly, Inc. v Bullock,* 489 US 1 (1989); *Lee v Weisman,* 120 L Ed 2d 467 (1992). *Board of Education of Kiryas Joel Village School District v Grumet,* 129 L Ed 2d 546 (1994).

16. *Lee v Weisman,* 120 L Ed 2d 467 (1992).

17. Concurring in *Board of Education of Kiryas Joel Village School District v Grumet*, C.D.O.S., June 27, 1994.

18. *Walz v Tax Commission*, 397 US 664 (1970); *Lemon v Kurtzman*, 403 US 602 (1971). For a review of these and other cases, see John Swomley, *Religious Liberty and the Secular State: The Constitutional Context* (Prometheus Books, 1987).

19. *Engel v Vitale*, 370 US 421 (1962).

20. *Lee v Weisman*, 120 L Ed 2d 467 (1992).

21. *Edwards v Aguillard*, 482 US 578 (1987).

22. *Marsh v Chambers*, 463 US 783 (1983).

23. *Witters v Washington Department of Service for Blind*, 474 US 481 (1986).

24. Donald L. Drakeman, *Church-State Constitutional Issues: Making Sense of the Establishment Clause* (Greenwood Press, 1991), p. 125.

25. *Mueller v Allen*, 463 US 388 (1983).

26. *Wolman v Walter*, 433 US 229 (1977).

27. *Zobrest v Catalina Foothills School District*, 125 L Ed 2d 1 (1993).

28. *Walz v Tax Commission*, 397 US 644 (1970).

29. *Frazee v Illinois Department of Employment Security*, 489 US 829 (1989).

30. *Wisconsin v Yoder*, 406 US 205 (1972).

31. *Employment Division, Department of Human Resources of Oregon v Smith*, 494 US 872 (1990).

32. *Lukumi Babalu Aye, Inc. v City of Hialeah*, 125 L Ed 2d 472 (1993).

33. *Lamb's Chapel v Center Moriches Union Free School District*, 124 L Ed 2d 352 (1993).

34. *Bob Jones University v United States*, 461 US 574 (1983).

35. *Hernandez v Commissioner*, 489 US 1027 (1989).

36. *Congressional Record* 139, no. 65 (May 11, 1993).

37. *Weekly Compendium of Presidential Documents* 2377 (November 16, 1993).

38. John Stuart Mill, "Essay on Liberty" (1859), in *The English Philosophers from Bacon to Mill*, ed. Arthur Burtt (Modern Library, 1939), p. 961.

39. *West Virginia State Board of Education v Barnette*, 319 US 624 (1943).

40. *Hustler Magazine v Falwell*, 485 US 46 (1988); *United States v Schriummer*, 279 US 644 (1928).

41. For a thoughtful statement of a somewhat contrary point of view, see Walter Berns, *First Amendment and the Future of American Democracy* (Basic Books, 1976). For a review of the classics and a call for a review of the civil liberties tradition to deal with issues such as the regulation of campaign finance and other matters designed to equalize the competition in the marketplace of ideas, see Mark A. Graber, *Transforming Free Speech: The Ambiguous Legacy of Civil Libertarianism* (University of California Press, 1991).

42. *R.A.V. v St. Paul*, 120 L Ed 2d 305 (1992).

43. *Gitlow v New York*, 268 US 652 (1925).

44. *Brown v Hartlage*, 456 US 45 (1982), in which the Supreme Court reversed a decision of the Kentucky Court of Appeals based on the bad tendency doctrine.

45. *Schenck v United States*, 249 US 47 (1919).

46. *Whitney v California*, 274 US 357 (1927).

47. *Nebraska Press Association v Stuart*, 427 US 539 (1976). See also Fred W. Friendly, *Minnesota Rag: The Dramatic Story of the Landmark Supreme Court Case That Gave New Meaning to Freedom of the Press* (Random House, 1981).

48. *Hazelwood School District v Kuhlmeier*, 484 US 260 (1988).

49. *Lanzetta v New Jersey*, 306 US 451 (1939).

50. *Winters v New York*, 333 US 507 (1948); *Burstyn v Wilson*, 343 US 495 (1952).

51. *Regan v Time, Inc.*, 468 US 641 (1984).

52. *R.A.V. v St. Paul*, 120 L Ed 2d 305 (1992).

53. *Dun & Bradstreet v Greenmoss Builders*, 472 US 749 (1985), citing *First National Bank of Boston v Bellotti*, 435 US 765, 766 (1978). See also Edward V. Heck and Albert C. Ringelstein, "The Burger Court and the Primacy of Political Expression," *The Western Political Quarterly* 40 (September 1987), pp. 411–23.

54. *Board of Trustees, State University of New York v Fox*, 492 US 469 (1989).

55. Lee C. Bollinger, *Images of a Free Press* (University of Chicago Press, 1991), p. 63.

56. *Lovell v Griffin*, 303 US 444 (1938).

57. *Richmond Newspapers, Inc. v Virginia*, 448 US 555 (1980). For a comprehensive history, see David A. Anderson, "The Origins of the Press Clause," *UCLA Law Review* (February 1983), pp. 455–537.

58. *Philadelphia Newspapers v Hepps*, 475 US 767 (1986); Richard Labunski, *Libel and the First Amendment: Legal History and Practice in Print and Broadcasting* (Transaction Books, 1987).

59. *Cohen v Cowles Media Co.*, 501 US 663 (1991).

60. *Dun & Bradstreet v Greenmoss Builders*, 472 US 749 (1985). See also William W. Van Alstyne, *Interpretations of the First Amendment* (Duke University Press, 1984), pp. 50–67.

61. *Hazelwood School District v Kuhlmeier*, 484 US 260 (1988).

62. *Richmond Newspapers, Inc. v Virginia*, 448 US 555 (1980); David M. O'Brien, *The Public's Right to Know: The Supreme Court and the First Amendment* (Praeger, 1981).

63. *United States v Nixon*, 418 US 683 (1974). See also Daniel N. Hoffman, *Governmental Secrecy and the Founding Fathers: A Study in Constitutional Controls* (Greenwood Press, 1981).

64. *Gentile v State Bar of Nevada*, 501 US 1030 (1991).

65. Susanna Barber, *News Cameras in the Courtroom: A Free Press-Fair Trial Debate* (Ablex Publishing Corporation, 1987), p. 9.

66. *Milwaukee Pub. Co. v Burleson*, 255 US 407 (1921).

67. *Lamont v Postmaster General*, 381 US 301 (1965).

68. *Rowan v Post Office Department*, 397 US 728 (1970).

69. *Southeastern Promotions, Ltd. v Conrad*, 420 US 546 (1975).

70. *California v LaRue*, 409 US 109 (1972); see also *Barnes v Glen Theatre, Inc.*, 501 US 560 (1991).

71. Lucas A. Powe Jr., *American Broadcasting and the First Amendment* (University of California Press, 1987).

72. *Federal Communications Commission v League of Women Voters of California*, 468 US 364 (1984).

73. Bruce Fein, "Cable Discretion and the First Amendment," *The Washington Times*, December 2, 1992, p. G1.

74. Edmund L. Andres, "Robotic Telephone Sales Calls Come under Fire in Congress," *The New York Times*, October 30, 1991, p. A1.

75. James Barron, "Watch What You Say on the Cordless Phone," *The New York Times*, November 9, 1991, p. 9.

76. *Sable Communications v Federal Communications Commission*, 492 US 115 (1989).

77. *Federal Communications Commission v Pacifica Foundation et al.*, 438 US 726 (1978). The Court, however, has refused to review a decision of the Court of Appeals for the District of Columbia, which declared unconstitutional a complete 24-hour ban on the televising of indecent materials.

78. Linda Greenhouse, "Supreme Court Roundup," *The New York Times*, March 3, 1992, p. A2.

79. Barnaby J. Feder, "Toward Defining Free Speech in the Computer Age," *The New York Times*, November 3, 1991, p. E5; Don Oldenburg, "Computers: Rights on the Line," and "The Law: Lost in Cyberspace," *The Washington Post*, October 1, 1991, p. E5.

80. *Amalgamated Food Employees v Logan Plaza*, 391 US 308 (1968).

81. *Frisby v Schultz*, 487 US 474 (1988).

82. *Boos v Barry*, 485 US 312 (1988).

83. *United States v O'Brien*, 391 US 367 (1968).

84. *Paris Adult Theatre v Slaton*, 413 US 49 (1973).

85. *United States v O'Brien*, 391 US 367 (1968).

86. *Clark v Community for Creative Non-Violence*, 468 US 288 (1984).

87. *R.A.V. v St. Paul*, 120 L Ed 2d 305 (1992).

88. *Clark v Community for Creative Non-Violence*, 468 US 288 (1984).

89. *Barnes v Glen Theatre, Inc.*, 501 US 560 (1991).

90. *The New York Times v Sullivan*, 376 US 254 (1964). See also Anthony Lewis, *Make No Law: The Sullivan Case and the First Amendment* (Random House, 1991), p. 140.

91. *Harte-Hanks, Inc. v Connaughton*, 491 US 657 (1989).

92. *Hustler Magazine v Falwell*, 485 US 46 (1988).

93. *Masson v New Yorker Magazine, Inc.*, 501 US 496 (1991).

94. Robert Scheer, "Pornography Commissioners Founder on the Limits of Sex," *Los Angeles Times*, May 1, 1986, p. 19.

95. *Brockett v Spokane Arcades, Inc.*, 472 US 491 (1985).

96. *Miller v California*, 413 US 15 (1973).

97. *Memoirs v Massachusetts*, 383 US 413 (1966).

98. *Jenkins v Georgia*, 418 US 153 (1974).

99. *Young v American Mini Theatres*, 427 US 51 (1976). See also *Renton v Playtime Theatres, Inc.*, 475 US 41 (1986).

100. "From Preamble to Indianapolis City-County Ordinance," cited by Joel B. Grossman, "The First Amendment and the New Anti-Pornography Statutes," *News for Teachers of Political Science* (American Political Science Association, 1985), p. 18. See also Catharine A. MacKinnon, *Only Words* (Harvard University Press, 1993).

101. Cass R. Sunstein, *The Partial Constitution* (Harvard University Press, 1993), p. 268.

102. Suzanne Stefanac, "Sex and the New Media," *The Recorder*, September 8, 1993, p. 14.

103. Barry Sussman, "With Pornography, It All Depends on Who's Doing the Looking," Washington Post-ABC News Poll, *The Washington Post National Weekly Edition*, March 24, 1986, p. 37.

104. "Anti-Pornography Laws and First Amendment Values," *Harvard Law Review* 98 (1984), p. 460. See also Donald Alexander Downs, *The New Politics of Pornography* (University of Chicago Press, 1990); Sunstein, *The Partial Constitution*, pp. 261–70.

105. *Butler v Her Majesty the Queen* 1 S.C.R. 452 (1992). See also "Pornography, Equality, and a Discrimination-Free Workplace: A Comparative Perspective," *Harvard Law Review*, 106 (March 1993), pp. 1075–92.

106. *Hudnut v American Booksellers*, 475 US 1001 (1986); *Sable Communications v Federal Communications Commission*, 492 US 115 (1989).

107. *Chaplinsky v New Hampshire*, 315 US 568 (1942).

108. *Cohen v California*, 403 US 115 (1971). See also *NAACP v Claiborne Hardware Co.*, 458 US 886 (1982); *R.A.V. v St. Paul*, 120 L Ed 2d 305 (1992).

109. *Cohen v California*, 403 US 115 (1971).

110. *United States v Eichman*, 496 US 310 (1990), repeated and reemphasized in *Simon & Schuster v New York State Crime Victims Board*, 116 L Ed 2d 476 (1991).

111. *R.A.V. v St. Paul*, 120 L Ed 2d 305 (1992).

112. David M. Hamlin, "Swastikas and Survivors: Inside the Skokie-Nazi Free Speech Case," *The Civil Liberties Review* (March/April 1978).

113. Lee C. Bollinger, *The Tolerant Society: Freedom of Speech and Extremist Speech in America* (Oxford University Press, 1986), pp. 24–32. See also Donald A. Downs, *Nazis in Skokie: Freedom, Community, and the First Amendment* (University of Notre Dame Press, 1985).

114. Bollinger, *Images of a Free Press*.

115. *Walker v Birmingham*, 388 US 307 (1967).

116. "Senate Passes Bill Making Blockades of Abortion Clinics a Federal Crime," *The New York Times*, May 13, 1994, pp. A1, A12.

117. *Pruneyard Shopping Center v Robins*, 447 US 74 (1980).

118. *National Association for the Advancement of Colored People v Alabama*, 357 US 449 (1958).

119. *Roberts v United States Jaycees*, 465 US 609 (1984).

120. J. Skelly Wright, "Politics and the Constitution: Is Money Speech?" *Yale Law Journal* 85 (1976), pp. 1001–21.

121. *Buckley v Valeo*, 424 US 1 (1976).

122. *Federal Election Commission v National Political Action Committee*, 470 US 480 (1985).

123. *West Virginia State Board of Education v Barnette*, 319 US 624 (1943).

124. See two works by Leonard W. Levy: *Legacy of Suppression* (Harvard University Press, 1960), and *Freedom of the Press from Zenger to Jefferson* (Bobbs-Merrill, 1966).

125. The Sedition Act of 1798, quoted in James Morton Smith, *Freedom's Fetters: The Alien and Sedition Laws and American Civil Liberties* (Cornell University Press, 1956), p. 442.

126. *Dennis v United States*, 341 US 494 (1950).

127. *Yates v United States*, 354 US 298 (1957).

128. *Brandenburg v Ohio*, 395 US 444 (1969).

CHAPTER 5

1. Sidney Verba and Gary R. Orren, *Equality in America: The View from the Top* (Harvard University Press, 1985), p. 1, on which this section is based. See also Jennifer L. Hochschild, *What's Fair? American Beliefs about Distributive Justice* (Harvard University Press, 1981).

2. Ellen Carol DuBois, *Feminism and Suffrage: The Emergence of an Independent Women's Movement in America, 1848–1869* (Cornell University Press, 1978); Joan Hoff-Wilson, "Women and the Constitution," *News for Teachers of Political Science* (American Political Science Association, Summer 1985), pp. 10–15.

3. James Vardaman, quoted in Alan P. Grimes, *Democracy and the Amendments to the Constitution* (D. C. Heath, 1979), p. 91. See also Nancy F. Cott, *The Grounding of Modern Feminism* (Yale University Press, 1987).

4. William Borah, quoted in Grimes, *Democracy*, p. 91.

5. Susan M. Hartmann, *From Margin to Mainstream: American Women and Politics since 1960* (Temple University Press, 1989); Susan Gluck Mezey, *In Pursuit of Equality: Women, Public Policy, and the Federal Courts* (St. Martin's Press, 1992).

6. *Plessy v Ferguson*, 163 US 537 (1896).

7. James MacGregor Burns and Stewart Burns, *A People's Charter: The Pursuit of Rights in America* (Knopf, 1991), pp. 305–18.

8. See David J. Garrow's prize-winning account, *Bearing the Cross: Martin Luther King, Jr., and the Southern Christian Leadership Conference* (Morrow, 1986).

9. Michael R. Belknap, *Federal Law and Southern Order: Racial Violence and Constitutional Conflict in the Post-Brown South* (University of Georgia, 1987), pp. 128–204.

10. Taylor Branch, *Parting the Waters: America in the King Years, 1954–1963* (Simon & Schuster, 1988). See also Harris Wofford, *Of Kennedys and Kings: Making Sense of the Sixties* (Farrar, Strauss and Giroux, 1980).

11. See Robert D. Loevy, *To End All Segregation: The Politics and Passage of the Civil Rights Act of 1964* (University Press of America, 1990).

12. Aldon D. Morris, *The Origins of the Civil Rights Movement: Black Communities Organizing for Change* (Free Press/Macmillan, 1985); James Farmer, *Lay Bare the Heart: An Autobiography of the Civil Rights Movement* (Arbor House, 1985); Branch, *Parting the Waters*.

13. Harold L. Hodgkinson, *The Demographics of American Indians: One Percent of the People, Fifty Percent of the Diversity* (Institute for Educational Leadership/Center for Demographic Policy, 1990), pp. 1–5.

14. Charles F. Wilkinson, *American Indians, Times, and the Law* (Yale University Press, 1987), p. 62; Vine Deloria, Jr., and Clifford M. Lytle, *The Nations Within: The Past and Future of American Indian Sovereignty* (Pantheon Books, 1984).

15. *Morton v Mancari*, 417 US 535 (1974); Theodore W. Taylor, *The Bureau of Indian Affairs* (Westview Press, 1984).

16. Office of Technology Assessment, quoted by Spencer Rich in "Native Americans, They Can Still Get Free Health Care If They're Indian Enough," *The Washington Post National Weekly Edition*, July 14, 1986, p. 34.

17. *County of Yakima v Yakima Indian Nation*, 116 L Ed 2d 687 (1992).

18. Theodora Lurie, "Shattering the Myth of the Vanishing American," *The Ford Foundation Letter* 22 (Winter 1991), p. 5.

19. The Bilateral Commission on the Future of the United States—Mexican Relations, *The Challenge of Interdependence* (University Press of America, 1989), p. 99.

20. U.S. Bureau of the Census, reported in *The New York Times*, September 7, 1988, p. 12.

21. Maurilio E. Vigil, *Hispanics in American Politics: Search for Political Power* (University Press of America, 1987).

22. Alan Pifer, *Annual Report of the Carnegie Corporation of New York* (1979), p. 16.

23. David Lesher and Gebe Martinez, "Latinos Claim 90s as Their Power Decade at Convention," *Los Angeles Times*, June 29, 1991, p. B9.

24. *1992 National Roster of Hispanic Elected Officials* (Washington, D.C.: National Association of Latino Elected and Appointed Officials, 1992), pp. 164–65.

25. Maria Newman, "Latino Meeting in O.C. to Focus on Remapping," *Los Angeles Times*, June 29, 1991, p. A1.

26. Celia W. Dugger, "U.S. Study Says Asian-Americans Face Widespread Discrimination," *The New York Times*, February 29, 1992, p. 1, reporting on U.S. Civil Rights Commission, *Civil Rights Issues Facing Asian Americans in the 1990s.*

27. Won Moo Hurh, *Korean Immigrants in America* (Fairleigh Dickinson University Press, 1984).

28. Antonio J. A. Pido, *The Filipinos in America: Macro/Micro Dimensions of Immigration and Integration* (Center for Migration Studies of New York, 1986).

29. *Minnestoa v Clover Leaf Creamery Co.*, 449 US 456 (1981).

30. *San Antonio School District v Rodriguez*, 411 US 1 (1973).

31. *Metro Broadcasting v Federal Communications Commission*, 497 US 547 (1990).

32. *Frontiero v Richardson*, 411 US 677 (1973).

33. *Califano v Webster*, 430 US 313 (1977).

34. *Mississippi University for Women v Hogan*, 458 US 718 (1982).

35. *Rostker v Goldberg*, 453 US 57 (1981).

36. *San Antonio School District v Rodriguez*, 411 US 1 (1973).

37. Sydney P. Freedberg, "Forced Exits? Companies Confront Wave of Age-Discrimination Suits," *The Wall Street Journal*, October 13, 1987, p. 37.

38. *San Antonio School District v Rodriguez*, 411 US 1 (1973).

39. *Washington v Davis*, 426 US 229 (1976). See also *Hunter v Underwood*, 471 US 522 (1985).

40. Justice Sandra Day O'Connor, concurring in *Hernandez v New York*, 114 L Ed 2d 395 (1991).

41. *Personnel Administrator of Massachusetts v Feeney*, 442 US 256 (1979).

42. C. Vann Woodward, *The Strange Career of Jim Crow* (Oxford University Press, 1968).

43. *Plessy v Ferguson*, 163 US 537 (1896).

44. *Brown v Board of Education of Topeka*, 347 US 483 (1954). See also J. W. Peltason, *Fifty-eight Lonely Men: Southern Federal Judges and School Desegregation* (University of Illinois Press, 1971), p. 248.

45. *Brown v Board of Education*, 349 US 294 (1955). For a comprehensive history of the events leading up to *Brown*, see Richard Kluger, *Simple Justice* (Knopf, 1976); Earl Black, *Southern Governors and Civil Rights: Racial Segregation as a Campaign Issue in the Second Reconstruction* (Harvard University Press, 1977), shows response, reaction, and eventually neutralization of race as a political issue following the *Brown* decision.

46. *Alexander v Board of Education*, 396 US 802 (1969).

47. Gary Orfield, *Must We Bus? Segregated Schools and National Policy* (Brookings Institution, 1979); Jennifer L. Hochschild, *The New American Dilemma: Liberal Democracy and School Desegregation* (Yale University Press, 1984).

48. *Swann v Charlotte-Mecklenburg Board of Education*, 402 US 1 (1971).

49. *Milliken v Bradley*, 418 US 717 (1974); Bernard Schwartz, *The School Busing Case and the Supreme Court* (Oxford University Press, 1986).

50. Gary Orfield, "Separate Societies: Have the Kerner Warnings Come True?" eds. Fred Harris and Roger Wilkins, *Quiet Riots: Race and Poverty in the United States—The Kerner Report Twenty Years Later* (Pantheon, 1988), p. 116. See also "Segregation's Threat to the Economy," *The New York Times*, December 19, 1993, p. A12.

51. William Celis, III, "Study Finds Rising Concentration of Black and Hispanic Students," *The New York Times*, December 14, 1993, p. A1.

52. Julie Johnson, "Deciding What to Do Next about Civil Rights," *The New York Times*, March 12, 1989, p. E5; Norman C. Amaker, ed., *Civil Rights and the Reagan Administration* (Urban Institute, 1988).

53. Quoted in Celis, "Study Finds Rising Concentration," p. A11.

54. V. O. Key, Jr., *Southern Politics* (Knopf, 1949), p. 555. For a history of the rise and fall of black disenfranchisement, see Steven F. Lawson, *Black Ballots: Voting Rights in the South, 1944–1969* (Columbia University Press, 1976).

55. *Smith v Allwright*, 321 US 649 (1944).

56. *Gomillion v Lightfoot*, 364 US 339 (1960).

57. *Harper v Virginia Board of Elections*, 383 US 663 (1966).

58. *Report of the United States Commission on Civil Rights* (Government Printing Office, 1959), pp. 103–104.

59. Harold W. Stanley, *Voter Mobilization and the Politics of Race: The South and Universal Suffrage, 1952–1984* (Praeger, 1987).

60. Abigail M. Thernstrom, *Whose Votes Count? Affirmative Action and Minority Voting Rights* (Harvard University Press, 1987), p. 15.

61. David J. Garrow, *Protest at Selma: Martin Luther King and the Voting Rights Act of 1965* (Yale University Press, 1978).

62. Thernstrom, *Whose Votes Count?* For a contrary view, see Bernard Grofman, Lisa Handley, and Richard Niemi, *Minority Representation and the Quest for Voting Equality* (Cambridge University Press, 1992).

63. *Presley v Etowah County Commission*, 117 L Ed 2d 51 (1992).

64. Ellen Perlman, "Feds on Remaps: No Go," *City and State*, July 29–August 11, 1991.

65. *Shaw v Reno*, 125 L Ed 2d 511 (1993); *Johson v De Grandy*, 129 L Ed 2d 775 (1994).

66. Richard L. Engstrom, "Racial Voter Dilution: The Concept and the Court," in Lorn S. Foster, ed., *The Voting Rights Act: Consequences and Implications* (Praeger, 1985), p. 13. Engstrom cites Harrell R. Rodgers, "Civil Rights and the Myth of Popular Sovereignty," *Journal of Black Studies* 12 (1981), pp. 53–70. See also Leonard A. Cole, *Blacks in Power: A Comparative Study of Black and White Elected Offficials* (Princeton University Press, 1976); Dianne M. Pinderhughes, *Race and Ethnicity in Chicago Politics: A Reexamination of Pluralist Theory* (University of Illinois Press, 1987), p. xvi. For a skeptical evaluation of the act, see Foster, ed., *Voting Rights Act.*

67. Katherine Tate, *From Protest to Politics* (Harvard University Press, 1993), p. 2.

68. Huey L. Perry, ed., "Recent Advances in Black Electoral Politics," symposium in *PS: Political Science and Politics* 23 (June 1990), pp. 133–60. See also Huey L. Perry, "Review Essay," *Publius* 18 (Fall 1988), p. 198, covering, among others, relevant work on these questions by Margaret Edds, *Free at Last: What Really Happened When Civil Rights Came to Southern Politics* (Adler and Adler, 1987).

69. Kenneth R. Mladenka, "Blacks and Hispanics in Urban Politics," *The American Political Science Review* 83 (March 1989), p. 188. See also Lawrence Bobo and Franklin D. Gilliam, Jr., "Race, Sociopolitical Participation and Black Empowerment," *The American Political Science Review* 84 (June 1990), pp. 377–93, for evidence that having an African American mayor enhances black participation in politics and a more trusting attitude toward civic affairs.

70. Thernstrom, *Whose Votes Count?* p. 243.

71. Perry, "Review Essay," p. 198.

72. J. Phillip Thompson III, reporting on findings of Carol M. Swaing, *Black Faces, Black Interests: The Representation of African Americans in Congress* (Harvard University Press, 1993) in *Political Science Quarterly* (Winter 1993–94), p. 743.

73. Charles V. Hamilton, "On Parity and Political Empowerment," in *The State of Black America, 1989*, ed. Janet Dewart (National Urban League, 1989), p. 119.

74. Justice William O. Douglas, dissenting in *Moose Lodge No. 107 v Irvis*, 407 US 163 (1972).

75. *New York State Club Association v New York City*, 487 US 1 (1988).

76. *Civil Rights Cases*, 109 US 3 (1883).

77. *Heart of Atlanta Motel v United States*, 379 US 421 (1964).

78. Paul Burstein, *Discrimination, Jobs, and Politics: The Struggle for Equal Employment Opportunity in the United States since the New Deal* (University of Chicago Press, 1985); Kathanne W. Greene, *Affirmative Action and Principles of Justice* (Greenwood Press, 1989).

79. *Meritor Savings Bank v Vinson*, 477 US 57 (1986); *Harris v Forklift Systems, Inc.* 126 L Ed 2d 295 (1993).

80. Hanes Walton, Jr., *When the Marching Stopped: The Politics of Civil Rights Regulatory Agencies* (State University of New York Press, 1988).

81. John O. Calmore, "To Make Wrong Right: The Necessary and Proper Aspirations of Fair Housing," in *State of Black America, 1989*, Dewart, p. 95.

82. Orfield, "Separate Societies," p. 105.

83. Charles M. Lamb, "Housing Discrimination and Segregation," *Catholic University Law Review* (Spring 1981), p. 370.

84. *Shelley v Kraemer*, 334 US 1 (1948).

85. Robert Reinhold, "Race Barriers in Housing Still High 11 Years after the Civil Rights Act," *The New York Times*, June 8, 1979, p. 1.

86. Joe T. Darden, Harriet Orcutt Duleep, and George C. Galster, "Civil Rights in Metropolitan America," *Journal of Urban Affairs* 14, no. 3/4 (1992), p. 473.

87. Timothy Noah, "Housing Report Says Racial Bias Remains Prevalent," *The Wall Street Journal*, August 30, 1991, reporting on findings of report prepared by the Urban Institute commissioned by the Department of Housing and Urban Development.

88. "The Racism Next Door: Segregated Housing Is Still a Blight in Most Neighborhoods," *Time*, June 30, 1986, p. 40. See also Alan Finder, "Housing Bias Still Pervades the New York Region," *The New York Times*, March 13, 1989, p. A16.

89. Justice John Marshall Harlan, dissenting in *Plessy v Ferguson*, 163 US 537 (1896).

90. *University of California Regents v Bakke*, 438 US 265 (1978).

91. Justice Byron White, concurring in *Wygant v Jackson Board of Education*, 476 US 267 (1986).

92. Justice Sandra Day O'Connor, majority opinion, and Justice Thurgood Marshall, dissenting in *Richmond v Croson*, 488 US 469 (1989).

93. Justice William J. Brennan, majority opinion, and Justice Sandra Day O'Connor, dissenting in *Metro Broadcasting v Federal Communications Commission*, 497 US 547 (1990).

94. *Shaw v Reno*, 125 L Ed 2d 511 (1993).

95. Justice Sandra Day O'Connor, majority opinion in *Richmond v Croson*, 488 US 469 (1989).

96. Ibid. Justices Anthony M. Kennedy and Antonin Scalia, who were part of the majority, opposed any kind of racial classification, even as a remedy. On the other side, Justice John Paul Stevens, who also voted with the majority, believed race may properly be taken into account under some circumstances, even when not a remedy for past discrimination. See also Gregg Ivers and Karen O'Connor, "Minority Set-Aside Programs in the States after *City of Richmond v J. A. Croson Co.*," *Publius* 20 (Summer 1990), pp. 63–78.

97. National Advisory Commission on Civil Disorders, *The Kerner Report* (Washington, D.C., Government Printing Office, 1968), p. 1.

98. Charles Murray, *Losing Ground: American Social Policy, 1950–1980* (Basic Books, 1984).

99. Summarized from Gary Orfield and Carol Ashkinaze, *The Closing Door: Conservative Policy and Black Opportunity* (University of Chicago Press, 1991), p. 13.

100. James Farmer, quoted in Rochelle L. Stanfield, "Black Complaints Haven't Translated into Political Organization and Power," *National Journal*, June 14, 1980, p. 465. Alphonso Pinkey, *The Myth of Black Progress* (Cambridge University Press, 1984), argues that the failure of blacks to make greater progress is due to white racism. William Julius Wilson, *The Declining Significance of Race*, 2d ed. (University of Chicago Press, 1984), argues to the contrary that most of the problems are those of class, not of race. See also Stuart Scheingold, "Constitutional Rights and Social Change: Civil Rights in Perspective," in *Judging the Constitution*, eds. Michael W. McCann and Gerald L. Houseman (Scott, Foresman and Company, 1989), pp. 73–91.

101. National Academy of Science, *A Common Destiny: Blacks and American Society* (National Academy Press, 1989).

102. Orfield, "Separate Societies," p. 103. See also Madeline Landau, "Race, Poverty and the Cities: Hyperinnovation in Complex Policy Systems," *Public Affairs Report, Bulletin of the Institute of Governmental Studies*, University of California, Berkeley, 30 (January 1989), p. 1; Margaret C. Simms, ed., *Black Economic Progress: An Agenda for the 1990's* (Joint Center for Political Studies, 1988); Nicholas Lehmann, *The Promised Land* (Knopf, 1991).

103. Orfield and Ashkinaze, *Closing Door*, p. 26.

104. William J. Wilson, *The Truly Disadvantaged: The Inner City, the Underclass, and Public Policy* (University of Chicago Press, 1987), particularly Chapter 5.

105. Orfield and Ashkinaze, *Closing Door*, pp. 221–34.

106. Edward G. Carmines and James A. Stimson, *Issue Evolution: Race and the Transformation of American Politics* (Princeton University Press, 1989), p. xiii.

107. Carmines and Stimson, *Issue Evolution*, p. xiv.

CHAPTER 6

1. Martin Edelman, *Democratic Theories and the Constitution* (State University of New York Press, 1984), p. 304; Judith N. Shklar, *American Citizenship: The Quest for Inclusion* (Harvard University Press, 1991), p. 3.

2. *Vance v Terrazas*, 444 US 252 (1980).

3. Arnold H. Leibowitz, "The Refugee Act of 1980: Problems and Congressional Concerns," *The Annals of the American Academy of Political and Social Sciences* (May 1983), pp. 163–71. See also Gil Loescher and John Scanlan, *Calculated Kindness: Refugees and America's Half-Open Door, 1945 to Present* (Free Press, 1986).

4. *Sale v Haitian Centers Council, Inc.*, 125 L Ed 2d 128 (1993).

5. *Plyer v Doe*, 457 US 202 (1982). See also Paul Yoshihashi, "Employer Sanctions and Illegal Workers," *The Wall Street Journal*, May 26, 1989, p. B1.

6. The National Research Council concluded that the number is 2–4 million; other studies have estimated it to be as high as 12 million. Many cite 6 million as the correct number; government officials use the figure 3.9 million. See Gaylord Shaw, "Number of Illegal Aliens in U.S. May Be as Low as 2 Million, New Study Contends," *Los Angeles Times*, June 25, 1985; Bilateral Commission on the Future of United States–Mexican Relations, *The Challenge of Interdependence: Mexico and the United States* (University Press of America, 1989), p. 185.

7. *Kleindienst v Mandel*, 408 US 753 (1972).

8. Senator Alan Simpson, quoted by Justice John Paul Stevens, in *McNary v Haitian Refugee Center*, 112 L Ed 2d 1005 (1991).

9. *Plyer v Doe* 457 US 202 (1982).

10. Bilateral Commission, *Challenge of Interdependence*, p. 77.

11. *Home Building & Loan Assn. v Blaisdell*, 290 US 398 (1934).

12. *Chicago, Milwaukee, and St. Paul Ry. v Minnesota*, 134 US 418 (1890).

13. Richard A. Epstein, *Taking: Private Property and the Power of Eminent Domain* (Harvard University Press, 1985).

14. *First English Evangelical v Los Angeles County*, 482 US 304 (1987).

15. *United States v 564.54 Acres of Land,* 441 US 506 (1979).

16. Ibid.

17. *Nollan v California Coastal Commission*, 483 US 825 (1987). See also *Dolan v City of Tigard*, discussed in *The New York Times*, June 25, 1994.

18. *Mathews v Eldridge*, 424 US 319 (1976), restated in *Connecticut v Doeher*, 115 L Ed 2d 1 (1991).

19. *Leary v United States*, 395 US 6 (1969); *Turner v United States*, 369 US 398 (1970).

20. *Meyer v Nebraska*, 262 US 390 (1923).

21. *Meachum v Fano*, 427 US 215 (1976).

22. *Cleveland Board of Education v Loudermill*, 470 US 532 (1985).

23. *Morrissey v Brewer*, 408 US 471 (1972).

24. Philip B. Kurland, *Some Reflections on Privacy and the Constitution* (University of Chicago Center for Policy Study, 1976), p. 9. A classic and influential article about privacy is S. D. Warren and L. D. Brandeis, "The Right to Privacy," *Harvard Law Review*, December 15, 1980, pp. 193–220.

25. *Roe v Wade*, 410 US 113 (1973).

26. *Planned Parenthood of Southeastern Pennsylvania v Casey*, 120 L Ed 2d 674 (1992).

27. *Ohio v Akron Center for Reproductive Health*, 111 L Ed 2d 405 (1990); *Hodgson v Minnesota*, 111 L Ed 2d 344 (1990); *Planned Parenthood of Southeastern Pennsylvania v Casey*, 120 L Ed 2d 674 (1992).

28. *Bowers v Hardwick*, 478 US 186 (1986).

29. The most comprehensive analysis of these complicated issues is Wayne R. LaFave, *Search and Seizure: A Treatise on the Fourth Amendment*, 2d ed. (West Publishing, 1987).

30. *County of Riverside v McLaughlin*, 114 L Ed 2d 49 (1991).

31. *California v Hodari D.*, 113 L Ed 2d 690 (1991).

32. *Mincey v Arizona*, 437 US 385 (1978), reaffirmed in *California v Acevedo*, 114 L Ed 2d 619 (1991).

33. *United States v Ross*, 456 US 798 (1982).

34. *Terry v Ohio*, 392 US 1 (1968); *United States v Sharpe*, 470 US 675 (1985); *Hayes v Florida*, 470 US 811 (1985).

35. *Minnesota v Dickerson*, 124 L Ed 2d 334 (1993).

36. *Adams v Williams*, 407 US 143 (1972).

37. *Chimel v California*, 395 US 752 (1969); *United States v Edward*, 415 US 800 (1974); *Illinois v Lafayette*, 462 US 640 (1983).

38. *Cupp v Murphy*, 412 US 291 (1973).

39. *Florida v Wells*, 495 US 1 (1990).

40. *Schneckloth v Bustamonte*, 412 US 218 (1973); *United States v Matlock*, 415 US 164 (1974).

41. *Almeida-Sanchez v United States*, 413 US 266 (1973); *United States v Ortiz*, 422 US 891 (1975).

42. *United States v Ramsey*, 431 US 606 (1977).

43. *Torres v Puerto Rico*, 442 US 465 (1979).

44. *Coolidge v New Hampshire*, 403 US 443 (1971); *Texas v Brown*, 460 US 730 (1983); *Arizona v Hicks*, 480 US 321 (1987).

45. *Michigan v Tyler*, 436 US 499 (1978); *Mincey v Arizona*, 437 US 385 (1978).

46. *Tennessee v Garner*, 471 US 1 (1985).

47. *Olmstead v United States*, 227 US 438 (1928).

48. *Florida v Riley*, 488 US 445 (1989).

49. *Katz v United States*, 389 US 347 (1967).

50. *Mapp v Ohio*, 367 US 643 (1961).

51. *United States v Leon*, 468 US 897 (1984).

52. *United States v Payner*, 447 US 727 (1980).

53. *Blau v United States*, 340 US 332 (1951).

54. *Mincey v Arizona*, 437 US 385 (1978).

55. *Miranda v Arizona*, 384 US 436 (1966). Liva Baker, *Miranda: Crime, Law and Politics* (Atheneum, 1983), explores every aspect of the decision, including subsequent controversy about its effects.

56. *Presier v Rodriguez*, 411 US 475 (1973).

57. 28 *United States Code* 2454.

58. *Stone v Powell*, 428 US 465 (1976).

59. *McCleskey v Zant*, 113 L Ed 2d 517 (1991); *Withrow v Williams*, 123 L. Ed. 2d 407 (1993). For a review of these decisions, see Jordan Steiker, "Innocence and Federal Habeas," *UCLA Law Review* 41 (December 1993), pp. 303–89.

60. Felix Frankfurter, dissenting in *United States v Rabinowitz*, 339 US 56 (1950).

61. *Johnson v Zerbst*, 304 US 458 (1938); *Gideon v Wainwright*, 372 US 335 (1963). Anthony Lewis, *Gideon's Trumpet* (Random House, 1964), has become a classic on this issue.

62. *United States v Salerno*, 481 US 739 (1987).

63. *United States v Enterprises, Inc.*, 112 L Ed 2d 795 (1991).

64. *Blanton et al. v North Las Vegas*, 489 US 538 (1989).

65. *J. E. B. v Alabama ex rel T. B.*, 128 L Ed 2d 89 (1994). *Batson v Kentucky*, 476 US 79 (1986); *Powers v Ohio*, 113 L Ed 2d 411 (1991); *Hernandez v New York*, 114 L Ed 2d 395 (1991); *Georgia v McCollum*, 120 L Ed. 2d 33 (1990).

66. *Rhodes v Chapman*, 452 US 337 (1981); *Wilson v Seither*, 115 L Ed 2d 271 (1991).

67. *Hutto v Davis*, 454 US 370 (1982).

68. *Solem v Helm*, 463 US 277 (1983).

69. *Benton v Maryland*, 395 US 784 (1969).

70. Jerome Frank, *Courts on Trial* (Princeton University Press, 1949), p. 122. See also Rita James Simon, ed., *The Jury System in America: A Critical Overview* (Sage Publications, 1975); John Guinther, *The Jury in America* (Facts-on-File Publications, 1988); Steven Brill, *Trial by Jury* (American Lawyer Books/Touchstone, 1989).

71. Harry Kalven, Jr., and Hans Zeisel, *The American Jury* (University of Chicago Press, 1971), p. 57.

72. William O. Douglas, dissenting in *United States v Mara*, 410 US 19 (1973).

73. Bryan Abas, "The Ruckus out of Rocky Flats—Empowering the People Through Grand Juries," *The Recorder*, February 1, 1994, p. 16.

74. "Race and the Criminal Process," *Harvard Law Review* 101 (May 1988), p. 1493.

75. Ibid., p. 1476.

76. Dean Alfred Blumstein and Joan Petersilia, quoted in Norval Morris, "Race and Crime: What Evidence Is There That Race Influences Results in the Criminal Justice System?" *Judicature* (August/September 1988), p. 112.

77. Morris, "Race and Crime," p. 112.

78. George Edwards, *The Police on the Urban Frontier* (Institute of Human Relations Press and the American Jewish Committee, 1968), p. 28.

79. Morris, "Race and Crime," p. 113.

80. *West Virginia State Board of Education v Barnette*, 319 US 624 (1943).

81. Robert H. Jackson, *The Supreme Court in the American System of Government* (Harvard University Press, 1955), pp. 81–82.

CHAPTER 7

1. Clinton Rossiter, *Conservatism in America* (Vintage, 1962), p. 72.

2. *Marbury v Madison*, 1 Cranch 137 (1803).

3. See, generally, Bernard Bailyn, *The Ideological Origins of the American Revolution* (Harvard University Press, 1967).

4. Robert A. Dahl, "Liberal Democracy in the United States," in *A Prospect of Liberal Democracy*, ed. William Livingtson (University of Texas Press, 1979), p. 64.

5. Ibid., pp. 59–60.

6. Franklin D. Roosevelt, State of the Union Address, January 11, 1944, *The Public Papers of the President of the United States, 1944* (Government Printing Office, 1962), pp. 371–94.

7. Bill Clinton, Address to Congress on Health Care, *The New York Times*, September 23, 1993, pp. A24–25.

8. For an analysis of one aspect of the underclass, see Paul M. Sniderman and Michael Hagen, *Race and Inequality: A Study in American Values* (Chatham House, 1985).

9. Harry S Truman, State of the Union Address, 1949, *The Public Papers of the President of the United States, 1949* (Government Printing Office, 1964), pp. 1–7.

10. David Spitz, "A Liberal Perspective on Liberalism and Conservatism," in *Left, Right and Center*, ed. Robert Goldwin (Rand McNally, 1965), p. 31.

11. See also Charles Peters and Philip Keisling, eds., *A New Road for America: The Neoliberal Movement* (University Press of America, 1984); Randall Rothenberg, *The Neoliberals: Creating the New American Politics* (Simon & Schuster, 1984).

12. Kevin Phillips, *The Politics of Rich and Poor: Wealth and the American Electorate in the Reagan Aftermath* (New York: Random House, 1990), pp. 220–21.

13. Michael Barone, *Our Country: The Shaping of America from Roosevelt to Reagan* (Free Press, 1990), p. xii.

14. Kenneth R. Hoover, *Ideology and Political Life* (Brooks/Cole, 1987), p. 34.

15. See the writings of Milton Friedman, *Capitalism and Freedom* (University of Chicago, 1962). See also Friedrich A. Hayek, *The Road to Serfdom*, (University of Chicago Press, 1944).

16. Barry Goldwater, *The Conscience of a Conservative* (Victor, 1960), p. 76.

17. Paula Poundstone, "He Didn't Even Like Girls," *Mother Jones* (May 1993), p. 37.

18. Walter H. Capps, *The New Religious Right: Piety, Patriotism, and Politics* (University of South Carolina Press, 1990).

19. Barry Goldwater with Jack Casserly, *Goldwater* (Doubleday, 1988), p. 387.

20. For a general discussion of this ideology, see Peter Steinfels, *The Neoconservatives* (Simon & Schuster, 1979). For a general text from this perspective, see Richard T. Saeger, *American Government and Politics: A Neoconservative Approach* (Scott, Foresman, 1982).

21. Ronald Reagan, Inaugural Address, 1981, *The Public Papers of the President of the United States: Ronald Reagan, 1981* (Government Printing Office, 1982), p. 1.

22. Kathleen Day, *S & L Hell: The People and the Politics Behind the $1 Trillion Savings and Loan Scandal* (W.W. Norton & Co., 1993).

23. See Edward A. Snyder, "The Effects of Higher Criminal Penalties on Antitrust Enforcement," *Journal of Law and Economics 33* (October 1990), pp. 439–62; also Brian Burrough and John Helyar, *Barbarians at the Gate: The Fall of RJR Nabisco* (Harper, 1990).

24. Dan Goodman, "Bleeding-Heart Conservatives," *Time*, May 18, 1992, p. 37.

25. Ronald Reagan, Address to the Nation on the Economy, February 5, 1981, *Public Papers of the Presidents: Ronald Reagan, 1981* (Government Printing Office, 1982), p. 81.

26. Sylvia Nasar, "Even among the Well-Off, the Rich Get Richer," *The New York Times*, March 5, 1992, p. A1.

27. Karl Marx, "Critique of the Gotha Program," in *Marx Selections*, ed. Allen W. Wood (Macmillan Publishing, 1988), p. 190.

28. Irving Howe, *Socialism and America* (Harcourt, 1985); Michael Harrington, *Socialism: Past and Future* (Arcade, 1989).

29. Eric R. A. N. Smith, *The Unchanging American Voter* (University of California Press, 1989), pp. 171–72.

30. Center for Political Studies, University of Michigan, *American National Election Study, 1990: Post Election Survey* (April 1991).

31. Herbert McClosky and Alida Brill, *Dimensions of Tolerance: What Americans Believe about Civil Liberties* (Russell Sage Foundation, 1983), pp. 274–75.

32. Dinesh D'Sousa, *Illiberal Education: The Politics of Race and Sex on Campus* (Free Press, 1991), p. 313.

CHAPTER 8

1. *Yniguez v Mofford*, 730 F. Supp. 309 (D. Ariz. 1990).

2. Albert Einstein, quoted in Laurence J. Peter, *Peter's Quotations* (William Morrow, 1977), p. 358.

3. Alexis de Tocqueville, *Democracy in America*, ed. J. P. Mayer, trans. George Lawrence (Doubleday and Company, 1969), p. 278.

4. Ibid. p. 280.

5. U.S. Bureau of the Census, *Statistical Abstract of the United States, 1982–83* (Government Printing Office, 1983), p. 488.

6. V. O. Key, Jr., *Politics, Parties, and Pressure Groups*, 5th ed. (Thomas Y. Crowell, 1964), p. 232.

7. Norman J. Ornstein, Thomas E. Mann, and Michael J. Malbin, *Vital Statistics on Congress, 1991–1992* (Congressional Quarterly, 1992), p. 10.

8. Tocqueville, *Democracy in America*, p. 68.

9. Holly Idelson, "Count Adds Seats in Eight States," *Congressional Quarterly Weekly Report* 48 (December 29, 1990), p. 4240.

10. U.S. Bureau of the Census, Release CB 91-24, January 25, 1991.

11. U.S. Bureau of the Census, U.S. Population Reports P 23, no. 185, *Population Profile of the United States, 1993* (Government Printing Office, 1993), p. 34.

12. U.S. Bureau of the Census, Release CB 91-24, January 25, 1991, and February 21, 1991.

13. U.S. Bureau of the Census, Release CB 91-66, February 21, 1991.

14. U.S. Bureau of the Census, U.S. Population Reports P 23, no. 185, *Population Profile of the United States, 1993*, p. 36.

15. Ibid., p. 3.

16. Dale Rogers Marshall, "The Continuing Significance of Race: The Transformation of American Politics," *American Political Science Review* 84 (June 1990), pp. 611–16.

17. Robert D. Ballard, "Introduction: Lure of the New South," in *Search of the New South: The Black Urban Experience in the 1970s and 1980s*, ed. Robert D. Ballard (University of Alabama Press, 1989), p. 5.

18. U.S. Bureau of the Census, U.S. Population Reports P 23, no. 185, *Population Profile of the United States: 1993*, p. 34.

19. Ibid., p. 5.

20. Ibid., pp. 34–35.

21. U.S. Bureau of the Census, Current Population Reports P 70, no. 34, *Household Wealth and Asset Ownership, 1991* (Government Printing Office, 1991), table H.

22. U.S. Bureau of the Census, 1992 Current Population Survey, P 20, no. 471, *The Black Population in the United States: March 1992*, p. 17.

23. U.S. Bureau of the Census, U.S. Population Reports P 23, no. 185, *Population Profile of the United States, 1993*, p. 34.

24. U.S. Department of Education, *Trends in Racial/Ethnic Enrollment in Higher Education: Fall 1978 through Fall 1988* (Government Printing Office, 1990), p. 15.

25. U.S. Bureau of the Census, U.S. Population Reports P 23, no. 185, *Population Profile of the United States: 1993*, p. 34.

26. Mark R. Levy and Michael S. Karmer, *The Ethnic Factor: How America's Minorities Decide Elections* (Simon & Schuster, 1973).

27. Mark Stern, "Democratic Presidency and Voting Rights," in *Blacks in Southern Politics*, eds. Lawrence W. Mooreland, Robert P. Steed, and Todd A. Baker (Praeger, 1987), pp. 50–51.

28 David Bositis, *Blacks and the 1993 Republican National Convention* (Joint Center for Political and Economic Studies, 1992), p. 5.

29. U.S. Bureau of the Census, U.S. Population Reports P 23, no. 185, *Population Profile of the United States, 1993*, p. 34.

30. See Frank R. Parker, *Black Votes Count: Political Empowerment in Mississippi After 1965* (University of North Carolina Press, 1990).

31. David Bositis, *Black State Legislators: A Survey and Analysis of Black Leadership in State Capitals* (Joint Center for Political and Economic Research, 1992) p. 3.

32. U.S. Bureau of the Census, U.S. Population Reports P 23, no. 185, *Population Profile of the United States, 1993*, pp. 34–39.

33. Gary D. Sandefur and Arthur Sakamoto, "American Indian Household Structure and Income," *Demography* 25 (February 1988), p. 74.

34. U.S. Bureau of the Census, *We, The First Americans* (Government Printing Office, 1989), pp. 5–7.

35. Richard Santillan and Carlos Munoz, Jr., "Latinos and the Democratic Party," in *The Democrats Must Lead*, eds. James MacGregor Burns, William Crotty, Lois Lovelace Duke, and Lawrence D. Longley (Westview Press, 1992), pp. 182–83.

36. Rodolfo O. de la Garza, Louis DeSipio, F. Chris Garcia, John Garcia, and Angelo Falcon, *Latino Voices: Mexican, Puerto Rican, and Cuban Perspectives on American Politics* (Westview Press, 1992), p. 13.

37. Ibid., p. 14.

38. U. S. Bureau of the Census, Current Population Reports, *The Hispanic Population in the United States* (Government Printing Office, 1992), p. 302.

39 de la Garza, *Latino Voices*, p. 14.

40. *The Hispanic Population in the United States*, Table 3A.

41. U.S. Bureau of the Census, *Statistical Abstract of the United States, 1992* (Government Printing Office, 1993), p. 10.

42. James West Davidson, William E. Gienapp, Christine Leigh Heyrman, Mark H. Lytle, and Michael B. Stoff, *Nation of Nations* (McGraw-Hill, 1990), pp. 833–34.

43. G. Thomas Edwards, *Sowing Good Seeds: The Northwest Suffrage Campaigns of Susan B. Anthony* (Oregon Historical Society Press, 1990), p. 136.

44. Paul Kleppner, *Continuity and Change in Electoral Politics, 1893-1928* (Greenwood Press, 1987), p. 172.

45. Carol Mueller, "The Gender Gap and Women's Political Influence," *Annals of the American Academy of Political and Social Sciences* 515 (May 1991), p. 25.

46. Self-reported turnout in the *American National Election Studies, 1978–88*, shows women voting at 2.2 percent less than men on average.

47. United Press International, "Is Year of the Woman for Real? Voters Will Settle the Matter," *Deseret News*, November 2, 1992, p. A4.

48. Diane L. Fowlkes, "Feminist Theory: Reconstructing Research and Teaching About American Politics and Government," *News for Teachers of Political Science* (Winter 1987), pp. 6–9. See also Andrea Dworkin, *Right-Wing Women* (Putnam's, 1983); Zillah R. Eisenstein, ed., *Feminism and Sexual Equality: Crisis in Liberal America* (Monthly Review Press, 1984); Ethel Klein, *Gender Politics* (Harvard University Press, 1984); Rebecca E. Klatch, *Women of the New Right* (Temple University Press, 1987).

49. "Women Carry Greatest Burden of Lowest Pay," *Deseret News*, November 12, 1991, p. A1.

50. U.S. Bureau of the Census, U.S. Population Reports P 23, no. 185, *Population Profile of the United States, 1993*, p. 27.

51. There is no difference in the proportion of men and women who graduate from high school, but men graduate from college at a higher rate than women. In 1991, 24.3 percent of men over the age of 25 had graduated from college, compared to 18.8 percent of women. U.S. Bureau of the Census, U.S. Population Reports P 23, no. 185, *Population Profile of the United States*, p. 15.

52. "Schooling Pays—But Women Still Lose," *Salt Lake Tribune*, November 15, 1991, p. A1.

53. E. J. Dionne, Jr., "Struggle for Work and Family Fueling Women's Movement," *The New York Times*, August 22, 1989, p. A1.

54. Jeffrey Schmalz, "Clinton Carves a Wide Path Deep into Reagan Country," *The New York Times*, November 4, 1992, p. B1.

55. Times Mirror Center for the People and the Press, *Jury Still Out on Clinton's Success* (August 5, 1993), p. 27.

56. Stephen C. LeSuer, *The 1838 Mormon War in Missouri* (University of Missouri Press, 1987), pp. 151-53.

57. John Conway, "An Adapted Organic Tradition," *Daedalus* 117 (Fall 1988), p. 382. For an extended comparison of the impact of religion on politics in the United States and Canada, see Seymour Martin Lipset, *Continental Divide: The Values and Institutions of the United States and Canada* (Routledge, 1990), pp. 74–89.

58. Robert N. Bellah, *Beyond Belief: Essays on Religion in a Post-Traditional World* (University of California Press, 1991), pp. 168–90.

59. Wade Clark Roof and William McKinney, *American Mainline Religion: Its Changing Shape and Future* (Rutgers University Press, 1987), pp. 82–85.

60. William H. Flanigan and Nancy H. Zingale, *Political Behavior of the American Electorate*, 8th ed. (CQ Press, 1994), p. 122.

61. Karl Cordell, "The Role of the Evangelical Church in the GDR," *Government and Opposition* 25 (Winter 1990), pp. 48–59.

62. Taylor Branch, *Parting the Waters: America in the King Years, 1954–63* (Simon & Schuster, 1988), p. 3.

63. Kevin Lange, "An Energized Religious Right? Strategies for the Clinton Era," *Christian Century* 110 (February 17, 1993), pp. 177–79.

64. Center for Political Studies, Inter-University Consortium for Political and Social Research, University of Michigan, *American National Election Study, 1992*.

65. Ibid.

66. Telephone survey of 113,000 households in the 48 contiguous states, April 1989-April 1990, Graduate School of the City University of New York.

67. Raymond E. Wolfinger, Fred I. Greenstein, and Martin Shapiro, *Dynamics of American Politics*, 2d ed. (Prentice Hall, 1980), p. 19.

68. U.S., Bureau of the Census, *Historical Statistics of the United States, Colonial Times to 1970* (Government Printing Office, 1976), p. 297; U.S. Bureau of the Census, *Statistical Abstract of the United States, 1993* (Government Printing Office, 1994), p. 457.

69. Stanley Fischer, "Symposium on the Slowdown in Productivity Growth," *Journal of Economic Perspectives* 2 (Fall 1988), pp. 3–7.

70. Organization for Economic Cooperation and Development (OECD), *National Accounts*, vol. 1, *Main Aggregates, 1960–89* (OECD, 1991), p. 145.

71. U.S. Department of Education, *Digest of Education Statistics, 1991* (Government Printing Office, 1991), p. 294.

72. U.S. Bureau of the Census, U.S. Population Reports P 60, no. 185, *Poverty in the United States: 1992*, p. vii.

73. U.S. Bureau of the Census, U.S. Population Reports P 23, no. 185, *Population Profile of the United States: 1993*, p. 28.

74. U.S. Bureau of the Census, *Report on Income and Poverty, 1992*, pp. v–viii.

75. Many of those classified as poor at the beginning of the 1980s climbed out of poverty over the course of the decade, but others fell into poverty during the same time. Overall, the proportion of the population classified as in

poverty increased during the 1980s. See David Wessel, "Low-Income Mobility Was High in the 1980s," *Wall Street Journal*, June 2, 1992, p. A.2.

76. In 1991, there were 31.7 million Americans over the age of 65 and 35.7 million people who fell below the poverty line. U.S. Bureau of the Census, U.S. Population Reports P 23, no. 178, *Sixty-Five Plus in America* (Government Printing Office, 1992), p.i.

77. Thomas Jefferson, "Autobiography," in *The Life and Selected Writings of Thomas Jefferson*, eds. Adrienne Koch and William Peden (Modern Library, 1944), p. 38.

78. Stanley Lebergott, *The Americans: An Economic Record* (W.W. Norton, 1984), p. 66.

79. U.S. Bureau of the Census, *Historical Statistics of the United States*, p. 224. Data for 1992 were obtained from U.S. Bureau of the Census, *Statistical Abstract of the United States, 1993*, p. 442. "Real" means that inflation has already been taken into account.

80. Daniel Bell, *The Coming of Post-Industrial Society: A Venture in Social Forecasting* (Basic Books, 1973), p. xviii.

81. U.S. Department of Education, *Digest of Education Statistics, 1991* (Government Printing Office, 1991), p. 11.

82. U.S., Bureau of the Census, *Statistical Abstract,1990*, p. 339.

83. *Griggs v Duke Power Company*, 401 US 424 (1971). See also *Wards Cove v Antonio*, 490 US 642 (1989).

84. Joan Biskupic, "Bush Signs Anti-Job Bias Bill amid Furor over Preferences," *Congressional Quarterly Weekly Report* 49 (November 23, 1991), p. 3463.

85. Stephen J. Rose, *American Profile Poster* (Pantheon Books, 1986), p. 9.

86. U.S. Bureau of the Census, Current Population Reports P60, no. 168, *Money, Income and Poverty Status in the United States, 1990* (Government Printing Office, 1991), p. 49.

87. Mattei Dogan and Dominique Pelassy, *How to Compare Nations: Strategies in Comparative Politics*, 2d ed. (Chatham House, 1990), p. 47.

88. Responses for subjective social class vary somewhat with wording of the question. The data on Great Britain are from the *Index to International Public Opinion, 1991-92* (Greenwood Press, 1992), p. 462.

89. Seymour Martin Lipset, *Continental Divide: The Values and Institutions of the United States and Canada* (Routledge, 1990), p. 170.

90. Rose, *American Profile Poster*, p. 24.

91. U.S. Bureau of the Census, Current Population Reports P 20, no. 446, *Voting and Registration in the Election of November 1992* (Government Printing Office, 1993).

92. U.S. Bureau of the Census, U.S. Population Reports P 23, no. 185, *Population Profile of the United States, 1993*, p. 43

93. *The New York Times*, September 23, 1993, pp. A24–25.

94. Seymour Martin Lipset, *Political Man* (Doubleday, 1963), pp. 283–86.

95. Thomas Jefferson to P. S. du Pont de Nemours, April 24, 1816, *The Writings of Thomas Jefferson*, ed. Paul L. Ford (G. P. Putnam's Sons, 1899), 10:25.

96. U.S. Bureau of the Census, U.S. Population Reports P 23, no. 185, *Population Profile of the United States, 1993*, p. 113

97. Ibid., p. 15.

98. World Development Report, *The Challenge of Development* (Oxford University Press, 1991), p. 261.

99. U.S. Bureau of the Census, *Statistical Abstract, 1992*, p. 144.

100. Herbert McClosky and John Zaller, *The American Ethos: Public Attitudes Toward Capitalism and Democracy* (Harvard University Press, 1984), p. 261.

101. John Gunther, *Inside U.S.A.* (Harper and Brothers, 1947), p. 911.

102. Alan Ehrenhalt, *The United States of Ambition: Politicians, Power, and the Pursuit of Office* (Times Books, 1991), p. 275.

103. Carl N. Degler, *Out of Our Past: The Forces That Shaped Modern America*, 3rd ed. (Harper & Row, 1984), p. 322.

CHAPTER 9

1. David S. Cloud. "As NAFTA Countdown Begins, Dealing Intensifies," *Congressional Quarterly Weekly Report* 51 (November 13, 1993), p. 3107.

2. Paul E. Peterson, "The Rise and Fall of Special Interest Politics," *Political Science Quarterly,* 105 (1990–91), p. 540.

3. Eleanor Flexner, *Century of Struggle* (Harvard University Press, 1975), pp. 7–8, 63–65.

4. Abigail Adams to John Adams, March 31, 1776, in *Feminism: The Essential Historical Writings,* Miriam Schneir, ed.(Vintage Books, 1972), p. 3.

5. *Roe v Wade*, 410 US 113 (1973).

6. Chuck Alston, "Lobbyists Storm Capitol Hill, Clash over Banking Bill," *Congressional Quarterly Weekly Report* 49 (August 24, 1991), pp. 2313-18.

7. James Parks, "*COPE* Endorsements, 1968-1992,"AFL-CIO, Department of Information, personal communication, January 6, 1994.

8. U.S. Department of Labor, *Developments in Labor Management Relations and Economic Research Division, AFL-CIO* (Government Printing Office, 1993).

9. James MacGregor Burns and Stewart Burns, *A People's Charter: The Pursuit of Rights in America* (Knopf, 1991).

10. William R. Donohue, *The Politics of the American Civil Liberties Union* (TransAction, 1985).

11. Michael Lienesch, "Right-Wing Religion: Christian Conservatism as a Political Movement," *Political Science Quarterly* 97 (Fall 1982), pp. 403–25.

12. Richard E. Cohen and Carol Matlack, "All-Purpose Loophole," *National Journal* 21 (December 9, 1989), p. 2981. See also Carol Matlack, "Freedom to Buttonhole," *National Journal* 23 (January 26, 1991), pp. 220–22.

13. *Public Policy and Foundations: The Role of Politicians in Public Charities* (Center for Responsive Politics, 1987).

14. Frank Swoboda, "AFL-CIO Membership Is Shifting: Survey Shows Growing Strength Among Government, Service Unions," *The Washington Post*, October 31, 1991, p. A17.

15. There is a debate in the literature about whether group membership has grown. For the view that it has, see Frank R. Baumgartner and Jack L. Walker, "Survey Research and Membership in Voluntary Associations," *American Journal of Political Science* 32 (November 1988), pp. 908–27. For a different perspective, see Tom W. Smith, "Trends in Voluntary Group Membership: Comments on Baumgartner and Walker," *American Journal of Political Science* 34 (August 1990), pp. 646–61, which in turn led to Frank R. Baumgartner and Jack L. Walker, "Measurement Validity and the Continuity of Results in Survey Research," *American Journal of Political Science* 34 (August 1990), pp. 662–70.

16. William P. Browne, "Organized Interests and Their Issue Niches: A Search for Pluralism in a Policy Domain," *Journal of Politics* 52 (May 1990), pp. 477–509.

17. Mancur Olson, *The Logic of Collective Action* (Harvard University Press, 1965), p. 34.

18. Robert Salisbury, "Interest Representation: The Dominance of Institutions," *American Political Science Review* (March 1984), p. 66.

19. Thomas B. Edsall, *The New Politics of Inequality* (Norton, 1984), p. 110.

20. V. O. Key, Jr., *Public Opinion and American Democracy* (Knopf, 1961), pp. 504–7.

21. R. Kenneth Godwin, *One Billion Dollars of Influence: The Direct Marketing of Politics* (Chatham House, 1988).

22. Joan Biskupic, "NRA, Gun-Control Supporters Take Aim at Swing Votes," *Congressional Quarterly Weekly Report* 49 (March 9, 1991), p. 604.

23. Lucius J. Barker, "Third Parties in Litigation: A Systemic View of the Judicial Function," *Journal of Politics* (February 1967), pp. 41–69; Jethro K. Lieberman, *Litigious Society*, rev. ed. (Basic Books, 1983).

24. Gregory A. Calderia and John R. Wright, "Organized Interests and Agenda Setting in the U.S. Supreme Court," *American Political Science Review* 82 (December 1988), pp. 1109–27. See also Gregory A. Calderia and John R. Wright, "Amici Curiae before the Supreme Court: Who Participates, When, and How Much?" *Journal of Politics* 52 (August 1990), pp. 782–806.

25. Karen O'Connor, *Women's Organizations' Use of the Courts* (Lexington Books, 1980).

26. Lee Epstein and C. K. Rowland, "Debunking the Myth of Interest Group Invincibility in the Courts," *American Political Science Review* 85 (March 1991), pp. 205–17.

27. Phil Kuntz, "Cranston Case Ends on Floor with a Murky Plea Bargain," *Congressional Quarterly Weekly Report* 49 (November 23, 1991), pp. 3432–38.

28. Ethan Bronner, *Battle for Justice: How the Bork Nomination Shook America* (Norton, 1989), pp. 50–55.

29. Jeffrey H. Birnbaum and Alan S. Murray, *Showdown at Gucci Gulch: Lawmakers, Lobbyists, and the Unlikely Triumph of Tax Reform* (Random House, 1987).

30. Evan Thomas, "Peddling Influence," *Time*, March 3, 1986, p. 28.

31. David Mayhew, *Congress: The Electoral Connection* (Yale University Press, 1974), p. 45.

32. One indication of the importance of transmitting information may be the frequency of contact by lobbyists. See John R. Wright, "Contributions, Lobbying, and Committee Voting in the U.S. House of Representatives," *American Political Science Review* 84 (June 1990), pp. 418–38.

33. Herbert E. Alexander, *PACs: What They Are, How They Are Changing Political Campaign Financing Patterns* (Grass Roots Guides, 1979), p. 3.

34. For evidence of the impact of PAC expenditures on legislative committee behavior and legislative involvement generally, see Richard L. Hall and Frank W. Wayman, "Buying Time: Moneyed Interests and the Mobilization of Bias in Congressional Committees," *American Political Science Review* 84 (September 1990), pp. 797-820.

35. Factors that predict the formation of PACs include company size and the degree of regulation for corporations. See Craig Humphries, "Corporations, PACs and the Strategic Link between Contributions and Lobbying Activities," *Western Political Quarterly* 44 (June 1991), pp. 353–72.

36. Federal Election Commission, press release, March 4, 1993.

37. Edwin M. Epstein, "Business and Labor under the Federal Election Campaign Act of 1971," in *Parties, Interest Groups, and Campaign Finance Laws*, ed. Michael J. Malbin (American Enterprise Institute for Public Policy Research, 1980), p. 112. See also Gary Jacobson, *Money in Congressional Elections* (Yale University Press, 1980).

38. Charles Keating, quoted in David J. Jefferson, "Keating of American Continental Corporation Comes Out Fighting," *The Wall Street Journal*, April 18, 1989, p. B2.

39. Senator Charles C. Mathias, statement in the *New York Times*, February 27, 1986, p. A31.

40. Gary J. Andres, "Business Involvement in Campaign Finance: Factors Influencing the Decision to Form a Corporate PAC," *PS: Political Science and Politics* (Spring 1985), p. 213.

41. David B. Magleby and Candice J. Nelson, *The Money Chase: Congressional Campaign Finance Reform* (Brookings, 1990), p. 20. See also Brooks Jackson, *Honest Graft: Big Money and the American Political Process* (Knopf, 1988), p. 131.

42. "Foreign Firms' U.S. Units Allowed to Operate PACs," *The Wall Street Journal*, June 18, 1991, p. A20.

43. Amy Dockster, "Nice PAC You've Got Here . . . A Pity If Anything Should Happen to It: How Politicians Shake Down the Special Interests," *Washington Monthly*, January 27, 1987, p. 24, quoted in Margaret Cates Nugent and John R. Johannes, eds., *Money, Elections, and Democracy: Reforming Congressional Campaign Finance* (Westview Press, 1990), p. 1.

44. Bernadette A. Budde, quoted in *National Journal*, November 24, 1979, p. 1983.

45. Hall and Wayman, "Buying Time," pp. 797–820. A different study of the House Ways and Means Committee found campaign contributions to be part of the representatives' policy decisions, but even more important was the number of lobbying contacts. See Wright, "Contributions, Lobbying, and Committee Voting," pp. 417–38.

46. For a study of the differences in individual and PAC contributions to incumbents, challengers, and open seat candidates, see Magleby and Nelson, *Money Chase*, chap. 4. See also John Theilmann and Al Wilhite, "The Determinants of Individuals' Campaign Contributions to Congressional Candidates," *American Politics Quarterly* 17 (July 1989), pp. 312–31.

47. Norman J. Ornstein, Thomas E. Mann, and Michael J. Malbin, *Vital Statistics on Congress, 1991–92* (Congressional Quarterly, 1992), pp. 99–100.

48. Federal Commission Press Release, April 29, 1993, p. 3. See also *Buckley v Valeo*, 424 US 1 (1976).

49. Frank J. Sorauf, *Money in American Elections* (Scott, Foresman/Little, Brown, 1988), pp. 64–65.

50. Ronald Reagan, "Remarks to Administration Officials on Domestic Policy," December 13, 1988, *Weekly Compilation of Presidential Documents* 24 (December 1988), pp. 1615-20.

51. Thomas L. Gais, Mark A. Peterson, and Jack L. Walker, "Interest Groups, Iron Triangles, and Representative Institutions in American National Government," *British Journal of Political Science* 14 (April 1984), pp. 161–85.

52. Sylvia Tesh, "In Support of 'Single-Interest' Politics," *Political Science Quarterly* (Spring 1984), pp. 27–44.

53. Alexander, *PACs*, p. 5.

54. Report and Recommendations of the California Commission on Campaign Financing, *The New Gold Rush: Financing California's Legislative Campaigns* (Center for Responsive Government, 1985), pp. 177–97. For a study of state lobby regulation, see Cynthia Opheim, "Explaining the Differences in State Lobby Regulation," *Western Political Quarterly* 44 (June 1991), pp. 405–21.

55. Magleby and Nelson, *Money Chase*, pp. 72–97.

56. See Jackson, *Honest Graft*; Robert Kuttner, "Protection Racket," review of *Honest Graft*, by Brooks Jackson, *The New Republic*, March 16, 1989, pp. 40–42.

57. David B. Magleby, "More Bang for the Buck: Campaign Spending in Small-State U.S. Senate Elections," paper presented to the Western Political Science Association Annual Meeting, Salt Lake City, Utah, 1989.

58. Michael J. Malbin, "Campaign Financing and the 'Special Interest,'" *Public Interest* (Summer 1979), pp. 21–42. But for a somewhat different view, see David Cohen and Wendy Wolff, "Freeing Congress from the Special Interest State: A Public Interest Agenda for the 1980s," *Harvard Journal of Legislation* 17, no. 2 (1980), pp. 253–93.

CHAPTER 10

1. John E. Mueller, "Choosing among 133 Candidates," *Public Opinion Quarterly* 34 (Fall 1970), pp. 395–402.

2. E. E. Schattschneider, *Party Government* (Holt, Rinehart and Winston, 1942), p. 1.

3. See, for example, David W. Brady and Charles S. Bullock IV, "Party and Faction Within Legislatures," in *Handbook of Legislative Research*, eds. Gerhard Loewenberg, Samuel C. Patterson, and Malcolm E. Jewell (Harvard University Press, 1985), chap. 4.

4. Charles O. Jones, *The Trusteeship Presidency: Jimmy Carter and the United States Congress* (Louisiana University Press, 1988). See also Charles O. Jones, "Ronald Reagan and the U.S. Congress: Visible Hand Politics," and Paul E. Peterson and Mark Rom, "Lower Taxes, More Spending and Budget Deficits," in *The Reagan Legacy*, ed. Charles O. Jones (Chatham House, 1988), pp. 30–59, 213–40, for discussions of the role of party in Congress during the last two administrations.

5. L. Sandy Maisel, *Parties and Elections in America: The Electoral Process* (Random House, 1987), chap. 5.

6. Peverill Squire, ed., *The Iowa Caucuses and the Presidential Nominating Process* (Westview Press, 1989).

7. *The Book of the States, 1990–1991* (Council of State Governments, 1990), p. 234.

8. Byron E. Shafer, *Bifurcated Politics* (Harvard University Press, 1988).

9. William H. Riker, "The Two-Party System and Duverger's Law: An Essay on the History of Political Science," *American Political Science Review* (December 1982), pp. 753–66. For a classic analysis, see Schattschneider, *Party Government*.

10. Steven J. Rosenstone, Roy L. Behr, and Edward H. Lazarus, *Third Parties in America: Citizen Response to Major Party Failure* (Princeton University Press, 1984). See also Xandra Kayden and Eddie Mahe, Jr., *The Party Goes On: The Persistence of the Two Party System in the United States* (Basic Books, 1985), pp. 143–44.

11. V. O. Key, "A Theory of Critical Elections," *Journal of Politics* 17 (February 1955), pp. 3–18.

12. Walter Dean Burnham, *Critical Elections and the Mainsprings of American Politics* (Norton, 1970), pp. 1–10.

13. E. E. Schattschneider, *The Semisovereign People: A Realist's View of Democracy in America* (Holt, Rinehart and Winston, 1975), pp. 78–80.

14. Benjamin Franklin, George Washington, and Thomas Jefferson, quoted in Richard Hofstadter, *The Idea of a Party System* (University of California Press, 1969), pp. 2, 123.

15. William E. Gienapp, *The Origins of the Republican Party, 1852–1856* (Oxford University Press, 1987).

16. David W. Brady, "Elections, Congress and Public Policy Changes: 1886–1960," in *Realignment in American Politics: Toward a Theory*, eds. Bruce A. Campbell and Richard J. Trilling (Texas University Press, 1980), p. 188.

17. Gerald Pomper, "Classification of Presidential Elections," *Journal of Politics* 29 (1967), p. 538.

18. For an examination of American attitudes toward parties over the breadth of American history, see Austin Ranney, *Curing the Mischiefs of Faction: Party Reform in America* (University of California Press, 1975).

19. Federal Election Commission, "Summary of 1989–90 Political Party Finances," March 15, 1991, August 6, 1991, and October 31, 1991.

20. See John E. Chubb and Paul E. Peterson, eds., *The New Direction in American Politics* (Brookings Institution, 1985).

21. Edmund Burke, "Thoughts on the Cause of the Present Discontents," in *Burke: Select Works*, ed. E. J. Payne (Clarendon Press, 1878), 1:86.

22. Joseph A. Schumpeter, *Capitalism, Socialism and Democracy* (Harper and Row, 1975), p. 283.

23. The early Republican efforts and advantages over the Democrats are well documented in Thomas B. Edsall, *The New Politics of Inequality* (Norton, 1984); Gary C. Jacobson, "The Republican Advantage in Campaign Finances," in *New Direction in American Politics*, eds. Chubb and Peterson, p. 6.

24. See L. Sandy Maisel, *From Obscurity to Oblivion: Running in the Congressional Primary*, rev. ed. (University of Tennessee Press, 1986).

25. John F. Bibby, *Politics, Parties, and Elections in America* (Nelson-Hall, 1992). For further data on these roles, see Cornelius P. Cotter, James L. Gibson, John F. Bibby, and Robert J. Huckshorn, *Party Organizations in American Politics* (Praeger, 1984).

26. See James L. Gibson, Cornelius P. Cotter, John F. Bibby, and Robert J. Huckshorn, "Assessing Party Organizational Strength," *American Journal of Political Science* 27 (May 1983), pp. 193–222; Cotter et al., *Party Organi-*

zations in American Politics.

27. Paul S. Herrnson, *Party Campaigning in the 1980s: Have the National Parties Made a Comeback as Key Players in Congressional Elections?* (Harvard University Press, 1988), p. 122.

28. On the influence of local parties, see Xandra Kayden and Eddie Mahe, Jr., *The Party Goes On* (Basic Books, 1985).

29. Michael J. Malbin, "The Conventions, Platforms, and Issue Activists," in *The American Elections of 1980*, ed. Austin Ranney (American Enterprise Institute, 1982), pp. 116-41.

30. See Bruce E. Keith, David B. Magleby, Candice J. Nelson, Elizabeth Orr, Mark C. Westlye, and Raymond E. Wolfinger, *The Myth of the Independent Voter* (University of California Press, 1992), p. 148.

31. See David E. Rosenbaum, "Parties' Core Differences in Platforms," *The New York Times*, August 16, 1992, p. 19.

32. Katja Bullock, director of information, White House Office of Personnel, interview with David Magleby, April 9, 1992. A listing of many of these positions is presented in a book published by the U.S. Government, *Policy and Supporting Positions* (Government Printing Office, November 9, 1988).

33. Angus Campbell, Philip E. Converse, Warren E. Miller, and Donald E. Stokes, *The American Voter* (Wiley, 1960), pp. 121–28.

34. Keith et al., *Myth of the Independent Voter*.

35. See Byron E. Shafer, *The End of Realignment: Interpreting American Electoral Eras* (University of Wisconsin Press, 1991).

36. Independent-leaning Democrats and Independent-leaning Republicans are classified with the parties toward which they lean. Data reported here are from the 1992 American National Election Study.

37. Hedrick Smith, *The Power Game: How Washington Works* (Random House, 1988), p. 671.

38. See David B. Hill and Norman R. Luttbeg, *Trends in American Electoral Behavior*, 2d ed. (Peacock, 1983), p. 2; Nie et al., *Changing American Voter*, p. 47.

39. Nine percent of all voters were Pure Independents in 1956 and 1960. Keith et al., *Myth of the Independent Voter*, p. 51. In 1992 the same percent were pure Independents. 1992 American National Election Study.

40. For the "pessimistic view" of the party condition, see Martin P. Wattenberg, *The Decline of American Political Parties, 1952–1988* (Harvard University Press, 1990). See also Alan Ware, *The Breakdown of Democratic Party Organization, 1940–1980* (Clarendon Press, 1985).

41. For the "optimistic view," see Ralph M. Goldman, *Search for Consensus: The Story of the Democratic Party* (Temple University Press, 1979), pp. 366–73; Kayden and Mahe, *Party Goes On*; Larry Sabato, *The Party's Just Begun: Shaping Political Parties in America's Future* (Scott, Foresman, 1988); Joseph A. Schlesinger, "The New American Political Party," *American Political Science Review* (December 1985), pp. 1152–69; David E. Price, *Bringing Back the Parties* (Congressional Quarterly Press, 1984).

42. "With Democrats in the White House, Partisanship Hits New High," *Congressional Quarterly Weekly Report* 51 (December 18, 1993), pp. 3432–34.

43. Herrnson, *Party Campaigning in the 1980s*, pp. 80–81.

44. Ibid., p. 14.

CHAPTER 11

1. Vanderbilt Television News Archives videotape, Vanderbilt University Library, Nashville, Tenn.

2. "It's Reagan 2 to 1 in Poll by ABC After the Debate," *Chicago Tribune*, October 29, 1980, sec. 1, p. 10.

3. Robert Coles, *The Moral Life of Children* (Atlantic Monthly Press, 1986); Robert Coles, *The Political Life of Children* (Atlantic Monthly Press, 1986).

4. Coles, *Political Life of Children*, pp. 59–60

5. Pamela Johnston Conover, "The Influence of Group Identifications on Political Perception and Evaluation," *Journal of Politics* (August 1984), pp. 760–85; Henry E. Brady and Paul M. Sniderman, "Attitude Attribution: A

Group Basis for Political Reasoning," *American Political Science Review* (December 1985), pp. 1061–78.

6. Shawn W. Rosenberg, "Sociology, Psychology, and the Study of Political Behavior: The Case of the Research on Political Socialization," *Journal of Politics* (May 1985), pp. 715–31.

7. Russell J. Dalton, "Reassessing Parental Socialization: Indicator Unreliability versus Generational Transfer," *American Political Science Review* (June 1980), pp. 421–31.

8. Edgar Litt, "Civic Education Norms and Political Indoctrination," *American Sociological Review* 28 (February 1963), pp. 69–75. See also: Elizabeth

Leonie Simpson, *Democracy's Stepchildren* (Jossey-Bass, 1971); M. Kent Jennings and Richard G. Niemi, *The Political Character of Adolescence* (Princeton University Press, 1974); Stanley Allen Renshon, "Personality and Family Dynamics in the Political Socialization Process," *American Journal of Political Science* (February 1975), pp. 63–80; Frances Fitzgerald, *America Revised* (Atlantic-Little, Brown, 1979).

9. Kenneth Feldman and Theodore M. Newcomb, *The Impact of College on Students*, vol. 2 (Jossey-Bass, 1969), pp. 16–24, 49–56.

10. Alexander N. Astin et al., *The American Freshmen: National Norms for 1990* (UCLA Graduate School of Education, 1991).

11. See Randall Herbert Balmer, *Mine Eyes Have Seen the Glory: A Journey into the Evangelical Subculture in America* (Oxford University Press, 1993).

12. Suzanne Koprince Sebert, M. Kent Jennings, and Richard G. Niemi, "The Political Texture of Peer Groups," in Jennings and Niemi, *Political Character of Adolescence*, p. 246.

13. Benjamin Page and Robert Shapiro, *The Rational Public* (University of Chicago Press, 1992) p. 237.

14. George J. Church, "What in the World Are We Doing?" *Time*, October 18, 1993, p. 42.

15. Walter Lippmann, *Public Opinion* (Harcourt Brace, 1922; Macmillan, 1961).

16. David Mayhew, *Congress: The Electoral Connection* (Yale University Press, 1974); Richard F. Fenno, Jr., *Home Style: House Members in Their Districts* (Little, Brown,1978).

17. Warren E. Miller and Donald E. Stokes, "Constituency Influence in Congress," *American Political Science Review* 57 (March 1963), pp. 45–46; Robert S. Erikson, Norman R. Luttbeg, and Kent L. Tedin, *American Public Opinion*, 4th ed. (Macmillian, 1991), p. 282.

18. Everett C. Ladd and John Benson, "The Growth of News Polls in American Politics," in *Media Polls in American Politics*, eds. Thomas Mann and Gary Orren (Washington, D.C.: Brookings Institution, 1992), pp. 19–31.

19. Scott L. Althaus, "The Conservative Nature of Public Opinion," paper presented to the American Political Science Association Annual Meeting, Washington, D.C., 1993, pp. 2–3.

20. Harold Mendelsohn and Irving Crespi, *Polls, Television, and the New Politics* (Chandler, 1970), chap. 2.

21. Thomas E. Mann and Raymond E. Wolfinger, "Candidates and Parties in Congressional Elections," *American Political Science Review* 74, no. 3 (September 1980), pp. 617–40.

22. Erikson, Luttbeg, Tedin, *American Public Opinion*, p. 295.

23. Neil S. Newhouse and Christine L. Matthews, "NAFTA Revisited: Most Americans Just Weren't Deeply Engaged," *Public Perspective* 5 (January/February 1994), pp. 31–32.

24. 1960–90 American National Election Studies, Center for Political Studies, University of Michigan, Ann Arbor.

25. Harold Stanley, *Voter Mobilization and the Politics of Race: The South and Universal Suffrage, 1952–1984* (Praeger, 1987), p. 61.

26. Frank R. Parker, *Black Votes Count: Political Empowerment in Mississippi After 1965* (University of North Carolina Press, 1990), p. 3.

27. Bernard Grofman and Lisa Handley, "The Impact of the Voting Rights Act on Black Representation in Southern State Legislatures," *Legislative Studies Quarterly* 16 (February 1991), pp. 111–28.

28. For a discussion of the differences in the turnout between presidential and midterm elections, see James E. Campbell, "The Presidential Surge and Its Midterm Decline in Congressional Elections, 1868–1988," *Journal of Politics* 53 (May 1991), pp. 477–87.

29. Raymond E. Wolfinger and Steven J. Rosenstone, "The Effect of Registration Laws on Voter Turnout," *American Political Science Review* (March 1978), p. 24.

30. Raymond E. Wolfinger and Steven J. Rosenstone, *Who Votes?* (Yale University Press, 1980), p. 78.

31. Ibid., p. 88.

32. David E. Rosenbaum, "Democrats Keep Solid Hold on Congress," *The New York Times*, November 9, 1988, p. A24.

33. Paula Ries and Anne J. Stone, eds., *The American Women 1992–93: A Status Report* (Women's Research and Education Institute, 1992), p. 415.

34. Congressional Research Service, "Voter Turnout in the Presidential Election of 1992: The States," January 26, 1993, pp. 4–5. See also G. Bingham Powell Jr., "American Voter Turnout in Comparative Perspective," *American Political Science Review* 80 (March 1986), pp. 17–43.

35. Grofman and Handley, "Impact of the Voting Rights Act," pp. 118–22.

36. Ruy A. Teixeira, "Will the Real Nonvoter Please Stand Up?" *Public Opinion* (July/August 1988), pp. 41–59.

37. Raymond E. Wolfinger, David P. Glass, and Peverill Squire, "Predictors of Electoral Turnout: An International Comparison," *Policy Studies Review* 9 (Spring 1990), pp. 567–68. The impact of registration requirements is not greater for poorly educated persons as was once thought. See Jonathan Nogler, "The Effect of Registration Laws on U.S. Voter Turnout," *American Political Science Review* 85 (December 1991), p. 1402.

38. Rosenbaum, "Democrats Keep Solid Hold in Congress," p. A24.

39. Wolfinger and Rosenstone, *Who Votes?* pp. 90–91.

40. Ibid., p. 102. See also Sandra Baxter and Marjorie Lansing, *Women and Politics: The Invisible Majority* (University of Michigan Press, 1980), pp. 106–7.

41. Baxter and Lansing, *Women and Politics*. See also Claire Knoche Fulenwider, *Feminism in American Politics: A Study of Ideological Influence* (Praeger, 1980). On age as a key correlation with high turnout, see Lee Sigelman, Philip W. Roeder, Malcolm E. Jewell, and Michael A. Baer, "Voting and Nonvoting: A Multi-Election Perspective," *American Journal of Political Science* (November 1985), pp. 749–65.

42. Austin Ranney, "Nonvoting Is Not a Social Disease," *Public Opinion* (October/November 1983), pp. 16–19.

43. Thomas Byrne Edsall, *The New Politics of Inequality* (W. W. Norton, 1984), p. 181.

44. Wolfinger and Rosenstone, *Who Votes?* p. 109.

45. 1992 American National Election Study, Center for Political Studies, University of Michigan, Ann Arbor.

46. Frances Fox Piven and Richard A. Cloward, "Prospects for Voter Registration Reform: A Report on the Experiences of the Human SERVE Campaign," *PS: Political Science and Politics* (Summer 1985), pp. 582–92.

47. E. E. Schattschneider, *The Semisovereign People* (Dryden Press, 1975), p. 96.

48. Stephen Earl Bennett and David Resnick, "The Implications of Nonvoting for Democracy in the United States," *American Journal of Political Science* 84 (August 1990), pp. 771–802.

49. The classic work on party identification remains Angus Campbell, Philip E. Converse, Warren E. Miller, and Donald E. Stokes, *The American Voter* (Wiley, 1960). For a more recent defense of this theory of partisanship, see Warren E. Miller, "Party Identification Realignment, and Party Voting: Back to Basics," *American Political Science Review* 85 (June 1991): 557–680.

50. Bruce E. Keith, David B. Magleby, Candice J. Nelson, Elizabeth Orr, Mark C. Westlye, and Raymond E. Wolfinger, *The Myth of the Independent Voter* (University of California Press, 1992), pp. 60–75; 1992 American National Election Study, Center for Political Studies, University of Michigan, Ann Arbor.

51. Michael B. MacKuen, Robert S. Erikson, and James A. Stimson, "Macropartisanship," *American Political Science Review* 83 (December 1989), pp. 1125–42.

52. Martin P. Wattenberg, *The Rise of Candidate-Centered Politics: Presidential Elections of the 1980s* (Harvard University Press, 1991), p. 1.

53. Barry Goldwater, quoted in Theodore H. White, *The Making of the President, 1964* (Athenaeum Publishers, 1965), p. 217.

54. Ibid., pp. 200–201.

55. William H. Flanigan and Nancy H. Zingale, *Political Behavior of the American Electorate*, 8th ed. (Congressional Quarterly Press, 1994), p. 173.

56. J. Merril Shanks and Warren E. Miller, "Policy Direction and Performance Evaluation: Complementary Explanations of the Reagan Elections," paper presented to the American Political Science Association Annual Meeting, New Orleans, 1985; Warren E. Miller and J. Merril Shanks, "Alternative Interpretations of the 1988 Election: Policy Direction, Current Conditions, Presidential Performance, and Candidate Traits," paper presented to the American Political Science Association Annual Meeting, Atlanta, 1989.

57. Amihai Glazer, "The Strategy of Candidate Ambiguity," *American Political Science Review* 84 (March 1990), pp. 237–41.

58. Robert S. Erikson and David W. Romero, "Candidate Equilibrium and the Behavioral Model of the Vote," *American Political Science Review* 84 (December 1990), p. 1122.

59. Morris P. Fiorina, *Retrospective Voting in American National Elections* (Yale University Press, 1981).

60. Miller and Shanks, "Alternative Interpretations of the 1988 Election."

61. Voter Research and Survey, Exit Poll of Voters, November 3, 1992.

63. John R. Hibbing and John R. Alford, "The Educational Impact of Economic Conditions: Who Is Held Responsible?" *American Journal of Political Science* (August 1981), pp. 423–39; Morris P. Fiorina, "Who is Held Responsible? Further Evidence on the Hibbing-Alford Thesis," *American Journal of Political Science* (February 1983), pp. 158–64.

64. Robert M. Stein, "Economic Voting for Governor and U.S. Senator: The Electoral Consequences of Federalism," *Journal of Politics* 52 (February 1990), pp. 29–53.

65. M. Stephen Weatherford, "Economic Voting and the 'Symbolic Politics' Argument: A Reinterpretation and Synthesis," *American Political Science Review* (March 1983), pp. 158–74.

CHAPTER 12

1. Marjorie Margolies-Mezvinsky and Barbara Feinman, *A Woman's Place: Freshmen Women Who Changed the Face of Congress* (Crown, 1994), pp. 194, 198.

2. Elaine S. Povich, "Budget Vote Gets Her National Spotlight, Local Glares," *The Chicago Tribune*, September 9, 1993, p. 1.

3. Ibid.

4. Thomas L. Friedman, "Clinton Wary of Cutting Entitlements," *The New York Times*, December 14, 1993, p. A12.

5. *1987 Census of Governments*, vol. 1, no. 2 (Government Printing Office, 1988), p. 1.

6. For an insightful examination of electoral rules, see Bernard Grofman and Arend Lijphart, eds., *Electoral Laws and Their Political Consequences* (Agathon Press, 1986).

7. Arend Lijphart, "The Political Consequences of Electoral Laws, 1945–85," *American Political Science Review* 84 (June 1990), pp. 481–95.

8. George Rabinowitz and Stuart Elaine MacDonald, "The Power of the States in U.S. Presidential Elections," *American Political Science Review* (March 1986), pp. 65–87.

9. See, as examples, David Mayhew, *Congress: The Electoral Connection* (Yale University Press, 1974); Richard F. Fenno Jr., *Home Style: House Members in Their Districts* (Little, Brown, 1978); James E. Campbell, "The Return of Incumbents: The Nature of Incumbency Advantage," *Western Political Science Quarterly* (September 1983), pp. 434–44.

10. Gary King and Andrew Gelman, "Systemic Consequences of Incumbency Advantage in U.S. House Elections," *American Journal of Political Science* 35 (February 1991), pp. 110–37.

11. See Gary C. Jacobson, *The Politics of Congressional Elections*, 3d ed. (Harper-Collins, 1992), chap. 6; Alan I. Abramowitz, "Economic Conditions, Presidential Popularity, and Voting Behavior in Midterm Congressional Elections," *Journal of Politics* (February 1985), pp. 31–43.

12. Alan Ehrenhalt, *The United States of Ambition: Politicians, Power, and the Pursuit of Office* (Times Books, 1991).

13. Mayhew, *Congress*, p. 46.

14. Linda L. Fowler and Robert C. McClure, *Political Ambition: Who Decides To Run for Congress* (Yale University Press, 1989); David T. Canon, "Political Conditions and Experienced Challengers in Congressional Elections, 1972–1984," paper presented to the American Political Science Association Annual Meeting, New Orleans, August 29–September 1, 1985.

15. Keith Drehbiel and John R. Wright, "The Incumbency Effect in Congressional Elections: A Test of Two Explanations," *American Journal of Political Science* (February 1983), p. 140.

16. See, for example, Alan I. Abramowitz, "Party and Individual Accountability in the 1978 Congressional Election," in *Congressional Elections*, ed. L. Sandy Maisel and Joseph Cooper (Russell Sage Foundation, 1981); Thomas E. Mann and Raymond E. Wolfinger, "Candidates and Parties in Congressional Elections," *American Political Science Review* (September 1980), pp. 617–32.

17. Gary C. Jacobson and Samuel Kernell, *Strategy and Choice in Congressional Elections* (Yale University Press, 1981).

18. David B. Magleby and Candice J. Nelson, *The Money Chase: Congressional Campaign Finance Reform* (Brookings Institution, 1990), p. 37.

19. Albert D. Cover, "One Good Term Deserves Another: The Advantages of Incumbency in Congressional Elections," *American Journal of Political Science* 21 (August 1977), pp. 523–42; Morris P. Fiorina, *Congress: Keystone of the Washington Establishment* (Yale University Press, 1978); Mayhew, *Congress*, pp. 52–53.

20. Mayhew, *Congress*, p. 61 Richard F. Fenno Jr., *Congressmen in Committees* (Little, Brown, 1973); Steven S. Smith and Christopher J. Deering, *Committees in Congress* (Congressional Quarterly Press, 1984).

21. See Fenno, *Home Style*.

22. Glenn R. Parker, "The Role of Constituent Trust in Congressional Elections," *Public Opinion Quarterly* 53 (Summer 1989), pp. 175–96.

23. *Thursted* v *Gregoire* 841 F. Supp. 1068.

24. Candice J. Nelson, "Campaign Finance in Presidential and Congressional Elections," *The Political Science Teacher* (Summer 1988), p. 6.

25. Alan I. Abramowitz, "Explaining Senate Election Outcomes," *American Political Science Review* (June 1988), pp. 385–403.

26. David B. Magleby, "More Bang for the Buck: Campaign Spending in Small–State U.S. Senate Elections," paper presented to the Western Political Science Association Annual Meeting , Salt Lake City, March 30–April 1, 1989.

27. Thomas E. Patterson, *The Mass Media Election: How Americans Choose Their President* (Praeger, 1980).

28. Robert D. Loevy, *The Flawed Path to the Presidency, 1992: Unfairness and Inequality in the Presidential Selection Process* (State University of New York Press, 1994).

29. Paul T. David and James W. Caesar, *Proportional Representation in Presidential Nominating Politics* (University Press of Virginia, 1980).

30. The descriptions of these types of primaries are drawn from James W. Davis, *Presidential Primaries*, rev. ed. (Greenwood Press, 1984), chap. 3. See pp. 56–63 for specifics on each state (and Puerto Rico). This material is used with the permission of the publisher.

31. *The Book of the States, 1992–1993* (Council of State Governments, 1992), pp. 273–74.

32. Stephen J. Wayne, *The Road to the White House 1992: The Politics of Presidential Elections*, 4th ed. (St. Martin's Press, 1992).

33. Jeff Fishel, *Presidents and Promises* (Congressional Quarterly Press, 1984).

34. William Safire, "Gore Flattens Perot," *The New York Times*, November 11, 1993, p. A27.

35. Jules Witcover uses the image of a marathon to describe the 1976 presidential campaign in *Marathon: The Pursuit of the Presidency, 1972–1976* (Viking, 1977).

36. Robert S. Erikson, "Economic Conditions and the Presidential Vote," *American Political Science Review* 83 (June 1989), pp. 567–75. Class-based voting has also become more important. See Robert S. Erikson, Thomas O. Lancaster, and David W. Romers, "Group Components of the Presidential Vote, 1952–1984," *Journal of Politics* 51 (May 1989), pp. 337–46.

37. On the key factor of personal attributes in presidential campaigning, see David P. Glass, "Evaluating Presidential Candidates: Who Focuses on Their Personal Attributes?" *Public Opinion Quarterly* (Winter 1985), pp. 517–34. See also Herbert B. Asher, *Presidential Elections and American Politics*, 4th ed. (Dorsey Press, 1988).

38. Sidney Kraus, *The Great Debates: Kennedy vs Nixon, 1960* (Indiana University Press, 1962). See also Myles Martel, *Political Campaign Debates* (Longman, 1983).

39. See Robert Hunter, ed., *Electing the President: A Program for Reform, Final Report of the Commission on National Election* (Center for Strategic and International Studies, 1986); James L. Sundquist, *Constitutional Reform* (Brookings Institution, 1986); Edward N. Kearny, "Presidential Nominations and Representative Democracy: Proposals for Change," *Presidential Studies Quarterly* (Summer 1984), pp. 348–56.

40. Barbara Norrander and Greg W. Smith, "Type of Contest, Candidate Strategy, and Turnout in Presidential Primaries," *American Politics Quarterly* (January 1985), p. 28.

41. Walter Shapiro, "The Primary Lessons of 1988," *Time*, June 20, 1988, p. 19.

42. John G. Geer, "Voting in Presidential Primaries," paper presented to the American Political Science Association Annual Meeting, Washington, D.C., September 1984. See also Albert R. Hunt, "The Media and Presidential Campaigns," in *Elections American Style*, ed. A. James Reichley (Brookings Institution, 1987), pp. 52–74.

43. Gwen Ifill, "Clinton Turning His Effort to the Battle for New York," *The New York Times*, March 26, 1992, p. A18.

44. Steven J. Brams and Peter Fishburn, *Approval Voting* (Birkhauser, 1983).

45. George S. McGovern, "Considerations on Our Political Processes," *Presidential Studies Quarterly* (Summer 1984), pp. 341–47.

46. Gary R. Orren and Nelson W. Polsby, eds., *Media and Momentum: The New Hampshire Primary and Nomination Politics* (Chatham House, 1987).

47. American Enterprise Institute memorandum, spring 1986, p. 10.

48. "A National Agenda for the Eighties," *Report of the President's Commission for a National Agenda for the Eighties* (Government Printing Office, 1980), p. 97, proposes holding only four presidential primaries, scheduled about one month apart.

49. Nelson Polsby, *Consequences of Party Reform* (Oxford University Press, 1983), p. 118.

50. Thomas E. Cronin and Robert Loevy, "The Case for a National Primary Convention Plan," *Public Opinion* (December/January 1983), pp. 50–53.

51. Malcolm S. Forbes, Jr., "Helpful, Useful Antique," *Forbes*, February 6, 1989, p. 27.

52. Neal R. Peirce and Lawrence Longley, *The People's President: The Electoral College in American History and the Direct-Vote Alternative*, 2d ed. (Yale University Press, 1981), describes and advocates the direct-vote alternative. Nelson W. Polsby and Aaron B. Wildavsky, *Presidential Elections*, 7th ed. (Free Press, 1988), favors the present system.

53. For a broader discussion of the plan and the problem, see Thomas E. Cronin, "Choosing a President," *The Center Magazine* (September/October 1978), pp. 5–15; William R. Keech, *Winner Take All: Report of the Twentieth Century Fund Task Force on Reform of the Presidential Election Process* (Holmes & Meier, 1978).

54. Magleby and Nelson, *Money Chase*, pp. 13–14.

55. Neil O. Staebler, quoted in Herbert E. Alexander and Brian A. Haggerty, *The Federal Election Campaign Act: After a Decade of Political Reform* (Citizen's Research Foundation, 1981), p. 13.

56. *Buckley v Valeo*, 424 US 1 (1976).

57. For a discussion of recent legislation, see Herbert E. Alexander and Monica Bauer, *Financing the 1988 Election* (Westview, 1991); Frank J. Sorauf, *Money in American Elections* (Scott, Foresman, 1988).

58. David Ignatius, "Return of the Fat Cats," *Washington Post*, November 20, 1988, p. D5; Charles R. Babcock, "$100,000 Donations Plentiful Despite Post-Watergate Restrictions," *The Washington Post*, September 22, 1988, p. A27.

59. Beth Donovan, "Parties Turned Soft Money Law into Hard and Fast Spending," *Congressional Quarterly Weekly Report* 51 (May 15, 1993); pp. 1196–97.

60. Magleby and Nelson, *Money Chase*, p. 30.

61. Herbert Alexander, interview with author, April 5, 1994; Federal Election Commission, press release, March 4, 1993, p. 1.

62. Robert Biersack, Federal Election Commission, interview with author, November 17, 1993.

63. See Alan I. Abramowitz, "Incumbency Campaign Spending, and the Decline of Competition in U.S. House Elections," *Journal of Politics* 53 (February 1991), p. 34.

64. Magleby and Nelson, *Money Chase*, p. 196.

65. Ibid., p. 53; Federal Election Commission, press release, March 4, 1993, pp. 22–40.

66. Sorauf, *Money in American Elections*, pp. 64–65.

67. H. Ross Perot, quoted in *Wit and Wisdom of Ross Perot*, ed. Sarah Dana-Hall (Wit and Wisdom Books, 1992), pp. 22–23.

68. Jeffrey Schmalz, "Clinton Carves a Wide Path into Reagan Country," *The New York Times*, November 4, 1992, p. B1.

CHAPTER 13

1. William Rivers, *The Other Government* (Universe Books, 1982); Douglas Cater, *The Fourth Branch of Government* (Houghton Mifflin, 1959); Dom Bonafede, "The Washington Press: An Interpreter or a Participant in Policy Making?" *National Journal*, April 24, 1982, pp. 716–21; Michael Ledeen, "Learning to Say 'No' to the Press," *Public Interest* (Fall 1983), p. 113.

2. Leslie G. Moeller, "The Big Four: Mass Media Actualities and Expectations," in *Beyond Media: New Approaches to Mass Communication*, eds. Richard W. Budd and Brent D. Ruben (Transaction Books, 1988), p. 15.

3. Times Mirror Center for the People and the Press, "Campaign '92: The Politics of the Economy," press release, January 16, 1992.

4. Ibid.

5. See Ray Hiebert, Donald Ungarait, and Thomas Bohn, *Mass Media VI* (Longman, 1991), chap. 11.

6. See Robert A. Rutland, *Newsmongers: Journalism in the Life of the Nation, 1690–1972* (Dial Press, 1973).

7. Frank Luther Mott, *American Journalism*, 3d ed. (Macmillan, 1962), p. 123.

8. See Culver Smith, *The Press, Politics, and Patronage* (University of Georgia Press, 1977).

9. James Pollard, *Presidents and the Press* (Macmillan, 1947), pp. 351–59.

10. Thomas C. Leonard, *The Power of the Press* (Oxford University Press, 1986), p. 93.

11. Whitelaw Reid, quoted in Mott, *American Journalism*, p. 412.

12. Frances Perkins, quoted in James MacGregor Burns, *Roosevelt: The Lion and the Fox* (Harcourt Brace, 1956), p. 205.

13. Edward W. Chester, *Radio, Television and American Politics* (Sheed and Ward, 1969), p. 62.

14. Ben H. Bagdikian, *The Media Monopoly* (Beacon Press, 1983).

15. See Doris A. Graber, *Mass Media and American Politics* (Congressional Quarterly Press, 1989); Gina M. Garramone and Charles K. Atkin, "Mass Communication and Political Socialization: Specifying the Effects," *Public Opinion Quarterly* 50 (Spring 1986), pp. 76–86.

16. Shanto Iyengar and Donald R. Kinder, *News That Matters* (University of Chicago Press, 1987).

17. Richard Davis, *The Press and American Politics: The New Mediator* (Longman, 1992), p. 100.

18. For a discussion of advocacy journalism, see Morris Janowitz, "Professional Models in Journalism: The Gatekeeper and the Advocate," *Journalism Quarterly* (Winter 1975), pp. 618–25.

19. Peter Stoler, *The War Against the Press: Politics, Pressure, and Intimidation in the 80s* (Dodd, Mead, 1986).

20. Harvey G. Zeidenstein, "News Media Perceptions of White House News Management," *Presidential Studies Quarterly* 24 (Summer 1984), pp. 391–98.

21. See, for example, Jack Dennis, "Preadult Learning of Political Independence: Media and Family Communications Effects," *Communication Research* 13 (July 1986), pp. 401–33; Olive Stevens, *Children Talking Politics* (Martin Robertson, 1982).

22. Elihu Katz and Paul Lazarsfeld, *Personal Influence: The Part Played by People in the Flow of Mass Communications* (Free Press, 1955).

23. See another classic, Angus Campbell, Philip E. Converse, Warren E. Miller, and Donald E. Stokes, *The American Voter* (Wiley, 1960).

24. See the classic works, Paul Lazarsfeld, Bernard Berelson, and Hazel Gaudet, *The People's Choice: How the Voter Makes Up His Mind in a Presidential Campaign*, 3d ed. (Columbia University Press, 1968); Bernard Berelson, Paul Lazarsfeld, and William McPhee, *Voting: A Study of Opinion Formation in a Presidential Campaign* (University of Chicago Press, 1954).

25. Stuart Oskamp, ed., *Television as a Social Issue* (Sage Publications, 1988); James W. Carey, ed., *Media, Myths, and Narratives: Television and the Press* (Sage Publications, 1988).

26. Doris A. Graber, *Processing the News: How People Tame the Information Tide*, 2d ed. (Longman, 1988), pp. 107–13.

27. Times Mirror Center for the People and the Press, "Times Mirror News Interest Index," press releases, January 16, 1992, and February 28, 1992.

28. John K. Robinson and Mark R. Levy, eds., *The Main Source: Learning from Television News* (Sage Publications, 1986).

29. Graber, *Processing the News,* p. 115.

30. Times Mirror Center for the People and the Press, "Times Mirror News Interest Index," press release, January 16, 1992.

31. Fred Smoller, "The Six O'Clock Presidency: Patterns of Network News Coverage of the President," *Presidential Studies Quarterly* 26 (Winter 1986), p. 34.

32. See Nelson Polsby, *Consequences of Party Reform* (Oxford University Press, 1983), pp. 142–46. See also Stanley Rothman and S. Robert Lichter, "Media and Business Elites: Two Classes in Conflict!" *The Public Interest* (Fall 1982), pp. 119–25.

33. David Broder, "Beware of the 'Insider' Syndrome: Why Newmakers and News Reporters Shouldn't Get Too Cozy," *Washington Post*, December 4, 1988, Outlook Section; see also Broder, "Thin-Skinned Journalists," *Washington Post*, January 11, 1989, p. A21.

34. See, for example, William A. Rusher, *The Coming Battle for the Media* (William Morrow, 1988).

35. *Public Opinion* (August/September 1985), p. 7.

36. See, for example, Michael Parenti, *Inventing Reality* (St. Martin's Press, 1986); Todd Gitlin, *The Whole World Is Watching: Mass Media in the Making and Unmaking of the New Left* (University of California Press, 1980).

37. Daniel P. Moynihan, "The Presidency and the Press," *Commentary* (March 1971), p. 43.

38. S. Robert Lichter, Stanley Rothman, and Linda S. Lichter, *The Media Elite* (Adler and Adler, 1986).

39. See, for example, Michael J. Robinson and Margaret A. Sheehan, *Over the Wire and on TV: CBS and UPI in Campaign '80* (Russell Sage Foundation, 1983); Lichter, Rothman, and Lichter, *Media Elite.*

40. Among others researching this topic, see Doris A. Graber, "Say It with Pictures: The Impact of Audio-Visual News on Public Opinion Formation," paper presented to the Midwest Political Science Association Annual Meeting, Chicago, April 1987; Benjamin I. Page, Robert Y. Shapiro, and Glenn R. Dempsey, "What Moves Public Opinion?" *American Political Science Review* 76 (March 1987), pp. 23–43.

41. Shanto Iyengar, Mark D. Peters, and Donald R. Kinder, "Experimental Demonstrations of the 'Not-So-Minimal' Consequences of Television News Programs," *American Political Science Review* (December 1982), pp. 848–58.

42. Maxwell E. McCombs and Donald L. Shaw, "The Agenda-Setting Function of the Mass Media," *Public Opinion Quarterly* 36 (1972), pp. 176–87; Iyengar, Peters, and Kinder, "Experimental Demonstrations," pp. 848–58; Maxwell E. McCombs and Sheldon Gilbert, "News Influence on Our Pictures of the World," in *Perspectives on Media Effects*, eds. Jennings Bryant and Dolf Gillman (Lawrence Erlbaum, 1986); Iyengar and Kinder, *News That Matters.*

43. Walter Mondale, quoted in Robinson and Sheehan, *Over the Wire and on TV*, p. xiii.

44. Iyengar and Kinder, *News That Matters.*

45. Robert M. Entman, "How the Media Affect What People Think: An Information Processing Approach," *Journal of Politics* 51 (May 1989), pp. 346–70.

46. Shanto Iyengar, "Television News and Citizens Explanations of National Affairs," *American Political Science Review* 81 (September 1987), pp. 815–32; Iyengar and Kinder, *News That Matters*, pp. 82–89.

47. David B. Magleby, *Direct Legislation: Voting on Ballot Propositions in the United States* (Johns Hopkins University Press, 1984).

48. Steven J. Simmons, *The Fairness Doctrine and the Media* (University of California Press, 1978).

49. Norman E. Isaacs, *Untended Gates: The Mismanaged Press* (Columbia University Press, 1985), p. 143.

50. Ibid.

51. S. Robert Lichter and Linda S. Lichter, "Covering the Convention Coverage," *Public Opinion* (September/October 1988), p. 41.

52. Davis, *Press and American Politics*, p. 279.

53. Frank I. Luntz, *Candidates, Consultants, and Campaigns* (Basil Blackwell, 1988), chap. 7.

54. Michael J. Robinson, "Where's the Beef? Media and Media Elites in 1984," in *The American Elections of 1984*, ed. Austin Ranney (Duke University Press, for the American Enterprise Institute, 1985), pp. 172–77.

55. Richard Armstrong, *The Next Hurrah: The Changing Face of the American Political Process* (Beech Tree Books, 1988), pp. 19–21.

56. See, for example, Kathleen Hall Jamieson, *Packaging the Presidency*, 2d ed. (Oxford University Press, 1992).

57. Larry J. Sabato, *The Rise of Political Consultants* (Basic Books, 1981).

58. Mimi Hall and Judy Keen, "Hillary Clinton's Image Undergoes a Change," *USA Today*, July 16, 1992, p. A4.

59. See in general, Sabato, *Rise of Political Consultants;* James David Barber, *The Pulse of Politics: Electing Presidents in the Media Age* (Norton, 1980). See also Fred Barnes, "The Myth of Political Consultants," *The New Republic*, June 16, 1986, p. 16.

60. Quoted in Sabato, *Rise of Political Consultants*, p. 144.

61. Thomas E. Patterson, *The Mass Media Election: How Americans Choose Their President* (Praeger, 1980), chap. 12.

62. See John H. Aldrich, *Before the Convention* (University of Chicago Press, 1980), p. 65, a study of candidates' choices and strategies. See also Patterson, *Mass Media Election.*

63. John Foley et al., *Nominating a President: The Process and the Press* (Praeger, 1980), p. 39. For the press's treatment of incumbents, see James Glen Stovall, "Incumbency and News Coverage of the 1980 Presidential Election Campaign," *Western Political Quarterly* (December 1984), p. 621.

64. Thomas E. Patterson and Robert McClure, *The Unseeing Eye: The Myth of Television Power in National Elections* (Putnam, 1976); Patterson, *Mass Media Election*, chap. 13.

65. Edwin Diamond and Stephen Bates, *The Spot: The Rise of Political Advertising on TV* (MIT Press, 1984). For a historical look at political advertising, see Jamieson, *Packaging the Presidency.*

66. Priscilla Southwell, "Voter Turnout in the 1986 Congressional Elections: The Media as Demobilizer?" *American Politics Quarterly* 19 (January 1991), pp. 96–108.

67. David B. Magleby, "Direct Legislation in the American States," in *Referendums Around the World: The Growing Use of Direct Democracy*, eds. David Butler and Austin Ranney (AEI Press, 1994), pp. 218–257.

68. Patterson, *Mass Media Election*, pp. 115–17.

69. Raymond Wolfinger and Peter Linguiti, "Tuning In and Tuning Out," *Public Opinion* 4 (February/March 1981), pp. 56–60.

70. Walter Lippmann, *Public Opinion* (Macmillan, 1938), p. 364.

71. Davis, *Press and American Politics*, p. 205.

72. Bernard Cohen, *The Press and Foreign Policy* (Princeton University Press, 1963); Gary Orren, "Thinking About the Press and Government," in *Impact: How the Press Affects Federal Policymaking*, ed. Martin Linsky (Norton, 1986), pp. 1–20.

73. Lewis Wolfson, *The Untapped Power of the Press* (Praeger, 1985), p. 79.

74. Stephen Hess, *The Government/Press Connection* (Brookings Institution, 1984), p. 106.

75. Lloyd Cutler, "Foreign Policy on Deadline," *Foreign Policy* (Fall 1984), p. 114.

76. Michael B. Grossman and Martha Joynt Kumar, *Portraying the President* (Johns Hopkins University Press, 1981), pp. 255–63; Smoller, "Six O'Clock Presidency," pp. 31–49.

77. Michael J. Robinson and Kevin R. Appel, "Network News Coverage of Congress," *Political Science Quarterly* (Fall 1979), pp. 407–18; Charles Tidmarch and John C. Pitney, Jr., "Covering Congress," *Polity* (Spring 1985), pp. 463–83.

78. Susan Heilmann Miller, "News Coverage of Congress: The Search for the Ultimate Spokesperson," *Journalism Quarterly* (Autumn 1977), pp. 459–65.

79. See Stephen Hess, *Live from Capitol Hill: Studies of Congress and the Media* (Brookings Institution, 1991), pp. 102–10.

80. Richard Davis, "Whither the Congress and the Supreme Court? The Television News Portrayal of American National Government," *Television Quarterly* (1987), pp. 55–63.

81. For a discussion of the Supreme Court and public opinion, see Thomas R. Marshall, *Public Opinion and the Supreme Court* (Unwin Hyman, 1989); Gregory Caldiera, "Neither the Purse nor the Sword: Dynamics of Public Confidence in the Supreme Court," *American Political Science Review* (December 1986), pp. 1209–28.

82. For a discussion of the relationship between the Supreme Court and the press, see Richard Davis, "Lifting the Shroud: News Media Portrayal of the U.S. Supreme Court," *Communications and the Law* (October 1987), pp. 43–58; Elliot E. Slotnick, "Media Coverage of Supreme Court Decision Making: Problems and Prospects," *Judicature* (October/November 1991), pp. 128–42.

83. Thomas E. Patterson, "The Press and Its Missed Assignment," in *The Elections of 1988*, ed. Michael Nelson (Congressional Quarterly Press, 1989), pp. 107–8.

84. Times Mirror Center for the People and the Press, "Campaign '92: The Politics of the Economy," press release, January 16, 1992.

85. Theodore White, quoted in Herbert Schmertz, "The Making of the Presidency," *Presidential Studies Quarterly* (Winter 1986), p. 25.

CHAPTER 14

1. Cited in Janet Hook and staff, "Democrats Hail 'Productivity,' But Image Problems Remain," *Congressional Quarterly Weekly Report*, December 11, 1993, p. 3355.

2. *The Gallup Poll Monthly* (April, 1993), pp. 22–23.

3. See *Wesberry v Sanders,* 376 US 1 (1964).

4. *Davis v Bandemer,* 478 US 109 (1986).

5. *Shaw v Reno,* 125 LEd 2d 511 (1993).

6. Norman I. Ornstein, Thomas E. Mann, and Michael J. Malbin, eds., *Vital Statistics on Congress, 1993–1994* (Congressional Quarterly Press, 1994), pp. 35–37.

7. For a brief discussion of the speakership in the 1990s, see Barbara Sinclair, "House Majority Party Leadership in an Era of Legislative Constraint," in *The Postreform Congress,* ed. Roger H. Davidson (St. Martin's Press, 1992), pp. 91–111.

8. Thomas P. O'Neill, with William Novak, *Man of the House: The Life and Political Memoirs of Speaker Tip O'Neill* (Random House, 1987), p. 273.

9. Steven S. Smith, "The Senate in the Postreform Era," in *Postreform Congress,* ed. Roger H. Davidson (St. Martin's Press, 1992), pp. 169–92.

10. For an insightful set of essays on Senate leadership, see Richard A. Baker and Roger H. Davidson, eds., *First Among Equals: Outstanding Senate Leaders of the Twentieth Century* (Congressional Quarterly Press, 1991).

11. Stephen Hess, *The Ultimate Insiders: U.S. Senators and the Media* (Brookings Institution, 1986).

12. Robert Dole, quoted in Steven V. Roberts, "Wheels Are Spinning over the Senate Rules," *The New York Times,* February 26, 1986, p. 8.

13. David Boren, quoted in John Dillon, "Shrinking Feeling Sweeps Down Crowded Congressional Halls," *Christian Science Monitor,* February 16, 1993, p. 3.

14. David L. Boren, "Why I am Leaving the Senate," *The New York Times* (May 13, 1994, p. A15)

15. Robert C. Byrd, quoted in David J. Vogler, *The Politics of Congress* (Allyn and Bacon, 1983), p. 77.

16. Ornstein, Mann, and Malbin, *Vital Statistics on Congress, 1993–1994*, p. 157.

17. David C. Kozak, *Contexts of Congressional Decision Behavior* (University Press of America, 1984).

18. Robert A. Bernstein, *Elections, Representation, and Congressional Voting Behavior* (Prentice Hall, 1989).

19. Harold W. Stanley and Richard G. Niemi, *Vital Statistics on American Politics,* 4th ed. (Congressional Quarterly Press, 1994), p. 216.

20. R. Douglas Arnold, *The Logic of Congressional Action* (Yale University Press, 1990).

21. Ornstein, Mann, and Malbin, *Vital Statistics on Congress, 1993–1994,* pp. 126–27.

22. Christine DeGregorio, "Professionals in the U.S. Congress: An Analysis of Working Styles," *Legislative Studies Quarterly* (November 1988), pp. 459–76. For a more critical view, see, as his title suggests, Michael J. Malbin, *Unelected Representatives* (Basic Books, 1980).

23. David W. Rhode, "Electoral Forces, Political Agendas, and Partisanship in the House and Senate," in *Postreform Congress,* ed. Roger H. Davidson, pp. 27–47.

24. Mark A. Peterson, *Legislating Together: The White House and Capitol Hill from Eisenhower to Reagan* (Harvard University Press, 1990).

25. Woodrow Wilson, *Congressional Government* (Houghton, Mifflin & Co., 1885; reprint Johns Hopkins University Press, 1981), p. 69.

26. Steven S. Smith and Christopher J. Deering, *Committees in Congress* (Congressional Quarterly Press, 1984). Two recent journal articles reflect a broad view of the subject: James M. Snyder, "Committee Power, Structure-Induced Equilibria, and Roll Call Votes," *American Journal of Political Science* 36 (February 1992), pp. 31–39; Melissa P. Collie and Brian E. Roberts, "Trading Places: Choice and Committee Chairs in the U.S. Senate, 1950–1986," *The Journal of Politics* 54 (February 1992), pp. 231–45.

27. Richard F. Fenno, Jr., *Congressmen in Committees* (Little, Brown, 1972). See also Glen R. Parker and Suzanne L. Parker, *Factions in House Committees* (University of Tennessee Press, 1985).

28. Thomas S. Foley, quoted in Janet Hook, "A Jolt for the Seniority System," *Congressional Quarterly Weekly Report*, March 26, 1994, p. 715.

29. Joel D. Aberbach, *Keeping a Watchful Eye: The Politics of Congressional Oversight* (Brookings Institution, 1990).

30. For studies of the role of congressional investigations, see James Hamilton, *The Power To Probe: A Study of Congressional Investigations* (Vintage, 1976);

Morris S. Ogul, *Congress Oversees the Bureaucracy* (University of Pittsburgh Press, 1976); Loch Johnson, *A Season of Inquiry: The Senate Intelligence Investigation* (University of Kentucky Press, 1985).

31. David J. Vogler, *The Politics of Congress,* 5th ed. (Allyn and Bacon, 1988), p. 213.

32. Burdett Loomis, *New American Politician: Elected Entrepreneurs and the Changing Style of Political Life* (Basic Books, 1988).

33. John Rhodes, *The Futile System* (EPM Publications, 1976), p. 15. See also Gregg Easterbrook, "What's Wrong with Congress?" *The Atlantic Monthly,* December 1984, pp. 57–84.

34. See, for example, Philip M. Stern, *The Best Congress Money Can Buy* (Pantheon, 1988).

35. James L. Sundquist, *Constitutional Reform and Effective Government,* rev. ed. (Brookings Institution, 1992); James MacGregor Burns, *The Power To Lead* (Simon & Schuster, 1984).

36. S. I. Hayakawa, quoted in *U.S. News and World Report,* December 20, 1982, p. 24. See also the Twentieth Century Fund Task Force on Political Action Committees, *What Price PACs?* (Twentieth Century Fund, 1984).

37. Richard S. Schweiker, quoted in David S. Broder, "Who Took the Fun out of Congress?" *The Washington Post National Weekly Edition,* February 17, 1986, p. 10. See also Stern, *Best Congress Money Can Buy.*

38. James Madison, *The Federalist,* No. 57. in Jacob E. Cooke, ed., *The Federalist* (Meridian Books, 1961), p. 385.

CHAPTER 15

1. Glenn A. Phelps, *George Washington and American Constitutionalism* (University Press of Kansas, 1993).

2. John Steinbeck, *America and Americans* (Bonanza Books, 1966), p. 46.

3. Louis Fisher, *Constitutional Conflicts Between Congress and the President,* 3d ed. (University Press of Kansas, 1991), p. 285.

4. Gerald Ford, informal talk at the Hinckley Institute of Politics, University of Utah, Salt Lake City, Utah, February 1982.

5. Our analysis here borrows and benefits from ideas in James A. Thurber, "The Roots of Divided Democracy," in *Divided Democracy,* ed. James A. Thurber (Congressional Quarterly Press, 1991).

6. Roger H. Davidson and Walter J. Oleszek, *Congress and Its Members,* 4th ed. (Congressional Quarterly Press, 1994), p. 239. See also Mark A. Peterson, *Legislating Together* (Harvard University Press, 1990); David R. Mayhew, *Divided We Govern: Party Control, Lawmaking, and Investigations, 1946–1990* (Yale University Press, 1991).

7. For a different point of view, see Benjamin I. Page and Mark P. Petracca, *The American Presidency* (McGraw-Hill, 1983), chap. 1.

8. Theodore J. Lowi, *The Personal President* (Cornell University Press, 1985).

9. G. Calvin Mackenzie, *The Politics of Presidential Appointments* (Free Press, 1981).

10. "Leadership in Jeopardy: The Fraying of the Presidential Appointments System," *National Academy of Public Administration Report* (November 1985), p. 3.

11. *United States v Curtiss-Wright Export Corp.,* 299 US 304 (1936).

12. For provocative debate on presidential war powers and "prerogative power," see David Gray Adler, "The President's War-Making Power," and Robert Scigliano, "The President's Prerogative Power," both in *Inventing the American Presidency,* ed. Thomas E. Cronin (University Press of Kansas, 1989), pp. 119–53, 236–56, respectively.

13. See, in general, Bob Woodward, *The Agenda: Inside the Clinton White House* (Simon & Shuster, 1994).

14. See Robert J. Spitzer, *The President and Congress: Executive Hegemony at the Crossroads of American Government* (McGraw-Hill, 1993); Lester G. Seligman and Cary R. Covington, *The Coalitional Presidency* (Dorsey Press, 1989).

15. William J. Keefe, *Congress and the American People,* 3d ed. (Prentice Hall, 1988), p. 151.

16. Robert J. Spitzer, "Regular Veto" in *Encyclopedia of the American Presidency,* eds. Leonard W. Levy and Louis Fisher (Simon & Schuster, 1994), p. 1555. See also Spitzer, *President and Congress.*

17. See Paul Brace and Barbara Hinckley, *Follow the Leader* (Basic Books, 1992).

18. See Sidney M. Milkis, *The President and the Parties: The Transformation of the American Party System Since the New Deal* (Oxford University Press, 1993).

19. See Woodward, *The Agenda.*

20. Ibid.; Howard E. Shuman, *Politics and the Budget,* 2d ed. (Prentice Hall, 1988).

21. For an analysis of the role of the vice-president as a potential adviser to the president, see Thomas E. Cronin, "Rethinking the Vice Presidency," in *Rethinking the Presidency,* ed. Thomas E. Cronin (Little, Brown, and Co., 1982), pp. 324–48; Report of the Twentieth Century Fund Task Force on the Vice-Presidency, *A Heartbeat Away* (Priority Press, 1988).

22. See, for example, Ann Devoy and Daniel Williams, "Vice-President in Charge of the World," *The Washington Post National Weekly Edition,* December 13–19, 1993, pp. 11–12.

23. Useful books on the vice-presidency are Jules Witcover, *Crapshoot: Rolling the Dice on the Vice Presidency* (Crown, 1992); Paul Light, *Vice Presidential Power* (Johns Hopkins University Press, 1984); Joel Goldstein, *The Modern Vice Presidency* (Princeton University Press, 1982).

24. See, for example, Donnie Radcliffe, *Hillary Rodham Clinton: A First Lady for Our Time* (Warner Books, 1993); also Connie Burck, "Hillary the Pol," *The New Yorker,* May 30, 1994, pp. 58–96.

25. A. M. Rosenthal, "The First Ladyship," *The New York Times,* March 11, 1994, p. A19.

26. See Stephen Skowronek, *The Politics Presidents Make: Leadership from John Adams to George Bush* (Harvard University Press, 1993), chaps. 1–3.

27. Mark Hertsgaard, *On Bended Knee: The Press and the Reagan Presidency* (Farrar, Straus and Giroux, 1988). See also John A. Maltese, *Spin Control* (University of North Carolina Press, 1992).

28. Thomas Griffith, "Goodbye to All That," *Time,* April 18, 1988, p. 47.

29. Richard Ellis and Aaron Wildavsky, "'Greatness' Revisited: Evaluating the Performance of Early American Presidents in Terms of Cultural Dilemmas," *Presidential Studies Quarterly* (Winter 1991), p. 17. See also the book by the same authors, *Dilemmas of Presidential Leadership from Washington through Lincoln* (Transaction Press, 1990).

30. Ellis and Wildavsky, "'Greatness' Revisited," p. 17.

31. Ibid., p. 18.

32. Ibid., p. 28.

33. Paul Kennedy, *The Rise and Fall of the Great Powers* (Random House, 1987), p. 534.

34. Richard Rose, *The Postmodern President: George Bush Meets the World,* 2d ed. (Chatham House, 1991); Barbara Kellerman and Ryan J. Barilleaux, *The President as World Leader* (St. Martin's Press, 1991); Richard Rose and Robert Thompson, "The President in a Changing International System," *Presidential Studies Quarterly* (Fall 1991), pp. 751–70.

CHAPTER 16

1. Henry J. Abraham, *The Judicial Process,* 5th ed. (Oxford University Press, 1986), p. 197.

2. Alexis de Tocqueville, *Democracy in America,* ed. Phillips Bradley (Knopf, 1944), 1:278–80.

3. Harold J. Laski, *The American Democracy* (Viking, 1948), p. 110.

4. Joseph F. DiMento and Dean W. Hestermann, "Ordering the Elephants To Dance: Consent Degrees and Organizational Behavior," *Journal of Urban and Contemporary Law* 43 (1993), p. 303.

5. *Luther v Borden,* 7 Howard 1 (1849).

6. *Chicago Grand Trunk Railway Co. v Wellman,* 143 US 339 (1892).

7. Karen Orren, "Standing to Sue, Interest Group Conflict in the Federal Courts," *The American Political Science Review* (September 1976), pp. 723–41.

8. Phillip J. Cooper, *Hard Judicial Choices: Federal District Court Judges and State and Local Officials* (Oxford University Press, 1988), p. 15.

9. Jeremiah Smith, quoted in Paul E. Freund, *On Understanding the Supreme Court* (Little, Brown, 1949), p. 3.

10. This discussion is based on H. L. A. Hart, *The Concept of Law* (Oxford University Press, 1961), chap. 7.

11. For one of the great classics, see Benjamin N. Cardozo, *The Nature of the Judicial Process* (Yale University Press, 1921).

12. This discussion is based on Hart, *Concept of Law,* Chap. 7.

13. John Marshall Harlan, quoted in Hart, *Concept of Law,* pp. 121–22.

14. C. K. Rowland, "The Federal District Courts," in *The American Courts: A Critical Assessment,* eds. John B. Gates and Charles A. Johnson (Congressional Quarterly Press, 1991), pp. 61–80.

15. Christopher E. Smith, *United States Magistrates in the Federal Courts: Subordinate Judges* (Praeger, 1990); Christopher E. Smith, "From U.S. Magistrates to U.S. Magistrate Judges: Developments Affecting the Federal District Courts' Lower Tier of Judicial Officers," *Judicature* 75 (December/January 1992), pp. 210–15.

16. Dissenting views of Representatives Robert F. Drinan and Thomas N. Kindness, quoted in Smith, *United States Magistrates in the Federal Courts,* p. 183.

17. Steven Puro and Roger Goldman, "U.S. Magistrates: Changing Dimensions of First-Echelon Federal Judicial Officers," in *The Politics of Judicial Reform,* ed. Philip L. Dubois (Heath, 1982). See also Caroll Seron, "Magistrates and the Work of Federal Courts: A New Division of Labor," *Judicature* (April/May 1986), pp. 353–59; Christopher E. Smith, "Who Are the U.S. Magistrates?" *Judicature* (October/November 1987), pp. 143–50.

18. *Peretz v United States,* 115 L Ed 2d 808 (1991).

19. Donald R. Songer, "The Circuit Courts of Appeals," in *American Courts,* eds. Gates and Johnson, pp. 35–57.

20. Deborah J. Barrow and Thomas G. Walker, *A Court Divided: The Fifth Circuit Court of Appeals and the Politics of Judicial Reform* (Yale University Press, 1988); Arthur D. Hellman, ed., *Reconstructing Justice: The Innovations of the Ninth Circuit and the Future of the Federal Courts* (Cornell University Press, 1991).

21. *Bordenkircher v Hayes,* 434 US 357 (1978). See also James Eisenstein, *Counsel for the United States: U.S. Attorneys in the Political and Legal Systems* (Johns Hopkins Press, 1978); *Wayte v United States,* 470 US 598 (1985).

22. Joan Biskupic, "For Court Advocate, a Nominee Who Seeks 'Different Solutions,'" *The Washington Post,* April 19, 1993, p. A21; John G. Roberts, Jr., "The New Solicitor General and the Power of the Amicus," *The Wall Street Journal,* May 5, 1993, p. A21.

23. Karen O'Connor, "The Amicus Curiae Role of the U.S. Solicitor General in Supreme Court Litigation," *Judicature* (December/January 1983), pp. 256–64; Jeffrey A. Segal, "Amicus Curiae Briefs by the Solicitor General During the Warren and Burger Courts," *Western Political Quarterly* 41 (March 1988), pp. 134–44.

24. For a critical analysis, see Lincoln Caplan, *The Tenth Justice: The Solicitor General and the Rule of Law* (Knopf, 1987). For a defense, see former Solicitor General Charles Fried, *Order and Law: Arguing the Reagan Revolution—*

A Firsthand Account (Simon & Schuster, 1991). For a more neutral and scholarly account, see Rebecca Mae Salokar, *The Solicitor General: The Politics of Law* (Temple University Press, 1992).

25. Joan Biskupic, "Politics Still Plays a Role in Solicitor General's Office," *The Washington Post,* February 22, 1994, pp. A1, A7.

26. David Leitch, "The Deal for Walter Dellinger," *The Recorder,* June, 1993, p. 6.

27. Charley Roberts, "Federal Defender Program To Be Studied," *Los Angeles Daily Journal,* August 19, 1991, p. 7; 61 U.S.L.W. 2627 (April 20, 1993).

28. Naftali Bendavid, "D-Day for Advocates of the Poor," *The Recorder,* February 22, 1994, p. 10.

29. Neil D. McFeeley, *Appointment of Judges: The Johnson Presidency* (University of Texas Press, 1987), p. 1.

30. Stephen LaBaton, "Shifting List of Prospects To Be Justice," *The New York Times,* May 9, 1993, p. A12; Paul M. Barrett, "More Minorities, Women Named to U.S. Courts," *The Wall Street Journal,* December 23, 1993, p. B 1.

31. Harold W. Chase, *Federal Judges: The Appointing Process* (University of Minnesota Press, 1972), pp. 3–47; Paul Simon, "The Senate's Role in Judicial Appointments," *Judicature* (June/July 1986), pp. 55–58; Elliot E. Slotnick, "Federal Judicial Recruitment and Selection Research: A Review Essay," *Judicature* (April/May 1988), pp. 317–24.

32. Naftali Bendavid, "Diversity Marks Clinton Judiciary," *The Recorder,* December 30, 1993, p. 11

33. Lettie McSpadden Wenner and Lee F. Dutter, "Contextual Influences on Court Outcomes," *Western Political Quarterly* 41 (March 1988), pp. 115–34; Ronald Stidham and Robert A. Carp, "Exploring Regionalism in the Federal District Courts," *Publius* 18 (Fall 1988), pp. 113–25.

34. "More Doubts About the ABA" [editorial], *The Wall Street Journal,* April 11, 1989; see also Gordon J. Humphrey, "End ABA Role as Hanging Judge," *The Wall Street Journal,* March 22, 1989, p. A14; *Public Citizen v Department of Justice,* 491 US 440 (1989).

35. Daniel Klaidman, "Liberals Hit Clinton on Judge Picks," *The Recorder,* October 27, 1993, pp. 1–14; Neil A. Lewis, "New York City Bar Told To Stop Rating Judges," *The New York Times,* June 4, 1991, p. A14.

36. Charles M. Cameron, Albert D. Cover, and Jeffrey A. Segal, "Senate Voting on Supreme Court Nominees: A Neo-Institutional Model," *American Political Science Review* 84, no. 2 (June 1990), p. 532.

37. George Watson and John Stookey, "Supreme Court Confirmation Hearings: A View from from the Senate," *Judicature* (December/January 1988), p. 193; see also John Massaro, *Supremely Political: The Role of Ideology and Presidential Management in Unsuccessful Supreme Court Nominations* (State University of New York Press, 1990).

38. Sheldon Goldman, "Bush's Judicial Legacy: The Final Imprint," *Judicature* 76 (April/May 1993), p. 291.

39. Quoted in Stephen Labaton, "Clinton Expected To Change Makeup of Federal Courts," *The New York Times,* March 8, 1993, p. A1.

40. Bendavid, "Diversity Marks Clinton Judiciary," p. 11; David G. Savage and Ronald J. Ostrow, "Women, Minorities, Outpace White Men for Jobs on Bench," *Los Angeles Times,* January 11, 1994, p. A 11.

41. Robert A. Carp and C. K. Rowland, *Policymaking and Politics in the Federal District Courts* (University of Tennessee Press, 1983), p. 82.

42. Abraham Lincoln, quoted in J. W. Peltason, *Federal Courts in the Political Process* (Doubleday, 1955), p. 41. See also Laurence H. Tribe, *God Save This Honorable Court: How How the Choice of Supreme Court Justices Shapes Our History* (Random House, 1985); Henry J. Abraham, *Justices and Presidents: A Political History of Appointments to the Supreme Court,* 3d ed. (Oxford University Press, 1992).

43. Theodore Roosevelt to Henry Cabot Lodge, *Selections from the Correspondence of Theodore Roosevelt and Henry Cabot Lodge* (Scribner's, 1925), 1:518–19.

44. Sheldon Goldman, "Reagan's Judicial Legacy: Completing the Puzzle and Summing Up," *Judicature* 72, no. 6 (April/May 1989), pp. 318–30.

45. Leo V. Hennessy, "Redrawing the Political Map? An Impact Analysis of the Reagan Appointments on the U.S. Courts of Appeals," paper presented to the Southern Political Science Association, November 7–9, 1991.

46. Jill Abramson, "Conservative Legal Groups Plan Efforts To Keep Bush Administration on Reagan's Judicial Path," *The Wall Street Journal*, November 21, 1988, p. A16.

47. Robert A. Carp, Donald Songer, C. K. Rowland, Ronald Stidham, and Lisa Richey-Tracey, "The Voting Behavior of Judges Appointed by President Bush," *Judicature* (April/May 1993), pp. 298–302.

48. David G. Savage, *Turning Right: The Makings of the Rehnquist Supreme Court* (John Wiley & Sons, 1992), pp. 451–58.

49. William Howard Taft to Horace Taft, November 14, 1929, quoted in Henry Pringle, *The Life and Times of William Howard Taft* (Farrar, 1939), 2:967.

50. Sue Davis, "Federalism and Property Rights: An Examination of Justice Rehnquist's Legal Positivism," *The Western Political Quarterly* (June 1986), pp. 250–64.

51. Albert P. Melone, "The Senate's Confirmation Role in Supreme Court Nominations and the Politics of Ideology versus Impartiality," *Judicature* 75 (August/September 1991), pp. 68–79, argues that the Senate should ask nominees pertinent ideological questions and nominees have an obligation to be forthcoming. For the contrary view, see William Bradford Reynolds, "The Confirmation Process: Too Much Advice and Too Little Consent," *Judicature* 75 (August/September 1991), pp. 80–82.

52. David M. O'Brien, *Judicial Roulette: Report of the Twentieth Century Fund Task Force on Judicial Selection* (Priority Press Publications, 1988), pp. 10–11.

53. Mark Silverstein, "The People, the Senate and the Court: The Democratization of the Judicial Confirmation System," *Constitutional Commentary* 9 (Winter 1992), p. 58.

54. Donald Santarelli, quoted in Jerry Landauer, "Shaping the Bench," *The Wall Street Journal*, December 10, 1970, p. 1. See also Peltason, *Federal Courts in the Political Process*, p. 32.

55. *Ex parte McCardle*, Wallace 506 (1869).

56. Richard Johnson, *The Dynamics of Compliance* (Wiley, 1967), pp. 33–41, as summarized in David Adamany, "Legitimacy, Realigning Elections, and the Supreme Court," *Wisconsin Law Review* (1973), p. 792.

57. Tony Mauro, "Jumping into the Pool," *The Recorder*, September 14, 1993, p. 6.

58. Sidney Ulmer, "The Supreme Court's Certiorari Decisions: Conflict as a Predictive Variable," *American Political Science Review* (December 1984), pp. 901–11.

59. Elder Witt, "Reagan Crusade Before Court Unprecedented in Intensity," *Congressional Quarterly,* March 15, 1986, p. 616.

60. Gregory A. Caldeira and John R. Wright, "Organized Interest and Agenda Setting in the U.S. Supreme Court." *American Political Science Review* 82 (December 1988), p. 1110.

61. Donald R. Songer and Reginald S. Sheehan, "Interest Groups' Success in the Courts: Amicus Participation in the Supreme Court," *Political Research Quarterly* 46 (June 1993), pp. 339–54.

62. *University of California Regents v Bakke,* 438 US 265 (1978); *Webster v Reproductive Health Services,* 492 US 490 (1989); *Roe v Wade,* 410 US 113 (1973). See also Susan Behuniak-Long, "Friendly Fire: Amici Curiae and *Webster v Reproductive Health Services,*" *Judicature* 74 (February/March 1991), pp. 261–70.

63. Tony Mauro, "The Supreme Court as Quiz Show," *The Recorder*, December 8, 1993, p. 10

64. Ibid.

65. Joyce O'Connor, "Selections from Notes Kept on an Internship at the U.S. Supreme Court, Fall 1988," *Law, Courts, and Judicial Process*, newsletter published by Department of Political Science, Purdue University, 6 (Spring 1989), p. 44.

66. Sandra Day O'Connor, quoted in Mauro, "Jumping into the Pool," p. 7.

67. O'Connor, "Selections from Notes Kept on an Internship," p. 46.

68. Justice Anthony M. Kennedy, Jr., address to Pasadena Bar Association, June 1991, quoted in Richard C. Reuben, "Kennedy Remembers William Brennan," *The Los Angeles Daily Journal*, July 2, 1991, p. 7.

69. William H. Rehnquist, *The Supreme Court: How It Was, How It Is* (William Morrow, 1987), pp. 289–90.

70. *National League of Cities v Usery,* 426 US 833 (1976).

71. *Garcia v San Antonio Metropolitan Transit Authority,* 469 US 528 (1985). The description following is taken from Bob Woodward and Scott Armstrong, *The Brethren* (Simon & Schuster, 1979), pp. 406–10.

72. *Maryland v Wirtz,* 392 US 183 (1968).

73. Daniel M. Berman, *It Is So Ordered: The Supreme Court Rules on School Segregation* (Norton, 1986), p. 114; Walter F. Murphy, *Elements of Judicial Strategy* (University of Chicago Press, 1964), p. 66; David M. O'Brien, *Storm Center: The Supreme Court in American Politics,* 2d ed. (W. W. Norton, 1990), pp. 262–72.

74. Clarks Evans Hughes, quoted in Donald E. Lively, *Foreshadows of the Law: Supreme Court Dissents and Constitutional Development* (Praeger, 1992), p. xx.

75. Oliver Wendell Holmes to Harold J. Laski, *Holmes-Laski Letters,* ed. Mark De Wolfe Howe (Atheneum, 1963), 2:124, 125.

76. Again the following description is from Woodward and Armstrong, *The Brethren*, pp. 409–10.

77. Robert J. Steamer, *Chief Justice: Leadership and the Supreme Court* (University of South Carolina Press, 1986). See also White Burkett Miller Center of Public Affairs, *The Office of Chief Justice* (University of Virginia, 1984).

78. Sue Davis, "The Supreme Court: Rehnquist's or Reagan's," *The Western Political Quarterly* 44 (March 1991), p. 98.

79. David G. Savage, "The Rehnquist Court," *Los Angeles Times Magazine,* September 29, 1991, p. 13; David W. Rohde and Harold J. Spaeth, "Ideology, Strategy and Supreme Court Decisions: William Rehnquist as Chief Justice," *Judicature* 72 (December/January 1989), pp. 247–50. See also Joseph F. Kobylka, "Leadership on the Supreme Court of the United States: Chief Justice Burger and the Establishment Clause," *The Western Political Quarterly* 42 (December 1989), pp. 545–68.

80. David Danelski, "The Influence of the Chief Justice in the Decisional Process of the Supreme Court," in *The Federal Judicial System: Readings in Process and Behavior,* eds. Thomas P. Jahnige and Sheldon Goldman (Holt, Rinehart and Winston, 1968), p. 148.

81. Stephen L. Wasby, *The Impact of the United States Supreme Court* (Dorsey Press, 1970).

82. J. W. Peltason, *Fifty-Eight Lonely Men: Southern Federal Judges and School Desegregation* (University of Illinois Press, 1971), p. 19.

83. *Immigration and Naturalization Service v Chadha,* 468 US 919 (1983).

84. Cooper, *Hard Judicial Choices,* pp. 347–50.

85. Peter W. Huber, *Liability: The Legal Revolution and Its Consequences* (Basic Books, 1988).

86. Arthur S. Miller, "In Defense of Judicial Activism," in *Supreme Court Activism and Restraint,* eds. Stephen C. Halpern and Charles M. Lamb (Heath, 1982), p. 177. See also, by the chief justice of the West Virginia Supreme Court, Richard Neely, *How Courts Govern America* (Yale University Press, 1981).

87. *United States v Carolene Products,* 304 US 144 (1938). Variations on this basic position have been restated in dozens of recent books. Halpern and Lamb, eds., *Supreme Court Activism and Restraint,* and Mark Tushnet, *Red, White, and Blue: A Critical Analysis of Constitutional Law* (Harvard University Press, 1988), provide balanced analysis from all perspectives. For another analysis of this great debate, see Lief H. Carter, *Contemporary Constitutional Lawmaking* (Pergamon Press, 1985). See David J. Richards, *Toleration and the Constitution* (Oxford University Press, 1986); Stephen Macedo, *The New Right v the Constitution* (Cato, 1986); Leslie F. Goldstein, "Judicial Review and Democratic Theory: Guardian Democracy vs. Representative Democracy," *The Western Political Quarterly* 40 (September 1987), pp. 391–412, also contains a bibliography.

88. Stephen Macedo, "Hurray for Judge Thomas' Conservative Activism," *The Wall Street Journal,* July 11, 1991, p. A11; L. Gordon Crovitz, "Reverse a Precedent, Protect the Constitution," *The Wall Street Journal,* July 10, 1991, p. A13.

89. J. W. Peltason, "The Supreme Court: Transactional or Transformational Leadership," in *Essays in Honor of James MacGregor Burns,* eds. Michael R. Beschloss and Thomas E. Cronin (Prentice Hall, 1988), pp. 165–80;

Mark Silverstein and Benjamin Ginsburg, "The Supreme Court and the New Politics of Judicial Power," *Political Science Quarterly* (Fall 1987), pp. 371–88.

90. *Planned Parenthood v Casey*, 121 L Ed 2d 674 (1992).

91. Marshall, *Public Opinion and the Supreme Court*, p. 193. See also Thomas R. Marshall, "The Supreme Court and the Grass Roots: Whom Does the Court Represent Best?" *Judicature* 46 (June/July 1992), pp. 22–28. See also Michael Comiskey, "The Rehnquist Court and American Values," *Judicature* 27 (March/April 1994), pp. 261–67.

92. Gerald N. Rosenberg, *The Hollow Hope: Can Courts Bring About Social Change?* (University of Chicago Press, 1991), p. 343.

93. Rehnquist, *Supreme Court*, p. 98.

CHAPTER 17

1. Al Gore, *Creating a Government That Works Better and Costs Less: The Report of the National Performance Review* (Plume-Penguin, 1993). See also John J. Dilulio, Jr., Gerald Garvey, and Donald F. Kettle, *Improving Government Performance: An Owner's Manual* (Brookings Institution, 1993).

2. See James Q. Wilson, "Mr. Clinton, Meet Mr. Gore," *Wall Street Journal*, October 28, 1993, p. A18.

3. For a study of bureaucracies and their strategies to keep as much autonomy as possible, see James Q. Wilson, *Bureaucracy: What Government Agencies Do and Why They Do It* (Basic Books, 1989).

4. Dennis Palumbo and Steven Maynard-Moody, *Contemporary Public Administration* (Longman, 1991), p. 26.

5. For an analysis of the use and abuse of the civil service system in the early twentieth century, see Stephen Skowronek, *Building a New American State* (Cambridge University Press, 1982).

6. For discussions of the representative character of the federal bureaucracy, see Samuel Krislov and David H. Rosenbloom, *Representative Bureaucracy and the American Political System* (Praeger, 1981).

7. For a discussion of these and the whole range of administrative agencies, see Harold Seidman and Robert Gilmour, *Politics, Position and Power: From the Positive to the Regulatory State*, 4th ed. (Oxford University Press, 1986), chap. 11. On government corporations, see John T. Tierney, "Government Corporations and Managing the Public's Business," *Political Science Quarterly* (Spring 1984), pp. 73–94.

8. A history of the old Hatch Act is provided in James Eccles, *The Hatch Act and the American Bureaucracy* (Vantage Press, 1981).

9. For the 1994 revisions of this act, see Jeanne Ponessa, "The Hatch Act Rewrite," *Congressional Quarterly Weekly Report*, November 13, 1993, pp. 3146–3147.

10. For an examination of Max Weber's ideas on bureaucracy, see Brian Fry, *Mastering Public Administration: From Max Weber to Dwight Waldo* (Chatham House, 1989).

11. See the useful discussion in Hugo Heclo, "Issue Networks and the Executive Establishment," in *The New American Political System*, ed. Anthony King (American Enterprise Institute, 1978), pp. 87–124.

12. John W. Gardner, testimony before the U.S. Senate Committee on Government Operations, *Executive Reorganization Proposals, Hearings* (Government Printing Office, 1971), pp. 57–58. See also R. Douglas Arnold, *Congress and the Bureaucracy* (Yale University Press, 1979).

13. W. Michael Blumenthal, "Candid Reflections of a Businessman in Washington," *Fortune*, January 29, 1979, p. 41.

14. Gerald R. Ford, *A Time to Heal: The Autobiography of Gerald R. Ford* (Harper and Row/Reader's Digest, 1979), p. 272.

15. David Osborne and Ted Gaebler, *Reinventing Government: How the Entrepreneurial Spirit Is Transforming the Public Sector* (Addison-Wesley, 1992).

16. Gore, *Creating a Government*.

17. E. S. Savas, *Privatization: The Key to Better Government* (Chatham House, 1987).

18. Osborne and Gaebler, *Reinventing Government*, pp. 45–46.

19. Anthony Frank, quoted in interview in *USA Today*, January 8, 1992, p. 7A.

20. For useful studies of these functions of OMB, see Larry Berman, *The Office of Management and Budget and the Presidency, 1921–1979* (Princeton University Press, 1979); Howard Shuman, *Politics and the Budget* (Prentice Hall, 1988). Of course, OMB does not always win, nor is it always right. See David Stockman, *The Triumph of Politics* (Harper and Row, 1986).

21. Morris P. Fiorina, "Flagellating the Federal Bureaucracy," *Society* (March/April 1983), p. 73.

22. Francis E. Rourke, "Whose Bureaucracy Is This, Anyway?" *PS: Political Science and Politics* (December 1993), p. 691.

23. James Q. Wilson, *Bureaucracy* (Basic Books, 1989), p. 268. See also James W. Fesler and Donald Kettl, *The Politics of the Administrative Process* (Chatham House, 1991), pp. 99–102.

CHAPTER 18

1. Edith Hamilton, *The Echo of Greece* (W. W. Norton, 1957), p. 47.

2. Adapted from Kenneth M. Dolbeare and Patricia Dolbeare, *American Ideologies* (Markham Publishing, 1971).

3. John F. Kennedy, *Profiles in Courage* (Pocket Books, 1956), p. 108.

4. See Thomas E. Cronin, "Thinking and Learning about Leadership," *Presidential Studies Quarterly* (Winter 1984), pp. 22–34.

5. See Bernard Crick, *In Defense of Politics*, rev. ed. (Pelican Books, 1983); Stimson Bullitt, *To Be a Politician*, rev. ed. (Yale University Press, 1977).

6. William J. Brennan, commencement address, Brandeis University, Waltham, Mass., May 18, 1986.

7. Arthur M. Schlesinger, Jr., *The Disuniting of American* (W. W. Norton, 1993), p. 134.

8. Lewis H. Lapham, "Who and What Is American?" *Harper's Magazine*, January 1992, p. 48.

9. John W. Gardner, *Self-Renewal*, rev. ed. (Norton, 1981), p. xiv.

10. Walt Whitman, "By Blue Ontario's Shore," *Leaves of Grass*, ed. Harold W. Blodgett and Sculley Bradley (New York University Press, 1965), p. 353.

PHOTO CREDITS

Chapter 15: **370** UPI/Bettmann   **374** The Granger Collection   **381** Sygma   **384** The Bettmann Archive   **385** AP/Wide World Photos   **387** UPI/Bettmann   **391** Reuters/Bettmann   **393** John Ficara/Sygma   **395** Reuters/Bettmann

Chapter 16: **402** AP/Wide World Photos   **411** UPI/Bettmann   **414** *(top)* UPI/Bettmann; *(bottom)* AP/Wide World Photos   **415** *(top)* Reuters/Bettmann; *(bottom)* Reuters/Bettmann   **422** Supreme Court Historical Society

Chapter 17: **428** Courtesy Sun Micro Systems   **430** John Marnaras/ Woodfin Camp & Associates   **434** AP/Wide World Photos   **441** UPI/Bettmann   **444** Reuters/Bettmann   **448** Larry Downing/Sygma   **449** AP/Wide World Photos

Chapter 18: **454** Bill Auth/Uniphoto   **455** The Granger Collection   **456** Jim Clark   **460** UPI/Bettmann   **461** UPI/Bettmann   **463** *(top)* Courtesy Louise Arnold; *(bottom)* The Granger Collection

INDEX

THE UNITED STATES
A Political Map

States drawn in proportion to
number of electoral votes

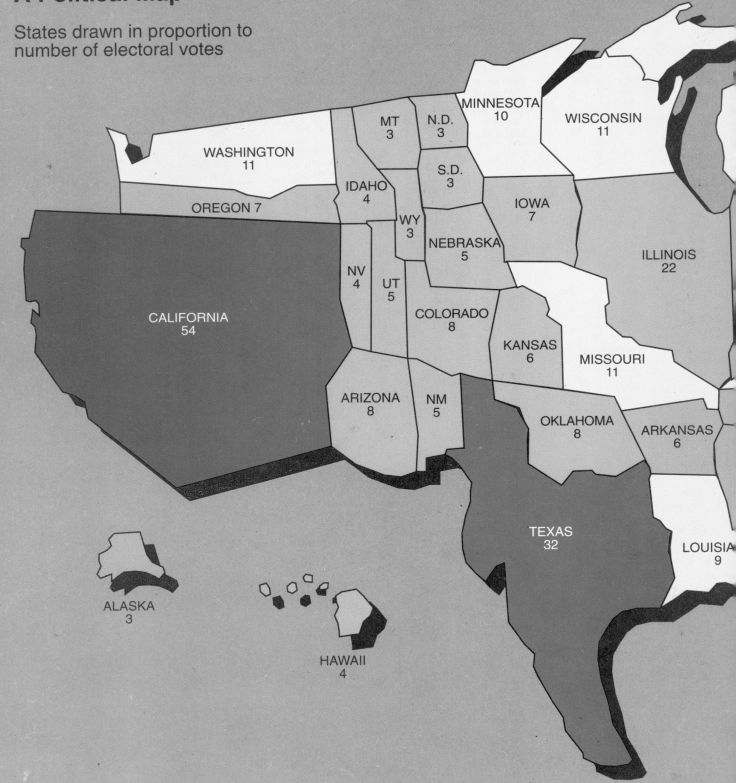